VOYAGES

in World History

AP® Edition

VOYAGES in World History

Third Edition

Valerie Hansen
Yale University

Kenneth R. Curtis
California State University Long Beach

Cengage Learning

Australia • Brazil • Mexico • Singapore • United Kingdom • United States

CENGAGE Learning

***Voyages in World History*, Third Edition—AP® Edition**
Valerie Hansen / Kenneth R. Curtis

Product Director: Paul R. Banks
Product Manager: Scott Greenan
Development Editor: Jan Fitter
Senior Marketing Manager: Andrea Kingman
Senior Content Project Manager: Carol Newman
Senior Art Director: Cate Rickard Barr
Manufacturing Planner: Fola Orekoya
IP Analyst: Alexandra Ricciardi
IP Project Manager: Betsy Hathaway
Production Service and Compositor: Cenveo® Publisher Services
Text and Cover Designer: Melissa Welch, Studio Montage
Cover Image: Caravan in the Desert (oil on canvas), Girardet, Eugene Alexis (1853–1907)/Private Collection/Photo © The Fine Art Society, London, UK/Bridgeman Images

Senior Content Developer, Advanced and Elective Products Program: Ashley Jack
Senior Content Developer, Advanced and Elective Products Program: Philip Lanza

Library of Congress Control Number: 2015956743

ISBN: 978-1-305-65956-8

Cengage Learning
20 Channel Center Street
Boston MA 02210
USA

Cengage Learning is a leading provider of customized learning solutions with employees residing in nearly 40 different countries and sales in more than 125 countries around the world. Find your local representative at **www.cengage.com**.

Cengage Learning products are represented in Canada by Nelson Education, Ltd.

To learn more about Cengage Learning Solutions, visit **www.cengage.com.**

To find online supplements and other instructional support, please visit **www.cengagebrain.com.**

Printed in Canada
Print Number: 01 Print Year: 2015

Brief Contents

Contents

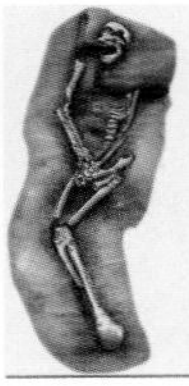

Photo credit: The Schoyen Collection, MS 1989 www.schoyencollection.com

Photo credit: Landov

Photo credits: Sanford Low, anthropologist/filmmaker // bpk, Berlin/(name of museum)/(name of photographer)/Art Resource, NY

Photo credit: Kharbine-Tapabor/The Art Archive at Art Resource, NY

CHAPTER 8
Hindu and Buddhist States and Societies in Asia, 100–1000 212

Traveler: *Ennin*

CHAPTER 9
Islamic Empires of Western Asia and Africa, 600–1258 244

Traveler: *Khaizuran*

CHAPTER 10
The Multiple Centers of Europe, 500–1000 274
Traveler: *Gudrid and Thorfinn Karlsefni*

CHAPTER 11
Expanding Trade Networks in Africa and India, 1000–1500 306
Traveler: *Ibn Battuta*

Photo credits: Historiated initial from the beginning of a chapter on seafaring and trade, copy of an original 14th century law collection "Jonsbok" (vellum), Icelandic School, (14th century)/Arni Magnusson Institute, Reykjavik, Iceland/Bridgeman Images // Superstock

Photo credits: © Cultural Relics Press // RMN-Grand Palais/Art Resource, NY

CHAPTER 14
The Mongols and Their Successors, 1200–1500 *400*
Traveler: *William of Rubruck*

Photo credit: INTERFOTO/Alamy

Photo credits: Clipart courtesy FCIT, from *Narrative and Critical History of America* (New York: Houghton, Mifflin, and Company, 1886)I:156 // Courtesy of the Ricci Institute for Chinese-Western Cultural History at the University of San Francisco Center for Asia Pacific Studies

Photo credits: Public Domain // Hulton Archive/Getty Images

CHAPTER 19 The Atlantic System: Africa, the Americas, and Europe, 1550–1807 558

Traveler: *Olaudah Equiano*

CHAPTER 20 Empires in Early Modern Asia, 1650–1837 588

Traveler: *Rammohun Roy*

Photo credits: Portrait of an African, c.1757–60 (oil on canvas), Ramsay, Allan (1713–84) (attr. to)/Royal Albert Memorial Museum, Exeter, Devon, UK/Bridgeman Images // Portrait of Rammohun Roy (1774–1833) 1832 (oil on canvas), Briggs, Henry Perronet (1792–1844)/© Bristol Museum and Art Gallery, UK/Bridgeman Images

CHAPTER 21
European Science and the Foundations of Modern Imperialism, 1600–1820 *618*
Traveler: *Joseph Banks*

CHAPTER 22
Revolutions in the West, 1750–1830 *648*
Traveler: *Simón Bolívar*

CHAPTER 23
The Industrial Revolution and European Politics, 1765–1880 682

Traveler: *Mikhail Bakunin*

CHAPTER 24
The Challenge of Modernity in China, Japan, and India, 1800–1910 714

Traveler: *Fukuzawa Yûkichi*

CHAPTER 25
State Building and Social Change in the Americas, 1830–1910 *744*

Traveler: *Pauline Johnson-Tekahionwake*

CHAPTER 26
The New Imperialism in Africa and Southeast Asia, 1830–1914 *776*

Traveler: *King Khama III*

Photo credits: Library of Congress Prints and Photographs Division[C-USZ62-48793] // From *Memoirs of Halide Adviar* Edib (N.J.: Gorgias Press). Reprinted by permission of Gorgias Press.

CHAPTER 29
The Second World War and the Origins of the Cold War, 1939–1949

CHAPTER 30
The Cold War and Decolonization, 1949–1975

Photo credits: Epa/Australia War Museum/Landov // Stefano Rellandini/Reuters/Corbis

CHAPTER 31 Toward a New World Order, 1975–2000 *932*

Traveler: *Nelson Mandela*

CHAPTER 32 Voyage into the Twenty-First Century *966*

Traveler: *Ai Weiwei*

Photo credits: David Turnley/Historical Premium/Corbis // Peter Macdiarmid/Getty Images

MAPS

VISUAL EVIDENCE IN PRIMARY SOURCES

MOVEMENT OF IDEAS THROUGH PRIMARY SOURCES

WORLD HISTORY IN TODAY'S WORLD

Preface

What makes this book different from other world history textbooks?

- Each chapter opens with a narrative about a traveler, whose real-life story is woven throughout the chapter. The *interactive map activity*, available through MindTap™, continues the story of the traveler online, allowing students to click on each important location the traveler visited to learn more about the historical, cultural, and political significance of the journey.
- Shorter than most world history textbooks, this survey still covers all of the major topics required in a world history course, as well as others we have found to be of interest to our students.
- The book's theme of movement highlights cultural contact and discovery and is reinforced in each chapter through the opening map, highlighting a specific traveler's journey, as well as through the unique chapter features, including *Movement of Ideas Through Primary Sources* and *Visual Evidence in Primary Sources*, which teach analytical skills and provoke critical thinking by inviting students to compare viewpoints.
- Brief *Context & Connections* inserts within the chapter text provide specific linkages and comparisons with other regions and periods, and the broader chapter-ending *Context and Connections* essay helps students understand the connections among different regions and periods, as well as global effects and trends.
- A robust digital support package includes numerous ways for students to further engage with the main themes of the text. The interactive environment of MindTap™ helps students exercise their critical thinking skills through a variety of activities and in a variety of formats.
- A beautiful, engaging design features an on-page glossary, a pronunciation guide, and chapter-opening focus questions. These tools help students grasp and retain the main ideas of the chapters.

This world history textbook will, we hope, be enjoyable for students to read and for teachers to teach. We have focused on thirty-two different people and the journeys they took, starting forty thousand years ago with Mungo Man in Australia (Chapter 1) and concluding in the twenty-first century with Chinese artist Ai Weiwei. Each of the thirty-two chapters introduces multiple focus points. First, the traveler's narrative introduces the home society and the civilizations visited, demonstrating our theme of the movement of people, ideas, trade goods, and artistic motifs and the results of these contacts. We introduce other evidence, often drawn from primary sources (marked in the running text with italics), to help students reason like historians. Each chapter also covers changes in political structure, the spread of world religions, and prevailing social structure and gender relations. Other important topics include cultural components and the effects of technology and environment.

The chapter-opening narratives enhance the scope and depth of the topics covered. The travelers take us to Tang China with the Japanese Buddhist monk Ennin, to Africa and South Asia with the hajj pilgrim Ibn Battuta, to Peru with the cross-dressing soldier and adventurer Catalina de Erauso, across the Atlantic with the African Olaudah Equiano, and to Europe during the Industrial Revolution with the Russian anarchist Mikhail Bakunin. Their vivid accounts are important sources about these long-ago events that shaped our world. Almost all of these travel accounts are available in English translation, listed in the suggested readings at the end of each chapter. Students new to world history, or to history in general, will find it easier, we hope, to focus on the experience of thirty-two individuals before focusing on the broader trends in their societies and their place in world history.

Instead of presenting a canned list of dates, each chapter covers the important topics at a sensible and careful pace, without compromising coverage or historical rigor. Students compare the traveler's perceptions with alternative sources, and so awaken their interest in the larger developments. Our goal was to select the most compelling topics and engaging illustrations from the entire record of human civilization and to present them in a clear flowing narrative in order to counter the view of history as an interminable compendium of geographical place, names, and facts.

We have chosen a range of travelers, both male and female, from all over the world. These individuals help cast our world history in a truly global format, avoiding the Eurocentrism that prompted the introduction of world history courses in the first place. Some travelers were well born and well educated, while others were not.

Our goal in focusing on the experience of individual travelers is to help make students enthusiastic about world history, while achieving the right balance between the traveler's experience and the course material. We measure our success by all the encouragement we have received both from teachers who teach the course and from students.

We aspire to answer many of the unmet needs of teachers and students in world history. Because our book is not encyclopedic, and because each chapter begins with a narrative of a trip, our book is more readable than its competitors, which strain for all-inclusive coverage. They pack so many names and facts into their text that they leave little time to introduce beginning students to historical method, which we do explicitly at the start of Chapter 2 and continue to do in subsequent chapters. Because our book gives students a chance to read primary sources in depth, particularly in the Movement of Ideas Through Primary Sources feature, teachers can spend class time teaching students how to reason historically—not just imparting the details of a given national history. Each chapter includes focus questions that make it easier for teachers new to world history to facilitate interactive learning.

Features of the AP® Edition

This AP® Edition incorporates the changes to the AP® course in effect for Fall 2016. In addition to the changes of the text, there are now specific AP® features. These include:

- On the second page of each chapter, the Key Concepts most relevant to that chapter are identified and expressed as a question to help students guide their reading.
- In each chapter, there are 5–7 marginal notes that serve to remind students of the course themes. Each theme is represented by one or more notes per chapter.
- Each Movement of Ideas through Primary Sources feature is followed by one or more discussion questions, each of which focuses on one of the Historical Thinking Skills. Students are thus able to apply the skill to a specific document.
- At the end of each chapter, there is a set of Multiple-Choice Questions in AP® format, each focusing on a primary or secondary source. These are followed by two Short-Answer Questions.
- At the end of the text, there is a bank of 15 Document-Based Questions and 10 Long Essay Questions, each accompanied by an introduction that helps the student learn to approach this type of question.
- At the beginning of the text, there is a correlation of the AP® Key Concepts to the pages of the text.
- At the beginning of the book, students will find sections on Preparing for and Taking the AP® Exam. These sections describe the different kinds of questions that will be on the exam, with examples and strategies for approaching each.

Theme and Approach

Our theme of movement and contact is key to world history because world historians focus on connections among the different societies of the past. The movement of people, whether in voluntary migrations or forced slavery, has been one of the most fruitful topics for world historians, as are the experiences of individual travelers. Their reactions to the people they met on their journeys reveal much about their home societies as well as about the societies they visited.

Our focus on individual travelers illustrates the increasing ease of contact among different civilizations with the passage of time. This theme highlights the developments that resulted from improved communications, travel among different places, the movement of trade goods, and the mixing of peoples. Such developments include the movement of world religions, mass migrations, and the spread of diseases like the plague. *Voyages* shows how travel has changed over time—how the distance covered by travelers has increased at the same time that the duration of trips has decreased. As a result, more and more people have been able to go to societies distant from their own.

Voyages and its integrated online components examine the different reasons for travel over the centuries. While some people were captured in battle and forced to go to new places, others visited different societies to teach or to learn the beliefs of a new religion like Buddhism, Christianity, or Islam. This theme, of necessity, addresses questions about the environment: How far and over what terrain did early people travel? How did sailors learn to use monsoon winds to their advantage? What were the effects of technological breakthroughs like steamships, trains, and airplanes—and the use of fossil fuels to power them? Because students can link the experiences of individual travelers to this theme, movement provides the memorable organizing principle for the book, a principle reinforced in the interactive online journeys offered by the *interactive map activity* on MindTap.

Having a single theme allows us to provide broad coverage of the most important topics in world history. Students who use this book will learn how empires and nations grew in power or influence, and how their ways of organizing their governments differed. Students need not commit long lists of rulers' names to memory; instead they focus on those leaders who created innovative political structures. This focus fits well with travel, since the different travelers were able to make certain journeys because of the political situation at the time. For example, William of Rubruck was able to travel across all of Eurasia because of the unification brought by the Mongol empire, while the size and strength of the Ottoman empire facilitated Evliya Çelebi's travels to Vienna and Egypt and across Southwest Asia.

Many rulers patronized religions to increase their control over the people they ruled, allowing a smooth introduction to the teachings of the major world religions. Volume 1 introduces the major religions and explains how originally regional religions moved across political borders to become world religions. Volume 2 provides context for today's complex interplay of religion and politics and the complex cultural outcomes that occurred when religions expanded into new world regions. The final two chapters analyze the renewed contemporary focus on religion, as seen in the rise of fundamentalist movements in various parts of the world. Our focus on travelers offers an opportunity to explore their involvement with religion, and *Voyages'* close attention to the religious traditions of diverse societies, often related through the travelers' tales, will give students a familiarity with the primary religious traditions of the world.

The topic of gender is an important one in world history, and throughout, *Voyages* devotes extensive space to the experience of women. Although in many societies literacy among women was severely limited, especially in the premodern era, we have included as many women travelers as possible. In addition, extensive coverage of gender and comparison across chapters of women's experiences in different societies allow students to grasp the experience of ordinary women.

Features

We see the features of this book as an opportunity to help students better understand the main text and to expand that understanding as they explore the integrated online features. Here, we describe the features in the printed book. Details about online features are found in the Ancillaries section on the next page.

Chapter Opening Introduction and Map

The beginning of each chapter should capture the student's attention at the outset. The opening section provides a biographical sketch for the chapter's traveler, a portrait, and a passage from his or her writings (or, if not available, a passage about the individual). A map illustrates the route of the traveler using imaginative graphics.

Movement of Ideas Through Primary Sources

This feature offers an introduction, an extensive excerpt from one or more primary sources, and discussion questions that connect the sources to one or more of the Historical Thinking Skills of the AP® course. The chosen passages emphasize the movement of ideas, often by contrasting different perspectives on an idea or a religious teaching. The feature aims to develop the core historical skill of analyzing original sources. Topics include "*The Analects* and the Qin Emperor's Stone Texts," "The Five Pillars of Islam," as described in the Hadith of Gabriel and by a contemporary Chinese encyclopedia, and an Iranian narrative of political and commercial competition in early modern Southeast Asia, "Iranians and Europeans at the Court of Siam."

Visual Evidence in Primary Sources

The goal of this feature is to train students to examine an artifact, a work of art, or a photograph and to glean historical information from the find or artwork. A close-up photograph of a recently discovered Chinese terracotta wrestler, for example, shows students how the figure differs from the famous terracotta warriors, and they are asked as well to compare the Chinese wrestler with a Greek example in a later chapter. Portraits of George Washington and Napoleon Bonaparte lead students to analyze the symbolism they contain and how the portraits serve as representations of political power. Discussion questions help students analyze the evidence as they examine the source.

World History in Today's World

This brief feature picks an element of modern life with roots in the period under study. We chose topics interesting to students (for example, "Recreating the World's Oldest Beer" and "From 'Shell Shock' to Post-Traumatic Stress Disorder"), and we highlight their relationship to the past. This feature should provide material to trigger discussion and help instructors explain why world history matters, since students often have little sense that the past has anything to do with their own lives.

Changes in the Third Edition

Every chapter of this new edition has been carefully checked and revised for readability and clarity of language. In every chapter, topics and subtopics have been added or elaborated on, and recent scholarship has been incorporated throughout the text. Some highlights of specific changes in the second edition follow.

- A new feature has been added: roughly eight to ten Context & Connections inserts within the running text of each chapter. These inserts relate to the surrounding text and describe developments or comparisons that link to other regions and periods to help show students how world history interrelates across time and space. The Context & Connections inserts often include key terms from other chapters, which are highlighted in color with their chapter reference to help emphasize recurring themes and ideas. These inserts complement, but are distinct from, the end-of-chapter Context and Connections essays.
- A total of ten Visual Evidence in Primary Sources and seven Movement of Ideas Through Primary Sources features have been replaced or significantly changed.
- Approximately 30 percent of the illustrations have been replaced with new images, with an eye toward visual interest and engagement.
- A new section at the start of Chapter 2—"Complex Societies and the Discipline of History"—introduces students to historical method and the nature of sources.
- Chapter 4's new traveler, China's Grand Historian Sima Qian, lived during the Han dynasty and wrote a record from the legendary past to 100 B.C.E., after the Qin dynasty (221–207 B.C.E.) unified the empire for the first time.
- Chapter 7 has a new traveler, Egeria, a Spanish pilgrim who from 381 to 384 traveled from the Roman empire's western edge to Jerusalem, Egypt, and Constantinople. Chapter 8 explicitly compares her experience with that of the Japanese Buddhist pilgrim Ennin, and Chapter 9 contrasts their pilgrimages with the hajj of Islam.
- Chapter 12 includes a new section, "The Changing Lives of Women in China's Commercial Revolution," which further illustrates the life of women in Song China.
- In Chapter 14, a new historical analysis of the fall of Constantinople will help students understand the global nature of world history.
- Chapter 15's new traveler is Bernardino de Sahagún, a Franciscan friar who compiled the *General History of the Things of New Spain*, also known as the Florentine Codex, by interviewing the native Nahua people of central Mexico in their own language and recording their answers in Nahuatl with a Spanish summary.
- In Chapter 17, the first main section has been refocused to concentrate on the Ottoman and Safavid empires and their relations. In addition, the chapter's concluding Context and Connections essay now analyzes early modern developments in light of recent scholarship on the role of climate change.
- The new traveler in Chapter 20, Rammohun Roy, a prominent Indian reformer and figure in the Bengal Renaissance, offers an Indian's

perspective on the transition from Mughal to British rule.
- Coverage of Mexico from 1910 through Carranza has been moved from Chapter 27 to Chapter 25, providing enhanced continuity in the coverage of Mexican history.
- Chapter 27 has a new traveler, the anarchist and feminist Emma Goldman, who brings to the narrative a broader critique of the Bolshevik system in Russia and an in-depth look at a radical view of women's issues in the early twentieth century.
- The survey of contemporary global affairs in Chapter 32 has been thoroughly updated and also includes greater emphasis on women's leadership.

Ancillaries

Teacher Resources

MindTap™

MindTap for *Voyages in World History*, Third Edition is a personalized, online digital learning platform providing students with an immersive learning experience that builds critical thinking skills. Through a carefully designed chapter-based learning path, MindTap allows students to easily identify the chapter's learning objectives, improve their writing skills by completing unit-level essay assessments, read short and manageable sections from the e-book, and test their content knowledge with a chapter test that employs Aplia™ questions (see Chapter Test description on the next page).

- ***Fast Track to a 5*** Mindtap begins with a full unit of AP® World History examination prep. It includes guidelines on how to prepare for and take the exam, a full AP® diagnostic test, several chapters of content review and practice aligned with the College Board course outline, and two full AP® practice tests. Students can pace their work in this AP® review unit according to their progress in the rest of the MindTap course.
- ***Setting the Scene*** Each subsequent chapter of the MindTap begins with a brief video that introduces the chapter's major themes in a compelling, visual way that encourages students to think critically about the subject matter.
- ***Interactive Traveler Map*** A unique interactive map activity expands upon each chapter's story of the traveler, allowing students to follow along the journey and click on each stop to learn more about where the traveler went and why it was historically significant. Opening learning objectives, posed as questions, help students focus on what to take away from each unique traveler experience, and place the journey in the context of the chapter's overarching lesson.
- ***Review Activities*** Reading comprehension assignments were designed to cover the content of each major heading within the chapter.
- ***Chapter Test*** Each chapter within MindTap ends with a summative chapter test. It covers each chapter's learning objectives and is built using Aplia critical thinking questions. All chapter tests include at least one map-based activity. Aplia provides automatically graded critical thinking assignments with detailed, immediate explanations on every question. Students can also choose to see another set of related questions if they did not earn all available points in their first attempt and want more practice.
- ***Reflection Activity*** Every chapter ends with an assignable, gradable reflection activity, intended as a brief writing assignment through which students can apply a theme or idea they've just studied.
- ***Unit Activities*** Chapters in MindTap are organized into multi-chapter units. Each unit includes a brief set of higher-stakes activities for teachers to assign, designed to assess students on their writing and critical thinking skills and their ability to engage larger themes, concepts, and material across multiple chapters.
- ***Classroom Activities*** MindTap includes a brief list of in-class activity ideas for teachers. These are designed to increase student collaboration, engagement, and understanding of selected topics or themes. These activities, including class debate scenarios and primary source discussion guides, can enrich the classroom experience for both teachers and students.

MindTap also includes a variety of other tools that will make history more engaging for students:

- ***The Instructor's Resource Center*** provides a large collection of searchable, curated readings intended for use in World History. Individual readings may be assigned to students along with a brief assessment to enhance their learning experience.

- ***ReadSpeaker*** reads the text out loud to students in a voice they can customize.
- ***Note-taking and highlighting*** are organized in a central location that can be synced with EverNote on any mobile device a student may have access to.
- ***Questia*** allows teachers to search a database of thousands of peer-reviewed journals, newspapers, magazines, and full-length books—all assets can be added to any relevant chapter in MindTap.
- ***Kaltura*** allows teachers to insert inline video and audio into the MindTap platform.
- ***ConnectYard*** allows teachers to create digital "yards" and communicate with students based upon their preferred social media sites—without "friending" students.

Instructor Companion Website

This website is an all-in-one resource for class preparation, presentation, and testing for teachers. Accessible through Cengage.com/login with your faculty account, you will find a Teacher's Resource Guide, PowerPoint presentations (descriptions below), and test bank files (please see the Cognero® description below).

AP® Teacher Resource Guide This resource guide, which is available printed or online will help teachers navigate the redesigned AP® course. This manual contains for each chapter: AP® focus on historical periods, historical thinking skills, thematic learning objectives, key concepts, essential historical details from the concept outline, chapter summary, and suggested activities and discussion topics for teaching to the redesigned AP® World History exam.

PowerPoint® Lecture Tools These presentations are ready-to-use, visual outlines of each chapter. They are easily customized for your lectures. There are presentations of only lectures or only images, as well as combined lecture and image presentations. Also available is a per-chapter JPEG library of images and maps.

Cengage Learning Testing, Powered by Cognero®: The test bank for *Voyages in World History*, Third Edition is accessible through Cengage.com/login with your faculty account. This test bank contains multiple-choice and essay questions for each chapter, correlated to the college edition. Cognero® is a flexible, online system that allows you to author, edit, and manage test bank content for *Voyages in World History*, Third Edition. Create multiple test versions instantly and deliver through your LMS from your classroom, or wherever you may be, with no special installs or downloads required.

The following format types are available for download from the Instructor Companion Website: Blackboard, Angel, Moodle, Canvas, and Desire-2Learn. You can import these files directly into your LMS to edit, manage questions, and create tests. The test bank is also available in PDF format from the Instructor Companion Website.

AP® World History Testbank in Cognero

Available in Cognero, this testbank contains more than 300 questions keyed to the redesigned AP® exam. These questions are organized into six periods, mirroring those on the AP® exam. Each of the six period tests contain 45 multiple-choice, 4 short-answer, 1 document-based, and 2 long essay questions, all in AP® format.

Fast Track to a 5: Preparing for the AP® World History Exam

This test preparation manual fully aligns with the redesigned AP® World History exam in both content and format and is keyed to the second and third editions of *Voyages*. Available in both print and online, it includes an introduction on strategies for addressing each type of question, a diagnostic test, review chapters arranged by the periods of the course with content review questions, AP® format questions of all types found on the exam for each part, and two complete practice tests in AP® format. It can be purchased with the text or separately.

Student Resources

MindTap™

The learning path for *Voyages in World History*, Third Edition MindTap incorporates a set of resources designed to help students develop their own historical skills. These include interactive, auto-gradable tutorials for map skills, essay writing, and critical thinking. They also include a set of resources developed to aid students with their research skills, primary and secondary source analysis, and knowledge and confidence around proper citations.

Fast Track to a 5: Preparing for the AP® World History Exam This test preparation manual fully aligns with the redesigned AP® World History exam in both content and format and is keyed to the second and third editions of *Voyages*. Available in both print and online, it includes an introduction on strategies for addressing each type of question, a diagnostic test, review chapters arranged by the periods of the course with content review questions, AP® format questions of all types found on the exam for each part, and two complete practice tests in AP® format.

***Writing for College History,* 1e [ISBN: 9780618306039]** Prepared by Robert M. Frakes, Clarion University. This brief handbook for survey courses in American history, Western civilization/European history, and world civilization guides students through the various types of writing assignments they encounter in a history class. Providing examples of student writing and candid assessments of student work, this text focuses on the rules and conventions of writing for the college history course. Available for purchase.

***The History Handbook,* 2e [ISBN: 9780495906766]** Prepared by Carol Berkin of Baruch College, City University of New York and Betty Anderson of Boston University. This book teaches students both basic and history-specific study skills such as how to read primary sources, research historical topics, and correctly cite sources. Substantially less expensive than comparable skill-building texts, *The History Handbook* also offers tips for Internet research and evaluating online sources. Available for purchase.

***Doing History: Research and Writing in the Digital Age,* 2e [ISBN: 9781133587880]** Prepared by Michael J. Galgano, J. Chris Arndt, and Raymond M. Hyser of James Madison University. Whether you're starting down the path as a history major or simply looking for a straightforward and systematic guide to writing a successful paper, you'll find this text to be an indispensable handbook to historical research. This text's "soup to nuts" approach to researching and writing about history addresses every step of the process, from locating your sources and gathering information, to writing clearly and making proper use of various citation styles to avoid plagiarism. You'll also learn how to make the most of every tool available to you—especially the technology that helps you conduct the process efficiently and effectively. Available for purchase.

Acknowledgments

It is a pleasure to thank the many instructors who read and critiqued the manuscript through its development in this and previous editions, as well as those who reviewed and class-tested MindTap and our other digital offerings:

Zachary Alexander, Snead State Community College
Barbara Allen, La Salle University
Mark Baker, California State University Bakersfield
Jessica Weaver Baron, Saint Mary's College
Albert Bauman, Hawai'i Pacific University
Natalie Bayer, Drake University
Christopher Bellito, Kean University
Robert Bond, Cuyamaca College
Marjan Boogert, Manchester College
Timothy Boyd, University of Buffalo
Maryann Brink, University of Massachusetts-Boston
Paul Buckingham, Morrisville State College
Jochen Burgtorf, California State University Fullerton
Celeste Chamberland, Roosevelt University
Annette Chamberlin, Virginia Western Community College
Patty Colman, Moorpark College
Tracey-Anne Cooper, St. John's University
Marcie Cowley, Grand Valley State University
Matthew Crawford, Kent State University
Brian Daugherity, Virginia Commonwealth University
Courtney DeMayo, Heidelberg University
Katie Desmond, Feather River College
Salvador Diaz, Santa Rosa Junior College
Audra Diptee, Carleton University
Kimberly Dowdle, Jackson State University
Jeffrey Dym, Sacramento State University
Don Eberle, Bowling Green State University
Jayme Feagin, Georgia Highlands College
Angela Feres, Grossmont College
Christopher Ferguson, Auburn State University
Christina Firpo, California Polytechnic State University
Nancy Fitch, California State University Fullerton
Candace Gregory-Abbott, California State University Sacramento
Eric Gruver, Texas A&M University
Kenneth Hall, Ball State University
Tracy Hoskins, Taylor University
Victor Jagos, Scottsdale Community College
Ellen J. Jenkins, Arkansas Tech University
Phyllis Jestice, University of Southern Mississippi
Gustavo Jimenez, Los Angeles Mission College
Michael Kinney, Calhoun Community College
Mark Lentz, University of Louisiana-Lafayette
Jodie Mader, Thomas More College
Susan Maneck, Jackson State University
Christopher Mauriello, Salem State University
Derek Maxfield, Genesee Community College
Scott Merriman, Troy University
Alexander Mirkovic, Arkansas Tech University
Houston Mount, East Central University
Stephen Neufeld, California State University Fullerton

Mari Nicholson-Preuss, University of Houston
Bill Palmer, Marshall University
Peter Patsouris, Three Rivers Community College
Sean Perrone, Saint Anselm College
Julio Pino, Kent State University
Dave Price, Santa Fe College
Elizabeth Propes, Tennessee Technological University
Carey Roberts, Arkansas Tech University
Anne Rose, Grand Valley State University
LaQuita Saunders, Arkansas State University
Charles Scruggs, Genesee Community College
Scott Seagle, Chattanooga State Community College
Tatiana Seijas, Miami University
Julia Sloan, Cazenovia College
Al Smith, Modesto Junior College
Jeffrey Smith, Lindenwood University
David Stefancic, Saint Mary's College
Pamela Stewart, Arizona State University
Kirk Strawbridge, Mississippi University for Women
Julie Tatlock, Mount Mary College
Philip Theodore, Mississippi Gulf Coast Community College
Lisa Tran, California State University Fullerton
Sarah Trembanis, Immaculata University
Sarah Tucker, Washburn University
Kimberly Vincent, North Carolina State University
Timothy Wesley, Pennsylvania State University
Robert Wilcox, Northern Kentucky University
James Williams, University of Indianapolis
Deborah Wood, Genesee Community College
Kent Wright, Arizona State University

Valerie Hansen would also like to thank the following for their guidance on specific chapters: Haydon Cherry, Yale University; Stephen Colvin, London University; Fabian Drixler, Yale University; Benjamin Foster, Yale University; Karen Foster, Yale University; Paul Freedman, Yale University; Phyllis Granoff, Yale University; Thomas R. H. Havens, Northeastern University; Stanley Insler, Yale University; Mary Miller, Yale University; Frederick S. Paxton, Connecticut College; Stuart Schwartz, Yale University; Koichi Shinohara, Yale University; Francesca Trivellato, Yale University; and Anders Winroth, Yale University.

The study of world history is indeed a voyage, and Kenneth Curtis would like to thank the following for helping identify guideposts along the way. First, thanks to colleagues in the World History Association and the Advanced Placement World History program, especially Omar Ali, University of North Carolina Greensboro; Ross Dunn, San Diego State University; Alan Karras, University of California, Berkeley; Patrick Manning, University of Pittsburgh; Laura Mitchell, University of California, Irvine; Heather Salter-Streets, Washington State University; and Merry Wiesner-Hanks, University of Wisconsin-Milwaukee. Ken would especially like to commemorate the scholarly stimulation, friendship, and generous spirit of the late Jerry Bentley of the University of Hawai'i. He would also like to acknowledge the support of his colleagues in the history department at California State University Long Beach, especially those who aided with sources, translations, or interpretive guidance: Houri Berberian, Craig Hendricks, Ali Igmen, Andrew Jenks, Timothy Keirn, Margaret Kuo, Sharlene Sayegh, and Donald Schwartz.

The authors would also like to thank the many publishing professionals at Cengage Learning who facilitated the publication of this book, in particular: Jan Fitter, whose desire to get it right shaped this and previous editions; our original editor, Nancy Blaine, for guiding us through the entire process from proposal to finished textbook, and her able successor, Cara St. Hilaire, who supervised the revisions; Jean Woy, for the extraordinary historical judgment she brought to bear on the first edition and her continuing guidance; Cate Rickard Barr, for managing another stellar design; Carol Newman, for shepherding the book through the final, chaotic prepublication process; Charlotte Miller, who oversaw creation of the book's distinctive maps; and Kate MacLean, who coordinated the multimedia components that accompanies the MindTap.

In closing, Valerie Hansen would like to thank Brian Vivier for doing so much work on Volume 1; the title of "research assistant" does not convey even a fraction of what he did, always punctually and cheerfully. She dedicates this book to her children, Lydia, Claire, and Bret Hansen Stepanek, and their future educations.

In recognition of his father's precious gift of curiosity, Ken dedicates this book to the memory of James Gavin Curtis.

About the Authors

Valerie Hansen

Valerie Hansen teaches Chinese and world history at Yale University, where she is professor of history. Her main research goal is to draw on nontraditional sources to capture the experience of ordinary people. In particular, she is interested in how sources buried in the ground, whether intentionally or unintentionally, supplement the detailed official record of China's past. Her books include *The Open Empire: A History of China to 1600* (2000) and *The Silk Road: A New History* (2012). In the past decade, she has spent three years in China: 2005–2006 in Shanghai on a Fulbright grant, and 2008–2009 and 2011–2012 teaching at Yale's joint undergraduate program with Peking University. She is currently working on a book about the world in the year 1000 and the many unexpected connections that tied different regions together for the first time.

Kenneth R. Curtis

Kenneth R. Curtis received his Ph.D. from the University of Wisconsin-Madison in African and Comparative World History. His research focuses on colonial to postcolonial transitions in East Africa, with a particular focus on the coffee economy of Tanzania. He is professor of History at California State University Long Beach, where he has taught world history at the introductory level, in special courses designed for future middle and high school teachers, and in graduate seminars. He has worked to advance the teaching of world history at the collegiate and secondary levels in collaboration with the World History Association, the California History/Social Science Project, and the College Board's Advanced Placement World History program.

Note on Spelling

Students taking world history will encounter new names of people, terms, and places from languages that use either different alphabets or no alphabet at all (like Chinese) and that have multiple variant spellings in English. As a rule, we have opted to give names in the native language of whom we are writing about, not in other languages.

Our goal has been to avoid confusing the reader, even if specific decisions may not make sense to expert readers. To help readers, we provide a pronunciation guide on the first appearance of any term or name whose pronunciation is not obvious from the spelling. A few explanations for specific regions follow.

The Americas

Only after 1492 with the arrival of Columbus and his men did outsiders label the original residents of the Americas as a single group. For this reason, any word for the inhabitants of North and South America is inaccurate. We try to refer to individual peoples whenever possible. When speaking in general terms, we use the word *Amerindian* because it has no pejorative overtones and is not confusing.

Many place names in Spanish-speaking regions have a form in both Spanish and in the language of the indigenous peoples; whenever possible we have opted for the indigenous word. For example, we write about the *Tiwanaku* culture in the Andes, not *Tiahuanaco*. In some cases, we choose the more familiar term, such as *Inca* and *Cuzco*, rather than the less familiar spellings *Inka* and *Cusco*. We retain the accents for modern place names.

East Asia

For Chinese, we have used the pinyin system of romanization. However, on the first appearance of a name, we alert readers to nonstandard spellings, such as Chiang Kai-shek and Sun Yat-sen, that have already entered English.

For other Asian languages, we have used the most common romanization systems (McCune-Reischauer for Korean, Hepburn for Japanese). Because we prefer to use the names that people called themselves, we use *Chinggis Khan* for the ruler of the Mongols (not *Genghis Khan*, which is Persian) and the Turkish *Timur the Lame* (rather than *Tamerlane*, his English name).

West Asia and North Africa

Many romanization systems for Arabic and related languages like Ottoman Turkish or Persian use an apostrophe to indicate specific consonants (*ain* and *hamza*). Because it is difficult for a native speaker of English to hear these differences, we have omitted these apostrophes. For this reason, we use *Quran* (not *Qur'an*).

Correlation of Key Concepts for the AP® World History Course to *Voyages in World History*, 3e

Key to Thematic Learning Objectives:
ENV – Interaction Between Humans and the Environment
CUL – Development and Interaction of Cultures
SB – State Building, Expansion, and Conflict
ECON – Creation, Expansion, and Interaction of Economic Systems
SOC – Development and Transformation of Social Structures

World History Curriculum		Chapter & Page References
Period 1: Technological and Environmental Transformations, to c. 600 B.C.E.		Chapters 1, 2, 3, 4, 5
Key Concept 1.1 Big Geography and the Peopling of the Earth	The term *Big Geography* draws attention to the global nature of world history. Throughout the Paleolithic period, humans migrated from Africa to Eurasia, Australia, and the Americas. Early humans were mobile and creative in adapting to different geographical settings from savanna to desert to tundra. Humans also developed varied and sophisticated technologies.	Chapter 1
	I. Archeological evidence indicates that during the Paleolithic era, hunting-foraging bands of humans gradually migrated from their origin in East Africa to Eurasia, Australia, and the Americas, adapting their technology and cultures to new climate regions. **[ENV-1, 4, 6 | CUL-6 | ECON-1, 10]**	• Mungo Man (pp. 2–4) • The First Anatomically Modern Humans in Africa, ca. 200,000 B.C.E. (pp. 4–7) • How Modern Humans Populated Asia, Australia, and Europe (pp. 7–15) • The Settling of the Americas, ca. 14,000–12,000 B.C.E. (pp. 15–18) • Context and Connections: Migrations as a Sign of Human Development (p. 26)

Key Concept 1.2 The Neolithic Revolution and Early Agricultural Societies	In response to warming climates at the end of the last Ice Age, about 10,000 years ago, some groups adapted to the environment in new ways, while others remained hunter-foragers. Settled agriculture appeared in several different parts of the world. The switch to agriculture created a more reliable, but not necessarily more diversified, food supply. Farmers also affected the environment through intensive cultivation of selected plants to the exclusion of others, the construction of irrigation systems, and the use of domesticated animals for food and labor. Populations increased; village life developed, followed by urban life with all its complexity. Patriarchy and forced labor systems developed, giving elite men concentrated power over most of the other people in their societies. Pastoralism emerged in parts of Africa and Eurasia. Like agriculturalists, pastoralists tended to be more socially stratified than hunter-foragers. Pastoralists' mobility facilitated technology transfers through their interaction with settled populations.	Chapters 1, 2, 3, 4, 5
	I. Beginning about 10,000 years ago, the Neolithic Revolution led to the development of more complex economic and social systems. **[ENV-1, 2, 4, 5, 6 | SB-6 | ECON-1, 10]**	• The Emergence of Agriculture, 9400–3000 B.C.E. (pp. 18–25) • Gilgamesh (pp. 28–30) • The Emergence of Complex Society in Mesopotamia, ca. 3100–1590 B.C.E. (pp. 30–35) • Egypt During the Old and Middle Kingdoms, ca. 3100–1500 B.C.E. (pp. 40–45) • The Origins of Complex Society in South Asia, 2600–500 B.C.E. (pp. 62–72) • The First Complex Societies of Mesoamerica, 5000 B.C.E.–500 C.E. (pp. 118–123)

	II. Agriculture and pastoralism began to transform human societies. **[ENV-1, 2, 5 | SB-1, 6, 8, 9 | ECON-1, 5, 10, 12 | SOC-1, 2]**	• The Emergence of Complex Society in Mesopotamia, ca. 3100–1590 B.C.E. (pp. 30–35) • The International System, 1500–1150 B.C.E. (pp. 45–49) • Syria-Palestine and New Empires in Western Asia, 1200–500 B.C.E. (pp. 52–57) • The Origins of Complex Society in South Asia, 2600–500 B.C.E. (pp. 62–72) • The Origins of Chinese Civilization, 1200–221 B.C.E. (pp. 90–100) • The First Complex Societies of Mesoamerica, 5000 B.C.E.–500 C.E. (pp. 118–123) • The Peoples of the Andes, 3100 B.C.E.–1000 C.E. (pp. 132–134)
Key Concept 1.3 The Development and Interactions of Early Agricultural, Pastoral, and Urban Societies	From about 5,000 years ago, urban societies developed, laying the foundations for the first civilizations. The term *civilization* is normally used to designate large societies with cities and powerful states. While there were many differences between civilizations, they also shared important features. They all produced agricultural surpluses that permitted significant specialization of labor. All civilizations contained cities and generated complex institutions, including political bureaucracies, armies, and religious hierarchies. They also featured clearly stratified social hierarchies and organized long-distance trading relationships. Economic exchanges intensified within and between civilizations, as well as with nomadic pastoralists.	Chapters 2, 3, 4, 5

	I. Core and foundational civilizations developed in a variety of geographical and environmental settings where agriculture flourished, including Mesopotamia in the Tigris and Euphrates River Valleys, Egypt in the Nile River Valley, Mohenjo-Daro and Harappa in the Indus River Valley, Shang in the Yellow River or Huang He Valley, Olmecs in Mesoamerica, and Chavín in Andean South America. **[ENV-2, 4]**	• The Emergence of Complex Society in Mesopotamia, ca. 3100–1590 B.C.E. (pp. 30–35) • Egypt During the Old and Middle Kingdoms, ca. 3100–1500 B.C.E. (pp. 40–45) • Syria-Palestine and New Empires in Western Asia, 1200–500 B.C.E. (pp. 52–57) • The Origins of Complex Society in South Asia, 2600–500 B.C.E. (pp. 62–72) • The Origins of Chinese Civilization, 1200–221 B.C.E. (pp. 90–100) • The First Complex Societies of Mesoamerica, 5000 B.C.E.–500 C.E. (pp. 118–123) • The Peoples of the Andes, 3100 B.C.E.–1000 C.E. (pp. 132–134)
	II. The first states emerged within core civilizations in Mesopotamia and the Nile Valley. **[ENV-1, 2, 4, 6 | SB-1, 2, 3, 4, 6, 9 | ECON-1, 3, 4, 5, 10 | SOC-2]**	• Egyptian Expansion During the Middle Kingdom, 2040–1782 B.C.E. (pp. 44–45) • The International System, 1500–1150 B.C.E. (pp. 45–49) • The Assyrian Empire, 911–612 B.C.E. (pp. 56–57)
	III. Culture played a significant role in unifying states through laws, language, literature, religion, myths, and monumental art. **[ENV-2 | CUL-1, 2, 3, 4, 6, 8, 9 | SB-1, 2, 5, 9, 10 | ECON-2, 8, 11, 12 | SOC-1, 2, 3, 4]**	• The Emergence of Complex Society in Mesopotamia, ca. 3100–1590 B.C.E. (pp. 30–35) • The Beginnings of Writing, 3300 B.C.E. (pp. 35–40) • Egypt During the Old and Middle Kingdoms, ca. 3100–1500 B.C.E. (pp. 40–45) • The International System, 1500–1150 B.C.E. (pp. 45–49) • Syria-Palestine and New Empires in Western Asia, 1200–500 B.C.E. (pp. 52–57) • The Origins of Complex Society in South Asia, 2600–500 B.C.E. (pp. 62–72) • The Origins of Chinese Civilization, 1200–221 B.C.E. (pp. 90–100) • The First Complex Societies of Mesoamerica, 5000 B.C.E.–500 C.E. (pp. 118–123) • The Peoples of the Andes, 3100 B.C.E.–1000 C.E. (pp. 132–134)

Period 2: Organization and Reorganization of Human Societies, c. 600 B.C.E. to c. 600 C.E.		Chapters 2, 3, 4, 5, 6, 7, 8, 10, 11
Key Concept 2.1 The Development and Codification of Religious and Cultural Traditions	As states and empires increased in size and contacts between regions multiplied, people transformed their religious and cultural systems. Religions and belief systems provided a social bond and an ethical code to live by. These shared beliefs also influenced and reinforced political, economic, and occupational stratification. Religious and political authority often merged as rulers (some of whom were considered divine) used religion, along with military and legal structures, to justify their rule and ensure its continuation. Religions and belief systems also generated conflict, partly because beliefs and practices varied greatly within and among societies.	Chapters 2, 3, 4, 7, 8
	I. Codifications and further developments of existing religious traditions provided a bond among people and an ethical code to live by. **[CUL-1, 2, 4, 5 | SB-7 | SOC-3, 5]**	• Syria-Palestine and New Empires in Western Asia, 1200–500 B.C.E. (pp. 52–57) • The Origins of Complex Society in South Asia, 2600–500 B.C.E. (pp. 62–72) • The Rise of Christianity, ca. 30–284 (pp. 194–200) • The Rise of Hinduism, 300–900 (pp. 216–217)
	II. New belief systems and cultural traditions emerged and spread, often asserting universal truths. **[ENV-2 | CUL-1, 2, 3, 4, 8, 9 | SB-2, 4 | ECON-8 | SOC-3, 4, 5]**	• The Rise of Buddhism (pp. 72–74) • The Mauryan Empire, ca. 320–185 B.C.E. (pp. 74–83) • The Zhou Dynasty, 1045–256 B.C.E. (pp. 95–96) • Confucianism (pp. 96–97) • Daoism (pp. 97–100) • Culture and Politics in Athens, 480–404 B.C.E. (pp. 163–164) • Athens as a Center for the Study of Philosophy (pp. 165–166) • The Rise of Christianity, ca. 30–284 (pp. 194–200) • Religious Changes of the Late Empire (pp. 201–202) • Christianity in North Africa (pp. 203–205) • Buddhism, Hinduism, and Indian Rulers, 100–1000 (pp. 215–219) • Buddhism, Hinduism, and Southeast Asian Rulers, 300–1000 (pp. 219–225) • Buddhism and the Revival of Empire in China, 100–1000 (pp. 225–235)

	III. Belief systems generally reinforced existing social structures while also offering new roles and status to some men and women. For example, Confucianism emphasized filial piety, and some Buddhists and Christians practiced a monastic life. **[CUL-1, 3, 5 | SOC-1, 5]**	• Confucianism (pp. 96–97) • Religious Changes of the Late Empire (pp. 201–202) • Christianity in North Africa (pp. 203–205) • Buddhism in China, 100–589 (pp. 225–227)
	IV. Other religious and cultural traditions, including shamanism, animism, and ancestor veneration persisted. **[ENV-2]**	• Early Chinese Writing in the Shang Dynasty, ca. 1200 B.C.E. (background on ancestor worship) (pp. 93–94) • Buddhism in China, 100–589 (pp. 225–227)
Key Concept 2.2 The Development of States and Empires	As the early states and empires grew in number, size, and population, they frequently competed for resources and came into conflict with one another. In quest of land, wealth, and security, some empires expanded dramatically. In doing so, they built powerful military machines and administrative institutions that were capable of organizing human activities over long distances, and they created new groups of military and political elites to manage their affairs. As these empires expanded their boundaries, they also faced the need to develop policies and procedures to govern their relationships with ethnically and culturally diverse populations, sometimes to integrate them within an imperial society and sometimes to exclude them. In some cases, these empires became victims of their own successes. By expanding their boundaries too far, they created political, cultural, and administrative difficulties that they could not manage. They also experienced environmental, social, and economic problems when they overexploited their lands and subjects and permitted excessive wealth to be concentrated in the hands of privileged classes.	Chapters 3, 4, 5, 6, 7, 8, 10

	I. The number and size of key states and empires grew dramatically as rulers imposed political unity on areas where previously there had been competing states. **[ENV-4 | SB-2, 5, 10]**	• The Mauryan Empire, ca. 320–185 B.C.E. (pp. 74–83) • Sima Qian (pp. 88–90) • Qin Rulers Unify China, 359–207 B.C.E. (pp. 100–107) • The Han Empire, 206 B.C.E.–220 C.E. (pp. 107–110) • Extending Han Rule to Mongolia, Vietnam, and Korea (pp. 110–112) • Han Expansion to the North, Northwest, and South (pp. 112–114) • Teotihuacan, ca. 200 B.C.E.–600 C.E. (pp. 121–123) • Maya Government and Society (pp. 125–126) • War, Politics, and the Decline of the Maya (pp. 127–131) • The Northern Peoples, 500 B.C.E.–1200 C.E. (pp. 131–132) • The Peoples of the Andes, 3100 B.C.E.–1000 C.E. (pp. 132–134) • Herodotus (pp. 144–147) • The Rise of the Achaemenids in Iran, 1000-330 B.C.E. (pp. 147–155) • Ancient Greece and the Mediterranean World, 2000–334 B.C.E. (pp. 155–166) • Alexander the Great and His Successors, 334–30 B.C.E. (pp. 166–172) • The Parthians and the Sasanians, Heirs to the Persians, 247 B.C.E.–651 C.E. (pp. 172–176) • Egeria (pp. 178–180) • The Roman Republic, 509–27 B.C.E. (pp. 181–194) • The Loss of the Western Provinces and the Rise of the Eastern Empire, 284–476 (pp. 200–208) • The Rise of Hinduism, 300–900 (pp. 216–219)

II. Empires and states developed new techniques of imperial administration based, in part, on the success of earlier political forms. **[ENV-2, 8 | SB-1, 2, 4, 6, 8, 9, 10 | ECON-3]**	• Life and Society in the Mauryan Dynasty, ca. 300 B.C.E. (pp. 75–78) • Mauryan Control Outside the Capital (pp. 78–80) • South Asia's External Trade (pp. 84–85) • Qin Rulers Unify China, 359–207 B.C.E. (pp. 100–107) • The Han Empire, 206 B.C.E.–220 C.E. (pp. 107–110) • Extending Han Rule to Mongolia, Vietnam, and Korea (pp. 110–112) • The Military Success of the Persian Empire, 550–486 B.C.E. (pp. 149–151) • Darius's Administration (pp. 154–155) • The Rise of the Greek City-State, 800–500 B.C.E. (pp. 160–161) • The Conquest of the Mediterranean World, 272–146 B.C.E. (pp. 182–185) • Travel and Knowledge of the Outside World (pp. 192–194)
III. Unique social and economic dimensions developed in imperial societies in Afro-Eurasia and the Americas. **[CUL-8 | SB-1, 2, 4, 5, 9, 10 | ECON-2, 3, 5, 6 | SOC-1, 2, 3, 4]**	• Life and Society in the Mauryan Dynasty, ca. 300 B.C.E. (pp. 75–78) • Teotihuacan, ca. 200 B.C.E.–600 C.E. (pp. 121–123) • Darius's Administration (pp. 154–155) • Visual Evidence in Primary Sources: The Parade of Nations at Darius's Palace in Persepolis (pp. 156–157) • Culture and Politics in Athens, 480–404 B.C.E. (pp. 163–164) • Athens as a Center for the Study of Philosophy (pp. 165–166) • The Conquest of the Mediterranean World, 272–146 B.C.E. (pp. 182–185) • Roman Society Under the Republic (pp. 185–186) • The Loss of the Western Provinces and the Rise of the Eastern Empire, 284–476 (pp. 200–208) • The Long Decline of the Tang Dynasty, 755–907 (on Chang'an; pp. 230–235) • Justinian and the Legacy of Rome, 476–565 (pp. 277–278) • Germanic-Speaking Europeans Before 500 (pp. 283–284) • The Merovingians, 481–751 (pp. 284–286)

	IV. The Roman, Han, Persian, Mauryan, and Gupta empires encountered political, cultural, and administrative difficulties that they could not manage, which eventually led to their decline, collapse, and transformation into successor empires or states. **[ENV-2, 4, 5 | SB-2, 3, 4, 6, 8 | SOC-4]**	• Mauryan Control Outside the Capital (pp. 78–80) • Ruling by Example: The Ceremonial State (pp. 80–81) • Conflict and Contact: The Han Dynasty and the Xiongnu Nomads, 201–60 B.C.E. (pp. 111–112) • The Loss of the Western Provinces and the Rise of the Eastern Empire, 284–476 (pp. 200–208)
Key Concept 2.3 Emergence of Interregional Networks of Communication and Exchange	With the organization of large-scale empires, the volume of long-distance trade increased dramatically. Much of this trade resulted from the demand for raw materials and luxury goods. Land and water routes linked many regions of the Eastern Hemisphere. The exchange of people, technology, religious and cultural beliefs, food crops, domesticated animals, and disease pathogens developed alongside the trade in goods across extensive networks of communication and exchange. In the Americas and Oceania localized networks developed.	Chapters 3, 6, 7, 8, 11
	I. Land and water routes became the basis for interregional trade, communication, and exchange networks in the Eastern Hemisphere. **[ENV-2, 3, 4 | SB-10 | ECON-12]**	• South Asia's External Trade (pp. 84–85) • The Phoenicians and the World's First Alphabet (on Mediterranean sea lanes) (pp. 158–160) • Ennin (on Silk Routes) (pp. 212–215) • Buddhist Kingdoms Along the Trade Routes (pp. 219–221) • Reconstructing the History of Sub-Saharan Africa Before 1000 (pp. 308–312)
	II. New technologies facilitated long-distance communication and exchange. **[ENV-2, 6 | CUL-6 | SB-10 | ECON-12]**	• Buddhist Kingdoms Along the Trade Routes (pp. 219–221) • The Geography and Languages of Sub-Saharan Africa (on camels; pp. 308–309) • The Spread of Bantu Languages (pp. 309–311)

	III. Alongside the trade in goods, the exchange of people, technology, religious and cultural beliefs, food crops, domesticated animals, and disease pathogens developed across extensive networks of communication and exchange. **[ENV-2, 3, 7 | CUL-1, 2, 6 | SB-4 | ECON-1, 8, 10, 12]**	• Religious Changes of the Late Empire (pp. 201–202) • Christianity in North Africa (pp. 203–205) • Buddhism, Hinduism, and Indian Rulers, 100–1000 (pp. 215–219) • Buddhism, Hinduism, and Southeast Asian Rulers, 300–1000 (p. 219–225) • Buddhism and the Revival of Empire in China, 100–1000 (pp. 225–235) • Buddhism and the Tang Blueprint for Rule in Korea and Japan, to 1000 (pp. 235–240)
Period 3: Regional and Interregional Interactions, c. 600 C.E. to c. 1450		Chapters 5, 8, 9, 10, 11, 12, 13, 14, 15
Key Concept 3.1 Expansion and Intensification of Communication and Exchange Networks	Although Afro-Eurasia and the Americas remained separate from one another, this era witnessed a deepening and widening of networks of human interaction within and across regions. The results were unprecedented concentrations of wealth and the intensification of cross-cultural exchanges. Innovations in transportation, state policies, and mercantile practices contributed to the expansion and development of commercial networks, which in turn served as conduits for cultural, technological, and biological diffusion within and between various societies. Pastoral or nomadic groups played a key role in creating and sustaining these networks. Expanding networks fostered greater interregional borrowing, while at the same time sustaining regional diversity. The prophet Muhammad promoted Islam, a new monotheistic religion, at the start of this period. It spread quickly through practices of trade, warfare, and diffusion characteristic of this period.	Chapters 5, 8, 9, 10, 11, 12, 13, 14, 15

I. Improved transportation technologies and commercial practices led to an increased volume of trade, and expanded the geographical range of existing and newly active trade networks. **[ENV-3, 6, 8 | CUL-6 | SB-1, 2, 4, 5, 6, 9 | ECON-2, 5, 10, 11, 12]**	• The Origins of Islam and the First Caliphs, 610–750 (pp. 246–255) • The Unified Abbasid Caliphate, 750–945 (pp. 255–263) • Byzantium, the Eastern Roman Empire, 476–1071 (pp. 277–282) • Trans-Saharan Trade Networks (pp. 318–319) • The Delhi Sultanate and the Hindu Kingdoms of Southern India (pp. 330–335) • China Divided: The Jin and the Southern Song, 1127–1234 (pp. 343–344) • The Currency of the Song Dynasty (p. 346) • Vietnam, Korea, Japan, and the World Beyond (pp. 360–365) • Population Growth and Urbanization (pp. 372–373) • The Import of Learning and Technology from the Islamic World, 1150–1250 (pp. 380–381) • Continuing Expansion of Trade Outside Europe (pp. 393–394) • From Nomads to World Conquerors, 1200–1227 (pp. 402–407) • The Chinese Voyages to South and Southeast Asia and Africa, 1405–1433 (pp. 427–430) • The Mexica Settlement of Tenochtitlan (pp. 438–439) • The Inca Expansion (pp. 443–445)
II. The movement of peoples caused environmental and linguistic effects. **[ENV-3, 5, 6 | CUL-6 | SB-4]**	• The Polynesian Voyages of Exploration, 1000 B.C.E.–1350 C.E. (pp. 134–141) • Viking Raids on Great Britain (pp. 289–291) • The Geography and Languages of Sub-Saharan Africa (pp. 308–309) • The Spread of Bantu Languages (pp. 309–311) • East Africa, India, and the Trade Networks of the Indian Ocean (pp. 327–335)

III. Cross-cultural exchanges were fostered by the intensification of existing, or the creation of new, networks of trade and communication. **[CUL-1, 2, 3, 4, 6, 7, 8, 9 | SB-4, 9, 10 | ECON-10, 12 | SOC-3, 5, 8]**	• Buddhism and the Revival of Empire in China, 100–1000 (pp. 225–235) • Buddhism and the Tang Blueprint for Rule in Korea and Japan, to 1000 (pp. 235–240) • The Origins of Islam and the First Caliphs, 610–750 (pp. 246–255) • The Unified Abbasid Caliphate, 750–945 (pp. 255–263) • Byzantium, the Eastern Roman Empire, 476–1071 (pp. 277–282) • The Germanic-Speaking Peoples of Western Europe, 481–1000 (pp. 282–288) • Trans-Saharan Trade Networks (pp. 318–319) • Ibn Battuta (pp. 306–308) • Reconstructing the History of Sub-Saharan Africa Before 1000 (pp. 308–312) • The Kingdom of Mali and Its Precursors in Sub-Saharan Africa (pp. 312–322) • Islamic North Africa and the Mamluk Empire (pp. 322–326) • East Africa, India, and the Trade Networks of the Indian Ocean (pp. 327–335) • The Collapse of the Northern Song, 1126–1127 (pp. 341–343) • Book Publishing and the Education Boom (pp. 353–358) • Korea Under the Koryo Dynasty (pp. 364–365) • Religious Life During the Song (pp. 358–360) • Continuing Expansion of Trade Outside Europe (pp. 393–394) • The Hundred Years' War and Monarchy in England and France (pp. 396–397) • The Rise of the Ottomans, 1300–1400 (pp. 420–421) • Intellectual and Geographic Exploration in Europe, 1300–1500 (pp. 447–452)

	IV. There was continued diffusion of crops and pathogens, including epidemic diseases like the bubonic plague, throughout the Eastern Hemisphere along the trade routes. **[ENV-5, 7, 8 | ECON-10, 12]**	• The Emergence of Japan (pp. 238–240) • Byzantium, the Eastern Roman Empire, 476–1071 (pp. 277–282) • The Outbreak of Plague in Damascus, 1348 (p. 326) • Changes in Agriculture and the Rise of the South (pp. 345–346) • Map 13.2 Trade Routes and Movement of the Plague (p. 394)
Key Concept 3.2 Continuity and Innovation of State Forms and Their Interactions	State formation in this era demonstrated remarkable continuity, innovation, and diversity in various regions. In Afro-Eurasia, some states attempted, with differing degrees of success, to preserve or revive imperial structures, while smaller, less centralized states continued to develop. The expansion of Islam introduced a new concept — the Caliphate — to Afro-Eurasian statecraft. Pastoral peoples in Eurasia built powerful and distinctive empires that integrated people and institutions from both the pastoral and agrarian worlds. In the Americas, powerful states developed in both Mesoamerica and the Andean region.	Chapters 8, 9, 10, 12, 13, 14
	I. Empires collapsed and were reconstituted; in some regions new state forms emerged. **[CUL-2, 4, 5 | SB-1, 2, 3, 4, 5, 6, 9, 10 | ECON-3, 12 | SOC-1, 4]**	• Buddhism and the Revival of Empire in China, 100–1000 (pp. 225–235) • The Emergence of Japan (pp. 238–240) • The Origins of Islam and the First Caliphs, 610–750 (pp. 246–255) • The Unified Abbasid Caliphate, 750–945 (pp. 255–263) • Context and Connections: The Legacy of the Abbasid Empire (pp. 271–272) • Byzantium, the Eastern Roman Empire, 476–1071 (pp. 277–282) • The Delhi Sultanate and the Hindu Kingdoms of Southern India (pp. 330–335) • The Five Dynasties Period and the Song Dynasty, 907–1276 (pp. 340–344) • Land Use and Social Change, 1000–1350 (p. 376) • From Nomads to World Conquerors, 1200–1227 (pp. 402–407) • The United Mongol Empire After Chinggis, 1229–1260 (pp. 407–415) • The Mexica Settlement of Tenochtitlan (pp. 438–439)

	II. Interregional contacts and conflicts between states and empires encouraged significant technological and cultural transfers, including transfers between Tang China and the Abbasids, transfers across the Mongol empires, transfers during the Crusades, and transfers during Chinese maritime activity led by MingAdmiral Zheng He. **[CUL-6 | SB-4, 6, 8, 10 | ECON-10]**	• Baghdad, City of Learning (pp. 256–258) • Religious Life During the Song (Neo-Confucianism; pp. 358–359) • The Postal Relay System (pp. 408–414)
Key Concept 3.3 Increased Economic Productive Capacity and Its Consequences	Changes in trade networks resulted from and stimulated increasing productive capacity, with important implications for social and gender structures and environmental processes. Productivity rose in both agriculture and industry. Rising productivity supported population growth and urbanization but also strained environmental resources and at times caused dramatic demographic swings. Shifts in production and the increased volume of trade also stimulated new labor practices, including the adaptation of existing patterns of free and coerced labor. Social and gender structures evolved in response to these changes.	Chapters 8, 9, 10, 11, 12, 13, 14, 15
	I. Innovations stimulated agricultural and industrial production in many regions. **[ENV-8, 9 | ECON-1, 3, 5, 10, 12]**	• The East African Coast (pp. 327–330) • Changes in Agriculture and the Rise of the South (pp. 345–346) • Iron and Steel (pp. 346–347) • Agricultural Innovation (pp. 370–372) • Population Growth and Urbanization (pp. 372–373)
	II. The fate of cities varied greatly, with periods of significant decline, and with periods of increased urbanization buoyed by rising productivity and expanding trade networks. **[ENV-4, 5, 7 | SB-4, 5, 9 | ECON-2, 3, 5, 12]**	• The Impact of the Plague and the Arab Conquests, 541–767 (pp. 279–281) • The Kingdom of Ghana, ca. 700–1000 (p. 313) • Jenne-jeno: A Different Path to Complex Society (pp. 313–315) • Cairo: Baghdad's Successor as the Cultural Capital of the Islamic World (pp. 325–326) • The Outbreak of Plague in Damascus, 1348 (p. 326) • Population Growth and Urbanization (pp. 372–373)

III. Despite significant continuities in social structures and in methods of production, there were also some important changes in labor management and in the effect of religious conversion on gender relations and family life. **[CUL-4, 5 | SB-2, 4, 6, 7, 10 | ECON-3, 5, 6 | SOC-1, 2, 4, 5, 8]**	• Buddhism and Regional Kingdoms in Korea (pp. 236–238) • The Life and Teachings of Muhammad, ca. 570–632 (pp. 246–249) • The Impact of the Plague and the Arab Conquests, 541–767 (pp. 279–281) • Charlemagne and the Carolingians, 751–ca. 1000 (pp. 286–288) • The Peoples Living in Russia (pp. 299–302) • Society and Family Life (pp. 311–312) • Trans-Saharan Trade Networks (pp. 318–319) • Society in Mali (pp. 319–322) • The Mamluk Empire, 1250–1517 (pp. 323–325) • Footbinding (p. 349) • The Changing Lives of Women in China's Commercial Revolution (pp. 349–353) • Day-to-Day Religious Life (pp. 359–360) • Agricultural Innovation (pp. 370–372) • Population Growth and Urbanization (pp. 372–373) • Land Use and Social Change (p. 376) • Mongol Society (pp. 403–404) • The Conquests of Khubilai Khan and Their Limits (pp. 424–426) • The First Ming Emperors, 1368–1405 (p. 426) • Nahua Society (pp. 440–441) • Inca Religion and Andean Society (pp. 442–443) • Inca Rule of Subject Populations (pp. 445–447) • The Portuguese Slave Trade After 1444 (pp. 451–452)

Period 4: Global Interactions, c. 1450 to c. 1750		Chapters 15, 16, 17, 18, 19, 20, 21
Key Concept 4.1 Globalizing Networks of Communication and Exchange	The interconnection of the Eastern and Western hemispheres made possible by transoceanic voyaging marked a key transformation of this period. Technological innovations helped to make transoceanic connections possible. Changing patterns of long-distance trade included the global circulation of some commodities and the formation of new regional markets and financial centers. Increased interregional and global trade networks facilitated the spread of religion and other elements of culture as well as the migration of large numbers of people. Germs carried to the Americas ravaged the indigenous peoples, while the global exchange of crops and animals altered agriculture, diets, and populations around the planet.	Chapters 15, 16, 17, 18, 19, 20
	I. In the context of the new global circulation of goods, there was an intensification of all existing regional patterns of trade that brought prosperity and economic disruption to the merchants and governments in the trading regions of the Indian Ocean, Mediterranean, Sahara, and overland Eurasia. **[SB-9 | ECON-3, 12, 13]**	• The Portuguese Slave Trade After 1444 (pp. 451–452) • Maritime Trade Connections: Europe, the Indian Ocean, and Africa, 1500–1660 (pp. 471–480) • African History and Afro-Eurasian Connections, 1550–1700 (pp. 560–565) • Africa and the Americas: The Plantation Complex (pp. 565–576) • Economic and Military Competition in the Atlantic Ocean, 1650–1763 (pp. 576–579)
	II. European technological developments in cartography and navigation built on previous knowledge developed in the classical, Islamic, and Asian worlds, and included the production of new tools, innovations in ship designs, and an improved understanding of global wind and currents patterns — all of which made transoceanic travel and trade possible. **[ENV-3, 6 | CUL-6 | ECON-10, 12]**	• The Portuguese Slave Trade After 1444 (pp. 451–452) • Ricci in China: Catholicism Meets Neo-Confucianism, 1582–1610 (pp. 491–493)

III. Remarkable new transoceanic maritime reconnaissance occurred in this period. **[ENV-3, 6 | CUL-6 | SB-6, 9 | ECON-3, 12, 13]**	• Maritime Trade Connections: Europe, the Indian Ocean, and Africa, 1500–1660 (pp. 471–480) • The Portuguese Slave Trade After 1444 (pp. 451–452) • The Iberian Conquest of Mexico, Peru, and Brazil, 1492–1580 (pp. 452–464)
IV. The new global circulation of goods was facilitated by royal chartered European monopoly companies that took silver from Spanish colonies in the Americas to purchase Asian goods for the Atlantic markets. Regional markets continued to flourish in Afro-Eurasia by using established commercial practices and new transoceanic shipping services developed by European merchants. **[SB-3, 4, 9, 10 | ECON-3, 5, 6, 9, 11, 12, 13 | SOC-2, 7, 8]**	• The Dutch East India Company, 1600-1660 (pp. 474–477) • The Apogee and Decline of Ming China, 1500–1644 (pp. 482–483) • From Conquest to Control (pp. 533–537) • Brazil, the Dutch, New France, and England's Mainland Colonies (pp. 542–550) • Africa and the Americas: The Plantation Complex (pp. 565–576) • Economic and Military Competition in the Atlantic Ocean, 1650–1763 (pp. 576–579) • The Age of Three Emperors, 1661–1796 (p. 593) • Qing Trade and Foreign Relations (pp. 597–598) • Aurangzeb and the Decline of Mughal Authority, 1658–1757 (pp. 604–606)
V. The new connections between the Eastern and Western hemispheres resulted in the Columbian Exchange. **[ENV-5, 7, 8 | SB-3 | ECON-1, 5, 10, 12 | SOC-2, 7, 8]**	• The Portuguese Slave Trade After 1444 (pp. 451–452) • The Columbian Exchange (pp. 464–465) • Africa and the Atlantic Ocean, 1483–1660 (pp. 477–480) • The Apogee and Decline of Ming China, 1500–1644 (p. 482) • The Americas in Global Context: The Spanish Empire, 1600–1700 (pp. 532–542) • Brazil, the Dutch, New France, and England's Mainland Colonies (pp. 542–550) • Comparisons Across the Colonial Americas (pp. 550–555) • Olaudah Equiano (pp. 558–560) • Africa and the Americas: The Plantation Complex (pp. 565–576)

VI. The increase in interactions between newly connected hemispheres and intensification of connections within hemispheres expanded the spread and reform of existing religions and created syncretic belief systems and practices. **[CUL-2, 4, 5 | ECON-8]**	• Portugal's Entry into the Indian Ocean, 1498–1600 (pp. 471–474) • The Rise of Mughal India, 1526–1627 (pp. 480–481) • Eurasian Intellectual and Religious Encounters, 1500–1620 (pp. 486–494) • Ottoman Power and Safavid Challenge (pp. 501–511) • Religion and Politics in Western Europe (pp. 511–520) • Colonial Society: Gender and Race on the Margins of Empire (pp. 537–542) • Aurangzeb and the Decline of Mughal Authority, 1658–1757 (pp. 604–606)
VII. As merchants' profits increased and governments collected more taxes, funding for the visual and performing arts, even for popular audiences, increased along with an expansion of literacy. **[CUL-8, 9 | SB-1, 9]**	• Visual Evidence in Primary Sources: An Ivory Mask from Benin, West Africa (pp. 478–479) • Tradition and Innovation: Korea, Vietnam, Japan, and Siam, 1500–1650 (pp. 483–486) • Challenges to Catholicism, 1517–1620 (pp. 487–490) • Stability and Prosperity in Early Tokugawa Japan, 1630–1710 (pp. 612–613)

Key Concept 4.2 New Forms of Social Organization and Modes of Production	Although the world's productive systems continued to be heavily centered on agricultural production throughout this period, major changes occurred in agricultural labor, the systems and locations of manufacturing, gender and social structures, and environmental processes. Adapting to the Little Ice Age, farmers increased agricultural productivity by introducing new crops and using new methods in crop-and-field rotation. Economic growth also depended on new forms of manufacturing and new commercial patterns, especially in long-distance trade. Political and economic centers within regions shifted, and merchants' social status tended to rise in various states. Demographic growth — even in areas such as the Americas, where disease had ravaged the population — was restored by the 18th century and surged in many regions, especially with the introduction of American food crops throughout the Eastern Hemisphere. The Columbian Exchange led to new ways of humans interacting with their environments. New forms of coerced and semicoerced labor emerged in Europe, Africa, and the Americas, and affected ethnic and racial classifications and gender roles.	Chapters 15, 16, 17, 18, 19, 20
	I. Beginning in the 14th century, there was a decrease in mean temperatures, often referred to as the Little Ice Age, around the world that lasted until the 19th century, contributing to changes in agricultural practices and the contraction of settlement in parts of the Northern Hemisphere. **[ENV-4, 8 | ECON-1]**	• Context & Connections: Climate Change and the Seventeenth Century (pp. 528–529)

II. Traditional peasant agriculture increased and changed, plantations expanded, and demand for labor increased. These changes both fed and responded to growing global demand for raw materials and finished products. **[SB-9 | ECON-1, 3, 5, 6, 10 | SOC-2, 7, 8]**	• The Portuguese Slave Trade After 1444 (pp. 451–452) • The Structure of Empire and the Encomienda System (pp. 461–464) • Africa and the Atlantic Ocean, 1483–1660 (pp. 477–480) • From Conquest to Control (pp. 533–537) • The Portuguese and Brazil (pp. 542–544) • Mainland English Colonies in North America (pp. 546–550) • Comparisons Across the Colonial Americas (pp. 550–555) • Africa and the Americas: The Plantation Complex (pp. 565–576) • The World of Women in Qing China (pp. 593–595) • Russian Imperial Expansion, 1725–1800 (pp. 599–601) • Aurangzeb and the Decline of Mughal Authority, 1658–1757 (pp. 604–606)
III. As social and political elites changed, they also restructured ethnic, racial, and gender hierarchies. **[SB-4 | ECON-3, 6 | SOC-1, 2, 4, 7]**	• Tradition and Innovation: Korea, Vietnam, Japan, and Siam, 1500–1650 (pp. 483–486) • Religious Conflict and Political Control in France and England, 1500–1715 (pp. 517–520) • From Conquest to Control (pp. 533–537) • The Power of the Qing Dynasty, 1644–1796 (pp. 591–598)

Key Concept 4.3 State Consolidation and Imperial Expansion	Empires expanded and conquered peoples around the world, but they often had difficulties incorporating culturally, ethnically, and religiously diverse subjects, and administrating widely dispersed territories. Agents of the European powers moved into existing trade networks around the world. In Africa and the greater Indian Ocean, nascent European empires consisted mainly of interconnected trading posts and enclaves. In the Americas, European empires moved more quickly to settlement and territorial control, responding to local demographic and commercial conditions. Moreover, the creation of European empires in the Americas quickly fostered a new Atlantic exchange network that included the transatlantic slave trade and transpacific exchange network. Around the world, empires and states of varying sizes pursued strategies of centralization, including more efficient taxation systems that placed strains on peasant producers, sometimes prompting local rebellions. Rulers used public displays of art and architecture to legitimize state power. African states shared certain characteristics with larger Eurasian empires. Changes in African and global trading patterns strengthened some West and Central African states — especially on the coast; this led to the rise of new states and contributed to the decline of states on both the coast and in the interior.	Chapters 15, 16, 17, 18, 19, 20, 21

	I. Rulers used a variety of methods to legitimize and consolidate their power. **[CUL-4, 8 | SB-1, 2, 4, 5, 7, 9, 10 | ECON-3, 8 | SOC-3, 5, 7]**	• The Aztec Empire of Mexico, 1325–1519 (pp. 436–441) • Empires of Southern and Eastern Asia, 1500–1660 (pp. 480–486) • Islam, Sikhism, and Akbar's "Divine Faith," 1500–1605 (pp. 490–491) • Evliya Çelebi (pp. 498–501) • Ottoman Power and Safavid Challenge (pp. 501–511) • Religious Conflict and Political Control in France and England, 1500–1715 (Versailles) (pp. 517–520) • Between East and West: Russians, Jews, and Armenians (pp. 520–525) • Colonial Society: Gender and Race on the Margins of Empire (pp. 537–542) • African History and Afro-Eurasian Connections, 1550–1700 (pp. 560–565) • The Power of the Qing Dynasty, 1644–1796 (pp. 591–598) • Enlightenment and Reform (pp. 644–645)
	II. Imperial expansion relied on the increased use of gunpowder, cannons, and armed trade to establish large empires in both hemispheres. **[ENV-6] [SB-1, 2, 3, 4, 9 | ECON-3, 12]**	• The Iberian Conquest of Mexico, Peru, and Brazil, 1492–1580 (pp. 452–464) • Maritime Trade Connections: Europe, the Indian Ocean, and Africa, 1500–1660 (pp. 471–480) • Empires of Southern and Eastern Asia, 1500–1660 (pp. 480–486) • The Ottoman Empire, 1500–1650 (pp. 502–505) • The Rise of the Russian Empire, 1500–1725 (pp. 520–524) • The Shifting Balance of Power in Western Eurasia by 1750 (pp. 525–527) • The Power of the Qing Dynasty, 1644–1796 (pp. 591–598)

	III. Competition over trade routes, state rivalries, and local resistance all provided significant challenges to state consolidation and expansion. **[SB-2, 3, 4, 7, 8, 9, 10 | ECON-3]**	• Evliya Çelebi (pp. 498–501) • Ottoman Power and Safavid Challenge (pp. 501–511) • The Habsburgs: Imperial Ambitions and Political Realities, 1519–1648 (pp. 512–517) • African History and Afro-Eurasian Connections, 1550–1700 (pp. 560–565) • African Culture and Resistance to Slavery (pp. 569–572) • Qing Trade and Foreign Relations (pp. 597–598)
Period 5: Industrialization and Global Integration, c. 1750 to c. 1900		Chapters 18, 19, 20, 21, 22, 23, 24, 25, 26
Key Concept 5.1 Industrialization and Global Capitalism	Industrialization fundamentally altered the production of goods around the world. It not only changed how goods were produced and consumed, as well as what was considered a "good," but it also had far-reaching effects on the global economy, social relations, and culture. Although it is common to speak of an "Industrial Revolution," the process of industrialization was a gradual one that unfolded over the course of the 18th and 19th centuries, eventually becoming global.	Chapters 20, 21, 23, 24, 25, 26
	I. Industrialization fundamentally changed how goods were produced. **[ENV-9 | SB-5 | ECON-2, 4, 5, 9 | SOC-2, 3, 4]**	• The Industrial Revolution: Origins and Global Consequences, 1765–1870 (pp. 685–691) • Challenges to Reform in the Russian and Ottoman Empires, 1825–1881 (pp. 705–711) • Context and Connections: Global Repercussions of the Industrial Revolution (pp. 712–713) • The Rise of Modern Japan, 1830–1905 (pp. 726–733) • Sectionalism and Civil War in the United States (econ. expansion & industrialization) (pp. 750–755) • Political and Economic Motives (pp. 779–780)

II. New patterns of global trade and production developed and further integrated the global economy as industrialists sought raw materials and new markets for the increasing amount and array of goods produced in their factories. **[ENV-9 | CUL-6 | SB-9 | ECON-3, 4, 12]**	• Foundations of British Rule, 1739–1818 (pp. 606–610) • The Industrial Revolution: Origins and Global Consequences, 1765–1870 (pp. 685–691) • Context and Connections: Global Repercussions of the Industrial Revolution (pp. 712–713) • Confederation in Canada (pp. 747–749) • Sectionalism and Civil War in the United States (cotton export) (pp. 750–755) • Western and Eastern Africa (pp. 784–788) • Southern Africa (pp. 788–790) • The New Imperialism in Southeast Asia, Austronesia, and the Pacific (pp. 793–797) • A Case Study of the New Imperialism: Rubber (pp. 797–800)
III. To facilitate investments at all levels of industrial production, financiers developed and expanded various financial institutions. **[CUL-3 | ECON-3, 4, 9, 11, 13]**	• "Enlightened" Ideas: Politics, Economics, and Society (pp. 640–643) • Origins of the Industrial Revolution, 1765–1850 (pp. 686–688) • Victorian Britain, 1815–1867 (pp. 693–695) • Political and Economic Motives (pp. 779–780)
IV. There were major developments in transportation and communication, including railroads, steamships, telegraphs, and canals. **[ENV-6 | ECON-12]**	• Global Dimensions of the Industrial Revolution, 1820–1880 (pp. 688–691) • Emancipation and Reaction in Russia (pp. 705, 708–710) • The Origins of Indian Nationalism, 1885–1906 (pp. 738–741) • Sectionalism and Civil War in the United States (railroads & canals, pp. 750–755) • Context and Connections: The Americas: Hemispheric and Global Connections (pp. 774–775) • The New Imperialism (first 4 paragraphs, pp. 778–779)

	V. The development and spread of global capitalism led to a variety of responses. **[CUL-3 | SB-1, 2, 4, 9 | ECON-3, 7, 9 | SOC-3]**	• Mikhail Bakunin (pp. 682–685) • The Industrial Revolution: Origins and Global Consequences, 1765–1870 (pp. 685–691) • Nineteenth-Century Ideologies: Liberalism, Socialism, Romanticism, Anarchism, and Nationalism (pp. 691–693) • Victorian Britain, 1815–1867 (pp. 693–695) • New Paradigms of the Industrial Age: Marx and Darwin (pp. 702–705) • Challenges to Reform in the Russian and Ottoman Empires, 1825–1881 (pp. 705–711) • "Self-Strengthening" and the Boxer Rebellion, 1842–1901 (pp. 720–726) • The Meiji Restoration, 1867–1890 (pp. 728–731) • The Gilded Age (pp. 755–757)
	VI. The ways in which people organized themselves into societies also underwent significant transformations in industrialized states due to the fundamental restructuring of the global economy. **[ENV-5, 9 | SB-4, 9 | ECON-5 | SOC-1, 2, 3]**	• Reform and Revolution in Nineteenth-Century Europe, 1815–1880 (pp. 691–701)
Key Concept 5.2 Imperialism and Nation-State Formation	As states industrialized during this period, they also expanded their existing overseas colonies and established new types of colonies and transoceanic empires. Regional warfare and diplomacy both resulted in and were affected by this process of modern empire building. The process was led mostly by Europe, although not all states were affected equally, which led to an increase of European influence around the world. The United States and Japan also participated in this process. The growth of new empires challenged the power of existing land-based empires of Eurasia. New ideas about nationalism, race, gender, class, and culture also developed that facilitated the spread of transoceanic empires, as well as justified anti-imperial resistance and the formation of new national identities.	Chapters 20, 23, 24, 25, 26

	I. Industrializing powers established transoceanic empires. **[ENV-9 | SB-1, 2, 3, 9, 10 | ECON-3 | SOC-7]**	• Joseph Banks (pp. 618–620) • Oceania and Australia, 1770–1820 (pp. 635–639) • Qing China Confronts the Industrial World, 1800–1850 (pp. 717–718) • British India, 1818–1905 (pp. 733–741) • King Khama III (pp. 776–778) • The New Imperialism (pp. 778–784) • Africa and the New Imperialism (pp. 784–793) • The New Imperialism in Southeast Asia, Austronesia, and the Pacific (pp. 793–797) • Insular Southeast Asia, Austronesia, and the Pacific (pp. 795–797) • Case Studies in Imperialism (pp. 797–801)
	II. Imperialism influenced state formation and contraction around the world. **[CUL-3 | SB-1, 2, 3, 4, 6, 10 | ECON-4 | SOC-7]**	• The Russian Empire, 1725–1800 (pp. 599–603) • The Rise of Modern Japan, 1830–1905 (pp. 726–733) • The Indian Revolt of1857 and Its Aftermath (p. 735) • Conservatives, Liberals, and the Struggle for Stability in Mexico (pp. 758–761) • The Fates of Indigenous Societies (pp. 765–772) • Southern Africa (pp. 788–790) • African Resistance to Conquest (pp. 791–793)
	III. New racial ideologies, especially social Darwinism, facilitated and justified imperialism. **[CUL-3, 4 | SB-4 | ECON-8 | SOC-6]**	• Charles Darwin, Evolution, and Social Darwinism (pp. 704–705) • Japanese Imperialism, 1890–1910 (pp. 731–733) • The Indian Revolt of 1857 and Its Aftermath (p. 735) • Ideology and Personal Ambition (pp. 780–784) • Southern Africa (pp. 788–790)

Key Concept 5.3 Nationalism, Revolution, and Reform	The 18th century marked the beginning of an intense period of revolution and rebellion against existing governments and the establishment of new nation-states around the world. Enlightenment thought and the resistance of colonized peoples to imperial centers shaped this revolutionary activity. These rebellions sometimes resulted in the formation of new states and stimulated the development of new ideologies. These new ideas in turn further stimulated the revolutionary and antiimperial tendencies of this period.	Chapters 18, 19, 21, 22, 23, 24, 25, 26
	I. The rise and diffusion of Enlightenment thought that questioned established traditions in all areas of life often preceded revolutions and rebellions against existing governments. **[CUL-2, 3, 4, 7 | SB-4, 7 | ECON-7 | SOC-1, 2, 3, 6, 7]**	• The Portuguese and Brazil (background on maroon communities) (pp. 542–544) • African Culture and Resistance to Slavery (pp. 569–572) • Abolition of the British Slave Trade, 1772–1807 (pp. 582–585) • The European Enlightenment, 1700–1800 (pp. 640–645) • Rebellion and Independence in America, 1763–1797 (pp. 651–655) • The French Revolution, 1789–1815 (pp. 655–667) • The Latin American Wars of Independence, 1800–1824 (pp. 669–676) • Nineteenth-Century Ideologies: Liberalism, Socialism, Romanticism, Anarchism, and Nationalism (pp. 691–693) • Victorian Britain, 1815–1867 (pp. 693–695) • Germany: Nationalism and Unification, 1848–1871 (pp. 700–701) • Challenges to Reform in the Russian and Ottoman Empires, 1825–1881 (pp. 705–711) • From Empire to Republic in Brazil (pp. 763–765)

II. Beginning in the 18th century, peoples around the world developed a new sense of commonality based on language, religion, social customs, and territory. These newly imagined national communities linked this identity with the borders of the state, while governments used this idea to unite diverse populations. **[CUL-2, 3, 4, 7 | SB-4 | SOC-3, 7]**	• The Age of Napoleon, 1795–1815 (pp. 661–667) • Revolutionary Outcomes and Comparisons to 1830 (pp. 676–679) • Nineteenth-Century Ideologies: Liberalism, Socialism, Romanticism, Anarchism, and Nationalism (pp. 691–693) • The Unification of Italy, 1848–1870 (pp. 699–700) • Germany: Nationalism and Unification, 1848–1871 (pp. 700–701) • The Origins of Indian Nationalism, 1885–1906 (pp. 738–741) • Insular Southeast Asia, Austronesia, and the Pacific (pp. 795–797)
III. Increasing discontent with imperial rule propelled reformist and revolutionary movements. **[CUL-2, 4 | SB-1, 2, 4, 7, 9 |**	• Rebellion and Independence in America, 1763–1797 (pp. 651–655) • The French Revolution, 1789–1815 (pp. 655–667) • The Haitian Revolution, 1791–1804 (pp. 667–669) • The Latin American Wars of Independence, 1800–1824 (pp. 669–676) • The Taiping Rebellion, 1850–1864 (pp. 718–720) • "Self-Strengthening" and the Boxer Rebellion, 1842–1901 (pp. 720–726) • The Indian Revolt of 1857 and Its Aftermath (pp. 735–738) • The Fates of Indigenous Societies (pp. 765–768) • Southern Africa (pp. 788–790)
IV. The global spread of European political and social thought and the increasing number of rebellions stimulated new transnational ideologies and solidarities. **[CUL-3, 5 | SB-4, 8 | ECON-7 | SOC-1, 2, 3, 4]**	• "Enlightened" Ideas: Politics, Economics, and Society (pp. 640–643) • Louis XVI and the Early Revolution, 1789–1792 (pp. 655–660) • Nineteenth-Century Ideologies: Liberalism, Socialism, Romanticism, Anarchism, and Nationalism (pp. 691–693) • Karl Marx, Socialism, and Communism (pp. 702–704) • Gender and Women's Rights (pp. 772–773)

Key Concept 5.4 Global Migration	Migration patterns changed dramatically throughout this period, and the numbers of migrants increased significantly. These changes were closely connected to the development of transoceanic empires and a global capitalist economy. In some cases, people benefited economically from migration, while other people were seen simply as commodities to be transported. Migration produced dramatically different sending and receiving societies and presented challenges to governments in fostering national identities and regulating the flow of people.	Chapters 19, 20, 23, 24, 25, 26
	I. Migration in many cases was influenced by changes in demography in both industrialized and unindustrialized societies that presented challenges to existing patterns of living. **[ENV-3, 4, 5, 6, 7, 8 | SB-5 | ECON-2, 4, 12 | SOC-8]**	• Effects of the Atlantic Slave Trade on West Africa (pp. 572–576) • The Age of Three Emperors, 1661–1796 (pp. 593–595) • The Taiping Rebellion, 1850–1864 (pp. 718–720) • Context and Connections: Asia in the Modern World (pp. 742–743) • The Gilded Age (pp. 755–757) • Spanish-Speaking South America (pp. 762–763) • Immigration, Abolition, and Race (pp. 769–772)
	II. Migrants relocated for a variety of reasons. **[ENV-3, 5 | ECON-5, 6 | SOC-2, 8]**	• Effects of the Atlantic Slave Trade on West Africa (pp. 572–576) • Global Dimensions of the Industrial Revolution, 1820–1880 (pp. 688–691) • Spanish-Speaking South America (pp. 762–763) • Immigration, Abolition, and Race (pp. 769–772) • Mainland Southeast Asia (pp. 793–795)
	III. The large-scale nature of migration, especially in the 19th century, produced a variety of consequences and reactions to the increasingly diverse societies on the part of migrants and the existing populations. **[ENV-3, 4 | CUL-9 | SOC-1, 8]**	• Spanish-Speaking South America (pp. 762–763) • Immigration, Abolition, and Race (pp. 769–772) • Mainland Southeast Asia (pp. 793–795)

Period 6: Accelerating Global Change and Realignments, c. 1900 to the Present		Chapters 27, 28, 29, 30, 31, 32
Key Concept 6.1 Science and the Environment	Rapid advances in science altered the understanding of the universe and the natural world and led to the development of new technologies. These changes enabled unprecedented population growth, which altered how humans interacted with the environment and disrupted delicate ecological balances at local, regional, and global levels.	Chapters 27, 29, 30, 31, 32
	I. Researchers made rapid advances in science that spread throughout the world, assisted by the development of new technology. **[ENV-6, 8, 9 | CUL-6, 7 | ECON-1, 12]**	• From Leonid Brezhnev to Mikhail Gorbachev (computer technology) (pp. 935–937) • Japan and the "Asian Tigers" (pp. 954–956) • Health and the Environment (pp. 982–985)
	II. During a period of unprecedented global population expansion, humans fundamentally changed their relationship with the environment. **[ENV-3, 5, 9 | SB-4 | ECON-4]**	• Enduring Challenges in the Middle East (competition over oil & other resources) (pp. 949–954) • Map 31.2 Middle East Oil and the Arab-Israeli Conflict (p. 952) • Health and the Environment (pp. 982–985)
	III. Disease, scientific innovations, and conflict led to demographic shifts. **[ENV-7 | CUL-7 | SB-9, 10 | SOC-6]**	• The Postwar Settlements (influenza epidemic) (p. 817) • The Allies on the Offensive, 1942–1945 (casualties) (pp. 878–884) • The Sixties: The Rising Expectations of Surging Youth (birth control) (pp. 922–923) • Health and the Environment (pp. 982–985) • Population Movement and Demography (pp. 986–988)

Key Concept 6.2 Global Conflicts and Their Consequences	At the beginning of the 20th century, a European-dominated global political order existed, which also included the United States, Russia, and Japan. Over the course of the century, peoples and states around the world challenged this order in ways that sought to redistribute power within the existing order and to restructure empires, while those peoples and states in power attempted to maintain the status quo. Other peoples and states sought to overturn the political order itself. These challenges to, and the attempts to maintain, the political order manifested themselves in an unprecedented level of conflict with high human casualties. In the context of these conflicts, many regimes in both older and newer states struggled with maintaining political stability and were challenged by internal and external factors, including ethnic and religious conflicts, secessionist movements, territorial partitions, economic dependency, and the legacies of colonialism.	Chapters 27, 28, 29, 30, 31, 32
	I. Europe dominated the global political order at the beginning of the 20th century, but both land-based and transoceanic empires gave way to new states by the century's end. **[SB-2, 7, 8, 9, 10 | ECON-4]**	• World War I as Global "Total" War (pp. 809–817) • The Postwar Settlements (pp. 817–825) • Civilians and Total War in Asia and the Colonial World (pp. 887–889) • Spheres of Influence: Old Empires and New Superpowers (pp. 907–921)
	II. Emerging ideologies of anti-imperialism contributed to the dissolution of empires and the restructuring of states. **[CUL-3, 4, 9 | SB-1, 2, 4, 7, 9, 10 | ECON-7, 8, 9 | SOC-3, 4, 7]**	• Fascism, Communism, and Authoritarianism (pp. 846–854) • Anticolonial Nationalism in Asia, Africa, and the Caribbean (pp. 858–865) • Spheres of Influence: Old Empires and New Superpowers (pp. 907–921) • Context and Connections: Beyond the "Age of Extremes"? (legacy of communism) (pp. 963–964)
	III. Political changes were accompanied by major demographic and social consequences. **[SB-4, 7, 9, 10 | ECON-2 | SOC-8]**	• The Mandate System in Africa and the Middle East (pp. 822–825) • The Holocaust (pp. 889–893) • The Bandung Generation, 1955–1965 (pp. 916–919) • The Rwandan Genocide and Congolese Conflict (pp. 947–949)

IV. Military conflicts occurred on an unprecedented global scale. **[CUL-3, 8 | SB-1, 2, 3, 4, 8, 9, 10 | ECON-3, 4, 9 | SOC-7]**	• World War I as Global "Total" War (pp. 809–817) • The Great Depression, 1929–1939 (pp. 843–846) • The Road to War (pp. 865–869) • Total War and Civilian Life (pp. 885–893) • Origins of the Cold War, 1945–1949 (pp. 893–898) • Context and Connections: Total War in World History (pp. 898–899) • The Cold War and Revolution, 1949–1962 (pp. 903–907) • Spheres of Influence: Old Empires and New Superpowers (pp. 907–921)
V. Although conflict dominated much of the 20th century, many individuals and groups — including states — opposed this trend. Some individuals and groups, however, intensified the conflicts. **[CUL-3, 9 | SB-1, 2, 7, 8, 9, 10 | ECON-3 | SOC-3, 4]**	• Gandhi and the Indian National Congress (pp. 858–862) • Vietnam: The Cold War in Southeast Asia, 1956–1974 (pp. 919–921) • 1968: A Year of Revolution (pp. 923–926) • Death and Dictatorship in Latin America, 1967–1975 (p. 927) • *Détente* and Challenges to Bipolarity (p. 929) • Nelson Mandela (pp. 932–934) • Visual Evidence in Primary Sources: Tanks and Protests in Moscow and Beijing (pp. 940–941) • South African Liberation (pp. 945–947) • Afghanistan and Al-Qaeda (p. 951) • Deng Xiaoping's China and Its Imitators (pp. 956–958) • Global Security (pp. 978–982)

Key Concept 6.3 New Conceptualizations of Global Economy, Society, and Culture	The 20th century witnessed a great deal of warfare and the collapse of the global economy in the 1930s. In response to these challenges, the role of the state in the domestic economy fluctuated, and new institutions of global governance emerged and continued to develop throughout the century. Scientific breakthroughs, new technologies, increasing levels of integration, changing relationships between humans and the environment, and the frequency of political conflict all contributed to global developments in which people crafted new understandings of society, culture, and historical interpretations. Institutions of global governance both shaped and adapted to these social conditions.	Chapters 27, 28, 29, 30, 31, 32
	I. States responded in a variety of ways to the economic challenges of the 20th century. **[CUL-3 | SB-1, 2, 4, 9 | ECON-3, 4, 9]**	• Stalin and "Socialism in One Country" (pp. 831, 834) • The Great Depression in the Industrialized World (pp. 843–844) • Mussolini and the Rise of Fascism (pp. 847–848) • The People's Republic of China, 1949–1962 (pp. 903–905) • Death and Dictatorship in Latin America, 1967–1975 (p. 927) • The United States in the Post-Vietnam Era, 1975–1990 (p. 935) • Post-Soviet Struggles for Democracy and Prosperity (pp. 939–942) • Japan and the "Asian Tigers" (pp. 954–956) • Deng Xiaoping's China and Its Imitators (pp. 956–958) • Neoliberalism, Inequality, and Economic Globalization (pp. 959–963) • Emerging Economic Players (pp. 969–976)

II. States, communities, and individuals became increasingly interdependent, a process facilitated by the growth of institutions of global governance. **[ENV-3, 9 | CUL-3 | SB-2, 4, 9, 10 | ECON-3, 4, 9, 11, 13 | SOC-4]**	• The Paris Peace Conference (pp. 817–821) • The New United Nations and Postwar Challenges, 1945–1947 (pp. 893–895) • The United States, the Soviet Union, and the Origins of a Bipolar World (pp. 895–898) • Context and Connections: Idealism Amid Cold War Constraints (pp. 930–931) • The European Union (pp. 958–959) • Neoliberalism, Inequality, and Economic Globalization (pp. 959–963) • Emerging Economic Players (pp. 969–976) • Women's Leadership and Gender Issues (pp. 998–990)
III. People conceptualized society and culture in new ways; rights-based discourses challenged old assumptions about race, class, gender, and religion. In much of the world, access to education, as well as participation in new political and professional roles, became more inclusive in terms of race, class, and gender. **[CUL-2, 3, 4, 5, 9 | SB-4 | ECON-4 | SOC-1, 3, 5, 6]**	• Emma Goldman on Women's Rights (pp. 834–836) • The Rise of Modern Turkey (pp. 856–857) • A Time of Upheaval, 1966–1974 (pp. 921–929) • South African Liberation (pp. 945–947) • Women's Leadership and Gender Issues (pp. 998–990)
IV. Popular and consumer culture became more global. **[CUL-9 | ECON-4]**	• Global Art and Culture (pp. 993–996)

Preparing for the AP® Exam

Advanced Placement is a challenging yet stimulating experience. Whether you are taking an AP course at your school or are working on AP independently, the stage is set for a great intellectual journey. As the school year progresses and you burrow deeper and deeper into the coursework, you can see the broad concepts, events, conflicts, resolutions, and personalities that have shaped the history of our complex world. Examining the cultural, political, and economic developments that have brought great change while acknowledging the continuities that remain throughout world history is a thrilling task. Fleshing out those forces of change and continuity in world history is exciting. More exciting still is recognizing references to those forces in the media and how history has shaped current world events.

But as spring approaches and the College Board examination begins to loom on the horizon, Advanced Placement can seem quite intimidating given the enormous scope and extent of the information you need to know. If you are intimidated by the College Board examination, you are certainly not alone.

The best way to approach an AP examination is to master it, not let it master you. If you manage your time effectively, you will eliminate one major obstacle—learning a considerable amount of factual material along with the analytical skills needed to be a true world historian. In addition, if you can think of these tests as a way to show off how your mind works, you have a leg up: attitude *does* help. If you are not one of those students, there is still a lot you can do to sideline your anxiety. Focused review and practice time will help you master the examination so that you can walk in with confidence and get a 5.

Before the Exam

By February, long before the exam, you need to make sure that you are registered to take the test. Many schools take care of the paperwork and handle the fees for their AP students, but check with your teacher or the AP coordinator to make sure that you are on the registration list. (This is especially important if you have a documented disability and need test accommodations.) If you are studying AP independently, call AP Services at the College Board for the name of the local AP coordinator, who will help you through the registration process.

The evening before the exam is not a great time for partying. Nor is it a great time for cramming. If you like, look over class notes or drift through your textbook, but concentrate on the broad outlines, not the small details, of the course. You might also want to skim through this book and read the AP tips. Then relax. Get your things together for the next day. Sharpen a fistful of no. 2 pencils with good erasers for the multiple-choice section of the test and set out several black or dark-blue ballpoint pens for the free-response questions. You should bring a watch in order to pace yourself since you will not be allowed to use the clock or timer functions on your smart phone. Get a piece of fruit or a snack bar and a bottle of water for the break. Depending on your testing site, you may need your Social Security number, photo identification, and an admission ticket. After you have set aside all of those items, put your mind at ease, go to bed, and get a good night's sleep. An extra hour of sleep is more valuable than an extra hour of study.

On the day of the examination, make certain to eat breakfast—fuel for the brain. Studies show that students who eat a hot breakfast before testing get higher grades. You will be given a ten-minute break between Section I and Section II; the World History exam lasts for over three hours, so be prepared for a long morning. You do not want to be distracted by a growling stomach or hunger pangs. Be sure to wear comfortable clothes, taking along a sweater in case the heating or air-conditioning is erratic. When you get to the testing location, make certain to comply with all security procedures. Cell phones are not allowed, so leave yours at home or in your locker if at all possible. Be careful not to drink a lot of liquids, necessitating trips to the bathroom, which take up valuable test time.

Remember, preparation is key! Best wishes on your journey to success—go out and get that 5.

Taking the AP® World History Exam

The AP World History exam consists of four parts in two sections. Section I includes Parts A and B. Section I Part A consists of 55 multiple-choice questions that you will have 55 minutes to answer; all questions will be organized into sets of two to five questions that follow an item of stimulus material (a primary or secondary source). Section I Part B consists of four short-answer questions that you will answer in 50 minutes. Section II includes its own Parts A and B. Section II Part A is the document-based question (DBQ) assessing your ability to apply your understanding of the documents while using historical thinking skills. You will be given 55 minutes to read the documents and answer the question. Section II Part B consists of two long essay questions that both focus on the same historical thinking skill as it applies to two time periods; you will choose to respond to one of these in the allotted 35 minutes. Both Parts A and B of Section II require students to develop a thesis supported by relevant evidence and strengthened with analysis and synthesis. Your proctor will monitor the time, but you need to keep an eye on your watch and pace yourself so you can do your best on all parts of the exam. Remember that watch alarms and smart phones are not allowed.

Here is a chart to help you visualize the breakdown of the exam:

Section	**Multiple-Choice Questions**	**Short-Answer Questions**	**Document-Based Question (Essay)**	**Long Essay Question (Essay)**
Weight	40% of exam	20% of exam	25% of exam	15% of exam
Number of Questions	55	4	1	Long Essay Question: choose one of the two question options
Time Allowed	55 minutes	50 minutes	90 minutes for reading and writing	
Suggested Pace	~1 minute per question	~12 minutes per question	15 minutes for reading and planning and 40 minutes to write	35 minutes to plan and write

The Themes and Historical Thinking Skills

In order to be successful on the exam, the AP World History course requires you to use all of the historical thinking skills that you have worked all year in class to develop. These skills are essential for any historian, but they are particularly critical in world history because of the large amount of content in the course. The themes and historical thinking skills were created to provide a framework upon which you can hang all of the information you have learned throughout the year. Additionally, the College Board has developed thematic learning objectives that aid students in identifying broad historical trends and offer them the opportunity to develop historical thinking skills in the process of traversing through the themes. All questions on the AP World History Exam will require students to apply one or more historical thinking skills to at least one of the thematic learning objectives, so it is a good idea to familiarize yourself with both.

A practical exercise that should become a habit is to ask yourself, "What theme does this piece of historical information fall under?" "What historical thinking skill am I using right now to process this information and make meaning out of it?"

This will help you to see the larger historical trends and global connections that twine through our past and present and into the future.

Below are the themes and historical thinking skills for the AP World History course. Please examine them carefully and use them throughout this review book as an essential reference tool and guideline. A complete list of the Thematic Learning Objectives and Overarching Questions can be found following the overview of the types of questions on the AP World History Exam.

Themes

1. Interaction Between Humans and the Environment (ENV)
   - Demography and disease
   - Migration
   - Patterns of settlement
   - Technology
   - Use of natural resources
2. Development and Interaction of Cultures (CUL)
   - Religions
   - Belief systems, philosophies, and ideologies
   - Science and technology
   - The arts and architecture
3. State Building, Expansion, and Conflict (SB)
   - Political structures and forms of governance
   - Empires
   - Nations and nationalism
   - Revolts and revolutions
   - Regional, transregional, and global structures and organizations
   - Diplomacy
4. Creation, Expansion, and Interaction of Economic Systems (ECON)
   - Agricultural and pastoral production
   - Trade and commerce
   - Labor systems
   - Industrialization
   - Capitalism and socialism
5. Development and Transformation of Social Structures (SOC)
   - Gender roles and relations
   - Family and kinship
   - Racial and ethnic constructions
   - Social and economic classes

These themes are constant topics throughout the course, and you should be working with them from the beginning of the year. Throughout the course keep asking yourself where you see elements of both continuity and change—in particular societies, across regions, and throughout time—as they relate to each of these themes. It is also a good idea to begin using the themes as a way to make comparisons between societies over the course of human history.

Historical Thinking Skills

One of the broader goals of AP World History is to train you to think like an historian. That raises the question, "How do historians think?" The answer is found in the historical thinking skills. As a student in any rigorous history course, you should be able to do the following skill types:

Skill Type I: Analyzing Historical Sources and Evidence

- Skill 1—Analyzing Evidence: Content and Sourcing: Make conclusions about the past by using a variety of diverse sources.
- Skill 2—Interpretation: Analyze the perspectives and points of view involved in recording and describing history.

Skill Type II: Making Historical Connections

- Skill 3—Comparison: View the similarities and differences among societies or among developments within one society.
- Skill 4—Contextualization: Connect large historical processes to individual situations in history.
- Skill 5—Synthesis: Understand the past by using multiple historical thinking skills and disciplines other than history.

Skill Type III: Chronological Reasoning

- Skill 6—Causation: Evaluate the causes and effects for what has occurred in the past.
- Skill 7—Patterns of Continuity and Change over Time: Analyze history through an investigation of what has stayed the same and what has changed.
- Skill 8—Periodization: Describe the turning points in history and how they help historians categorize periods of history.

Skill Type IV: Creating and Supporting a Historical Argument

- Skill 9—Argumentation: Answer a question by making a clear and persuasive argument.

To be successful on the AP World History exam, you need to master these historical thinking skills as well as the content. The historical thinking skills are the tools you need to unlock the meaning from the content in the multiple-choice section as well as in the free-response portions of the exam. For example, on the DBQ you will use several different historical thinking skills, from analyzing primary documents to understanding diverse interpretations. Any time you write a thesis you are constructing an argument. Long Essay Questions may ask you to demonstrate your ability to assess continuity and change or to compare societies in a variety of ways. In the multiple-choice section, you will apply the historical thinking skills when you examine graphs, maps, and primary source information and you will often deal with multiple-choice questions that require an understanding of diverse interpretations or ask you to address an author's point of view.

The historical thinking skills are also the tools you use in the classroom every day to think critically about the content of the course. These are the tools of historians that you train with all year; by the time of the exam you should be ready to demonstrate your understanding of these historical thinking skills as well as the content of the AP World History course.

Strategies for the Multiple-Choice Section

As mentioned in the chart above, the multiple-choice section of the test makes up 40% of your total score. Thus, it is important that you spend time learning how to master this section—especially its timing. Here are some rules of thumb to help you work your way through the multiple-choice questions:

- **Read the question carefully**. Pressured for time, many students make the mistake of reading the questions too quickly or merely skimming them. By reading a question carefully, you may already have some idea about the correct answer. You can then look for it in the responses. Careful reading is especially important in EXCEPT or NOT questions because, unlike the typical multiple-choice question, all the answers are right except for one.
- **Eliminate any answer you know is wrong**. You can write on the multiple-choice questions in the test book. As you read through the responses, draw a line through any answer you know is wrong.
- **Read all of the possible answers, then choose the most accurate response**. AP exams are written to test your precise knowledge of a subject. Sometimes there are a few probable answers but one of them is more accurate.
- **Mark and skip tough questions**. If you are hung up on a question, mark it in the margin of the question book. You can come back to it later if you have time. Make sure you skip that question on your answer sheet too.
- **Apply the historical thinking skills and the course themes to help you answer stimulus-based questions**. All of the multiple-choice questions will ask you to use a primary source, a secondary source, or a historical issue including a document, an image, a map, a graph or a chart to help answer the question. Examine the wording of the question for clues as to what thinking skill and theme you should be using.
- **Watch your time carefully!** You can spend too much time pondering potential answers—especially when you have multiple sources to synthesize. Watch the time and don't get bogged down. Instead, mark the best answer and then flag the question for review should you have time remaining at the end.

Types of Multiple-Choice Questions

Although you will encounter various types of multiple-choice questions in Section I Part A of the exam, one characteristic they all have in common is that each question is tied to some type of stimulus. The answer to each question may not come directly from the stimulus, in which case you will need to combine your knowledge of the content of the course (thematic learning objectives and concept outline) with your ability to apply historical thinking skills. Additionally, although the stimulus will typically represent one period (or one region or society) in world history, the questions accompanying the stimulus may ask you to make connections to information from a different time period (or region).

Here are some suggestions for how to approach each kind of stimulus you are likely to encounter on the exam.

Photograph/Illustration/Cartoon Questions

These questions require you to interpret a picture in order to answer the question. A good approach is to examine the picture and any given source information before you read the question and possible responses. Look for symbolism in the image; symbols are especially used in cartoons and paintings. Ask yourself what the artist or photographer is trying to convey. After you have read the question, re-examine the image for clues to answer correctly.

Gandhi's Salt March in 1930

Dinodia Photos/Alamy

1. The people in the above image would most likely support which of the following?
   (A) Continued monopoly of a natural resource
   (B) A civil war
   (C) Manufacturing salt in Great Britian
   (D) Nonviolent civil disobedience

ANSWER: D. The above photo shows Mohandas K. Gandhi and his supporters marching to the sea to make salt from ocean water. The act portrayed nonviolent civil disobedience, since the manufacture of salt was a legal monopoly of the British Indian government.

Historical Thinking Skill: Analyzing Evidence: Content and Sourcing

Theme: Development and Interaction of Cultures; State Building, Expansion, and Conflict; Creation, Expansion, and Interaction of Economic Systems; Development and Transformation of Social Structures

Chart/Graph Questions

These questions require you to examine the data on a chart or graph. While these questions are not difficult, spending too much time interpreting a chart or graph can slow you down. Therefore, for these kinds of stimulus, it is preferable to read the question and all of the possible answers first so that you know what you are looking for as you look over the stimulus. Often, you can even eliminate obviously incorrect responses quickly by reading the question first, making the final answer selection easier.

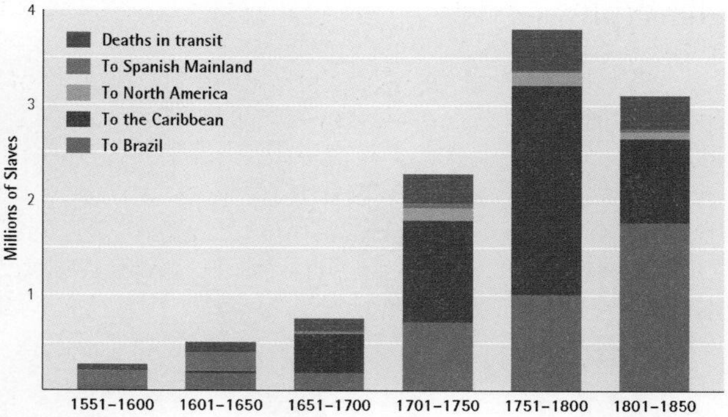

2. Which of the following statements does the above chart best support?
   (A) The transatlantic slave trade remained at the same level from 1551 to 1850.
   (B) The period 1801–1850 witnessed the largest forced migration of African slaves.
   (C) Most slaves came from East Africa.
   (D) Beginning in 1651, the majority of slaves were brought to the Caribbean and Brazil.

ANSWER: D. After analyzing the chart, Option A can be eliminated because the measurement bars are not level in *any* period. Option B is incorrect because the total number of Africans in transit was highest in the period 1751–1800 and declined some in the period 1801–1850. Option C is incorrect in that there is no way to tell from the table what percentage of the slaves came from a specific region in Africa. Because the bars for transit of slaves to the Caribbean and Brazil are longest beginning in 1651, Option D is the correct answer.

Historical Thinking Skills: Analyzing Evidence: Content and Sourcing; Synthesis

Themes: Interaction between humans and the environment; creation, expansion, and interaction of economic systems

Interpreting a Map

For history students, maps are used to describe not only geography but also to convey information about the social, political, cultural, and/or economic organization of human societies. When you are asked to interpret a map, your best bet is to read the title and the key to the map first to get an idea of what information you will find on the map. Then, read through the questions and the answer choices before going back to the map to find the correct answer.

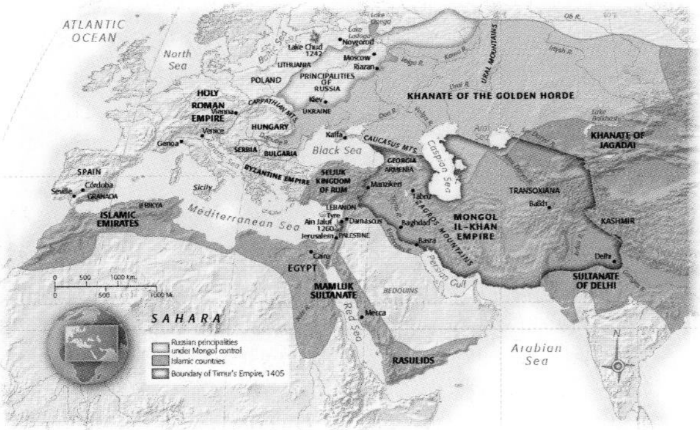

3. This map of western Eurasia in the 1300s shows
   (A) the coexistence of Mongol domains and Islamic sultanates.
   (B) the khanate of the Great Khan, which Khubilai Khan ruled.
   (C) the Mongol takeover of all of western Eurasia.
   (D) the Mongol takeover of all of the Islamic world.

ANSWER: A. The map shows both Mongol khanates and Islamic kingdoms. The answer cannot be B because the domains of the Great Khan were in Central and East Asia. It cannot be C or D because we see other kingdoms that the Mongols did not control, including those of Western Europe.

Historical Thinking Skills: Analyzing Evidence: Content and Sourcing; Interpretation; Synthesis; Contextualization

Theme: State building, expansion, and conflict

Interpreting a Primary Source

Historians rely on primary sources to gather information about the past. When presented with primary sources on the AP World History Exam, be sure to note the origin of the source (both time and place) in order to help you situate the source within your knowledge of history. Although authors' names are cited whenever possible, it is likely that you won't be familiar with the author, so attention to the details of time and place in which the source was created can help you better understand the source itself. For these kinds of questions, you should look over the source information first. Next, read through each multiple-choice question before thoroughly reading the entire source carefully. Because textual sources often accompany a longer set of multiple-choice questions (three to five per source), it will save time if you consider the questions first so that you know what information to focus on from the source. Sometimes you might be presented with two short sources and may be asked to compare or identify the reason for differences between the two.

Code of Nesilim 8. If anyone blind a male or female slave or knock out their teeth, he shall give ten half-shekels of silver, he shall let it go to his home.

–Hittite legal code from c. 1650-1500 B.C.E.

Hammurabi's code 17. If any one find runaway male or female slaves in the open country and bring them to their masters, the master of the slaves shall pay him two shekels of silver.

–Babylonian law code from c. 1750 B.C.E.

http://www.fordham.edu/halsall/ancient

4. It appears from the above excerpts of two ancient law codes that
   (A) slaves were considered property.
   (B) male and female slaves were considered equal in value.

(C) slaves had legal rights.
(D) silver was a common medium of exchange for slaves.

ANSWER: B. Although answers A, C, and D are also partially evident from the textual evidence, it is evident from the excerpts that both societies viewed the value of male and female slaves equally. Thus, B is the best answer.

Historical Thinking Skills: Argumentation; Comparison; Contextualization; Interpretation; Synthesis

Theme: Development and transformation of social structures

Interpreting a Secondary Source

Secondary sources reveal the work historians do to interpret and develop analytical theories about the past. A secondary source presents the historian's argument along with the historical evidence to support it. You might be asked to identify appropriate historical evidence to either support or challenge the argument presented in the source. Sometimes you will be presented with two short excerpts from two historians that might present opposing views or interpretations of the same topic and then asked to compare the two and/or identify the differences between the authors' interpretations. As with primary source-based multiple-choice questions, a strategy to help you use your time effectively is to read the questions first to get an idea of what to look for in the source excerpts. Be sure to read the entire excerpt carefully before selecting an answer.

Short-Answer Questions

You are required to write responses to a total of four short-answer questions in 50 minutes for Part B of Section I of the AP World History Exam. Your score on this portion will count for 20% of your final exam score. Each short-answer question asks the student to do three things, and at least two of the four questions will require using or interpreting a stimulus (the same types of stimulus material seen in the multiple-choice section: primary and secondary sources, graphs, charts, maps, images, etc.). Each short-answer question will also directly assess one or more thematic learning objectives, as well as require you to demonstrate one or more historical thinking skills. Although you do not need to develop and defend a thesis for these types of questions, you may not simply write a "bulleted" response. Instead, word your response to each part of each short-answer question in a complete sentence (or a few concise sentences), taking care to fit your entire response within the indicated space (box) in the response booklet. Be sure to include the correct number of clear, appropriate examples as required in the question in your response. The scoring of the short-answer questions is fairly straightforward: you earn one point for each successfully answered part of each question.

Consider the following example of a short-answer question:

1. Answer Parts A, B, and C.
   (A) Explain ONE cause for the expansion of Islam in the period 600 C.E. to 1450 C.E.
   (B) Explain ONE effect of the spread of Islam in Sub-Saharan Africa in the period 600 C.E. to 1450 C.E.
   (C) Identify ONE similarity in the spread of Islam in Sub-Saharan Africa in the period 600 C.E. to 1450 C.E. to the spread of Christianity in Latin America and the Caribbean in the period 1450 C.E. to 1750 C.E.

ANSWER: For Part A, there are a number of acceptable reasons for the spread of Islam, such as the expansion of trade networks across the Saraha Desert and Indian Ocean, or the political expansion of the Caliphates. A good response would not only identify one of these reasons but also directly connect and thoroughly explain how the reason identified actually contributed to the spread of the religion.

A good response to Part B could include the discussion of the transformation of indigenous culture to reflect the newly introduced religion (construction of mosques, for example), or an increase in commercial relations between African states (Swahili city-states, West African kingdoms, etc.) and Muslim merchants coinciding with the conversion of local merchants and/or leaders. Regardless of the identified effect, a good response would need to directly connect the spread of Islam to the effect, explaining how the arrival of Islam led to the effect.

A good response to Part C could include discussing of how conversion to the newly introduced religion was not total or complete: many people in both Latin America and Sub-Saharan Africa continued indigenous religious practices, or that in both places indigenous beliefs were incorporated into the practice of the new religion among converts.

Strategies For Section II

In Section II of the AP World History exam, you are required to write essays for one document-based question (DBQ) and one long essay question. Part A of Section II is the DBQ, and it represents 25 percent of your final score. For the DBQ, you are given 15 minutes for reading the documents and organizing and outlining your material and 40 minutes for writing the essay. The DBQ is scored out of 7 points.

Part B of Section II is the long essay question, and it represents 15 percent of your final score. For Part B, you will be presented with two questions that assess the same historical thinking skill as applied to different time periods, so you will have to choose which question you will answer. You will have 35 minutes to plan and respond to whichever of the two long essay questions you choose. The long essay question is scored out of 6 points.

The key to success on each of these essays is understanding and internalizing the components of each type of essay's scoring rubric. That's what we will focus on here.

AP Tip

For each essay in Section II, the AP examination has built in time for you to develop an outline. Time spent on an outline is important for a number of reasons:

- It prevents you from writing an essay that is unorganized because you begin writing whatever comes into your head at the moment.
- It allows you to determine your analytical thesis after seeing the evidence you can gather to support your argument.
- It provides you with an opportunity to brainstorm before writing the essay.

Once you have outlined your essay, it is time to put pen to paper. Remember that examination readers are looking for a clear thesis backed up with specifics. Concentrate on setting out accurate information in straightforward, concise prose. You cannot mask vague information with elegant prose.

The Document-Based Question (DBQ)

As its name implies, the DBQ presents you with a wide variety of primary-source information in the form of five to seven documents. Primary sources are original material created during the time period under study, and they include everything from maps, photographs, and illustrations to excerpts of speeches, essays, books, and personal letters.

All free-response essays require you to utilize your knowledge of the topic, but with the DBQ your essay must additionally be based on the documents provided. Your goal is to link each document to the question and then use that information in an analytical and evaluative essay. Thus, the following are necessary for a quality DBQ essay according to the AP World History rubric:

- **Thesis and Argument Development (0–2 points)** One point is earned for the presentation of a thesis that makes a historically defensible claim. The thesis must respond specifically to all parts of the question and must do more than restate or rephrase the question. The thesis must consist of at least one sentence located in either the introduction or the conclusion.

  The second point is earned by developing and supporting a cohesive argument that recognizes and accounts for historical complexity by illustrating relationships among historical evidence such as contradiction, corroboration, and/or qualification.
- **Document Analysis (0–2 points)** One point is awarded for using at least six of the documents to support the thesis or a relevant argument. The second point is earned by explaining the significance of the author's point of view, the author's purpose, the historical context, and/or the audience for at least four of the documents.

- **Using Evidence Beyond the Documents (0–2 points)** One point is earned for contextualization. Situate the argument by explaining the broader historical events, developments, or processes immediately relevant to the question. This requires using knowledge not found in the documents. This does not mean you simply include a phrase or reference but rather that you include an explanation of multiple sentences or a full paragraph.

  The second point is awarded for providing an example or additional piece of evidence beyond those found in the documents to support or qualify the argument. You must explain how the evidence supports or qualifies the argument. The example must be different from the evidence used to earn other points.
- **Synthesis (0–1 point)** This final point is earned from the extension of the argument by explaining the connections between the argument and ONE of the following:
  - a development in a different historical period, situation, era, or geographical area
  - a course theme and/or approach to history that is not the focus of the essay, such as political, economic, social, cultural, or intellectual history
  - a different discipline or field of inquiry, such as economics, government and politics, art history, or anthropology

Take a look at this sample DBQ, one containing six documents.

1. Using the following documents, analyze the roles of class and gender in China before 1450 C.E.

Document 1

A woman's duties are to cook the five grains, heat the wine, look after her parents-in-law, make clothes, and that is all! She has no ambition to manage affairs outside the house. She must follow the "three submissions." When she is young, she must submit to her parents. After her marriage, she must submit to her husband. When she is widowed, she must submit to her son.

Source: Liu Hsiang, "Biographies of Admirable Women," account of the life of the mother of Confucian philosopher Mencius written three centuries after she lived, 33 B.C.E.

Document 2

Source: Sima Qian, also called the Grand Historian, completed a history of the world, much of it about his native China, sometime around 90 B.C.E. He wrote *Records of the Grand Historian* with such empathy and detail that it continues to be extremely popular whenever a new edition is issued by a Chinese publisher.

Document 3

On the third day after the birth of a girl the ancients observed three customs: first to place the baby below the bed; second to give her a potsherd with which to play; third to announce her birth to her ancestors by an offering. Now to lay the baby below the bed plainly indicated that she is lowly and weak, and should regard it as her primary duty to humble herself before others. To give her potsherds with which to play indubitably signified that she should practice labor and consider it her primary duty to be industrious. To announce her birth before her ancestors clearly means that she ought to esteem as her primary duty the continuation of the observance of worship in the home.

Source: Ban Zhao, female Chinese scholar, advisor on state matters to Empress Deng, and imperial historian, 106 C.E.

Document 4

Xu Chong returned home and permitted his daughter to become a nun. Lingshou thereupon cut off her hair, discarded secular ornaments, and received the rules of monastic life from Fotudeng and nun Jingjian. She established Foundling of Wisdom Convent, and Fotudeng presented her with a cut-flower embroidered vestment, a seven-strip monastic robe, and an elephant-trunk-shaped water ewer. In the religious communities of that time there was no one who did not honor her. The Emperor honored her and promoted her father to the official court position of undersecretary of the Yellow Gate and administrator of the Qinghe Commandery.

Source: Shi Baochang, Lives of the Nuns, a biography of a Buddhist nun, 516 C.E.

Document 5

The king occupies the most honorable position and receives Heaven's precious decrees. Like Heaven and Earth, he acts to shelter and support, thus serving as the father and mother of the masses. As his children, as his subjects, they must be loyal and filial. Should they dare to cherish wickedness and have rebellious hearts, however, they will run counter to Heaven's constancy and violate human principle. Therefore, this is called plotting rebellion.

Source: Chinese legal code, seventh century.

Document 6

When a farmer falls on bad times, he has to sell his field and his hut. If it is a good year, he might be able to pay his debts by selling out. But no sooner will the harvest be in than his storage bins will be empty again, and he will have to try and contract a new debt promising his labor for the next year. Each time he indentures himself he incurs higher interest rates, and soon will be destitute again.

If it is a bad year, and there is a famine, then the situation is hopeless. Families break up, parents separate, and all try to sell themselves into slavery. But in a bad year nobody will buy them....

The gentry however, live off their rents, with no troubles and no cares. Wealth and poverty are very clearly divided.

Source: Extract from a scholar's account of the day-to-day realities of country life, late eighth century.

Document 7

When the lord Khan is seated on his imperial throne, the empress resides on his left, and one step below sit two of the other wives whom he keeps. At the bottom of the stairs are all the other women of his family. All of the women who are married have on their heads something shaped like a human foot, which is a good forearm and a half long. On the lower portion of the so-called foot are crane's feathers fashioned into a peak, and the entire "foot" is ornamented with great pearls. Whatever large and beautiful pearls there are in the world, they are to be found on the decorations of those ladies.

Source: Odoric of Pordenone, a Roman Catholic missionary working in China, report of travels, 1330.

The first step is an analysis of each document in order to come up with evidence in order to create your thesis. What is the meaning of the document? What or who is the source, and how does that affect their point of view? The source provides important clues in the position being put forth in the document. As you analyze the meaning or significance of the document, jot down margin notes—generalizations that relate to the document and the prompt. For example:

- **Margin note for Document 1** *Duty is based on gender.*
- **Margin note for Document 2** *There is a benefit in knowing the history of your culture.*
- **Margin note for Document 3** *Duty is based on gender.*
- **Margin note for Document 4** *If the father permits it, women can become nuns and escape the prescribed duties of a woman.*

- **Margin note for Document 5** *According to the law code, the king is to be a paternal leader, and—important for the king—citizens are to be loyal followers.*
- **Margin note for Document 6** *There are difficulties for the farmers in escaping the cycle of poverty, while the gentry benefits from the system.*
- **Margin note for Document 7** *Women in the royal household have an honored place and are dressed quite ornately.*

Once you have done this, you should consider the information you know about the prompt outside of the information presented in the documents. Combine the evidence from the documents with the outside information to create your thesis and the main points you are going to use to prove your thesis (your arguments). Each argument should specifically connect evidence from the document back to your main thesis, while incorporating outside information and analysis of the purpose, intended audience, historical context of the document, and/or author's point of view. For example, your thesis might argue that before 1450, social structure in China was a rigid system in which one's position and lifestyle were dictated by gender and class, as well as a moral duty to fulfill one's appointed role as understood through Confucian principles. You want to provide evidence in the context of your groupings, which could include class, gender, and duty. Thinking about point of view, two of the documents are especially useful. Written by a Han Confucian scholar, Mengzi (Mencius), Document 1 describes his mother's life. Mengzi is upholding the Confucian social system and the traditional ideals to which he has dedicated his life. As a published Confucian scholar, he would want to spread values that support the strict social and gender structure of Han society. His gender and class also matter; as an upper-class male, he was part of the social class that propagated the ideas about gender roles, particularly for the upper-class females with whom upper-class males would come into contact. Document 5, the excerpt from the Tang law code, imposes expectations of good citizenship and loyalty on Chinese subjects. Those in power would want to encourage such behavior to maintain their position of authority.

As part of your planning, you will also want to consider one or more other historical events or processes that may have influenced the topic, and what your strategy will be to earn the synthesis point (see how to earn the point on the previous page). Finally, write your thesis, making sure it answers the prompt and shows your argument. Make sure your thesis has an argument and does not just repeat the prompt. With good planning at the beginning, your DBQ should be in great shape.

Additional DBQs are provided in the appendix of the textbook. Use these DBQs to practice going through the process of writing a DBQ, and you will feel very comfortable and confident on the exam.

Long Essay Questions

The AP World History exam concludes with the long essay question. You will be required to choose to respond to one of the two possible prompts. Both prompts assess the same historical thinking skill but use different time periods or topics, so which option to select really depends on how much accurate, relevant historical evidence you can confidently include in your essay given that you should spend no more than 35 minutes for planning and writing it

Your essay for this question must come entirely from your knowledge of world history—sorry, no documents to support your answer this time! However, the topics of the questions are limited to topics or examples detailed in the concept outline developed by the College Board for AP World History. Again, the prompt will assess your ability to demonstrate one of the historical thinking skills, such as comparison, causation, continuity and change over time, or periodization. Long essay questions are graded with a six-point rubric as follows:

- **Thesis (0–1 point)** An acceptable thesis must make a historically defensible claim and directly and specifically address all parts of the question and must do more than restate or rephrase the question. The thesis must consist of at least one sentence located in either the introduction or the conclusion.
- **Argument Development: Using the Targeted Historical Thinking Skill (0–2 points)** These two points are awarded depending on the method used to develop and support the argument.
  - **Comparison** One point is earned by describing similarities AND differences among

historical individuals, events, developments, or processes. Depending on the prompt, the second point is earned by explaining the reasons for similarities AND differences among historical individuals, events, developments, or processes OR by evaluating the relative significance of historical individuals, events, developments, or processes.

- **Causation** One point is earned by describing causes AND/OR effects of a historical event, development, or process. The second point is earned by explaining the reasons for the causes AND/OR effects of a historical event, development, or process. Note: If the prompt requires a discussion of both causes and effects, responses must address both causes and effects in order to earn both points.
- **CCOT** One point is earned by describing historical continuity AND change over time. The second point is earned by explaining the reasons for historical continuity AND change over time.
- **Periodization** One point is earned by describing the ways in which the historical development specified in the prompt was different from and similar to developments that preceded AND/OR followed it. The second point is earned by explaining the extent to which the historical development specified in the prompt was different from and similar to developments that preceded AND/OR followed it. Note: For both points, if the prompt requires evaluating a turning point, then responses must discuss developments that preceded AND followed it. For both points, if the prompt requires evaluating the characteristics of an era, then responses can discuss developments that EITHER preceded OR followed it.

- **Argument Development: Using Evidence (0–2 points)** One point is earned for addressing the topic of the question with specific examples of relevant evidence. The second point is earned by utilizing specific examples of evidence to fully and effectively substantiate the stated thesis or a relevant argument. Note: To fully and effectively substantiate the stated thesis or a relevant argument, responses must include a broad range of evidence that, through analysis and explanation, justifies the stated thesis or a relevant argument.
- **Synthesis (0–1 point)** This final point is earned from extending the argument by explaining the connections between the argument and ONE of the following:
  - a development in a different historical period, situation, era, or geographical area.
  - a course theme and/or approach to history that is not the focus of the essay, such as political, economic, social, cultural, or intellectual history.
  - a different discipline or field of inquiry, such as economics, government and politics, art history, or anthropology.

Be sure that in your preparations you practice a few times with each type of skill so that you will feel confident applying any of the skills.

To conclude, here are some tips for writing AP World History essays:

- **Thesis** Be sure that your thesis statement is in either the introduction or the conclusion of your essay. You need to present your main argument in the first paragraph or the last paragraph so it is clear what you are proving in your essay.
- **Grammar** You will not lose points for spelling or grammar errors, but it is important to write as coherently as possible. Remember, if the reader cannot understand what you are trying to say or cannot follow your arguments, it will be harder to get the necessary information across for points. It is also important to write as legibly as time permits so all of your good ideas can be understood.
- **Dates** Do not panic if you cannot remember a specific date; try to use a broader description such as "early nineteenth century" or "around the sixth century" if you cannot remember the exact date.
- **Quality over quantity** Remember: quality, not quantity. Writing a great deal does not mean you are writing what needs to be in your essay. Focus on making sure you are hitting all the rubric points rather than writing long introductions and conclusions. Make your argument, prove it with evidence, and wrap up. You want to have time to do both essays well.

Thematic Learning Objectives

As mentioned earlier, the College Board has identified five themes present throughout each of the six time periods defined in the concept outline for AP World History. To further assist students in the study of world history, the College Board has also created thematic learning objectives—a series of tasks students should be able to do with related content, categorized by theme. You should make reviewing the thematic learning objectives a regular part of your study of world history throughout the school year, because every question on the AP exam serves to measure your understanding of at least one of these objectives. Because all of the learning objectives can be applied to content in multiple time periods, reviewing them can also be a way of tracing continuity and change over time, as well as periodization. You can use the learning objectives as a way of helping you organize and remember content.

Note how many of the thematic learning objectives are embedded within a historical thinking skill, such as comparison, causation, continuity and change over time, etc. Remember, all questions on the AP exam are not only based on the following learning objectives but also require the use of historical thinking skills.

Theme 1: Interactions between Humans and the Environment (ENV)

Overarching Questions	**Learning Objectives—*Students are able to...***
1. How have people used diverse tools and technologies to adapt to and affect the environment over time?	**ENV-1:** Explain how early humans used tools and technologies to establish communities.
	ENV-2: Explain and compare how hunter-forager, pastoralist, and settled agricultural societies adapted to and affected their environments over time.
2. How and to what extent has human migration and settlement been influenced by the environment during different periods in world history?	**ENV-3:** Explain the environmental advantages and disadvantages of major migration, communication, and exchange networks.
	ENV-4: Explain how environmental factors influenced human migrations and settlements.
	ENV-5: Explain how human migrations affected the environment.
	ENV-6: Explain how people used technology to overcome geographic barriers to migration over time.
3. How has the environment changed as a consequence of population growth and urbanization?	**ENV-7:** Assess the causes and effects of the spread of epidemic diseases over time.
	ENV-8: Assess the demographic causes and effects of the spread of new foods and agricultural techniques.
4. How have processes of industrialization and global integration been shaped by environmental factors, and, in turn, how has their development affected the environment over time?	**ENV-9:** Analyze the environmental causes and effects of industrialization.

Theme 2: Development and Interaction of Cultures (CUL)

Overarching Questions	**Learning Objectives—*Students are able to...***
1. How and why have religions, belief systems, philosophies, and ideologies developed and transformed as they spread from their places of origin to other regions?	**CUL-1:** Compare the origins, principal beliefs, and practices of the major world religions and belief systems.
	CUL-2: Explain how religious belief systems developed and spread as a result of expanding communication and exchange networks.
	CUL-3: Explain how major philosophies and ideologies developed and spread as a result of expanding communication and exchange networks.
2. How have religions, belief systems, philosophies, and ideologies affected the development of societies over time?	**CUL-4:** Analyze the ways in which religious and secular belief systems affected political, economic, and social institutions.
	CUL-5: Explain and compare how teachings and social practices of different religious and secular belief systems affected gender roles and family structures.
3. How were scientific and technological innovations adapted and transformed as they spread from one society or culture to another?	**CUL-6:** Explain how cross-cultural interactions resulted in the diffusion of technologies and scientific knowledge.
	CUL-7: Analyze how new scientific, technological, and medical innovations affected religions, belief systems, philosophies, and major ideologies.
4. In what ways do the arts reflect innovation, adaptation, and creativity of specific societies?	**CUL-8:** Explain how economic, religious, and political elites defined and sponsored art and architecture.
	CUL-9: Explain the relationship between expanding exchange networks and the emergence of various forms of transregional culture, including music, literature, and visual art.

Theme 3: State Building, Expansion, and Conflict (SB)

Overarching Questions	Learning Objectives—*Students are able to...*
1. How have different forms of governance been constructed and maintained over time?	**SB-1:** Explain and compare how rulers constructed and maintained different forms of governance.
	SB-2: Analyze how the functions and institutions of governments have changed over time.
2. How have economic, social, cultural, and environmental contexts influenced the processes of state building, expansion, and dissolution?	**SB-3:** Analyze how state formation and expansion were influenced by various forms of economic organization, such as agrarian, pastoral, mercantile, and industrial production.
	SB-4: Explain and compare how social, cultural, and environmental factors influenced state formation, expansion, and dissolution.
	SB-5: Assess the degree to which the functions of cities within states or empires have changed over time.
	SB-6: Assess the relationships between states with centralized governments and those without, including pastoral and agricultural societies.
3. How have conflicts, exchanges, and alliances influenced the processes of state building, expansion, and dissolution?	**SB-7:** Assess how and why internal conflicts, such as revolts and revolutions, have influenced the process of state building, expansion, and dissolution.
	SB-8: Assess how and why external conflicts and alliances have influenced the process of state building, expansion, and dissolution.
	SB-9: Assess how and why commercial exchanges have influenced the processes of state building, expansion, and dissolution.
	SB-10: Analyze the political and economic interactions between states and non-state actors.

Theme 4: Creation, Expansion, and Interaction of Economic Systems (ECON)

Overarching Questions	Learning Objectives—*Students are able to...*
1. How and to what extent have modes of production and commerce changed over time?	**ECON-1:** Evaluate the relative economic advantages and disadvantages of foraging, pastoralism, and agriculture.
	ECON-2: Analyze the economic role of cities as centers of production and commerce.
	ECON-3: Assess the economic strategies of different types of states and empires.
	ECON-4: Analyze how technology shaped the processes of industrialization and globalization.
2. How have different labor systems developed and changed over time?	**ECON-5:** Explain and compare forms of labor organization, including families and labor specialization within and across different societies.
	ECON-6: Explain and compare the causes and effects of different forms of coerced labor systems.
	ECON-7: Analyze the causes and effects of labor reform movements, including the abolition of slavery.
3. How have economic systems and the development of ideologies, values, and institutions influenced each other over time?	**ECON-8:** Analyze the relationship between belief systems and economic systems.
	ECON-9: Explain and compare the ways in which economic philosophies influenced economic policies and behaviors.
4. What is the relationship among local, regional, and global economic systems; how have those relationships changed over time?	**ECON-10:** Analyze the roles of pastoralists, traders, and travelers in the diffusion of crops, animals, commodities, and technologies.
	ECON-11: Explain how the development of financial instruments and techniques facilitated economic exchanges.
	ECON-12: Evaluate how and to what extent networks of exchange have expanded, contracted, or changed over time.
	ECON-13: Analyze how international economic institutions, regional trade agreements, and corporations—both local and multinational—have interacted with state economic authority.

Theme 5: Development and Transformation of Social Structures (SOC)

Overarching Questions	Learning Objectives—*Students are able to...*
1. How have distinctions based on kinship, ethnicity, class, gender, and race influenced the development and transformations of social hierarchies?	**SOC-1:** Analyze the development of continuities and changes in gender hierarchies, including patriarchy.
	SOC-2: Assess how the development of specialized labor systems interacted with the development of social hierarchies.
	SOC-3: Assess the impact that different ideologies, philosophies, and religions had on social hierarchies.
2. How, by whom, and in what ways have social categories, roles, and practices been maintained or challenged over time?	**SOC-4:** Analyze the ways in which legal systems have sustained or challenged class, gender, and racial ideologies.
	SOC-5: Analyze ways in which religious beliefs and practices have sustained or challenged class, gender, and racial ideologies.
	SOC-6: Analyze the extent to which philosophies, medical practices, and scientific theories sustained or challenged class, gender, and racial ideologies.
	SOC-7: Analyze the ways in which colonialism, nationalism, and independence movements have sustained or challenged class, gender, and racial ideologies.
3. How have political, economic, cultural, and demographic changes affected social structures over time?	**SOC-8:** Analyze the extent to which migrations changed social structures in both the sending and receiving societies.

VOYAGES
in World History

1 The Peopling of the World, to 4000 B.C.E.

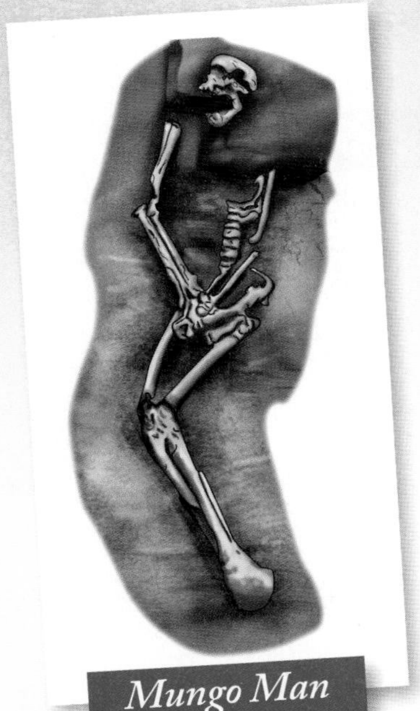

Mungo Man

From the earliest moments of human history, our ancestors were on the move. Archaeologists continue to debate when the earliest anatomically modern humans moved out of Africa and how they populated the rest of the world. One of the most distant places our ancient forebears reached—probably around 50,000 years ago—was Australia. In 1974, a team of archaeologists from Australia National University discovered the remains of a male near Mungo (muhn-GO) Lake in the southeastern Australian state of New South Wales. He is known as **Mungo Man**; Mungo Woman is the cremated remains of a female that the team's lead archaeologist, J. M. Bowler, found at the site several years earlier. Here, Bowler describes the moment he spotted Mungo Man's skull sticking out of the ground:

> *Prolonged and heavy rains during 1973 had swept across the eroded dune surface, uncovering a new crop of archaeologic and other prehistoric finds. At a point some 500 m [1,600 ft] east of the Lake Mungo I cremation/burial site [of Mungo Woman] the late afternoon sun was highlighting a small white object protruding through the sandy surface.… Closer examination revealed the object to be the exposed left side of a carbonate-encrusted human cranium. The central area of exposed bone protruded some 2–3 cm above the eroded surface. Much of the bone was coated with a thin layer of calcrete which was pinkish in color, a feature not known from carbonate of similar age elsewhere.…**

*J. M. Bowler and A. G. Thorne, "Human Remains from Lake Mungo: Discovery and Excavation of Lake Mungo III," in *The Origin of the Australians*, ed. R. L. Kirk and A. G. Thorne (Atlantic Highlands, N.J.: Humanities Press Inc., 1976), p. 128.

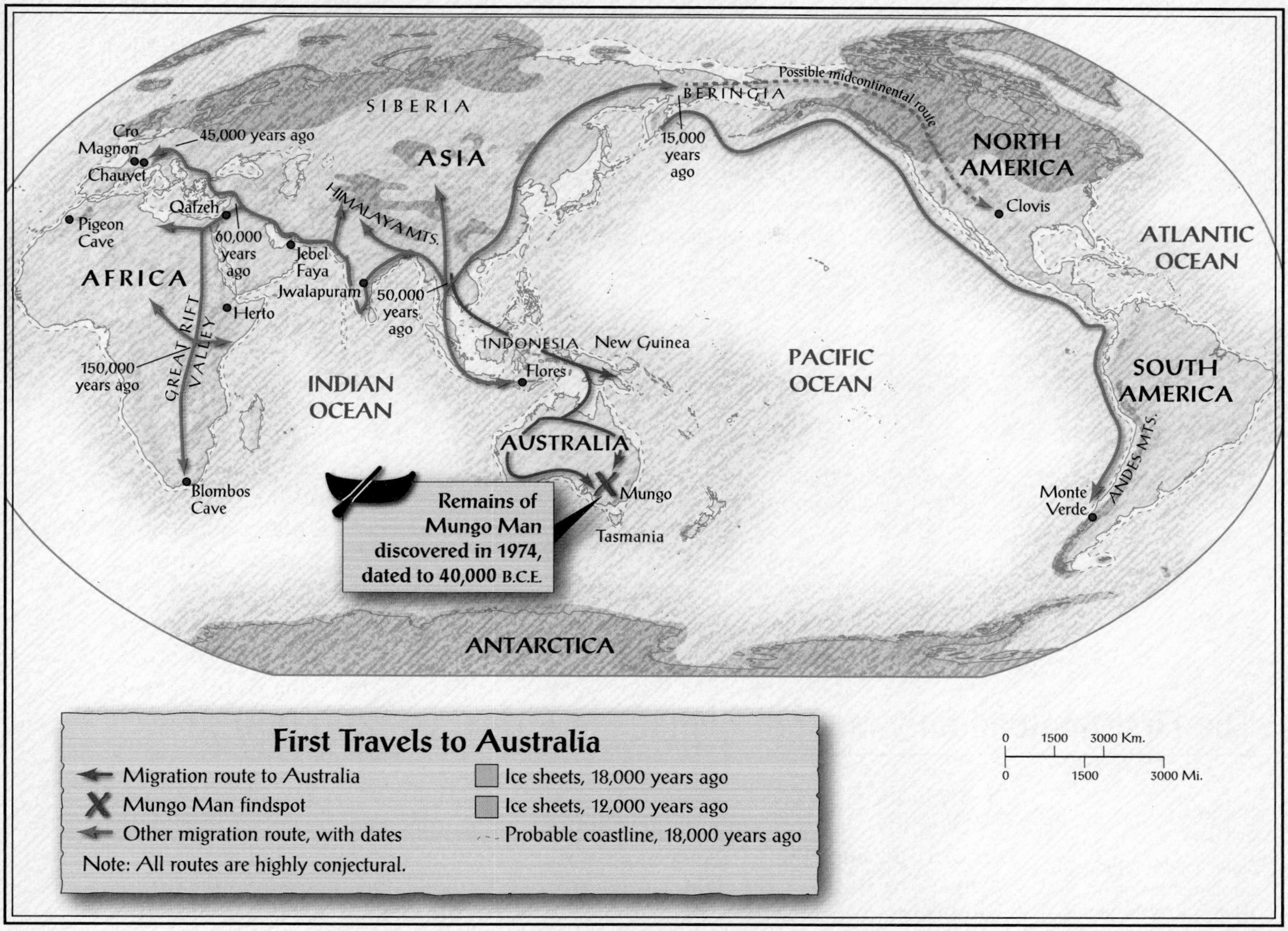

Even on that first day, Professor Bowler noticed that the soil around the burial had a pinkish tinge, which turned out to be the remains of **ocher** (OH-kerh), a reddish-brown mineral element ancient peoples used to color the soil. The site dates to 40,000 B.C.E., some 10,000 years after Australia was first settled. (As is common among world historians, this book uses B.C.E. [Before Common Era] for dates prior to the year 1 of the first century, and C.E. [Common Era] for dates from the year 1 forward. Older books use B.C. [Before Christ] and A.D. [Anno Domini, In the Year of Our Lord].) The peopling of Australia marked an important phase in the history of humankind: people had advanced to the point where they could plan into the future. They could construct boats or rafts to take them across the 60 miles (100 km) of water separating Australia from the Eurasian landmass at the time.

By 200,000 B.C.E., anatomically modern people had fully developed in Africa. Starting between 80,000 and 60,000 B.C.E., our ancestors arrived in Asia. They later

Mungo Man
Remains of a male found near Mungo Lake in the southeastern Australian state of New South Wales, dated to about 40,000 B.C.E.

ocher
A reddish-brown iron-based pigment that ancient peoples used to color the soil and to decorate cave walls.

reached Australia and Europe at the same time. The Western Hemisphere was settled much later.

Since none of these early peoples could read and write, no documents survive. But archaeological evidence, including cave paintings and ancient tools, makes it possible to reconstruct the early history of humanity. In addition, new information derived from genetic material called deoxyribonucleic acid (DNA) has allowed scientists to reconstruct the peopling of the world with unprecedented accuracy.

KEY CONCEPT QUESTIONS

- What were the key ways that human groups adapted to their environment during the Paleolithic era? (**Key Concept 1.1**)
- Why did humans migrate from their origin in East Africa to Eurasia, Australia, and the Americas? (**Key Concept 1.1**)
- In what regions did the Neolithic Revolution occur, and how did it differ around the world? (**Key Concept 1.2**)

The First Anatomically Modern Humans in Africa, ca. 200,000 B.C.E.

Homo sapiens sapiens
Biological term for modern human beings belonging to the genus *Homo*, species *sapiens*, and subspecies *sapiens*.

hominins
Term referring to all humans and their ancestors but not to chimpanzees, gorillas, or orangutans.

When the species ***Homo sapiens sapiens*** (HO-mo SAY-pee-uhnz SAY-pee-uhnz), anatomically modern humans, first appeared in central and southern Africa some 200,000 years ago, they lived side by side with other animals and other **hominins**, a general term referring to humans and their ancestors. But in important respects, they were totally different from their neighbors, for they learned to change their environment with radically new tools and skills. Their departure from Africa, their first art works, their hunting prowess, and their trade networks are all signs of recognizably human behavior. One fascinating puzzle remains to be solved: If they were anatomically the same as modern humans, why did they only start to behave in recognizably human ways after 50,000 B.C.E.? Early analysts wondered if leaving Africa somehow forced our ancestors to behave differently, but a series of discoveries in recent years, particularly in South Africa, provide evidence of modern behaviors long before 50,000 B.C.E.

Predecessors to the First Anatomically Modern Humans

Because ancient human remains are rare, in 1997 paleontologists (pay-lee-on-TAHL-oh-gists), scientists who study life in the distant past, were extremely pleased to excavate three skulls dating to 160,000 B.C.E. at the Herto site of Ethiopia. Compared to those of later modern humans, the skulls found at the Herto site are slightly larger, the faces are longer, and the brows more pronounced. The Herto skulls (from two adults and one child) represent either the earliest modern humans or their immediate predecessors and thus decisively demonstrate that the *Homo sapiens sapiens* species arose first in Africa. Concluding that all modern people are descended from this group, one of the excavating archaeologists commented: *"In this sense, we are all African."**

Scientists use the concept of **evolution** to explain how all life forms, including modern humans, have come into being. In the nineteenth century, Charles Darwin proposed that natural selection is the mechanism underlying evolutionary change. He realized that variations exist within a species and that certain variations increase an individual's chances of survival. We know that genetic mutations, or permanent, transmissible changes to genetic material, cause DNA to change, and so all variations, beneficial or not, are passed along to offspring. Because those individuals within a population who possess beneficial traits—perhaps a bigger brain or more upright posture—are more likely to survive, they will have more offspring. And because traits are inherited, these offspring will also possess the beneficial traits. Individuals lacking those traits will have few or no offspring. As new mutations occur within a population, its characteristics will change and a new species can develop from an earlier one, typically over many thousands or even millions of years. The species closest to modern human beings today is the chimpanzee, whose cells contain nuclei with DNA that overlaps with 98.4 percent of human DNA. But humans and chimpanzees have developed separately for some seven million years.

evolution
Model proposed by Charles Darwin to explain the development of new species through genetic mutation and natural selection.

Biologists use four different subcategories when classifying animals: family, genus (JEAN-uhs, the Latin word for "group" or "class"), species, and subspecies. Members of the primate family, modern humans belong to the genus *Homo* ("person" in Latin), the species *sapiens* ("wise" or "intelligent" in Latin), and the subspecies *sapiens*, so the correct term for modern people is *Homo sapiens sapiens*. Members of the same species can reproduce, while members of two different species cannot. Since modern humans are now the only living subspecies in the *Homo sapiens* species, scholars often abbreviate the name to *Homo sapiens*. Here, we will continue to say *Homo sapiens sapiens* because we are discussing periods when other subspecies were alive.

The Herto site was on the edge of a shallow, freshwater lake that was home to crocodiles, fish, and hippopotamuses, and buffalo lived on the land. The site's residents used stone tools to remove flesh from the hippopotamus, and the only child's skull had tool marks as well, an indication that flesh had been removed from it. Some scientists have speculated that the Herto residents practiced cannibalism, but it is just as likely that they left marks on the skull as part of the ritual preparation of the dead.

Anatomically Modern Humans

The finds at Herto indicate that, sometime around 200,000 years ago, anatomically modern humans appeared in Africa. Their build, the size of their brains, and their physical appearance were very similar to ours.

Analysis of genetic material has provided crucial information that supplements what we can learn by analyzing archaeologically excavated remains. When

*J. N. Wilford, "In Ancient Skulls from Ethiopia, Familiar Faces," *New York Times*, June 12, 2003, pp. A1, A8.

a man and a woman have a child, most of their DNA recombines to form a new sequence unique to their baby, but some DNA passes directly from the mother to the child in mitochondrial DNA, or mtDNA. By analyzing mtDNA, geneticists have identified a single female ancestor, known as **mitochondrial Eve**, whom all living humans have in common. Mitochondrial Eve lived in West Africa near modern Tanzania. Eve may not have been the first anatomically modern female; she was the first anatomically modern female whose daughters gave birth to daughters, and so on through the generations, allowing her mtDNA to pass to every person alive today. The total number of anatomically modern humans alive during Eve's lifetime was surprisingly small: about 10,000 or 20,000 people. That number seems to have held steady for more than 100,000 years, until the development of agriculture (discussed later in this chapter) made it possible to support a larger population.

mitochondrial Eve
The first female ancestor shared by all living humans, who was identified by analysis of mitochondrial DNA.

The Beginnings of Modern Human Behavior

Scientists debate when these members of our species first began to act like modern humans. The ability to plan ahead is the most important indicator of human behavior, and additional clues lie in the ability to modify tools to improve them, the existence of trade networks, the practice of making art, the ritual of burying the dead, and the ability to speak. Early *Homo sapiens sapiens* had larynxes, but they did not begin to speak until sometime between 100,000 and 50,000 B.C.E. We cannot know precisely when because the act of speaking produces no lasting evidence in the archaeological record. Instead, paleontologists have identified certain human activities, such as organizing hunting parties to trap large game, as sufficiently complex to require speech. Speech may have begun because of a genetic mutation; scientists have identified a single gene on the Y chromosome (*FOXP2*) that only men carry. This finding suggests that women would have had to learn language by interacting with men, but many skeptical scientists await further confirmation of the language gene's existence.

Our forebears may have begun to leave Africa around 100,000 B.C.E., perhaps even earlier. In 2011, archaeologists found tools at the Jebel Faya site in modern United Arab Emirates that date to about 125,000 B.C.E. and resemble those made in Africa by anatomically modern humans. But the tools are so simple that scientists cannot be certain that modern humans made them. Because water levels differed at this time, only 3 miles (5 km) of water separated the Arabian peninsula from Africa. Some scientists doubt that any modern humans left Africa before 50,000 B.C.E., the date of the first conclusive evidence of humans outside Africa.

AP® THEMES
How did ancient humans adapt to their environments?

Several sites in South Africa have produced evidence of distinctly human behavior dating to around 75,000 B.C.E. Animal remains at the sites indicate that anatomically modern humans had developed spears and arrows sufficiently powerful to kill local antelope and seals. The Pinnacle Point site, outside Cape Town, has produced small stone blades that ancient humans attached to wooden arrow shafts. These remained in use for over 11,000 years, demonstrating that generations of humans passed the blade-making technology down to their children, a possible sign that the blade makers could speak and certain evidence that they had greater cognitive powers than earlier hominins.

Even more revealing, the humans living on the site of Blombos Cave, also in South Africa, showed a capacity for symbolic thinking, as evidenced in the production of red ocher art objects. (See the feature "Visual Evidence in Primary Sources: The First Art Objects in the World.")

How Modern Humans Populated Asia, Australia, and Europe

To be able to migrate out of Africa and displace existing populations in Asia and Europe, modern humans had to behave differently from their forebears. Long-distance migration required forward planning and most likely speech. As the modern humans left Africa, they modified existing tools to suit new environments, and they devised boats or rafts to cross bodies of water. After crossing into Asia between 80,000 and 60,000 years ago, they proceeded to modern Indonesia, Papua New Guinea, and Australia, which they reached 50,000 years ago, the same time that they reached Europe. Europe was colder than Asia, and it was inhabited by Neanderthals, whom the modern humans displaced by 40,000 years ago. They traveled to the Americas last, reaching there by at least 14,000 B.C.E., if not earlier.

The Settling of Asia, 80,000–60,000 B.C.E.

Many archaeologists propose that the peoples living near the coast of Africa, near Djibouti and Somalia, crossed a land bridge to the Arabian peninsula (water levels were lower then) and continued to hug the coast of the Indian Ocean, eating shellfish and tropical fruit as they made their way south. The first humans to leave Africa probably did so without realizing they were leaving one landmass and going to another: they simply followed the coastline in search of food. It is most likely that multiple generations traveled short distances and kept on moving into new environments.

AP® THEMES

What environmental factors influenced the first humans to leave Africa?

The earliest concrete archaeological evidence of the migration from Africa to Asia comes from Jwalapuram, India, where tools—but no human remains—dating to 74,000 B.C.E. have been found. The 215 stone tools and a piece of ocher are nearly identical to those found in Africa, an important clue to the origins of the travelers. Pieces of a human skull, found at Tam Pa Ling, Laos, and dating to 61,000–44,000 B.C.E., suggest a possible route from Southeast Asia to Australia, confirmed by a recent study of aboriginal peoples living in Australia, whose DNA suggested that the first wave of settlers arrived around 50,000 B.C.E. from New Guinea and the Philippines. These were Mungo Man's forebears.

The Settling of Australia, ca. 50,000 B.C.E.

The farthest *Homo sapiens sapiens* traveled from Africa was to Australia. One of the most isolated places on earth, Australia provides a rich environment for animals, such as kangaroos, that are found nowhere else in the world. No animals from Eurasia, except for rodents and modern humans, managed to reach Australia.

Although oceans then lay about 250 feet (76 m) below modern levels, the body of water dividing Australia from the Greater Southeast Asian landmass was

The First Art Objects in the World

One site in Africa—Blombos Cave in South Africa—has produced some of the earliest art objects in the world. The Blombos Cave site, on the coast about 186 miles (300 km) east of Cape Town, dates to 100,000 B.C.E. and was occupied for long periods after that.

The occupants of Blombos Cave fished and hunted and made sets of fine bone tools, all of the same size. First they cut bone with stone tools and then polished it with leather and abrasive powder. They also mixed ocher with animal fat and some charcoal in two abalone shells (shown opposite) to make the earliest known paint and the earliest known container for human use in the world.* What did they use the ocher for? To color the earth? As a type of makeup? To make cave paintings? Whatever its use, it was entirely decorative, evidence of an early human desire to make something beautiful. The paint box also demonstrates the ability to plan ahead since early artists placed the ocher and tools for applying it in the shells for whenever they were needed.

The Blombos also produced nineteen snail shells, about the size of a kernel of corn, each with a hole through it (opposite, bottom). Traces of wear at the ends of the shells indicate that they were originally strung together to make a strand of beads, worn perhaps on the wrist or at the neck. The beads also show traces of ocher. The beads, archaeologists speculate, may have functioned at Blombos as they do among the Ju/'hoansi people who live in the Kalahari Desert in Botswana and who are sometimes called Bushmen. Speakers of a language with many click sounds, the Ju/'hoansi present ostrich shell beads to other groups with whom they hope to form alliances.

The scientist who discovered these shells argued convincingly that these are very early signs of human creativity. A recent discovery suggests that they may be more than that. In 2007, archaeologists excavating the Pigeon Cave site in Morocco found similar shells dated between 91,000 and 74,000 years ago. These beads also have holes, abrasion marks at the ends where they were strung together, and traces of ocher. They are not from exactly the same species of snail as those from Blombos Cave, but the two species of snail look identical to the naked eye (one can see the differences between them only with a microscope). Other undated finds of similar shells in Israel and Algeria suggest that a trading network that spanned Africa and Israel may have existed as early as 82,000 years ago.

The shell tool kit, the bone tools, and the beads from Blombos reveal that their makers were able to produce beautiful objects because they had extra time and energy after meeting basic subsistence needs. These early objects clearly display the artistic impulses of their makers and suggest that *Homo sapiens sapiens* engaged in the recognizably human activity of making art objects as early as 75,000 B.C.E. and possibly even before.

---

*John Noble Wilford, "In African Cave, Signs of an Ancient Paint Factory," *New York Times*, October 13, 2011.

This abalone shell contains a lump of ocher, the red mineral possibly used as a pigment for cave paintings.

Image courtesy of Prof Christopher Henshilwood

This abalone shell contained tools made from quartzite chips and different types of animal bone used to prepare and apply the paint. ***Which evidence from the archaeological record (including, but not limited to, the objects shown here) do you find most convincing as the earliest indication of people becoming recognizably human? Why?***

This shell bead (notice the hole) was found in Blombos Cave, some 186 miles (300 km) from Cape Town, where the cave's occupants hunted and fished around 75,000 B.C.E. The reddish tinge to the shell is from ocher, suggesting that the bead either was deliberately colored or came into contact with the skin of someone who was wearing ocher makeup. (Prof Christopher Henshilwood, University of Bergen, Norway)

at least 60 miles (100 km) across. So these humans must have constructed rafts or boats, a process requiring complex skills such as cutting timber and lashing pieces of wood together. These ancient travelers probably first made boats for fishing, which they did with nets, and then used the boats to travel longer distances. Although these changes took place gradually, it took only a single generation to travel all the way from Southeast Asia to Australia. No evidence of the means of transportation survives, but it seems most likely that our ancestors traveled by canoe or dugout boat, hugging the shore whenever possible. Those who settled in Australia may have been blown off course in a storm and landed there unintentionally. In Chapter 5, we will learn about the settlement of the Americas; there, too, scientists suppose that early humans traveled down the west coast of the Americas all the way to Chile in similar boats. Yet no watercraft from this time have been found, possibly because any remains have disintegrated.

AP® THEMES

What do the burial practices of early humans indicate about the development of belief in an afterlife?

Once they reached Australia, the early settlers did not stay on the coast but moved inland rapidly, reaching the site of Mungo, in southeast Australia, by 50,000 years ago. There, J. M. Bowler found the grave of Mungo Man near an ancient campsite marked by hearths. The living arranged the body of Mungo Man carefully, positioning his hands over his crotch. Mungo Man was buried in a grave colored by reddish ocher, the same mineral element used to make the ocher implement at Blombos Cave. Bowler explained, *"Small lumps of ochre were recovered but it is likely the bulk of the ochre was scattered over the cadaver as a powder."**

The living, then, deliberately colored the soil around the grave. Burials, which began as early as 100,000 B.C.E., are another important indicator of human behavior because they suggest the presence of religious beliefs. The defining characteristic of **religion** is the belief in a divine power or powers that control or influence the environment and people's lives. The most reliable evidence is a written text demonstrating religious beliefs, but early humans did not write. They did, however, bury their dead, most likely because they believed in an afterlife, a major component of many religious belief systems.

religion

Belief system that holds that divine powers control the environment and people's futures.

Nearby was a woman (Mungo Woman), whose burnt remains constitute the earliest known example of human cremation. The bones of Mungo Woman underwent a multistep process: the living burned her bones, crushed them, burned them a second time, and then buried them—possibly because they wanted to ensure that her spirit never returned to bother the living. Or perhaps they cremated the dead in the hope that their souls could proceed safely to the next world. Like the residents of Blombos, those of the Mungo site also wore and traded shell beads, and they established long-distance trade networks linking Australia with Tasmania and New Guinea.

The Settling of Europe, 50,000–25,000 B.C.E.

Homo sapiens sapiens were sufficiently versatile that they could adjust to new, even cold, habitats, and their improved hunting skills allowed them to move to new places. Early humans followed two routes into Europe: one went around the Mediterranean Sea, and the other followed the Danube River into eastern Europe. Starting around 50,000 B.C.E., the humans living in

*J. M. Bowler and A. G. Thorne, "Human Remains from Lake Mungo: Discovery and Excavation of Lake Mungo III," in *The Origin of the Australians*, ed. R. L. Kirk and A. G. Thorne (Atlantic Highlands, N.J.: Humanities Press Inc., 1976), p. 129.

Europe began to organize hunts of migrating animals in the fall to provide meat during the winter. They continued to refine the advanced hunting technologies of their African forebears, who had formed large, organized hunting parties that killed big game with sharp-pointed spears. In addition to hunting, the migrants also gathered wild plants.

The earliest *Homo sapiens sapiens* found so far in Europe are called Cro Magnon (CROW MAG-nahn), after the site, dating to around 38,000 B.C.E., where their remains were first located in southwest France. Their practices show that they were better able to think about the future than earlier hunting groups. Cro Magnon bands traveled to rivers and coasts to catch fish. As they moved in search of more game and fish, they built new types of houses and developed better clothes. One of their most important innovations was the bone needle, which they used to sew snug-fitting fur clothing to protect them from the cold winters of Europe.

An Ancient Artist at the Chauvet Caves of France Traces of charcoal from the battling woolly rhinoceros (*lower right*) have been dated to about 30,000 B.C.E., making this one of the earliest cave paintings found anywhere in the world. The panel also portrays the same horse in four different poses, rare sketches done by an individual artist. Many of the paintings in the Chauvet caves display this artist's distinctive style. (AP Images/Jean Clottes)

The Worship of Goddesses?

What were the religious beliefs of the residents of Europe between 26,000 and 23,000 B.C.E.? Over twenty female figurines have been found at sites in Austria, Italy, Ukraine, Malta, the Czech Republic, and most often France. Made from mammoth ivory tusk, soapstone, and clay, the figurines range in size from 2 inches (5 cm) to a foot (30 cm) tall. The wide distribution of the figurines poses an interesting problem: Did different groups learn independently to make similar objects, or did one group first craft a model, which was then diffused to other places? Modern archaeologists require striking similarities before they can be persuaded of diffusion. It seems likely in this case that people in different places crafted women according to their own conceptions and that diffusion did not take place.

Some of the women are shown with extremely wide hips and pendulous breasts. Almost none have feet. They may have been placed upright in dirt or on a post. Their facial features remain vague, a suggestion that they are not portraits of particular individuals. Some appear to be pregnant, others not. Some have pubic hair, and one, from Monpazier, France, has an explicitly rendered vulva.

Some have suggested that the figurines are fertility icons made by men or women who hoped to have children. Others propose that the images are self-portraits because no mirrors existed at this early time. If women portrayed their own bodies as they looked to themselves, they would have shown themselves with pendulous breasts and wide hips. Still other archaeologists take these figurines as a sign of a matriarchal society, in which women served as leaders, or a matrilineal society, in which people traced descent through their mother (as opposed to a patriarchal society, in which descent is traced through the father). Since most of these figurines were found in the nineteenth century and were taken to museums or private collections, we do not know their original archaeological context and cannot conclude more about their function.

The one exception is a cave site at Laussel in the Dordogne region of France, where five different pictures were carved onto the cave walls and could not be easily removed. One picture, Woman with a Horn, was carved into the face of a block of stone. This rendering has the large breasts and wide hips of the smaller freestanding figurines, but her right hand is unusual in that it holds a horn, perhaps from a bison.

The Laussel cave had other relief carvings of a similar woman, a younger man in profile, a deer, and a horse. One relief showing a woman on top and another figure below has been interpreted alternatively as two people copulating or a woman giving birth to a child. Several vulvas and phalluses were shown in the same cave. The conjunction of these different images strongly suggests that the Woman with a Horn was worshiped, along with the other carvings and statues of body parts, probably to facilitate conception or easy childbirth.

❯ Historical Thinking Skill:

INTERPRETATION **Why have many historians interpreted prehistoric images and figurines of women, such as the Woman with a Horn, as depictions of a goddess figure?**

❯ Historical Thinking Skill:

ANALYZING EVIDENCE **What details from the Woman with a Horn carving signal to historians that the woman is pregnant?**

Woman with a Horn, Laussel Cave, Dordogne River Valley, France. An Ancient Pregnancy? Standing 17.5 inches (44 cm) high, this block of stone, along with five others, came from a rock shelter occupied by people between 25,000 and 21,000 B.C.E. Similar carvings of women with wide hips and pendulous breasts have been found throughout the Dordogne River Valley region in France, but only this woman holds a horn, which might be from a bison. Interpreting the markings on the horn as calendrical records (perhaps of moon sightings), some analysts propose that her hand on her stomach indicates that she may be pregnant. (Musée d'Aquitaine, Bordeaux, Italy/Erich Lessing/Art Resource, NY)

The Cro Magnon also produced the extraordinary cave paintings of Chauvet (SHOW-vay) in southern France (dated to 30,000 B.C.E.), which show the different animals they hunted: mammoths (various types of extinct elephants), lions, and rhinoceroses. Some paintings are decorated with patterns of dots or human handprints. Other cave sites, such as the well-known Lascaux (las-KOH) (15,000 B.C.E.) site in southwestern France, show horses, bison, and wild goats, suggesting that ancient hunters targeted different animals during different seasons. (See also the feature "Movement of Ideas Through Primary Sources: The Worship of Goddesses?")

Coexisting with Neanderthals

When they entered Europe some 60,000 years ago, the *Homo sapiens sapiens* encountered groups of premodern humans called **Neanderthals** (nee-AHN-dehr-talls) who had been living in Europe for over 100,000 years and who were descended from earlier hominins. Named for the site in West Germany where their remains were first found, Neanderthals were shaped differently from modern humans: their skulls were longer, their faces protruded more, and their bones were bigger and heavier. Neanderthals belonged to a different species: *Homo neanderthalensis*.

Neanderthals
Group of premodern humans who lived between 100,000 and 25,000 B.C.E. in western Asia and Europe, eventually replaced by *Homo sapiens sapiens*.

Contrary to the classification of Neanderthals as a separate species, meaning that they did not mate with *Homo sapiens sapiens*, recent DNA evidence from modern humans suggests that Neanderthals and *Homo sapiens sapiens* did mate. The human genome is composed of 20,000–25,000 genes in DNA; it holds all the instructions contained in our genes that determine growth from the first cell to a fully developed newborn and beyond. The mapping of the human genome has revealed that the DNA of humans living in Eurasia, but not in Africa, contains 1–4 percent Neanderthal DNA, suggesting that humans mated with Neanderthals only after they left Africa. Many of these genes, which relate to skin and hair, may have helped humans adjust to the colder living conditions in Europe.

● **CONTEXT&CONNECTIONS** Modern scientists believe that comparing the DNA of *Homo sapiens sapiens* with that of the Neanderthals will make it possible to distinguish which chromosomes are in active use and which are simply part of our genetic legacy. They are also making progress in reconstructing the genomes of humans who died long ago; in 2014, one team announced that they had successfully read the DNA from a single thighbone of a man who died 45,000 years ago. ●

Neanderthal tools included long stone flakes, which they chipped off large stone cores. They painted themselves and their dwellings. They buried the dead and decorated their graves with clumps of pigment such as ocher. The Neanderthals used fire to cook large animals that they killed. In addition to meat, they ate fish and possibly mushrooms, and they cleaned their teeth with toothpicks. The tartar on some Neanderthal teeth shows that they ingested vegetable matter, too, most likely in the stomachs of herbivores they hunted and killed. (Modern Inuit peoples "regarded this [stomach contents] as a special treat," explains Chris Stringer of London's Natural History Museum.*)

*Z. Zorich, "Neanderthal Smorgasbord," *Archaeology* 67 (Jan/Feb 2014): 16.

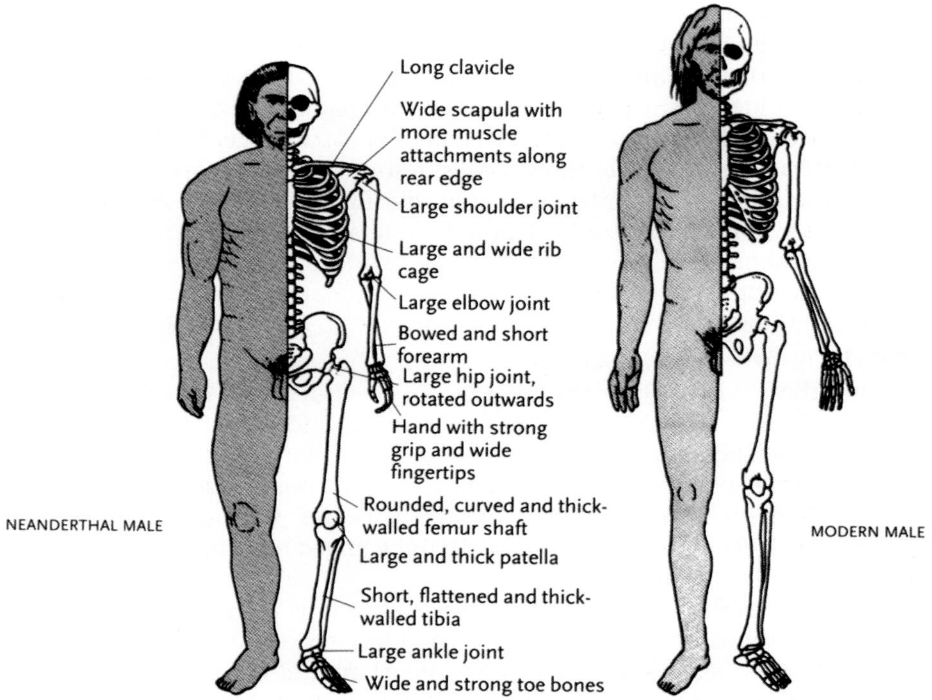

Neanderthal Versus Modern Human Note the differences between a Neanderthal male and modern human male. The Neanderthal's stocky build was better suited to Europe's colder climate. (copyright Thames & Hudson)

• **CONTEXT&CONNECTIONS** The dog was domesticated sometime after the Neanderthals died out, between 30,000 and 18,000 years ago. Previously scientists believed that dogs broke off from wolves and became a separate species in East Asia, but as they study ancient DNA samples from canines recovered archaeologically, they are refining their techniques. They can now pinpoint the emergence of the dog to Europe. And where earlier analysts saw the domestication of the dog as related to the emergence of agriculture, they now realize that it predated that shift by thousands of years. The first wolves to be tamed joined the humans because it was easier to get meat by hunting with human bands than it was on their own. Some even propose, though they are partially joking, that the early dogs domesticated the humans (and not the other way round) because the humans helped the dogs more than the dogs helped the humans. •

Neanderthal skeletons display massive injuries that resulted from hunting large game using short spears with small blades. Most died around the age of forty. Whatever the activity, anatomically modern humans performed the same task at a higher level than Neanderthals: their graves were more elaborate, their tools more finely worked, and their art more complex. Humans could also protect themselves better because they developed longer spears that they could throw. By 40,000 years ago, the Neanderthals had died out, leaving only *Homo sapiens sapiens* in Europe.

Indeed, most experts thought that by 40,000 years ago, *Homo sapiens sapiens* was the only human species on earth, since all other species, including the Neanderthals, had died out. But a discovery announced in October 2004 forced everyone to reconsider this view.

Archaeologists working on the island of Flores in western Indonesia announced that they had discovered bones from a previously unknown human species they called *Homo floresiensis* (HO-mo flor-ehs-ee-EHN-suhs; "Human from Flores"). The remains date from 38,000 to 12,000 B.C.E. The most complete skeleton, intact except for missing arms, came from a female who stood only 42 inches (106 cm) tall.

The excavating archaeologists propose that the new species was a descendant of the hominins who were the predecessors of *Homo sapiens*. Because other pygmy animals, such as pygmy elephants, developed on the island, these scientists suggest that the process of island dwarfing could also have produced smaller-than-usual hominins. The island is currently home to a group of human pygmies, who could be the descendants of the earlier population.*

Yet some scientists have loudly voiced their skepticism, largely because the stone tools found at the site are much more sophisticated than any associated with earlier hominins. They suggest, instead, that the skeleton may be that of a small *Homo sapiens sapiens* afflicted with a disorder called microcephaly (my-cro-SEPH-uh-lee) that results in a shrunken brain and other deformities. This controversial find shows how a single discovery can prompt radical revision of the scientific consensus on human evolution. Even if *Homo floresiensis* gains recognition as a new hominin species, it died out by 12,000 B.C.E., leaving *Homo sapiens sapiens* as the sole surviving human species on the planet.

The Settling of the Americas, ca. 14,000–12,000 B.C.E.

Homo sapiens sapiens reached the Americas much later than they did any other landmass. The earliest confirmed human occupation in the Western Hemisphere dates to about 12,000 B.C.E., some 40,000 years after the settling of the Eurasian landmass and Australia. Accordingly, all human remains found so far in the Americas belong to the *Homo sapiens sapiens* species. Scholars are not certain which routes the early settlers took, when they came, or if they traveled over land or by water.

One theory is that humans reached America on a land bridge from Siberia to Alaska: **Beringia** (bear-in-JEE-uh). Today Beringia is covered by a shallow 50-mile-wide (80-km-wide) stretch of the Bering Sea. As the earth experienced different periods of extended coldness and glaciation, called Ice Ages, the ocean level declined and the ancient Beringia land bridge emerged, measuring over 600 miles (1,000 km) from north to south. What are now islands of the Bering Sea then stood as giant peaks on the Beringia landmass.

Beringia
Landmass now submerged below water that connected the tip of Siberia with the northeastern corner of Alaska.

● **CONTEXT&CONNECTIONS** The early humans may have stayed on Beringia for thousands of years; this would explain the long time gap between the settlement of Eurasia and the Americas. ●

*J. N. Wilford, "Report Reignites Feud over 'Little People' as Separate Species," *New York Times*, August 22, 2006, p. F2.

The first migrations to the Americas may have occurred in 14,000 B.C.E. or even earlier, and they certainly took place by about 12,000 B.C.E., when ice still covered most of Beringia. Much of North America also lay under sheets of ice over 10,000 feet (3,000 m) thick. Some scientists believe that an ice-free corridor between ice masses allowed movement through today's Canada. Others hypothesize that the ancient settlers hugged the coast, traveling in boats covered by animal skins stretched tight over a wooden pole frame. Boats would have allowed them to proceed down the coast from Beringia to South America, disembarking and pitching temporary camps where no ice had formed.

Monte Verde, Chile: How the First Americans Lived, 12,000 B.C.E.

The best evidence for this first wave of migration comes from far down the west coast of the Americas, from a settlement called **Monte Verde, Chile**, which lies only 9 miles (14 km) away from the Pacific coast, south of the 40th parallel. Forming a bony spine running along the western edge of the Americas, the Rocky Mountains and the Andes Mountains formed a barrier that kept the first settlers in the coastal zones west of the mountain chain.

Monte Verde, Chile
Earliest site in the Americas, where evidence of human occupation has been found dating to 12,000 B.C.E.

● **CONTEXT&CONNECTIONS** Early humans probably traveled down the west coast of North and South America in small boats, probably not too different from those used by early humans to go to Australia. ●

Monte Verde is the most important ancient site in the Americas for several reasons. First, without a doubt it contains very early remains. Lying under a layer of peat, it also preserves organic materials like wood, skin, and plants that almost never survive. Finally, and most important, professional archaeologists have scrupulously recorded which items were found at each level, following the key principle of **stratigraphy**—that, at an undisturbed site, any remains found under one layer are earlier than anything from above that layer.

stratigraphy
Archaeological principle that, at an undisturbed site, material from upper layers must be more recent than that from lower layers.

Monte Verde's undisturbed state made it an excellent place from which to collect samples for carbon-14 testing. **Carbon-14** is an isotope of carbon present at a fixed percentage in a living organism. Because this percentage declines after death, one can determine the approximate age of an archaeological sample by analyzing the percentage of carbon-14 in it. Carbon-14 dates always include a plus/minus range because they are not completely accurate: the farther back in time one goes, the less accurate the dating is. (This book gives only one date for ease of presentation.) Carbon-14 analysis of evidence from Monte Verde gave an approximate date of 12,000 B.C.E. for the lowest level definitely occupied by humans.

Carbon-14
Isotope of carbon whose presence in organic material can be used to determine the approximate age of archaeological samples.

Although no human remains have been found at Monte Verde so far, the footprints of a child or a young teenager were preserved on the top of a level dated to 12,000 B.C.E. This finding provides indisputable evidence of human occupation. The twenty to thirty residents of Monte Verde lived in a structure about 22 yards (20 m) long that was covered with animal skins; the floor was also covered with skins. The residents used poles to divide the structure into smaller sections, probably for family groups, and heated these sections with fires in clay hearths. There they prepared food that they had gathered: wild berries, fruits, and wild potato tubers. An even lower layer with stone tools has been dated to approximately 31,000 B.C.E., but the evidence for human occupation is less convincing than the human footprints from the higher level. If people lived at the site at this time, then the Americas may have been settled much earlier than the 14,000 B.C.E. date that is widely accepted today.

A separate building, shaped like a wishbone, stood about 100 feet (30 m) away from the large structure. The residents hardened the floor of this building by mixing sand, gravel, and animal fat to make a place where they could clean bones, produce tools, and finish animal hides. Healers may have treated the ill in this building, too, since the floor contained traces of eighteen different plants, some chewed and then spit out, as though they had been used as medicine.

The unusual preservation of wood at Monte Verde means that we know exactly which tools the first Americans used. The site's residents mounted stone flakes onto wooden sticks, called hafts. They also had a small number of more finely worked spear points. Interestingly, Monte Verde's residents used many round stones, which they could have easily gathered on the beach, for slings or bolos. A bolo consists of a long string made of hide with stones tied at both ends. Holding one end, early humans swung the other end around their heads at high speed and then released the string. If on target, the spinning bolo wrapped itself around the neck of a bird or other animal and killed it. The residents of Monte Verde hunted mastodon, a relative of the modern elephant that became extinct about 9000 B.C.E. They also foraged along the coast for shellfish, which could be eaten raw. In the initial stages of migration, the settlers found a coastal environment much more hospitable than an inland one because they could forage for many different types of food at the beach. Hunting parties could leave for long periods to pursue mastodon and other large game, confident that those left behind had ample food supplies.

● **CONTEXT&CONNECTIONS** The main weapon used to kill large game at Monte Verde and other early sites was the atlatl (AHT-latt-uhl), a word from the Nahuatl (NAH-waht) language spoken in central Mexico. The atlatl was a powerful weapon, capable of piercing thick animal hide, and was used for thousands of years. ●

A Powerful Ancient Weapon: The Atlatl The residents of the Monte Verde site used the atlatl spear-thrower to kill game. The atlatl had two parts, a long handle with a cup or hook at the end, and a spear tipped with a sharp stone point. The handle served as an extension of the human arm, so that the spear could be thrown farther with much greater force. (Illustration by Eric Parrish from Dixon, James E., *Bones, Boats and Bisons: Archaeology and the First Colonization of Western North America*, first edition, Albuquerque, NM, University of New Mexico Press, 1999, page 153, figure 6-1)

The Rise of Clovis and Other Regional Traditions, 11,000 B.C.E.

By 11,000 B.C.E., small bands of people had settled all of the Americas. They used a new weapon in addition to the atlatl: wooden sticks with sharp slivers of rock, called microblades, attached to the shaft. Studies of different sites have determined that while the people in these regions shared many traits in common, different technological traditions also existed in different North American regions. Each left behind distinct artifacts (usually a spear point of a certain type).

Clovis technological complex
The characteristic stone spear points that were in use around 11,000 B.C.E. across much of modern-day America.

Like the residents of Monte Verde, these later peoples combined hunting with the gathering of wild fruits and seeds. They lived in an area stretching from Oregon to Texas, with heavy concentration in the Great Plains, and hunted a wide variety of game using atlatl tipped with stone spear points. Archaeologists call these characteristic spear points the **Clovis technological complex**, named for Clovis, New Mexico, where the first such spear points were found. It is difficult to estimate the number of residents at a given location, but some of the Clovis sites are larger than earlier sites, suggesting that as many as sixty people may have lived together in a single band.

The Clovis spear points impress all viewers with their beauty: their makers chose glassy rocks of striking colors to craft finely worked stone points. Foraging bands covered large stretches of territory, collecting different types of stone and carrying them far from their areas of origin. The Clovis peoples buried some of these collections in earth colored by ocher, the same mineral used by the ancient peoples of South Africa and Australia. (See the feature "World History in Today's World: The Unquenchable Demand for Ivory.")

● **CONTEXT&CONNECTIONS** Archaeologists working at later Clovis sites throughout the Great Plains have also found a different type of stone blade lodged in bison bones. It seems that, as mammoth and mastodon became extinct, the residents shifted to hunting bison. ●

The migrations to the Americas ended when the world's climate warmed quickly at the end of the Wisconsin Ice Age. After 8300 B.C.E., the sea level rose, so that by 7000 B.C.E. most of Beringia lay under water once again. The only regions of the world that had not yet been settled were the islands of the Pacific (see Chapter 5). After 7000 B.C.E., the ancestors of modern Amerindians dispersed over North and South America, where they lived in almost total isolation from the rest of the world until after 1492.

The Emergence of Agriculture, 9400–3000 B.C.E.

agriculture
The planting of seeds and harvesting of crops using domesticated animals.

The development of **agriculture**, when people planted the first seeds and harvested the resulting crops using domesticated animals to help with their work, marked a crucial breakthrough in the history of humankind. Before it, all ancient peoples were hunters and gatherers, constantly in motion, whether following herds of wild animals or gathering wild berries and plants. Over thousands of years, early peoples in different parts of the globe experimented first by gathering certain plants and planting their seeds, which anthropologists refer to as cultivation, and raising and killing selected animals, a process called domestication.

Eventually some of these peoples began to plant seeds in specific locations and to raise tame animals that could help them harvest their crops. Only when

WORLD HISTORY IN TODAY'S WORLD

The Unquenchable Demand for Ivory

In 1989, because Africa's population of elephants was dwindling dangerously quickly, the Convention on International Trade in Endangered Species banned all trade in ivory. Although poaching continues in some countries, the ban has largely succeeded in protecting Africa's elephant population, and, as a result, South Africa and its neighboring countries face the unprecedented situation of having too many elephants. As the elephant and human populations both increase, elephants trample villages and crops growing in the fields. The problem of elephant overpopulation is so severe that the Botswana government has even permitted the hunting of elephants to resume.

Despite the ban, the demand for ivory, mostly from China, continues to grow. The newly rich, many prospering from China's booming economy, often purchase large pieces of ivory, such as a single tusk, with detailed art scenes engraved on them. These objects can cost more than a million dollars, a price that includes several years of carving by high-level craftsmen. Their trade is over one thousand years old.

Where do the Chinese obtain this ivory? Sometimes ivory that has been obtained without killing elephants comes on the market. For example, when an elderly elephant dies, its tusks can be removed, and some African governments sell authorized stockpiles of legal ivory.

Global warming has produced another source of ivory far to the north of Africa, in the Sakha region of Siberia, in the Russian arctic. This region used to be covered in ice, but in recent years some of the permafrost has begun to melt, exposing the frozen carcasses of mammoths that roamed the region over ten thousand years ago, with the last dying out about four thousand years ago. Often their tusks stick out of the ice before the rest of their body, and the men involved in the trade can earn more than $60,000 for a single tusk, which can weigh 150 pounds, or just under 70 kg. Although experts can distinguish between the two types of ivory, mammoth ivory can be used for all the same purposes as elephant ivory. The sale of mammoth tusks is also illegal, and Russian border guards in helicopters do patrol the area, confiscating illegally obtained tusks. Armed with snowmobiles, GPS devices, and satellite phones, the mammoth tusk hunters have the advantage, and the number of tusks recovered from the permafrost is bound to increase in coming years as the demand for ivory shows no signs of flagging.

Source: Brook Larmer, "Of Mammoths and Men," *National Geographic* April (2013): 44–63.

a society committed to both processes did it become an agricultural society. Many others continued to forage for all their food. For example, in the spring, hunter-gatherers in New Guinea planted the seeds of a particularly desirable crop, such as bananas, and then moved on, returning in the fall to harvest the ripened fruit. This is cultivation but not agriculture, because they did not raise crops or animals full time.

For those who adopted agriculture, the cultivation of crops caused a dramatic increase in human populations, who first lived in small farming villages and then in towns. Archaeologists have found evidence of cultivation that arose independently in at least nine places, all at different times: western Asia, the east African highlands, China's Yangzi River Valley, Pakistan's Indus River Valley, Southeast Asia, New Guinea, central Mexico, the Andes, and sub-Saharan Africa (see Table 1.1 and Map 1.1). The crops grown in each place had a strong, lasting influence on that society's diet; even today Chinese people eat rice and wheat products, while corn remains important in Mexico. The ancient peoples also domesticated animals with very different results. The main meat source for people living in the Andes was the domesticated guinea pig (they did not eat llama), while the residents of New Guinea and Mexico followed a predominantly vegetarian diet.

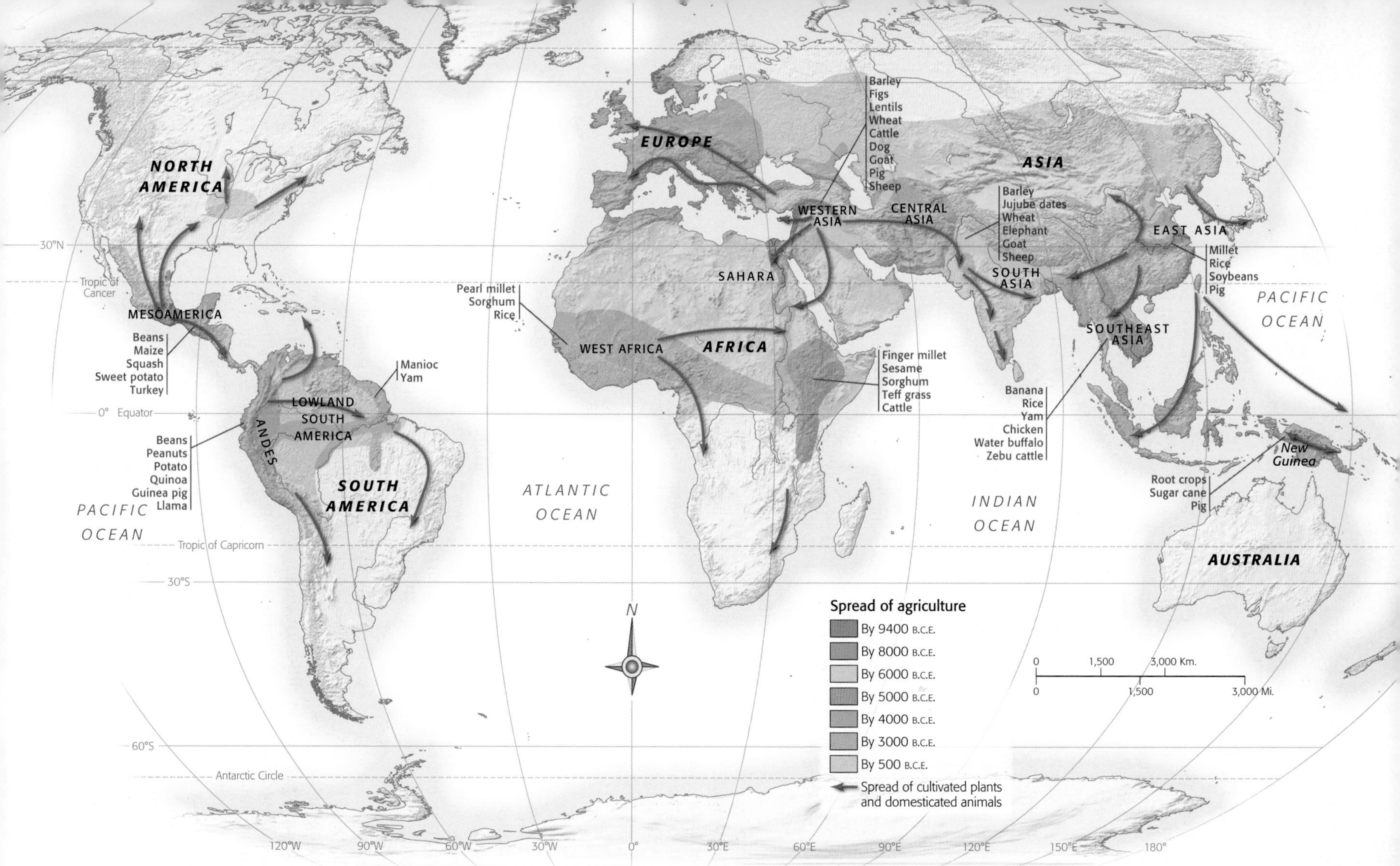

Map 1.1 Early Agriculture Agriculture developed independently at different times in the different regions of the world. In some places, like western Asia, residents gradually shifted to full-time cultivation of crops and raising domesticated animals, while in others, like New Guinea, they continued to hunt and gather.

Table 1.1 Dates and locations of earliest cultivation

Date of Earliest Cultivation	Place	Crops and Animals
9400 B.C.E.	West Asia	Fig, barley, lentil, wheat, cattle, dog, goat, pig, sheep
8000 B.C.E.	Yangzi River Valley China	Rice, millet, soybeans, pig, dog
8000 B.C.E.	East African highlands	Finger millet, sesame, sorghum, teff grass, cattle
7000 B.C.E.	Indus River Valley, Pakistan	Wheat, barley, jujube date, elephant, sheep, goat
5000 B.C.E.	Southeast Asia	Banana, rice, yam, water buffalo, chicken, zebu cattle
5000 B.C.E.	New Guinea	Root crops, sugar cane, pig
5000 B.C.E.	Central Mexico	Beans, maize, squash, sweet potato, turkey
4000 B.C.E.	Peruvian Andes	Beans, peanuts, potato, quinoa, guinea pig, llama
3000 B.C.E.	Sub-Saharan Africa	Pearl millet, sorghum, rice

The Domestication of Plants and Animals, ca. 9400–7000 B.C.E.

The first people in the world who learned how to plant seeds, domesticate animals, and cultivate crops were the **Natufians** (NAH-too-fee-uhnz), who lived in Palestine and southern Syria by 12,500 B.C.E. (see Map 1.2). Hunters and gatherers, they harvested fields of grain, particularly wild barley and emmer wheat. They also picked fruits and nuts and hunted wild cattle, goats, pigs, and deer.

Natufians
The first people to cultivate crops and domesticate animals, ca. 9400 B.C.E., who lived in Palestine and southern Syria.

The Natufians used small flint blades mounted on wooden handles to cut down the stands of wild barley and emmer wheat, and they ground the harvested grain in stone mortars with pestles. Because they knew how to make advanced stone tools, archaeologists class them as **Neolithic**, literally "New Stone Age," people who, unlike earlier peoples, practiced agriculture. Gradually the Natufians began to modify their way of life so that they could support a growing population.

Neolithic
"New Stone Age," the archaeological term for societies that used stone tools and practiced agriculture.

Around 9400 B.C.E., the Natufians began to cultivate their first crop: figs. In 2006, archaeologists found nine dried figs that had been preserved after being burnt in a fire. These figs, because of a mutation, had no fertile seeds but tasted sweet; unless someone planted a branch from a fig tree in the ground, this type of fig would have died out the following season. Since the figs did not die out, we know that someone deliberately planted them. The Natufians did not have to stay near the fig trees they planted; they could continue to hunt and gather as before and simply had to visit the fig trees from time to time to collect the fruit and plant new branches.

The next crop they cultivated—grain—had a far greater impact because it replaced basic elements in their diet. At first, the Natufians gathered wild grain where it grew naturally. But wild grain had two flaws: the stems were so weak that their seeds easily fell to the ground, and thick husks made it difficult to remove the kernels of grain from inside the seeds. The Natufians gradually started to weed

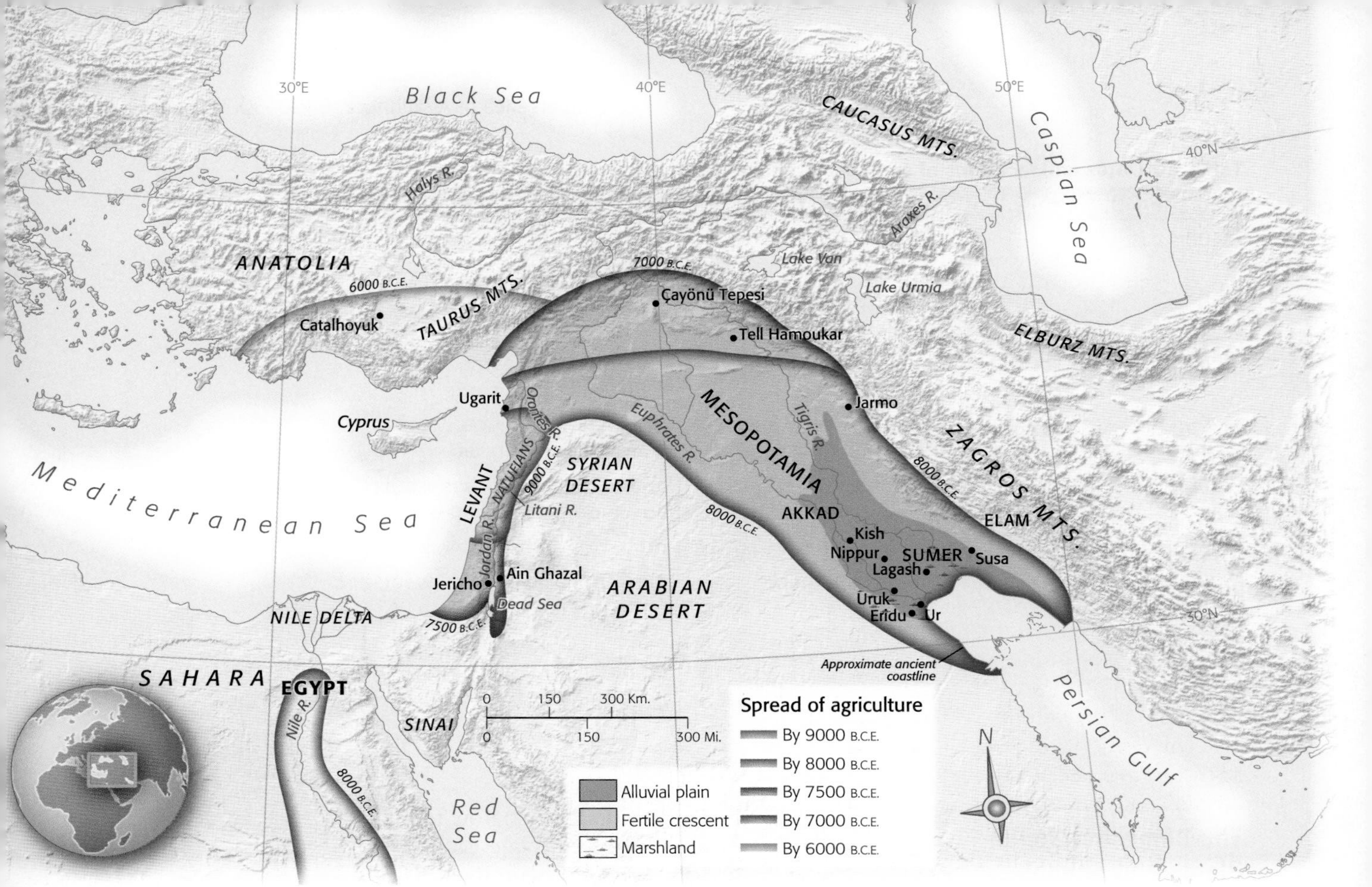

Map 1.2 Ancient Southwestern Asia The Natufians, who lived in Palestine and southern Syria, began to harvest wild crops around 12,500 B.C.E. and gradually learned how to raise animals and plant crops over the next several thousand years. Agriculture eventually spread beyond the Levant and Mesopotamia to southern Anatolia, where agriculturalists built the world's earliest town at Catalhoyuk.

these naturally occurring stands of grain and to plant extra seeds in them. The Natufians picked seeds from tall plants and favored plants whose kernels had thinner husks, which eventually fostered the growth of grain that was easier to harvest and winnow. The wheat and barley they planted began to diverge from their wild prototypes.

People took thousands of years to master the two major components of farming: domesticating animals and planting crops. The first step to domesticating wild animals was simply to stop killing young female animals. Then people began to watch over wild herds and kill only those animals that could no longer breed. Eventually, the Natufians began to feed the herds in their care. After several thousand years, villagers had domesticated goats, sheep, and cattle. All these animals produced meat, and sheep produced wool that was woven into cloth.

Most of the Natufians lived in houses dug halfway into the ground, 10–20 feet (3–6 m) across, with a fireplace. The size of excavated Natufian sites suggests that groups as large as 150 or 250 people—far larger than the typical hunting and gathering band of 30 or 40—lived together in settlements as large as 10,800 square feet (1,000 sq m). The shift to agriculture almost always caused a dramatic increase in population.

By 8000 B.C.E. many peoples throughout the eastern Mediterranean, particularly near the Zagros (ZAH-groes) Mountains in modern Turkey, had begun to cultivate wheat and barley (see Map 1.2). Unlike the Natufians, these peoples did not live near pre-existing stands of wild wheat and barley but rather in dryer, less fertile conditions. Peoples living in marginal areas, not the most fertile areas with the heaviest rainfall, tended to plant crops because they had to innovate. Once they had begun to cultivate crops, the larger size of their villages forced them to continue farming because agriculture could support a larger population than foraging.

The First Larger Settlements, 7000–3000 B.C.E.

Between 8300 and 7500 B.C.E., the largest Natufian settlement was **Jericho** (JEHR-ih-koh), near the Jordan River in the present-day West Bank, where as many as one thousand people may have lived in an area of 8–10 acres (.03–.04 sq km). Residing in mud-brick dwellings with stone foundation bases, the residents of Jericho planted barley and wheat, possibly along with figs and lentils, at the same time they continued to hunt wild animals. The more grains they ate, the more their bodies needed salt, which they collected by evaporating water from the Dead Sea.

Jericho The first walled settlement, built between 8300 and 7500 B.C.E., with a population of around one thousand people.

The residents of Jericho dug a wide ditch and built a wall at least 8 feet (2.5 m) high around their settlement to protect their accumulated resources from wild animals, human enemies, or possibly both. They also built a 28-foot (8.5-m) tower inside the wall that may have served as a lookout post. The ditches, the wall, and the tower all show the ruler's ability to mobilize laborers and supplies for large-scale construction.

AP® THEMES

How does the layout of Jericho reflect the role of its ruler in ensuring the security of the inhabitants?

Although the site of Jericho suggests that the rise of agriculture contributed to an increase in population and, thus, large settlements, some analysts argue the opposite. They see the rise of large settlements as causing the shift to agriculture. Gobekli Tepe, a site near Jericho but in Turkey, supports the view that the population increased before the shift to agriculture. The excavating archaeologist summarizes the site's significance: "This is the first human-built holy place,"* meaning that this was a ritual site. As sophisticated as the site is, it contains no evidence of agriculture. The residents hunted many different wild animals but domesticated none of their own. Gobekli Tepe was occupied about 9000 B.C.E., and evidence of early cultivation has been found 20 miles (32 km) away, dating just 500 years later, suggesting that the residents built this elaborate cult center before they began to cultivate seeds and domesticate the first animals.

Around 7250 B.C.E., more than one thousand people lived at the site of Ain Ghazal (AYN GUH-zahl) near Amman, Jordan, which also covered 10 acres (.04 sq km) and had tripled in size by 6000 B.C.E. The residents of Ain Ghazal detached the heads of some of the dead and buried them in pits under their houses—perhaps these were ancestors they especially revered—but they threw away other intact corpses without removing their heads. Two ritual pits held groups of unusual human figurines, made from plaster around a tree-branch core; some were as tall

*Andrew Curry, "Gobekli Tepe: The World's First Temple," *Smithsonian Magazine* (2008), http://www.smithsonianmag.com/history/gobekli-tepe-the-worlds-first-temple-83613665/?no-ist.

Marcia Chambers/dbimages/Alamy

Gobekli Tepe This site holds more than sixty limestone pillars that bear carvings of animals, mostly predators like lions, boars, and snakes. The tallest, some originally in the shape of a T, stood over 16 feet (5 m) and weighed between 7 and 10 tons (6.3 to 9 metric tons). What do you notice about the layout of the site? Do you agree that it must have been a ritual center?

as 3 feet (.9 m), with distinctive shell eyes. These practices all suggest that the living believed they could communicate with the dead.

- **CONTEXT&CONNECTIONS** In the absence of written texts, archaeologists have to speculate about the nature of religious beliefs. The next chapter will introduce a text that describes in detail the journey of the hero to the world of dead. Nothing comparable survives from Ain Ghazal. •

By 7000 B.C.E. early farmers were living in villages in western Turkey and the region of the Levant (the eastern shore of the Mediterranean in today's Lebanon and Israel). Their residents could depend on rainfall to support their crops, and they continued to forage as they raised their own herds. By far the largest settlement in the region was at **Catalhoyuk** (CHAH-tal-her-yerk) in south-central Anatolia, where some five thousand people were living in 6000 B.C.E.

Catalhoyuk
The world's largest early settlement, with a population of 5,000 in 6000 B.C.E., located in modern Turkey.

Catalhoyuk did not resemble earlier settlements. Unlike Jericho, it had no external wall or surrounding moats. The residents lived in mud-brick dwellings touching each other, and the exteriors of the houses on the perimeter of the town formed a continuous protective wall. The settlement had no streets, and the houses had no doors at ground level. Instead, residents walked on top of the roofs to get from one place to another. Entering houses through a hole in the roof, they climbed down a ladder to get inside.

The Earliest Depictions of People? The Plaster Statues of Ain Ghazal, Jordan Dating to 6500 B.C.E., these figures were probably used in rituals and commemorated the dead. Their makers fashioned a core of reeds and grass, covered it with plaster, and then painted clothes and facial features on it. The eyes, made from inlaid shells with painted dots, are particularly haunting.

• **CONTEXT&CONNECTIONS** Many more people lived at Catalhoyuk than at Natufian sites, and their dwellings were much more complex, too. •

Frequently whitewashed, the walls of the Catalhoyuk dwellings depicted animals, hunters, gods, and even the earliest known landscape painting of a volcano exploding. Of the more than one hundred rooms that have been excavated, forty had plaster models of bull or ram heads mounted on the walls or paintings showing women giving birth to rams or bulls. These rooms may have served as shrines where residents worshiped bulls and rams.

The different types of houses at Catalhoyuk indicate that some residents had more wealth than others. The wealthy buried their dead with jewelry and tools, while the poor interred only their dead bodies.

AP® THEMES
What different kinds of economic activities did the people of Catalhoyuk engage in?

• **CONTEXT&CONNECTIONS** These differences became even more pronounced in complex societies, the subject of the next chapter, and archaeologists use them to distinguish complex societies from those that came before. •

At the same time that they worked in the fields, some families worked bone tools, wove cloth, or made clay pots, which they could trade for other goods, especially obsidian, a naturally occurring volcanic glass. Ancient peoples treasured obsidian because they could use it to make sharp knives and beautiful jewelry.

CONTEXT AND CONNECTIONS

Migrations as a Sign of Human Development

Mungo Man and Mungo Woman are among the earliest exemplars of human behavior. Their discovery shows that, by 50,000 B.C.E., when they arrived in Australia, *Homo sapiens sapiens* were certainly behaving like modern humans—planning for the future, imagining an afterlife, and engaging in multistep activities, such as planning long-distance journeys. Anatomically modern humans had arisen in western Africa sometime around 200,000 B.C.E., and they began to behave in recognizably human ways tens of thousands of years later, when they hunted large game, crafted the world's first art objects, built large trade networks, and started to speak.

Our forebears had to build small boats or rafts to cross some 60 miles (100 km) of ocean to reach Australia, but they did not have to adapt to a different climate. However, when *Homo sapiens sapiens* entered Europe in 50,000 B.C.E., they had to adjust to colder temperatures, and they mated with the Neanderthals already living there, leaving traces in the DNA of people living in Europe and Asia today. The trip into the Americas, which also required some migrants to travel by boat, occurred in 14,000 B.C.E. at the latest.

The total worldwide population of humans remained low—an estimated 10,000–20,000—as they settled all of the world's regions except for the islands of the Pacific. The population only began to increase after the introduction of agriculture. Many peoples of the world continued to hunt and gather as the major way of securing food. The Natufians were the first to shift to agriculture, around 8400 B.C.E., and their settlements at Jericho and Ain Ghazal were larger than any earlier human settlements. Archaeologists are not certain that agriculture predated all larger settlements; the existence of the ritual site of Gobekli Tepe suggests that people were capable of forming larger settlements even without the benefits of intensive cultivation or the domestication of animals. Catalhoyuk, the largest early settlement, was the result of the spread of agriculture to Turkey. In a few places in the world, the development of agriculture would lead to the rise of a complex society, as we will see in Chapters 2 through Chapters 5.

The remains of Mungo Man testify to the settlement of Australia, one of the most distant journeys ancient humans took. The movement of humans from Africa to almost every corner of the globe was a long one, requiring over 100,000 years. One theme is constant: our ancestors were always on the move. They followed herds, crossed rivers, traveled by boat, and ultimately covered enormous distances at a time when their most powerful weapon was a stone hand ax and the fastest means of locomotion was running. From their beginnings, humans have always been voyagers who traveled the world.

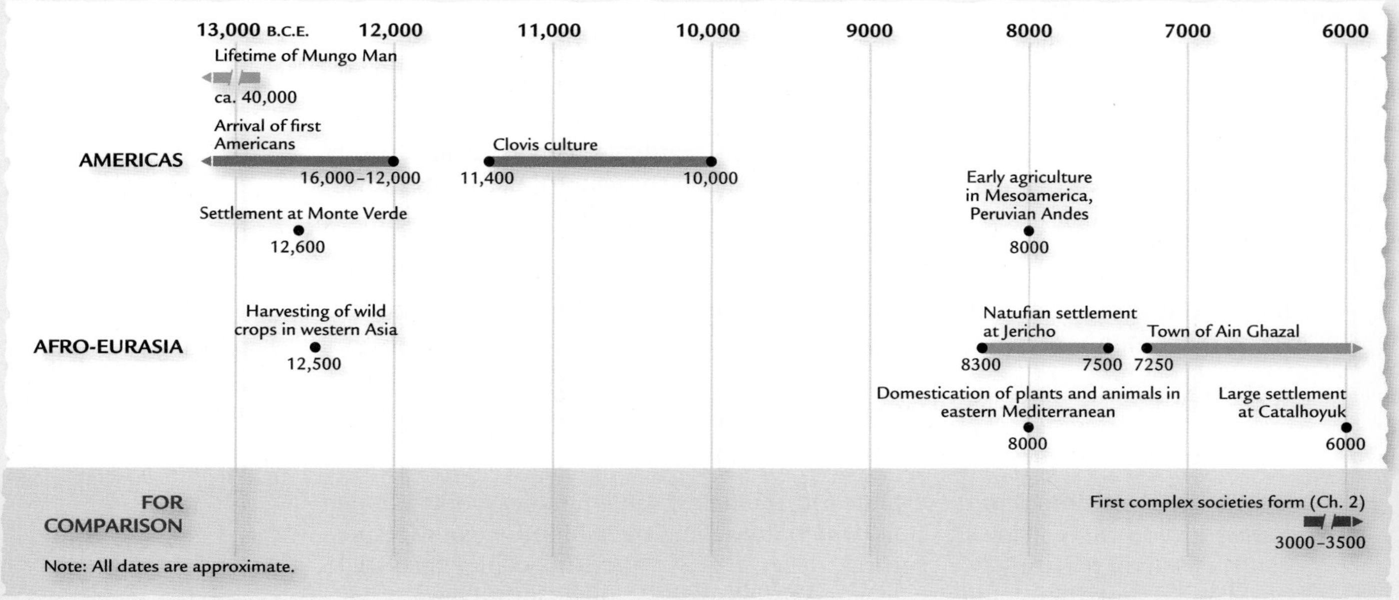

Key Terms

Mungo Man (3)
ocher (3)
Homo sapiens sapiens (4)
hominins (4)
evolution (5)
mitochondrial Eve (6)
religion (10)
Neanderthals (13)
Beringia (15)
Monte Verde, Chile (16)
stratigraphy (16)
carbon-14 (16)
Clovis technological complex (18)
agriculture (18)
Neolithic (21)
Natufians (21)
Jericho (23)
Catalhoyuk (24)

For Further Reference

Cook, Jill. *Ice Age Art: Arrival of the Modern Mind*. London: British Museum Press, 2013.

Davidson, Iain, and William Noble. "Why the First Colonisation of the Australian Region Is the Earliest Evidence of Modern Human Behaviour." *Archaeology in Oceania* 27, no. 3 (October 1992): 135–142.

Dillehay, Tom D., et al. "Monte Verde: Seaweed, Food, Medicine, and the Peopling of South America." *Science* 320, no. 5877 (May 2008): 784–789.

Dixon, E. James. *Bones, Boats, and Bison*. Albuquerque: University of New Mexico Press, 1999.

Fagan, Brian M. *The Great Journey: The Peopling of Ancient America*. Gainesville: University Press of Florida, 2004.

Haynes, G. *Early Settlement of North America: The Clovis Era*. New York: Cambridge University Press, 2002.

Klein, Richard, with Blake Edgar. *The Dawn of Human Culture*. New York: John Wiley, 2002.

Scarre, Chris. *The Human Past: World Prehistory and the Development of Human Societies*. 3rd ed. New York: Thames and Hudson, 2013.

Stiebing, William H. *Ancient Near Eastern History and Culture*. New York: Pearson/Longman, 2009.

Stringer, Chris. *Lone Survivors: How We Came to be the Only Humans on Earth*. New York: Times Books, 2012.

Tattersall, Ian. *The World from Beginnings to 4000 B.C.E.* New York: Oxford University Press, 2008.

Wells, Spencer. *Deep Ancestry: Inside the Genographic Project*. Washington, D.C.: National Geographic, 2006.

AP® Review Questions for Chapter 1

Multiple-Choice Questions

QUESTIONS 1–4 REFER TO THE FOLLOWING MAP.

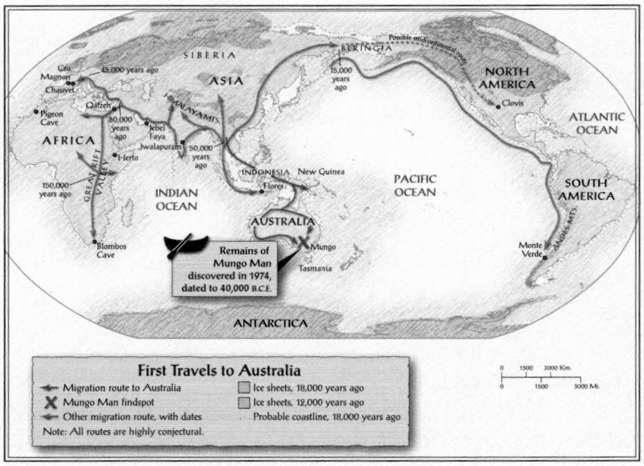

1. Based on the map, where has the earliest evidence for human beings been found?
   (A) Southwest Asia
   (B) Northern Europe
   (C) Southeast Asia
   (D) Eastern Africa

2. What made the migration of humans to Oceania and the Americas possible?
   (A) A warming trend made arid lands more fertile.
   (B) Ice ages made regions accessible through land bridges.
   (C) Early sailing technology made the Americas accessible to Asian tribes.
   (D) Paleolithic Europeans probably sailed across the Atlantic to the Americas.

3. Which of the following conclusions can be drawn from the map?
   (A) Europe and Australia were settled at about the same time.
   (B) The Americas were settled before Australia.
   (C) Monte Verde was settled at an earlier date than Clovis.
   (D) Europe and the Americas were settled at the same time.

4. Which of the following would be an argument against the theory that the populations of the Americas and Oceania arrived during the last ice age?
   (A) A Paleolithic site in the Americas established 400 years after the Roman empire
   (B) The lack of Paleolithic sites in North America
   (C) A Paleolithic site that predates the last ice age
   (D) Hunting technology located in northern Siberia

QUESTIONS 5–8 REFER TO THE FOLLOWING PASSAGE.

Anthropologists . . . have found evidence that the women of the so-called upper Paleolithic era were far more accomplished, economically powerful, and sartorially gifted than previously believed.

As the researchers see it, subtle but intricate details on a number of the figurines offer the most compelling evidence yet that Paleolithic women had already mastered a revolutionary skill long thought to have arisen much later in human history: the ability to weave plant fibers into cloth, rope, nets, and baskets.

—Natalie Angier, "Furs for Evening, but Cloth Was the Stone Age Standby," *New York Times*, 1999

5. The existence of Venus figurines like the ones described above indicate which of the following?
   (A) Paleolithic societies were essentially patriarchic.
   (B) Women and men shared the same occupations and activities.
   (C) Women held significant amounts of power and status.
   (D) Paleolithic societies lacked what we term today as culture.

6. Based on the Venus figurines, anthropologists infer which of the following?
   (A) Women had mastered the skills needed for weaving.
   (B) Hunting and reliability of food sources were the primary concerns.
   (C) Fear of neighboring tribes led to the establishment of religion.
   (D) Severe shifts in the climate disrupted food supplies.

7. The author seems surprised by the finding of the anthropologists for which of the following reasons?
   (A) Paleolithic societies created no technologies at all.
   (B) Paleolithic societies mastered technologies earlier than once believed.
   (C) Paleolithic societies showed no concern over the fertility of women and animals.
   (D) Paleolithic societies made extensive preparations before going to war.

8. If the author's claim is correct, which of the following is a valid inference based on the passage?
   (A) Women were responsible for more than just gathering in Paleolithic societies.
   (B) Women were quickly losing status to men and their weapons technology.
   (C) Women were responsible for creating all technology in Paleolithic societies.
   (D) Women were held in equal status with children in Paleolithic societies.

QUESTIONS 9–10 REFER TO THE FOLLOWING PASSAGE.

The discovery of farming techniques has usually been assumed to have been made by men, but it is in fact very much more likely to have been made by women. On the basis of anthropological evidence for societies still living traditional foraging lifestyles and those living by simple, non-mechanised farming, taken in conjunction with direct archaeological evidence, it seems probable that it was women who made the first observations of plant behavior, and worked out, presumably by long trial and error, how to grow and tend crops.

—Margaret Ehrenberg,
Women in Prehistory, 1989

9. The author portrays the findings of anthropologists and archaeologists as surprising for which of the following reasons?
   (A) Women were the ones who benefited the most from the rise of agriculture.
   (B) Women were primarily concerned with hunting.
   (C) Men usually provided more calories than women by hunting.
   (D) The development of agriculture has usually been attributed to men.

10. The author argues that women were in the best position to start agriculture for which reason?
   (A) Women spent the most time in the woods hunting.
   (B) Men were only partially responsible for gathering.
   (C) As gatherers, women spent more time around plants.
   (D) Women and men spent equal amounts of time domesticating animals.

Short-Answer Questions

1. Answer parts A and B.
   A. Identify and explain TWO ways that Paleolithic societies adapted to their environment.
   B. Explain ONE reason why the transition to agriculture was a slow process that developed over time.

2. Answer parts A and B.
   A. Explain ONE reason why agriculture began in Asia before other regions.
   B. Explain TWO reasons why agriculture developed in Africa later than in Asia.

2 The First Complex Societies in the Eastern Mediterranean, ca. 4000–550 B.C.E.

Gilgamesh Killing the Human-headed Bull of Heaven

The *Epic of Gilgamesh* (GIL-ga-mesh), one of the earliest recorded works of literature, captures the experience of the people of Mesopotamia (mess-oh-poh-TAME-ee-ah), who established one of the first complex societies in the world. **Mesopotamia** (Greek for "between the rivers") is the region between the Tigris (TIE-gris) and Euphrates (you-FRAY-teez) Rivers in today's Iraq and eastern Syria. The *Epic of Gilgamesh* indicates that the people in this region remembered what life was like before the rise of cities. It describes the unlikely friendship between two men: Enkidu (EN-kee-doo), who lives in the wild like an animal, and **Gilgamesh**, the king of the ancient city Uruk (OO-rook), located in modern-day Warka in southern Iraq. Ruler of the walled city during a time between 2700 and 2500 B.C.E., Gilgamesh enjoys the benefits of a complex society: wearing clothing, drinking beer, and eating bread. Early in the epic, when a hunter complains to Gilgamesh that Enkidu is freeing the animals caught in his traps, Gilgamesh sends the woman Shamhat, a priestess at the main temple of Uruk, to introduce Enkidu to the pleasures of life:

Enkidu, born in the uplands,
Who feeds on grass with gazelles,
Who drinks at the water hole with beasts, . . .
Shamhat looked upon him, a human-man,
A barbarous fellow from the midst of the steppe:
Shamhat loosened her garments,
She exposed her loins, he took her charms, . . .
After he had his fill of her delights,
He set off towards his beasts.

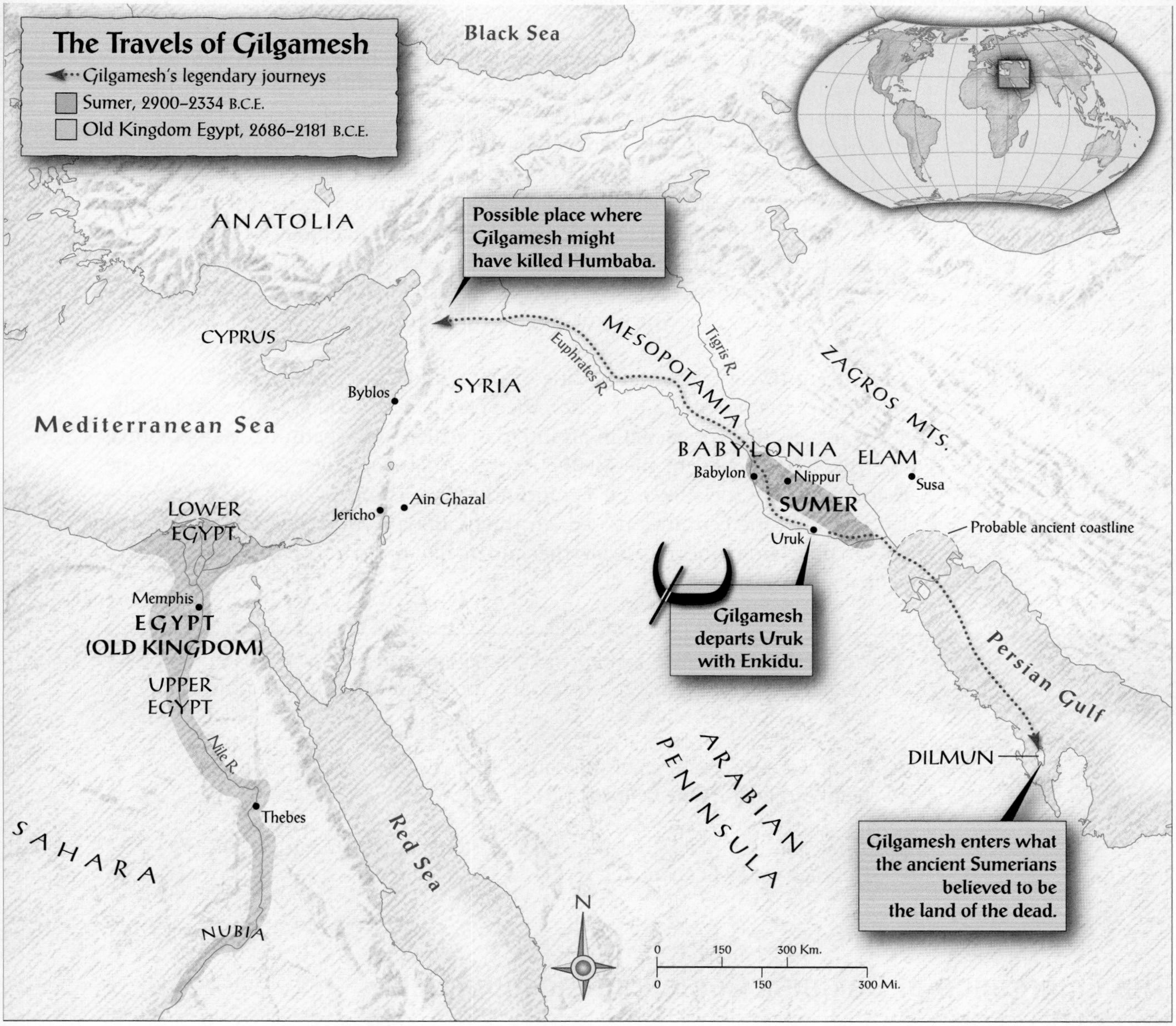

When they saw him, Enkidu, the gazelles shied off,
The wild beasts of the steppe shunned his person. . . .
Enkidu was too slow, he could not run as before,
*But he had gained reason and expanded his understanding.**

---

*Excerpt from *The Epic of Gilgamesh*, translated by Benjamin R. Foster. Copyright © 2001 by W.W. Norton & Company. Used by permission of W.W. Norton & Company, Inc.

Mesopotamia
Greek for "between the rivers": the region between the Tigris and Euphrates Rivers in today's Iraq and eastern Syria.

Gilgamesh
Name of a historic king of Uruk (modern-day Warka, Iraq) who ruled between 2700 and 2500 B.C.E. Also the name of an epic about him.

After his encounter with Shamhat, Enkidu immediately adopts the ways of those living in complex societies and becomes Gilgamesh's close friend. First written around 2100 B.C.E., *Gilgamesh* is not a strict chronicle of the historic king's life, but the romanticized version of a legendary king's life, complete with appearances by different gods who control human fate.

The hero of the epic is constantly in motion. Gilgamesh makes two long journeys, traveling overland by foot and across water on a small boat he guides with a pole. First, he travels with Enkidu to kill the ferocious monster Humbaba, who guards a cedar forest somewhere to the west. Then, after Enkidu dies, Gilgamesh voyages to the land of the dead, where he learns about a flood surprisingly like that described in the Hebrew Bible.

Gilgamesh reveals much about one of the world's first complex societies. This chapter traces the rise of the first cities, then city-states, then kingdoms, and finally regional powers that interacted in an international system spanning Mesopotamia, Egypt, the eastern coast of the Mediterranean, Anatolia, Crete, and Greece in the Aegean Sea. These societies were significantly more complex than those that preceded them. As the centuries passed, an international system developed, allowing envoys to travel from one ruler to another and merchants to transport goods throughout the region.

KEY CONCEPT QUESTIONS

- How did the core civilizations in Mesopotamia and Egypt use laws, language, literature, religion, myths, and monumental architecture to unify their regions? **(Key Concept 1.3)**
- What were the features of the early systems of exchange in the eastern Mediterranean? **(Key Concept 1.3)**
- What were the main characteristics of monotheism among the ancient Hebrews? **(Key Concept 1.3)**

The Emergence of Complex Society in Mesopotamia, ca. 3100–1590 B.C.E.

complex society
Society characterized by a large urban center with specialized labor and social stratification, as well as the belief that rulers and deities were entitled to the surpluses the society produced.

As we have seen in the previous chapter, the settlements of the eastern Mediterranean increased in size gradually, reaching some five thousand people living in Catalhoyuk by 6000 B.C.E. Eventually some villages became larger than the surrounding villages and thus became centers. In time, these centers grew to house twenty thousand inhabitants or more. By 3100 B.C.E. even larger urban centers had formed in southern Mesopotamia, where the first city of forty or fifty thousand people was located at Uruk. Here complex society took shape.

Scholars define a **complex society** as a large urban center with a population in the tens of thousands whose residents pursue different occupations, the mark of specialized labor. Some have higher social positions than others, an indication of social stratification. Some earlier definitions of complex society required the presence of a writing system, but today the term also covers urban societies without writing systems. In recent years, analysts have stressed that, unlike Neolithic societies, early complex societies had much larger surpluses—of both material goods and labor—which were often the product of agriculture. The people living in complex societies believed that their rulers, their gods, and their gods' human representatives, the priests, were entitled to a large share of these surpluses.

Complex Societies and the Discipline of History

The shift from a simpler society to a complex one took thousands of years. Complex societies interest historians because they had larger populations than simple societies and their residents often left behind written records that allow historians to study how they changed over time. Although historians sometimes write about societies with no writing systems (as we have seen in the previous chapter and will see again in future chapters), they generally specialize in analyzing written materials, which they divide into primary sources and secondary sources. The *Epic of Gilgamesh* is a primary source because it took shape in ancient Mesopotamia and was first written down around 2100 B.C.E. This chapter draws on other primary sources like Hammurabi's laws, which explain the logic of the Babylonian legal system; the Egyptian *Book of the Dead*, which sheds light on ancient Egyptian beliefs; and also the Hebrew Bible, which according to Hebrew tradition tells of the origins of the Jews. Passages from primary sources are italicized to help you in your reading. Historians always prefer information from primary sources because later observers have not altered it in any way.

Historians have to consider all types of information about past societies, not just written documents. Visual evidence from paintings and other objects often provides a valuable supplement, especially in societies with limited literacy (true of almost all the societies considered in Volume 1). The Visual Evidence feature gives you a chance to develop your ability to analyze information that was not written down.

This book, *Voyages in World History*, is a secondary source: it did not originate with those who made history, but was written to teach history. This is true of all the books listed at the end of each chapter under "For Further Reference"; these works reflect the best scholarship on the topics treated in the chapter. We have checked the content of *Voyages* with the world's experts, and the information is reliable. This is not true of a random search on the Internet; you might find something accurate, but much misinformation circulates.

For some world regions, historians work to establish basic facts such as the names of kings or when they reigned, but nowadays most historians study societies where the basic chronology is already known. In those cases, they bring new questions to the past that reflect our changing concerns. Ultimately, historians always rely on the primary sources, but they read their sources carefully, checking the meanings of different words and grappling with unfamiliar grammar and ambiguous or uncertain language. They consult with fellow historians and others in different disciplines and exercise ingenuity in trying to pin down the meaning of the sources. They mine the sources for evidence, the information they derive from the sources, which they weave to create historical arguments. Successive generations return to the same evidence with new questions about the past, questions that are of interest today, and rediscover unnoticed information in the sources. (See "World History in Today's World: Recreating the World's Oldest Brew," page 34, for a specific example of how historians working with brewers are making beer as the ancient Mesopotamians did.) All this is part of interpretation, the art of history.

This book focuses on movement and contact, which are key to world history because world historians focus on connections among the different societies of the past. The movement of people, whether in voluntary migrations or forced slavery, has been one of the most fruitful topics for world historians. In addition, we increasingly live in a world where each of us meets people from many different societies. If we know something about their history and their traditions, we can better understand why they behave as they do and perhaps avoid conflict.

The world's first complex societies appeared in Mesopotamia and Egypt at about the same time, before 3000 B.C.E. Both societies produced written records about this time, making them particularly intriguing to historians. This chapter considers Mesopotamia first.

City Life in Ancient Mesopotamia

The first settlers came to southern Mesopotamia from the eastern Mediterranean and western Turkey. They found the environment harsh. Each year not enough rain fell to support intensive farming, and no wild grain grew naturally in the marshlands. In addition, the Tigris and Euphrates Rivers tended to flood in the late summer, when crops were ripening, and the floodwaters often washed away the settlers' homes.

AP® THEMES

How did the first settlers in Mesopotamia alter their environment to suit their needs?

The settlers responded by digging channels for the river's floodwater, through which they could move the water to fields far from the river. Using irrigation, these early farmers permanently settled the lower Mesopotamian plain between 6000 and 5000 B.C.E.

Their first villages were small, but by 4000 B.C.E. some villages had grown into walled urban centers of over ten thousand people. The urban centers came to depend on surplus food grown by the residents of the surrounding villages, which was stored in temples. In turn, the cities provided the villages with military protection from raids by neighboring cities.

• **CONTEXT&CONNECTIONS** Like the ancient city of *Jericho* (key term in Chapter 1), which was built some four thousand years earlier, these new settlements had walls around them, but they housed a population ten times larger than Jericho's population of one thousand. •

city-state

A city whose ruler governs both the city center and the surrounding countryside.

Historians use the term **city-state** for a city whose ruler governs both the city center and the surrounding countryside. Kings descended from prominent families, like Gilgamesh, ruled these city-states, often with the support of temple priests and in consultation with other prominent families (see page 37). The first kings were probably successful military leaders who continued to rule in peacetime.

Ancient texts simply call Gilgamesh's city of Uruk "the city," because no other city rivaled Uruk in size or importance between 3400 and 3000 B.C.E., the dates of the Uruk period. One of the most ancient cities to be excavated by archaeologists, Uruk meets the definition of a complex society: its population numbered between forty and fifty thousand, and its inhabitants had specialized occupations and were divided by social level. The surrounding countryside provided a large surplus of grain that the ruler and temple leadership distributed to the residents of the city.

The opening section of *Gilgamesh* provides a vivid description of the region's greatest city:

Go up, pace out the walls of Uruk,
Study the foundation terrace and examine the brickwork.

Is not its masonry of kiln-fired brick?
And did not seven masters lay its foundations?
One square mile of city, one square mile of gardens,
One square mile of clay pits, a half square mile of Ishtar's dwelling,
*Three and a half square miles is the measure of Uruk!**

Uruk, then, contained roughly 1 square mile each of land occupied by residences, farmland, and clay pits, with the remaining half square mile taken by the temple of Ishtar, the city's guardian deity. However, the most complete version of the *Gilgamesh* epic is a retelling of the original story, dating to 700 B.C.E., and historians must use archaeological data to supplement the information it provides about early Uruk. Although the epic claims that the walls were made from fired bricks, the actual walls were made from sun-dried mud brick. In roughly 3000 B.C.E., the city had a wall 5 miles (9.5 km) long. Enclosing approximately 1,000 acres (400 hectares), it was by far the largest city in the world at the time. Much of it consisted of open farmland.

Unlike Neolithic farmers, whose tools were made from bone, wood, or stone, Mesopotamian farmers had much more durable tools made of **bronze**, an alloy of copper and tin. In addition to axes used to cut down trees and clear fields, they used bronze plow blades to dig their furrows and bronze sickles to harvest their grain.

bronze
An alloy of copper and tin used to make the earliest metal tools.

• **CONTEXT&CONNECTIONS** Different ancient peoples discovered how to use different metals for different purposes, and historians pay close attention to these differences because they had long-reaching aftereffects. Because the Mesopotamians and other Eurasian peoples used bronze and then later iron, earlier historians thought that all societies went through a Bronze Age before reaching an Iron Age. We now know that this was not a universal pattern: the people living in Mesoamerica and the Andes never used iron, and conversely, people living in Africa discovered iron without using bronze beforehand. Accordingly, world historians avoid the terms *Bronze Age* and *Iron Age*. •

Archaeologists are not certain where the **wheel** was invented. One of the most important tools used by the Mesopotamians, it first appeared sometime around 3500 B.C.E. in a wide area extending from Mesopotamia to the modern European countries of Switzerland, Slovenia, Poland, and Russia. The earliest wheeled vehicles were flat wooden platforms that moved on two logs pulled by laborers. By 3000 B.C.E. the Mesopotamians were using narrow carts, usually with four solid wooden wheels, to move loads, both within city-states and over greater distances. By 2500 B.C.E. they had begun to add spokes to wheels, which allowed for much greater speed.

wheel
An important innovation in transport dating to 3500 B.C.E.

• **CONTEXT&CONNECTIONS** Interestingly, the ancient peoples living in Mexico knew about the wheel but never used it. •

Built in the floodplain of the Euphrates, Uruk had no tall trees suitable for lumber, little stone, and almost no mineral deposits. The epic tells of Gilgamesh and Enkidu's overland journey to the wooded home of the monster Humbaba to

---

*Excerpt from *The Epic of Gilgamesh,* translated by Benjamin R. Foster. Copyright © 2001 by W.W. Norton & Company. Used by permission of W.W. Norton & Company, Inc.

WORLD HISTORY IN TODAY'S WORLD

Recreating the World's Oldest Brew

"*Enkidu did not know how to eat bread / Nor had he ever learned to drink beer!*"* exclaims the author of *Gilgamesh*, introducing Enkidu as a man of the wild with no experience of life in complex society. *Gilgamesh* vividly describes Enkidu's first taste of beer:

> *Enkidu drank seven juglets of the beer.*
> *His mood became relaxed, he was singing joyously,*
> *He felt light-hearted and his features glowed.**

Unlike Enkidu and all those living outside cities, Sumerians of all social levels drank beer constantly, usually through straws. Beer, unlike water, was sanitary, carrying no waterborne diseases. Temple-goers offered clay jars of beer to the gods, and Sumerians regularly gave wedding presents ranging from 5 to 10 gallons (20–40 L) of beer, or one-third to two-thirds of a modern keg.

Although no detailed recipes survive from Mesopotamia, a hymn to the goddess of beer-making specifies the multiple steps in the process: baking bread in an oven to get yeast in a usable form, sprinkling malt placed on the ground with water, preventing stray dogs from eating it, soaking the malt in clay jars, adding cooked grain, sweetening with honey and flavoring with herbs, leaving it in a clay pot to ferment, and finally skimming off the beer.

This is not, unfortunately, enough information to make the beer. To attempt that, in an innovative experiment, one microbrewery, the Great Lakes Brewing Company, has sought out the expert advice of archeologists at the Oriental Institute of the University of Chicago, which provided facsimile clay pots modeled on ancient vessels. The team has had some breakthroughs. The project members succeeded in fermenting barley on the roof of the microbrewery, and a local bakery provided bread that produced the active yeast they needed. So far the beer tastes sour and is undrinkable, but the experimenters are not discouraged because the collaboration has been so stimulating.

The brewers have asked the archeologists new questions that had not occurred to them. One University of Chicago doctoral student, in an apt characterization of historical method, summarized how the collaboration worked: "We keep going back to the evidence and finding new hints that can help us choose between different interpretations." Who knows? With a little more experimenting, the brewery and the archeologists may succeed in recreating the world's oldest beer.

---

*Excerpts from *The Epic of Gilgamesh*, translated by Benjamin R. Foster.

Source: Steven Yaccino, "For Its Latest Beer, a Craft Brewer Chooses an Unlikely Pairing: Archaeology," *New York Times*, Tuesday, June 18, 2013, p. A16.

obtain lumber, and the real-life inhabitants of Uruk shipped wood in carts or by boat first from the highlands of northern Mesopotamia, near the Zagros (ZAH-groes) Mountains, and later from the forests of Lebanon.

At Uruk, archaeologists have found extensive evidence of occupational diversity and social stratification, both important markers of a complex society. Large quantities of broken pottery found in the same area suggest that potters lived and worked together, as did other craftworkers like weavers and metal-smiths. Because people received more or less compensation for different tasks, some became rich while others stayed poor. Poorer people lived in small houses made of unfired mud bricks and mud plaster, while richer people lived in fired-brick houses with kitchens and many rooms. They hosted guests in large reception rooms in which they served lavish meals washed down with generous quantities of beer. (See the feature "World History in Today's World: Recreating the World's Oldest Brew.")

• **CONTEXT&CONNECTIONS** The differences between wealthy and poor were more pronounced in Uruk than in earlier settlements such as *Catalhoyuk*, around 6000 B.C.E. (Chapter 1), where graves, not houses, displayed the greatest disparities. And Uruk contains more evidence than previous sites of how people who were neither rich nor poor, but somewhere in the middle, lived. •

The Beginnings of Writing, 3300 B.C.E.

People living in southern Mesopotamia developed their writing system sometime around 3300 B.C.E., making it the earliest in the world. Scholars call the language of the first documents Sumerian, after **Sumer**, a geographical term referring broadly to the ancient region of southern Mesopotamia. It is not always easy to determine whether a given sign constitutes writing in ancient script. Markings on pottery, for example, look like writing but may be only the mark of the person who made the pot. A sign becomes writing only when someone other than the writer associates a specific word or sound with it.

Sumer
A geographical term from Akkadian meaning the ancient region of southern Mesopotamia.

We can track the invention of writing in Mesopotamia because the residents used clay, a material that, once baked, was virtually indestructible. At first, sometime between 4000 and 3000 B.C.E., the ancient Sumerians used small clay objects of different shapes to keep track of merchandise, probably animals being traded or donated to a temple. Eventually they began to incise lines in these objects to stand for a certain number of items. Later, they placed these small objects in a bag made from a clay sheet and incised these bags, while still soft, on the outside to indicate their contents. These markings did not yet constitute written language because they could be understood in different ways; one had to cut open the clay bag, after it had hardened, to find out what was inside. In recent years, archeologists have used CT-scanning technology to examine the contents of these clay bags without having to destroy the outer bag, but they have not yet deciphered the markings on them.

AP® THEMES
How did the development of record keeping facilitate the growth of commerce?

The transition to written language came when people drew a picture on a flat writing tablet that represented a specific animal and could not be mistaken for anything else. The first documents in human history, from a level dating to 3300 B.C.E., depict the item being counted with a tally next to it to show the number of items. Temple accountants needed writing to record increasingly sophisticated transactions, like the number and type of animal or the amount of grain donated on successive days.

By 3300 B.C.E., a full-blown writing system of more than seven hundred different signs had emerged. Some symbols, like an ox head representing an ox, are clearly pictorial, but many others are not. The word *sheep*, for example, was a circle with an *X* inside it (see Figure 2.1).

Over time, the marks lost their original shapes, and by 700 B.C.E. each symbol represented a certain sound; that is, it had become phonetic. We call this later writing **cuneiform** (cue-NAY-i-form), meaning "wedge-shaped," because it was made by a writing implement in the triangular shape of a wedge pressed into clay. These early records, most of them temple accounts, allow us to understand early Sumerian religion and how the ancient Sumerians distributed their surplus wealth.

cuneiform
The term, meaning "wedge-shaped," for the writing system of Sumer in its late stages, when the script became completely phonetic.

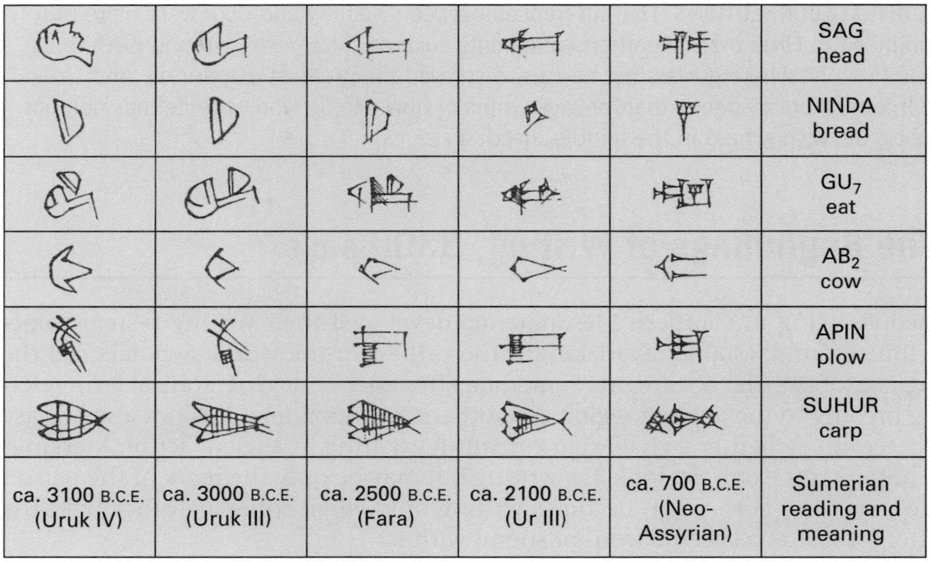

FIGURE 2.1 **Cuneiform** The Mesopotamians first made small pictures, or pictographs, to write, but these symbols gradually evolved into combinations of lines that scribes made by pressing a wedge-shaped implement into wet clay. The cuneiform forms from 700 B.C.E. hardly resemble their original pictographic shapes from 3100 B.C.E. (From J. N. Postgate, *Early Mesopotamia: Society and Economy at the Dawn of History*, Routledge, 1992, p. 63. Reprinted with permission of Taylor and Francis Books Ltd.)

Sumerian Religion

The people of ancient Sumer believed that various gods managed different aspects of their hostile environment. The most powerful god, the storm-god, could control storms and flooding. Like human beings, the Sumerian gods had families who sometimes lived together in harmony and sometimes did not.

The largest building in Uruk was the temple to Ishtar, the protective deity of Uruk and the storm-god's daughter. Sumerian temple complexes sometimes housed a thousand priests, priestesses, and supporting laborers. The largest structure inside each temple was a ziggurat, a stepped platform made from bricks. Throughout the year both rich and poor participated in different festivals and ceremonies presided over by priests and priestesses.

The human king played an important role in Sumerian religion because he was believed to be the intermediary between the gods and human beings. The epic describes Gilgamesh as two-thirds divine and one-third human, an indication that the Sumerians did not believe that parents contributed equal shares to their offspring. He was sufficiently attractive that Ishtar proposed marriage to him. He brusquely turned her down, pointing out that each of her previous lovers had come to a bad end.

Ishtar persuaded her father to retaliate by sending the Bull of Heaven to punish Gilgamesh and destroy Uruk. Gilgamesh's friend Enkidu killed the bull, to the delight of Uruk's residents but to the dismay of the gods, who then convened in council. The storm-god decided that Enkidu must die.

Before he died, Enkidu dreamed of the world of the dead:

To the house whence none who enters comes forth,
On the road from which there is no way back,
To the house whose dwellers are deprived of light,
Where dust is their fare and their food is clay.
They are dressed like birds in feather garments,
*Yea, they shall see no daylight for they abide in darkness**

This description provides certain evidence—not available for earlier, preliterate societies—that the Sumerians believed in an afterworld.

• **CONTEXT&CONNECTIONS** For earlier periods from which no written records survive, archaeologists must surmise belief in the afterworld on the basis of burial practices such as those at Ain Ghazal (see Chapter 1), where some of the dead were buried underneath the houses of the living and where the earliest depictions of people may be statues of the deceased made to remind the living of those whom they had lost. •

When Enkidu dies, the heartbroken Gilgamesh renounces life in complex society: *"Now that you are dead, I will let my hair grow matted / I will put on a lion skin and roam the steppe!"** Resolving to escape death himself, he travels a great distance over mountains and desert to reach the entrance to the underworld, believed to be near modern-day Bahrain. At the end of his journey, Gilgamesh meets Utanapishtim (OO-tah-nah-pish-teem), who tells him that a great flood occurred because the storm-god became angry with humankind and that Utanapishtim escaped when another divinity secretly informed him in time to build a boat. Gilgamesh realizes that he, like all human beings, must die, and returns to Uruk to rule the city-state.

Sumerian Government

The ruler of each city-state claimed to rule with the support of the local guardian deity, but an early version of *Gilgamesh* makes clear that he actually ruled in consultation with one or more assemblies. Faced with a demand from a neighboring kingdom to surrender, Gilgamesh consults with two separate assemblies, one of elders and one of younger men. While the elders oppose Gilgamesh's decision to go to war, the younger men support him.

During the Early Dynastic period, between 2900 and 2334 B.C.E., settlers moved out of Uruk to build new city-states closer to supplies of lumber and precious metals. Because transportation was slow and communication difficult, these satellite cities had their own rulers but maintained trade ties with the mother cities and with each other. Higher city walls, growing numbers of bronze weapons, and increasing artistic depictions of battle victories indicate regular warfare among these city-states.

*Excerpts from *The Epic of Gilgamesh*, translated by Benjamin R. Foster. Copyright © 2001 by W.W. Norton & Company. Used by permission of W.W. Norton & Company, Inc.

Documenting the Violence of War: The Standard of Ur This object tells a story of war in different panels read from bottom to top. Notice the trampled bodies of the enemy under the feet of the donkeys on the bottom frame. The battle continues in the middle, and, on the top, officials present prisoners to a larger-than-life size king. (The Trustees of the British Museum/Art Resource, NY)

Sargon of Akkad
(r. 2334–2279 B.C.E.) The first ruler to unify Mesopotamia. Changed the language of administration to Akkadian.

empire
A large territory in which one people rule over other subject peoples with different languages and different religious traditions.

The first ruler to conquer all the city-states and unify the region was **Sargon of Akkad** (r. 2334–2279 B.C.E.). Sargon (SAHR-gone) and the Akkadians ruled the world's first **empire**. He and his descendants ruled over southern Mesopotamia for slightly over one hundred years. Researchers there have made new discoveries of obsidian, volcanic black glass used to make razor-edged knives (see Chapter 5). Its presence shows that the Akkadians created trading networks that extended as far as central Turkey; when their empire broke apart, these networks contracted sharply. As surviving inscriptions indicate, Sargon changed the language of administration from Sumerian to Akkadian (uh-KAY-dee-uhn), named for his home city of Akkad (AHK-cad), and Akkadian replaced Sumerian as the language of daily life.

The Babylonian Empire, 1894–1595 B.C.E.

After the fall of the Akkadian empire, Mesopotamia again broke into several different kingdoms. Sometime around 2200 B.C.E., a new city, Babylon, located north of Uruk on the Euphrates, gained prominence. Babylon was a small city-state ruled by a succession of kings until the great military and legal leader Hammurabi (ham-u-ROB-ee) (r. 1792–1750 B.C.E.) unified much of Mesopotamia.

Hammurabi is famous, even today, for the laws that he issued. Many people have heard of a single provision in Hammurabi's law—"an eye for an eye"—but few realize that the original document contained nearly three hundred articles on a host of topics, including the treatment of slaves, divorce, criminal punishments, and interest rates on loans. Although Hammurabi's laws are often called a "code," the texts of many surviving decisions indicate that judges did not actually consult them. The king carved different legal cases onto stone tablets as proof of his divine rule and as model cases for future kings to study.

AP® THEMES
How did Hammurabi's code reinforce existing social class and gender divisions?

The laws recognized three different social groups, who received different punishments for the same crime. The most privileged group included the royal family, priests, merchants, and other free men and women who owned land. In the middle were commoners and peasants, and at the bottom were slaves.

The original wording of the famous eye-for-an-eye clause says, *"If an awālu [freeman] should blind the eye of another awālu [freeman], they shall blind his eye."** This is the law of exact retaliation: if you bring harm to someone else, the identical wound shall be your punishment. It operated only among social equals, however. If a freeman destroyed the eye of a commoner, he paid only a moderate fine. If he destroyed the eye of a slave or broke one of his bones, then he had to pay the owner half of the slave's value, an even lesser amount. The laws stipulated the payment of fines in fixed amounts of silver or grain because coins did not yet exist.

As trade increased in the years after 2000 B.C.E., the Babylonian law codes governing commerce became more detailed. The main trading partners of the Babylonians lay to the southeast and included communities in the Persian Gulf and modern-day Afghanistan, who exported copper, the blue semiprecious mineral lapis lazuli, and other metals and precious stones in exchange for Mesopotamian textiles.

Hammurabi's laws also provide insight into marriage and the roles and status of women. Marriage had to be recorded in a written contract to be legally valid. Women were entitled to a share of their father's and/or mother's property, either as a gift when they married or as a share of the father's wealth upon his death. Punishment for adultery was severe: if a wife was found "lying with" someone other than her husband, she and her lover were tied together and thrown into water to drown; she was permitted to live if her husband allowed it.

At the same time, the law afforded women certain legal rights. If a woman was accused of adultery and denied it (and was not found with a lover), she could take an oath of innocence before a god and return to her husband's house unpunished. A wife could initiate divorce on the grounds that her husband failed to support her or had committed adultery. If the judge found that her husband had taken a lover but she had not, the divorce would be granted.

The tablets reveal only how Hammurabi hoped his laws would operate, not how they actually did. Historians call this a prescriptive source because it reports what should happen, and they value descriptive sources that tell what actually did happen. One case, recorded shortly before Hammurabi's reign on a clay tablet found at Nippur, is valuable precisely because it shows how the legal system actually functioned. Three men—a barber, a gardener, and a third person whose occupation is not mentioned—killed a temple official named Lu-Inanna. They confessed to the victim's wife, but she, for unstated reasons, failed to report the crime.

Eventually the murderers were apprehended and the case came before the assembly of Nippur. A group of about ten men, including a bird-hunter, a porter, and a gardener, argued against the murderers: *"They who have killed a man are not worthy of life. Those three males and that woman [the widow] should be killed in front of the chair of Lu-Inanna."* An official and a gardener, whose different social ranks show the mixed composition of the assembly, spoke on the wife's behalf: *"Granted*

*Martha T. Roth, *Law Collections from Mesopotamia and Asia Major* (Atlanta: Scholars Press, 1997), p. 121.

*that the husband... had been killed, but what had the woman done that she should be killed?"** The assembly decided that the murderers should be punished but that the wife was innocent.

Southern Mesopotamia came to be known as Babylonia. Yet Hammurabi's dynasty was short-lived. It officially ended in 1595 B.C.E., when the Hittites (see page 48) sacked the city. Although the pace and extent of trade continued to increase, between 3300 and 1500 B.C.E. Mesopotamia remained politically apart from the other kingdoms of the eastern Mediterranean, as well as from Egypt, its neighbor to the west.

Egypt During the Old and Middle Kingdoms, ca. 3100–1500 B.C.E.

pharaoh The god-king who ruled the unified kingdom of Egypt from at least 3100 B.C.E.

Complex society arose in Egypt at about the same time as in Mesopotamia—3100 B.C.E.—but under much different circumstances. The people of Egypt never lived in city-states but rather in a unified kingdom made possible by the natural geography of the Nile River Valley. Their god-king was called the **pharaoh**. Although Egypt did not have the large cities so characteristic of early complex societies, its society was highly stratified, with great differences between the poor and the rich. Large construction projects, like the building of the pyramids, required the same kind of occupational specialization so visible in Mesopotamian cities. The less tangible aspects of complex societies—the belief that the ruler governed with the support of the gods and that his subjects owed him their surplus—were also present in ancient Egypt.

In certain periods, Egypt was unified under strong rulers. Historians call these periods "kingdoms." In other times, called "intermediate periods," the presiding pharaoh did not actually govern the entire region. The pharaohs of the Old Kingdom (2686–2181 B.C.E.) ruled the Nile Valley from the Delta to the first impassable rapids; those who ruled during the Middle Kingdom (2040–1782 B.C.E.) controlled an even larger area.

The Central Role of the Nile

The Egyptian climate is mild, and the country is protected by natural barriers: deserts on three sides and the Mediterranean Sea on the fourth. Fed by headwaters coming from Lake Victoria and the Ethiopian highlands, the Nile flows north, and its large delta opens onto the Mediterranean. Along the river are six steep, perilous, unnavigable rapids called cataracts (see Map 2.1). Lying 620 miles (1,000 km) upstream, the First Cataract formed a natural barrier between Egypt and **Nubia**, an ancient kingdom, sometimes called Kush, that straddled modern Egypt and Sudan (see page 47). Egypt was divided into three parts: Lower Egypt (the Delta region north of present-day Cairo), Upper Egypt (which ran from the First Cataract to the Delta), and Nubia.

Nubia Region south of the First Cataract on the Nile, in modern-day Egypt and Sudan; was an important trading partner of Egypt.

Because almost no rain falls anywhere along the Nile, farmers had to tap the river to irrigate their fields, which were near the river. Two types of soil filled the

---

*Samuel Noah Kramer, *History Begins at Sumer: Thirty-Nine Firsts in Recorded History* (Philadelphia: University of Pennsylvania Press, 1981), p. 58.

banks of the Nile: "the black land," averaging one-quarter mile (.65 sq km) on both sides, consisted of very fertile soil, each year renewed by the river's deposits of silt; beyond the black land lay the red land, which was less fertile. Beyond the red land lay uncultivable desert.

● **CONTEXT&CONNECTIONS** The Nile, with its annual summer floods, was a much more reliable source of water than the Tigris and Euphrates in Mesopotamia; thus the Egyptians had no equivalent of the vengeful Mesopotamian storm-god who ordered the flood in *Gilgamesh*. ●

The Egyptians began to cultivate the floodplain of the Nile between 4400 and 4000 B.C.E. Their calendar had three seasons, each 120 days long: "Inundation," "Emergence of the Fields from Waters," and "Drought." During "Emergence," farmers used irrigation to move the Nile waters to their fields and planted seeds, which they harvested during the "Drought" season.

Egyptian Government and Society: Unity Without City-States

Egyptians were writing by 3100 B.C.E., using **hieroglyphs** (pictorial and phonetic symbols). The surviving record does not explain how writing developed in Egypt because the Egyptians used a perishable writing material made by pressing together the inner stems of **papyrus** (pah-PIE-rus), a reed that grew along the banks of the Nile. The dried fibers bonded to form a lightweight, convenient writing material that was far more fragile than the clay tablets of Mesopotamia. Most of the surviving sources for Egyptian history were carved into stone.

● **CONTEXT&CONNECTIONS** Egyptian hieroglyphs are so different from Sumerian writing that the two societies probably developed writing independently. ●

Ancient historians credited the legendary founder of the First dynasty (3200–3000 B.C.E.), Narmer (NAR-mer), with consolidating the

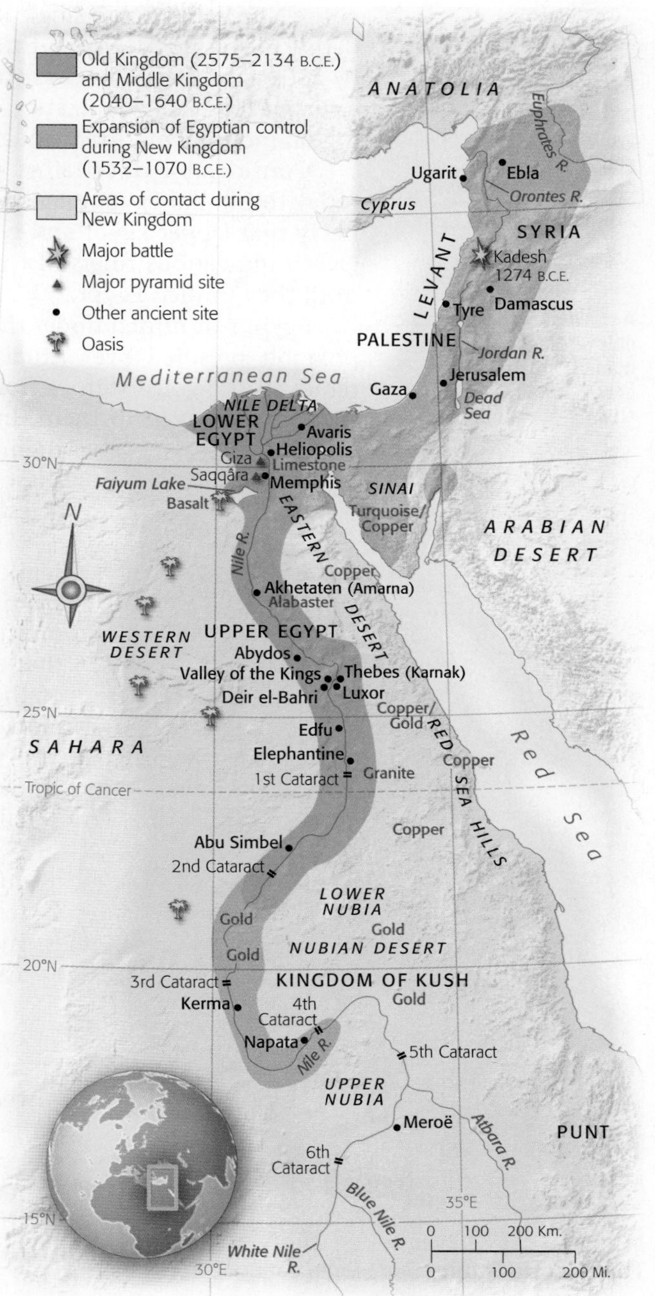

Map 2.1 Ancient Egypt and Nubia The Nile River lay at the heart of ancient Egypt, but one could not sail all the way from its headwaters in Lake Victoria and the Ethiopian highlands to the Delta at the Mediterranean. Because no boat could cross the sheer vertical rapids called cataracts, the First Cataract formed a natural barrier between Egypt and Nubia, the region to the south where many gold fields were located.

hieroglyphs
The writing system of ancient Egypt, which consisted of different symbols, some pictorial and some phonetic, used on official inscriptions.

papyrus
A convenient but perishable writing material made from a reed that grew naturally along the Nile.

entire Nile Valley into a single kingdom. One of the earliest records is a piece of slate dating to around 3100 B.C.E. that uses hieroglyphs to indicate the king's name. Later, by 2500 B.C.E., Egyptians were using two writing systems: pictorial hieroglyphs, and a cursive form, called hieratic ("priestly"). Hieroglyphs were reserved for public writing on monuments and plaques.

Considerable uncertainty persists in our knowledge of Egypt. Many scholars today think that Egypt may have been unified as early as 3500–3200 B.C.E. It seems likely that Upper Egypt and Lower Egypt originally formed two separate regions. Over time various rulers of Upper Egypt gradually conquered more of the Delta until they unified Egypt.

Egypt was united under the rule of one man, the pharaoh. As a god-king, the pharaoh presided over rituals to the Egyptian gods. In theory, the pharaoh removed the gods' statues from their shrines in each temple, dressed them, fed them, and prayed to them. In the evening he fed them again before returning them to their shrines. In practice, the pharaoh performed these rites in the capital and delegated his duties to priests throughout Egypt.

Since the pharaoh's family members shared his semidivine status, pharaohs often married their closest kin, including their sisters and mothers. They also took multiple wives. The frequency of intermarriage meant that a single woman could simultaneously be the wife of the serving pharaoh, the mother of the future pharaoh, and the daughter of the previous one. For example, the wife of King Tutankhamen (too-tunk-AH-muhn), Ankhesenamen (ON-kays-ah-muhn), was also his half-sister.

Since the pharaoh was often occupied with ritual duties, his chief adviser, the vizier, handled all matters of state. The vizier was assisted by a variety of higher- and lower-ranking officials, many of whom came from the same small group of families.

Egypt was divided into some forty districts, each ruled by a governor with his own smaller establishment of subordinate officials and scribes. Scribes were among the few Egyptians who could read and write. Legendary for its record keeping, the Egyptian government employed a large number of scribes to keep detailed papyrus records of every conceivable item. The demand for scribes was so great that the government often hired people from nonofficial families, and some of these managed to be promoted to higher office, a rare chance for social mobility in Egyptian society.

Craftspeople and farmers formed the illiterate majority of Egyptian society. Slavery was not widespread. Those who worked the land gave a share of their crop to the pharaoh, the owner of all the land in Egypt, and also owed him labor, which they performed at fixed intervals on roads and royal buildings.

The Rosetta Stone This stone, dating to 196 B.C.E., provided the key to deciphering Egyptian hieroglyphs because it gives the same government regulations in ancient Greek, a phonetic version of Egyptian called demotic, and hieroglyphs. In fact, the stone contains a fourth, often-overlooked inscription: "Captured in Egypt by the British Army in 1801." The British took the stone from the French, who had found it, which is why the stone is in the British Museum today. (Erich Lessing / Art Resource, NY)

The Old Kingdom and Egyptian Belief in the Afterlife, 2686–2181 B.C.E.

The five hundred years of the Old Kingdom (2686–2181 B.C.E.) marked a period of prosperity and political stability for Egypt. No invasions occurred during this time. The Old Kingdom is also called the Pyramid Age because government officials organized the construction of Egypt's most impressive monuments at this time.

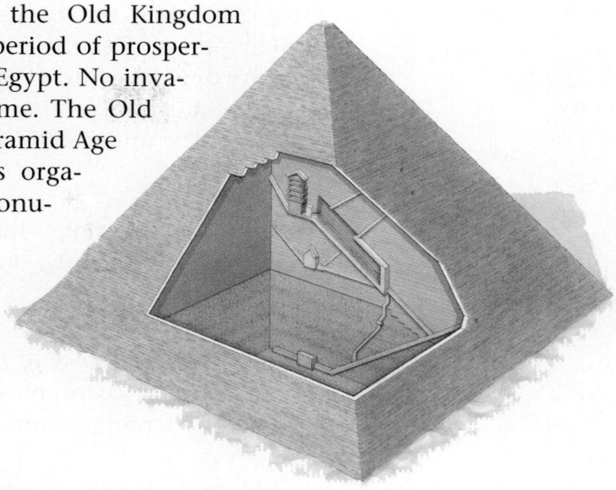

Great Pyramid of Khufu (Cheops): How Did the Egyptians Do It? This cut-away diagram shows the inside of the Great Pyramid, which had three chambers: the pharaoh's, his wife's, and one unfinished room at ground level. This is the only pyramid that contained two staircases, one going up and one going down. The pyramid originally had a smooth covering of casing stones, none of which survives today. (Maltings Partnership/Getty Images)

Egyptians believed that each person had a life-force (*ka*) that survived on energy from the body. When the body died, Egyptians preserved it and surrounded it with food so that the life-force could continue. The Great Pyramid was built between 2589 and 2566 B.C.E. to house the life-force of the pharaoh Khufu (KOO-fu), also called Cheops (KEY-ops).

Covering an area of 571,211 square feet (53,067 sq m), the Great Pyramid stands 480 feet (147 m) tall. It contains an estimated four million stone blocks ranging from 9.3 tons (8,445 kg) to 48.9 pounds (22.2 kg) in weight,* which the builders moved by means of a system of ramps and poles. They managed to construct a perfectly level base by pouring water into a grid of channels. Approximately fifteen to twenty thousand laborers, both male and female, worked on the pyramids each year during the Inundation season. None of these laborers were slaves. About five thousand skilled workers and craftsmen worked full-time, while the rest rotated in and out.

The size of his funerary monument provides a tangible measure of each ruler's power. The government had to organize the labor of all the workers and coordinate the shipment of large stones to the site of the pharaoh's tomb. Such projects required a level of social organization and occupational specialization characteristic of early complex societies.

• **CONTEXT&CONNECTIONS** Even today, the pyramid of Khufu is the tallest pyramid in the world (see table in Chapter 5, page 122). •

The earliest surviving Egyptian mummy dates to 2400 B.C.E., just after the time of the Great Pyramid, and happens to be one of the best preserved, with his facial features and even a callus on his foot still visible. During the Old Kingdom, only the pharaoh and his family could afford to preserve their corpses for eternity, but in later centuries, everyone in Egypt, whether rich or poor, hoped to travel to the next world with his or her body intact. One recently unwrapped mummy had a wooden toe attached to his foot with pieces of leather, the world's oldest known artificial prosthesis. Detailed descriptions of mummification date to around

*Anthony P. Sakovich, "Counting the Stones: How Many Blocks Comprise Khufu's Pyramid?" *KMT: A Modern Journal of Ancient Egypt* 13, no. 3 (Fall 2002): 53–57.

450 B.C.E., when the Greek traveler Herodotus (he-ROD-uh-tuhs) visited Egypt (see Chapter 6). (See the feature "Visual Evidence in Primary Sources: Reading the Mummy of Hornedjitef: High Priest at Karnak" on page 50.)

Egyptians believed that the dead had to appear before Osiris (oh-SIGH-ruhs), the god of the underworld, who determined who could enter the realm of eternal happiness.

• **CONTEXT&CONNECTIONS** The Egyptian view of the afterlife was much more optimistic than the dark realm described in *Gilgamesh*. •

Compiled in the sixteenth century B.C.E., yet drawing on materials dating back to 2400 B.C.E., the *Book of the Dead* contained detailed instructions for what the deceased should say on meeting Osiris. At the moment of judgment, the deceased should deny having committed any crime:

I have not committed evil against men.
I have not mistreated cattle.
I have not committed sin in the place of truth [that is, a temple or burial ground].
I have not blasphemed a god. . . .
I have not made (anyone) sick.
I have not made (anyone) weep.
I have not killed. . . .
I have not held up water in its season [that is, denied floodwaters to others].
*I have not built a dam against running water. . . .**

The list reveals the offenses thought most outrageous by the Egyptians: diverting water from the irrigation channels belonging to one's neighbor constituted a major infraction.

During the First Intermediate Period (2180–2040 B.C.E.), Old Kingdom Egypt broke apart into semi-independent regions ruled by rival dynasties the pharaoh could not control. Nor could the pharaoh collect as much revenue as his predecessors, possibly because sustained drought reduced agricultural yields.

Egyptian Expansion During the Middle Kingdom, 2040–1782 B.C.E.

In 2040 B.C.E. the ruler based in Thebes (modern-day Luxor) reunited Egypt and established what became known as the Middle Kingdom (2040–1782 B.C.E.), the second long period of centralized rule. Egypt's trade with other regions increased dramatically. Like Mesopotamia, Egypt had few natural resources and was forced to trade with distant lands to obtain wood, gold, silver, and semiprecious stones, including the treasured purple stone porphyry. Its main trading partners were modern-day Syria and Lebanon to the north and Nubia to the south. At the

*Excerpt from the *Book of the Dead* from James B. Pritchard (ed.), *Ancient Near Eastern Texts Relating to the Old Testament*, Third Edition With Supplement.

height of the Middle Kingdom, the pharaoh sent his armies beyond Egypt for the first time, conquering territory in Palestine and Nubia (see Map 2.1). Various Middle Kingdom rulers conquered and governed the regions south of the First and Second Cataracts.

The capital of the kingdom of Kush, another name for Nubia, lay south of the Third Cataract. During the Middle Kingdom, trade goods coming from sub-Saharan Africa, including panther and other rare animal skins, gold, ivory from elephant tusks, and slaves, traveled through Nubia, overland around the cataracts, and down the Nile to Egypt.

By 1720 B.C.E., the Middle Kingdom had weakened, most likely because a group of immigrants from Syria and Palestine, whom the Egyptians called Hyksos (HICK-sos) (literally "chieftains of foreign lands"), settled in the Delta. Historians call the years from 1782 to 1570 B.C.E. the Second Intermediate Period. The Hyksos had horse-drawn chariots with spoked wheels as well as strong bows made of wood and bone, while the Egyptians had no carts and only wooden bows. The Hyksos formed an alliance with the Nubians and ruled Egypt from 1650 to 1570 B.C.E.

The International System, 1500–1150 B.C.E.

Around 1500 B.C.E., western Asia entered a new stage of increasingly sophisticated material cultures and extensive trade. During the third period of centralized rule in Egypt, the New Kingdom (1570–1069 B.C.E.), Egypt had more dealings with the other kingdoms of the eastern Mediterranean than in previous periods. Pharaohs of the Eighteenth dynasty (1570–1293 B.C.E.) exchanged diplomatic envoys with rulers in Crete, Cyprus, and Anatolia and brought captured foreigners from the Mediterranean and Nubia to serve in the Egyptian army and to work as slaves.

Egypt's main rivals in the region were the Hittites (see page 48), who were based in Anatolia, Turkey, and Syria (see Map 2.2). Egypt reached its greatest extent at this time, governing a swath of territory that included Palestine, Lebanon, Syria, and Nubia. For five hundred years, the states of the eastern Mediterranean enjoyed a period of relative tranquility as they intensified their trade and diplomatic contacts to form what has been called the first international system.

New Kingdom Egypt and Nubia, 1570–1069 B.C.E.

During the New Kingdom period, Egypt continued to expand into Nubia. After eliminating the kingdom of Kush as a rival, Egypt destroyed its capital and extended control all the way to the Fourth Cataract. Nubia's most valuable natural resource was gold, which the pharaohs required in large amounts.

> **AP® THEMES**
> How did Egyptian religious beliefs help shape the relationship between Egypt and Nubia?

The pharaohs of the Eighteenth dynasty venerated the sun-god Amun-Ra (AH-muhn–RAH) above all other deities because they believed that he had enabled them to expel the Hyksos from Egypt and establish their dynasty. They built an enormous temple at Karnak to house the image of Amun-Ra.

The Egyptians believed that the most appropriate offerings to Amun-Ra were made from gold because gold was the color of the sun. Being indestructible, gold also represented immortality. Living people who wore gold became like gods, and

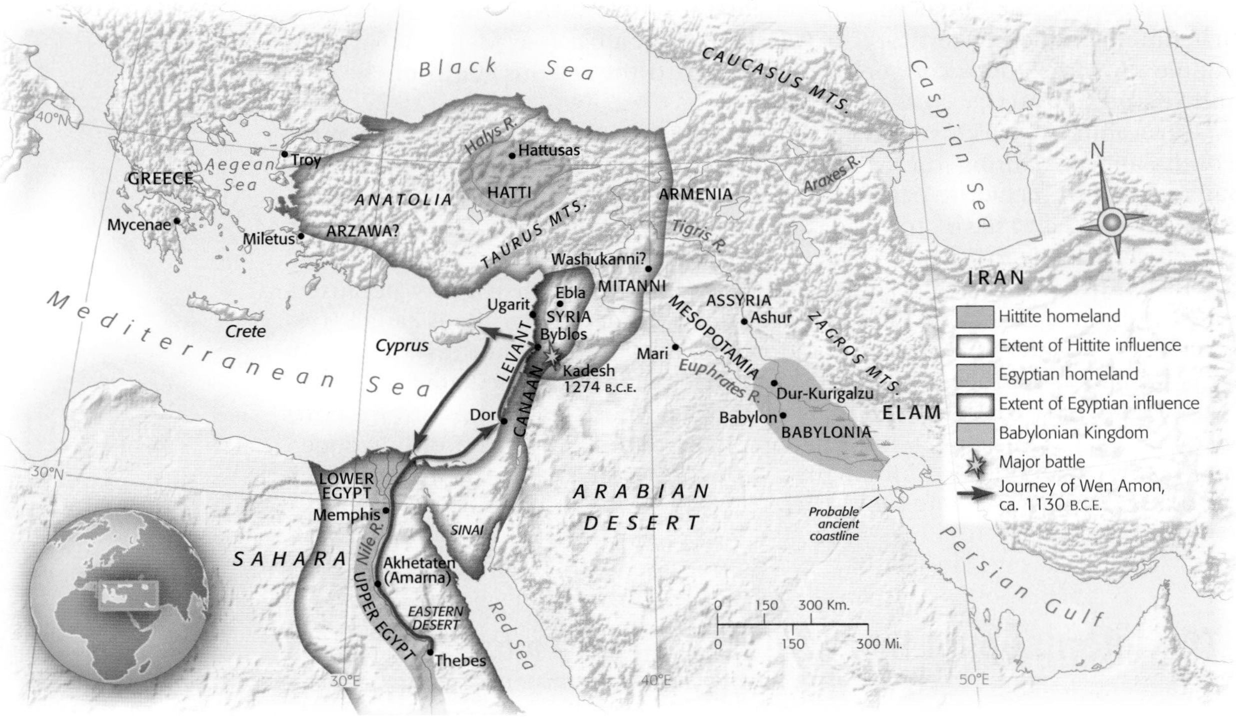

Map 2.2 The International System, ca. 1500–1250 B.C.E. Wen-Amun's journey from Egypt to Lebanon and Cyprus in around 1130 B.C.E. (see page 49) shows the ease with which individuals moved in the region of the eastern Mediterranean. International credit networks made it possible for Egyptian merchants to send gold, silver, linen, and papyrus to Lebanon, meaning that Wen-Amun did not have to return to Egypt to collect them.

the Egyptians buried the dead with multiple gold ornaments in the hope that they would live forever. While Egypt had some gold mines (see Map 2.1), Nubia had many more, and New Kingdom pharaohs were able to exploit these mines to the fullest extent.

After conquering Nubia, the pharaohs of the Eighteenth dynasty worked to transform Nubia into an Egyptian society: they brought the sons of Nubian chiefs to Egypt, where they studied the Egyptian language and worshiped Egyptian deities like Amun-Ra. When they returned home, they served the Egyptians as administrators.

Egypt continued to trade with Nubia and other regions during the reign of Hatshepsut (hat-SHEP-soot) (r. 1473–1458 B.C.E.), the only woman pharaoh of the Eighteenth dynasty. Older women, whether mothers or aunts, occasionally served as regents when the pharaoh was too young to rule on his own, but Hatshepsut ruled for a full fifteen years as pharaoh. She imported gold, ebony, and cedar to add new rooms at Amun-Ra's temple at Karnak and build a spectacular new temple in the Valley of the Kings, where the New Kingdom pharaohs were buried. She was particularly proud of an expedition that she dispatched to Punt (in modern-day Ethiopia), which brought exotic goods such as monkeys and myrrh trees back to Egypt

Near the end of the Eighteenth dynasty, Akhenaten (ah-ken-AHT-n) (r. 1352–1336 B.C.E.) introduced an important change to Egyptian religion. Rather than accepting Amun-Ra as the supreme deity, he worshiped a different form of the sun-god, whom he called the "living sun-disk," "Aten" (AHT-n) in Egyptian. In the past analysts erroneously thought Akhenaten worshiped Aten as the only god. In fact, he continued to worship other gods as well, even though Aten clearly ranked highest among them. After Akhenaten's death, Egyptians restored Amun-Ra to his position as the most important deity.

During the New Kingdom period, Egypt established a series of alliances with the various powers in the region and occasionally went to war with them. An extraordinary find of 350 letters concerning diplomatic matters makes it possible to reconstruct the international system of the time. Akhenaten addressed the rulers of Babylonia, Assyria, and Anatolia, who governed kingdoms as powerful as Egypt, as "brother," an indication that he saw them as his equals, while he reserved the term *servant* for smaller, weaker kingdoms in Syria and Palestine.

Many of the letters concern marriage among royal families. Akhenaten tried to persuade other rulers to send their daughters to marry Egyptian men, but he did not ask for their sons because Egyptians would not allow Egyptian women to marry non-Egyptians. Even though the arrangement was unequal, the rulers usually sent their daughters because they wanted gold, and only Egypt had gold (obtained from Nubia).

The Kingdom of Nubia, 800 B.C.E.–350 C.E.

Much weaker after 1293 B.C.E., when the Eighteenth dynasty ended, Egypt eventually lost control of Nubia. For several centuries no centralized power emerged in Nubia, but around 800 B.C.E. a political center formed at Napata, the administrative center from which the Egyptians had governed Nubia during the New Kingdom.

Seeing themselves as the rightful successors to the pharaohs of the Eighteenth dynasty, the rulers of Nubia conquered Egypt under King Piye (r. 747–716 B.C.E.). King Taharqo (690–664 B.C.E.) ruled over Nubia at its peak. The builder of an elaborate cult center to Amun-Ra, King Taharqo also revived the building of pyramids, a practice that had long since died out in Egypt. His pyramid was the largest ever built by the Nubians, standing 160 feet (49 m) tall. The Nubians continued to erect pyramids even after 300 B.C.E., when they shifted their capital from Napata to Meroë. By 300 B.C.E. the Nubians had developed their own writing system, called Meroitic (mer-oh-IT-ick), which combined hieroglyphs with hieratic script. Scholars know how to pronounce the Meroitic script because it is phonetic, but they cannot understand it because its structure differs from all living languages.

The royal cemetery at Meroë contains the pyramids of thirty kings and eight queens. As was common throughout sub-Saharan Africa, the Nubian dynasties practiced matrilineal succession in which the king was succeeded by his sister's son. (In a patrilineal system, the son succeeds the father.) If the designated successor was too young to rule, the king's sister often ruled in his place. Nubian queens did everything the male kings did, including patronizing temples, engaging in diplomacy, and fighting in battle.

Nubia, Land of Pyramids Modern Sudan has more pyramids—a total of 223—than Egypt. Modeled on those of Old Kingdom Egypt, the Nubian tombs are steeper and originally had a layer of white plaster on their exterior. Starting in the mid-700s B.C.E. and continuing to 370 C.E., the Nubian rulers of Kush built pyramids over their tombs, which were in the ground—unlike the Egyptian tombs, which were constructed above ground and inside the pyramids. (Martin Gray/National Geographic Creative)

The kingdom of Meroë thrived because it was able to tax the profitable trade between sub-Saharan Africa and the Mediterranean. However, it broke apart in the fourth century C.E., possibly because the trade was diverted to sea routes it did not control.

Hittites
A people based in Anatolia, Turkey, and Syria who spoke the Indo-European language of Hittite and learned to work iron around 2000 B.C.E. The Hittite Empire reached its greatest extent between 1322 and 1220 B.C.E. and ended around 1200 B.C.E.

• **CONTEXT&CONNECTIONS** Located south of Egypt, Nubia had little contact with the different states of the eastern Mediterranean to the north of Egypt. Accordingly, it did not actively participate in the system of international alliances that had begun to take shape as early as 1500 B.C.E. •

The Hittites, 2000–1200 B.C.E., and the Durability of Trade

During the New Kingdom period, Egypt's rulers frequently wrote to the rulers of a powerful new kingdom based in Anatolia and Syria, the **Hittites**. The language of the Hittites belonged to the Indo-European language family, meaning that its structure resembled that of Latin, Greek, and Sanskrit (see Chapter 3). The Hittites were the first speakers of an Indo-European language to establish a complex society in western Asia.

The Hittites were able to do so because, sometime around 2000 B.C.E., they learned how to work **iron**. With a much higher melting point (2,786 degrees Fahrenheit, 1,530 degrees Celsius) than other metals, iron could not be melted and then poured into molds like bronze. Metalsmiths heated iron and hammered it into the shape of the tool or weapon needed, a process that removed impurities in the metal. Much stronger than bronze weapons, the iron weapons of the Hittites were highly prized.

iron
A metal used to make farm tools and weapons; iron smelting was an important technology because iron implements were much more durable than those made of bronze.

The Hittite Empire reached its greatest extent between 1322 and 1220 B.C.E., when the Hittites controlled all of Anatolia and Syria. In the thirteenth century B.C.E., the Hittite ruler wrote to the ruler of the Assyrians to apologize for not sending any unworked iron. Instead he sent a single blade, an indication of iron's value at the time.

The Hittites had another advantage over their enemies: they had mastered the art of chariot warfare. Two horses pulled a chariot that carried three men (a driver and two warriors). In the Battle of Kadesh in 1285 B.C.E., when the Hittites faced the Egyptians, the ruler commanded 2,500 chariots. The two sides reached an agreement, and the Hittites sent a princess to marry the pharaoh.

AP® THEMES

How did environmental factors and technological developments help the Hittites expand their empire?

The Hittite kingdom came to an end in 1200 B.C.E. when their capital fell to outsiders. Historians are not certain who the invaders were, but they note a period around 1200–1150 B.C.E. of prolonged instability throughout western Asia. Egyptian sources mention attacks by "sea peoples," and Egypt lost control of both Syria-Palestine to the north and Nubia to the south.

In the centuries after 1200 B.C.E., Egypt continued to enjoy extensive trade relations with the Mediterranean, as we can see in the earliest detailed account of an actual voyage, recorded on a torn papyrus dating to 1130 B.C.E.* In that year, an Egyptian priest named Wen-Amun (one-AH-muhn) traveled down the Nile to its mouth, where he caught a ship across the Mediterranean to Lebanon to buy cedar for the Amun-Ra temple at Karnak. (See the feature "Visual Evidence in Primary Sources: Reading the Mummy of Hornedjitef: High Priest at Karnak.")

After being robbed of all his money, Wen-Amun committed theft himself at a port in modern-day Lebanon. When the victims reported the theft to their king, he detained Wen-Amun. The ruler made a proposal: if Wen-Amun sent to his home temple for funds, he would be allowed to depart. The credit network of the local merchants was sufficiently sophisticated that Wen-Amun was able to write home to request that another ship bring him gold, silver, ten linen garments, and five hundred rolls of papyrus to cover the cost of the lumber. Eventually, Wen-Amun managed to make his way back home, but because the papyrus breaks off abruptly, we do not know whether he managed to deliver the lumber. Still, his many adventures demonstrate that, even during this time of instability, the international system of the period functioned smoothly enough that people could obtain credit and travel in the eastern Mediterranean.

*Lionel Casson, *Travel in the Ancient World* (Baltimore: Johns Hopkins University Press, 1994), p. 39.

Reading the Mummy of Hornedjitef: High Priest at Karnak

Mummies possess an undying fascination because we always want to know about the person wrapped up inside the linen straps. Often, though, crucial information is missing because the mummy has been separated from its coffin or accompanying burial goods. One extraordinary example, held in the British Museum, survives with its exterior and interior cases intact, as well as a papyrus text, 18 inches (.45 m) tall and 16 feet (4.9 m) long, from the *Book of the Dead*, instructing the deceased how to travel to the next world.

The biography on the interior coffin gives the name of the deceased, Hornedjitef (ca. 240 B.C.E.), and all his official titles. As a high priest at the temple of Amun at Karnak, Hornedjitef was one of the few people who could handle the statue of Amun, which was carried outside the temple during processions. Hornedjitef's tomb text does not mention his family, but most of the Amun temple priests married and had children.

Because the museum staff did not want to damage Hornedjitef's mummy, they did not unwrap it. Instead, they performed a nondestructive CT scan. Hornedjitef's body was intact; a few missing teeth and wear on the rest provide a key indicator that he was between fifty and sixty at the time of death. (The cause of death is unknown.) His spinal column was misshapen by chronic arthritis, which must have been extremely painful.

The scan revealed the precise location of several items: rings on Hornedjitef's left hand and left big toe, protective amulets on his neck, and a scarab, which had slipped away from its proper placement over his heart. Before he was buried, his organs were removed through an incision in the abdomen so that they could be dried and treated with preservatives; the embalmers then wrapped the organs in their own linen cases and replaced them in their original locations. His wrapped stomach, lungs, and heart were all visible on the CT scan. (In earlier periods, embalmers buried the wrapped body parts in a separate container called the canopic chest; Hornedjitef had one, but it contained broken pottery and no body parts—perhaps the embalmers included the chest simply to observe tradition.) Using a hook, the embalmers removed his brain through the nasal cavity and filled the skull about halfway with resin. Scientists at the British Museum recently X-rayed a mummy from slightly before Herodotus's time and discovered exactly where the embalmers broke the nose of the deceased so that they could take out his brain.

As was fitting for a man of his high station, Hornedjitef received the most expensive treatment offered to the dead by embalmers. After removing his organs, they rinsed the body and covered it with natron (NAY-tron), a crystallized form of potassium carbonate that kept the corpse dry. After forty days, bandagers spent two weeks wrapping the body in linen before placing it in a coffin.

In the less expensive option, the embalmers simply injected the body with cedar oil, which caused the internal organs to decay and to be expelled through the anus. Bandaging and burial followed. The poorest Egyptians could only afford to have the internal organs expelled and the corpse buried unbandaged. This information comes from Herodotus, and recent testing of mummies has shown that it is accurate.

This funerary mask does not show Hornedjitef at death, but the younger man he hoped to be reborn as.

This wooden case is made of sycamore.

This is a list of the planets and the stars.

This shows the sky goddess Nut with her hands stretched above her head.

This artificial beard is attached to his funerary mask with straps. Priests shaved off all their body hair, including beards, because body hair was believed to be unclean.

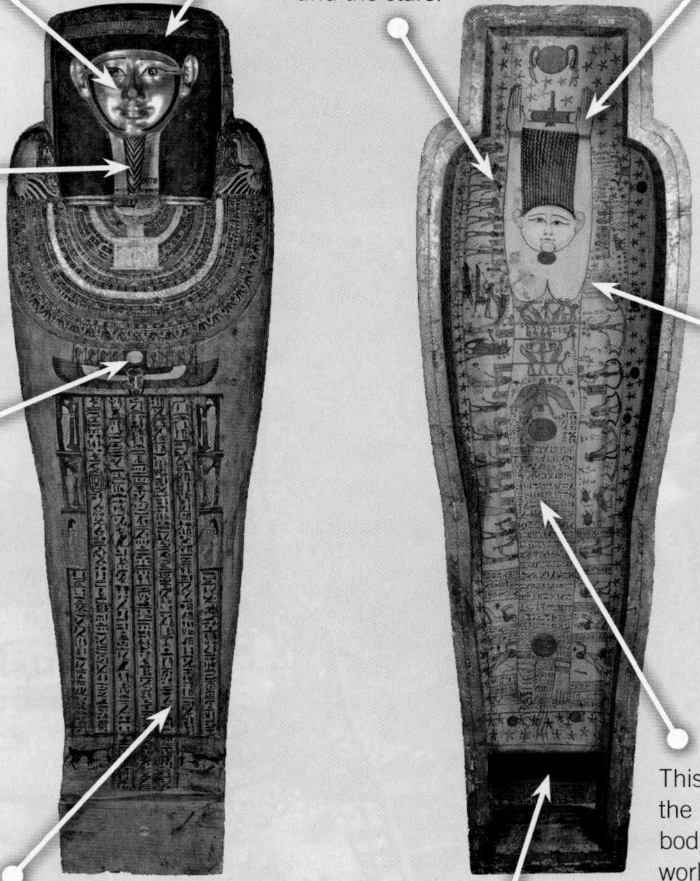

This section lists the constellations and protective gods and shows scenes of the zodiac.

This winged scarab beetle represents the sun god, who grants life. The eight baboons standing on the beetle's wings worship the sun god.

This spell to unite the soul and the body in the underworld comes from Chapter 89 of the *Book of the Dead.*

This space is for the feet of the mummy.

This text gives Hornedjitef's biography in hieroglyphs. As "overseer of the abattoir" at the Karnak temple to Amun, he ensured that the meat from animals killed at the temple was used correctly in ceremonies. ***Historians always consider the issue of typicality. Why is it not appropriate to use the information from Hornedjitef's mummy to analyze the burial customs of the Egyptian poor?*** (British Museum)

Syria-Palestine and New Empires in Western Asia, 1200–500 B.C.E.

Several kingdoms occupied the land along the eastern shore of the Mediterranean where modern-day Palestine, Israel, Lebanon, and Syria are located. They participated in the international system, but always as minor players in a world dominated by kings of larger powers. Around 1000 B.C.E. a smaller complex society arose in the eastern Mediterranean that was notable for its innovation in religion.

monotheism Belief in only one god.

This lightly populated and politically weak region was the homeland of the ancient Hebrews or Israelites. The Hebrews were the first people in the eastern Mediterranean to practice **monotheism**, or belief in only one god, whom they called Yahweh (YAH-way) in Hebrew (God in English). Belief in a single god underlay the religious teachings recorded in the Hebrew Bible (called the Old Testament by Christians). Hebrew monotheism would profoundly shape both Christian and Islamic teachings (see Chapters 7, 9, and 10).

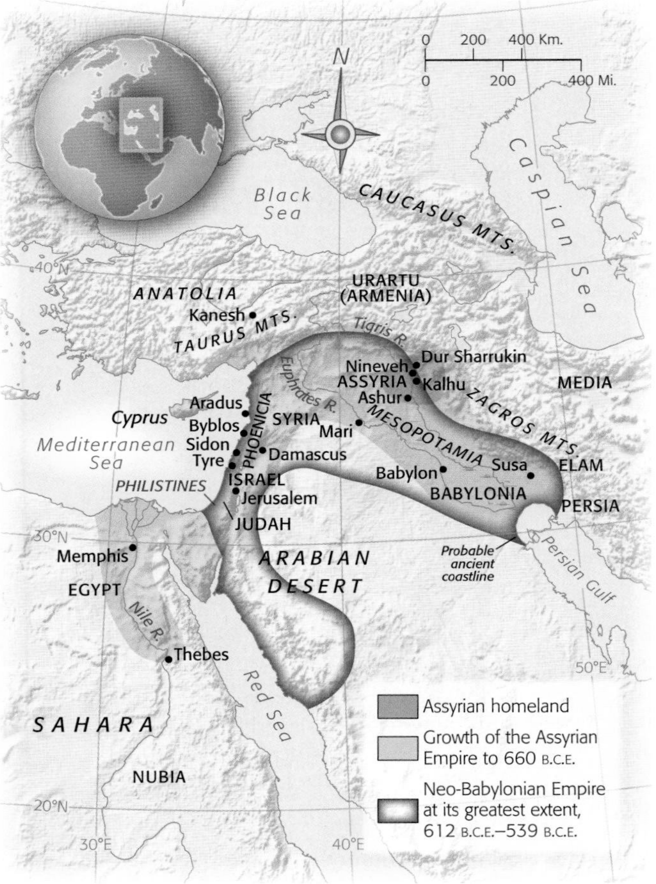

Map 2.3 The Levant and the Assyrian and Neo-Babylonian Empires First the Assyrians and then the Neo-Babylonians controlled the Levant, the region bordering the eastern Mediterranean. The most populated section was Israel and Palestine, occupying the strip of land 30–70 miles (50–110 km) wide and 250 miles (400 km) north to south along the coast.

Weighing Archaeology and the Bible to Reconstruct the Ancient Hebrew Past

The Hebrew Bible was written sometime around 700 B.C.E., most likely when the Jews were exiled in Babylon (see Map 2.3), and its current text dates to around 500 B.C.E. Historians and archaeologists of Israel and Palestine disagree sharply about the value of the Bible as a historical source. The maximalists, a group of archeologists based at the Hebrew University in Jerusalem, believe that archeological evidence confirms what the Hebrew Bible says: King David and his son Solomon ruled a region around modern Jerusalem around 1000 B.C.E. The minimalists, based at Tel Aviv University, reject the claim about the House of David; instead, they see the rival kingdoms of Israel and Judea as arising in 900 B.C.E., with no evidence linking them to anything in the Hebrew Bible.

The first book of the Hebrew Bible, Genesis, traces the history of the ancient Hebrews from the earth's creation. The Hebrew Bible contains a later version of the flood story that closely resembles that in *Gilgamesh*. Archaeologists have not found evidence of a single flood as described in either *Gilgamesh* or the Hebrew Bible; most think the flood narrative collapses repeated floods in the Tigris and

Euphrates Valley into a one-time calamity. (See the feature "Movement of Ideas Through Primary Sources: The Flood Narrative in the *Epic of Gilgamesh* and the Hebrew Bible.")

The most important event in their history, the ancient Hebrews believed, was God's choice of Abraham to be the leader of his people. Abraham, like his direct ancestor Noah, spoke directly to God and agreed to be the leader. God, in turn, made Abraham promise that all his descendants would be circumcised. The Hebrew Bible teaches that Abraham, aged one hundred, and his wife Sarah, ninety, had no children. But as God promised, Sarah gave birth to a son, Isaac. Abraham had one son, Ishmael, with Sarah's maid Hagar, but Sarah sent Hagar away after the birth of Isaac.

God then subjected Abraham to the most severe test of all: he asked him to sacrifice his son Isaac as an offering. (Muslims believe that Abraham's son Ishmael, not Isaac, was designated for sacrifice.) At the moment when Abraham was about to obey and kill Isaac, the Bible records, God, speaking through an angel, commanded: *"Do not lay your hand on the boy or do anything to him; for now I know that you fear God, since you have not withheld your son, your only son, from me"** (Genesis 22:12). Although it cannot be verified, the Bible's dramatic account of Isaac's rescue reflects a crucial change in Israelite religious observance. In an earlier time, the ancient Hebrews might have sacrificed children. By later times, when the Isaac story was recorded, the Hebrews had abandoned child sacrifice. The Hebrew Bible gives no dates for the events it describes; if they occurred, it was sometime before 1300 B.C.E., when the archaeological record starts.

After the ancient Hebrews came to Israel, the book of Exodus claims that they went to Egypt and then returned to Israel under the leadership of the patriarch Moses. Since no archaeological evidence confirms that a single migration out of Egypt occurred, many scholars suggest that the Exodus may have been a series of migrations. Archaeology does tell us that in 1300 B.C.E. approximately twelve to fifteen thousand people lived in three hundred small villages on previously unoccupied hillsides in the southern Levant; by 1100 B.C.E. the population had mushroomed to eighty thousand. No urban centers existed. Most of the residents had tools made of bronze, flint, and occasionally iron. One piece of evidence suggests that the residents were the Israelites: "the consistent absence of pig bones in excavated remains," a sign that they observed the taboo on eating pork recorded later in the Hebrew Bible.†

Archaeologists have found evidence that sometime between 1000 and 900 B.C.E., complex society first took shape in the region. The main evidence, as in Mesopotamia, is the formation of large urban centers with massive walls. At this time what had been a loose tribal confederacy became a small kingdom, complete with a bureaucracy and intermediate-level cities. The population of the Levant around 1000 B.C.E. has been estimated at 150,000, and its largest city, Jerusalem, reached its maximum population of 5,000 in 700 B.C.E. In 2008 archaeologists

---

*All quotations from the Bible are from the New Revised Standard Version. Revised Standard Version of the Bible, Copyright © 1952 [2nd edition, 1971] by the Division of Christian Education of the National Council of the Churches of Christ in the United States of America. Used by permission. All rights reserved.

†William G. Dever, *What Did the Biblical Writers Know and When Did They Know It? What Archaeology Can Tell Us About the Reality of Ancient Israel* (Grand Rapids: William B. Eerdmans, 2001), pp. 127, 113.

The Flood Narrative in the *Epic of Gilgamesh* and the Hebrew Bible

The striking similarities in the two versions of the flood story demonstrate that the Hebrew Bible drew on oral traditions circulating throughout Mesopotamia. The most complete version of the *Epic of Gilgamesh* was written in 700 B.C.E., but it drew on written versions dating to at least 2100 B.C.E. and even earlier oral traditions. Like the *Epic of Gilgamesh*, the Bible had a long history of oral transmission before being recorded in its current version around 500 B.C.E. Some of its oldest content may have circulated orally as early as 1200 B.C.E., when the ancient Hebrews first settled what is now modern Israel.

The two accounts of the flood differ most notably in their depiction of the divine. In the *Epic of Gilgamesh*, multiple gods squabble and the god Enki warns Utanapishtim that the storm-god Enlil is sending the flood to destroy his home city of Shuruppak. In the Bible, one god decides to punish all of humanity except for Noah (played in the 2014 film by Russell Crowe) and his family.

❯ **Historical Thinking Skill:**
COMPARISON **What might explain the similarities between the two flood stories?**

❯ **Historical Thinking Skill:**
COMPARISON **What might explain the differences between the two flood stories?**

Sources: The Epic of Gilgamesh, translated by Benjamin R. Foster. pp. 85–89; Genesis 6:11–19; Genesis 7:17–18; Genesis 8:1–3; Genesis 8:6–12. All quotations from the Bible are from the New Revised Standard Version.

The Flood Story in *Gilgamesh*

Instructions to Utanapishtim for Building the Ark

O Man of Shuruppak, son of Ubar-Tutu,
Wreck house, build boat,
Forsake possessions and seek life,
Belongings reject and life save!
Take aboard the boat seed of all living things.
The boat you shall build,
Let her dimensions be measured out:
Let her width and length be equal,
Roof her over like the watery depths.

The Length of the Flood

Six days and seven nights
The wind continued, the deluge and windstorm leveled the land…
The sea grew calm, the tempest stilled, the deluge ceased.

The End of the Flood

When the seventh day arrived,
I [Utanapishtim] brought out a dove and set it free.
The dove went off and returned,
No landing place came to its view so it turned back.
I brought out a swallow and set it free,
The swallow went off and returned,
No landing place came to its view, so it turned back.
I brought out a raven and set it free,
The raven went off and saw the ebbing of the waters.
It ate, preened, left droppings, did not turn back.
I released all to the four directions,
I brought out an offering and offered it to the four directions.
I set up an incense offering on the summit of the mountain,
I arranged seven and seven cult vessels,
I heaped reeds, cedar, and myrtle in their bowls.

The Flood Story In the Bible

Instructions to Noah for Building the Ark

Now the earth was corrupt in God's sight, and the earth was filled with violence. And God saw that the earth was corrupt; for all flesh had corrupted its ways upon the earth. And God said to Noah, "I have determined to make an end of all flesh, for the earth is filled with violence because of them; now I am going to destroy them along with the earth. Make yourself an ark of cypress wood; make rooms in the ark, and cover it inside and out with pitch. This is how you are to make it: the length of the ark three hundred cubits, its width fifty cubits, and its height thirty cubits.* Make a roof for the ark, and finish it to a cubit above; and put the door of the ark in its side; make it with lower, second, and third decks. For my part, I am going to bring a flood of waters upon the earth, to destroy from under heaven all flesh in which is the breath of life; everything that is on the earth shall die. But I will establish my covenant with you; and you shall come into the ark, you, your sons, your wife, and your sons' wives with you. And of every living thing, of all flesh, you shall bring two of every kind into the ark, to keep them alive with you; they shall be male and female."†

---

* A cubit measures about 1.5 feet (.5 m) long. The ark was approximately 450 feet (137 m) long, 75 feet (23 m) wide, and 45 feet (14 m) tall.

†All quotations from the Bible are from the New Revised Standard Version. Revised Standard Version of the Bible, Copyright © 1952 [2nd edition, 1971] by the Division of Christian Education of the National Council of the Churches of Christ in the United States of America. Used by permission. All rights reserved.

The Length of the Flood

The flood continued forty days on the earth; and the waters increased, and bore up the ark, and it rose high above the earth. The waters swelled and increased greatly on the earth; and the ark floated on the face of the waters. . . .

But God remembered Noah and all the wild animals and all the domestic animals that were with him in the ark. And God made a wind blow over the earth, and the waters subsided; the fountains of the deep and the windows of the heavens were closed, the rain from the heavens was restrained, and the waters gradually receded from the earth. At the end of a hundred fifty days the waters had abated.

The End of the Flood

At the end of forty days Noah opened the window of the ark that he had made and sent out the raven; and it went to and fro until the waters were dried up from the earth. Then he sent out the dove from him, to see if the waters had subsided from the face of the ground; but the dove found no place to set its foot, and it returned to him to the ark, for the waters were still on the face of the whole earth. So he put out his hand and took it and brought it into the ark with him. He waited another seven days, and again he sent out the dove from the ark; and the dove came back to him in the evening, and there in its beak was a freshly plucked olive leaf; so Noah knew that the waters had subsided from the earth. Then he waited another seven days, and sent out the dove; and it did not return to him any more.

excavating an urban center southwest of Jerusalem found two large gates, one on the walls and the other inside them. The maximalists propose this site was the ancient city of Shaarayim, meaning "Two Gates," which is mentioned several times in the Bible. Their discovery of a pottery shard with ancient Hebrew characters also points to the presence of Israelites.

Many archaeologists see both positions in the maximalist/minimalist debate as too extreme. Professor Aren Maeir of Israel's Bar-Ilan University explains: "We're not here to prove or disprove the Bible. We're here to illustrate the cultures in which the biblical text was formed."

The Assyrian Empire, 911–612 B.C.E.

The two kingdoms of Israel and Judah remained separate and independent until 721 B.C.E., when the Assyrians, whose homeland was in northern Mesopotamia, conquered southern Mesopotamia, Egypt, and the kingdoms of Israel and Judah. Like the Hittites, the Assyrians had iron weapons. In addition, their cavalry was particularly powerful because it was the first true army on horseback. The cavalry soldiers rode bareback since neither saddles nor stirrups had been invented.

Unlike the various conquerors of the eastern Mediterranean before them, the Assyrians did not simply send in armies and subjugate enemy territory. Because the Assyrian ruler saw himself as the representative of the gods, he asked the rulers of foreign territories to submit voluntarily to him and his deities. Those who surrendered he treated gently, but his troops were infamous for their cruel treatment of those who resisted. Soldiers skinned captives alive, removed their eyes or cut off their hands and feet, and impaled others on stakes. These atrocities served as a warning to those who had not yet been conquered: if they surrendered quickly, they could avoid such barbarities. Such treatment was justified, the Assyrians believed, because the subject populations were resisting the gods, not just a human king.

Once the Assyrians had conquered a given region, they forcibly resettled the conquered rulers and skilled craftsmen to another part of the empire. The original intent in the ninth century was to fill up the lightly populated sections of the empire; later, resettlement was simply a demonstration of the ruler's power. Several hundred thousand people were resettled in this way, including many people from Israel and Judah who were sent to Assyria.

● **CONTEXT&CONNECTIONS** The rulers of the Assyrian Empire were the first in the eastern Mediterranean to resettle subject populations. Their successors, the Neo-Babylonians, continued the practice and resettled many subject peoples, including the Hebrews, in their capital at Babylon. ●

The last Assyrian king, Asshurbanipal (as-shur-BAH-nee-pahl) (r. 668–627 B.C.E.), built one of the world's earliest libraries, which consisted of over 1,500 texts for his own private use. In the 1850s, British excavators found the most complete set of clay tablets of the *Gilgamesh* epic, and the basis of all modern translations, in the ruins of Asshurbanipal's palace

The Babylonian Captivity and the Recording of the Bible, 612–539 B.C.E.

The Neo-Babylonians conquered the Assyrians and established their capital at Babylon. Their most powerful ruler was Nebuchadnezzar II (r. 605–562 B.C.E.), who rebuilt the city of Babylon, repaired its temples, and constructed magnificent hanging gardens. Nebuchadnezzar II (nab-oo-kuhd-NEZ-uhr) extended his empire all the way to Syria, Palestine, and Lebanon. The Neo-Babylonian deportation of thousands of Hebrews to Babylon is known today as the Babylonian Exile or Babylonian Captivity.

The exiled Hebrews living in Babylon were not allowed to return to Israel, but otherwise they had some freedom of movement, and some seem to have prospered as merchants or farmers. The exiled community reached a new understanding of their past. Many of the tales they told, including those about Noah and Abraham, had episodes in which God punished the ancient Hebrews for failing to follow his instructions, and they interpreted the Assyrian and Neo-Babylonian conquests in the same light. The Israelite community, the prophets explained, had strayed from righteousness, which they defined as ethical behavior.

During these years, the exiles recorded the core of the modern Hebrew Bible, from Genesis to 2 Kings. In earlier periods, the ancient Hebrews worshiped several different deities, including the storm-god, called El or Ba'al (BAHL), his wife, a fertility goddess, and a second storm-god named Yahweh. Now, the first five books of the Bible, recorded during the Captivity and known either as the Torah in Hebrew or the Pentateuch in Greek, stressed that Yahweh is the only god and that he will not tolerate the worship of any other gods. This pure monotheism was the product of specific historical circumstances culminating in the Babylonian Exile and the recording of the Bible. The word **Jew**, derived from the Hebrew *Yehudhi*, literally means a member of the nation of Judah. After 538 B.C.E., it came to refer to all Hebrews.

Jew
A term (derived from Hebrew) that originally meant a member of the nation of Judah and later came to refer to all Hebrews.

● **CONTEXT&CONNECTIONS** The Neo-Babylonians were the last dynasty to rule from Babylon. In 539 B.C.E. *Cyrus* (Chapter 6), the leader of the Persians, conquered Mesopotamia, and the entire Neo-Babylonian empire came under Persian rule. In 538 B.C.E. Cyrus allowed the Hebrews to return to Judah, bringing the Babylonian Captivity to an end. ●

CONTEXT AND CONNECTIONS

The Place of Mesopotamia and Egypt in World History

The *Epic of Gilgamesh* contrasts the experience of the king Gilgamesh, who governs a complex society, with that of his friend Enkidu, who grew up in the wild. Composed at a time in which people in complex societies lived adjacent to those in the wild, the epic vividly portrays the sharp differences between life inside and outside the world's first city-states. As the chapter opening shows, once Enkidu sleeps with the priestess named Shamhat, he immediately becomes a member of a complex society; the next morning, the gazelles that had been his original companions avoid him. Both men go on a long journey to kill the monster Humbaba. When Enkidu dies, Gilgamesh dons fur clothing and enters the wild, leaving the life of complex society behind—until he realizes that he, too, ultimately will die. Chastened, he returns to rule his city-state.

Those living in the cities ate bread and drank beer made from cultivated grain, the fruits of the world's first agricultural societies, which arose in West Asia starting in 12,500 B.C.E., the time of the Natufians (see Chapter 1). In city-states like Gilgamesh's Uruk, people with similar occupations resided together in different neighborhoods, as did members of similar social strata. Complex society had a more abstract side: the people living in Mesopotamian city-states believed that they owed payments of grain to the gods and to their intermediary, the king, and the king, in turn, had an obligation to govern them. They also knew the qualities of a good

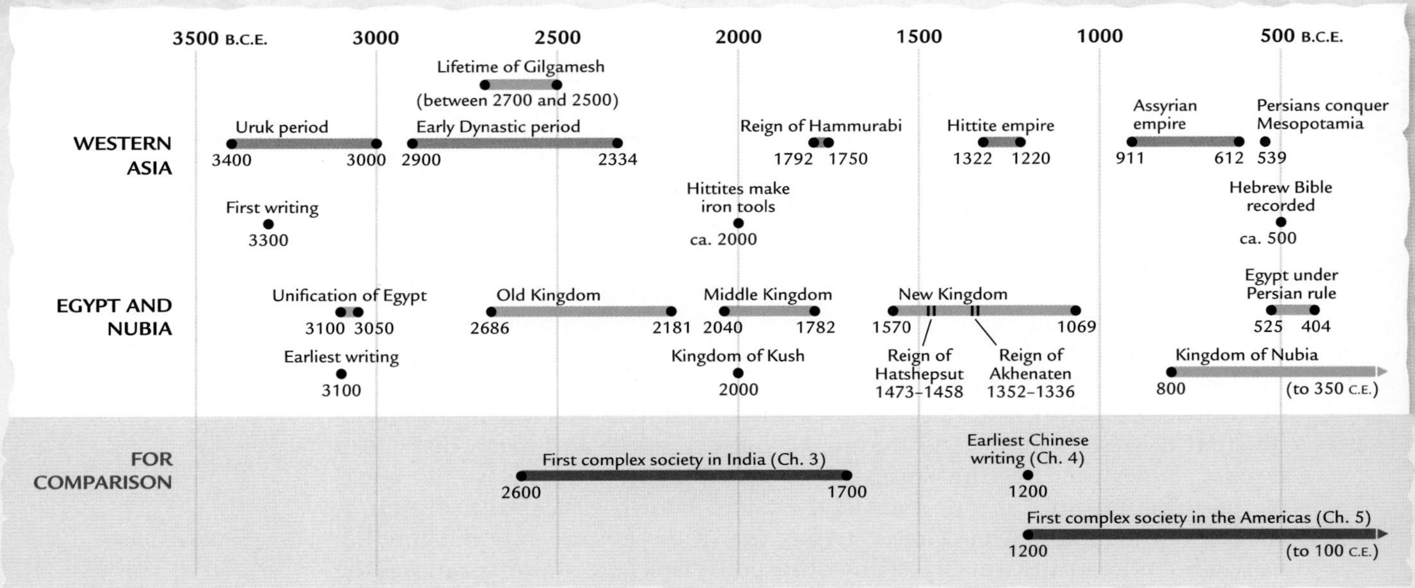

king, qualities that Gilgamesh lacks at the beginning of the epic and slowly acquires as he matures.

Cuneiform, used in Mesopotamia, and hieroglyphs, used in Egypt, were the world's two earliest writing systems. But the complex society of the Egyptians differed from that of the Mesopotamians. Sometime around 3500 B.C.E., the earliest pharaohs unified the Nile Valley, and city-states never existed in Egypt. As the different types of burial show, Egyptians had different occupations and occupied different social levels, both marks of complex society. The corpses of high-ranking priests such as Hornedjitef received the most extensive mummification and survive intact even today. At the pinnacle of Egyptian society, the pharaoh collected both taxes and labor from his subjects; over ten thousand laborers worked on the final resting place of pharaoh Khufu (Cheops), one of the world's largest and longest-lasting monuments.

Both the Mesopotamians and the Egyptians believed in multiple deities. Yet the *Gilgamesh* story of a flood sent by the storm-god Enlil was also told in a different form by the ancient Hebrews living in West Asia, who invoked only one god, Yahweh, whose deeds are recounted in the Bible.

Complex societies are historically significant because they attained much higher population densities than those of peoples who did not pursue agriculture full-time. These societies also produced some of the largest and most important monuments in human history, whether the ziggurats of Mesopotamia or the pyramids of Egypt and Nubia. The coming chapters will analyze the varying experiences of peoples living in other regions of the world: in India (Chapter 3), in China (Chapter 4), and in Mexico, the Andes, the modern-day United States, and the islands of the Pacific (Chapter 5). As different as these places were and are, there are underlying commonalities. Before the rise of agriculture, the region's residents lived by foraging. Their populations were low, and they lived in bands of less than one hundred people. In most cases they left few lasting traces. In each place, the transition to complex society produced radically different results, each with far-reaching implications for the world we live in today.

Key Terms

Mesopotamia (29)
Gilgamesh (30)
complex society (30)
city-state (32)
bronze (33)
wheel (33)
Sumer (35)
cuneiform (35)
Sargon of Akkad (38)
empire (38)
pharaoh (40)
Nubia (40)
hieroglyphs (42)
papyrus (42)
Hittites (48)
iron (49)
monotheism (52)
Jew (57)

For Further Reference

Andrews, Carol. *Egyptian Mummies*. Cambridge, Mass.: Harvard University Press, 2004.

Brewer, Douglas J. *Ancient Egypt: Foundations of a Civilization*. 1st ed. Harlow, England; New York: Pearson/Longman, 2005.

Casson, Lionel. *Travel in the Ancient World*. Baltimore: Johns Hopkins University Press, 1994.

Cline, Eric H. *1177* B.C. *The Year Civilization Collapsed*. Princeton: Princeton University Press, 2014.

Dever, William G. *The Lives of Ordinary People: Where Archaeology and the Bible Intersect*. Grand Rapids, Mich.: William B. Eerdmans Publishing Company, 2012.

Fisher, Marjorie, et al. *Ancient Nubia: African Kingdoms on the Nile*. Cairo: American University Press, 2012.

Kramer, Samuel Noah. *History Begins at Sumer: Thirty-nine Firsts in Recorded History*. Philadelphia: University of Pennsylvania Press, 1988.

Manzanilla, Linda, ed. *Emergence and Change in Early Urban Societies*. New York: Plenum Press, 1997.

Postgate, J. N. *Early Mesopotamia: Society and Economy at the Dawn of History*. New York: Routledge, 1992.

Richards, Janet, and Mary Van Buren, eds. *Order, Legitimacy, and Wealth in Ancient States*. New York: Cambridge University Press, 2000.

Shaw, Ian. *The Oxford History of Ancient Egypt*. New York: Oxford University Press, 2004.

Taylor, John H., and Daniel Antoine. *Ancient Lives, New Discoveries: Eight Mummies, Eight Stories*. London: British Museum Press, 2014.

van de Mieroop, Marc. *A History of the Ancient Near East, ca. 3000–323* B.C. Malden, Mass.: Blackwell Publishing, 2007.

AP® Review Questions for Chapter 2

Multiple-Choice Questions

QUESTIONS 1–3 REFER TO THE FOLLOWING PASSAGE.

I have not committed evil against men.
I have not mistreated cattle.
I have not committed sin in the place of truth [that is, a temple or burial ground].
I have not blasphemed a god. . . .
I have not made (anyone) sick.
I have not made (anyone) weep.
I have not killed. . . .
I have not held up water in its season [that is, denied floodwaters to others].
I have not built a dam against running water. . . .

—*The Book of the Dead,* Egyptian religious scripture, 1550 B.C.E.

1. The existence of documents like the one excerpted above demonstrates that the Egyptians
   (A) relied on the desert for protection rather than defensive walls.
   (B) had a strong central authority.
   (C) had developed a concept of the afterlife.
   (D) relied on oaths to keep the military loyal to the pharaoh.

2. Which of the following statements can be inferred based on the passage?
   (A) The Egyptians had developed large-scale public works and urban planning.
   (B) The Egyptians relied solely upon cattle to meet their needs for food.
   (C) Military actions such as war were outlawed.
   (D) Gender equality was the norm in Egyptian society.

3. The above passage tells us what about Egyptian religious life?
   (A) The Egyptian afterlife was devoid of gods.
   (B) Moral action was enforced by religious ideals.
   (C) Egyptians lacked the essential framework for deep religious understanding.
   (D) Egyptians borrowed heavily from Mesopotamian religions.

QUESTIONS 4–6 REFER TO THE FOLLOWING MAP.

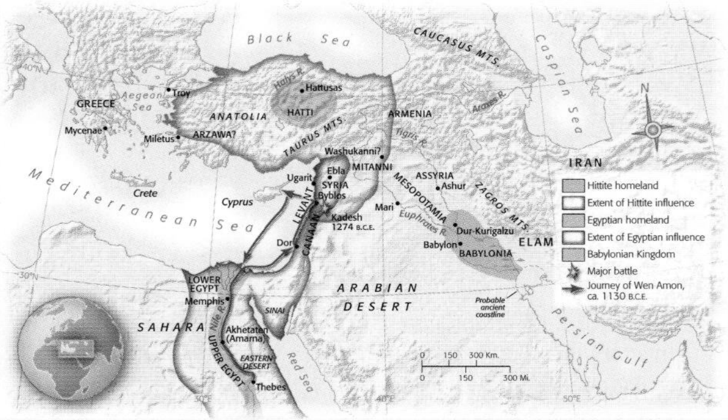

4. Which of the following concepts is illustrated by the map?
   (A) Social hierarchies, including patriarchy, intensified as states expanded.
   (B) Trade expanded throughout this period from local to regional to interregional.
   (C) Pastoralists were often the developers and disseminators of new weapons.
   (D) As civilizations expanded, people had to balance their need for resources with environmental constraints.

5. Which of the following explains the degree of interaction that the Hittite and Egyptian civilizations had with each other?
   (A) Disagreements between the civilizations rarely led to war.
   (B) Competition over land and other resources sometimes led to conflict between civilizations.
   (C) Interaction between early civilizations was limited to trade.
   (D) Although many civilizations were close to each other, they rarely exchanged goods and ideas.

6. Which of the following is a valid inference based on the information in the map?
   (A) Environmental constraints limited interregional trade.
   (B) The Indus Valley civilization was the dominate trade partner.
   (C) The close proximity of the three civilizations led to exchanges through war and trade.
   (D) Of all the early river valley civilizations, the Hittites were the oldest.

QUESTIONS 7–10 REFER TO THE FOLLOWING TWO PASSAGES.

O Man of Shuruppak, son of Ubar-Tutu,
Wreck house, build boat,
Forsake possessions and seek life,
Belongings reject and life save!
Take aboard the boat seed of all living things.
The boat you shall build,
Let her dimensions be measured out:
Let her width and length be equal,
Roof her over like the watery depths.

—The Flood Story in the *Epic of Gilgamesh*, instructions to Utanapishtim from the gods for building the ark, 2100 B.C.E.

And God saw that the earth was corrupt; for all flesh had corrupted its ways upon the earth. And God said to Noah, "I have determined to make an end of all flesh, for the earth is filled with violence because of them; now I am going to destroy them along with the earth. Make yourself an ark of cypress wood.... For my part, I am going to bring a flood of waters upon the earth, to destroy from under heaven all flesh in which is the breath of life; everything that is on the earth shall die. But I will establish my covenant with you; and you shall come into the ark, you, your sons, your wife, and your sons' wives with you. And of every living thing, of all flesh, you shall bring two of every kind into the ark, to keep them alive with you; they shall be male and female."

—The Flood Story in the Hebrew Bible, instructions to Noah for building the ark, between 1200 and 500 B.C.E.

7. Which of the following best explains the similarities in these two flood stories?
   (A) The two cultures independently developed flood stories.
   (B) The *Epic of Gilgamesh* incorporated the flood story from the Hebrew Bible.
   (C) Both societies attempted to unite their societies using literature and religion.
   (D) Both societies borrowed from stories circulated as part of an older tradition.

8. The two flood accounts differ in which of the following ways?
   (A) The Mesopotamian account omits any mention of gods or deities.
   (B) The Hebrew account focuses on multiple gods and goddesses.
   (C) The Mesopotamian account introduces the concept of a single god.
   (D) The Hebrew account introduces the concept of monotheism to the flood story.

9. Writing systems like the one used in the writing of *Gilgamesh* were originally developed for which of the following purposes?
   (A) To divine the will of the gods in religious rituals
   (B) To be used in early record keeping
   (C) As ornamentation on monumental architecture like the ziggurats
   (D) As a method to help students memorize poetry and other forms of literature

10. The two flood stories demonstrate which of the following conclusions concerning early civilizations?
   (A) Early civilizations rarely experienced environmental disasters.
   (B) Religion and morality did not impact each other.
   (C) Sedentary living sometimes meant facing severe environmental challenges.
   (D) Gods and goddesses were present but did not interfere in human affairs.

Short-Answer Questions

If a man has destroyed the eye of a member of the aristocracy, they shall destroy his eye. If he has broken another man's bone, they shall break his bone. If he has destroyed the eye of a commoner or broken the bone of a commoner, he shall pay one mina of silver. If he has destroyed the eye of another man's slave or broken the bone of a man's slave, he shall pay one-half of the slave's value.

—The Code of Hammurabi, eighteenth century B.C.E.

1. Using this excerpt, answer parts A, B, and C.
   A. Identify ONE reason for the creation of this passage.
   B. Explain how ONE of the following aspects is addressed in the passage:
      - Social class
      - Private property
   C. Explain ONE reason why the code described in this passage was a necessary development in early civilizations.

2. Answer parts A, B, and C.
   A. Briefly explain ONE reason why social classes developed in civilizations.
   B. Identify and explain ONE impact sedentary living had on the role and status of women.
   C. Identify and explain ONE long-term effect civilization had on social hierarchies.

3 Ancient India and the Rise of Buddhism, 2600 B.C.E.–100 C.E.

Ashoka and his Wife

Archaeological Survey of India

For the first eight years he was king, **Ashoka** (r. 268–232 B.C.E.) led his armies on a series of campaigns in north and central India that culminated in a ferocious struggle in Kalinga (kuh-LING-uh) in modern-day Orissa on India's eastern coast. Victorious at last but appalled by the losses on both sides, Ashoka (uh-SHO-kuh) made a decision that would affect world history long after his Mauryan (MORE-ee-ahn) Dynasty (ca. 320–185 B.C.E.) came to an end: he chose to embrace the teachings of Buddhism.

Because the ancient Indians used perishable materials like palm leaves for writing, we have no written documents before the third century B.C.E. from South Asia (including the modern countries of India, Pakistan, Bangladesh, Nepal, Sri Lanka, Bhutan, and the Maldives). However, throughout his reign, Ashoka had his ideas carved on both large and small stones, called rock edicts, and later on stone pillars. Thus Ashoka's inscriptions provide the fullest record of a single individual's thoughts and movements in South Asia before the modern era. Shortly after conquering Kalinga, in an inscription carved in 260 B.C.E., Ashoka explained his decision to follow Buddhism:

When he had been consecrated eight years the Beloved of the Gods, the king Ashoka, conquered Kalinga. A hundred and fifty thousand people were deported, a hundred thousand were killed and many times that number perished. Afterwards, now that Kalinga was annexed, the Beloved of the Gods very earnestly practiced dharma, desired dharma, and taught dharma. On conquering Kalinga the Beloved of the Gods felt remorse, for, when an independent country is conquered the slaughter, death, and deportation of the people is extremely grievous to the Beloved of the Gods, and weighs heavily

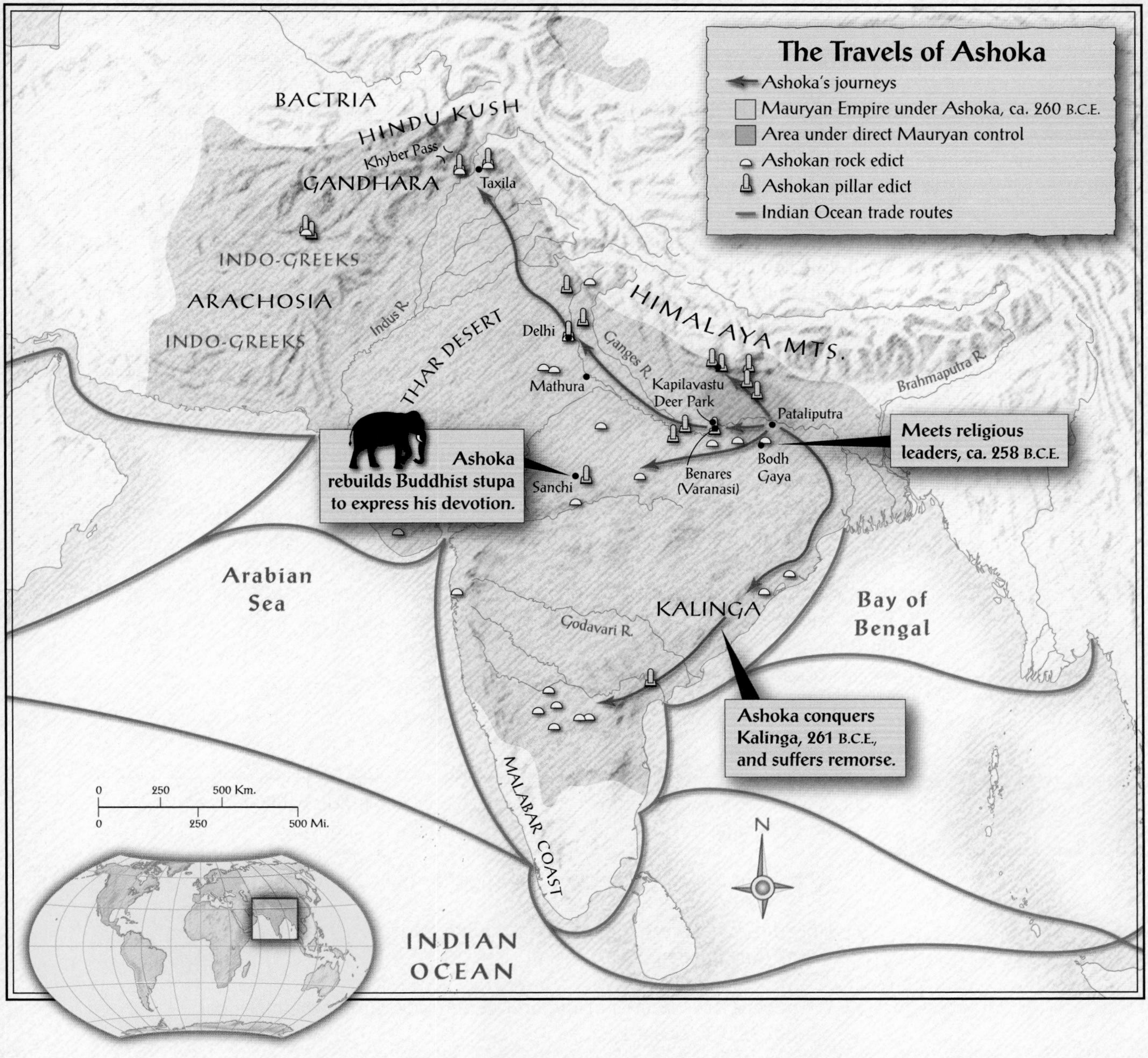

*on his mind. Today if a hundredth or a thousandth part of those people who were killed or died or were deported when Kalinga was annexed were to suffer similarly, it would weigh heavily on the mind of the Beloved of the Gods.**

---

*Excerpt from *Aśoka and the Decline of the Mauryas*, ed. Romila Thapar, 1973, pp. 255–256. Reprinted with permission of Oxford University Press India, New Delhi.

Ashoka
(r. 268–232 B.C.E.) The third king of the Mauryan dynasty (ca. 320–185 B.C.E.), the first Indian ruler to support Buddhism.

dharma
A Sanskrit term meaning correct conduct according to law or custom; Buddhists, including Ashoka, used this concept to refer to the teachings of the Buddha.

The concept of **dharma** occurs repeatedly in Ashoka's inscriptions. He uses the word to mean the teachings of the Buddha, but more broadly it means correct conduct according to law or custom, which is how many people in South Asia would have understood it. Dharma was also an important concept in Hinduism, the major religion that arose in India after Buddhism declined. (The main coverage of Hinduism, discussed briefly in this chapter, is in Chapter 8.)

Ashoka governed an unusually large area. Riding on an elephant, he traveled along the trunk roads that radiated out like spokes on a bicycle wheel from his capital at Pataliputra (puh-TAH-lee-poo-truh). For much of its history South Asia was divided into separate regions governed by various rulers; only a few dynasties, like the Mauryan, succeeded in uniting the region for brief periods. Although not politically unified, Indians shared a common cultural heritage: living in highly developed cities, many spoke Sanskrit or related languages, recited religious texts in those languages, and conceived of society in terms of distinct social ranks.

In contrast to rulers of the city-states of ancient Mesopotamia, the kingdom of ancient Egypt, and the Neo-Assyrian and Neo-Babylonian empires (see Chapter 2), South Asian rulers exercised much less direct control over their subjects. They lacked the power to resettle conquered peoples in new places. Instead, leaders like Ashoka ruled by example, often patronizing religion to show what good monarchs they were. Indeed, religion provided one of the major unifying forces in the often-disunited South Asia. This chapter first discusses the ancient Vedic religion of India and then the exciting alternatives that appeared around the fifth century: Buddhism and Jainism (JANE-is-uhm). It concludes by discussing the Indian Ocean trade network.

KEY CONCEPT QUESTIONS

- What were the key cultural and social aspects of Indus Valley civilization? **(Key Concept 1.3)**
- What were the core beliefs of the Buddha? **(Key Concept 2.1)**
- How did Ashoka attempt to use Buddhism to strengthen the Mauryan state? **(Key Concept 2.2)**
- What were the features of Indian Ocean trade during the classical period? **(Key Concept 2.3)**

The Origins of Complex Society in South Asia, 2600–500 B.C.E.

We can glimpse the origins of South Asian social structures and religious traditions from archaeological evidence in the Indus River Valley dating to between 2600 and 1700 B.C.E. One of the most important urban sites lies near the modern Pakistan village of Harappa (ha-RAHP-pa). The Harappan culture extended over a wide area that included parts of present-day Pakistan, India, and Afghanistan (see Map 3.1). The people of the Indus Valley society used the same script, but because archaeologists have not deciphered their writing system, we do not know what cultural forces bound them together. We learn more about ancient Indian society from evidence dating to 1500 B.C.E., when people in India, though never politically unified, came to share certain religious beliefs and conceptions of society. The pattern they established at that time held for much of Indian history.

Complex Society in the Indus River Valley, 2600–1700 B.C.E.

The South Asian landmass, often called a subcontinent, can be divided into three geographical regions: the high and largely uninhabited mountains to the north (the Himalayas); the heavily populated plains of the subcontinent's two great rivers, the Indus to the west and Ganges (GUN-geez) (Ganga) to the east; and the southern peninsula, which is not as densely settled. The headwaters of the Indus and Ganges Rivers start in the high Himalayas and drain into the sea, with the Indus flowing into the Arabian Sea and the Ganges into the Bay of Bengal. The earliest farmers planted wheat and barley on the hillsides of what is now western Pakistan. The domestication of plants and animals, sometime around 7000 B.C.E., made it possible for the people to create larger settlements in the valley of the Indus River. The first crops cultivated were wheat, barley, and the jujube date, while the first animals to be domesticated were elephants, sheep, and goats.

India's pattern of rainfall differed from that in Mesopotamia and Egypt. Much of the annual rainfall came in several months in late summer or fall, called the **monsoon** season, and a second period came in the winter months. Indus Valley farmers had to build water storage tanks and measure out the water carefully until the next monsoon came. Like the Mesopotamians and the Egyptians, the Indus Valley residents learned to make pottery and to work metal, usually copper and bronze.

monsoon
A term referring both to seasonal winds in South Asia blowing northeast in spring and early summer and southwest in fall and winter, and to the heavy seasonal rains they bring.

In the 1920s British and Indian archaeologists began to excavate huge mounds of brick and debris near the town of Harappa in the **Indus River Valley**. They uncovered the remains of a large urban settlement built from mud brick, complete with walls, drainage systems, open plazas, and avenues several yards (meters) across. Subsequent excavations have revealed that at its height Harappa had an area of over 380 acres (150 hectares) and a population between forty and eighty thousand. Archaeologists have found over fifteen hundred settlements belonging to the Indus River Valley society, the largest complex society of its time on the Indian subcontinent. Mohenjo-daro (mo-HEN-juh DAH-ro), the second-largest site of the Harappan settlements, was perhaps the most impressive. Unlike other cities of the ancient world, the cities of the Indus River Valley provided drinking water, bathing facilities, and sewer drains to all their residents, not just a privileged few.

Indus River Valley
Site of the earliest complex society on the Indian subcontinent (2600–1700 B.C.E.), characterized by brick cities, drainage systems, open plazas, and broad avenues.

We know frustratingly little about the people who occupied the Harappan sites because their script has yet to be deciphered. Seals with the same signs have been found at different sites throughout the Indus River Valley, suggesting that the region shared a common writing system. Archaeologists have identified 400 to 450 signs. But this number is puzzling; 400 signs is more than an alphabet (most alphabets contain fewer than 50 letters) yet fewer than a pictorial writing system (the earliest, simplest phase of Sumerian writing had 700 signs). Scholars wonder whether these mysterious signs stood for an individual word, syllable, or sound. Since no key giving their meaning in another language has yet been found, they are almost impossible to decipher.

A seal made in the Indus River Valley was found at the Mesopotamian city-state of Ur from a level occupied in 2600 B.C.E. The ancient peoples of the Indus River

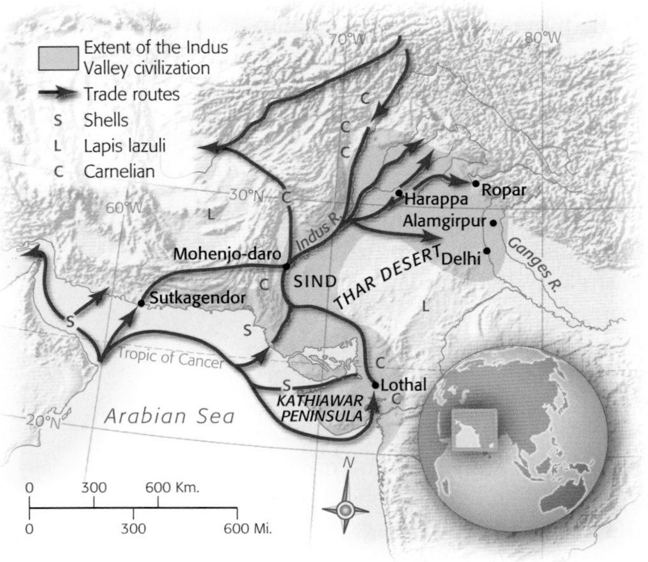

Map 3.1 **Indus River Valley Society** Between 2600 and 1700 B.C.E., the Indus River Valley society covered a large area in modern-day India and Pakistan. The most important sites were at Mohenjo-daro and Harappa. The region exported carnelian and lapis lazuli to Mesopotamia and to the northeast and imported shells in return.

Valley were heavily involved in trade, and the people of Mesopotamia were among their most important trading partners. The residents of ancient Mesopotamia imported carnelian and lapis lazuli from the Indus Valley, and shells traveled in the opposite direction (see Map 3.1).

• **CONTEXT&CONNECTIONS** Recently, scientists analyzed the DNA of aboriginal peoples living in Australia and confirmed that the first wave of settlers arrived around 50,000 B.C.E. from New Guinea and the Philippines; these were *Mungo Man's* forebears (key term in Chapter 1). More unexpectedly, the DNA analysis showed that a second wave of settlers had arrived from India sometime around 2200 B.C.E., at the peak of the Indus Valley civilization.•

The DNA evidence indicates that the Harappan peoples developed ships capable of traveling not just to nearby Mesopotamia but all the way across the Indian Ocean to Australia. The new settlers brought two new technologies with them: smaller and finer stone tools that could be used on the tips of weapons and methods of removing toxins from cycad nuts by washing and then fermenting the nuts. The settlers also introduced the wild dingo dog. Because the two technologies originated in South Asia, which matches the DNA evidence, scientists hypothesize that the settlers came directly from South Asia and most likely did not pass through Southeast Asia.

The absence of written documents makes it difficult to reconstruct either the social structure or the religious practices of the residents of the Indus River Valley. As in Mesopotamia, craftsmen who made similar goods seem to have lived in the same residential quarter. There is clear archaeological evidence of social stratification, one of the hallmarks of cities and complex societies. The people who had more possessions than others lived in bigger houses and were buried in graves with more goods.

AP® THEMES
What may have led to outbreaks of new diseases in Harappan society?

Beginning in 1900 B.C.E., the large urban sites of the Harappan society become smaller. The characteristic Indus River pottery vessel types give way to new shapes and decorative patterns. Some of the pots have graffiti markings in Indus Valley script, indicating that the script remained in use. The decline of the Indus Valley civilization has several possible causes. Lower rainfall for over one hundred years suggests that climate change was a factor. In addition, the increasing density of urban settlement made the population more susceptible to disease, particularly new diseases, such as leprosy and tuberculosis, which entered the subcontinent from the north and which skeletons from the Harappan site display.

With incontrovertible evidence of social stratification,, occupational specialization, and large urban centers, the Indus River Valley sites certainly meet our definition of a complex society. Although the people were probably not united under a single ruler, they shared a common system of weights and measures, standardized brick size, and urban planning. Shared cultural practices in the absence of political unification characterized later South Asian societies as well.

The Spread of Indo-European Languages

Our understanding of the South Asian past becomes much clearer with the first textual materials in the Indo-European language of **Sanskrit**. Linguists place languages whose vocabulary and grammatical structures are most closely related into the same language family. If you have studied French or Spanish, you know that many words are related to their English counterparts. English, French, and Spanish all belong to the Indo-European language family, as do ancient Greek, Latin, Hittite, and Sanskrit. The Indo-European languages contain many core vocabulary words related to English, such as the words for mother, father, and brother (see Table 3.1). If you study a non-Indo-European language, like Chinese or Arabic, few words will resemble any word in English, and word order may be different.

Sanskrit
A language, such as Latin, Greek, and English, belonging to the Indo-European language family and spoken by Indo-Aryan migrants to north India around 1500–1000 B.C.E.

The "Great Bath" at Mohenjo-daro, Pakistan One of the most impressive ruins from the Harappan period (2600–1700 b.c.e.), the Great Bath is misnamed. Measuring 40 feet (12 m) high and 23 feet (7 m) wide, it was a water tank—not a pool or a bathing area. It held water for the ritual use of the city's residents, who bathed in a nearby building. (Borromeo / Art Resource, NY)

Can You Decipher the Harappan Seals of Mohenjo-daro, Pakistan? These five seals have Indus Valley writing above several figures (*clockwise from top left*): a unicorn, a rhinoceros, an elephant, a water buffalo, and a short-horned bull. A water fountain, possibly with a square sieve on top, stands below the unicorn's mouth; the water buffalo and the bull eat from feeding troughs on the ground. No one has yet deciphered the symbols of the Indus Valley writing system.

Sometime in the distant past, thousands of years ago, a group of herding peoples who spoke Indo-European languages began to leave their homeland, possibly the Pontic steppe north of the Black Sea. The distribution of Indo-European languages over Eurasia shows how far these peoples went: Russia, most of Europe, Iran, and north India, but not southern India or East Asia (see Map 3.2). Those going east passed through Iran and arrived in north India sometime between 1500 and 1000 B.C.E., where they spoke Sanskrit. The modern inhabitants of the region speak a range of Indo-European languages descended from Sanskrit, including Hindi (HIN-dee), while those in south India speak Dravidian (druh-VID-ee-uhn) languages, which belong to a different language family.

• **CONTEXT&CONNECTIONS** When linguists first discovered the similarities among Latin, Greek, and Sanskrit in the early nineteenth century, they assumed that the speakers of Indo-European languages invaded and wiped out the indigenous peoples. Modern scholars have since proposed variations on the original conquer-and-destroy model. Perhaps, when the Indo-European speakers migrated into a new region, their superior technology convinced the local peoples to adopt the newcomers' language. Linguists engage in a similar debate about the distribution of *Bantu* languages in Africa (Chapter 11), and there too, they increasingly favor models of assimilation rather than forced conquest. •

Table 3.1 Related Words in Various Indo-European Languages

English	Latin	Greek	Sanskrit
mother	mater	meter	matar
father	pater	pater	pitar
brother	frater	phrater	bhratar
sister	soror	(unrelated)	svasar
me	me	me	ma
two	duo	duo	duva
six	sex	hex	shat
seven	septem	hepta	sapta

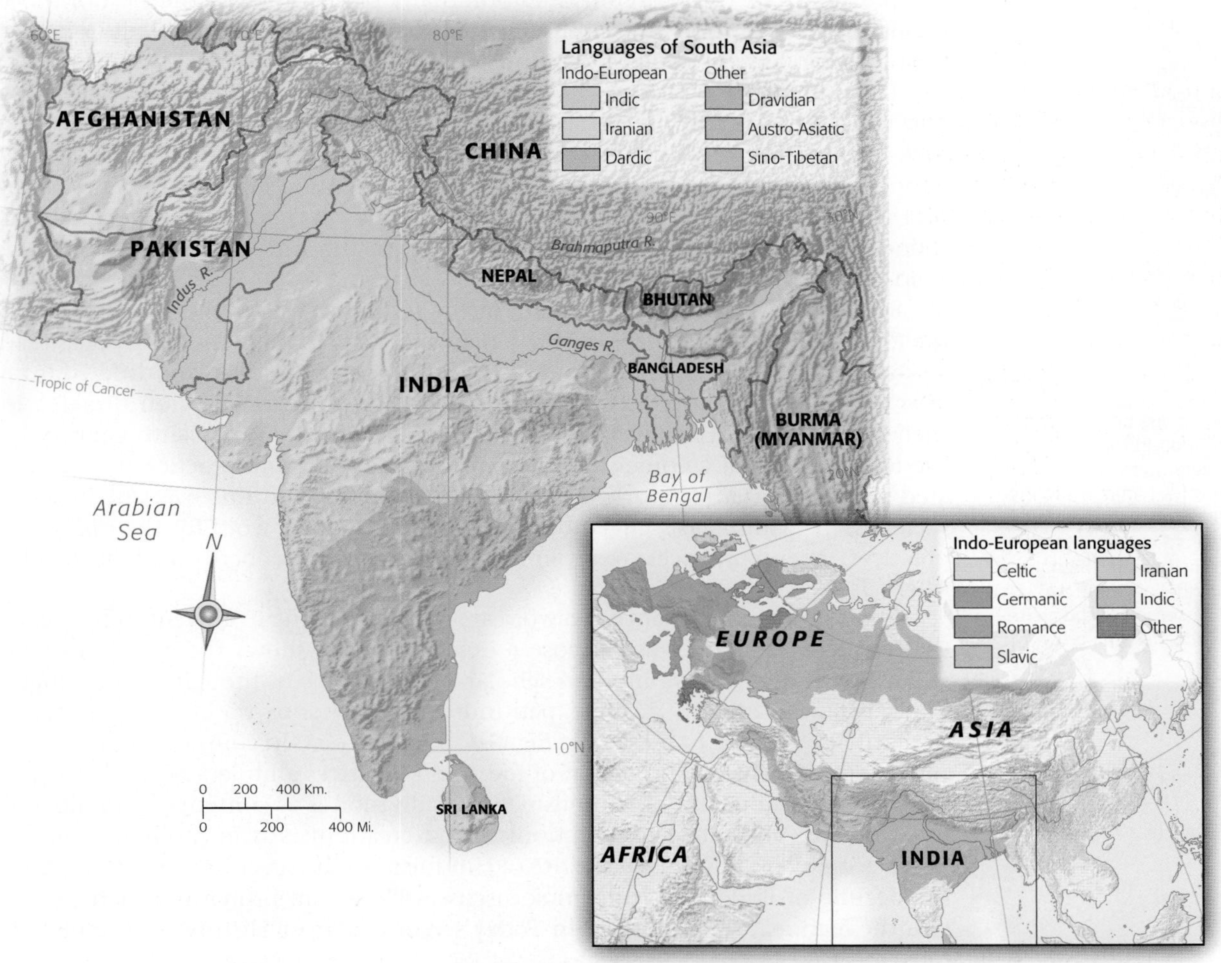

Map 3.2 Distribution of Languages in Modern South Asia Most people living in the northern regions of modern South Asia speak Indo-European languages, including Hindi and Urdu, while those living in the south speak Dravidian languages like Tamil and Telegu. The dominance of Indo-European languages in much of today's Eurasia is the result of migrations occurring over three thousand years ago.

The Indo-European Migrations and Vedic Culture, 1500–1000 B.C.E.

The Indo-European migrants left us the ***Rig Veda*** (RIG VAY-duh), a collection of 1,028 hymns that were preserved because the priests who sang them passed them down orally from one generation to the next. Touching on many everyday activities, including sex and gambling, they date to around 1500 to 1000 B.C.E., the probable time of the Indo-European migrations to South Asia, yet they were not written down until more than two thousand years later, perhaps in 1000 C.E.

Rig Veda A collection of 1,028 Sanskrit hymns, composed around 1500–1000 B.C.E. but written down around 1000 C.E. One of the most revealing sources about Indo-Europeans who settled in north India.

Linguists have concluded that the Sanskrit of the older hymns varies slightly from the later hymns, making it possible to determine the order of their composition. The earlier hymns mention many place names to the west of those included in the later hymns, an indication that the migrants came first to northwest India and later to all of north India.

These migrants sometimes called themselves "Aryan," a Sanskrit word whose meaning is "noble" or "host." While modern researchers think that many and varied peoples spoke Indo-European languages, the propagandists of Nazi Germany wrongly imputed a racial unity to what was a linguistic group. Always mindful that we know nothing of their appearance, it is best to refer to these migrants as Indo-Aryans because their language belonged to the Indo-Aryan branch of the Indo-European language family.

Scholars have named the religion of the Indo-Aryans Vedic (VAY-dick), from the *Rig Veda*. The roots of Hinduism, a major religion in modern South Asia, lie in **Vedic religion**, but the religious practices of the early Indo-Aryans differed from later Hinduism, discussed in Chapter 8. Scholars of Indian religion disagree in their definitions of Hinduism, a word coined only in the nineteenth century by the British rulers of colonial India to refer to traditions and practices not associated with Islam, Jainism, or Christianity. In the past—and this was true in other societies, like China, as well—Indian worshippers had no word for their religious practices; these practices were simply something they performed at regular intervals.

Vedic religion

Religious belief system of Indo-European migrants to north India; involved animal sacrifice and elaborate ceremonies to ensure that all transitions in the natural world—day to night, or one season to the next—proceeded smoothly.

Analytically, this absence of a word among those living in ancient India means that modern scholars must impose a definition that allows them to pin down what they study. Among modern scholars, two schools of thought predominate. The centralists "identify a single, pan-Indian . . . orthodox tradition, transmitted primarily in Sanskrit," and see the *Rig Veda* as a core text. In contrast, the pluralists "envision a decentered profusion of ideas and practices all tolerated and incorporated under the big tent of Hinduism."* This division is as contentious in modern India as the split between evolutionists and creationists is in modern America. Because many pluralists date the rise of Hinduism to the seventh century C.E., after the decline of Buddhism, this book discusses Hinduism primarily in Chapter 8. (See the feature "World History in Today's World: Whose History of Hinduism Is Correct?")

The deities mentioned in the *Rig Veda* include the war-god, Indra (IN-druh), the god of fire, the sun-god, and the god of death, as well as many minor deities. Rituals honoring these gods could last several days and involve intricate sequences of steps, including animal sacrifice. The Brahmin (BRAH-min) priests who performed them were paid handsomely by local rulers.

The *Rig Veda* provides a few valuable hints about social organization. The original Indo-European migrants were **nomads**. Carrying their tents with them, they usually did not farm but tended their herds full-time. The most important animal in their society was the horse, which pulled the carts that transported their families and possessions across Eurasia. According to some hymns, some people began to cultivate grain after settling in India.

nomads

A term for people who migrate seasonally from place to place to find grass for their animals. They do not usually farm but tend their herds full-time.

One early hymn, addressed to Indra, gives a clear sense of the diverse occupations of the Indo-European speakers: "*Our thoughts bring us to diverse callings, setting people apart: the carpenter seeks what is broken, the physician a fracture, and the*

*Richard H. Davis, "Introduction: A Brief History of Religions in India," in *Religions of Asia in Practice: An Anthology*, ed. Donald S. Lopez, Jr. (Princeton: Princeton University Press, 2002), p. 6.

Whose History of Hinduism Is Correct?

Historians of religion often have a different understanding of a given religious tradition than do its adherents. Studying documents and art objects from specific periods, historians see all religions as changing over time, and they often have evidence revealing that different groups—the illiterate and literate, men and women, rich and poor—understand the teachings of a religion in divergent ways. In contrast, believers sometimes maintain that since their own understanding of a religious tradition has been true since the founding of the religion, it is the only correct view. Pluralists see Hinduism as an evolving, changing set of beliefs, while the centralists lean toward the view that the Vedas have always been the primary texts of Hinduism, which they believe existed since time immemorial.

These two views have collided head-on in India. In 2010, Penguin Press published a book entitled *The Hindus: An Alternative History,* by a professor of religion at the University of Chicago, Wendy Doniger. The book offers a pluralist perspective, presenting materials in languages other than Sanskrit, the language of India's high tradition, to highlight the experiences of women and untouchables. Because Hindus debate certain core beliefs of Hinduism, such as vegetarianism, nonviolence, and the caste system, Doniger argues that there is no single, correct teaching, or orthodoxy.

In 2011 a small Hindu group, called Shiksha Bachao Andolan (Save Education Movement), led by a retired school principal, filed a civil claim against Penguin in Indian courts. "The book is in bad taste right from the beginning," the principal told BBC. "If you see the front page [cover], the picture there is also objectionable since it portrays a deity in a vulgar pose." The book cover features a painting of the blue-skinned deity Krishna riding on a horse made up of multiple bare-breasted women.

Choosing to settle out of court, in February 2013, Penguin India recalled all remaining copies of the book and promised to destroy them. The publisher justified its decision by citing an Indian law, aimed at those deliberately inciting religious violence, that makes it a criminal offense to deliberately insult or outrage "religious feeling." Further, Penguin maintained that Hindu activists might threaten the safety of its employees. The publisher's decision dismayed many intellectuals, who launched a protest by sending one copy of a well-known book to Penguin to be destroyed. But many observers, including Professor Doniger, felt that the wording of the law gave the publisher little choice.

Source: Soutik Biswas, "Why Did Penguin Recall a Book on Hindus?" *BBC News India,* February 12, 2014. http://www.bbc.co.uk/news/world-asia-india-26148875.

*Brahmin priest seeks one who presses Soma."** Soma was an intoxicating beverage, possibly made from ephedra (AY-fay-druh) leaves, that was drunk at ceremonies. This poem shows that Vedic society included carpenters, doctors, Brahmin priests, and people who prepared the ritual drink.

The position of women in Vedic society was probably not much lower than that of men. Girls could go out unsupervised in public. Both girls and boys received an education in which they memorized hymns and studied their meaning, yet only male specialists recited hymns in public ceremonies. One hymn instructs educated girls to marry educated husbands. Girls could sometimes even choose their own husbands, provided they had obtained permission from their mother and father. Women could inherit property, and widows could remarry.

*From *The Rig Veda: An Anthology of One Hundred and Eight Hymns,* selected, translated, and annotated by Wendy Doniger O'Flaherty (Penguin Classics, 1981). Copyright © Wendy Doniger O'Flaherty, 1981. Reprinted with permission of Penguin Group/UK.

Changes After 1000 B.C.E.

The later hymns, composed perhaps around 1000 B.C.E. as the former nomads settled down to a life of agriculture, indicate that social roles in Vedic society became more fixed, and women's freedom declined. Eventually people came to be classed into four different social groups, called **varna** (VAR-nuh), that were determined by birth. The literal meaning of *varna* is "color," reflected in the modern English word *varnish*. One hymn, "The Hymn of the Primeval Man," explains that when the gods dismembered a cosmic giant, they created each varna from a different part of his body:

varna

From the Sanskrit word for "color": the four major social groups of ancient Indian society, ranked in order of purity (not wealth or power): Brahmin priests at the top, then warriors, then farmers and merchants, and finally dependent laborers.

> *When they divided the man, into how many parts did they apportion him?*
> *What do they call his mouth, his two arms and thighs and feet?*
> *His mouth became the Brahmin; his arms were made into the Warrior, his thighs the People, and from his feet the Servants were born.**

AP® THEMES

How did religious beliefs influence the social hierarchy in Vedic society?

This passage sets out the major social groups of late Vedic society, ranked in order of purity (not wealth or power): Brahmins were the purest because they conducted Vedic rituals; the warrior category included the kings who sponsored the rituals. The farmers and merchants ("the People") were supposed to farm the land and tend the herds. The fourth varna of dependent laborers, many of whom were the region's original residents, served all the varna above them. Like all documents, however, this hymn has a distinct point of view: a Brahmin priest composed it, and it is not surprising that he placed Brahmins at the top of the social hierarchy.

India's caste system has changed greatly over the last three thousand years. There is no exact equivalent in Indian languages of the English word *caste*, which comes from the sixteenth- to seventeenth-century Portuguese word *castas*, meaning breed or type of animal or plant. Most Indians would say that the word ***jati*** (JAH-ti), sometimes translated as "subcaste," comes closest. People often socialize within their own jati and share meals together. Many, but not all, people in modern South Asia find their spouse through an arranged marriage with someone from the same jati.

jati

A term, sometimes translated as "subcaste," for groups of five thousand to fifteen thousand people in modern India. Many, but not all, Indians marry someone from the same jati and share meals on equal footing only with people of the same jati.

● **CONTEXT&CONNECTIONS** Most outside observers tend to exaggerate the rigidity of caste in modern India. Castelike groups exist within other modern societies, too, although we often fail to recognize how many people in non-Indian societies, including the United States, also tend to marry spouses from similar social and economic backgrounds.●

Different changes took place in the centuries after about 1000 B.C.E., when the later poems in the *Rig Veda* were composed. Iron came into widespread use, and as in Mesopotamia, iron tools proved much more effective for clearing land than bronze or copper ones, enabling the residents of the lower Ganges Valley to clear much of the forest cover between 1000 and 500 B.C.E. so that they could intensively pursue agriculture. Higher agricultural yields prompted an increase in population and a boom in trade, as shown by the appearance of the first coins around 500 B.C.E.

---

*From *The Rig Veda: An Anthology of One Hundred and Eight Hymns*, selected, translated, and annotated by Wendy Doniger O'Flaherty (Penguin Classics, 1981).

• **CONTEXT&CONNECTIONS** Indian coins appeared at the same time as in China (see Chapter 4) and the Persian empire (see Chapter 6). Called punch-marked coins, the Indian coins were made by cutting silver bars into slices, weighing them, and cutting off corners until the coin reached the desired shape. Assayers, or the craftsmen who tested the coins, stamped them with their personal symbols to vouch for their quality. Because Indian coins from this time do not resemble either Chinese or Persian examples, historians conclude that coinage did not diffuse from one center to the other two but arose independently in the three regions. •

This period also saw other challenges to the old order. Composed between 900 and 600 B.C.E., the *Upanishad* (oo-PAHN-ih-shahd) texts claim to be linked to the Vedic tradition but introduce entirely new ideas. These texts turn inward, away from costly sacrificial rituals. One new and exciting idea was that souls transmigrated: according to the doctrine of **karma**, people's acts in this life determined how they would be reborn in the next. New gods appeared and are still worshiped by Hindus today. Unlike the gods of the *Rig Veda*, these gods intervene actively in human affairs and sometimes assume human form.

karma
The sum of one's deeds in this and all earlier existences that determines one's rebirth in the next life.

The *Mahabharata* (muh-HAH-bah-ruh-tuh) and the *Ramayana* (ruh-MAH-yuh-nuh), the two great Sanskrit epics, began to be composed at this time, although they were recorded only in the fourth century C.E. The *Mahabharata*, over 100,000 verses in length, describes a long-running feud between two clans. Its major theme is dharma, or right conduct. The epic vividly enacts some of the most basic conflicts in the human psyche as the characters struggle to understand what it means to be good and what the consequences of evil actions might be. We see men and women struggling with the question of whether it even matters if a person is actively trying to change the world, or whether perhaps everything is simply fated to be the way it is.

One part of the *Mahabharata*, the *Bhagavad Gita* (bug-GAH-vud GEEH-tuh), was often read as an independent work. Composed around 200 C.E., it tells the story of a battle between two armies. One leader hesitates before the battle: his dharma is to fight, but he will not be able to escape from the cycle of death and rebirth if he kills any of his relatives fighting on the other side. The deity Krishna, in human form as a chariot driver, argues that each person should fulfill his dharma, or his given role, in life. Then Krishna appears as a deity and urges the warrior to devote himself fully to worshiping him. Krishna's teaching later became a key tenet in Hinduism.

The *Ramayana* tells of a great king, Rama (RAH-muh), whose wife is abducted by a demon king. Rama fights and gets Sita (SEE-tuh) back, but he greets her coldly because, although a married woman, she has lived alone with her captors. Only after she jumps into a flaming pyre and the fire-god lifts her from the flames does he accept that she has remained faithful to him. In the centuries after their initial composition, both the *Mahabharata* and the *Ramayana* spawned many versions throughout South Asia and even Southeast Asia, and today's television versions captivate millions of viewers.

Jainism
An Indian religion founded around the same time as Buddhism that emphasizes right faith, right knowledge, and right conduct: a key tenet is not to harm any living beings.

Different teachers continued to debate new religious concepts in succeeding centuries. Between the sixth and fourth centuries B.C.E., **Jainism**, an Indian religion with some two million followers today, took shape. Mahavira, the founder of the Jains (JANES), went from place to place for twelve years, testing himself and debating ideas with other ascetics. For eleven of those years he wandered naked before reaching liberation from the bondage of human life. He died, it is thought, in his seventies after voluntarily renouncing food and water. Jains believe in right faith, right knowledge, and right conduct, and they emphasize the obligation to harm no living beings. They abstain from eating and drinking when it is dark so that they will not kill any insects by mistake.

The Rise of Buddhism

Buddha
The founder of the Buddhist religion, Siddhartha Gautama (ca. 630–550 B.C.E.); also called the Buddha, or the enlightened one.

Also living in this time of religious ferment was the founder of the Buddhist religion, Siddhartha Gautama (sid-DAR-tuh gow-TA-muh), or the Buddha. The word ***Buddha*** literally means "the enlightened or awakened one." The religion that he founded became one of the most influential in the world, and Ashoka's decision to support Buddhism marked a crucial turning point in the religion's history. Buddhism spread to modern-day Sri Lanka (the island of Ceylon), Central Asia, Southeast Asia, and eventually to China and Japan.

● **CONTEXT&CONNECTIONS** Today Japan, Tibet, and Thailand have significant Buddhist populations, and growing Buddhist communities live in Europe and North America.●

We know many details about the Buddha's life but cannot be sure which are facts and which myths because all our sources date to several centuries after his death and were recorded by Buddhist monks and nuns. The Buddha's stated goal was to teach people how to break out of the endless cycle of birth, death, and rebirth.

The Life of the Buddha

Born along the southern edge of the Himalaya Mountains in today's Nepal, the Buddha lived to almost eighty and died in the 550s B.C.E. The legend of his life, known to all practicing Buddhists, recounts that his mother dreamed of a white elephant with a lotus flower in his trunk. The wise men she consulted explained that she would give birth to either a great monarch or a great teacher. One seer predicted that, if he learned about human problems, he would become a teacher; this prediction prompted his parents to raise him inside a walled palace precinct so that he would never see any signs of suffering or illness. He grew up, married, and fathered a child.

One day when he was driving inside the palace park with his charioteer, he saw an extremely elderly man, then a man who was very ill, and then a corpse being taken away to be cremated. A fourth encounter, with a wandering ascetic who wore a simple robe but who looked happy, gave Siddhartha hope, and he resolved to follow the ascetic's example. For six years he subjected himself to all kinds of self-mortification. Then he decided to stop starving himself and meditated under a tree, later known as the Tree of Wisdom (also called a bodhi tree), for forty-nine days. He gained enlightenment and explained how he had done so.

The Teachings of the Buddha

According to much later Buddhist tradition, the Buddha preached his first sermon in the Deer Park near Benares (buh-NAR-us) in the Ganges Valley to five followers, who, like him, were seeking enlightenment. First he identified two incorrect routes to knowledge: extreme self-denial of those who strenuously fasted and complete self-gratification of those who did exactly as they pleased.

The Buddha preached that his listeners should avoid both extremes by leaving family life and following him.

He explained that one could escape from the endless cycle of birth, death, and rebirth by following a clear series of steps, called the Noble Eightfold Path. Like a doctor, the Buddha diagnosed suffering in the First Noble Truth, analyzed its origins in the Second Noble Truth, stated that a cure exists in the Third Truth, and explained that cure in the Fourth Noble Truth: to follow the Noble Eightfold Path. This path consists of right understanding, right resolve, right speech, right action, right livelihood, right effort, right mindfulness, and right meditation. When people follow the Noble Eightfold Path and understand the Four Noble Truths, their suffering will end because they will have escaped from the cycle of life and rebirth by attaining **nirvana**, literally "extinction."

Buddhism shared with Jainism much that was new. Both challenged Brahminic authority, denied the authority of the Vedic hymns, and banned animal sacrifices. Vedic religious practice did not address the question of individual liberation; the goal of Vedic ritual was to make sure that the cosmos continued to function in an orderly way. In contrast, the Buddha preached that salvation was entirely the product of an individual's actions, without regard to his or her varna ranking, a teaching that attracted many followers.

The people who heard the Buddha preach naturally wanted to know how they could attain nirvana. He urged them to leave their families behind so that they could join him as monks in the Buddhist order. Those who followed him went from place to place, begging for their daily food from those who did not join the order. They lived nowhere permanently except during the monsoon months, when it was not practical to live by begging.

Only those monks who joined the Buddhist order could attain nirvana, the Buddha taught. His first followers were all men, but Buddhist sources record that the Buddha's aunt asked to join the Buddhist order. The Buddha refused her until his star disciple Ananda (uh-NAN-duh) intervened and persuaded him to change his mind. Later women did become Buddhist nuns, but they were always subordinate to men.

Those outside the Buddhist order could not attain nirvana, but they could gain merit by donating food and money, the Buddha taught. Many kings and merchants gave large gifts in the hope of improving their lives, either in this world or in future rebirths.

This teaching marked a major departure from the pre-existing Vedic religion. According to the *Rig Veda*, Brahmins stood at the top of the ritual hierarchy, and those who ranked below them could do nothing to change their position. The Buddhists took a radically different view: a merchant, a farmer, or even a laborer who made a donation to the Buddhist order could enhance his or her standing. From its very earliest years, Buddhism attracted merchant support, and communities of Buddhists often lived near cities, where merchants had gathered.

The Buddha forbade his followers to worship statues or portraits of him. Instead, they worshiped at the four sites that had been most important during the Buddha's life: where he was born, where he gained enlightenment, where he preached the first sermon, and where he died. Before his death the Buddha had instructed his followers to cremate him and bury his ashes under a bell-shaped monument built over a burial mound, called a stupa (STEW-pah). Recent excavations in Lumbini, Nepal, have uncovered a temple dedicated to the Buddha's mother that is built around a tree, most likely symbolizing the bodhi tree under

AP® THEMES

How do the teachings of the Buddha compare to Hindu teachings?

nirvana

A Sanskrit word that literally means "extinction," as when the flame on a candle goes out. In Buddhism the term took on broader meaning: those who followed the Eightfold Path and understood the Four Noble Truths would gain true understanding.

which the Buddha attained enlightenment. The Lumbini temple dates to the sixth century B.C.E., when the Buddha died. In keeping with his instructions, this early temple had no portrayals of the Buddha.

The first generation of Buddhists divided the Buddha's remains under many different stupas, where they honored him by circling the stupa in a clockwise direction, a practice called circumambulation (pradaksina) (pra-DUCKSH-ee-nah). To gain merit, they walked a fixed number of circuits with their right arm, thought to be more pure than the left, facing the stupa. They also left flowers, incense, and clothing on the stupas, where they lit lamps and played music as an expression of their devotion. (See the feature "Visual Evidence in Primary Sources: The Buddhist Stupa at Kanaganahalli.")

●**CONTEXT&CONNECTIONS** As the second phase of construction at Kanaganahalli shows, beginning in the first and second centuries C.E., sculptors began to make images of the Buddha. One group in north India portrayed the Buddha as a young man, while another, active in the Gandhara (gahn-DAHR-ah) region of modern Pakistan and Afghanistan, was influenced by later copies of Greek statues brought by the armies of *Alexander of Macedon*, or Alexander the Great, in the fourth century B.C.E. (Chapter 6).●

A Mix of Sculptural Traditions from Gandhara, Afghanistan This Gandharan statue's posture is classically Buddhist: his legs are crossed so that both feet face up, the left hand grasps his robe, and the right makes a gesture meaning to dispel fear. But the facial expression, hair, and overall posture are drawn from Greco-Roman models already familiar to Gandharan sculptors for several centuries. Neither Buddhist nor Greco-Roman, the spokes in the halo behind the Buddha's head probably represent the sun's rays. Image copyright (© The Metropolitan Museum of Art. Image source: Art Resource, NY)

The Mauryan Empire, ca. 320–185 B.C.E.

The support of Ashoka, the third ruler of the **Mauryan dynasty**, founded by Ashoka's grandfather, transformed Buddhism into the most influential religion of its day. Ashoka's adoption of Buddhism as the state religion promoted cultural unity and strengthened his political control. The Mauryans came to power at a time when trade was increasing throughout the region, and Buddhism was able to succeed because it appealed to merchants. The Mauryans created the first large state in India, extending over all of north India (see the map on page 61).

Mauryan dynasty (ca. 320–185 B.C.E.) A dynasty that unified much of the Indian subcontinent. Relying on trunk roads, it exercised more control in the cities than in the countryside.

Historians continue to debate the amount of control the Mauryan empire exercised over the regions it conquered. Local rulers may have retained considerable power. In addition to archaeological excavations, our major sources are the partial report of a Greek ambassador named Megasthenes (ME-gas-thuh-nees), written after 288 B.C.E., and Ashoka's rock edicts.

Life and Society in the Mauryan Dynasty, ca. 300 B.C.E.

In 320 B.C.E. the grandfather of Ashoka, a general named Chandragupta (chuhn-druh-GOOP-tuh) Maurya (r. ca. 320–297 B.C.E.), defeated another general and gained control of his territory and his capital Pataliputra (modern-day Patna [PUTT-nuh]), located on the Ganges. In 302 B.C.E. Seleucus I (seh-LOO-kuhs) (321–281 B.C.E.), a general who succeeded Alexander the Great in Mesopotamia (see Chapter 6), sent an ambassador named Megasthenes to the Mauryan court at Pataliputra. Megasthenes stayed for fourteen years. Unfortunately, his original work does not survive; we know it only from passages quoted by later Greek and Roman writers.

Megasthenes wrote a work entitled *Indika* (IN-dick-uh), which provides a detailed description of Pataliputra in approximately 300 B.C.E., some thirty years before Ashoka ascended to the throne. Archaeological excavations early in the twentieth century around Patna revealed clear evidence of large fortification walls, and the city occupied some 20 square miles (50 sq km). Pataliputra's size impressed Megasthenes deeply.

Within the capital the Mauryans exercised considerable control. Most of their officials supervised trade and commerce, the major source of Mauryan revenue. Market officials in the capital collected taxes and regulated weights and measures to ensure that no one was cheated. They levied fines on merchants who passed off old goods as newly made.

> **AP® THEMES**
> What role did the Mauryan capital Pataliputra play in commercial activities?

The passages from Megasthenes that have come down to us include no personal anecdotes. His account of the officials who watched over foreigners comes closest to describing his own life in Pataliputra:

> *Those of the second branch attend to the entertainment of foreigners. To these they assign lodgings, and they keep watch over their modes of life by means of those persons whom they give to them for assistants. They escort them on the way when they leave the country, or, in the event of their dying, forward their property to their relatives. They take care of them when they are sick, and if they die bury them.**

We may surmise that city officials gave Megasthenes a servant.

According to Megasthenes, the military section of the government was the same size as the urban section: thirty men, divided into six branches, each with its own area of responsibility—navy, supplies, infantry, cavalry, war chariots, and elephants. If true, and we have no independent source to verify this information, this is a tiny number of officials: still, historians value Megasthenes's reports for their plausibility and detail. Elephants, used by the military, fascinated Megasthenes, who devoted many lines to their capture, training, loyalty to their masters, and general care; when on active duty, he reports, they consumed rice wine and large quantities of flowers.

Megasthenes's descriptions of Indian society have long puzzled analysts. He identifies seven ranks within Indian society: (1) philosophers, (2) farmers, (3) herdsmen, (4) artisans, (5) soldiers, (6) spies, and (7) councillors. This overlaps only slightly with the *Rig Veda*'s varna, with its four ranks of Brahmin,

---

*J. W. McCrindle, *Ancient India as Described by Megasthenes and Arrian* (London: Trübner, 1877), p. 87.

The Buddhist Stupa at Kanaganahalli

The earliest portraits of Ashoka found so far come from the Kanaganahalli (kuh-nuh-guh-na-HAH-lee) site, southeast of Bombay, and were published in 2013. Unlike other portraits of the Mauryan ruler, the stone tablet from this site has a label that reads "King Ashoka," so there is no doubt at all about who is portrayed (see photo on page 60).

The site fully illustrates the shift from the early period of Buddhism, when devotees did not worship images of the Buddha, to the later period, when they did. Construction at the site began at the end of the Mauryan period, sometime before 185 B.C.E., and continued through the third and fourth centuries C.E.

The first phase of construction saw the creation of a large earthen mound, which was covered with small pebbles, blocks of limestone, and soil. Inside the mound were either actual ashes of the Buddha after his cremation or similar looking objects, such as glass beads, that served as substitutes. Buddhists believe that visiting a stupa holding someone's remains brings them closer to the deceased, and Buddhist followers often constructed stupas for the Buddha in multiple places in ancient India.

The original mound was 52 feet (16 m) in diameter and 25 feet (7.5 m) high. Buddhist believers showed their reverence to the Buddha, and hoped to gain merit, by circumambulating the stupa clockwise.

A pathway led worshippers around the stupa, where different scenes illustrating the life of the Buddha were placed at eye level. In the first phase of construction, the sculptors exercised great ingenuity in showing the Buddha's footprints over the seat of a throne or an empty space below an umbrella, but never directly the Buddha himself, because in his dying instructions, the Buddha forbade his followers to worship representations of him.

As visitors viewed the stone pictures, local monks and guides told stories, which were based on local folktales. For example, in one tale, some monkeys crossed a river to steal fruit from an orchard. When the orchard owner returned unexpectedly, they panicked and fled to the river, where their king had magically stretched his body between two trees to form a bridge for them to cross. In the Buddhist retelling of this tale, the monkey king was actually the Buddha in an earlier reincarnation who sacrificed himself to help others.

In later periods, builders added more earth and stones so that the diameter of the mound extended 85 feet (26 m), with an impressive circumference over 300 feet (94 m). At its full height the stupa reached 56 feet (17 m), but it collapsed in later times and measured only a few meters tall when the site was rediscovered. The builders in the second phase retained the original walkway as a lower walkway and added a new floor above it to create an upper walkway. They also placed larger structures that held statues of the Buddha at the four points of the cardinal directions, east, west, north, and south. At the height of the monument's popularity, ten different buildings stood outside the circular mound: a monastery, smaller stupas, and places where visitors could worship the Buddha's footprints.

Later Buddhist monuments, such as the Indonesian site of Borobudur (see the Chapter 8 feature, "Visual Evidence in Primary Sources: Borobudur: A Buddhist Monument in Java, Indonesia"), also offered the experience of walking around a round space and viewing scenes with Buddhist content. Unlike Kanaganahalli, Borobudur was not a stupa because it did not contain any Buddhist remains.

The stupa mound was first built over the remains of the Buddha in the third century B.C.E. and attained its largest size—85 feet (26 m) in diameter, with an impressive circumference over 300 feet (94 m) and height of 56 feet (17 m)—one hundred years later.

As devotees walked around the stupa, they saw scenes from the life of the Buddha (specifically, birth, renunciation, enlightenment, first sermon, and great departure); pictures of different kings, including Ashoka, who patronized Buddhism; and tales recounting the Buddha's earlier lives.

The limestone panel illustrations on the top walkway were about 10 feet (3 m) tall, while those on the lower walkway were half that size.

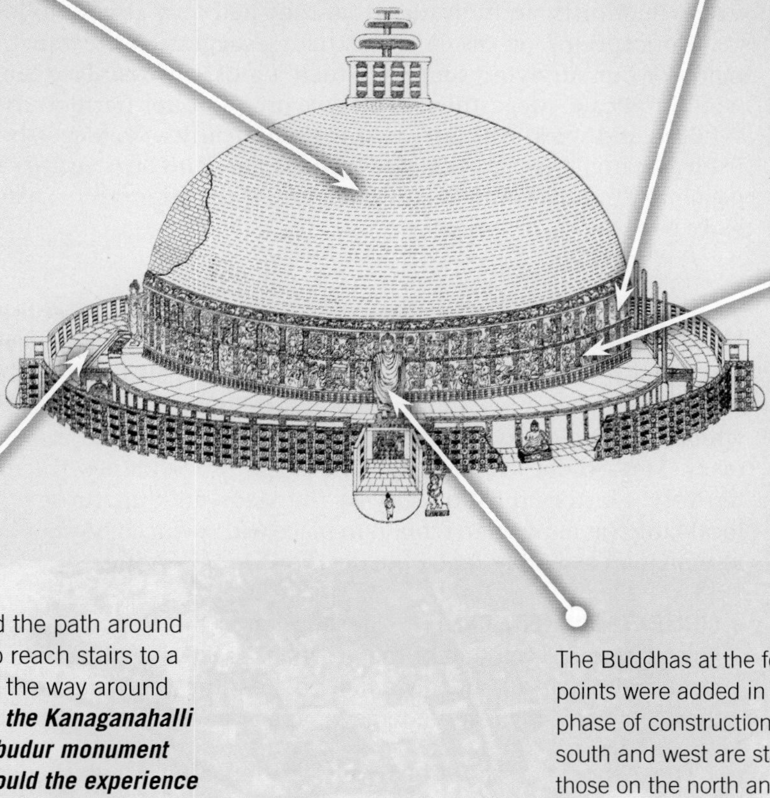

Archaeological Survey of India

Worshipers followed the path around the burial mound to reach stairs to a walkway that led all the way around the stupa. ***Compare the Kanaganahalli stupa and the Borobudur monument (page 224). How would the experience of visitors to these two sites have differed?***

The Buddhas at the four cardinal points were added in the second phase of construction: those on the south and west are standing, while those on the north and east are seated.

warriors, merchants and farmers, and dependent servants. Three of Megasthenes's groups (herdsmen, artisans, and spies) do not even appear in the varna ranking.

The top-ranking group, according to Megasthenes, was the smallest: the king's advisers, military generals, and treasury officials, who were *"the most respected on account of the high character and wisdom of [their] members."** The placement at the top of the ranking suggests that this was the group Megasthenes spoke to directly.

Ranking second were the "philosophers," or religious practitioners. They performed sacrifices and funerals, and Megasthenes explains that the Brahmins among them married and had children but lived simply. Another group of religious practitioners underwent various privations, such as abstaining from sexual intercourse or sitting in one position all day. The Jains would have belonged to this group. Finally, a third group followed the Buddha, *"whom they honor as a god on account of his extraordinary sanctity."** Megasthenes devotes only a few sentences to the Buddhists, an indication that they had only a small following in 300 B.C.E.

Conceptions of caste, Megasthenes suggests, were much more fluid than many of our surviving sources, which almost always place Brahmins at the top, would indicate. Megasthenes lists five other groups (farmers, herdsmen, artisans, soldiers, and spies) without ranking them in any way. Megasthenes concludes his list by saying, *"No one is allowed to marry out of his own caste, or to exercise any calling or art except his own,"** an indication of the strength of caste identities in this early period.

AP® THEMES

What strategies did Mauryan rulers use to govern territories outside of the capital?

Mauryan Control Outside the Capital

The Mauryans exercised close supervision over the rural areas in the immediate vicinity of the capital, but not over all of north India. Control also extended to the trade routes linking the capital with outlying trade centers, along which the Mauryans could have dispatched officials to markets to collect sales taxes. Megasthenes reports that the kingdom contained three different types of territory: territory ruled directly by the Mauryan king, those territories where the local king was allowed to remain in place with reduced powers, and local republics, in which an assembly made the decisions for everyone.

• **CONTEXT&CONNECTIONS** This description of the Mauryans suggests an empire quite different from that of the Assyrians (see Chapter 2). Whereas the Mauryans exercised direct rule in only a limited area, the Assyrians were so powerful that they could forcibly resettle large groups of people throughout their empire. •

The Ashokan inscriptions were written after Megasthenes left India (most likely between 260 and 232 B.C.E.). They were placed in the capital, in northwest India in the Punjab (PUHN-juhb) region, on the east and west coasts, and in central India (see the map on page 61).

Mauryan control was greatest in the region about Pataliputra. The dynasty's control also extended to the trade routes linking the capital with outlying trade centers, along which the Mauryans could have dispatched officials to markets to

*J. W. McCrindle, *Ancient India as Described by Megasthenes and Arrian* (London: Trübner, 1877), pp. 43, 105, 44.

Lion Pillar of Emperor Ashoka (c.264-223 BC) (photo), Indian School/Lauria Nandangarh, Bihar, India/Bridgeman Images

An Ashokan Column from Vaishali, Bihar, India This pillar, made of polished red sandstone, stands 27.5 feet (8.5 m) high. Capped with a lion, it was visible in all four directions. This and the other stone columns Ashoka commissioned are the first monuments worked in stone anywhere in ancient India. Some scholars have wondered if Ashoka knew of other stone monuments in neighboring regions like Iran.

collect sales taxes. But the regions lying in between the trade routes were controlled lightly, if at all.

The Mauryan empire remained a decentralized one in which local people continued to speak their own languages. Ashoka drafted the texts of his inscriptions in his native language of Magadhi (muh-GUH-dee), a language related to Sanskrit. They were then translated into the different vernaculars used in north India, which are all descended from Sanskrit.

• **CONTEXT&CONNECTIONS** Some of Ashoka's inscriptions were translated into Greek and Aramaic, a western Asian language, because the residents of the northwest spoke both languages. •

Ashoka drafted short, medium, and lengthy versions of each edict so that his local officials could decide which one to use. Officials sometimes left out passages from the original to save space, Ashoka realized, and the officials at Kalinga did not even put up the text cited at the beginning of this chapter about Ashoka's bloody conquest of the region, possibly because they did not want to antagonize the local population. The text survives in the long version in the capital, an important reminder that central governments may issue prescriptive orders but local officials do not necessarily implement them.

The inscriptions report that Ashoka sent officials to inspect outlying regions every three to five years. He claims to have built new roads, along which his men planted trees and dug wells. Ashoka and the other Mauryan rulers did not mint their own coins; rulers in each locality did.

Ruling by Example: The Ceremonial State

Ashoka was the first major Indian ruler to support Buddhism. The ideal ruler followed Buddhist teachings and made donations to the Buddhist order, which he did not join. Nor did he renounce his family. The Buddhists called such a ruler a **chakravartin** (chah-kruh-VAR-tin), literally "turner of the wheel," a broad term indicating that the sovereign ruled over a wide territory. Ashoka's inscriptions fully express his ideal of ruling by example. Every measure he took had the same goal: to encourage his subjects to follow dharma, which he described in this way:

chakravartin

Literally "turner of the wheel," a Buddhist term for the ideal ruler who patronized Buddhism but never became a monk.

> *There is no gift comparable to the gift of dharma, the praise of dharma, the sharing of dharma, fellowship in dharma. And this is—good behavior towards slaves and servants, obedience to mother and father, generosity towards friends, acquaintances, and relatives and towards shramanas [shrah-MUH-nuhz; Buddhists and other renunciants] and Brahmins, and abstention from killing living beings.**

• **CONTEXT&CONNECTIONS** Many subsequent rulers, particularly in South and Southeast Asia, followed Ashoka's example. •

In the tenth year of his reign, around 258 B.C.E., Ashoka decided to increase his devotion to Buddhism even further. Presumably along with learned Buddhists, he conducted a series of meetings with non-Buddhist "ascetics" engaged in different austerities, as well as with Brahmin priests, who continued to sacrifice animals. Ashoka discussed the teachings of the Buddha and gave them gifts to encourage them to convert to Buddhism. He used the same combination of persuasion and gift giving with elderly people and with ordinary people in the countryside. (See the feature "Movement of Ideas Through Primary Sources: The First Sermon of the Buddha and Ashoka's Fourth Major Rock Edict.")

Historians call this type of rule a "**ceremonial state**" to contrast it with empires in which rulers exercised more direct control. The ruler of a ceremonial state sponsored religious observances and contributed money for the construction of religious edifices in the hope that his subjects would recognize his generosity

ceremonial state

State whose ruler sponsored religious observances and construction of religious edifices in the hope that his subjects would willingly acknowledge him as ruler. Usually contrasted with rulers who depended on sheer force to govern.

---

*Excerpt from *Aśoka and the Decline of the Mauryas*, ed. Romila Thapar, 1973, pp. 254–255. Reprinted with permission of Oxford University Press India, New Delhi.

and willingly acknowledge him as their leader. Ashoka's inscriptions permit us to see how his devotion to Buddhism increased over time. As we have seen, the huge number of deaths in the battle of Kalinga (260 B.C.E.) filled him with remorse, and he made a decision to follow the teachings of the Buddha. In the following year he promised to uphold the five most important precepts—not to kill, steal, commit adultery, lie, or drink alcohol—and became a **lay Buddhist** (*upasaka*). Anyone could become a lay Buddhist; one simply had to vow to uphold the five precepts. Four distinct groups formed the early Buddhist order: monks and nuns were ordained, while male and female lay Buddhists were not.

lay Buddhist
A Buddhist devotee who observes the five precepts not to kill, steal, commit adultery, lie, or drink alcohol, but continues to live at home and does not join the Buddhist order.

Ashoka visited the Deer Park in Benares as well as the site of the Buddha's birth in present-day Nepal, where he built a stone fence and erected a stone pillar in memory of the Buddha (the newly discovered temple built around a bodhi tree lies under the Ashokan monument).

Ashoka's style of governing was very personal. One inscription describes how seriously he took the business of ruling and explains that his officials were free to interrupt him with public business no matter what he was doing. It tells us that some officers could speak directly to the king and that there was a council, but not how it functioned.

● **CONTEXT&CONNECTIONS** Ashoka claimed to exercise influence over lands far from north India. One inscription composed between 256 and 254 B.C.E. claims that Ashoka brought about "*victory by dharma*" far beyond his frontiers, as far west as the realms of Greek rulers in Egypt and Greece, and as far south as the island of Ceylon, modern Sri Lanka. Modern scholars concur that he may have sent missionaries, particularly to Sri Lanka, where oral accounts record their names. ●

We must keep in mind that Ashoka wrote his inscriptions and had them carved into huge, dramatic monuments to remind his subjects that he had the right to rule over them. The only external confirmation of their veracity comes from later Buddhist sources, which mention Ashoka's devotion to Buddhism. If Ashoka had violated his Buddhist vows, or if a certain region had risen up in rebellion during his reign, we can be sure that the inscriptions would not mention it. One recent analysis suggests that the inscriptions be seen as "pieces of political propaganda, as the campaign speeches of an incumbent politician who seeks not so much to record events as to present an image of himself and his administration to the world."*

After Ashoka's death in 232 B.C.E., the Mauryan empire began to break apart; the Mauryans lost control of the last remaining section, the Ganges Valley, around 185 B.C.E. A series of regional kingdoms gained control, as was the usual pattern for much of South Asian history.

● **CONTEXT&CONNECTIONS** In the second century B.C.E. a local chieftain unified the island of Ceylon for the first time. After being named king, he followed Ashoka's example and built a giant stupa as a monument to the Buddha. Also in the second century B.C.E., another patron of Buddhism, a ruler of Greek descent, unified a large territory in Afghanistan and Pakistan whose eastern edge included the former Mauryan capital at Pataliputra. These two rulers' patronage of Buddhism marked the first time Buddhism spread beyond the immediate territory of India. ●

---

*John S. Strong, "Images of Asoka: Some Indian and Sri Lankan Legends and Their Development," in *King Asoka and Buddhism: Historical and Literary Studies*, ed. A. Seneviratne (Kandy, Sri Lanka: Buddhist Publication Society, 1994), p. 99.

The First Sermon of the Buddha and Ashoka's Fourth Major Rock Edict

After gaining enlightenment under the Tree of Wisdom at Bodh Gaya, the Buddha preached his first sermon at the Deer Park at Benares. The Buddha's sermon presented the main teachings of Buddhism in a capsule form that could be translated into other languages when Buddhism spread beyond India to East and Southeast Asia. Because the language is easy to understand, this would have worked well as a spoken sermon, with repetition of important concepts to ensure the comprehension of his five followers, or bhikkhus (BEAK-kooz), whom he addressed. This text was transmitted orally by Buddhists in north India. Hundreds of monks met, first following the Buddha's death and then one hundred years later, to make sure that they were reciting the standard version of the sermon. The text was committed to writing only in the first century B.C.E. by monks in modern-day Sri Lanka, evidence that Buddhism had spread to south India and beyond by that time.

The Fourth Major Rock Edict provides a summary of Ashoka's beliefs. Some overlap with the Buddha's teachings in the First Sermon, while others differ. Although Ashoka himself embraced Buddhism, he reached out to both Buddhist and non-Buddhist subjects by erecting pillar and rock inscriptions throughout India. The location of his edicts provides a rough indication of how far Buddhist teachings reached during his reign.

Historical Thinking Skill:
ANALYZING EVIDENCE **What evidence can you cite from the first sermon of the Buddha to indicate this source was originally orally transmitted?**

Historical Thinking Skill:
CONTEXTUALIZATION **Using the Fourth Major Rock Edict as evidence, how has Ashoka incorporated Buddhist values into Mauryan society?**

Historical Thinking Skill:
CONTEXTUALIZATION **Why did many rulers during the period 600 B.C.E., to 600 C.E. shape policies around local religious beliefs?**

Sources: From "The First Sermon of Buddha," from Walpola Rahula, *What the Buddha Taught*, Grove Atlantic, 1974, pp. 92–94. Copyright © 1959, 1974 by Wapola Rahula. Used by permission of Grove/Atlantic, Inc.; *Aśoka and the Decline of the Mauryas*, ed. Romila Thapar, 1973, pp. 251–252. Reprinted with permission of Oxford University Press India, New Delhi. (Some changes in spelling and capitalization made for the sake of consistency.)

The First Sermon of the Buddha

Thus I have heard. The Blessed One was once living in the Deer Park at Isipatana (the Resort of Seers) near Varanasi (Benares). There he addressed the group of five bhikkhus:

Bhikkhus, these two extremes ought not to be practiced by one who has gone forth from the household life. What are the two? There is devotion to the indulgence of sense-pleasures, which is low, common, the way of ordinary people, unworthy and unprofitable; and there is devotion to self-mortification, which is painful, unworthy and unprofitable.

Avoiding both these extremes, the Tathagatha [the Buddha] has realized the Middle Path: it gives vision, it gives knowledge, and it leads to calm, to insight, to enlightenment, to nirvana. And what is that Middle Path ... ? It is simply the Noble Eightfold Path, namely, right view, right thought, right speech, right action, right livelihood, right effort, right mindfulness, right concentration. . . .

The Noble Truth of suffering (*dukkha*) is this: Birth is suffering; aging is suffering; sickness is suffering; death is suffering; sorrow and lamentation, pain, grief and despair are suffering; association with the unpleasant is suffering; dissociation from the pleasant is suffering; not to get what one wants is suffering—in brief, the five aggregates of attachment are suffering.

The Noble Truth of the origin of suffering is this: It is this thirst (craving) which produces re-existence and re-becoming, bound up with passionate greed. It finds fresh delight now here and now there, namely, thirst for sense-pleasures; thirst for existence and becoming; and thirst for non-existence (self-annihilation).

The Noble Truth of the cessation of suffering is this: It is the complete cessation of that very thirst, giving it up, renouncing it, emancipating oneself from it, detaching oneself from it.

The Noble Truth of the path leading to the cessation of suffering is this: It is simply the Noble Eightfold Path, namely right view; right thought; right speech; right action; right livelihood; right effort; right mindfulness; right concentration.

"This is the Noble Truth of Suffering (*dukkha*)"; such was the vision, the knowledge, the wisdom, the science, the light, that arose in me with regard to things not heard before. . . .

As long as my vision of true knowledge was not fully clear . . . regarding the Four Noble Truths, I did not claim to have realized the perfect Enlightenment that is supreme in the world. . . . But when my vision of true knowledge was fully clear ... regarding the Four Noble Truths, then I claimed to have the perfect Enlightenment that is supreme in the world. . . . And a vision of true knowledge arose in me thus: My heart's deliverance is unassailable. This is the last birth. Now there is no more re-becoming (rebirth).

This the Blessed One said. The group of five bhikkhus was glad, and they rejoiced at his words.

The Fourth Major Rock Edict

In the past, the killing and injuring of living beings, lack of respect towards relatives, Brahmins and shramanas had increased. But today, thanks to the practice of dharma on the part of the Beloved of the Gods, the king Ashoka, the sound of the drum has become the sound of dharma, showing the people displays of heavenly chariots, elephants, balls of fire, and other divine forms. Through his instruction in dharma abstention from killing and non-injury to living beings, deference to relatives, Brahmins and shramanas, obedience to mother and father, and obedience to elders have all increased as never before for many centuries. These and many other forms of the practice of dharma have increased and will increase.

The Beloved of the Gods, the king Ashoka, his sons, his grandsons and his great grandsons will advance the practice of dharma, until the end of the world and will instruct in the law, standing firm in dharma. For this, the instruction in the law, is the most valuable activity. But there is no practice of dharma without goodness, and in these matters it is good to progress and not to fall back. For this purpose, the inscription has been engraved—that men should make progress in this matter, and not be satisfied with their shortcomings. This was engraved here when the Beloved of the Gods, the king Ashoka, had been consecrated twelve years.

South Asia's External Trade

India's geographic proximity to western Asia meant that outsiders came to South Asia in very early times, and conversely, Indian culture, particularly Buddhist teachings, traveled out from India on the same paths. In ancient times travelers seeking to enter South Asia had a choice of routes. Although the Himalaya Mountains in the north and extensive mountains in the northeast prevented large-scale overland trade, regular cultural contacts and the movement of valuable goods always continued. Land routes through the Hindu Kush (KOOSH) in the northwest, including the Khyber (KAI-ber) Pass, allowed contacts between South Asia and Central Asia through what is today Afghanistan. These are the routes that allowed the expansion of Indo-European languages and that Megasthenes used when he came to India.

However, the most important mode of communication between South Asia and the rest of the world was by sea. By 2200 B.C.E., if not earlier, mariners from South and Southeast Asia had arrived in Australia. By 100 C.E., if not earlier, they had learned to capture the monsoon winds blowing northeast in the spring and early summer, and southwest in the fall and winter, to carry on regular commerce and cultural interaction with surrounding lands. If one caught the winds going west on a summer departure, one could return in the following winter as they blew east. Merchants traveling the Indian Ocean usually sailed in small boats called **dhows** (DOWZ). With their teak planks held together by coconut fiber twine and tightly caulked, dhows had greater flexibility during storms than boats made from nailed wooden planks.

dhows
Small sailboats used in the Indian Ocean made from teak planks laid edge to edge, fastened together with coconut fiber twine, and caulked to prevent leaking.

● **CONTEXT&CONNECTIONS** Finds of Harappan artifacts in the archaeological assemblages of early *Sumer* (Chapter 2) testify to the importance and age of these ancient sea routes across the Indian Ocean, connecting India with Mesopotamia, the Arabian Peninsula, East Africa, and Australia (see Map 3.1 on page 64). ●

Because no written descriptions of the ancient trade exist, archaeologists must reconstruct the trade on the basis of excavated commodities. Natural reserves of the semiprecious blue stone lapis lazuli exist only in the Badakhshan (BAH-duck-shan) region of northern Afghanistan, so we know that by 2600 B.C.E., if not earlier, trade routes linked Badakhshan with ancient Sumer, where much lapis lazuli has been found. Similarly, the red-orange semiprecious stone carnelian traveled from mines in Gujarat (GOO-juh-ruht), India, to Mesopotamian sites. The presence of Harappan seals and clay pots at Sumer reveals that the trade included manufactured goods as well as minerals. These goods traveled overland or by boat down the Indus River to the Arabian Sea, where they hugged the coast as they traveled west to the Persian Gulf. Ancient sea routes across the Indian Ocean connected India with Mesopotamia, the Arabian peninsula, and East Africa.

We learn much about the Indian Ocean trade during the first century C.E. from an unusual work called the *Periplus* (PAY-rih-plus) (literally "around the globe"), written in colloquial Greek by an anonymous merchant living in Egypt around 50 C.E. By the first century C.E., navigators from Egypt had learned how to harness the monsoon winds and travel by boat to India. The *Periplus* describes the routes sailors took from Egypt and the goods they traded at Indian ports, where they obtained clothing and textiles, semiprecious stones, wine, copper, tin, lead, and spices. The contents of the earliest shipwreck found so far in the Indian Ocean, off the coast of Sri Lanka an and dating to the first century before or after the Common Era, supplement this list: marine archaeologists found lumps of unworked glass, stone grindstones, ceramics, and iron, which *Periplus* identifies as one of India's major exports.

Written explicitly for merchants, the *Periplus* is organized as a guidebook: port by port, down the East African coast, around the Arabian peninsula, and then to India, the most important trading destination. In African and Arabian ports sailors could purchase ivory or gum resins like frankincense and myrrh, which were prized for their fragrance, but India offered far more goods than either Arabia or Africa. The author says almost nothing about social structure and little about government; he is much more interested in which commodities were for sale.

The *Periplus* summarizes the import trade on India's southwestern Malabar (MAH-lah-bar) coast. At the markets one could buy a yellow gem called peridot (PAY-ree-doh), clothing and textiles, coral, raw glass, copper, tin, lead, and wine. The author instructs his readers to bring money, and lots of it, to the southwestern coast because there were few opportunities for barter. Thousands of Roman silver and gold coins have been found on the south coast but not farther north, suggesting that the traders could barter in the north but had to pay Roman coins in the south (see Chapter 7). The author continues his discussion of the southwest coast by explaining the goods the region exported. Most of the items on the list, like pepper, pearls, ivory, and precious stones, are valuable even today.

Aimed at non-Indian readers, the *Periplus* gives the misleading impression that the Indian Ocean trade was controlled by foreigners, possibly because its author was a Greek living in Egypt who used Roman coins to purchase Indian goods. In fact, though, Indian merchants played an active role.

At the end of the *Periplus*, the author describes one final destination:

> *Beyond this region, by now at the northernmost point, where the sea ends somewhere on the outer fringe, there is a very great inland city called Thina from which silk floss, yarn, and cloth are shipped by land... and via the Ganga River.... It is not easy to get to this Thina; for rarely do people come from it, and only a few.**

Thina? The spelling makes sense when one realizes that ancient Greek had no letter for the sound "ch," so the author had to choose either a "th" or an "s" for the first letter of the place whose name he heard from Indian traders. He opted for Thina. *China* was pronounced "CHEE-na" in Sanskrit (and is the source of our English word *China*).

The author thought Thina was a city, not a country, but he knew that silk was made there and exported. The *Periplus* closes with the admission that China lay at the extreme edge of the world known to the Greeks: "*What lies beyond this area, because of extremes of storm, bitter cold, and difficult terrain and also because of some divine power of the gods, has not been explored.*" The India described in the *Periplus*, then, was a major trade center linking the familiar Roman empire with the dimly understood China.

---

*Lionel Casson, *The Periplus Maris Erythraei Text with Introduction, Translation, and Commentary* (Princeton: Princeton University Press, 1989), pp. 91 (Thina); 93 (regions beyond China).

The Significance of Ancient India in World History

Ashoka's decision to patronize Buddhism in 260 B.C.E. marked a key juncture in world history: after Buddhism became the state religion of the Mauryan dynasty, it spread throughout the Ganges, northern Indus, and Godavari River Valleys. A century later, as kings in Sri Lanka and Afghanistan emulated Ashoka's example as a chakravartin ruler, Buddhism extended even farther. Eventually it would become a major world religion with adherents in South, Southeast, and East Asia (see Chapter 8).

The residents of the Indian subcontinent adopted agriculture sometime around 7000 B.C.E. Like the inhabitants of Mesopotamia (see Chapter 2), the people of the Indus River Valley's complex society did not have a single ruler but multiple rulers in different cities. The ruins of these ancient cities had distinct neighborhoods for people of varying occupations and social levels, but because the Indus River Valley script has not been deciphered, we do not know how the residents conceived of these different social groupings. Most distinctive, the sophisticated water system of their largest settlement at Mohenjo-daro provided clean water for drinking and bathing as well as sewage facilities for all residents, regardless of social level.

The introduction of Sanskrit by Indo-Aryan migrants between 1500 and 1000 B.C.E. brings Indian ideas about social rank into clearer focus. The hymns of the *Rig Veda* explain the system of four ranked varna for different occupations. Local kings ruled by patronizing Brahmin priests who performed complex rituals on their behalf, a hallmark of complex societies whose members believed that their rulers were entitled to the surplus they produced.

In a ceremonial state, the king patronized priests in the hope that his subjects would support his rule because of his ties to religious specialists. Ashoka's exercise of chakravartin rule made the Mauryans a full-fledged ceremonial state. Both Egypt and ancient Mesopotamia also had elements of ceremonial states: the pharaoh was thought to be a god-king whose rituals ensured the well-being of his kingdom, and the rulers of ancient Sumer made regular offerings to the temples in their city-states.

The Greek ambassador Megasthenes reported that the kingdom had three types of territory: that ruled directly by the Mauryan king, that governed by local rulers with reduced powers who acknowledged the sovereignty of the Mauryan king, and local republics. Even under Ashoka, one of ancient India's most powerful rulers, India was not politically united, but its different regions maintained shared cultural traditions. This pattern held for many periods in South Asian history.

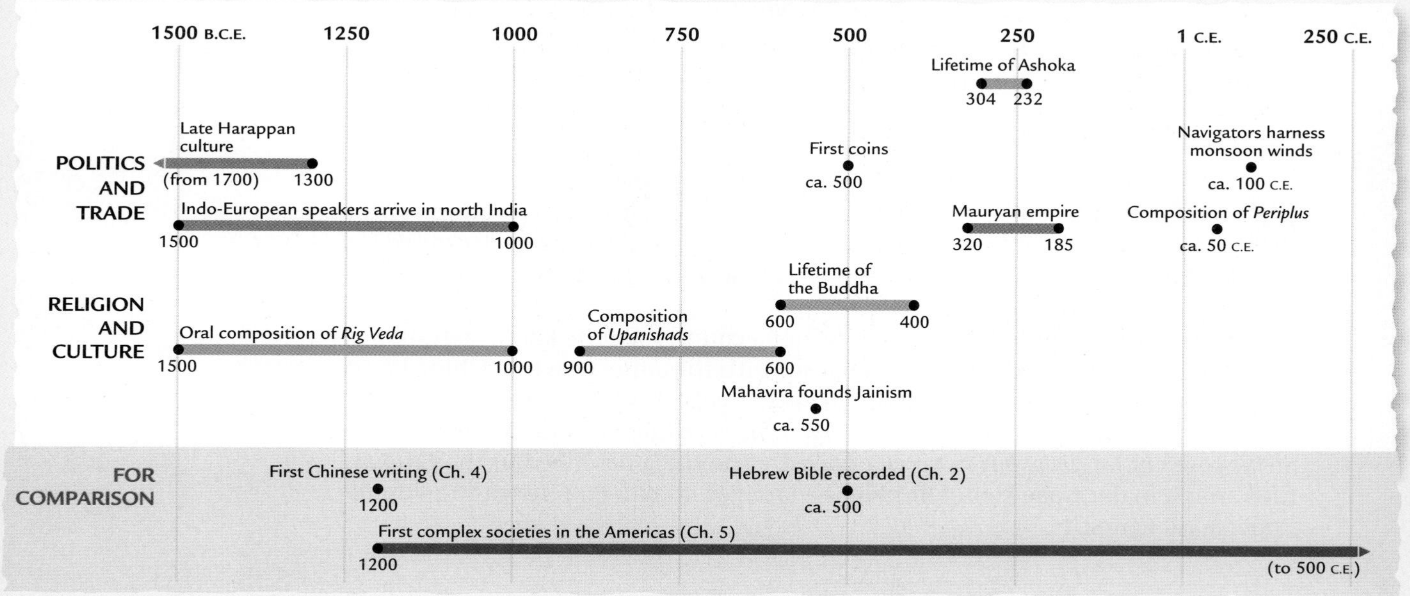

Although surrounded by water on two sides and bounded by mountains to the north, ancient India had extensive contacts with its neighbors. Trade of carnelian, lapis lazuli, and shells with Mesopotamia dated back to at least 2500 B.C.E. Sometime before the year 100 C.E., the understanding of the monsoon winds made it possible for ships to sail to India from Egypt and to sail west of India to China. In China, as the next chapter will show, only a few decades after Ashoka put up his stone pillars, a different ruler erected stones carved with texts asserting his virtue, but he exercised far greater control over his subjects than did Ashoka.

Key Terms

Ashoka (62)
dharma (62)
monsoon (63)
Indus River Valley (63)
Sanskrit (65)
Rig Veda (67)
Vedic religion (68)
nomads (68)
varna (70)
jati (70)
karma (71)
Jainism (71)
Buddha (72)
nirvana (73)
Mauryan dynasty (74)
chakravartin (80)
ceremonial state (80)
lay Buddhist (81)
dhows (84)

For Further Reference

Basham, A. L. *The Wonder That Was India: Survey of the Culture of the Indian Sub-continent Before the Coming of the Muslims*. New York: Grove Press, 1959.

Davis, Richard. *Global India Circa 100 CE: South Asia in Early World History*. Ann Arbor: Association for Asian Studies, Inc., 2009.

Fussman, Gerard. "Central and Provincial Administration in Ancient India: The Problem of the Mauryan Empire." *Indian Historical Review* 14 (1987–1988): 43–72.

Kenoyer, Mark. *Ancient Cities of the Indus Valley Civilization*. Karachi, Pakistan: Oxford University Press, 1998.

McIntosh, Jane R. *The Ancient Indus Valley: New Perspectives*. Santa Barbara: ABC-CLIO, 2007.

Mines, Diane. "Caste in India." *Key Issues in Asian Studies*. Vol 3. Ann Arbor: Association of Asian Studies, 2009.

Pearson, Michael. *Eyes Across the Water: Navigating the Indian Ocean*. Pretoria, South Africa: Unisa Press, 2010.

Pugach, Irina, et al. "Genome-wide data substantiate Holocene Gene Flow from India to Australia." *Proceedings of the National Academy of Sciences of the United States of America* 110.5 (2013): 1803–1808.

Thapar, Romila. *Aśoka and the Decline of the Mauryas*. New York: Oxford University Press, 2012.

Thapar, Romila. *Early India: From the Origins to AD 1300*. Berkeley: University of California Press, 2003.

Films

The Little Buddha.

AP® Review Questions for Chapter 3

Multiple-Choice Questions

QUESTIONS 1–3 REFER TO THE FOLLOWING PASSAGE.

The Noble Truth of suffering is this: Birth is suffering; aging is suffering; sickness is suffering; death is suffering; sorrow and lamentation, pain, grief and despair are suffering. . . .

The Noble Truth of the origin of suffering is this: It is this thirst which produces re-existence and re-becoming, bound up with passionate greed. . . .

The Noble Truth of the cessation of suffering is this: It is the complete cessation of that very thirst, giving it up, renouncing it, emancipating oneself from it, detaching oneself from it.

The Noble Truth of the path leading to the cessation of suffering is this: It is simply the Noble Eightfold Path, namely right view; right thought; right speech; right action; right livelihood; right effort; right mindfulness; right concentration.

—The Buddha's First Sermon, sixth century B.C.E., northern India

1. Which of the following statements accurately describes the Buddha's core teachings?
   (A) Release from desire comes from performing the duties associated with a person's caste.
   (B) The ending of desire releases a person from suffering.
   (C) Brahmin rituals, as described in the Vedas, are essential for maintaining order in the universe.
   (D) Devotion to an individual god or goddess will lead the devotee to a pleasant afterlife.

2. Based on the above passage, what Hindu concept was adopted by the Buddhists?
   (A) The significance of reincarnation
   (B) The social structure of caste
   (C) The importance of the Ganges River
   (D) The need for priests to act as spiritual mediators

3. Which of the following accurately explains the difference between Buddhism and Hinduism based on your knowledge of world history?
   (A) The Buddhists believe nonliving objects contain a soul, while Hindus do not.
   (B) Unlike Hinduism, Buddhism does not assign unique responsibilities for castes and promotes spiritual egalitarianism.
   (C) Buddhism emphasizes the important role of gods and goddesses on the path toward enlightenment.
   (D) Buddhism preaches a stronger enforcement of caste distinctions than Hinduism.

QUESTIONS 4–7 REFER TO THE FOLLOWING PASSAGE.

In the past, the killing and injuring of living beings, lack of respect towards relatives . . . had increased. But today, thanks to the practice of dharma [correct conduct] on the part of the Beloved of the Gods, the king Ashoka, the sound of the drum has become the sound of dharma, showing the people displays of heavenly chariots, elephants, balls of fire, and other divine forms. Through his instruction in dharma abstention from killing and non-injury to living beings, deference to relatives, Brahmins and shramanas, obedience to mother and father, and obedience to elders have all increased as never before for many centuries. These and many other forms of the practice of dharma have increased and will increase.

—Emperor Ashoka of the Mauryan Dynasty, The Fourth Major Rock Edict, fourth century C.E.

4. The excerpt above most directly reflects which of the following statements concerning Emperor Ashoka?
   (A) Ashoka's adoption of Brahminism as the basis of his law code
   (B) Ashoka's use of Buddhist principles to direct and rule over the empire
   (C) Ashoka's reliance on military action to maintain social order
   (D) Ashoka's inability to create a centralized government and bureaucracy

5. Which of the following concepts best explains the above passage?
   (A) Religions and belief systems provided a social bond and an ethical code to live by.
   (B) Religious and political authority often merged as rulers used religion to justify their rule.
   (C) Vedic teachings contributed to the development of the social and political roles of caste.
   (D) Religions and belief systems generated conflict.

6. Which of the following situations demonstrates a different model of governing from the one described in the above passage?
   (A) Constantine's use of Christianity to unite the Roman empire
   (B) The Han dynasty organizing the civil service with Confucian principles
   (C) Mongol khans allowing conquered regions to practice their chosen religions
   (D) Persian emperors using Zoroastrianism to bolster their rule

7. Based on the provided passage, what inference can we make concerning religious diversity during Ashoka's rule?
   (A) Ashoka outlawed all religions except for ones officially sanctioned by the state.
   (B) Only Brahmins were allowed to keep their religion and not convert to Buddhism.
   (C) Other religions were tolerated and protected.
   (D) Only Buddhism was allowed to send out missionaries.

QUESTIONS 8–10 REFER TO THE FOLLOWING MAP.

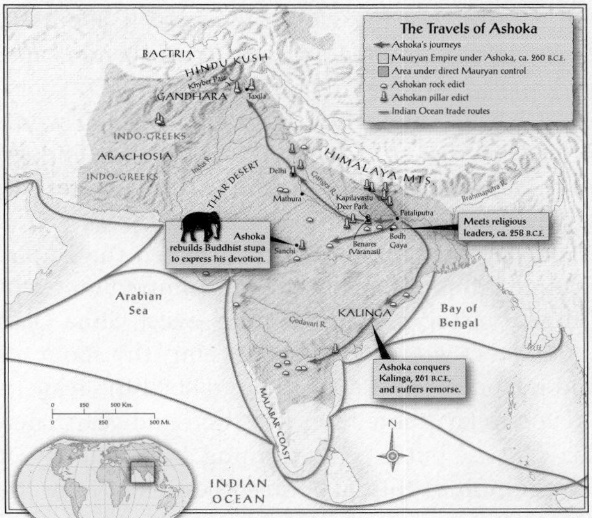

8. Based on the above map, Ashoka attempted to unite his empire using which of the following methods?
   (A) Reinforcing and building military garrisons
   (B) Expanding the road systems and other forms of infrastructure
   (C) Building new cities on the coast to promote trade
   (D) Visiting and building Buddhist sites

9. From the map, which of the following is a valid inference?
   (A) The Mauryan empire had direct contact with European regions.
   (B) The Mauryans' connection to land and sea routes promoted the spread of Buddhism.
   (C) The Mauryan empire relied completely on the Malabar Coast for trade.
   (D) Brahminism remained a powerful religious force in the southern portion of the empire.

10. Which of the following inferences can be supported by the map?
   (A) The rock and pillar edicts were located only in the south of the empire.
   (B) The edicts of Ashoka were heavily influenced by China.
   (C) The rock and pillar edicts in the north needed to be written in Greek.
   (D) Kalinga continued to rebel against Ashoka's rule.

Short-Answer Questions

When they divided the man, into how many parts did they apportion him?

What do they call his mouth, his two arms and thighs and feet?

His mouth became the Brahmin; his arms were made into the Warrior, his thighs the People, and from his feet the Servants were born.

—The Hymn of the Primeval Man, the *Rig Veda*, ca. 1000 B.C.E.

By birth one is not an outcaste,
By birth one is not a Brahmin;
By deeds alone one is an outcaste,
By deeds alone one is a Brahmin

—Siddhartha Gautama or the Buddha, ca. 350 B.C.E.

1. Using the excerpts, answer parts A, B, and C.
   A. Explain how ONE of the following aspects of life in South Asia was influenced by the points of view expressed above:
      - Religion
      - Occupation
      - Political structures
   B. Explain ONE way in which the quote from the Buddha contradicts the point of view expressed in the Hymn of the Primeval Man.
   C. Explain ONE reason Buddhism is considered a universal religion based on the quote from the Buddha.

2. Answer parts A and B.
   A. Explain ONE reason why Buddhism expanded under Ashoka.
   B. Explain TWO ways Ashoka helped spread the Buddhist message.

4 Blueprint for Empire: China, 1200 B.C.E.–220 C.E.

Sima Qian, the Grand Historian

Landov

Sima Qian (ca. 145–86 B.C.E.), or the Grand Historian, completed a history of the world, much of it about his native China, sometime around 90 B.C.E. Working before paper came into widespread use, the Grand Historian wrote on bamboo and wooden slips and produced a text 526,500 words long. He divided the slips into 130 different bundles, enough to fill an entire cart. His *Records of the Grand Historian* starts in the legendary past and covers the period up to 100 B.C.E., after the Qin (CHIN) dynasty (221–207 B.C.E.) unified the empire for the first time, unquestionably the most important event in all of Chinese history. A master prose stylist, Sima Qian (SUH-mah CHEE-en) wrote with genuine empathy about his subjects and included racy details that grabbed the reader's attention. Even today, more than two thousand years later, whenever a Chinese publisher is running out of money, it issues a new edition of this guaranteed bestseller. Here the Grand Historian concludes his biography of the general Meng Tian (MUHNG TYEN) (d. 210 B.C.E.), who oversaw the construction of the Great Wall:

> *I have travelled to the northern border and returned by the Direct Road. As I went along I saw the towers of the Great Wall, which Meng Tian had constructed for the Qin. He cut through the mountains and filled up the valleys, opening up a direct road. Truly he made free with the strength of the common people! Qin had only recently destroyed the feudal states; the hearts of the people of the world were not yet at rest and the wounded were not yet healed. Tian was a renowned general, yet he did not take this opportunity to urge that the ills of the common people be attended to.**

---

*Burton Watson, *Ssu-ma Ch'ien Grand Historian of China* (New York: Columbia University Press, 1958), p. 192.

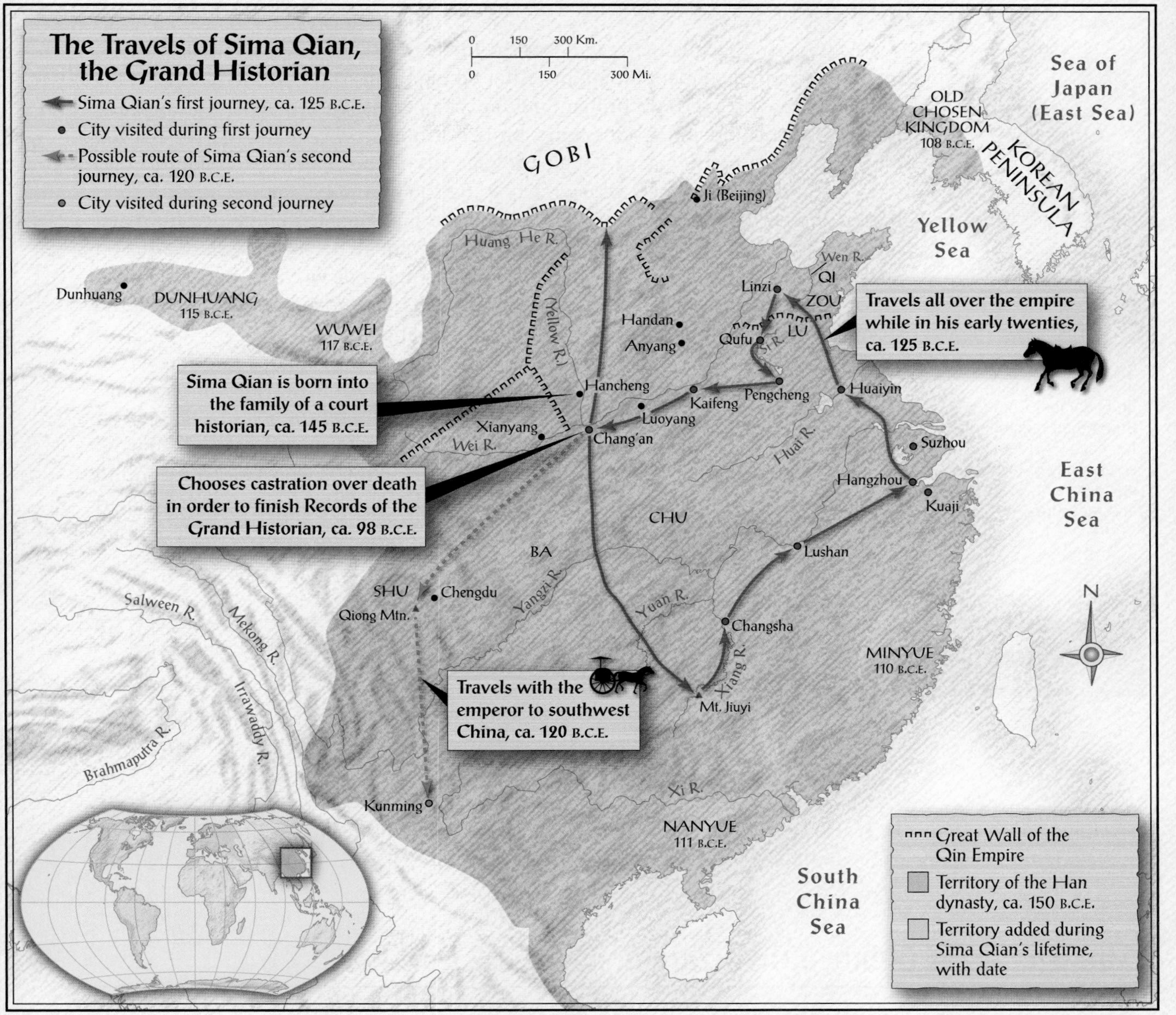

Here the Grand Historian draws on his own experience to describe the watchtowers of the Great Wall, a place he visited while touring the different regions of China when in his early twenties.

Sima Qian explains how, in 221 B.C.E., the **First Emperor of the Qin dynasty** (259–210 B.C.E.) united China for the first time and implemented a blueprint for empire that helped keep China together for much of the next two thousand years. Sima Qian, himself the child of a court historian who also recorded eclipses and other unusual astronomical events, grew up in the capital at Chang'an and learned to write history from his father. His father began *Records of the Grand Historian* but died before he could complete it, so Sima took over from him.

Sima Qian

(145–86 B.C.E.) Author of *Records of the Grand Historian*, a history of China from ancient legendary times to the first century B.C.E.. Lived during the Han dynasty.

First Emperor of the Qin dynasty

Founder of the Qin dynasty (221–207 B.C.E.) and the first ruler to unify ancient China. Eliminated regional differences by creating a single body of law and standardizing weights and measures.

As the *Records* explain, the Qin was the first dynasty to vanquish all of its rivals, including six independent kingdoms. After taking the throne, the First Emperor led the Qin armies on a series of brilliant military campaigns. They fought with the same weapons as their enemies—crossbows, bronze armor, shields, and daggers—but the Qin army was a meritocracy. A skilled soldier, no matter how low-ranking his parents, could rise to become a general, while the son of a noble family, if not a good fighter, would remain a common foot soldier for life. The First Emperor eliminated regional differences by creating a single body of law for all his subjects, standardizing all weights and measures, and even mandating a single axle width for ox- and horse-drawn carts. He coined a new title, *First Emperor* (*Shi Huangdi*), because he felt that the word *king* did not accurately convey his august position.

On his deathbed, the First Emperor urged that his descendants rule forever, or "ten thousand years" in Chinese phrasing. Instead, peasant uprisings brought his dynasty to an end in three years, as *The Records of the Grand Historian* recounts. The succeeding emperors of the Han dynasty denounced Qin brutality but used Qin governance to rule for four centuries. Subsequent Chinese rulers who aspired to reunify the empire always looked to the Han as their model. Unlike India, which remained politically disunited for most of its history (see Chapter 3), the Chinese empire endured for over two thousand years.

KEY CONCEPT QUESTIONS

- How did the Shang dynasty and Confucianism contribute to the development of Chinese culture during the classical age? **(Key Concept 2.1)**
- How did the Qin dynasty build and administer its empire? **(Key Concept 2.2)**
- What aspects of the Qin dynasty did the Han adopt, and what aspects did they modify? **(Key Concept 2.2)**
- How did the Han promote political unity, and how successful were they in maintaining it? **(Key Concept 2.2)**

The Origins of Chinese Civilization, 1200–221 B.C.E.

Agriculture developed independently in several different regions in China starting around 8000 B.C.E. In each region, as elsewhere in the world, people began to harvest grain occasionally before progressing to full-time agriculture. By 1200 B.C.E., several independent cultural centers had emerged. One, the Shang (SHAHNG) kingdom based in the Yellow River (Huang He) Valley, developed the Chinese writing system. Many elements of Chinese civilization—the writing system, the worship of ancestors, and the Confucian and Daoist systems of belief—developed in the years before China was united in 221 B.C.E.

Early Agriculture, Technology, and Cuisine to 1200 B.C.E.

Three major climatic zones extend across China (see the map on page 89). The water-laden monsoon winds off the ocean drop much of their moisture on south China, with little rain falling on the north. Less than 20 inches (50 cm) of rain falls each year on the region north of the Huai (HWHY) River; about 40 inches (1 m) per year drops on the middle band along the Yangzi River; and over 80 inches (2 m) a year pours on the southernmost band of China and Hong Kong.

Sometime around 8000 B.C.E., the residents of the Huai and Yangzi River Valleys began to deliberately cultivate rice. Pinning down the exact date is difficult because wild and domesticated varieties of rice considerably resemble one another. Archaeologists concur that rice was the first crop to be domesticated in China and that agriculture spread from central China north to the Yellow River Valley, where millet was first grown around 7000 B.C.E. Millet is a grain that can be made into gruel, baked as bread, or cooked as noodles. Wheat and millet cultivation extended as far north as Manchuria and as far south as the Yangzi River Valley.

The climate of the Yellow River was probably hotter and wetter than it is today. Elephants and rhinoceros both lived there as late as 1000 B.C.E. North China was particularly suited for early agriculture because a layer of fine yellow dirt, called loess (LESS), covers the entire Yellow River Valley, and few trees grow there.

AP® THEMES

How did the environmental conditions in the Yellow River Valley contribute to the development and spread of agriculture in China?

As in Mesopotamia, Egypt, and India, some communities turned to full-time agriculture while others continued to forage for food (see Chapters 2 and 3).

● **CONTEXT&CONNECTIONS** The crops grown in China differed from those grown in other world regions: after cultivating figs, the Natufians focused on wheat and barley, the major crops grown in both Egypt and Mesopotamia, and the local peoples developed a cuisine based on bread and beer (see Chapters 1 and 2). The Indians grew wheat and barley, too, and cultivated rice as well, and this was the pattern in China. Chinese food is famous for rice, but even now in the north, as earlier, people eat gruel, bread, and noodles more often than rice. ●

The different implements found in various regions suggest great cultural diversity within China between 8000 and 2000 B.C.E. Around 4500 B.C.E., those living in the Yangzi River delta raised silkworms and spun silk. Around 3000 B.C.E., craftsmen in the same region sanded chunks of jade to make exquisite jade tubes. On the Shandong Peninsula, in the northeast, two early urban centers emerged around 2500 B.C.E., with three layers of smaller settlements around them, suggesting an interlocking city system.

These different peoples started out as small, egalitarian tribal groups who farmed intermittently. They evolved to larger settled groups with clearly demarcated social levels living in large urban settlements, demonstrating all the elements of complex society described in Chapter 2. Although agriculture first arose in the Yangzi River Valley, the first complex society arose to the north, in the Yellow River Valley.

● **CONTEXT&CONNECTIONS** Like the Mesopotamians, the early Chinese lived inside walled cities. Whereas the Mesopotamians made their walls of kiln-fired bricks, the first Chinese city dwellers made their walls of sun-dried loess, whose heavy clay content made it particularly suitable as a construction material. ●

Starting around 2000 B.C.E., the Chinese made machetes, shovels, and plowblades from bronze. Ancient Chinese bronze casters mastered the exacting technology of mixing copper, tin, and lead in differing ratios to cast harder and softer bronze objects: daggers had to be hard, while mirrors could only be polished sufficiently to see one's reflection if they were soft.

The early Chinese conducted frequent rituals in which they made offerings of food and drink. Whether for ritual offerings or daily use, they used two types of vessels for foodstuffs: flat bronze vessels for grain (usually wheat or millet)

WORLD HISTORY IN TODAY'S WORLD

The World's Oldest Soup

What did the Chinese eat in the distant past? For years historians have sought answers in written documents. One of the most informative sources, dated to the Han dynasty, records a poem that the living recited to the newly dead in hopes of enticing them to return to life:

O soul come back! Why should you go far away?
All your household have come to do you honor: all kinds of good food are ready:
Rice, broom-corn, early wheat, mixed all with yellow millet;
Bitter, salt, sour, hot, and sweet: they are dishes of all flavors.
Ribs of the fatted ox cooked tender and succulent;
Sour and bitter blended in the soup of Wu; ...
Jade-like wine, honey-flavored, fills the winged cups;
Ice-cooled liquor, strained of impurities, clear wine, cool and refreshing;
*Here are laid out the patterned ladles, and here is sparkling wine.**

As appealing as this menu is, it does not reveal what people actually ate in the past. Only archeological finds can do this. As part of the recent expansion of the Xi'an airport, archeologists excavated the ground underneath a new wing. There, they found the world's oldest meat soup, a cloudy, green liquid with thirty-seven bones in it, held in a bronze vessel dating to the fourth or third century B.C.E. The bones were from a puppy under one year old, evidence that people ate dog soup. Dog soup used to be particularly popular in south China, but now, as pet ownership is skyrocketing, many Chinese find the idea of dog soup just as off-putting as pet owners in other countries.

A related archaeological discovery from Xinjiang (SHIN-jyahng) in northwest China consists of intact noodles made from millet. After conducting a variety of experiments to determine how the inhabitants prepared the millet, archeologists concluded that they used it to make noodles, cakes, and porridge. Today the Chinese usually make these items from wheat. As archeological techniques continue to improve, we can look forward to restaurants serving exact copies of dishes eaten long ago. Of course, fidelity to the past is no guarantee of good taste!

*David Hawkes, *Songs of the South* (New York: Penguin, 1985), pp. 227–228.

Sources: China Daily, March 31, 2011; Lauren Hilgers, "Ancient Chinese Takeout," *Archaeology* 65 (2012): 28.

and baskets and wooden and pottery vessels for meat and vegetables. This division of foods between starch and dishes made from cut-up meat and vegetables continues among Chinese chefs to the present day. Combining component parts in various ways to produce a slightly different product each time, the chef tosses precut meat and vegetables into a wok, stir-fries them, and uses an array of sauces to make a large number of dishes, each with a different name and recognizable taste.

Shang dynasty cooks used many of the same tools as today's cooks—knives, stirring utensils, and bronze cooking pots. However, rather than stir-frying, they steamed and braised food. Those who presided over Shang rituals used chopsticks, one of the hallmarks of East Asian culture, to move food from large serving vessels to smaller plates. People then ate the food with their hands. Ordinary diners began to use chopsticks as eating utensils sometime around 200 B.C.E., the time of the first stir-fried food. (See the feature "World History in Today's World: The World's Oldest Soup.")

Early Chinese Writing in the Shang Dynasty, ca. 1200 B.C.E.

Chinese characters constitute the world's writing system with the longest history of continuous use. Archaeologists cannot be certain when the Chinese first spoke Chinese, because the only certain evidence about ancient language is the presence of writing. The first recognizable Chinese characters appeared on bones dating to around 1200 B.C.E. The bones came from near the modern city of Anyang (AHN-yahng) in the central Chinese province of Henan (HUH-nahn), the core region of China's first historic dynasty, the **Shang dynasty** (1766–1045 B.C.E.). The discovery and deciphering of these bones, first found in 1899, mark one of the great intellectual breakthroughs in twentieth-century China.

Shang dynasty
China's first historic dynasty. The earliest surviving records date to 1200 B.C.E., during the Shang. The Shang king ruled a small area in the vicinity of modern Anyang, in Henan province, and granted lands to allies in noble families.

Many ancient peoples around the world used oracles to consult higher powers, and scholars call the excavated bones "**oracle bones**" because the Shang ruler used them to forecast the future. To do so the Shang placed a heated poker on cattle shoulder blades and turtle shell bottoms, or plastrons, and interpreted the resulting cracks. They then recorded on the bone the name of the ancestor they had consulted, the topic of inquiry (which ranged from the cause of toothaches to the likelihood of military victory), and the outcome.

oracle bones
The earliest surviving written records in China, scratched onto cattle shoulder blades and turtle shell bottoms, or plastrons, to record the diviners' interpretations of the future.

Since 1900 more than 200,000 oracle bones, both whole and fragmented, have been excavated in China. The quantities are immense—1,300 oracle bones concern rainfall in a single king's reign. Their language is grammatically complex. Shang dynasty characters, like their modern equivalents, have two elements: a radical, which suggests the broad field of meaning, and a phonetic symbol, which indicates sound. Like Arabic numerals, Chinese characters retain the same meaning even if pronounced differently: 3 means the number "three" even if some readers say "trois" or "drei."

● **CONTEXT&CONNECTIONS** China's writing system differed from Mesopotamia's, Egypt's, and India's in that the Chinese never developed a phonetic script. Chinese students have to learn thousands of characters before they can read, even if today they use a phonetic script to input characters into their text messages. ●

During the Shang dynasty only the king and his scribes could read and write characters. Presenting the world from the king's vantage point, some oracle bones treat affairs of state, like the outcomes of battles, but many more touch on individual matters, such as his wife's pregnancy or his own aching teeth. The major religion of the

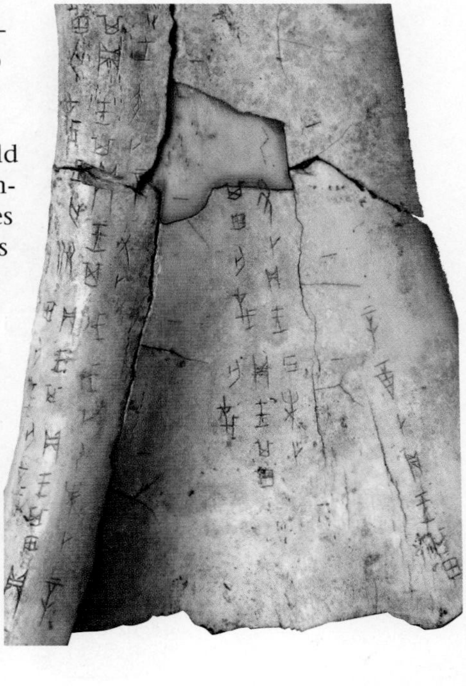

The Earliest Records of Chinese Writing Starting around 1200 B.C.E., ancient Chinese kings used the clavicle bones of cattle (as shown here) and the bottom of turtle shells to ask their ancestors to advise them on the outcomes of future events, including battles, sacrifices, their wives' pregnancies, and even their own toothaches. After applying heat, the fortune-tellers interpreted the resulting cracks and wrote their predictions—in the most ancient form of Chinese characters—directly on the bones and turtle shells. (Lowell Georgia/Eureka/Corbis)

ancestor worship
The belief in China that dead ancestors could intercede in human affairs on behalf of the living. Marked by frequent rituals in which the living offered food and drink to the ancestors in the hope of receiving help.

time was **ancestor worship**. The Shang kings believed that their recently dead ancestors could intercede with the more powerful long-dead on behalf of the living.

Shang Dynasty Relations with Other Peoples

Working with oracle bones and careful analysis of Shang archaeological sites, historians of China have pieced together how Shang government and society functioned between 1200 and 1000 B.C.E. Before the bones were studied, the main source for early Chinese history was Sima Qian's *Records of the Grand Historian*, which gave the founding date of the Shang dynasty as 1766 B.C.E. and listed the names of the Shang kings but provided little detail about them. Sima Qian believed that there could be only one legitimate ruler of China at any time, as would later historians, and he omitted any discussion of regional rulers who coexisted with the Shang and other dynasties.

● **CONTEXT&CONNECTIONS** Even if modern historians do not share all of Sima's assumptions, the *Records of the Grand Historian* provides a detailed chronology for early Chinese history, something that historians of South Asia do not have. Mesopotamian and Egyptian sources list dynasties and sometimes individual rulers, but never with the detail that the Grand Historian provides. ●

In fact, though, the Shang exercised direct control over a relatively small area, some 125 miles (200 km) from east to west, and Shang kings, who did not have a fixed capital, sometimes traveled as far as 400 miles (650 km) to fight enemy peoples. Beyond the small area under direct Shang control lived many different non-Shang peoples whose names appear on the oracle bones but about whom little is known.

Many oracle bones describe battles between the Shang and their enemies. When the Shang defeated an enemy, they took thousands of captives. The fortunate worked as laborers, and the less fortunate were killed as an offering. One oracle bone asks the ancestors' opinion about the number of human sacrifices necessary—ten? twenty? thirty?—a chilling reminder of these casualties.

Shang subjects interred their kings in large tombs with hundreds of sacrificed corpses. Even in death they observed a hierarchy. Placed near the Shang king were those who accompanied him in death, with their own entourages of corpses and lavish grave goods. Royal guards were also buried intact, but the lowest-ranking corpses, most likely prisoners of war, had their heads and limbs severed.

Early Chinese Bronzeworking The ancient Chinese combined copper, tin, and lead to make intricate bronze vessels like this wine container, which dates to circa 1050 B.C.E. and was found buried in the hills of Hunan (HOO-nan), in southern China. Analysts are not sure of the relationship between the tiger-like beast and the man it embraces. The man's serene face suggests that the beast is communicating some kind of teaching—not devouring him. (Musée Cernuschi, Paris, France/Scala/Art Resource, NY)

The Shang were but one of many peoples living in China around 1200 B.C.E. Yet since only the Shang left written records, we know much less about the other peoples. Fortunately an extraordinary archaeological find at the Sanxingdui (SAHN-shing-dway) site near Chengdu (CHUHNG-dew), in Sichuan (SUH-chwan) province, offers a glimpse of one of the peoples contemporary with the Shang. Inside the ancient city walls, archaeologists found two grave pits filled with bronze statues, bronze masks, and elephant tusks that had been burnt and cut into sections. Like the Shang, the people at the Sanxingdui site lived in small walled settlements.

Whereas the Shang made no human statues, the bronze metallurgists at Sanxingdui did. Unlike the Shang, the people at Sanxingdui do not seem to have practiced human sacrifice, and they did not have a writing system.

The Zhou Dynasty, 1045–256 B.C.E.

In 1045 B.C.E. a new dynasty, the **Zhou dynasty**, overthrew the Shang. The Grand Historian Sima Qian wrote the earliest detailed account of the Zhou (JOE) conquest, long after the fact. Claiming that 48,000 Zhou troops were able to defeat 700,000 Shang troops because the Shang ruler was corrupt and decadent, Sima Qian alleged that the last Shang ruler killed his enemies and roasted them on a rack or cut them into mincemeat before eating them. Historians question his account because of his clear bias against the Shang. Sima Qian set a pattern followed by all subsequent historians: vilifying the last emperor of a fallen dynasty and glorifying the founder of the next.

Zhou dynasty
The successor dynasty to the Shang that gained the Mandate of Heaven and the right to rule, according to later Chinese historians. Although depicted by later generations as an ideal age, the Zhou witnessed considerable conflict.

According to Sima Qian, the Zhou king was able to overthrow the Shang because he had obtained the **Mandate of Heaven**. Worshiped by the Zhou ruling house but not previously by the Shang, Heaven represented the generalized forces of the cosmos, rather than the abode of the dead. China's rulers believed that Heaven would send signs—terrible storms, unusual astronomical events, famines, even peasant rebellions—before withdrawing its mandate. But because the recipient of the Mandate of Heaven could only be known after the fact, it often served as a retrospective justification for overthrowing a dynasty by force.

Mandate of Heaven
The Chinese belief that Heaven, the generalized forces of the cosmos (not the abode of the dead), chose the rightful ruler. China's rulers believed that Heaven would send signs before withdrawing its mandate.

Many other states coexisted with the Zhou dynasty (1045–256 B.C.E.), the most important being the Qin, who would first unify China. The long period of the Zhou dynasty is usually divided into the Western Zhou, 1045–771 B.C.E., when the capital was located in the Wei (WAY) River Valley, and the Eastern Zhou, from 771 to 256 B.C.E., because the second Zhou capital was east of the first. Even when China was divided into different regions, the Zhou rulers claimed to rule a unified empire.

During Zhou rule, the people writing Chinese characters gradually settled more and more territory at the expense of other peoples. Because the final centuries of the Zhou were particularly violent, the period from 481 to 221 B.C.E. is commonly called the Warring States Period. Yet constant warfare brought benefits, such as the diffusion of new technology. As in India, the spread of iron tools throughout China enabled people to plow the land more deeply and to settle in new areas. Agricultural productivity increased, and the first money—in the shape of knives and spades—circulated around 500 B.C.E., also at roughly the same time as the punch-marked coins of India, indicating that economies of China and India were equally developed.

Changes in warfare brought massive social change. Since the time of the Shang, battles had been fought with chariots, and only boys who grew up in wealthy households had the time and the resources to learn how to guide a galloping horse pulling a chariot with three men into battle. But in the sixth and fifth centuries B.C.E., as they went farther south, armies began to fight battles in muddy terrain where chariots could not go. The most successful generals were those, regardless of family background, who could effectively lead armies of ten thousand foot soldiers into battle. At this time ambitious young men studied strategy and general comportment with tutors, one of whom became China's most famous teacher, **Confucius** (551–479 B.C.E.).

Confucius

(551–479 B.C.E.) A teacher who made his living by tutoring students. Known only through *The Analects*, the record of conversations with his students that they wrote down after his death.

Confucianism

Confucius was born in 551 B.C.E. in Shandong (SHAHN-dohng) province. His family name was Kong (KOHNG); his given name, Qiu (CHEE-OH). Confucius's students have left us the only record of his thinking, a series of conversations he had with them, which are called *The Analects*, meaning "discussions and conversations."

When we pick up a copy of *The Analects* today, whether the Chinese original or an English translation, we must remember that bound books did not exist during Confucius's lifetime. Invented in the second century B.C.E., paper came into widespread use only in the third century C.E. Before then, the most commonly used writing materials were slips cut from wood, often bamboo. Ranging in length from 8 to 30 inches (20 to 75 cm), the slips were tied together with strings to make something resembling a modern placemat.

A series of recent archeological discoveries has completely changed the way that scholars envision the writings of early teachers like Confucius. Almost all these discoveries date to 300 B.C.E., about two hundred years after Confucius died, and they consist of wooden slips preserved in water or in mud. Some of the excavated texts are close copies of texts already known to scholars, while others are completely new. They suggest a rich and varied tradition of stories about Confucius, only a small fraction of which appear in *The Analects*.

In the received version of *The Analects*, Confucius claims that he did not introduce any new ideas, maintaining that he was seeking simply to return the disordered empire to an earlier time. *"I transmit but do not innovate; I am truthful in what I say and devoted to antiquity"* (7.1).* These words, or close variations, occur in the writings of thinkers who lived at the same time or just after Confucius and in the *Records of the Grand Historian* as well. Before the use of paper, individual sentences had a life of their own. Sentences floated from one text to the next, which is why we find so many similar sentences in texts attributed to different authors.

Modern scholars concur that *The Analects* assumed its final form sometime between 200 and 100 B.C.E., some three hundred years after the death of Confucius. In the past, though, everyone was convinced that because *The Analects* accurately recorded Confucius's conversations with his students, they deserved serious study and often memorization.

Confucianism

The term for the main tenets of the thought of Confucius, which emphasized the role of ritual in bringing out people's inner humanity (a quality translated variously as "benevolence," "goodness," or "man at his best").

Confucianism is the term used for the main tenets of Confucius's thought. The optimistic tone of *The Analects* will strike any reader. Acutely aware of living in a politically unstable era, Confucius did not advocate violence. Instead, he emphasized the need to perform ritual correctly. Ritual is crucial because it allows the gentleman, the frequent recipient of Confucius's teachings, to express his

---

*Excerpts from *Confucius Analects with Selections from Traditional Commentaries*, 7.1, translated by Edward Slingerland. Copyright © 2003. Used by permission of Hackett Publishing Company, Inc., Indianapolis.

inner humanity (a quality sometimes translated as "benevolence," "goodness," or "man at his best"). Since Confucius is speaking to his disciples, he rarely explains what kind of rituals he means, but he mentions sacrificing animals, playing music, and performing dances.

Confucius's teachings do not resemble a religion so much as an ethical system. Filial piety, or respect for one's parents, is its cornerstone. If children obey their parents and the ruler follows Confucian teachings, the country will right itself because an inspiring example will lead people toward the good. (See the feature "Movement of Ideas Through Primary Sources: *The Analects* and the Qin Emperor's Stone Texts.")

Confucius was also famous for his refusal to comment on either the supernatural or the afterlife:

> *Zilu [ZUH-lu; a disciple] asked how to serve the spirits and gods.*
> *The Master [Confucius] said: "You are not yet able to serve men, how could you serve the spirits?"*
> *Zilu said: "May I ask you about death?"*
> *The Master said: "You do not yet know life, how could you know death?"**

● **CONTEXT&CONNECTIONS** If we define religion as the belief in the supernatural, then Confucianism does not seem to qualify. It differs from the religious systems of the ancient Mesopotamians, Egyptians, and Indians, who all believed in higher deities. But if we consider religion as the offering of rituals at different turning points in one's life—birth, marriage, and death—then Confucianism qualifies as a religion. ●

Daoism

Many of Confucius's followers were also familiar with the teachings of **Daoism** (DOW-is-uhm) (alternate spelling Taoism), the other major belief system of China before unification in 221 B.C.E. Both Confucius and the leading Daoist teachers spoke about the "Way," a concept for which they used the same word, *dao* (DOW), and the Chinese at the time did not necessarily think of Daoism and Confucianism as distinct belief systems.

Daoism A Chinese belief system dating back to at least 300 B.C.E. that emphasized the "Way," a concept expressed in Chinese as "dao." The Way of the early Daoist teachers included meditation, breathing techniques, and special eating regimes.

For Confucius, the Way denoted using ritual to bring out one's inner humanity. In contrast, the Way of the early Daoist teachers included meditation, breathing techniques, and special eating regimes. They believed that if one learned to control one's breath or the life-force present in each person, one could attain superhuman powers and possibly immortality. Some said that immortals shed their human bodies much as butterflies cast off pupas. Such people were called Perfect Men. One early Daoist text, *Zhuangzi* (JUAHNG-zuh), named for the author of its teachings, Master Zhuang, describes such people: *"The Perfect Man is godlike. Though the great swamps blaze, they cannot burn him; though the great rivers freeze, they cannot chill him."*†

Funny and ironic, *Zhuangzi* describes many paradoxes, and the question of knowledge—of how we know what we think we know—permeates the text. One

---

*Excerpt from *The Analects of Confucius*, translated by Simon Leys. Copyright © 1997 by Pierre Ryckmans. Used by permission of W.W. Norton & Company, Inc.

†*Chuang Tzu: Basic Writings*, trans. Burton Watson (New York: Columbia University Press, 1964), p. 41.

The Analects and the Qin Emperor's Stone Texts

Unlike Buddhism, which has the first sermon of the Buddha (see Chapter 3), Confucianism has no short text that summarizes its main teachings. Throughout history students carefully studied *The Analects* because it was thought to be the only text that quoted Confucius directly. Each chapter contains ten to twenty short passages, often dialogues between Confucius and a student, and each passage is numbered. The first chapter introduces the most important Confucian teachings, including the importance of ritual and respect for one's parents, or filial piety.

Two hundred fifty years after Confucius died, the Qin emperor put up seven different inscriptions on stone tablets all over the empire in which he described his own accomplishments and explained how he was able to govern his subjects, whom he called the "black-haired people." Look carefully at his phrasing: you will see that he uses many of the same terms that appear in *The Analects*.

Historical Thinking Skill:
CONTEXTUALIZATION Given the historical context of China when Confucianism developed, why would Confucian teachings focus so much on maintaining harmony?

Historical Thinking Skill:
COMPARISON What similarities do you find between the Qin emperor's inscription and Ashoka's Rock Edicts from Chapter 3?

Historical Thinking Skill:
CONTEXTUALIZATION Based on the Qin emperor's stone texts, how has the Qin emperor incorporated Confucian values into Chinese society?

Sources: From *Confucius Analects with Selections from Traditional Commentaries*, translated by Edward Slingerland. Copyright © 2003. Used by permission of Hackett Publishing Company, Inc., Indianapolis; "The Inscription on Mt. Lang-yeh," translated by Martin Kern, *The Stele Inscriptions of Ch'in Shih Huang Text and Ritual in Early Chinese Imperial Representation.* New Haven: American Oriental Society, 2000, pp. 25–26, 29–31.

Chapter One of *The Analects*

1.1 The Master said: "To learn something and then to put it into practice at the right time: is this not a joy? To have friends coming from afar: is this not a delight? Not to be upset when one's merits are ignored: is this not the mark of a gentleman?"

1.2 Master You said: "A man who respects his parents and his elders would hardly be inclined to defy his superiors. A man who is not inclined to defy his superiors will never foment a rebellion. A gentleman works at the root. Once the root is secured, the Way unfolds. To respect parents and elders is the root of humanity."

1.3 The Master said: "Clever talk and affected manners are seldom signs of goodness."

1.4 Master Zeng said: "I examine myself three times a day. When dealing on behalf of others, have I been trustworthy? In intercourse with my friends, have I been faithful? Have I practiced what I was taught?"

1.5 The Master said: "To govern a state of middle size, one must dispatch business with dignity and good faith; be thrifty and love all men; mobilize the people only at the right times."

1.6 The Master said: "At home, a young man must respect his parents; abroad, he must respect his elders. He should talk little, but with good faith; love all people, but associate with the virtuous. Having done this, if he still has energy to spare, let him study literature."

1.7 Zixia said: "A man who values virtue more than good looks, who devotes all his energy to serving his father and mother, who is willing to give his life for his sovereign, who in intercourse with friends is true to his word—even though some may call him uneducated, I still maintain he is an educated man."

1.8 The Master said: "A gentleman who lacks gravity has no authority and his learning will remain shallow. A gentleman puts loyalty and faithfulness foremost; he does not befriend his moral inferiors. When he commits a fault, he is not afraid to amend his ways."

1.9 Master Zeng said: "When the dead are honored and the memory of remote ancestors is kept alive, a people's virtue is at its fullest."

1.10 Ziqing asked Zigong: "When the Master arrives in another country, he always becomes informed about its politics. Does he ask for such information, or is it given him?"

Zigong replied: "The Master obtains it by being cordial, kind, courteous, temperate, and deferential. The Master has a way of enquiring which is quite different from other people's, is it not?"

1.11 The Master said: "When the father is alive, watch the son's aspirations. When the father is dead, watch the son's actions. If three years later, the son has not veered from the father's way, he may be called a dutiful son indeed."

1.12 Master You said: "When practicing the ritual, what matters most is harmony. This is what made the beauty of the way of the ancient kings; it inspired their every move, great or small. Yet they knew where to stop: harmony cannot be sought for its own sake, it must always be subordinated to the ritual; otherwise it would not do."

1.13 Master You said: "If your promises conform to what is right, you will be able to keep your word. If your manners conform to the ritual, you will be able to keep shame and disgrace at bay. The best support is provided by one's own kinsmen."

1.14 The Master said: "A gentleman eats without stuffing his belly; chooses a dwelling without demanding comfort; is diligent in his office and prudent in his speech; seeks the company of the virtuous in order to straighten his own ways. Of such a man, one may truly say that he is fond of learning."

1.15 Zigong said: "'Poor without servility; rich without arrogance.' How is that?"

The Master said: "Not bad, but better still: 'Poor, yet cheerful; rich, yet considerate.'"

Zigong said: "In the *Poems*, it is said: 'Like carving horn, like sculpting ivory, like cutting jade, like polishing stone.' Is this not the same idea?"

The Master said: "Ah, one can really begin to discuss the *Poems* with you! I tell you one thing, and you can figure out the rest."

1.16 The Master said: "Don't worry if people don't recognize your merits; worry that you may not recognize theirs."

The Inscription of the First Emperor

Now, in His twenty-sixth year,
The Emperor created a beginning:
He rectified the rules and measures
As the guidelines for the ten thousand beings.
In order to illuminate the human affairs
He united and led to concord father and son.
Sage, wise, humane, and right:
He made manifest and clear the Way and its inner pattern!
…
He worries for and takes pity on the black-haired people,
From daybreak to dawn He is never remiss.
He eliminates uncertainties, fixes the laws,
And all know what to avoid.
The chiefs of the regions are assigned separate duties,
The various rulings are measured and smooth.
Whatever one undertakes or rejects is invariably proper,
There is nothing that does not conform to the scheme.
The Emperor, He brightly shines,
He looks down on and inspects the four quarters.
The honored and the humble, the noble and the mean,
They never exceed their position and rank.
Evil and depravity are not tolerated,
All are committed to honesty and goodness.
To all affairs tiny or great they dedicate their utmost effort,
No one dares to be idle or negligent.
Distant and near, down to regions remote and obscure,
They are single-minded in their efforts, reverential and respectful.
They are upright and straight, solid and loyal –
Duties and responsibilities have constancy.

anecdote describes how Zhuang dreamt he was a happy butterfly. When he awoke he was himself, *"But he didn't know if he was Zhuang Zhou [Zhuangzi] who had dreamt he was a butterfly, or a butterfly dreaming he was Zhuang Zhou."**

Zhuangzi often mocks those who fear death because they cannot know what death is actually like; he dreams that a talking skull asks him, *"Why would I throw away more happiness than that of a king on a throne and take on the troubles of a human being again?"** Zhuang could poke fun at death, but the general Daoist view of death pictured it as a series of underground prisons from which no one could escape.

The other well-known Daoist classic, *The Way and Integrity Classic*, or *Daodejing* (DOW-deh-jing), combines the teachings of several different masters into one volume. It urges rulers to allow things to follow their natural course, or *wuwei* (WOO-way), often misleadingly translated as "nonaction": *"Nothing under heaven is softer or weaker than water, and yet nothing is better for attacking what is hard and strong, because of its immutability."*†

Qin Rulers Unify China, 359–207 B.C.E.

While Confucian and Daoist thinkers were proposing abstract solutions to end the endemic warfare, a third school, the Legalists, took an entirely different approach based on their experience governing the Qin homeland in western China. In 359 B.C.E., the statesman Shang Yang (SHAHNG yahng), the major adviser to the Qin ruler, implemented a series of reforms reorganizing the army and redefining the tax obligations of all citizens. Those reforms made the Qin more powerful than any of the other regional states in China. The First Emperor implemented Shang Yang's blueprint for rule both as the regional ruler of the Qin and as emperor after the unification of China in 221 B.C.E.

Prime Minister Shang Yang's Reforms 359–221 B.C.E.

In 359 B.C.E., Prime Minister Shang Yang sent officials to register every household in the Qin realm, creating a direct link between each subject and the ruler. Once a boy resident in the Qin region reached the age of sixteen or seventeen and a height of 5 feet (1.5 m), he had to serve in the military, pay land taxes (a fixed share of the crop), and perform labor service, usually building roads, each year. To encourage people to inform on each other, Shang Yang divided the population into mutual responsibility groups of five and ten: if someone committed a crime but was not apprehended, everyone in the group was punished.

AP® THEMES
How did the application of Legalist policies affect the existing social hierarchy in China under Qin rule?

Most people in ancient China took it for granted that the son of a noble was destined to rule and the son of a peasant was not, but the Legalists disagreed. Renouncing a special status for "gentlemen," they believed that the ruler should recruit the best men to staff his army and his government. In keeping with

---

**Chuang Tzu: Basic Writings*, trans. Burton Watson (New York: Columbia University Press, 1964), pp. 45 (butterfly); 115 (talking skull).

†*Tao Te Ching: The Classic Book of Integrity and the Way*, trans. Victor Mair (New York: Bantam Books, 1990), p. 54.

Legalism, Qin officials recognized no hereditary titles, not even for members of the ruler's family.

Instead the Qin officials introduced a strict meritocracy, which made their army the strongest in China. A newly recruited soldier might start at the lowest rank, but if he succeeded in battle, he could rise in rank and thereby raise the stature of his household. Because Qin rules tolerated no value judgments, which could be biased, a soldier had to present the heads of all those enemy soldiers he had killed before he could advance. The more heads he presented, the higher he rose in the army. This reorganization succeeded brilliantly because each soldier had a strong incentive to fight. Starting in 316 B.C.E., the Qin polity began to conquer neighboring lands and implement Shang Yang's measures in each new region.

Legalism

A school of thought, originating in the fourth century B.C.E. and associated with Qin dynasty rulers, that emphasized promotion for officials and soldiers alike on the basis of merit and job performance, not heredity.

● **CONTEXT&CONNECTIONS** This strictly enforced meritocracy was unique in the ancient world. In the 1700s B.C.E., at the time of Hammurabi's code, the Babylonian population was divided into three groups: the privileged who owned land, commoners and peasants, and slaves. Similarly, after 1000 B.C.E., ancient Indian society had four *varna* groups (key term in Chapter 3): Brahmin priests, warriors, farmers and merchants, and dependent laborers. Some people managed to rise higher than their social group, but most believed that people were born unequal. The belief in inequality prevailed in Warring States China, too, but the Legalists rejected this widespread view in favor of their new merit-based system. The successors to the Qin did not adopt the same type of meritocracy, but subsequent dynasties gradually became more meritocratic. The fullest expression of Chinese meritocracy was the civil service examinations, which came to full fruition around 1000 C.E. (see Chapter 12). ●

Legalist philosophers valued the contributions of the farmer-soldiers most highly because they paid taxes and were the backbone of the army. Accordingly, Legalist thinkers ranked peasants just under government officials, or scholars, who could read and write. Because artisans made objects peasants needed, like baskets and tools, they ranked third, and merchants, who neither worked the land nor manufactured the goods they traded, ranked at the bottom of society.

This ranking is prescriptive, reflecting how Legalist thinkers thought society should be, not descriptive, how it actually was. Any Chinese peasant would gladly have changed places with a merchant because merchants did not perform arduous physical labor and could afford better clothes and food. Although the Legalist ranking, like the explanation of varna in the Indian "Hymn of the Primeval Man" (see Chapter 3), did not reflect reality, it persisted throughout Chinese history.

The Policies of the First Emperor, 221–210 B.C.E.

In 246 B.C.E., the First Emperor ascended to the Qin throne. He succeeded his father, who had not originally been in line to the throne. The Grand Historian presents a complicated series of allegations purporting to explain how the Qin emperor came to the throne. He intimates that the future emperor's mother had been pregnant by another man when she married, meaning that the First Emperor's father was not his birth father. After giving birth to the First Emperor, his mother *"did not cease her wanton behavior."* The birth father of her child, frightened that someone might discover their affair, decides that she needs another lover. He tells her about a servant who stuck *"his unusually large penis . . . through the center of a wheel"* made of wood and walked around showing off his unusual endowment.* According to Sima Qian, that servant became the second secret lover of the First Emperor's mother. The Grand Historian offers no backup for this outrageous gossip. He may have included it to entertain his readers, and it is likely that he copied it from an earlier source. *Records of the Grand Historian* appears to be a compendium of material collected from other works, not a single-author work.

In 221 B.C.E. the Qin ruler defeated his final rival, the ruler of Qi (modern-day Shandong) and then named himself First Emperor (r. 221–210 B.C.E.). His blueprint for empire would help keep China together for much of the next two thousand years, but Sima Qian portrayed him as one of the worst tyrants in Chinese history, who murdered his opponents, suppressed all learning, and adamantly opposed Confucian virtues. This view of the First Emperor still prevails today, but the evidence *from* his reign (as opposed to that composed *after* it) suggests that the First Emperor conceived of himself as a virtuous ruler along Confucian lines.

After 221 B.C.E., the stone tablets the emperor placed on high mountaintops recorded his view of his reign. The tablets invoked Confucian learning, and like the first ruler of the Zhou, the First Emperor hoped to be perceived as the virtuous founder of a new dynasty. One of the inscriptions claims, "*The way of filial piety is brilliantly manifest and shining!*"† According to Confucian teachings, the ruler's main role was to lead his subjects in ritual, and the Qin emperor assumed this role each time he put up a stone tablet.

● **CONTEXT&CONNECTIONS** Unlike *Ashoka's* pillar and stone inscriptions in different languages (Chapter 3), all the Qin inscriptions were written in Chinese because the Qin enforced linguistic standardization throughout their empire. Also unlike the Ashokan inscriptions, which were located by crossroads where his subjects could see them, the Qin tablets were placed on remote mountaintops where the intended audience of ancestors could view them. And whereas Ashoka's inscriptions were phrased colloquially, the Qin inscriptions were rigidly formal, consisting of thirty-six or seventy-two lines, each with exactly four characters. ●

AP® THEMES

How did the placement of these stone monuments reinforce the Qin emperor's authority?

The Qin emperor placed these monuments in the far corners of his realm to demonstrate that he directed all of his subjects, both those in the Qin homeland and those recently conquered, in correct ritual observance. The inscriptions use the characteristic Chinese technique of manufacture: their authors placed component parts, or characters, in various combinations to produce a slightly different text for each inscription. Although Ashoka's inscriptions were completed within the Qin emperor's lifetime, northern India lay some 1,000 miles (1,600 km) from the western edge of the Qin emperor's realm, and there is no evidence that the Mauryans inspired the First Emperor. (See the feature "Movement of Ideas Through Primary Sources: *The Analects* and the Qin Emperor's Stone Texts," page 98.)

● **CONTEXT&CONNECTIONS** Ruling a unified China from 221–207 B.C.E., the First Emperor had far greater power over his subjects than did India's Ashoka, who ruled slightly earlier, in 268–232 B.C.E. Ashoka governed a *ceremonial state* (Chapter 3)

---

*Burton Watson, *Records of the Grand Historian: Qin Dynasty* (New York: Columbia University Press, 1993), p. 163.

†Excerpt from Martin Kern, *The Stele Inscriptions of Ch'in Shih-huang: Texts and Ritual in Early Chinese Imperial Representation* (New Haven: American Oriental Society, 2000), pp. 13, 17. Reprinted with permission of the American Oriental Society, http://www.umich.edu/~aos/.

and erected monuments to win his subjects' support. The First Emperor also used monuments, but he was able to list everyone in his realm in household registers, collect taxes directly from them, and require able-bodied males to perform labor service and serve in the military. ●

Qin dynasty sources demonstrate clearly that the First Emperor exercised far more control over his subjects than had his predecessors. Using government registers listing all able-bodied men, the First Emperor initiated several enormous public works projects, including 4,000 miles (6,400 km) of roads, roughly as many as the Romans built, and long walls of pounded earth, the most readily available building material. The Qin emperor also used conscript labor to build his tomb, where he was buried in 210 B.C.E.

The core of the tomb, where the Qin emperor himself was buried, has yet to be excavated, but the Grand Historian describes it: "*Artisans were ordered to install mechanically triggered crossbows set to shoot any intruder. With mercury the various waterways of the empire, the Yangzi and Yellow Rivers, and even the great ocean itself were created and made to flow and circulate mechanically.*"* Sima Qian also claimed that the son of the Qin founder ordered that the craftsmen who worked on the tomb be buried alive so that the tomb's exact location would remain secret. Archaeologists have not found human remains, but they continue to announce new discoveries. (See the feature "Visual Evidence in Primary Sources: The Terracotta Warriors of the Qin Founder's Tomb.")

Many Qin subjects left their homes either to perform labor service on these different projects or to serve in the army, which had several hundred thousand conscripts and traveled as far north as modern-day Mongolia and as far south as Vietnam (as discussed later in this chapter). The central government sent supplies overland to its armies on the roads it built, but when the armies traveled too far, it became difficult to sustain their supply lines, and many died far from home in unsuccessful military campaigns. Their suffering prompted Sima Qian to remark that the emperor "*made free with the strength of the common people*" (see the chapter-opening quotation).

Legalism and the Laws of the Qin Dynasty

The Qin ruler saw the establishment of laws as one of his most important accomplishments. Viewing law as a tool for strengthening the realm, the Legalists advocated treating all men identically, regardless of birth, because they believed that only the systematic application of one set of laws could control man's inherently evil nature. Subjects could not use law to challenge their ruler's authority because the only law for Legalists was the law of the ruler. They did not acknowledge the existence of a higher, divine law.

AP® THEMES
How do Qin laws compare to the Mesopotamian laws of Hammurabi?

● **CONTEXT&CONNECTIONS** The Legalist conception of law differed markedly from the Buddhist idea of dharma (Chapter 3), so often invoked in Ashoka's inscriptions. For Ashoka, dharma meant the correct way to do things, and by extension, law or custom. The Mauryan ruler could not determine the content of dharma, but the Qin emperor could and did issue new laws. ●

*Maxwell K. Hearn, "The Terracotta Army of the First Emperor of Ch'in," in *The Great Bronze Age of China: An Exhibition from the People's Republic of China*, ed. Wen Fong (Metropolitan Museum of Art: New York, 1980), p. 357.

The Terracotta Warriors of the Qin Founder's Tomb

The Qin emperor's tomb, sometimes called the eighth wonder of the world, was discovered in 1973 by a farmer digging a well. The enormous tomb is so big that archaeologists have to dig test pits to probe its dimensions. Test pit 1, a section of which is shown here, contains over seven thousand soldiers of four types—foot soldiers, archers, charioteers, and soldiers riding on horseback. Because the Qin emperor expected the afterlife to be exactly the same as his life, his tomb formed a miniaturized world in which he could pursue his usual activities, including commanding his troops in battle.

The terracotta warriors do not resemble the figurines placed in any Chinese tomb before or since, prompting much speculation about the identity of their creators. One intriguing possibility, recently proposed, is that the emperor used his plumbers, because the soldiers' legs greatly resemble clay water pipes found in the ruins of the Qin palace.

One estimate suggests that it took eleven years for eighty-five foremen, each supervising some ten men, to make the entire army of over seven thousand figures.* How did the Qin craftsmen make so many different soldiers in such a short time? As chefs in today's Chinese restaurants work with ingredients, they arranged thousands of prefabricated parts in various combinations to make a slightly different product each time. Archaeologists have identified two types of feet, three types of shoes and four types of boots, two types of legs, eight types of torso, and two types of armor used to make the mass-produced soldiers, whose bodies range from 5 feet 11 inches to 6 feet 5 inches (180 to 195 cm) tall.

Once a soldier's body was completed, a craftsman used clay to make his facial features. All the soldiers have individual faces, as if the craftsmen worked from living models. Yet the faces are idealized: no soldier has any wounds or scars. When the soldiers were completed, craftsmen painted them with bright colors, most of which have flaked off on the surrounding dirt.

One of archaeologists' most recent discoveries is clay wrestlers and tumblers who performed for the emperor's pleasure in the next world. These statues differ from the terracotta warriors; wearing only loincloths, they bare their torsos and legs, revealing more musculature and more anatomy than do the warriors. Some analysts detect the influence of the ancient Greeks, whose art traveled to northwestern India with Alexander of Macedon in the 300s B.C.E. and could conceivably have moved to China from there.

---

*Lothar Ledderose, *Ten Thousand Things: Module and Mass Production in Chinese Art* (Princeton: Princeton University Press, 2000), pp. 69–70.

This ordinary soldier's head was made by combining molded forms of the front and the back and smoothing them together. Like all Chinese, he did not cut his hair, considered to be a gift from his parents, but bound it in intricate patterns on the back and top of his head. ***How do the terracotta warriors illustrate the Chinese technique of using prefabricated component parts to mass-produce multiple objects that differ from each other?***

His headdress indicates that this figure is an officer. This group of nine statues includes at least three officers who stand at the front of their unit so that they can lead their subordinates into battle.

A roof of wooden beams was originally built over the entire army and then covered with mats, a layer of sand and chalk, and finally a layer of dirt.

This missing head reveals how the hollow statues were made.

CuboImages srl/Alamy

Each Qin soldier wore a uniform consisting of a gown to the knees, leather armor on the upper torso, short pants, leg guards, and a headdress (never a helmet).

This officer's hands originally held weapons, most likely wooden spears or staffs, which have since disintegrated.

Compare and contrast the statue of the boxer in Chapter 6 (page 169) with this terracotta wrestler and decide whether you find the claim of Greek influence persuasive. (O. Louis Mazzatenta/ National Geographic Image Collection)

The Great Wall Then and Now Few people realize that the Great Wall that we see today (*right*) was built during the Ming dynasty (1368–1644), not during the Qin dynasty (221–207 B.C.E.). The Qin emperor ordered the construction of the Great Wall by linking together many pre-existing dirt walls. In the fifteenth through seventeenth centuries C.E., the Ming built with stone along the foundations of the Qin dirt walls. The remains of the Qin wall, which was made largely from pounded earth, survive in only a few places in China (*left*).

Qin dynasty
(221–207 B.C.E.) The first dynasty to rule over a unified China; heavily influenced by Legalist teachings that promoted soldiers and officials strictly on the basis of accomplishment, not birth.

In place for only fourteen years, the **Qin dynasty** (221–207 B.C.E.) did not have time to develop a governmental system for all of China, but it did create a basic framework. The First Emperor appointed a prime minister as the top official in his government. Different departments in the capital administered the emperor's staff, the military, and revenue. The Qin divided the empire into over forty military districts called commanderies, each headed by a governor and a military commander. They in turn were divided into districts, the smallest unit of the Qin government, which were governed by magistrates with the help of clerks.

Although later historians described Qin laws as arbitrary and overly harsh, contemporary evidence shows that the Qin laws were surprisingly detailed, clearly the product of a government deeply concerned with following legal procedures carefully. Archaeologists working in Shuihudi (SHWAY-who-dee) town, in Hubei (WHO-bay) province, found a partial set of Qin dynasty laws dating to 217 B.C.E. in the tomb of a low-ranking clerk. Written on bamboo slips, this set of complex model cases points to the existence of established procedures for officials to follow before reaching a judgment. One text begins as follows:

> *Report. A, the wife of a commoner of X village, made a denunciation, saying, "I, A, had been pregnant for six months. Yesterday, in the daytime, I fought with the adult woman C of the same village. I, A, and C grabbed each other by the hair. C threw me, A, over and drove me back. A fellow-villager, D, came to the rescue and separated C and me, A. As soon as I, A, had reached my house, I felt ill and my belly hurt; yesterday evening the child miscarried."**

The text provides detailed instructions for investigating such a case. The legal clerk had to examine the fetus and consult with the local midwife; he also had to interrogate A and the members of her household to determine her condition.

The Shuihudi tomb also contained sections of the Qin legal code that make fine distinctions: the penalties for manslaughter (inadvertently killing someone) were lighter than those for deliberate murder. The determination of manslaughter hinged on whether the assailant had used an object lying at hand or had concealed his weapon, which indicated intent to murder. The fine legal distinctions among different types of murder resemble those in Hammurabi's laws (see Chapter 2). However, whereas in Babylon an assembly decided whether the accused was guilty of murder, in China the presiding official or clerk determined an individual's guilt.

Qin punishments were grisly. One could have one's foot cut off or one's nose severed for various offenses, and many of those sentenced to hard labor were not "complete," meaning that they were missing a limb. But if we consider the punishments in use elsewhere in the world at the time, such as Roman crucifixion, the Qin punishments were not unusual.

The Han Empire, 206 B.C.E.–220 C.E.

The Qin dynasty came to a sudden end in 207 B.C.E. with the suicide of the First Emperor's son. The following year, in 206 B.C.E., a new emperor founded the **Han dynasty**. Although the Han founder always depicted the Qin as a brutal dynasty, he drew on many Legalist precedents to create a blueprint that allowed him and his descendants to rule for four hundred years. The Han modified the Qin structure of central and local government and developed a mechanism that linked education with bureaucratic advancement for the first time in Chinese history. The dynasty's support of learning encouraged the spread of Confucianism throughout the empire, and the Chinese of that era schooled not only their sons but also, when they could, their daughters. Yet because the Han continued many policies of the Qin, it was a Legalist dynasty with a Confucian veneer.

Han dynasty
(206 B.C.E.–220 C.E.) The immediate successor to the Qin dynasty. Han rulers denounced Legalist governance but adopted much of the Qin blueprint for empire. Because of its long rule, the Han dynasty was a model for all subsequent dynasties.

*A. F. P. Hulsewé, *Remnants of Ch'in Law: An Annotated Translation of the Ch'in Legal and Administrative Rules of the Third Century* B.C., *Discovered in Yün-meng Prefecture, Hu-pei Province, in 1975* (Leiden: E. J. Brill, 1985), p. 205.

Han Government and the Imperial Bureaucracy

After the death of the First Emperor, some regions, sensing weakness at the center, rebelled against the unpopular second Qin emperor. Eventually one man, formerly a low-ranking official under the Qin named Liu Bang (LEO bahng) (r. 206–195 B.C.E.), emerged as leader of the successful rebels and founded the Han dynasty in 206 B.C.E. Liu Bang was one of only two emperors to be born as a commoner (the other founded the Ming dynasty in 1368). When he and his forces entered the Qin capital, he assured the capital's residents:

> *You elders have long suffered under the harsh laws of Qin.... I make an agreement with you that the law shall consist of only three sections: He who kills others shall die; he who harms others or steals from them shall incur appropriate punishment. For the rest, all other Qin laws shall be abolished.**

Like a modern politician's campaign promise, this statement does not provide an accurate description of Han law, which actually retained many provisions of Qin law.

When the Han forces took power, they faced the immediate problem of staffing a government large enough to govern the empire. They adopted the Legalist structure of a central government with the emperor at the head and a prime minister (sometimes called a chancellor) as the top official. Underneath the prime minister were three main divisions: collection of taxes, supervision of the military, and recruitment of personnel.

The Han dynasty ruled for four hundred years, with only one interruption when Wang Mang (WAHNG mahng) founded his own short-lived dynasty (9–23 C.E.). During the first two hundred years of the Han, called the Former Han or the Western Han (206 B.C.E.–9 C.E.), the capital was in Chang'an (CHAHNG-ahn). After Wang Mang was deposed, the Later Han (25–220 C.E.) governed from the new capital of Luoyang (LWAW-yahng).

The Han empire exercised varying amounts of control over the 60 million people under its rule. Immediately after taking over, the Han founder ceded about half of Qin territory to independent kings. He divided the remaining territory into one hundred commanderies and subdivided them into fifteen hundred prefectures, where a magistrate registered the population, collected revenues, judged legal disputes, and maintained irrigation works.

The Han was the first Chinese dynasty to require that officials study classical writings on ritual, history, and poetry, as well as *The Analects*. Han officials embraced the Confucian view that knowledge of these classic texts would produce more virtuous, and thus better, officials, and they usually appointed the sons of men known to them because they believed their acquaintances' sons would make suitable officials.

In 140 B.C.E., one of the most powerful Han emperors came to the throne, Emperor Wu (also known as Han Wudi) (r. 140–87 B.C.E.). The father of the Grand Historian and the Grand Historian himself worked in his court as historians. Their primary task was to record astronomical events, like eclipses, and any other signs from Heaven that might indicate the loss of the Mandate of Heaven.

---

*Hugh Scogin, "Between Heaven and Man: Contract and the State in Han Dynasty China," *Southern California Law Review* 63, no. 5 (1990): 1386.

Imperial Academy
Established in 124 B.C.E. by the Han emperor, Emperor Wu (r. 140–87 B.C.E.), to encourage the study of Confucian texts.

In 124 B.C.E., Emperor Wu established the **Imperial Academy** to encourage the study of Confucian texts. Within one hundred years the number of students at the Academy ballooned to several thousand. Ambitious young men already in the government realized that knowledge of Confucian texts could advance their careers. Before promoting them, the central government tested their knowledge of the Confucian classics, an important forerunner of the civil service examinations in later centuries, which all candidates had to pass before they could take office in any position.

The invention of paper furthered the study of Confucian texts. The earliest examples of Chinese paper found by archaeologists date to the second century B.C.E. Ragpickers who washed and recycled old fabric left fibers on a screen to dry and accidentally discovered how to make paper. Initially, the Chinese used paper for wrapping fragile items, not as a writing material. But by 200 C.E. paper production had increased so much that people used paper, not bamboo slips, for letter writing and books.

With the adoption of paper as the primary writing material, the culture of learning in China shifted from an oral to a written one. In the early years, Han dynasty teachers taught students to memorize texts and recite them orally, but by the end of the dynasty they were reading books. When one poet in the first century B.C.E. submitted a written poem to the court as a gift, the emperor could not imagine that someone would commit a poem to writing without first reciting it in person. By the end of the dynasty, though, writing literary works on paper without reciting them had become commonplace.

● **CONTEXT&CONNECTIONS** Paper was one of China's most important inventions because it was cheap to produce, durable, and lightweight. Only Egyptian *papyrus* (Chapter 2) was equally light, but papyrus did not grow everywhere. Every society that used stone, wood, or animal skins as writing material shifted to paper almost immediately after encountering it; paper spread from China to the Islamic world in the eighth century C.E. and to Europe in the eleventh century. ●

The Grand Historian worked in the court of Emperor Wu for some twenty years without incident. Then, in 99 B.C.E., a non-Chinese force to the north defeated the Han armies, and a general named Li Ling surrendered. Sima Qian had known him since they were boys, and he defended the general's actions, which resulted in the Grand Historian's being charged with treason, punished by either death or castration. The Grand Historian opted for the shame of castration—Confucians believed that, because your body is a gift from your parents, allowing damage to your body insults your parents. He explained his decision saying, "*But the reason I have not refused to bear these ills and have continued to live, dwelling in vileness and disgrace without taking leave, is that I grieve that I have things in my heart that I have not been able to express fully, and I am ashamed to think that after I am gone my writings will not be known to posterity.*"* Sima chose to finish his history because it was a joint project, initiated by his father and completed by himself.

*Burton Watson, *Records of the Grand Historian: Qin Dynasty* (New York: Columbia University Press, 1993), p. 235.

Ban Zhao's *Lessons for Women*

Ban Zhao
(45–120 C.E.) A historian and the author of *Lessons for Women*, a book that counseled women to serve men and advocated education for girls starting at the age of seven.

A century later, another literary family was active in the Later Han capital of Luoyang. One powerful poet and historian had three children: twin boys and a daughter. His daughter, **Ban Zhao** (BAHN jow) (ca. 45–120 C.E.), was the most famous woman writer of her day. She is best known for her work *Lessons for Women*, which Chinese girls continued to read for centuries after her death.

Ban Zhao wrote *Lessons for Women* when in her mid-fifties. It contained everything she would like to have known when she married at age fourteen. Ban Zhao's main theme is clear: women exist to serve their husbands and their in-laws, whom they should always obey and with whom they should never quarrel. Yet the ideal woman was also literate. She began her book by advising her readers to copy down her instructions, sure evidence that they could read and write. Writing at a time when the literacy rate among men did not exceed ten percent, she criticized men who taught only their sons to read:

> *Yet only to teach men and not to teach women—is that not ignoring the essential relation between them? ... It is the rule to begin to teach children to read at the age of eight years.... Only why should it not be that girls' education as well as boys' be according to this principle?**

This is an eloquent call to teach girls to read at the same age as boys (age seven; eight in Chinese reckoning includes the time in the womb).

We must remember that Ban Zhao differed from her contemporaries. For one, like the Grand Historian, she had studied with her father the historian and completed his manuscript after he died. When married, she bore children, but she was widowed at a young age and became a tutor to the women at the imperial court. When a woman took power as regent, Ban Zhao advised her on matters of state. Ban Zhao and the female regent did not have typical careers. Still, their unusual lives show that it was possible for women to take on male roles under certain circumstances.

● **CONTEXT&CONNECTIONS** Think back on the chapters you have read so far in this book: can you name any women from other societies whose names are known to history? In addition to Ban Zhao, we have encountered only one: Hatshepsut. This reveals one of the major challenges of writing about early world history: how can we recover the experience of ordinary women when so few surviving records document their experiences? We often know about only women from elite families like Ban Zhao's or women rulers like Hatshepsut. Still, it is important to learn as much as we can about the experiences of women who have left their names in the historical record, even as we remember that they were not representative of the women living in their time. ●

Extending Han Rule to Mongolia, Vietnam, and Korea

As the Qin and Han Dynasties left their successors with a blueprint of how to govern the empire, the territories they conquered established boundaries that would define Chinese territory for centuries to come. Compare Qin dynasty China (see the map on page 89) with Han dynasty China (see Map 4.1). The most visible

*Nancy Lee Swann, *Pan Chao: Foremost Woman Scholar of China* (New York: American Historical Association, 1932), pp. 84–85.

difference is that the Han rulers controlled a narrow stretch of territory in the northwest, now Gansu (GAHN-sue) province and the Xinjiang Autonomous Region. Han armies also extended the empire's borders northeast to control much of the Korean peninsula and south to modern-day Vietnam.

Xiongnu
Nomadic people north of China whose military strength derived from brilliant horsemanship. Regularly defeated the Han armies in battle until 60 B.C.E., when their federation broke apart.

Conflict and Contact: The Han Dynasty and the Xiongnu Nomads, 201–60 B.C.E.

The Han dynasty gained much of this territory during its wars between 201 and 60 B.C.E. with the **Xiongnu** (SHEE-AWNG-new), a northern nomadic people who moved across modern-day Mongolia in search of grass to feed their

Map 4.1 The Han Empire at Its Greatest Extent, ca. 50 B.C.E. The Han dynasty inherited all the territory of its predecessor, the Qin dynasty, and its powerful armies conquered new territory to the north in the Korean peninsula, to the west in the Taklamakan Desert, and to the south in modern-day Vietnam.

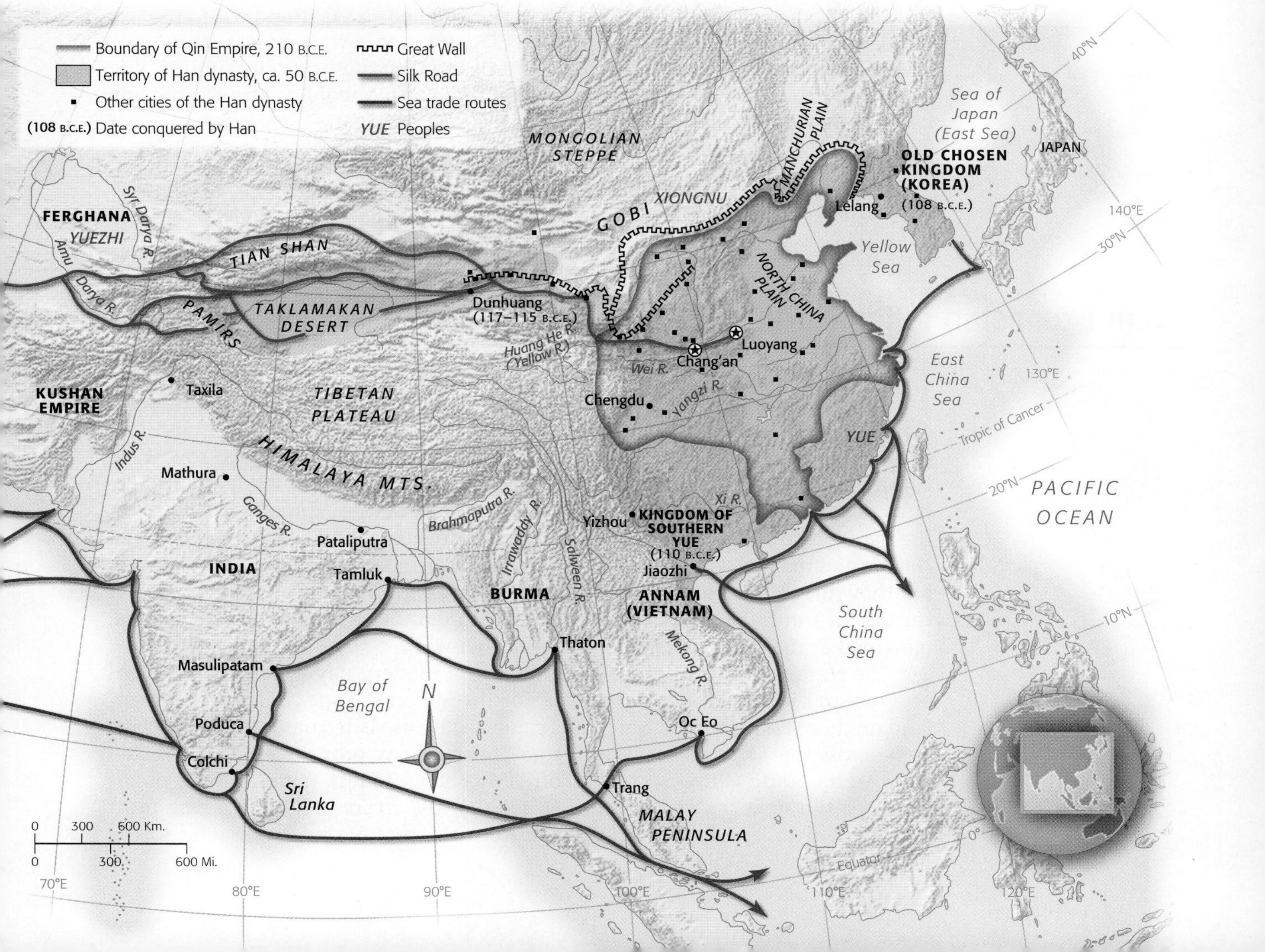

sheep and horses. Only the Xiongnu had an army sufficiently powerful to threaten the Han, and they tried to conquer Chinese territory for the first century and a half of Han rule. Their military strength derived from their quick-footed horses and brilliant horsemanship, which enabled them to defeat the Chinese in battle after battle.

Having formed a confederation of the different tribal peoples living in Mongolia in Qin times, the Xiongnu fought their first battle with the Han soon after the founding of the dynasty. The Xiongnu won and after a temporary peace continued to launch military campaigns into China. In peace agreements the Han reached with the Xiongnu, the Chinese drafters referred to the two powers as "brother" countries, a fiction that allowed the Chinese to see themselves as the older brother even though they were militarily weaker.

AP® THEMES
What role did the Xiongnu play in commerce along the Silk Road?

In 139 B.C.E. Emperor Wu dispatched an envoy named Zhang Qian (JAHNG chee-en) to Central Asia to persuade the Yuezhi (YOU-EH-juh) people to enter into an alliance against the Xiongnu. Zhang Qian reached the Yuezhi only after being held hostage by the Xiongnu for ten years. Although he failed to secure an alliance against the Xiongnu, he visited local markets and, to his surprise, saw Chinese goods for sale, certain evidence that merchants carrying Chinese goods had preceded him. Today most Chinese regard Zhang Qian as the person who discovered the Silk Road (see Chapter 8). The Xiongnu supplied the Chinese with animals, hides, and semiprecious gems, particularly jade; in return the Chinese traded silk. The Chinese never succeeded, at least within the Chinese heartland, in breeding horses as strong as those the Xiongnu bred in the Mongolian steppe, probably because they did not have comparable grasslands.

• **CONTEXT&CONNECTIONS** In 60 B.C.E. the huge Xiongnu confederation broke apart, ending the Xiongnu threat. Other nomadic peoples living in the grasslands to the north, like the Mongols (see Chapter 12), would intermittently threaten later dynasties. •

Han Expansion to the North, Northwest, and South

In certain periods, the Han dynasty was weak, but in other periods, particularly during the long reign of Emperor Wu, the army was so strong that the emperor conquered new lands. Once the Han army had conquered a region, it established garrisons in the major towns. Chinese officials and merchants in these towns led Chinese-style lives, eating Chinese food and speaking Chinese, while the indigenous peoples largely continued to live as they had before. The officials living in the garrison towns exercised only tenuous control over the indigenous peoples. Han armies managed to take parts of the Taklamakan Desert, Korea, and Vietnam, but they ruled these borderlands only briefly. After 127 C.E., only a Han garrison at the city of Dunhuang (DUHN-hwahng), the outermost point of Chinese control, remained as the staging point for going farther west.

The region south of China, extending from modern-day Fujian (FOO-jee-en) province to Vietnam, differed from the northwest because one could reach it overland or, more easily, by sea. Much like camel caravans visited oases in their voyage west across the Taklamakan Desert, small boats, many propelled by oars, visited ports on the South China Sea, which offered a chance to rest, trade, and buy provisions for the next leg of the journey. Like all the rivers in Vietnam, the most important river, the Red River, drained from the mountains in the west to the

A Korean National Treasure This basket was found in the Chinese garrison town of Lelang, near Pyongyang in modern North Korea. Measuring 16 inches (39 cm) long and 9 inches (22 cm) high, the central band uses lacquer paint to depict ninety-four different paragons of filial piety (a detail is shown here). These figures performed various good deeds for the benefit of their parents. The basket documents the spread of Confucianism to the Korean peninsula in the first and second centuries C.E. (Werner Forman/Art Resource, NY)

South China Sea. High mountain chains separated the different river valleys, making overland transport much more difficult than sea travel.

When the Qin armies conquered Vietnam before 207 B.C.E., they established centers of Chinese control in garrison towns. After 207 B.C.E., an independent kingdom also ruled by a Chinese leader, called the Southern Kingdom of Yue (Nam Viet), took over from the Qin. The kingdom was home to fishermen and traders who specialized in unusual goods like ivory tusks, pearls, tortoise shells, and slaves. The Han armies defeated this ruler in 110 B.C.E.

While Vietnam marked the southern extent of Han territory, Korea marked the northern extent. Korea did not receive as much rainfall as Vietnam, and its climate was much cooler. Large, dense forests covered the region, and most early settlements were along rivers or on the coast, where residents could easily fish. Before 300 B.C.E., the region was home to several tribal confederations; then, during the third century B.C.E., the Old Choson (JOE-sohn) kingdom united much of the Korean peninsula north of the Han River, in what is today's North Korea. Qin armies defeated the Old Choson kingdom, and Han armies again conquered the region in 108 B.C.E., soon after gaining control of China.

Officials and merchants lived in a garrison city located in modern-day Pyongyang (BYOHNG-yahng), but the people outside the garrison were much less affected by the Chinese presence. Large, wealthy graves suggest that the people living on the Korean peninsula believed that the dead would travel to another realm. In one region they were buried with large bird wings so that they could fly to the next world.

In later periods (see Chapter 8), these three regions—northwest China, Vietnam, and Korea—would all join the Chinese cultural sphere and adopt the Chinese writing system. But during the Qin and Han dynasties, Chinese influence was limited because the Chinese presence consisted only of military garrisons.

CONTEXT AND CONNECTIONS

The Significance of Ancient China in World History

In his huge compendium, the Grand Historian documents how, following the lead of the First Emperor, the Qin and Han dynasties created a blueprint for imperial rule that lasted for two thousand years. In the centuries after the fall of the Han, China was not always unified. But subsequent Chinese rulers always aspired to reunify the empire and conceived of China's physical borders as largely those of the Han dynasty at its greatest extent.

Held together by the Qin/Han blueprint for rule, China remained unified for most of its long history. Even before the Qin unified China, the Chinese shared a cuisine, belief in the tenets of Confucianism, and a common writing system, which has remained in use, with some modifications, for over three thousand years. These commonalities made China easier to unify than neighboring India. Just as a Chinese chef combines different precut ingredients to make distinctive dishes, other ancient innovations often made use of component parts to make final products that all varied slightly.

The Qin dynasty begun by the First Emperor introduced a centralized administration headed by the emperor, recorded the population in household registers, systematized weights and measures, and promoted officials strictly on the basis of merit. The Qin also had a ceremonial state, as the emperor's sacrifices showed, but the administrative measures affected everyone living in Qin territory and had far greater impact than any actions of the Mauryan dynasty in India (see Chapter 3).

The Han dynasty made one important change: officials had to pass examinations testing their knowledge of Confucianism before they could attain higher office. The Han extended its military control far to the west, establishing more sustained contacts with the peoples living along the Silk Road. Use of this route continued in later periods, peaking in the sixth through eighth centuries (see Chapter 8).

China's path to complex society followed the same pattern as in Mesopotamia, Egypt, and India, all societies on the Eurasian landmass (see Chapters 2 and 3). Agriculture arose first in river valleys. In about 8000 B.C.E. the Chinese began to cultivate rice in the Yangzi and Huai River Valleys and, one thousand years later, millet and wheat in the Yellow River Valley. Chinese farmers domesticated cattle, oxen, and horses to work the land, and they made agricultural implements—plows, shovels, machetes—first of stone and then, around 2000 B.C.E., of bronze. They used wheeled carts to carry things. In both China and India, iron replaced bronze around 500 B.C.E., the time when the first coins circulated. The next chapter will examine the experience of people living in the Americas and the Pacific islands, whose history took an entirely different course.

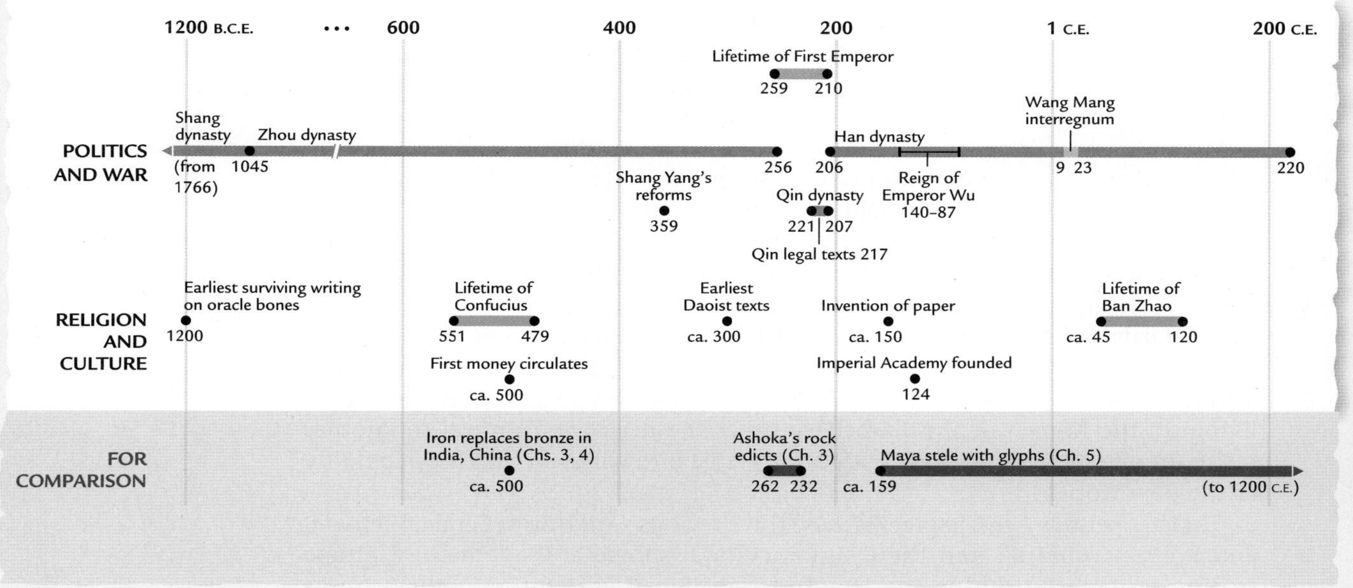

Key Terms

Sima Qian (90)
First Emperor of the Qin dynasty (90)
Shang dynasty (93)
oracle bones (93)
ancestor worship (94)
Zhou dynasty (95)
Mandate of Heaven (95)
Confucius (96)
Confucianism (96)
Daoism (97)
Legalism (101)
Qin dynasty (106)
Han dynasty (107)
Imperial Academy (109)
Ban Zhao (110)
Xiongnu (111)

For Further Reference

Eckert, Carter, et al. *Korea Old and New: A History*. Cambridge, Mass.: Harvard University Press, 1990.

Hansen, Valerie. *The Open Empire: A History of China to 1600*. New York: W. W. Norton, 2000.

Hunter, Michael., "Sayings of Confucius, Deselected.," Princeton University Ph.D. Dissertation, 2012.

Ledderose, Lothar. *Ten Thousand Things: Module and Mass Production in Chinese Art*. Princeton: Princeton University Press, 2000.

Liu, Li, and Xingcan Chen. *Archaeology of Ancient China: From the Late Paleolithic to the Early Bronze Age*. New York: Cambridge University Press, 2012.

Nickel, Lucas. "The First Emperor and Sculpture in China." *Bulletin of the School of Oriental and African Studies* 76.3 (2013): 413–447.

Nylan, Michael, and Michael Loewe. *China's Early Empires: A Re-Appraisal*. New York: Cambridge University Press, 2010.

Stark, Miriam. *Archaeology of Asia*. Hoboken, N.J.: Wiley-Blackwell, 2005.

Tarling, Nicholas, ed. *The Cambridge History of Southeast Asia*. Cambridge, England: Cambridge University Press, 1999.

Twitchett, Denis, and Michael Loewe, eds. *The Cambridge History of China*. Vol. 1, *The Ch'in and Han Empires 221* B.C.–A.D. *220*. New York: Cambridge University Press, 1986.

Films

The First Emperor of China from the Canadian Film Board.
USA orders: 800–542–2164.

AP® Review Questions for Chapter 4

Multiple-Choice Questions

QUESTIONS 1–4 REFER TO THE FOLLOWING PASSAGE.

The Master said: "At home, a young man must respect his parents; abroad, he must respect his elders. He should talk little, but with good faith; love all people, but associate with the virtuous. Having done this, if he still has energy to spare, let him study literature."

The Master said: "A gentleman who lacks gravity has no authority and his learning will remain shallow. A gentleman puts loyalty and faithfulness foremost; he does not befriend his moral inferiors. When he commits a fault, he is not afraid to amend his ways."

Master Zeng said: "When the dead are honored and the memory of remote ancestors is kept alive, a people's virtue is at its fullest."

—Chapter One of *The Analects* by Confucius, fifth century B.C.E.

1. The teachings in the above passage are based on which of the following principles?
   (A) The Mandate of Heaven
   (B) Legalist belief
   (C) The Dao
   (D) Filial piety

2. The author of the above passage would agree with which of the following statements?
   (A) Society achieves harmony when egalitarianism is achieved.
   (B) True harmony happens when an individual leaves public life to meditate and become one with the Dao.
   (C) Society is based on a series of superior/inferior relationships and people act according to their station in life.
   (D) People are stubborn and evil and only understand harsh rule and stiff penalties.

3. Which of the following is a valid inference based on the passage above?
   (A) Ancestor worship was an important part of life in classical China.
   (B) The concept of balance and yin/yang was used to bring harmony to society.
   (C) Reincarnation played an important role in Chinese views of the afterlife.
   (D) The need to maintain order in society meant the emperor had absolute authority.

4. Which of the following would be a Daoist response to Confucius's claim?
   (A) Humans are untrustworthy and only respond to harsh punishments.
   (B) Meditating on the Dharma promotes moral actions.
   (C) True harmony is achieved when an individual finds harmony with nature.
   (D) Government is the ideal institution for promoting moral behavior.

QUESTIONS 5–7 REFER TO THE FOLLOWING MAP.

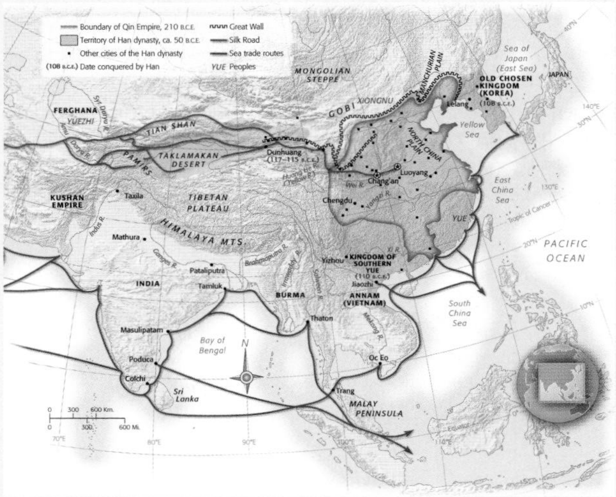

5. Which of the following best explains the expansion of the Han dynasty into Central Asia?
   (A) The need to control Indian Ocean kingdoms
   (B) The emergence of interregional networks of exchange
   (C) Innovations in maritime technologies
   (D) The spread of Buddhism

6. Which of the following is a valid conclusion based on the map?
   (A) The Han attempted to occupy the Tibet Plateau.
   (B) The Qin dynasty's borders exceeded those of the Han dynasty.
   (C) Land and water routes were the basis for Han involvement in interregional trade.
   (D) The Han were unable to control the Korean peninsula.

7. Using data from the map, which of the following is the most likely reason for building the Great Wall?
   (A) Regulate Indian Ocean and South Sea trade routes
   (B) Defend against and control steppe nomads
   (C) Defend against Japanese pirates
   (D) Limit the expansion of the Kushan empire

QUESTIONS 8–10 REFER TO THE FOLLOWING PASSAGE.

If a wife be unworthy, then she possesses nothing with which to serve her husband. If a husband does not control his wife, then the rules of conduct manifesting his authority are abandoned and broken. If a wife does not serve her husband, then the proper relationship between men and women and the natural order of things are neglected and destroyed.

—Ban Zhao, Chinese female scholar, ca. 45–120 C.E., *Lessons for Women*

8. Using the passage above, which of the following concepts was typical of the time period?
   (A) Belief systems tended to challenge traditional social structures.
   (B) Elites of various types were chosen to run bureaucracies.
   (C) Belief systems generally reinforced existing social structures.
   (D) Governments extracted surplus resources through complex bureaucratic systems.

9. The passage above reveals that
   (A) Ban Zhao is questioning traditional gender roles in the Han.
   (B) Ban Zhao is writing from and supporting traditional Confucian ideals.
   (C) Ban Zhao believes Daoism is a threat to the Confucian concept of harmony.
   (D) Ban Zhao believes that women must assert themselves to promote harmony.

10. Using the excerpt above, which of the following is a valid inference?
   (A) Disharmony at home has an impact on the harmony of society.
   (B) The emperor should encourage harmony through harsh laws.
   (C) Nonaction leads to harmony in social relationships.
   (D) Buddhism provided a better model of marriage and social interaction.

Short-Answer Questions

1.1. The Master said: "To learn something and then to put it into practice at the right time: is this not a joy? To have friends coming from afar: is this not a delight? Not to be upset when one's merits are ignored: is this not the mark of a gentleman?"

1.2. Master You said: "A man who respects his parents and his elders would hardly be inclined to defy his superiors. A man who is not inclined to defy his superiors will never foment a rebellion. A gentleman works at the root. Once the root is secured, the Way unfolds. To respect parents and elders is the root of humanity."

—Chapter One of *The Analects* by Confucius, fifth century B.C.E.

1. Using the excerpt above, answer parts A, B, and C.
   A. Identify ONE characteristic expressed by Confucius in this passage.
   B. Briefly explain ONE effect of this teaching on family relationships.
   C. Briefly explain how a Daoist would respond to this teaching.

2. Answer parts A, B, and C.
   A. Briefly explain the Legalist view on governing.
   B. Briefly explain how a Confucian would respond to the Legalist view.
   C. Briefly explain how a Daoist would respond to the Legalist view.

5 The Americas and the Islands of the Pacific, to 1200 C.E.

Mau Piailug with His Star Chart

Sanford Low, anthropologist/filmmaker

In 1976 a group of Hawai'ians decided to celebrate the bicentennial of U.S. independence by crossing the Pacific from Hawai'i to Tahiti using the twin-hulled sailing canoes and navigation techniques of their ancestors. The greatest challenge was finding someone who could navigate without the assistance of a single instrument or map. Eventually, a former Peace Corps volunteer suggested that they contact his wife's cousin on the Micronesian island of Satawal (SAH-tah-wohl) in the Caroline island chain. The cousin, **Mau Piailug** (MOW pee-EYE-lug) (1932–2010), had learned from his grandfather the art of navigating by using the stars, ocean currents, cloud patterns, and flight paths of birds. He frequently led short trips from one island in the Carolines to another.

The 3,337-mile (5,370-km) trip from Hawai'i to Tahiti was far longer than any trip Piailug had previously navigated, but after sailing for thirty-two days the voyagers' vessel, the *Hokule'a*, arrived safely in Tahiti, where 15,000 people, one-fifth of the island's population, turned out to celebrate the successful voyage. In a documentary film made that year, Piailug explained (through a translator) his feelings about the voyage:

Our navigation is different from yours. I don't need a map or a sextant. I just use my head. I observe the ocean and the sky and I remember the words of my teachers.

The trip to Tahiti was very important for me. I know that people of Tahiti and Hawai'i once navigated as we do. They didn't use instruments. They navigated by the stars and the waves. I made the trip to show those people what their ancestors used to know and what we still know.

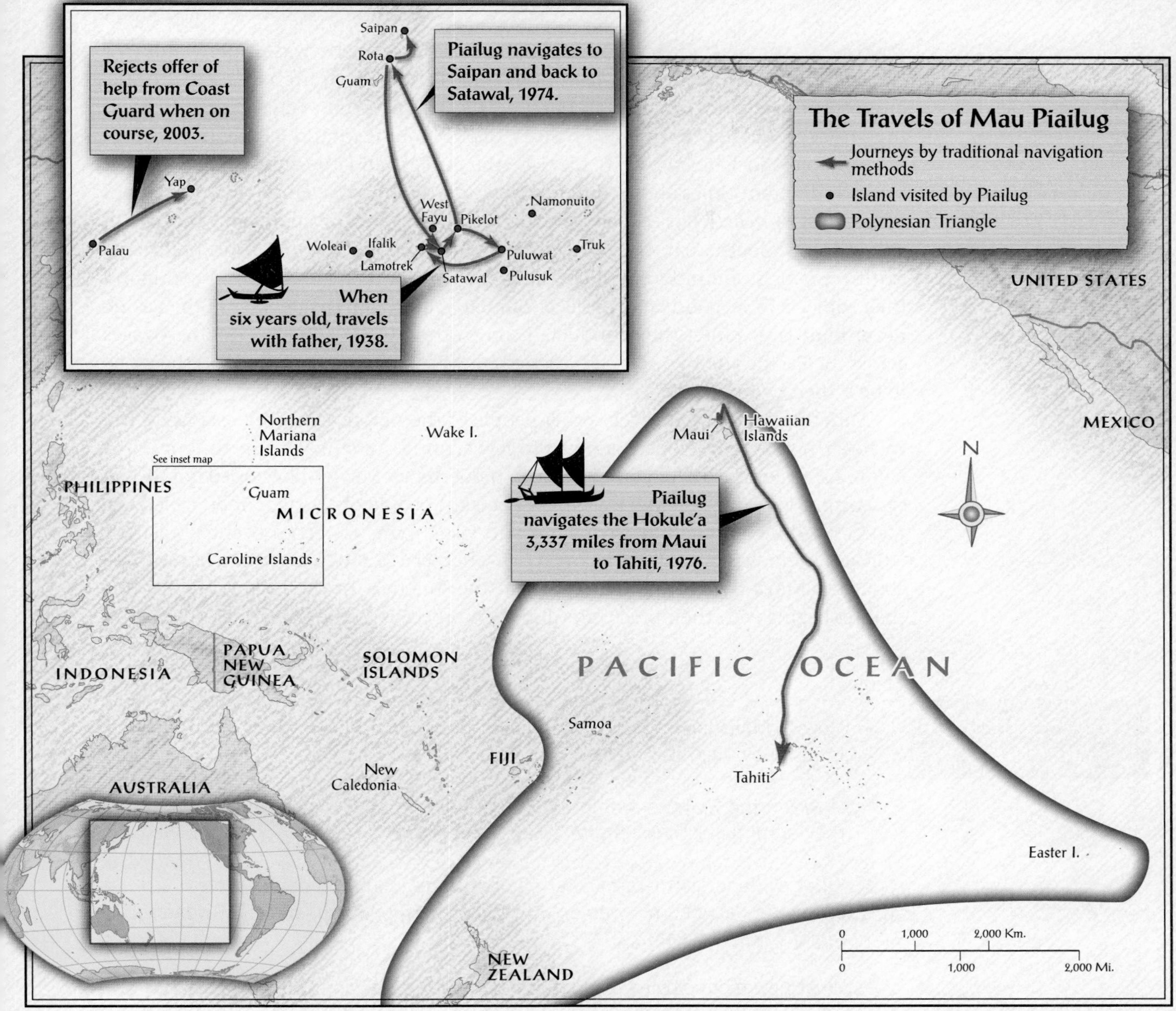

*The trip to Tahiti was very good because it will remind those people of what their ancestors did and make them want to learn about it.**

Mau Piailug's homeland of Micronesia belonged to the vast area of the globe—North and South America and the islands of the Pacific—that developed in almost total isolation from Eurasia because, after approximately

---

*Mau Piailug speaking through a translator in the film *The Navigators: Pathfinders of the Pacific*, directed by Sanford Low and Boyd Estus (Documentary Educational Resources [DER], 1976), 59 mins. Excerpt available online at http://www.der.org/films/navigators-preview.html. Reprinted by permission of Documentary Educational Resources.

Mau Piailug
(1932–2010) Native of Satawal island in the Caroline islands who studied traditional Polynesian navigation as a child and successfully guided a reconstructed double-hulled canoe from Hawai'i to Tahiti in 1976.

7000 B.C.E., the Beringia ice bridge linking Alaska to Siberia was under water (see Chapter 1). Drawing on oral testimony like Piailug's, on archaeological finds, and on surviving documents, archaeologists and historians have exercised great ingenuity in reconstructing the history of the American and Pacific peoples.

Complex societies arose in Mexico, the Andes, and the modern-day United States at different times and in different ways than in Eurasia. Hundreds, sometimes thousands, of years elapsed between the first cultivation of plants and the rise of cities. Archaeologists pay close attention to the American peoples who built large earthworks or stone monuments because their rulers had the ability to command their subjects to work on large projects. Similarly, although the peoples of the Pacific never built large cities, they conducted some of the world's longest ocean voyages across the Pacific and by 1350 had reached New Zealand, the final place on the globe to be settled by humans.

Differing from almost every other people of the Americas and the islands of the Pacific, the Maya developed one of the few writing systems used in the Americas before 1500. Some earlier peoples living in modern-day Mexico developed notational systems; much later, the Mexica (MAY-shee-kah) people of Mexico, often called the Aztecs, used a combination of pictures and visual puns to record events, but their writing system was not fully developed (see Chapter 15). Since historians know more about the Maya than any other society in the Americas or the Pacific islands, this chapter begins with their precursors and then proceeds to the Maya themselves.

KEY CONCEPT QUESTIONS

- How did Mesoamerican techniques of imperial administration differ from those used in Eurasia? **(Key Concept 2.2)**
- How did the Mayans promote political unity in their region, and how did they administer their empire? **(Key Concept 2.2)**
- What evidence is there of interregional trade, communication, and exchange between Mesoamerica, the northern peoples, and the Andean region? **(Key Concept 2.3)**
- What new technologies facilitated Polynesian expansion? **(Key Concept 2.3)**

The First Complex Societies of Mesoamerica, 5000 B.C.E.–500 C.E.

Unlike in Mesopotamia, Egypt, India, and China, agriculture in the Americas arose not in river valleys but in a plateau region, the highlands of Mexico, around 5000 B.C.E. The residents of Mexico continued to hunt and gather for thousands of years as they slowly began to cultivate corn, potatoes, cocoa beans, and other crops that grew nowhere else in the world. Large urban centers, one of the markers of complex society, first appeared in Mexico around 1200 B.C.E.

The Development of Agriculture, 5000–1500 B.C.E.

The people of Tehuacán (tay-wah-KAHN) in the modern state of Puebla (PWAY-bla), Mexico, initially harvested wild grasses with tiny ears of seeds. Their grinding stones, the first evidence of cultivation in the Americas, date to 5000 B.C.E. Just as the Natufians of western Asia had gradually domesticated wheat by harvesting certain wild plants with desirable characteristics (see Chapter 1), the residents of Tehuacán selected different grasses with more rows of seeds until they eventually developed a domesticated variety of maize sometime around 7000 B.C.E. (Specialists prefer the term *maize* to *corn* because it is more specific.) Unlike the early farmers of western Asia, the people of Tehuacán used no draft animals.

Mesoamerica
The region that includes the southern two-thirds of modern Mexico, Guatemala, Belize, El Salvador, Honduras, Nicaragua, and Costa Rica.

Maize spread from the Tehuacán Valley throughout the region of **Mesoamerica** (see Map 5.1). Mesoamerica is bounded by barren desert north of modern Mexico.

Map 5.1 Complex Societies in the Americas, ca. 1200 B.C.E. Starting around 1200 B.C.E., complex societies arose in two widely separated regions in the Americas. In modern-day Mexico the Olmec hewed giant heads from basalt; in modern-day Peru, the Chavín built large temples decorated with statues combining human and animal body parts.

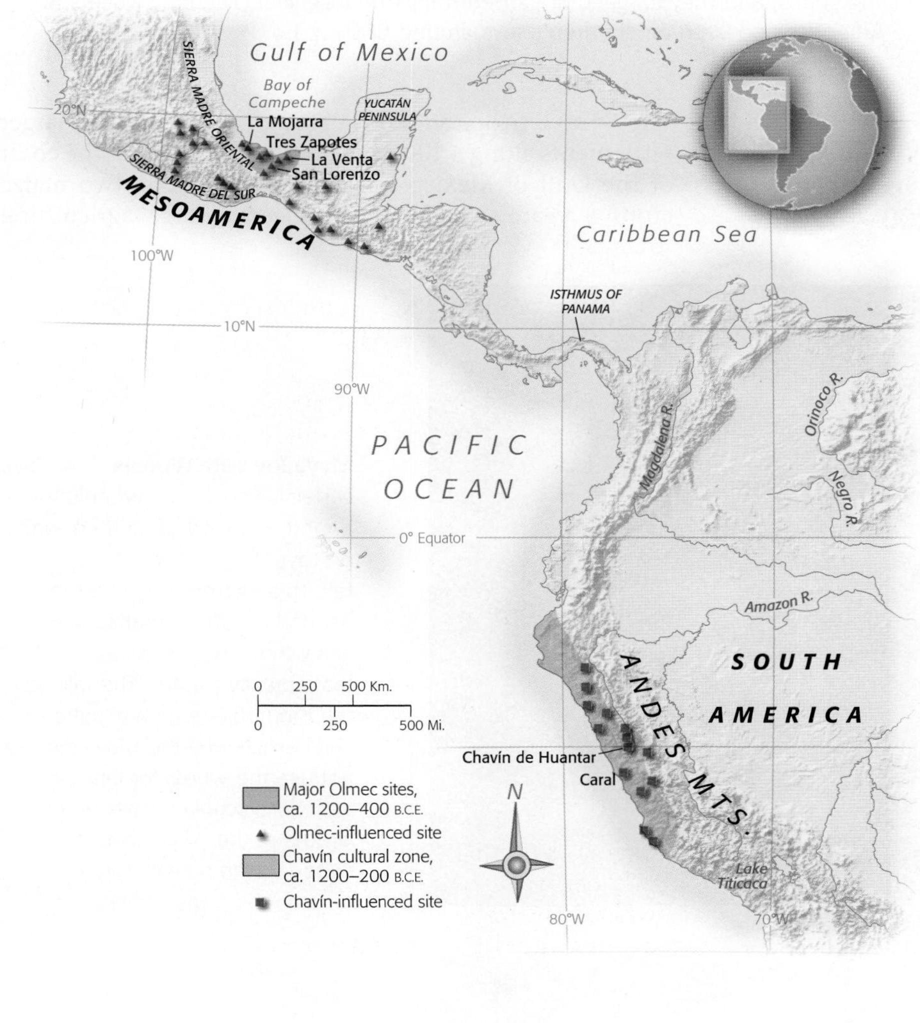

More rain falls in the east than in the west; because of the uneven rainfall, the inhabitants used irrigation channels to move water west. Maize later reached north to Canada and south to the tip of South America.

Once planted, maize required little tending until the harvest. The hard dried kernels were ground or boiled and mixed with ground limestone into a paste, called nixtamal (NISH-ta-mal), that was used to make unleavened cakes. As the proportion of cultivated crops in the diet increased, the Mesoamericans gradually abandoned hunting and gathering. Eating little meat because they raised no domesticated animals, they cultivated squash and beans along with maize, three foods that together offered the same nutritional benefits (amino acids and vitamin B_{12}) as meat. The systematized cultivation of maize made it possible to support larger populations. By 2500 B.C.E., the population of Mesoamerica had increased by perhaps twenty-five times; the largest settlements had several hundred residents. By 1500 B.C.E., the Mesoamericans had adopted full-time agriculture.

• **CONTEXT&CONNECTIONS** If an ancient farmer from anywhere in Mesopotamia, China, or India had visited at this time, he or she would have been amazed to see that no one in Mesoamerica employed the familiar tools of farming—the plow, the wheel, or draft animals. Instead of the plow, the Mesoamericans used different types of digging sticks, and they dragged or carried things themselves. (The only wheels in the Americas appeared on children's toys around 500 C.E.) •

Olmec
A complex society (1200–400 B.C.E.) that arose on the Gulf of Mexico coast from modern-day Veracruz to Tabasco. Known particularly for the massive colossal heads hewn from basalt.

The Olmec and Their Successors, 1200–400 B.C.E.

The **Olmec** peoples (1200–400 B.C.E.) built the first larger settlements along a 100-mile (160-km) stretch on the coast of the Gulf of Mexico (see Map 5.1). Raising two maize crops a year, the Olmec produced a large agricultural

Photograph K3670 © Justin Kerr

Maya Toy with Wheels The Maya certainly knew how wheels functioned, but they used them only on toys. Five inches (12.5 cm) tall, this example, unlike the handful of others that survive, has wheels with separate axels that actually rotate. (The tail was the mouthpiece for a whistle.) Not certain why the Maya did not use the wheel for farming or transport, scholars have speculated that the wheel was not suited to the heavily forested terrain where the Maya lived.

surplus, and the population also increased because of the nutritional benefits of the nixtamal diet.

Surviving colossal heads testify to the Olmec rulers' ability to mobilize their subjects for large labor projects. The Olmec used stone hammers to hew these heads from basalt. They are 5–10 feet (1.5–3.0 m) tall, and the largest weighs over 40 tons (36 metric tons). The nearest source of basalt lay more than 50 miles (80 km) to the northwest, and archaeologists surmise that Olmec laborers, lacking the wheel, carried the rock overland and built rafts to transport it along local rivers.

The peoples of Mesoamerica developed the **Long Count**, a calendar that ran cumulatively, starting from a day far in the mythical past (whose equivalent is August 11, 3114 B.C.E.) and ending on December 21, 2012, when the world did not, as some expected, come to an end. The Long Count came into use in the fifth and fourth centuries B.C.E., when the successors to the Olmec built several monuments bearing Long Count dates. The inscriptions of Long Count dates use a mix of bars and dots to show the different units of the calendar: 400 years, 200 years, 1 year, 20 days, and 1 day.

Long Count
A calendar that ran cumulatively, starting from a day equivalent to August 11, 3114 B.C.E., and continuing to the present. Came into use in the fifth and fourth centuries B.C.E., when inscriptions of bars and dots showed different calendar units.

Teotihuacan, ca. 200 B.C.E.–600 C.E.

At the same time that the peoples along the coast were developing the Long Count and using glyphs, a huge metropolis arose at **Teotihuacan** (tay-oh-tee-WAH-kahn). Founded around 200 B.C.E., the city continued to grow until the year 650 C.E. Estimates of its population range between 40,000 and 200,000, certainly enough to qualify as a complex society. (See the feature "Visual Evidence in Primary Sources: The Imposing Capital of Teotihuacan.")

Teotihuacan
The largest city in the Americas before 1500, covering 8 square miles (20 sq km), located some 30 miles (50 km) northeast of modern-day Mexico City. Was occupied from around 200 B.C.E. to 650 C.E. and had an estimated population at its height of 40,000–200,000.

• **CONTEXT&CONNECTIONS** Teotihuacan's population made it the largest city in the Americas before 1500 but smaller than contemporary Rome's 1 million (see Chapter 7) or Luoyang's 500,000 during the *Han dynasty* (key term in Chapter 4). •

On Teotihuacan's neatly gridded streets, ordinary people lived in one-story apartment compounds, divided among several families, whose painted white exteriors had no windows and whose interiors were covered with colorful frescoes. A plumbing system drained wastewater into underground channels along the street, eventually converging in aboveground canals. As is characteristic of complex societies, the compounds show evidence of craft specializations: for example, one was a pottery workshop.

One residential district in the city has atypical rounded houses instead of the more common apartment compounds and contains pottery similar to that in the Veracruz region on the Gulf coast. Since this type of dwelling has been found in many sites along the Gulf of Mexico, archaeologists surmise that this was a community of migrant workers from the Veracruz region that continued to make the characteristic pottery of their homeland.

We do not know whether Teotihuacan served as the capital of an empire, but it was certainly a large city-state. Sometime around 600 C.E. a fire, apparently caused by an internal revolt, leveled sections of the city, causing the residents to gradually move away.

The Imposing Capital of Teotihuacan

The three magnificent pyramids of Teotihuacan, 30 miles (50 km) northeast of Mexico City, impress visitors even today. Lined with smaller pyramids, the broad Avenue of the Dead runs from the Pyramid of the Moon past the Pyramid of the Sun to the Feathered Serpent Pyramid. All of these names, including *Teotihuacan*, which means "the abode of the gods," were given by Nahuatl-speaking settlers from the north after their arrival sometime in the twelfth century (see Chapter 15).

Since we do not know what the original residents of the city called these structures and since no one has deciphered the few glyphs that appear on scattered stones, archaeologists have exercised great ingenuity in trying to understand the city's layout. Teotihuacan is unusual in that none of the city's rulers built monuments to themselves. Because deities of later peoples, like the Maya, were often associated with stars and planets, most concur that the city's orientation must have been astronomical, based on the different phases of Venus, the morning star honored by so many peoples in the Americas.

The discovery of more than two hundred skeletons under the Feathered Serpent Pyramid has shed new light on the building's purpose. The group with the most valuable jewelry appears to have the highest social status; another group that wears less valuable shell beads seems to rank lower. A third group of women had even less jewelry, while a fourth group consisted of uniformed men buried with large quantities of projectile points, most likely an army. The people in these groups assume different postures, some with their hands tied behind their backs, as if they had been killed before burial, possibly with the accompanying obsidian knives, blades, and piercing implements. Because looters dug two large trenches leading to the center of the Feathered Serpent Pyramid, archaeologists cannot be certain who was originally buried there, but the mass burials and valuable grave goods make it likely that this was the ruler's tomb. The dead buried at Teotihuacan, like the terracotta warriors of the Qin founder (see Chapter 4), appear to have served as a sacrificial army for the deceased ruler, who was buried circa 200 C.E. at the time when the Feathered Serpent Pyramid was completed.

The World's Largest Pyramids

Name	Site	Date	Material	Height
Great Pyramid	Giza, Egypt	2580 B.C.E.	stone	480 ft (146 m)
La Danta	El Mirador, Guatemala	200 B.C.E.	cut stone and rock fill	230 ft (70 m)
Pyramid of the Sun	Teotihuacan	200 C.E.	volcanic rubble and earth	216 feet (66 m)
Tarharqa's Pyramid	Nuri, Nubia	664 B.C.E.	stone	160 feet (49 m)
Pyramid of the Moon	Teotihuacan	200 C.E.	volcanic rubble and earth	140 feet (43 m)
Pirámide Mayor	Caral	2600 B.C.E.	brick and earth	60 ft (18 m)

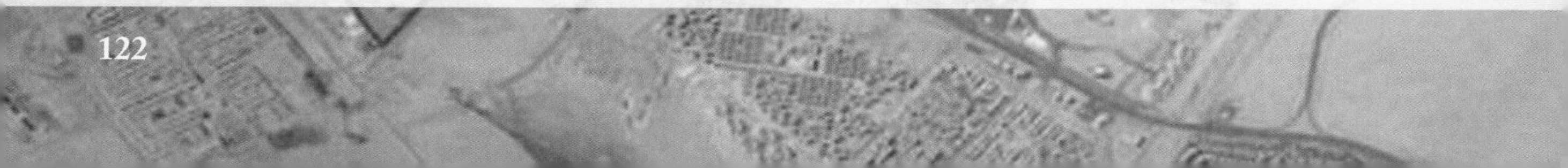

With sides over 700 feet (213 m) long at the base, and over twenty stories high, the Pyramid of the Sun is one of the two largest structures in the Americas constructed before 1500 (the other is La Danta). The recent discovery of a greenstone mask points to a ruler's burial there since similar masks have been found only in other rulers' tombs.

The Citadel, opposite the Feathered Serpent Pyramid, was the political center of the city. ***Compare and contrast the site of Teotihuacan with descriptions of the urban centers of other early complex societies in the Americas (Caral, Olmec, Maya in this chapter) and in Eurasia (Sumer, Chapter 2; Indus River Valley, Chapter 3; Shang dynasty, Chapter 4)***.

The Feathered Serpent Pyramid, also called the Quetzalcoatl Temple, has staircases up the side of the monument with stone facades and elaborate serpent heads dividing the different terraces.

Georg Gerster/Science Source

The Avenue of the Dead, 50 yards (50 m) wide, extends for more than 3 miles (5.2 km) and connects the different pyramids of Teotihuacan.

Laborers made the Pyramid of the Moon in the same way that they made the Pyramid of the Sun: they piled up earth and rubble to form a pyramid shape, leveled off horizontal terraces, and then faced the surface with adobe and stone.

This modern ring road, the Periférico, was built in the 1960s to steer traffic away from the monuments.

The Maya, 300 B.C.E.–1200 C.E.

Maya
Indigenous people living in modern-day Yucatán, Belize, Honduras, and Guatemala. Their complex society reached its height during the classic period, when they used a fully developed written language.

The **Maya**, like the other peoples of the Americas, differed from the Eurasian empires in that they created a remarkable complex society unaided by the wheel, plow, draft animals, or metal tools. Some scholars see the Olmec as a mother culture that gave both the Teotihuacan and Maya peoples their calendar, their writing system, and even their enormous flat-topped stepped pyramids—perhaps temples, perhaps palaces—of limestone and plaster packed with earth fill. Others disagree sharply, arguing that the Olmec, Teotihuacan, and Maya were neighboring cultures that did not directly influence each other. These ongoing debates combine with new discoveries to make Maya studies a lively field.

Some scholars also thought the Maya were a peace-loving people governed by a religious elite, until inscriptions dating between 250 and 910 C.E. were deciphered in the 1970s. Scholars today recognize the Maya's unrelenting violence but see it as no different from that of the Assyrian empire and Shang dynasty China.

The Major Periods of Maya History and Maya Writing

Scholars specializing in Maya studies refer to the period from 250 to 910 as the classic age, because there are written inscriptions on monuments, and the period before 250 as the preclassic age. Recent discoveries are forcing scholars to reconsider these labels.

The urban complex of El Mirador and fifty surrounding satellite cities occupies 2,500 square miles (6,500 sq km) of jungle spanning northern Guatemala and the Campeche state in southwestern Mexico. The settlement, which covers 6 square miles (15.5 sq km), dates to 300 B.C.E.–200 C.E. and thus existed before the classic period. With an estimated population of at least one hundred thousand, El Mirador challenges the earlier view that all preclassic sites were small. The city had the enormous La Danta pyramid, compelling evidence of the ruler's ability to command labor (see the table "The World's Largest Pyramids"). The city's sophisticated system of water collection allowed the residents to attain much higher agricultural yields than their neighbors and fueled great prosperity. Because archaeologists are not certain whether the residents of El Mirador had a writing system (they have found some isolated glyphs), El Mirador is still considered a preclassic site. The city was abandoned sometime around 200 C.E.

In some Maya cities, such as Tikal (TEE-kal), but not in others, such as Copán (co-PAHN), construction of monuments and inscriptions stopped between 550 and 600, possibly because of a political or ecological crisis. This half-century marks the division between the early classic period (250–550) and late classic period (600–800), when the building of monuments resumed. The latest Maya monument with an inscription is dated to 909, marking the end of the terminal classic period (800–909).

One of the great intellectual breakthroughs of the twentieth century was the decipherment of the Mayan script. (Scholars today use the word *Maya* to refer to the people and *Mayan* for the language they spoke.) Mayan glyphs did not look like any of the world's other writing systems. They were so pictorial that many doubted they could represent sounds. After twenty years of research and study, however, scholars realized in the 1970s that one could write a single Mayan word several different ways: entirely phonetically, entirely pictorially, or using a combination of both phonetic sounds and pictures. It is as if one could write *hat* in English by drawing a picture of a hat or writing h + a + t, h + @ + t, or simply h + @. Since 1973 Mayanists have learned to read about 85 percent of all surviving glyphs.

Maya Government and Society

Copán provides a good example of a typical Maya city-state, including a population divided into sharply demarcated groups: the ruling family, the nobility, ordinary people, and slaves. Copán reached its peak in the eighth century.

Copán
A typical Maya city-state. At its peak in the eighth century, Copán had a population of 18,000–20,000 divided into sharply demarcated groups: the ruling family, the nobility, ordinary people, and slaves.

The ruler of Copán, who was also the commander of the army, ranked higher than everyone else. He decided when to ally with other city-states and when to fight them, as well as how to allocate the different crops and taxes received from the populace. When a ruler died, a council of nobles met to verify that his son or his younger brother was fit to rule. If a ruler died without an heir, the council appointed someone from one of the highest-ranking noble families to succeed him.

One ruler's tomb contained a deer-shaped vessel with traces of theobromine, a caffeine-like molecule found only in chocolate. Mesoamericans started preparing drinks made from pounded seeds from the cacao (*ka-ka-wa* in Mayan) tree as early as 600 B.C.E. and certainly by the early fifth century, the time of this ruler's tomb. The Maya did not sweeten the cacao drink but added spices and crushed chile peppers to make a variety of drinks they prized for their foam. The Maya believed that cacao could cure a variety of ills, including hemorrhoids and nervous tension.

AP® THEMES
How were members of the upper classes of Maya society differentiated from members of lower classes?

Ranking just below the members of the ruling family, the nobles of Maya society lived in large, spacious houses such as those found in the section of Copán known as the House of the Officials. One typical compound there contains between forty and fifty buildings surrounding eleven courtyards. In judging a man's prominence, the Maya considered all of his relatives on both his father's and mother's side. The Mayan word for "nobles" means "he whose descent is known on both sides."

Literate in a society where few could read or write, scribes came from the highest ranks of the nobility. When the king's armies did well in battle, the scribes enjoyed the best treatment that the king could give them. When the king's armies lost, they were often taken prisoner.

Only those scribes with mathematical skills could maintain the elaborate calendar. Around 350 C.E., Maya ritual specialists were the first mathematicians in the world to use zero as a place-holder. They devised an extraordinarily sophisticated numerical system. Astronomers observed the stars and planets so closely that they could predict eclipses. They were particularly skilled in tracking the movements of Venus, which during some seasons appeared first in the evening before any stars, and in others was the last to disappear in the morning. The Maya used their knowledge of celestial bodies to determine auspicious days for inaugurating rulers, conducting elaborate religious ceremonies, or starting wars.

AP® THEMES
How did commerce contribute to the success of the Maya urban centers?

The most prosperous ordinary people became merchants specializing in long-distance trade. Salt was the one necessity the Maya had to import because their diet did not provide enough sodium to prevent a deficiency. They collected salt from the Yucatán beaches and shipped it in canoes along the ocean's shore and on interior rivers until it had to be carried by hand. Some of the items traded were luxury goods like jade, shells, and quetzal bird feathers, which flickered blue, gold, or green in the light. The craft specialists who transformed these raw materials into finely worked goods lived in the small houses of ordinary people. The Maya first encountered gold around the year 1000 and learned to work it, yet they made few items out of metal. They preferred green jade, which they carved and smoothed with saws made of coated string and different types of sandpaper.

obsidian
A naturally occurring volcanic glass used by different peoples in the Americas to make fine art objects, dart tips, and knife blades sharper than modern scalpels. The most important good traded by the Maya.

The most important trade good in the Maya world was **obsidian**, a naturally occurring volcanic glass. The best material available to the Maya for making tools, obsidian could also be worked into fine art objects. Obsidian shattered easily, though, so the Maya also made tools from chert, a flintlike rock that was more durable.

● **CONTEXT&CONNECTIONS** Obsidian was not unique to the Americas; the Akkadians used it to make knives as well, and they traded the knives across large distances (see Chapter 2). ●

Since Copán's urban inhabitants could not raise enough food to feed themselves, farmers who lived outside the city provided residents with maize and smaller amounts of beans, squash, and chili peppers. City dwellers had fruit gardens and were able occasionally to hunt wild game.

Because the Maya had no draft animals, most cultivators worked land within a day or two's walk from the urban center. Their fields marked the limit of each city-state's direct political control. Aerial photographs of the Yucatán, Mexico, and Belize have revealed raised fields dating back to the time of the Maya, which were farmed season after season. Much of the agricultural work was done by slaves. The lowest-ranking people in Maya society, slaves were prisoners of war who had been allowed to live and forced to work in the fields.

The Religious Beliefs of the Maya

Many Maya rituals featured the spilling of royal blood. No surviving text explains exactly why the Maya thought blood sacred, but blood offerings clearly played a key role in their belief system. Surviving paintings from throughout the Maya region depict women pulling thorny vines through their tongues and kings sticking either a stingray spine or a pointed bone tool through the tips of their penises.

Popul Vuh
One of the few surviving sources in the Mayan language, this oral epic features a series of hip ballgames between the gods and humans. Originally written in Mayan glyphs, it was recorded in the Roman alphabet in the 1500s.

One of the few Mayan sources that survives, an oral epic named ***Popul Vuh*** (POPE-uhl voo), or "The Council Book," features a series of games in which players on two teams moved the ball by hitting it with their hips and tried to get it past their opponents' end line. The Maya believed that the earth was recreated each time the hip ballgame was played, and the side seen as being tested by the gods, usually prisoners of war, always lost, after which their blood was spilled in an elaborate ceremony. (See the feature "Movement of Ideas Through Primary Sources: The Ballgame in *Popul Vuh*.")

Written down in the Roman alphabet in the 1550s, the *Popul Vuh* preserves only a part of the Maya's rich legends, but scholars have used it in conjunction with surviving texts to piece together the key elements of the Maya belief system. All Maya gods, the *Popul Vuh* explains, are descended from a divine pair. The Lizard House, the father, invented the Mayan script and supported all learning, while his wife, Lady Rainbow, was a deity of weaving and medicine who also helped women endure the pain of childbirth. Their descendants, the Maya believed, each presided over a different realm: separate gods existed for merchants, hunters, fishermen, soldiers, and the ruling families. Maya rulers sacrificed their prisoners of war as offerings to these deities.

The Maya communicated with the dead using various techniques. Caves served as portals between the world of the living and the Xibalba Underworld described in *Popul Vuh*. One cave is 2,790 feet (850 m) long; its walls are decorated with drawings of the Hero Twins, the ballgame, and sexual acts. The Maya who visited this and other caves employed enemas to intoxicate themselves so they could see the dead. They performed these enemas by attaching bone tubes, found in large quantities at Maya sites, to leather or rubber bags filled with different liquids. Surviving drawings make it impossible to identify the liquids, but anthropologists speculate that the enema bags were filled with wine, chocolate, or hallucinogens made from the peyote cactus.

● **CONTEXT&CONNECTIONS** The Maya understanding of the realm of the dead differed from the other societies discussed in previous chapters. *Gilgamesh* (Chapter 2) tells of the hero's journey to the underworld, but only he manages to visit the underworld, see what it is like, and return to the realm of the living. The Chinese, particularly the *Daoists* (Chapter 4), envisioned the afterlife as a series of underground prisons, but they did not believe that the living could travel to the realm of the dead whenever they desired. ●

War, Politics, and the Decline of the Maya

Scholars have devoted considerable energy to sorting out the relationships among the sixty or so Maya city-states. A few key phrases appear in inscriptions: some rulers are said to be someone else's king, indicating that they accepted another king as their overlord. It is not clear what ties bound a subordinate ruler to his superior: marriage ties, loyalty oaths, military alliances, or perhaps a mixture of all three.

Because rulers vied continuously to increase their territory and become each other's lord, the Maya city-states devoted significant resources to war. Armies consisted of foot soldiers whose weapons included spears with obsidian points, slingshots, and darts propelled by a spear-thrower. The Maya did not have the bow and arrow. On the most informal level of conflict, a group of soldiers might steal into enemy territory to take captives, while in formal battles, two opposing armies of infantry faced off and showered each other with darts or stones from slingshots. Traps and ambushes were common, and the fighters used both daggers and spears in hand-to-hand combat.

The goal of all Maya warfare was to obtain captives. In inscriptions rulers brag about how many captives they held, because they wanted to appear powerful. Low-born captives, if spared ritual sacrifice, were assigned to work in the fields, while prisoners of higher status, particularly those from noble families, might be held in captivity for a long time, sometimes as much as twenty years. However, many ordinary soldiers captured in warfare, and especially higher-ranking prisoners, could expect to suffer ritual bloodletting. Maya victors removed the fingernails of war captives, cut their chests open to tear out their hearts, and publicly beheaded them as sacrifices to their deities.

AP® THEMES
How did the sacrifice of captives reinforce the authority of Maya rulers?

At the peak of Maya power in 750, the population reached 8 to 10 million. Sometime around the year 800, the Maya city-states entered an era of decline, evident because site after site has produced unfinished monuments abruptly abandoned by stoneworkers. So sudden was the decline that workers at some sites stopped carving after completing a single face of a square monument.

The Ballgame in *Popul Vuh*

The complicated plot of the Maya oral epic *Popul Vuh* involves two sets of ball-playing twins: after disturbing the gods with their play, one pair go to the Xibalba (SHE-bal-ba) Underworld (derived from the Mayan word for "fear," "trembling"), where they die at the hands of One and Seven Death, the head lords of Xibalba. The severed head of one of these twins hangs on a tree from which its spittle magically impregnates Lady Blood, who gives birth to the second set of twins, Hunahpu (HOO-nah-pooh) and Xbalanque (sh-bal-on-kay). These Hero Twins, far more skillful than their father and uncle, at first trick the gods of the Underworld repeatedly and then defeat them in the ballgame described in the episode below. Eventually they also die, but because the gods grant them another life, they rise at the end of the narrative to become the sun and the moon, creating the upper world or cosmos.

The earliest archaeological evidence of the game comes from the Olmec site of El Manatí, located 6 miles (10 km) east of San Lorenzo, where a dozen rubber balls dating to around 500 B.C.E. were found. Almost every Maya city-state had a ball court, usually in the shape of an L, with walls around it, located near a major temple. The Maya played this soccer-like game with heavy rubber balls measuring 12 or 18 inches (33 or 50 cm) across. The Maya combined the liquid rubber from latex trees with sap from morning glory flowers to make rubber for different purposes: sandal soles had to be durable, rubber bands to attach blades to shafts had to be resilient, and balls had to be bouncy. Sometimes the ball-makers used a human skull to make a hollow, less lethal, ball. The game spread throughout the Maya core region and as far north as Snaketown near Phoenix, Arizona, the home of an early Anasazi people who had two ball courts and rubber balls.

Since ball courts and balls do not provide enough information to understand how the game was played, anthropologists are closely studying the modern hip ballgames in the few villages near Mazatlán (ma-zat-LAN), Sinaloa (sin-A-loh-a) State in northwestern Mexico, where the game is still played. Two opposing teams of three to five players try to get the ball past the other team's end line. After serving with their hands, they propel the heavy rubber balls with their hips. Although players cover their hips with padding, the hips of modern players develop calluses and often become permanently bruised a deep-black color. We cannot be sure that everyone who played the game knew the story of the Hero Twins, but many players probably understood the game as a contest between two teams, one representing good, life, or the Hero Twins, and the other evil, death, or Xibalba, which was ultimately victorious.

This passage from the *Popul Vuh* describes the first test the twins must endure.

> **Historical Thinking Skill:**
> INTERPRETATION **Based on this account of the Mayan underworld, what is the relationship between the human ball players and the gods?**

> **Historical Thinking Skill:**
> SYNTHESIS **How are modern historians using contemporary activities to speculate on how the game was played in pre-Columbian times?**

First they entered Dark House.

And after that, the messenger of One Death brought their torch, burning when it arrived, along with one cigar apiece.

"'Here is their torch,' says the lord. 'They must return the torch in the morning, along with the cigars. They must return them intact,' say the lords," the messenger said when he arrived.

"Very well," they said, but they didn't burn the torch—instead, something that looked like fire was substituted. This was the tail of the macaw, which looked like a torch to the sentries. And as for the cigars, they just put fireflies at the tips of those cigars. . . .

"We've defeated them," said the sentries, but the torch was not consumed—it just looked that way. And as for the cigars, there wasn't anything burning there—it just looked that way. When these things were taken back to the lords:

"What's happening? Where did they come from? Who begot them and bore them? Our hearts are really hurting, because what they're doing to us is no good. They're different in looks and different in their very being," they said among themselves. And when they had summoned all the lords:

"Let's play ball, boys," the boys were told. . . .

"Well, this is the one we should put in play, here's our rubber ball," said the Xibalbans....

"Very well," said Hunahpu. When it was sent off by Xibalba, the ball was stopped by Hunahpu's yoke [hip-pad].

And then, ... the White Dagger came out from inside the ball. It went clattering, twisting all over the floor of the court.

"What's that!" said Hunahpu and Xbalanque. "Death is the only thing you want for us! . . . Truly, take pity on us, or else we'll just leave," the boys told them. . . .

"Well, don't go, boys. We can still play ball, but we'll put yours into play," . . .

And after that, they specified the prize:

"What should our prize be?" asked the Xibalbans.

"It's yours for the asking," was all the boys said.

"We'll just win four bowls of flowers," said the Xibalbans. . . .

"Very well," said the boys, and then their ball was dropped in. The boys were their equals in strength and made many plays, since they only had very good thoughts. Then the boys gave themselves up in defeat, and the Xibalbans were glad when they were defeated:

"We've done well. We've beaten them on the first try," said the Xibalbans. "Where will they go to get the flowers?" they said in their hearts.

"Truly, before the night is over, you must hand over our flowers and our prize," the boys, Hunahpu and Xbalanque, were told by Xibalba.

"Very well." . . . they said when they accepted their charge.

And after that, the boys entered Razor House, the second test of Xibalba.

Archaeologists have different explanations for the Maya decline. In the seventh and eighth centuries, blocs of allied city-states engaged in unending warfare. The drain on resources may have depopulated the Maya cities. Agriculture depleted the nutrients in the fields close to the political centers. In some places, a sustained drought between 800 and 1050 may have dealt the final blow to the ecosystem.

Maya culture revived during the postclassic period (910–1500), and the city of Chichen Itza (CHEE-chen IT-za) in the northern Yucatán, which flourished between 1000 and 1200, combined classic elements of Maya and central Mexican architecture and city planning. The ball court at Chichen Itza measures 545 feet (166 m) by 223 feet (68 m), making it the largest ball court in the Americas. Although Maya culture did not die out after 1500, the Maya never again matched the social stratification, specialized occupations, and large urban centers of the classic period.

Celebrating a Maya Victory in Battle This colorful fresco in a Maya tomb in Bonampak, Mexico, commemorates the victory of the ruler, who wears an elaborate headdress and a jacket made from jaguar skin. He relentlessly thrusts his spear downward and grasps the hair of a prisoner whose outstretched hand implores his captor. These murals, which reveal so much about the lives of the Maya, were suddenly abandoned around 800, a time when work on many other monuments stopped abruptly, marking the end of the classic era. (Charles Lenars/Corbis)

• **CONTEXT&CONNECTIONS** Perhaps because of their distinctive language, the Maya managed to keep their identity even after the Spanish conquest of the early 1500s. (Their lack of gold was another advantage; the Spanish had no reason to conquer them.) About ten million Mayan speakers are alive today in Guatemala, Honduras, Belize, El Salvador, and Mexico, and there are immigrant communities in various American cities such as Philadelphia and New Haven, Connecticut. •

The Northern Peoples, 500 B.C.E.–1200 C.E.

Complex society arose north of the Rio Grande, in the area occupied by the modern United States and Canada, relatively late—after the decline of the Maya—and possibly as a result of contact with Mesoamerica. The North Americans planted maize as the Mesoamericans did. The first complex societies in North America, both dating to after 700 C.E., were the Mississippian culture in the central United States and the Anasazi (AH-nah-sah-zee) culture in the southwest United States.

Until about 500 B.C.E., the peoples living to the north continued to hunt and gather in small bands of around sixty people, much like the residents of Monte Verde, Chile (see Chapter 1). Then, from 500 B.C.E.to 100 C.E., the Adena (uh-DEE-nuh) created earthworks along the Ohio River Valley in Ohio and Illinois. Some Adena mounds are perfect circles; others are shaped like animals.

The Adena did not farm, but their successors, the Hopewell peoples (200 B.C.E.–500 C.E.), cultivated maize, beans, and squash and built larger earthworks in the valleys of the Ohio, Illinois, and Mississippi Rivers. The taller and more elaborate Hopewell earthworks formed clusters of circles, rectangles, and polygons.

The Adena and Hopewell settlements were not large urban centers, but these earthworks demonstrate that their leaders could organize large-scale labor projects. Archaeologists have reconstructed the Hopewell trade routes by locating the sources of unusual items, such as alligator teeth and skulls from Florida, mapping the sites where those items appear, and then inferring the trade routes by linking the items' sources with their various destinations. The Hopewell trading networks, more extensive than those of the Adena, extended from the Rocky Mountains to the Atlantic Ocean; with their neighbors to the south in modern-day Mexico, they traded conch shells, shark teeth, and obsidian.

Occupying over a hundred different sites concentrated in the Mississippi River Valley, the **Mississippian peoples** (800–1450) built the first large urban centers that characterize complex society in the north. Mississippian towns followed a Maya plan, with temples or palaces on earthen mounds around a central plaza. The Mississippian peoples were the first in the Americas to develop the bow and arrow, sometime around 900.

Mississippian peoples
The first northern people (800–1450) to build large urban centers in the Mississippi River Valley.

The largest surviving mound, in the Cahokia (kuh-HOKE-ee-uh) Mounds of Collinsville, Illinois (just east of St. Louis), is 100 feet (30 m) high and 1,000 feet (300 m) long. Its sheer magnitude testifies to the power the leaders had over their subjects. Cahokia, with a population of thirty thousand, held eighty-four other mounds, some for temples, some for mass burials. One mound contained the corpses of 110 young women, evidence of a sacrificial cult to either a leader or a deity.

The other major complex society of the north appeared in modern-day Colorado, Arizona, Utah, and New Mexico: the Anasazi. Their centers also show signs of contact with the Maya, most notably in the presence of ball courts. During the Pueblo period (700–1300), the Anasazi built two kinds of houses: pit houses carved out of the ground and pueblos made from bricks, mortar, and log roofs. One pueblo structure in Chaco, New Mexico, had eight hundred rooms in five stories and was home to one thousand residents. After 1150 the Anasazi began to build their pueblos next to cliff faces, as at Mesa Verde, Colorado. They used irrigation to farm, and their craftspeople made distinctive pottery, cotton and feather clothing, and turquoise jewelry.

Like so many other urban centers in the Americas, Cahokia Mounds and Mesa Verde declined suddenly after 1200, when their populations dispersed, and archaeologists do not know why.

The Peoples of the Andes, 3100 B.C.E.–1000 C.E.

Several complex societies arose, flourished, and collapsed between 3100 B.C.E. and 1000 C.E. in the Andean region, which includes modern-day Peru, Bolivia, Ecuador, Argentina, and Chile in South America. These complex societies predated the first Mesoamerican complex society of the Olmec by nearly two thousand years, indicating that the two regions developed independently of each other. All the Andean complex societies built city-states with large urban centers, though never on the scale of Teotihuacan.

The Andean mountain chain runs up the center of the Andean region, which extends east to the edge of the dense Amazon rainforest and west to the Pacific coast (see Map 5.1). In the east, rain falls heavily, and the residents moved rainwater to their fields by a system of channels; to the west, almost none falls.

The main diet staple was potatoes, supplemented by squash, chili peppers, beans, and sometimes maize, which could grow only at lower altitudes. The earliest strains of domesticated squash date to about 4000 B.C.E. Sometime around 4000 B.C.E., the Andeans domesticated the llama and the alpaca. Both animals could carry loads of approximately 100 pounds (50 kg) over distances of 10–12 miles (16–20 km) a day. The Andeans never rode these animals, used them for farming, or raised them to eat. Their main source of animal protein was the domesticated guinea pig.

Caral
The earliest complex society (3100–1800 B.C.E.) in the Americas, whose main urban center was located at Caral in modern-day Peru, in the Andes.

The earliest large urban settlement in the Americas, at the site of **Caral** (KA-ral) in the Andes, lies some 100 miles (160 km) north of Lima, the capital of modern Peru, and only 14 miles (22 km) from the Pacific coast. People have known about the site since the early twentieth century because its structures are clearly visible from the air, but only in 2001 did archaeologists realize that it dated to 3100 B.C.E.

The Caral site contains five small pyramid-shaped structures and one large one: the Pirámide Mayor (pi-RAH-me-day my-your), which stands 60 feet (18 m) tall and covers 5 acres (.02 km) (see the table "The World's Largest Pyramids," page 122). Inside the pyramid, archaeologists found a set of thirty-two carved flutes made from condor and pelican bone with decorations showing birds and monkeys, possibly deities.

• **CONTEXT&CONNECTIONS** Caral, like Uruk in Mesopotamia or Harappa in India, showed clear signs of social stratification. The three thousand or so residents included wealthy people living in large dwellings on top of the pyramids, craftsmen in smaller houses at their base, and unskilled laborers in much simpler dwellings around the perimeters of the town. •

With some twenty smaller communities in the immediate vicinity, Caral was probably a city-state, not an early empire. The history of the site reflects the rise-and-fall pattern so common to the early cities of the Americas and also to the Indus Valley (see Chapter 3). Agricultural improvements led to dramatic urban growth, followed by sudden decline. Usually no direct evidence reveals why a given city was abandoned, but drought and overfarming may have contributed. Caral was abandoned in 1800 B.C.E.

In 1200 B.C.E., nearly two thousand years after Caral was first occupied, a major urban center arose at **Chavín** (cha-VEEN), about 60 miles (100 km) north of Caral (see Map 5.1). Chavín has large temples, some in the shape of a U, and impressive stone sculptures, which combine elements of different animals such as jaguars, snakes, and eagles with human body parts to create composite human-animal sculptures, possibly of deities.

Chavín
Andean complex society (1200–200 B.C.E.) in modern-day Peru. Best known for its temples and large stone sculptures of animals.

In 350 B.C.E., during the last years of the Chavín culture, several distinct regional cultures arose on the south coast of Peru that are most famous for the Nazca (NAZ-ka) lines, a series of earthworks near the modern town of Nazca. The Nazca people scraped away the dark surface layer of the desert in straight-edged trenches to reveal a lighter-colored soil beneath, creating precise straight lines as long as 6 miles (10 km), as well as elaborate designs of spiders, whales, and monkeys, possibly offerings to or depictions of their gods. No one knows how people working on the ground created these designs, which are still visible from the air today. No large cities of the Nazca people have been found, but the Nazca lines, like the earthworks of the Adena and Hopewell peoples, show that their rulers were able to mobilize large numbers of laborers.

AP® THEMES
How did the geography of the Andes shape the formation of states in the region?

Occupied between 600 and 1000, the biggest Andean political center was at Tiwanaku (tee-wan-a-koo), 12 miles (20 km) south of Lake Titicaca (tit-tee-ka-ka), southern Bolivia, at the high altitude of 11,800 feet (3,600 m) above sea level. The rulers of the Tiwanaku city-state, archaeologists surmise, exercised some kind of political control over a large area extending through modern-day Bolivia, Argentina, northern Chile, and southern Peru. At its peak, Tiwanaku was home to some forty thousand people. Its farmers could support such a large population because they used a raised-field system: the irrigation channels they dug around their fields helped to keep the crops from freezing on chilly nights.

Sometime around 700 to 800, the Andean peoples, alone among the peoples living in the Americas, learned how to work metal intensively. Unlike the Maya, who worked with only gold, the Andeans discovered how to extract metallic ore from rocks and heat different metals to form alloys. They made bronze both by combining copper with tin, as was common in Eurasia, and also by combining copper with arsenic. One site in Peru, in continuous use after 700, had draft furnaces in which families melted fuel and metal ore together, producing slag with copper in it, which they extracted

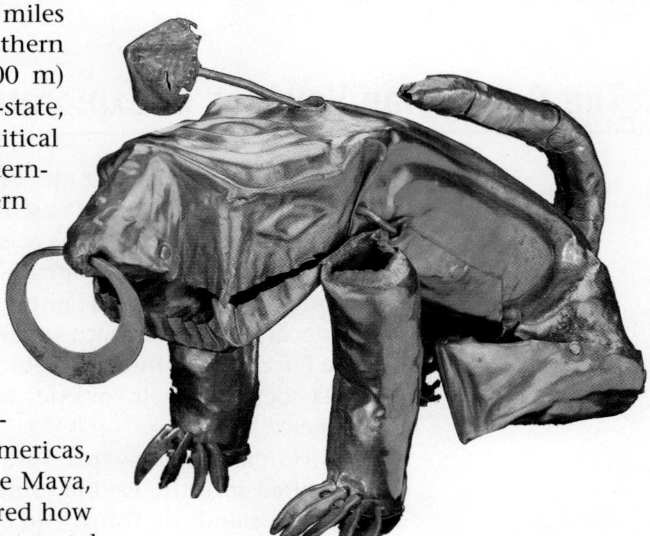

Andean Metalworking This jaguar-shaped container was used to carry lime powder made from crushed shells, which the Andeans ate as they chewed coca leaves as they performed rituals. Note the ring in the jaguar's nose, which is made from an unusual alloy of platinum and gold: the Andeans, the most skilled metalworkers in the Americas, never worked iron.
(Calima jaguar lime container – Museo del Oro, Colombia)

The World's First Telephone? Over 1200 years old, this telephone made by the Chimu people used two cup-shaped gourds connected by a piece of intact twine measuring 75 feet (23 m) long. When someone spoke into one of the cups, someone at the other end could place the cup to his or her ear to hear what was being said. The Chimu ruler, occupying a royal chamber, could have used this device to issue requests to servants or orders to lower officials. (National Museum of the American Indian, Smithsonian Institution. Photo by Travis Rathbone.)

and worked into ingots, small sheets, or "ax money"—ax-shaped pieces of metal tied together in bundles and placed in tombs as an offering for the dead. Andean metalsmiths combined gold, copper, and silver to make an alloy that had a lower melting point than its constituents but was easier to work than pure gold. Metalsmiths combined different quantities to achieve different colors.

● **CONTEXT&CONNECTIONS** Andean graves have produced the only ancient metal tools found so far in the Americas. Most Andean metal was used to make decorations worn by people or placed on buildings, not for tools or weapons, which challenges yet another preconception prompted by the complex societies of Eurasia. In Mesopotamia, Egypt, India, and China, people switched to metal tools—first *bronze*, then *iron* (Chapter 2)—as soon as they learned to mine metal ore and make alloys. But the Andean peoples continued to use tools of wood and stone and reserved metal for different purposes. ●

Andean engineering extended well beyond metallurgy. The peoples in Chimu society (900–1470) who lived in northern Peru were great engineers: they constructed an elaborate system of irrigation canals to water the deserts of their home region so that they could plant crops. They also made a very early form of the telephone.

The Polynesian Voyages of Exploration, 1000 B.C.E.–1350 C.E.

The societies of the Americas discussed above, including the Maya, were land-based. Their residents used canoes for trips on inland waterways and for occasional voyages hugging the ocean shore, but they focused their energies on farming and building cities. In contrast, the peoples of the Pacific, who lived on the islands inside the Polynesian Triangle, spent much of their lives on the sea. Like the residents of the Americas, they developed in isolation from and quite differently from the Eurasians. Although their urban centers never became the large cities of complex societies, their societies were stratified and their leaders relied on their subjects for labor.

Humans had reached Australia in about 50,000 B.C.E. (see Chapter 1), and they ventured into the Pacific sometime after that. Starting around 1000 B.C.E., when the Fiji islands of Tonga and Samoa were first settled, early voyagers crossed the Pacific Ocean using only the stars to navigate and populated most of the Pacific islands. Their voyages resulted in one of the longest yet least-documented seaborne migrations in human history.

Polynesian Triangle
An imaginary triangle with sides 4,000 miles (6,500 km) long linking Hawai'i, Easter Island, and New Zealand and containing several thousand islands.

The Settlement of the Polynesian Triangle

The islands of the Pacific fall into two groups: those lying off Australia and Indonesia—Micronesia (mike-ro-NEE-zhuh), Melanesia (mel-uh-NEE-zhuh), and New Guinea—and those within the **Polynesian Triangle**, an imaginary

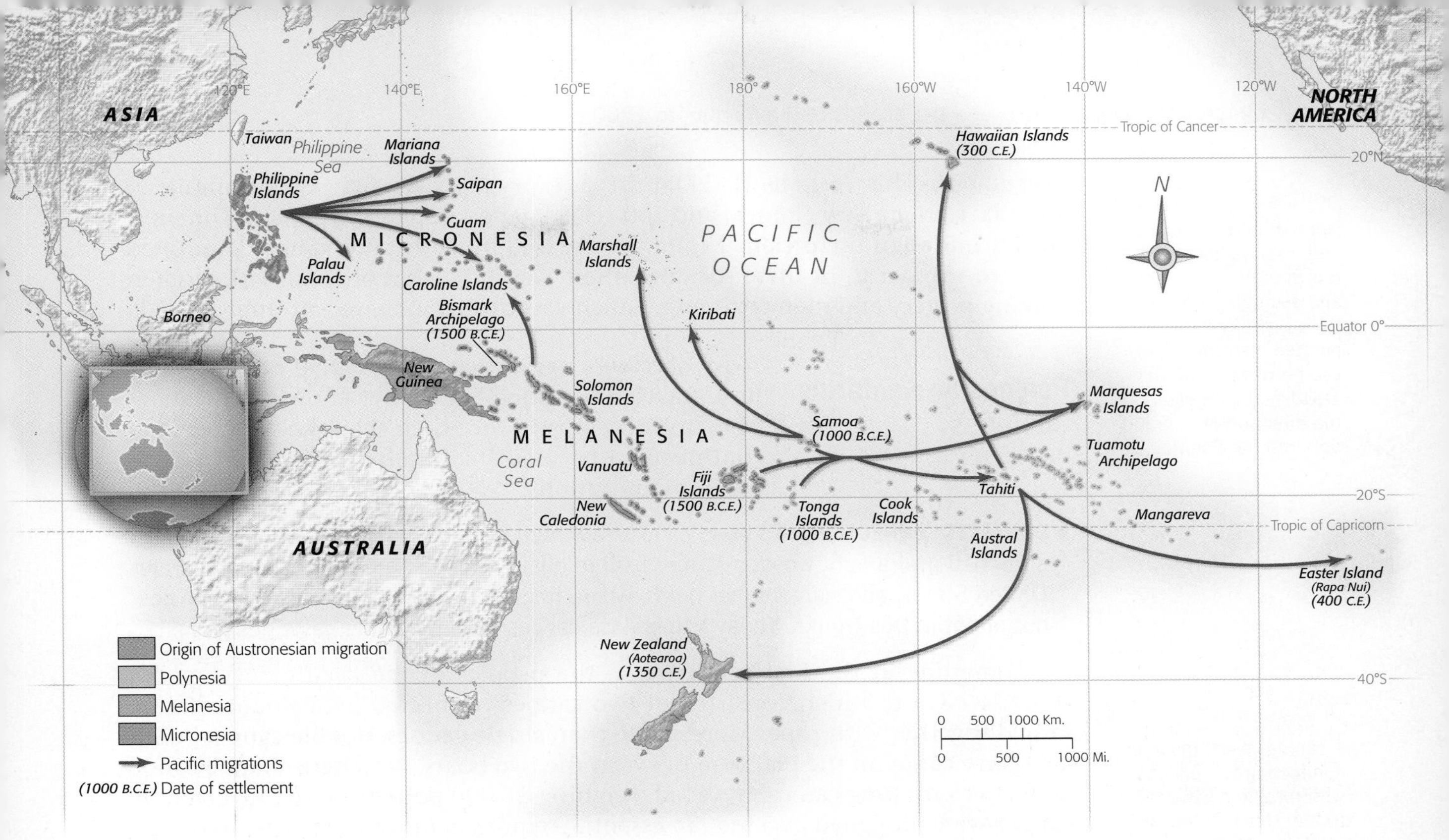

Map 5.2 Pacific Migration Routes Before 1500 Starting around 1000 B.C.E., the peoples living in Micronesia and Melanesia began to go to islands lying to the east in the Pacific Ocean. At first, they took canoes to the islands they could see with the naked eye. But later they traveled thousands of miles without navigational instruments, reaching Hawai'i before 300, Easter Island by 400, and New Zealand in 1350.

triangle linking Hawai'i, Easter Island, and New Zealand (see Map 5.2), with several thousand islands ranging in size from tiny uninhabited atolls to the largest, New Zealand, with an area of 103,695 square miles (268,570 sq km). The triangle's vast area can hold the continental United States twice over with room to spare.

The islands lying close to Indonesia and Australia were settled first. The discovery of Mungo Man in Australia, which dates to circa 40,000 B.C.E., showed that ancient peoples could go from one island to the next in small craft (see Chapter 1). Since the islands of Micronesia and Melanesia were close together, the next island was always within sight. But as these ancient settlers ventured farther east, the islands became farther apart; between Easter Island and Peru lie 2,250 miles (3,600 km) of open ocean. Sometime before 300 the first settlers reached Hawai'i, and after the year 400 they had reached Easter Island, or Rapa Nui (RA-pah nwee). Their final destination, in 1350, was New Zealand.

All the spoken languages within the Polynesian Triangle belong to the Oceanic language family. Languages within the Oceanic family differ only slightly among themselves; while the Hawai'ians say "kabu," meaning "forbidden" or "prohibited," the Tahitian pronunciation is "tabu." (This word has entered English as *taboo*.)

Archaeologists have reconstructed the route of ancient migration, which started from Asia's Pacific coast and traveled east, by tracing the movement of a distinctive pottery with lines and geometric decorations made with a pointed

Lapita pottery
Named for a site in Melanesia, a low-fired brown pottery with lines and geometric decorations made with a pointed instrument. In use between 1500 and 1000 B.C.E., it reveals the direction of migration into the Pacific.

instrument. This **Lapita** (la-PEE-tuh) **pottery** appears first in Melanesia in 1500 B.C.E., then New Guinea, and 500 years later on Tonga and Samoa. The similarities in design on ancient Lapita pottery and modern tattoos have prompted some to wonder if, in these societies, there was a division of labor with women making pottery and men tattooing, which was true in more recent times.

Polynesian Seafaring Societies

Most observers agree that the original settlers must have traveled by canoe but do not know when canoes were first developed. Once their shape was perfected, it continued to be used for hundreds of years with no major modifications.

● **CONTEXT&CONNECTIONS** To build canoes, different peoples have used various coverings stretched over a light wooden frame: bark in heavily wooded areas like the temperate United States, and skins farther north, where trees were scarce. They also dug canoes out of entire tree trunks. Today's fiberglass canoes have the same basic design. ●

double canoe
A sailing vessel made by connecting two canoes with rope to a wooden frame. Used by the ancestors of modern Polynesians for ocean voyages. Capable of speeds of 100–150 miles (160–240 km) per day.

Sometime in the first century C.E., the peoples of the Pacific developed a **double canoe**, which consisted of two canoes connected by a wooden frame lashed together with rope. More stable than single canoes, double canoes could also carry cargo on the platform between the two boats. A modern double canoe 50 feet (15 m) long can carry a load weighing 18,000 pounds (8,165 kg). Double canoes were propelled by a sail, an essential requirement for long ocean voyages, and could reach speeds of 100–150 miles (160–240 km) per day. (See the feature "World History in Today's World: Single- and Double-Hulled Canoes.")

Europeans first described the villages of Tahiti and Hawai'i in the eighteenth century, and many historians assume that Polynesian life in earlier centuries resembled their descriptions. The predominantly male chiefs and their kin lived lives of leisure, supported by gifts of food from the lower-ranking populace. Ordinary people tended crops in fields, which were often irrigated, and also hunted wildlife, mostly small birds.

The settlement of the Pacific resulted from both deliberate voyages and accidental exploration. Early settlers of both sexes must have traveled in boats, because otherwise the settlers could not have reproduced and populated the different islands. The settlers carried dogs and small rats because these animals became their main sources of protein. They found some islands when they were blown off course, most likely in storms.

The voyagers also carried plants, most likely in pots, to all the islands they reached. The staple crops of the Polynesian diet, breadfruit and taro, dispersed throughout the Pacific. Breadfruit, a seedless fruit with the texture of bread when baked, can be quite filling; taro is an edible starchy root plant that is pounded before being eaten.

● **CONTEXT&CONNECTIONS** The distribution of two other plants points to early contacts between the Polynesian islands and South America: the sweet potato and the coconut. The sweet potato originated in South America and later spread throughout the Pacific; the coconut, in contrast, appeared first in Asia and later in Latin America. In addition, excavated chicken bones show that chickens lived in Chile between approximately 1304 and 1424. Prior to this find, many scholars believed that European settlers introduced chickens to the Americas in the 1500s (see Chapter 15), but the similarities between the Chilean and Polynesian chickens suggest that the first American chickens came from Polynesia. ●

WORLD HISTORY IN TODAY'S WORLD

Single- and Double-Hulled Canoes

The Pacific nation of Fiji has more than 300 islands spread across 200,000 square miles (518,000 sq km) of ocean. Islanders can go from one island to another by ferry, but the rising cost of running ferries across such a large area is becoming prohibitive as the price of gasoline goes up. Some islands have ferry service only once or twice a year, and even that depends on government subsidies of up to 48 percent of the cost; the rest of the time islanders travel in their own fiberglass motor boats. A typical fishing boat can easily incur an annual gas bill of more than $4,000 a year.

The high costs have prompted some islanders to return to the traditional canoes of their ancestors, the use of which declined in the 1800s. Equipped with sails and stabilized by a double outrigger, these single-hulled canoes may be making a comeback.

Traditional canoes had some flaws: if too much water entered the hull, the vessel would capsize because there was no way to bail water out. One sixty-one-year-old boat builder, who lost his brother in such an accident, is now designing safer canoes that have Styrofoam inside the hulls, adding floatation and helping to prevent capsizing. The modern canoe builder uses nails and rope rather than the traditional coconut husks. The cost of building these new boats is not high: islanders can recycle water bottles as flotation (instead of the Styrofoam) and use the islands' local trees and other natural resources.

With the help of several nongovernmental organizations (NGOs), the boat designers are hoping to introduce a double-hulled canoe for longer trips, also powered by wind. These can hold some forty people and 4–10 tons (3.6–9 metric tons) of goods, which is particularly important to those who travel to other islands to sell goods at market. The designers also hope that tourists will prefer the traditional boats to more modern sailboats. Since tourism revenues make up one-quarter of Fiji's total gross domestic product, the potential is great, and the designers and NGOs hope that their craft will provide steady employment for those who build the boats. An additional benefit is that the art of building the boats—and using the stars to navigate—will not be lost forever.

Source: Ginanne Brownell, "Looking Forward, Fiji Turns to Its Canoeing Past," *New York Times*, February 3, 2012.

National Library of Australia

A Double Canoe on the Pacific This painting of masked rowers in the Sandwich Islands is one of the earliest Western paintings of a double canoe, the primary mode of transportation throughout the Pacific. Notice that a wooden frame connected two canoes of identical size. The sail gave the canoes additional speed.

The Polynesians may have followed large sea mammals, possibly orca or bottlenose dolphins, as they migrated for long periods over great distances. The first European observers were struck by the Polynesians' ability to travel sometimes up to several hundred miles to go deep-sea fishing.

Traditional Polynesian Navigation Techniques

etak
Traditional Polynesian system of navigation that uses the stars, clouds, waves, and bird flight patterns to steer on sea voyages.

In 1983, seven years after he guided the *Hokule'a* to Tahiti, Mau Piailug taught the traditional system of navigation, called **etak**, to an American named Steve Thomas. Piailug began by making a circular diagram from stones and palm fronds to teach Thomas the most important fifteen stars. Each star rose at one point and set on another on the circle; Piailug knew the trajectories through the night sky of over 150 stars. The start and end point for each star functioned exactly like the points on a compass: north, north by northeast, and so forth (see the photo on page 116).

Studying the skies and allowing for seasonal change, Polynesian navigators used the stars each night to determine their location. Piailug told Thomas which stars would be overhead for different journeys within the Caroline islands, to the Philippines in the west, and to Guam in the north. "*Then,*" Thomas reports, "*to my astonishment, he recorded the courses from Satawal [Piailug's home island] to Pikelot [a nearby island], then north to Hawai'i; from Hawai'i he delineated courses to North America, South America, Tahiti, the Marquesas, Samoa, and Japan. He told me he learned this wofanu [star course] from his grandfather.*"*

At the age of fifteen or sixteen, Piailug was formally initiated as a navigator: because no one after him received this recognition, Thomas called Piailug the last navigator. Although Piailug had not himself followed these different routes, the knowledge of these star courses enabled him to sail all the way from Hawai'i to Tahiti on his first attempt.

In its use of the stars, etak resembled navigation systems in use elsewhere, but the conceptual framework of etak was totally different. In Piailug's mind, his boat never moved through the water. Instead, the islands and water came to the boat and then went past it.

As every sailor knows, the stars are not always visible. Piailug summed up etak's main points: "*In good weather look to the stars. In bad weather look to the waves.*"† Very subtle changes in the waves contained valuable information. As Thomas explains, "*He tried to get me to see a kind of 'tightness' in the water—tiny ripples flowing on the surface, almost like the wrinkles on a weatherbeaten face.*"* Although Thomas could not detect it, he later checked navigational instruments and it turned out that Piailug was absolutely correct: the current was from the west. Using the etak system, Piailug used eight different patterns of ocean swells to determine his direction.

Clouds also contained valuable information. One morning Thomas and Piailug woke up early before the sun was up.

---

*Steve Thomas, *The Last Navigator: A Young Man, an Ancient Mariner, and the Secrets of the Sea* (New York: H. Holt, 1987).

†"By Canoe from Hawaii: Tahiti Trip to Celebrate Bicentennial," *Los Angeles Times*, May 30, 1976, p. D8.

*On the walk up the beach, Piailug stopped to squat in the darkness. A large dark cloud was about to engulf the island, and he casually asked if I thought it would rain. I scrutinized the cloud carefully, wanting to give the right answer. I could feel a wave of cool air against my chest as the cloud approached, but if it was going to rain, I reasoned, this wave would be even cooler and would be followed by a distinctive smell. I said it wouldn't rain. He grunted approvingly.**

Piailug read the clouds just as he read the waves, and he was pleased when Thomas learned to do the same.

Once navigation by the stars brought boats close to land, etak navigators used other means to reach the islands. Certain birds nest on land and then fly far out to sea each day to look for fish before returning to their nests in the evening. Boobies, for example, fly 30–50 miles (50–80 km) each day. Thomas learned that once sailing vessels sighted such birds, they would wait *"for dawn or dusk, and carefully observe the flight paths of the birds,"** which they could then follow to their destination.

The Polynesian system occasionally broke down. Typhoons caused the most problems; on one occasion, when a typhoon destroyed his vessel, Piailug and his crew waited five days in the water before they were rescued; a shark attacked and killed one of the crew. When Piailug was seventy-one, he led a short 250-mile (400-km) voyage between two nearby islands. When he failed to show up two weeks after the date of his expected return, his family asked the Coast Guard for help. Once located, the voyagers explained that they had encountered a typhoon whose strong winds delayed them. But Piailug knew their exact location: they were some 30 miles (50 km) from home and, exhausted as they were, they made their way back on their own. *"I wasn't worried. I knew right away that it was the weather,"* said Junior Coleman, a Hawai'ian who had earlier sailed with Piailug. *"I told people to remember who is involved here. He's the Yoda of the Pacific."*†

Piailug may have died, but the etak system of navigation did not die with him. Today members of the Polynesian Voyaging Society teach etak in Hawai'i's public schools as they continue to use it on long-distance voyages all over the Pacific.

The Mystery of Easter Island

Etak navigation techniques may have brought the ancestors of the Polynesians to the island chains of Hawai'i and Tahiti, but no one knows how they reached Easter Island, the easternmost inhabited island in the Pacific, which lies 1,300 miles (2,100 km) southeast of its nearest neighbor, Pitcairn Island, and 2,250 miles (3,600 km) off the coast of Chile. These distances are less than the 2,400 miles (3,800 km) between Hawai'i and Tahiti, but since Easter Island is a single island only 14 miles (23 km) across at its widest point and not part of an island chain, it would have been extremely difficult for ancient navigators to locate. It was probably settled in 300 by a small party of Polynesians blown far off their original course. Since linguists believe that the Easter Island language retains many more archaic features than that of its neighbors, the early settlers probably

*Steve Thomas, *The Last Navigator: A Young Man, an Ancient Mariner, and the Secrets of the Sea* (New York: H. Holt, 1987). Copyright © 1987, 2009 by Steve Thomas. All rights reserved. Reprinted by permission.

†Mau Piailug obituary, *Washington Post*, July 21, 2010.

had little contact with the other peoples of Oceania after they arrived on Easter Island.

Moai Figures, Easter Island The giant stone figures, or moai, of Easter Island portray ancestral leaders. When alive, the leaders commissioned a statue of themselves that remained horizontal. After they died, the statues were placed in an upright position, and eye inlays of coral and other rock were inserted into the eye sockets. The chunk of red stone on the top of this moai represents a headdress.

Easter Island has two names, neither of which is original. Most English speakers refer to it as Easter Island because a Dutch navigator first glimpsed the island on Easter Day, 1722. In the nineteenth century Polynesian sailors named the island Rapa Nui after the Polynesian Island Rapa, 2,400 miles (3,850 km) to the west, and this is the name currently in use by Polynesian speakers.

The people of Easter Island, like those elsewhere in the Pacific, subsisted on a diet of sweet potatoes, taro, and sugarcane supplemented by chicken, their only domesticated animal. Their garbage pits contain bones of dolphin, porpoise, and tuna, an indication that they also engaged in deep-sea fishing.

All early European visitors to Easter Island noticed the huge statues of volcanic tufa stone, called **moai** (MOH-ai), that dot the island, some taller than 70 feet (21 m). The islanders—who had no metal, only tools of stone, wood, and bone—began to construct the statues during the island's most prosperous period, starting in 1000, when the population reached some fifteen thousand. The most recent count of the moai statues is 887. Some stand on platforms that hold up to fifteen statues. The average weight is around 10 tons (9 metric tons), but the heaviest weighs a massive 270 tons (245 metric tons; it was never moved from its quarry). No two statues are identical. Some have designs showing tattoos and loincloths.

Local oral traditions hold that the statues portray ancestral leaders. The island was divided into small bands, whose leaders built the monuments as an expression of their power. Competition would account for the variation in height of the monuments; as leaders sought to outbuild one another, they erected ever-higher statues.

How could a Stone Age people with no metal tools make statues of such size and transport them? Earlier analysts proposed that the statues must have been brought by outsiders from South America or even outer space, but modern scholars concur that these statues were built and erected by indigenous peoples with no outside assistance. Sculptors used stone choppers and water to hew each statue's basic shape from the soft volcanic rock.

moai
The name for the 887 statues, probably of ancestral leaders, made from tufa volcanic rock and erected on Easter Island around 1000. The largest are more than 70 feet (21 m) high and the heaviest weighs 270 tons.

In 1998, Jo Anne Van Tilburg designed an experiment as innovative as the Polynesian Voyaging Society's sailing from Hawai'i to Tahiti. She found that between fifty and seventy people working five hours a day for a week could move a 12-ton (11-metric-ton) statue 9 miles (14.4 km). Some think that once the stone was at its destination, the Easter Islanders made a series of ramps from dirt, each steeper than the next, to move the statues into a standing position; others think they must have used ropes to hoist the statues into place. Tilburg's findings suggest that the islanders used a wooden frame, giant logs that functioned as rollers, or both to pull the statues from the quarry to their destinations. Although the island has no trees now, it did in the past. One of the largest was a type of palm tree that grew over 65 feet (20 m) tall.

Sometime around 1600 the Easter Islanders stopped making moai. In the end, the different chiefs made war against each other so intensively and for so long, pausing only to create these monuments, that they used up their resources. The activities of the Easter Islanders resulted in the total degradation of their environment: no trees or large animals remained in the eighteenth century. The only large bones available on the island were those of humans, which the islanders worked into fishhooks, and they used human hair to make ropes, textiles, and fishnets, a chilling demonstration of survival with few natural resources.

• **CONTEXT&CONNECTIONS** In 1877, after contact with outsiders, only 111 people lived on Easter Island; today 5,000 people live on the island, of whom only 2,000 are indigenous. •

The Impact of Humans on New Zealand

New Zealand was the final island in the Pacific to be settled by humans. The first artifacts made by humans appear in a layer of volcanic ash dating to circa 1350. Studies of mitochondrial DNA (see Chapter 1) show that the indigenous Maori people of New Zealand were descended from some seventy different female ancestors in a founding population of more than one hundred settlers.

These settlers had a profound effect on the New Zealand environment. Like the Easter Islanders, they demonstrated that environmental damage is not simply a modern development. Within a century after their arrival, twenty different species of birds had died out, and hunters had killed more than 160,000 giant moa birds. Surviving skeletal remains indicate that some twenty different species of moa once flourished on the island; the tallest stood over 10 feet (3 m) tall. After the residents had eliminated the large birds, they preyed on large mammals like seals and sea lions until those populations were also depleted. The hunters then targeted smaller animals. As the supply of wild animals dwindled, the residents became more dependent on cultivation, destroying an estimated 40 percent of the island's forest cover.

AP® THEMES

How did human migrations negatively impact the environments of New Zealand and Easter Island?

When the first Europeans arrived in the seventeenth and eighteenth centuries, they found many small warring bands leading an arduous existence that was the unintended result of their ancestors' overhunting and overfishing.

CONTEXT AND CONNECTIONS

The Different Path to Complex Societies in the Americas and the Pacific

When Mau Piailug steered the *Hokule'a* all the way from Hawai'i to Tahiti without using a single navigational instrument, his journey illustrated an important historical reality: the peoples of the Americas and the Pacific islands took paths to complex society different from those taken by peoples of Eurasia. The peoples who migrated to the Americas and the Pacific islands lived in almost total isolation from Eurasia until around 1500. During the long period of separation, they developed very different ways of adapting to their environments: they farmed differently than Eurasians, they used metal differently, and they navigated differently. Still, some of their societies had occupational diversity, social stratification, and large urban centers, the hallmarks of complex society.

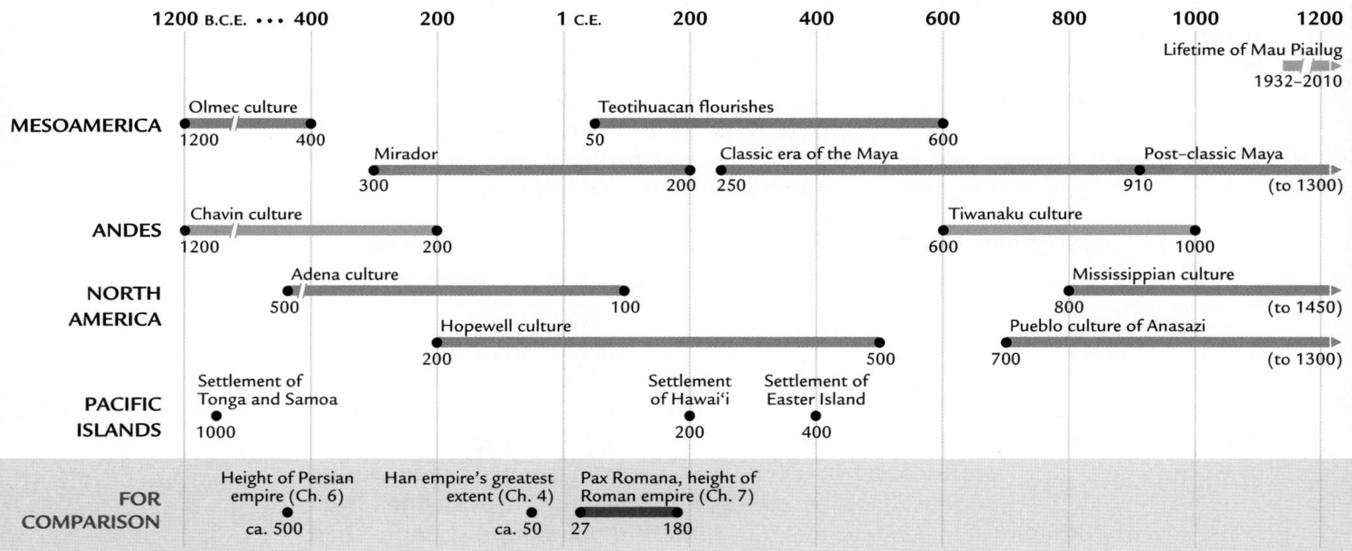

Chapters 2–4 of this book analyze the rise of agriculture and of complex societies first in West Asia, then India, and then China. In each of these regions, agriculture arose in river valleys, and early farmers used tools and domesticated draft animals to raise their crops. Not so in the Americas. The peoples of Mesoamerica cultivated the earliest maize in the highlands and then moved down into river valleys; they never used the wheel, plow, or draft animals. The Andean peoples to the south domesticated both the alpaca and the llama, but they did not employ them as farm animals; the only animals they raised to eat were guinea pigs.

Another important difference lay in the use of metal. Western Asian, Indian, and Chinese metallurgists learned to work bronze, which has a lower melting point, before iron. After they learned how to smelt iron, they made farm tools, particularly plow blades, from iron, which markedly increased agricultural productivity. In the Americas, by comparison, the Maya first worked gold around 1000, but they made few implements from it, preferring knives of obsidian and ornaments of green jade and bird feathers. The Andean peoples had greater experience with metalworking: they made bronze from copper and tin, as the Eurasian peoples did, but also by mixing copper and arsenic, a combination not used in Eurasia. They even worked alloys made from gold and platinum, but they never used iron. The Andean peoples reserved metal for ceremonial and decorative purposes. Like the peoples of Mesoamerica and the north, the Andean peoples preferred tools of wood, bone, and stone. The peoples of the Pacific also used wood, bone, and stone tools for farming and for large-scale projects like carving the moai statues of Easter Island from volcanic tufa stone and placing them upright.

As we have seen in this chapter, the peoples living on various continents developed radically different systems of navigation: as Mau Piailug demonstrated, skilled navigators could cross the Pacific by making use of the information in the stars, waves, clouds, and bird flight patterns. As Chapters 10 and 15 will show, Viking navigators around the year 1000 and European navigators around the year 1500 also used some of these same clues. And while Piailug thought his boat stayed still and the water moved, the Europeans believed that their boats moved and the water stayed still. Whatever their thinking, they crossed the oceans in boats.

The settlement of New Zealand in 1350 by the Polynesian peoples marked the close of the first long chapter in world history: the settlement of all the globe's habitable regions, which began with the departure of the first anatomically modern humans from Africa over a hundred thousand years ago (see Chapter 1). After 1350, no unoccupied land was left other than Antarctica, where humans can survive only with the help of modern technology. After that date, whenever people migrating from their homeland to anywhere else in the world encountered indigenous peoples, conflict almost always resulted.

Key Terms

Mau Piailug (118)
Mesoamerica (119)
Olmec (120)
Long Count (121)
Teotihuacan (121)
Maya (124)
Copán (125)
obsidian (126)
Popul Vuh (126)
Mississippian peoples (131)
Caral (132)
Chavín (133)
Polynesian Triangle (134)
Lapita pottery (136)
double canoe (136)
etak (138)
moai (140)

For Further Reference

Baldwin, Neil. "Can You Hear Me Now?" *Smithsonian*, December 2013, pp. 66–67.

Brown, Chip. "El Mirador, the Lost City of the Maya." *Smithsonian*, May 2011, pp. 36–49.

Coe, Michael D. *The Maya*. 8th ed. New York: Thames and Hudson, 2011.

Coe, Michael D. *Mexico: From the Olmecs to the Aztecs*. New York: Thames and Hudson, 1984.

Fash, William L. *Scribes, Warriors and Kings: The City of Copán and the Ancient Maya*. Rev. ed. New York: Thames and Hudson, 2001.

Finney, Ben. *Hokule'a: The Way to Tahiti*. New York: Dodd, Mead, and Company, 1979.

Finney, Ben. *Voyage of Rediscovery: A Cultural Odyssey Through Polynesia*. Berkeley: University of California Press, 1994.

Flenley, John, and Paul Bahn. *The Enigmas of Easter Island: Island on the Edge*. New York: Oxford University Press, 2002.

Howe, K. R. *The Quest for Origins: Who First Discovered and Settled the Pacific Islands?* Honolulu: University of Hawai'i Press, 2003.

Lewis, David. "Mau Piailug's Navigation of Hokule'a from Hawaii to Tahiti." *Topics in Culture Learning* 5 (1977): 1–23.

Martin, Simon, and Nikolai Grube. *Chronicle of the Maya Kings and Queens: Deciphering the Dynasties of the Ancient Maya*. 2d ed. New York: Thames and Hudson, 2008.

Oliphant, Margaret. *The Atlas of the Ancient World: Charting the Civilizations of the Past*. New York: Barnes and Noble Books, 1998.

Schele, Linda, and Mary Ellen Miller. *The Blood of Kings: Dynasty and Ritual in Maya Art*. Fort Worth: Kimball Art Museum, 1986.

Sugiyama, Saburo. *Human Sacrifice, Militarism, and Rulership: Materialization of State Ideology at the Feathered Serpent Pyramid, Teotihuacan*. New York: Cambridge University Press, 2005.

Films

The Navigators: Pathfinders of the Pacific

Nova: "Lost King of the Maya"

Nova: "Secrets of Lost Empires: Easter Island"

AP® Review Questions for Chapter 5

Multiple-Choice Questions

QUESTIONS 1–4 REFER TO THE FOLLOWING PASSAGE.

Motechuhzoma guided them [the Spaniards] to it. . . . When they arrived at the treasure house called Teucalco, the riches of gold and feathers were brought out to them: ornaments made of quetzal feathers, richly worked shields, disks of gold, the necklace of the idols, gold nose plugs, gold greaves, and bracelets and crowns . . . little gold bells, the royal crowns and the royal finery—everything that belonged to the king and was reserved for him only. . . . On the evening before the fiesta of Toxcatl, celebrants began to model a statue of the god Huizilopochtli. Early the next morning . . . they gathered in front of the idol in single file and offered it gifts of food, such as seed cakes or human flesh.

—The Annals of Tlatelolco, An Aztec Account of the Conquest of Mexico, 1528

1. The description above is evidence of which of the following concepts?
   (A) The use of luxury items to show status
   (B) Early monotheism in the Americas
   (C) Expanded use of wheel technology acquired from the Maya
   (D) The greater influence of local military elites compared with the religious elites
2. The passage demonstrates that the American civilizations
   (A) lacked the social organization found in most Eurasian and African civilizations.
   (B) limited the influence of religious institutions on the state.
   (C) developed some knowledge of metalworking.
   (D) were heavily reliant on the buffalo.
3. Based on the passage, which conclusion can be drawn concerning Aztec society?
   (A) Aztecs lacked the social structure to organize large groups of people.
   (B) The Aztecs had a central authority similar to Eurasian empires.
   (C) Aztec elites were crueler than elites in Asia.
   (D) Amerindian empires developed early versions of democracy.
4. This passage is evidence that Amerindian empires were similar to Eurasian empires in which of the following ways?
   (A) Used religion and rituals to legitimize political authority
   (B) A strong division between religious and political authority
   (C) Domination of all parts of society by religious elites
   (D) Acceptance of multi-religious society

QUESTIONS 5–8 REFER TO THE FOLLOWING PASSAGE.

On the walk up the beach, Piailug stopped to squat in the darkness. A large dark cloud was about to engulf the island, and he casually asked if I thought it would rain. I scrutinized the cloud carefully, wanting to give the right answer. I could feel a wave of cool air against my chest as the cloud approached, but if it was going to rain, I reasoned, this wave would be even cooler and would be followed by a distinctive smell. I said it wouldn't rain. He grunted approvingly. . . . To my astonishment, he recorded the courses from Satawal [Piailug's home island] to Pikelot [a nearby island], then north to Hawai'i; from Hawai'i he delineated courses to North America, South America, Tahiti, the Marquesas, Samoa, and Japan. He told me he learned this wofanu [star course] from his grandfather.

—Steven Thomas, *The Last Navigator: A Young Man, an Ancient Mariner, and the Secrets of the Sea*, 1987, a travel narrative

5. The techniques like those described by Steven Thomas in the passage above most clearly demonstrate
   (A) early Polynesians relied exclusively on technology to make long ocean voyages.
   (B) a deep understanding of the ocean and the climate made ocean travel possible.
   (C) a severe lack of technology made ocean travel impossible.
   (D) the isolation of most Polynesians.
6. Which of the following most resembles the techniques used in the passage above?
   (A) The use of the compass by the Chinese to determine direction
   (B) The increasing use of caravans on the Silk Road
   (C) The irrigation works used by river valley civilizations for crops
   (D) Sailors understanding the monsoon patterns of the Indian Ocean

7. Based on the provided passage, which of the following is an accurate statement concerning the migration of the Pacific Islanders?
   (A) The Pacific Islanders developed sophisticated forms of navigation.
   (B) Pacific Islanders lacked the necessary knowledge to cross the ocean.
   (C) People in the South Pacific relied on Chinese forms of navigation.
   (D) Sailing was used only in religious rituals.

8. The knowledge in the South Pacific seems to have been transmitted primarily through
   (A) cave paintings.
   (B) forms of record keeping similar to those in Eurasia.
   (C) oral tradition.
   (D) pictographs.

QUESTIONS 9–10 REFER TO THE FOLLOWING MAP.

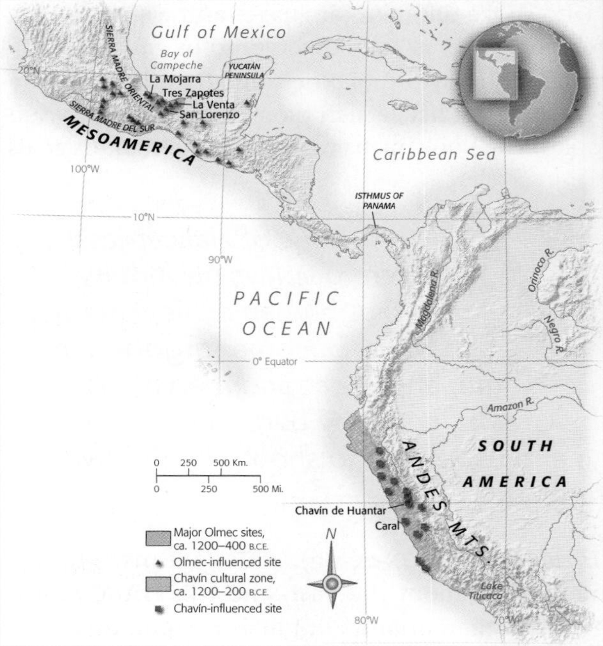

9. Which conclusion can be drawn from the map above?
   (A) Early American complex societies were highly centralized empires.
   (B) Early American societies adapted to a variety of geographies and climates.
   (C) There were significant cultural exchanges between the Olmec and Chavin.
   (D) The early American societies originated from the Mayan city-states.

10. The Chavin adapted to their geography by
   (A) raising a large standing army to deal with invaders.
   (B) enslaving lowland regions to grow food and other necessities.
   (C) developing innovative farming techniques and roads.
   (D) relying on cattle and horses to perform labor-intensive jobs.

Short-Answer Questions

1. Using the above image, answer parts A and B.
   A. Identify and explain the importance of the technology used in this toy.
   B. Identify and explain TWO possible reasons for this technology not being used on a larger scale.

2. Answer parts A and B.
   A. Identify the geographic feature(s) that dominated Inca society and ONE type of challenge the feature(s) presented to the people.
   B. Explain ONE way the Inca dealt with the challenges presented by their geographic location.

6 New Empires in Iran and Greece, 2000 B.C.E.–651 C.E.

Herodotus

Herodotus (heh-ROD-uh-tuhs) (ca. 485–425 B.C.E.) was born to a well-to-do literate family in Halicarnassus (HAH-lee-kar-nuh-suhs) (modern Bodrum), a city on the southwest coast of modern-day Turkey, which was home to a large Greek-speaking community. His hometown was part of the Persian empire ruled by the **Achaemenids** (ah-KEH-meh-nid), which was far more diverse than any previous empire. It governed multiple peoples spread across Afro-Eurasia who spoke different languages and worshiped disparate religions, and so fully deserves to be called a world empire. Herodotus wrote his life's great work, *The Histories*, in Greek about his Persian rulers and their many subject peoples. The book opens with a statement of his goals:

> *Herodotus of Halicarnassus here displays his inquiry, so that human achievements may not become forgotten in time, and great and marvelous deeds—some displayed by Greeks, some by barbarians—may not be without their glory; and especially to show why the two peoples fought with each other.**

Herodotus chose the title *Historia* (hiss-TOR-ee-uh), which means "inquiry" or "investigation," not necessarily about the past, and this is the root of our word *history*. He calls the Persians "barbarians," but he is scrupulously even-handed: as the Greeks have performed "great and marvelous deeds," so too have the Persians.

---

*From *The Histories* by Herodotus, translated by Aubrey de Sélincourt, revised with introductory matter and notes by John Marincola (Penguin Classics 1954, second revised edition 1996). Translation copyright 1954 by Aubrey de Sélincourt. Used by permission of Viking Penguin, a division of Penguin Group (USA) Inc., and David Higham Associates.

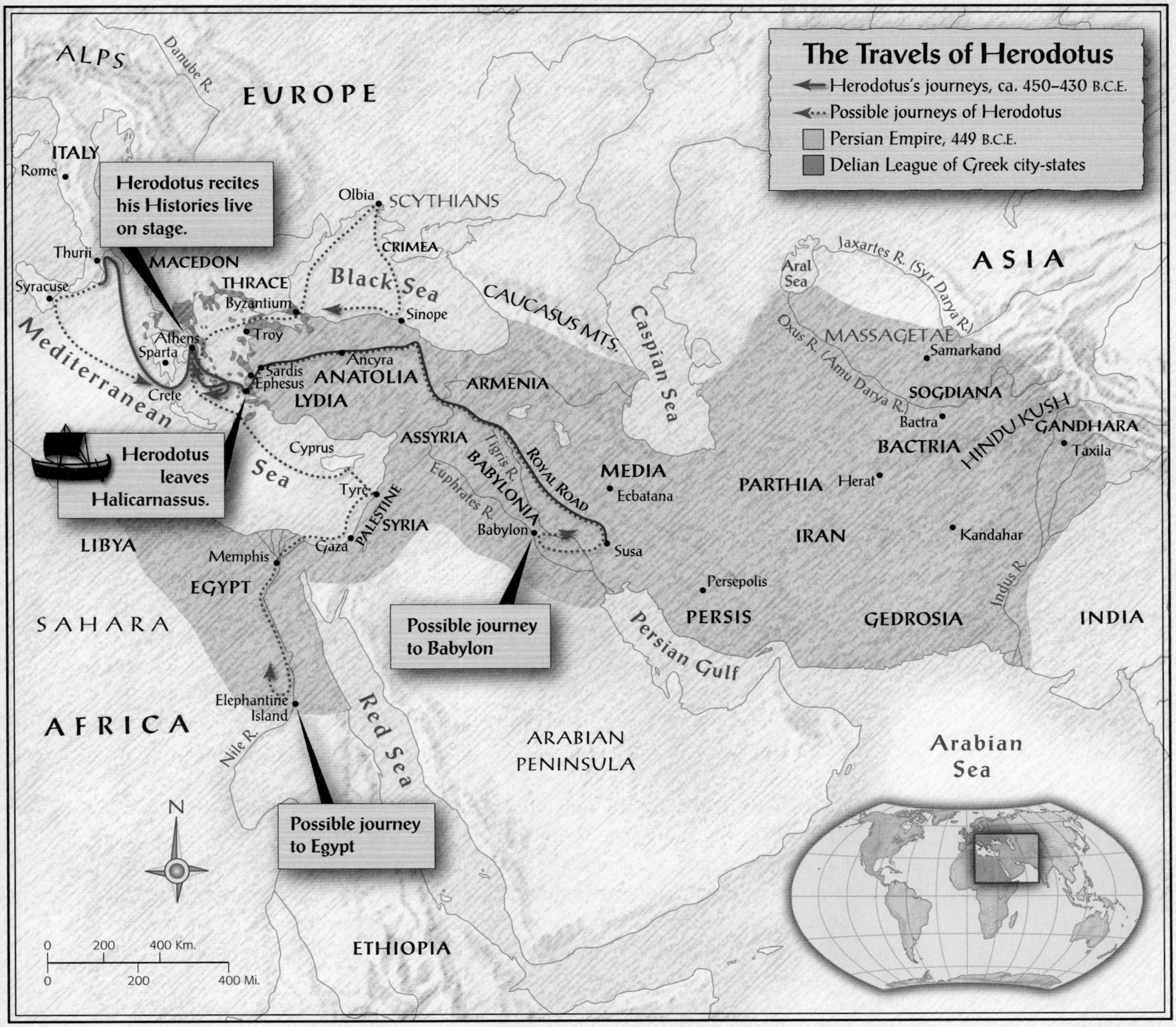

Before recording his work, Herodotus performed sections before live audiences. The world's first stand-up historian, he narrated the events of the past to keep his audience entertained. Characteristically, he launched into one of his most gripping anecdotes immediately following the introduction to his work: an account of how a king forced his bodyguard to hide behind a door and see the queen naked so that he would appreciate her beauty. Contrary to the king's plan, the queen saw the bodyguard, realized that he had glimpsed her nude, and summoned him. She gave him an ultimatum: "*Kill Candaules* [her husband the king] *and seize the throne, with me as*

Herodotus

(ca. 485–425 B.C.E.) A Greek-speaking historian born in Halicarnassus. Author of *The Histories*, an investigation of the history, folklore, geography, plants, and customs of the known world. Known as the "father of history."

Achaemenids

The ruling dynasty in Iran between 550 and 330 B.C.E. The Achaemenids, whose founder was from the region of Persia in the southwest of modern-day Iran, ruled the Persian empire and at its height in the fifth century B.C.E. governed a population estimated at 30 to 35 million people.

*your wife; or die yourself on the spot."** The bodyguard killed the king. The audience realized that the usurper's descendants would pay a price, but they did not yet know what—and so Herodotus's narrative began. The narrative pull is as strong as that of the Grand Historian Sima Qian, who is sometimes called China's Herodotus (see Chapter 4).

Unlike other historians of his time, Herodotus makes it clear when he is including a hearsay account rather than his own observations and openly expresses doubt about some of the taller tales he presents. For this reason, the Roman orator Cicero (SIS-erh-oh) (106–43 B.C.E.) called Herodotus the father of history, a label he retains to this day.

Not a first-person travel account, *The Histories* presents the history, folklore, geography, plants, and customs of the known world in Herodotus's day. In addition to visiting Greece, he must have traveled along the Aegean coast of Turkey and to Italy. *The Histories* claims he visited Egypt, the Crimean peninsula, Sicily, Babylon, and North Africa (see the map on page 145). Herodotus recorded his book sometime after 431 B.C.E. and died soon after, most likely around 425 B.C.E., in the town of Thurii in Italy.

Herodotus devoted his life to explaining the success of the Persian empire, easily the largest and certainly the most powerful empire of its time. From 550 to 330 B.C.E. the Achaemenid dynasty governed a region extending from North Africa to the Indus Valley and from the Arabian Sea as far east as Samarkand in Central Asia. Between 30 and 35 million people lived in the Persian empire.† Up to around 500 B.C.E., the greatest western Asian empires—the Akkadians, the Babylonians, the Assyrians—had been based in the Tigris and Euphrates River Valleys (see Chapter 2); for more than a thousand years after 500 B.C.E., some of the largest empires were in Iran.

The Greeks were among the few who managed to defeat the powerful Persian army and resist conquest. In Athens, during the sixth and fifth centuries B.C.E., a new political system emerged, a system the Athenians called *democracy*, or rule by the people, the ancestor of modern democratic governments. Some thirty thousand men, but no slaves and no women, made decisions affecting the estimated three hundred thousand people living in Athens, 1 percent or less of the total population of the Persian empire.

The Achaemenid rulers developed a flexible type of empire that allowed them to conquer and rule the many different peoples of western Asia for more than two centuries, until the Macedonian king Alexander the Great defeated the Persians in 331 B.C.E. When Alexander came to power, he took over Persian conceptions and structures of kingship intact. Unable to match the Achaemenid dynasty's feat of governing for two centuries, his empire broke apart after only thirteen years. Many different governments rose and fell in western Asia, but those that ruled the most territory

---

*From *The Histories* by Herodotus, translated by Aubrey de Sélincourt, revised with introductory matter and notes by John Marincola (Penguin Classics 1954, second revised edition 1996). Translation copyright 1954 by Aubrey de Sélincourt. Used by permission of Viking Penguin, a division of Penguin Group (USA) Inc., and David Higham Associates.

†M. Aperghis, "Population—Production—Taxation—Coinage: A Model for the Seleukid Economy," in *Hellenistic Economies*, ed. Z. H. Archibald et al. (London: Routledge, 2001), p. 77.

for the longest periods of time—the successor states to Alexander, the Parthians, and the Sasanians—were all monarchies that drew much from the Persian empire.

Note that many of the answers this chapter proposes must be based on the work of Greek writers, including Herodotus, because so few sources in Persian survive.

KEY CONCEPT QUESTIONS

- What techniques of imperial administration did the Persians develop in order to construct and administer their empire? **(Key Concept 2.2)**
- What were the core ideas in Greco-Roman philosophy and science, and how were those ideas put into practical application? **(Key Concept 2.1)**
- How did Alexander's empire serve as a basis for interregional trade, communication, and exchange? **(Key Concept 2.3)**
- What aspects of Persian political forms did the Parthians and Sasanians adapt? **(Key Concept 2.2)**

The Rise of the Achaemenids in Iran, 1000–330 B.C.E.

In approximately 1000 B.C.E., one group of Indo-European migrants arrived in the region of modern-day Iran. These tribal people were largely nomads who did not plant crops but moved their sheep and camel flocks from pasture to pasture seeking fresh grass. The tall mountains of Iran contain streams that drain into the high plateaus; many end in either salt lakes or trickle out into the desert.

Farming was only possible by digging irrigation channels, and the first people who did so lived in the region of Persis in southwestern Iran. (*Iran* is the name of the larger geographic unit, while the English word *Persia* refers to the smaller Persis, which was the cultural heartland of the larger Iran.)

● **CONTEXT&CONNECTIONS** The language of the migrants to Iran, Indo-Iranian, belonged to the same language family as *Sanskrit* (key term in Chapter 3), and their caste system resembled that of Vedic India (see Chapter 3) but had only three ranks: priests, rulers or warriors, and ordinary herders or farmers. Their herding way of life took maximum advantage of the high plateau environment of Iran, which had no major river valley comparable to the Nile, the Indus, or the Yellow Rivers. ●

Starting in 550 B.C.E. the Achaemenids created an empire far larger than any the world had seen before. The dynasty's founding ruler was from Persis and spoke Persian. The Achaemenid realm was larger than several later empires whose rulers came from the region of Persia. It contained some of the world's most advanced cities, such as Babylon and Susa, and some of its most barren stretches, like the deserts of Central Asia. The key innovation in Persian rule was the use of **satraps**: after conquering a region, the Persians appointed a local governor, or satrap (SAH-trap), who was responsible for collecting taxes from the defeated and forwarding them to the capital at Susa.

satraps
The third Achaemenid ruler, Darius, divided his empire into provinces called *satrapies*, each administered by a governor, or satrap. The officials under the satrap were recruited locally, a hallmark of the Persian system.

• **CONTEXT&CONNECTIONS** This flexible system of satrapies suited the many different peoples of western Asia far better than the system used by the Qin and Han empires, which had identical districts all over China (see Chapter 4). •

Zoroastrianism

The Avesta

A book, probably dating to circa 1000 B.C.E. and first recorded in writing around 600 C.E., whose title means "The Injunction of Zarathushtra," the founding prophet of Zoroastrianism. Contains hymns attributed to Zarathushtra himself, which provide our best guide to his original thought.

Zoroastrianism

Iranian religion named for Zarathushtra (in Persian; Zoroaster in Greek), who taught that a host of good deities and evil demons, all in perpetual conflict, populate the spiritual world.

Ahura Mazda

The name of the supreme deity of Zoroastrianism, the Lord of Truth, who created heaven and earth, day and night, and darkness and light.

Our best source for understanding the early migrants to Iran is ***The Avesta*** (uh-VEST-uh), a book that contains the core teachings of their religion, **Zoroastrianism** (zo-roe-ASS-tree-uhn-iz-uhm). Describing pastoral nomads active in eastern Iran, *The Avesta* portrays ancient Iran as having no cities or any political unit larger than a tribe.

• **CONTEXT&CONNECTIONS** Like *Vedic religion* (Chapter 3), Zoroastrianism featured hymn singing and the performance of elaborate rituals, but unlike the ancient Indian religion, it also held that the world was governed by two opposing forces: good and evil. •

Zoroastrianism is named for its founding prophet Zarathushtra (za-ra-THOOSH-tra) (in Persian; Zoroaster in Greek), who lived in the region of Herat, a city in the Iranian highland plateau now located in modern Afghanistan. Scholars have no way to determine when Zarathushtra lived, and informed estimates diverge widely. Sometime around 1000 B.C.E. seems a reasonable compromise. Three thousand years old, Zoroastrianism is one of the world's most ancient religions still practiced today.

Written in an extremely ancient form of Indo-Iranian, *The Avesta*, which means "The Injunction of Zarathushtra," contains a group of hymns attributed to the prophet Zarathushtra himself. First recorded sometime around 600, these hymns provide our best guide to Zarathushtra's original thought.

Zarathushtra believed in a supreme deity, **Ahura Mazda** (ah-HURR-uh MAZZ-duh), the Lord of Truth. Ahura Mazda gave birth to twin entities, the good spirit and the evil spirit. Zoroastrianism is dualistic because it posits two equal, opposing entities: a host of good deities and evil demons, all in perpetual conflict.

Each person, whether male or female, Zarathushtra taught, had to prepare for the day of judgment when everyone would appear before Ahura Mazda. Zarathushtra firmly believed in the ability of human beings to shape their world by choosing between the good and the bad. People who chose the good had to think good thoughts, do good deeds, and tell the truth. Herodotus remarked that young boys were taught to "*speak the truth*,"* the fundamental Zoroastrian virtue. Whenever anyone lied or did a bad deed, the evil spirit gained ground.

Much of Zoroastrian ritual involved fire altars. The Zoroastrians built three permanent fire altars, each dedicated to a different caste group and tended by male hereditary priests called Magi (MAHJ-eye). Towns had fire altars, as did individual households, and worshipers fed fires five times a day, when they recited prayers.

The practice of reciting prayers ensured the transmission of the sacred hymns for a full two thousand years before they were written down. The ancient core texts of Zoroastrianism are still recited by one of the most active communities of Zoroastrian believers today, the Parsis of modern Bombay (Mumbai), India. The Parsis (also spelled Parsees, which means "Persian") left Iran after the Islamic conquest and moved to India sometime between the eighth and tenth centuries C.E.

---

*From *The Histories* by Herodotus, translated by Aubrey de Sélincourt, revised with introductory matter and notes by John Marincola (Penguin Classics 1954, second revised edition 1996). Translation copyright 1954 by Aubrey de Sélincourt. Used by permission of Viking Penguin, a division of Penguin Group (USA) Inc., and David Higham Associates.

The Parsis recite two core prayers. The prayers stress that people should choose the Lord of Truth, Ahura Mazda, because *"Just as the lord in accord with truth must be chosen, so also the judgment in accord with truth. Establish a rule of actions stemming from an existence of good thinking for the sake of the Wise One [Ahura Mazda] and for the lord whom they established as pastor (Zarathushtra) for the needy dependents."* The second prayer continues this theme: *"Truth exists as the very best good thing. It exists under your will. Desire the truth for what is the very best truth."** In short, truth is the highest good, and everyone has the ability to follow and promote the truth.

AP® THEMES

What similarities do you find between the beliefs of Zoroastrians and those of the ancient Hebrews?

The funerary practices of the Zoroastrians differed from those of almost all other ancient peoples. Whereas most peoples buried their dead, Zoroastrians, believing that dead flesh polluted the ground, left corpses outside so that scavenging birds and dogs could eat the flesh; then they collected the cleaned bones and buried them.

The Military Success of the Persian Empire, 550–486 B.C.E.

In 612 B.C.E., an Iranian tribe called the Medes captured the Assyrian capital and brought Assyrian rule to an end. The Medes began to expand beyond Iran's borders into western Asia. In 550 B.C.E. the tribal leader **Cyrus** (r. 558–530 B.C.E.), from Persis, defeated the Medes and founded the Achaemenid dynasty, named for his ancestor Achaemenes. When Cyrus founded his dynasty, his soldiers from Persis were obliged to serve in the king's army and to provide their own equipment. They were not paid but were entitled to a share of the spoils from the cities they conquered.

Cyrus
(r. 558–530 B.C.E.) Founder of the Achaemenid dynasty in Iran. A native of Persis, Cyrus staffed his administration with many Persians as well as Medes, the tribe he defeated when he took power.

As Cyrus's army conquered new territory, the army of citizen-soldiers became a paid full-time army staffed by Persians and other Iranians, the conquered peoples, and large contingents of Greek mercenaries. The most prestigious unit, the king's bodyguard, was called the Immortals, Herodotus explains, because *"If a man was killed or fell sick, the vacancy he left was at once filled, so that its strength was never more nor less than 10,000."*† No records of the size of the army survive in Persian; Greek observers, prone to exaggerate, give figures as high as 2.5 million men, but the army certainly numbered in the hundreds of thousands, if not millions.

To bind their empire together physically and supply the army, the Persians maintained an extensive network of roads. Some were simple caravan tracks through the desert, while others, usually in or just outside the main cities like Babylon, were paved with bricks or rock. The main road, the Royal Road, linked the cities near the Aegean coast with the capital at Susa.

A system of government couriers made excellent use of these roads, as Herodotus remarks:

> *The service is a Persian invention, and it goes like this, according to what I was told. Men and horses are stationed a day's travel apart, a man and a horse for*

---

*The translation from *The Avesta* of the prayers is courtesy of Stanley Insler, Edward E. Salisbury Professor of Sanskrit and Comparative Philology at Yale University (e-mail dated September 4, 2002).

†From *The Histories* by Herodotus, translated by Aubrey de Sélincourt, revised with introductory matter and notes by John Marincola (Penguin Classics 1954, second revised edition 1996). Translation copyright 1954 by Aubrey de Sélincourt. Used by permission of Viking Penguin, a division of Penguin Group (USA) Inc., and David Higham Associates.

*each of the days needed to cover the journey. These men neither snow nor rain nor heat nor gloom of night stay from the swiftest possible completion of their appointed stage.**

Traveling at a breathtaking 90 miles (145 km) each day, government couriers could cover the 1,600 miles (2,575 km) of the Royal Road in less than twenty days; ordinary travelers took three months. The couriers were crucial to the army's success because generals could communicate across large expanses of territory.

The Persian army achieved a long string of military conquests. Cyrus began from his base in Persis, and by 547–546 B.C.E., his troops moved north and west into Anatolia (modern-day Turkey), and its enormously wealthy region called Lydia. There, around 600 B.C.E., people minted **Lydian coins**, the first metal coins used anywhere in the world.

Lydian coins
The first metal coins in the world, dating to around 600 B.C.E. Made from electrum, a naturally occurring alloy of gold and silver collected from the riverbeds in Lydia, a region on the Aegean coast of modern-day Turkey.

Cyrus conquered the various Ionian ports on the eastern Aegean and Syria, Palestine, and Babylon. He did not attempt to change their cultures but made offerings to local gods and allowed his subjects to continue to worship as they had before, a key reason for the success of the Persian empire.

The Cyrus Cylinder, a 9-inch (23-cm) long football-shaped piece of clay that is one of the most famous primary sources from the ancient world, documents Cyrus's policy. The cylinder has an inscription of forty-five lines on its exterior in Babylonian, the language spoken in Babylon in 539 B.C.E., when Cyrus's army took the city from the neo-Babylonians, ended the Babylonian Captivity, and allowed the Hebrews to return home (see Chapter 2). Acknowledging the power of the Babylonian deity Marduk, the text identifies Cyrus as *"king of the universe, the great king, the powerful king, king of Babylon, king of Sumer and Akkad, king of the four quarters of the world, son of Cambyses."*† (Cyrus had just conquered Babylon, and the Sumerians and Akkadians ruled Babylon thousands of years earlier.) Cyrus orders that the statues of deities that had been captured by the Neo-Babylonians be returned to their original temples. Most important, he continues: *"I collected together all of their people and returned them to their settlements."*† Although the cylinder mentions only Babylonia, Assyria, and Iran, and does not mention the ancient Hebrews by name, this statement allowed all the peoples originally resettled by the Neo-Babylonians to return to their homes, including Jerusalem, as the Bible records. (See the feature "World History in Today's World: The Cyrus Cylinder.")

The Cyrus Cylinder records that Cyrus acknowledged the rule of Marduk when he was in Babylon, showing that deities were perceived as having an identity within a given country and that no god was seen as the sole god. As Marduk was the god of the Babylonians, and Ahura Mazda of the Persians, so too was Yahweh the deity of the ancient Israelites.

- **CONTEXT&CONNECTIONS** Although the *Jews* (Chapter 2) practiced their own religion while in Babylon, they encountered and absorbed some of the beliefs of those living

---

*From *The Histories* by Herodotus, translated by Aubrey de Sélincourt, revised with introductory matter and notes by John Marincola (Penguin Classics 1954, second revised edition 1996). Translation copyright 1954 by Aubrey de Sélincourt. Used by permission of Viking Penguin, a division of Penguin Group (USA) Inc., and David Higham Associates.

†John Curtis, *The Cyrus Cylinder and Ancient Persia: A New Beginning for the Middle East* (London: The British Museum, 2013), translation of the inscription by I. L. Finkel on pp. 42–43.

The Cyrus Cylinder

When the British Museum asked Iranian authorities which items they wanted to borrow for a 2010 exhibit, the Iranians requested only the Cyrus Cylinder. And when the British Museum announced that the cylinder would visit five different American museums in 2013, newspapers heralded the document as the world's earliest bill of human rights.

Is this accurate?

In 1971 the shah of Iran celebrated the 2500th anniversary of the Persian empire. Claiming to be the direct descendant of Cyrus, the shah issued commemorative coins heralding the cylinder as an early charter of human rights and implying that he was a similarly generous ruler. Within a decade, the Iranian revolution of 1979 overthrew the shah, and most Iranians associated the cylinder with the excesses of his regime. Their attitude shifted during the Iran-Iraq War of 1980–1988, a prolonged and difficult war with their historic enemy, because the Cyrus Cylinder documents an Iranian victory over Iraq.

Similarly, many Jewish observers applaud the Cyrus Cylinder because Cyrus granted the Israelites religious freedom. Those who call it an early declaration of human rights did not realize that Cyrus's immediate predecessors, the Assyrians and Neo-Babylonians, also allowed subject peoples to practice their beliefs. In truth, none of the ancient kingdoms of West Asia had imposed their religion on subject peoples. But whereas the Assyrians and Neo-Babylonians had forcibly resettled conquered peoples and exiled the Israelites to Babylon, Cyrus allowed them to return home, ending their exile.

In short, the Cyrus Cylinder documents an important relaxation in the treatment of conquered peoples, not a bill of rights. Both Iranian sources and the Bible record Cyrus's order just as *the Epic of Gilgamesh* and the Bible offer variant accounts of the flood story. For this reason it deserves our attention as important historical evidence.

Source: John Curtis, *The Cyrus Cylinder and Ancient Persia: A New Beginning for the Middle East* (London: The British Museum, 2013).

around them. Scholars of Judaism and Zoroastrianism have recently been able to decipher difficult-to-understand passages because of similar wording in Jewish and Zoroastrian texts. Modern scholarship indicates that the Hebrew concepts of the afterlife and of the Devil arose after the sixty-year Babylonian Captivity, and some attribute these new ideas to the influence of Zoroastrianism. ●

The Persian army was not invincible. In 530 B.C.E. in Central Asia, Herodotus reports, the Persians were able initially to gain the advantage against the Massagetae (mass-uh-GET-aye) tribes by offering them wine so that they fell drunk, but the fierce Massagetae recovered and defeated the Persians in hand-to-hand combat. Cyrus died while campaigning in Massagetae territory.

Cyrus's survivors did not place his bones outside so animals would clean them before burial as Zoroastrian teachings required. Instead, they put his intact corpse in a gold coffin covered in textiles and resting on a gold platform, which they placed inside an undecorated square limestone building on top of seven stepped layers resembling a ziggurat (see Chapter 2). Surviving today as a UNESCO World Heritage Site, this monument constitutes a major piece of evidence for those who argue that the Achaemenid rulers were not Zoroastrians even though they worshipped Ahura Mazda as the supreme deity. Achaemenid inscriptions never mention Zarathustra by name, suggesting that his teachings may not have circulated throughout ancient Iran. Other scholars who think that the Achaemenids were Zoroastrian explain Cyrus's burial as a departure from usual burial practices because he was the ruler, not an ordinary believer.

Darius's Coup, 522 B.C.E.

Darius I

(r. 522–486 B.C.E.) The third Achaemenid Persian ruler, who succeeded to the throne by coup. He conquered much territory in Eurasia but was unable to defeat the Scythians north of the Black Sea or the Greeks. He also reformed the empire's administrative structure.

When Cyrus's son Cambyses (kam-BUY-sees) died in 522 B.C.E., a priest named Gaumata (GOW-mah-tah) pretended that Cambyses was still alive and governed in his place. In the same year **Darius I** (r. 522–486 B.C.E.) led a group of six co-conspirators who killed the pretender. At the time of the murder the conspirators had not yet agreed on the political system they would implement. Herodotus (ca. 485–425 B.C.E.) recounted their lively discussion about the best form of government. While one suggested the democracy of the Greek city-state of Athens, another spoke up for rule by a few, or oligarchy (OLL-ih-gahr-key), the governing system of the city-state of Sparta. Darius (dah-RYE-uhs), the future king, vigorously defended rule by one man, or monarchy:

> *One ruler: it is impossible to improve upon that—provided he is the best. His judgment will be in keeping with his character; his control of the people will be beyond reproach; his measures against enemies and traitors will be kept secret more easily than under other forms of government....*
>
> *To sum up: where did we get our freedom from, and who gave it us? Is it the result of democracy, or oligarchy, or of monarchy? We were set free by one man, and therefore I propose that we should preserve that form of government, and, further, that we should refrain from changing ancient ways, which have served us well in the past.**

Herodotus could not possibly have known what was said in a secret conversation that occurred long before his birth in Persian, a language that he did not speak. He must have created this dialogue to enliven his narrative. Persuaded by Darius that monarchy was the best system, the conspirators agreed to choose the future king by seeing whose horse neighed first after the sun came up. Darius's wily groom made sure that his master's horse did so, and Darius became *king of kings*, the Persian term for the ruler of the empire.

Darius commemorated his accession to power in an extraordinary inscription at Behistun, the site of a steep cliff. Blocks of cuneiform text in different languages around the large rock relief brag of the murder of the imposter-king. At the simplest level, Darius's message was obvious: if you oppose me, this is what will happen to you. Darius justified Gaumata's murder by appealing to a higher authority:

> *There was not a man, neither a Persian nor a Mede nor anyone of our family, who could have taken the kingdom from Gaumata the Magian. The people feared him greatly.... Then I prayed to Ahura Mazda. Ahura Mazda bore me aid.... Then I with a few men slew that Gaumata.... Ahura Mazda bestowed the kingdom upon me.*†

---

*From *The Histories* by Herodotus, translated by Aubrey de Sélincourt, revised with introductory matter and notes by John Marincola (Penguin Classics 1954, second revised edition 1996). Translation copyright 1954 by Aubrey de Sélincourt. Used by permission of Viking Penguin, a division of Penguin Group (USA) Inc., and David Higham Associates.

†Richard N. Frye, *The Heritage of Persia* (New York: World Publishing Company, 1963), p. 85.

Darius's Victory: The Stone Relief at Behistun, Iran In 522 B.C.E., Darius ordered this stone relief commemorating his victory over his rivals to be carved over 300 feet (100 m) above the road below. In it, Darius triumphantly places his left foot on the deposed priest Gaumata, who lies dead on his back with his arms dramatically pointing vertically upward. The eight tribal leaders that Darius defeated are shown on the right; the larger figure with the pointed hat was added later. Above the human figures floats the winged deity Ahura Mazda, who looks on approvingly. (Wojtek Buss/age fotostock/Robert Harding)

Darius distributed translations of the inscription throughout the empire, and his account largely matches Herodotus's except for a few details. Most of Darius's subjects were illiterate, though; even Darius had to have the Old Persian text read aloud to him.

● **CONTEXT&CONNECTIONS** Darius's inscription differs from those of *Ashoka* of the *Mauryan dynasty* (Chapter 3) and the *First Emperor of the Qin dynasty* (Chapter 4), both of whom had inherited the throne from their fathers. Darius, however, had killed the reigning king, and his distant family ties to Cyrus did not entitle him to the throne, so he had to justify taking power by claiming Ahura Mazda's support. In addition, Darius's use of languages differed from that of the Qin founder, who used a single language, confident that he could communicate with his subjects in Chinese. The text framing the Behistun relief appears in three languages, because Darius, like Ashoka, ruled a multilingual empire in which people living in the same place spoke different languages. ●

Justifying his rule by invoking Ahura Mazda, Darius also married Artystone (AR-tih-stoe-nay), daughter of Cyrus and half-sister of Cambyses, to bolster his claim to the Persian throne. Darius had several wives, but his favorite was Artystone, who possessed her own palace and wielded genuine authority within her own estate. She organized banquets and trips, and sometimes the king would even take her with him on military campaigns.

Darius's Administration

During Darius's reign, the empire expanded to include Thrace in northern Greece and the Indus Valley in present-day Pakistan, but not the Scythian peoples living north of the Black Sea or the Greeks in Athens (discussed next). Fully aware of the challenges of governing his large empire, Darius instituted a series of far-reaching administrative reforms that held the Persian empire together for the better part of two centuries. He established a flexible administrative and taxation system and implemented a uniform law code for all his subjects.

AP® THEMES

What innovations did Darius introduce into the Persian system of governance?

Seeing himself as transmitting Ahura Mazda's laws to all his subjects, Darius appointed judges for life to administer those laws in his name. Just as on the day of judgment Ahura Mazda would judge each person's good and bad deeds, Persian judges were supposed to examine lawsuits carefully.

As they reformed the courts, the Persians also changed the system of taxation. Herodotus explains:

> *During the reign of Cyrus and Cambyses there was no fixed tribute at all, the revenue coming from gifts only; and because of his imposition of regular taxes, and other similar measures, the Persians called Darius a huckster, Cambyses a master, and Cyrus a father; the first being out for profit wherever he could get it, the second harsh and arrogant, and the third, merciful and ever working for their well-being.**

We must remember that Cyrus had died nearly a century before Herodotus was writing and that Cambyses was reputed to be insane, a judgment with which Herodotus enthusiastically concurred. The view of Darius as a huckster contains an important element of truth: in seeking to put his empire on sound financial footing, Darius revolutionized the way the Persians collected taxes.

Darius introduced satrapies, and the officials under the satrap were recruited locally, a hallmark of the Persian system. Darius required each satrap to submit a fixed amount of revenue each year. The taxes due from many of the different regions were assessed in silver, but Darius allowed several regions to pay some of their taxes in other items: Egypt, the empire's breadbasket, was required to forward 120,000 bushels of grain each year. The Indians, Herodotus explains, paid in gold dust, which they collected from riverbeds, while the Ethiopians submitted an annual quota of "*two quarts of unrefined gold, two hundred logs of ebony, and twenty elephant tusks.*"†

Newly translated documents from the royal ritual center of Persepolis reveal that the Achaemenid ruler donated food and wine to priests of Ahura Mazda. Surprisingly, Darius also made contributions to Babylonian deities as well,

---

*Josef Wiesehöfer, *Ancient Persia from 550 BC to 650 AD*, trans. Azizeh Azodi (New York: I. B. Tauris, 2001), p. 63, citing Herodotus, *The Histories*, trans. Aubrey de Sélincourt, further rev. ed. (New York: Penguin Books, 1954, 1996), p. 89, Book III.

†From *The Histories* by Herodotus, translated by Aubrey de Sélincourt, revised with introductory matter and notes by John Marincola (Penguin Classics 1954, second revised edition 1996). Translation copyright 1954 by Aubrey de Sélincourt. Used by permission of Viking Penguin, a division of Penguin Group (USA) Inc., and David Higham Associates.

providing further evidence that the Achaemenid rulers worshipped Ahura Mazda but were not Zoroastrians. Carved stone friezes at Persepolis (per-SEH-poe-lis), the site of the royal ritual center some 200 miles (360 km) west of Susa, illustrate beautifully the diversity of Darius's empire. (See the feature "Visual Evidence in Primary Sources: The Parade of Nations at Darius's Palace at Persepolis.")

After Darius died in 486 B.C.E., his son Xerxes (ZERK-sees) succeeded him. But in 465 B.C.E., Xerxes's younger son killed both his father and his elder brother. Royal assassinations occurred frequently over the next one hundred years, but the administrative structure the Persians originated allowed them to hold on to their empire until 331 B.C.E., when Alexander defeated them (see page 167).

Ancient Greece and the Mediterranean World, 2000–334 B.C.E.

A branch of the Indo-European speakers reached the Greek peninsula around 2000 B.C.E. The Greek speakers, as well as the Phoenicians (foe-NEE-shuns), were active traders in the Mediterranean. Although historians sometimes speak of the Phoenician and Greek "empires," neither people had a centralized administration governing many different peoples. Instead, both lived in scattered city-states, whose residents had sailed across the seas to establish new outposts that retained their ties to the mother city-state.

Although we tend to think of Greece as a single Greek-speaking entity, whether in earlier times or today, there was no unified nation called "Greece" in the ancient world. Greek speakers saw themselves as citizens of the city-state where they lived, such as Athens or Sparta. By the year 500 B.C.E. Athens emerged as the largest of over one hundred different Greek city-states, and only Athens had a democracy in which all free male citizens, some 10 percent of the city's population, could participate equally. In addition to being a military power, Athens was also a cultural center renowned for its drama, art, and philosophy.

Greek Expansion in the Mediterranean, 2000–1200 B.C.E.

When the Indo-European speakers arrived in Greece, they found that the rocky land of the Greek peninsula, the Aegean coast of Turkey, and the islands of the Mediterranean offered little grass for their herds. No major rivers flowed in these areas. As the Indo-European migrants shifted from herding to farming, they used irrigation channels to distribute water over their fields. They usually planted barley, which was sturdier than wheat, in the lowlands, olive trees in the foothills, and grapes on the hillsides.

The earliest trading centers of the Mediterranean have left ample archaeological evidence. Between 2000 and 1500 B.C.E., the Mediterranean island of Crete was home to a civilization with lavish palaces, well-built roads, bronze metallurgy, and a writing system called Linear A, which has not been deciphered. The archaeologist who discovered the site in the early twentieth century named the residents

The Parade of Nations at Darius's Palace at Persepolis

To document his accomplishments, Darius built an enormous audience hall in Persepolis in modern-day Iran. The hall held 10,000 people and was 62,500 square feet (5,800 sq m), with a roof supported by columns more than 60 feet (20 m) high. Although the original wooden buildings, which were lavishly decorated with curtains, tiles, and paintings, no longer stand, the surviving stone reliefs show the many different peoples of the Persian empire coming to pay homage to their ruler.

The stairways leading to the audience hall have been called "perhaps the most perfect flight of stairs ever built."* Alongside the staircases, stone masons carved reliefs of twenty-three distinct peoples bringing gifts to the king to celebrate the coming of spring, one of the most important ritual occasions in the Zoroastrian calendar. On one side of the staircase the masons depicted the peoples of the empire as seen from the left, and on the facing side, as seen from the right. Each view of the procession occupies three tiers stretching 300 feet (92 m) long, making the frieze the largest mirror image in the world.

The top register, now partially destroyed, shows different regiments in the Persian army: the Persians and the Medes have different headdresses. The soldiers lead the king's horse, two empty chariots, a tent, and the throne for the king. The king himself is not shown.

On the lower tiers, trees divide the friezes into frames that show a small group of men from each place, wearing their native dress and led by a Persian or Median envoy. They carry local products as gifts for the king and guide a native animal. The animals reflect the great reach of the empire: horses from Syria, a humped bull and a wild donkey from Pakistan, a two-humped camel from Central Asia, and an antelope and a giraffe from Ethiopia. The animals are more detailed than the people, whose faces are the same and can be distinguished only by their clothing and different hairstyles.

The portraits capture the essence of the Persian empire. Each subject people occupies the same amount of space in the tableau; tall animals like giraffes are scaled down so that they take as much space as smaller animals like sheep and horses. Each group wears its national dress and offers its own distinctive gifts, while participating in a single procession designed to honor the Persian ruler.

The timing of the monument reveals something important about the Persian concept of empire. Darius began construction in 515 B.C.E., soon after he came to power, and the complex provided vivid testimony of his conquests of many different peoples. Xerxes completed the monument after the Greeks defeated the Persians in 480 B.C.E., but the Persian vision of empire remained unchanged.

The facing page shows a small section of the frieze taken from the left side of the staircase.

---

*R. Ghirshman and E. Herzfeld, *Persepolis: The Achaemenian Capital* (Tehran: Mirdashti Farhangsara, 1999), p. 33.

These Scythians, from the region north of the Black Sea, wear their characteristic pointed hoods and offer a fine horse. ***How does the Parade of Nations illustrate the diversity of the Persian empire?***

This magnificent two-humped Bactrian camel follows Central Asians bearing cups and other gifts from the region east of the Caspian Sea.

These seven men from the impoverished Assyrian empire, defeated in 612 B.C.E., offer low-cost objects: a pair of rams, animal skins, and bowls.

Fine Art Value/Corbis

The Ionians, from the Aegean coast of modern-day Turkey, offer folded bolts of cloth and bowls, most likely of gold.

These trees, like vertical lines in a comic strip, divide the different delegations in the Parade of Nations from one another. Each delegation is led by either a fully robed Mede, as in the bottom panel, or a bare-chested Persian guide, as directly above.

This Armenian groom keeps a close watch on this fine steed, while the countrymen behind him carry bolts of cloth.

the Minoans (mih-NO-uhns) after the king Minos (MY-nohs) who, Greek legends recounted, ruled a large empire with many ships. Archaeologists have found pottery made in the Minoan style all over the Mediterranean and western Asia, evidence of a wide-reaching Minoan trade network.

The Minoan civilization came to an abrupt end in 1500 B.C.E., probably because the Minoans were conquered by the Mycenaeans (1600–1200 B.C.E.). The Mycenaeans (my-sen-EE-uhns) used Linear B script, which remained undeciphered until 1952. In that year, an architect and amateur cryptographer, Michael Ventris, realized what no one else had: Linear B was a dialect of Greek. He used his high school ancient Greek to decipher four thousand surviving clay tablets, which reveal much about the palace accounting system but little about Mycenaean society.

Two epic poems, *The Odyssey* and *The Iliad*, are often credited to the Greek poet Homer (ca. 800 B.C.E.), but this may simply be a name attached to an oral tradition. The poems describe the Trojan Wars that took place centuries earlier between the Greeks and the Trojans living across the Aegean Sea in modern-day Turkey. Archaeologists are not certain whether the Trojan Wars occurred. If they did, it was during the time of the Mycenaean civilization. When the international system broke down in 1200 B.C.E. (see Chapter 2), Linear B fell into disuse, and the final archaeological evidence of Mycenaean culture dates to no later than 1200 B.C.E.

The Phoenicians and the World's First Alphabet

Phoenicians

A seagoing people who, around 900 B.C.E., expanded outward from their base on the Mediterranean coast of modern-day Lebanon. Their alphabet, which used only letters with no pictorial symbols, is the ancestor of the Roman alphabet.

Around this time, another seafaring people, the **Phoenicians**, appeared in the western Mediterranean. The Greeks called this people "red men," *Phoinikes*, or Phoenicians in English, most likely because they produced an extremely rare reddish-purple dye made from the glands of snails. The Phoenicians began to expand outward from their homeland in modern-day Lebanon around 900 B.C.E. They used a new type of writing system: an alphabet of twenty-two consonants. Readers supplied vowels on their own. (Consider the many abbreviations we use when texting.) Unlike cuneiform, this alphabet had no pictorial symbols and depicted only sounds.

● **CONTEXT&CONNECTIONS** The phonetic alphabet was surely one of the most influential innovations in the ancient world because it was much faster to learn an alphabet than to memorize a symbolic script like *cuneiform* (Chapter 2) or Chinese characters. All of the writing systems in the ancient world that existed before Phoenician required students and scribes to learn a new symbol for each word. The still-undeciphered *Indus River Valley* script (Chapter 3) had symbols, and the first Indian alphabets date to Ashoka's reign. Chinese remains a character-based language even today. Cuneiform eventually evolved into a phonetic alphabet, but only after the development of the Phoenician alphabet. ●

By 814 B.C.E., the Phoenicians had established one outpost at Carthage (KAR-thudge) (modern-day Tunis in Tunisia) and subsequently built others along the North African coast and the southern coast of modern-day Spain (see Map 6.1). Herodotus described a Phoenician voyage circumnavigating Africa sometime around 600 B.C.E.: "*Every autumn they [the voyagers] put in where they were on the African coast, sowed a patch of ground, and waited for next year's harvest. Then, having*

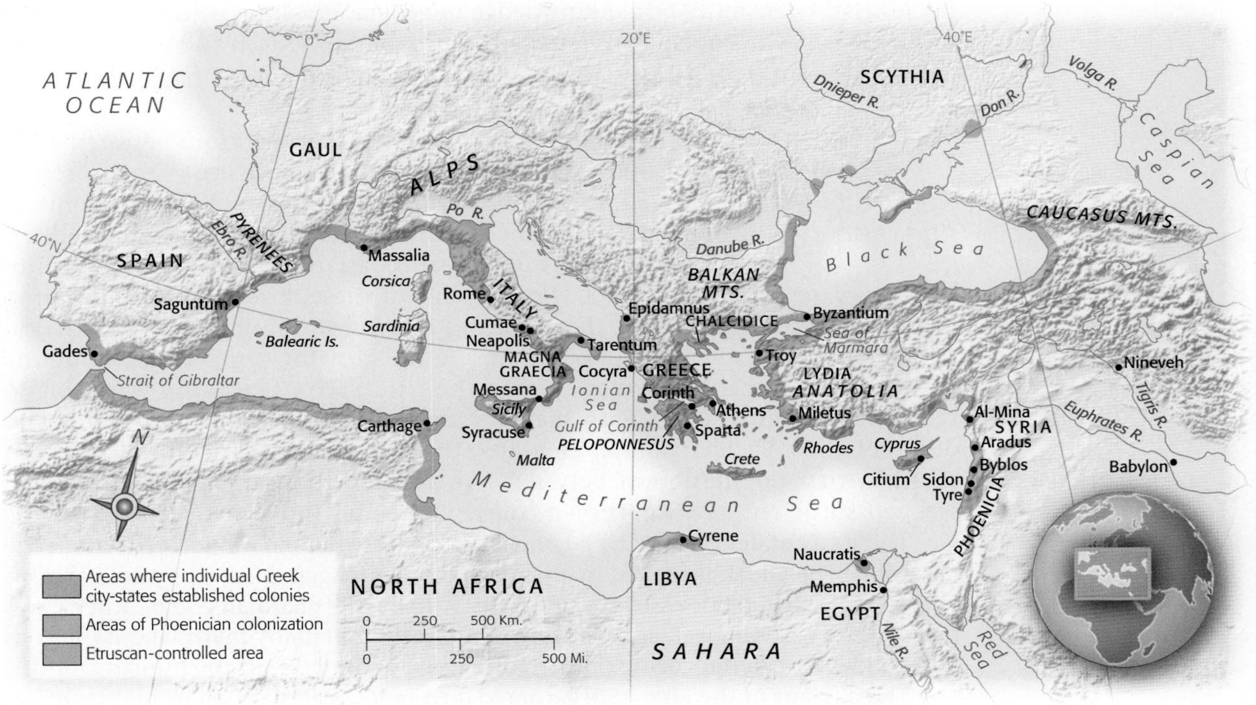

Map 6.1 Greek and Phoenician Settlement in the Mediterranean Starting in 900 B.C.E., the Phoenicians expanded westward into the Mediterranean from their base along the eastern shore; they settled on the island of Sardinia and the North African shore. In 800 B.C.E., settlers from different Greek-speaking city-states left their homelands and formed more than 250 city-states in the eastern Mediterranean and Black Seas.

*got in their grain, they put to sea again, and after two full years rounded Gibraltar in the course of the third, and returned to Egypt."**

The Phoenicians founded new colonies by sending groups of men and women to coastal towns around the Mediterranean and even beyond. We learn this from a Greek account about the Phoenician explorer Hanno, who set off from Carthage in 500 B.C.E. with sixty vessels and thirty thousand men and women. Hanno passed a river and two large gulfs and then captured three "gorillas," probably chimpanzees or baboons. Then he turned back. The vagueness of the description makes it difficult to know how far the Phoenicians traveled, but they may have reached Sierra Leone on the west coast of Africa.

The veracity of both of these accounts—the Phoenician circumnavigation of Africa and the Phoenician visits to West Africa—is much debated because of the lack of independent confirmation, but it is certain that the oceangoing

AP® THEMES

What role did the Phoenicians play in the development of trade networks in the Mediterranean?

---

*From *The Histories* by Herodotus, translated by Aubrey de Sélincourt, revised with introductory matter and notes by John Marincola (Penguin Classics 1954, second revised edition 1996). Translation copyright 1954 by Aubrey de Sélincourt. Used by permission of Viking Penguin, a division of Penguin Group (USA) Inc., and David Higham Associates.

Phoenicians transmitted their knowledge of geography along with their alphabet to the Greeks. The Phoenicians retained control of the western and southern Mediterranean until their defeat by ancient Rome in 202 B.C.E. (see Chapter 7).

The Rise of the Greek City-State, 800–500 B.C.E.

AP® THEMES

What similarities do you find in the way geography shaped the development of Greek states to the way geography shaped the development of early Andean states?

No materials in ancient Greek survive from between 1200 and 900 B.C.E. A new era in Greek history starts around 800 B.C.E., when various regions—including mainland Greece, the islands of the Aegean and the eastern Mediterranean, and the Aegean coast of Turkey—coalesced into city-states (*polis*; plural, *poleis*). The residents of these different places began to farm more intensively, and the resulting increase in agricultural production permitted a diversification of labor among the growing population: while the vast majority of people farmed around the cities, a tiny minority were able to settle inside walled cities with markets for agricultural goods and temples to different gods. Each city-state, including the surrounding agricultural area, was small, with a population of between five and ten thousand people, but each was self-sufficient, having its own courts, law code, and army (see Map 6.1).

These city-states each had a guardian deity whose temple was located within the city walls. The Greeks believed in a pantheon of many gods headed by Zeus and his wife Hera. Each god possessed specific traits: Athena, the guardian god of Athens, was a goddess of wisdom, war, and weaving. The Greeks told many myths about the gods and goddesses, often focusing on their attempts to intervene in the human world.

The citizens of the city-state gathered during festivals to offer animal sacrifices to the gods, with whom they communicated through prayers and oracles. The most celebrated oracle was at Delphi, on the Gulf of Corinth where, before making any important decisions, individuals and city-states consulted Apollo's priests to learn what would happen in the future. People traveled all over the Aegean to pray for medical cures and to participate in temple festivals such as the Olympic games, which were held every four years starting in 776 B.C.E. at the temple to Zeus at Olympia in the Peloponnese.

The citizens of the city-states of Greece went out to establish more than 250 different city-states along the coasts of the Mediterranean and Black Seas (see Map 6.1). Like Mesopotamian city-states, the Greek city-states remained linked to the mother city through trade. Ships carried olive oil, wine, and pottery produced by the Greeks to other regions, where they obtained lumber to make more ships.

During this period, the Greeks adopted the Phoenician alphabet and added vowels. Their first inscriptions date to 730 B.C.E. This new alphabet underlies many modern alphabets, including that of English, because the vowels and consonants could be used to represent the sounds of any language.

During the eighth and seventh centuries B.C.E., most Greek city-states were governed by powerful landowning families, but around 600 B.C.E. several city-states enacted reforms. Sparta became one of the first to grant extensive rights to its citizens. Only the descendants of original Spartans could be citizen-soldiers, who fought full-time and were not permitted to farm or engage in business. A second group, called "dwellers around," were descended from the first peoples to be conquered by the Spartans; entitled to own land, they also worked as craftsmen and traders but could not vote. The lowest-ranking group, full-time state slaves (Helots), cultivated the land of the citizens. Because their husbands were often away at war, Spartan women ran their estates and had more freedom than women in other city-states, yet they could not vote.

Future Spartan citizens joined the army as young children and received an austere military upbringing; only when they had successfully completed military training could they become citizens. Citizens (but not the state slaves) exercised a limited veto over the policies enacted by a council of elders who ruled in conjunction with two kings as an oligarchy.

It took more than one hundred years for Athens to establish democracy. The most famous reformer, Solon (SOH-luhn), became the civilian head of state of Athens in 594 B.C.E. and launched a reform that abolished the obligation to pay one-sixth of one's crop as tax to the state. He also cancelled debts, which made it possible for former debtors to acquire and farm their own land. Athenian citizens formed four assemblies, defined by how much property they owned.

In 508 B.C.E., a group of aristocrats extended Solon's reforms further and established direct democracy. All citizens above the age of twenty—roughly thirty thousand men, or 10 percent of the population, but no women or slaves—could join the assembly, the lawmaking body. Supporters of Athenian democracy proclaimed the importance of liberty, both private liberty to live as one desired and political liberty to participate in decision making. Freedom of speech in the private sphere meant that men could speak their minds freely at home; in the political sphere it guaranteed that men could say anything they liked at the assembly. Political equality meant that all citizens enjoyed equal opportunity to speak before the assembly, even though not everyone had the same social position or the same amount of property. Many, however, were too busy to attend the frequent meetings, which occurred as often as forty times a year. Nevertheless, these important ideals continued even after Athenian democracy came to an end in 322 B.C.E. and reemerged some two thousand years later after 1850, when European thinkers urged the adoption of representative democracy, in which one person spoke for others, a departure from the assembly of ancient Athens.

● **CONTEXT&CONNECTIONS** As earlier chapters have discussed, other societies had assemblies: consider the two councils, one of elders and one of younger men, that *Gilgamesh* (Chapter 2) consulted before he went to war. Athens differed, though, in that these assemblies—and no monarch—ruled. ●

Women could not serve as soldiers or become citizens. The women who enjoyed the greatest security were married; only children born to such couples were legitimate. Athenian men had many other sexual partners, both male and female: prostitutes whom they visited occasionally, concubines whom they supported financially, and slaves who could not say no to their owners.

Roughly two-fifths of Athens's population, some 120,000 people, were slaves, who also did not participate in the assembly. Many different types of slaves existed. Those who had skills and lived with their masters had less arduous lives than those who worked in the fields or in the hazardous silver mines.

The Greco-Persian Wars, 490–479 B.C.E.

The Athenian army was particularly effective because it consisted of citizen-soldiers with a powerful commitment to defend their home city-state. Greek soldiers, called hoplites (HAHP-lites), could defeat the Persians in hand-to-hand combat because they had better shields, stronger armor, and more effective formations. The soldiers were divided into units, called phalanxes, eight men deep. If the first row of soldiers was broken, the row behind them pressed forward to meet the attack.

The first important Athenian victory came at the battle of Marathon in 490 B.C.E., when the Persian ruler Darius sent a force to punish the Athenians for supporting an uprising against the Persians by the Greeks living on the east coast of the Aegean. The Athenian forces of eleven thousand men attacked the Persian army of twenty-five thousand when they were foraging for food and, in a stunning reversal of what every informed person expected, won a decisive victory on the plain of Marathon. Herodotus's tally of the casualties underlines the immensity of the Athenian victory: the Athenians lost 192 men; the Persians, 6,400.

• **CONTEXT&CONNECTIONS** The English word *marathon* comes from a later legend about a messenger running over 20 miles (32 km) from Marathon to Athens to announce the victory. Exhausted by his effort, he then died, according to the legend. •

After Darius died in 486 B.C.E., his son Xerxes (r. 486–465 B.C.E.) decided to avenge his father's defeat and gathered a huge army that he hoped would frighten the Greeks into surrendering. But Sparta and Athens for the first time organized a coalition of the Greek city-states that fought the Persians for control of a mountain pass north of Athens at Thermopylae (thuhr-MOP-uh-lie). The Greeks were eventually routed, but three hundred Spartans stood firm and fought to their deaths. The victorious Persians then sacked the deserted city of Athens.

The Greeks regrouped, and Athenian naval commanders secured a surprising Greek victory at Salamis. In recounting this battle, Herodotus highlighted the role of **Artemisia** (ar-TEM-ee-zee-uh) (flourished 480 B.C.E.), the woman ruler of Halicarnassus (Herodotus's hometown), who had become queen upon the death of her husband and who, like all conquered peoples in the Persian empire, fought alongside the Persians. Artemisia commanded five of the Persians' 1,207 triremes (TRY-reems), three-story boats powered by rowers on each level. *"She sailed with the fleet,"* Herodotus explains, *"in spite of the fact that she had a grown-up son and that there was consequently no necessity for her to do so."** Expecting her adult son would lead the fleet, Herodotus nevertheless thought it perfectly understandable for a woman to command, even if she had small children at home.

Artemisia (flourished 480 B.C.E.) The woman ruler of Halicarnassus, on the Aegean coast of modern-day Turkey, who fought with the Persians against the Greeks at the Battle of Salamis.

• **CONTEXT&CONNECTIONS** Artemisia fascinated Herodotus because unlike well-off Athenian women, who stayed indoors and devoted themselves to managing their households, she led her country's ships into battle. Chinese women, too, occasionally led troops: the oracle bones record that one of the wives of the *Shang-dynasty* king (Chapter 4) who ruled around 1200 B.C.E. led armies on the battlefield. The famous woman warrior Mulan, depicted in a Disney film, actually existed (she lived before the sixth century C.E.), but she belonged to a northern non-Chinese people. Herodotus also devotes an unusual amount of space to the legendary all-female Amazon warriors. Most scholars had assumed the Amazons never existed, but excavations of Scythian graves in modern Russia have uncovered graves of women soldiers who were buried with their armor and their horses. So the Scythians had women fighters, too, but not all-women armies as Herodotus recorded. •

---

*From *The Histories* by Herodotus, translated by Aubrey de Sélincourt, revised with introductory matter and notes by John Marincola (Penguin Classics 1954, second revised edition 1996).

Among the most ferocious opponents that the Persians faced, the Scythians posed a challenge for Herodotus: should he dispassionately describe their violent customs or should he condemn them? This is how Herodotus described the Scythian practice of scalping their dead enemies: the Scythian soldier *"strips the skin off the head by making a circular cut round the ears and shaking out the skull; he then scrapes the flesh off the skin with the rib of an ox, and when it is clean works it in his fingers until it is supple, and fit to be used as a sort of handkerchief."** Herodotus opted for an objective, nonsensationalistic tone that is an early forerunner to modern anthropological analysis.

Herodotus employed contrasts to heighten his comparisons between Greeks and non-Greeks. The Athenians enjoyed the benefits of democracy while the Persians suffered under the tyranny of Xerxes. Greek men were strong while Persian men were weak, which is why Xerxes had to depend on Artemisia. In the inverted world of the war, the only Persian commander worthy of mention in Herodotus's eyes is the Greek woman Artemisia.

Contrary to all expectations, the Greeks defeated the Achaemenids. Defeat, however, had little impact on the Persian empire except to define its western edge. Xerxes returned home to an empire just as large as his father's, and no Persian ruler after Xerxes ever succeeded in adding Greece to his empire.

Hand-to-Hand Combat in Ancient Greece A naked Greek soldier, armed with only a shield and a spear, bests his Persian opponent, who wears a long-sleeved tunic and trousers. In fact, Greek soldiers did not fight naked; they wore armor. Vases depicting Greeks defeating Persians were extremely popular in the fifth century B.C.E.
(Erich Lessing / Art Resource, NY)

Culture and Politics in Athens, 480–404 B.C.E.

During the century after the defeat of the Persians, Athens experienced unprecedented cultural growth. The new literary genres of both Greek tragedy and Greek comedy took shape after 472 B.C.E., when the playwright Aeschylus (525–456 B.C.E.) wrote *The Persians*, the earliest Greek tragedy surviving today. Set in the Persian capital at Susa, the play opens with a chorus of elderly men speculating about Xerxes's attempted invasion of Greece because they have had no news for so long. One-quarter of the way through the play, a lone messenger arrives and mournfully announces: *"A single stroke has brought about the ruin of great Prosperity, the flower of Persia fallen and gone. Oh oh!"*†

*From *The Histories* by Herodotus, translated by Aubrey de Sélincourt, revised with introductory matter and notes by John Marincola (Penguin Classics 1954, second revised edition 1996). Translation copyright 1954 by Aubrey de Sélincourt. Used by permission of Viking Penguin, a division of Penguin Group (USA) Inc., and David Higham Associates.

†Reprinted with the permission of Simon & Schuster, Inc., from *The Persians* by Aeschylus, translated by Anthony J. Pedlecki. Copyright © 1970 by Prentice-Hall, Inc. All rights reserved.

Writing only eight years after the war, Aeschylus (ESS-kih-luhs), himself a veteran, exaggerates the losses to make the audience sympathize with the Persians and emphasizes the shared humanity of the Persians and the Greeks. Xerxes's mother, the queen, struggles to understand why the Persians have lost: they have violated natural law, she eventually realizes, by trying to conquer what did not belong to them. *The Persians* is the first of over one hundred surviving tragedies written during the fifth century B.C.E. by three great playwrights—Aeschylus, Sophocles (sof-uh-KLEEZ) (496–406 B.C.E.), and Euripides (you-RIP-uh-deez) (ca. 485–406 B.C.E.)—that show individuals, both male and female, coming to terms with their fates.

In 478 B.C.E., the Athenians formed the Delian (DEE-lih-yuhn) League, a group of city-states whose stated purpose was to drive the Persians from the Greek world. After several victories in the 470s eliminated the Persian threat, some of the league's members withdrew. Athens invaded these cities and forced them to become its subjects, and in 454 B.C.E. the Athenians moved the league's treasury to Athens, ending all pretense of an alliance among equals. This was the closest that Athens came to having an empire, but its possessions were all Greek-speaking, and its control was short-lived.

In 449 B.C.E. Pericles (PER-eh-kleez) (ca. 495–429 B.C.E.), a general and Athens' most popular leader, used the league's funds to finance a building campaign to make Athens as physically impressive as it was politically powerful. The centerpiece of the city's reconstruction, the Parthenon, was both a temple to Athena, the city's guardian deity, and a memorial to those who had died in the wars with Persia. Once completed, the Parthenon expressed the Athenians' desire to be the most advanced people of the ancient world. Built between 447 and 432 B.C.E., the Parthenon was a two-roomed building surrounded by columns over 34 feet (10 m) tall; one of the interior rooms held a magnificent statue of Athena, now lost. Beautiful friezes inside the roofs and above the columns portrayed the legendary battles of the Trojan War, in which the Greek forces (symbolizing the Athenians and their allies) defeated the Trojans (the ancient counterpart of the Persian enemy).

The Spartans, however, felt that they, not Athens, should be the leader of the Greeks. Since the 460s, tensions had been growing between the two city-states, and from 431 to 404 B.C.E. Athens and Sparta, and their allied city-states, engaged in the Peloponnesian War. Sparta, with the help of the Persians, finally defeated Athens in 404 B.C.E.

● **CONTEXT&CONNECTIONS** Much as the protracted wars among the city-states resulted in the decline of the *Maya* (Chapter 5), the protracted Peloponnesian War wore both Sparta and Athens down, creating an opportunity for the rulers of the northern region of Macedon to conquer Greece (see page 166). ●

Thucydides
(460–395 B.C.E.) Author of *History of the Peloponnesian War*, a pioneering work.

In writing about the Peloponnesian War, the historian **Thucydides** (ca. 460–ca. 400 B.C.E.) pioneered a more scientific approach to history by focusing exclusively on human, not divine, actors. Himself a general, he saw the study of history as a science; as doctors studied the health of a human being, historians studied their political behavior. Later historians in the ancient world, like Plutarch (see page 170), saw Thucydides as the best of the ancient Greek historians and Herodotus as the worst because he overly favored the Persians and included unbelievable and dubious anecdotes. In recent years, though, scholars have realized that Thucydides exercised some creativity (unable to know exactly what historical actors said, he admitted to creating dialog) and that Herodotus's digressions often turn out to be accurate.

© Olga Lipatova/Shutterstock.com

The Caryatids at the Parthenon of Athens The visitor passes this distinctive porch just before reaching the Parthenon, which stands at the top of a high hill. Over 6.5 feet (2 m) tall, these five different female figures (a sixth is now in the British Museum) hold up the roof above them; their elaborate hairstyles add crucial bulk to their necks so that they can support the weight. Artfully, the porch covers a 15-foot (4.5-m) long beam that served as the main support for the entire temple, built around 420 B.C.E. Known as the Caryatids (cary-AT-ids), these imposing statues are among the most memorable sights of Athens.

Athens as a Center for the Study of Philosophy

Even during these years of conflict, Athens was home to several of the best-known philosophers in history: Socrates (469–399 B.C.E.) taught Plato (429–347 B.C.E.), and Plato in turn taught Aristotle (384–322 B.C.E.). Their predecessors, the earliest Greek philosophers, were active around 600 B.C.E. Members of this school argued that everything in the universe originated in a single element: some proposed water; others, air. Their findings may seem naive, but they were the first to believe in rational explanations rather than crediting everything to divine intervention, and the Athenian philosophers developed this insight further.

Socrates

(469–399 B.C.E.) A great philosopher who believed that virtue was the highest good. He developed a method of instruction still in use today, in which teachers ask students questions without revealing the answers.

The Athenian philosopher **Socrates** (SOCK-ruh-teez) wrote nothing down, so we must depend on the accounts of his student Plato (PLAY-toe). Socrates perfected a style of teaching, now known as the Socratic (suh-KRAT-ick) method, in which the instructor asks the student questions without revealing his own views. Many of the dialogues reported by Plato stress the Greek concept of *aretê* (virtue or excellence), which people can attain by doing right. Socrates believed that wisdom allows one to determine the right course of action.

Immediately after Sparta defeated Athens in the Peloponnesian War, a small group of men formed an oligarchy in Athens in 404–403 B.C.E., but they were overthrown by a democratic government. Late in Socrates's life, some in the democratic government suspected the philosopher of opposing democracy because he had associated with those in the oligarchy. In 399 B.C.E. they brought him to trial on vague charges of impiety (not believing in the gods) and corrupting the city's youth. Found guilty by a jury numbering in the hundreds, Socrates did not apologize but insisted that he had been right all along. His death in 399 B.C.E. from drinking poisonous hemlock, the traditional means of execution, became one of the most infamous executions in history. Democratic rule in Athens ended in 322 B.C.E.

Plato
(429–347 B.C.E.) A student of Socrates and a teacher of Aristotle who used the Socratic method in his teaching, which emphasized ethics. He believed that students should use reason to choose the correct course of action.

Plato continued Socrates's method of teaching by asking questions. He founded the Academy, a gymnasium where he could teach students a broad curriculum emphasizing ethics. Gymnasiums had begun simply as an open ground for soldiers to train, but they had evolved into schools where young boys engaged in exercise and studied texts. Plato taught that people could choose the just course of action by using reason to reconcile the conflicting demands of spirit and desire. Reason alone determined the individual's best interests. Plato admitted boys to the Academy as well as some girls. Some scholars contend that all well-off Greek women could read and write, while others think that only a small minority could.

Aristotle
(384–322 B.C.E.) A Greek philosopher who encouraged his students to observe the natural world and explain logically how they proceeded from their starting assumptions. This system of reasoning shapes how we present written arguments today.

Plato's student **Aristotle** (ah-riss-TOT-uhl) was not a native of Athens but was born in Macedon. He studied with Plato for twenty years, returning to Macedon after Plato's death in 347 B.C.E. There he later served as a tutor to Alexander, the son of the Macedonian ruler Philip (382–336 B.C.E.). Aristotle did not share Socrates's and Plato's optimism that knowledge alone would result in ethical behavior because he did not accept their view that human nature was good. He emphasized, instead, that people had to study hard so that they could gain control over their desires.

Observing the round shadow the earth cast on the moon during eclipses, Aristotle concluded that the earth was a sphere and lay at the center of the universe. He urged his students to observe live animals in nature and was one of the first to realize that whales and dolphins were mammals, a discovery ignored for nearly two thousand years. Aristotle required that his students identify their starting assumptions and explain logically how they proceeded from one point to the next. This system of reasoning remained influential in the Islamic world and Europe long after his death and continues to shape how we present written arguments today.

Alexander the Great and His Successors, 334–30 B.C.E.

Alexander of Macedon
(r. 336–323 B.C.E.) Also known as Alexander the Great; son of Philip of Macedon. He defeated the last Achaemenid ruler in 331 B.C.E. and ruled the former Persian empire until his death.

In the course of his lifetime Aristotle witnessed the decline of Athens, which never recovered from the costs of the Peloponnesian War, and the rise of his native region of Macedon. Philip and his son **Alexander of Macedon** (also called Alexander the Great) were autocrats untouched by the Athenian tradition of democracy: as generals they governed conquered territory as if the inhabitants were part of their professional army. As Alexander's army conquered territory, his Greek-speaking soldiers encountered many different peoples living in West, Central, and South Asia. Some settled in these regions and built communities that resembled those they had left behind in Greece.

Philip and Alexander: From Macedon to Empire, 359–323 B.C.E.

Lying to the north of Greece, Macedon, where Greek was spoken, was a peripheral and barren region with no cities and little farming. It became a powerful kingdom under Philip II (r. 359–336 B.C.E.), who reorganized the army into a professional fighting force of paid soldiers. Philip and Alexander built empires by amassing wealth from the peoples they conquered.

Philip created, and Alexander inherited, an army more powerful than any of its rivals. Philip trained his army to use close-packed infantry formations and armed some of the infantry with pikes 17 feet (5 m) long. Alexander's infantry carried the same long pikes, and the infantry phalanx had fifteen thousand men who fought in rows and were almost invincible; 1,800 cavalry aided them by attacking the enemy on either side.

Following his father's assassination in 336 B.C.E., Alexander defeated the Persian forces in 331 B.C.E., and in 330 B.C.E. one of the Persian satraps killed the last Achaemenid emperor, Darius III (r. 336–330 B.C.E.), which allowed Alexander to take over the Persian empire intact; he did not alter the administrative structure of satrapies. A brilliant military strategist, Alexander led his troops over 11,000 miles (18,000 km) in eight years, going as far as Egypt and north India, but did not significantly expand the territory of the Persian empire (see Map 6.2).

Alexander constantly wrestled with the issue of how to govern. Should he rule as a Macedonian or adopt the Persian model? To the horror of his Macedonian troops, he donned Persian clothing and expected them to prostrate themselves before him as the Persian subjects had honored their king. When his senior advisers protested, Alexander made one of many compromises during his thirteen-year reign: he required the Persians, but not the Macedonians, to prostrate themselves. Like the Persian kings, Alexander married women to cement his political alliances; his wife Roxana (ROCKS-ahn-nah) was a native of Samarkand, one of the cities that most vigorously resisted his rule.

The Hellenistic Legacy of Alexander the Great

Alexander died in Babylon in 323 B.C.E. The aftereffects of his conquests lasted far longer than his brief thirteen-year reign. Initially the greatest impact came from his soldiers. Thousands traveled with him, but thousands more chose to stay behind in different parts of Asia, often taking local wives. These men introduced Greek culture over a large geographic region.

Many scholars use the term *Hellenization* to describe the process by which societies, peoples, and places during Alexander's rule became more Greek (the Greek word for Greece is *Hellas*). Recent historians have questioned this depiction of Alexander as primarily a carrier of Greek culture, noting how much he emulated the Persians. Alexander portrayed himself as a defender of the Persian rulers' tradition and adopted many of their practices, sometimes to the dismay of his Greek followers. Recently discovered leather scrolls show that four years after defeating the Persians, Alexander's government issued orders under his name in the same format and language as their former rulers used. The borders of his empire overlapped almost entirely with those of the Persian empire, and his army, administration, and tax system were all modeled on those of the Persians. After his death, Alexander's empire broke into three major sections, each

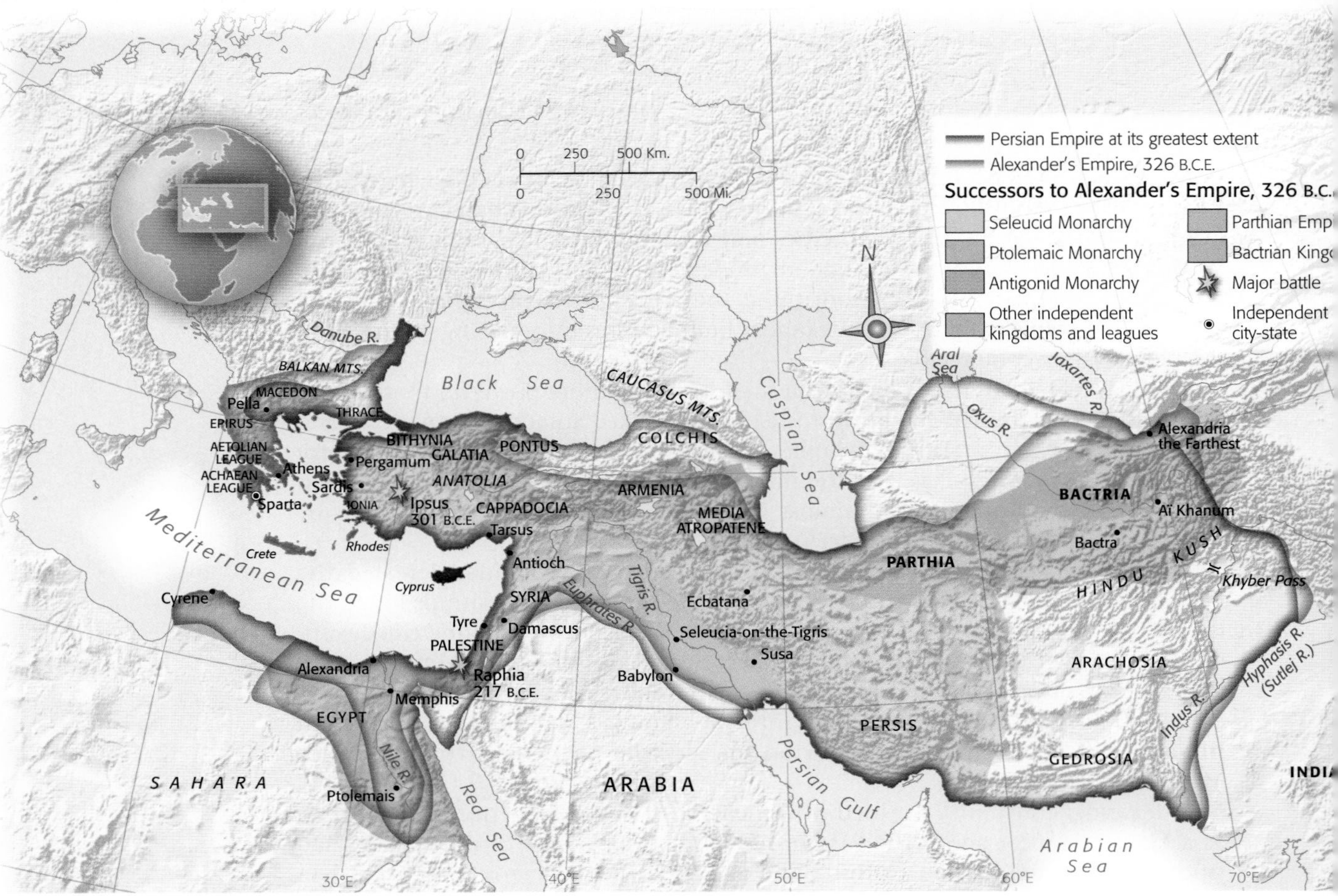

Map 6.2 The Empires of Persia and Alexander the Great The Achaemenids (550–330 B.C.E.), the Parthians (247 B.C.E.–224 C.E.), and the Sasanians (224–651) all formed powerful dynasties in Iran. The largest (shown with a brown border) was that of the Achaemenids. After conquering it in 330 B.C.E., Alexander of Macedon enlarged its territory only slightly. Under the Achaemenids, this large region remained united for over two hundred years; under Alexander, for only thirteen. After Alexander's death, the empire split into three separate empires.

ruled by a successor dynasty that followed Persian practice. (See the feature, "Movement of Ideas Through Primary Sources: Alexander's Hellenistic Policies in Central Asia.")

Hellenism

Formerly seen as a one-way stream of influence in which non-Greek peoples adopted Greek language, education, sculpture, architecture, and other customs, but more recently understood as a two-way process, with non-Greeks and Greeks influencing each other.

Some historians also question the utility of the concept of **Hellenism** as a one-way stream of influence in which non-Greek peoples adopted the Greek language, education, sculpture, architecture, and other customs because of the prestige of Greek culture—often after the demise of Alexander's empire when the Greeks had no political power. These scholars argue that Hellenism was a two-way process, with non-Greeks emulating Greeks, but with the Greeks also absorbing non-Greek ways.

Archaeologists have unearthed an entire Greek city, founded in 300 B.C.E. by Alexander's successor Seleucus (seh-LOO-kuhs), in the Afghan town of Ai Khanum (aye-EE KAH-nuhm), with all the characteristic buildings of a Greek town. The city's planners mounded dirt into an acropolis, or citadel, some 200 feet (60 m) high. A semicircular structure provided a place for the city's residents to watch theater. Other elements of the city, though, drew on different cultural traditions. Like other similar settlements, Ai Khanum included the local Iranian peoples along with descendants of Alexander's soldiers. The palace had long rows of Greek columns, but the layout, with its huge open spaces, was clearly Persian, modeled on Darius I's palace at Susa, which nicely illustrates how non-Greeks contributed to a Hellenistic city.

After Alexander's death, three of his generals each ruled one of his empire's main sections (see Map 6.2): Egypt went to Ptolemy (TOHL-uh-mee), Greece and Macedon to Antigonas (an-TIG-uh-nass), and vast western and central Asian territories to Seleucus, who sent Megasthenes as his ambassador to the Mauryans in 302 B.C.E. (see Chapter 3). Each general founded a regional dynasty named for himself: the Ptolemies (TOHL-uh-meze), the Antigonids (an-TIG-uh-nidz), and the Seleucids (seh-LOO-sidz). These successor regimes continued to administer their territories using the Persian system of administration.

The city of Alexandria in Egypt, founded by Alexander in 332 B.C.E., became a major center of learning within the territory of the Ptolemies. There the Ptolemies welcomed scholars in many different fields, whose interactions produced many important scientific breakthroughs.

A Hellenistic Statue of a Boxer at Rest Found in Rome, this bronze statue perfectly illustrates the spread of Hellenism beyond the territory held by Alexander of Macedon after his death. Continuing Greek traditions celebrating the individual, the sculptor shows the fighter just as he is taking a break. His gloves identify him as a boxer, as do his cauliflower ears, bruises, and gashes all over his body. Blood, crafted from a copper inlay that is a different shade from his bronze body, drips from a cut on his right leg, heightening the immediacy of our encounter with this athlete who lived over two thousand years ago. (DEA / A. DAGLI ORTI / Getty Images)

• **CONTEXT&CONNECTIONS** Because of a long-standing Greek belief that dead bodies should not be touched, Greek scientists did not dissect human cadavers; Aristotle dissected only animal remains. In Alexandria, though, Greek scholars performed dissections on deceased prisoners, possibly inspired by Egyptian experts skilled in mummification (see Chapter 2). Like the palace at Ai Khanum, the practice of dissection shows the two-directional merging of Greek and regional culture. •

Alexandria was a center of mathematical learning. Euclid (ca. 325–ca. 265 B.C.E.) wrote a book entitled *The Elements*, the world's first systematic explanation of geometry, which presented the theorems in logical order. Drawing on Euclid's teachings, sometime around 240 B.C.E., the slightly younger Greek astronomer Eratosthenes (eh-ruh-TOSS-thih-nees), devised an ingenious experiment by which he concluded that the earth's circumference must be 24,427 miles (39,311 km),

Alexander's Hellenistic Policies in Central Asia

About four hundred years after the death of Alexander, the historian Plutarch (ca. 46–ca. 120) wrote two essays about him. The first appeared in Plutarch's *Lives*, an innovative collection of biographies that each paired one Greek with one Roman (in this case, Alexander the Great with the Roman leader Julius Caesar). The second, "On the Fortune of Alexander," appears in a collection of essays on moral topics. Writing as a Greek speaker under Roman rule, Plutarch is often remembered for his account of Hellenism, or Alexander's efforts to spread Greek culture to the non-Greek peoples of Central Asia. In fact, Plutarch devotes considerable attention to Alexander's efforts to win the support of the locals and not simply to force his policies on them, as Plutarch felt that Xerxes had.

› **Historical Thinking Skill:**
ARGUMENTATION **Of the many actions Plutarch cites Alexander as taking in the process of conquest, which action(s) does Plutarch indicate contributed to Alexander's successes?**

› **Historical Thinking Skill:**
INTERPRETATION **How might Plutarch's position as a historian experiencing Roman rule have influenced his perception of Alexander the Great?**

Sources: Plutarch, *Greek Lives*, trans. Robin Waterfield (New York: Oxford University Press, 1998), pp. 355–356; Plutarch, *Moralia*, trans. Frank Cole Babbitt, vol. 4 (Cambridge, Mass.: Harvard University Press, 1957), pp. 397–401 (with some modifications to enhance readability).

"Alexander," from Plutarch's *Lives*

Alexander was worried about his troops refusing to continue with the campaign, so leaving the main body where it was, and taking only the best of them—20,000 foot-soldiers and 3,000 cavalrymen—with him into Hyrcania [the region south of the Caspian Sea], he won them over by telling them that at the moment the easterners could see them face to face, but that if all they did was cause havoc in Asia and then leave, the enemy would regard them as no better than women and not hesitate to attack them. Nevertheless, he left it up to them to leave if they wanted to, and asked that if they did so they should testify that in his attempt to make the whole world subject to the Macedonians, he had been left behind with his friends and those who were prepared to continue with the campaign. This is almost a verbatim quote from a letter of his to Antipater, and he goes on to say that after he had finished speaking they all shouted out loud, calling on him to take them wherever he wanted in the world. Once these elite troops had met this test of their loyalty, it proved easy to win over the main body of the army, which readily followed his lead.

After this, then, he began to assimilate his way of life even more closely with that of the locals, and also tried to get them to adopt Macedonian customs. He was of the opinion that while he was away on a lengthy expedition political stability would follow from fusion and co-operation, achieved through goodwill, rather than from the use of force. This is also why he issued instructions that 30,000 selected children were to learn Greek and to be trained in the use of Macedonian weaponry, and appointed a large number of people to oversee this project. Moreover, although what happened with Roxana occurred because he fell in love with her beauty and grace when he saw her dancing at a banquet, the marriage was also held to fit in quite well with the policy he was pursuing. For the easterners were reassured by the bond the marriage formed, and they particularly appreciated the self-restraint he demonstrated in refusing to lay a finger even on the only woman he ever fell for until it had been sanctioned by law.

"On the Fortune of Alexander"

Alexander did not follow the advice to treat the Greeks as if he were their leader, and other peoples as if he were their master; to have regard for the Greeks as for friends and kindred, but to conduct himself toward other peoples as though they were plants or animals; for to do so would have been to cumber his leadership with numerous battles and banishments and festering seditions. But, as he believed that he came as a heaven-sent governor to all, and as a mediator for the whole world, those whom he could not persuade to unite with him, he conquered by force of arms, and he brought together into one body all men everywhere, uniting and mixing in one great loving-cup, as it were, men's lives, their characters, their marriages, their very habits of life. He bade them all consider as their fatherland the whole inhabited earth, as their stronghold and protection his camp, as akin to them all good men, and as foreigners only the wicked; they should not distinguish between Greek and foreigner by Greek cloak and shield, or sword and jacket; but the distinguishing mark of the Greek should be seen in virtue, and that of the foreigner in iniquity; clothing and food, marriage and manner of life they should regard as common to all, being blended into one by ties of blood and children....

But methinks I [Plutarch] would gladly have been a witness of that fair and holy marriage-rite, when Alexander brought together in one golden-canopied tent an hundred Persian brides and an hundred Macedonian and Greek bridegrooms, united at a common hearth and board. He himself, crowned with garlands, was the first to raise the marriage hymn as though he were singing a song of truest friendship over the union of the two greatest and most mighty peoples; for he, of one maid the bridegroom, and at the same time of all the brides the escort, as a father and sponsor united them in the bonds of wedlock.

Indeed at this sight I should have cried out for joy, "O dullard Xerxes, stupid fool that spent so much fruitless toil to bridge the Hellespont! This is the way that wise kings join Asia with Europe; it is not by beams nor rafts, nor by lifeless and unfeeling bonds, but by the ties of lawful love and chaste nuptials and mutual joy in children that they join the nations together."

Hellespont The Dardanelles strait that connects the Aegean Sea to the Sea of Marmara in northwestern Turkey.

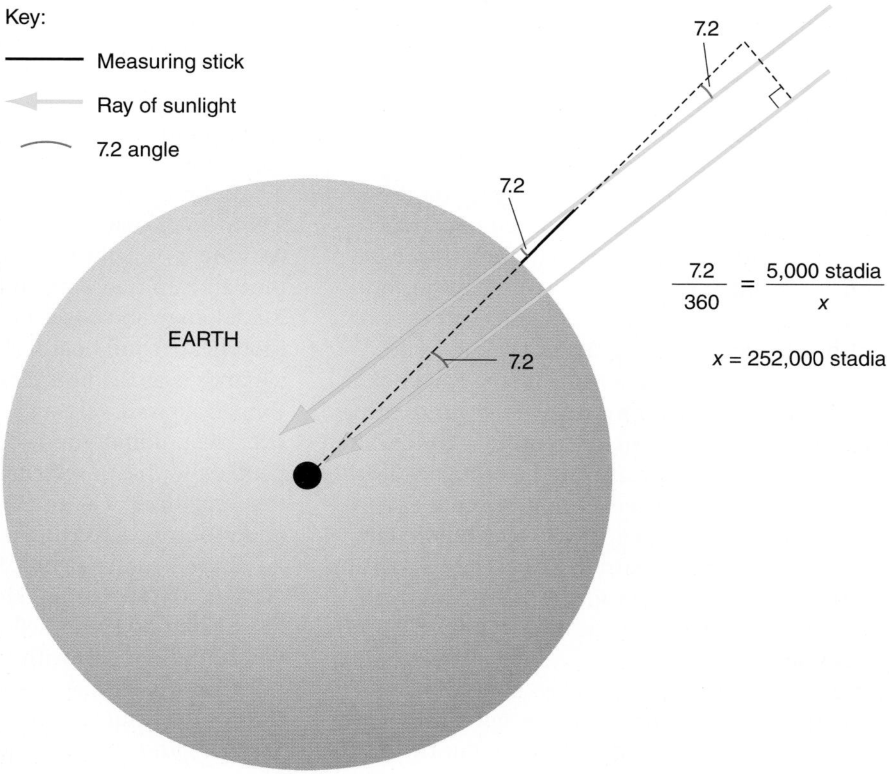

Figure 6.1 **Eratosthenes's Measurement of the Earth** Eratosthenes knew that, on June 21, a ray of light entering a well at the city of Syene cast no shadow because the sun was directly above. At Alexandria, 5,000 stadia away, also at noon, a parallel sun ray cast a shadow of 7.2 degrees on the ground next to a measuring stick. Using the law of congruent angles, Eratosthenes reasoned that 1/50th of the earth's circumference was 5,000 stadia, and therefore the circumference of the earth was 250,000 stadia. His result (24,427 miles, or 39,311 km) was less than 2 percent from the correct figure. (Illustration by Lydia Stepanek)

an error of less than 2 percent from the actual circumference of 24,857 miles (40,000 km) (see Figure 6.1). Eratosthenes' brilliant experiment taught the Greeks that the known world occupied only a small section of the earth's northern hemisphere. Since Aristotle, the Greeks had believed that the earth was spherical, but they had no idea how big it was Eratosthenes answered that question.

The Parthians and the Sasanians, Heirs to the Persians, 247 B.C.E.–651 C.E.

A people based in northern Iran, the Parthians, took Iran from the Seleucids by 140 B.C.E. The **Parthians** (247 B.C.E.–224 C.E.) and then the **Sasanians** (224–651 C.E.) governed Iran for nearly nine hundred years. The two dynasties frequently emulated the Persians; they built monuments like theirs, retained their military and tax structures, and governed the different peoples under them flexibly. The Parthians followed the Persian precedent closely, while the Sasanians experimented more.

The homeland of a seminomadic people who lived in northern Iran, Parthia had been a satrapy within both the Persian and Seleucid empires. In 247 B.C.E., according to a legend, Arsaces I formed a conspiracy to found his own dynasty with six other men. It was no coincidence that he had exactly the number of conspirators that his role model Darius had. The dynastic founder and his successors eventually conquered the Tigris and Euphrates River Valleys and the Iranian plateau extending up to the Indus River Valley in Pakistan (see Map 6.2). The Parthians were Zoroastrians, celebrated for collecting all the surviving holy texts, but they allowed their subjects to practice their own religions.

Parthians
(247 B.C.E.–224 C.E.) The ruling dynasty of Iran, who defeated the Seleucids and took over their territory in 140 B.C.E. Famous for their heavily armored cavalry, they posed a continuous problem for the Roman empire.

The Parthians were celebrated for their fine and fast horses, which were heavily protected by armor. Parthian archers tricked the enemy by pretending to retreat and then turning backward on their mounts to shoot, in a display of archery prowess still known as the Parthian shot. Starting in the first century B.C.E. and continuing through the first and second centuries C.E., the Romans (see Chapter 7) attacked the Parthians at periodic intervals, but the powerful Parthian military always kept them at bay.

Sasanians
The ruling dynasty (224–651 C.E.) of Iran who defeated the Parthians and ruled for more than four centuries until the Islamic conquest of Iran. Introduced innovations such as nonsatrap royal lands and government support of Zoroastrianism.

Parthian soldiers were retainers to the nobles, for whom they performed military service. The king, who called himself "king of kings" in the Persian tradition, stood at the top of Parthian society, and the upper nobility ranked just below him but above the lower nobility. Though not slaves, the retainers had to perform a certain amount of labor and to pay a fixed amount of goods to the nobles they served. Doctors, artists, singing storytellers, and traders formed a middle level between the nobles and the retainers.

Trade was important to the Parthians because they occupied the territory between the Greco-Roman world and their Asian trading partners. In times of peace with Rome the Parthians traded spices and textiles for Roman metals and manufactured goods.

The Parthians ruled for nearly five hundred years, far longer than the two-hundred-year reign of the Persians, and their rule came to an end in 224 when Ardashir, one of their satraps, overthrew them and founded the Sasanian empire (named for his ancestor, Sasan). After defeating the Parthians, the Sasanians incorporated the Parthian forces into their army, of which the armored cavalry continued to be the strongest section. The Sasanian rulers led their powerful army to conquer all the territory of the former Parthian empire, in addition to lands to the east and the northeastern Arabian peninsula.

Sasanian society remained as hierarchical as in earlier times under the Persians. The upper nobility was divided into four ranks, with the king's direct relatives ranking highest and those unrelated to the king lowest. Royal women continued to exercise considerable power, like their earlier Persian counterparts; some of the most powerful rulers' mothers were called "queen of queens." Under the upper nobility were a lower group of nobles, some of whom received their lands and positions directly from the king. The middle ranks included craftsmen, traders, doctors, and singers. At the bottom of society were the cultivators, who had to give a share of their crop to the nobles in addition to the taxes they paid.

AP® THEMES
What was the relationship between social rank and economic or political role in Sasanian society?

Once the Sasanians conquered a region, they divided the territory into two types of land: some was reserved for the king, while that portion entrusted to a

The Sasanian Palace, Ctesiphon, Iran These ruins demonstrate the ingenuity and great skill of the brickmasons, who came from all over the empire and were resettled there by the emperors. The vaulted arch stands 118 feet (36 m) high, making it one of the world's largest brick arches. Its open doorways and fine brickwork inspired Islamic architects, who incorporated these same features into early mosques. [Gerard Degeorge/AKG Images]

satrap was divided into smaller districts. Only on the royal lands could the king establish cities. Like western Asian rulers before him, going back to the Assyrians and the Neo-Babylonians, the king populated the cities with deported peoples, most often skilled craftsmen, drawn from prisoners of war. Under the Sasanians, the resettled peoples could not leave their assigned cities, but they were well paid and were free to marry local women, practice their own religions, and speak their native languages. These skilled craftsmen received high pay for their work as weavers and as builders and engineers who constructed roads and bridges.

After defeating an army of Byzantines (see Chapter 10), the most successful of the Sasanian rulers Khusro (HOOSS-roh) I (r. 531–579) captured many residents of Antioch and forced them to build a copy of their native city that he named "Khusro's Better than Antioch." Located outside the Sasanian capital at Ctesiphon, the new city was complete with Roman baths and a stadium, or hippodrome, for chariot and horse racing, where the Sasanians staged elaborate ceremonies just like those their envoys had witnessed in the Byzantine capital.

● **CONTEXT&CONNECTIONS** As the city of Khusro's Better than Antioch showed, the Sasanian rulers were intensely aware that they governed a region surrounded by other powerful empires. The Sasanian ruler sat on a throne that had three empty thrones around it: for the rulers of Rome, China, and the Eurasian grasslands to the north. One of Khusro's successors honored the Roman emperors by ranking them higher than the other kings simply because they had given him refuge when he was trying to overthrow his predecessor. ●

Aware that many different peoples lived within their empire, the Sasanians encouraged the translation of certain books from Sanskrit, Greek, and Syriac (the language spoken in Mesopotamia). They appointed officials to supervise Zoroastrian observances in each province at the local level, and the state constructed fire altars all over the empire. These government policies made Sasanian Iran actively Zoroastrian, and the Sasanians had difficulty managing the great religious diversity of their subjects.

By the third century C.E. two new religions, each with sizable followings, appeared in Iran: Christianity (see Chapter 7) and Manichaeism (mah-nih-KEE-iz-uhm). Mani (mah-NEE) (216–ca. 274) was an Iranian preacher born in Mesopotamia who believed that his Manichaean teachings incorporated all the teachings of earlier prophets, including Zarathushtra, the Buddha, and Jesus Christ. Like Zoroastrianism, his was a dualistic system in which the forces of light and dark were engaged in a perpetual struggle. Ordinary people could strengthen the forces of light by supporting the Manichaean clergy, who ate only vegetarian food provided by the laity, lived celibate lives, and conducted Manichaean rituals.

● **CONTEXT&CONNECTIONS** Zoroastrianism and Manichaeism typify how world religions differ on the issue of priestly celibacy. These two religions originating in Iran take radically different views of celibacy. While the Manichaean clergy were always required to observe celibacy and not simply when performing rituals, the Zoroastrians never required priestly celibacy, even for rituals, viewing sex as an important activity for humans that was even more crucial for priests because their family lines needed to continue. At the moment of creation, the world was pure, but then it entered into the current age in which good and bad struggle for supremacy. Ultimately, when evil is defeated, the world will return to its original state. Until then, every family should maintain its strength. ●

The Sasanians saw both the Christians and the Manichaeans as threats because they had their own religious hierarchy and refused to perform Zoroastrian rituals. Some rulers directly persecuted members of the two churches. The third major religious community, the Jews, fared better under the Sasanians and were allowed to govern their own communities as long as they paid their taxes.

Adherence to the Persian model of a flexible satrap-based empire allowed the Sasanians to rule for over four centuries, until 651, when their capital at Ctesiphon fell to the Islamic armies of the caliphate (see Chapter 9). A major world empire would not be based again in Iran until 1501 when the Safavids took power, but just as Greek practices exerted influence after the death of Alexander, the term, **Persianate**, matching *Hellenistic,* refers to elements of the various Persian empires that lived on after the fall of the Sasanians. These legacies include ideals of rulership, a rich cultural life at the ruler's court, truth-telling and justice, music, cuisine, and the recitation of Persian verses and epic poems.

Persianate
Elements of the various Persian empires that lived on after the fall of the Sasanians, including ideals of rulership, truth-telling and justice, and the recitation of Persian verses and epic poems.

CONTEXT AND CONNECTIONS

The Persians and Greeks in the History of Empires

Born in the decade of the most intense fighting between Athens and the Persian empire, Herodotus devoted his life to understanding the conflict between the two. Although, as a Greek, Herodotus sympathized with the Athenians, he attributed the Persians' success in other conquests and in expanding their empire to their monarchical form of government and to the innovative policies of their early rulers: Cyrus, Darius I, and Xerxes. Herodotus went all over the Mediterranean to learn about the various peoples who resisted conquest by the Persians and those who succumbed to them. He earned his way as a stand-up historian: in front of live audiences, he recounted the stories that he later included in *The Histories*.

The division of the empire into satrapies allowed the Persians to govern 30–35 million subjects in an expanse centered on modern-day Iran that included modern Egypt, Turkey, and Uzbekistan. The Persian empire was larger than any earlier or contemporary empire, and the rulers tolerated their subjects' diverse languages and religions. This flexible empire differed strongly from Chinese models, which assumed that all subjects spoke Chinese and shared the same religious orientation (see Chapters 4 and 8).

The Persian rulers granted religious freedom as long as their subjects paid their taxes to the center. Unlike in the Roman, Chinese, and Islamic empires, to be discussed in Chapters 7, 8, and 9, the Persian rulers did not force or even encourage their subjects to worship Ahura Mazda. Nor did the Persian kings require their subjects to use the Persian language. The Persians' tax system embodied this flexibility: while much of the empire paid taxes in silver, some regions substituted grain, gold dust, ebony logs, and even elephant tusks. The empire's subjects all served in the Persian army, which was formed of separate divisions for each of the regions in the empire. It was the most powerful military force of its day.

The peoples who avoided conquest by the Persians intrigued Herodotus: he wrote about both the fierce Massagetae who bested Cyrus and the Athenians who turned back successive Persian invasions. The Athenians are notable for their many breakthroughs: the teaching methods of Socrates, the educational ideals of Plato, the scientific inquiries of Aristotle, the plays of Aeschylus, and the histories of both Herodotus and Thucydides. Athens' participatory democracy was an important forerunner to modern democratic governments, although the

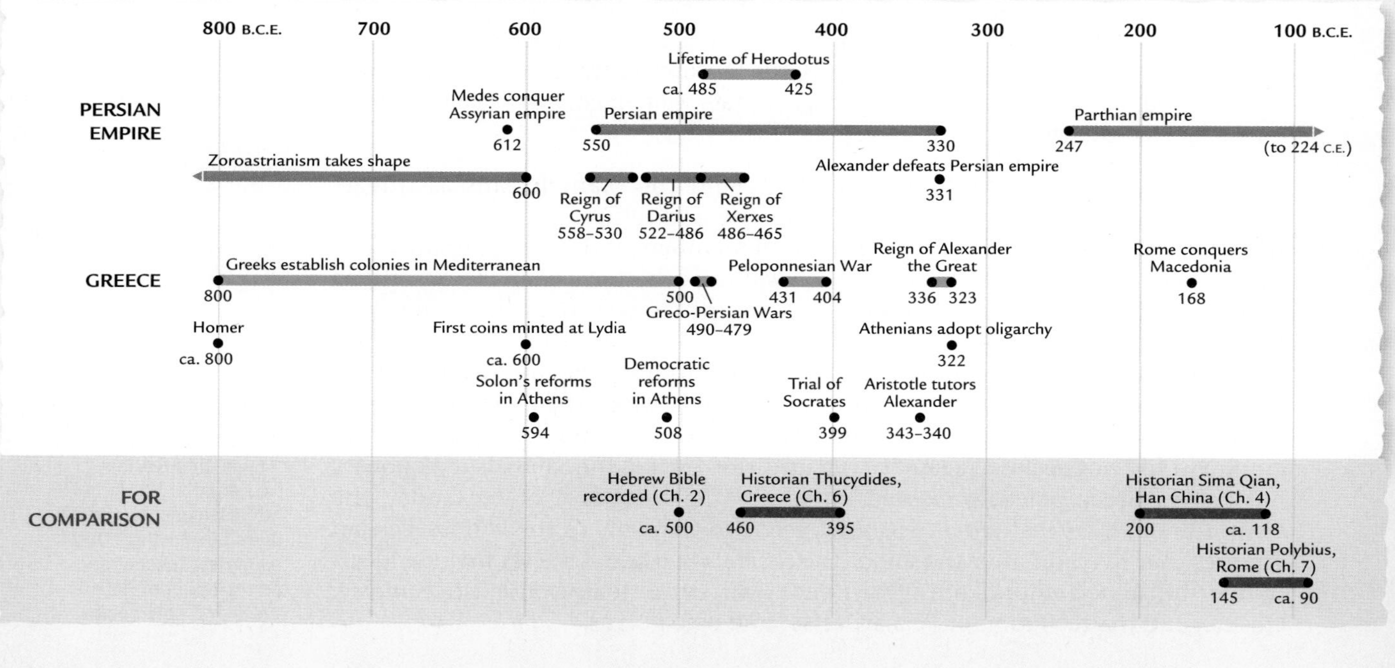

vote was limited to only 10 percent of the population, all men. At most, only three hundred thousand people in the ancient world experienced Athenian democracy, at a time when a hundred times that many people lived under Persian rule.

This chapter has introduced more women than any previous chapter, several of them by name—Artystone, Artemisia, Roxana—as well as unnamed others in both Greek and Persian societies. The increase in documentation, more than in earlier periods, and Herodotus's interest in all people, whether male or female, explain our growing knowledge of women. In Persian kingdoms, the queen of queens played an important if subordinate role to her husband, the king of kings, and Artemisia led ships in naval battles. In ancient Greece, some girls attended schools, and some portion of women could read and write.

Because of the success of the Greek and Iranian states, many peoples with no ties to either culture emulated them in the centuries after their empires no longer existed. The three states that succeeded Alexander—the Ptolemies, the Antigonids, and the Seleucids—are often called Hellenistic, but the term covers peoples outside those kingdoms, like those at Ai Khanum, too. Similarly, after 651 C.E., non-Persian peoples living in non-Persian states who adopted the cultural practices of the Persians are called Persianate. For over a thousand years, the model of a flexible empire based on satrapies was so successful that the Persians, Alexander, the successor states, the Parthians, and the Sasanians all used it to govern their empires. During this time, a very different empire and a powerful military rival to both the Parthians and the Sasanians arose in Rome, as the next chapter will explain. The Romans defeated the last of the Antigonids in 168 B.C.E. and won Egypt from the Ptolemies in 30 B.C.E., but they never conquered the Iranian plateau, testimony to the lasting power of the Persian model for empire.

Key Terms

Herodotus (146)
Achaemenids (146)
satrap (147)
The Avesta (148)
Zoroastrianism (148)
Ahura Mazda (148)
Cyrus (149)
Lydian coins (150)
Darius I (152)
Phoenicians (158)
Artemisia (162)
Thucydides (164)
Socrates (165)
Plato (166)
Aristotle (166)
Alexander of Macedon (166)
Hellenism (168)
Parthians (173)
Sasanians (173)
Persianate (175)

For Further Reference

Allen, Lindsay. *The Persian Empire: A History*. London: The British Museum Press, 2005.

Bernard, Paul. "The Greek Colony at Aï Khanum and Hellenism in Central Asia." In *Afghanistan: Hidden Treasures from the National Museum, Kabul*, ed. Fredrik Hiebert and Pierre Cambon. Washington, D.C.: National Geographic, 2008, pp. 81–105.

Casson, Lionel. *Travel in the Ancient World*. Baltimore: Johns Hopkins University Press, 1994.

Davies, W. D., et al. *The Cambridge History of Judaism*. Vol. 1: *Introduction: The Persian Period*. New York: Cambridge University Press, 1984.

Gruen, Erich S. *Rethinking the Other in Antiquity*. Princeton: Princeton University Press, 2011.

Hornblower, Simon, and Antony Spawforth. *The Oxford Companion to Classical Civilization*. 2d ed. New York: Oxford University Press, 2014.

Kuhrt, Amélie. "The Achaemenid Persian Empire (c. 550–c. 330 B.C.E.): Continuities, Adaptations, Transformations." In *Empires: Perspectives from Archaeology and History*, ed. Susan Alcock. New York: Cambridge University Press, 2009, pp. 93–124.

Markoe, Glenn E. *Peoples of the Past: Phoenicians*. Berkeley: University of California Press, 2000.

Martin, Thomas R. *Ancient Greece from Prehistoric to Hellenistic Times*. 2d ed. New Haven: Yale University Press, 2013.

Nylan, Michael. "Golden Spindles and Axes: Elite Women in the Achaemenid and Han Empires." In *Early China/Ancient Greece: Thinking Through Comparisons*, ed. Steven Shankman and Stephen W. Durrant. Albany: State University of New York Press, 2002.

Yarshater, Ehsan. *Encyclopaedia Iranica*. Boston: Routledge & Kegan Paul, 1982–continuing.

AP® Review Questions for Chapter 6

Multiple-Choice Questions

QUESTIONS 1–3 REFER TO THE FOLLOWING PASSAGE.

Herodotus of Halicarnassus here displays his inquiry, so that human achievements may not become forgotten in time, and great and marvelous deeds—some displayed by Greeks, some by barbarians—may not be without their glory; and especially to show why the two peoples fought with each other.

—Herodotus, Greek historian, fifth century B.C.E., *The Histories*

1. According to the passage, which of the following was a motivation for writing *The Histories*?
   (A) To celebrate the superiority of the Greeks over the barbarians
   (B) To divide the world's societies into levels of success and failure
   (C) To identify and explain historical causes for events in the past
   (D) To celebrate the greatness of the Persian empire

2. Herodotus claims that *The Histories* is based on which of the following?
   (A) A gathering of facts presented with no context
   (B) Inquiry into past events and interpretation of their meaning or significance
   (C) Reliance on tradition to guide the conclusions he draws about the past
   (D) Simple retelling of the stories and legends told to him by others

3. The events described by Herodotus can best be described as which of the following?
   (A) A civilization addressing the challenges of a culturally diverse society
   (B) The decline of Greek civilization due to environmental constraints
   (C) The result of the structure of the Persian bureaucracy
   (D) The use of religion to promote political legitimacy

QUESTIONS 4–7 REFER TO THE FOLLOWING PASSAGE.

After this, then, he [Alexander] began to assimilate his way of life even more closely with that of the locals, and also tried to get them to adopt Macedonian customs. He was of the opinion that while he was away on a lengthy expedition political stability would follow from fusion and co-operation, achieved through goodwill, rather than from the use of force. This is also why he issued instructions that 30,000 selected children were to learn Greek and to be trained in the use of Macedonian weaponry, and appointed a large number of people to oversee this project.

—Plutarch, Greek historian, first century C.E., *Lives*

4. The passage from Plutarch demonstrates that Alexander used which strategy to unite his empire?
   (A) Excluding local elites from imperial institutions
   (B) Imposing theocratic rule over towns by religious leaders
   (C) Incorporating local subjects into imperial institutions
   (D) Using the threat of violence to maintain order within the empire

5. To build greater unity within his empire, Alexander attempted which of the following?
   (A) Incorporating Macedonian and Greek ideals into the local culture
   (B) Encouraging his soldiers to assimilate to the local culture
   (C) Creating a cultural barrier to keep Greek and conquered peoples separated
   (D) Decentralizing political authority and allowing regions greater autonomy

6. The policies established by Alexander continued to affect which region into the Postclassical Era?
   (A) East Asia
   (B) The Mediterranean region
   (C) South Asia
   (D) West Africa

7. Similar to other empires of the time period, Alexander's empire encountered which of the following?
   (A) Difficulty incorporating a culturally diverse population in the empire
   (B) Success in eliminating all cultural rivals
   (C) The refusal of local cultures to allow religion a place in public life
   (D) Suppression of trade throughout Eurasia

QUESTIONS 8–10 REFER TO THE FOLLOWING IMAGE.

8. The large size of the city of Ctesiphon demonstrates which of the following concepts?
   (A) The decline of urban living in the Sasanian empire
   (B) The reliance on seaports to promote interregional trade
   (C) The continuing role of cities as important trade and administrative centers
   (D) The reliance of empires on foreign elites to run bureaucracies

9. The large arches and exceptional brickwork illustrate which of the following concepts?
   (A) The use of monumental architecture to help legitimize imperial rule
   (B) The continued reliance on foreign architecture to build Persian cities
   (C) The exporting of Persian styles to the Greek city-states
   (D) The depopulation of many regions during the time period

10. The palace in Ctesiphon demonstrates which of the following characteristics of the Classical Era?
   (A) Urban centers ceased to play important economic roles.
   (B) Cities tended to play only religious roles in the life of empires.
   (C) Architecture was used to reinforce social hierarchies.
   (D) Important cities were located only on the sea coast.

Short-Answer Questions

1. Answer parts A and B.
   A. Identify and explain TWO policies used by Alexander to unify his empire.
   B. Identify and explain ONE impact of these policies on conquered regions.

2. Answer parts A and B.
   A. Identify and explain TWO geographic features that influenced Greek development.
   B. Identify and explain ONE way the geography influenced political life in Classical Greece.

7 The Roman Empire and the Rise of Christianity, 509 B.C.E.–476 C.E.

Egeria

Kharbine-Tapabor / The Art Archive at Art Resource, NY

Sometime in the late 370s, a wealthy Spanish woman named **Egeria** set off for Jerusalem, where she stayed for three years from 381 to 384. She traveled near the end of a one-thousand-year-long period during which Rome ruled the Mediterranean region. For much of this time the empire was home to different religions. Earlier, the empire had banned Christianity, but in 313 the Roman emperor reversed this policy. In 380, when Egeria was probably on her way to Jerusalem, the emperor went one step further and declared Christianity the official religion of the empire. On her trip, Egeria crossed from the empire's western edge in Spain to the eastern edge in Jerusalem, and she visited the new capital at Constantinople (modern-day Istanbul) as well. Just as she was about to leave for home, in late 383, Egeria wrote from Jebel Mûsâ on the Sinai Peninsula:

*I want you to be quite clear about these mountains, reverend ladies my sisters, which surrounded us as we stood beside the church looking down from the summit of the mountain. . . . From there we were able to see Egypt and Palestine, the Red Sea and the Parthenian Sea (the part that takes you to Alexandria) [the eastern Mediterranean], as well as the vast lands of the Saracens [the Sinai Peninsula, Petra, and el Hisma]—all unbelievably far below us.**

---

*John Wilkinson, *Egeria's Travels* (Warminster, England: Aris & Phillips LTD, 2002), pp. 110–111.

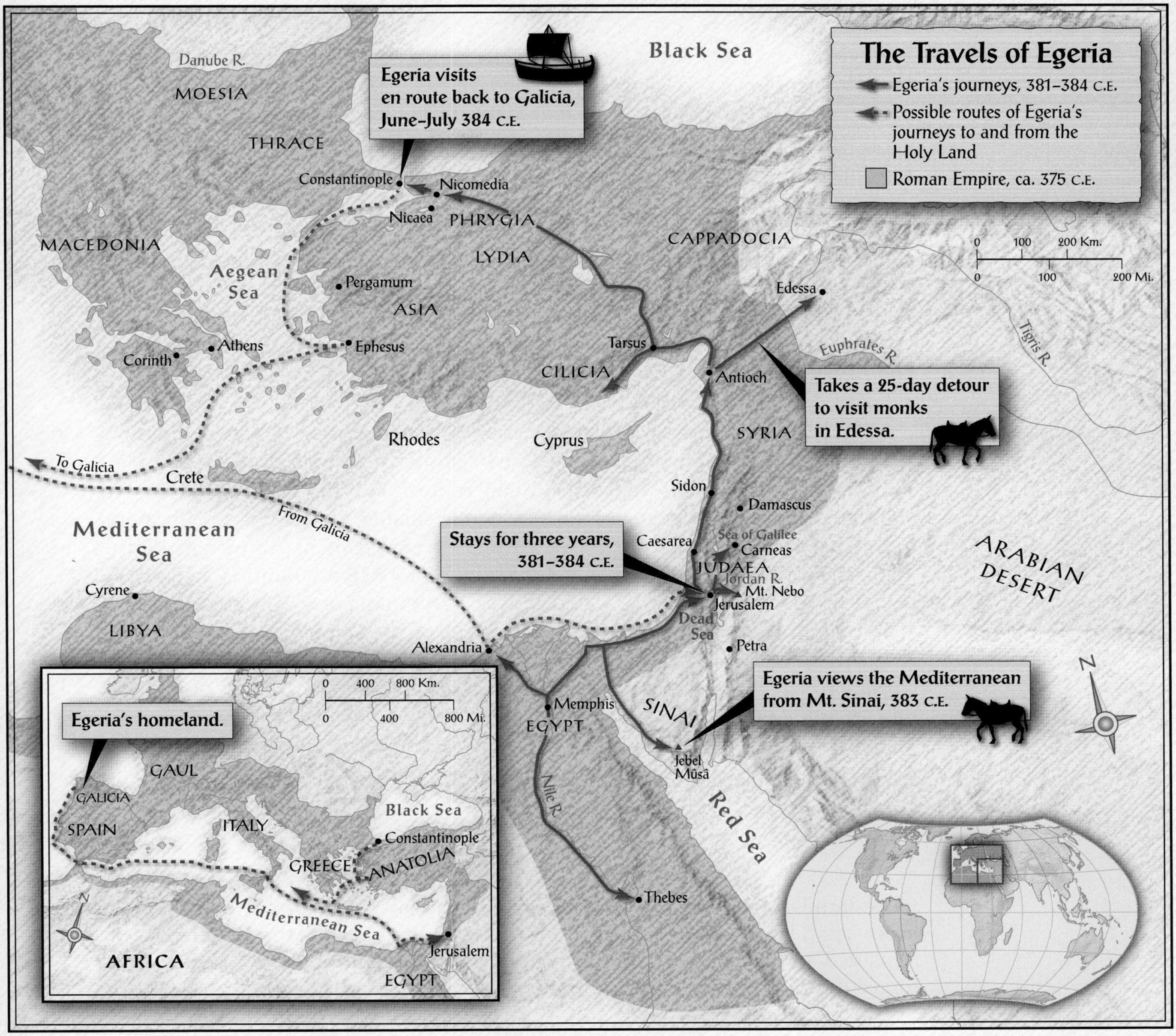

In this excerpt, Egeria addresses her readers *"reverend ladies my sisters,"* suggesting that she was writing to a group of close friends who were members of a female Christian order, probably not nuns because nunneries did not yet exist in western Europe. The first Christian monasteries and nunneries were founded in the early 300s in Egypt, which is one of the reasons Egeria wanted to visit the region.

Egeria
A Christian pilgrim from Spain who visited Jerusalem, Egypt, and parts of modern Turkey between 381 and 384. The dates of her birth and death are unknown.

Much is unknown about Egeria. Only the middle section of her account (the part about modern Israel and Egypt) survives today, having been discovered in the library of a small Italian monastery at the end of the 1800s. That section does not give her name, but a letter written circa 650 from a Spanish monk named Valerius does, allowing the identification of the author as Egeria.

Egeria's purpose in travel was religious: she wanted to visit places and to talk to local Christians about events in the Bible, which she knew thoroughly. Her ability to travel so far and for so long also indicates that she came from a wealthy background. She writes in expressive, colloquial Latin, including the occasional Greek phrase, just as someone might speak it, complete with multiple grammatical errors. Scholars at the time would have taken such Latin as the mark of a poorly educated man, but Egeria was female, and basic literacy would have put her among a small group of elite women.

Travel around and across the Mediterranean was common in Egeria's lifetime. Officials, soldiers, and couriers of the Roman empire proceeded along a network of straight paved roads that ringed the Mediterranean Sea, the heart of the Roman empire. Large boats crisscrossed the sea, while smaller vessels hugged its shore. Individual travelers often purchased passage on government ships transporting grain across the Mediterranean and enjoyed the protection of Rome's navy.

At its founding in 509 B.C.E., Rome was a republic, but a century of political chaos culminated in the adoption of monarchy as the empire's new political system in 27 B.C.E. In the beginning of the Common Era, the new religion of Christianity spread on roads and waterways throughout the Mediterranean region. By 138 C.E., more than two hundred years before Egeria's trip, Rome had conquered the entire Mediterranean region, including western Asia, North Africa, and much of Europe.

• **CONTEXT&CONNECTIONS** Rome's only rival in size was the *Han dynasty* in China (key term in Chapter 4), which had a similar number of subjects (around 55 million people). •

In 330, the empire, increasingly unable to defend itself from powerful tribes in western Europe, moved to a new capital in the east. Even long after the empire broke apart more than a century following Egeria's death, the Mediterranean remained a coherent geographical region with shared cultural and linguistic ties forged during the nearly one thousand years of Roman rule.

KEY CONCEPT QUESTIONS

› What cultural characteristics did Rome possess that allowed it to administer such a large empire? **(Key Concept 2.2)**

› What administrative and social institutions did Rome create in order govern its empire, and how did those institutions change with the transition from republican Rome to imperial Rome? **(Key Concept 2.2)**

› What were the core beliefs of Christianity, and why were those beliefs so appealing to people in the Roman empire? **(Key Concept 2.1)**

› What were the political, cultural, and administrative reasons for the collapse of the Western Roman empire? **(Key Concept 2.2)**

The Roman Republic, 509–27 B.C.E.

In its early years Rome was but one of many city-states on the Italian peninsula, but one with an unusual policy toward defeated enemies: once a neighboring city-state surrendered to Rome, Rome's leaders offered its citizens a chance to join forces with them. As a result of this policy, more and more men joined Rome's army, and it became almost unstoppable. By 272 B.C.E. Rome had conquered the Italian peninsula. In 202 B.C.E., after defeating Carthage, it dominated the western Mediterranean, and in 146 B.C.E., after defeating a Greek coalition it again defeated Carthage. Only with the conquest of all the successor states to Alexander of Macedon in 133 B.C.E. did it gain control of the entire Mediterranean.

Those conquests were the crucial first step in the formation of the Mediterranean as a geographical region. The Greek historian **Polybius** (poh-LIH-bee-us) (ca. 200–ca. 118 B.C.E.), who was sent to Rome indefinitely as a hostage, provides the most detailed explanation of Rome's success in his book, *The Rise of the Roman Empire*. After 146 B.C.E., Rome's armies continued to win territory, but the violence and civil wars of the first century B.C.E. brought an end to the republic in 27 B.C.E.

Polybius
(ca. 200–ca. 118 B.C.E.) A Greek historian who was deported to Rome, where he wrote *The Rise of the Roman Empire*. Believed the task of the historian was to distinguish underlying causes of events.

Early Rome to 509 B.C.E.

The city of Rome lies in the middle of the boot-shaped peninsula of Italy. One chain of mountains, the Apennines (AP-puh-nines), runs down the spine of Italy, while the Alps form a natural barrier to the north. Italy's volcanic soil is more fertile than Greece's, and many different crops flourished in the temperate Mediterranean climate. Several large islands, including Sardinia and Corsica, lie to the west of Italy; immediately to the south, the island of Sicily forms a natural stepping stone across the Mediterranean to modern-day Tunisia, Africa, only 100 miles (160 km) away.

Written sources reveal little about Rome's origins. The earliest surviving history of Rome, by Livy, dates to the first century B.C.E., nearly one thousand years after the site of Rome was first settled in 1000 B.C.E. The city's original site lay 16 miles (26 km) from the Tyrrhenian Sea at a point where the shallow Tiber River could be crossed easily. The seven hills of the settlement formed a natural defense, and from the beginning people gathered there to trade.

AP® THEMES
What environmental characteristics helped establish Rome as a center for commerce?

Romans grew up hearing a myth, also recorded by Livy, about the founding of their city by two twin brothers, Romulus and Remus, grandsons of the rightful king. An evil king who had seized power ordered a servant to kill them, but the servant abandoned them instead. Raised by a wolf, the twins survived, and Romulus went on to found Rome in 753 B.C.E. This legend is not unique to Rome; it is a Romanized version of a western Asian myth. At this time, Rome consisted of small communities surrounded by walls.

• **CONTEXT&CONNECTIONS** During the sixth and fifth centuries B.C.E., when the Persian and the Greek empires were vying for power, Rome was an obscure backwater. Greek colonists had settled in southern Italy, and their cities were larger and far better planned than Rome. •

The Romans learned city planning, sewage management, and wall construction from their Etruscan neighbors to the north. The Etruscans modified the Greek alphabet to write their own language, which the Romans in turn adopted around 600 B.C.E. to record their first inscriptions in their native Latin, a language in the Indo-European family.

The Early Republic and the Conquest of Italy, 509–272 B.C.E.

The earliest form of government in the Roman city-state was a monarchy. The first kings governed in consultation with an assembly composed of men from Rome's most prominent and wealthiest families, the patricians (puh-TRISH-uhns), who owned large landholdings and formed a privileged social group distinct from the plebians (pluh-BEE-uhns), or commoners. Each time the king died, the patrician assembly chose his successor, not necessarily his son; the early kings included both Etruscans and Latins.

Roman republic
Roman government between 509 and 27 B.C.E. Ruled by two elected executives who consulted regularly with the senate.

Roman senate
Roman governing body during the Roman republic, composed of some three hundred patricians. Later became an advisory body.

After overthrowing an Etruscan king, the Romans founded the **Roman republic** in 509 B.C.E. In a republic, unlike in a direct democracy like the assembly of Athens, the people choose the officials who govern. The power to rule was entrusted to two elected executives, called consuls, who served a one-year term. The consuls consulted regularly with an advisory body, the **Roman senate**, which was composed entirely of patricians, and less often with the plebian assembly, in which all free men, or citizens, could vote. The Romans never allowed a simple majority to prevail; initially they gave more weight to the voice of the patrician senate than to the plebian assembly, but eventually the plebian assembly achieved equal participation.

After 400 B.C.E., the republic continuously fought off different mountain peoples from the north who hoped to conquer Rome's fertile agricultural plain. The Celts or Gauls were residents of the Alps region who spoke Celtic, also an Indo-European language. In 387 B.C.E., Rome suffered a crushing military defeat at the hands of the Gauls, who took the city and left after plundering it for seven months.

In the fourth century B.C.E. Rome recovered and began to conquer other city-states. To speakers of Latin among their defeated enemies, the Romans offered all the privileges of citizenship and the accompanying obligations; those who did not speak Latin had to pay taxes and serve as soldiers but could not participate in the political system.

● **CONTEXT&CONNECTIONS** This policy of actively incorporating conquered peoples differed from the Persian empire to the east, which never granted the conquered peoples the same privileged status as Persians and Medes. ●

AP® THEMES
What elements of other Mediterranean cultures did the Roman people adopt?

The Romans learned much from the different peoples they conquered. They worshiped their own gods and found parallels between their gods and those of the Greeks; they adopted elements of Greek law. They also constructed roads linking Rome with their new possessions. Their policies led to military success, and by 321 B.C.E. Roman troops had gained control of the entire Italian peninsula except for the south (the toe and heel of the Italian boot), a region of heavy Greek settlement. Almost fifty years passed before Rome conquered the final Greek city-state in Italy.

The Conquest of the Mediterranean World, 272–146 B.C.E.

Carthage
A city in modern-day Tunisia originally founded by the Phoenicians. Rome's main rival for control of the Mediterranean.

In 272 B.C.E., the year that Rome gained control of the Italian peninsula, six different powers held territory around the coastline of the Mediterranean, and the residents of these different regions had no shared cultural identity. To the east, the three successors to Alexander still occupied territory: the Antigonids in Macedon, the Seleucids in Syria, and the Ptolemies in Egypt. In addition, two separate leagues of city-states controlled the Greek peninsula. Finally, **Carthage** controlled the north coast of Africa between today's Tunis and Morocco, the southern half of modern-day

A Modern Reconstruction of the Port of Carthage The city's most prominent feature was its protected port. During peace, ships used the port behind the seawall, but during war, all the ships could retreat behind the city walls into the interior circular harbor, where they were well protected. (The circular building is a winter storage area.)

Spain, Corsica, Sardinia, and half of Sicily. An oligarchy (see page 152), Carthage prospered by taxing trade. Rome and Carthage, the only two actively expansionist states among these different powers, collided in 264 B.C.E.

In that year Rome sent troops to support one city-state in Sicily against a different city-state allied with Carthage, triggering the first of the **Punic Wars**. (The Latin word for Phoenicians was *Poeni*, the origin of the English word *Punic* [PYOO-nik].) Whereas Rome had an army of citizens who fought when they were not farming, Carthage's army consisted almost entirely of mercenary troops paid to fight. Previously a land power, Rome built its first navy of sailing ships powered by multiple levels of oarsmen. After more than twenty years of fighting—some on land, some on sea—Rome won control of Sicily in 241 B.C.E., but Carthage continued to dominate the Mediterranean west of Sicily.

Punic Wars
Three wars that Rome and Carthage fought between 264 and 146 B.C.E., all won by Rome.

Rome and Carthage faced each other again in the Second Punic War (sometimes called the Hannibalic War) from 218 to 202 B.C.E. This war matched two brilliant generals: Carthage's **Hannibal** (ca. 247–ca. 182 B.C.E.) with Rome's Scipio Africanus (SIP-ee-o ah-frih-KAHN-us) (236–183 B.C.E.). Writing about events that occurred before he was born, Polybius believed that the historian should distinguish the underlying causes of war from both the pretexts and the actual battle that began the fighting. The underlying cause of the Second Punic War, Polybius argued, dated back to Hannibal's childhood and his father's anger at losing the First Punic War.

Hannibal
(ca. 247–ca. 182 B.C.E.) A brilliant military strategist who led Carthage's armies over the Alps into Italy during the Second Punic War but lost to Rome in 202 B.C.E.

From New Carthage (modern-day Cartagena) in Spain, Hannibal led a force of 50,000 infantry, 9,000 cavalry, and 37 elephants on a five-month march across southern France and then through the Alps. Polybius believed that the historian had to do on-site research; as he said, *"I... have personally explored the country, and have crossed the Alps myself to obtain first-hand information and evidence."** Polybius found Hannibal's decision to cross the Alps audacious: *"These conditions were so unusual as to be almost freakish,"* Polybius learned from interviews with the locals. *"The new snow lying on top of the old, which had remained there from the previous winter,...gave way easily, both because it was soft, having just fallen, and because it was not yet deep."** Many of Hannibal's men froze or starved to death, and Polybius estimated that less than half the original army, and a single elephant, survived the fifteen-day march through the Alps.

Carthage's army included Africans, Spaniards, Celts, Phoenicians, Italians, and Greeks. The varied composition of Hannibal's force intimidated the Romans. Polybius reported: *"The troops were drawn up in alternate companies, the Celts naked, the Spaniards with their short linen tunics bordered with purple—their national dress—so that the line presented a strange and terrifying appearance."**

● **CONTEXT&CONNECTIONS** Like the Qin army in China (see Chapter 4), the Roman commanders enforced a complex policy of rewards and punishments. ●

Polybius attributed much of the Romans' success to the rules governing their army. Men who fought bravely in battle could win a spear, cup, or lance. The punishments for failure to fight were severe. If a group of men deserted, their commander randomly selected one-tenth of the deserters to be beaten to death, condemning each, explains Polybius, *"whereupon all the soldiers fall upon him with clubs and stones, and usually kill him in the camp itself."**

Diminished as their numbers were by the trip across the Alps, Hannibal's army entered Italy and won several major battles in succession. Finally, though, when the two armies met in 202 B.C.E. at Zama, on the North African coast, Rome defeated Carthage and gained control of the entire western Mediterranean. After the Second Punic War, Roman forces fought a series of battles in the east, subduing the three successor states to Alexander to secure control of the eastern Mediterranean by 133 B.C.E.

In 146 B.C.E. Rome defeated Carthage a third time. After he had taken the city, Scipio Aemilianus (SIP-ee-o ay-mill-YAN-us), the commander of Roman forces, ordered it leveled and the survivors sent to Rome to be sold as slaves. The Roman senate passed a bill forbidding anyone to rebuild Carthage and in place of Carthage's empire established the province of Africa (the origin of the continent's name) along the North African coast. As we have seen in previous chapters, conquering rulers frequently exacted a high price from the people of a newly subjugated territory, but the order to destroy a city and enslave all its inhabitants marked a noteworthy level of brutality.

Each conquest brought new territory to be administered by the Roman empire. By the time of the First Punic War, conquered territories, including Sicily, Sardinia, and Spain, were ruled as military districts by a governor appointed by the senate. The residents of these military districts did not receive citizenship. Like the Persian satraps, each Roman governor was in charge of an extremely large area; the district

---

*From *The Rise of the Roman Empire* by Polybius, translated by Ian Scott-Kilvert, selected with an introduction by F.W. Walbank (Penguin Classics, 1979), pp. 221–222, 227–228, 271, 332–333.

of North Africa took in 5,000 square miles (13,000 sq km) stretched along the Mediterranean coastline of the three modern nations of Libya, Tunisia, and Algeria. The governor had a tiny staff: one official to watch over the province's finances and an advisory panel of the governor's friends and high-ranking clients. The low number of officials meant that the Roman governor almost always left the conquered peoples' previous governmental structures in place. The greatest challenge for the provincial governors was collecting taxes to be forwarded to Rome.

• **CONTEXT&CONNECTIONS** Unlike the Persian *satraps* (Chapter 6), who retained control over tax collection, the Roman governors divided their provinces into regions and auctioned off the right to collect taxes in each region to the highest bidder, who became a "tax farmer." •

Tax farmers agreed to provide the governor with a certain amount of revenue; anything above that was theirs to keep. The residents of provinces suffered because the tax farmers took much more than they were entitled to. Most of the men who applied for the position of tax farmer belonged to a new commercial class of entrepreneurs and businessmen, called equites (EH-kwee-tays) because they were descended from soldiers who rode on horseback.

Roman Society Under the Republic

In 168 B.C.E., the family of the general Scipio Africanus persuaded the authorities to allow Polybius to stay with them. Polybius befriended the general's younger grandson, Scipio Aemilianus (ay-mil-ee-AH-nus) (ca. 185–ca. 129 B.C.E.) and offered to help him launch a career in politics.

• **CONTEXT&CONNECTIONS** As a native speaker of Greek, Polybius embodied the best of the Greek tradition. Reserving the term *Hellenism* (Chapter 6) for the kingdoms arising after *Alexander of Macedon* (Chapter 6) or settlements like Ai Khanum in Central Asia, historians do not usually call ancient Rome Hellenistic, but many Romans, including the Scipios, admired ancient Greece and adopted elements of Greek culture in their lives. •

The relationship between Scipio Aemilianus and Polybius illustrates how influential Romans gained clients, or dependents not in their families. Clients were often newcomers to a city, traders, or people who wanted to break from their own families. Patrons had the same obligation to help their clients as the head of the family had to help his own family members. They gave their clients food and money or assistance with legal matters, and clients in turn demonstrated loyalty by accompanying their patrons to the Forum, the marketplace where the residents of every Roman town gathered daily to transact business and discuss government affairs.

Scipio Aemilianus, like most important patrons in Rome, belonged to an eminent patrician family. Both his father and mother were the children of consuls. When he met Polybius, he was living with his adoptive father, who was the head of his family, or the **paterfamilias** (pah-tehr-fah-MIL-lee-us). In Roman society the paterfamilias made all decisions affecting his wife, children, and son's wives, including, for example, the decision of whether the family could afford to raise a newborn baby or should deny it food and expose it to the elements. When the head of the family died, the sons might decide to split up the immediate family or to stay together under a new paterfamilias.

paterfamilias
The legal head of the extended family in Rome who made all decisions and was the only person who could own property.

AP® THEMES

How did the Roman legal system reinforce the patriarchal structure of Roman society?

The Romans had two forms of marriage. Marriage among more prominent families, like the Scipios, required a formal contract stipulating that the father would recognize as heirs any children resulting from the match. More often a man and a woman simply moved in together and were recognized as married. Women were allowed to inherit, own, and pass on property in their own right, but under the stewardship of a male guardian, usually the paterfamilias. Roman men took only one wife, but the shorter life spans of the ancient world meant that remarriage among the widowed was common. Either the husband or wife could initiate divorce, which was accomplished by simple notification; the main legal issue was the settlement of property.

Cornelia

(ca. 190–100 B.C.E.) The mother of the Gracchus brothers, two reformers who sought to help Rome's poor; Cornelia exercised considerable political influence even though she, like all Roman women, did not hold public office.

Roman women devoted considerable energy to educating their children, whose marriages they often helped to arrange. The biographer of **Cornelia**, the widowed aunt of Scipio Aemilianus, praised her for being *"proper in her behavior"* and *"a good and principled mother."** She refused to marry the ruler of Ptolemaic Egypt, one of the post-Alexander kingdoms, so that she could devote herself to her twelve children, of whom only three survived to adulthood. Late in her life, *"she had a wide circle of friends . . . and her hospitality meant that she was never short of dinner guests. She surrounded herself with Greek and Roman scholars, and used to exchange gifts with kings from all over the world. Her guests and visitors used particularly to enjoy the stories she told of the life and habits of her father, Africanus."** Cornelia's example shows how Roman women were able to exert considerable influence even though they were formally barred from holding public office.

Well-off Roman households like the Scipios also owned slaves, who were usually captured in military campaigns abroad, brought to Rome, and sold to the highest bidder. Those who worked the fields or inside the homes of their masters were more fortunate than those who toiled in gold and silver mines, where mortality rates were high. Some estimate that a ratio of three free citizens to one slave prevailed in the republic, one of the highest rates in world history. Roman slaves rarely obtained their freedom, but those who did gained the full rights of citizens. However, a child born to a slave mother, regardless of the father's status, remained a slave unless freed by the owner.

The Late Republic, 146–27 B.C.E.

Polybius and his contemporaries were well aware of the strains on Roman society that came with the rapid acquisition of so much new territory. Soon after the victories of 146 B.C.E., the political system of the republic proved unable to resolve the tensions that the expanding empire brought.

In the early years of the republic, most Roman soldiers lived on farms, which they left periodically to fight in battles. As the Roman army fought in more distant places, like Carthage, soldiers went abroad for long stretches at a time and often sold off their fields to rich landowners, who invested in large-scale agricultural enterprises that grew fruit or vegetables, pressed olive oil, or produced wine. With few freedmen for hire, the rich landowners turned increasingly to slaves, and privately held estates, called *latifundia* (lat-uh-FUN-dee-uh), grew larger and larger. As the gulf between the well-off owners of *latifundia* estates and ordinary people who had lost their land widened, many landless people moved to Rome, where they joined the ranks of the city's poor because they had no steady employment.

*Plutarch, *Roman Lives: A Selection of Eight Roman Lives*, trans. Robin Waterfield (New York: Oxford University Press, 1999), pp. 83, 115.

Cornelia's son Tiberius Gracchus (ty-BEER-ee-us GRAK-us) (ca. 169–133 B.C.E.) was one of the first to propose economic reforms to help the poor. Each time Rome conquered a new region, the government set aside large amounts of public land, much of it controlled by the wealthy landed families of the city. Tiberius wanted to give portions of this land to the poor. A gang of senators and their supporters killed him, and this was the first time since the founding of the republic that participants in a political dispute used murder as a weapon. His younger brother Gaius Gracchus (GUY-us GRAK-us) launched an even broader program of reform. He, too, died in mob fighting that broke out between the reformers and their opponents.

Polybius and his contemporaries were shocked by the sudden violent turn in Roman politics, but the violence increased in the first century B.C.E. To raise an army, one general, Marius (157–86 B.C.E.), did the previously unthinkable: he enlisted volunteers from among the working poor in Rome, waiving the traditional requirement that soldiers had to own land. Unlike the traditional farmer-soldiers, these troops had to be paid, and the leader who recruited them was obliged to support them for their entire lives. The troops eagerly looked forward to military campaigns because they received a share of the plunder each time they won a battle. Their loyalties were to the commander who recruited and paid them, not the republic.

After Marius died, Sulla, another general with his own private army, came to power. In 81 B.C.E. Sulla arranged for the senate to declare him **dictator**. In earlier periods, the senate had the power to name a dictator for a six-month term during a crisis, but Sulla used the position to secure his hold on the government. After Sulla's death in 78 B.C.E., different generals vied to lead Rome. The senate continued to meet and to elect two consuls, but the generals, with their private armies, controlled the government, often with the senate's tacit consent.

dictator

A position given by the Roman senate before the first century B.C.E. to a temporary commander that granted him full authority for a limited amount of time, usually six months.

Large privatized armies staffed by the clients and slaves of generals conquered much new territory for Rome in the first century B.C.E. They defeated the much-weakened Seleucids in 64 B.C.E. in Syria, bringing the dynasty to an end, but they never defeated the powerful Parthian cavalry. The most successful Roman commander was **Julius Caesar** (100–44 B.C.E.), who conquered Gaul, an economically prosperous region that included northern Italy and present-day France. Although the Romans looked down on the peoples of Gaul as barbarians, or less civilized people who could not read and write, the Gauls participated actively in trade and had a strong economy. After his term as governor ended in Gaul, Caesar led his armies to Rome, and in 49 B.C.E. the senate appointed him dictator.

Julius Caesar

(100–44 B.C.E.) Rome's most successful military commander in the first century B.C.E. who was named dictator by the senate in 49 B.C.E.

Caesar named himself dictator for life in 44 B.C.E., antagonizing even his allies, and a group of senators killed him. Caesar's death, however, did not end Rome's long civil war. In his will, Caesar had adopted as his heir his great-nephew Octavian (63 B.C.E.–14 C.E.), the future Augustus. In 30 B.C.E. Octavian conquered Egypt, ending the rule of the Ptolemies and making Egypt a province of the Roman empire.

The Roman Principate, 27 B.C.E.–284 C.E.

In 27 B.C.E. Octavian became the sole ruler of Rome. He had eliminated all his rivals and brought nearly a century of political chaos and civil war to a close. When the republic came to an end, he had to devise a new political system capable of governing the entire Mediterranean region. He never named himself emperor. Instead he called himself *"princeps"* (PRIN-keps), or first citizen.

The new political structure he devised, in which he held almost all power over the empire, is called the **Roman principate** (PRIN-sih-pate) (government of the princeps). The principate remained in place until 284 C.E. Historians call the period between 27 B.C.E., when Octavian took power, and 180 C.E. the *Pax Romana* (PAHKS ro-MAHN-uh), or Roman Peace, because the entire Mediterranean region benefited from these centuries of stability. People moved easily across the empire, which became even more integrated as a result.

Roman principate

The system of government in Rome from 27 B.C.E. to 284 C.E., in which the princeps, a term meaning "first citizen," ruled the empire as a monarch in all but name.

The Political Structure of the Principate

Octavian wanted to establish a regime that would last beyond his own life. Yet he did not want to name himself perpetual dictator or king for fear that he would antagonize the Roman political elite. In 27 B.C.E. the senate awarded him a new title, **Augustus**, meaning "revered," the name by which he is usually known.

Augustus

The name, meaning "revered," that Octavian (63 B.C.E.–14 C.E.) received from the senate when he became princeps, or first citizen, of Rome in 27 B.C.E.

Augustus transferred the power to tax and control the armies from the senate to the princeps. Fully aware that the armies were dangerously big, Augustus ordered many soldiers demobilized and used his own private funds to buy land for them—some in Italy, some in the provinces. Augustus asserted the right to appoint all military leaders and the governors of the important provinces, thus ensuring that no one could form an army in the provinces and challenge him in Rome.

AP® THEMES

How did the internal conflict that Caesar faced influence changes Augustus made to Roman government?

The one issue that Augustus did not resolve was who would succeed him: with no son of his own, he named his wife's son from a previous marriage as his heir. By chance, the three princeps who ruled from 98 to 161 did not have sons and so were able to choose their successors while still in office. The two centuries of Pax Romana brought great prosperity to the empire and to the men who governed it, as we can see from the size and grandeur of the emperor Hadrian's palace just outside modern Rome. (See the feature "Visual Evidence in Primary Sources: The Emperor Hadrian's Villa.")

The last century of the principate was not as smooth. Between 211 and 284, the empire had thirty-six emperors, of whom nineteen were murdered, were executed, or died in battle against their successors.

The Social Changes of the Principate

Ever since the second century B.C.E., when the government classified Sicily and other new conquests as provinces, men in the provinces had not received the privileges of citizens. They did not have access to Roman courts, and they could not participate in the political system of Rome. In the first century C.E. Augustus deliberately increased the number of citizens by awarding Roman citizenship to discharged soldiers, many of whom lived outside Rome. On Augustus's death in 14 C.E. about 4 million people had become citizens, and the number continued to increase until, in 212, the emperor granted citizenship status to all free men anywhere in the empire.

Roman law also changed during the course of the principate. Even though the Roman justice system never treated everyone equally, the sharp differences of the republic among patricians, equites, and plebians gradually faded. Two new social groups subsumed the earlier divisions: the elite *honestiores* (hoh-NEST-ee-or-eez) and the *humiliores* (HUGH-meal-ee-or-eez), or the humble. Courts tended to treat the two groups very differently, allowing the wealthy to appeal their cases to Rome while sentencing the humble to heavier punishments for the same crime.

The years of the principate also saw some gradual changes in the legal position of women. The age of the large family headed by the paterfamilias had passed. Most people lived in small families consisting of a couple, their children, and whatever slaves or servants they had. On marriage, women moved in with their husbands but technically remained in their father's families and so retained the right to reclaim their dowries when their husbands died. Dowries were small, often about a year of the father's income, because daughters were entitled to a share of their father's property on his death, which granted them financial independence during the marriage.

Although they had greater control over their property than women in most other societies, Roman women continued to assume a subordinate role in marriage, possibly because many were much younger than their husbands. Men tended to marry in their late twenties and early thirties, women in their teens or early twenties. Most families arranged their children's marriages to form alliances with families of equal or better social standing.

Some marriages turned out to be quite affectionate, as made clear by one well-known writer in the first century who was also a lawyer, **Pliny the Younger** (ca. 61–113). Pliny (PLIH-nee) wrote to his wife's aunt about his wife Calpurnia:

Pliny the Younger
(ca. 61–113) Roman lawyer and official famous for his letters describing life during the principate, especially the eruption of Mount Vesuvius in 79 C.E.

> *She is highly intelligent and a careful housewife, and her devotion to me is a sure indication of her virtue. In addition, this love has given her interest in literature: she keeps copies of my works to read again and again and even learn by heart. She is so anxious when she knows that I am going to plead in court, and so happy when all is over!...*
>
> *Please accept our thanks for having given her to me and me to her as if chosen for each other.**

Pliny married Calpurnia, his third wife, in his forties, while she was still a teenager. Pliny's letter shows that Calpurnia was literate, as were many prominent Roman women.

Pliny also wrote about the famous eruption of Mount Vesuvius, which he witnessed from his home in the Bay of Naples in the early afternoon on August 24, 79 C.E. Many of the residents of nearby Pompeii (POMP-ay) did not recognize the danger and stayed in the town, as did Pliny's uncle, Pliny the Elder. He described the cloud of smoke on the first day as "*white, sometimes blotched and dirty, according to the amount of soil and ashes carried with it.*"* The fumes were poisonous, and Pliny the Elder died, like many of the inhabitants, on the second day when a mass of gas hit the city. Before he died, Pliny the Elder completed his *Natural History*, a general work on different topics ranging from artists to technological breakthroughs that remained influential through the 1500s when a priest used it as a model for his own study of the peoples and history of Mexico before the arrival of the Spanish.

Pompeii and nearby Herculaneum are Italy's most popular archaeological sites, attracting 2.5 million visitors each year, as many people as perform the annual hajj pilgrimage to Mecca (see Chapter 9). They come because the site offers

---

*Excerpt from *The Letters of the Younger Pliny*, translated with an introduction by Betty Radice (Penguin Classics 1963, reprinted 1969), pp. 126–127, 166.

The Emperor Hadrian's Villa

In 118, one year after taking the throne, Emperor Hadrian (r. 117–138) began construction on a lavish villa that took ten years to complete. It is a major tourist site today 15 miles (24 km) east of Rome. Hadrian is most famous for the wall he built in Great Britain, which marked the northern edge of the empire, and he was fortunate to reign during the Pax Romana (27 B.C.E.–180 C.E.), a long period of peace and prosperity.

An admirer of the buildings of Greece and Egypt, the emperor commissioned copies of famous monuments for his 300-acre (120-hectare) estate, which had palaces, baths, and gardens irrigated by an elaborate system of canals and fountains. Hadrian particularly liked Greece and hoped to make Athens the cultural heart of his empire. One of the most lovely reflecting pools, shown here, features copies of the Caryatids, the women holding up the porch roof near the Parthenon (see Chapter 6).

The emperor did not like living in the city of Rome and spent much of the year, particularly as he grew older, at his villa. In recent years archaeologists have realized that the area underground was as extensive as the above-ground villa. They recently sent a remote-controlled robot to explore an underground tunnel that turned out to be 19 feet (3 m) wide, allowing traffic to move in two directions. They propose that the emperor's thousands of slaves who waited on him, his officials, and his family members used these tunnels to travel from one building to another, so that no one could see them.

Hadrian's sculptors made a group of four women flanked by two men on the edge. Their reflections in the water are particularly beautiful.

In ancient times these Caryatids also supported a ceiling, which no longer exists. ***How do these Caryatids differ from those at the Parthenon (see page 164)?***

Norman Barrett/Alamy

This lake was fed by a water tank located behind a nearby hill; the water traveled by aqueduct to the lake.

This pool, measuring 393 feet (120 m) long by 59 feet (18 m wide), was named for a branch of the Nile and decorated with elements copied from both Greece and Egypt. The emperor used to hold summer banquets by the pool, which was famous for its wild parties at night.

Scala/Art Resource, NY

House of the Faun, Pompeii, Italy One of the loveliest surviving villas at Pompeii is the House of the Faun, named for the figure in the fountain. The well-off residents of Pompeii, a provincial Roman town, lived in luxurious villas like this one with lush gardens, exquisite tiled fountains, and hot and cold running water, which ran through lead pipes. Ordinary people who stored their household water in large containers, or cisterns, were much less likely to suffer lead poisoning.

a vivid glimpse of life in a provincial town during the first century C.E. Pompeii possessed all the important features of a typical Roman city: a theater, temples to Roman and non-Roman gods, baths, a gymnasium, an amphitheater, shops, paved streets, and a forum where the residents met each day and carried out their business transactions. The site of Pompeii provides a valuable reminder of the high living standards Romans enjoyed, even those living in a provincial town.

The city's twenty thousand residents participated in a highly commercialized economy in which they bought and sold baked bread, wine, and local agricultural products. Over 150 buildings with counters and evidence of cooking, most likely take-out stands or wine bars, have been found so far at the site. Others were restaurants for the wealthy, complete with reclining sofas, that served delicacies. One favorite delicacy was a dormouse that was caught in a jar and fattened up until ready to be eaten; rolled in honey and poppy seeds, the small rodents were first baked and then fried. Restaurants and tavern owners posted their menus on the wall, an indication that their customers knew how to read.

The excavations at Pompeii have been ongoing since the mid-1700s, affording researchers access to an unparalleled amount of information about life in a provincial town. Many of the local houses and shops were operated by slaves who had obtained their freedom, prompting historians to rethink their understanding of slavery. It seems that fewer people were slaves in the principate than during the republic. Roman law specified that a master could set aside property to be managed by a slave and that he was not liable for the slave's losses unless he actively participated in the enterprise managed by the slave.

Travel and Knowledge of the Outside World

Romans had been traveling for business and pleasure ever since the conquests of the second century B.C.E., and travel continued to increase throughout the principate and contributed to the further integration of the Mediterranean world. The empire reached its largest extent in the second century C.E., with an estimated population of 55 million people living in an area of 2 million square miles (5 million sq km). Rome controlled not only the entire Mediterranean coast of North Africa, western Asia, and Europe, but also large amounts of territory inland from the Mediterranean (see Map 7.1).

Roman roads connected the different parts of the empire, and sea transport, although more dangerous, remained even cheaper. Travelers needed to carry only one type of currency, Roman coins. Just two languages could take them anywhere

Map 7.1 The Roman Empire at Its Greatest Extent Some 55 million people lived in the Roman empire in the second century C.E. A network of roads and shipping lanes bound the different regions together, as did a unified currency. Two common languages—Latin in the western Mediterranean and Greek in the eastern Mediterranean—helped to integrate the Mediterranean world even more closely.

within the empire: Latin was used throughout the western Mediterranean and in Rome itself, while Greek prevailed in the eastern Mediterranean.

• **CONTEXT&CONNECTIONS** The study of geography flourished throughout the empire. The geographer Ptolemy (ca. 100–170) (not related to the Ptolemy royal family in Egypt) devoted his life to collecting the longitudinal and latitudinal coordinates for eight thousand places. We do not know whether he made an actual map, but his work marked the high point of geographic knowledge in the Roman empire. China and Southeast Asia stood at the eastern edge of the world known to the Romans; the Canary Islands in the Atlantic Ocean at the western end. To the north lay the British Isles and the Scythian region (north of the Black Sea in Russia); to the south, below Ethiopia, lay Africa. Although he made some errors, Ptolemy knew where more places were located on the globe than did any geographer elsewhere in the world. His comprehensive knowledge of geography remained influential in the Islamic world (see Chapter 9) and Europe until 1500 (see Chapters 10 and 13). •

The Rise of Christianity, ca. 30–284

During these years, the people who moved easily and widely throughout the Mediterranean world spread religious teachings. The Romans had their own gods, to whom officials offered regular sacrifices, and they worshiped many deities originating in other parts of the empire. Christianity began as a faith professed by a small group of Jews in the province of Judaea (joo-DAY-uh) and began to spread throughout the Mediterranean. The emperor Constantine's decision to support Christianity in 313 proved to be the crucial step in its extension throughout the Mediterranean world.

Roman Religion and Judaism

Throughout the republic and the principate, the state encouraged the worship of many different gods in the Roman polytheistic religion. Most Romans worshiped major deities, like Jupiter, the most powerful of all the gods, or Mars, the god of war, both of which have given their names to planets. Many of these gods had Greek counterparts; for example, Jupiter was the same as the Greek Zeus. Officials frequently spent tax monies to support public cults, sometimes honoring a deity and sometimes deifying current or former princeps.

In addition to their public obligations to state-supported gods, many people throughout the Mediterranean privately worshiped in mystery cults that promised adherents immortality and a closer personal relationship with the divine.

• **CONTEXT&CONNECTIONS** Cult deities not originally from Rome included Isis (EYE-sis), the Egyptian goddess of the dead, thought to have power to cure the sick, and Mithra (MIH-thruh), the Iranian sun-god sent by *Ahura Mazda* (Chapter 6) to struggle against evil. Gathering in small groups to sacrifice bulls, the worshipers of Mithra believed that the souls of the dead descended into earth before ascending into heaven. •

Unlike almost everyone else in the Roman empire, Jews were monotheistic (see Chapter 2). Worshiping a single god, never depicted in images or paintings, Jews refused to worship any of the Roman gods or former princeps, a stance the

Roman government tolerated. Their center of worship was the Jerusalem Temple, which housed their scriptures and survived the Roman conquest of Judaea in 63 B.C.E.

• **CONTEXT&CONNECTIONS** During holy days, Jewish priests lived at the temple, where they performed rituals. Because they were separated from their wives during these times, refraining from sexual intercourse came to be equated with a ritually pure state. Great supporters of family life, Jews never required their priests to be celibate as the Manichaeans did. •

The discovery of the Dead Sea Scrolls, a group of texts on leather, papyrus, and copper, has revealed the diversity of beliefs among Jewish groups. The scrolls mention a Teacher of Righteousness, a figure who the authors believed would bring salvation, called a Messiah (muh-SIGH-uh) in Hebrew. Many Jewish groups at the time believed that a Messiah would come, yet they disagreed about how to identify him.

The Life and Teachings of Jesus, ca. 4 B.C.E.–30 C.E.

Almost every surviving record about early Christianity written before 100 C.E., whether about the life of **Jesus** or the early ministry, is written by a Christian believer. The earliest sources about Jesus' life, and so the most reliable, are the four gospels of Mark, Matthew, Luke, and John, written between 70 and 110.

Jesus
(ca. 4 B.C.E.–30 C.E.) Jewish preacher believed by Christians to be the Messiah, the figure who would bring salvation and, through atonement, eternal life to those who believed in him.

• **CONTEXT&CONNECTIONS** Historians use the gospels to piece together the chronology of Jesus' life, all the while remembering that, like sources about the Buddha, they were written by devotees, not outsiders (see Chapter 3). •

The gospels relate that Jesus was born in Bethlehem around 4 B.C.E. to a well-off Jewish family who lived near the Sea of Galilee, where residents made a good living fishing. They say little about his life before about 26 C.E., when his cousin John the Baptist immersed him in the waters of the River Jordan. John, who claimed to be a prophet, urged Jews to undergo a one-time baptism in preparation for the kingdom of God.

• **CONTEXT&CONNECTIONS** Although baptism later took on a specific meaning within Christianity, the Greek word *baptein* simply means "to wash in water" or "to immerse," and many ancient religions viewed bathing in water as a way to prepare believers for various rituals. Jewish tradition held that washing with water could cleanse someone of impurities—for example, when someone had touched a corpse—and the Jew could repeat the washing as often as needed. Modifying this tradition, at around the time Jesus lived, several Jewish groups required converts to undergo a single ritual bathing before they could enter the temple as Jews. •

In 28 and 29 C.E. Jesus began preaching publicly in Galilee and, like John, urged Jews to repent and undergo baptism. This marked the beginning of his life as a religious teacher. Illness was a sign of Satan's presence, Jesus taught, and many of the miracles recorded in the gospels are anecdotes about his curing the sick. Historians, particularly those who do not subscribe to the teachings of a given belief system, are often skeptical about whether the events described in miracle tales actually occurred. But they realize that many religious figures were able to win converts because of them.

As he explained in the Sermon on the Mount, Jesus welcomed the poor and downtrodden: *"Blessed are the poor in spirit, for theirs is the kingdom of heaven"** (Matthew 5:3). Jesus summed up his teachings succinctly in response to someone who asked him what the most important commandment was:

> *"You shall love the Lord your God with all your heart, and with all your soul, and with all your mind." This is the great and first commandment. And a second is like it: "You shall love your neighbor as yourself." (Matthew 22:36–39)**

Jesus also taught his followers that God would send a Messiah to usher in a new age. *Christos*, which literally means "having been anointed," was the Greek word for Messiah, and Jesus came to be known as Jesus Christ because his followers believed that he was the Messiah. Jesus' teachings attracted converts because his egalitarian message promised salvation to all, including the poor, and welcomed all to follow his teachings, regardless of their background.

Jesus also wanted to challenge and reform the abuses he saw. His criticisms provoked the Jewish community leaders, who may also have feared that he would lead the residents of Palestine, where there was already a great deal of unrest, in an uprising against Roman rule. They asked the Roman governor, Pontius Pilate, to convict Jesus on the grounds that he claimed to be king of the Jews and thus posed a political threat to Rome. In 30 C.E., fearful of possible disorder, Pilate agreed to crucify Jesus. At the time of his death Jesus had been actively preaching for only three years.

On the third day after he died, Christians believe, and the gospels concur, that Jesus was resurrected, or raised from the dead. As the gospel of John explains: *"God so loved the world that he gave his only Son, so that everyone who believes in him may not perish but may have eternal life"** (John 3:16). This teaching, that Jesus died so that all believers will be able to overcome death, is called atonement, and it became one of the most important teachings of the Christian church.

The Early Church and the Travels of Paul

Jesus' disciples devised a structure for the early church. They established churches in Christian communities. Bishops headed these churches; below them were deacons and deaconesses, a position of genuine authority for the many women who joined the church.

Paul
(ca. 5–ca. 64) An influential early Christian leader who traveled widely in modern-day Turkey, Cyprus, and Greece to teach about early Christianity.

The teachings of an early Christian leader, Paul, were highly influential. **Paul** (ca. 5–ca. 64) was born to a wealthy family of Roman citizens living in Tarsus in modern-day Turkey. As described in the book of Acts, the turning point in Paul's life came when Jesus appeared to him in a vision, probably in the year 38 C.E., as he traveled to Damascus, where he became a Christian and was baptized. The Christian leadership in Jerusalem, however, never granted that Paul's vision was equal to their own experience of knowing Jesus personally and hearing him teach. Understandably suspicious of him, they sent Paul to preach in his native Tarsus in 48 C.E.

*All quotations from the Bible are from the New Revised Standard Version. Revised Standard Version of the Bible, Copyright © 1952 [2nd edition, 1971] by the Division of Christian Education of the National Council of the Churches of Christ in the United States of America. Used by permission. All rights reserved.

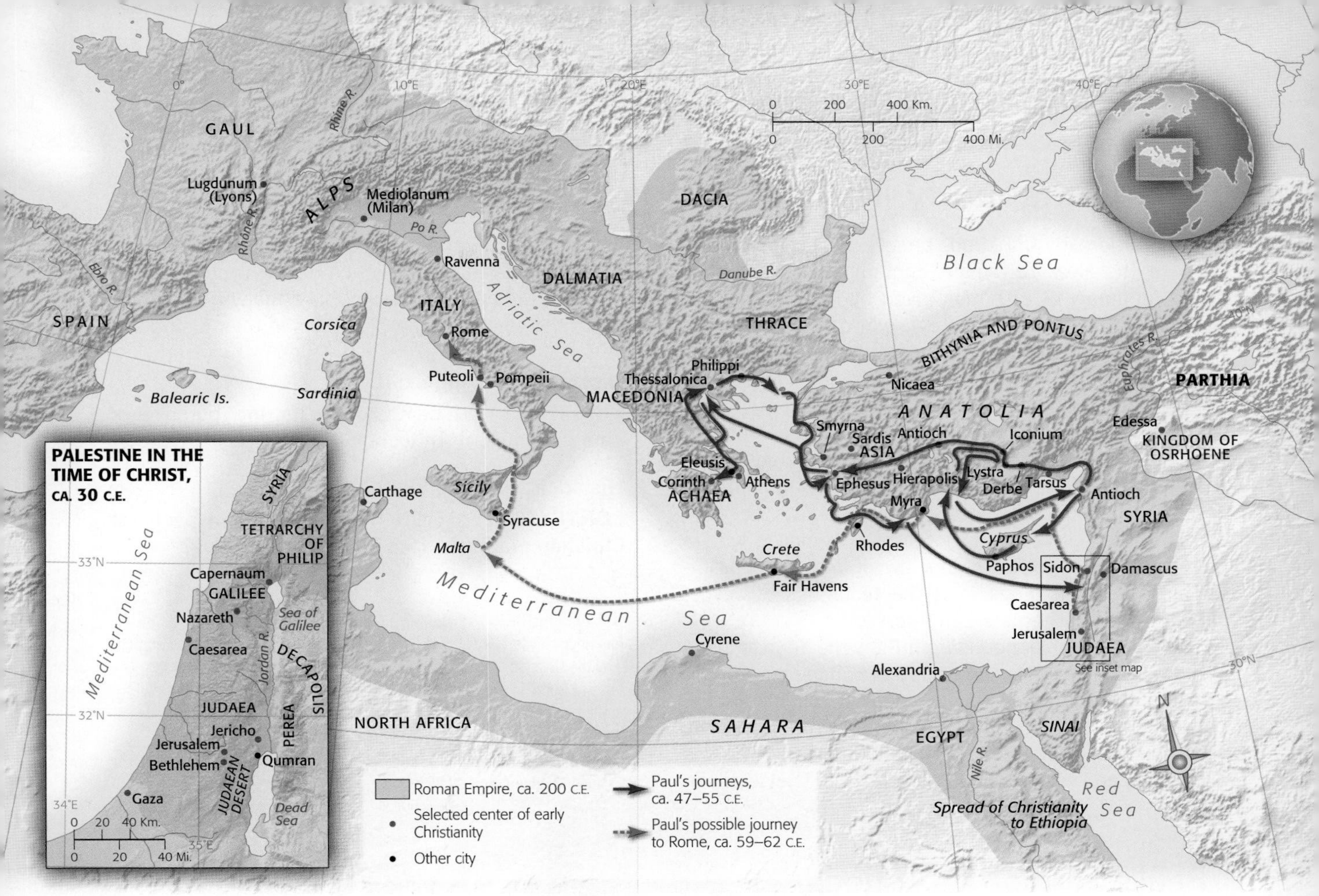

Map 7.2 The Spread of Christianity During his lifetime, Jesus preached in the Roman province of Judaea. After his death, Paul and other missionaries introduced Christian teachings to the eastern Mediterranean. By the late 300s, Christianity had spread throughout the Mediterranean, and pilgrims traveled all the way from Rome to Jerusalem and Egypt—including Egeria, who began her journey in Spain—to visit the earliest Christian monasteries.

Paul initially focused on converting the Jewish communities scattered throughout the eastern half of the Mediterranean. His letters, written in Greek with the sophistication of an educated Roman, carried the teachings of Christianity to many fledgling Christian communities as did his preaching. (See the feature "Movement of Ideas Through Primary Sources: Early Christianity in the Eastern Provinces.") Whereas Jesus had preached to the poor and to slaves, Paul's potential audience consisted of more prosperous people. He did not call for the abolition of slavery or propose any genuine social reform. Accepting the right of the Roman empire to exist, he, like Jesus before him, urged his audiences to pay their taxes.

Paul took advantage of the ease of travel within the Roman empire to propagate his views. By the time he died, circa 64, a Christian community had arisen in many of the cities he visited in modern-day Turkey, Cyprus, and Greece. In Rome, according to Christian tradition, Jesus' apostle Peter (d. ca. 65) headed the Christian community (see Map 7.2). A Jewish uprising in Judaea in 66 prompted the Roman

Early Christianity in the Eastern Provinces

What did early Christians believe? The book of Acts in the New Testament contains this very interesting summary of a sermon given by Paul in Pisidian Antioch (in modern-day Turkey), one of the first cities he visited in 46. Local Jews constituted the bulk of his audience, and Paul expected them to be familiar with the predictions about the coming of prophets in the Old Testament, which they read in a Greek translation of the original Hebrew Bible. His sermon concludes with a statement of the important doctrine of atonement: Jesus died so that the sins of everyone who believed in his teachings could be forgiven. He closes with a pointed contrast between the law of Moses, or traditional Jewish teachings, and the teachings of Jesus, which he says offer more benefits.

The second selection is from Pliny the Younger, who was not a Christian. He served as a provincial governor in a region of present-day Turkey, south of the Black Sea, between 111 and 113. In one letter, he wrote to ask the emperor Trajan exactly how he should determine who was a Christian and who deserved punishment. The details in his letter offer a vivid description of the impact of Christianity on local religious practice during a period when it was officially banned. Unlike Pliny, many Roman officials did not persecute the Christians in their districts.

Historical Thinking Skill:
ANALYZING EVIDENCE **What is the purpose of Paul's Sermon at Antioch?**

Historical Thinking Skill:
CONTEXTUALIZATION **What specific aspects of Christian practices does Pliny find troubling?**

Paul's Sermon at Antioch

You Israelites, and others who fear God, listen. The God of this people Israel chose our ancestors and made the people great during their stay in the land of Egypt, and with uplifted arm he led them out of it. . . . Then they asked for a king . . . ; he [God] made David their king. In his testimony about him he said, "I have found David, son of Jesse, to be a man after my heart, who will carry out all my wishes." Of this man's posterity God has brought to Israel a Savior, Jesus, as he promised; before his coming John had already proclaimed a baptism of repentance to all the people of Israel. And as John was finishing his work, he said, "What do you suppose that I am? I am not he. No, but one is coming after me; I am not worthy to untie the thong of the sandals on his feet."

My brothers, you descendants of Abraham's family, and others who fear God, to us the message of this salvation has been sent. Because the residents of Jerusalem and their leaders did not recognize him nor understand the words of the prophets that are read every sabbath, they fulfilled those words by condemning him. Even though they found no cause for a sentence of death, they asked Pilate to have him killed. When they had carried out everything that was written about him, they took him down from the tree, and laid him in a tomb. But God raised him from the dead; and for many days he appeared to those who came up with him from Galilee to Jerusalem, and they are now his witnesses to the people. And we bring you the good news that what God promised to our ancestors, he has fulfilled for us, their children, by raising Jesus; as also it is written in the second psalm,

"You are my son; today I have begotten you."

. . . Let it be known to you therefore, my brothers, that through this man [Jesus] forgiveness of sins is proclaimed to you; by this Jesus everyone who believes is set free from all those sins from which you could not be freed by the law of Moses.

Pliny the Younger to Emperor Trajan

For the moment this is the line I have taken with all persons brought before me on the charge of being Christians. I have asked them in person if they are Christians, and if they admit it, I repeat the question a second and third time, with a warning of the punishment awaiting them. If they persist, I order them to be led away for punishment;* . . .

Others, whose names were given to me by an informer, first admitted the charge and then denied it; they said that they had ceased to be Christians two or more years previously, and some of them even twenty years ago. . . . They also declared that the sum total of their guilt or error amounted to no more than this: they had met regularly before dawn on a fixed day to chant verses alternately among themselves in honor of Christ as if to a god, and also to bind themselves by oath, not for any criminal purpose, but to abstain from theft, robbery, and adultery, to commit no breach of trust and not to deny a deposit when called upon to restore it. This made me decide it was all the more necessary to extract the truth by torture from two slave-women, whom they call deaconesses. I found nothing but a degenerate sort of cult carried to extravagant lengths.

I have therefore postponed any further examination and hastened to consult you. The question seems to me to be worthy of your consideration, especially in view of the number of persons endangered; for a great many individuals of every age and class, both men and women, are being brought to trial, and this is likely to continue. It is not only the towns, but villages and rural districts too which are infected with contact with this wretched cult. I think though that it is still possible for it to be checked and directed to better ends, for there is no doubt that people have begun to throng the temples which had been almost entirely deserted for a long time; the sacred rites which had been allowed to lapse are being performed again, and flesh of sacrificial victims is on sale everywhere, though up till recently scarcely anyone could be found to buy it.

*The Latin text has puniri, which Radice translates as "execute," but "punishment" is more accurate.

authorities to intervene with great brutality: they destroyed the Jerusalem Temple in 70, and many Jews fled the city. After this year, Rome, Antioch, and Alexandria all became centers of the Christian church, which continued to be banned. The church grew steadily during the first, second, and third centuries C.E.

The Loss of the Western Provinces and the Rise of the Eastern Empire, 284–476

The Pax Romana ended in the third century. In 226 Rome faced new enemies on its northern borders, as a tribal people called the Goths launched a series of successful attacks in the region of the Danube River. The attacks by neighboring peoples continued in the following centuries. As a result, different Roman rulers repeatedly restructured the Roman empire and shifted the capital east. During these same centuries, they lifted the ban on Christianity and increasingly offered government support to the religion, which led to its further spread. In her letters, perhaps because she was writing to her women friends in Spain and did not want to alarm them, Egeria mentions no obstacles to travel, and she seems to have traveled in relative safety even as an unaccompanied woman.

After 400, the western half of the empire suffered continuous economic decline even as the eastern half flourished. Although the Romans lost chunks of their empire and ultimately even the city of Rome to barbarian invaders, the region of the Mediterranean remained a cultural unit bound by a common religion—Christianity—and the same two languages—Latin and Greek—that had been in use since the time of the republic.

Political Changes of the Late Empire

The principate came to a formal end early in the reign of Diocletian (r. 284–305). Diocletian (dy-oh-KLEE-shun) increased the size of Rome's armies by a third so that they could fight off their various enemies, including the Sasanians, the dynasty established in Iran in 224. In 260, the Sasanians had captured and humiliated the Roman emperor Valerian by forcing him to crouch down so that the Sasanian emperor could step on his back as he mounted his horse. This was the first time that a foreign army had ever captured a Roman emperor. Realizing that the new threats made the empire too large to govern effectively, Diocletian divided the empire into an eastern and western half and named a senior emperor and a junior emperor to govern each half. This new structure of government, which replaced the principate, is called the tetrarchy (TEH-trar-kee) because there were four different emperors.

Constantine
(272–337, r. 312–337) Roman emperor who issued the Edict of Milan, the first imperial ruling to allow the practice of Christianity, and who shifted the capital from Rome to the new city of Constantinople (modern-day Istanbul, Turkey).

However, **Constantine** (272–337, r. 312–337), the son of one of the junior emperors named by Diocletian, defeated each of the other emperors in battle until he was the sole ruler of the reunited empire. In 330, to place himself near threatened frontiers, Constantine established a new capital 800 miles (1,300 km) to the east of Rome at Byzantium (bizz-AN-tee-um) on the Bosphorus. The new capital took on the name Constantinople in Greek, or "City of Constantine" (modern-day Istanbul, Turkey). The Latin name of the city was "New Rome."

At the time the population of Byzantium was around fifty thousand, while that of Rome was over 1 million. The move was strategic: it was difficult to maintain control of the empire from a base in Rome, and the emperors of the tetrarchy had already established individual capitals outside of Rome. Constantinople, located near the Danube and the Euphrates frontiers, could be defended more easily than Rome.

When Constantine died in 337, he left the empire to his three sons, who immediately began fighting for control. After the last son died in 364, no ruler succeeded in reuniting the empire for more than a few years at a time. In 395 the emperor formally divided the empire into western and eastern halves.

Religious Changes of the Late Empire

Diocletian launched the last attack on Christianity in 303. In addition to ordering that Christian scriptures be destroyed and churches torn down, he called for the punishment of all practicing Christians. Because the Christians worshipped a single god and refused to honor any Roman gods, including deceased emperors, Diocletian's government saw them as a dangerous threat.

The Earliest Christian Art in the World? This painting on plaster dates to 232 C.E., a time when Christianity was banned throughout the Roman empire. It comes from a house church, or a place of Christian worship concealed in a devotee's dwelling, in the town of Dura Europos in modern Syria. Christ (top) heals a paralyzed man who lies on his bed unable to move (right) and then stands up, carrying his bed on his back (left). Located near the baptismal bath in the church, it emphasized to new converts Christ's ability to heal and to perform miracles. (Yale University Art Gallery)

In 311 Constantine defeated one of the other claimants to the throne. Initially he claimed to have had a vision of the Roman sun-god Apollo and the Roman numeral for 30, which is written XXX; he interpreted the vision to mean that Apollo chose him to rule for the next thirty years. However, Constantine later began to worship the Christian God along with Roman deities, and according to his biographer, a Christian bishop, what Constantine actually saw in his vision in 311 was a Christian cross.

Whatever the precise nature of Constantine's own beliefs, we know for certain that he ended Diocletian's persecution of Christianity in 313. With his co-emperor, Constantine issued the Edict of Milan, which officially allowed the practice of Christianity.

● **CONTEXT&CONNECTIONS** Like *Ashoka's* decision to support Buddhism (Chapter 3), this decision proved crucial to the spread of Christianity. ●

In 325 Constantine summoned different church leaders to Nicaea (ny-SEE-uh) (modern-day Iznik, Turkey). The council drew up a basic statement of faith, the

Nicene (ny-SEEN) Creed. In subsequent centuries the church convened many similar meetings to ensure doctrinal agreement among the different Christian branches. In 380 Theodosius I, the last emperor to rule over both the eastern and western halves of the empire, issued the Edict of Thessalonica declaring Christianity, as defined by the Council at Nicaea, the official religion of the empire. In the following year Theodosius banned the worship of pagan deities.

In the 300s Christian pilgrimages, often to Jerusalem, became increasingly popular as more and more people could afford to travel great distances to visit important religious sites. In the early 300s, the emperor Constantine's mother traveled to Jerusalem, where she ordered the dismantling of pagan temples and the building of Christian churches. She also sponsored one of the world's earliest archaeological excavations to find the spot where Jesus had been crucified, which itself became a tourist site.

The appearance of new maps and guides testifies to the frequency of travel. Some simply listed each place on a given road and the distance to the next city; others portrayed the information visually. When papyrus was not available, the Romans used **parchment**, which was made by scraping the hair from the stretched skins of sheep, goats, or calves and then cleaning it. One of the longest surviving texts on parchment, the Peutinger Map, occupies a piece of parchment 13 inches (34 cm) wide and over 22 feet (6.75 m) long. It depicts the full 64,600 miles (104,000 km) of the empire's road system

parchment
Writing material made by stretching, scraping, and cleaning animal skin.

Egeria traveled at this time (see the map on page 179). She went to Egypt, the Sinai, Jordan, and modern-day Turkey to visit the important sites of Judaism and early Christianity.

In this era, when the first monasteries and nunneries were just forming in Egypt, Egeria's trip was an alternative form of Christian devotion. Travel was difficult, and putting up with poor sleeping conditions, unsanitary food, and uncertainties on the road was a way to demonstrate one's faith. Road conditions were sufficiently safe that she usually traveled alone, but for a particularly dangerous stretch in Egypt she hired an escort of armed soldiers. Egeria traveled by foot or by a four-wheeled wagon pulled by mule. The devout Egeria wanted to go to Egypt to see the monasteries there because they were a new institution.

After a three-year stay in Jerusalem, Egeria returned home via Constantinople. On her way, she decided to take a 25-day detour to continue her journey before returning home: *"by the will of God, I wished to go to Mesopotamia of Syria [modern-day Edessa, Turkey], to visit the holy monks who were said to be numerous there and to be of such exemplary life that it can scarcely be described."** The bishop at Edessa greeted Egeria warmly, *"My daughter, I see that you have taken on yourself, because of your piety, the great task of journeying from very distant lands to these places."** His tone hints at her high social status; he himself took her on a tour of the city's sites. Egeria is grateful, but she also expects such a reception, which she received everywhere she went. Because her account breaks off abruptly, she does not tell her friends how her journey ended, but the monk Valerius says that she returned safely to Spain.

**Egeria: Diary of a Pilgrimage*, trans. George E. Gingras (New York: Newman Press, 1970), pp. 75–76.

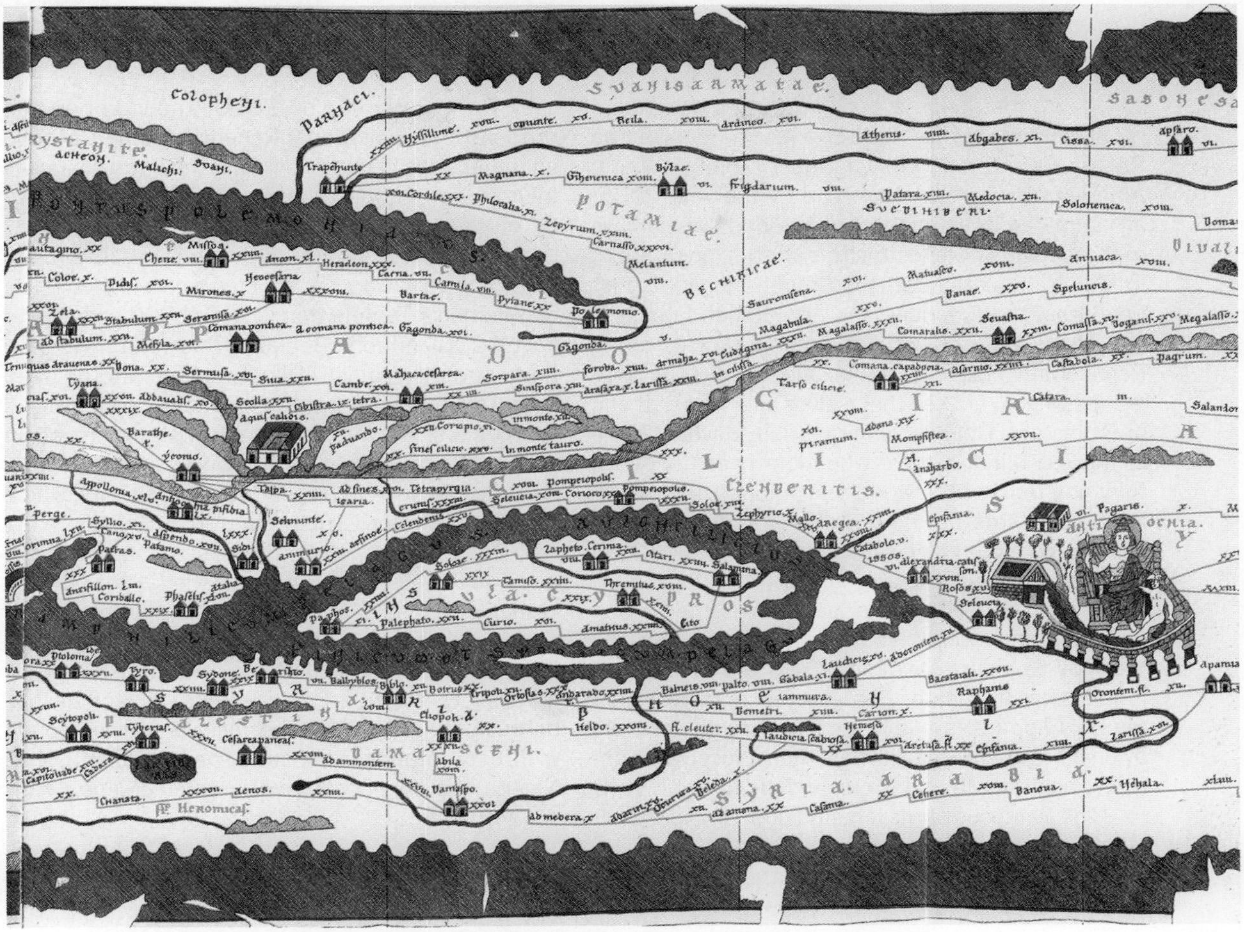

akg-images

The Peutinger Map: The Roman Equivalent of the Michelin Guide? This detail from the Peutinger Map shows Syria, where many Christians, including Egeria, traveled in the late 300s and 400s. (This is a twelfth- or thirteenth-century copy of a map dating to the 300s.) The cartographer devised symbols for the different types of lodging at each stopping place: a square building with a courtyard, for example, indicated the best kind of hotel. Modern guidebooks use exactly the same type of system.

Christianity in North Africa

As Egeria's itinerary shows, North Africa had already become an important center of Christianity by the fourth century. (See the feature "World History in Today's World: Christianity Shifts Southward.") Early in the 300s, an Egyptian Christian founded the first monastic community whose members worked in the fields and prayed each day. Before this time, Christians who wanted to devote themselves full-time to a religious life had lived alone as hermits. In later centuries, monasteries became so popular that they spread from Egypt all over the Mediterranean.

Christianity Shifts Southward

Today Christianity is declining in its traditional heartland in the Mediterranean region of the Roman Empire and growing most rapidly in Latin America, Africa, and Asia, and by the year 2025, an estimated three-quarters of all Christians will live in those regions. Reflecting this shifting orientation, in March 2013 the Catholic Church named its first pope from the Americas: the Argentinian Francis.

The word "Christian" is a broad term covering Roman Catholics, Protestants, and members of other groups who do not see themselves as either Catholic or Protestant. Not everyone is equally devout. Some of the 2.6 billion people who identify as Christian, fully one-third of the world's population, were baptized as infants but do not attend services, while others, more pious, go several times a week.

The fastest-growing groups among Latin American and African Christians are Pentecostals, named after the Christian feast that commemorated the Holy Spirit's appearance to some of Jesus' followers after his death. Pentecostalists believe that the Holy Spirit communicates directly with believers by enabling them to speak in tongues, receive prophecies, heal the ill, and exorcise demons.

The Pentecostal movement is thriving in Brazil. Many Brazilians have left the Catholic Church and joined the Brazilian Pentecostalists. In 1970, 90 percent of Brazilians reported to the census that they were Catholic; by 2010, the number had dropped to 65 percent. Recently, some Catholic churches have begun to emulate the Pentecostalists by holding group exorcisms and masses in which devotees speak in tongues.

One Pentecostal group, the Universal Church of the Kingdom of God, constructed a copy in Sao Paolo of Solomon's Temple that seats 10,000 people and cost $200 million. Because this church is only thirty-seven years old, it has reached into the deep past to claim greater legitimacy: built around 1000 B.C.E. Solomon's Temple was destroyed in 587 B.C.E. by the Neo-Babylonians who forcibly resettled the Jews in the Babylonian Captivity, which the Persian ruler Cyrus ended in 539 B.C.E. as is recorded by the Cyrus Cylinder (see Chapter 6).

The Pentecostalists are also the fastest-growing branch of Christianity in Africa, where 46 percent of the population is Christian (as opposed to 9 percent in 1900). The Pentecostalists' enthusiasm is contributing to a new, worrisome trend: violent clashes between Christians and Muslims, who are competing with each other for converts, have broken out in Nigeria, the Ivory Coast, Sudan, and the Central African Republic.

Sources: chartsbin.com; Simon Romero, "A Laboratory for Revitalizing Catholicism," *New York Times*, February 13, 2014.

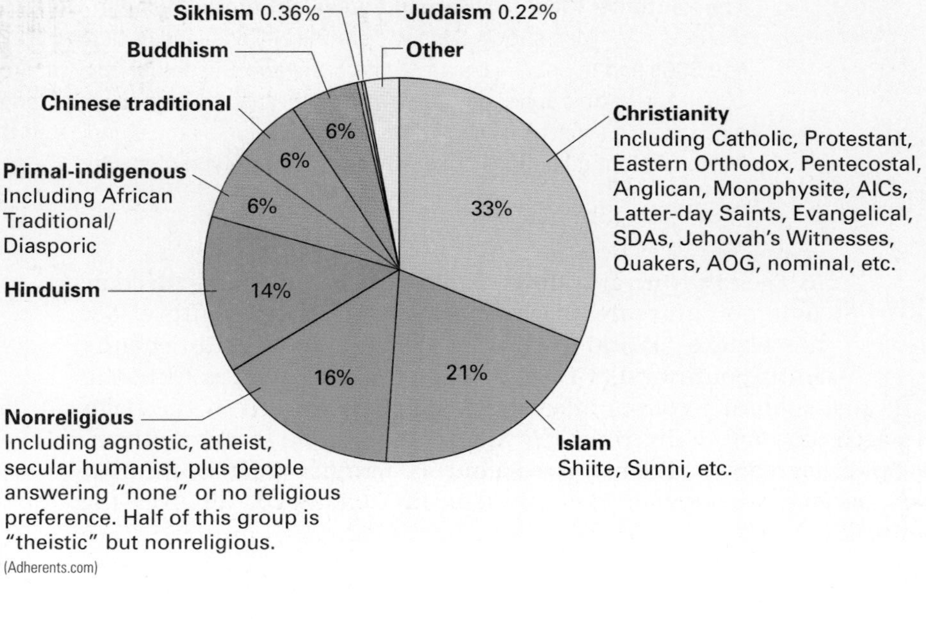

(Adherents.com)

One important Christian center lay to the east of Egypt in **Aksum**, in modern-day Ethiopia, whose rulers converted soon after Constantine issued the Edict of Milan. Their kingdom profited by taxing the trade from Egypt that went via the Red Sea to India. Merchants, who exported ivory from Africa and imported frankincense and myrrh from Arabia, encountered Christians while on trading voyages to the Mediterranean and introduced the religion to their countrymen.

The pre-Christian inscriptions commissioned by the rulers of Aksum mention local deities, including the southern Arabian goddess of the evening star, while the later ones mention the Lord of Heaven. One inscription, in Greek, names the Father, the Son, and the Holy Ghost, a definite indication of the ruler's support for Christianity. The Aksum Christians looked to the Egyptian church for leadership; the first bishop of Aksum and all his successors received their appointments from Egyptian bishops.

To the west of Egypt was another Christian center at Hippo, now Annaba, Algeria, home to one of the most important thinkers in early Christianity, **Augustine** (354–430). Augustine wrote over 5 million words in his lifetime. His book *The Confessions* detailed his varied experiences, which included fathering a child when not married and belonging to the Manichaean order (see Chapter 6). Augustine was one of the first Christians to see sexual activity as sinful, and he became celibate after his conversion to Christianity, rising to become a bishop in the church. His views on sexuality influenced many later Christians, particularly those in the Roman church, which required celibacy of all priests, and not just bishops, around 1100 (see Chapter 13).

Stone Stele at Aksum, Ethiopia Supported by a counterweight placed underground, this stone tower stands 67 feet (21 m) tall. It represents a building ten stories high, with closed windows and a door bolted shut. Some two hundred stone towers like this were built in the 300s and 400s, when the rulers of Aksum converted to Christianity, but unlike coins from the same period that show the cross, these towering monuments give no hint that the rulers who built them had converted to Christianity. (ve. Location: 70.Photo Credit)

Aksum
A center of Christianity in Ethiopia, one of the first places in the world outside the Roman empire to convert to Christianity in the early 300s.

Augustine
(354–430) Author of *The Confessions* and a prominent early Christian thinker who encouraged Christians to confess their sins.

Invasions by Neighboring Peoples

During the 400s, armies of Germanic-speaking peoples repeatedly defeated the overstretched Roman army. These peoples, including the Vandals, the Visigoths and Ostrogoths (both branches of the Goths), and other tribes (see Map 7.3), lived north and west of the empire and spoke a variety of languages in the Germanic language family, but they had no writing system (see Chapter 10).

Although Roman authors referred to the conquering armies by their tribal names, implying that they were quite different from the Romans, archaeologists in recent decades have found little material evidence of distinct invasions, prompting

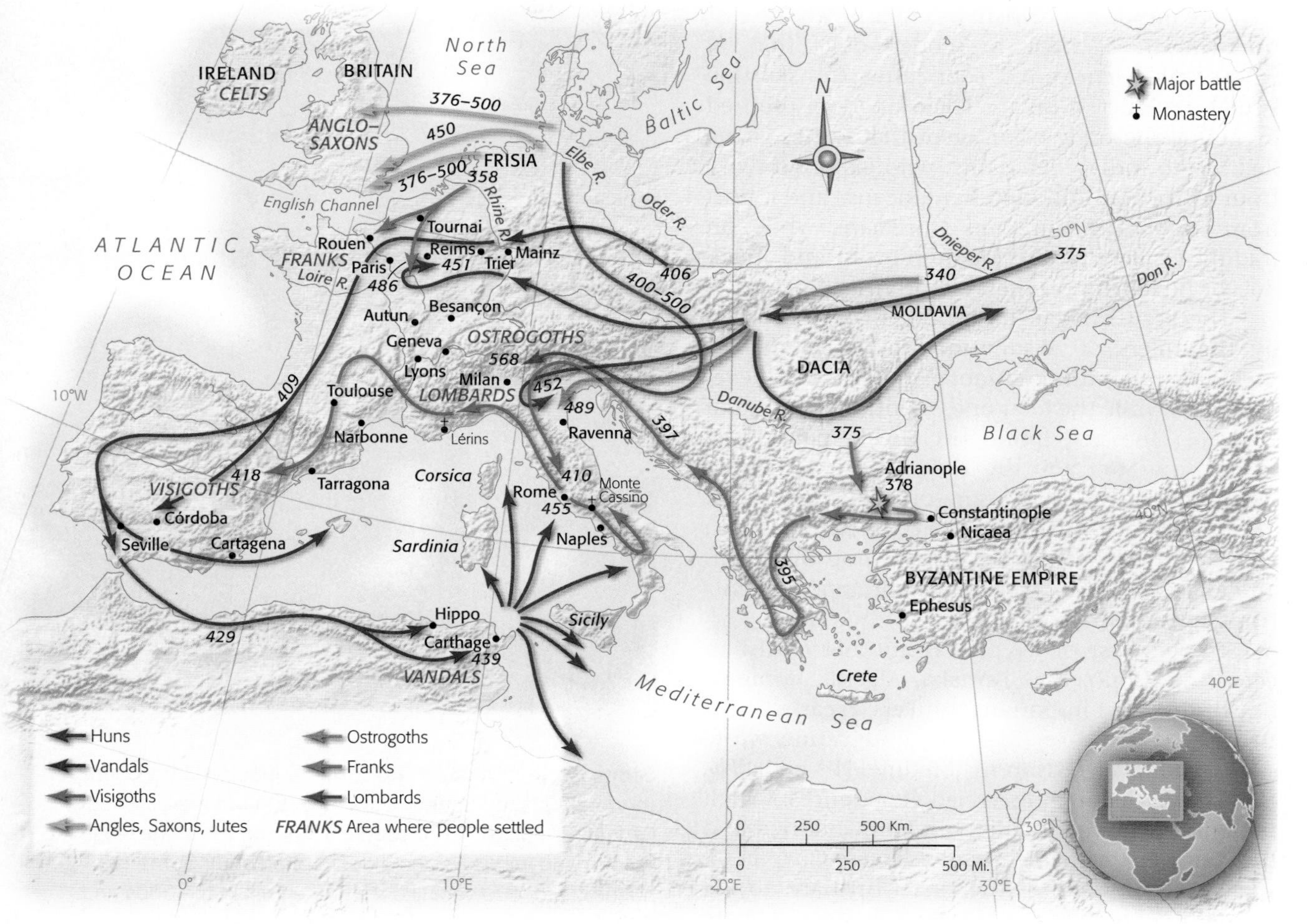

Map 7.3 The Migrations of Germanic-Speaking Peoples Although the Romans looked down on these pre-literate peoples living on their borders, the Germanic-speaking armies proved surprisingly powerful and launched wave after wave of attacks on the empire and Rome itself. In 410, invaders the Romans called Visigoths came from the east and sacked Rome. In 430 migrants called Vandals attacked the city of Hippo on the North African coast. They went on to cross the Mediterranean and loot Rome for two weeks in 455. Terms like *Vandals* and *Visigoths* do not fully reflect the makeup of the invading groups, which were confederations of many different peoples, not just one.

a revision of earlier views of tribal hordes invading civilized Rome. Scholars, led by Walter Goffart, now realize that the Goths and Vandals had lived alongside the Romans for centuries and adopted many of their customs. They now think that the migrations were not large-scale invasions by a single people, and only the leaders belonged to whatever groups the written sources name. The bulk of their followers belonged to multiple peoples with different customs, which is why they leave no distinctive footprint behind in the archaeological record.

Highly mobile and ferocious fighters, these peoples had little to defend and could devote their energies to attacking the long Roman frontier. In 410 the group Romans called Visigoths sacked Rome for three days and then retreated; this was the first time since the fourth-century B.C.E. attack of the Gauls that foreign armies had entered the city.

Economic Change in the Empire

The 400s were a time, particularly in the western half of the empire, of economic decline, most visible in Britain. Before 400 the wealthy lived in beautiful villas (similar to the House of the Faun in Pompeii pictured earlier in this chapter), local potteries produced a variety of high-quality pots, and coins circulated throughout the region. Suddenly, after 400, "There were no towns, no villas, and no coins."* The Roman central government, chronically short of revenues, minted devalued coins that contained far less metal than indicated by their face value. With fewer coins in use, people living in regions where the use of coins had been common, like Britain, began to trade material goods for other goods. The pottery wheel, which had been common, disappeared almost overnight, and the quality of ceramics plummeted. Modern-day France and Germany suffered similar changes, but regions farther to the east, such as Egypt and Syria, where Egeria had traveled, continued to prosper.

Roman historians today agree that the changes occurred, but they disagree about why. One group attributes the economic decline directly to the invasions by neighboring peoples and the resulting damage. As we have seen, the invaders were a mixed force, but they were perceived as being non-Roman, and so they are called barbarian, an originally Greek word that represented the babbling of non-Greek languages. The invading forces differed from the Roman armies in a crucial respect: like the Romans, they received a share of whatever they looted, but they were not paid as the Romans were.

• **CONTEXT&CONNECTIONS** The word *barbarian* was not always pejorative; remember that *Herodotus* (Chapter 6) promised at the outset of *The Histories* to recount the "*great and marvelous deeds*" of both the Greeks and the barbarians. •

In the 300s and 400s the Roman government taxed both land and population, and when the economy was still strong, people paid their taxes in coins. But as the economy declined, they began to pay their taxes in grain, and it was increasingly difficult for the empire to pay its armies. Without pay, the imperial forces stopped fighting, which only increased Rome's vulnerability.

AP® THEMES
What contributed to the economic decline of the Roman empire?

A different group of historians sees the damage inflicted as a contributing cause, but not as the main cause of the Western empire's decline. According to this school, the Roman system functioned remarkably smoothly, and the economy grew accordingly, largely because the empire was well run. For all of Rome's prosperity, there were no dramatic inventions to produce an agricultural surplus—nothing like the first use of irrigation or the introduction of iron farm tools.

---

*Bryan Ward-Perkins, "Specialized Production and Exchange," In *The Cambridge Ancient History. Volume XIV. Late Antiquity: Empires and Successors, A.D. 425-600*, ed. Averil Cameron et al. (New York: Cambridge University Press, 1970), p. 350.

The different regions specialized in different products, which were sold across the empire, and the government kept the economy functioning by keeping peace and maintaining order. The barbarian invasions revealed how high-functioning but also how fragile the Roman economy was. And the division of the empire into eastern and western halves allowed the east to prosper precisely because it did not have to prop up the western half.

● **CONTEXT&CONNECTIONS** The sudden end of an empire is a common event in history. Chapters 3 and 5 describe the collapse of the Harappan and Mayan societies, which are not documented in primary sources. The Harappan writing system remains undeciphered, and the Mayan inscriptions on stone monuments come to a halt as abruptly as wheel-thrown pottery disappears in the Roman sites of Britain. When historians have no documents, they weigh different explanations—perhaps ecological crisis, perhaps overcrowding and disease outbreaks, perhaps overfarming. For Rome, documentation survives, but historians are still not certain why the economy in the western half of the empire collapsed. It makes sense that the damage caused by the barbarians brought down the finely wrought structure of the Roman empire with its many different parts. ●

Vandals
Leaders of a Germanic-speaking force that attacked North Africa in 430 and sacked Rome for two weeks in 455.

The Eastward Shift of the Empire's Center

In 430, the last year of Augustine's life, **Vandals** led a force of eighty thousand men from different Germanic-speaking tribes across the Mediterranean and laid siege to Hippo. Augustine described what he witnessed:

> *whole cities sacked, country villas razed, their owners killed or scattered as refugees, the churches deprived of their bishops and clergy, and the holy virgins and ascetics dispersed; some tortured to death, some killed outright, others, as prisoners, reduced to losing their integrity, in soul and body, to serve an evil and brutal enemy.**

For Augustine, the invasions indicated the breakdown of the Roman empire and the end of the civilized world.

After taking Hippo, the invaders went on to conquer all of North Africa and the Mediterranean islands of Sardinia, Corsica, and Sicily. Even though it is not accurate to call them all Vandals (this was a confederation like all the barbarian groups), their fighting techniques and looting were so brutal that the word *vandal* came to mean any deliberate act of destruction. In 455, the marauders moved north to Italy and sacked Rome for two weeks.

For the next twenty years different Germanic-speaking groups gained control of the city and placed puppet emperors on the throne. In 476, the final emperor of the Western empire was deposed and not replaced. This year marks the end of the Western empire, and many earlier historians dated the fall of the Roman empire to 476. Most recent historians, however, note that the eastern half of the empire continued to flourish economically and the Eastern Roman empire, or the Byzantine empire, continued to be governed from Constantinople for another thousand years (see Chapter 10).

---

*Peter Brown, *Augustine of Hippo: A Biography* (London: Faber and Faber Limited, 2000), p. 430.

The Roman Empire's Lasting Imprint on the Mediterranean

By the 400s, the cultural center of the Mediterranean world, thoroughly Christianized by this time, had simply shifted once again—away from the Latin-speaking world centered on Rome to the Greek-speaking world. Egeria may have been a native of the Latin-speaking west, but she voyaged to the Holy Land in the Eastern empire to see where Biblical tales had occurred and where the new monasteries were taking shape. She encountered Greek speakers everywhere she went, and usually someone knew enough Latin to translate for her.

The cultural center of the Mediterranean was in Greece in 168 B.C.E. when Polybius was deported to Rome. Looking back on the rise of Rome, he compared the Roman empire with the empires of the Persians and Alexander the Great (see Chapter 6). He focused on the size of these three empires, noting correctly that the Roman empire was larger than the other two. Because of its different policies about citizenship and religion, the Roman empire also had greater lasting impact.

Three different governments—a republic, a principate, and a tetrarchy—ruled Rome for nearly one thousand years, and their approach to citizenship broadened over time. During the republic, the Roman government granted citizenship only to the Latin-speaking peoples of Italy. All conquered regions outside of Italy became military districts ruled by a governor. He, like the satrap of the Persian empire, was responsible for collecting taxes and forwarding them to the center.

In the early years of the principate, Augustus granted citizenship to discharged soldiers living outside of Rome, and subsequent emperors continued to increase the number of citizens until, in 212, all free men were granted citizenship. As citizens they were obliged to pay taxes; in return they gained access to the Roman legal system. The equal treatment of all citizens, whether in the heartland or outside it, was unique to the Romans: the Persian rulers, Alexander of Macedon, and the Han Dynasty always treated the subject peoples of their empires differently.

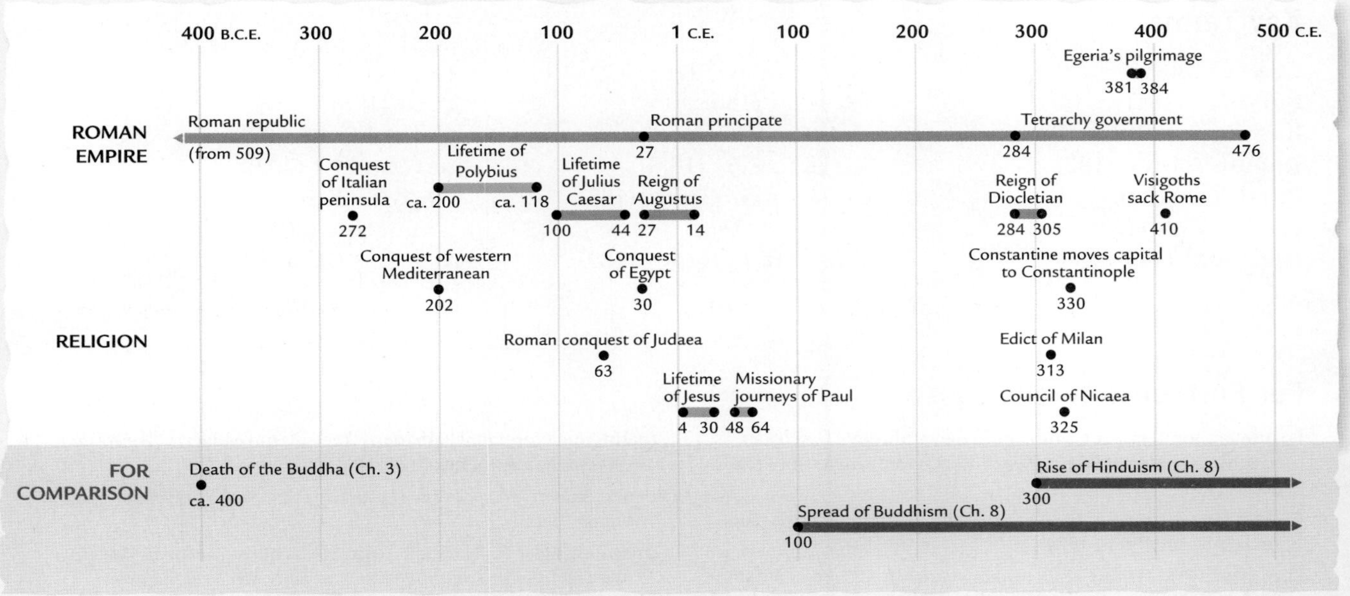

During the republic and the principate, the Roman government supported the worship of different Roman deities and current or deceased princeps. Jesus lived in the early years of the principate, and even though after his death the government banned Christianity, the roads and waters around the Mediterranean provided wonderfully effective channels for the spread of Christian teachings. Constantine's decision to worship the Christian God and to rescind Diocletian's ban on Christianity was a crucial measure bringing the further spread of Christianity throughout the empire.

In the years after 313, Constantine encouraged church leaders to reach agreement about doctrinal matters, and the Council of Nicaea drew up the Nicene Creed and excommunicated (expelled) those who disagreed with it. In 380 Emperor Theodosius issued the Edict of Thessalonica, which made Christianity the official religion of the Roman empire and banned all other religions.

At this time, Egeria was probably already on her way to the Holy Land (we cannot be certain because the beginning of her account is missing). The ease of travel in the empire, even in the late 300s, facilitated pilgrimages and contributed further to the spread of Christianity, which was well established in North Africa in the 400s, as shown by the inscriptions of Aksum and Augustine's *Confessions*. The religious policies of the Romans differed from those of the Persians, who had built Zoroastrian altars throughout their large empire but allowed their subjects to worship their own religions. Similarly, Alexander of Macedon tolerated the worship of Greek and local deities. The granting of citizenship to subject peoples, the widespread use of Greek and Latin, and the imperial orders supporting Christianity were critical policies of the Roman empire that left a lasting legacy for the Mediterranean region long after the empire ended. Chapter 8 will analyze how decisions made by many different rulers led to the spread of two different religions, Buddhism and Hinduism, throughout Asia. Chapter 9 will explore the rise of Islam, which replaced Christianity in large sections of the former Roman empire in western Asia and North Africa only a few centuries after the eastward shift of the capital to Constantinople.

Key Terms

Egeria (180)
Polybius (181)
Roman republic (182)
Roman senate (182)
Carthage (182)
Punic Wars (183)
Hannibal (183)
paterfamilias (185)
Cornelia (186)
dictator (187)
Julius Caesar (187)
Roman principate (188)
Augustus (188)
Pliny the Younger (189)
Jesus (195)
Paul (196)
Constantine (200)
parchment (202)
Aksum (205)
Augustine (205)
Vandals (208)

For Further Reference

Boardman, John, Jasper Griffin, and Oswyn Murray. *The Oxford History of the Roman World*. New York: Oxford University Press, 2001.

Casson, Lionel. *Travel in the Ancient World*. Baltimore: Johns Hopkins University Press, 1974.

Ellis, Steven J. R. "Eating and Drinking Out." In *A Cultural History of Food*. Vol. 1. *Classical Antiquity*, ed. Paul Erdkamp. New York: Berg, 2012, pp. 95–112.

Etherington, Norman. "Barbarians Ancient and Modern." *American Historical Review* 16, no. 1 (2011): 31–57.

Etienne, Robert. *Pompeii: The Day a City Died*. New York: Harry N. Abrams, 1992.

Garipzanov, Ildar H., Patrick J. Geary, et al. *Franks, Northmen, and Slavs: Identities and State Formation in Early Medieval Europe*. Turnhout, Belgium: Brepols Publishers, 2008.

Goffart, Walter. *Barbarian Tides: The Migration Age and the Later Roman Empire*. Philadelphia: University of Pennsylvania Press, 2006.

Green, Bernard. *Christianity in Ancient Rome: The First Three Centuries*. New York: T & T Clark International, 2010.

Heather, Peter. *Empires and Barbarians*. London: Macmillan, 2009.

Lynch, Joseph H. *Early Christianity: A Brief History*. New York: Oxford University Press, 2010.

Roberts, John. *The Oxford Dictionary of the Classical World*. New York: Oxford University Press, 2007.

Roberts, Paul. *Life and Death in Pompeii and Herculaneum*. New York: Oxford University Press, 2013.

Smith, Morton. *Jesus the Magician*. New York: Harper and Row, 1978.

Ward, Allen M., et al. *A History of the Roman People*. Upper Saddle River, N.J.: Pearson, 2009.

Wilken, Robert L. *The Christians as the Romans Saw Them*. New Haven: Yale University Press, 2003.

AP® Review Questions for Chapter 7

Multiple-Choice Questions

QUESTIONS 1–4 REFER TO THE FOLLOWING PASSAGES.

Therefore the law was our disciplinarian until Christ came, so that we might be justified by faith. But now that faith has come, we are no longer subject to a disciplinarian, for in Christ Jesus you are all children of God through faith. As many of you as were baptized into Christ have clothed yourselves with Christ. There is no longer Jew or Greek, there is no longer slave or free, there is no longer male and female; for all of you are one in Christ Jesus.

—The Letter to the Galatians, the Christian New Testament, first century, Roman empire

Let a woman learn in silence with full submission. I permit no woman to teach or to have authority over a man; she is to keep silent. For Adam was formed first, then Eve; and Adam was not deceived, but the woman was deceived and became a transgressor.

—I Timothy, the Christian New Testament, first century, Roman empire

1. Based on the *first* passage, how did Christian ideas concerning gender roles in the period from 600 B.C.E. to 600 C.E. differ from those of traditional Roman society?
   (A) They removed all rights for women.
   (B) They believed that men were inferior to women.
   (C) They believed women and men were equal because of Christianity.
   (D) They ignored the issue of patriarchy.

2. The *first* passage is evidence for which of the following statements?
   (A) New belief systems and cultural traditions emerged and spread, often asserting universal truths.
   (B) The core ideas in Greco-Roman philosophy and science emphasized logic, empirical observation, and the nature of political power and hierarchy.
   (C) Belief systems generally reinforced existing social structures.
   (D) Ancestor veneration persisted in many religions.

3. The second passage disagrees with the first in what way?
   (A) The second passage gives even greater freedoms to women.
   (B) Non-Jewish Christians are considered inferior to Jewish Christians in the second passage.
   (C) The second passage supports slavery.
   (D) Women are portrayed as inferior to men in the second passage.

4. Taken together, what do these two passages imply about universal religions?
   (A) Universal religions radically altered social structures permanently.
   (B) The social disruptions caused by universal religions tended to be short-lived.
   (C) Universal religions rarely succeeded in converting a population.
   (D) Universal religions were rarely associated with merchant activity.

QUESTIONS 5–7 REFER TO THE FOLLOWING PASSAGE.

She [Cornelia] had a wide circle of friends . . . and her hospitality meant that she was never short of dinner guests. She surrounded herself with Greek and Roman scholars, and used to exchange gifts with kings from all over the world. Her guests and visitors used particularly to enjoy the stories she told of the life and habits of her father, Africanus.

—Plutarch, Roman philosopher, *Roman Lives: A Selection of Eight Roman Lives*, ca. first century C.E.

5. Based on the passage, which of the following best explains the status of women in the Roman empire?
   (A) Women gave up all their rights to their husbands after marriage.
   (B) Husbands and wives were seen as equal partners.
   (C) Women could play important social, political, and cultural roles.
   (D) Women were not allowed to have contact with men outside their families.

6. Which of the following would challenge the role of women portrayed in the passage?
   (A) Women often ran the family estates.
   (B) Women in Rome only had legal protection through their husbands.
   (C) Women were allowed to own property even after marriage.
   (D) Many temples used priestesses.

7. In what way does Plutarch's description of Cornelia describe patriarchy in Rome?
   (A) Patriarchy was present and completely dictated the lives of women.
   (B) Patriarchy was nonexistent because of the impact of Christianity.
   (C) Patriarchy was present, but some women found ways to raise their status on their own.
   (D) Patriarchy led to the eventual suppression of the rights of men as well.

FOR QUESTIONS 8–10, REFER TO THE FOLLOWING MAP.

8. Which of the following conclusions can be drawn from this map?
   (A) The Roman empire occupied a region with few cultural and geographic differences.
   (B) The unity of the Roman empire relied solely on land routes.
   (C) The Roman empire contained a variety of geographic and cultural regions.
   (D) The heart of the Roman empire was located in North Africa.

9. Which of the following describes the role geography played in the Roman empire?
   (A) The location of the empire gave it access to multiple trade networks.
   (B) Rome's geographic features isolated it from other empires in the region.
   (C) Due to its location and climate, Rome relied on grain from Persia.
   (D) Mountain ranges and deserts kept the empire safe from invasions.

10. Based on the map, which of the following is a legitimate inference?
    (A) Rome expanded into sub-Saharan Africa.
    (B) The Mediterranean Sea was a major conduit for trade.
    (C) The eastern half of the empire was dominated by German populations.
    (D) Arab culture was dominant in both the western and eastern halves.

Short-Answer Questions

...whole cities sacked, country villas razed, their owners killed or scattered as refugees, the churches deprived of their bishops and clergy, and the holy virgins and ascetics dispersed; some tortured to death, some killed outright, others, as prisoners, reduced to losing their integrity, in soul and body, to serve an evil and brutal enemy.

—St. Augustine of Hippo, North Africa, on the invasion of the Vandals, ca. 410 C.E.

1. Use the passage above to answer parts A and B.
   A. Identify ONE reason why Augustine saw the above event as the fall of the empire.
   B. Identify TWO reasons that would contradict Augustine's view.

2. Answer parts A and B.
   A. Briefly explain TWO reasons for the Roman empire choosing Christianity as the imperial religion.
   B. Briefly explain ONE long-term effect of Rome's adoption of Christianity.

8 Hindu and Buddhist States and Societies in Asia, 100–1000

Portrait of Ennin

Edwin O. Reischauer, trans., *Ennin's Diary: The Record of a Pilgrimage to China in Search of the Law* (New York: The Ronald Press, 1955), p. 6.

In 838, at the age of forty-five, the Japanese monk **Ennin** (EN-nin) (793–864) joined a Japanese delegation that was the last of nearly twenty official delegations sent to China by the Japanese government. The Japanese emperors wanted to learn the reasons for the success of the Tang dynasty (618–907), the most powerful empire in East Asia and a model for all rulers. The Tang dynasty blueprint for rule drew on the earlier Qin/Han blueprint (see Chapter 4) but added other elements, most importantly state support for Buddhism. The Japanese delegation of 651 people included 200 rowers powering four wooden boats, officials, and monks like Ennin, who hoped to study with knowledgeable teachers and to obtain copies of books not available in Japan. Eleven days after the four ships departed from Japan, it began to rain:

> *The east wind was blowing fiercely, and the waves were raging high. The ship was suddenly dashed up onto a shoal. In trepidation we immediately lowered sail, but the corners of the rudder snapped in two places, while the waves from both east and west battered the ship and rolled it back and forth. Since the blade of the rudder was stuck in the ocean floor, and the ship was about to break up, we cut down the mast and cast away the rudder. The ship straightway floated with the waves. When the waves came from the east, the ship leaned over to the west, and when they came from the west, it inclined to the east. They washed over the ship to a number beyond count. All on board put their faith in the Buddha and in the deities, and there was none but did pray.**

---

*Edwin O. Reischauer, trans., *Ennin's Diary: The Record of a Pilgrimage to China in Search of the Law* (New York: The Ronald Press, 1955), p. 6.

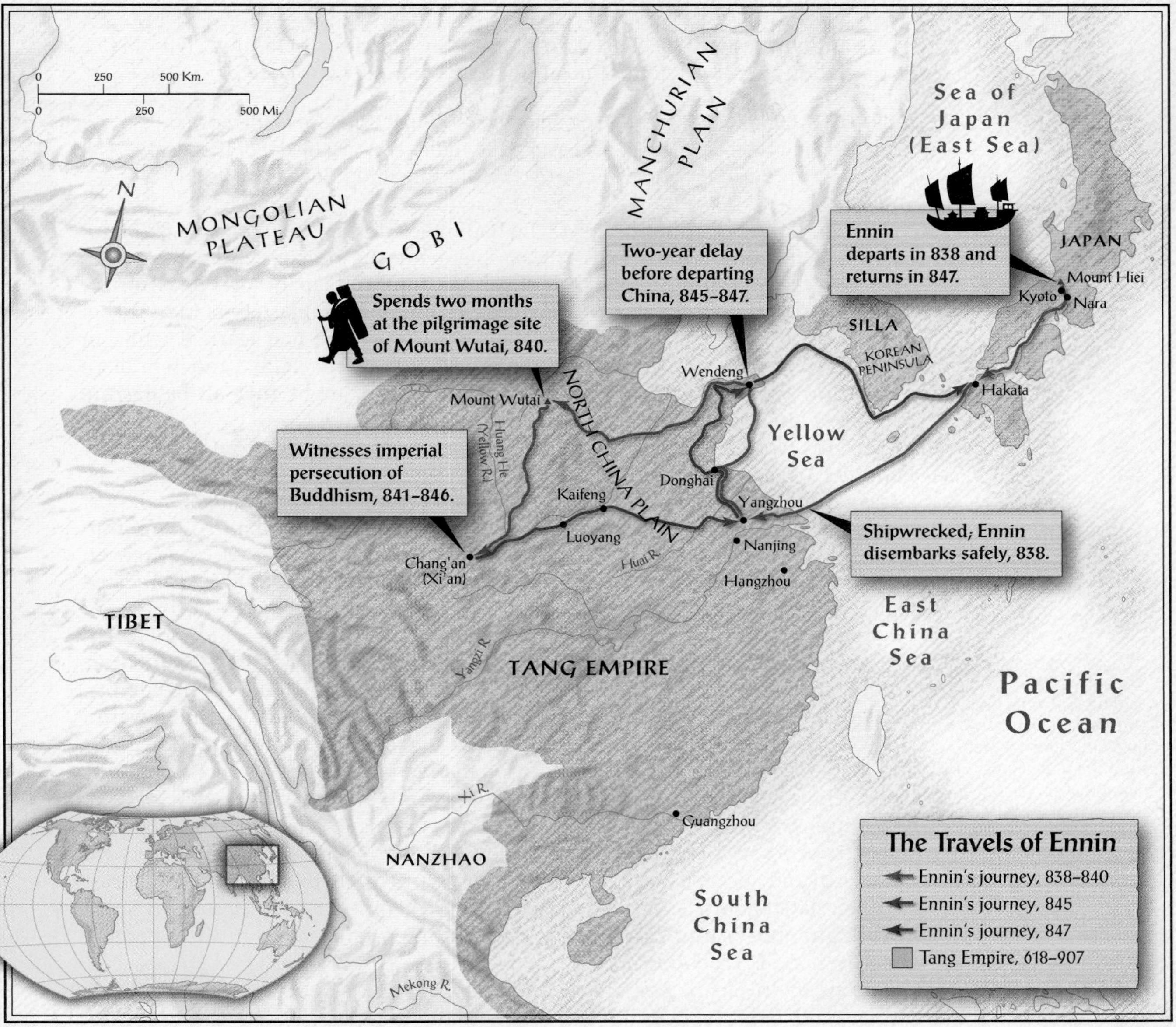

Eventually the ship drifted to the Chinese coast, near the city of Yangzhou, and the Japanese reached shore safely. This was only the first of several shipwrecks Ennin survived, and he had many other setbacks during his seven-year stay in China: he had to wait for months for officials to grant him permission to visit the monastery where he wanted to study, and most frightening of all, he experienced an anti-Buddhist persecution.

As this chapter explains, Buddhism represented an important element of the revised Chinese blueprint for empire. After reuniting China, the Sui (SWAY) (589–617) and Tang (TAHNG) emperors introduced important additions to the

Ennin
(793–864) A Japanese monk who traveled to China between 838 and 847 to obtain original Buddhist texts.

Qin/Han synthesis of Legalist and Confucian policies, including civil service examinations, a new system of taxation, and a complex law code.

• **CONTEXT&CONNECTIONS** The Tang emperors, like the Japanese emperor who sent Ennin in the delegation, also aspired to fulfill *Ashoka's* model of the ideal *chakravartin* king (key terms in Chapter 3) who patronized Buddhism. •

When Ennin went home in 847, he had traveled over 3,000 miles (4,800 km). Ennin's detailed account of his trip supplements the official Chinese histories because it reveals so much about Buddhism in China and Japan. After he returned, Ennin became the third abbot of an enormous Buddhist monastery at Mount Hiei outside Kyoto, where he introduced new rituals that he had learned while in China. He was one of the most famous teachers in the Pure Land school of Buddhism, active in both China and Japan, which taught that all beings are capable of attaining Buddhahood, or enlightenment.

On his travels through China, Ennin encountered monks from many other Buddhist countries, including north and south India, Sri Lanka, Central Asia, Korea, and his homeland of Japan. The people traveling in this larger Buddhist world—which stretched from India and Nepal, where the Buddha had taught, to Japan and Korea and included China and Central Asia—had two languages in common: Sanskrit and Chinese. Ennin did not speak Chinese, but like all educated Japanese, he could read and write Chinese characters.

Silk Routes
Overland routes through Central Asia connecting China and India, as well as the sea routes around Southeast Asia, along which were transmitted teachings, technologies, and languages.

The overland routes through Central Asia—and the sea routes around Southeast Asia and extending to Japan and Korea—are known today as the **Silk Routes**. These routes were conduits not just for pilgrims like Ennin but also for merchants, soldiers, and refugees fleeing dangerous areas. Information about distant, powerful states traveled along these same routes. Travelers told of powerful rulers in India and China, whose accomplishments inspired chieftains in border areas to imitate them. These Asian leaders introduced new writing systems, law codes, ways of recruiting government officials, and taxation systems, often modifying them to suit their own societies. Some, like the rulers of Korea, Japan, and Tibet, patronized Buddhism and adopted Tang policies. Others, particularly in South and Southeast Asia, emulated South Asian monarchs and built temples to deities such as Shiva (SHIH-vah) and Vishnu (VISH-new), the most important deities in the emerging belief system of **Hinduism**.

Hinduism
Temple-based religious system that arose between 300 and 700 in India. Hinduism has two dimensions: public worship in temples to deities such as Shiva and Vishnu, and daily private worship in the home.

As rulers in Japan, Korea, and Tibet adopted the Tang blueprint, they gave money and land to Buddhist monks and monasteries, providing the crucial impetus for the belief system to spread throughout East and Southeast Asia between 200 and 1000. The individual decisions of these rulers resulted in the religious reorientation of the region. In 100, a disunited India was predominantly Buddhist, while the unified China of the Han dynasty embraced Legalist, Confucian, and Daoist beliefs. By 1000, the various kingdoms of India and Southeast Asia had become largely Hindu, while China, Japan, Korea, and Tibet had become Buddhist.

• **CONTEXT&CONNECTIONS** This religious shift did not occur because one ruler of an intact empire, such as *Constantine* in ancient Rome (Chapter 7), recognized a single religion. It was the result of many decisions taken in different places by multiple rulers, all of whom sought to strengthen their governments and so increase their power. •

KEY CONCEPT QUESTIONS

- How did the spread of Hinduism and Buddhism transform the religious and cultural traditions of each faith? **(Key Concept 2.3)**
- How did Hinduism and Buddhism influence the development of societies in Southeast Asia? **(Key Concept 2.3)**
- How did the Sui and Tang dynasties combine traditional sources of power and legitimacy with innovations better suited to their needs? **(Key Concept 3.2)**
- To what extent did Chinese traditions influence Korea and Japan? **(Key Concept 3.2)**

Buddhism, Hinduism, and Indian Rulers, 100–1000

By the year 100, India had broken up into different regional kingdoms, all much smaller than the Mauryan empire ruled by Ashoka (see Chapter 3) but bound by common cultural ties of Buddhism, social hierarchy, and respect for classical Sanskrit learning. Despite the claims of Ashokan inscriptions, the first evidence of the spread of Buddhism beyond South Asia dates to the regional Kushan empire (ca. 50–260), located in Pakistan, Afghanistan, and northwest India. The most important Kushan ruler, Kanishka (r. ca. 120–140), launched a missionary movement that propelled the new Greater Vehicle teachings of Buddhism into Central Asia and China.

Between 100 and 1000, Buddhism gained many adherents outside India but increasingly lost ground to new deities inside India. A Chinese monk who in the early 600s traveled to north India noticed Buddhism in decline everywhere, and he recorded, often regretfully, the rise of a new religion taught by Brahmins. By the year 1000, in many regions in India, particularly south India, the largest religious institutions were temples to Hindu deities such as Vishnu and Shiva. We know this religion as Hinduism, a name not used until the nineteenth century, when British scholars of Indian religion coined the term for the religious practices of Indians who were not Zoroastrian, Christian, or Muslim. As one scholar of religion says of the worshippers of different Hindu deities, "Before this [the 1800s] not only did these groups not have a name for themselves as a religious unity but for the most part they did not consider that they were members of a single religious collectivity."*

The Rise of Greater Vehicle Teachings in Buddhism

Buddhism changed a great deal between Ashoka's time in the third century B.C.E. and Kanishka's reign in the second century C.E. Most importantly, Buddhist teachings no longer required an individual to join the Buddhist order to gain enlightenment. New interpreters of Buddhism referred to their own teachings as the Greater Vehicle (Mahayana) and denigrated those of earlier schools as the Lesser Vehicle (Hinayana, also called Theravada, meaning "the Tradition of the Elders").

*Richard H. Davis, "Introduction: A Brief History of Religions in India," in *Religions of Asia in Practice: An Anthology*, ed. Donald S. Lopez, Jr. (Princeton: Princeton University Press, 2002), p. 5.

● **CONTEXT&CONNECTIONS** The Buddha had taught that he was not a deity and that his followers should not make statues of him. Yet Indians began to worship statues of the Buddha in the first and second centuries C.E. (see Chapter 3). ●

bodhisattvas
Buddhist term denoting a being headed for Buddhahood who postpones it to help others.

They also began to pray to **bodhisattvas** (BODE-ee-saht-vahz) for easier childbirth or the curing of illness. A bodhisattva—literally, a being headed for Buddhahood—refers to someone on the verge of enlightenment who chooses, because of his or her compassion for others, to stay in this world for this and future lives and help other sentient beings (the Buddhist term for all living creatures, including humans) to attain nirvana.

The proponents of the Greater Vehicle schools emphasized that Buddhists could transfer merit from one person to another: if someone paid for a Buddhist text to be recited, for example, he or she acquired a certain amount of merit that could be transferred to someone else, perhaps an ill relative.

During the early centuries of the Common Era, Buddhist monasteries appeared throughout India. Since monastic rules forbade the monks from working in the fields, most monasteries hired laborers to do their farming for them. One monastery erected a giant stone begging bowl by its front gate, where the monastery's supporters placed large gifts for the monks and nuns.

King Kanishka certainly supported the Buddhist order, and rich merchants probably did as well. Many Buddhist texts encouraged donors to make gifts of gold, silver, lapis lazuli, crystal, coral, pearls, and agate. These valuable items, often referred to as the Seven Treasures, were traded overland between India and China. The blue mineral lapis lazuli could be mined only in present-day Afghanistan, and one of the world's best sources of pearls was the island of Sri Lanka, just south of India.

● **CONTEXT&CONNECTIONS** The Buddhists, like the Christians at the Council of Nicaea (see Chapter 7), met periodically to discuss their teachings, and Buddhist sources credit Kanishka with organizing the Fourth Buddhist Council, whose primary task was to determine which versions of orally transmitted texts were authoritative. Because the few writing materials available in ancient India, such as leaves and wooden tablets, decayed in the tropical climate, monks who specialized in specific texts taught their disciples to memorize them. ●

The earliest Buddhists to arrive in China, in the first and second centuries C.E. (discussed later in this chapter), were missionaries from the Kushan empire. The Kushan dynasty was only one of many regional dynasties in India during the first to third centuries C.E. After 140, Kanishka's successors fought in various military campaigns, and Chinese sources report the arrival of refugees fleeing the political upheavals in north India. In 260 the Sasanians (see Chapter 6) defeated the final Kushan ruler, bringing the dynasty to an end.

Gupta dynasty
(ca. 320–600) Indian dynasty based in north India; emulated the earlier Mauryan dynasty and revived the use of the Sanskrit language. The Gupta kings pioneered a new type of religious gift: land grants to Brahmin priests and Hindu temples.

The Rise of Hinduism, 300–900

In the centuries after the fall of the Kushan dynasty, various dynasties arose in the different regions of South Asia, still culturally united even as it was politically divided. One of the most important was the **Gupta dynasty**, which controlled much of north India between 320 and 600. An admirer of the Mauryan dynasty (ca. 320–185 B.C.E.), Chandragupta (r. 319/320–ca. 330), the founder of the Gupta (GOOP-tah) dynasty, took the same name as the Mauryan founder and governed from the former capital at Pataliputra (modern-day Patna).

The Gupta (GOOP-tah) rulers sponsored writers who used Sanskrit, which they saw as the language of higher learning. People living in different parts of India spoke regional languages; Pali was a grammatically simpler language descended from Sanskrit.

● **CONTEXT&CONNECTIONS** The Gupta period was the great age of *Sanskrit* (Chapter 3), and India's most famous epics, the *Ramayana* and *Mahabharata*, both composed in Sanskrit, were written down in the fourth century. In subsequent centuries, Sanskrit and Pali spread to Southeast Asia and China. ●

During his travels in China, Ennin experienced several Buddhist rituals with Sanskrit chanting, and he encountered several different teachers of Sanskrit, all from India. He believed they had a deeper knowledge of Buddhist teachings since they could read them in the original Sanskrit, and he himself started to study the language, with limited success.

In an important innovation, the Gupta rulers issued land grants to powerful families, Brahmins, monasteries, and even villages. These grants gave the holder the right to collect a share of the harvest from the cultivators who worked the land. Scribes developed a decimal system that allowed them to record the dimensions of each plot of land. During the Gupta reign, they also started to use a small circle to hold empty places—the ancestor of the modern zero. The astronomer and mathematician Brahmagupta (brah-mah-GOOP-tah) (598–ca. 670) understood positive and negative numbers and gave rules in rhymed verse for multiplying and dividing by zero.

● **CONTEXT&CONNECTIONS** On the other side of the globe, the *Maya* (Chapter 5) started to use zero at roughly the same time. ●

The Gupta rulers made many grants of land to Brahmins, members of the highest-ranking varna (see Chapter 3), who conducted rituals honoring Hindu deities like Vishnu and Shiva. The two deities, who appear only briefly in the *Rig Veda* of ancient India, became increasingly important in later times. Both took many forms with various names. Some Hindus claimed that the Buddha was actually an earlier incarnation of Vishnu.

AP® THEMES

How did Hindu beliefs and practices impact the political characteristics and social hierarchy of Gupta India?

Brahmin priests played an important role in Hindu worship, but unlike the Brahmins of Vedic times, who had conducted large public ceremonies with animal sacrifices, the Brahmins of the Gupta era performed offerings to Vishnu and Shiva at temples. These public ceremonies allowed local rulers to proclaim their power for all visiting the temple to see. The second dimension of Hindu worship was private worship in the home, in which devotees daily sang songs of love or praise to their deities. This strong personal tie between the devotee and the deity is known as **bhakti**. The main evidence for the rise of bhakti devotionalism is a large corpus of poems written in regional languages such as Tamil, a language of great antiquity spoken in the southernmost tip of India.

bhakti

Literally "personal devotion or love," a term for Hindu poetry or cults that emphasize a strong personal tie between the deity and a devotee, and did not use priests as intermediaries.

The Beginnings of the Chola Kingdom, ca. 900

In 907, the Tamil-speaking Chola (CHOH-lah) kings established their dynasty in south India. They were among the most powerful leaders who patronized Hindu temples.

● **CONTEXT&CONNECTIONS** In their capital at Tanjore, the Chola rulers bestowed huge land grants on the Shiva temple, hoping that their subjects would associate the generosity of the royal donors with the power of the deity, just as Ashoka's subjects associated him with the power of the Buddha in his *ceremonial state* (Chapter 3). ●

The Tanjore temple to Shiva, like many other Hindu temples, had an innermost chamber, called the womb room, that housed a stone lingam, to which

Brihadeshwara Temple at Tanjore, with Womb Room
Rajaraja I (r. 985–1014) built this imposing temple (*below*) to Shiva at Tanjore. The temple's ornate exterior contrasts sharply with the austere interior. The innermost sanctuary of the Hindu temple, the womb room (*right*), held the lingam, on which devotees placed offerings, like the flowers shown here. A Hindu goddess sits on the peacock on the wall. Many temples allowed only Hindus, sometimes only Hindu priests, to enter the womb room.

Occidor Ltd/Robert Harding/Getty Images

D 200 COLLECTION/Balan Madhavan/Alamy

Hindu priests made ritual offerings. *Lingam* means "sign" or "phallus" in Sanskrit. On a concrete level, the lingam in the womb room symbolized the creative force of human reproduction; on a more abstract level, it stood for all the creative forces in the cosmos.

The Shiva temple lands lay in the agricultural heartland of south India and, when irrigated properly, produced a rich rice harvest whose income supported the thousands of Brahmins who lived in the temple. These Brahmins performed rituals in the temple, memorized and transmitted different texts, and taught local boys in temple schools. The Chola kings controlled the immediate vicinity of the capital and possibly the other large cities in their district. Many villages surrounding the cities were self-governing, but since their temples were subordinate to the larger temple in the Chola capital, they also acknowledged the Chola kings as their spiritual overlords.

One of the most successful Chola rulers was Rajaraja (RAH-jah-rah-jah) I (r. 985–1014), who conquered much of south India and sent armies as far as Srivijaya (sree-VEE-jeye-ah) (modern Indonesia, on the southern Malay Peninsula and Sumatra). Although he did not conquer any territory there, as a direct result of these contacts, local rulers encouraged South Asian priests literate in Sanskrit to move to Southeast Asia to build Hindu temples and teach them about Chola governance.

Buddhism, Hinduism, and Southeast Asian Rulers, 300–1000

The term *Southeast Asia* encompasses a broad swath of land in subtropical Asia and over twenty thousand islands in the Pacific. In most periods, travel among islands and along the shore was easier than overland travel, which was limited to some of the region's major rivers. Most of the region's sparse population (an estimated fifteen people per square mile [six people per sq km] in the seventeenth century,* and even lower in earlier centuries) lived in isolated groups separated by forests and mountains, but the coastal peoples went on sea voyages as early as 1000 B.C.E.

Like India, Southeast Asia received heavy monsoon rains in the summer, and farmers stored rainwater in tanks for use throughout the year. While people in the lowlands raised rice in paddies, the different highland societies largely practiced slash-and-burn agriculture. Once farmers had exhausted the soil of a given place, they moved on, with the result that few states with fixed borders existed in Southeast Asia.

With no equivalent of caste, the shifting social structure of the region was basically egalitarian. From time to time, a leader unified some of the groups, dedicated a temple to either the Buddha or a Hindu deity, and tried to strengthen his new state.

Buddhist Kingdoms Along the Trade Routes

Merchants and religious travelers going from India to China (and back) by boat traveled along well-established routes (see Map 8.1). Before 350, ships

*Anthony Reid, "Introduction: A Time and a Place," in *Southeast Asia in the Early Modern Era: Trade, Power, and Belief* (Ithaca: Cornell University Press, 1993), p. 3.

Map 8.1 The Spread of Buddhism and Hinduism to Southeast Asia Sea routes connected Southeast Asia with both India and China, facilitating travel by missionaries to the region and by devotees from the region. The regions closest to China, particularly Vietnam, became predominantly Buddhist, like China, while the rulers of other regions, including Cambodia, patronized both Buddhism and Hinduism, as did most rulers in India.

usually landed at a port on the Isthmus of Kra, and travelers crossed the 35-mile (56-km) stretch of land dividing the Andaman Sea from the Gulf of Thailand by foot before resuming their sea voyages.

AP® THEMES

How did the predictable monsoon winds facilitate the growth of commerce in Southeast Asia?

Prevailing winds determined the schedule for merchants and pilgrims. During the spring and summer, while the Eurasian landmass heated up, the monsoon winds blew toward India; during the fall and winter, as the landmass cooled, they blew away from India. In Southeast Asia, ships waiting for the winds to change—sometimes with several hundred crew and passengers—needed food and shelter for three to five months, and port towns grew up to accommodate their needs. Local rulers discovered that they could tax the travelers, and merchants found a market for Southeast Asian aromatic woods and spices in both China and India.

Sometime after 350, the mariners of Southeast Asia discovered a new route between China and India, passing through either the Strait of Malacca or the Sunda Strait. Merchants and monks disembarked in the kingdom of Srivijaya, waited for the winds to shift, and then continued through the South China Sea to China. Srivijaya's ruler welcomed Buddhist travelers and made extensive contributions to local Buddhist monasteries as well as non-Buddhist deities. The Srivijayan kings called themselves "Lord of the Mountains" and "Spirit of the Waters of the Sea," titles from the local religious traditions. The kingdom of Srivijaya flourished between 700 and 1000. The kingdom traded with many regional kingdoms in central Java, where the world's largest Buddhist monument, at Borobudur (boh-roh-BUH-duhr), provides a powerful example of religious architecture connected with early state formation. (See the feature "Visual Evidence in Primary Sources: Borobudur: A Buddhist Monument in Java, Indonesia.")

The huge scale of Borobudur testifies to the wealth of the kingdom, which clearly benefited from its position on the main sea route between Tang dynasty China and the Islamic world. Archaeologists' discovery of a dhow wrecked in 826 near the island of Beilitung, Indonesia, offered an unusual snapshot of the sea trade between Tang dynasty China and the Islamic world. It held over sixty thousand vessels, mostly ceramic, but also some of silver and gold, all made in China.

● **CONTEXT&CONNECTIONS** Like all *dhows* (Chapter 3), the Beilitung vessel had a triangular sail but no nails or wooden dowels: its wooden planks were sewn together with coconut fiber. ●

The pottery vessels were mass produced in five different Chinese kilns. The large quantities of identical or similar items, such as 763 identical pots for ink, suggest that they were to be sold in foreign markets, perhaps in the port of Basra on the Arabian Sea. Some of the motifs, like lotus leaves, were Buddhist; others, like inscriptions from the Quran in Arabic, were Islamic. The sea route from Guangzhou, where this ship most likely departed, to the Persian Gulf was the "longest in regular use by mankind before the European expansion in the sixteenth century," according to a historian of early maritime trade.*

Buddhist and Hindu Kingdoms of Inland Southeast Asia, 300–1000

Although the interior kingdoms of Southeast Asia had much less contact with ocean travelers, Buddhist images made in stone appeared throughout interior Southeast Asia between 300 and 600. In the pre-Buddhist period, all the different societies of the region recognized certain individuals as "men of prowess" who used military skill and intelligence to rise to the leadership of their tribes or, sometimes, their region. However, no group held together for very long. People were loyal to a given individual, not to a dynasty, and when he died, they tended to seek a new man of prowess to support.

Many people conceived of a natural world populated by different spirits usually thought to inhabit trees, rocks, and other physical features. Specialists conducted rituals that allowed them to communicate with these spirits.

This was the world into which literate outsiders came in the fourth, fifth, and sixth centuries C.E. Most of the visitors, some identified as Brahmins, came from India. Southeast Asians also traveled to India, where they studied Sanskrit and returned after they memorized both sacred texts and laws. Inscriptions often refer to men literate in Sanskrit as ***purohita***, a Sanskrit word meaning a chief priest, who conducted rituals for leaders and served as advisers,

purohita
A Sanskrit name, meaning "chief priest," for the learned men who brought Hinduism and Buddhism from India to Southeast Asia.

*George Fadlo Hourani and John Carswel, *Arab Seafaring in the Indian Ocean in Ancient and Early Medieval Times* (Princeton: Princeton University Press, 1995), p. 61.

Borobudur: A Buddhist Monument in Java, Indonesia

The largest Buddhist monument in the world lies not in the homeland of the Buddha in India but over 1,000 miles (1,600 km) to the southeast at Borobudur on the island of Java in Indonesia. The Shailendra (SHAI-len-drah) kings (ca. 775–860) built the monument out of volcanic rock sometime in the eighth or ninth century, just as they were consolidating their rule. When they moved their capital to a different location in east Java, they abandoned the magnificent complex, and it lay unknown until the early nineteenth century, when Sir Thomas Raffles, founder of Singapore, saw it covered with mold and lichen plants in the middle of a dense forest.

Since no surviving documents explain the meaning of the elements of the monument, analysts must study the different sections of the enormous structure to reconstruct its possible meaning. Rising over 100 feet (31.5 m) above the ground, the monument rests on a large squarish base measuring 400 feet (122 m) on each side. The overall effect resembles the ziggurat temples of Mesopotamia. Staircases at the center of each level lead up to the next, and visitors walk around each level for a total of 3 miles (5 km) until they reach the top.

The lowest level of the monument, originally below ground, depicts an underground hell for those who do not obey Buddhist teachings. The four square terraces above contain over 2,500 panels, most showing scenes from the earlier lives of the Buddha. Monks and guides probably explained the meaning of these scenes to pilgrims. Near the top, the visitor reaches the three terraces holding seventy-two bodhisattvas, each sitting under a bell-shaped stone with holes to look through. At the top of the monument stands an empty stupa, which may have originally held a relic.

Borobudur was a pilgrimage site for people all over Southeast Asia. Pilgrims brought simple clay objects in the shape of stupas and buried them underground at the site. Archaeologists have unearthed 2,397 clay stupas and 252 clay tablets with writing on them. Pilgrims also buried clay pots and sheets of silver covered with written Buddhist charms, either to keep away evil spirits or to bring good health. The many languages on the tablets indicate that people came from great distances to see Borobudur and to make offerings to the Buddha who came to be worshiped so far from his original home.

Most analysts concur that the monument was designed to lead pilgrims from the underworld, shown in the base, up through the five platforms showing human existence, through the world of the seventy-two bodhisattvas, to the single Buddha on top who had attained enlightenment. While the content of the different panels is clearly inspired by Buddhism, the design of the monument, with its multiple ascending levels, is distinctly local. No other Buddhist monument is like it.

Borobudur is made of 2 million separate blocks of yellow-brown andesite, volcanic rock found throughout Java. Each year over 70 inches (2 m) of rain falls on the rocks, creating the perfect environment for moss and lichen to thrive. Between 1973 and 1983, with UNESCO support, workers dismantled the monument, removed and cleaned each of the blocks, and restored the monument for the third time since its rediscovery in the early 1800s.

This is one of seventy-two bodhisattvas on the top three circular terraces of the monument, underneath a central stupa at the top, which is 460 feet (43 m) above the ground.

This stupa's cover is missing, allowing a view of this serene bodhisattva. All the others are covered.

Luca Tettoni/Robert Harding

All of the stones today are grayish-black, but they were originally covered with a layer of white plaster and then painted different eye-catching colors.

Below this level are four square levels holding 1,460 6-foot-wide stone panels, each showing a different scene from Buddhist songs, poems, sacred texts, and the earlier lives of the Buddha. ***How does the visitor's experience at Borobudur differ from that at Kanaganahalli (see Chapter 3)?***

The heavy stone monument rests on an unstable core of earth. After construction first started, the monument sagged, prompting a reconfiguration of the subterranean level, which now is surrounded by a terrace to prevent it from slipping even further. Some observers have compared the resulting uneven profile to a cake that did not rise properly.

Using a Statue to Trace the Spread of Buddhism This image, found in southern Cambodia, bears the oldest inscription in Pali, a Sanskritic language, found so far in all of Southeast Asia. The text dates the image to the late 600s, but it does not say where in India the Buddhist missionaries came from. By examining the style of the statue's hair and robe closely, historians of art can identify the sculptural school of Sarnath, India, whose art is being copied and thus pinpoint the homeland of the purohita who came to Cambodia.

administrators, and teachers. The teachings of bhakti encouraged devotees to study with a purohita teacher, so that they could get closer to the divinity they worshiped.

In addition to Hindu teachings, men literate in Sanskrit also brought teachings we now identify as Buddhist to the rulers of Southeast Asia. We can see how they came together in the person of Jayavarman II (JAI-ah-var-mahn) (ca. 770–850), who ruled the lower Mekong basin in Cambodia between 802 and 850. Before the Mekong River empties into the South China Sea, much of its waters flow into Tonle Sap (the Great Lake). The lake served as a holding tank for the monsoon rains, which were channeled into nearby rice fields.

Historians view Jayavarman II's reign as the beginning of the Angkor period (802–1431), named for the **Angkor dynasty**, whose rulers spoke the Khmer (KMEHR) language. Jayavarman II was a devotee of the Hindu deity Shiva, believed to preside over the entire universe, with other less powerful deities having smaller realms. Similarly, Jayavarman II presided over the human universe as the overlord, while the chieftains in the surrounding region had their own smaller, but inferior, realms. Jayavarman II did not have to conquer them militarily to win their allegiance, because they acknowledged him as a bhakti teacher who could bring them closer to Shiva.

Devotees of Shiva built temples on sites where local spirits were thought to live. If the spirit inhabited a rock, that rock could be worshiped as the lingam. In a Hindu ceremony to request children, devotees poured a sacred liquid over the lingam, a practice that echoed earlier fertility cults. The largest temple in the kingdom, built in the early twelfth century, came to be known as Angkor Wat (ang-core WAHT). Built in the early twelfth century, it used motifs borrowed from Hinduism to teach its viewers that they were living during a golden age, when peace reigned and the Angkor dynasty controlled much of modern-day Cambodia. Jayavarman II also invoked Buddhist terminology by calling himself a chakravartin ruler, as did all subsequent Angkor kings and many other Southeast Asian rulers, who adopted this combination of Hindu and Buddhist imagery.

A recent innovation in aerial surveying, called lidar, which analyzes both light and radio waves, has allowed scholars to see below the forest cover so that they can produce accurate elevation maps. The new maps show the extent of the Angkor Wat urban settlement as 13 square miles (34 sq km) in area, four times bigger than previously thought.

● **CONTEXT&CONNECTIONS** Like the decline of the Harappan and Maya states (see Chapters 3 and 5), the sudden collapse of the Angkor state in the 1300s and 1400s has puzzled scholars. New information suggests that overpopulation may have been the cause, while other scholars, citing evidence from sediment cores, think long-term drought is a more likely cause because it would have damaged the city's complex system of canals and rivers. ●

With the exception of Vietnam, which remained within the Chinese cultural sphere, Southeast Asia faced toward India, where Buddhism and Hinduism often coexisted. Buddhism and Hinduism came to Southeast Asia not because of conquest but because local rulers aspired to create new states as powerful as those they heard existed in India.

Angkor dynasty
Khmer-speaking dynasty in what is now Cambodia founded by Jayavarman II. His combination of Hindu and Buddhist imagery proved so potent that it was used by all later Angkor kings.

Buddhism and the Revival of Empire in China, 100–1000

With the fall of the Han dynasty in 220, China broke up into different regions, each governed by local military leaders. When the first Buddhist missionaries from the Kushan empire arrived in China during the first and second centuries C.E., they faced great difficulties in spreading their religion. Buddhist teachings urged potential converts to abandon family obligations and adopt a celibate lifestyle, yet Confucian China was one of the most family-oriented societies in the world. The chakravartin ideal of the universal Buddhist ruler, though, appealed to military leaders of regions no longer united under the Han dynasty. During the Sui Dynasty, which reunited China, and its long-lived successor, the Tang dynasty, Chinese emperors introduced important additions to the Qin/Han blueprint for empire, additions that remained integral to Chinese governance until the end of dynastic rule in the early 1900s.

Buddhism in China, 100–589

The first Chinese who worshiped the Buddha did so because they thought him capable of miracles; some sources report that his image shone brightly and could fly through the air. The earliest Chinese document to mention Buddhism, from 65 C.E., tells of a prince worshiping the Buddha alongside the Daoist deity Laozi (see Chapter 4), indicating that the Chinese initially thought the Buddha was a Daoist deity.

The Han dynasty ended in 220, and no other regional dynasty succeeded in uniting the empire until 589. During this long period of disunity, called the Six Dynasties (220–589), Buddhist miracle workers began to win the first converts.

● **CONTEXT&CONNECTIONS** Historians of Buddhism treat these miracle accounts in the same way as historians of Christianity do biblical accounts (see Chapter 7). Nonbelievers may be skeptical that the events occurred as described, but people at the time found these tales compelling (and modern devotees continue to do so), and they are crucial to our understanding of how these religions gained their first adherents. ●

One of the most effective early missionaries was a Central Asian man named **Fotudeng** (d. 349), who claimed that the Buddha had given him the ability to bring rain, cure the sick, and foresee the future. In 310, Fotudeng managed to convert a local ruler named Shi Le (274–333). Shi Le asked Fotudeng to perform a miracle to demonstrate the power of Buddhism. A later biography explains what happened: *"Thereupon he took his begging bowl, filled it with water, burned incense, and said a spell over it. In a moment there sprang up blue lotus flowers whose brightness and color dazzled the eyes."**

Fotudeng
(d. 349) Central Asian Buddhist missionary who persuaded the ruler Shi Le to convert to Buddhism; Shi Le's decision to grant tax-free land to Buddhist monasteries was a crucial first step in the establishment of Buddhism in China.

*Arthur Wright, "Fo-t'u-teng: A Biography," in Arthur F. Wright and Robert M. Somers (ed.), *Studies in Chinese Buddhism* (New Haven: Yale University Press, 1990), p. 47.

A Buddhist symbol, the lotus is a beautiful flower that grows from a root coming out of a dirty lake bottom; similarly, Fotudeng explained, human beings could free their minds from the impediments of worldly living and attain enlightenment. As usual with miracle tales, we have no way of knowing what actually happened, but Fotudeng's miracle so impressed Shi Le that he granted the Buddhists tax-free land so they could build monasteries in north China.

The son of a Xiongnu (SHEE-awng-new) chieftain (see Chapter 4), Shi Le could never become a good Confucian-style ruler because he spoke but could not read or write Chinese. Buddhism appealed to him precisely because it offered an alternative to Confucianism. He could aspire to be a chakravartin ruler.

AP® THEMES
How did Buddhist practices challenge established gender roles and family structures in China?

Fotudeng tried to persuade ordinary Chinese to join the new monasteries and nunneries, but most people were extremely reluctant to take vows of celibacy. If they did not have children, future generations would not be able to perform ancestor worship for them. A Buddhist book written in the early sixth century, *The Lives of the Nuns*, portrays the dilemma of would-be converts. When one young woman told her father that she did not want to marry, he replied, *"You ought to marry. How can you be like this?"* She explained, *"I want to free all living beings from suffering. How much more, then, do I want to free my two parents!"** But her father was not persuaded by her promise that she could free him from the endless cycle of birth, death, and rebirth. Many families made a compromise; they allowed one child to join the Buddhist order and transfer merit to the other children, who married and had children.

Buddhist missionaries found that they could use miracles to convert uneducated people like Shi Le, but they needed accurate Chinese translations of Buddhist texts in Sanskrit to impress China's scholars. No dictionaries or other translation aids existed. The first understandable translations in Chinese appeared only in the year 400, long after Buddhists had been active in China, when a monk who knew both Chinese and Sanskrit founded a translation bureau with teams of bilingual translators. Buddhists continued to win converts during the fifth and sixth centuries.

• **CONTEXT&CONNECTIONS** Buddhists gained support because their teachings offered more hope about the afterlife than did *Confucian* and *Daoist* teachings (Chapter 4). •

The original Indian belief in the transmigration of souls as expressed in the *Upanishads* (oo-PAHN-ih-shahdz; see Chapter 3) presumed that someone's soul in this life stayed intact and could be reborn in a different body. But the Buddhists propounded the no-self doctrine, which taught that there is no such thing as a fixed self. Each person is a constantly shifting group of five aggregates—form, feelings, perceptions, karmic constituents, and consciousness—that change from one second to the next. Accordingly, there is no self that can be reborn in the next life. This idea proved extremely difficult for people to grasp and was much debated as a result. Gradually, Chinese Buddhists abandoned the strict no-self doctrine and began to describe a series of hells, much like the indigenous Chinese concept of the underground prison, where people went when they died. (See the feature "Movement of Ideas Through Primary Sources: Teaching Buddhism in a Confucian Society.")

**Lives of the Nuns: Biographies of Chinese Buddhist Nuns from the Fourth to Sixth Centuries: A Translation of the Pi-ch'iu-ni chuan*, compiled by Shih Pao-ch'ang, trans. Kathryn Ann Tsai (Honolulu: University of Hawai'i Press, 1994), pp. 20–21.

By the year 600, Buddhism was firmly implanted in the Chinese countryside. A history of Buddhism written in that year explained that three types of monasteries existed. In the largest 47 monasteries, completely financed by the central government, educated monks conducted regular Buddhist rituals on behalf of the emperor and his immediate family. In the second tier were 839 monasteries that depended on powerful families for support. The final category included over thirty thousand smaller shrines that dotted the Chinese countryside. Dependent on local people for contributions, the monks who worked in these shrines were often uneducated. The number of monks never exceeded more than 1 percent of China's total population, which was about 50 million in 600.

China Reunified, 589–907

After more than three hundred years of disunity, the founder of the Sui dynasty reunified China in 589. Then, in less than thirty years, the **Tang dynasty** succeeded the Sui. The Sui and Tang emperors embraced the chakravartin ideal, for they hoped Buddhism would help to bind their many subjects together. The Tang emperors ruled more territory than any dynasty until the mid-eighteenth century, and Chinese openness to the influences of Central Asia made Tang art and music particularly beautiful.

Tang dynasty
Dynasty (618–907) that represented a political and cultural high point in Chinese history. The Tang emperors combined elements of the Qin/Han blueprint for empire with new measures to create a model of governance that spread to Tibet, Korea, and Japan.

Consciously modeling himself on the great chakravartin ruler Ashoka, whose support for the Buddhist order was well known in China, the Sui founder gave money for the construction of monasteries all over his empire. However, when the emperor's son came to power, he led his armies on a disastrous campaign in Korea. He was soon overthrown by one of his generals, who went on to found the Tang dynasty. After only eight years of rule, in 626, the Tang founder's son, Emperor Taizong, overthrew his father in a bloody coup. Taizong then was able to fulfill the chakravartin ideal by making generous donations of money and land to Buddhist monasteries.

A talented general, Emperor Taizong led his armies on successive campaigns and extended Tang China's borders deep into Central Asia. The expansion to the northwest marked the period of China's greatest activity on the Silk Road in overland contact with Central Asia. Scholars disagree about why Tang China expanded to the northwest. One view is that the Chinese central government wanted to protect trade, which these scholars see as most important. A newer view sees the threat of invasion by different nomadic peoples of Central Asia, particularly the Turks (a distant ancestor of the inhabitants of modern Turkey), as the main motivation for sending armies to the northwest. The high point of the Silk Road trade coincided with the presence of Chinese armies, who bought goods from the local people using their pay, which they often received in bolts of silk since coin shortages were constant. Payments to the soldiers stationed in Central Asia by the central government constituted a massive subsidy to local producers.

One of Taizong's greatest accomplishments was a comprehensive law code, the *Tang Code*, that was designed to help local magistrates govern and adjudicate disputes, a major part of their job. It taught them, for example, how to distinguish between manslaughter and murder and specified the punishments for each.

• **CONTEXT&CONNECTIONS** Tang dynasty governance continued many Han dynasty innovations, particularly respect for Confucian ideals coupled with *Legalist* punishments and regulations (Chapter 4). •

equal-field system
The basis of the Tang dynasty tax system as prescribed in the *Tang Code*. Dividing households into nine ranks on the basis of wealth, officials allocated each householder a certain amount of land.

The *Tang Code* also laid out the **equal-field system**, which was the basis of the Tang dynasty tax system. Under the equal-field system, the government

Teaching Buddhism in a Confucian Society

Monks frequently told stories to teach ordinary people the tenets of Buddhism. The story of the Indian monk Maudgalyayana (mowd-GAH-lee-yah-yah-nah) survives in a Sanskrit version, composed between 300 B.C.E. and 300 C.E., and a much longer Chinese version from a manuscript dated 921. This story has enormous appeal in China (it is frequently performed as Chinese opera or on television) because it portrays the dilemma of those who wanted to be good Confucian sons as well as good Buddhists. Maudgalyayana may have been filial, but he was unable to fulfill his Confucian obligations as a son because he did not bear a male heir. The Buddhist narrator takes great pains to argue that he can still be a good son because Confucian offerings have no power in a Buddhist underworld.

In the Sanskrit version, Maudgalyayana, one of the Buddha's disciples, realizes that his mother has been reborn in the real world and asks the Buddha to help her to attain nirvana. Maudgalyayana and the Buddha travel to find the mother, who attains nirvana after hearing the Buddha preach.

In the Chinese version, the protagonist retains his Indian name but acts like a typical Chinese son in every respect. The tale contrasts the behavior of the virtuous, if slightly dim, Maudgalyayana with his mother, who never gave any support to her local monastery and even kept for herself money that her son had asked her to give the monks. As a filial son, he cannot believe her capable of any crime, and he searches through all the different compartments of the Chinese hell to find her. Unrepentant to the very end of the tale, she explains that traditional Confucian offerings to the ancestors have no power in the underworld. Only offerings to the Buddhist order, such as paying monks to copy Buddhist texts, can help to ease her suffering. At the end of the story, the Buddha himself frees her from the underworld, a grim series of hells that do not exist in the Sanskrit original.

› **Historical Thinking Skill:**
COMPARISON What are the similarities between the Sanskrit and Chinese versions of the story?

› **Historical Thinking Skill:**
COMPARISON What might explain the differences between the two versions of the story?

› **Historical Thinking Skill:**
ANALYZING EVIDENCE Based on the Chinese version of the story, what are the main features of the Buddhist underworld?

Sources: John Strong, "Filial Piety and Buddhism: The Indian Antecedents to a 'Chinese' Problem," in *Traditions in Contact and Change: Selected Proceedings of the XIVth Congress of the International Association for the History of Religions*, ed. Peter Slater and Donald Wiebe (Winnipeg, Man.: Wilfrid Laurier University Press, 1980), p. 180; from *Tun-huang Popular Narratives*, by Victor H. Mair. Copyright © 1983 Cambridge University Press. Reprinted with permission of Cambridge University Press.

Sanskrit Version

From afar, [Maudgalyayana's mother] Bhadrakanya [bud-DRAH-kahn-ee-ya] saw her son, and, as soon as she saw him, she rushed up to him exclaiming, "Ah! At long last I see my little boy!" Thereupon the crowd of people who had assembled said: "He is an aged wandering monk, and she is a young girl—how can she be his mother?" But the Venerable Maha Maudgalyayana replied, "Sirs, these skandhas* of mine were fostered by her; therefore she is my mother."

Then the Blessed One, knowing the disposition, propensity, nature and circumstances of Bhadrakanya, preached a sermon fully penetrating the meaning of the Four Noble Truths. And when Bhadrakanya had heard it, she was brought to the realization of the fruit of entering the stream.

***skandhas** The five aggregates—form, feelings, perceptions, karmic constituents, and consciousness—which in Buddhism are the basis of the personality.

Chinese Version

This is the place where mother and son see each other: . . .
Trickles of blood flowed from the seven openings of her head.
Fierce flames issued from the inside of his mother's mouth,
At every step, metal thorns out of space entered her body;
She clanked and clattered like the sound of five hundred broken-down chariots,
How could her waist and backbone bear up under the strain?
Jailers carrying pitchforks guarded her to the left and the right,
Ox-headed guards holding chains stood on the east and the west;
Stumbling at every other step, she came forward,
Wailing and weeping, Maudgalyayana embraced his mother.
Crying, he said: "It was because I am unfilial,
You, dear mother, were innocently caused to drop into the triple mire of hell;
Families which accumulate goodness have a surplus of blessings,
High Heaven does not destroy in this manner those who are blameless.
In the old days, mother, you were handsomer than Pan An,*
But now you have suddenly become haggard and worn;
I have heard that in hell there is much suffering,
Now, today, I finally realize, 'Ain't it hard, ain't it hard.'
Ever since I met with the misfortune of father's and your deaths,
I have not been remiss in sacrificing daily at your graves;
Mother, I wonder whether or not you have been getting any food to eat,
In such a short time, your appearance has become completely haggard."
Now that Maudgalyayana's mother had heard his words,

***Pan An** A well-known attractive man.

"Alas!" she cried, her tears intertwining as she struck and grabbed at herself:
"Only yesterday, my son, I was separated from you by death.
Who could have known that today we would be reunited?
While your mother was alive, she did not cultivate blessings,
But she did commit plenty of all the ten evil crimes;†
Because I didn't take your advice at that time, my son,
My reward is the vastness of this Avici Hell.††
In the old days, I used to live quite extravagantly,
Surrounded by fine silk draperies and embroidered screens;
How shall I be able to endure these hellish torments,
And then to become a hungry ghost for a thousand years?
A thousand times, they pluck the tongue from out of my mouth,
Hundreds of passes are made over my chest with a steel plough;
My bones, joints, tendons, and skin are everywhere broken,
They need not trouble with knives and swords since I fall to pieces by myself.
In the twinkling of an eye, I die a thousand deaths,
But, each time, they shout at me and I come back to life;
Those who enter this hell all suffer the same hardships.
It doesn't matter whether you are rich or poor, lord or servant.
Though you diligently sacrificed to me while you were at home,
It only got you a reputation in the village for being filial;
Granted that you did sprinkle libations of wine upon my grave,
But it would have been better for you to copy a single line of sutra."

†**ten evil crimes** The ten worst offenses according to Buddhist teachings.

††**Avici Hell** The lowest Buddhist hell, for those who had committed the worst offenses.

conducted a census of all inhabitants and drew up registers listing each household and its members every three years. Dividing households into one of nine ranks, it allocated to each householder a certain amount of land. It also fixed the tax obligations of each individual. Historians disagree about whether the equal-field system took effect throughout all of the empire, but they concur that Tang dynasty officials had an unprecedented degree of control over their 50 million subjects.

Emperor Taizong made Confucianism the basis of the educational system. By reserving the highest 5 percent of posts in the government for those who had passed written examinations on the Confucian classics, the Tang set an important precedent (see Chapter 12). Taizong combined the chakravartin ideal with Confucian policies to create a new model of rulership for East Asia.

One Tang emperor extended the chakravartin ideal to specific government measures: **Emperor Wu** (r. 685–705), the only woman to rule China as emperor in her own right. Many English-language books incorrectly refer to her as Empress Wu, even though she called herself emperor.

Emperor Wu
(r. 685–705) The sole woman to rule China as emperor in her own right; she called herself emperor and founded a new dynasty, the Zhou (690–705), that replaced the Tang dynasty until her death in 705, when the Tang dynasty was restored.

● **CONTEXT&CONNECTIONS** Like the female pharaoh Hatshepsut (see Chapter 2), Emperor Wu portrayed herself as a legitimate dynastic ruler and used the same title as male rulers. ●

The chakravartin ideal appealed to Emperor Wu because an obscure Buddhist text, *The Great Cloud Sutra*, prophesied that a kingdom ruled by a woman would be transformed into a Buddhist paradise. (The word *sutra* means the words of the Buddha recorded in written form.) Emperor Wu ordered the construction of Buddhist monasteries in each part of China so that *The Great Cloud Sutra* could be read aloud. She issued edicts forbidding the slaughter of animals or the eating of fish, both violations of Greater Vehicle teachings.

Documents and portrayals of the time do not indicate that Emperor Wu was particularly aware of being female, but the recent discovery of the biography of a female official buried in the official's grave has revealed that a small group of women scribes worked in the imperial palace. Beginning life as a slave, the deceased official learned to read and write in the palace school, where a small number of women studied so that they could draft documents on matters concerning the emperor's family. Emperor Wu happened to read the slave's poetry and appointed her as private secretary. The official's career does not challenge prevailing views of limited literacy among women, but it does show that some unusual women worked as Chinese bureaucrats even if most such women remain nameless.

In 690, after serving five years as a Tang emperor, Emperor Wu proclaimed a new dynasty named the Zhou, and in 693 she officially proclaimed herself a chakravartin ruler. In 705 she was overthrown in a palace coup that restored the Tang dynasty.

The Long Decline of the Tang Dynasty, 755–907

Historians today divide the Tang dynasty into two halves: 618–755 and 755–907. In the first half, the Tang emperors enjoyed extensive military victories in Central Asia, unprecedented control over their subjects through the equal-field system, and great internal stability. The first signs of decline came in the early 700s, when tax officials reported insufficient revenues from the equal-field system. In 751, the Tang sent an army deep into Central Asia, to Talas (modern-day Dzhambul, Kazakhstan), to fight an army sent by the Abbasid caliph, ruler of much of the Islamic world (see Chapter 9). The Tang army lost the battle, which marked the end of Tang expansion into Central Asia. When the Tang dynasty withdrew its troops, the Central Asian economy declined, a sign of its dependence on government payment of soldiers' salaries.

The defeat drew little notice in the capital, where all officials were transfixed by the conflict between the emperor and his leading general, who was rumored to be having an affair with the emperor's favorite consort, a court beauty named Precious Consort Yang. In 755 General An Lushan led a mutiny of the army against the emperor. The Tang dynasty suppressed the rebellion in 763 but never regained full control of the provinces. The equal-field system collapsed, and the dynasty had to institute new taxes that produced much less revenue.

Although the Tang dynasty was weaker after 755 than before, it remained quite powerful, especially in comparison to its neighbors in Korea, Japan, and Tibet. When, after 838, Ennin traveled around China, he encountered officials who zealously enforced the complex rules governing travelers. He initially tried to follow all the regulations, but when he realized that his hosts might not permit him to stay, he lied to them and said that he had missed a boat home. When ordained, all Buddhist monks took a vow promising to uphold the five precepts, which included not lying (see page 81), but Ennin invoked the Buddhist teaching of expedient means to justify his decision: it was more important for him to study Buddhism than to obey the emperor's regulations. His unusual candor makes his account particularly reliable: historians value a primary source whose author admits to being flawed. (See the feature "World History in Today's World: Buddhism Declines in Thailand.")

China's wealth struck Ennin early in his travels. Just after his arrival, as he and his companions made their way to Yangzhou, they saw *"boats of the salt bureau laden with salt,"* tied three or four across, and stretching for over 10 miles (16 km). *"This unexpected sight is not easy to record. It was most extraordinary."** The Japanese monk had simply never seen so much salt, a costly commodity, in the same place, and he could not conceive of a government that could control so many boats.

Ennin also visited the Tang capital of Chang'an. With a population of at least 500,000, the city may have been the largest in the world (its only possible rival was Baghdad, in modern-day Iraq). Chang'an was laid out on a formal grid (see Figure 8.1). Designed to awe all those who saw them, the major boulevards stretched 500 feet (150 m) across—the width of a modern forty-lane highway. The city had two markets, one to the west for mostly foreign goods, one to the east for domestic goods. In 843 Ennin heard about a fire in the Eastern Market that *"burned over four thousand houses.... Public and private money and gold, silver, silks, and drugs were all destroyed"**—an indication of both the market's population density and the goods for sale. Making a statement about imperial power, Chang'an was not designed for the comfort of its inhabitants. The Tang dynasty established a secondary capital at Luoyang, farther to the east and closer to the Grand Canal, so that during droughts, when it was impossible to ship grain to Chang'an, the government could move to Luoyang.

AP® THEMES

What economic roles did the cities of Chang'an and Luoyang serve for China under Tang rule?

---

*Edwin O. Reischauer, trans., *Ennin's Diary: The Record of a Pilgrimage to China in Search of the Law* (New York: The Ronald Press, 1955), pp. 20, 333.

WORLD HISTORY IN TODAY'S WORLD

Buddhism Declines in Thailand

What makes someone a Buddhist? The answer is less than straightforward because there is no clear marker of belief such as baptism in Christianity or the Five Pillars of Islam (see Chapters 7 and 9). Buddhists take vows (many fewer for lay Buddhists than for monks and nuns), but someone who has not taken any vows at all may still regard himself or herself as a Buddhist. For this reason, analysts can only estimate how many people in a given country are Buddhist; one figure proposes 376 million Buddhists worldwide, with 100 million in China and 90 million in Japan. Third on the list, with 55 million, is Thailand.

Scholars of Buddhism almost always cite Thailand as the country where Buddhist belief is strongest. In addition to the three hundred thousand men and women who now serve as monks and nuns for their entire lives, many young Thai men join monasteries for a year as novices before returning to the secular world to find jobs and build families. Every morning monks and novices go into nearby villages to visit households and beg for the day's food, a practice going back to the time of the Buddha, who depended on offerings from lay people as he and his followers went from place to place (they stayed put only during the monsoon season).

In recent years, though, the degree of observance among Thais has dropped noticeably. One prominent monk summarized the situation pithily: "Consumerism is now the Thai religion." Today there are half as many monks and novices as in 1980. Novices, who used to spend a full year at a monastery, sometimes stay for just a week and are called "factory monks" because they leave the monasteries as rapidly as goods coming off assembly lines. In villages where there are only one or two monks, they find it embarrassing to go and beg for their daily food; instead they order take-out food.

Part of the decline is due to the rise of social media, which has publicized incidents in which Buddhist monks violate their vows. Online videos show monks drinking alcohol, watching pornography, and partying with men and women. Charges of monks improperly spending funds are also common.

It is not clear how, or if, the Thai Buddhists can win back adherents. One monk suggests that Buddhism should appeal to the newly wealthy because it can relieve stress. He also proposed that monks should preach about Buddhist teachings in nontraditional venues: "You can get dharma in department stores, or even over the Internet." So far, though, Thai Buddhists have made few such efforts at outreach.

Source: Thomas Fuller, "Monks Lose Relevance as Thailand Grows Richer," *New York Times*, December 19, 2012.

● **CONTEXT&CONNECTIONS** Chang'an, although it probably had roughly the same number of residents as Rome (somewhere between 500,000 and 1,000,000), was a very different city. As large as the Tang dynasty capital was, its only public spaces were markets. Unlike Romans who went to the forum daily, the socially prominent in Chang'an avoided the markets because they thought merchants were unclean; the only officials who entered the markets were those who checked scales and who recorded the low, middle, and high prices of a long list of goods every two weeks. Unlike in Rome, there was no amphitheater, hippodrome, or public bath. Like Rome, though, the main streets of the Tang capital had wide drainage channels to remove the rainwater pouring off roofs. ●

woodblock printing
Printing technique developed by the Chinese in which printers made an image in reverse on a block of wood and then pressed the block onto sheets of paper. An efficient way to print texts in Chinese characters.

Among the goods for sale in Chang'an's markets were printed books and calendars, the product of a new technology that originated in China and altered the course of world history. In China devout Buddhists, seeking merit for themselves and their families, paid monks to copy memorized texts. Sometime in the eighth century, believers realized that they could make multiple copies of a prayer or picture of a deity if they used **woodblock printing**.

Figure 8.1 Layout of Chang'an and Heian (Kyoto) Many rulers in East Asia followed Tang models very closely. Compare the city plans of Chang'an, the Tang capital, and Kyoto, the Heian capital in Japan. Both cities had square walls enclosing a gridded street plan, and the imperial palace was located in the north. Even though the emperor who founded Kyoto called the eastern half Luoyang (the secondary capital) and the western half Chang'an, Kyoto, lacking both a city wall and two central markets, was much smaller than either Chinese capital. (Figure 8.1 from Patricia Ebrey, Anne Walthall, and James Palais, East Asia, 2d ed. Copyright © 2009 by Wadsworth, a part of Cengage Learning, Inc. Reproduced by permission, www.cengage.com/permissions.)

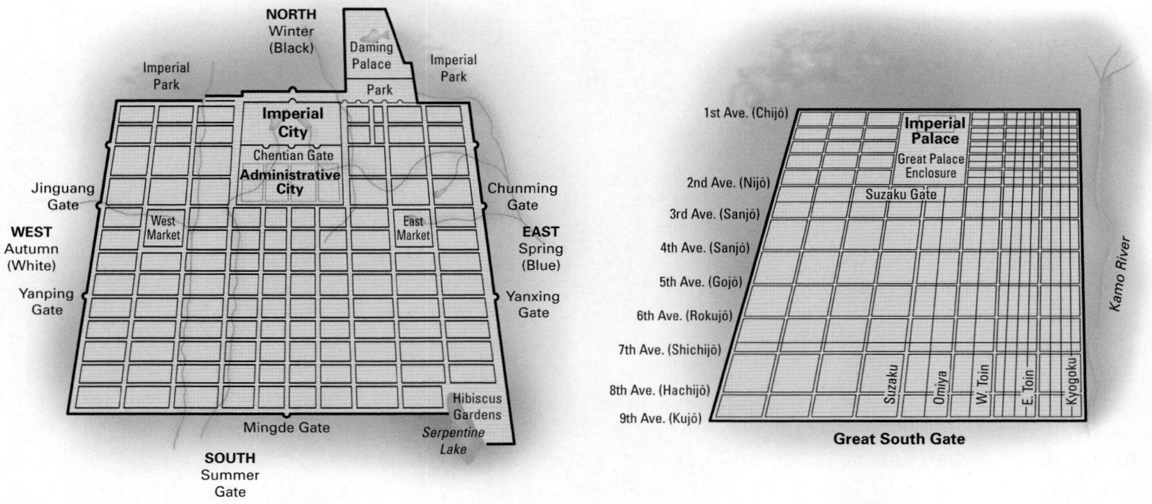

At first Buddhists printed multiple copies of single sheets; later they used glue to connect the pages to form a long book. The world's earliest surviving printed book, from 868, is a Buddhist text, *The Diamond Sutra*. During the Tang dynasty, almost all printing was religious, and Ennin bought both printed books and hand-copied manuscripts throughout his stay in China so that he could bring them to Japan, where books were scarce.

In 841, a new emperor, Emperor Wuzong, came to the throne and tried immediately to increase tax revenues by collecting taxes from the 300,000 tax-exempt monks and nuns. The emperor ordered monks and nuns under fifty to leave the monasteries and return to lay life so that they could raise their own tax-paying families. Ennin agreed to return to lay life so that he could return to Japan. He put on non-Buddhist clothes and started to let his shaved head grow hair.

As happy as he was to return home, his main concern was *"that I shall not be able to take with me the holy teachings I have copied."** If Chinese officials caught him with Buddhist books, they would surely confiscate them and possibly prevent him from going home. Ennin entrusted his books for safekeeping to a Korean friend who had been the interpreter for the Japanese when they first arrived; many Koreans lived in Tang China, and they were not as closely watched as the Japanese

*Edwin O. Reischauer, trans., *Ennin's Diary: The Record of a Pilgrimage to China in Search of the Law* (New York: The Ronald Press, 1955), p. 363.

The World's First Printed Book Even though the fifteenth-century Gutenberg Bible is much more famous (see Chapter 15), this copy of *The Diamond Sutra*, printed with woodblocks in 868, is the world's earliest printed book. Chinese printing technology reproduced line drawings and characters equally well, and printers could make as many copies as they liked simply by inking the woodblock and pressing individual sheets of paper on it. The more copies they made, they believed, the more merit they earned. *The Diamond Sutra*'s dedication explains that a Buddhist believer commissioned the text to generate merit for his parents, a major motivation for the development of Chinese printing.

Ennin was. Luckily for Ennin, in 846, just before his departure, the emperor Wuzong died. The new emperor permitted monasteries to reopen and monks to return to them. Ennin departed with most of his library intact.

After Ennin returned home in 847, no Tang emperor managed to solve the problem of dwindling revenues. In 907, when a rebel deposed the last Tang emperor, who had been held prisoner since 885, China broke apart into different regional dynasties and was not reunited until 960 (see Chapter 12). Even so, the Tang dynasty remained a powerful symbol for its neighbors and subsequent dynasties. It had stayed in power for nearly three centuries and governed more territory than any previous Chinese empire by combining support for Buddhist clergy and monasteries with strong armies, clear laws, and civil service examinations.

The Tibetan Empire, ca. 617–ca. 842

The rulers of the Tibetan plateau were among the first to adopt the Tang model of governance. Most of the Tibetan plateau lies within today's People's Republic of China, but historically it was a borderland not always under Chinese control. Located between the Kunlun Mountains to the north and the Himalayan Mountains to the south, the Tibetan plateau is high, ranging between 13,000 and 15,000 feet (4,000 and 5,000 m). Its extensive grasslands are suitable for raising horses, and barley can be grown in some river valleys.

- **CONTEXT&CONNECTIONS** The inhabitants of the Tibetan plateau used knotted cords and tallies to keep records because they had no writing system; the *Inca*, who ruled an empire in Peru in the 1400s, used a similar system, called *quipu*, of recordkeeping (Chapter 15). •

Sometime between 620 and 650, during the early years of the Tang, a ruler named **Songtsen Gampo** (srong-btsan sgam-po) (ca. 617–649/650) unified Tibet for the first time and founded the Yarlung dynasty (ca. 617–ca. 842). Hoping to build a strong state, he looked to both India and China for models of governance. In 632, he sent an official to India to study Buddhism, who returned and introduced a new alphabet, based on Sanskrit, that enabled Tibetans to write their language for the first time.

Songtsen Gampo (ca. 617–649/650) Founder of the Yarlung dynasty in Tibet who introduced Buddhism and an alphabet to his subjects.

Songtsen Gampo learned that the Tang emperor had provided Chinese brides for the leaders of several peoples living in western China and demanded that he be given a Chinese bride, too. At first Emperor Taizong refused, but when a Tibetan army nearly defeated the Tang forces in Sichuan, Emperor Taizong sent Songtsen Gampo a bride in 641. Later sources credit this woman, the princess of Wencheng (ONE-chuhng) (d. 684), with introducing Buddhism to Tibet and call her a bodhisattva because of her compassion for Tibetans. Her husband requested that the Tang court send to his court men who could read and write, and he dispatched members of his family to Chang'an to study Chinese. The Chinese sent craftsmen to teach Tibetans how to make silk and paper and how to brew wine.

The Tibetan army took advantage of Tang weakness during the An Lushan rebellion and in 763 briefly invaded the capital of Chang'an before retreating. They conquered territory in western China, which they ruled for nearly a century until 842, when the confederation of peoples who had supported the Yarlung dynasty suddenly broke apart. The Tibetan experience demonstrates the utility of the Sui/Tang model of governance for a people in the early stages of state formation.

Buddhism and the Tang Blueprint for Rule in Korea and Japan, to 1000

In Korea and Japan, as in Tibet, rulers adopted the Tang blueprint for rule, including Buddhism, because they hoped to match the accomplishments (particularly the military success) of the Tang dynasty. Certain elements of the blueprint, like the patronage of Buddhism, were easy for them to adopt, but others, like the equal-field system, did not suit either Korean or Japanese society.

Three Kingdoms period
The period of Korean history from 313 to 668 when the Koguryo, Paekche, and Silla kingdoms all fought for control of the Korean peninsula and exercised profound cultural influence on Japan.

● **CONTEXT&CONNECTIONS** Because of the Han dynasty military garrisons in Korea (see Chapter 4), Koreans had some contact with China as early as the Qin and Han Dynasties, while their neighbors to the east in Japan, who were surrounded by water, did not. The Japanese learned about many Chinese innovations from the Koreans. ●

Buddhism and Regional Kingdoms in Korea

The northern part of the Korean peninsula remained under Chinese dominance until 313 (see Chapter 4), when the king of the northern Koguryo (KOH-guh-ree-oh) region overthrew the last Chinese ruler. Because the Chinese presence had been limited to military garrisons, it had little lasting influence.

During this time, Korea was divided into different small chiefdoms on the verge of becoming states (see Map 8.2). The three most important ones were Koguryo (traditionally 37 B.C.E.–668 C.E.), Paekche (PECK-jeh; traditionally 18 B.C.E.–660 C.E.), and Silla (SHE-luh; traditionally 57 B.C.E.–935 C.E.). These "traditional" dates are based on much later legends, not contemporary evidence, which indicates that the three states largely coalesced after 300. The **Three Kingdoms period** started in 313, when the Koguryo kingdom expelled the last Chinese armies, and lasted until 668, when the Korean peninsula was unified for the first time.

Map 8.2 Korea and Japan, ca. 550 The Japanese island of Kyushu lies some 150 miles (240 km) from the Korean peninsula, and the island of Tsushima provided a convenient stepping stone to the Japanese archipelago for those fleeing the warfare on the Korean peninsula. The Korean migrants introduced their social structure (with its bone-rank system) and Buddhism to Japan.

After 300, these three kingdoms constantly vied with each other for territory and influence. Their campaigns extended all the way to the Japanese archipelago, where the Korean armies introduced new iron weapons like swords and spear points. In the centuries before gunpowder, heavy armor was a powerful military technology that protected soldiers from flying arrows and spears.

The Korean rulers adopted crucial elements of the Tang blueprint for rule during the Three Kingdoms period. They learned to read and write using Chinese characters and read them aloud using Korean pronunciation. Adopting Chinese-style written laws, they established Confucian academies where students could study Chinese characters, Confucian classics, and other works in Chinese. They also introduced Buddhism.

Before the adoption of Buddhism, the residents of the Korean peninsula prayed to local deities or nature spirits for good health and good harvests. The vast majority lived in small agricultural villages and grew rice. The ruling families of the Koguryo and Paekche kingdoms adopted Buddhism in the 370s and 380s for the same reasons: their rulers hoped to strengthen their dynasties. Like Chinese rulers, the Koguryo and Paekche kings combined patronage for Buddhism with support for Confucian education.

The circumstances accompanying the adoption of Buddhism by the **Silla** royal house illustrate how divided many Koreans were about the new religion. King Pophung (r. 514–540), whose name means "King who promoted the Dharma," wanted to patronize Buddhism but feared the opposition of powerful families who had passed laws against it. Sometime around 527, he persuaded one of his courtiers to build a shrine to the Buddha. However, since such activity was banned, the king had no choice but to order the courtier's beheading. The king and his subject prayed for a miracle. An early history of Korea describes the moment of execution: *"Down came the sword on the monk's neck, and up flew his head spouting blood as white as milk."* The miracle, we are told, silenced the opposition, and Silla became Buddhist in that year.*

Silla
Korean kingdom that adopted Buddhism and united with the Tang dynasty in 660 to defeat the Koguryo and Paekche kingdoms, unifying Korea for the first time in 668.

By the middle of the sixth century, having adopted pro-Buddhist policies, all three Korean kingdoms sent government officials and monks to China to learn how to govern. The three ruling dynasties built Buddhist monasteries in major cities and in the countryside, but ordinary people continued to worship the same local deities they had in pre-Buddhist times.

A Formidable Korean Warrior This mounted cavalry soldier, a ceramic figurine from the Korean peninsula made in the fifth or sixth century C.E., displays the most up-to-date weaponry and armor of his time. Observe his saddle, the armor covering his legs (which consists of small plates of iron sewn together in parallel rows), and, in particular, the stirrups, a brand-new innovation that gave riders much greater control over their mounts. (Courtesy, National Museum of Korea)

From 598 into the 640s, the Sui and Tang Dynasties led several attacks on the Korean peninsula, all unsuccessful. In 660 the Silla kingdom allied with the Tang dynasty in hopes of defeating the Koguryo and Paekche kingdoms. Paekche was allied with the Japanese, and the Silla-Tang armies defeated the Paekche forces first in 660 and then in a major naval battle at Paekchon River in 663. The combined Silla-Tang forces did not reach Japan, but the defeat of Japan's navy—the greatest before 1600—caused the loss of four hundred Japanese ships and several thousand Japanese sailors.

After defeating the Paekche, the Silla-Tang armies conquered the Koguryo dynasty. By 675 the Silla forces had pushed Tang armies back to the northern edges of the Korean peninsula. This victory unified the Korean peninsula for the first time under Korean rule and ushered in a period of stability that lasted for two and a half centuries. Silla kings offered different

*Ilyon, *Samguk Yusa: Legends and History of the Three Kingdoms of Ancient Korea*, trans. Tae-Hung Ha and Grafton K. Mintz (Seoul: Yonsei University Press, 1972), p. 188.

types of support to Buddhism, with several following the example of Ashoka and the Sui founder in building pagodas throughout their kingdom.

bone-rank system
Korean social ranking system used by the Silla dynasty that divided Korean families into seven different categories, with kings coming from only the top group.

Some elements of the Tang blueprint were not appropriate for the highly stratified Korean society of the seventh and eighth centuries. The **bone-rank system** classed all Korean families into one of seven categories. The true-bone classification was reserved for the highest-born aristocratic families, which included those eligible to be king. Below them were six other ranks in descending order.

The Silla rulers found that the redistribution of land every three years according to the equal-field system was not workable and that they could govern better if they granted entire villages forever to members of the true-bone families. In turn, the true-bone families paid the salaries of government officials, who then appointed other officials from the true-bone families. Civil service examinations became an important element of Korean society, but unlike in Tang China, were limited to candidates from the highest-ranking families.

The Silla kingdom entered a period of decline after 780. From that time on, different branches of the royal family fought each other for control of the throne, and no one managed to rule for long.

The Emergence of Japan

Japan is an island chain, or archipelago, of four large islands and many smaller ones. Like Korea, which is only 150 miles (240 km) away, Japan had no indigenous writing system, so archaeologists must piece together the island's early history from archaeological materials and later sources like the *Chronicle of Japan* (*Nihon shoki*) (knee-HOHN SHOW-kee), a year-by-year account written in 720. The royal Yamato (YAH-mah-toe) house, the *Chronicle* claims, was directly descended from the sun-goddess Amaterasu (AH-mah-TAY-rah-suh). The indigenous religion of Japan, called Shinto (SHIN-toe), included the worship of different spirits of trees, streams, and mountains, as well as deceased rulers.

In the 300s and 400s, multiple chieftains, including the Yamato clan's, ruled the different regions of Japan. Cultural influence from Korea to Japan accelerated in the fifth and sixth centuries, when many Koreans fled the political instability of the disunited peninsula. In addition to military practices, the Korean refugees introduced techniques of governance relying on Chinese characters, law codes, and Buddhist teachings. These changes affected all social groups.

The kings of the Yamato clan gave titles modeled on the Korean bone-rank system to powerful Japanese clans who were their military allies. They also allied with the Korean kingdom of Paekche against the Silla kingdom, which was geographically closest and so posed the greatest threat to Japan. Once the Paekche royal house adopted Buddhism, it began to pressure its clients, the Yamato clan, to follow suit. In 538, the Paekche ambassador brought a gift of Buddhist texts and images for the Yamato chief, but the most powerful Japanese families hesitated to support the new religion. The conflict among supporters and opponents of Buddhism lasted for nearly fifty years, during which the Paekche rulers continued to send Buddhist writings, monks, and nuns.

Soga clan
Powerful Japanese family of Korean descent that ruled in conjunction with the Yamato clan from 587 to 645; introduced Buddhism to Japan.

The main supporters of Buddhism in Japan were the **Soga clan**, who were most likely of Korean ancestry and who supplied the Yamato rulers with wives. In 587, armed conflict broke out between the clans opposed to Buddhism and the Soga family, led by the thirteen-year-old prince Shotoku (SHOW-toh-ku) (574–622), too young to govern in his own right, and his mother, the regent. Prince Shotoku vowed that if the Soga clan was victorious, the government would support

Buddhism. The pro-Buddhist forces won, and the Japanese court converted to Buddhism in 587.

Aware of the founding of the Sui dynasty and the subsequent reunification of China, Prince Shotoku sent the first Japanese delegation to China in 600. A large mission could have as many as five hundred participants, including officials, Buddhist monks, students, and translators. Some Japanese stayed in China for as long as thirty years before they returned home to teach their countrymen what they had learned.

Acutely aware of China's military campaigns in Korea, successive Japanese rulers made several attempts to implement the Tang blueprint for rule. They sought to strengthen their country and also to enhance their own rule, because a Chinese-style emperor had much more power than a chieftain. The 663 defeat of their Paekche allies galvanized the Japanese rulers, who realized that, if they did not adopt Chinese-style reforms, they could easily suffer the same fate. In 701, a Japanese ruler attempted to enforce the Tang blueprint for rule: he successfully issued a written law code, assigned rice-paddy land to individual households, and redistributed land every six years.

The changing design of Japanese capitals clearly illustrates the extent of Chinese influence. Before 710 the Japanese had occupied thirty-six capitals in 250 years. Houses were made with thatched roofs and wooden pillars buried directly in the dirt, where they rotted after only a few years. Every time a ruler died, the new ruler shifted the capital, partially to escape the ghost of the deceased emperor. After 710 the Japanese adopted Chinese building practices, using tiled roofs and stone bases for timber columns so that they did not rot. They built a new capital at Nara, their first Chinese-style city with gridded streets, walls, and gates, which gives its name to the Nara period (710–784).

Then in 784, they shifted the capital to modern Kyoto, where it remained for over one thousand years. One-fourth the area of Tang dynasty Chang'an, the city had a population of 120,000, one-eighth that of its Chinese model. Like Chang'an, Kyoto was built to impress: its avenues were half as wide as Chang'an's. The cost of construction proved so onerous that some emperors suspended building simply to ease the burden on the residents, and the city was filled with large empty spaces. Kyoto was called Heian (HEY-on), and the Heian period lasted from 784 to 1185 (see Figure 8.1, page 233).

Contact with China brought genuine risks, too. Starting in the 720s and then accelerating rapidly in the 730s, multiple smallpox epidemics

Christopher Rennie/Robert Harding Picture Library Ltd / Alamy

Horyuji Pagoda, Nara, Japan Built before 794, this five-story pagoda is possibly one of the oldest wooden buildings in the world. Like the stupa at the Indian site of Sanchi, it was built to hold relics of the Buddha. Not certain how the building survived multiple earthquakes without sustaining any damage, architects speculate that the central pillar is not directly connected to the ground below, allowing it to float slightly above the ground.

broke out. Commentators knew that the disease originated in China and Korea. In earlier centuries Japan's population was dispersed over a wide area, so epidemic diseases could not spread. But the building of Chinese-style cities and growing population density resulting from the introduction of rice agriculture created the optimal conditions for epidemics. Japan's population reached around 5 million in the year 700, and some 25 percent of its people died in the epidemics.

AP® THEMES

What elements of Chinese culture and style of governance did Korean and Japanese rulers reject in forming their own policies?

In 749 a woman named Koken ascended to the throne when her father died of smallpox, and she herself died in 770 of the same disease. A devout Buddhist who became a nun, Empress Koken decided to generate Buddhist merit by printing 1 million copies of a Buddhist prayer (pronounced in Sanskrit but written in Chinese characters) and placing the prayers in small wooden pagodas. She buried 100,000 pagodas each in ten different monasteries. Her act illustrates both the lasting power of the chakravartin ideal and the appeal of the brand-new technology of woodblock printing. She was the eighth woman to rule Japan as emperor, but when she died, the imperial family decided not to allow any more woman emperors because of persistent rumors of her sexual involvement with a Buddhist monk (similar rumors circulated about Emperor Wu of the Tang).

In the years after 800, the Japanese gradually departed from the Tang blueprint for rule. Although the *Tang Code* prescribed a militia staffed by farmer-soldiers who left their fields to fight part-time in battle, the emperor and his courtiers preferred to hire full-time bodyguards, who were the precursors of the samurai warriors. The government no longer redistributed land every six years; instead powerful families amassed large, permanent estates. The vast majority of the Japanese population continued to farm, while only a tiny minority, numbering in the thousands, lived in the capital and served the emperor as courtiers.

We know much more about the courtiers than any other group in early Japan because they produced almost all surviving records. Like them, Ennin wrote entirely in Chinese characters, which he pronounced in Japanese. During his travels in China, because he could not speak Chinese, he wrote everything down in Chinese characters. He called this "brush-talking."

Yet because Japanese, like Korean, was in a different language family, Chinese characters did not capture the full meaning of Japanese. In the ninth century, at the same time that Ennin was brush-talking in China, the Japanese developed an alphabet, called **kana** (KAH-nah), that allowed them to write Japanese words as they were pronounced.

kana

An alphabet developed in the ninth century that allowed the Japanese to write the pronunciation of words in Japanese.

In 1000, a Japanese woman named Murasaki Shikibu (MOO-rah-sock-ee SHE-key-boo) used kana to write one of the world's most important works of literature, *The Tale of Genji*, which some view as the world's first novel. The book relates the experiences of a young prince as he grows up. While the highest members of Japan's aristocracy could read and write—men using both Chinese characters and kana and women more often only kana—the vast majority of their countrymen remained illiterate.

By 1000, Japan, like Korea, had joined a larger East Asian cultural realm, in which people read and wrote Chinese characters and ate with chopsticks as the Chinese did. Although its rulers were predominantly Buddhist, they supported Confucian education, and their capital looked like Chang'an even if it was much smaller. After a brief period of using the *Tang Code* as a model of governance, the Japanese emperors abandoned the equal-field system and civil service exams in favor of a more Japanese system in which the emperor and his courtiers lived in the capital while they farmed out all military tasks to full-time warriors.

The Place of Buddhism and Hinduism in World History

In the year 100, the only Buddhists in the world lived in India and Sri Lanka; by the year 1000, Buddhist teachings had spread throughout the entire region encompassing South, Southeast, Central, and East Asia. When the Japanese monk Ennin traveled in China between 838 and 847, he encountered Buddhist monks from north and south India, Sri Lanka, Central Asia, Japan, Korea, and of course, China. Between 380 and 400, the Roman woman Egeria had traveled as a Christian pilgrim to Jerusalem to see where Jesus had lived and to visit monasteries in Turkey (see Chapter 7). Ennin's reasons for going on pilgrimage differed. His purpose was not to see where the Buddha had lived (in any case, the Buddha had lived in India, not in China), but to study and obtain books so that he could understand complex Buddhist teachings more completely.

Chinese monasteries hosted Indian monks who taught Sanskrit, the language of many texts from India, but as the centuries passed, more and more Buddhist texts were translated into Chinese. A beginning student of Sanskrit, Ennin read these texts in Chinese. Like Greek and Latin in the Christian world, Sanskrit and Chinese were spoken and written throughout the Buddhist world. Unable to speak Chinese, Ennin found that he could brush-talk by writing Chinese characters to communicate with almost every Buddhist he met.

Buddhism became a major world religion during the same centuries as Christianity did. No single event in Buddhist history marked a turning point like the Edict of Milan in 313 or the decree of 380 that declared Christianity the official religion of the Roman empire (see Chapter 7). Instead, drawn by the chakravartin ideal, different Asian rulers made a series of individual decisions to support Buddhism.

First, sometime around 120, Kanishka, the Kushan ruler of north India, launched a missionary movement to introduce the teachings of Greater Vehicle Buddhism to Central Asia and China. Then, during the fourth and sixth centuries, rulers in different places converted to Buddhism: the Xiongnu leader Shi Le in north China, the rulers of the three Korean kingdoms of Koguryo, Silla,

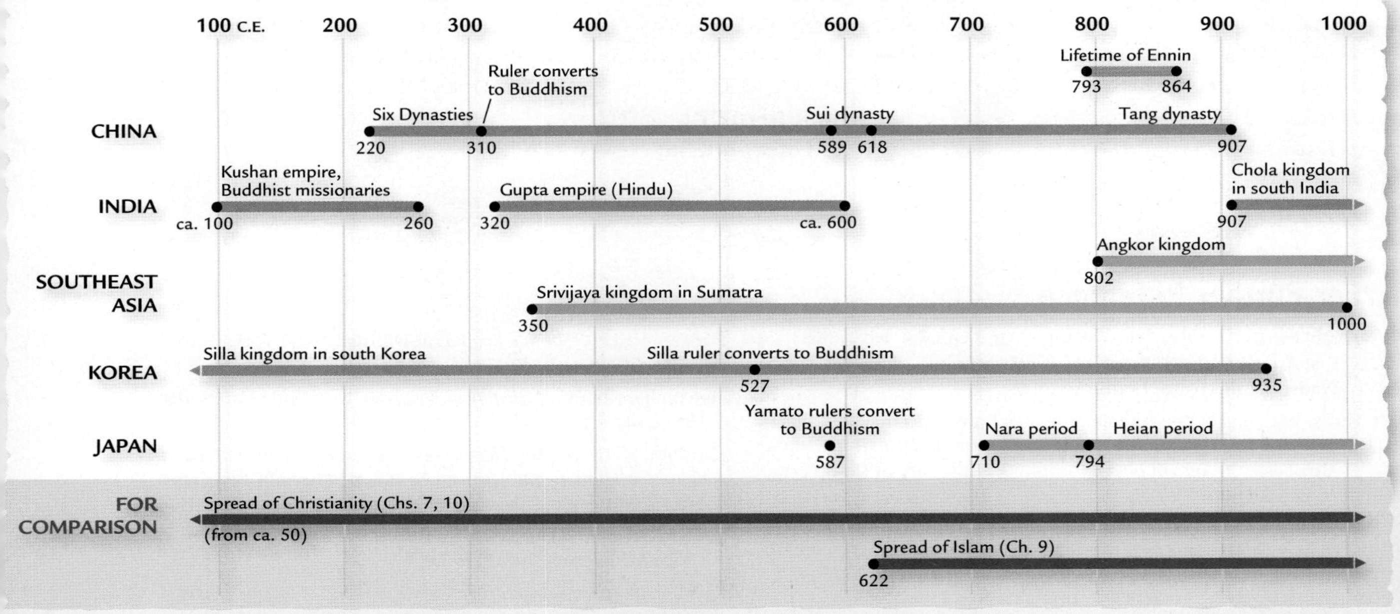

and Paekche, and the Yamato rulers of Japan. After the Sui emperor reunified the Chinese empire in 589, he financed the construction of Buddhist monasteries all over his empire.

Many of these events involved an element of belief, as individual rulers embraced Buddhist teachings, and some—like the Empress Koken of Japan—even became Buddhist nuns or monks. But these decisions also turned on nonreligious elements. The Tang blueprint for rule, as written in the *Tang Code*, offered a guide for the heads of smaller, weaker states who wished to become rulers as powerful as the Tang emperor. Rulers in Korea, Tibet, and Japan all issued local versions of the *Tang Code*.

In India, as more rulers endowed Hindu temples and patronized Brahmin priests, Hinduism gained in importance as Buddhism declined. Southeast Asian rulers combined both Hindu and Buddhist elements and sponsored magnificent religious monuments like Angkor Wat in Cambodia.

At the time of Ennin's visit, Buddhism had become so influential that the Chinese Emperor Wuzong ordered thousands of monks and nuns, who did not pay taxes, to return to lay life and generate income for his revenue-starved dynasty. On his death in 846, his successor immediately overturned all of his hostile measures, and Ennin was able to retrieve from his Korean interpreter friend the books he cared about so deeply and take them to Japan.

By the year 1000, Buddhism, Hinduism, and Christianity had all spread far beyond the lands of their origin. Each is one of the largest religions in the world today, and many Hindus and Buddhists live in Asia. In the next chapter we will consider yet another world religion that had spread over a large region by 1000 and that would have an equally profound impact on world history: Islam.

Key Terms

Ennin (214)
Silk Routes (214)
Hinduism (214)
bodhisattva (216)
Gupta dynasty (216)
bhakti (217)
purohita (221)
Angkor dynasty (225)
Fotudeng (225)
Tang dynasty (227)
equal-field system (227)
Emperor Wu (230)
woodblock printing (232)
Songtsen Gampo (235)
Three Kingdoms period (236)
Silla (237)
bone-rank system (238)
Soga clan (238)
kana (240)

For Further Reference

Ebrey, Patricia Buckley, Anne Walthall, and James B. Palais. *East Asia: A Cultural, Social, and Political History*. 2d ed. Boston: Wadsworth/Cengage Learning, 2009.

Farris, William Wayne. "Ancient Japan's Korean Connection." In *Sacred Texts and Buried Treasures: Issues in the Historical Archaeology of Ancient Japan*. Honolulu: University of Hawai'i Press, 1998, pp. 55–122.

Hansen, Valerie. "The Devotional Use of Buddhist Art in Ennin's Diary." *Orientations* 45.3 (April 2014): 76–82.

Hansen, Valerie. *The Open Empire: A History of China to 1600*. New York: Norton, 2000.

Hansen, Valerie. *The Silk Road: A New History*. New York: Oxford University Press, 2012.

Holcombe, Charles. *A History of East Asia*. New York: Cambridge University Press, 2011.

Kapstein, Matthew. *The Tibetan Assimilation of Buddhism: Conversion, Contestation, and Memory*. New York: Oxford University Press, 2000.

Keown, Damien. *Buddhism: A Very Short Introduction*. New York: Oxford University Press, 1996.

Krahl, Regina. *Shipwrecked: Tang Treasures and Monsoon Winds*. Washington, D.C.: Smithsonian Books, 2011.

Ricklefs, M.C., et al. *A New History of Southeast Asia*. New York: Palgrave Macmillan, 2010.

Thapar, Romila. *Early India from the Origins to* AD *1300*. Berkeley: University of California Press, 2003.

Waley, Paul, and Nicolas Fiévé. "Kyoto and Edo-Tokyo: Urban Histories in Parallels and Tangents." In *Japanese Capitals in Historical Perspective*, ed. Paul Waley and Nicolas Fiévé. London: Routledge Curzon, 2003.

Worrall, Simon. "Made in China." *National Geographic Magazine* (June 2009): 112–123.

AP® Review Questions for Chapter 8

Multiple-Choice Questions

QUESTIONS 1–4 REFER TO THE FOLLOWING PASSAGE.

Confucius said, "The barbarians with a ruler are not so good as the Chinese without one." . . .

Mou Tzu said: ". . . According to the Buddhist scriptures, above, below, and all around, all beings containing blood belong to the Buddha-clan. Therefore I revere and study these scriptures. Why should I reject the Way of Yao, Shun, Confucius? Gold and jade do not harm each other, crystal and amber do not cheapen each other."

—*The Disputation of Error*, by an unknown Buddhist author, the Southern Dynasties, ca. fifth century C.E.

1. Which of the following is a likely purpose of this passage?
   (A) A tool for answering Confucian critics of Buddhism
   (B) An explanation of how Daoist and Buddhist teachings contradict each other
   (C) An explanation of the superiority of the Buddhist dharma to all other religions
   (D) A response to Brahmin critiques of Buddhist moral teachings

2. The views expressed in the passage are best seen as evidence for which of the following?
   (A) The universal message of the Buddhist faith
   (B) The eclipse of Mahayana schools by the Theravada sect
   (C) The rejection of Buddhism by the Tang dynasty
   (D) The uniformity of Buddhist doctrine over time and place

3. Which of the following conclusions about the period from 600 B.C.E. to 600 C.E. is most supported by the passage?
   (A) Missionary religions tended to reinforce traditional class and gender roles.
   (B) Expansion and intensification of trade networks increased the exchange of luxury goods.
   (C) The movement of peoples caused environmental and linguistic effects.
   (D) New belief systems and cultural traditions emerged asserting universal truths.

4. Which is the most likely explanation for the harsh portrayal of the Confucian scholar?
   (A) Confucians were accepting of Buddhist doctrines and rituals.
   (B) Confucians worked with Buddhists to squash Daoist beliefs.
   (C) Confucians considered Buddhism inferior because of its non-Chinese origins.
   (D) Confucians were suspicious of family life as an appropriate model for attaining harmony.

QUESTIONS 5–7 REFER TO THE FOLLOWING MAP.

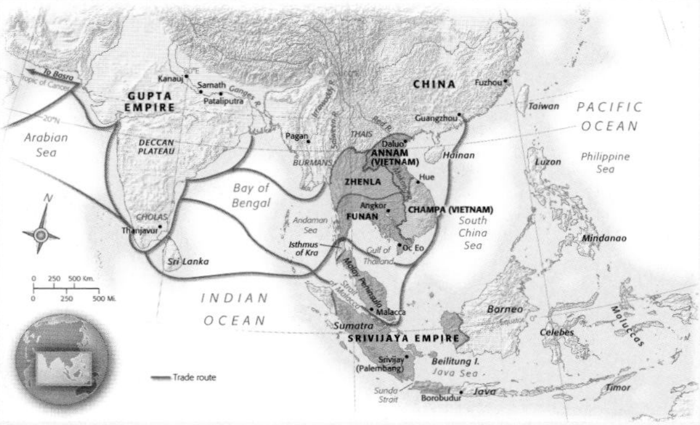

5. Which of the following was a direct result of the trade pattern shown on the map?
   (A) The spread of Buddhism and Hinduism to Southwest Asia
   (B) The adoption of Christianity by local elites
   (C) The spread of Buddhism and Hinduism to Southeast Asia
   (D) The spread of indigenous religions from Southeast Asia to South Asia

6. Which of the following led directly to the cultural diffusion represented on the map?
   (A) The growth of interregional networks
   (B) The expansion of South Asian empires into Southeast Asia
   (C) Muslim merchant activity prior to the fifth century C.E.
   (D) Confucian support of merchant activity over farming

7. Which of the following is an accurate conclusion that can be drawn from the map?
   (A) Southeast Asia was isolated compared to other regions in the time period.
   (B) Southeast Asia was affected by both South and East Asian cultures.
   (C) Southeast Asia rejected all forms of South Asian religion.
   (D) Southeast Asia adopted only Confucianism.

QUESTIONS 8–10 REFER TO THE FOLLOWING PASSAGES.

The Master said, "In serving his parents a filial son renders the utmost reverence to them while at home. In supporting them he maximizes their pleasure. When they are sick he takes every care. At their death he expresses grief. Then he sacrifices to them with full solemnity. If he has fulfilled these five requirements, then he is truly able to serve his parents."

— *The Classic of Filial Piety*, a Confucian classic from the twelfth century C.E.

Though you diligently sacrificed to me while you were at home,
It only go you a reputation in the village for being filial,
Granted that you did sprinkle libations of wine upon my grave,
But it would have been better for you to copy a single line of sutra.

—Story of the Indian monk Maudgalyayana, author unknown, Sanskrit manuscript from between 300 B.C.E. and 300 C.E.

8. The tone of the *first* passage best reflects which development in Chinese society?
   (A) The acceptance of Legalism as the official policy of the government
   (B) The spread of Daoist meditative practices
   (C) The adoption of the Buddhist doctrine of Nirvana
   (D) The dominance of Confucian ideals concerning social relationships

9. The two passages disagree over which of the following conclusions?
   (A) The appropriateness of practicing Confucian rituals
   (B) The possibilities of attaining Nirvana in future lifetimes
   (C) The requirements for acquiring and keeping the Mandate of Heaven
   (D) The drawbacks of monastic life in Buddhism

10. The ideas addressed in the passages above are best explained in the context of which of the following statements?
   (A) The continuity of gender roles from the Classical Era into the Postclassical Era
   (B) The effect of religious conversion on family life
   (C) The decreasing influence of the Tang dynasty in Central Asia
   (D) The justification of new forms of coercive labor by religions

Short-Answer Questions

Now Buddha was a man of the barbarians who did not speak the language of China and wore clothes of a different fashion. His sayings did not concern the ways of our ancient kings, nor did his manner of dress conform to their laws. He understood neither the duties that bind sovereign and subject nor the affections of father and son. If he were still alive today and came to our court by order of his ruler, Your Majesty might condescend to receive him. . . . How then now that he is long dead, could his rotten bones . . . be rightly admitted to the palace? Your servant is deeply ashamed and begs that this bone be given to the proper authorities to be cast into fire and water that this evil may be rooted out.

—Han Yu, Chinese scholar, *Memorial on the Bone of the Buddha*, 819 C.E.

1. Use the passage above to answer parts A, B, and C.
   A. Identify the point of view expressed by Han Yu. Then briefly explain how ONE of the following aspects of the Tang dynasty influenced the point of view expressed above:
      - Religion or belief system
      - Relationships with regions outside of China
      - Political institutions
   B. Briefly explain ONE example of how Buddhism was perceived in Tang China.
   C. Briefly explain ONE example of how Buddhism was incorporated into Chinese culture.

2. Answer parts A, B, and C.
   A. Briefly explain ONE influence of Chinese culture on Japan.
   B. Provide ONE piece of evidence that supports this view.
   C. Some historians contend that China is essentially a Confucian society and not a Buddhist one. Provide ONE additional piece of evidence that supports this view.

9 Islamic Empires of Western Asia and Africa, 600–1258

Abbasid Singing Girl

Khaizuran (ca. 739–789) grew up as a slave girl but became the favored wife of the supreme religious and political leader of the Islamic world, the caliph Mahdi (MAH-dee), who reigned from 775 to 785 as the third ruler of the Abbasid (ah-BAHS-sid) caliphate (750–1258). As the wife of Mahdi and the mother of the caliph who succeeded him, Khaizuran (HAY-zuh-rahn) played an active role in court politics. A slave dealer brought her, while still a teenager, to Mecca, where she met Mahdi's father. He had come to perform the hajj pilgrimage, the religious obligation of all Muslims. When he inquired where she was from, she said:

> *Born at Mecca and brought up at Jurash (in the Yaman).**

This is one of the few statements by Khaizuran that is preserved in the written record. Of course we would like to know more, but she left no writings of her own. The written record almost always says more about men than about women, and as previous chapters have shown, more about prominent and literate women than about ordinary and illiterate ones. To understand the experience of everyone in a society, historians must exercise great ingenuity in using the evidence at hand. Khaizuran provides a rare opportunity to study the life of an ordinary Muslim woman who rose to become a leader in her own right.

In its support for Islam, the Abbasid dynasty played a role in world history similar to that of the Roman empire, which patronized Christianity (see Chapter 7), and the Tang dynasty in China, which supported Buddhism (see Chapter 8). Under the Abbasids, Islam became a world religion with millions of adherents in Africa, Europe, and Asia. At the peak of their power, around the year 800, the

---

*Nabia Abbott, *Two Queens of Baghdad: Mother and Wife of Harun al-Rashid* (London: Al Saqi Books, 1986, reprint of 1946 original), p. 26, citing Jahiz (pseud.), *Kitab al-Mahasin wa Al-Addad*, ed. van Vloten (Leiden: E. J. Brill, 1898), pp. 232–233.

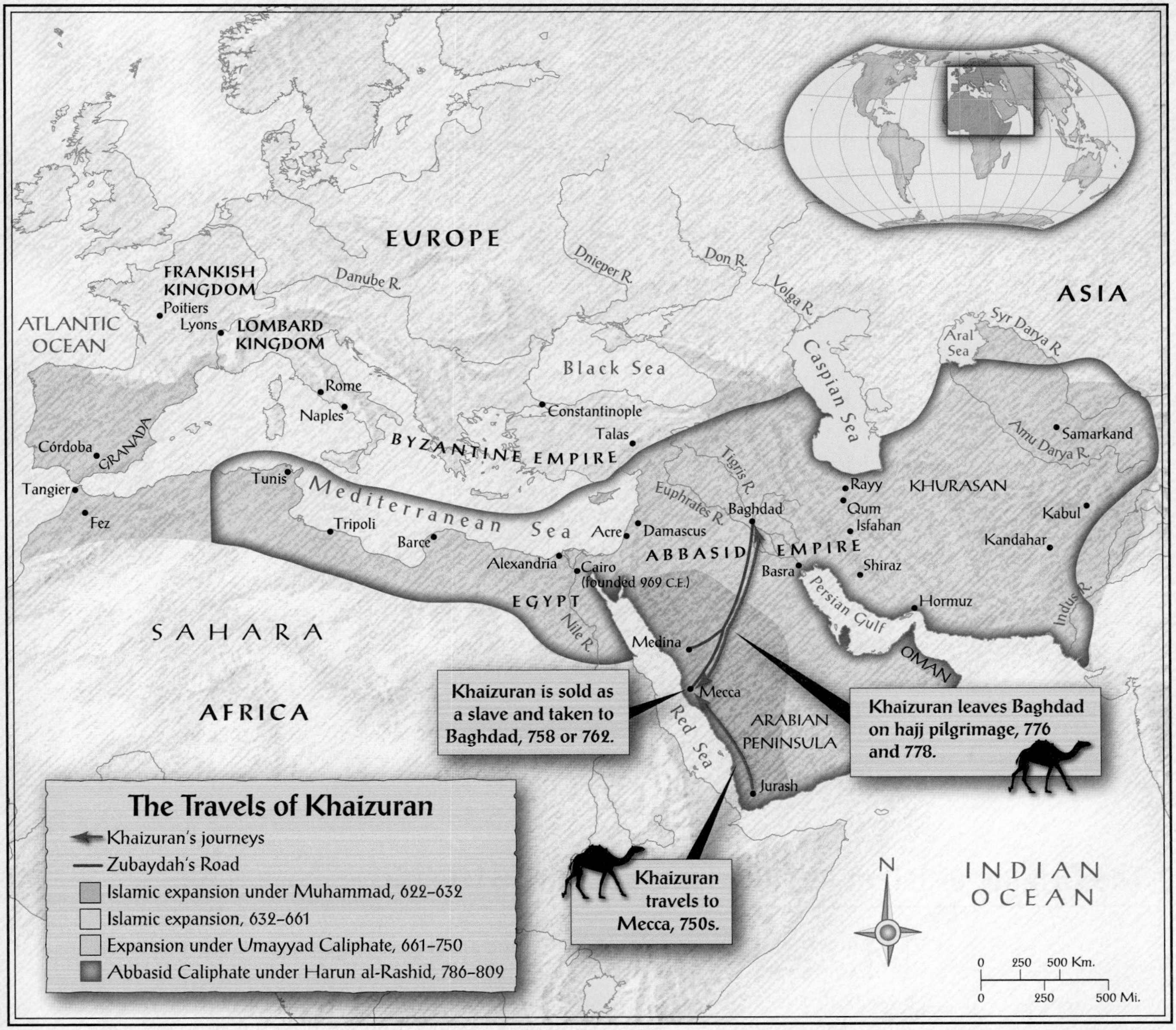

Abbasids governed some 35 or 40 million people living in North Africa and Southwest Asia.*

But the Abbasid empire differed in a crucial way from either the Roman or the Tang empire. When the Roman emperor Constantine issued the Edict of Milan in 313, he recognized a religion already popular among his subjects. And when the

Khaizuran

Slave girl (ca. 739–789) who became the wife of the caliph Mahdi (r. 775–785), the third ruler of the Abbasid caliphate. Khaizuran played an active role in court politics.

*Charles Issawi, "The Area and Population of the Arab Empire: An Essay in Speculation," in *The Islamic Middle East, 700–1900: Studies in Economic and Social History*, ed. A. L. Udovitch (Princeton: Darwin Press, 1981), pp. 375–396; estimated population on p. 392.

early Tang emperors supported Buddhism, they did so because many Chinese had come to embrace it. Yet the Roman and Tang emperors could withdraw their support for these religions, and they sometimes did.

In contrast, the Abbasid rulers were religious leaders who claimed a familial relationship with the prophet **Muhammad** (ca. 570–632) through his uncle Abbas (ah-BAHS). They could not withdraw their support from the Islamic religious community because they headed that very religious community. At the same time, they were also political leaders; the founder of the Abbasid dynasty seized power from the Umayyad (oo-MY-uhd) dynasty in 750. Even when the Abbasid caliphs no longer served as political leaders, they retained their religious role. Others could be king, but the Abbasids had a unique claim to being caliph.

Muhammad
(ca. 570–632) Believed by Muslims to be the last prophet who received God's revelations directly from the angel Gabriel. The first leader of the Muslim community.

This chapter will examine the history of Islam, from the first revelations received by Muhammad to the final collapse of the Abbasid empire in 1258.

KEY CONCEPT QUESTIONS

- How do the beliefs and practices of Islam reflect interactions among the peoples of the Arabian peninsula? **(Key Concept 3.1)**
- How did the caliphate develop after the death of Muhammad? **(Key Concept 3.2)**
- How did the Abbasid caliphate blend different cultural traditions? **(Key Concept 3.2)**
- What new forms of governance emerged in the Islamic world following the collapse of the Abbasid caliphate? **(Key Concept 3.2)**

The Origins of Islam and the First Caliphs, 610–750

Muhammad began to preach sometime around 613 and won a large following among the residents of the Arabian peninsula before his death in 632. The man who succeeded to the leadership of the Islamic religious community was called the **caliph** (KAY-lif), literally "successor." The caliph exercised political authority because the Muslim religious community was also a state, complete with its own government and a powerful army that conquered many neighboring regions. The first four caliphs were chosen from different clans on the basis of their ties to Muhammad, but after 661 all the caliphs came from a single clan, or dynasty, the Umayyads, who governed until 750.

caliph
Literally "successor." Before 945, the caliph was the successor to Muhammad and the supreme political and religious leader of the Islamic world. After 945, the caliph had no political power but served as the religious leader of all Muslims.

The Life and Teachings of Muhammad, ca. 570–632

Muhammad was born into a family of merchants sometime around 570 in Mecca, a trading community in the Arabian peninsula far from any major urban center. At the time of his birth, the two major powers of the Mediterranean world were the Byzantine empire (see Chapter 10) and the Sasanian empire of the Persians (see Chapter 6).

On the southern edge of the two empires lay the Arabian peninsula, which consisted largely of desert punctuated by small oases. Traders traveling from Syria to Yemen frequently stopped at the few urban settlements, including Mecca and Medina, near the coast of the Red Sea. The local peoples spoke Arabic.

The population was divided between urban residents and the nomadic residents of the desert, called Bedouins (BED-dwins), who tended flocks of sheep, horses, and camels and were divided into different clans. Even though they no longer followed a nomadic way of life, many city people maintained a strong clan identity. Extensive trade networks connected the Arabian peninsula with Palestine and Syria, and followers of both Judaism and Christianity lived in its urban centers.

All Arabs, whether nomadic or urban, worshiped protective deities that resided in an individual tree, a group of trees, or sometimes a rock with an unusual shape. One of the most revered objects was a large black rock in a cube-shaped shrine, called the Kaaba (KAH-buh), at Mecca.

AP® THEMES

How did the environment and geography of the Arabian peninsula shape settlement patterns and networks of exchange?

● **CONTEXT&CONNECTIONS** The Kaaba was associated with Abraham, the patriarch described in the Hebrew Bible (see Chapter 2). In the 400s, one Egyptian observer, himself possibly an Arab, wrote that the Arabs believed they were descended from Abraham's son Ishmael (not Isaac, the man the *Jews* (key term in Chapter 2) believed to be their ancestor) and that they refrained from eating pork. These *monotheists* (Chapter 2), the Egyptian noted, were neither Jews nor Christians.* ●

While in his forties and already a wealthy merchant, Muhammad had a series of visions in which he saw a figure. Muslims believe that God spoke to Muhammad through the angel Gabriel, after which Muhammad called on everyone to submit to God. The religion founded on belief in this event is called Islam, meaning "submission" or "surrender." The Arabic word *allah* means "the god" and, by extension, "God." Early Muslims had contact with Jews, and their understanding of God considerably overlapped with Jewish and Christian conceptions.

Muslims do not call Muhammad the founder of Islam because God's teachings, they believe, are timeless. Muslims consider Muhammad the last messenger of God, however, and historians place the beginning date for Islam in the 610s because no one thought of himself or herself as Muslim before Muhammad received his revelations. Muhammad's earliest followers came from his immediate family: his wife Khadijah (kah-DEE-juh) and his cousin Ali, whom he had raised since early childhood.

● **CONTEXT&CONNECTIONS** Muhammad taught that his predecessors included all the Hebrew prophets from the Hebrew Bible as well as *Jesus* (Chapter 7) and his disciples. The Quran "singles out Noah, Abraham, Moses, and Jesus as prophets with whom God established a strong covenant."† God granted Jesus the ability to perform miracles, the Quran teaches, but Jesus was not divine. Scholars of religion refer to Judaism, Christianity, and Islam as Abrahamic religions because they all recognize figures from the Hebrew Bible, such as Abraham, as important. All three of the Abrahamic religions have a specific text they see as holy, whether the Hebrew Bible of the Jews, the New and Old Testaments of the Christians, or the Quran of the Muslims. ●

---

*Patricia Crone, *Meccan Trade and the Rise of Islam* (Piscataway, N.J.: Gorgias Press, 2004), p. 190, n104.

†Neal Robinson, "Jesus," in *Encyclopaedia of the Qur'an*, Gen. ed. Jane Dammen McAuliffe (Leiden, the Netherlands: Brill Online Reference Works, 2015).

Certificate of Pilgrimage to Mecca Many pilgrims to Mecca purchased a document to show that they had completed the pilgrimage. The one here, written on paper, testifies that the bearer—a woman named Maymuna, possibly a native of North Africa—completed the pilgrimage to Mecca in 1433 and thus fulfilled the Fifth Pillar of Islam. The certificate shows the Kaaba at Mecca (in the second frame from the top), the Prophet Muhammad's tomb at Medina (fourth frame from the top), and the sole of Muhammad's sandal (bottom frame). The certificate also includes several passages from the Quran about the hajj.

Unlike the existing religion of Arabia, but like the Abrahamic religions of Christianity and Judaism, Islam was monotheistic; Muslims worshiped only one God. Muhammad also stressed the role of individual choice: each person had the power to decide to worship God or to turn away from God. Those who submitted to God became the first Muslims. Men who converted to Islam had to undergo circumcision, a practice already widespread throughout the Arabian peninsula.

Islam developed within the context of Bedouin society, in which men were charged with protecting the honor of their wives and daughters. Accordingly, women often assumed a subordinate role in Islam. In Bedouin society, a man could repudiate his wife by saying "I divorce you" three times. Although women could not repudiate their husbands in the same way, they could divorce an impotent man.

Muhammad recognized the traditional right of men to repudiate their wives but introduced several measures aimed at improving the status of women, including limiting the number of wives a man could take to four. His supporters explained that Islamic marriage offered this limited number of secondary wives far more legal protection than multiple secondary wives had enjoyed before Muhammad's reforms. He also banned the Bedouin practice of female infanticide. Finally, he instructed his female relatives to veil themselves when receiving visitors.

● **CONTEXT&CONNECTIONS** Although many in the modern world think the veiling of women an exclusively Islamic practice, women in various societies in the ancient world, including Byzantines, Greeks, Mesopotamians, and Arabs, wore veils as a sign of high station. ●

Feuding among different clans was a constant problem in Bedouin society. In 620, a group of non-kinsmen from Medina, a city 215 miles (346 km) to the north, pledged to follow Muhammad's teachings in hopes of ending the feuding. Because certain clan leaders of Mecca had become increasingly hostile to Islam, even threatening to kill Muhammad, in 622 Muhammad and his followers moved to Medina. Everyone who submitted to God and accepted Muhammad as his messenger became a member of the umma (UM-muh), the community of Islamic believers.

This migration, called the *hijrah* (HIJ-ruh), marked a major turning point in Islam. All dates in the Islamic calendar are calculated from the year of the hijrah (Anno Hegirae, a Latin term usually abbreviated A.H.). The Islamic calendar calculated each year as twelve lunar months of 29.5 days each, with no adjustment for the remaining days (each solar year has 365.25 days). As a result, Islamic years often straddle two Common Era years, and each day falls at a slightly different time each calendar year. For example, the first day of the month of Ramadan, when Muslims fast during daytime, falls ten or eleven days earlier than it did the previous year.

AP® THEMES

How did the development of Islam change gender roles in Bedouin society?

● **CONTEXT&CONNECTIONS** Although believers see Muhammad's teachings as the direct product of his hearing the word of God, historians note the considerable borrowings from early Judaism in early Islam. The practice of fasting during the day and eating after sundown was a Jewish observance of holy days that Muhammad extended for the entire month of Ramadan. Initially Muhammad and his followers prayed five times a day toward Jerusalem, the holy city of the Jews; only later, in accordance with Muhammad's teachings, did they switch to praying toward Mecca. Sometime around 620, the Quran and later sources report, Muhammad had a night vision in which he traveled first to Jerusalem and then to the seven circles of heaven where he met Abraham, Moses, Jesus, and other prophets who acknowledged him as a prophet. Still, contemporary Jews found Muhammad's versions of Jewish teachings difficult to accept, and Muhammad expelled one group of Jews from Medina, an indication of the tensions between the two groups. ●

Muhammad began life as a merchant, became a religious prophet in middle age, and assumed the duties of a general at the end of his life. In 624, Muhammad and his followers fought their first battle against the residents of Mecca. Muhammad said that he had received revelations that holy war, whose object was the expansion of Islam—or its defense—was justified. He used the word ***jihad*** (GEE-hahd) to mean struggle or fight in military campaigns against non-Muslims. In addition to its basic meaning, modern Muslims also use the term in a more spiritual or moral sense to indicate an individual's striving to fulfill all the teachings of Islam.

jihad

(Arabic root for "striving" or "effort") A struggle or fight against non-Muslims.

In 630, Muhammad's troops conquered Mecca and removed all tribal images from the pilgrimage center at the Kaaba. Muhammad became ruler of the region and exercised his authority by adjudicating among feuding clans. The clans, Muhammad explained, had forgotten that the Kaaba had originally been a shrine to God dedicated by the prophet Abraham (Ibrahim in Arabic) and his son Ishmael.

● **CONTEXT&CONNECTIONS** Muslims do not accept the version of Abraham's sacrifice given in the Old Testament, in which the elderly couple, Abraham and Sarah, have a son, Isaac, whom Abraham spares at God's command (see Chapter 2). In contrast, Muslims believe that Abraham offered God another of his sons: Ishmael, whose mother was the slave woman Hajar (Hagar in Hebrew). ●

hajj

The pilgrimage to Mecca, required of all Muslims who can afford the trip. The pilgrimage commemorates that moment when, just as he was about to sacrifice him, Abraham freed Ishmael and sacrificed a sheep in his place.

The pilgrimage to Mecca, or **hajj** (HAHJ), commemorates that moment on Mount Arafat when Abraham freed Ishmael and sacrificed a sheep in his place. Later, Muslims believe, Ishmael fathered his own children, the ancestors of the clans of Arabia.

The First Caliphs and the Sunni-Shi'ite Split, 632–661

Muhammad preached his last sermon from Mount Arafat outside Mecca and then died in 632. He left no male heirs, only four daughters, and did not designate a successor, or caliph. Clan leaders chose Abu Bakr (ah-boo BAHK-uhr) (ca. 573–634), an early convert and the father of Muhammad's second wife, to lead their community based on what he and his advisers remembered of Muhammad's teachings. Although not a prophet, Abu Bakr held political and religious authority and also led the Islamic armies. Under Abu Bakr's skilled leadership, Islamic troops conquered all of the Arabian peninsula and pushed into present-day Syria and Iraq.

When Abu Bakr died only two years after becoming caliph, the Islamic community again had to determine a successor. This time the umma chose Umar ibn al-Khattab (oo-MAHR ib-in al-HAT-tuhb) (ca. 586–644), the father of Muhammad's third wife. Muslims brought their disputes to Umar, as they had to Muhammad. As the number of cases increased, the caliph appointed **qadi**, or jurists, who listened to the aggrieved parties, often after the close of Friday prayers in the Islamic house of worship, or mosque.

qadi
A Muslim jurist.

Quran
The book that Muslims believe is the direct word of God as revealed to Muhammad. Written sometime around 650.

hadith
Testimony recorded from Muhammad's friends and associates about his speech and actions. Formed an integral part of the Islamic textual tradition, second in importance only to the Quran.

Five Pillars of Islam
The primary obligations of each Muslim as listed by Muhammad (specified in Table 9.1).

Sunnis
The larger of the two main Islamic groups that formed after Ali's death. Sunnis, meaning the "people of custom and the community," hold that the leader of Islam should be chosen by consensus and that legitimate claims to descent are only through the male line. Sunnis do not believe that Ali and Fatima's descendants can become caliph.

During Muhammad's lifetime, a group of Muslims had committed all of his teachings to memory, and soon after his death they began to compile them as the **Quran** (also spelled Koran), which Muslims believe is the direct word of God as revealed to Muhammad. In addition, early Muslims recorded testimony from Muhammad's friends and associates about his speech and actions. In the Islamic textual tradition, these reports, called **hadith** (HAH-deet) in Arabic, are second in importance only to the Quran (kuh-RAHN).

Umar reported witnessing an encounter between Muhammad and the angel Gabriel in which Muhammad listed the primary obligations of each Muslim, which have since come to be known as the **Five Pillars of Islam**. (See Table 9.1 and the feature "Movement of Ideas Through Primary Sources: The Five Pillars of Islam.")

When Umar died in 644, the umma chose Uthman to succeed him. Unlike earlier caliphs, Uthman was not perceived as impartial. He gave all the top positions to members of his own Umayyad clan, which angered many. In 656, a group of soldiers mutinied and killed Uthman. With their support, Muhammad's cousin Ali, who was also the husband of his daughter Fatima, became the fourth caliph. Ali was unable to reconcile the different feuding groups, and in 661 he was assassinated. Ali's martyrdom became a powerful symbol for all who objected to the reigning caliph's government.

The political division that occurred with Ali's death led to a permanent religious split in the Muslim community. The **Sunnis**, the "people of custom and the community," held that the leader of the Islamic community could be chosen by

Table 9.1 The Five Pillars of Islam

1. To bear witness to Allah as the sole god and to accept Muhammad as his messenger
2. To pray five times a day in the direction of Mecca
3. To pay a fixed share of one's income to the state in support of the poor and needy
4. To refrain from eating, drinking, and sexual activity during the daytime hours of the month of Ramadan
5. Provided one has the necessary resources, to do the hajj pilgrimage to Mecca

consensus and that the only legitimate claim to descent was through the male line. In Muhammad's case, two of his fathers-in-law succeeded him, since he left no sons. Although Sunnis accept Ali as one of the four rightly guided caliphs that succeeded Muhammad, they do not believe that Ali and Fatima's children, or their descendants, can become caliph because their claim to descent is through the female line of Fatima.

Opposed to the Sunnis were the "shia" or "party of Ali," usually referred to as **Shi'ites** in English, who believed that the grandchildren born to Ali and Fatima should lead the community. They denied the legitimacy of the three caliphs before Ali, who were related to Muhammad only by marriage, not by blood. The breach between Sunnis and Shi'ites became the major fault line within Islam; it still exists today.

Shi'ites
The "shia" or "party of Ali," one of the two main groups of Islam, who support Ali's claim to succeed Muhammad and believe that the grandchildren born to Ali and Fatima should lead the community. Shi'ites deny the legitimacy of the first three caliphs.

Early Conquests and the Spread of Islam, 632–661

The early Muslims forged a powerful army that attacked non-Muslim lands, including the now-weak Byzantine and Sasanian empires, with great success. When the army attacked, the front ranks of infantry advanced using bows and arrows and crossbows. Their task was to break into the enemy's frontlines so that the mounted cavalry, the backbone of the army, could attack.

In the first stage of conquest, the troops seized all the movable property of the conquered people and reserved a fixed share, called *zakat* (literally "purification," officially set at one-fifth), for the commander. The remaining four-fifths were distributed among the troops and provided a powerful incentive to keep on fighting. The caliph headed the army, which was divided into units of one hundred men and subunits of ten.

Once the Islamic armies pacified a new region, a process that sometimes took generations, the regional governor had to implement a more regular system of taxation. The Muslims levied the same tax rates on conquering and conquered peoples alike, provided that the conquered peoples converted to Islam. Islam stressed the equality of all believers before God, and all Muslims, whether born to Muslim parents or converts, paid two types of taxes: one on the land, usually fixed at one-tenth of the annual harvest, and the zakat tax, which evolved into a property tax with different rates for different possessions. Because the revenue from the zakat was to be used to help the needy or to serve God, it is often called an "alms tax" or "poor tax." Exempt from the alms tax, each individual non-Muslim paid a head tax, called a *jizya*, usually set at a higher rate than the taxes paid by Muslims.

Islamic forces conquered city after city and ruled the entire Arabian peninsula by 634. Crossing overland from the Sinai Peninsula, Islamic armies controlled Egypt by 642, and by 650 they controlled an enormous swath of territory from Libya to Central Asia. In 650, they vanquished the once-powerful Sasanian empire.

• **CONTEXT&CONNECTIONS** The new Islamic state in Iran aspired to build an empire as large and long-lasting as that of the *Sasanians* (Chapter 6), which had governed modern-day Iran and Iraq for more than four centuries. •

The caliphate's armies divided conquered peoples into three groups. Those who converted became Muslims. Those who continued to adhere to Judaism or Christianity were given the status of "protected subjects" (*dhimmi* in Arabic), because they too were "peoples of the book" who honored the same prophets from the Hebrew Bible and the New Testament that Muhammad had. Non-Muslims and unprotected subjects formed the lowest group. Dhimmi status was later extended to Zoroastrians as well.

The Five Pillars of Islam

One of the most important Islamic texts, the Hadith of Gabriel, is associated with the second caliph, Umar, who described an encounter he had witnessed between the prophet Muhammad and the angel Gabriel. The Hadith of Gabriel summarizes the core beliefs of Islam as they were understood in Muhammad's lifetime. The Five Pillars proved crucial to the expansion of Islam because these concise teachings encapsulated its most important practices. One did not have to learn Arabic or memorize the entire Quran to be a Muslim; nor did one require access to a mosque or to educated teachers.

The second passage, from a Chinese book entitled *The Encyclopedic History of Institutions*, completed in 801 by the author Du You (735–812), shows how quickly the news of Muhammad's teachings spread throughout Eurasia. Du You's cousin Du Huan was his main informant. In 751 the Abbasids and the Tang dynasty intervened in a local power struggle at Talas (Dzhambul, Kazakhstan), and Du Huan was taken prisoner by the Abbasid army. Du You's encyclopedia entry combines stereotypes about the immense wealth of the Islamic world with information about Muslim practice. Interestingly, without mentioning the Five Pillars by name, he touches on several. Du You highlights Muslim teachings that differ from Buddhism. Unlike the Buddhists who believed that it was wrong to kill animals, the Muslims sacrificed animals to mark holy days. Du You draws attention to the difference by using the word "meritworthy"; in Buddhism, the sacrifice of animals would have lowered the sacrifice's total amount of merit and increased his or her chance of being reborn as an animal or demon ranking lower than humans in the next life.

❯ Historical Thinking Skill:

ANALYZING EVIDENCE **What is the purpose of the Hadith of Gabriel?**

❯ Historical Thinking Skill:

COMPARISON **Based on these two sources, how do Muslims of the two societies practice their faith?**

❯ Historical Thinking Skill:

CONTEXTUALIZATION **How might the political relationship between China and the Abbasid caliphate have shaped Du You's description of the Islamic world?**

Sources: Hadith of Gabriel as translated in Vincent J. Cornell, "Fruit of the Tree of Knowledge: The Relationship Between Faith and Practice in Islam," in *The Oxford History of Islam*, ed. John L. Esposito (New York: Oxford University Press, 1999), pp. 75–76 (brackets removed to enhance readability); Hyunhee Park, *Mapping the Chinese and Islamic Worlds: Cross-Cultural Exchange in Pre-modern Asia* (New York: Cambridge University Press, 2012), pp. 26–28, translation of Du You, *Tongdian* 193: 5279.

From the Hadith of Gabriel

Umar ibn al-Khattab reported: One day, while we were sitting with the Messenger of God (may God bless and preserve him), there came upon us a man whose clothes were exceedingly white and whose hair was exceedingly black. No dust of travel could be seen upon him, and none of us knew him. He sat down in front of the Prophet (may God bless and preserve him), rested his knees against the Prophet's knees and placed his palms on the Prophet's thighs. "Oh Muhammad, tell me about Islam," he said. The Messenger of God (may God bless and preserve him) replied: "Islam means to bear witness that there is no god but Allah, that Muhammad is the Messenger of Allah, to maintain the required prayers, to pay the poor-tax, to fast in the month of Ramadan, and to perform the pilgrimage to the House of God at Mecca if you are able to do so."

"You are correct," the man said. We were amazed at his questioning of the Prophet and then saying that the Prophet had answered correctly. Then he said, "Tell me about faith." The Prophet said: "It is to believe in Allah, His angels, His books, His messengers, and the Last Day, and to believe in Allah's determination of affairs, whether good comes of it or bad."

"You are correct," he said. "Now tell me about virtue [*ihsan*]." The Prophet said: "It is to worship Allah as if you see Him; for if you do not see Him, surely He sees you." . . . Then the man left. I remained for a while, and the Prophet said to me: "Oh, Umar, do you know who the questioner was?" "Allah and His Messenger know best," I replied. He said: "It was the angel Gabriel, who came to you to teach you your religion."

From Du You's *The Encyclopedic History of Institutions*

The gentlemen and women of this place [Arabia] are tall and well-built. They wear fine and clean garments, and their manners are gentle and elegant. When women go outdoors, they must cover up their faces with veils. Five times a day all the people, whether humble or noble, pray to Heaven. They eat meat as a religious observance, and they consider killing animals merit-worthy. They wear silver belts decorated with silver knives. They prohibit wine and music. When they quarrel, they do not come to blows.

There is also a prayer hall that holds tens of thousands. Every seven days the king attends the prayers, mounts a high seat and expounds the religious law to the people, saying: "Men's life is very hard; this is a way of Heaven that would not change. If you commit one of the following crimes—lewdness, kidnapping, robbery, mean actions, slander, self-gratification at the expense of others, cheating the poor and oppressing the humble—your sins are among the most heinous. Those who are killed in battle by the enemy will be reborn in Heaven; those who kill the enemy will enjoy unlimited good fortune (on Earth)."

A large territory came under the king's rule, and the number of those who follow him is increasing incessantly. The law is lenient, and funerals are frugal.

Within the city walls, in the villages, all of the earth's products are here. Nothing is lacking. It is the hub of the four quarters. Thousands of varieties of merchandise have been brought here in immense quantities and are sold at very low prices. Silk and embroideries, pearls and shells are piled up in the markets. Camels and horses, donkeys and mules jam the streets and alleys. Dwelling houses and other buildings are carved of stone-honey [earth bricks?] and resemble Chinese carriages. On each festival, the nobles are presented with glass work, porcelain, brass, bottles and jugs in enormous quantities. . . .

Now the Arabs have destroyed and swallowed forty to fifty states, all of which are subject to them. They divide their soldiers into many places to protect them, and their territory extends all the way to the Western Sea.

• **CONTEXT&CONNECTIONS** The granting of dhimmi status to certain non-Muslim believers is a special characteristic of Islam. Almost all religions distinguish between believers and those outside their religion, but very few grant privileges to some nonbelievers but not to others. •

The Umayyad Caliphate, 661–750

Although the Islamic community had not resolved the issue of succession, by 661 Muslims had created their own expanding empire whose religious and political leader was the caliph. After Ali was assassinated in 661, Muawiya (mu-ah-WEE-ya), a member of the Umayyad clan like the caliph Uthman, unified the Muslim community. In 680, when he died, Ali's son Hussein tried to become caliph, but Muawiya's son defeated him and became caliph instead. Since only members of this family became caliphs until 750, this period is called the Umayyad dynasty.

The Umayyads built their capital at Damascus, the home of their many Syrian supporters, not in the Arabian peninsula. Initially they used local languages for administration, but after 685 they chose Arabic as the language of the empire.

• **CONTEXT&CONNECTIONS** In Damascus, the Umayyads erected the Great Mosque on the site of a church housing the relics of John the Baptist (see Chapter 7). Architects modified the building's Christian layout to create a large space where devotees could pray toward Mecca. •

The Great Mosque was the first Islamic building to have a place to wash one's hands and feet, a large courtyard, and a tall tower, or minaret, from which Muslims issued the call to prayer. Since Muslims honored the Ten Commandments, including the Second Commandment, *"You shall not make for yourself a graven image,"** the Byzantine workmen depicted no human figures or living animals. Instead their mosaics showed landscapes in an imaginary paradise (see the photo on page 255).

The Conquest of North Africa, 661–750

Maghrib
The African coastal region facing the Mediterranean whose residents largely converted to Islam by the 1100s.

Under the leadership of the Umayyads, Islamic armies conquered the part of North Africa known as the **Maghrib**—modern-day Morocco, Algeria, and Tunisia—between 670 and 711, and then crossed the Strait of Gibraltar to enter Spain. Strong economic and cultural ties dating back to the Roman empire bound the Maghrib to western Asia.

• **CONTEXT&CONNECTIONS** The Maghrib's fertile fields provided the entire Mediterranean with grain, olive oil, and fruits. Slaves and gold moved from the interior of Africa to the coastal ports, where they, too, were loaded into ships crossing the Mediterranean. •

Arab culture and the religion of Islam eventually took root in North Africa, expanding from urban centers into the countryside. By the tenth century, Christians had become a minority in Egypt, outnumbered by Muslims, and by the twelfth century, Arabic had replaced both Egyptian and the Berber languages of the Maghrib

---

*All quotations from the Bible are from the New Revised Standard Version. Revised Standard Version of the Bible, Copyright © 1952 [2nd edition, 1971] by the Division of Christian Education of the National Council of the Churches of Christ in the United States of America. Used by permission. All rights reserved.

Portraying Paradise on Earth: The Umayyad Mosque of Damascus The most beautiful building in the Umayyad capital of Damascus was the mosque, where some twelve thousand Byzantine craftsmen incorporated mosaics, made from thousands of glass tiles, into the building's structure. Notice how the trees grow naturally from the columns at the bottom of the photograph and how the twin windows allow viewers to glimpse the beautiful flowers on the ceiling above. These compositions portray the paradise that Muhammad promised his followers would enter after their deaths. (B. O'Kane/Alamy)

as the dominant language. Annual performance of the hajj pilgrimage strengthened the ties between the people of North Africa and the Arabian peninsula. Pilgrim caravans converged in Cairo, from which large groups then proceeded to Mecca.

Islamic rule reoriented North Africa. Before it, the Mediterranean coast of Africa formed the southern edge of the Roman empire, where Christianity was the dominant religion and Latin the language of learning. Under Muslim rule, North Africa lay at the western edge of the Islamic realm, and Arabic was spoken everywhere.

The Unified Abbasid Caliphate, 750–945

In 744, a group of Syrian soldiers assassinated the Umayyad caliph, prompting an all-out civil war among all those hoping to control the caliphate. In 750, a section of the army based in western Iran, in the Khurasan (HWER-us-sahn) region, triumphed and then shifted the capital some 500 miles (800 km) east from Damascus to Baghdad, closer to their base of support. Because the new caliph claimed descent from Muhammad's uncle Abbas, the new dynasty was called the Abbasid dynasty and their empire the **Abbasid caliphate**. Under Abbasid rule, the Islamic empire continued to expand east into Central Asia (see Map 9.1, page 262). At its greatest extent, it included present-day Morocco, Tunisia, Egypt, Saudi Arabia, Iraq, Iran, southern Pakistan, and Uzbekistan. In Spain, however, the leaders of the vanquished Umayyad clan established a separate Islamic state.

Abbasid caliphate
Dynasty of rulers (750–1258) who ruled a united empire from their capital at Baghdad until the empire fragmented in 945. They continued as religious leaders until 1258, when the last Abbasid caliph was killed by the Mongols.

Baghdad, City of Learning

The new Abbasid capital was built by the second Abbasid caliph Mansur (r. 754–775). Baghdad was on the Tigris River in the heart of Mesopotamia, near the point where the Tigris and Euphrates Rivers come closest together (see Chapter 2). Several canals linked the two rivers. Mansur explained his choice:

> *Indeed, this island between the Tigris in the East and the Euphrates in the West is the harbor of the world. All the ships that sail up the Tigris... and the adjacent areas will anchor here.... It will indeed be the most flourishing city in the world.**

Baghdad more than fulfilled his hopes. Located at the crossroads of Africa, Europe, and Asia, it was home to half a million residents including the majority Muslim community and smaller communities of Christians, Jews, and Zoroastrians. The city's residents lived side by side, celebrated each other's festivals, and spoke Arabic, Persian, Greek, and Hebrew.

Mansur, we learn from the historian Masudi, *"was the first caliph to have foreign works of literature translated into Arabic,"* including Aristotle's works, the geography of Ptolemy, the geometry and physics of Euclid, various mathematical treatises, *"and all the other ancient works.... Once in possession of these books, the public read and studied them avidly."*† Caliphs, officials, and private individuals collected large numbers of books, sometimes holding several hundred thousand volumes in a single collection. Local scholars benefited from the support of both the caliph and the city's residents, who paid for the manuscripts to be copied and studied them in their schools. The city's cosmopolitan environment encouraged scholars to study the scientific and mathematical discoveries of Greece, India, and Mesopotamia.

Historians call their collective efforts, which lasted several centuries, the **translation movement**. In translating astronomy, medical, mathematical, and geography books from ancient Greek, Sanskrit, and Persian into Arabic, they created a body of scientific knowledge unsurpassed in the world. Certain works by ancient Greek scholars, such as the medical scholar Galen, survive only in their Arabic translations. When, beginning in the eleventh and twelfth centuries, Europeans once again became interested in the learning of the Greeks, they followed Fibonacci's lead and adopted Arabic numerals (see page 382).

translation movement
Between 750 and 1000, the effort by Islamic scholars, many living in Baghdad, to translate books on astronomy, medicine, mathematics, and geography from ancient Greek, Sanskrit, and Persian into Arabic.

Islamic scholars also made many scientific and mathematical discoveries of their own. The great mathematician al-Khwarizmi (al-HWAR-iz-mee) (d. 830) combined the Indian and Babylonian number systems to create the world's first

---

*Jacob Lassner, *The Topography of Baghdad in the Early Middle Ages* (Detroit: Wayne State University Press, 1970), p. 127, citing the Islamic writer Ya'qubi.

†Paul Lunde and Caroline Stone, trans., *The Meadows of Gold: The Abbasids by Mas'udi* (New York: Kegan Paul International, 1989), p. 388.

workable decimal system. Al-Khwarizmi invented algebra (from the Arabic word *al-jabr*, meaning "transposition"). He also developed a system of computation that divided complex problems into shorter steps, or algorithms (the word *algorithm* is derived from al-Khwarizmi's name).

One of the Five Pillars of Islam is to pray five times a day facing toward Mecca. Islamic scholars developed increasingly sophisticated instruments to determine this position for prayer. The **astrolabe** allowed observers to calculate their location on earth once they had set the appropriate dials for the date, the time of day, and the angle of the sun's course through the sky. The astrolabe also functioned as a slide rule, one of the world's first hand-held mathematical calculators. It became the most significant computational tool of its time.

astrolabe
Computational instrument that allowed observers to calculate their location on earth to determine the direction of Mecca for their prayers. Also functioned as a slide rule.

• **CONTEXT&CONNECTIONS** In another significant technological advance, a paper-making factory was opened in Baghdad in 794–795 that produced the first paper in the Islamic world, using Chinese techniques (see Chapter 4). Muslim scholars had previously written on either *papyrus* (Chapter 2), a dried plant grown in Egypt, or the scraped and cleaned animal skin called *parchment* (Chapter 7). Both were much more costly than paper, and the new writing material spread quickly throughout the empire. By 850, Baghdad housed one hundred paper-making workshops. •

Determining the Direction of Mecca: The Astrolabe This astrolabe, made in 1216, is a sophisticated mathematical device. After holding the astrolabe up to the sun to determine the angle of the sun's rays and thus fix the viewer's latitude on earth, one inserted the appropriate metal plate (this example has three) into the mechanism, which allowed one to chart the movement of the stars.

Erich Lessing/Art Resource, NY

AP® THEMES

How did the expansion of the caliphate contribute to the spread of new technologies and scientific knowledge?

The low cost of paper greatly increased the availability of books. Manuals on agriculture, botany, and pharmacology contributed to the ongoing spread of agricultural techniques and crops from one end of the empire to the other. Cookbooks show the extent to which the empire's residents embraced Asian foodstuffs like rice, eggplant, and processed sugar. Cotton for clothing, grown by Persians at the time of the founding of the Abbasid dynasty, gradually spread to Egypt and, by the twelfth century, to West Africa.

Abbasid Governance

Baghdad, the city of learning, was the capital of an enormous empire headed by the caliph, who presided over the military, the bureaucracy, and the judiciary. His chief minister, or vizier, stood at the head of a bureaucracy based in the capital. In the provinces, the caliph delegated power to regional governors, who were charged with maintaining local armies and transmitting revenues to the center; however, they often tried to keep revenues for themselves.

In the early centuries of Islamic rule, local populations often continued their pre-Islamic religious practices. For example, in 750 fewer than 8 percent of the people living in the Abbasid heartland of Iran were Muslims. By the ninth century, the Muslim proportion of the population had increased to 40 percent, and in the tenth century to a majority 70 or 80 percent of the population.

The caliphate offered all of its subjects access to a developed judicial system that implemented Islamic law. The caliph appointed a qadi for the city of Baghdad and a qadi for each of the empire's provinces. These judges were drawn from the learned men of Islam, or **ulama** (also spelled *ulema*), who gained their positions after years of study. The ulama took no special vows and could marry and have families. Some ulama specialized in the Quran, others scrutinized records of Muhammad's sayings in the hadith to establish their veracity, and still others concentrated on legal texts. Scholars taught at schools, and on Fridays, at the weekly services, the ulama preached to the congregation (women and men sat separately, with the men in front), and afterward they heard legal disputes in the mosques.

ulama
Learned Islamic scholars who studied the Quran, the hadith, and legal texts. They taught classes, preached, and heard legal disputes.

The judiciary enjoyed an unusually high position, for even members of the caliph's immediate family were subject to their decisions. In one example, an employee who bought goods for Zubaydah, the wife of the caliph Harun al-Rashid, refused to pay a merchant. When the merchant filed suit a judge ordered the queen's agent to pay the debt. The angry queen ordered the judge transferred and Harun complied with his wife's request, but only after he himself paid the money owed to the merchant.

• **CONTEXT&CONNECTIONS** A comparison with other contemporary empires demonstrates the power of the judiciary in the Abbasid empire: no Chinese subject of the *Tang dynasty*, for example, would have dared to sue the emperor (Chapter 8). •

Abbasid Society

When compared with its Asian and European contemporaries (see Chapters 8 and 10), Islamic society appears surprisingly egalitarian. It had divisions, of course: rural/urban, Muslim/non-Muslim, free person/slave. Apart from gender differences, however, none of these divisions were insurmountable. Rural people could move to the city, non-Muslims could convert to Islam, and slaves could be freed.

In the royal ranks, however, much had changed since the time of Muhammad, whose supporters treated him as an equal. The Abbasid rulers rejected the egalitarianism of early Islam to embrace the lavish court ceremonies of the Sasanians. To the horror of the ulama, the caliph received visitors from behind a curtained throne, and visitors had to kiss the ground in front of his throne even though only God, the learned Muslims felt, should receive such a form of submission. Equally reprehensible in the eyes of the ulama, his subjects addressed the caliph as "the shadow of God on earth," a title modeled on the Sasanian "king of kings." At the right of the caliph's curtained throne stood an executioner, ready to kill any visitor who might offend the caliph.

The one group in Islamic society to inherit privileges on the basis of birth were those who could claim descent from Muhammad's family. All the Abbasid caliphs belonged to this group, and their many relatives occupied a privileged position at the top of Baghdad society. Descent from Muhammad did not bring any financial advantage; it simply commanded more respect.

Below the royal family, two large groups enjoyed considerable prestige and respect: the ulama, on the one hand, and the cultured elite on the other, including courtiers surrounding the caliph, bureaucrats staffing his government, and educated landowners throughout the empire. These groups often patronized poets, painters, and musicians, themselves also members of the cultured elite.

Like the caliph's more educated subjects, ordinary people varied in the extent of their compliance with the religious teachings of Islam. In the cities they worked carrying goods, and in the countryside they farmed. Most farmers prayed five times a day and attended Friday prayers at their local mosques, but they could not always afford to go on the hajj.

Farmers aspired to send their sons to study at the local mosque for a few years. Here, before starting work full-time as cultivators, they acquired the rudiments of Arabic so that they could recite the Quran. Families who educated their daughters did so at home. Boys who demonstrated scholarly ability hoped to become members of the ulama, while those gifted in mathematics might become merchants.

Muhammad and two of his immediate successors had been merchants, and trade continued to enjoy a privileged position in the Abbasid caliphate. Merchants were supposed to adhere to a high standard of conduct: to be true to their word and to sell merchandise free from defects. Many merchants contributed money for the upkeep of mosques or to help the less fortunate. Because Islamic law forbade usury (charging interest on loans), Muslim merchants used credit mechanisms like checks, letters of credit, and bills of exchange. While the most successful merchants became bankers and traders who specialized in large-scale transactions that spanned the empire, other merchants ran single shops or peddled their goods, some of which they made themselves, from town to town.

AP® THEMES

How did Islamic beliefs and practices support commerce and the merchant class?

The shift of the capital to Baghdad in the eighth century brought a dramatic increase in trade within the empire and beyond. Long-distance merchants sent ships to India and China that were loaded with locally produced goods—such as Arabian horses, textiles, and carpets—and nonlocal goods, such as African ivory and Southeast Asian pearls. The ships returned with spices, medicines, and textiles. Islamic merchants were at home in a world stretching from China to Africa.

● **CONTEXT&CONNECTIONS** As early as the ninth century, ships traveled routinely between the Arabian Sea and southern Chinese ports, and the China-Basra route was the longest regularly traveled sea route in the world before 1500 (see Chapter 8). Aladdin, the famous fictional hero of a tale from *The Thousand and One Nights*, was born in China and adopted by an African merchant. ●

Slavery

Much long-distance trade involved the import of slaves from three major areas: Central Africa, Central Asia, and central and eastern Europe, by far the largest source (see Map 9.1, page 262). The Arabs referred to the region of modern Poland and Bohemia as the "slave country." (The English word *slave* is derived from the Latin word for *slav*, because so many slaves were originally Slavic.)

Under the Abbasids, the coastal cities of East Africa, particularly those north of Madagascar, became Muslim, not because they were conquered by invading armies but because traveling merchants introduced Islam to them. The merchants came to the coast to buy slaves and other products, including gold and ivory. In many cases, the rulers converted first, and the population later followed.

Like Khaizuran, some Islamic slaves worked as servants or concubines. The caliph's household purchased thousands of slaves each year. The women entered the secluded women's quarters, or harem, in the palace. Other slaves labored in the fields, as soldiers, or—most dangerous of all—in mines.

Although Islamic teaching stressed the equality of all believers, slavery predated Muhammad and continued. Even when slaves converted to Islam, they remained slaves unless expressly freed by their masters. However, all levels of society, from the caliph with his hundreds of female slaves down to the petty trader who could afford only one, respected the teaching that children born to a slave woman and a free Muslim father should be raised as free Muslims, provided that the father acknowledged the child as his. As a result, these children were granted identical rights as their siblings born to free Muslim mothers.

Harun al-Rashid was himself the child of a slave mother, Khaizuran. As a child, she learned to read and write because educated slaves could command a higher price on the slave market. When the caliph Mansur gave her to his son Mahdi sometime in the late 750s, Mahdi took an immediate liking to the young girl, who was "*slender and graceful as a reed,*"* the root meaning of her name *khaizuran*.

Politics of the Harem

Like most ordinary people living within the Abbasid empire, Khaizuran had grown up in a nuclear family headed by her father and his one wife, her mother. Islamic law permitted Muslim men to marry as many as four wives, but most men could afford to support only one. The caliphs took the four wives Islamic law entitled them to, and their enormous incomes permitted them to support unlimited numbers of concubines as well.

When Khaizuran joined the royal household, she left behind her life in the streets of Mecca, where women had some freedom of movement, and entered a world whose customs were completely unfamiliar. The higher a woman's class, the greater the degree of seclusion, and royal wives were the most secluded of all. An army of eunuchs, or castrated men, guarded the secluded women's quarters and prevented illicit contact with any men. Khaizuran was free to leave the palace only on rare occasions, and then only under escort.

Only after she was certain of her status as one of the future caliph's favorites did Khaizuran reveal that her mother, two sisters, and a brother were still alive in Yemen. The caliph Mansur immediately summoned them to live in the palace and

*Nabia Abbott, *Two Queens of Baghdad: Mother and Wife of Harun al-Rashid* (London: Al Saqi Books, 1986, reprint of 1946 original), p. 26, citing Jahiz (pseud.), *Kitab al-Mahasin wa Al-Addad*, ed. van Vloten (Leiden: E. J. Brill, 1898), pp. 232–233,.

arranged for Khaizuran's sister to marry another of his sons. The sister subsequently gave birth to a daughter, whose nickname was "little butter ball," or Zubaydah.

Khaizuran's relations with her son Hadi soured soon after he, and not his brother Harun, became caliph in 785. Hadi was particularly upset to discover that his mother was meeting with his generals and courtiers on her own. He chastised her, saying: "*Do not overstep the essential limits of womanly modesty.... It is not dignified for women to enter upon affairs of state. Take to your prayer and worship and devote yourself to the service of Allah. Hereafter, submit to the womanly role that is required of your sex.*"*But Khaizuran did not back down. Hadi then asked his generals how they would feel if their mothers interfered in politics, and they all agreed, "*Not any one of us would like that.*"* This description by the historian al-Tabari (al–TAH-bah-ree) (d. 923) suggests that all the commanders felt the same: that no woman, and certainly not Khaizuran, should intervene in matters of state. However, contrary to the expectation of these men, Khaizuran did intervene. Hadi died suddenly, in mysterious circumstances, and Khaizuran made sure that Harun succeeded him as caliph. (No one knows exactly how.)

● **CONTEXT&CONNECTIONS** Two thousand years earlier, Hatshepsut ruled as pharaoh in Egypt (see Chapter 2); from 690 to 705 C.E., Wu was the emperor of China (see Chapter 8); and Khaizuran's contemporary Irene reigned as the Byzantine emperor from 797 to 802 (see Chapter 10). Each of these women came to power under unusual circumstances, usually when a young child ascended to the throne following the death of the ruler, and each chose a title (pharaoh or emperor) reserved for men. In the Islamic world, the word *calipha* (the female form of caliph) usually referred to the wife of the caliph, but it could also indicate a female ruler. The one woman in the Islamic world who ruled on her own right was the calipha Sitt al-Mulk. She became leader of the *Mamluk empire*, the state that succeeded the Abbasids in Egypt (Chapter 11), for a single month in 1021, until a new heir could be named, when she became regent. ●

Unlike her mother and her famous aunt Khaizuran, Zubaydah grew up entirely within the women's quarter of the palace. After her marriage to the caliph, she devoted herself to public works. While in Mecca, she contributed 1,700,000 dinars, or nearly eight tons of gold, from her own funds to construct a giant reservoir. She also ordered wells dug to provide hajj pilgrims with fresh water. The resulting stone water tunnels ran above and below ground for 12 miles (20 km), a genuine feat of engineering. Finally, she made extensive repairs to the road linking Kufa, a city outside Baghdad, with Mecca and Medina, which is called **Zubaydah's Road** even today. (See the feature "Visual Evidence in Primary Sources: Zubaydah's Road.")

Zubaydah's Road
The pilgrimage road linking Kufa with Mecca and Medina that was rebuilt and improved by Queen Zubaydah.

The Breakup of the Abbasid Empire, 809–936

Like her mother-in-law Khaizuran, Zubaydah tried to manipulate the succession after Harun's death in 809, but she sided with the losing son, who was defeated by his brother Mamun in 813. The empire Mamun won, however, was not as prosperous as it appeared. Even during Harun's reign the caliphs were often forced to seek emergency loans. The central government frequently ran short of money because regional governors did not forward the taxes they collected to the caliph. The frequent civil wars between

*Nabia Abbott, *Two Queens of Baghdad: Mother and Wife of Harun al-Rashid* (London: Al Saqi Books, 1986, reprint of 1946 original), p. 26, citing Jahiz (pseud.), *Kitab al-Mahasin wa Al-Addad*, ed. van Vloten (Leiden: E. J. Brill, 1898), pp. 89–90, 92.

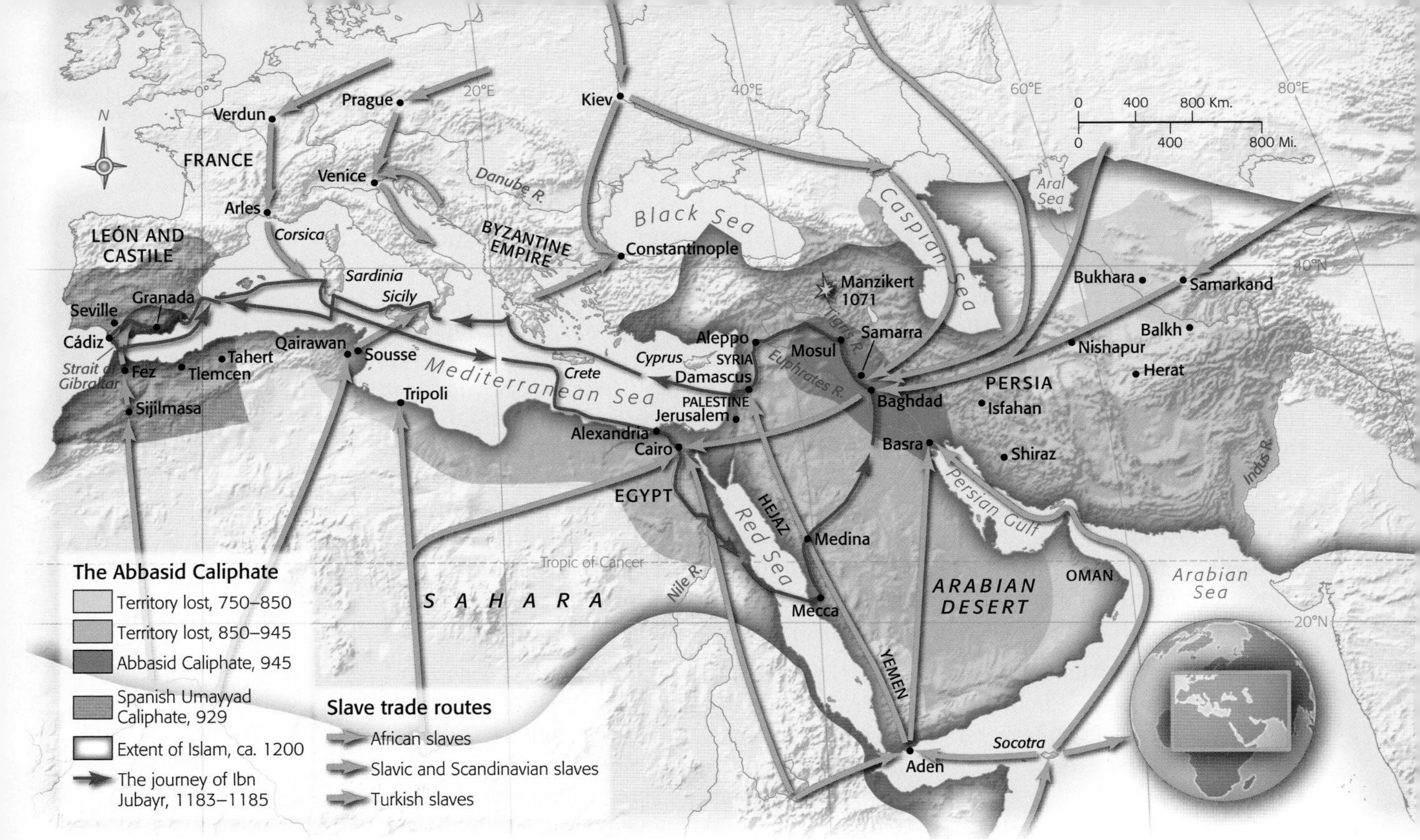

Map 9.1 The Breakup of the Abbasid Empire Between 750 and 945, the Abbasid caliphate lost huge chunks of territory in North Africa, the Arabian peninsula, Iran, and Central Asia, yet a shared Islamic identity held the former empire together, as Ibn Jubayr learned in his 1183–1185 journey (see pages 266–268). The people living in the empire's core around Baghdad imported slaves, many of whom converted to Islam, from Africa, northern Europe, and Central Asia.

rivals for the caliphate destroyed the irrigation works that underpinned the agrarian economy, and because no one rebuilt them, tax revenues continuously declined (see Map 9.1).

As a temporary expedient, the caliph occasionally appointed a tax farmer (see Chapter 7) to collect a fixed amount in a region where the caliph's bureaucrats had trouble raising revenue. In these cases, the caliph still retained direct political control. If tax farmers failed to raise the necessary revenues, the caliph might go a step further and make an **iqta grant**, ceding all political control to the man who promised to collect taxes and pay a certain amount. The iqta (ICK-tah) grant holder ruled the area, and the caliph retained only nominal control. In 789 and 800, Harun granted independence to two Islamic states in North Africa in exchange for annual tax payments; his successors made similar arrangements with other regions.

iqta grant
A grant given by the caliph to someone who promised to collect taxes and pay the caliph a certain amount of money from their region, over which the caliph retained only nominal control.

● **CONTEXT&CONNECTIONS** Iqta grants were a dangerous innovation, far riskier than any grants the Persians had made to *satraps* (Chapter 6) or the Romans had made to tax farmers, because the iqta holders had no reason to support the empire. ●

Until the middle of the tenth century, none of the iqta holders directly challenged the authority of the caliph. Then, in 936, the caliph took the final step and ceded all his power to an Iraqi grant holder, giving him the title *commander of commanders*. The grant holder disbanded the entire Abbasid army and replaced it with an army loyal to himself. He eliminated the Abbasid bureaucracy as well, sentencing the last vizier to life imprisonment in a dungeon.

This new arrangement did not last long. In 945, the Buyids, a group of Shi'ite Iranian mercenaries based in the mountains south of the Caspian Sea, conquered Baghdad and took over the government. Rather than depose the caliphs and risk alienating their Muslim subjects, the Buyids retained them as figureheads who led the Islamic caliphate but had no political power. The caliph received a small allowance so that he could reside in his crumbling palace in Baghdad, and Islamic preachers continued to cite his name in their Friday prayers. The extensive territory of the Abbasid empire proved ungovernable as a single political unit, and it broke up into different regions, all still part of the Islamic cultural and religious world.

AP® THEMES

How did the role of Baghdad change as the power of Abbasid rulers waned?

The Rise of Regional Centers, 945–1258

Muslims found it surprisingly easy to accept the new division of political and religious authority. The caliphs continued as the titular heads of the Islamic religious community, but they were entirely dependent on temporal rulers for financial support. No longer politically united, the Islamic world was still bound by cultural and religious ties, including the obligation to perform the hajj. Under the leadership of committed Muslim rulers, Islam continued to spread throughout South Asia and the interior of Africa. Rulers all over the Islamic world continued to patronize Islamic scholars, and Islamic scholarship and learning, particularly in the field of geography, continued to thrive.

Regional Islamic States

In 1055, Baghdad fell to yet a different group of soldiers from Central Asia, the Turkish-speaking Seljuqs (also spelled Seljuks, and pronounced sell-JOOKs). Other sections of the empire broke off and, like Baghdad, experienced rule by different dynasties. Yet two centuries of Abbasid rule had transformed all regions of the former empire into Islamic realms whose residents, whether Sunni or Shi'ite, observed the tenets of Islam. Their societies retained the basic patterns of Abbasid society. When Muslims traveled anywhere in the former Abbasid territories, they could be confident of finding mosques, being received as honored guests, and having access to the same basic legal system (even if some legal schools differed in their interpretations). As in the Roman empire, where Greek and Latin prevailed, just two languages could take a traveler through the entire realm: Arabic, the language of the Quran and high Islamic learning, and Persian, the Iranian language of much poetry, literature, and history.

Sometime around 1000, the city of Córdoba in Islamic Spain replaced Baghdad as the leading center of Islamic learning. The Umayyad capital from around 750 to 1031, Córdoba attracted many visitors because of its gardens, fountains, paved streets, and most of all, its running water (the first in Europe since the fall of Rome). Córdoba played a crucial role in the transmission of learning from the Islamic world to Christian Europe. Craftsmen learned how to make paper in the eleventh century and transmitted the technique to the rest of Europe. Córdoba's residents, both male and female, specialized in copying manuscripts and translated treatises from Arabic into Latin for European audiences.

Zubaydah's Road

Zubaydah devoted considerable resources to the project that brought her lasting fame: the road linking Kufa, a city outside Baghdad, with Mecca and Medina. Although the road existed before her reign, she made so many improvements to it that it came to be called Darb Zubaydah, or Zubaydah's Road.

When Saudi archaeologists surveyed the desert in the 1970s, they found identifiable traces of a roadway 18 yards (17 m) wide. The road's builders had faced the challenge of designing a road for pedestrians even though it ran through long stretches of sand, some muddy ground, and rough lava fields. They cleared the road of stones, paved the sections of the road that went through the mud, and smoothed rough lava fields before covering them with soft sand on which pilgrims could easily walk. One archaeologist has called the project "the finest and most remarkable and extensive road system in the earlier period of Islamic history."*

Because Zubaydah was particularly concerned about poorer pilgrims who traveled the difficult route on foot, she added nine new rest stations at

*Saad A. al-Rashid, *Darb Zubaydah: The Pilgrim Road from Kufa to Mecca* (Riyad: Riyad University, 1980), p. 330.

The stones of the lava field were so sharp that they hurt the feet of the pilgrims and their camels.

After clearing the road, engineers covered it with a smooth layer of sand for the convenience of the pilgrims and their camels, who traveled over 700 miles (1,100 km).

Al Sahra Desert Resort, www.alsahra.org

convenient intervals between existing stations, for a total of fifty-four rest stops. All the new stations had a pool, and they often included some kind of shelter and sometimes even a small mosque. This painting, from an illustrated thirteenth-century manuscript of collected anecdotes, shows what a resting place on the Darb Zubaydah might have looked like.

The nimbus, or cloud, behind the head was originally an Iranian artistic convention used to show royalty. In this picture, however, the nimbus seems purely decorative, since all the human figures have one.

This figure uses a bellows to light a fire below a cooking pot. ***What preparations did hajj travelers going overland or by sea have to make, and how did their experiences differ from those of Buddhist pilgrims like Ennin (see Chapter 8) or Christian pilgrims like Egeria (see Chapter 7)?***

This is a shrine, most likely to a prominent Islamic teacher whose grave lies inside it, where Muslims came to pray.

Two camels bray with their mouths open. Although often ill-tempered, camels were the one draft animal that could withstand the hot, dry climate of the desert.

Inside a tent made from beautiful textiles, these two men lean on portable wooden furniture as they converse with each other.

Three camels feed from saddlebags placed on the ground. Able to survive for up to nine days without water, camels can carry loads over 300 pounds (140 kg).

al-Bakri

A Muslim geographer based in Córdoba whose *Book of Routes and Realms* is one of the earliest written sources about Africa.

The study of geography also flourished in the eleventh and twelfth centuries as Muslims learned about the most distant places within the Islamic community. The geographer **al-Bakri** (see Chapter 11), based in Córdoba, provided a rare, detailed description of Central Africa. His geographic work, entitled *The Book of Routes and Realms*, reported that the Central African kingdom of Ghana had a capital city with separate districts for Muslims and for local religious practitioners who prayed to images. He explained that when rulers converted to Islam, their subjects, as in the case of the country of Mali, did not always follow suit.

This religious division between rulers who converted to Islam and subjects who did not held true in another major area that was brought into the Islamic world in the eleventh and twelfth centuries: Afghanistan, Pakistan, and north India. For example, when Muslim conquerors moved into north India from their base in Afghanistan, they tore down Hindu temples during the actual conquest, but once they gained power they allowed Hindu temples to remain, even as they made contributions to mosques. Ordinary Indians continued to worship Hindu deities, while the ruling family, which was based in Delhi and were thus known as the Delhi sultanate, observed the tenets of Islam (see Chapter 11).

During this long period of division, Muslim cartographers made some of the most advanced maps of their day. Working in Sicily, the geographer al-Idrisi (1100–1166) engraved a map of the world on a silver tablet 3 yards by 1.5 yards (3 m by 1.5 m) in size. Although the map was destroyed during his lifetime, the book al-Idrisi wrote to accompany his map is so detailed that scholars have been able to reconstruct much that appeared on his original map, which like all Islamic maps, looks upside down to modern viewers because he oriented the map to the south. His map showed the outlines of the Mediterranean, Africa, and Central Asia with far greater accuracy than contemporary maps made elsewhere in the world.

Ibn Jubayr's Hajj in 1183

By the twelfth century, since the realm of Islam was no longer unified, devout Muslims had to cross from one Islamic polity to the next as they performed the hajj. Local Islamic rulers might take advantage of the pilgrims by charging them extra taxes, but sometimes they also facilitated the pilgrims' journey. Pilgrims were often unsure of the correct rituals to perform in Mecca, and as the number of pilgrims increased over the centuries, a new genre of book, called "travels" (*rihla* in Arabic), appeared that described the trip to Mecca and the most important rituals performed there, which bound Muslims from distant places together.

● **CONTEXT&CONNECTIONS** Pilgrimage was part of other religious traditions. *Egeria* (Chapter 7) traveled from Spain to Jerusalem to see the locations where Jesus had performed miracles, as well as to Egypt to see the first monasteries built there. Similarly, *Ennin* (Chapter 8) went to Mount Wutai in China so that he could obtain written copies of Buddhist texts whose Japanese versions were garbled and difficult to understand. Egeria and Ennin both made individual decisions to go on pilgrimage, and they chose their destinations to fulfill their own personal goals. No Christian or Buddhist teaching encouraged all believers to make a certain pilgrimage in the way that the Five Pillars enjoined Muslims, as long as they could afford it, to visit Mecca. ●

Ibn Jubayr

(1145–1217) Spanish courtier from Granada, Spain, who went on the hajj pilgrimage in 1183–1185. Wrote *The Travels* describing his trip to Mecca—the most famous example of a travel book, called a *rihla* in Arabic.

The most famous account of the hajj is *The Travels of Ibn Jubayr* (1145–1217), a courtier from Granada, Spain, who went on the hajj in 1183–1185. **Ibn Jubayr**

Table 9.2 The Most Important Ritual Practices Performed by Hajj Pilgrims

1. To take off one's ordinary clothing and enter a state of purity by putting on the simple pilgrims' clothing
2. To circumambulate the Kaaba seven times in a clockwise direction
3. To participate in the Standing at Arafat, asking God for forgiveness, and then to spend the night there
4. To participate in the symbolic stoning of the devil on three separate days at three different locations where, Muslims believe, the Prophet Ishmael was tempted by Satan
5. To offer an animal sacrifice at Mina
6. To repeat the circumambulation at the Kaaba
7. To pray at the site where Ishmael and Abraham prayed after the Kaaba was built
8. To leave the state of purity by having one's head shaved or trimmed and then putting on one's own clothes

Sources: Created by author from multiple sources: Vincent J. Cornell, "Fruit of the Tree of Knowledge," in *Oxford History of Islam*, ed. John L. Esposito (New York: Oxford University Press, 1999), pp. 84–86; www.religionfacts.com; *Encyclopedia of Islam*. 3d ed.; *Encyclopaedia of the Qu'ran.*

(IH-buhn joo-BAH-eer) decided to go to Mecca to repent for drinking seven cups of wine, a drink forbidden to all Muslims. He financed his trip with a gift of seven cups of gold coins received from the governor of Granada, his superior, who felt contrite about having forced Ibn Jubayr to drink so much. Ibn Jubayr's book serves as a guide to the sequence of hajj observances that had been fixed by Muhammad; Muslims today continue to perform the same rituals (see Table 9.2).

- **CONTEXT&CONNECTIONS** After thirty days' sail across the Mediterranean, Ibn Jubayr arrived in the port of Alexandria, Egypt, then under the rule of Saladin (1137/38–1193), the founder of the Ayyubid dynasty (1171–1250) in Egypt, who was the most skilled Muslim commander to fight the *Crusaders* (Chapter 13). ●

Ibn Jubayr praised Saladin's generosity as a host but criticized the port officials for requiring the pilgrims to pay the zakat tax on the goods they carried. From Egypt, he traveled south with other pilgrims and crossed the Red Sea; on his arrival, he once again had to pay a tax. Before 945, all territory was under Abbasid rule and there were no border crossings; after 945, Muslim travelers, even those going on the hajj, had to pay the costs of leaving one country and entering another.

Muslims could fulfill their obligation to go on the hajj only once a year: on the eighth, ninth, and tenth days of the twelfth month in the Islamic lunar calendar. After Ibn Jubayr arrived in Mecca, he waited for some eight months before the month of the hajj arrived. To prepare for the hajj, he put on the two pieces of unsewn cloth permitted to the male pilgrim. (Because women pilgrims were obliged to cover all but their face, hands, and feet, they required more cloth.) While Sunni and Shi'ite rules differed slightly, all concurred that pilgrims should refrain from having sex, eating meat, and cutting their hair or nails during the hajj.

- **CONTEXT&CONNECTIONS** Sexual abstinence was part of the holy state into which all hajj pilgrims entered when they donned the special clothing for pilgrims. Similarly, during the daytime in the month of Ramadan, Muslims fast and refrain from sex. Unlike Manichaean and Christian doctrines (see Chapters 6 and 10), Islamic teachings never required celibacy, viewing sex as a normal part of family life. ●

British Library, London

Ihram Clothing During the Hajj This Iranian watercolor from the early 1400s shows male hajj pilgrims wearing the prescribed ritual dress of two pieces of white clothing. Inside the gates of the walled city of Mecca, the pilgrims circumambulate the Kaaba, behind which two winged angels look on. Other angels fly in the golden clouds above.

The number of Muslims going on the hajj had increased dramatically over time. By 1184, Ibn Jubayr writes that the total number of pilgrims from Iraq alone *"formed a multitude whose number only God Most High could count."** The more unruly pilgrims (often from Yemen, in Ibn Jubayr's opinion) forced the Meccan authorities to replace the Kaaba's wooden covering with a strong iron dome.

The authorities had another pressing concern. Even in 632, when there were fewer than one hundred hajj pilgrims, a malaria epidemic broke out as a result of crowding and people coming together from different places. Over the centuries the authorities have always been worried about outbreaks of disease, and today is no different. (See the feature "World History in Today's World: Preventing Disease Among Hajj Pilgrims.")

Once pilgrims arrived in Mecca, they walked around the Kaaba seven times in a counterclockwise direction. On the eighth day of the month Ibn Jubayr and all the other pilgrims departed for Mina, which lay halfway to Mount Arafat. The hajj celebrated Abraham's release of his son Ishmael. The most important rite, **The Standing**, commemorated the last sermon given by the prophet Muhammad.

Fear of bandits prevented the pilgrims from spending the night at Arafat as was customary. When they arrived at Mount Arafat early in the morning of the ninth day, they first climbed the mountain and then descended to the plain, where they remained on their feet throughout the Standing:

> *When, on Friday, the midday and afternoon prayers were said together, the people stood contrite and in tears, humbly beseeching the mercy of Great and Glorious God. The cries of "God is Great" rose high, and loud were the voices of men in prayer. Never has there been seen a day of such weeping, such penitence of heart, and such bending of the neck in reverential submission and humility before God.**

The Standing
The rite that marks the culmination of the hajj, when pilgrims meditate and pray (they are not required to stand) at the site where Muhammad gave his last sermon.

As soon as the sun had set, the pilgrims proceeded quickly in the dark toward a mosque some three hours away for final prayers. They spent the rest of the night there.

**The Travels of Ibn Jubayr*, trans. R. J. C. Broadhurst (London: Jonathan Cape, 1952), pp. 191, 180.

WORLD HISTORY IN TODAY'S WORLD

Preventing Disease Among Hajj Pilgrims

In recent years, the number of Muslims participating in the annual pilgrimage to Mecca has reached almost three million (one million Saudis and almost two million non-Saudis), but in 2013 the number fell sharply to under two million. Why? Fear of Middle East respiratory syndrome, or MERS, an often fatal respiratory virus.

The first outbreak occurred in Saudi Arabia in 2012, and most of those who have fallen ill live in West Asia, whether in Saudi Arabia, Jordan, Qatar, or the United Arab Emirates. Scientists are not certain where the disease originated or how it spreads. It may be associated with camels; some of those taken ill have either been in close contact with camels or drunk camel's milk. Twice as many men have fallen ill as women, and some speculate that the veil, worn by all Saudi women and many female Muslim visitors, helps prevent infection.

In their attempt to manage the vast numbers of pilgrims, the Saudi authorities closely limit how many can come, granting one thousand visas for each one million Muslims who live in a given country. Twenty-three percent, or 1.57 billion, of the world's population is Muslim, and Islam is the world's second largest religion (see page 204). The four countries with the largest Muslim populations are far from Mecca, and their citizens must fly to Saudi Arabia: Indonesia with 210 million, Pakistan 178 million, India 177 million, and Bangladesh 149 million. Egypt (80 million) and Nigeria (76 million) are fifth and sixth on the list, reflecting that Africa is the world region with the largest number of recent converts to Islam. Growing rapidly, the number of Muslims is projected to reach 26 percent of the world's population by 2030.

In efforts to prevent outbreaks of illness, the Saudi authorities have banned the import of any fresh food and will spray mosquito repellent in the temporary quarters for those from countries where dengue fever is frequent. They plan to give antibiotics to anyone coming from a country where meningitis occurs and to distribute polio vaccine to 500,000 others. But the uncertainty about the origins of MERS and the mechanisms of its spread makes it difficult to prevent. Hajj authorities express cautious optimism because MERS did not break out during the hajj of either 2012 or 2013. However, they have not yet publicized the hundreds of cases occurring in the first half of 2014 in Jeddah, the location of the airport where most pilgrims landed in October 2014.

Sources: Denise Grady, "Investigation Follows Trail of a Virus in Hospitals," *New York Times*, June 20, 2013; Donald G. McNeil, "Guarding Against Disease Among Pilgrims to Mecca," *New York Times*, May 27, 2014; Pew Research Center, "The Future of the Global Muslim Population," January 15, 2011, http://www.pewforum.org/interactives/muslim-population-graphic/.

When the pilgrims arrived back at Mina the next day, their religious observance shifted suddenly from solemn piety to raucous celebration. They first threw stones at the wall where Muslims believe Satan tempted Ishmael, and they then slaughtered sheep to celebrate Abraham's substitution of a sacrificial ram for his son Ishmael. The change of pace was abrupt, and disturbances often broke out at Mina. Ibn Jubayr saw *"dissension and riot between the negro inhabitants of Mecca and the Turks of Iraq in which there were some hurts. Swords were drawn, arrow notches were put to the bow-string, and spears were thrown, while some of the goods of the merchants were plundered."**

After the religious observances were completed, giant bazaars sprang up in which Ibn Jubayr saw *"wares ranging from precious jewels to the cheapest strings of beads, together with other articles and various merchandises of the world."** The hajj may have been a religious duty, but it also had a distinctly commercial side: merchants from all over the Islamic world found a ready market among the pilgrims.

**The Travels of Ibn Jubayr*, trans. R. J. C. Broadhurst (London: Jonathan Cape, 1952), pp. 184, 184–185.

Mecca's New Look The illuminated clock face of the Royal Mecca Clock Tower, completed in 2011, looms high above the enclosure housing the cube-shaped shrine of the Kaaba, which means "cube" in Arabic. The Arabic writing on the clock face says "God is the Greatest." Because Muhammad instructed all Muslims who could afford the trip to make the pilgrimage to Mecca, many Muslims believe that all pilgrims should experience the same travel conditions. But in recent years new luxury high-rise apartments have been built near the Kaaba, offering the well-to-do a better view and more comfortable rooms than those available to ordinary hajj pilgrims. (Salah Malkawi/The New York Times/Redux)

Finally, Ibn Jubayr, like almost all pilgrims, went to see Muhammad's tomb and mosque at Medina, even though this was not an obligatory part of the hajj. From Medina to Baghdad, Ibn Jubayr traveled along Zubaydah's Road, which he covered at a rapid 30 miles (50 km) per day: "*These tanks, pools, wells, and stations on the road from Baghdad to Mecca are monuments to Zubaydah.... But for her generous acts in this direction this road could not have been traversed.*"* Ibn Jubayr then traveled to Baghdad

---

**The Travels of Ibn Jubayr*, trans. R. J. C. Broadhurst (London: Jonathan Cape, 1952), p. 216.

and visited the palace where the family members of the figurehead caliph *"live in sumptuous confinement in those palaces, neither going forth nor being seen."** Because of several months' delay caused by a shipwreck, Ibn Jubayr arrived back in Spain more than two years after his departure in 1185. Ibn Jubayr's rihla offers a precious eyewitness account that portrays the Islamic world in the late twelfth century, when the Abbasid caliphs continued as figureheads in Baghdad but all real power lay with different regional rulers.

• **CONTEXT&CONNECTIONS** Having the Abbasid ruler serve as caliph came to an abrupt end in 1258, when the Mongols invaded Baghdad and ended even that minimal symbolic role for the caliph (see Chapter 14). •

---

*The Travels of Ibn Jubayr, trans. R. J. C. Broadhurst (London: Jonathan Cape, 1952), p. 236.

CONTEXT AND CONNECTIONS

The Legacy of the Abbasid Empire

When Muhammad instructed his followers to perform the annual hajj pilgrimage, provided that they had the means to do so, the Islamic world was limited to the west coast of the Arabian peninsula. In the eighth century, after Islamic armies conquered much of western Asia and North Africa, Khaizuran was able to fulfill her hajj obligation by traveling from the palace in Baghdad for only a few weeks, while other pilgrims living at the edges of the Abbasid empire, whether in Central Asia, Africa, or Ibn Jubayr's Spain, measured their journeys in years.

Almost all Muslims were subjects of the Abbasid caliph, whom they recognized as both the political head of state and the religious head of the caliphate. No other

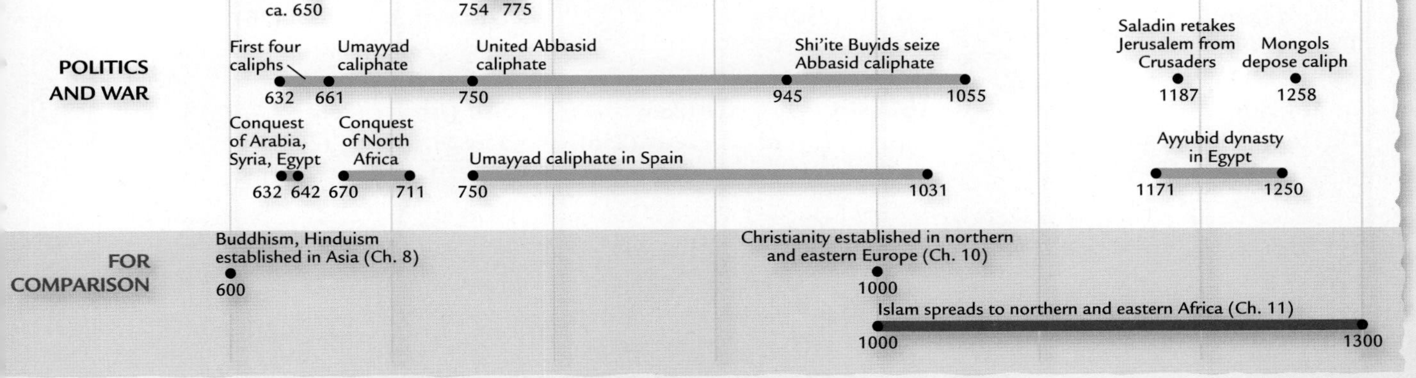

head of a major state in the world at That time served concurrently as both religious and political leader. The Roman emperor headed the government based at Constantinople, while the church had different leaders in Rome, Constantinople, and other cities (see Chapter 10). Similarly, the Tang emperor led the government of China, and Buddhist abbots headed their communities, as Ennin discovered on his pilgrimage from Japan (see Chapter 8).

The political structure holding the Abbasid empire together was fragile. Short of revenues, the Abbasid rulers made iqta grants to powerful men in the provinces who became more independent than either the satraps of the Achaemenid empire (see Chapter 6) or the provincial governors or tax farmers of the Roman Empire (see Chapter 7). In 936 one iqta holder took all political power from the caliph and received the title *commander of commanders.* Nine years later the Buyids seized power from him, and the Abbasid empire fragmented into different regions bound by linguistic, cultural, and religious ties.

The Abbasids used two languages to govern: the Arabic of the heartland of Islam and the Persian of the Sasanians who preceded them in Iran (see Chapter 6). Because both languages continued to be spoken after 945, they enabled people to communicate across the Islamic world, just as Latin and Greek connected inhabitants of the Roman empire and Sanskrit and Chinese connected the Buddhists of Asia (see Chapters 7 and 8). The Abbasid caliphs continued as figureheads until 1258, when the Mongols invaded Baghdad (see Chapter 14).

In the late fourth century Christian pilgrims like Egeria traveled to Jerusalem and Egypt; similarly, Ennin went to China in the mid-800s to visit important Buddhist sites. But they were both unusual; everyone who greeted them was surprised to meet a woman from Spain in the Holy Land or a monk from Japan in China. Both Khaizuran and Ibn Jubayr differed in that they traveled as members of a group who were carrying out Muhammad's instructions to perform the hajj.

Although primarily a religious obligation, the hajj had a profound effect on trade, navigation, and technology in the years after 945, as Ibn Jubayr discovered in the late 1100s. The hajj, and the resulting trade, pushed Muslims to adopt or to discover the fastest and most efficient means of transport from different places to Mecca and to equip their vessels with the best astronomical instruments, maps, and navigational devices. Despite the hardships, all Muslims, like Ibn Jubayr, viewed a trip to Mecca, no matter how distant, as an obligation to be fulfilled if at all possible. The result was clear: ordinary Muslims were far better traveled and more knowledgeable than their contemporaries in other parts of the world.

In the years after 945, multiple political and cultural centers arose that challenged Baghdad's position in the previously united Islamic world. As the next chapter will show, something similar happened in Europe as new political and cultural centers first appeared and then overtook the Byzantine capital at Constantinople.

Key Terms

Khaizuran (245)
Muhammad (246)
caliph (246)
jihad (249)
hajj (249)
qadi (250)
Quran (250)
hadith (250)
Five Pillars of Islam (250)
Sunnis (250)
Shi'ites (251)
Maghrib (254)
Abbasid caliphate (256)
translation movement (256)
astrolabe (257)
ulama (258)
Zubaydah's Road (261)
iqta grant (262)
al-Bakri (266)
Ibn Jubayr (266)
The Standing (268)

For Further Reference

Bennison, Amira K. *The Great Caliphs: The Golden Age of the 'Abbasid Empire*. New Haven: Yale University Press, 2009.

Berkey, Jonathan Porter. *Formation of Islam: Religion and Society in the Near East, 600–1800*. New York: Cambridge University Press, 2003.

Burke III, Edmund. "Islam at the Center: Technological Complexes and Roots of Modernity." *Journal of World History* 20, no. 2 (June 2009): 165–186.

Clarence-Smith, William Gervase. *Islam and the Abolition of Slavery*. London: Hurst and Company, 2006.

Crone, Patricia. *Meccan Trade and the Rise of Islam*. Piscataway, N.J.: Gorgias Press, 2004.

Freeman-Grenville, G. S. P. *The East African Coast: Select Documents from the First to the Earlier Nineteenth Century*. Oxford, England: Clarendon Press, 1962.

Gutas, Dmitri. *Greek Thought, Arabic Culture: The Graeco-Arabic Translation Movement in Baghdad and Early 'Abbāsid Society (2nd–4th/8th–10th Centuries)*. New York: Routledge, 1998.

Hodgson, Marshall. *Venture of Islam*. Vols. 1–3. Chicago: University of Chicago Press, 1977.

Hourani, George F. *Arab Seafaring*. Exp. ed. Princeton: Princeton University Press, 1995.

Kennedy, Hugh. *The Prophet and the Age of the Caliphates*. 2d ed. London: Pearson Education Limited, 2004.

Park, Hyunhee. *Mapping the Chinese and Islamic Worlds: Cross-Cultural Exchange in Pre-modern Asia*. New York: Cambridge University Press, 2012.

Porter, Venetia. *Hajj: Journey to the Heart of Islam*. London: The Trustees of the British Museum, 2012.

Turner, Howard R. *Science in Medieval Islam: An Illustrated Introduction*. Austin: University of Texas Press, 1995.

AP® Review Questions for Chapter 9

Multiple-Choice Questions

QUESTIONS 1–2 REFER TO THE FOLLOWING PASSAGE.

Which is better for the community, to choose its own leader or guide, or for the Prophet to have chosen him for us? Had the Prophet chosen him, that would of course have been preferable to the community's own choice, but since he did not, it is well for it that he left the choice in its own hands. . . . Had God laid down the procedure for the nomination of the Imam [Caliph] in a detailed formula with his own precise directions and clear signs, that would indeed have been a blessing. But since He did not make specific provision [for the office of Caliph], it is preferable for us to have been left in our present situation. How can anyone oblige or constrain God to establish an Imam according to a formula simply because in your view such a solution would be more advantageous and less troublesome, and better calculated to avoid error and problems.

—al-Jahiz (d. 868 C.E.), *The Uthmanis*

1. The claim of the author is a response to
   (A) Islam's inability to incorporate new ethnic groups into their religious community.
   (B) disagreement among Muslim scholars concerning the powers of the caliph.
   (C) Islam's lack of a clear procedure concerning the succession of power.
   (D) the corrupt nature of the caliph and his officials.

2. It can be inferred that the author is addressing
   (A) tensions between Arab and Persian Muslims.
   (B) power struggles between military and bureaucratic elites in the government.
   (C) the Umayyad's seizing of the caliphate after the death of Ali.
   (D) Sunni and Shia disagreement concerning the choosing of the caliph.

QUESTIONS 3–5 REFER TO THE FOLLOWING PASSAGE.

This common Arabic language bureaucratic culture was a major source of unity. This unity was expressed at a formal level by the recognition of the theory of the caliphate. The ideal of the caliphate lived on after the demise of its political authority. . . . Among the other dynasties, there were none who did not acknowledge the rights of a caliph in the khutba, the Friday sermon in which political allegiances were made public. . . . But whatever the practical reservations, no dynasty dispensed entirely with the idea of the caliphate or proclaimed an absolute independence. The grant of a title by the caliph remained a sign of political legitimacy and a sign that the recipient was now an accepted ruler.

— Dr. Hugh Kennedy, *The Prophet and the Age of the Caliphates: The Islamic Near East from the 6th to the 11th Century*, 2004

3. According to Dr. Hugh Kennedy, Islam was divided into many states but still maintained its unity by
   (A) the caliph in Baghdad demanding that he be recognized as the military and religious leader.
   (B) regional Muslim leaders acknowledging the authority of the caliph and pledging their loyalty to him.
   (C) ignoring the caliph and relying on economic relationships to maintain unity.
   (D) replacing the caliphate with the position of the sultan.

4. Which of the following statements best describes Dar al-Islam in the late Postclassical period based on the above passage?
   (A) Religious unity and social and political divisions
   (B) Cultural and economic unity and religious divisions
   (C) Religious and cultural unity with political divisions
   (D) Political unity and cultural disunity

5. The passage applies most directly to which of the following types of leaders from the Postclassical period?
   (A) Muslim religious scholars
   (B) Sultanates in South Asia
   (C) Non-Muslim bureaucratic elites
   (D) Byzantine emperors

QUESTIONS 6–7 REFER TO THE FOLLOWING IMAGE.

6. Which of the following statements best explains the motif used in the mosaic?
   (A) The garden paradise motif was an allusion to the oases of the Hijaz.
   (B) The mosaic is a representation of the Garden of Eden.

(C) Vegetation is the focus because representing humans and animals in art is prohibited.
(D) It is meant to celebrate the growing power of the caliphate.

7. The Umayyad use of mosaics in their mosques demonstrates which of the following?
(A) The Umayyads were willing to borrow from neighboring cultures.
(B) The Umayyad caliphate chose to culturally isolate itself from its neighbors.
(C) The early caliphs did not see mosques as the appropriate setting for high art.
(D) It replaced calligraphy as the primary artistic medium in the Islamic world.

QUESTIONS 8–10 REFER TO THE FOLLOWING PASSAGE.

...the Turks who dwell in tents in the desert and keep herds: they are the Bedouins of the non-Arabs.... Uninterested in craftsmanship or commerce, medicine, geometry, fruit-farming, building, digging canals, or collecting taxes, they care only about raiding, hunting, horsemanship, skirmishing with rival chieftains, taking booty, and invading other countries. In this way they have acquired a mastery of these skills, which for them take the place of craftsmanship and commerce and constitute their only pleasure, their glory, and the subject of all their conversation.

—al-Jahiz (d. 868 C.E.), "The Peculiarities of the Turks"

8. Which of the following statements best represents the attitude of the author toward the Turks?
(A) Disinterested, because the Turks have no skills of value
(B) Admiring, because of the prowess of the Turks on the battlefield
(C) Fearful, because the Turks are irrational and unpredictable in warfare
(D) Uncertain, because the skills of the Chinese may equal or surpass those of the Turks

9. al-Jahiz's attitude toward the Turks explains why the Abbasid caliphate
(A) feared the Turks and created substantial defenses against them in Central Asia.
(B) saw the Turks as inferior and incapable of threatening the empire's in Central Asia.
(C) preferred hiring Chinese and Greek soldiers to protect their borders.
(D) used Turkish slaves within their military force.

10. The most likely explanation for the Arabs' increased contact with the Turks is
(A) the Turkish conquest of the Arabian peninsula.
(B) Islamic expansion into Central Asia.
(C) increased Arab activity on the Indian Ocean trade circuits.
(D) expansion of the trans-Saharan trade.

Short-Answer Questions

In short, we have regards to the qualifications regarding sultans and their role public welfare.... but the political power in these days is a consequence solely of military power, and whoever holds military power and professes his allegiance to the caliph. And whosoever exercises independent authority, while he shows allegiance to the caliph by mentioning his name in the mosque and on the coinage, he is a sultan, whose orders and judgements are executed in the several parts of the earth by valid political power.

—Abū Ḥāmid Muḥammad ibn Muḥammad al-Ghazālī,
Muslim scholar in eastern Persia, ca. 1058–1111

1. Use the passage above to answer A, B, and C.
   A. Identify the point of view expressed by al-Ghazālī. Then briefly explain how ONE of the following aspects influenced it:
   - Traditional role of the caliph
   - The power of the sultans
   - The spread of Islam across much of Asia

   B. Briefly explain how the point of view expressed in the passage affected the power of the caliph.
   C. Based on the passage, briefly explain ONE example of a regional Muslim state.
2. Answer A, B, and C.
   A. Briefly explain ONE influence of Islam on slavery.
   B. Briefly explain ONE influence of Islam on women.
   C. To what extent did Islam challenge and maintain older social structures?

10 The Multiple Centers of Europe, 500–1000

Gudrid and Thorfinn Karlsefni

Historiated initial from the beginning of a chapter on seafaring and trade, copy of an original 14th century law collection "Jonsbok" (vellum), Icelandic School, (14th century)/Arni Magnusson Institute, Reykjavik, Iceland/Bridgeman Images

Sometime around the year 1000, Leif Eriksson (LEAF ERIC-son) sailed with some forty companions from Greenland across the North Atlantic to Newfoundland in today's Canada. His former sister-in-law **Gudrid** and her second husband **Thorfinn Karlsefni** followed in a subsequent voyage. The travelers were originally from Norway in the Scandinavian region of Europe, which also includes Sweden, Finland, and Denmark. Europe in the year 1000 differed dramatically from Europe in 500. In 500, Europe contained only one major empire, Byzantium, with its capital at Constantinople (modern Istanbul, Turkey). Five hundred years later, Europe was home to multiple centers—modern-day France and Germany, Scandinavia, and Russia—that are still the most important European powers today.

Competition among these multiple centers provided a powerful stimulus, as the Scandinavian voyages to the Americas amply demonstrate. An account recorded several hundred years later, but based on oral history, reports that, after the Scandinavians arrived in the Americas, Karlsefni set off to explore with a man named Snorri:

Karlsefni sailed south along the coast. . . . Karlsefni and his men sailed into the estuary and named the place Hope (Tidal Lake). Here they found wild wheat growing in fields on all the low ground and grape vines on all the higher ground. Every stream was teeming with fish. They dug trenches at the high-tide mark, and when the tide went out there were halibut trapped in all the trenches. In the woods there was a great number of animals of all kinds.

They stayed there for a fortnight [two weeks], enjoying themselves and noticing nothing untoward. They had their livestock

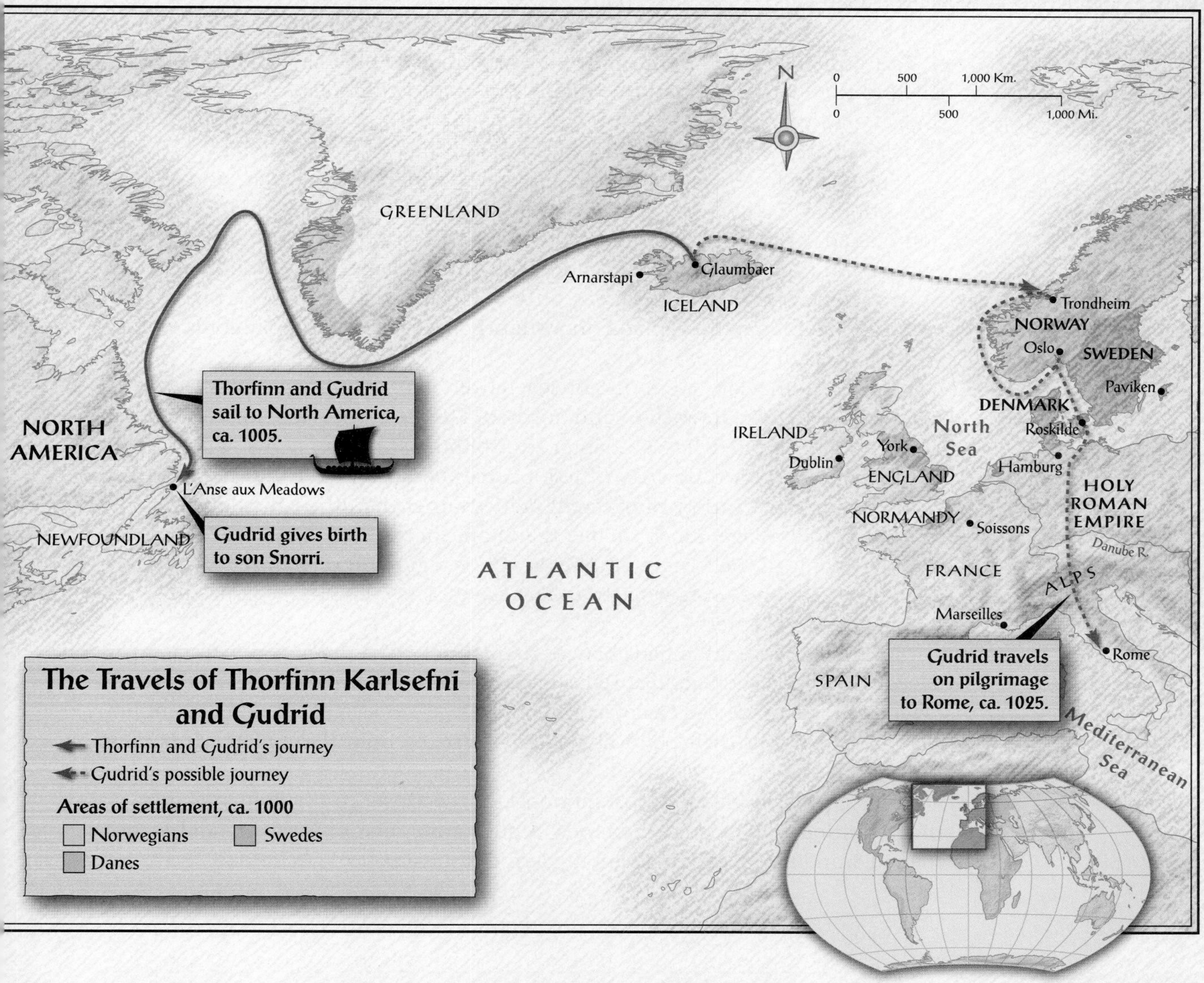

with them. But early one morning as they looked around they caught sight of nine skin-boats; the men in them were waving sticks which made a noise like flails [tools used to thresh grain], and the motion was sunwise [clockwise].

Karlsefni said, "What can this signify?"

*"It could well be a token of peace," said Snorri. "Let us take a white shield and go to meet them with it."**

---

*From *The Vinland Sagas*, translated with an introduction by Magnus Magnusson and Hermann Pálsson (Penguin Classics, 1965).

Gudrid and Thorfinn Karlsefni

A couple originally from Iceland who settled in about 1000 in Greenland and then Canada and later returned to Iceland.

Karlsefni and Snorri went out to meet the men in boats, who stared at them and then left. Although this incident is recorded in a later source, archaeological evidence shows that the Scandinavians built at least one settlement at the Canadian town of L'Anse aux Meadows in today's Newfoundland.

Possessing faster and more maneuverable wooden boats than any of their contemporaries, the Scandinavians went as far as Russia, Greenland, Iceland, and Canada. Although we are accustomed to think of the distance between Europe and the Americas as enormous, the direct voyage from Greenland to the northeastern coast of Canada was only 1,350 miles (2,200 km). Hugging the coast of Greenland and Canada on a slightly longer route, a boat could remain within constant sight of land.

The Scandinavians were one of several different groups speaking Germanic languages who lived in western and northern Europe at the time the Western half of the Roman empire fell (see Chapter 7). Around 500, the residents of the Eastern Roman empire looked down on these peoples because they could not read and write, worshiped a variety of different deities rather than the Christian God, and lived in simple villages much smaller than Rome or the eastern capital of Constantinople. People of the Eastern empire saw these regions as uncivilized backwaters, good only as sources of raw materials and slaves. They did not recognize the vitality of these new centers.

By 1000, the situation had changed dramatically. The rise of regional states paralleled the rise of the Buddhist states of East Asia that borrowed the Tang dynasty blueprint for empire (see Chapter 8). These new European states, like Byzantium, were Christian, but their political structures differed from those of Rome because they were based on the war-band.

This chapter begins in Constantinople, the successor to the Roman empire. As the Byzantine empire contracted, new centers arose: first in Germany and France, then in Scandinavia, and finally in modern-day Russia.

KEY CONCEPT QUESTIONS

- How did the Byzantine empire respond to pressures from neighboring states? **(Key Concept 3.2)**
- How did the Merovingians and Carolingians build upon traditional sources of power and legitimacy? **(Key Concept 3.2)**
- How did the Scandinavians use technology to adapt to their environment? **(Key Concept 3.1)**
- What role did the spread of Christianity have on the development of the earliest states in Russia? **(Key Concept 3.1)**

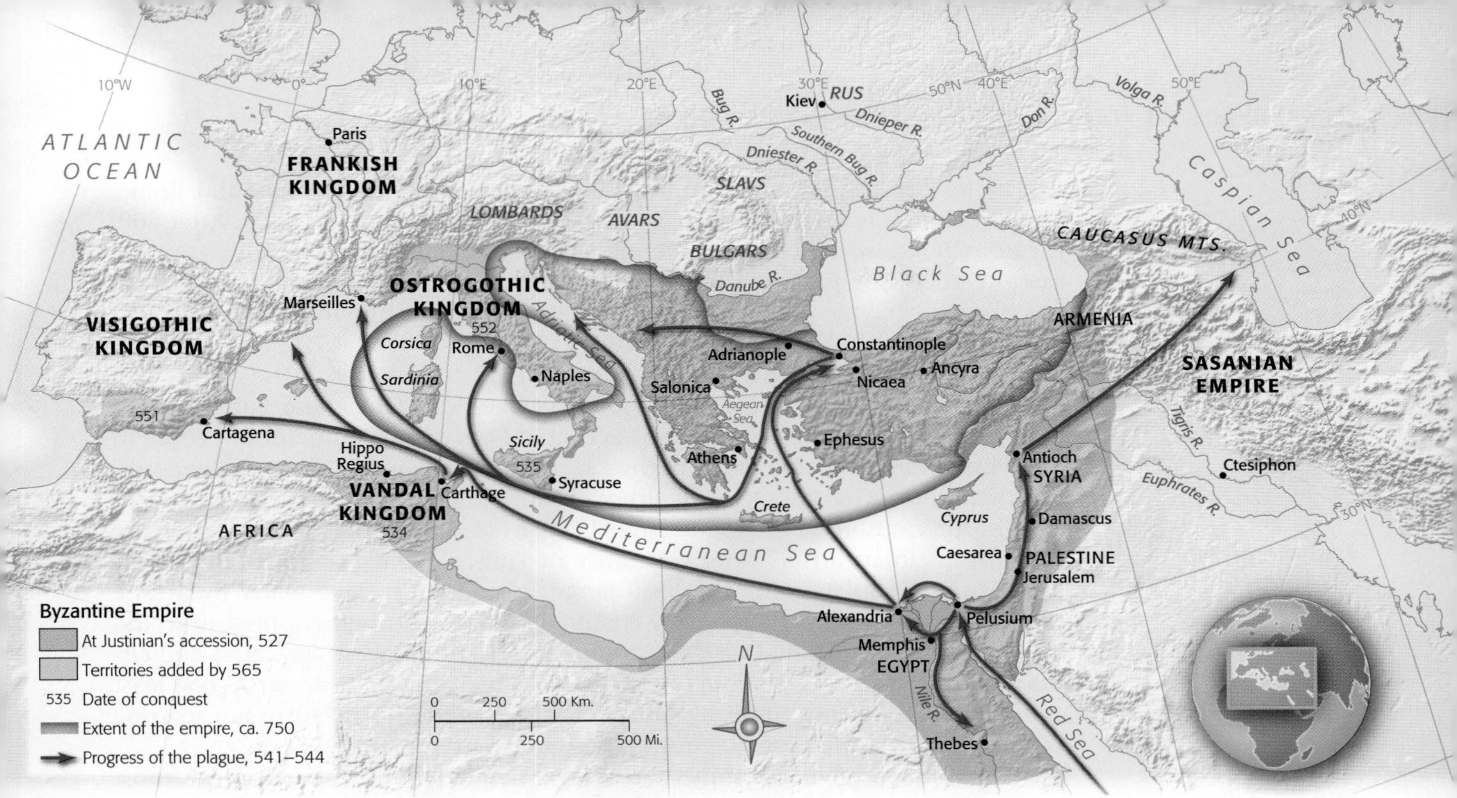

Map 10.1 The Byzantine Empire The Byzantine empire grew dramatically during the reign of Justinian (r. 527–565), expanding its territory in North Africa, the Balkans, and Italy. Yet the plague struck for the first of at least fifteen times in 541–544, killing 7 million of his 26 million subjects.

Byzantium, the Eastern Roman Empire, 476–1071

To distinguish it from the Western empire based in Rome, historians call the Eastern Roman empire, with its capital at Constantinople, the **Byzantine empire**, or simply Byzantium (see Map 10.1). The Byzantine empire lasted for over a thousand years after the Western empire ended, despite continuous pressure from surrounding peoples. Far worse than any attack by a foreign power, the bubonic plague struck the empire in 541 and then at regular intervals for two more centuries. The massive decline in population, coupled with the disruption of Mediterranean shipping, resulted in a sharp economic downturn. Through all these events the empire's scholars continued to preserve Greek learning, systematize Roman law, and write new Christian texts. Over the centuries, however, the amount of territory under Byzantine rule shrank, providing an opportunity for other European centers to develop.

Byzantine empire (476–1453) Eastern half of the Roman Empire after the loss of the Western half in 476. Sometimes simply called Byzantium.

Justinian and the Legacy of Rome, 476–565

Constantinople, the city named for the emperor Constantine, had been a capital of the Eastern Roman empire since 330 (see Chapter 7). After 476 the Eastern emperor had no counterpart in Rome. The Christian church at this time had

patriarchs
In the 400s and 500s, the highest-ranking bishop of the four major Christian church centers at Constantinople, Alexandria, Jerusalem, and Antioch.

pope
In the 400s and 500s, the pope was the highest-ranking bishop in Rome, and by 1000, the pope was recognized as leader of the Catholic Church in Rome.

Justinian Corpus of Civil Law
Consisting of the Code, the Digest, and the Institutes, this compendium preserved the core of Roman law for succeeding ages.

five major centers: Constantinople, Alexandria, Jerusalem, Antioch, and Rome. The top church bishops in the first four cities were called **patriarchs**. After 500, the church led from Rome became increasingly separate from the church in the east. By 1000, the patriarch of Constantinople had become head of the Orthodox church of Byzantium, while the highest-ranking bishop in Rome was called the **pope**.

Culturally the residents of the Eastern and Western halves of the empire had much in common: educated people often spoke both Greek and Latin, almost everyone was Christian, and citizens accepted Roman law. Sometimes people in the West referred to those living in the Eastern half as "Greeks" since nearly everyone there spoke Greek, not Latin, although not always as their mother tongue.

The first outbreak of plague in 541 occurred during the long reign of the emperor Justinian I (r. 527–565). A native of Thrace, the region north of Greece, Justinian grew up speaking the local language and Latin. Like many Byzantine emperors, Justinian was chosen by his predecessor, who had adopted him and raised him in Byzantium. In 520, Justinian met his future wife: an actress and circus performer named Theodora (497–548), who had already given birth to at least one child. She did not fulfill Byzantine ideals of modesty, yet Justinian married her, and the two ruled together for more than twenty years.

Early in their reign, a commission of legal scholars completed one of the most important legal works ever written: the **Justinian Corpus of Civil Law**. Working for five years from 529 to 534, the commission gathered together all the valid laws of the Roman empire, and reduced some 3 million laws, many no longer in effect, to a manageable body 1,500 pages long in its modern edition. The texts of the laws and the extensive legal commentary were written in Latin, still the official language of the central government, but the laws issued by Justinian himself were in Greek, which was rapidly becoming the administrative language of the empire. The Justinian Corpus preserved the core of Roman law not simply for sixth-century jurists but for all time.

Justinian and Theodora faced challenges to their rule, particularly from the residents of Constantinople who occasionally rioted against them. In 532, after suppressing one such outbreak, as an expression of gratitude they sponsored an enormous church called Hagia Sophia (hah-GHEE-ah so-FEE-ah), the Church of Holy Wisdom. This church had a majestic dome. *"A spherical-shaped dome standing upon this circle makes it exceedingly beautiful,"* marveled the historian Procopius (pro-COE-pee-uhs), *"from the lightness of the building, it does not appear to rest upon a solid foundation, but to cover the place beneath as though it were suspended from heaven by the fabled golden chain."**

Justinian and Theodora managed the empire's relations with its neighbors with considerable success. Unlike his predecessors, Justinian challenged the Vandals, one of the peoples who led the conquest of North Africa in the fifth century (see Chapter 7). His successful military campaigns in Northwest Africa, coastal Spain, and Italy added territory to the empire. Yet on the eastern front, the armies of the Sasanian empire in Iran captured Antioch, the third-largest city in the Byzantine empire, revealing how vulnerable the Eastern empire was.

*Medieval Sourcebook (http://www.fordham.edu/halsall/source/procop-deaed1.html), trans. W. Lethaby and H. Swainson, from Procopius, *De Aedificiis*, in *The Church of St. Sophia Constantinople* (New York: 1894), pp. 24–28.

Louis Haghe/Philip de Bay/Corbis

The Striking Dome of Hagia Sophia Built in a mere five years, the dome of the Hagia Sophia cathedral in Constantinople (modern Istanbul, Turkey) is more than 100 feet (30 m) in diameter and over 180 feet (55 m) tall. Forty windows at the bottom of the dome give the impression that it floated in the air, and later observers believed that such a beautiful dome could only have been made with divine help.

The Impact of the Plague and the Arab Conquests, 541–767

The fighting on both the Eastern and Western frontiers subsided immediately after the first recorded outbreak of the bubonic plague in 541. Many people, including Justinian himself, became terribly ill. In modern usage, the term ***plague*** refers to two distinct illnesses, bubonic plague and pneumonic plague, which form two phases of an outbreak. First, fleas that have drunk the blood of infected rodents transmit the bubonic plague to people. Lymph glands on the neck, under the arm, and on the groin swell up and turn black. The pneumonic plague spreads as one bubonic plague victim sneezes or coughs onto another person. Pneumonic plague is almost always fatal. One contemporary observer, Procopius, observed that the disease first appeared in towns along the coast and then moved inland, but he did not know why. Only in the late nineteenth century did scientists realize that black rats living on ships were the main agents responsible for spreading the disease.

plague Refers to two distinct illnesses, bubonic plague and the almost always fatal pneumonic plague, forming two phases of an outbreak.

The first outbreak hit the Egyptian port of Pelusium (pell-OOZE-ee-uhm) on the mouth of the Nile in 541 and spread across the Mediterranean to

WORLD HISTORY IN TODAY'S WORLD

The Plague Bacteria Lives On

The plague is not a disease of the past. Outbreaks still occur, as in 2014, when a dog, apparently infected by fleas, transmitted the plague to four people in Denver. No one died there, but the death toll can be high. One recent occurrence killed twenty people in a Madagascar village in a single week.

In 1994, in the largest recent instance of the plague, the Indian city of Surat experienced an outbreak that caused more than one hundred thousand of the city's residents to flee. Although neighboring cities dreaded a massive epidemic, that particular strain responded to tetracycline. The final death toll was 56, far lower than most had feared.

The plague bacillus that struck the Byzantines in 541 is one of 155 known strains. Scientists managed to extract the genome from two teeth of a victim buried in a southern German graveyard. After analyzing the genome carefully, they have concluded that this particular strain, which originated in Asia, no longer survives.

Other strains, like the bacterial descendants of the Black Death plague that struck Europe in 1348 (see Chapter 13), continue to evolve. Most of the time these strains of plague lie dormant in rodents, usually rats, but when a new variant appears, it jumps to humans, and an outbreak occurs. The strain that caused the 1994 outbreak in Surat was related to the Black Death.

As it moves from victim to victim, the plague bacterium will change up to 10 percent of its genes, making it that much more resistant to existing medicines and posing a real threat to humans. Fortunately, tetracycline has cured the Black Death strains that have appeared since the end of World War II, and most of the known strains respond to tetracycline or other antibiotics, which were discovered in the 1930s and 1940s. Still, the Black Death bacillus has survived for more than 700 years, providing strong evidence of its ability to adapt and evolve.

Source: Donald G. McNeil, Jr., "No Longer Leading Killer, Plague Still Raises Fears," *New York Times*, January 28, 2014.

Constantinople in the following year. Ports such as Carthage, Rome, and Marseilles were affected in 543. At least fifteen outbreaks followed between 541 and 767, when the plague finally came to an end.

In the absence of accurate population statistics, historians have to estimate the deaths resulting from the plague. The deaths in the large cities were massive: some 230,000 out of 375,000 died in Constantinople alone. High estimates put the death toll from the plague at one-quarter of the empire's population during Justinian's reign: of 26 million subjects, only 19 million survived. (See the feature "World History in Today's World: The Plague Bacteria Lives On.")

Before the plague, the Byzantine empire had been an urban society in which powerful people met at the marketplace each day to discuss their affairs, enjoying theater and circus performances alongside their poorer neighbors. By 600, such an urban type of life had become a memory. Starting in 541 and continuing to sometime in the ninth century, the population declined, cities shrank, the economy contracted, and tax revenues plummeted. In these centuries of declining tax revenues, the government minted far fewer coins than earlier, and a barter economy replaced the partially monetized economy. Craftsmen and merchants gave up their occupations to become farmers.

Another consequence of these catastrophes was that the government could no longer afford to pay its soldiers. Instead, militias were formed by part-time soldiers who farmed the land during peacetime. When Islamic expansion began around 640 (see Chapter 9), the Byzantine empire lost large chunks of territory in Armenia and Africa to caliphate armies.

In contrast to the multiple officials of Roman times, the basic administrative unit of the Byzantine empire during the seventh and eighth centuries was the *theme* (Greek plural: *themata*), headed by a single governor. This governor heard legal disputes, collected taxes, and commanded the local militia.

Society had also changed from Roman times. The high and low in rank led almost identical lives. Fewer people knew Latin. Some people possessed more land than others, but they now worked the land alongside their poorer dependents. Slavery declined as well because no one could afford to feed slaves. Most of the people in the countryside were legally independent peasants who farmed the land intensively, often with two oxen and a plow, and grew only enough food for their own families.

The final outbreak of plague hit Constantinople in 747 and ended in 767. In the following years, a slow revival began. The government minted more small coins, and trade and commerce increased slightly. The writing of manuscripts resumed, especially in monasteries, where scribes devised a new, smaller minuscule script that allowed them to write more words on a piece of parchment, the most common writing material at the time (see Chapter 7). Literacy was mainly concentrated among monks and nuns. Although monasteries had little land and not much wealth, like the monasteries of Egypt (see Chapter 7), they offered an appealing alternative to family life.

Religion and State, 767–1071

The Byzantine emperor ruled the empire, while the patriarch of Constantinople presided over the church, which held property throughout the empire. While the Christian emperors sometimes tried to impose their own views on the church, they also served as patrons, as Justinian's financing of the Hagia Sophia demonstrates.

Byzantine opinion during the eighth century was sharply divided over the use of images in Christian worship. The **iconoclasts**, literally "image-breakers," advocated the removal of all icons, or images, but permitted prayers directed to crosses.

iconoclasts
Members of a movement calling for the destruction of images of Jesus, Mary, and the saints because they were believed to violate the Second Commandment of the Hebrew Bible.

● **CONTEXT&CONNECTIONS** Like the Umayyad caliphs in Spain, who also banned images (see Chapter 9), the iconoclasts justified their position by citing the Second Commandment of the Hebrew Bible, forbidding the worship of graven images. ●

Iconoclasm was deeply controversial among Byzantines. When one Byzantine emperor ordered the removal of an image of Jesus from the main entrance to his palace, an angry crowd of women killed the man who took the portrayal down. The iconoclast movement also appalled many Christians in western Europe who frequently prayed to the statues of saints.

AP® THEMES
Why did differences in the beliefs and practices of Christians of western Europe and those of Christians in the Byzantine empire develop?

In 780, Irene, the widow of the emperor Leo IV, came to power in her mid-twenties, serving as regent for her nine-year-old son. Few expected Irene to rule for long, but she surprised her opponents by tackling some of the major issues facing the empire. Hoping to work out a compromise to end the iconoclast controversy, Irene summoned a church council, a meeting that included Constantinople's patriarch and bishops from all over the Christian world. In 787, the Second Council of Nicaea met and condemned iconoclasm. Images that had been removed from different churches were returned.

During her reign, Irene, by agreeing to make various large payments of both books and money, managed to keep the Abbasid armies from taking the city of

Icon of Christ The iconoclasts opposed the use of icons like this intensely colored example, which shows Jesus holding the Gospel in his left hand and making a blessing with his right. The painter mixed his pigments in beeswax and then applied them to the wood to make a painting in encaustic. Coming to Byzantium from Egypt, this technique was prized for its lifelike eyes and skin tones. Jesus' face has two distinct halves: where the side on our left appears to judge the viewer, the side on our right is more compassionate. Was the artist trying to portray the human and divine sides of Jesus? (Jean-Luc MANAUD/Gamma-Rapho/Getty Images)

Constantinople. But she could not prevent the powerful Islamic forces from making incursions into the empire's shrunken territory.

Irene and her son did not share power easily. First he tried to seize power from her, then they ruled together, and then, in 797, she tried to overthrow him. Her allies blinded her son, possibly without her knowledge, and he died soon after.

● **CONTEXT&CONNECTIONS** Irene became the first woman to rule the Byzantine empire in her own right and called herself emperor (not empress), just as *Emperor Wu* had in China a century earlier (key term in Chapter 8). Both women rulers wanted to be accepted as the equals of male rulers, but they did not see themselves as champions of women's rights, a concept that first appeared only in the late 1700s. ●

In 802, her courtiers deposed the elderly Irene and installed a general as her successor. The empire that Irene relinquished was less than a third the size it had been in the mid-sixth century. Justinian had ruled an empire that controlled the eastern half of the Mediterranean, but Islamic forces had conquered large blocks of territory throughout the seventh century. The Byzantine empire had shrunk largely to the borders of modern-day Turkey, and its population was only 7 million. A new state outside the Byzantine empire, Charlemagne's Francia, had staked a claim as the legitimate heir to the Roman empire (as discussed later in this chapter).

In the centuries after 800, Byzantium, though small, continued to be an important intellectual center where scholars studied, copied, and preserved Greek texts from the past, analyzed Roman law, and studied Christian doctrine. In 1071, the Byzantines suffered a massive defeat at the battle of Manzikert (modern-day Malazgirt, Turkey) at the hands of the Seljuq Turks, who captured the emperor himself. After 1071, the Byzantine emperors continued to rule a much smaller empire with a much-weakened army.

The Germanic-Speaking Peoples of Western Europe, 481–1000

After the fall of the Western Roman empire, the Byzantines often referred to the peoples living in the north of Europe as *barbarians*, a Greek word meaning "uncivilized." The largest group was the Franks, who lived in the **Frankish kingdom**. Although uncivilized in Byzantine eyes, they commanded powerful armies who defeated the Byzantine armies in battle. The Franks were ruled first by the kings of the Merovingian dynasty (481–751) and then by the Carolingians (751–ca. 1000). And in 800, the pope crowned the king of the Franks, Charlemagne, the emperor of Rome.

● **CONTEXT&CONNECTIONS** Unlike the Byzantine emperors, who governed an empire divided into regular administrative districts called *themata*, the Merovingian and Carolingian monarchs ruled as the leaders of war-bands, the most important unit of Frankish society. ●

Frankish kingdom
The homeland of the Franks, including much of modern-day France, Germany, and the land in between.

Germanic-Speaking Europeans Before 500

Many different peoples lived in the regions of northern and central Europe and crowded the borders of the Western Roman empire before it fell in 476. They spoke a group of related languages now classed as Germanic, about which little is known because none was written down. Even so, analysts have been able to sketch some broad similarities among these peoples, usually on the basis of archaeological evidence. Those who lived near the Rhine Valley are called Franks.

The basic unit of society was the extended family, which was headed by the father, who might have more than one wife, as well as children and slaves. The number of cattle an individual possessed determined the person's rank. Freemen looked down on slaves, who were usually war captives.

Beyond the immediate family were larger kinship groups consisting of several households bound by family ties on both the male and female sides. These groups feuded often and developed a complex set of rules for determining the correct handling of disputes. The best source for understanding the practices of these peoples is the Salic Law, a list of punishments for different crimes recorded early in the sixth century. Although written in Latin, the Salic Law shows little Roman influence. One of the most important legal concepts was that of **wergeld** (literally "man-payment"), which set the monetary value of a human life. Wergeld (WEAR-geld) payments served to prevent an endless cycle of killing and counter-killing among feuding families. Different wergeld penalties were specified for men and women, both free and unfree. For example, the section of the Salic Law "On Killing Pregnant Women" says the following:

wergeld
Literally "man-payment," an important legal concept that set the monetary value of a human life. The function of wergeld payments was to prevent an endless cycle of killing and counter-killing among feuding families.

1. *He who kills a pregnant woman shall be liable to pay twenty-four thousand denarii [600 solidi, or 6 pounds, or 2.73 kg, of gold]. And if it is proved that the fetus was a boy, he shall also be liable to pay six hundred solidi for the child.*
2. *He who kills a girl less than twelve years old or up to the end of her twelfth year shall be liable to pay two hundred solidi [2 pounds, or .9 kg, of gold].*
3. *He who kills a woman of mature age up to her sixtieth year, as long as she is able to bear children, shall be liable to pay twenty-four thousand denarii [600 solidi, or 6 pounds, or 2.73 kg, of gold].**
4. *But if she is killed afterwards when she is no longer able to bear children he shall be liable to pay two hundred solidi [2 pounds, or .9 kg, of gold].*

AP® THEMES
What does the Salic Law reveal about the roles of women in Germanic society?

Penalties were levied in either silver denarius coins or gold solidus coins and varied depending on whether a woman had reached or passed childbearing age,

---

*Katherine Fischer Drew, *The Laws of the Salian Franks* (Philadelphia: University of Pennsylvania Press, 1991), p. 127.

and if pregnant, whether she was carrying a male or female child. These payments were the sole form of punishment: no one was imprisoned or banished.

war-bands
The most important social unit among Germanic-speaking peoples. In times of war, warriors formed bands behind a leader, who gave them horses, armor, a place to live, and a share of plunder.

In times of war, groups of warriors called **war-bands** gathered behind a leader, whose main claim to their allegiance was the distribution of plunder. A successful leader rewarded his men liberally with the spoils of victory, fed and clothed them, and provided them with horses, armor, and a place to live. His supporters, in turn, fought next to him in battles and banqueted with him when at peace.

This society was extremely fluid, because war-bands could form rapidly and collapse equally quickly. Members of a war-band distinguished themselves from others by wearing a certain kind of clothing, having similar hairstyles, or carrying similar weapons. They often believed that they and the other members of the war-band had a common ancestor, sometimes a god, from whom they all claimed descent. According to custom, freemen were obliged to fight in wars while slaves were not. The freemen in these bands often gathered in assemblies, called Thing (TING), to settle internal disputes or to plan military campaigns.

The Merovingians, 481–751

Merovingian dynasty
A Frankish dynasty (481–751) in modern-day France and Germany whose founder, Clovis (r. 481–511), converted to Christianity and ruled as a war-band leader.

The most important leader to emerge from the constantly evolving alliances of Frankish society was Clovis (r. 481–511), who established the **Merovingian dynasty** that ruled what are now France and Germany from 481 to 751. He combined great military successes, such as defeating the Visigoths of Spain, with skillful marriage alliances to build a dynasty that lasted two centuries, far longer than any earlier dynasty in the region.

The Merovingian army consisted of different war-bands linked by their loyalty to Clovis. One incident, recounted by the chronicler Gregory of Tours (538/39–ca. 594), vividly illustrates the ties between Clovis and his followers. In 486, Clovis and his men removed many items from the treasuries of several churches, including a *"vase of marvelous size and beauty"* from Soissons. The bishop of the robbed church requested the vase's return. After Clovis and his followers had divided the goods they had stolen, Clovis addressed his men: *"I ask you, O most valiant warriors, not to refuse to me the vase in addition to my rightful part."** Most of his men agreed, but one man crushed the vase with his battle-ax because he felt that Clovis, although their leader, was not entitled to more than his fair share. The humiliated Clovis returned the pieces of the broken vase to the bishop.

One year later, Clovis summoned his troops for a review so that he could inspect their spears, swords, and axes, the iron weapons that helped to make his armies invincible. When he reached the man who had destroyed the vase, he threw the soldier's ax to the ground. As the soldier bent down to pick it up, Clovis grabbed his head and smashed it down on the weapon. *"Thus,"* he said, *"didst thou to the vase at Soissons."** This incident shows that, though called a king, Clovis was a war-band leader who ruled his men only as long as he commanded their respect, and he had to use brute strength coupled with rewards to do so.

One sign of the Merovingian king's role as a war-band leader was his hair, which only he was allowed to grow long. If someone challenged his hold on power and succeeded in overthrowing him, the challenger forced the king to shave off his hair—a visible reminder that he had lost leadership—and the challenger took power.

---

*Medieval Sourcebook (http://www.fordham.edu/halsall/source/gregtours1.html), "The Incident of the Vase at Soissons," in *Readings in European History*, ed. J. H. Robinson (Boston: Ginn, 1905), pp. 51–55.

The Franks, a tiny minority of perhaps two hundred thousand people, lived among 7 million Latin-speaking Christian Gallo-Romans in modern-day France and Germany. The Gallo-Romans were the Christian subjects of the fallen Roman empire who spoke Latin. Like many of his subjects, Clovis worshiped both Roman and local deities. A few years before his death in 511, Clovis's wife, Clotilde, persuaded him to convert to Roman Christianity and acknowledge the pope's authority. With his conversion, Clovis eliminated the primary cultural barrier between the Frankish peoples and the Gallo-Romans they governed.

● **CONTEXT&CONNECTIONS** Like the Roman emperor *Constantine* (Chapter 7), Clovis promised to convert if Jesus Christ brought him victory in a battle; when his enemy surrendered, he was baptized, along with three thousand of his men. ●

When Clovis died, he had divided his realm among his four sons, according to Frankish custom. They and their descendants continued to rule until the mid-eighth century.

Under the Romans, large landowners had lived with their slaves in widely dispersed estates. Under the Merovingians, the basic farming unit changed to the village. Former villa owners lived with others in small settlements near streams or forests and engaged in slash-and-burn agriculture, changing plots whenever a field's productivity gave out. Ordinary people consumed a diet composed largely of hunted animals, fish caught in rivers, or plants foraged from the forest.

In the sixth century, monasteries—small communities under the supervision of the local bishop—gradually spread to western Europe from the eastern Mediterranean (see Chapter 7). Many were modeled on a monastery founded in 529 near Rome by Benedict of Nursia (ca. 480–545), who composed a concise set of practical rules for running a monastery. Benedictine monks devoted themselves full-time to manual labor and the worship of God, usually through public prayer conducted eight times each day. Unlike monks in more extreme monasteries, they ate an adequate diet and received enough sleep. The adult members of the community selected their leader, or abbot, who was to obey the local bishop.

In 590, an Irish monk named Saint Columbanus (543–615) arrived in the Merovingian kingdom and founded many monasteries that encouraged monks to be even more devout and disciplined. Columbanus (coh-luhm-BAHN-us) taught that laypeople could contribute land and money to monasteries, read religious texts (or have them read aloud), and recite psalms from the Hebrew Bible. Irish monks copied, and so preserved, many manuscripts that would have otherwise been lost.

Bishops were among the few educated men in Merovingian society. Some had served as priests, others had worked for the king; still others had been monks or abbots in monasteries, and some had no ties to the church but belonged to an important lay family. Many learned to read and write by studying with other bishops or in monasteries.

Most Merovingian bishops had married before assuming office. The popes in Rome frequently urged them to treat their wives as their sisters and stop sleeping with them. In some cases, bishops slept surrounded by their male assistants so that everyone could see that they maintained their vows of celibacy.

The head cleric of the Western church, the pope was elected by the clergy in Rome. When the Byzantines lost control of northern and central Italy to a Germanic-speaking people called the Lombards in 568, the popes needed military protection because they had no armies of their own. The popes eventually turned to the Carolingians for help.

The Carolingians were a powerful family living in the Merovingian realm. Charles Martel (688–741), a palace official, succeeded in building a powerful army in Austrasia, the northern section of the Merovingian realm. The **Carolingian dynasty** is named for Martel even though he never called himself king. (Carolus is Latin for Charles.)

Carolingian dynasty
(751–ca. 1000) An important aristocratic family that overthrew the Merovingian rulers in 751. Their most powerful ruler was Charlemagne. After his death, the empire split into three sections, each under a different Carolingian ruler.

• **CONTEXT&CONNECTIONS** After defeating local rivals, Charles Martel gathered his armies to prevent an invasion by the Umayyad caliphate (see Chapter 9). In 732 they defeated the Umayyad troops at the Battle of Tours, effectively preventing further Muslim expansion from Spain into Europe. •

Charlemagne and the Carolingians, 751–ca. 1000

Charles Martel's grandson Charlemagne, or Charles "the Great" ("le Magne" in old French), was even more successful than he was. In 751, the Carolingian dynasty overthrew the Merovingian rulers. Charlemagne (r. 768–814) was the most powerful Carolingian ruler. Recognition by the pope demonstrated that the Carolingian realm exceeded Byzantium in importance, at least in Rome's eyes. By 800, Europe had two powerful centers: Byzantium, which had inherited the legacy of Rome, and the new kingdom of the Franks.

AP® THEMES
How did Charlemagne's alliance with the pope help legitimize his power over his empire in Europe?

Charlemagne became king of the Franks in 768 and then launched a series of wars against the neighboring Germanic-speaking peoples. The pope in Rome supported him against the Lombards, and Charlemagne rapidly conquered northern and central Italy, some parts of Spain, and much of Germany (see Map 10.2).

• **CONTEXT&CONNECTIONS** In 800, during Irene's reign as Byzantine emperor, the pope crowned Charlemagne emperor of Rome, using the pretext that Irene could not be emperor because she was female. The Byzantines were horrified. They thought of Charlemagne as the unlettered leader of primitive peoples, not as a monarch comparable to their own. When Charlemagne accepted the title, the Frankish kingdom, in a great blow to the Byzantines, styled itself the legitimate heir to the Roman empire. The alliance between the Carolingians and the pope allowed both to increase their power over their rivals, whether the countries surrounding the Franks or the church in Byzantium. •

Diverging from its roots in the war-band, Carolingian society was divided into two groups: the powerful (potentes in Latin) and the powerless (paupers, literally "the poor"). The powerful owned their own land and could command others to obey them. Although some paupers owned land, they had no one to command. Among the powerless were slaves, a minority of the laborers in the countryside.

During Charlemagne's many conquests, his armies took vast numbers of prisoners from enemy forces, which they sold as slaves to buyers, sometimes in distant lands. Writers in the eighth and ninth centuries used the word *captive,* not *slave,* for these prisoners of war. Charlemagne's Christian advisers urged him to stop the sale of Christian slaves to non-Christians, but he continued the practice. One of Europe's main exports to the Abbasids under Charlemagne and his successors was slaves (see Chapter 9).

Despite his title of emperor and his conquests, Charlemagne was still very much a war-band leader. He was much less educated than the Byzantine or Abbasid rulers of his day. His biographer, Einhard, reports that "*he also attempted to learn how to write, and, for this reason, used to place wax-tablets and notebooks under the pillows on his bed, so that, if he had any free time, he might accustom his hand to*

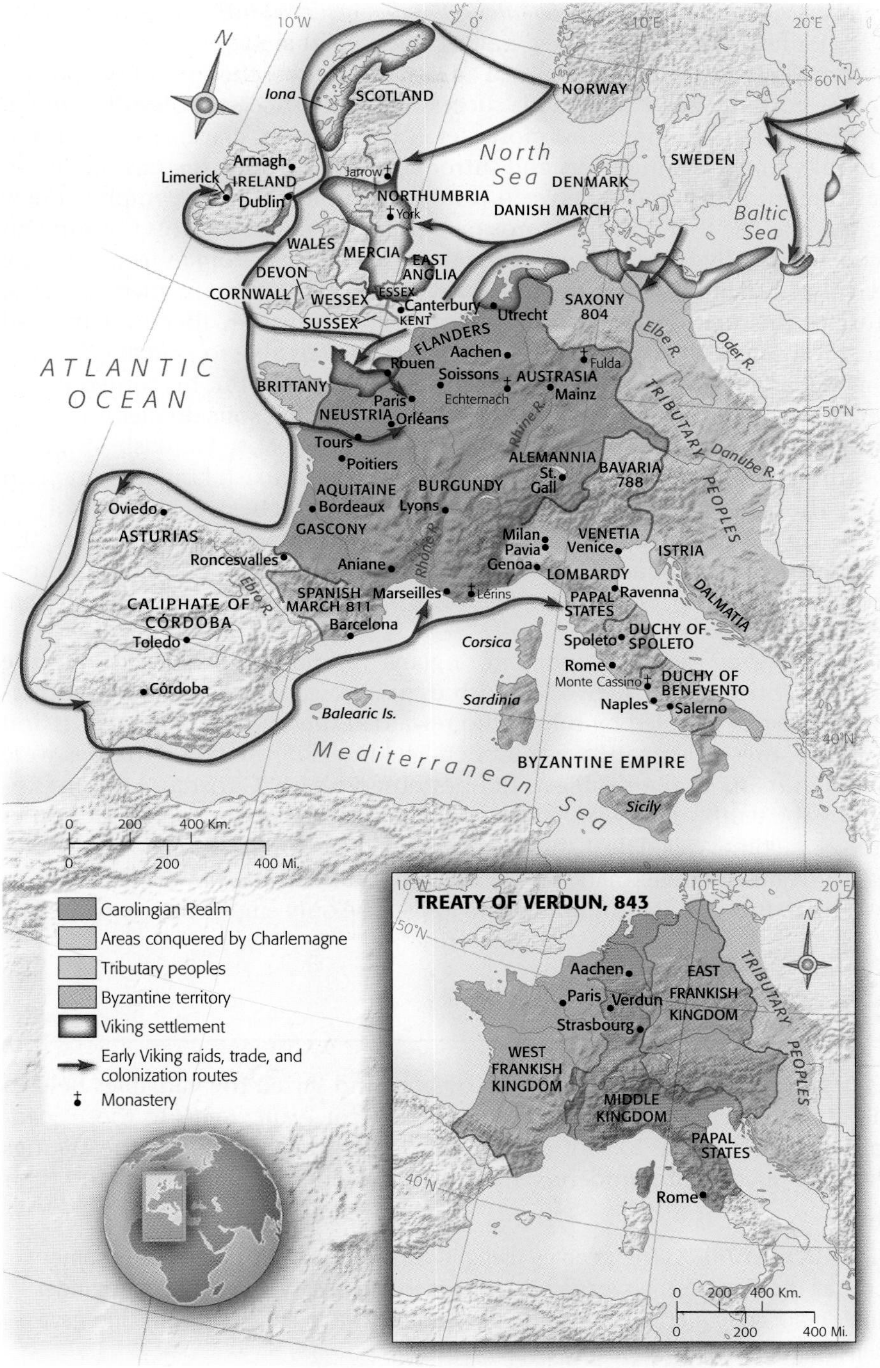

Map 10.2 The Carolingian Realms After coming to power in 768, Charlemagne continuously expanded the area under Carolingian rule. The unified empire did not last long. In 843, his grandsons divided his realm into three separate regions. The West Frankish kingdom eventually became modern-day France, while the East Frankish kingdom developed into modern Germany. The two states regularly vied for control of the territory between them.

*forming letters. But his effort came too late in life and achieved little success."** Unable to sign his name, Charlemagne liked having books read aloud to him.

Nevertheless, Charlemagne founded an academy where the sons of the powerful could be educated, and he and his successors established schools at the imperial court and in monasteries. Most monasteries had a special place, or scriptorium, where monks copied manuscripts and introduced innovations such as the use of lowercase lettering and spaces between words. As in the Byzantine empire, a new script came into use that fit more words on a page of parchment; this Carolingian minuscule eventually became the basis of today's lowercase Roman fonts. During this revival of learning, monastic authors wrote Latin grammars, medical texts, and liturgies (instructions for church ceremonies). However, literacy remained extremely restricted, with only a tiny number of officials able to read and write.

When Charlemagne died in 814, he left his empire intact to his son Louis the Pious (r. 814–840), but when Louis died in 840, his feuding sons divided the kingdom into thirds with the Treaty of Verdun (843). The West Frankish kingdom would eventually become modern France, and the East Frankish kingdom, modern Germany. The East and West kingdoms continuously fought over the territory of the Middle kingdom, which today contains portions of France, Germany, Italy, the Netherlands, and Switzerland. The Carolingians ruled until 911 in the area of modern Germany and until 987 in the region of modern France, when they were succeeded by new dynasties.

Historians often describe the Carolingians as more centralized than the Merovingians, but in fact the two Frankish dynasties were more alike than different. Both dynasties were led by rulers who rewarded their followers with gifts and whose main source of revenue was plunder. The rulers of the two dynasties were Christian, but many of their subjects did not observe basic Christian teachings.

Thus by the tenth century, when Carolingian rule came to an end, the region of the Franks, sometimes called the Latin West, was no longer united. Its major sections—modern-day France and Germany—were beginning to become powerful centers in their own right. By 1000, Byzantium was no longer the only empire in Europe.

The Age of the Vikings, 793–1066

Viking
Term used for those Scandinavians who left home to loot coastal towns and who were most active between 793 and 1066.

In 793, a group of ***Viking*** raiders came by boat and seized the valuables held in an island monastery off the English coast. The term *Viking* refers to those Scandinavians who left home to loot coastal towns. For three centuries the Vikings were the most successful plunderers in Europe, and no one could withstand their attacks.

• **CONTEXT&CONNECTIONS** The peoples living in Scandinavia had many of the same customs as the Franks: their leaders commanded the loyalty of war-bands, plunder was their main source of income, and they gradually adopted Christianity and gave up their traditional gods. •

Some Scandinavian boatmen eventually settled in Iceland, Greenland, England, Scotland, Ireland, and Russia; ultimately, however, they abandoned the Atlantic

---

*Paul Edward Dutton, *Charlemagne's Courtier: The Complete Einhard* (Orchard Park, N.Y.: Broadview Press, 1998), II: 25.

coast of Canada. Between 800 and 1000, Vikings formed several new states, creating still more centers in Europe (see Map 10.3).

Viking Raids on Great Britain

The Viking homeland was north of Charlemagne's realm, in Scandinavia, a region consisting of modern-day Norway, Sweden, and Denmark, whose residents spoke languages in the Germanic language family. The region had a cold climate

Map 10.3 The Viking Raids, 793–1066 From their homeland in Scandinavia, the Vikings launched their first raid on Lindisfarne on the North Sea in 793 and moved on to attack Iceland, Greenland, France, Spain, and Russia for more than two hundred years. They often settled in the lands they raided. In around 1000, they even reached North America.

with a short growing season, and many of its residents hunted walrus and whale for their meat or maintained herds on farms.

Since the Scandinavians conducted their raids by sea, the greatest difference between the Viking and the Frankish war-bands was the large wooden Viking **longboat** held together by iron rivets and washers. These craft ranged between 50 and 100 feet (15 and 30 m) long. The combination of oars and sails made these boats, along with Polynesian canoes, the fastest mode of transport in the world before 1000. Longboats had a shallow draft, which made them ideal for inland raids. The first Viking targets were the monasteries of the British Isles in England, Ireland, and Scotland, which lay closest to the southwestern coast of Norway.

longboat
Boat used by the Vikings to make raids; made of wood and equipped with both oars and sails, they were the fastest mode of transport before 1000.

● **CONTEXT&CONNECTIONS** Like the ancient Polynesians (see Chapter 5), the Scandinavian navigators did not use navigational instruments. Instead, they used the shapes of different landmasses for orientation. Unlike the Polynesians, however, the Scandinavians did not designate certain individuals as navigators or transmit geographical knowledge secretly; all men knew how to steer the longboats, and they announced their discoveries to everyone in their war-band. ●

Before 500, Britain was home to a group of Romanized peoples, but after 500 these groups were absorbed by the Anglo-Saxons, a general term for the many groups speaking Germanic languages who migrated to Britain from present-day Denmark and northern Germany. Anglo-Saxon society resembled society on the continent, having a sharp distinction between free and unfree, with a legal system emphasizing the concept of wergeld.

The Anglo-Saxons converted to Christianity during the sixth and seventh centuries. Bede (ca. 672–735) became their most famous Christian thinker. He also wrote a history of the Anglo-Saxons that dated events before Christ's birth as B.C.

The Longboats of the Scandinavians Sewn between 1066 and 1082, the Bayeux tapestry (held in northern France) is an embroidered piece of linen that stretches 231 feet (70 m). This detail shows the longboats moving rapidly under full sail, so that the men do not need to row. They used oars to maneuver, not to row long distances. Notice that two boats are large enough to transport horses. (Duke William and his fleet cross the Channel to Pevensey, detail from the Bayeux Tapestry, before 1082 (wool embroidery on linen) (detail of 115620)/Musee de la Tapisserie, Bayeux, France/The Bridgeman Art Library)

and those after as A.D., a system still in use in most of the world today. Historians prefer B.C.E. (Before the Common Era) and C.E. (Common Era) because they do not presume belief in the Christian God.

The English names for the days of the week also came into use at this time. Tuesday, Wednesday, Thursday, and Friday each uses the name of a Scandinavian god. Thursday, or Thor's day, is named for the vigorous god who ruled the sky and controlled thunder, wind, rain, and the harvest. Friday is named for Frey, the powerful god of fertility. Odin, or Wodin—the root of the modern Wednesday—was the powerful god of war, thought to have created the first man and the first woman. Odin's son Tiu gave his name to Tuesday. Sunday, Monday, and Saturday date to 321 C.E., when the Romans adopted the seven-day week, and Emperor Constantine named the days for different astronomical bodies: the sun, the moon, and the planet Saturn.

Anglo-Saxon monasteries made appealing targets for Viking raiders because they contained much detailed metalwork, whether reliquaries that held fragments of saints' bones or bejeweled gold and silver covers for illustrated manuscripts. News of the 793 attack on the Lindisfarne monastery on England's northeast coast traveled throughout Christian Europe. A native of north England, Alcuin (735–804), one of the most educated men at Charlemagne's court, wrote to the bishop at Lindisfarne: *"I can only cry from my heart before Christ's altar: 'O Lord, spare thy people… lest the heathen say, 'Where is the God of the Christians?'"** Alcuin saw the attack as a sign that non-Christians, or heathens, were more powerful than the Christians who could not repel the raiders. The raiders also captured many slaves, keeping some for use in Scandinavia and selling others to the Byzantine and Abbasid empires.

In 866, a large Viking army arrived in England, just north of London, and established a long-term base camp. Between 866 and 954, the Scandinavians held tenuous control in a region of northern and eastern England called the **Danelaw**. The residents paid an annual indemnity to their conquerors, and the Scandinavians settled throughout the Danelaw, Ireland, and Scotland. Alfred I (r. 871–899), who called himself "king of the Anglo-Saxons," managed to survive in the face of Viking attacks. After his death, various English, Anglo-Saxon, and Scandinavian leaders vied with each other for control of England, but no one succeeded for very long. In the tenth century, some Scandinavians settled in Normandy ("Northman's land") in northern France. From this base William the Conqueror launched a successful invasion of England in 1066, and his descendants ruled England for more than a hundred years.

Danelaw
Region including much of northern and eastern England, over which the Scandinavians maintained tenuous control between 866 and 954.

Scandinavian Society

Since the Scandinavians left only brief written texts, historians must draw on archaeological evidence and orally transmitted epics. Composed in Old Norse, a Germanic language, these epics were written down between 1200 and 1400. Two fascinating works entitled *Erik the Red's Saga* and *The Greenlanders' Saga*, together called ***The Vinland Sagas***, recount events around the year 1000. The Scandinavians called the Americas Vinland, meaning either grape land or fertile land. Like all oral sources, these epics must be used cautiously; both glorify certain ancestors while denigrating others, and both exaggerate the extent of Christian belief while minimizing the extent of non-Christian practices.

The Vinland Sagas
Term for *Erik the Red's Saga* and *The Greenlanders' Saga*, composed in Old Norse, that recount events around the year 1000. Both were written down between 1200 and 1400.

*Anders Winroth, *The Conversion of Scandinavia: Vikings, Merchants, and Missionaries in the Remaking of Northern Europe*. (New Haven: Yale University Press, 2012), p. 25.

The peoples of Scandinavia lived on small farms with their servants in communities of large, extended families of parents, children, grandchildren, and unmarried siblings. Women had considerable authority in Scandinavian society. They had property rights equal to those of their husbands and could institute divorce proceedings.

Leif Eriksson's sister-in-law Gudrid plays such a major role in *Erik the Red's Saga* that some have suggested it should have been named for her, and not for Leif's father Erik. She married three times, once to Leif Eriksson's brother, was widowed twice, and possibly went to Rome on a pilgrimage at the end of her life. In the saga, whereas Gudrid is virtuous, Leif's illegitimate sister Freydis (FRY-duhs) is a murderer who will stop at nothing to get her way. Both women, however one-dimensional, are intelligent, strong leaders.

Like the Germanic-speaking peoples living on the European continent, the Scandinavians formed war-bands. Leaders gave gifts to members of their bands, who fought beside them for shares of plunder.

AP® THEMES

What contributed to the development of a network of exchange between Scandinavian people and other societies of Europe and Asia by 1000?

In the years before 1000, new trade routes appeared linking Scandinavia with the Abbasid empire (see Chapter 9). Muslims bought slaves and furs from Scandinavians with silver dirham coins, over 200,000 of which have been found around the Baltic Sea. A single ceramic jar buried in the 990s and found on the Swedish island of Gotland produced over 1,900 silver coins, including 1,300 from the Islamic world and 600 from Germany, direct evidence of the trade routes linking Scandinavia with West Asia.

Gift exchange among rulers was common: envoys like Ibn Fadlan often brought expensive items to the rulers of neighboring powers and brought back gifts to the rulers who sent them on their missions. (See the feature "Movement of Ideas Through Primary Sources: Ibn Fadlan's Description of a Rus Burial," page 300.) Regifting was also frequent: rulers valued rare materials from foreign places, such as spices and gems, much more than local goods, such as furs. These valued items traveled huge distances across Eurasia as envoys carried them to one ruler's court, and he in turn regifted them to another monarch, and so on until they reached their final destination, where centuries later archaeologists uncovered them.

• **CONTEXT&CONNECTIONS** The most unusual item of foreign manufacture found in Scandinavia so far is a sixth-century bronze figurine of the *Buddha* (Chapter 3), found on the Swedish island of Helgö, where archaeologists also uncovered a bronze ladle from Egypt. Comparably distinctive Scandinavian goods have not yet surfaced in India or China, most likely because the main exports from Scandinavia—furs, whalebone, walrus tusk, and slaves—usually do not survive centuries of burial. One important exception is amber, or fossilized tree resin. Muslim geographers report that the Chinese preferred amber from the Baltic because of its darker color, and recent laboratory tests have shown that several amber items buried in a 1018 tomb of a princess in north China originated in Scandinavia. •

At this time, Scandinavian society produced a leader who played a role comparable to King Clovis of the Merovingians: Harald Bluetooth (r. 940–985) unified the multiple tribes living in Denmark. (The IBM engineer who designed the Bluetooth communication protocol hoped that it would unify disparate computer and phone systems.) In 965 Harald became the first Scandinavian ruler to convert to Christianity, and the rulers of Norway and Sweden did so around 1030.

In recent years, historians have come to understand these conversions in a new light: the leaders of war-bands such as Harald converted to Christianity because its ban on pagan ritual prevented their rivals from creating gift-giving networks linked to the worship of pre-Christian deities. Once Harald became Christian, he could command the support of all the church clergy. And because Christianity was a prestigious foreign religion, Harald gained prestige, too.

Pre-Christian Scandinavian Religion

Women played an especially active role in pre-Christian religion because some served as seers who could predict the future. Once when famine hit a Greenland community, *Erik the Red's Saga* relates, a wealthy landowner hosted a feast to which he invited a prophetess. She asked the women of the community who among them knew *"the spells needed for performing the witchcraft, known as Warlock songs."* Gudrid reluctantly volunteered, and *"sang the songs so well and beautifully that those present were sure they had never heard lovelier singing."* When she finished, the seer explained that the famine would end soon, since *"many spirits are now present which were charmed to hear the singing."**

As the weekday names suggest, the Scandinavians worshiped many gods. One traveler described a pre-Christian temple in Sweden that held three images. In the center was Thor, the most powerful deity, who controlled the harvest and weather. On either side of him stood the war-god Odin and the fertility goddess, Frey. Scandinavian burials often contain small metal items associated with Thor, such as hammers.

Burial customs varied. In some areas burials contained many grave goods, including full-size boats filled with clothing and tools, while in other areas the living cremated the dead and burned all their grave goods. (See the feature "Movement of Ideas Through Primary Sources: Ibn Fadlan's Description of a Rus Burial," page 300.) When people converted to Christianity, they were not supposed to bury grave goods, but many were reluctant to follow this prohibition for fear that the dead might starve or freeze as a result.

Werner Forman/Universal Images Group/Getty Images

What Can a Buddhist Statue Reveal? Compare this image of the Buddha, found on a Swedish island, with the statue in Chapter 8 of the Buddha from Cambodia with a Pali inscription on it (page 224). The Buddha here sits in lotus position on top of a lotus flower. Although this image is undated and has no writing on it, art historians have used the same technique as with the Cambodian statue—comparing it with other images found in India—to determine where and when it was made. The lines of the Buddha's robe indicate that it was crafted in north India, sometime in the sixth century, about a hundred years earlier than the Cambodian Buddha. But whereas the Cambodian Buddha allows us to trace the spread of Buddhism into Southeast Asia, this Buddha does not indicate the spread of Buddhism into Scandinavia. No other images have been found, and no inscriptions or later texts mention Buddhist teachers. Thus, this Buddha illuminates the exchange of gifts among rulers, not the spread of Buddhism.

*From *The Vinland Sagas*, translated with an introduction by Magnus Magnusson and Hermann Pálsson (Penguin Classics, 1965).

The Scandinavian Migrations to Iceland and Greenland, 870–980

As in Merovingian and Carolingian society, slaves and former slaves ranked at the bottom of society. In the saga, when a former slave proposes to Gudrid, her father is furious and rants at the suitor: *"I never expected to hear such a suggestion from you—that I should marry my daughter to the son of a slave! My lack of money must be very obvious to you!"** The proposal prompts him to give up his farm and leave for Greenland, where he hopes to find more fertile land. This was the impetus for migration: more fertile land than was available in Scandinavia, which was becoming increasingly crowded.

In the first wave, between 870 and 930, Scandinavians went to Iceland. In 930 they established a Thing, which had the power to pass laws and to hear disputes. Some have called Iceland's Thing the world's first legislature, but wealthy landowners had a greater say than the poor.

● **CONTEXT&CONNECTIONS** Like the Polynesian explorers on the Pacific islands, the Scandinavian settlers had a huge impact on Iceland's environment. They brought pigs, horses, cattle, sheep, and goats with them, a combination that one historian likened to "a bulldozer moving across this subarctic landscape."† ●

The Vinland Sagas describe events occurring in Iceland sometime around 980, when Erik the Red was exiled by the Thing because he killed two men. Erik sailed west 200 miles (320 km) to Greenland and, after his term of exile ended, returned to recruit followers to go with him there. In 985 or 986, Erik led a fleet of fourteen boats to Greenland. His 400–500 followers included higher-ranking war-band members as well as freemen, servants, and slaves.

The Scandinavians established two settlements on Greenland, the Eastern and Western Settlements. The settlers lived much as they had on Iceland, grazing animals on the narrow coast between the ocean and the interior ice, fishing for walrus, whales, and seals, and hunting polar bears and reindeer. They had to trade furs and walrus tusks to obtain the grain, wood, and iron they needed to survive. The Greenlanders established their own Thing assembly, which voted to adopt Christianity soon after 1000.

The Scandinavians in Vinland, ca. 1000

Around 1000, Leif Eriksson, the son of Erik the Red, decided to lead an exploratory voyage because he had heard of lands lying to the west of Greenland from a man named Bjarni Herjolfsson (bee-YARN-ee hair-YOLF-son), who had been blown off course in a storm. It is possible that others had preceded Bjarni to the Americas, but *The Vinland Sagas* do not give their names, so we should probably credit **Bjarni Herjolfsson**—and not Christopher Columbus—with being the first European to sail to the Americas. First Leif and then Thorfinn Karlsefni made several voyages to the Americas, landing in modern-day L'Anse aux Meadows, Newfoundland, Canada, and possibly going farther south to Maine. The Scandinavians arrived in North America after the end of the Maya

Bjarni Herjolfsson
The first European, according to *The Vinland Sagas*, to sail to the Americas, most likely sometime in the 990s.

---

*From *The Vinland Sagas*, translated with an introduction by Magnus Magnusson and Hermann Pálsson (Penguin Classics, 1965).

†Thomas McGovern interview, *Nova: The Vikings*, 2000, transcript available at http://www.pbs.org/wgbh/nova/transcripts/2708vikings.html.

classic era and before the great Mississippian cities of the Midwest were built (see Chapter 5). (See the feature "Visual Evidence in Primary Sources: The Scandinavian Settlement at L'Anse aux Meadows.")

The sagas report that Leif's brother-in-law, Thorfinn Karlsefni, decided to lead a group of sixty men and five women to settle in Vinland. Their first year went well because they found much wild game. Then *"they had their first encounter with* ***Skraelings****"** (literally "wretches"), the term that the Scandinavians used for indigenous peoples. At first the Skraelings traded furs for cow's milk or scraps of red cloth, because Karlsefni would not allow his men to trade their iron weapons. But relations soon deteriorated, and the Scandinavians and the Skraelings fought each other in several battles involving hand-to-hand combat. *Erik the Red's Saga* reports that the Skraelings *"were using catapults. Karlsefni and Snorri saw them hoist a large sphere on a pole; it was dark blue in color. It came flying in over the heads of Karlsefni's men and made an ugly din when it struck the ground."** A Native American arrowhead found at L'Anse aux Meadows provides archaeological confirmation that the Scandinavians actually fought with the local inhabitants.

Skraelings
Term in *The Vinland Sagas* for the Amerindians living on the coast of Canada and possibly northern Maine, where the Scandinavians established temporary settlements.

The settlers in this story belonged to Karlsefni's war-band. Many had kin ties to him, whether direct or through marriage, and they probably gave him a share of the lumber they shipped to Greenland, much as they would have given him a share of any loot they collected in battle. Whenever the Scandinavians went to a new place, they captured slaves, and North America was no exception. Karlsefni enslaved two Skraeling boys, who lived with the Scandinavians and later learned their language. The boys told them about their homeland: *"that people lived in caves or holes in the ground. They said that there was a country across from their own land where the people went about in white clothing and uttered loud cries and carried poles with pieces of cloth attached."** This intriguing report is one of the earliest we have about Amerindians.

• **CONTEXT&CONNECTIONS** In the year 1000 the residents of both *Mesoamerica* and the Andes (Chapter 5) knew how to work gold, silver, copper, and even platinum. But no indigenous peoples anywhere in the Americas knew how to work *iron* (Chapter 2). The Scandinavians did, but iron knives and daggers did not provide enough power for them to win if outnumbered, as they were in L'Anse aux Meadows. •

The sagas succinctly explain why the newcomers decided to leave the Americas: *"Karlsefni and his men had realized by now that although the land was excellent they could never live there in safety or freedom from fear, because of the native inhabitants."** In later centuries, the Scandinavians sometimes returned to Canada to gather wood but never to settle. Sometime in the fifteenth century, they also abandoned their settlements on Greenland because a drop in global temperature made life there much more difficult.

• **CONTEXT&CONNECTIONS** The Vikings' westward voyages are significant because the Scandinavians were the first Europeans to settle in the Americas, but their encounter had no long-term consequences, a result utterly different from that of *Christopher Columbus's* voyages in the 1490s (Chapter 15). •

---

*From *The Vinland Sagas,* translated with an introduction by Magnus Magnusson and Hermann Pálsson (Penguin Classics, 1965).

The Scandinavian Settlement at L'Anse aux Meadows

In 1960, a Norwegian diplomat-turned-explorer, Helge Ingstad, and his archaeologist wife, Anne Stine Ingstad, explored the Canadian coastline hoping to find a place where, as *The Vinland Sagas* said, "*the country was flat and wooded, with white sandy beaches wherever they went; and the land sloped gently down to the sea.*"* This description fit an inlet near the town of L'Anse aux Meadows on the northern tip of Newfoundland, where Helge and Anne Ingstad found a small settlement.

Pollen analysis revealed that the climate in about 1000 was similar to today's and could have easily supported a settlement. Lumber, whether live trees or driftwood, was abundant. It was so cold that in most years the ice did not melt until June or July, an impossible climate for wild grapes. Caribou, wolves, and foxes lived on the land, while walruses, whales, and seals flourished in the bay. Still, the growing season was long enough for cloudberries, raspberries, blueberries, and red and black currants to thrive. Butternuts, a kind of a walnut, were found at the site but do not grow that far north. The Scandinavians probably traveled south to collect them and possibly the grapes mentioned so often in the sagas.

The small settlement contained eight houses that dated to between 980 and 1020, precisely the time of the Scandinavian exploration of Vinland. The most revealing artifact was a small ringed pin, identical in design to thirteen others found on Iceland and one of a few indications that it was a Scandinavian settlement.

Identical in structure to Icelandic buildings of the same period, the houses had walls and roofs made of sod that rested on wooden supports. Three were quite large halls, for perhaps fifty people, measuring 65 feet (20 m) long, with five smaller structures nearby. They formed three clusters of houses, each with a main dwelling for the group's leader and smaller, outlying houses for his dependents and slaves. Perhaps a total of eighty or ninety people lived at the site. Archaeologists found no large objects, an indication that the residents of the site systematically packed their possessions and left for home.

Many small artifacts indicate the kinds of tasks done on site. Needles and spindle whorls point to textile manufacture and mending, which, according to the sagas, were traditional women's work. The residents also collected iron ore, which forms naturally in bogs containing iron and manganese, and melted it in a furnace to obtain metal, which they hammered into nails for their boats. The place where the Scandinavians worked iron contained an anvil and a big stone for hammering iron. The presence of a single locally produced iron nail makes this the earliest site of ironworking in the Americas (since none of the indigenous peoples living in the Americas could work iron).

The settlement at L'Anse aux Meadows could not have been the main base camp for the Scandinavian settlers described in the sagas. On an exposed point, it was not in a protected cove, the preferred site for Viking landings. The shed for repairing ships was used only on a short-term basis, probably in winter, and the absence of any barns or enclosures for animals means that none of the site's residents engaged in any farming. Most likely the site was a launching point for expeditions further inland. Still, this site provides undeniable evidence that the Scandinavians lived at L'Anse aux Meadows, however briefly, before deciding to return home.

*From *The Vinland Sagas*, translated with an introduction by Magnus Magnusson and Hermann Pálsson (Penguin Classics, 1965).

I: The room where the war-band chieftain slept and received visitors. A small soapstone lamp was one of the few artifacts of Icelandic design found on the site. ***What other finds from the site of L'Anse aux Meadows indicated that it was a Scandinavian settlement and not an Amerindian site?***

Hall F: This, the largest and most important building at the site of L'Anse aux Meadows, belonged to the war-band chieftain. Like all of the Viking structures, it was made from sod and wooden pillars.

II: This large room, which had space for at least sixteen war-band retainers to sleep, also served as a banqueting hall. In the middle of the room was a fire pit 7.38 feet (2.25 m) long, just like those in Icelandic dwellings. ***Once you have read the other captions, describe what activities men and women did separately in the different rooms of Hall F and which they did together.***

IV: The stone oven and garbage midden in this room show that it served as the kitchen.

VI: Remains of damaged nails and slag, a byproduct of working iron, indicate that this side room was where the men repaired boats. They used the large fireplace to heat water to steam wooden planks into the right shape and then nailed them onto their long boats.

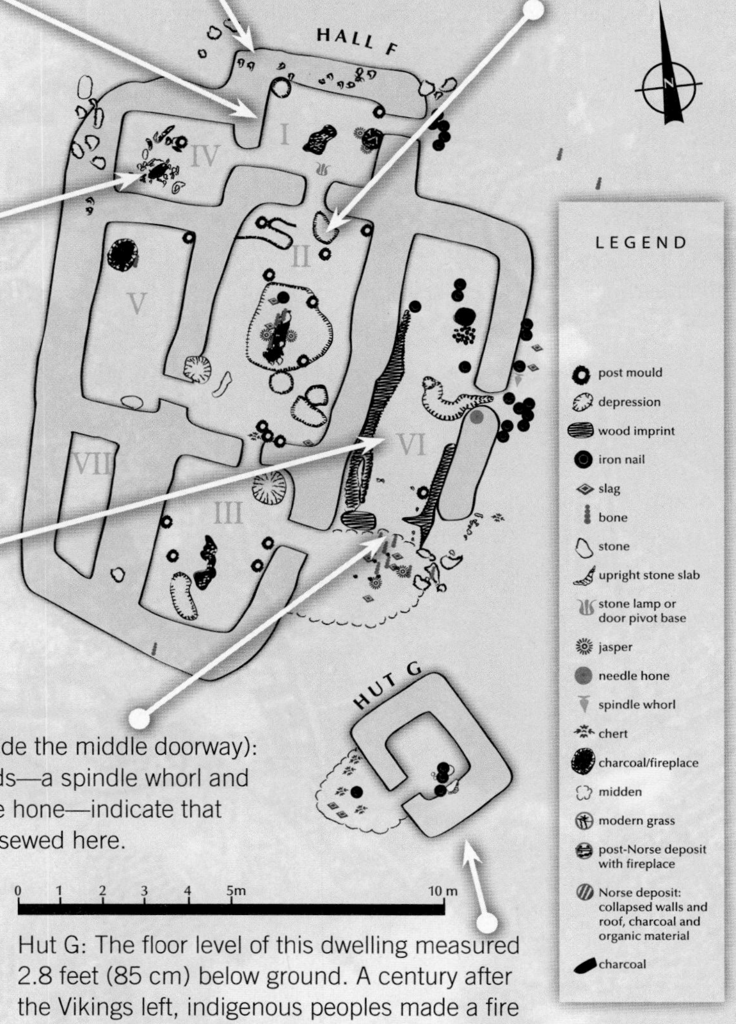

VI (outside the middle doorway): Two finds—a spindle whorl and a needle hone—indicate that women sewed here.

Hut G: The floor level of this dwelling measured 2.8 feet (85 cm) below ground. A century after the Vikings left, indigenous peoples made a fire on top of the collapsed structure.

Russia, Land of the Rus, to 1054

Rus
Name given to themselves by people who lived in the region stretching from the Arctic to the north shore of the Black Sea and from the Baltic Sea to the Caspian Sea.

Around 800, long before they set foot in Iceland, Greenland, or the Americas, early Scandinavians, mostly from Sweden, found that they could sail their longboats along the several major river courses, including the Volga and Dnieper Rivers, through the huge expanse of land lying to their east (see Map 10.4). Some of the peoples living in this region called themselves **Rus**, the root of the word *Russia*. This region offered many riches to the raiders, primarily furs and slaves. The Rus were a multiethnic group including Balts, Finns, and Slavs, with Scandinavians eventually the most prominent among them. The region of modern-day Russia also saw the rise of important centers before 1000, contributing to even more centers in Europe.

Map 10.4 Kievan Rus Before 970, the leaders of different war-bands controlled the region between the Baltic, Black, and Caspian Seas. In the 970s Prince Vladimir gained control of the trading post at Kiev and gradually expanded the territory under his rule to form the state of Kievan Rus.

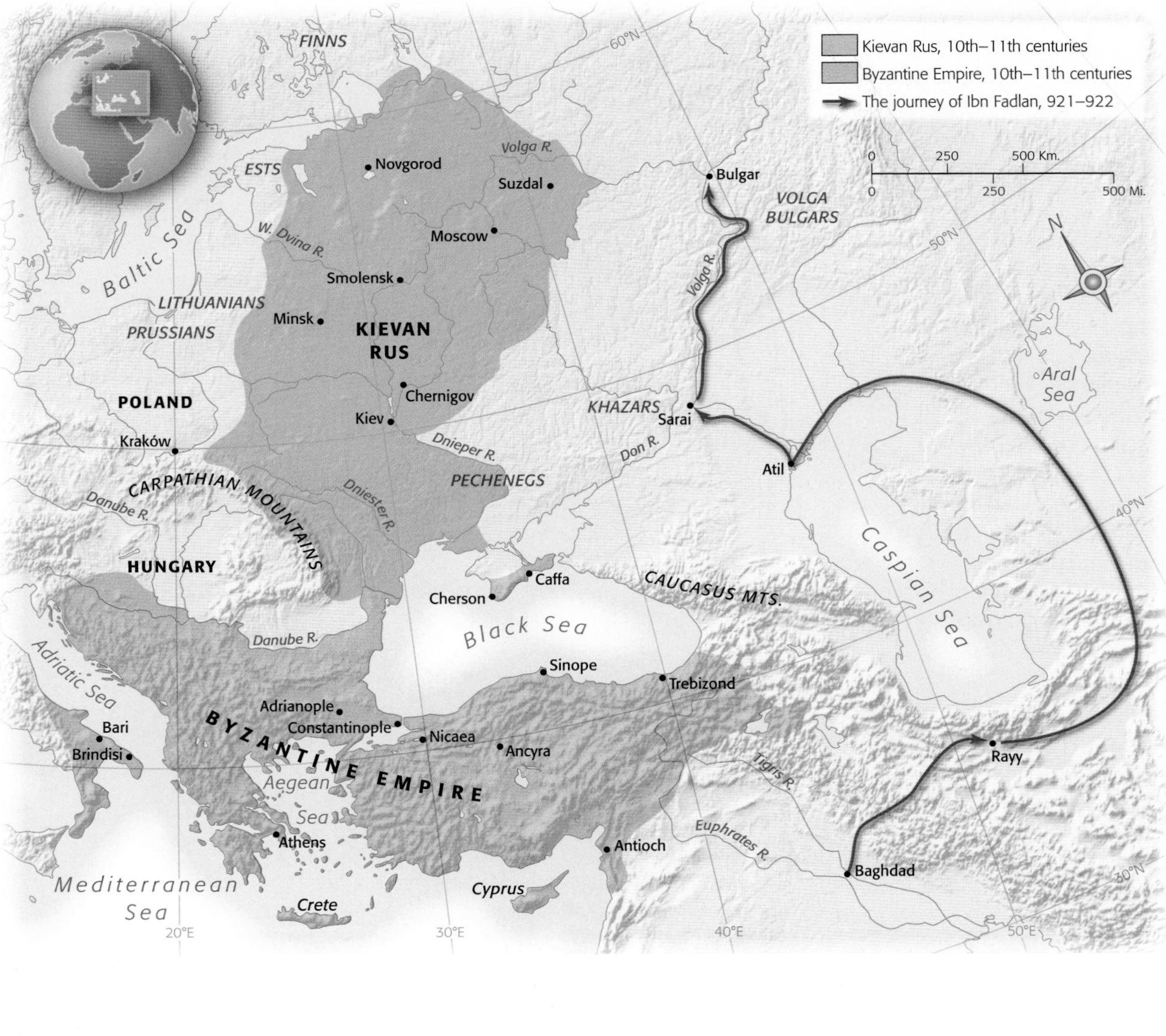

The Peoples Living in Russia

The region of Russia (which was much larger than today's modern nation) housed different ecosystems and different peoples deriving their living from the land. To the north, peoples exploited the treeless tundra and the taiga (sub-Arctic coniferous forest) to fish and to hunt reindeer, bear, and walrus. On the steppe grasslands extending far to the west, nomadic peoples migrated with their herds in search of fertile pasture.

AP® THEMES
What hindered the development of settled, agricultural societies in Russia?

In the forests, where most people lived, they raised herds and grew crops on small family farms. Too poor to dedicate much land to raising hay, they had no draft animals and could clear the land only with fire and hand tools. The lack of natural fertilizer from draft animals forced them to clear new lands every few years. These cultivators and foragers never could have survived had they depended entirely on their intermittent cultivation.

The various peoples living in Russia spoke many different languages, none of which were written down. In 500, the **Slavs** occupied much of the territory in the lower Danube River Valley near the Black Sea. As they moved north and east for the next five hundred years, they enlarged the area in which their language was spoken.

Slavs
The people who, around 500, occupied much of the lower Danube River Valley near the Black Sea. They moved north and east for the next five hundred years and enlarged the area where their language, an ancestor of Russian, Ukrainian, Polish, and Czech, was spoken.

All these peoples, whatever their ecological niche, lived on the edge of subsistence and were vulnerable to Scandinavian slave raiders. After 700, the Scandinavians established trade outposts on the southeast coast of the Baltic and on the Dnieper and Volga Rivers. By 800, they had learned how to navigate these rivers to reach the Black and Caspian Seas. Ibn Fadlan, an envoy from the Abbasid court, traveled from Baghdad up the Volga River and left a vivid description of the pre-Christian practices of the Rus. (See the feature "Movement of Ideas Through Primary Sources: Ibn Fadlan's Description of a Rus Burial.")

• **CONTEXT&CONNECTIONS** Much of what we know about Russia before 900 comes from Byzantine accounts and concerns the decisions of different rulers to convert to a given religion. By this time all of the world's major religions had taken shape. Most familiar with the religions of their neighbors, the rulers of eastern Europe chose among Judaism, Islam, Roman Christianity, or the Eastern Orthodox church of Byzantium. They chose to convert to a given religion for different reasons: often they sought to ally with a neighbor of a certain faith; or they may have believed that one religion's god was more powerful than another; or perhaps, like Harald Bluetooth, they hoped to strengthen ties with their followers through conversion. •

To the west, a nomadic people, the Magyars (known as the Hungarians to their neighbors) established a base in the Danube basin. Originally polytheistic, the Hungarians converted to Roman Christianity in 1000 to strengthen their ties to Germany, and their king was baptized by a German bishop. In contrast, the rulers of the Khazars, a formerly nomadic Turkic people living near Kiev, converted to Judaism, rather than the Christianity of their Byzantine enemies or the Islam of their Abbasid rivals. The Bulgars, a Turkic nomadic people previously subject to the Khazars (and the ancestors of the modern Bulgarians), formed their own Islamic state along the Volga River. The Bulgars paid the Khazars one sable pelt each year for every household they ruled, but they converted to Islam partially in hope of breaking away from the Khazars. After they received a visit by an envoy from the Abbasid caliph in 921–923, the ruler of the Bulgars assumed the title *emir*, and this state is therefore known as the Volga Bulgar Emirate.

Rus traders used the currency of the Abbasid empire: gold dinars and silver dirhams. Rus husbands gave their wives a gold or silver neckband for each ten thousand

Ibn Fadlan's Description of a Rus Burial

Although Ibn Fadlan, an envoy from the Abbasid court, looked down on the Rus as coarse and uncivilized, his account of a king's funeral is the most detailed description of pre-Christian Rus religious beliefs and practices surviving today. It is particularly moving because he was able to observe a young girl who died so that she could be buried with her lord. The Angel of Death who kills the girl may have been a priestess of either Frey or Odin, whose devotees sometimes engaged in sex as part of their fertility rites. While Ibn Fadlan clearly finds the Rus funerary practices strange, the Scandinavian he quotes at the end of this selection finds the Islamic practice of burial equally alien.

❯ Historical Thinking Skill:

COMPARISON **How do the funeral practices of the Rus differ between members of different social classes?**

❯ Historical Thinking Skill:

COMPARISON **What are the differences between the burial practices of the Rus culture and Muslim culture?**

❯ Historical Thinking Skill:

INTERPRETATION **What evidence do you find in this excerpt to indicate that the author, Ibn Fadlan, views the funeral practices of the Rus as inferior to his own culture's practices?**

Source: Excerpts/quotes from James E. Montgomery, "Ibn Fadlan and the Rusiyyah," *Journal of Arabic and Islamic Studies*, 2, 2000, pp. 1–25. Reprinted by permission of New York University Press.

I was told that when their chieftains die, the least they do is cremate them. I was very keen to verify this, when I learned of the death of one of their great men. They placed him in his grave and erected a canopy over it for ten days, until they had finished making and sewing his funeral garments.

In the case of a poor man they build a small boat, place him inside and burn it. In the case of a rich man, they gather together his possessions and divide them into three, one third for his family, one third to use for his funeral garments, and one third with which they purchase alcohol which they drink on the day when his slave-girl kills herself and is cremated together with her master. (They are addicted to alcohol, which they drink night and day. Sometimes one of them dies with the cup still in his hand.)

When their chieftain dies, his family ask his slave-girls and slave-boys, "Who among you will die with him?" and some of them reply, "I shall." Having said this, it becomes incumbent on the person and it is impossible ever to turn back. Should that person try to, he is not permitted to do so. It is usually slave-girls who make this offer.

When that man whom I mentioned earlier died, they said to his slave-girls, "Who will die with him?" and one of them said, "I shall." So they placed two slave-girls in charge of her to take care of her and accompany her wherever she went, even to the point of occasionally washing her feet with their own hands. They set about attending to the dead man, preparing his clothes for him and setting right all that he needed. Every day the slave-girl would drink alcohol and would sing merrily and cheerfully.

On the day when he and the slave-girl were to be burned I arrived at the river where his ship was. To my surprise I discovered that it had been beached and that four planks of birch and other types of wood had been placed in such a way as to resemble scaffolding. Then the ship was hauled and placed on top of this wood. They advanced, going to and fro around the boat uttering words which I did not understand, while he was still in his grave and had not been exhumed.

Then they produced a couch and placed it on the ship, covering it with quilts made of Byzantine silk brocade and cushions made of Byzantine silk brocade. Then a crone arrived whom they called the

"Angel of Death" and she spread on the couch the coverings we have mentioned. She is responsible for having his garments sewn up and putting him in order and it is she who kills the slave-girls. I myself saw her: a gloomy, corpulent woman, neither young nor old.

When they came to his grave, they removed the soil from the wood and then removed the wood, exhuming him still dressed in the *izar* [clothing] in which he had died.... They carried him inside the pavilion on the ship and laid him to rest on the quilt, propping him with cushions.... Next they brought bread, meat, and onions, which they cast in front of him, a dog, which they cut in two and which they threw onto the ship, and all of his weaponry, which they placed beside him....

At the time of the evening prayer on Friday, they brought the slave-girl to a thing they had constructed, like a door-frame. She placed her feet on the hands of the men and was raised above the door-frame. She said something and they brought her down. [This happened two more times.] They next handed her a hen. She cut off its head and threw it away. They took the hen and threw it on board the ship.

I quizzed the interpreter about her actions and he said, "The first time they lifted her, she said, 'Behold, I see my father and my mother.' The second time she said, 'Behold, I see all of my dead kindred, seated.' The third time she said, 'Behold I see my master, seated in Paradise. Paradise is beautiful and verdant. He is accompanied by his men and his male-slaves. He summons me, so bring me to him.'" ...

The men came with their shields and sticks and handed her a cup of alcohol over which she chanted and then drank.

Six men entered the pavilion and all had intercourse with the slave girl. They laid her down beside her master and two of them took hold of her feet, two her hands. The crone called the "Angel of Death" placed a rope around her neck in such a way that the ends crossed one another and handed it to two of the men to pull on it. She advanced with a broad-bladed dagger and began to thrust it in and out between her ribs, now here, now there, while the two men throttled her with the rope until she died.

Then the deceased's next of kin approached and took hold of a piece of wood and set fire to it.... A dreadful wind arose and the flames leapt higher and blazed fiercely.

One of the Rus stood beside me and I heard him speaking to my interpreter. I quizzed him about what he had said, and he replied, "He said, 'You Arabs are a foolish lot!'" So I said, "Why is that?" and he replied, "Because you purposely take those who are dearest to you and whom you hold in highest esteem and throw them under the earth, where they are eaten by the earth, by vermin and by worms, whereas we burn them in the fire there and then, so that they enter Paradise immediately." Then he laughed loud and long.

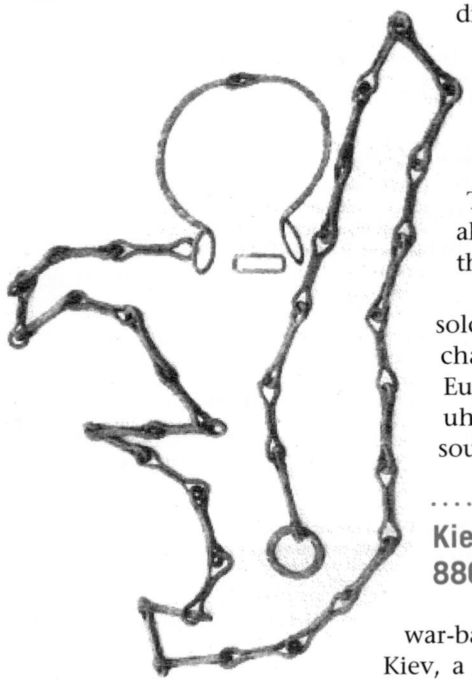

Tangible Evidence of the European Slave Trade European slave traders used this set of shackles, found in modern Bulgaria, to restrain a slave. They wrapped the long chain of iron links around his arms and legs and then connected it to the large ring, which they fastened around the captive's neck. Iron was expensive, though, so wooden and rope restraints would have been more common. (Museum Ruse, Krivina, Bulgaria/Visual Connection Archive)

dirhams the husband accumulated. Archaeologists have found many such neckbands, frequently decorated with small Thor's hammers like those found in Scandinavian graves. Arm and neck rings were also the primary gift from a war-band leader to his followers. The Rus, like the Scandinavians, used silver coins and other objects to buy and sell items, weighing them each time to judge their value. They incorporated silver coins into necklaces and other jewelry. They also began to make arm and neck rings in standard weights, a sign that the rings functioned as currency as well.

In addition to amber, swords, and wax, the main goods the Rus sold to the Islamic world were furs and slaves. Scandinavian merchants sold so many Slavs into slavery that, in the tenth century, the Europeans coined a new word for slaves: the Latin *sclavus* (SCLAV-uhs), derived from the Latin word for the Slavic peoples. This is the source of the English word *slave*.

Kievan Rus, 880–1054

Before 930, the Rus consisted of war-bands who paid tribute to rulers like the Khazars and the Volga Bulgar Emirate, who then allowed the Rus to sell slaves and furs in their territories. After 930, the Rus war-bands evolved into early states called principalities. The history of Kiev, a trading outpost on the Dnieper River, illustrates how this happened. Before 900, Kiev had a population of only one or two hundred residents who lived in villages. After 900, as trade grew, its population increased to several thousand, including specialized craftsmen who made goods for the wealthy. In 911, and again in 945, the Rus **Principality of Kiev** signed a treaty with Byzantium that specified the terms under which the Rus were to do business in Constantinople. Throughout the tenth century, the princes of Kiev eliminated their political rivals, including the Khazars and the Bulgars.

Principality of Kiev
A new state that began as a trading post on the Dnieper River and evolved into a principality around 900.

Since the middle of the ninth century, Byzantine missionaries had been active among the Rus and had modified the Greek alphabet to make the Cyrillic alphabet, which is named for Saint Cyril (827–869). Using this alphabet, they devised a written language, called Old Church Slavonic, into which they translated Christian scriptures.

In the 970s, Prince Vladimir emerged as leader of the Kievan Rus. Like the Khazar and Bulgar rulers, he had to decide which religion would best unify his realm. Our main source for this period, *The Primary Chronicle*, written down around 1100, explains that in 987 Vladimir decided to send ten *"good and wise men"* to compare the religions of the Volga Emirate, the Franks, and the Byzantines. When the men returned, they criticized both the Islamic practices of the Volga Emirate and the Christianity of the Franks. Of their visit to the Hagia Sophia church in Byzantium, however, Prince Vladimir's advisers reported the following:

> *We knew not whether we were in heaven or on earth. For on earth there is no such splendor or such beauty, and we are at a loss how to describe it.... We know only that God dwells there among men, and their service is fairer than the ceremonies of other nations. For we cannot forget that beauty.**

*Serge A. Zenkovsky, *Medieval Russia's Epics, Chronicles, and Tales* (New York: E. P. Dutton, 1974), pp. 67–68.

They urged Vladimir to convert to the Byzantine church.

Vladimir did not immediately accept their recommendation, but instead asked the reigning Byzantine emperor, Basil II (r. 963–1025), to send his sister Anna to him as his bride, Basil agreed because he desperately needed the assistance of Vladimir's troops to suppress a rebellion, and Vladimir promised to receive baptism from the priests accompanying Anna to the wedding. Once baptized, Vladimir then ordered, on penalty of death, all the inhabitants of Kiev to come to the riverbank, and surprised them all by performing a mass baptism, and so Kiev and all its inhabitants converted to Christianity.

The Growing Divide Between the Eastern and Western Churches

Prince Vladimir and his ten advisers conceived of the Christianity of the Franks and of the Byzantines as two separate religions, which we now call Roman Catholicism and Eastern Orthodoxy. The two churches used different languages, Latin in Rome and Greek in Constantinople, and grew further and further apart after 500. Since 751, the pope had been allied with the rulers of the Franks, not the Byzantine emperors.

By 1000, the practices of the Eastern and Western clergy diverged in important ways. Members of the Western church accepted the pope as head, while members of the Eastern church recognized the patriarch of Constantinople as leader. Orthodox Christians put yeast in the communion bread, while Roman Catholics ate unleavened bread. Eastern priests were required to have beards, while Western priests were not.

• **CONTEXT&CONNECTIONS** The Eastern and Western churches differed on the issue of celibacy. Western church councils decided that all priests should be celibate in light of *Augustine's* teachings about ritual purity (Chapter 7) and the need for priests to be pure when giving communion. In actual practice, not all Western priests were; for example, the Christian cleric *Peter Abelard* had sex with *Heloise* even though they were not married (Chapter 12). Eastern church councils took the opposite position: their decrees held that most ordinary priests would have married before they were ordained. (Only those living in monasteries would not marry.) Eastern priests, too, were supposed to be ritually pure when administering communion, but they could attain the necessary purity by temporarily abstaining from sex with their wives. The Eastern and Western churches concurred on two important points: already-ordained priests could not marry, and bishops had to be celibate. •

In 1054, a bishop in Bulgaria wrote to an Italian bishop criticizing certain practices of the Western church, such as using unleavened bread in communion and failing to fast on Saturdays. The pope responded by sending an envoy who carried two letters (one was 17,000 words long) to the patriarch in Constantinople defending these practices and asserting his right as the pope to lead the Western church. As the level of rhetoric escalated, the pope's envoy excommunicated the patriarch of Constantinople, and the patriarch did the same to the pope's envoy. Historians call this the Great Schism of 1054.

After 1054, the pope in Rome, whose wealth and influence made him the equal of European monarchs, led the Roman Catholic Church. In Constantinople, the patriarch led the Eastern Orthodox Church, the church of both the Byzantine empire and its close ally, the Kievan princes. (The dispute was resolved only in 1965, but the two churches stayed separate.)

The Rise of a Multicentered Europe

In 1000, Gudrid and her husband Thorfinn Karlsefni visited Greenland and the Scandinavian settlement in modern-day Canada before returning to Iceland to live permanently. At the end of her life, her descendants claimed, she may have traveled to Rome to visit the pope, the head of the Roman Catholic Church. She did not visit Constantinople, still an important regional center but no longer the unchallenged leader of Europe as it had been in 500. The intervening centuries had taken their toll on Byzantium; plague had struck at least fifteen times, and incursions from its neighbors had reduced the empire to less than half its original size.

In the centuries of Byzantine decline, two Frankish dynasties, the Merovingians and the Carolingians, tapped the dynamic energy of the war-band to form powerful new armies. The soldiers owed their allegiance to the military chiefs who shared the spoils of battle with them. The Merovingian king Clovis converted to Christianity in the early 500s, and Charlemagne was also Christian.

In 500, Constantinople had dominated Christian Europe much as Baghdad shaped the Islamic world before the Abbasid empire broke apart (see Chapter 9). Just as Córdoba and Cairo became important Islamic centers, so too did new centers challenge Byzantium's supremacy. The residents of Constantinople looked down on the rulers of the Frankish kingdom for their lower cultural level, but the pope saw Charlemagne as a powerful ally and crowned him as emperor of Rome, much to the dismay of the Byzantine ruler Irene.

Other regions in Europe converted to Christianity and became new centers as well. The Anglo-Saxons adopted Christianity in the 500s and 600s. Farther to the north, the Scandinavians converted around 1000, at the same time as the leaders of the Magyars and Kievan Rus. The decision of these individual rulers to adopt Christianity, whether the Roman Catholicism of Rome or the Orthodoxy of Constantinople, had long-term consequences as great as those resulting from the decisions of individual Asian rulers to patronize Buddhism or Hinduism (see Chapter 8). By the year 1000, almost all of Europe had become Christian, and it remained Christian for the next one thousand years.

At around this time, the first Europeans began to explore the north Atlantic. After being exiled by the Thing assembly in Iceland, Erik the Red went to Greenland, where he founded a settlement in 985 or 986. In the year 1000, using information from Bjarni Herjolfsson, Erik's son Leif led his followers all the way to L'Anse aux Meadows and possibly as far south as Maine. Challenged by the Skraelings, the Scandinavians decided to return to Greenland.

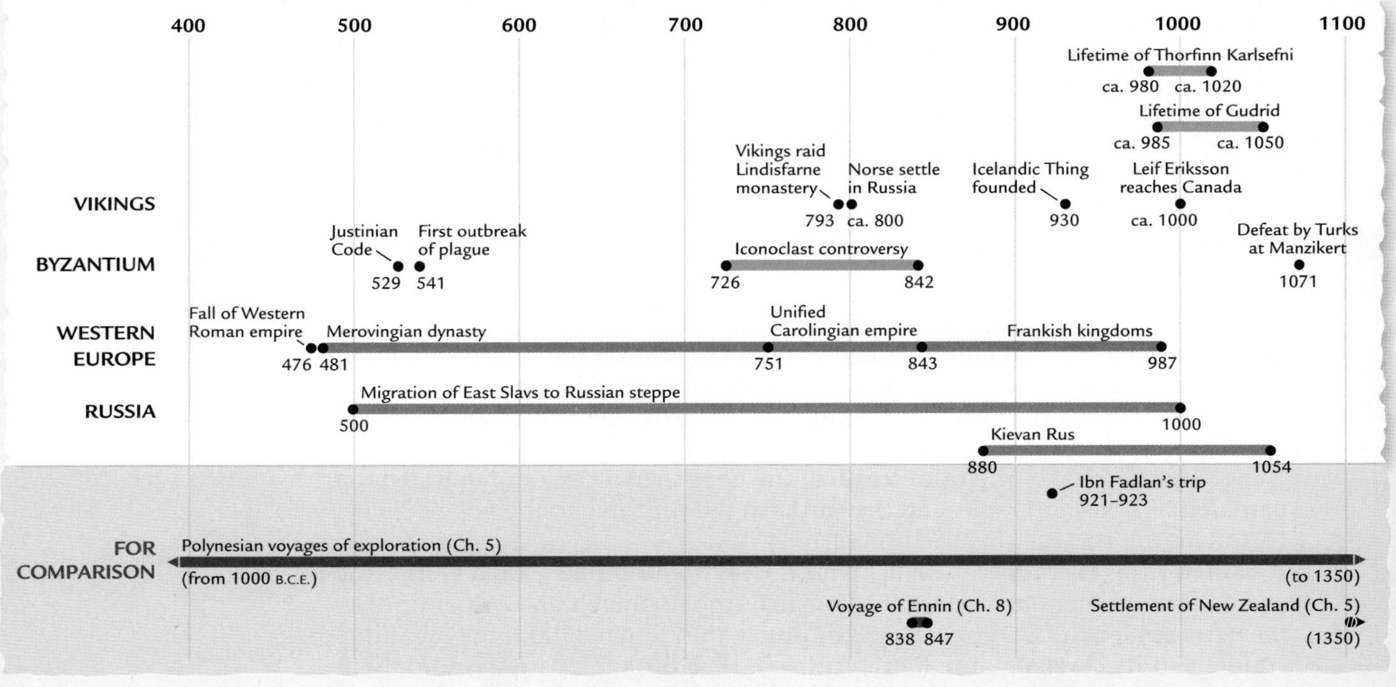

Their voyages amply demonstrated that it was easy to cross the Atlantic in their longboats, but because they did not stay in the Americas, their voyages—unlike Columbus's in the 1490s—had no lasting impact (see Chapter 15).

The world became dramatically bigger in the year 1000—not, of course, because the earth changed size, but in the sense that people living in Europe found out about Iceland, Greenland, and the Americas for the first time. As the next chapter will show, a similar development occurred in the Islamic world as people living there learned about sub-Saharan Africa, India, and China. An important source of their information was an intrepid traveler who managed to visit all of these lands in the course of a single lifetime.

Key Terms

Gudrid and Thorfinn Karlsefni (276)
Byzantine Empire (277)
patriarch (278)
pope (278)
Justinian Corpus of Civil Law (278)
plague (279)
iconoclasts (281)
Frankish kingdom (283)
wergeld (283)
war-band (284)
Merovingian dynasty (284)
Carolingian dynasty (286)
Viking (288)
longboat (290)
Danelaw (291)
The Vinland Sagas (291)
Bjarni Herjolfsson (294)
Skraelings (295)
Rus (298)
Slavs (299)
Principality of Kiev (303)

For Further Reference

Bagge, Sverre. *Cross and Scepter: The Rise of the Scandinavian Kingdoms from the Vikings to the Reformation*. Princeton: Princeton University Press, 2014.

Biraben, J. N., and Jacques Le Goff. "The Plague in the Early Middle Ages." In *Biology of Man in History: Selections from Annales Economies, Sociétés, Civilisations*, ed. Robert Forster et al. Baltimore: Johns Hopkins University Press, 1975, pp. 48–80.

Fitzhugh, William W., and Elisabeth I. Ward. *Vikings: The North Atlantic Saga*. Washington, D.C.: Smithsonian Institution Press, 2000.

Geary, Patrick. *Before France and Germany: The Creation and Transformation of the Merovingian World*. New York: Oxford University Press, 1988.

Lynch, Joseph H. *The Medieval Church: A Brief History*. New York: Longman, 1992.

Martin, Janet. *Medieval Russia 980–1584*. New York: Cambridge University Press, 1995.

McCormick, Michael. *Origins of the European Economy: Communications and Commerce* AD *300–900*. New York: Cambridge University Press, 2001.

McKitterick, Rosamond, ed. *The New Cambridge Medieval History*, vol. 2, c. 700–c. 900. New York: Cambridge University Press, 1995. (See particularly the essays by Michael McCormick.)

Parish, Helen. *Clerical Celibacy in the West: c. 1100–1700*. Burlington, Vt.: Ashgate, 2010.

Reuter, Timothy, ed. *The New Cambridge Medieval History*, vol. 3, c. 900–1024. New York: Cambridge University Press, 1999. (See particularly the essay by Thomas S. Noonan.)

Reuter, Timothy. "Plunder and Tribute in the Carolingian Empire." *Transactions of the Royal Historical Society*, 5th ser., 35 (1985): 75–94.

Rosenwein, Barbara H. *A Short History of the Middle Ages*, 3d ed. Toronto: University of Toronto Press, 2009.

Treadgold, Warren. *A History of the Byzantine State and Society*. Stanford: Stanford University Press, 1997.

Wallace, Birgitta L. "The Norse in Newfoundland: L'Anse aux Meadows and Vinland." *Newfoundland Studies* 19, no. 1 (2003): 5–43.

Wallace, Birgitta L. *Westward Vikings: The Saga of L'Anse aux Meadows*. St. John's, Newfoundland, Canada: Historic Sites Association of Newfoundland and Labrador, 2006.

Winroth, Anders. *The Conversion of Scandinavia: Vikings, Merchants, and Missionaries in the Remaking of Northern Europe*. New Haven: Yale University Press, 2012.

Films

Nova: "The Viking Deception"
Nova: "The Vikings"

AP® Review Questions for Chapter 10

Multiple-Choice Questions

QUESTIONS 1–3 REFER TO THE FOLLOWING PASSAGE.

Karlsefni sailed south along the coast.... Karlsefni and his men sailed into the estuary and named the place Hope (Tidal Lake). Here they found wild wheat growing in fields on all the low ground and grape vines on all the higher ground. Every stream was teeming with fish. They stayed there for a fortnight [two weeks], enjoying themselves and noticing nothing untoward. They had their livestock with them. But early one morning as they looked around they caught sight of nine skin-boats; the men in them were waving sticks which made a noise like flails [tools used to thresh grain], and the motion was sunwise [clockwise]. Karlsefni said, "What can this signify?" "It could well be a token of peace," said Snorri. "Let us take a white shield and go to meet them with it."

—*The Vinland Sagas*, Icelandic texts from the thirteenth century C.E.

1. Which of the following is supported by the passage?
   (A) In this time period, there was sustained interactions between the hemispheres.
   (B) Seaworthy vessels were not developed in Europe until the early Modern era.
   (C) European maritime activity was limited to the Mediterranean region.
   (D) There was temporary contact between the two hemispheres in this time period.

2. The passage helps us in understanding which of the following?
   (A) The limited scope of Viking activity
   (B) The inability of Muslim states to defend against Viking raids
   (C) The wide range of Viking raids across the region
   (D) The reliance of northern Europeans on land routes for trade

3. What is the most likely explanation for Viking sailing activity during the time period?
   (A) The Vikings relied on Islamic sailing technology for travel.
   (B) Similar to Central Asians, the Vikings traveled primarily by land routes.
   (C) Vikings adapted their sailing technology to work in many different environments.
   (D) Viking sailing vessels were relegated to the coasts.

QUESTIONS 4–7 REFER TO THE FOLLOWING PASSAGE.

We knew not whether we were in heaven or on earth. For on earth there is no such splendor or such beauty, and we are at a loss how to describe it.... We know only that God dwells there among men, and their service is fairer than the ceremonies of other nations. For we cannot forget that beauty.

—Rus advisors to Prince Vladimir describing the Hagia Sophia

4. The design of the Hagia Sophia supports which of the following statements?
   (A) There was a complete loss of Roman culture and technology after the Germanic invasions.
   (B) The grandeur of Roman culture continued into the Postclassical era.
   (C) The Arab and Turkish invasions of the region removed the last vestiges of Roman culture.
   (D) Gothic architecture was accepted by the Byzantine empire.

5. The building of the Hagia Sophia by Emperor Justinian illustrates which of the following concepts?
   (A) Imperial governments used religious institutions to legitimize their rule.
   (B) Religious and political institutions were constantly at odds with each other.
   (C) Religious institutions tended to dominate and control governments in most regions.
   (D) Religious institutions relied completely on the governments for their funds.

6. The passage above supports which of the following statements?
   (A) The adoption of Islam by the Rus
   (B) The adoption of Orthodox Christianity by the Rus
   (C) The pledging of loyalty by Russian princes to the pope
   (D) Isolation of the Rus until the early Modern era

7. Which of the following explains the impact of other regions on Rus culture?
   (A) Russia's close proximity to the Abbasid caliphate
   (B) The pope's policy of sending big missionary teams to the city of Kiev
   (C) Russia's proximity to the Byzantine empire
   (D) Kiev's position as a major stop on the Silk Road

QUESTIONS 8–10 REFER TO THE FOLLOWING IMAGE.

8. The Buddhist statue found on a Swedish island supports which of the following statements?
   (A) Viking elites looking for a religion to legitimize their power
   (B) The migration of European communities to the eastern Mediterranean
   (C) The conversion of entire regions to religions with universal messages
   (D) The expansion of trade networks in the Post-classical era

9. Which of the following events most likely brought the statue to Sweden?
   (A) New metallurgical techniques developed in Europe
   (B) The development of European trading cities in the Indian Ocean basins
   (C) Development of ritual gift giving in courts across Eurasia
   (D) Viking raids in western Sung territories

10. Which of the following describes the system that led to the statue going to Sweden?
    (A) The various trade networks acted as discrete and unconnected systems.
    (B) The various trade networks interacted only at the regional level.
    (C) Trade networks during the time period began to decay.
    (D) Various trade networks worked as a single system to transport goods.

Short-Answer Questions

1. Answer parts A and B.
   Some historians claim that the Byzantine empire remained a strong and viable state after the fall of the western half of the empire.
   A. Identify TWO pieces of evidence that would support this claim.
   B. Identify ONE piece of evidence that undermines this claim.

2. Answer parts A and B.
   Constantinople remained the primary center of Christian thought and culture from 600 to 1450.
   A. Identify ONE fact that supports this claim.
   B. Identify TWO reasons for the rise of other centers challenging Constantinople's authority.

11 Expanding Trade Networks in Africa and India, 1000–1500

Superstock

Muslim Traveler, ca. 1300

In 1325, a twenty-year-old legal scholar named **Ibn Battuta** (1304–1368/69*) set off on a hajj pilgrimage from his home in Tangier (tan-jeer), a Mediterranean port on the westernmost edge of the Islamic world (see Chapter 9). In Mecca, Ibn Battuta (IH-buhn bah-TOO-tuh) made a decision that changed his life: instead of returning home, he decided to keep going. A world traveler with no fixed destination and no set time of return, he followed trade routes that knitted the entire Islamic world together. These routes connected places like Mecca, which had been at the center of the Islamic world since Muhammad's first revelations, to others that had more recently joined that world, such as the sub-Saharan kingdom of Mali and the Delhi sultanate of north India. After his travels were over, Ibn Battuta dictated his adventures to a ghost writer. His account began:

My departure from Tangier, my birthplace, took place . . . in the year seven hundred and twenty-five [1325] with the object of making the Pilgrimage to the Holy House at Mecca and of visiting the tomb of the Prophet . . . at Medina. I set out alone, having neither fellow-traveller in whose companionship I might find cheer, nor caravan whose party I might join, but swayed by an over-mastering impulse within me, and a desire long-cherished in my bosom to visit these illustrious sanctuaries.†

---

*Because of differences in the calendars, Islamic years often straddle two Western years. Although most sources give the year in both the Islamic calendar and the Western, this chapter, like Chapter 9, will give only the Western equivalent.

†From H. A. R. Gibb, *The Travels of Ibn Battuta A.D. 1325–1354*, The Hakluyt Society, p. 8. The Hakluyt Society was established in 1846 for the purpose of printing rare or unpublished Voyages and Travels. For further information, please see their website at: www.hakluyt.com.

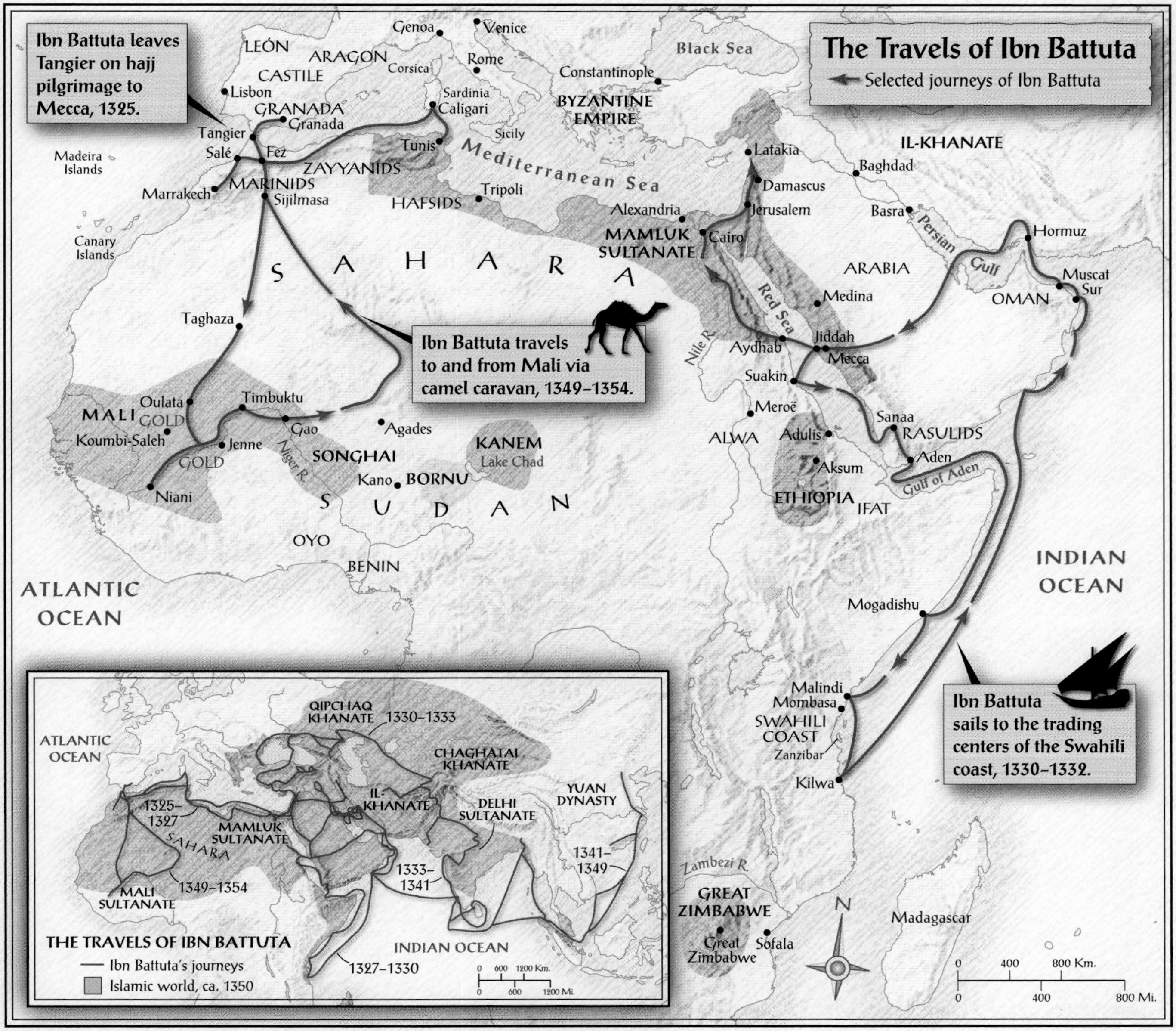

So begins the account of the longest known journey taken by any single individual before 1500. Proceeding on foot, riding camels and donkeys, and sailing by boat, Ibn Battuta covered an estimated 75,000 miles (120,000 km)—an extraordinary distance in the preindustrial world. Because the Five Pillars of Islam obligated all Muslims to give alms, not just to the poor and the sick but also to travelers, Ibn Battuta was able to continue his travels even when his own funds were exhausted.

After setting out alone, Ibn Battuta soon fell in with a caravan of traders on their way to Cairo. Because he always traveled with Islamic merchants on established caravan routes, his itinerary provides ample evidence of the extensive trade

Ibn Battuta

(1304–1368/69) Legal scholar from Tangier, Morocco, who traveled throughout the Islamic world between 1325 and 1354 and wrote *The Travels*.

networks connecting northern Africa, much of East and West Africa, and northern India. Many of the people he met accepted the teachings of the Quran, and he was able to communicate in Arabic everywhere he went. In each place he visited, he named the rulers, identified the highest-ranking judges, and then listed the important holy men of the town and their most important miracles. This narrow focus means that he rarely reported on some important topics, such as the local economy or the lives of women and non-Muslims.

Ibn Battuta was the first traveler to leave an eyewitness description of Africa south of the Sahara Desert, where he stayed in the kingdom of Mali. He visited Cairo—the capital city of the Mamluks (MAM-lukes) of Egypt, a powerful dynasty founded by military slaves—as well as several East African ports south of the equator. He remained for seven years in north India, then under Muslim rule, and visited many Indian Ocean ports. He did not, however, go to the interior of southern Africa or see the majestic site of Great Zimbabwe.

Many legs of Ibn Battuta's journey would not have been possible three hundred years earlier. In 1000 many parts of Africa were not connected to the broader Islamic world, including the rainforest of the West African coastlands and Central Africa, the densely populated Great Lakes region around Lake Victoria, and the southern African savanna. By 1450, however, expanding networks of trade had brought West and East Africa into increasing contact with the Islamic world of northern Africa and western Asia.

KEY CONCEPT QUESTIONS

- What environmental effects resulted from the Bantu migration in sub-Saharan Africa? **(Key Concept 3.1)**
- How did the trans-Saharan trade routes facilitate the rise of Sudanic trading cities in Africa? **(Key Concept 3.1)**
- What factors propelled the Mamluk empire to become a leader within the Islamic world? **(Key Concept 3.2)**
- What were the principal features of the Indian Ocean trade network? **(Key Concept 3.1)**

Reconstructing the History of Sub-Saharan Africa Before 1000

The Sahara Desert divides the enormous continent of Africa into two halves: sub-Saharan Africa in contrast to North and East Africa. In the seventh century, Islamic armies conquered North Africa, and East Africans had much contact with Muslim traders throughout the Abbasid period (750–1258). We know much less about sub-Saharan Africa before 1000 because few Muslims, the source of so much of our information, traveled there. Apart from Arabic accounts, historians of Africa must draw on archaeological excavation, oral traditions, and distribution of languages to piece together sub-Saharan Africa's history before 1000.

The Geography and Languages of Sub-Saharan Africa

Africa is a large continent, with an area greater than that of the United States (including Alaska), Europe, and China combined. As we saw in Chapter 1, the first anatomically modern humans crossed the Sinai Peninsula from Africa into western Asia by at least 150,000 years ago. The Nile River Valley was the site of Africa's earliest complex societies, first in Egypt and then in Nubia (see Chapter 2). Rome's greatest rival, Carthage (see Chapter 7), operated from a base in North Africa, and after its defeat in 202 B.C.E., Romans bought much of their grain from Egypt. In the 300s, Christianity spread throughout the Mediterranean to Egypt, northern Africa, and Ethiopia (see Chapter 7). After 650, Islam replaced Christianity in much of northern Africa, but not in Ethiopia.

A glance at Map 11.1 shows why only North and East Africa had such close contacts with the larger world: 3,000 miles (4,800 km) across and around 1,000 miles (1,600 km) from north to south, the Sahara Desert created a barrier between the coast and the sub-Saharan regions. The first traders to cross the Sahara did so riding camels. The single-humped camel they used originated in Arabia and reached North Africa sometime in the first century B.C.E. Domesticated in the third or fourth centuries C.E., camels were preferable to human porters because they could go for long periods without water and carry much heavier loads. Camels did not need roads and crossed the desert along sandy tracks.

Immediately to the south of the Sahara is a semidesert region called the **Sahel** (meaning "shore" in Arabic). South of the Sahel (SAH-hel), sufficient rain fell to support the tall grasses of the dry savanna and a band of wooded savanna farther south. Rainfall was heaviest in Central Africa, and rainforest stretched from the Atlantic coast to the Great Lakes region. The pattern repeated itself south of the rainforest: first a band of woodland savanna, then dry savanna, and then the Kalahari Desert near the tip of southern Africa.

Sahel
Semidesert region south of the Sahara.

Africans today speak nearly two thousand different languages, one-third of the total number of languages spoken in the world (see Map 11.1). Several languages spoken in North Africa, including Egyptian, Nubian, Ethiopian, and Arabic, have had written forms for a thousand years or longer (see Chapters 2, 7, and 9). But none of those spoken south of the Sahara were written down before 1800. Today, about five hundred of Africa's two thousand languages have written forms.

The Spread of Bantu Languages

Africa's languages cluster in several major groups. Arabic is spoken throughout the Islamic regions, while the **Bantu** languages are widely distributed throughout sub-Saharan Africa. The word for "people" in Bantu is "bantu," hence the name of the language group. Since many of these languages show surprising uniformity over a wide area, earlier analysts posited that the migration of a single people, all speaking an earlier form of the Bantu language, accounted for the modern distribution.

Bantu
Name for the languages of the Niger-Congo language family and the speakers of those languages.

More recently, however, African historians pioneered the use of a linguistic method called *glottochronology* to analyze the history of languages. By comparing vocabulary lists, linguists can count how many words in two languages are the same and how many have changed. The greater the number of shared words, the closer two languages are; the fewer the number, the more distant. Glottochronology can indicate which languages broke off from others and in what order but not always exactly when. Close analysis of the linguistic variation among modern Bantu languages suggests that multiple waves of change occurred. Accordingly, scholars today have discarded the theory of a single wave of Bantu migration.

A persuasive model for the spread of Bantu languages sees three different, and often overlapping, processes taking place over an extended period: the planting of the first crops, the development of metallurgy, and the spread of the

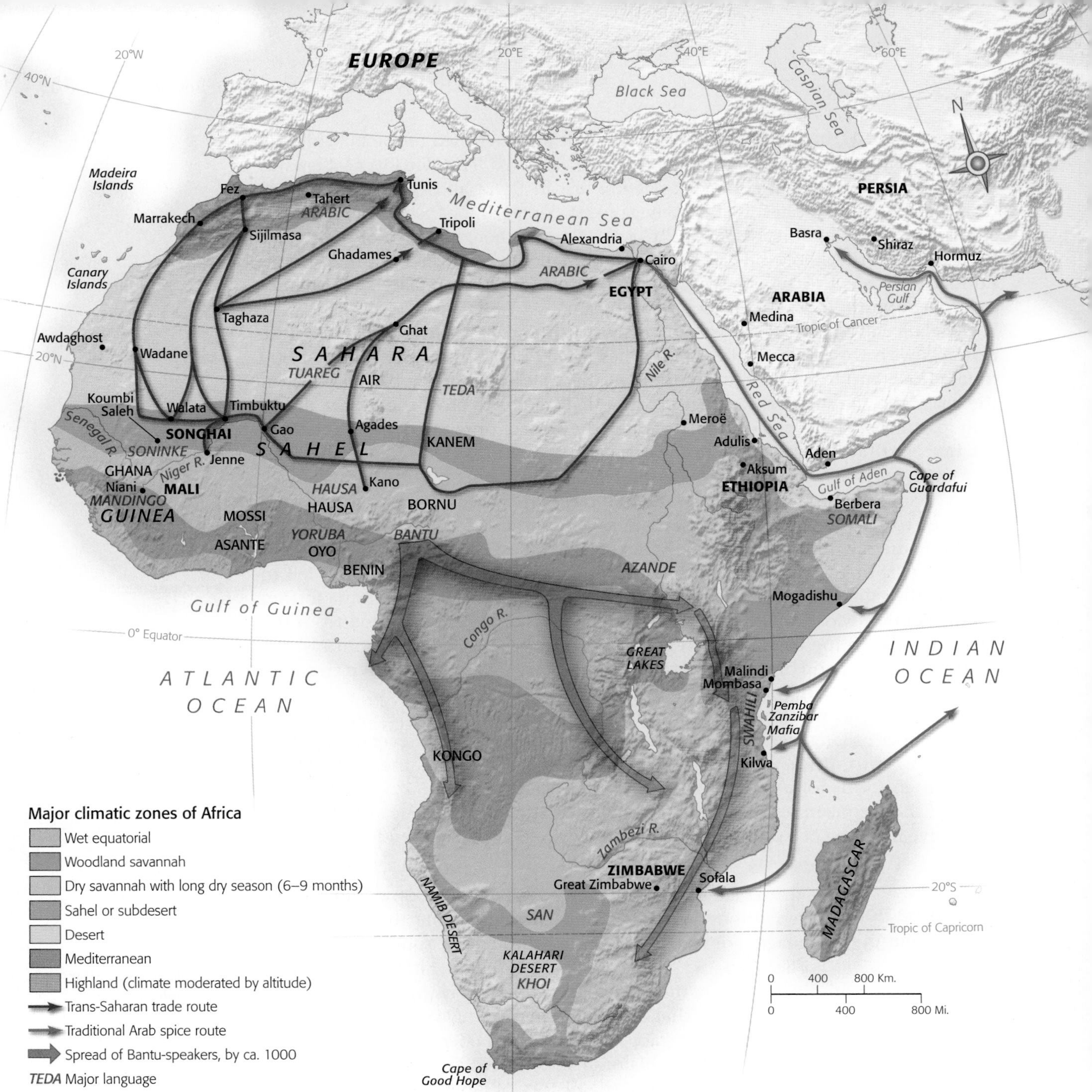

Map 11.1 African Trade Routes Before 1500 The Sahara Desert forms a natural boundary between Saharan Africa and sub-Saharan Africa. Overland camel routes across the Sahara Desert linked Mali with the Mediterranean coast, while Indian Ocean sea routes connected the important center of Great Zimbabwe in East Africa to the Islamic world and Asia.

Bantu languages. First, archaeological evidence shows that, sometime between 1000 and 500 B.C.E., different peoples began to cultivate crops. Those in the drier regions grew sorghum, millet, and rice, while those in the rainforest raised tubers such as yams. Like the Maya (see Chapter 5), many of these peoples engaged in slash-and-burn agriculture, with the result that they farmed the same place for only one or two seasons. As in other parts of the world, it took hundreds, possibly thousands, of years before people shifted to full-time agriculture.

AP® THEMES
What are the advantages of slash-and-burn agriculture?

During this transition to agriculture, different peoples learned how to work iron. Iron tools were much more effective than stone and wood tools in turning the earth and preparing it for seed. The first evidence of ironworking in Africa dates to about 600 B.C.E. Interestingly, people living north of the Sahara, along the Nile River in modern Sudan, and south of the Sahara in central Nigeria learned how to work iron at about the same time, but their differing metallurgical techniques indicate that they did so independently of each other.

● **CONTEXT&CONNECTIONS** In contrast to the usual pattern in Eurasia, most sub-Saharan African peoples started to work iron without any previous experience with copper. In Eurasia the usual pattern was first to combine copper and tin into *bronze* and then, as the *Hittites* did in 2000 B.C.E., build on that expertise to smelt iron (key terms in Chapter 2); the peoples of the Americas, though, never worked iron (see Chapter 5). ●

Africans built a greater variety of furnaces for smelting iron than people anywhere else in the world. Some furnaces had tall shafts; others used preheated air. These smelting techniques allowed Africans to make iron from much leaner ores than those used elsewhere. The technology for smelting iron spread throughout southern Africa by 300 C.E.

Although iron is an extremely useful metal that can be made into agricultural implements and military weapons, it is relatively soft and rusts. Steel is much stronger and more resistasnt to rusting. The difference between iron and steel is the amount of carbon in the metal: iron that has been worked by a blacksmith, or wrought iron, usually contains less than 0.2 percent carbon, while steel may contain up to 1.5 percent. African smelting furnaces often made iron with enough dissolved carbon to have the properties of steel.

In the same centuries that the sub-Saharan Africans were developing agriculture and refining their production of iron, the Bantu languages spread southward. It is likely that indigenous peoples adopted farming, iron-smelting, and the Bantu languages at different times in different regions. By 1000, agricultural peoples who used iron tools had settled throughout sub-Saharan Africa, many of them speaking Bantu languages. Their iron tools allowed them to move into and settle heavily forested areas such as the Great Lakes region.

oral histories
Historical accounts passed from one generation to the next. Particularly important in societies where no written accounts survive.

Society and Family Life

The final centuries of these changes overlap with the first written records. As early as the eighth century, Arab geographers began to record some preliminary notes, often on the basis of hearsay, about sub-Saharan Africa, and Arabic sources dominate the historical record through the sixteenth century, particularly for North and East Africa. The lack of indigenous historical records means that historians of sub-Saharan Africa must rely on **oral histories**. In Africa, royal storytellers, or **griots** (GREE-oh; a French word), often recited the events of the past to the monarchs

griots
Royal storytellers who served as advisers to the rulers of Mali and other West African states. (A *griotte* is a female storyteller.)

they advised; even today griots still recite stories, sometimes on the radio, and receive high payments for doing so. Exciting breakthroughs in African history have come when historians have linked events from oral histories with archaeological finds or Arabic-language sources. Ibn Battuta's account occupies pride of place among these Arabic sources because he went to so many places and wrote at such great length. (The English translation of his account fills nearly a thousand pages in four volumes.)

Historians have been able to reconstruct the past by carefully examining historic accounts and judiciously considering which aspects of social and economic life were least likely to change. Jan Vansina, a prominent historian of Africa, coined the term *upstreaming* for their task because it resembles standing on a riverbank, observing what is happening on the river flowing by, and making an intelligent guess about what occurred upstream.

Upstreaming has led historians to concur that certain generalizations probably hold true for most of sub-Saharan Africa before 1000. People lived in villages of several hundred to several thousand residents, and fertile areas were more heavily populated than barren regions like the Sahara Desert. Often the people of one village claimed descent from the same ancestor, whether legendary or historical, and historians use the term **lineage** or *clan* for such family units. (Historians today avoid the word *tribe* because of its negative associations and condescending use in the past.)

lineage
Group of people claiming descent from the same ancestor, whether legendary or historical, who are not necessarily biologically related but consider themselves a family unit.

Lineages and clans organized into villages were the bedrock of Africa's diverse societies. Men often dominated the tasks with the greatest prestige, like hunting or metallurgy, as well as anything requiring long-distance travel, such as military conquest, long-distance trade, and diplomatic negotiations. Women usually tilled the soil, gathered wild fruits and vegetables, made pottery, and prepared meals. Marriage patterns varied from village to village: a man might take a single wife or multiple wives, sometimes from within his own lineage, sometimes from other groups.

Men formed tight bonds with other men of the same age while undergoing initiations into adulthood. Younger men respected and obeyed more senior men. A man who fathered many children and attained great wealth was called a "great man." Great men earned their position at the top of village society, often by military prowess.

AP® THEMES
How did kinship ties and gender roles shape economic activities in sub-Saharan Africa prior to 1000?

Great men led villages, and if continually successful in battle, they might form larger political units such as a chieftaincy or a kingdom. During the lifetimes of the great men who led them, the villages they had conquered would submit gifts to them; after their deaths, however, the fragile political units they formed could easily break apart. In the course of his travels, Ibn Battuta met several great men who headed their own kingdoms, one of whom was the ruler of Mali.

The Kingdom of Mali and Its Precursors in Sub-Saharan Africa

Mali
Kingdom founded ca. 1230 by Sundiata in West Africa. Generated revenue by taxing the caravans of the trans-Saharan trade.

The kingdom of **Mali**, centered on the Niger River basin, occupied much of West Africa south of the Sahara Desert. It straddled the Sahel and the vast savanna grasslands to the south. Because this territory included some of the world's biggest gold mines, merchants crossed the Sahara to this region perhaps as early as 500. Urbanization began in the West African Sahel with the development of the trans-Saharan trade. Ghana (ca. 700–1000) was the first kingdom to take advantage of its location at an important node of trade, and the kingdom of Mali built on these earlier achievements in taxing trans-Saharan trade as a pathway to power. Ibn Battuta describes Mali's trade with the north in the 1350s: caravans brought slaves and gold from the south and exchanged them for cloth, pottery, and glass trinkets from the north.

The Kingdom of Ghana, ca. 700–1000

The Muslim geographer al-Bakri (d. 1094) provided the earliest and most detailed description of the kingdom of **Ghana** in his *Book of Routes and Realms* (see Chapter 9). Since al-Bakri never left his native Córdoba in Spain, he drew all of his information from earlier geographic accounts and from named informants who had been to the sub-Saharan trading kingdoms.

Ghana
The first empire in western Sudan. Prospered between 700 and 1000.

These kingdoms began as small settlements located at points where different routes crossed each other. Sijilmasa (sih-jil-MAHS-suh), located on the northern edge of the Sahara in modern Morocco, originated, al-Bakri reports, as a periodic market on a *"bare plain"* where local people came to buy and sell goods, like iron tools, only at certain times of year. He says the periodic market *"was the beginning of its being populated, then it became a town."** Sijilmasa grew into an important trade depot ruled by a royal lineage whose founder claimed descent from a family who sold iron tools at the earliest periodic market. Towns like Sijilmasa became city-states whose main source of revenue was the taxes their rulers collected from traders.

AP® THEMES
How did commerce facilitate the development of powerful kingdoms in sub-Saharan West Africa?

The kingdom of Ghana (1600 km, or 1000 miles, to the northwest of modern-day Ghana; see Map 11.1) was the first empire in the region of the western Sudan and arose through a similar process. In the mid-1000s, al-Bakri reported that the kingdom contained two cities: preachers and scholars lived in the Islamic one, which had twelve mosques where Friday prayers were said; and *"six miles"* away, the king and his *"sorcerers"* lived in the other. Al-Bakri's informants drew a sharp line between Muslims and *"polytheists,"* whose *"religion is paganism and the worship of idols."** The king did not convert to Islam, but he welcomed Muslim visitors.

The king taxed the goods going in and out of the cities he ruled. For each donkey load of goods, merchants paid a tax in gold, which was higher for more valuable goods like copper and lower for cheaper commodities like salt. The proceeds financed the king's military campaigns. The king, al-Bakri wrote, could raise an army of 200,000 men, of whom 40,000 were archers. Archaeologists have concluded that the kingdom did not have a fixed capital and that the king and his retinue regularly moved among different cities.

Jenne-jeno: A Different Path to Complex Society

Outside the kingdom of Ghana, 2 miles (3 km) southeast of Jenne, is the large urban site of Jenne-jeno (jen-NAY jenn-OH) in the **Middle Niger Valley** (see Map 11.1). Jenne-jeno's population in the 700s was between 15,000 and 27,000. Smaller surrounding towns of 500 to 1,500 people formed a nested hierarchy of villages, small towns, and medium-size towns.† Jenne-jeno, meaning "ancient Jenne" in the local Songhai language, is 220 miles (354 km) southwest of Timbuktu in Mali.

Middle Niger Valley
A recently discovered complex society, well established by the 700s, with large urban settlements but no distinct political center or full-time agriculture.

*Al-Bakri's *The Book of Routes and Realms,* as translated in *Corpus of Early Arabic Sources for West African History,* ed. N. Levtzion and J. F. P. Hopkins (New York: Cambridge University Press, 1981), pp. 65–66, 79–81.

†Susan Keech McIntosh and Roderick J. McIntosh, "Cities Without Citadels: Understanding Urban Origins Along the Middle Niger," in *The Archaeology of Africa: Food, Metals and Towns,* ed. Thurstan Shaw et al. (New York: Routledge, 1993), p. 633.

In the years leading up to 1000, Jenne-jeno had a large population, but it did not resemble cities anywhere else in the world. For one thing, archaeologists have found no evidence of a clear political center. Nor did the city have any prominent buildings made of stone. For this reason archaeologists did not recognize the Middle Niger Valley as a complex society until the 1980s.

They changed their minds when they realized how big the settlement was; it covered over 80 acres (32 hectares). Enormous mounds of debris standing over 26 feet (8 m) tall hold hundreds of thousands of broken pieces of dirt foundations and mud bricks, waste from ironworking, copper ornaments, clay figures used as toys, grinding stones, and fragments of pottery, all persuasive evidence of population density. The city's most prominent feature was its mud-brick wall 11.8 feet (3.6 m) across at the base.

• **CONTEXT&CONNECTIONS** The Middle Niger Valley society departs from the world's complex societies in other ways. The local people cultivated wet rice but never shifted to full-time agriculture, continuing to gather wild plants and hunt wild animals. There is no evidence of social stratification, but there is of occupational specialization: after 400 C.E., certain residents smelted iron outside the city and brought the partially worked metal to the city, where others, smiths, worked it into tools. •

As al-Bakri suggested, trade was crucial to the region. Early on, the exchanges were largely local, with residents trading dried fish, fish oil, and rice for iron. Over time the city imported commodities from farther away, such as copper and salt from the Sahara. The city reached its greatest extent around the year 1000 and prospered for several hundred years.

The ruler of Jenne-jeno converted to Islam sometime between 1200 and 1300, and the first mosque there was built around that time. Torn down and rebuilt on the same site over the years, the Great Mosque in the city of Jenne is both the largest mud-brick structure in the world and one of the world's most distinctive buildings. Rebuilt most recently in 1906–1907 using traditional construction techniques, it is made from mud bricks between 16 and 24 inches (40 and 60 cm) thick. Supported by more than ninety wooden pillars, the prayer hall holds three thousand people; the roof has built-in ceramic caps that can be removed to introduce cool air. Each of the mosque's unusual three minarets (normally mosques have four) has an ostrich egg, a symbol of purity, suspended above the highest point.

Archaeologists are not certain why the city of Jenne declined after 1300. It is possible that the Black Death (discussed later in this chapter) reached the city. Because no written records mention the plague, and because DNA analysis has yet to shed light on this issue, historians instead look to material evidence like the statue in the photo "Evidence of the Plague."

Some states in pre-1500 Africa, like Ghana, controlled large amounts of territory, but usually, like Jenne-jeno, they exercised direct political control over only a small core area. Kings normally had little independent political power, usually serving as mediators and consensus builders for councils of lineage and clan elders, who made the most important decisions at the local level.

• **CONTEXT&CONNECTIONS** Unlike *Mesopotamia* (Chapter 2), Egypt, India, China, or the Americas, where the first complex societies tapped agricultural surplus, most

African states arose through control and taxation of strategic natural resources like water or gold. For example, the loss of several key trading depots to a dynasty based in Spain drastically reduced the tax revenues paid to the kings of Ghana, and they lost their kingdom to a local lineage named the Sosso (SOO-soo) around 1150. ●

Evidence of Plague? This beautifully crafted statue, 10 inches (25 cm) tall, shows a seated man clasping a leg and resting his head sideways with his mouth open. Is he in pain? Mourning someone? Or simply lost in thought? Observers cannot be certain, and interpretations of the raised bumps on his back differ, too. One view sees them as a kind of tattoo or ritual scarification (there are three regular rows). Others note, though, that they resemble plague pustules, and the timing—the 1300s—is just right. It is very possible that the plague traveled along trade routes to Mali just as to other places, and deaths from the plague might have contributed to the demise of the Jenne state. (Image Asset Management Ltd./Alamy)

Sundiata and the Founding of the Mali Kingdom, ca. 1230

The best source about the rise of Mali is an oral epic, written down only in the twentieth century, that recounts the life and exploits of the kingdom's founder, Sundiata (soon-JAH-tuh) (r. ca. 1230). In the Malinke (muh-LING-kay) language spoken in Mali, the version of the tale *Sundiata* tells how the son of a local ruler overthrew the Sosso king Soumaoro (soo-mah-oh-roh) and united the different peoples of the region.

Each king of Mali had his own griot who had been taught the story of his dynastic predecessors and whose task was to compose new sections about the reigning king. The griots' extensive knowledge of the ancestral teachings granted them a prominent position in Mali society, and they often advised rulers on matters of state and diplomacy. Ibn Battuta's description is one of the earliest we have of the griots and their close relationship to the **sultan**. Ibn Battuta used the word *sultan* for the Mali king because his predecessors had converted to Islam sometime around 1000. Ibn Battuta described the Mali sultan's griots:

sultan
"Ruler" in Arabic. Any head of an Islamic state, often called *sultanates.*

> *Each of them is inside a costume made of feathers resembling the green woodpecker on which is a wooden head with a red beak.... They stand before the Sultan in this laughable get-up and recite their poems.... They say to the Sultan: "This platform, formerly such and such a king sat on it and performed noble actions, and so and so did such and such; do you do noble acts which will be recounted after you?"**

Once they were done reciting, the griots climbed up the platform on which the sultan was sitting and placed their head on the sultan's right shoulder, his left, and then his lap to show their respect.

---

*From H. A. R. Gibb, *The Travels of Ibn Battuta* A.D. *1325–1354*, The Hakluyt Society, pp. 379–380. The Hakluyt Society was established in 1846 for the purpose of printing rare or unpublished Voyages and Travels. For further information, please see their website at: www.hakluyt.com.

Gift of Mr. William W. Brill Photograph courtesy of the Herbert F. Johnson Museum of Art, Cornell University

A Modern Headdress from Mali When Ibn Battuta visited the sultan of Mali, he described griots who wore a feathered costume topped by a bird's head with a beak. Perhaps he saw something like this bird mask, made in the twentieth century out of feathers, porcupine quills, antelope horns, and mud, from the same region of Mali that he visited.

The story of Sundiata remains our most detailed source about the early years of Mali. Sundiata was born to a king and his hump-backed wife, and he walked only at the age of seven. These traits indicated to the audience that both mother and son possessed unusual spiritual powers. In the hope that Sundiata would someday succeed to the throne, his father assigned him his own griot. One day, when his exasperated mother yelled at Sundiata because he still depended on others for food, his griot sent word to the village blacksmith to send an iron bar so heavy that six men were needed to carry it. Sundiata easily picked up the bar with one hand and then stood up and walked. He grew into a strong and powerful warrior and later resolved to overthrow the oppressive rule of Soumaoro.

The *Sundiata* epic reveals much about African religions. Sundiata's enemy Soumaoro is a sorcerer who knows how to make small figurines, or fetishes, and recite spells to wound his enemies. Still, Soumaoro is not invincible. Sundiata's half-sister finds out that he must observe a taboo against touching a cock's spur, the sharp talon a rooster uses in fighting. If he violates the taboo, he will lose the mysterious power, or *jinn*, granted to him by his ancestors. The Arabic word for a spirit or ghost (also the root of the English word *genie*), jinn is a key concept in Islam. Sundiata attaches a cock's spur to an arrow that hits Soumaoro. *"The cock's spur no more than scratched him, but the effect was immediate and Soumaoro felt his powers leave him."** By the end of the epic, Sundiata rules the kingdom of Mali.

---

*Excerpt from D. T. Niane, *Sundiata: An Epic of Old Mali*, trans. G. D. Pickett (London: Longman, 1965), p. 65.

The epic illustrates how local African religion absorbed religious conceptions from Islam. Aside from the clue about jinn, *Sundiata* never explicitly mentions God or the power of Islam, even though al-Bakri's report about the Mali ruler's conversion to Islam dates to 1068, nearly two centuries before the events described in the epic occurred.

- **CONTEXT&CONNECTIONS** Possibly because they draw on a wide variety of sources, historians of Africa have thought more deeply about oral history than many of their colleagues who study other regions. But this book has introduced important oral sources from other regions, generally recorded long after the events they describe but long before our own time. This is true of the *Epic of Gilgamesh* (Chapter 2), the *Bible* (Chapter 2), and *The Vinland Sagas* (Chapter 10). In discussing these sources, we consider possible distortions caused by someone's point of view, or bias as historians call it. For example, the coverage of *Gudrid* (Chapter 10) is so extensive and positive that historians suspect her descendants composed *Erik the Red's Saga* to glorify her. ●

In recent decades, historians specializing in Africa who work with oral sources have gradually changed their approach. The first generation of historians, including Jan Vansina, believed that they could collect various oral accounts, reconcile the differences, and find out exactly what happened long ago. But more recently, historians have realized that differing accounts cannot always be matched up. In the 1500s, two different oral histories circulated in Mali; both versions tried to explain the source of Mali's greatness. One related how Sundiata tamed different spirits (this chapter has drawn on such an account), while the other told of the great deeds of Mansa Musa, a later ruler, without even mentioning Sundiata. Why the difference? The first account held that Sundiata's power over the spirit world underlay Mali's former greatness; the second, that Mansa Musa's support for Islam was the key.

How many of the events described in *Sundiata* can be confirmed by other sources? Arab chronicles record that the kingdom of Mali existed in the thirteenth century, and the Arab historian **Ibn Khaldun** (1332–1406) recorded the names of the Mali kings and the major events of their reigns. The most important Muslim historian of all time, Ibn Khaldun (IH-buhn hal-DOON) formulated an entirely original definition of history as the study of human society and its transformations. His painstaking work makes it possible to date Sundiata's reign to around 1230.

Ibn Khaldun
(1332–1406) Prominent Muslim historian born in Tunis in North Africa; he reported on the kings of Mali.

The process of state formation by a series of conquests that the *Sundiata* narrative describes is plausible: armies several thousand strong did fight with iron-tipped bows and other metal weapons. The Mali army consisted of different independent armies, each led by a local leader who decided in each instance which higher leader he would support. Mali leaders began to import horses from North Africa around 1000, but initially only the most important leaders fought on horseback. At its largest point, reached some one hundred years after Sundiata's reign, the kingdom of Mali extended more than 1,000 miles (1,600 km) east to west and included the basins of both the Senegal and Niger Rivers. By 1400, the kings of Mali led armies of mounted warriors into battle.

The Mali government's primary source of revenue was taxing trade. One of Sundiata's wealthiest successors was Mansa Musa (r. 1307–1332), who visited Cairo on his way to Mecca in 1324. (*Mansa* is a word in the Malinke language meaning "supreme ruler," and *Musa* is Arabic for Moses; *Mansa Musa* means King Moses.) Five hundred servants, each carrying a staff of gold weighing 6 pounds (2.7 kg), for a total of 3000 pounds (over 1 metric ton), walked in front of him. Our sources may exaggerate, of course. One hundred camels were required to

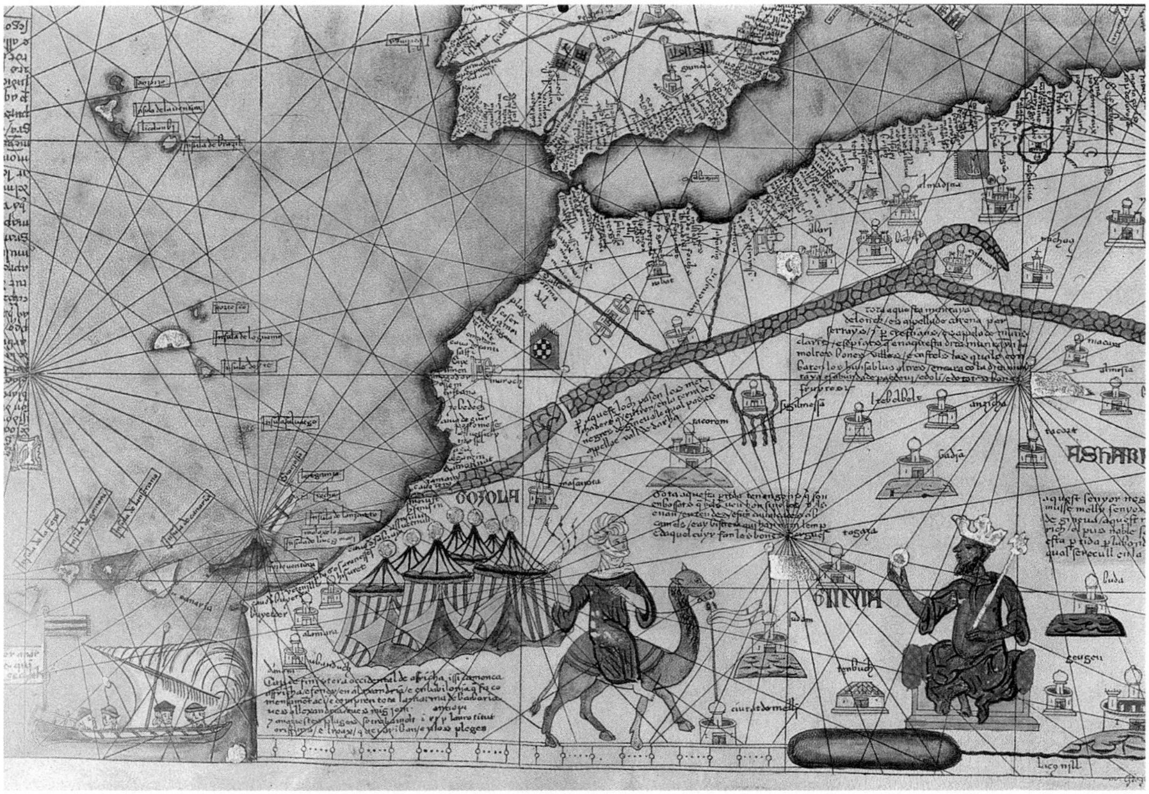

The Richest King in the Land? Mansa Musa of Mali In 1375, a European cartographer mapped Afro-Eurasia with unprecedented accuracy. This detail of the Catalan Atlas shows the blue Mediterranean Ocean, southern Spain, and North Africa. The mapmaker has also included written labels that identify the seated figure on the lower right as Mansa Musa, the richest king in the land because of the abundant gold in his country.

carry his travel money, which was some 700 pounds (315 kg) of gold, making Mansa Musa one of the most talked-about and most welcome travelers of his day.

Trans-Saharan Trade Networks

In 1352, twenty years after Mansa Musa's death, Ibn Battuta went to Mali. The only eyewitness description we have of the fabulously wealthy kingdom, his account provides our best source about the **trans-Saharan caravan trade network** connecting Mali with northern Africa. Traveling in caravans on well-established trade routes, Ibn Battuta witnessed a highly developed commercial network (see Map 11.1).

trans-Saharan caravan trade network A network of overland trade exchanging slaves and gold from sub-Saharan Africa for cloth, pottery, and glass trinkets from the Mediterranean.

Those crossing the desert usually bought camels and provisions at towns like Sijilmasa, whose rise al-Bakri described. After twenty-five days crossing the desert, Ibn Battuta's exhausted caravan arrived in Taghaza, one of the major salt-producing centers on the southern edge of the Sahara. *"It is a village with no attractions,"**

*From H. A. R. Gibb, *The Travels of Ibn Battuta* A.D. *1325–1354*, The Hakluyt Society, p. 947. The Hakluyt Society was established in 1846 for the purpose of printing rare or unpublished Voyages and Travels. For further information, please see their website at: www.hakluyt.com.

remarks Ibn Battuta, who describes only dwellings and a mosque with walls of salt blocks and roofs of camel skins. Salt structures were long-lasting because there were less than 8 inches (200 mm) of rain each year. The slaves who mined the salt lived on a monotonous diet of camel meat, dates from North Africa, and millet from Mali, so even they were enmeshed in a trading economy.

Salt is an essential nutrient for all human beings, and it is even more important in hot areas because it allows the body to replace salt lost by sweating. Pure salt was so valuable that it was used as a currency. *"The Blacks,"* Ibn Battuta remarks, *"trade with salt as others trade with gold and silver; they cut it in pieces and buy and sell with these."** As Ibn Battuta made his way south of the Sahara, he learned that travelers did not have to carry either food or silver coins because they could trade small amounts of salt, small glass trinkets, or spices for whatever food and lodging they required.

At the end of his stay in Mali, Ibn Battuta visited Timbuktu (tim-buk-TOO), a great trading city on the Niger River, whose ruler gave him a young male slave, a typical gift for an honored guest. The slave traders of Mali did not enslave people of their own country; they captured slaves in the forest belt to the south. When Ibn Battuta returned to Morocco, he traveled with a caravan carrying six hundred female slaves. One of the few reliable statistics available, Ibn Battuta's observation, combined with a handful of other sources, has led one historian to estimate that 5,500 slaves crossed the desert each year between 1100 and 1400.†

More women than men crossed the Sahara because more buyers wanted female slaves than male slaves. Once sold in the markets of Morocco, women slaves would work as servants and concubines for urban dwellers, or perhaps for the royal court. Since slave owners feared that male slaves might impregnate the female members of the household, they preferred castrated males, or eunuchs. In the premodern era, the operation to remove male slaves' genitals, whether partially or entirely, was perilous; only a lucky few survived.

Mali's other major export was gold. In the thirteenth and fourteenth centuries, two-thirds of all the gold entering Europe passed through the North African cities of Tunis, Fez, and Cairo. Working conditions in Mali's gold mines were grim: shafts could be over 60 feet (20 m) deep and frequently collapsed. Men dug out the ore while women extracted the gold. Both tasks were laborious, but the mining allowed subsistence farmers to augment their incomes.

Society in Mali

Ibn Battuta visited Mali because it was on an established caravan route and he was confident that he would be received there as he was throughout the Islamic world. Although al-Bakri reported that the first ruler of Mali to convert to Islam did so around 1000, his subjects, according to the geographer, did not. (See the feature "Movement of Ideas Through Primary Sources: Conversion to Islam in Fictional and Nonfictional Sources.")

*From H. A. R. Gibb, *The Travels of Ibn Battuta* A.D. *1325–1354*, The Hakluyt Society, p. 947. The Hakluyt Society was established in 1846 for the purpose of printing rare or unpublished Voyages and Travels. For further information, please see their website at: www.hakluyt.com.

†Ralph A. Austen, "The Trans-Saharan Slave Trade: A Tentative Census," in *The Uncommon Market: Essays in the Economic History of the Atlantic Slave Trade*, ed. Henry A. Gemery and Jan S. Hogendorn (New York: Academic Press, 1979), pp. 23–69; tables on pp. 31, 66.

Conversion to Islam in Fictional and Nonfictional Sources

Even though they are experts in assessing reliability, most historians prefer nonfictional sources: why bother with a source that announces at the outset that the author is consciously altering what actually happened? Still, in fields for which primary evidence is scarce, historians sometimes find valuable information in fictional sources. Very few sources describe the Islamicization of sub-Saharan Africa before 1100. Here, we compare a fictional source with a nonfictional source on the same topic to see what we can learn about early conversions to Islam in Africa.

The first account is from a collection of sailor's fictional tales composed in the mid-900s in the port of Siraf on the Arabian Sea. The plot of the story is so intricate as to defy belief. Caught in a storm, an Arab slave ship from Oman is shipwrecked in an African kingdom, most likely in modern Somalia or Kenya. The ship's captain abducts the ruler and sells him as a slave at Oman. Several years later the same ship is again blown off course to the same locale; and when the traders go before the ruler, they are amazed to see the king they had kidnapped. The king explains that he got away and fled to Cairo and escaped being kidnapped by slave traders two more times. Finally, he reached his former kingdom, where his countrymen welcomed him back and he once again took the throne. Clearly, there are too many coincidences and narrow escapes for the storyteller's account to be strictly factual, but his account of the king's conversion to Islam is utterly plausible.

At first glance, the second account, from the Islamic geographer al-Bakri, writing in 1068, appears to be more straightforward. It describes how a Muslim teacher persuaded a king in Mali to convert to Islam. Recall, though, that al-Bakri lived in Spain his entire life and thus did not himself see the Mali king's conversion or the rainfall that followed it. Historians always prefer eyewitness accounts because details can be distorted in the retelling. This second account captures what an educated Muslim geographer writing in Córdoba heard about the conversion of a distant ruler to Islam. Not an eyewitness account, it is a just-so tale that explains why the king of Mali was called "the Muslim."

› Historical Thinking Skill:

CONTEXTUALIZATION What are the ways that African rulers, such as the king in the Slaving Adventure tale and the king in Mali, came into contact with the Islamic faith?

› Historical Thinking Skill:

COMPARISON What are the similarities in the ways the two converted African rulers practiced their new Islamic faith?

Sources: G. S. P. Freeman-Grenville, *The East African Coast: Select Documents from the First to the Earlier Nineteenth Century* (Oxford: Clarendon Press, 1962), excerpt 5, "Buzurg Ibn Shahriyar of Ramhormuz: A Tenth-Century Slaving Adventure," pp. 9–13. Reprinted by permission of the Estate of G. S. P. Freeman-Grenville; N. Levtzion and J. F. P. Hopkins, eds., *Corpus of Early Arabic Sources for West African History* (New York: Cambridge University Press, 1981), excerpt 22, "Al-Bakri," pp. 82–83.

From Buzurg's "A Tenth-Century Slaving Adventure"

He [the king] answered: "After you had sold me in Oman, my purchaser took me to a town called Basrah"—and he described it. "There I learnt to pray and to fast, and certain parts of the Quran. My master sold me to another man who took me to the country of the king of the Arabs, called Baghdad"—and he described Baghdad. "In this town I learnt to speak correctly. I completed my knowledge of the Quran and prayed with the men in the mosques. I saw the Caliph, who is called al-Muqtadir [r. 908–932]. I was in Baghdad for a year and more, when there came a party of men from Khorasan [west Iran, modern Turkmenistan] mounted on camels. Seeing a large crowd, I asked where all these people were going.

"I was told: 'To Mecca.'

"'What is Mecca?' I asked.

"'There,' I was answered, 'is the House of God to which Muslims make the Pilgrimage.' And I was told the history of the temple.

"I said to myself that I should do well to follow the caravan. My master, to whom I told all this, did not wish to go with them or to let me go. But I found a way to escape his watchfulness and to mix in the crowd of pilgrims. On the road I became a servant to them. They gave me food to eat and got for me the two cloths needed for the *ihram* [the ritual garments used for the pilgrimage]. Finally, they instructing me, I performed all the ceremonies of the pilgrimage....

"And here I am, happy and satisfied with the grace God has given me and mine, of knowing the precepts of Islam, the true faith, prayers, fasting, the pilgrimage, and what is permitted and what is forbidden."

From al-Bakri's *The Book of Routes and Realms*, About the Malal Region (Modern-Day Mali)

Beyond this country lies another called Malal, the king of which is known as al-musulmani [the Muslim]. He is thus called because his country became afflicted with drought one year following another; the inhabitants prayed for rain, sacrificing cattle till they had exterminated almost all of them, but the drought and the misery only increased. The king had as his guest a Muslim who used to read the Quran and was acquainted with the Sunna [the model of behavior that all Muslims were expected to follow]. To this man the king complained of the calamities that assailed him and his people.

The man said: "O King, if you believed in God (who is exalted) and testified that He is One, and testified as to the prophetic mission of Muhammad (God bless him and give him peace), and if you accepted all the religious laws of Islam, I would pray for your deliverance from your plight and that God's mercy would envelop all the people of your country, and that your enemies and adversaries might envy you on that account."

Thus he continued to press the king until the latter accepted Islam and became a sincere Muslim. The man made him recite from the Quran some easy passages and taught him religious obligations and practices which no man be excused from knowing. Then the Muslim made him wait till the eve of the following Friday, when he ordered him to purify himself by a complete ablution, and clothed him in a cotton garment which he had.

The two of them came out towards a mound of earth, and there the Muslim stood praying while the king, standing at this right side, imitated him. Thus they prayed for a part of the night, the Muslim reciting invocations and the king saying "Amen."

The dawn had just started to break when God caused abundant rain to descend upon them. So the king ordered the idols to be broken and expelled the sorcerers from his country. He and his descendants after him as well as his nobles were sincerely attached to Islam, while the common people of his kingdom remained polytheists. Since then their rulers have been given the title of al-musulmani [the Muslim].

By the time of Ibn Battuta's visit, Mali had become a Muslim kingdom, but people in Mali did not behave as Ibn Battuta felt observant Muslims should. Although he wrote as though there was a single standard of behavior that prevailed throughout the Islamic world, there was not. Within the structure of Islam, no supreme authority existed that could establish such a standard, which explains why Islamic religious and cultural practices were (and are) so diverse.

AP® THEMES
How did the role of women in Mali differ from the role of women in other Muslim societies?

On his arrival in Mali, Ibn Battuta commented how unusual the kingdom was: *"No one takes his name from his father, but from his maternal uncle. Sons do not inherit, only sister's sons! This is something I have seen nowhere in the world except among the infidel Indians of al-Mulaibar [Malabar, on the east coast of India]."** In short, Mali society was matrilineal, with descent determined by the mother, not the father. Royal women had much more power than their North African counterparts, but the rulers were male.

Ibn Battuta disdainfully described the customs that did not seclude women. On one occasion he visited his caravan leader and his wife, who were hosting a male friend of the wife. Indignantly, Ibn Battuta inquired: *"Are you happy about this, you who have lived in our country and know the content of the religious law?"* His host defended himself, explaining that the local women *"are not like the women of your country,"** but the indignant Ibn Battuta refused to return to his host's house.

Ibn Battuta concluded his discussion of Mali with an *"account of what I found good,"* namely, its secure roads, its high attendance at Friday services, and most of all, the *"great attention to memorizing the Holy Quran."** He was deeply impressed by the example of several different children who had been placed in shackles because they had failed to memorize assigned passages from the Quran.

The kings of Mali continued to govern after Ibn Battuta's departure in 1353, but they faced rival armies as cavalry warfare became more common around 1400, by which time they had added helmets and chain mail armor to their equipment. The kings lost control of several major cities, such as Timbuktu in 1433, and around 1450 Songhai (SONG-high), a neighboring kingdom similarly wealthy from trans-Saharan trade, conquered Mali, ending Sundiata's dynasty.

Islamic North Africa and the Mamluk Empire

Mamluk empire
(1250–1517) Dynasty founded by mamluk military slaves in Cairo that re-established the caliphate in 1261.

By the time of Ibn Battuta's travels, North Africa had split into three separate kingdoms, each ruled by a sultan. Each year these sultanates sent thousands of pilgrims, like Ibn Battuta, to Cairo, where they joined pilgrims coming from North and West Africa to form even larger caravans for the final trip to Mecca. Cairo had become the cultural capital of the Islamic world in 1261, when the rulers of the **Mamluk empire** announced the re-establishment of the caliphate after Baghdad

*From H. A. R. Gibb, *The Travels of Ibn Battuta* A.D. *1325–1354*, The Hakluyt Society, p. 966. The Hakluyt Society was established in 1846 for the purpose of printing rare or unpublished Voyages and Travels. For further information, please see their website at: www.hakluyt.com.

fell to the Mongols in 1258 (see Chapter 9). Ibn Battuta traveled through Mamluk territory in Egypt, Syria, and Arabia and personally experienced the ravages of the plague, which struck Eurasia for the first time since the eighth-century outbreaks in Constantinople (see Chapter 10).

The Sultanates of North Africa

Three months after his departure from Tangier in 1325, Ibn Battuta arrived at the trading port of Tunis, the capital of one of the three sultanates in North Africa, with a population near one hundred thousand. Located on a point sticking out into the Mediterranean, it was ideally situated as a port for trade across the Strait of Gibraltar to southern Europe. European merchants traded fine textiles, weapons, and wine for animal hides and cloth from North Africa as well as gold and slaves transshipped from the interior.

In almost all of the North African states, a sultan headed the government. In exchange for taxes paid by the inhabitants (Muslims paid a lower rate than non-Muslims), the government provided military and police protection. In addition, the sultan appointed a **qadi**, or chief jurist, who was assisted by subordinate jurists, to settle disputes in court. Anyone who, like Ibn Battuta, had studied law at Islamic schools was eligible to be appointed a qadi. These courts implemented Islamic law, called **sharia** (sha-REE-ah), which consisted of all the rules that Muslims were supposed to follow. Interpretation of certain points varied among the jurists belonging to different legal schools. Before leaving home in Morocco, Ibn Battuta had studied the legal interpretations of the Maliki school, one of the four major Sunni legal schools that interpreted the sharia. (See the feature "World History in Today's World: Legal Reform in Morocco.")

qadi
A Muslim jurist whose decisions were based on sharia.

sharia
Islamic law: all the rules that Muslims were supposed to follow, compiled on the basis of the Quran, the hadith, and earlier legal decisions.

The chief jurist in Tunis, Ibn Battuta informs us, heard disputes every Friday after prayers in the mosque: *"People came to ask him to give a decision on various questions. When he had stated his opinion on forty questions he ended that session."** The qadi's decision, called a fatwa, had the force of law and was enforced by the sultan's government.

Although Ibn Battuta had come to Tunis as an individual pilgrim, he left the city as the qadi for a caravan of Berber pilgrims going on the hajj. The caravan functioned like a small, mobile sultanate, with the caravan leader making the important decisions about the route and Ibn Battuta serving as the traveling qadi. His new salary made it possible for him to marry the daughter of a fellow pilgrim, but the marriage did not last. *"I became involved in a dispute with my father-in-law which made it necessary for me to separate from his daughter,"** Ibn Battuta comments, without explaining further (see Chapter 9).

The Mamluk Empire, 1250–1517

Sometime in the spring of 1326, not quite a year after his departure from Tangier, Ibn Battuta arrived in the port city of Alexandria and went immediately to see the

---

*From H. A. R. Gibb, *The Travels of Ibn Battuta* A.D. *1325–1354*, The Hakluyt Society, pp. 14, 18. The Hakluyt Society was established in 1846 for the purpose of printing rare or unpublished Voyages and Travels. For further information, please see their website at: www.hakluyt.com.

WORLD HISTORY IN TODAY'S WORLD

Legal Reform in Morocco

In 2003, King Mohammed VI of Morocco addressed his country's parliament. Calling himself "commander of the faithful," and so evoking the time of the caliphs, the king announced that he could not "permit what God has forbidden, nor forbid what the Almighty has allowed." Positioning himself as a moderate between conservative Muslims and reformist feminists, he presented a new family code, which took advantage of the flexibility of Islamic law. Because justice is a key principle of Islamic law, the Islamic legal tradition does allow for change, particularly if the proposed reforms appear to bring justice to more people, in this case women.

The new code introduced several provisions that diverged from the Maliki school of Quranic law (the same legal tradition that Ibn Battuta studied) that prevails in Morocco today: the right to divorce by mutual consent, a limit on the number of wives a man can take, and an increase in the age of marriage for women from fifteen to eighteen.

The past decade has shown, though, that passing a new family code is not sufficient to change how people live. Many families, especially in the countryside, still want their daughters to marry at a younger age, and before 2010, in 90 percent of cases that came before the courts requesting an exception, judges permitted the bride to marry before the age of eighteen. One scholar who specializes in women and Islamic law explained, "Judges have to go by the reality on the ground."

While some Moroccans feel that the new code changed too much, feminists feel that laws unchanged by the code, particularly those governing inheritance, are unfair to women. Inheritance remains just as the Quran specifies: daughters are entitled to one-half the share their brothers receive. This practice may have made sense in a traditional Islamic society, where household heads were usually men, but in Morocco—as in many other modern Islamic countries—women also head households, and it presents a genuine hardship for female household heads to receive a smaller amount of money than their brothers.

Some women are not waiting for a new inheritance law to pass. One woman had to give up two-thirds of her inheritance to a half-brother that she and her mother learned about only after her father died: "My advice to all women," she explained, "is to make sure they put the stuff in the kids' names. And they have to do it while they're alive so the law doesn't take away the girls' rights."

Source: Aida Alami, "Gender Inequality in Morocco Continues, Despite Amendments to Family Law," *New York Times*, March 17, 2014.

city's most famous tourist attraction: the lighthouse overlooking the Mediterranean. Alexandria marked the westernmost point of the Mamluk empire, which ruled eastward all the way to Damascus.

mamluk
Non-Muslim slaves purchased by Islamic states in Afghanistan, North Africa, Spain, and Egypt and forced to convert to Islam before serving as warriors.

The word ***mamluk*** originally referred to a type of non-Muslim slave used by Islamic states as warriors. In the ninth and tenth centuries, Islamic rulers in Afghanistan, North Africa, Spain, and Egypt, unable to recruit sufficient numbers from among their own populace, purchased large numbers of Turks from Central Asia to staff their armies. The number of these slaves swelled in succeeding centuries.

Bought as children, the young mamluks studied Islam in preparation for their mandatory conversion. Living in isolation from the rest of the population, they continued to speak their own Turkic dialects and often could not read Arabic. They did no manual labor and could rise to high military rank. Once a mamluk soldier converted to Islam, he was freed, and his children would be born Muslim. This made his children ineligible for service as mamluks, a powerful check on the ability of any commander to develop his own power base.

Many of these mamluk slaves rose to high positions in the Ayyubid Dynasty of Egypt (1171–1250), which Saladin had founded and which Ibn Jubayr visited in 1183–1185 (see Chapter 9). Taking advantage of their growing power, the mamluk slave soldiers staged a coup in 1250 and founded the Mamluk dynasty. Only ten years later, in 1260, Mamluk generals masterminded one of the greatest military victories in premodern times; 12,000 Mamluk troops defeated 10,000 Mongol archers at the battle of Ain Jalut, north of Jerusalem in modern Israel (see Chapter 14). Originally from the Central Asian grasslands and intimately familiar with horses, many Mamluk soldiers were skilled in the same fighting techniques used by the Mongols. The Mamluk forces were one of the few armies in the world to defeat the Mongols in direct combat. As news of the defeat spread, the Mongols' enemies gained confidence that they could be defeated, and the Mamluks retained control of Syria and Egypt, creating the eastern border of the Mongol Empire.

Cairo: Baghdad's Successor as the Cultural Capital of the Islamic World

Although the Mamluks were neither originally Muslim nor native speakers of Arabic, they positioned themselves as the protectors of the Islamic world. In 1261, they announced the re-establishment of the caliphate in Cairo, three years after its destruction by the Mongols in 1258. Thousands of refugees poured into the city, particularly Islamic teachers. They taught in Cairo's many colleges, called *madrasas* in Arabic, the high number of which impressed Ibn Battuta.

The thirteenth and fourteenth centuries saw the rise throughout the Islamic world of a new type of Islamic mystic, or **Sufi**. Followers of individual Sufis believed that their teachers had *baraka*, or divine grace, and could help others gain direct access to God. When alive, these Sufi teachers usually formed their own lodges where they taught groups of disciples and hosted visitors. When they died, their tombs, believed to retain their occupant's *baraka*, became pilgrimage sites.

Sufi
An Islamic mystic who taught that the individual could experience God directly without the intercession of others.

• **CONTEXT&CONNECTIONS** In its emphasis on the direct communication between devotee and deity, Sufism resembled Hindu *bhakti* devotionalism (Chapter 8), but in Sufism teachers played a key role as intermediaries that Brahmin priests did not play in south India. •

Ibn Battuta stayed three days with a Sufi teacher named Burhan al-Din the Lame, whom he described as *"learned, self-denying, pious and humble."** Burhan al-Din urged Ibn Battuta to visit three teachers in India, Sind (modern Pakistan), and China. His advice is certain evidence of a Sufi network stretching all the way from Egypt to China, and Ibn Battuta eventually met all three men.

With a population between 400,000 and 500,000, Cairo was larger than most contemporary cities; only a few Chinese cities outranked it. As in Baghdad, when it was the Abbasid capital, the city's population fell into distinct social groups. At the top were the Mamluk rulers, military commanders, and officials who kept records and supervised the tax system. Independent of the military were the Islamic notables, or *ulama* (see Chapter 9). Merchants, traders, and brokers formed a third influential group, often as wealthy and respected as members of the Mamluk ruling class.

---

*From H. A. R. Gibb, *The Travels of Ibn Battuta* A.D. *1325–1354*, The Hakluyt Society, p. 23. The Hakluyt Society was established in 1846 for the purpose of printing rare or unpublished Voyages and Travels. For further information, please see their website at: www.hakluyt.com.

Below these elites were those who worked at respectable occupations: tradesmen, shopkeepers, and craftsmen. Farmers came next. At the bottom of society were the people whose occupations violated Islamic teachings, such as usurers (who lent money for interest) and slave dealers. Cairo residents looked down on their neighbors who sold wine or performed sex for a fee, and they shunned those whose occupations brought them into contact with human corpses or dead animals.

The Outbreak of Plague in Damascus, 1348

The sultan of the Mamluk empire provided camels, food, and water for the poorer hajj travelers and guaranteed the safety of the pilgrims. Ibn Battuta's group probably numbered some ten thousand, who went overland to Damascus (in modern-day Syria), the second-largest city in the Mamluk empire and a great cultural center in its own right, having been the capital of the Umayyads in the seventh century.

In Damascus, Ibn Battuta's route converged with Ibn Jubayr's (see Chapter 9), and his account borrowed, often without acknowledgment, as much as one-seventh of Ibn Jubayr's twelfth-century narrative. From Damascus, Ibn Battuta proceeded to Mecca. After some time there, he decided to continue east on his journey.

Some twenty years later, Ibn Battuta again passed through Damascus on his journey home. This time he was unwittingly traveling with the rats that transmitted one of the most destructive diseases to strike humankind: the plague. Historians reserve the term *Black Death* for the outbreak in the mid-1300s.

● **CONTEXT&CONNECTIONS** Europe, the Middle East, and North Africa had experienced no major outbreaks of *plague* since the eighth century losses that so hurt the *Byzantine empire* (Chapter 10). Immunity was therefore low and the effects devastating. ●

The first new outbreak in western Europe occurred in 1346 in the Black Sea port of Kaffa. From there the dreaded disease traveled to Italy and Egypt (see Map 13.2, page 394). In May or June 1348, Ibn Battuta first heard of the plague in Ghazza, Syria, where *"the number of dead there exceeded a thousand a day."** He returned to Damascus, where the city's residents stayed up all night praying at the Great Mosque, and then joined a barefoot march in hopes of lowering the death toll: *"The entire population of the city joined in the exodus, male and female, small and large; the Jews went out with their book of the Law and the Christians with their Gospel, their women and children with them; . . . the whole concourse of them in tears and humble supplications, imploring the favour of God through His Books and His Prophets."** Damascus lost two thousand people *"in a single day,"* yet Ibn Battuta managed to stay well.

Modern historians estimate that the plague wiped out 33 to 40 percent of the population in Egypt and Syria alone, where it took two to three hundred years for the populations to return to their pre-plague levels.

---

*From H. A. R. Gibb, *The Travels of Ibn Battuta* A.D. *1325–1354*, The Hakluyt Society, pp. 918, 144. The Hakluyt Society was established in 1846 for the purpose of printing rare or unpublished Voyages and Travels. For further information, please see their website at: www.hakluyt.com.

East Africa, India, and the Trade Networks of the Indian Ocean

The Indian Ocean touched three different regions, each with its own languages and political units: the East African coast, the southern edge of the Arabian peninsula, and the west coast of India. Much as rulers of the trading posts on the Sahara survived by taxing overland trade, the sultans of the **Indian Ocean trade network**—the city-states and larger political units encircling the Indian Ocean—taxed the maritime trade. Some sultanates consisted of only a single port city like Kilwa island in modern Tanzania; others were larger, like the Delhi sultanate, which controlled as much Indian territory as the Mauryan and Gupta dynasties of the past (see Chapters 3 and 8).

Indian Ocean trade network
Network traversed by dhows that connected the ports around the Indian Ocean in East Africa, Arabia, and western India.

Although politically decentralized, the Indian Ocean was bound together by frequent boat crossings to and from its different ports. Merchants who had grown up along the African coast had operations in Arabia or India, and much intermarriage among the residents of different coasts took place, contributing to a genuine mixing of cultures. Interior regions supplied goods to the coastal cities, but because so few outsiders visited them, we know much less about them.

The East African Coast

In January 1329, after leaving Mecca, Ibn Battuta sailed from the port of Aden to East Africa, most likely in a **dhow** (DOW). Among the earliest and most seaworthy vessels ever made, dhows served as the camels of the Indian Ocean trade. Because they had no deck, passengers sat and slept next to the ship's cargo. Traders frequently piloted their dhows along the coastline of East Africa, the Arabian peninsula, and India's west coast. Their expenses were low: dhows required little labor power because they harnessed the wind, and traders and their family members could staff their own boats.

dhow
Main vessel used in the Indian Ocean trade, made from teak planks laid edge to edge, fastened together with coconut fiber twine, and caulked to prevent leaking.

Everywhere Ibn Battuta traveled, he saw Indian, Persian, and Arabian ships and merchants. After leaving Aden, he sailed for fifteen days to reach the port city of Mogadishu, Somalia, which exported cotton textiles to Egypt and other destinations. Mogadishu's political structure resembled that of other African ports on the east and north coasts: headed by a sultan, the government maintained an army and administered justice through a network of qadis.

AP® THEMES
How did the spread of Islam throughout the Indian Ocean region reflect the expansion of trade networks?

The sultan spoke his native Somali in addition to a little Arabic. The farther Ibn Battuta traveled from the Islamic heartland, the fewer people he would find who knew Arabic. Still, he could always find an Arabic speaker because so many people from north Africa and the Arabian peninsula had settled on the east coast. Because Ibn Battuta's stay in Mogadishu was brief, he did not go inland, where he would have seen villages growing the strange, colorful foodstuffs he ate, fewer people of Arabian descent, and more non-Islamic religious practices.

Ibn Battuta proceeded to Kilwa (modern Kilwa Kivinye), a small island off the coast of modern Tanzania; there he saw *"a large city on the seacoast, most of whose inhabitants are Zinj, jet-black in colour. They have tattoo marks on their faces."** Ibn Battuta used the word *zinj*, meaning black, to refer to the indigenous peoples of

*From H. A. R. Gibb, *The Travels of Ibn Battuta* A.D. *1325–1354,* The Hakluyt Society, pp. 379–380. The Hakluyt Society was established in 1846 for the purpose of printing rare or unpublished Voyages and Travels. For further information, please see their website at: www.hakluyt.com.

The Dhows of the Indian Ocean Unlike most other boats, the dhows of the Indian Ocean were sewn and not nailed together. Boatmakers sewed planks of teak or coconut trees together with a cord and added a single sail. This boat design was so practical that it is still in use today. (LOOK Die Bildagentur der Fotografen GmbH/Alamy)

East Africa. The people he encountered may have already begun to speak the creole mixture that later came to be called Swahili (swah-HEE-lee), a Bantu language that incorporated many words from Arabic. (*Swahili* means "of the coast" in Arabic, and about one million people living in east Africa today identify themselves as Swahili.)

Ibn Battuta arrived at Kilwa during a period of prosperity. We know more about the history of Kilwa than about many other East African ports because of the survival of *The Chronicle of the Kings of Kilwa* in both Portuguese and Arabic versions. This work gives the name of individual rulers but not their dates. By matching the names of rulers in *The Chronicle* with Ibn Battuta's detailed account, historians have concluded that the Kilwa dynasty began in the 1200s. The kings of Kilwa were descended from Arabic-speaking settlers who came to the region from Yemen, further evidence of the ties linking the different societies on the Indian Ocean.

The sultan of Kilwa was a generous man, Ibn Battuta reports, who regularly gave gifts of slaves and ivory from elephant tusks, which he obtained in the interior: *"He used to engage frequently in expeditions to the land of the Zinj people, raiding them and taking booty."** These were Kilwa's main exports. Kilwa was located at the southernmost point where ships sailing with the trade winds landed on the coast. The dynasty that ruled Kilwa also controlled the small port of Sofala on the Zambezi

---

*From H. A. R. Gibb, *The Travels of Ibn Battuta* A.D. *1325–1354*, The Hakluyt Society, pp. 379–380. The Hakluyt Society was established in 1846 for the purpose of printing rare or unpublished Voyages and Travels. For further information, please see their website at: www.hakluyt.com.

River, some 800 miles (1300 km) to the south. Goods from the interior—primarily ivory, gold, resins, and slaves—traveled first to ocean ports, then to Kilwa, and from there to destinations overseas.

• **CONTEXT&CONNECTIONS** Like the other East African ports, Kilwa imported high-fired ceramics from China, glass from Persia, and textiles from China and India. •

Kilwa had an imposing palace built of stone, which was modeled on other Islamic palaces located across the Indian Ocean, with an octagonal swimming pool and more than one hundred rooms for visitors. The town's inhabitants lived in stone houses with indoor toilets, ate in kitchens equipped with Chinese porcelains, and wore imported silks and gold and silver ornaments. The town also had a mosque with beautiful columns decorated with Chinese bluish-green celadon bowls. Recent excavations at the nearby town of Shanga in Kenya have demonstrated that mosques in the region date back to the eighth century. All have the same floor plan, clear evidence that they were not designed by immigrants, as some early analysts thought, but by local people.

Kilwa was just one of about 400 settlements with stone (often coral) buildings along the east coast of Africa. One island near Kilwa, Songo Mnara, was occupied for about 150 years after Ibn Battuta's departure. The town's buildings are now a dirty gray, but made from bricks of coral, they were originally coated with a layer of gleaming white. The architectural details were carved from live *Porites*, or multifingered corals. One of the six mosques on the island contains a *mihrab*, a niche in the wall facing Mecca from which a teacher led prayers. Over the course of several renovations, it was gradually reoriented five or ten degrees closer to the direction of Mecca, evidence that the locals obtained more accurate compasses over the course of a century or so, most likely from China or from the Islamic world.

• **CONTEXT&CONNECTIONS** The Chinese discovered the *steel-needle compass* (Chapter 12) sometime between 850 and 1050; before that they had used magnetic lodestones to locate north. Chinese ships used the new navigation devices to travel farther to coastal ports in Southeast Asia and in India. From there, the new compasses traveled to the coast of East Africa, possibly with Chinese mariners or possibly with Muslim sailors who adopted Chinese compasses. •

Another small mosque on the beach at Songo Mnara contains an even more unusual element: a mihrab with a wall separating it from a larger prayer room. This may have been a separate mosque for women, who were kept apart from the man reciting the prayers.

• **CONTEXT&CONNECTIONS** Very few Islamic countries have had separate mosques for women; China is one of the few places with them. Almost everywhere else, women either stay home for prayers or pray in a separate area in the same mosque as men. •

Even if the beach mosque was not for women, other finds are prompting a rethinking of women's place in Swahili society. One prevailing theory, called the intimacy gradient, holds that the outer rooms of houses were masculine spaces, while the more enclosed, interior spaces at the back of the house were for women's more private activities, particularly childbirth and breastfeeding. But the front rooms of many houses on Songo Mnara contain beads (some of carnelian, a reddish mineral imported from India), an indication that women occupied those rooms, too. Ibn Battuta, so vocal in his criticism of the women of Mali, says nothing about the women he encountered in Kilwa and nearby, but that does not necessarily mean that women stayed in the back rooms. It is always risky, historians realize, to decide that something did not exist simply because a source fails to mention it.

Great Zimbabwe and Its Satellites, ca. 1275–1550

Although the interior of southern Africa supplied Kilwa and Songo Mnara with slaves, gold, and ivory, we know much less about the region because Ibn Battuta and other Muslim travelers never visited the interior. There, on the high plateau south of the Zambezi River, stood a state that reached its greatest extent in the early 1300s. Its center was the imposing archaeological site of **Great Zimbabwe** (see Map 11.1).

Great Zimbabwe
Large city in Zimbabwe surrounded by smaller outlying settlements, all distinguished by stone enclosures called "zimbabwe" in the local Shona language. The location of the largest stone structure built in sub-Saharan Africa before 1500.

Like other speakers of Bantu languages in sub-Saharan Africa, the people living on the Zimbabwe plateau cultivated sorghum with iron tools. Before 1000, most lived in small villages of houses made from wood beams. Sometime around 1000, some villagers became wealthy enough to build stone enclosures for themselves. By the thirteenth and fourteenth centuries, the population had reached ten thousand, and they built three hundred small stone enclosures over a large area on the plateau. The word for these enclosures in the local Shona language—*zimbabwe*, meaning "venerated houses"—is the source for the name of the modern nation of Zimbabwe where they are located.

The Elliptical Building of Great Zimbabwe is the largest single stone structure in sub-Saharan Africa built before 1500. One estimate holds that four hundred laborers could have built the wall of this building during the slack period of the agricultural season over the course of four years.

Since the people who lived there did not keep written records, archaeological finds provide our only information about local religion. Nothing points to Islamic beliefs, which were widespread on the coast. On the northern edge of the site, the Eastern Enclosure held six stylized birds carved from soapstone, which may depict ancestors or deities. The Zimbabwe people also made and probably worshiped phalluses and female torsos with breasts in the hope of increasing the number of children. (See the feature "Visual Evidence in Primary Sources: The Ruins of Great Zimbabwe.")

When excavated, the Great Zimbabwe site contained a hoard that one archaeologist has called "a cache of the most extraordinary variegated and abundant indigenous and imported objects ever discovered.... in the interior of south-central Africa." The hoard included pieces of broken, green, Chinese high-fired celadon ceramic pots and colorful Persian earthenware plates with script on them. Clearly the site's residents traded with the coastal towns and were part of existing trade networks.

Kilwa was most prosperous at exactly the same time that Great Zimbabwe was—in the thirteenth and fourteenth centuries when Ibn Battuta visited the city. When the Portuguese arrived on the East African coast after 1498, both Kilwa and the Great Zimbabwe site had already declined dramatically, but we do not know why.

The Delhi Sultanate and the Hindu Kingdoms of Southern India

Delhi sultanate
(1206–1526) Islamic state led by former mamluk slaves originally from Afghanistan, who governed north India from their capital at Delhi. At their height, in the early 1300s, they controlled nearly all of the Indian subcontinent.

When Ibn Battuta sailed away from Kilwa, he embarked on a fifteen-year journey along the trade routes linking Africa with India and China. In Central Asia, he learned that a Muslim leader in India, Muhammad bin Tughluq (r. 1324–1351), ruler of the powerful **Delhi sultanate** (1210–1526), was deliberately staffing his government with foreign-born Muslims. Sensing a chance of employment, Ibn Battuta headed for Delhi.

• **CONTEXT&CONNECTIONS** The Delhi sultanate, like the Mamluk empire of Egypt and Syria, was founded by Turkish military slaves from Central Asia (see Map 11.2). It was not the first Islamic dynasty in South Asia. In the eighth century, conquering caliphate armies had established Islamic states in the Sind region of modern Pakistan, but no Muslim ruler had yet managed to conquer the lands south of Delhi. •

In 1210, a group of mamluks overthrew the reigning sultan, who was from Afghanistan, and conquered large sections of northern India, considerably expanding the territory under Muslim control. Five different dynasties ruled between 1210 and 1524, and since the capital was always at Delhi, these dynasties are collectively known as the Delhi sultanate. Delhi remained the capital of many later northern Indian dynasties and is India's capital today. Although the Delhi Sultanates sometimes controlled almost all of the subcontinent, southern India remained under the control of the Cholas and other regional dynasties (see Chapter 8).

Map 11.2 The Delhi Sultanate Starting in 1210, a Muslim dynasty based in Delhi gained control of northern India and established its capital in Delhi, a city from which a total of five different Muslim dynasties governed. Collectively known as the Delhi sultanate, none of these dynasties conquered the southernmost tip of the subcontinent, where Hindu dynasties like the Cholas ruled.

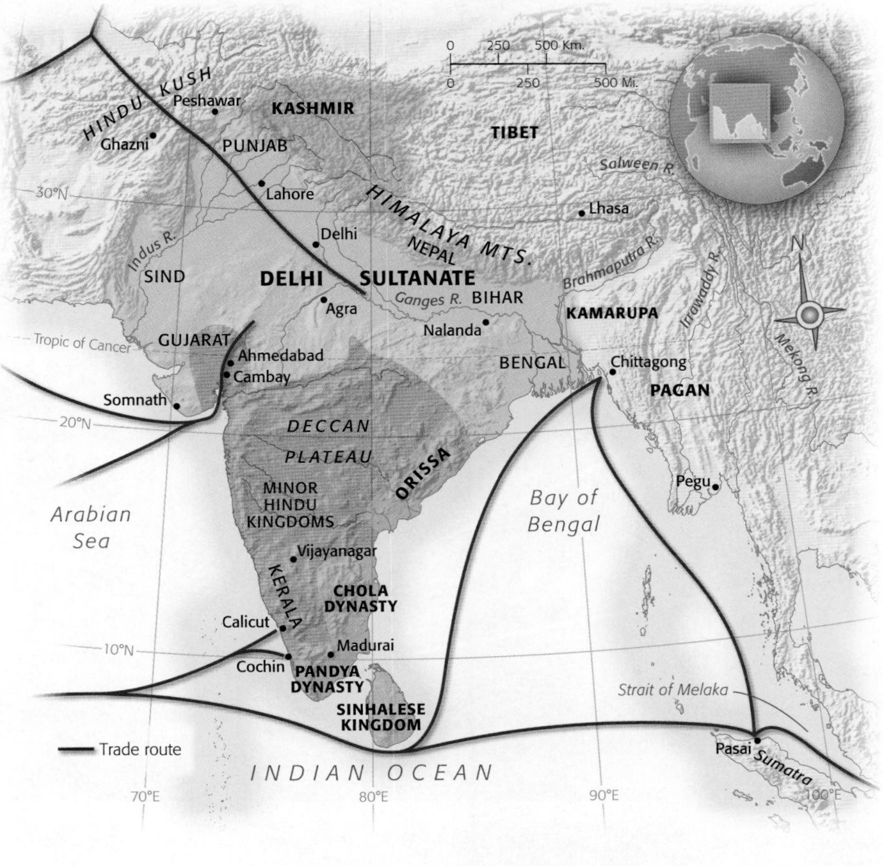

The Ruins of Great Zimbabwe

Located near Masvingo, Zimbabwe, the Great Zimbabwe site contains several large ruins and many smaller stone structures whose original purpose is undocumented and therefore still not well understood. The ruins, covering almost 1,800 acres (7.2 sq km), fall into three groups: the Hill Complex, the Valley Complex, and the Great Enclosure. The site was first settled before 1000, when the first stone structures were built, and continued to grow through the 1300s. Little evidence of cereal agriculture survives, indicating that the city's population depended largely on cattle for their food supply.

The Hill Complex, a group of stone buildings forming a ritual space, stood above a granite cliff 330 feet (100 m) long and 100 feet (30 m) high on the northern edge of the site.

In the Valley Complex, Enclosure 12 contained the largest hoard found on the site: over 220 pounds (100 kg) of iron hoes, 44 pounds (20 kg) of iron for wire, warthog and elephant tusks, thousands of Indian beads, and broken ceramic vessels from China and Iran.

With three entrances, the Great Enclosure contains the Elliptical Building, the Conical Tower, and mud and thatch huts where individual families lived.

The Elliptical Building has an outer wall that runs 800 feet (250 m) long and contains 182,000 cubic feet (5,150 cubic m) of stone. ***Which explanation—Garlake's or Huffman's—of this building's purpose is more plausible? Explain your reasoning.***

Georg Gerster/Science Source

Like other Bantu peoples, the Zimbabwe people living at the site knew how to work iron. Archaeologists have found nodules of iron ore from mines and alluvial gold collected from riverbeds. The site also contained a workshop where metalsmiths heated copper ingots in crucibles to make wire.

The Great Enclosure holds two large structures: the Elliptical Building and the solid Conical Tower inside it. The outer wall of the Elliptical Building is made of evenly cut granite blocks, fitted together without mortar, that are elegantly trimmed with an intricate (V-shaped) design on the top. What was the purpose of these two buildings? Two analysts, Peter S. Garlake and Thomas N. Huffman, propose radically different answers.

Garlake bases his analysis on close examination of the construction techniques used to make the different types of walls and the location of different artifacts. The sheer size of the Elliptical Building suggests to him that it was the palace of the ruler. Its walls, he contends, stood too high to be mere guard walls: they made a statement about the ruler's power to all his subjects.

Huffman, in contrast, examines the settlements of the Shona-speaking peoples who live near the site today. Since many of their houses are divided into areas for men to work and women to work, he wonders whether this might not be true of Great Zimbabwe as well. The one hundred smaller soapstone carvings of phalluses and female torsos with breasts found in the Elliptical Building resemble some figurines used in modern schools to teach adolescent girls about family life. The high walls of the Elliptical Building, Huffman believes, kept outsiders from observing the activities at a girls' initiation school.

Sources: P. S. Garlake, *Great Zimbabwe* (New York: Stein and Day, 1973); Thomas N. Huffman, "Where You Are the Girls Gather to Play: The Great Enclosure at Great Zimbabwe," in *Frontiers: Southern African Archaeology Today*, ed. M. Hall et al., *Cambridge Monographs in African Archaeology* 10 (Oxford: B. A. R., 1984), pp. 252–265.

The Conical Tower—possibly a symbolic granary—is a completely solid stone structure with an outer wall over 30 feet (9 m) high.

Eight bird statues like this, averaging 16 inches (40 cm) tall, were found at the site; each was placed on a pillar 3 feet (90 cm) tall. This bird, along with five others, was originally in the Eastern Enclosure, suggesting that it was a ritual center, while the other two stood alone in different locations. The birds are so striking that a stylized representation has appeared on every version of the national flag since 1968, even before Zimbabwe became independent in 1980.

Denny Allen/Gallo Images/Alamy

The birds resemble fish eagles, a common raptor in the region, but they have human toes and lips. Local people view all birds as messengers, and the eagles' size makes them suitable couriers for the most powerful men. ***Citing information from modern informants, Huffman proposes that the birds represent royal ancestors who can fly between gods and man. Do you find his reasoning compelling? Why or why not?***

Massimo Borchi/Latitude/Corbis

Qutb Minar One of Delhi's most recognizable landmarks, Qutb Minar is a high tower with inscriptions from the Quran written on the face of red and tan sandstone, measuring 237.8 feet (72.5 m) tall. Even before the founding of the first Delhi sultanate, a ruler based in Afghanistan initiated its construction, and the first Delhi sultan continued it. To the right stands a 23-foot (7 m) iron pillar, originally from the courtyard of a Jain temple, that dates to at least the 300s, if not earlier. As was common practice, the builders used pieces of destroyed Hindu and Jain temples to build both the tower and the nearby mosque.

● **CONTEXT&CONNECTIONS** In addition to mamluk slaves, the Delhi sultans imported another important institution from the Islamic world: *iqta grants* (Chapter 9), which had spread throughout the former Abbasid realm. Even in the late 1100s, the Afghani sultan who controlled Delhi asked the Abbasid caliphs to sign iqta grants giving him the right to tax and to govern the lands he had conquered. ●

In this region, the people in the government believed that the most qualified person, even if not related to the sultan, should become sultan. The first mamluk to seize power killed the reigning king and then named himself sultan in 1210. Every time the sultan died, a free-for-all broke out until a victor emerged as the new sultan. The Delhi sultanate thus witnessed many internal conflicts.

Fueled by a desire for plunder, the armies of Muhammad bin Tughluq, the son of a Turkish slave and an Indian woman, succeeded in conquering almost all of India. In a departure from the practices of earlier rulers, Muhammad bin Tughluq decided to hire only foreigners to administer his empire. His goal was to build up an aristocracy born outside of India who would be loyal to him should any Indian

Muslims try to overthrow him. He named Ibn Battuta to be the highest qadi in Delhi, a very high-ranking position, even though Ibn Battuta did not speak Persian, the language of the government. In fact, Ibn Battuta kept so busy attending court ceremonials and hunting expeditions that he heard no legal cases.

The Delhi sultanate granted Hindus the status of *dhimmi* ("protected subjects") even though they worshiped multiple gods. Hindus were obliged to pay the *jizya* tax, a head tax on non-Muslims, and they were not allowed to fight in the all-Muslim army. Their payment of taxes brought them some unusual rights: at least in some periods the Delhi sultanate repaired Hindu temples that had been damaged by Muslim troops in battle. They did not repair the temples of foreigners living in India, who did not pay the *jizya* tax. Muhammad bin Tughluq was infamous among Muslims for his support of Hinduism, and his successors did not grant Hindus all the benefits that he did.

Throughout Muhammad bin Tughluq's reign, south India remained largely Hindu. Hindu rulers gained control of urban centers in the south and established temple-centered kingdoms like that of the Cholas, who ruled until 1279 (see Chapter 8). The most important Hindu empire was based at **Vijayanagar** (veej-eye-NUH-guh-ru) (see Map 11.2). The Vijayanagar rulers (ca. 1336–1614) patronized Sanskrit learning and Hindu temples while creating a powerful army that enabled them to rule for more than two centuries.

Vijayanagar
(ca. 1336–1614) "City of victory" in Sanskrit. Important Hindu empire that was able to rule in central India for more than two centuries.

Ibn Battuta remained in Delhi for seven years before the sultan named him his emissary to China. When he departed in August 1341, he was traveling with fifteen Chinese envoys, over two hundred slaves, one hundred horses, and various lavish gifts of textiles, dishes, and weapons—all intended for the Mongol rulers of China.

As Ibn Battuta made his way down the west coast of India, he visited towns that resembled the ports on the African side of the Indian Ocean. A sultan governed each port, where qadis administered justice, and each town had a bazaar and a mosque. Ibn Battuta arrived in Calicut at the head of a large embassy, carrying Muhammad bin Tughluq's gifts for the ruler of China and accompanied by several concubines, one pregnant with Ibn Battuta's child. At the time of his visit, thirteen Chinese-built vessels were in the port. *"On the sea of China,"* Ibn Battuta comments, *"traveling is done in Chinese ships only."** These Chinese ships were enormous, over 100 feet (30 m) long and carrying six hundred sailors and four hundred armed men. Ibn Battuta much preferred the Chinese-built ships with their private cabins to open dhows.

On the day Ibn Battuta sailed, he discovered that the best staterooms, those with lavatories, were taken by Chinese merchants. He indignantly transferred to a smaller vessel, where he could have a room big enough for him to stay with his female companions, *"for it is my habit,"* he said, *"never to travel without them."** His traveling companions remained on the larger vessel.

A violent storm broke out that night, and the captains of the two ships removed their vessels from the shallow harbor to the safety of the sea. The smaller boat survived, but the big ship was totally destroyed. Ibn Battuta stood horror-struck on the beach, watching floating corpses whose faces he recognized. Having utterly failed to protect the envoys he accompanied, Ibn Battuta fled. Eight years more in India, the Maldive Islands, and China passed before he returned home to Morocco.

---

*From H. A. R. Gibb, *The Travels of Ibn Battuta* A.D. *1325–1354*, The Hakluyt Society, pp. 813–814. The Hakluyt Society was established in 1846 for the purpose of printing rare or unpublished Voyages and Travels. For further information, please see their website at: www.hakluyt.com.

Africa's Many Ties to the Rest of the World

As Ibn Battuta discovered, many roads to Mecca went through Africa. His account of his travels is one of the most important sources for sub-Saharan African history. With no indigenous written sources before 1800, historians of Africa have exercised great ingenuity in reconstructing the past by drawing on oral histories (some transmitted over the centuries by griots), archaeology, glottochronology, and upstreaming.

Africa's path to complex society did not follow the agricultural surplus and river valley pattern of Mesopotamia, Egypt, India, or China (see Chapters 2–4). Residents of the Middle Niger Valley built huge urban complexes financed by trading dried fish, fish oil, and rice for iron; later they diversified and traded for copper and salt as well. Whereas the other peoples of Eurasia had worked bronze before iron, and the peoples of the Americas never worked iron at all (see Chapter 5), iron was the first metal that Africans smelted, sometime around 600 B.C.E. As elsewhere in Africa, the peoples of the Middle Niger cultivated wet rice but never shifted to full-time agriculture.

By Ibn Battuta's time, kingdoms like Mali were profitably engaged in the trans-Sahara trade in slaves and gold. Ibn Battuta's travels along this and other existing trade routes brought him to much of the recently Islamicized world of the 1300s: to the ports of northern and eastern Africa and around the Indian Ocean to the Delhi sultanate, as well as across the Sahara. He encountered Islamic practices everywhere he went: rulers and the well-off received him generously; students learned to recite the Quran in Arabic; Friday prayers were conducted in mosques; and he could always find companions, often hajj pilgrims or merchants, to accompany him on another leg of his journey. With the fall of Baghdad to the Mongols in 1258 (see Chapter 14), the center of the Islamic world shifted to Cairo, where the Mamluks founded a new caliphate in 1261 and welcomed Muslim students, teachers, and artists. At the second most important center in the Mamluk empire, Damascus, Ibn Battuta witnessed an outbreak of plague, which traveled across Eurasia along pathways opened by the Mongols and kept open by their successor states (see Chapter 14).

Dependent as he was on Muslims to give him alms, Ibn Battuta never ventured beyond the realm of Islam. He did not visit the inland stone city of Great Zimbabwe, travel south of the islands of Kilwa and Songo Mnara, Tanzania, on the East African coast, or travel to southern Africa. These places lay beyond the two trade networks that he traced in his travels through Africa: the

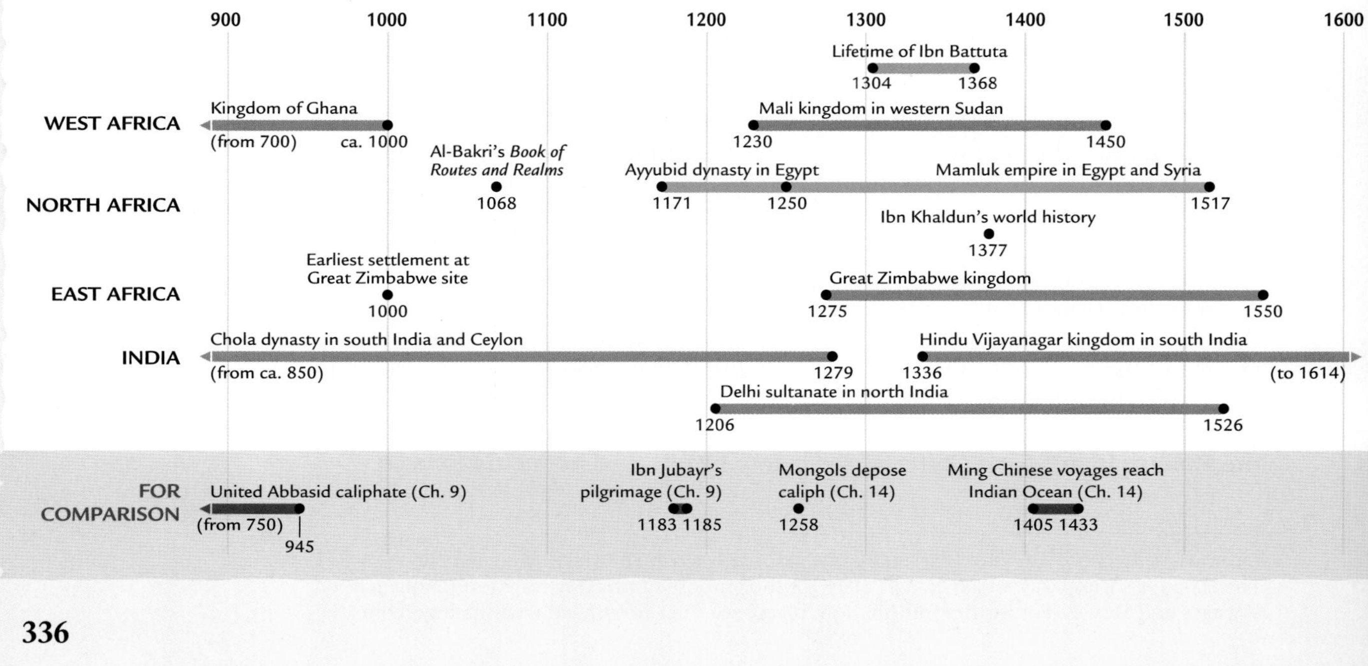

trans-Saharan caravan trade network and the Indian Ocean trade network. In the Sahara he found that he could trade salt, glass trinkets, and spices to pay for meals and his lodging; on the Indian Ocean, he sailed in dhows, the seagoing counterpart to the camels crossing the Sahara. Both networks provided channels for Africa's exports of slaves and gold to reach Europe and the Islamic world.

Ibn Battuta's account of his travels shows that, in the centuries before Columbus's voyages, just as the Europeans sailed to Iceland, Greenland, and the Americas and so learned about a larger world (see Chapter 10), so too did Muslim geographers document more places in Afro-Eurasia. From Burhan al-Din the Lame in Cairo, Ibn Battuta learned of a Sufi network extending all the way to China, the farthest point he traveled in his lifetime. As we will see in the next chapter, during these same centuries, the Chinese were also learning about Africa and Europe.

Key Terms

Ibn Battuta (308)
Sahel (309)
Bantu (309)
oral histories (311)
griot/griotte (311)
lineage (312)
Mali (312)
Ghana (313)
Middle Niger Valley (313)
sultan (315)
Ibn Khaldun (317)
trans-Saharan caravan trade network (318)
Mamluk empire (322)
qadi (323)
sharia (323)
mamluk (324)
Sufi (325)
Indian Ocean trade network (327)
dhow (327)
Great Zimbabwe (330)
Delhi sultanate (335)
Vijayanagar (335)

For Further Reference

Childs, S. Terry, and David Killick. "Indigenous African Metallurgy: Nature and Culture." *Annual Reviews Anthropology* 1993 (22): 317–337.

Clarence-Smith, William Gervase. *Islam and the Abolition of Slavery*. London: Hurst and Company, 2006.

Dunn, Ross. *The Adventures of Ibn Battuta: A Muslim Traveler of the 14th Century*. Berkeley: University of California Press, 2012.

Garlake, P. S. *Great Zimbabwe*. New York: Stein and Day, 1973.

Hale, Thomas A. *Griots and Griottes: Masters of Words and Music*. Bloomington: Indiana University Press, 2007.

Huffman, Thomas N. "Where You Are the Girls Gather to Play: The Great Enclosure at Great Zimbabwe." In *Frontiers: Southern African Archaeology Today*, ed. M. Hall et al. *Cambridge Monographs in African Archaeology* 10. Oxford, England: B. A. R., 1984, pp. 252–265.

Irwin, Robert. *Mamluks and Crusaders: Men of the Sword and Men of the Pen*. Burlington, Vt.: Variorum, 2010.

Isichei, Elizabeth. *A History of African Societies to 1870*. Cambridge, England: Cambridge University Press, 1997.

Jackson, David. *The Delhi Sultanate: A Political and Military History*. New York: Cambridge University Press, 1999.

Lapidus, Ira M. *Muslim Cities in the Later Middle Ages*. Cambridge, Mass.: Harvard University Press, 1967.

Letzvion, Nehemia, and Randall L. Pouwels, eds. *The History of Islam in Africa*. Athens: Ohio University Press, 2000.

McIntosh, Roderick J. *Ancient Middle Niger: Urbanism and the Self-Organizing Landscape*. New York: Cambridge University Press, 2005.

Newbury, David. "Contradictions at the Heart of the Canon: Jan Vansina and the Debate over Oral Historiography in Africa, 1960-1985." *History in Africa* 34 (2007): 213–254.

Patel, Samir S. "Stone Towns of the African Coast." *Archaeology* (January-February 2014): 42–49.

Schoenbrun, David Lee. *A Green Place, A Good Place: Agrarian Change, Gender, and Social Identity in the Great Lakes Region to the 15th Century*. Portsmouth, N.H.: Heineman, 1998.

Siddiqi, Iqtidar Husain. *Composite Culture Under the Sultanate of Delhi*. New Delhi: Primus Books, 2013.

Vansina, J. "New Linguistic Evidence and 'The Bantu Expansion.'" *Journal of African History* 36 (1995): 173–195.

Vansina, J. *Paths in the Rainforest: Towards a History of Political Tradition in Equatorial Africa*. Madison: University of Wisconsin Press, 1990.

AP® Review Questions for Chapter 11

Multiple-Choice Questions

QUESTIONS 1–3 REFER TO THE FOLLOWING PASSAGE.

The pilots of Oman pass by the channel of Berbera to reach the island of Kanbalu, which is in the Zanj sea. It has a mixed population of Muslims and Zanj idolaters. . . . The aforesaid Kanabalu is the farthest point of their voyages on the Zanj sea, and the land of Sofala. . . . The people of Siraf (a Persian port) also make this voyage. . . . The land of Zanj produces wild leopard skins. The people wear them as clothes, or export them to Muslim countries. . . . The sea of Zanj and that of Abyssinia (Ethiopia) lie on the right of the sea of India, and join up. They also export tortoise-shell for making combs, for which ivory is likewise used. . . . They have settled in that area, which stretches as far as Sofala, which is the farthest limit of land and the end of the voyages made from Oman and Siraf on the sea of Zanj.

—*Meadows of Gold*, Abu'l-hasan Ali al-Mas'udi, a Muslim writer, 943 C.E.

1. Which of the following can be justified from the passage above?
   (A) East Africa remained relatively isolated well into the tenth century.
   (B) Islam was present in East Africa by at least the tenth century.
   (C) Life in the Swahili states continued to center around traditional, regional religions.
   (D) The city-states of East Africa were highly centralized.

2. The author's knowledge of East Africa was most likely the result of
   (A) classical Greek and Roman texts.
   (B) trade on the Silk Routes.
   (C) East Africa participating in the Indian Ocean trade.
   (D) contacts made by the trans-Saharan trade in West Africa.

3. The interactions mentioned in the passage were caused by which of the following?
   (A) The expansion of trading networks in the Postclassical era
   (B) The increase in the frequency and intensity of warfare in the region
   (C) The spread of pathogens across multiple regions
   (D) The limited interaction of regional trade circuits

QUESTIONS 4–7 REFER TO THE FOLLOWING MAP.

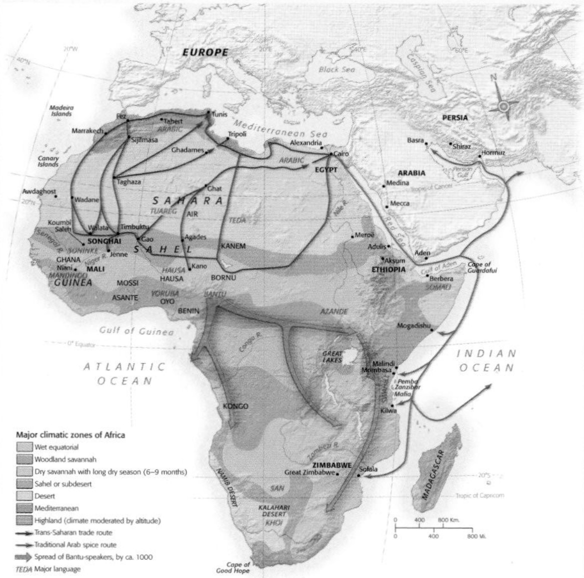

4. Which of the following statements is supported by the map?
   (A) Africa remained an isolated continent up to 1500 C.E.
   (B) North Africa had significant commercial activity while East Africa remained isolated.
   (C) Africa had significant interactions in several trade networks.
   (D) West Africa was more prosperous than East Africa.

5. Which of the following inferences can be made using the map?
   (A) Christianity dominated Africa in the Post-classical era.
   (B) There were significant Chinese migrations to East Africa.
   (C) The adoption of Arabic words by Bantu speakers created a new language.
   (D) European slaves were imported to North African kingdoms.

6. Which region played a limited or supporting role in interregional trade in Africa?
   (A) Central Africa
   (B) East Africa
   (C) West Africa
   (D) North Africa

7. The West African kingdoms of Mali and Songhai relied on which of the following commodities?
   (A) Silk and silver
   (B) Sugar and nutmeg
   (C) Gold and salt
   (D) Furs and textiles

QUESTIONS 8–10 REFER TO THE FOLLOWING PASSAGE.

The entire population of the city joined in the exodus, male and female, small and large; the Jews went out with their book of the Law and the Christians with their Gospel, their women and children with them...the whole concourse of them in tears and humble supplications, imploring the favour of God through His Books and His Prophets.

—Ibn Battuta, *The Travels of Ibn Battuta*, Damascus, 1348

8. The passage above most directly reflects which of the following characteristics of the Postclassical era?
   (A) There was continued diffusion of crops and pathogens, including epidemic diseases like the bubonic plague, throughout the Eastern Hemisphere along the trade routes.
   (B) Increased cross-cultural interactions resulted in the diffusion of literary, artistic, and cultural traditions, as well as scientific and technological innovations.
   (C) Some migrations and commercial contacts led to the diffusion of languages throughout a new region.
   (D) The expansion and intensification of long-distance trade routes often depended on environmental knowledge and technological adaptations to it.

9. The passage above reveals that by 1348
   (A) the city of Damascus had been completely converted to Islam.
   (B) Christianity remained the dominant religion in Syria.
   (C) public displays of religion were forbidden.
   (D) Damascus still had a religiously diverse population.

10. Which of the following is a valid inference based on this passage?
   (A) Islam forced conversions in regions and cities it conquered.
   (B) The crusaders kept the population of Damascus completely Christian.
   (C) Islam was tolerant of other religions.
   (D) Judaism remained the dominant religion in the eastern Mediterranean region.

Short-Answer Questions

Each of them is inside a costume made of feathers resembling the green woodpecker on which is a wooden head with a red beak.... They stand before the Sultan in this laughable get-up and recite their poems.... They say to the Sultan: "This platform, formerly such and such a king sat on it and performed noble actions, and so and so did such and such; do you do noble acts which will be recounted after you?"

—Ibn Battuta, Muslim traveler and scholar, on the Kingdom of Mali

1. Use the passage above to answer parts A, B, and C.
   A. What is the tone of the author in this passage, and what might account for it?
   B. Briefly explain ONE example, not described in the passage above, of diversity in the Islamic world.
   C. Briefly explain the circumstances that led to the spread of Islam in West Africa.

2. Answer parts A, B, and C.
   A. Briefly explain the relationship between the caliph and the sultan of Delhi.
   B. Briefly explain how Islam adapted its practices for the Hindu population in India.
   C. Compare the Delhi sultanate's use of religion with that of the Chola emperors.

12 China's Commercial Revolution, ca. 900–1276

Li Qingzhao

In 1127, **Li Qingzhao** (LEE CHING-jow) (ca. 1084–ca. 1151) and her husband Zhao Mingcheng (JOW MING-chung) (1081–1129), a low-ranking Chinese official, abandoned their home in Shandong (SHAN-dong) province and joined half a million refugees fleeing to the south. After Zhao's death only two years later, Li recorded her memoir, which depicts the long-term economic changes of the Song (soong) dynasty (960–1276), when China's prosperity made it the world's most advanced economy, and the short-term consequences of military defeat, when the Song emperors were forced to surrender all of north China to a non-Chinese dynasty named the Jin (GIN) (1115–1234). As Li explains, she and Zhao fled from their home in north China and traveled 500 miles (800 km) to the Yangzi River:

In 1126, the first year of the Jingkang [JEENG-kong] Reign, my husband was governing Zichuan [DZE-chwan; in Shandong province] when we heard that the Jin Tartars were moving against the capital. He was in a daze, realizing that all those full trunks and overflowing chests, which he regarded so lovingly and mournfully, would surely soon be his possessions no longer. . . . Since we could not take the overabundance of our possessions with us, we first gave up the bulky printed volumes, the albums of paintings, and the most cumbersome of the vessels. Thus we reduced the size of the collection several times, and still we had fifteen cartloads of books. When we reached Donghai

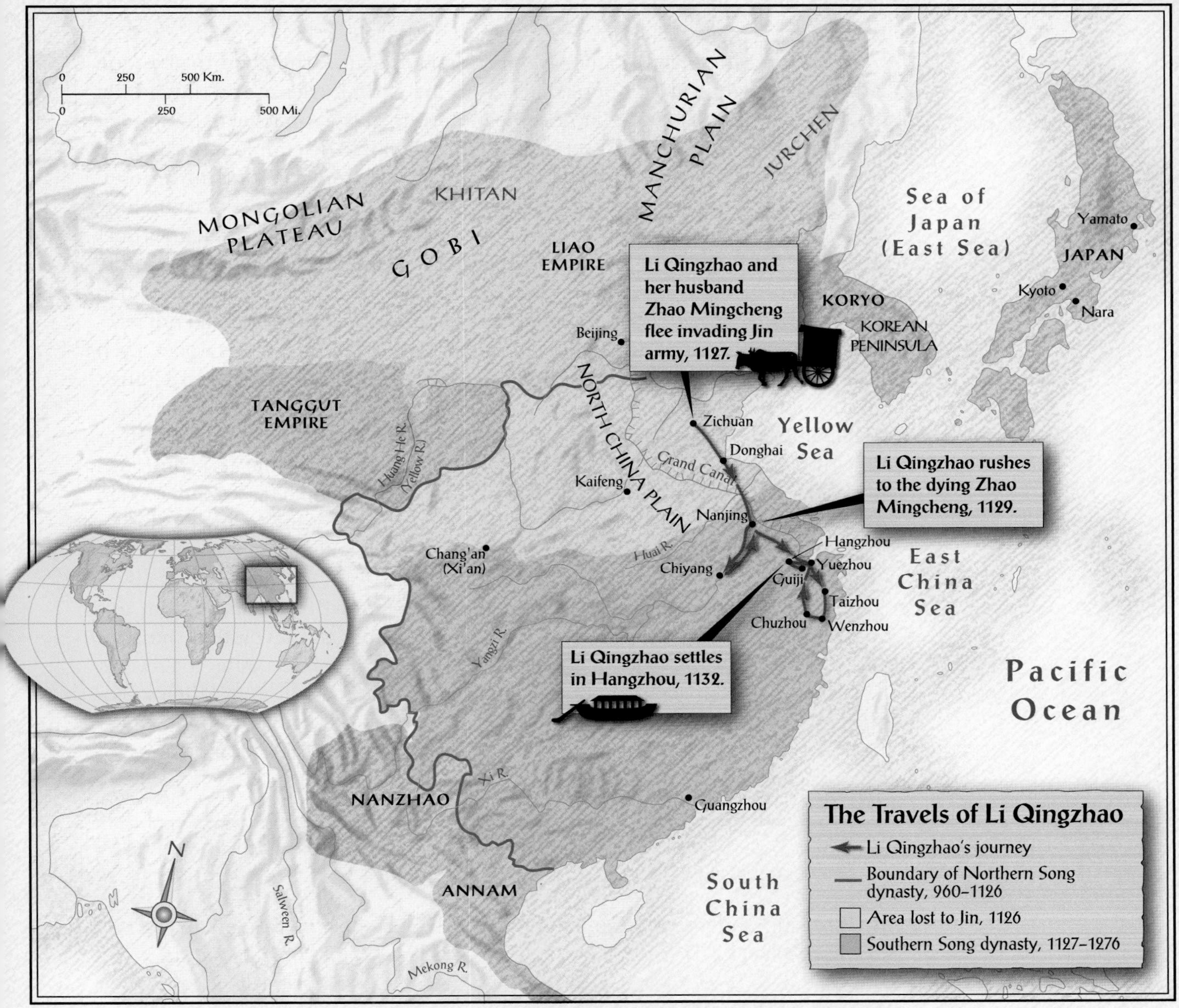

[DONG-high; Jiangsu], it took a string of boats to ferry them all across the Huai, and again across the Yangzi River to Jiankang [JI-AHN-kong; modern Nanjing, Jiangsu].*

*Reprinted by permission of the publisher from *Remembrances: The Experience of the Past in Classical Chinese Literature* by Stephen Owen, p. 90, Cambridge, Mass.: Harvard University Press, Copyright © 1986 by the President and Fellows of Harvard College.

Li Qingzhao
(ca. 1084–ca. 1151) Famous woman poet of the Song dynasty who wrote a first-person memoir about her marriage to Zhao Mingcheng.

After they reached Nanjing (NAHN-jeeng), Li explains, they had to abandon their last fifteen carts of books. Li was in her early forties at the time of her flight. She and her husband Zhao had been born into the top level of Song society, and their fathers had both served as high officials. The couple went by boat to south China, where they hoped they would be safe from the invading armies.

Li Qingzhao's memoir permits a glimpse of Chinese life at a time of wrenching political chaos. Seldom has the world seen such a mass panic as when the Jin armies defeated the Northern Song dynasty. While half a million other people made the same trip south as Li Qingzhao, her account stands out. For one thing, a woman wrote it. Highly educated in an age when the vast majority of women could not read, Li Qingzhao was the only woman of her time to achieve lasting fame as a poet. Even though only fifty of her poems survive today, many people consider her China's greatest woman poet, and she remains some people's favorite, male or female.

The fall of the Northern Song intensified a long-term migration from north to south China that had started centuries before Li Qingzhao's lifetime and continued centuries after it. Starting around 750, farmers realized they could grow more food in south China than in north China. In addition, during the years following the An Lushan rebellion of 755–763 (see Chapter 8), north China suffered continuous political instability that pushed people to migrate south.

These long-term migrations resulted in economic growth so dramatic that this period is called China's "commercial revolution." Before the revolution, most of China's farmers grew the food they ate and bought little at markets. After the revolution, farmers and craftsmen produced full-time for the market, and China's economic growth affected its neighbors in Korea, Japan, and Vietnam as well. Advances in technology and navigation contributed significantly to Chinese knowledge of foreign peoples across Afro-Eurasia.

KEY CONCEPT QUESTIONS

- What caused the Song to reconstitute its dynasty in the south? **(Key Concept 3.2)**
- What innovations contributed to the Chinese commercial revolution? **(Key Concept 3.1)**
- How did the commercial revolution influence the development of social structures in China? **(Key Concept 3.3)**
- To what degree did Japan, Korea, and Vietnam synthesize Chinese culture? **(Key Concept 3.2)**

The Five Dynasties Period and the Song Dynasty, 907–1276

After the Tang dynasty (618–907), permanently weakened by the An Lushan rebellion of 755, came to an end (see Chapter 8), China broke apart until 960, when the founder of the Song dynasty (960–1276) reunited the empire. The dramatic rise and fall of Chinese dynasties sometimes left the political structure basically unchanged, and this happened during the transition from the Tang dynasty to the Song. The new Song emperor presided over the central government. Almost all government officials were recruited by means of the civil service examinations, making the Song the world's first genuine bureaucracy. Despite the loss of north China to the Jin, Song officials successfully managed the transfer of the central government to a new capital in the south, where they presided over two centuries of unprecedented economic growth.

The Rise of the Northern Song Dynasty, 960–1126

The fifty-three years between the Tang and Song Dynasties is known as the Five Dynasties period (907–960) because during this time China was ruled by different regional governments, of which five were most important. The Five Dynasties, in turn, came to an end when a powerful general overthrew a boy ruler of one of the regions and founded the **Song dynasty** in 960. By 976, he had united both north and south China and made his capital in Kaifeng (KAI-fuhng), which, like China's earlier capitals, was in the Yellow River Valley.

Song dynasty
(960–1276) Dynasty that ruled a united China from the northern capital of Kaifeng from 960–1126 and only the southern half of the empire from 1127–1276.

The Song founder kept in place the old political structure, with the emperor at the top of a central bureaucracy that oversaw local government, but with one major difference. After unifying the empire in 976, the emperor summoned his most important generals and explained that the Tang dynasty had fallen apart because the regional governors, many of them also generals, exercised too much power. His generals agreed to retire, setting an important precedent. The Song initiated a period of greater civilian rule, with genuine power remaining in the hands of bureaucrats, not generals.

The Song government in the capital referred all matters of state to the same six ministries as existed in the Tang: Revenue, Civil Appointments, Rites, Works, Punishments, and War. The heads of these six ministries all reported to the grand councilor, the highest official in the government, who was named to office by the emperor. If the emperor chose, he could, like the Song founder, be active in government matters.

AP® THEMES
What changes to Chinese administration and bureaucracy did Song rulers introduce?

The largest administrative districts during the Tang had been the prefectures. During the Song dynasty officials grouped 220 such prefectures into more than twenty larger units called circuits. Each prefecture in a circuit was further divided into subprefectures headed by a magistrate, who was in charge of collecting taxes and implementing justice. Aided by two or three subordinate officials and a clerical staff, the magistrate depended on powerful local families to help him govern. At every level of the bureaucracy, officials were required to carry out the directives of the central government.

The Collapse of the Northern Song, 1126–1127

The Song dynasty faced a problem common to earlier dynasties: keeping peace with the nomads to the north, in this case the Kitan (KEE-tan), a nomadic people living in modern-day Mongolia. To counter this threat, the Song formed an alliance with the Jurchen (JER-chen), a forest-dwelling, fishing people based in Manchuria who proved to be skilled horsemen. They spoke Jurchen, an Altaic language similar in structure to Japanese. Originally a subject people of the Kitan, the Jurchen declared their independence by founding their own dynasty, the **Jin dynasty** ("gold" in Chinese), in 1115. The Song-Jurchen forces defeated the Kitan in 1125, yet as soon as victory was certain, the Jurchen leader ordered his troops to attack the Song. The Jurchen army, with its superior horses, defeated the Song handily and conquered Kaifeng.

Jin dynasty
(1115–1234) Dynasty of the Jurchen people of Manchuria that ruled north China from 1127–1234, when the Mongols defeated their armies.

To conquer the huge walled cities of north China like Kaifeng, the Jurchen had to use weapons fueled by **gunpowder**, a Chinese invention. Initially, the Chinese used gunpowder primarily for fireworks, but sometime around 900 they realized that they could use it as a weapon.

gunpowder
Mixture of potassium nitrate, sulfur, and charcoal used by the Chinese for fireworks and explosive weapons.

Chinese soldiers employed gunpowder in both simple and complex ways. In the most basic use, archers tied small bags of gunpowder onto their arrows, which then detonated on impact. In a technologically more complex use, at the siege of Kaifeng the Jurchen used the flame-thrower, which emitted a continuous stream of fire. They also built siege towers, taller than the city's walls, from which they could shoot incendiary bombs made of bamboo shells containing gunpowder and fragments of porcelain. Unable to devise an effective defense against this horrific new weapon, the residents of Kaifeng surrendered in January 1127.

The loss of the capital marked the end of the Northern Song dynasty (960–1126) and the beginning of the Southern Song dynasty (1127–1276). When the Jurchen captured Kaifeng, they took two emperors prisoner. One, Huizong (HWAY-dzong), the most artistically talented of all China's emperors, had reigned from 1101 to 1125 and then abdicated in favor of his eldest son. His Jurchen captors gave Huizong the humiliating title *Marquis of Muddled Virtue*, and his son, *Doubly Muddled Marquis*.

Despite their success, Jurchen armies could not conquer the region south of the Huai River. One of Huizong's ten living sons managed to escape from Kaifeng and was named emperor in May of 1127. Both his father and his brother would die in captivity, making him the first emperor of the Southern Song dynasty.

The Emperor as Painter Emperor Huizong (r. 1101–1125) is famous for his bird-and-flower paintings and his distinctive calligraphy, but recently art historians have carefully analyzed the brushstrokes used to depict bird feathers in several paintings labeled "imperially brushed" and have discovered that they were made by different artists, probably those in the imperial workshop. They argue that Huizong's idiosyncratic calligraphy, in fact, lent itself to replication by others.

Five-coloured Parakeet on a Blossoming Apricot Tree, Northern Song Dynasty, c.1110 (ink & colour on silk) (detail of 263786), Emperor Huizong (1082-1135) / Museum of Fine Arts, Boston, Massachusetts, USA / Maria Antoinette Evans Fund

Hangzhou (HAHNG-jo), in Zhejiang province, became the capital of the Southern Song. For the first time in history, China's capital lay south of the Yangzi. Historians refer to the period when the capital of a united China was in Kaifeng as the Northern Song (960–1126) and the period when the capital was in Hangzhou as the Southern Song (1127–1276). Although China was not united after 1126, the period of the Song dynasty covers its founding in 960 to its collapse in 1276.

The military defeat of the Northern Song triggered one of the greatest migrations in human history. Most of the people who left Kaifeng worked for the Song government: 20,000 officials, 100,000 clerks, and 400,000 soldiers, all with their families. In sum, more than 500,000 people, out of a population in north and south China of an estimated 100 million, crossed the Yangzi River in 1126 and 1127. Like Li Qingzhao, most never returned to north China.

China Divided: The Jin and the Southern Song, 1127–1234

Life in the south was extremely difficult for many northerners, who viewed the north and south as two distinct cultural regions. Northerners ate wheat and millet, often in the form of noodles or bread, while southerners ate rice. Worse, their spoken dialects were mutually incomprehensible. Hangzhou had been a small, regional city, and its population was hard-pressed to accept 500,000 new residents. Yet within a few years its 1 million residents had built it into a worthy successor to the Northern Song capital of Kaifeng.

Li Qingzhao's memoir provides a rare eyewitness account of the migration south. When she and her husband Zhao Mingcheng fled in 1127, they left behind belongings and artwork that filled ten rooms in their home, which was burnt to the ground by the Jurchen invaders a few months later. In the south, crisscrossed by many rivers and lakes, the couple moved more rapidly by boat.

The Southern Song emperor had taken temporary refuge in Nanjing, since there was no new capital yet. In the summer of 1129 when the emperor summoned Zhao Mingcheng to Nanjing for a personal audience, the couple were forced to separate, with Li Qingzhao remaining behind. Six weeks later, Li Qingzhao received a letter from her husband saying that he had contracted malaria. She frantically traveled the 100 miles (160 km) to Nanjing in twenty-four hours by boat, reaching his side just in time to watch him die of dysentery at age forty-nine.

Li Qingzhao closes her memoir with this sentence: "*From the time I was eighteen until now at the age of fifty-two—a span of thirty years—how much calamity, how much gain and loss I have witnessed!*"* Alone and widowed, Li Qingzhao wrote some of her most moving poems:

The wind subsides—the dust carries a fragrance of fallen petals;
It's late in the day—I'm too tired to comb my hair.
Things remain but he is gone, and with him everything.
On the verge of words, tears flow.

---

*Stephen Owen, *An Anthology of Chinese Literature, Volume 1: Beginnings to 1911* (New York, N.Y.: W. W. Norton & Company, Inc., 1997).

I hear at Twin Creek spring's still lovely;
How I long to float there on a small boat—
But I fear that at Twin Creek my frail grasshopper boat
*Could not carry this load of grief.**

Li Qingzhao gave voice to the losses suffered by the many people displaced by the Jurchen conquest.

In the south, the Southern Song dynasty governed some 60 million people from the capital at Hangzhou, where Li Qingzhao settled and eventually remarried. For more than a century and a half after 1127, China was divided. With a government structure modeled after the Song dynasty, 1 million Jurchen ruled a population of some 40 million Chinese in the north until 1234. After fourteen more years of fighting, the Southern Song and the Jurchen signed a peace treaty in 1142. But according to the humiliating terms of the treaty, the Southern Song, an "*insignificant state,*" agreed to pay the Jurchen, a "*superior state,*" tribute of 250,000 ounces of silver and 250,000 bolts of silk each year. Significantly, the Southern Song was the first Chinese dynasty that formally accepted another dynasty as its superior even as it continued to rule. One could sum up the new foreign policy of the Song as China among equals; earlier emperors conceived of all their neighbors as lesser countries.

● **CONTEXT&CONNECTIONS** The different empires that you have studied in earlier chapters had different understandings of the world outside their borders and their role in it. *Han dynasty* China had fought and been defeated by the *Xiongnu* (key terms in Chapter 4), but no other power threatened the hold of a ruling dynasty until the Kitan and then the Jurchen. Similarly, once Rome had defeated *Carthage* and Greece (Chapter 7), it became the only real player in the entire Mediterranean for some 500 years, which is why *Polybius* chose to write about its rise (Chapter 7). Iran differed from both Rome and China in a crucial respect: the *Parthians* and *Sasanians* (Chapter 6) came to power after Rome's rise, and Iranian rulers understood that their country was located among other powerful empires. In the same vein, the Sasanians placed three empty thrones around the emperor's to represent symbolically the rulers of Rome, China, and the Eurasian grasslands to the north. ●

The payments to the Jurchen placed an enormous burden on the Song state and its people, who were well aware that earlier dynasties had received tribute from weaker neighbors, not paid it. The payments, however, stimulated trade and economic growth because the Jurchen used the money to buy Chinese goods as the people of south China rebuilt their economy and became one of the richest societies in the world.

The Commercial Revolution in China

We do not usually think of a change that takes place over more than four hundred years as revolutionary, but the expansion of markets throughout China between 900 and 1300 brought such rapid economic growth that scholars refer to these changes as a commercial revolution. Before this revolution, farmers grew their own food in a largely self-sufficient barter economy in which government

---

*Excerpt from *Women Writers of Traditional China: An Anthology of Poetry and Criticism*, ed. Kang-i Sun Chang and Haun Saussy (Stanford, Calif.: Stanford University Press, 1999), p. 98.

officials closely monitored local markets. At the height of the commercial revolution in the Song dynasty, China's farmers sold cash crops such as tangerines and handicrafts such as pottery, baskets, and textiles at markets. They used their earnings to buy a variety of products, including food. Dependent on the marketplace for their incomes, they led totally different lives from those who had lived before the commercial revolution.

Changes in Agriculture and the Rise of the South

The origins of the commercial revolution go back centuries before Li Qingzhao's lifetime. In north China, where rainfall was lower, farmers planted wheat and millet; in south China, where rainfall was greater, farmers grew rice (see Chapter 4).

Before the commercial revolution, south China was universally viewed as a remote backwater whose many swamps provided a breeding ground for malaria and other diseases. When northerners moved south in search of more land, they settled in the highlands and drained the swamps. They used pumps and water wheels to regulate the flow of water into walled fields for rice. After planting rice seeds in small gardens, they transplanted the rice plants into a field drained of water. Once the plants had taken root, they flooded the fields with water until the crop ripened.

Government Support for New Technologies To encourage the spread of the most current agricultural techniques, the Song government printed and distributed copies of illustrated agricultural manuals that introduced new technologies. This painting shows a waterwheel powered by human pedaling. With this device and pumps, gates, and fences, Chinese farmers transformed south China's swamps into productive agricultural land.

Southern farmers experimented with different rice strains, and in the late tenth century they realized that a type of rice imported from Vietnam had a shorter growing season than indigenous rice, making it possible to harvest two crops a year rather than just one.

AP® THEMES
What was the impact of new agricultural techniques in Song China?

The shift to rice had a dramatic impact on China's population. In 742, 60 percent of the population of 60 million lived in north China. By 980, 62 percent were living in south China, where they cultivated the higher-yielding rice. With more food available, the overall population increased to 100 million in the year 1000. The increasing rice surplus freed others to grow cash crops or to produce handicrafts. Thus one of the most important changes in China's history was this shift south. During the Song dynasty, for the first time, the majority of China's population lived in the south, a trend that continues today.

The Currency of the Song Dynasty

As more and more people produced for markets, they needed a way to pay for their purchases. In response, Song authorities greatly increased the money supply, which at the start of the dynasty in 960 consisted of round bronze coins with square holes.

Li Qingzhao described her husband's many shopping trips during the Northern Song: *"On the first and fifteenth day of every month, my husband would get a short vacation from the Academy: he would 'pawn some clothes' for five hundred cash and go to the market at Xiangguo [SHE-AHNG-gwaw] Temple, where he would buy fruit and rubbings of inscriptions."** Many people in the Song enjoyed tangerines and oranges, which were grown in south China but were available at reasonable cost at markets all over the empire. Zhao also purchased rubbings of inscriptions, art objects that only the richest people could afford.

Sometime near the year 1000, the government introduced the world's first **paper money**. A string of one thousand bronze coins could weigh more than 8 pounds (4 kg), so paper money's lighter weight was an advantage. The new currency appeared at a time when China's paper-making technology was just reaching the Islamic world (see Chapter 9) and had not yet spread to Europe. While people continued to use coins, paper money expanded the money supply, further contributing to the economic growth of the commercial revolution.

paper money
Money that could be used instead of bronze coins; issued around 1000 by the Song dynasty, the first government in world history to do so.

How much paper money to print was intensely controversial: some wanted to print vast quantities; other officials urged caution. The debate came to a head in 1069, when the reigning emperor appointed a new grand councilor, named Wang Anshi (WAHNG AHN-shih). He instituted the **New Policies**, which included paying all government salaries in money and extending low-interest loans to poor peasants. But peasants could not earn enough money to pay back their loans, and by 1086 the reforms had failed.

New Policies
Reforms, implemented between 1069 and 1086, that included paying all government salaries in money and extending low-interest loans to poor peasants.

Iron and Steel

The commercial revolution led to the increased production of all goods, not just of rice and fruit. Iron production boomed as well. Song metallurgists made two kinds of iron: cast and wrought.

*Reprinted by permission of the publisher from *Remembrances: The Experience of the Past in Classical Chinese Literature* by Stephen Owen, p. 82, Cambridge, Mass.: Harvard University Press, Copyright © 1986 by the President and Fellows of Harvard College.

Wrought iron was malleable enough that blacksmiths could work it. At the smallest scale, part-time metal workers (often farmers during the winter) mined iron, collected fuel, and smelted the metal in individual blacksmith's workshops. If there were enough men working together, they might be able to afford a small blast furnace.

AP® THEMES
How did advances in metallurgy techniques contribute to the commercial revolution in Song China?

• **CONTEXT&CONNECTIONS** This scale of *iron* production (Chapter 2) was similar to Africa's, where people had mastered smelting iron in furnaces by 300 C.E. (see Chapter 11), but the Chinese had begun to make iron tools earlier, around 500 B.C.E. Also, as in Africa, Song-era metalsmiths learned how to produce steel, one of the strongest metals known. They heated sheets of iron together in a superheated furnace and then worked them by hand to make steel swords. Chinese metalsmiths also learned to fire their smelters with coke, a fuel made from preheated coal that produced high temperatures. •

The commercial revolution increased demand for iron goods so much that individual workshops could not meet it. Freed by the rice surplus from having to work as farmers, some metal workers began to work full time in factory-like spaces, some privately run, some owned by the government. Cast iron was poured into a mold and was so hard that it could not be worked with a hammer. Large-scale foundries, most near Kaifeng, cast iron armor and weapons for soldiers and iron tools and iron fittings, like nails and locks, for buildings and bridges (see page 351). Like the factories of the Industrial Revolution that came much later, these enterprises housed hundreds of workers who worked full-time to produce identical items in large quantities and at low prices. Song dynasty metalsmiths even crafted Buddhist pagodas from iron, section by section, that stood eight stories (24 m) high.

• **CONTEXT&CONNECTIONS** By 1078, China was producing 125,000 tons of iron, or 3.1 pounds per person, in the entire country. This ratio was matched in Europe only in 1700, on the eve of the Industrial Revolution, prompting historians to ask why, if the Song reached such an advanced stage of metal production, China did not experience a sustained industrial revolution. The answer most often given is that Britain's Industrial Revolution occurred under different circumstances. For example, the British invented machines run by steam to make up for a labor shortage, while the Song had no corresponding shortage of labor and therefore no need to develop labor-saving machinery. •

Urban Life amid Commercial Prosperity

Often, as they shared tea, Li Qingzhao and her husband played a drinking game that shows how close they were:

> *I happen to have an excellent memory, and every evening after we finished eating, we would sit in the hall called "Return Home" and make tea. . . . Pointing to the heaps of books and histories, we would guess on which line of what page in which chapter of which book a certain passage could be found. Success in guessing determined who got to drink his or her tea first. Whenever I got it right, I would raise the teacup, laughing*

*so hard that the tea would spill in my lap, . . . and I would get up, not having been able to drink anything at all. I would have been glad to grow old in such a world.**

Li Qingzhao and her husband clearly enjoyed each other's company, and he treated her as his intellectual equal. Urban prosperity gave them the leisure to share learning and leisure pursuits like this.

• **CONTEXT&CONNECTIONS** As newlyweds, Li Qingzhao and her husband lived in Kaifeng, one of the world's most prosperous cities and possibly the largest, rivaled only by Cairo, with a population of five hundred thousand. (At that time London and Paris each had far less than one hundred thousand residents.) Although Li Qingzhao does not write about crowding, Kaifeng's residents lived at a density of 32,000 people per square mile (12,000 per sq km) (see Table 12.1). With people so crowded, sanitation posed a genuine problem, and disease must have spread quickly. •

For people like Li Qingzhao and Zhao Mingcheng, Kaifeng was a city with many sensual pleasures for those who could afford them, and the wealth from the commercial revolution meant that many people could. Kaifeng alone had seventy-two major restaurants, each standing three floors high and licensed by the government. Even working people could afford to eat noodles or a snack at the many stands dotting the city. (See the feature "Visual Evidence in Primary Sources: The Commercial Vitality of a Chinese City.")

• **CONTEXT&CONNECTIONS** Although many food historians portray Song dynasty China as the birthplace of the public restaurant, ancient Rome also had public eating places, as shown by the more than 150 food stands in Pompeii (see Chapter 7). •

Table 12.1 The World's Largest Cities in the Year 1000

City	Modern Location	Population
Cairo	Egypt	500,000
Constantinople	Turkey	500,000
Kaifeng	China	500,000
Baghdad	Iraq	300,000
Córdoba	Spain	300,000
Angkor	Cambodia	200,000
Samarkand	Uzbekistan	200,000
Paris	France	20,000
London	United Kingdom	15,000

All figures for premodern populations are only rough approximations based on uncertain data; the actual populations may have been half or double the figures given here.

Sources: George Modelski, *World Cities, -3000 to 2000* (Washington, D.C.: Faros, 2000, 2003); James Heitzman and Wolfgang Schenkluhn, *The World in the Year 1000* (New York: University Press of America, 2004).

*Reprinted by permission of the publisher from *Remembrances: The Experience of the Past in Classical Chinese Literature* by Stephen Owen, p. 85, Cambridge, Mass.: Harvard University Press, Copyright © 1986 by the President and Fellows of Harvard College.

Footbinding

The southward migration eventually brought greater wealth to most people and eroded the distinctions among social groups. Although merchants continued to be at the bottom of the ideal social hierarchy—below scholars, peasants, and artisans—others envied their wealth. Meanwhile, many peasants turned into part-time and full-time artisans, and many of those making money selling goods at the market aspired to the high social position of the officials they saw above them.

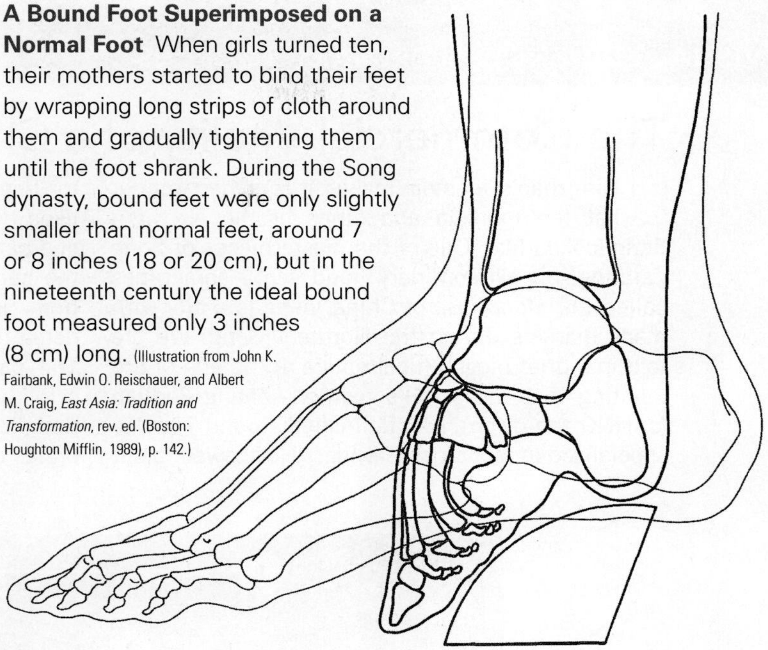

A Bound Foot Superimposed on a Normal Foot When girls turned ten, their mothers started to bind their feet by wrapping long strips of cloth around them and gradually tightening them until the foot shrank. During the Song dynasty, bound feet were only slightly smaller than normal feet, around 7 or 8 inches (18 or 20 cm), but in the nineteenth century the ideal bound foot measured only 3 inches (8 cm) long. (Illustration from John K. Fairbank, Edwin O. Reischauer, and Albert M. Craig, *East Asia: Tradition and Transformation*, rev. ed. (Boston: Houghton Mifflin, 1989), p. 142.)

Both in cities and the countryside, wealthy men sought second and third wives, called concubines, who they hoped would give them more children. Being able to support a large family including concubines and many children was a mark of prestige. Many observers complained about unscrupulous merchants who kidnapped women and sold them as concubines to newly wealthy men.

Brokers in women found that those with bound feet attracted a higher price than those with natural feet because men found unnaturally small feet sexually attractive. Li Qingzhao's mother did not bind her daughter's feet, but by 1300 the wives and daughters of officials throughout south China did. The practice appeared first in the tenth century, when dancers at the imperial court, who were probably in their late teens, had begun to wrap their own feet to make them smaller. By the Southern Song, women from good families began to wrap a daughter's feet in hopes of enhancing her chances of making a good match. The mothers started when the girls were young, around ten, so that their feet would never grow to their natural size. The initial binding was very painful, but eventually girls could resume walking, though always with difficulty and great discomfort. Footbinding transformed a woman's foot into a sexual object that only her partner was supposed to see, wash, or fondle.

AP® THEMES

How did the practice of footbinding reinforce gender inequalities in China?

The Changing Lives of Women in China's Commercial Revolution

At exactly the time when footbinding began to spread in the twelfth and thirteenth centuries, some women began to enjoy increased educational opportunities because of steady economic growth during the commercial revolution. Although they were not allowed to take the civil service exams, many women learned to read and write and how to manage their families' finances. We know a good deal about wealthy women in the Song dynasty from biographies, called epitaphs, that were placed in their tombs.

The epitaphs reveal what kind of woman was most admired in the twelfth and thirteenth centuries. Whereas Tang dynasty epitaphs emphasized women's physical appearance and ancestry, Song epitaphs frequently praised women for successfully

The Commercial Vitality of a Chinese City

Li Qingzhao's memoir makes the reader wonder what the markets and cities of the Northern Song looked like. One of the masterpieces of Song painting, an extraordinary hand scroll sometimes called the *Mona Lisa* of China, depicts a city with many markets during the Northern Song. We are told in a brief biographical notice at the end of the painting that the scroll's painter—Zhang Zeduan (JAHNG zeh-dwon), who flourished around 1150—specialized in technical drawing: "He showed talent for fine-lined architectural drawing, and especially liked boats and carts, markets and bridges, moats and paths." The artist intended that viewers look at the hand scroll slowly, rolling it out inch by inch, from right to left, and savoring the extraordinary detail that extends a full 17.25 feet (5.25 m) long. The painting, often referred to as the Qingming scroll, was completed sometime before 1186. Entitled *Peace Reigns over the River*, the scroll celebrates commercial life.

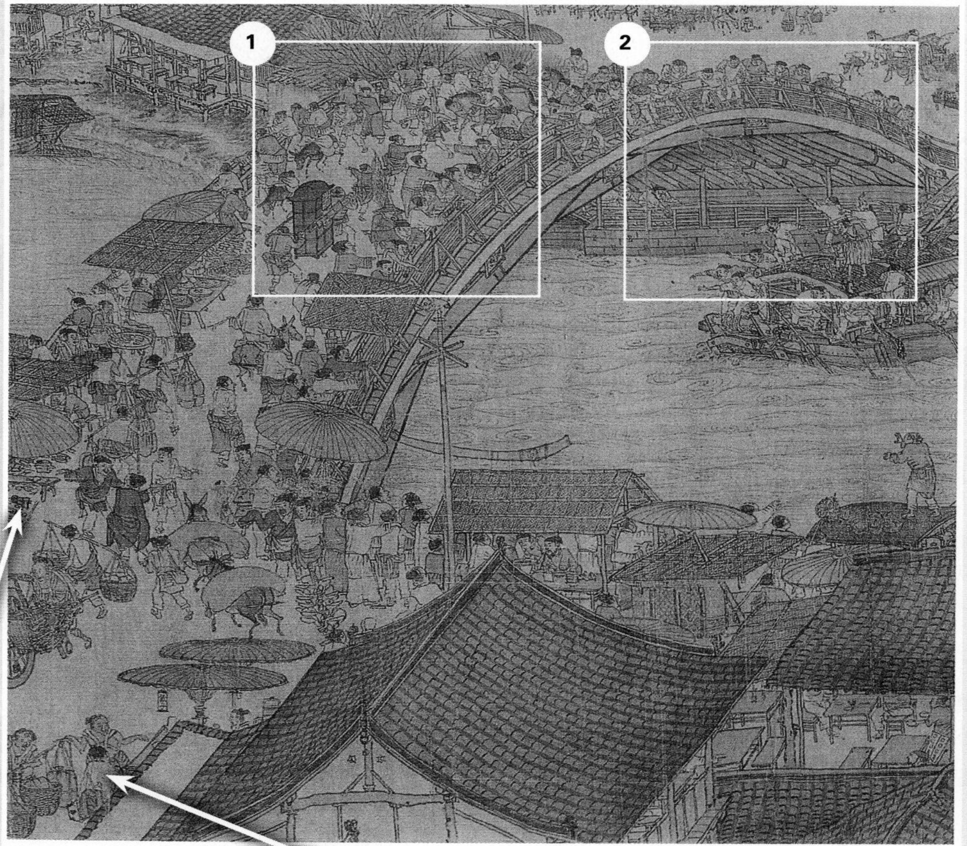

National Palace Museum, Beijing/Cultural Relics Press

This vendor has laid out his tools on a cloth for customers to see. ***What are people on the bridge buying and selling?***

Three lightly clothed carriers put down their loaded baskets outside a stand serving drinks under two large umbrellas.

The dramatic high point of the painting comes right in the middle of the scroll. At first one views a boat with sailors hurriedly pulling the mast down. Then, as the scroll unfurls, the viewer understands why: the boat is going under the rainbow bridge, yet its towline has snapped. In his efforts to keep the boat from crashing, one sailor grabs a rope thrown by a passerby standing on the bridge, just as the men at the ship's bow gesture frantically to the oncoming boat to stay out of the way.

The bridge scene vividly illustrates the major change of the commercial revolution: commerce had exploded out of restricted market districts to blanket the cities of the twelfth century. Restaurants and food stands line the side of the river, and they have even crept up the bridge where passersby can eat a snack purchased from a seated baker or can buy ropes or scissors from vendors who have laid out their goods on the ground. As the scroll ends, when one goes through a large gate and finally enters the city proper, it dawns on the viewer that all the commercial activity seen so far has taken place outside the city walls—a location where all markets were banned during the Tang dynasty.

The detail of the scroll is so mesmerizing that one can easily forget that one is looking at a painting by an artist and not at a photograph. Zhang Zeduan has fit the city into an artfully constructed composition, complete with the rainbow bridge at the exact midpoint of the scroll, and has depicted a city without dirt, illness, or crowding. Curiously, Zhang has nearly omitted women from his cityscape. Of more than five hundred people in the scroll, only twenty or so are female. Surely a real city would have had more women outside, even if women from prestigious families, like Li Qingzhao, often remained indoors.

A collision is about to occur on top of the bridge: an official riding a horse confronts someone (possibly a woman not visible to the viewer) in a sedan chair. Several feisty servants gesture emphatically to the horseman to get out of the way. ***As you continue to look at the scroll, consider why an artist painting an idealized cityscape would leave women out.***

1

National Palace Museum, Beijing/Cultural Relics Press

2

National Palace Museum, Beijing/Cultural Relics Press

A bystander on top of the bridge tosses a rope to the boat's frantic crew, who hope to avert a crash with a boat coming toward them from under the bridge.

The details of the bridge's construction—a round arch made from straight wooden beams wrapped together with iron—are clear from this angle. A wooden walkway at the water's edge allows pedestrians to pass underneath the bridge.

managing their household finances, a skill requiring knowledge of math. In 1250, one official wrote an epitaph for Lady Fang, the wife of his younger brother:

> *My brother was untalented at making a living but loved antiques and would spend every cent to collect famous paintings and calligraphies. Lady Fang calmly made secret economies and never complained of lacking anything. . . .*
>
> *Lady Fang was a widow for over ten years. During this time she arranged for her husband's tomb, completed marriage arrangements for her children, repaired the old house, and brought new fields into cultivation in order to continue the thread of our family and preserve the orphans.**

Note that the author commends her ability to manage her family's income after her husband's death. Funerary texts often praise widows for tutoring their young children at home and for making economies that allow their offspring to attend school when older.

As with remembrances of the dead in many different cultures, epitaphs often exaggerate the virtues of deceased women, reporting how they *should* behave, rather than how they actually lived. Few epitaphs, for example, mention widow remarriage, and even fewer refer to divorce, both of which society frowned on, even though both occurred. Sources, such as rule books for schools and all laws, that record how people should behave are called *prescriptive*; those that describe how people actually lived are called *descriptive*.

Because so many Song sources about women are prescriptive, Li Qingzhao's descriptive writings are particularly important to historians who want to understand how women lived during China's commercial revolution. Contrary to Confucian ideas that held women should not remarry after their husbands died, Li Qingzhao did remarry, and divorced within just one hundred days when her second husband, an official, was found guilty of corruption.

A new study of Li Qingzhao offers a compelling rereading of her memoir. Challenging the traditional view that it is simply a factual account of an idyllic marriage, Stanford University professor Ronald Egan places the memoir in its historic context and notes that Li Qingzhao wrote the afterword after her second marriage fell apart.

A new source—a letter that Li Qingzhao wrote to an acquaintance, who happened to be a high-ranking official—reveals the sad circumstances of her remarriage, in which her husband *"began to abuse me freely, and his blows came down daily."*† Women in the Song dynasty could divorce, but they could not initiate divorce. Song law also forbade family members to bring suit against higher-ranking family members, and a husband outranked a wife. Thus when Li Qingzhao brought a suit against her husband for misrepresenting his past performance on the exams, she was jailed. Freed nine days later, she was ultimately granted a divorce on the grounds that her husband had committed a crime (wives of all criminals received a divorce).

---

*Patricia Buckley Ebrey, "The Women in Liu Kezhuang's Family," *Modern China* 10, no. 4 (1984): citation on p. 437.

†Quoted in Ronald Egan, *The Burden of Female Talent: The Poet Li Qingzhao and Her History in China* (Cambridge: Harvard University Asia Center, 2013), p. 148.

Still, she had no regular income, and this was why she wrote the afterword. She hoped to reestablish her eligibility for a government pension due to her as Zhao Mingcheng's widow. She also hoped to regain her good name with his immediate family and more broadly throughout society. Her essay succeeded wonderfully in these goals; she qualified for the pension, and over the centuries, her marriage became one of China's most famous successful pairings, just as the memory of her unsavory second marriage and divorce faded away. Professor Egan's reexamination shows how a new piece of evidence (her letter) can lead to a completely persuasive rereading of a text that many people in China know by heart and thought there was nothing further to learn about.

● **CONTEXT&CONNECTIONS** Earlier chapters have introduced women rulers—the Egyptian pharaoh Hatshepsut, the Chinese emperor Wu, and the Byzantine emperor Irene (see Chapters 2, 8, and 10)—but surviving materials reveal little about them as individuals. *Egeria's* diary (Chapter 7) is unusual in that she, and not a male author, wrote it, but it remains very dry, with few personal details. The spread of woodblock printing in China led to the preservation of many more personal materials, like Li Qingzhao's memoir, her letter describing her divorce, and her poetry. Printing came later to Europe—not until the 1450s—but similarly personal letters survive written by *Heloise* (Chapter 13), an educated woman who bore the child of a man who deserted her and later reappeared in her life. Historians prize these materials because they allow us to understand women's point of view. ●

Book Publishing and the Education Boom

The commercial revolution brought an information revolution parallel to the Internet boom, caused by a deceptively simple innovation, woodblock printing. Before 700, creating a book was a slow, laborious process done by hand. The introduction of woodblock printing sped up book publishing dramatically and significantly lowered the cost of books.

As a result, many more men and women could afford books and learned to read. Because people had more disposable income, they could finance the education of their children. The rise in wealth and educational opportunity also prompted more people to take the government's civil service examination, the door to a job in the bureaucracy (see Chapters 4 and 8).

Woodblock Printing and the Invention of Movable Type

Using the same technique developed in the eighth century, Song dynasty printers used woodblocks to print individual sheets of paper (see Chapter 8). Printers could make hundreds of copies from the same block of wood. Folding each page in half, they sewed the sheets into bound chapters of thirty or so pages, which were stored in boxes.

Shortly after 1040, the Chinese bookmaker Bi Sheng (bee shung) invented **movable type**, in which each character is made separately and arranged on a frame to form a page. An eleventh-century description explains:

movable type
Printing method first developed in China after 1040 by printers who arranged reusable individual characters on the page.

Bi Sheng, a man of unofficial position, made moveable type. His method was as follows: he took sticky clay and cut in it characters as thin as the edge of a

> *coin. . . . When he wished to print, he took an iron frame. . . . In this he placed the types, set close together. . . . If one were to print only two or three copies, this method would be neither simple nor easy. But for printing hundreds or thousands of copies, it was marvelously quick.**

Since Chinese has thousands of different characters, making a different piece of type for each character was a slow and expensive process. For this reason, it was cheaper to carve woodblocks for smaller runs, such as a thousand books. Movable type made sense only for a few large-scale printing projects.

- **CONTEXT&CONNECTIONS** The world's earliest surviving book printed with movable type was made in Korea in 1377, at least seventy years before the German printer Johannes Gutenberg used movable type to print his much more famous Bible

*Tsien Tsuen-hsuin, *Chemistry and Chemical Technology, Part I: Paper and Printing*, vol. 1 of *Science and Civilisation in China*, ed. Joseph Needham (New York: Cambridge University Press, 1985), pp. 201–202.

The World's First Movable Type This model reconstructs the movable type Bi Sheng invented for printing in the 1040s. Because the printer had to cut out an individual clay type for each character, the cost of movable type was much higher than the traditional Chinese method of woodblock printing. For large print runs of over one hundred thousand, however, movable type made sense. (Ontario Science Centre)

(see Chapter 15). Titled *Jikji*, the work was originally a multiple-volume set of the conversations that famous *Buddhist* monks (Chapter 3) had with their students, much as *Confucius* did in *The Analects* (Chapter 4). Today only one volume of the set survives, in the National Library of France, which is controversial because many people in Korea think that it should be returned to the country where it was made. ●

The low cost of books combined with sustained economic growth produced an education boom that intensified the competition for government jobs. More and more families hired scholars who had failed the civil service examinations to serve as tutors for their sons and daughters, buying books and study aids in large numbers. Though only a few passed the exams, many boys gained basic literacy.

The Growth of Civil Service Examinations

The Song dynasty was the only government in the twelfth- and thirteenth-century world to recruit its bureaucrats via merit, as measured by a grueling series of examinations. At the time of the dynasty's founding in 960, civil service examinations had been in use for over a thousand years. But it was only in the Song era that the proportion of civil officials in the bureaucracy who had passed the examinations reached nearly 90 percent (versus 5 percent for the Tang). As a result, the Song era saw a decisive shift from government by aristocracy to government by merit-based bureaucracy.

● **CONTEXT&CONNECTIONS** Although examinations during the Song dynasty were not always fair, they were more equitable than the system of appointments on the basis of heredity or social position used elsewhere in the world. ●

During the Song dynasty, exam candidates took two rounds of exams, which were held every three years: the first in their home prefecture and the second in the capital. At the start of the dynasty, as in the Tang, examiners knew whose paper they were grading; after 1000, the candidates' names were covered up and the exam papers recopied so that examiners could not recognize anyone's handwriting. The emperor himself conducted the final stage, the palace examinations, in which those placing highest in the written exams were examined orally (Li Qingzhao's second husband had never passed these).

Success in the examinations brought a government-issued degree; each time the examinations were held during the Southern Song, some five hundred men received the highest rank of "**advanced scholar**." The degree did not guarantee employment. Those placing highest were given prestigious entry-level jobs, often drafting decrees for the emperor, but those with lower scores had to wait for a vacancy in the bureaucracy to open up, which could take years.

advanced scholar The highest degree given by the government to the top-scoring examination candidates.

The government examiners devised different types of exams over the centuries. Successful candidates had to demonstrate mastery of a classic text, often within the Confucian tradition, by explaining from which text an unidentified passage had been taken. They were asked to compose poetry, or essays with a fixed number of lines and a set number of words per line (like a sonnet in English). The candidates also wrote essays about problems the central government might face, such as inflation or defeating border peoples. Many of these literary skills did not relate directly to what officials would do once in office. Still, the exams tested a broad range of learning, and it was expected that they could identify the most educated and so, the examiners believed, the most virtuous men to become officials.

The examinations were not open to everyone. Local officials permitted only young men from well-established families to register for the first round of exams. Unlike farmers' sons, who were lucky to attend village school for a year or two, the sons of privileged families had the time and money to study for the exams, often at home with a tutor. Preparation required long years of study.

In the eleventh century, successful exam candidates tended to come from a small group of one hundred families living in the capital, Kaifeng. This was the elite into which Li Qingzhao and Zhao Mingcheng were born, and both of their fathers had been advanced scholars.

As the population grew and printed books became more widely available, examinations became more competitive. By 1270, 1 out of every 250 people took the exams, showing how the literacy rate had increased. Some historians believe that one in ten men, but many fewer women, could read.*

During the Song dynasty, children learned to read by using primers that taught a core vocabulary. One of the most popular, *The Three-Character Classic*, written circa 1200, consisted of rhyming lines of three Chinese characters each, which students had to learn by heart. The book reminded students of the five important Confucian relationships: father/son, husband/wife, elder brother/younger brother, friend/friend, ruler/subject:

Father and son should live in love, in peace the married pair:
Kindness the elder brother's and respect the younger's care.
Let deference due to age be paid, comrades feel friendship's glow,
Princes treat well their minister—they loyalty should show.
These moral duties binding are on all men here below.†

● **CONTEXT&CONNECTIONS** Because almost everyone studied *The Three-Character Classic*, this version of Confucianism had great influence, not only in China but also all over East Asia, where many students used this primer to learn to read Chinese characters (even if they pronounced them in Japanese or Korean). ●

shadow privilege
Privilege extended to sons and relatives of Song dynasty officials, allowing them to take a less competitive series of examinations.

Outwardly, the examinations were fair. In fact, however, the sons and relatives of high officials were eligible to take a less competitive series of examinations, often with a pass rate of 50 percent, an advantage called the **shadow privilege**. Since Zhao Mingcheng's father was grand councilor, the highest official in the bureaucracy, his shadow privilege extended to his sons, grandsons, sons-in-law, brothers, cousins, and nephews. In the twelfth and thirteenth centuries, as more men became eligible for the shadow privilege, fewer candidates took the open examinations. Even so, in some districts, competition remained intense, particularly in the southeast in Fujian province, whereby 1270 some seven hundred men competed for a single position as an advanced scholar. (See the feature "World History in Today's World: Chinese Students Take the SAT.")

As competition increased, so did the pressure to cheat. Some candidates paid others to take the exams in their place, or they copied others' answers or bribed

---

*Valerie Hansen, *The Open Empire: A History of China to 1600*. 2d ed (New York: W. W. Norton, 2015), p. 270.

†*The Three-Character Classic*, Pei-yi Wu, "Education of Children in the Sung," in *Neo-Confucian Education: The Formative Stage*, ed. Wm. Theodore de Bary and John W. Chaffee (Berkeley: University of California Press, 1989), p. 323.

ORLD HIST

Chinese Students Take the SAT

Imagine taking the SAT with ten thousand other people in a giant arena where Lady Gaga has performed to sell-out crowds. That is the scene in Hong Kong's Asia-World Expo Hall, the place where many Chinese students in Hong Kong go to take the SATs. In the 1200s, candidates for the civil service examinations complained about crowded halls in which hundreds competed for a single spot, but those crowds were minor compared to what today's high school seniors from China have to endure.

As long as China was a poor country, up to about ten years ago, high school seniors had only one option for going to college: getting a high enough score on the extremely competitive *gaokao* ("high exam") to qualify for a place in a Chinese university. Even now there are not enough spaces for all those who want to attend college; each year about 7 million students receive offers of admission, while some 2 million are turned away. In the past decade, more and more Chinese high school students have opted to study abroad, almost always in an English-speaking country. And they need to perform well on the SAT to do so.

The Chinese government has put one major hurdle in their way. No Chinese citizen is allowed to take the SAT within China. (Only holders of foreign passports may do so, at international schools.) All Chinese citizens must travel abroad to take the SAT, and Hong Kong is the closest destination. Even so, going there is not cheap: families regularly spend thousands of dollars on tutoring for their children, and a package of flight, hotel, and test registration costs at least $1,000.

The number of Chinese students at the undergraduate level in the United States has doubled since 2007; it's now 75,000. This is the highest number of students from a single country studying in the United States, and twice as many as from India, the runner up. One in four international students in the United States hails from China, and the number will probably continue to increase in the future. Alert to the Hong Kong authorities: the exam takers will soon need an even larger concert hall!

Sources: Various Internet sources; David Leonhardt, "Chinese Students Bolster U.S. College Budgets," *New York Times*, August 29, 2013.

graders. In one scandal in Sichuan province, officials grading the exams took bribes, changed the names on the exams, and secretly marked the booklets to which they were supposed to give passing grades. Crafty students also bought commercial aids, like miniature books with tiny characters the size of a fly, that they could smuggle into the examination halls.

Cheating and heightened competition prompted many men to turn away from the examinations and government service altogether. In 1101, when Li Qingzhao married, she assumed that her husband would become an official, and he did. One hundred years later, many families of equally prominent rank chose instead to educate their sons at private academies and to keep them at home to run their family estates once their education was completed. As a book critical of the examination system explained:

> *If the sons of a gentleman have no hereditary stipend to maintain and no permanent holdings to depend on, and they wish to be filial to their parents and to support children, then nothing is as good as being a scholar. . . . For those who cannot be scholars, then medicine, Buddhism and Daoism, agriculture, trade, or crafts are all possible.**

---

*Valerie Hansen, *The Open Empire: A History of China to 1600*. 2d ed (New York: W. W. Norton, 2015), p. 269.

This author uses the word *scholar* for everyone who earned a living by reading, writing, teaching, or editing. Many young men followed the book's advice. After studying at private academies, they returned to their family estates and pursued careers in writing, teaching, agriculture, or trade.

Religious Life During the Song

Prosperity allowed the Chinese to give money to practitioners of many different religions. Most Chinese did not adhere to a specific religion: they worshiped the deities and consulted the religious specialists they thought most powerful. Lay Chinese also made offerings to Buddhist and Daoist deities and to gods not associated with any organized religion. Many educated families were drawn to the teachings of Neo-Confucianism.

The most influential private academy, the White Deer Academy, was founded in 1181 by the thinker **Zhu Xi** (1130–1200). Zhu Xi's curriculum emphasized moral cultivation. He wanted his students to become true Confucian gentlemen, not civil service officials, and he thought the best guidelines were the Confucian classics, in particular four texts: *The Analects* (which contained Confucius's conversations with his students; see Chapter 4), *Mencius* (written by a follower of Confucius), and two chapters from a ritual manual. These writings are known collectively as *The Four Books*.

Zhu Xi
(1130–1200) The leading thinker of Neo-Confucianism, who wrote a commentary on *The Four Books*.

Zhu Xi (JOO she) criticized Buddhism as a non-Chinese religion and urged his followers to give up all Buddhist practices, yet Buddhist teachings about meditating and reaching enlightenment clearly influenced Zhu Xi's understanding of the transmission of the Way (see Chapter 4). He also claimed that studying and thinking on his own had allowed him to understand the Way as it had passed from Confucius to Mencius, from Mencius to a Tang dynasty thinker named Han Yu (768–824), and then to himself. He used the word *daotong*, or "transmission of the Way," for this process. Whereas earlier historians believed that Zhu Xi came up with this idea on his own, scholars have recently discovered other texts, not by members of Zhu Xi's school, that used the same word. Zhu Xi, then, adopted a word already in circulation for his own teaching. Similarly, he was not the first thinker to focus on the two chapters from the ritual manual included in *The Four Books*: Buddhist teachers in the early 1000s had noticed that these books contained ideas that overlapped with Buddhism, and the two chapters had already circulated in Buddhist monasteries as independent texts.

Because Zhu Xi's teachings were based on Confucianism but introduced major revisions, they are called **Neo-Confucianism**. Rather than focusing on ritual and inner humanity as Confucius had, Zhu Xi urged students to apprehend the principle in things. If students examined everything in the world around them (an all-inclusive concept that Zhu Xi called psychophysical stuff—*qi*—literally "air") and studied *The Four Books* carefully, Neo-Confucians believed that they could discern a coherent pattern underlying everything. Armed with that knowledge, an individual could attain sagehood, the goal of all Neo-Confucian education.

Neo-Confucianism
Teachings of the thinker Zhu Xi (1130–1200) and his followers that urged students to apprehend the principle in psychophysical stuff, or *qi*.

Zhu Xi and the other leading Neo-Confucian thinkers revived a literary genre called "records of conversations" to explain the most important concepts of their teaching. In form, the conversations between the teacher and student resembled the snippets of conversations between Confucius and his students captured in

The Analects. This genre fit well with the Neo-Confucian conviction that everyone was born with a mind that could learn and recognize the truth, whether from reading a given text or from listening to a teacher. The main difference between students and a sage was that the sage had perfected his understanding of Neo-Confucian ideas, while students were still learning.

The records of conversations influenced how Neo-Confucian students expressed their ideas, particularly in the essays they wrote for the civil service examinations. Because the candidates had studied the records of conversations so closely, the Neo-Confucian students used vernacular Chinese, which used more words than classical Chinese to make the same point. Students ignored the usual rules of composition so that they could express their ideas as their teachers did; their decision appalled the examiners, who initially gave low scores to examinations they identified as influenced by Neo-Confucianism.

The students' steadfast faith in the Neo-Confucian teachings, and their willingness to risk low scores, contributed to the spread of Neo-Confucian ideas throughout the empire. In the 1200s, as more and more people came to embrace Neo-Confucian thinking, examiners began to reward students for exactly this kind of writing, and in the 1240s and later, only students who wrote essays in the Neo-Confucian style could hope to do well on the civil service examinations.

● **CONTEXT&CONNECTIONS** Although the government went so far as to ban Zhu Xi's teachings during the last years of his life, by the fourteenth century his edition of *The Four Books* became the basis of the civil service examinations—an outcome Zhu Xi could never have anticipated. By the seventeenth century his teachings had also gained a wide following in Japan, Korea, and Vietnam. ●

Day-to-Day Religious Life

At the time that Zhu Xi and his followers were formulating their teachings, Neo-Confucian shrines spread throughout south China, and by the end of the Song dynasty, shrines to worthies had proliferated throughout the empire. A "worthy" was someone who embodied the Neo-Confucian virtues of being educated, honest, and concerned about his community's welfare. All worthies were male. These shrines provided a physical reminder of Neo-Confucian teachers and teachings to ordinary people who might not otherwise have encountered them. They often housed a portrait of the person to be worshiped. Local people gathered at shrines on certain holidays, and a member of the community led a prayer asking the worthy to descend, listen to the prayer, and receive offerings: bolts of cloth, food, and drinks like wine or tea.

Many other types of religion coexisted with the shrines to worthies. Li Qingzhao's account mentions ancestor worship in particular. When she and her husband parted, Zhao instructed her to *"carry the sacrificial vessels for the ancestral temple yourself; live or die with them; don't give them up."** Each household had an altar for ancestor worship. The wealthy put bronze vessels on their altars; ordinary people used pottery or wooden bowls and cups.

Much religious activity took place outside the home. Some religious practitioners going from market-town to market-town were associated with organized

---

*Reprinted by permission of the publisher from *Remembrances: The Experience of the Past in Classical Chinese Literature* by Stephen Owen, p. 90, Cambridge, Mass.: Harvard University Press, Copyright © 1986 by the President and Fellows of Harvard College.

religions, like Daoism and Buddhism, while others, like the spirit mediums, tended to work on their own. Believing that evil spirits caused illness, many people consulted religious specialists, such as exorcists, in the hope of curing sick family members.

Buddhist monasteries offered many women a place where they could go unaccompanied by men and listen to Buddhist texts recited aloud (see Chapter 8). Thousands forswore marriage and became monks and nuns living in monasteries and nunneries. Male clerics outnumbered women six to one during the Song dynasty.

Vietnam, Korea, Japan, and the World Beyond

AP® THEMES

What were the consequences, in terms of technological diffusion, of cross-cultural interactions between China, Vietnam, Korea, and Japan?

During the Song dynasty, as the commercial revolution led to technological breakthroughs, particularly in ocean exploration, the vastness of the larger world became apparent to educated Chinese. Chinese navigators continued to modify their designs for ships, whose large wooden construction profoundly impressed Ibn Battuta (see Chapter 11), and mapmaking also improved.

Foreign trade with surrounding powers played an important role in China's commercial revolution. Anyone traveling to Vietnam, Korea, or Japan in the thirteenth century would have seen signs of Chinese influence everywhere: people using chopsticks, Buddhist monasteries and Confucian schools, books printed in Chinese, and Chinese characters on all signposts and government documents. Chinese bronze coins, or local copies, circulated throughout the region, forming a Song dynasty currency sphere. But Vietnam, Korea, and Japan also had their own distinctive political structures and their own ways of modifying the collection of institutions, laws, education systems, and religions they had adopted from the Tang (see Chapter 8).

Technological Breakthroughs

Although Chinese ships traveled to Southeast Asia and India as early as the fifth century, they stayed close to the coastline because they did not have compasses. Already in the fourth century B.C.E. the Chinese had known that naturally magnetic lodestones would point north when placed on a board. The lodestones, however, eventually lost their magnetism and so were not suited to long sea voyages. Sometime between 850 and 1050, Chinese metallurgists realized that if they heated steel needles to a high temperature that we now call the Curie point and then cooled them rapidly, they could magnetize the needles. Placed in water on a float of some kind, the buoyant needles pointed north. In the twelfth and thirteenth centuries the use of a **steel-needle compass** made deep-water navigation possible, facilitating travel to distant places like Vietnam and Cambodia in Southeast Asia.

steel-needle compass
A navigational instrument made by floating a magnetized steel needle in water: since the magnetized needle pointed north, sailors knew where to go.

The World Beyond East Asia

Although access to foreign lands improved, Song knowledge of the outside world grew only slowly. By the twelfth century, Chinese mapmakers had achieved the precision of grid maps with each square covering the same amount of territory. But their maps showed little beyond China's borders. One map describes foreign peoples, but it does so in words, without showing their geographic positions.

● **CONTEXT&CONNECTIONS** In 1225, Muslim geographers knew more about Afro-Eurasia than did anyone in China. The transfer of geographic knowledge to China that started in the eleventh century continued through to the early 1400s, when the Muslim Chinese admiral *Zheng He* would lead an imperial fleet to South and Southeast Asia and later to East and North Africa (Chapter 14). ●

In *Records of the Grand Historian*, Sima Qian was the first Chinese historian to devote a major section to the peoples living outside of China, including the major enemy of the Han dynasty, the Xiongnu. Although each description varied, he usually included the estimated distance from the Chinese capital, whether the ruler was an ally of the Chinese, important local products, and any notable customs. The Chinese tradition of writing about foreign peoples culminated with the publication in 1225 of *The Description of Foreign Peoples* by **Zhao Rugua** (JAO RUE-gwah) (1170–1231), the director of the Department of Overseas Trade in Quanzhou. Zhao's book had two parts, one listing the various goods imported to China and the second briefly describing the different countries that traded with Song China. (See the feature "Movement of Ideas Through Primary Sources: Chinese Knowledge of the World's Islands in 1225.") Zhao gives particularly detailed information about the three states of East Asia most influenced by the Tang: Vietnam, Korea, and Japan (see Map 12.1).

Zhao Rugua

(fl. 1225) Author of *The Description of Foreign Peoples*, a compendium of information about China's closest trading partners in East Asia and distant places such as the east coasts of Africa and Spain.

Ly dynasty

(1009–1224) The independent rulers of Vietnam who adopted the *Tang Code* in 1042.

Vietnam During the Song Dynasty

Since Vietnam bordered China on the south, it received the most extensive Chinese influence. Zhao did not consider it a separate country. Under direct Chinese rule during the Han and Tang Dynasties, Vietnam became independent under the **Ly dynasty** (1009–1224). Because it was a tributary of China, its king acknowledged the superiority of the Chinese emperor and periodically sent delegations to present him with gifts. The Chinese emperor bestowed gifts on the emissaries in return.

The Chinese-educated scholars of the Ly (LEE) dynasty argued that their king, the southern emperor, ruled the southern kingdom of Vietnam because he, like the Chinese emperor, had the Mandate of Heaven (see Chapter 4). The Vietnamese kings credited local spirits with protecting the royal house and supported Buddhism. Since at least the fourth century, Buddhist monks had traveled back and forth between China and Vietnam, and Buddhist texts had circulated in both directions (see Chapter 8).

The Vietnamese king and his courtiers had received a Chinese-style education and could read and write Chinese. In 1042, the Ly emperor

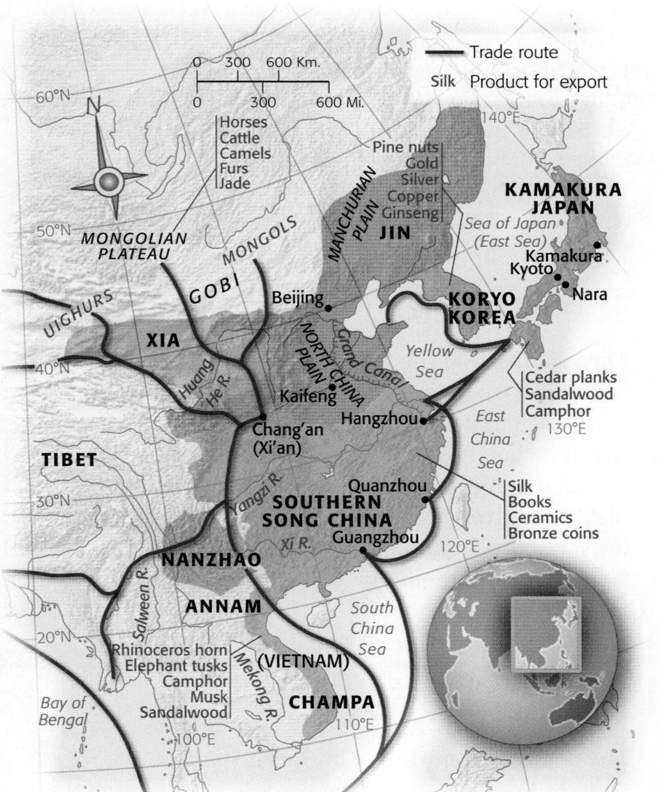

Map 12.1 China's Trade Relations with the External World, 1225 In 1225, most of Song dynasty China's foreign trade was with Japan, Korea, and Vietnam. China exported silk and high-quality ceramics, while these different societies traded different minerals, raw materials, and foodstuffs in return. Chinese bronze coins circulated throughout the region, creating a currency sphere.

Chinese Knowledge of the World's Islands in 1225

In his position as the director of the Department of Overseas Trade in China's largest international trade port, Quanzhou, on the southeast coast, Zhao Rugua met many foreign and Chinese traders and spoke with them directly about the Islamic heartland of Arabia and Mecca and the Islamic periphery; the southern coast of Europe; and the northern and eastern coasts of Africa. Zhao's knowledge of the non-Chinese was the product of the trading environment of Quanzhou. Almost every place he covers is located on a seacoast, and the goods he describes came to China on seagoing vessels. He combined the information he obtained firsthand with written records, including both earlier Chinese sources and Islamic geographers' accounts, which he probably learned about from Muslim travelers.

Writing more than one thousand years after the Grand Historian Sima Qian, Zhao was deeply influenced by the long Chinese tradition of writing about foreign peoples. As you read these descriptions of three different islands—northern Taiwan, Madagascar, and Sicily—identify Zhao's basic outline. What topics does he always include? Which does he sometimes include? What does he leave out?

Historical method presumes that people know more about closer places and recent events than those separated by greater distance or more time. Accordingly, Zhao should have known more about the island closest to Quanzhou—Taiwan, a mere 150 miles (240 km) away—than the distant islands of either Madagascar or Sicily. But because Taiwan's local pirates were so fierce, few Chinese actually sailed to the island. Zhao's description of Taiwan actually recycles a description from an earlier dynastic history written in the 600s.

Historical Thinking Skill:
ANALYZING EVIDENCE **What do you think is the purpose of Zhao's descriptions of these islands?**

Historical Thinking Skill:
ANALYZING EVIDENCE **Of the many descriptions of nature and the environment Zhao provides, which seem the most believable? Why?**

Source: Friedrich Hirth and W. W Rockhill, *Chau Ju-kua: His Work on the Chinese and Arab Trade in the Twelfth and Thirteenth Centuries, Entitled Chu-fan-chï* (St. Petersburg: Imperial Academy of Sciences, 1911), pp. 149, 153, 162–164. Passages checked against the original Chinese and updated as necessary.

The Islands of Pemba and Madagascar

This country is in the sea to the southwest. It is adjacent to a large island. There are usually on the great island great *peng* birds that are so large that they cover the sun when they fly by, and the sun's shadow shifts so much that it gives a different reading on the sundial. If the great *peng* bird finds a wild camel, it swallows it. If one should happen to find a *peng* feather, after cutting off the hollow quill, you can use it to make a water pail.

The products of the country are big elephants' tusks and rhinoceros horns.

To the West there is an island in the sea on which there are many wild people, with bodies as black as lacquer and with frizzy hair. Enticed by offers of food, they are caught and then carried off to be sold as slaves in the Arab countries where they command a high price. They work as gatekeepers. People say that they do not miss their families.

Northern Taiwan

The country of northern Taiwan is some five or six days' sail east of Quanzhou. . . . The king's residence is called Poluotan Cave; around it, it has three separate wooden palisades surrounded by running water and protected by thorn hedges, and the palace roof has many carvings of birds and animals.

Both sexes bind their hair with white linen string and coil it up in a knot at the back of the head; they make different kinds of clothes from hempen cloth and decorated feathers. None are the same.

They braid hats of rattan and decorate them with feathers. Their soldiers are armed with weapons of every kind, such as knives, pikes, bows and arrows, and swords; they use drums, and make armor from bear and leopard skins.

The carts in which the chiefs drive are carved with the statues of ferocious animals, and only several tens of men walk in front and behind. They have no regular tax collection, but when the ruler needs money he collects an equal amount from everyone.

They do not understand the solar and lunar divisions of the year, but simply record time by observing the phases of the moon.

Fathers and sons sleep together on the same bed. They evaporate seawater in the sun to make salt, and they brew rice into spirits. Whenever they happen to have any extraordinary delicacy, they first offer it to their leaders.

They have bear and wolf meat, and much pork and chicken, but no cattle, sheep, donkeys or horses. The soil of this country is rich and loamy. After burning the grass (the stubble of the previous crop), they flood the land and merely use a hoe to dig just a few inches deep before planting seeds.

They have no unusual goods; the locals tend to be robbers, which is why traders do not go there. Still, the locals, from time to time, collect yellow wax, locally mined gold, buffalo tails and jerked leopard meat and take it to the Philippines to sell it.

Sicily

The country of Sicily is near the border with Rome. It is a sea island one thousand *li* [a li is roughly .33 miles or .5 km] in breadth. The clothing, customs, and language of the people are the same as those of Rome. This country has a mountain with a very deep cavern in it that emits fire the four seasons of the year. When seen from afar it looks like smoke in the morning and fire in the evening; when seen up close it is a wildly roaring fire.

When the people of the country carry up on a pole a big stone weighing five hundred or a thousand *catties* [a cattie is roughly one pound or .5 kg] and fling it into the cavern, after a little while there is an explosion and [the stone] comes out in little pieces like pumice stone.

Once every five years fire and stones break out and flow down to the sea-coast and then flow back again. The trees in the woods through which this stream of fire flows are not burned, but the stones it meets in its course turn to ashes.

Koryo dynasty
(936–1392) Dynasty that gave its name to the modern country of Korea, whose founder adopted Tang governing models.

adopted a modified form of the *Tang Code* (see Chapter 8), and in 1075 the government held the first civil service examinations. The dynasty's control beyond the major administrative centers was weak. In much of the kingdom's territory, largely independent chieftains ruled groups who lived in bands in the highlands and submitted valued items like rhinoceros horns and elephant tusks to the king. At the time of Zhao's writing, the Vietnamese exported to China the same unprocessed goods, including rhinoceros horn, elephant tusks, camphor, musk, and sandalwood, that they had for the previous thousand years (see Map 12.1).

Korea Under the Koryo Dynasty

Like Vietnam, Korea did not strike Zhao Rugua as foreign: "*Their houses, utensils and implements, their mode of dressing and their methods of administration are,*" Zhao remarked, "*more or less copies of what we have in China.*"* In 936, the founder of the **Koryo dynasty** (936–1392) defeated his last rival and founded the dynasty that gave its name to the modern country of Korea. He modeled the structure of the central government on the Tang dynasty and divided the region into administrative districts like those in China.

The king used a Chinese-style exam to recruit officials and thereby reduce the influence of his main rivals, powerful families who formed a hereditary local aristocracy. This policy succeeded for over two hundred years until 1170, when aristocrats and their military supporters overthrew the Chinese-style administration. Military officers took over all government positions, and men of letters retreated to the countryside. Kings continued to rule as figureheads, but the top generals could and did replace them at will.

Trade with China, persisted even during these politically unstable times. Korea exported precious metals like gold, silver, and copper and edible goods like ginseng and pine nuts in exchange for Chinese silks, books, and high-quality ceramics (see Map 12.1). Korean potters built high-firing kilns in which they made pale green, inlaid celadon pots even more beautiful than Chinese export ware.

Korean Celadon Vase Sometime after 1150, Korean potters introduced an important innovation to Chinese celadon wares, with their characteristic green-gray glaze colored by iron pigments. After the vessels had hardened to the consistency of cheese, the potters cut holes in the surface of thrown pots and then filled them with a mixture of water and different colors of clay. They used black and white inlay to delineate the three cranes—each in a distinctive posture—a small grove of bamboos, and a partridge looking at the cranes. (Prunus vase with inlaid bamboo and cranes, Goryeo dynasty, early 13th century (stoneware with celadon glaze), Korean School (13th century)/Museum of Fine Arts, Boston, Massachusetts, USA/Bequest of Charles Bain Hoyt—Charles Bain Hoyt Collection/Bridgeman Images)

*Frederick Hirth and W. W. Rockhill, *Chau Ju-kua: His Work on the Chinese and Arab Trade in the Twelfth and Thirteenth Centuries, Entitled Chu-fan-chï* (St. Petersburg: Imperial Academy of Sciences, 1911), p. 167.

Koreans also embraced woodblock printing. In 1251, Korean printers created a library of Buddhist texts that includes over eighty thousand pages and is universally acknowledged to be the highest-quality set made anywhere in East Asia. Much more so than their Chinese counterparts, Korean printers adopted the technology of movable type. As we have seen, the world's first surviving book printed with movable type was made in Korea.

Transition to the Kamakura Shogunate in Japan

Zhao Rugua called Japan the "Land of the Rising Sun," because *"this country is situated near the place where the sun rises."** The Japanese, Zhao reported, exported cedar planks from trees as tall as 15 yards (15 m). *"The natives split them into planks, which they transport in large junks to our port of Quanzhou for sale."** So many Song dynasty coins flowed into Japan that Chinese coins became the unofficial currency of Japan, which did not mint its own coins at the time.

Although the Japanese emperors had earlier looked to China as a model (see Chapter 8), after 900 certain warrior clans gradually gained power and forced the emperor to retire to Kyoto, abandon Chinese-style government, and remain as a figurehead. In 1185, the Minamoto (ME-nah-MOE-toe) clan defeated its rivals and established a new capital at Kamakura, a city just outside modern Tokyo.

During the Kamakura period (1185–1333), political power rested in the hands of the **shogun**, or general, who claimed to govern on behalf of the emperor. The shogun did not conduct Chinese-style civil service examinations but appointed members of powerful clans to office. Still, scholars continued to study both Buddhist and Confucian texts, many of them imported from China and written in Chinese characters; they also used the kana alphabet to write Japanese (see Chapter 8).

The shogun patronized Buddhism, and the teachings of **Zen Buddhism** attracted many followers. Zen masters posed puzzling questions with no clear answer: for example, what is the sound of one hand clapping? As disciples meditated on these questions, their masters hoped that they would suddenly understand the teachings of the master and attain enlightenment.

shogun
"General" in Japanese; an all-powerful military leader governing on behalf of the emperor, who lived in Kyoto but exercised little actual power.

Zen Buddhism
A Japanese school of Buddhism that emphasized attaining enlightenment through meditation.

---

*Frederick Hirth and W. W. Rockhill, *Chau Ju-kua: His Work on the Chinese and Arab Trade in the Twelfth and Thirteenth Centuries, Entitled Chu-fan-chï* (St. Petersburg: Imperial Academy of Sciences, 1911), pp. 170, 149.

CONTEXT AND CONNECTIONS

The World of China's Commercial Revolution

When later Chinese looked back on the Song dynasty, they had many reasons to be proud. To be sure, the dynasty's military forces had suffered the massive loss in 1126 of all north China to the Jurchen, as Li Qingzhao so movingly recorded in her memoir of her first marriage. But as wealthy urbanites living in Kaifeng before 1127, she and her husband were able to enjoy all the fruits of the commercial revolution. The expansion of markets changed everyone's lives dramatically. Freed from the necessity to grow their own food, many cultivators began to produce goods for local markets. Government-issued coins and paper money, and even the treaty obligations of the Song to send annual payments north to buy peace, fueled the steady economic growth of China, quite possibly the world's richest country in the twelfth and thirteenth centuries. No country matched China's output of

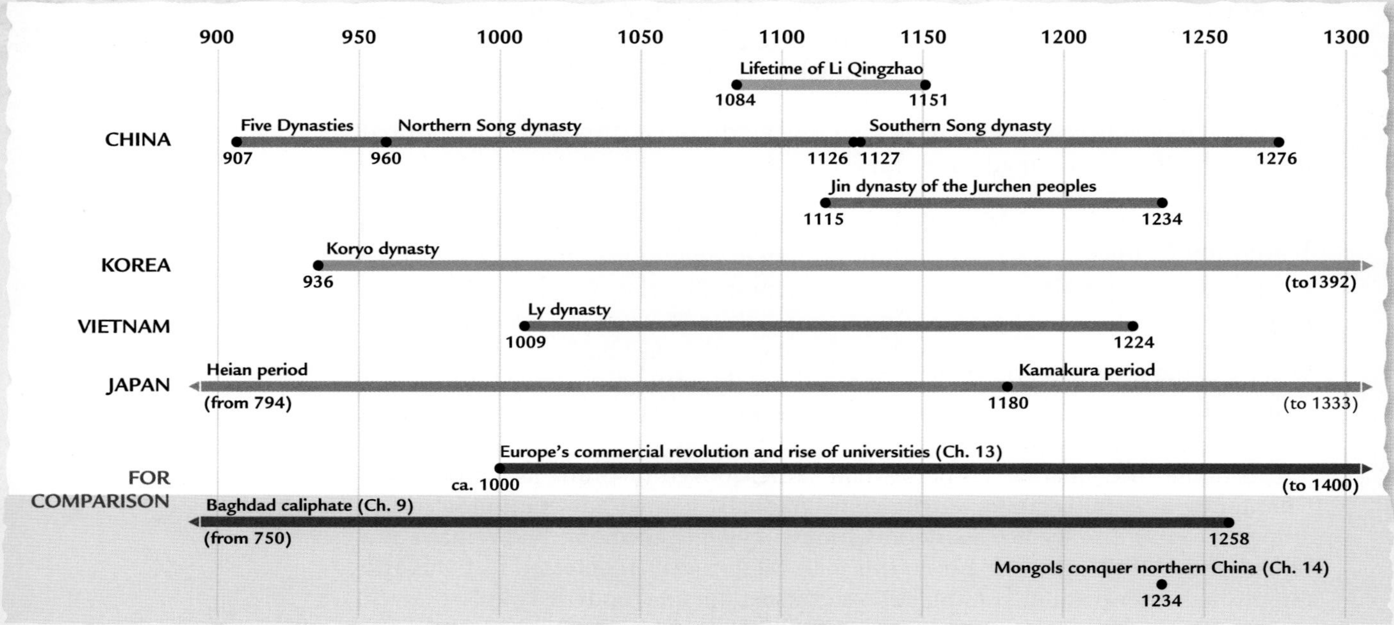

iron until Britain did so in 1700, just at the start of the Industrial Revolution.

The wealth had other far-reaching effects. It sustained an increase in the number of books that circulated, whether printed with woodblocks or, much less common, with movable type. Books spread throughout society, and libraries, both government and private, grew dramatically. Young children of both sexes learned to read, and boys from the upper strata studied for and took the civil service examinations. The top candidates received the degree of advanced scholar, an indicator of learning unique to China and likewise to Korea and Vietnam, the two societies that also administered Chinese-style civil service examinations. As we saw in the preceding chapter, the Islamic world had an equally sophisticated madrasa-based educational system but no comparable degrees.

Unlike any of its contemporaries, the Chinese bureaucracy recruited over 90 percent of new officials by exam and not by recommendation, as was the case in so much of the world. After 1200 some scholars turned away from official life and devoted themselves to studying the teachings of Zhu Xi and the other Neo-Confucians, who stressed how learning could help individuals to gain sagehood, the goal of their teachings.

The sustained economic growth fueled improvements in mapmaking, boat building, and navigational instruments. The makers of the world's first grid maps, the Chinese depicted foreign lands verbally rather than visually. Their ships, which Ibn Battuta encountered in India (see Chapter 11), were the envy of other countries for their size, adjustable sails, and watertight separate compartments. The use of steel-needle compasses on board allowed ships to sail on direct deep-water routes to Vietnam and Cambodia for the first time. News about even more distant places filtered back to China via the traders who came to her ports: in addition to hearing about Arabia, Zhao Rugua even learned about Spain, Sicily, and the slave traders of Africa (see Chapters 9 and 11). Knowing nothing of the nomadic peoples of the north, however, Zhao was completely unaware that as he was writing, a powerful confederation of Mongols was taking shape on the grasslands of Eurasia (see Chapter 14).

China's wealth affected the whole region of East Asia. Song-issued coins traveled all around to form a Song dynasty currency sphere that included Japan, Korea, and Vietnam. So many Chinese coins circulated in Japan that they became the country's unofficial currency.

China's commercial revolution made it possible for couples like Li Qingzhao and Zhao Mingcheng to live a civilized, cosmopolitan life in the Northern Song capital of Kaifeng, a city rivaled only by Cairo in size and attractions. During these same centuries, Europe experienced a period of comparable growth. In the next chapter, we will meet a similarly talented couple who lived through hardships far worse than those suffered by Li Qingzhao on the death of her husband.

Key Terms

Li Qingzhao (340)
Song dynasty (341)
Jin dynasty (341)
gunpowder (342)
paper money (346)
New Policies (346)
movable type (353)
advanced scholar (355)
shadow privilege (356)
Zhu Xi (358)
Neo-Confucianism (358)
steel-needle compass (360)
Zhao Rugua (361)
Ly dynasty (361)
Koryo dynasty (364)
shogun (365)
Zen Buddhism (365)

For Further Reference

Bol, Peter K. "The Sung Examination System and the Shih." *Asia Major*, 3d ser., 3, no. 1 (1990): 149–171.

Chaffee, John. *The Thorny Gates of Learning in Sung China: A Social History of Examinations*. Albany: SUNY Press, 1995.

De Weerdt, Hilde. *Competition over Content: Negotiating Standards for the Civil Service Examinations in Imperial China (1127–1279)*. Cambridge, Mass.: Harvard University Asia Center, 2007.

Ebrey, Patricia. *The Inner Quarters: Marriage and the Lives of Chinese Women in the Sung Period*. Berkeley: University of California Press, 1993.

Egan, Ronald. *The Burden of Female Talent: The Poet Li Qingzhao and Her History in China*. Cambridge: Harvard University Asia Center, 2013.

Farris, William Wayne. *Japan to 1600: A Social and Economic History*. Honolulu: University of Hawai'i Press, 2009.

Franke, Herbert. "The Chin Dynasty." In *Alien Regimes and Border States, 907–1368*, vol. 6 of *The Cambridge History of China*, eds. Denis C. Twitchett and Herbert Franke. New York: Cambridge University Press, 1994.

Hall, Kenneth R. *A History of Early Southeast Asia: Maritime Trade and Societal Development, 100–1500*. Lanham, Md.: Rowman and Littlefield, 2011.

Hansen, Valerie. *The Open Empire: A History of China to 1800*. 2d ed. New York: W. W. Norton, 2015.

Holcombe, Charles. *A History of East Asia from the Origins of Civilization to the Twenty-First Century*. New York: Cambridge University Press, 2011.

Temple, Robert. *The Genius of China: 3,000 Years of Science, Discovery, and Invention*. Rochester, Vt.: Inner Traditions, 2007.

AP® Review Questions for Chapter 12

Multiple-Choice Questions

QUESTIONS 1–3 REFER TO THE FOLLOWING PASSAGE.

In cases of robbery by force, when no property is obtained, the punishment is penal servitude for two years. When the stolen property is valued at up to a foot of silk, the punishment is penal servitude for three years. For each additional two lengths of silk, the punishment is one degree heavier. When the value has reached ten lengths of silk or someone has been injured, the sentence is strangulation. When killing has occurred, the sentence is decapitation.

—Tang Legal Code, 653 C.E.

1. The severity of the punishments in the Tang law code demonstrates which of the following?
   (A) The harshness of Chinese law compared to other contemporary civilizations
   (B) The continued dominance of Daoism within the imperial bureaucracy
   (C) The immense value of silk in the Postclassical era
   (D) Consistent contact with steppe nomads

2. The law code demonstrates that, in the Postclassical era, silk was
   (A) used as a form of currency or a way of calculating wealth.
   (B) used primarily as a commodity for religious rites.
   (C) used to promote the status of the merchant classes.
   (D) reserved only for use by religious elites.

3. The use of both physical punishments and fines in Tang China is an example of empires of the time period
   (A) rarely innovating upon their older, more established forms of statecraft.
   (B) building on older traditions to meet new economic and political situations.
   (C) abandoning their political traditions completely.
   (D) relying entirely on the laws and customs of conquered peoples.

QUESTIONS 4–6 REFER TO THE FOLLOWING PASSAGE.

Bi Sheng, a man of unofficial position, made moveable type. His method was as follows: he took sticky clay and cut it into characters as thin as the edge of a coin. . . . When he wished to print, he took an iron frame. . . . In this he placed the types, set close together. . . . If one were to print only two or three copies, this method would be neither simple nor easy. But for printing hundreds or thousands of copies, it was marvelously quick.

—Eleventh century description of Bi Sheng's invention found in Tsien Tsuen-hsuin, *Chemistry and Chemical Technology, Part I: Paper and Printing*, Vol. 1 of *Science and Civilisation in China*

4. Which of the following was a direct result of Bi Sheng's invention?
   (A) Increased book bans by Legalist officials
   (B) Motivation for the creation and development of paper
   (C) Increased efficiency of the imperial civil service
   (D) Significant decrease in the price of books

5. A long-term effect of Bi Sheng's creation was
   (A) a significant drop in literacy rates in China.
   (B) fewer official histories written by Confucian scholars.
   (C) the spread of printing press technology to Europe.
   (D) fewer qualified candidates sitting for the civil service exams.

6. Bi Sheng's technology allowed the Chinese and the Mongols to experiment with which of the following?
   (A) Paper money
   (B) Gunpowder weapons
   (C) Water-powered clocks
   (D) New types of fast-growing rice

QUESTIONS 7–10 REFER TO THE FOLLOWING IMAGE.

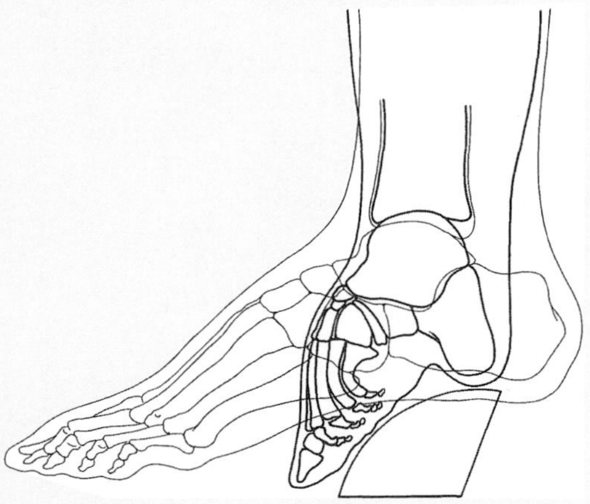

7. The practice of binding feet can be viewed in the context of the
   (A) Daoist search for harmony through nature.
   (B) Legalist requirements for harsh punishments.
   (C) Neo-Confucianism emphasis on patriarchal gender norms.
   (D) Buddhist commitments to renounce family life for monasticism.

8. Which of the following would be considered a challenge to the ideals supporting binding women's feet?
   (A) Buddhist nuns participating in religious rituals
   (B) The practice of having multiple wives and concubines
   (C) Women's responsibility for caring for the family and house
   (D) Preference for sons over daughters

9. Which of the following played a similar role to foot binding?
   (A) Women owning property in Muslim Arabia
   (B) The writings of female mystics in Medieval Europe
   (C) Women joining artisan guilds in Europe
   (D) Forbidding women from mixing with men outside of their family

10. In the Postclassical era, the binding of feet in Song China demonstrates which of the following?
   (A) Social hierarchies were eradicated by more egalitarian forms of thought.
   (B) Social hierarchies persisted in a limited number of regions.
   (C) Social hierarchies persisted throughout the Afro-Eurasian world.
   (D) Social hierarchies rarely put physical constraints on people.

Short-Answer Questions

Father and son should live in love, in peace the married pair:
Kindness the elder brother's and respect the younger's care.
Let deference due to age be paid, comrades feel friendship's glow.
Princes treat well their minister—they loyalty should show.
These moral duties binding are on all men here below.

—*The Three-Character Classic*, a Confucian primer, ca. 1200

1. Using the excerpt, answer parts A, B, and C.
   A. Identify the point of view expressed by the author. Then briefly explain how ONE of the following aspects of life in Tang China was influenced by the author's point of view:
      - Government and administration
      - Family life
   B. Briefly explain how a Daoist would respond to the document.
   C. Briefly explain ONE example of how Buddhism challenged the point of view of the author.

2. Answer parts A, B, and C.
   A. Briefly explain ONE effect of printing on life in the Postclassical era.
   B. Briefly explain ONE effect of Buddhism on China during the Tang era.
   C. Some historians contend that acceptance of Buddhism by the Tang led directly to a decline in the power and influence of the Confucian elite. Provide ONE additional piece of evidence that defends or refutes this interpretation.

13 Europe's Commercial Revolution, 1000–1400

Abelard and Heloise

Sometime around 1132, when he was in his early fifties, **Peter Abelard** (1079–1142/44) wrote an account of his own life entitled *The Story of His Misfortunes*. The title was apt. Abelard wrote about his love affair with **Heloise** (ca. 1090–1163/64), a woman at least ten years younger than he was, and its disastrous outcome. No dry affidavit, the *Story* seeks both to defend Abelard's conduct and to document God's goodness.

Over the course of their eventful lives (they lived at exactly the same time as Li Qingzhao and Zhao Mingcheng), Heloise and Abelard personally experienced the changes occurring in Europe between 1000 and 1400. Like China of the Song Dynasty (see Chapter 12), Europe underwent a dramatic commercial revolution, especially in agriculture. Most of the land in Europe was brought under cultivation in a process called *cerealization*. The economic surplus financed the first universities of Europe, new religious institutions, the Crusades, and trade with East Asia, all of which made the Europeans in 1400 richer and more knowledgeable about distant places than they had been in 1000.

Abelard, like many of his contemporaries, traveled so that he could study. He begins his *Story* with his childhood:

I was born on the borders of Brittany, about eight miles I think to the east of Nantes [NAHNT], in a town called Le Pallet [luh PAH-lay]. I owe my volatile temperament to my native soil and ancestry and also my natural ability for learning. My father had acquired some knowledge of letters before he was a knight, and later on his passion for learning was such that he intended all his sons to have instruction in letters before they were trained to arms. His purpose was fulfilled. I was his first-born, and being specially dear to him

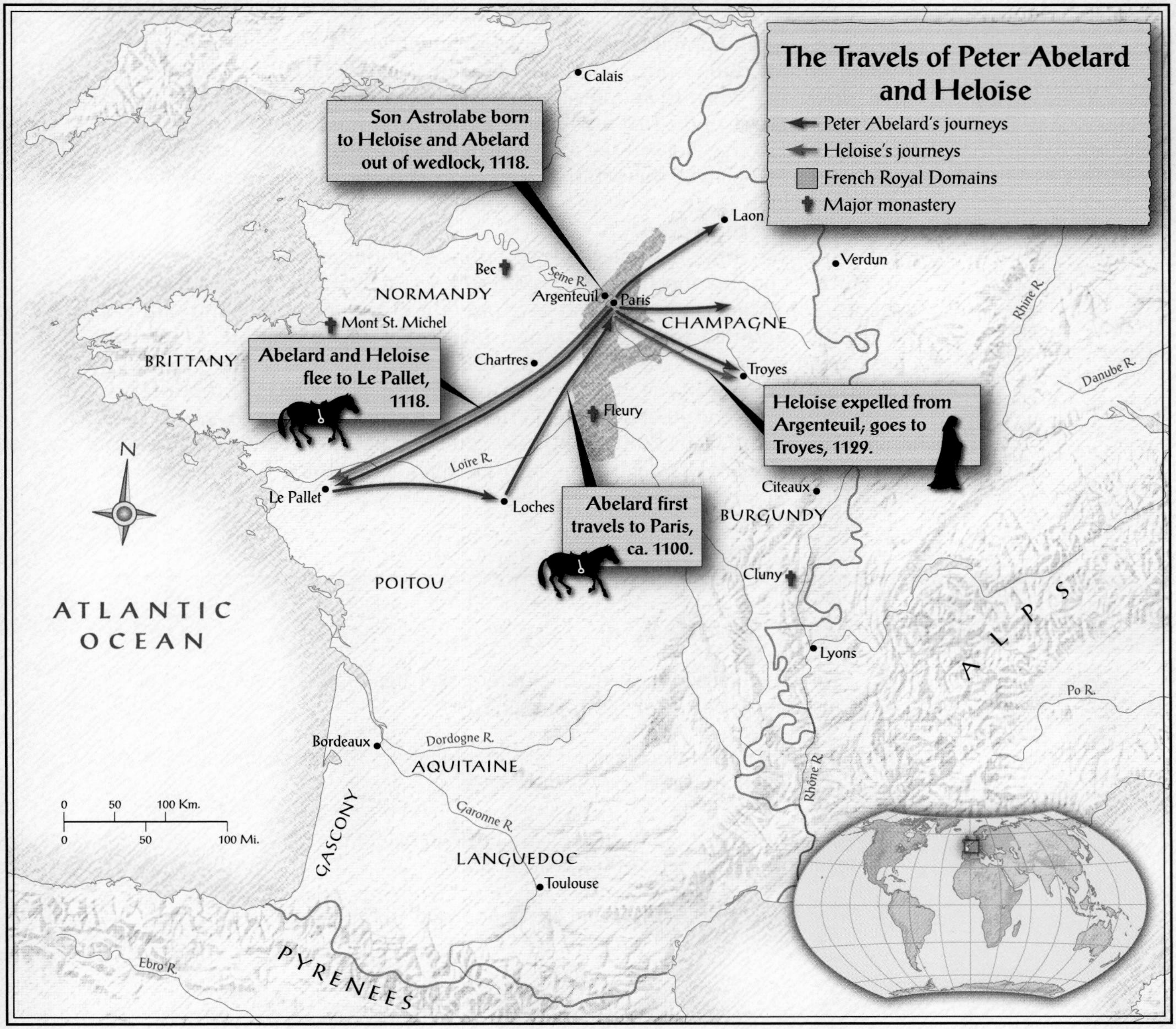

*had the greatest care taken over my education. For my part, the more rapid and easy my progress in my studies, the more eagerly I applied myself, until I was so carried away by my love of learning that I renounced the glory of a military life. . . . I began to travel about in several provinces disputing, like a true peripatetic philosopher, wherever I had heard there was a keen interest in the art of dialectic.**

---

*From *The Letters of Abelard and Heloise*, translated and introduced by Betty Radice (Penguin Classics, 1974), p. 3. Copyright © Betty Radice, 1974. Reproduced by permission of Penguin Books Ltd.

Peter Abelard
(1079–1142/44) Prominent scholastic thinker who wrote about his affair with Heloise in his autobiography, *The Story of His Misfortunes*.

Heloise
(ca. 1090–1163/64) French nun who exchanged many letters with Peter Abelard, her former lover and the father of her child Astrolabe.

Abelard's speaking abilities and ferocious intelligence made him one of the best-known philosophers and most famous teachers in Europe. He traveled from one French town to another until he arrived in the great intellectual center of Paris, where one of the first universities in the world was taking shape. Students from all over Europe flocked to hear his lectures before returning home to serve their kings as officials or their churches as clergy. Heloise's uncle hired Abelard to tutor his brilliant niece, one of the few women in Europe who received the same education as her male peers.

During this time, new methods of farming produced much higher yields, and Europe's population increased as a result. Many landowning families initiated new inheritance practices that gave only the eldest sons the right to inherit their father's estates, forcing the other sons to go into education, as Abelard chose to do voluntarily, or the church, which after undergoing many different reforms, became one of the most vibrant institutions in medieval European society. Both Heloise and Abelard joined church orders after the discovery of their affair. The century from 1300 to 1400 saw a temporary halt in growth caused by a massive outbreak of plague but also changes that strengthened European monarchies.

KEY CONCEPT QUESTIONS

- What innovations led to greater agricultural production in western Europe? **(Key Concept 3.3)**
- How did increased cross-cultural interactions lead to the development of European universities? **(Key Concept 3.1)**
- How did European economic prosperity influence the development of Christianity? **(Key Concept 3.1)**
- What were the technological and cultural transfers that occurred as a result of the Crusades? **(Key Concept 3.2)**
- What factors led to the decline of feudalism? **(Key Concept 3.2)**

The Cerealization and Urbanization of Europe

Europe experienced sustained economic prosperity between 1000 and 1300. The growth resulted not from migration to rice-growing regions as in China, but because Europeans reclaimed more land and farmed it more intensively than they had before. Europe's population grew dramatically, and as in China, the large agricultural surplus freed some people to pursue a variety of careers.

cerealization
Collective term for many agricultural practices that allowed Europeans between 1000 and 1300 to cultivate most of the land in Europe.

Agricultural Innovation

The agricultural innovations from 1000 to 1300 can be summed up in a single word: ***cerealization***. Like the term *industrialization*, the word *cerealization* indicates a broad transformation that profoundly affected everyone who experienced it. Before cerealization, much of the land in Europe was not cultivated regularly; afterward, most of it was.

This transformation did not occur at the same time throughout Europe. Northern France and England were the most advanced regions. Farmers before 1000 realized that land became less fertile if they planted the same crop year after year, so each year they allowed one-third to one-half of their land to lie fallow. After 1000, a few farmers began to rotate their crops so that they could keep their land under continuous cultivation. One popular rotation of turnips, clover, and grain took advantage of different nutrients in the soil each year. This practice, so crucial to increasing agricultural yield, spread only slowly.

European farmers also began to exploit sheep for their wool, while they could use both horses and oxen for transport. By 1200, horses, which worked harder and faster, gradually replaced oxen on European farms. The manure from these animals provided much-needed fertilizer. Before 1000, most of the plows used in Europe to prepare the earth for planting had wooden blades, which broke easily and could not penetrate far into the soil. Gradually farmers, particularly in northern France, added pieces of iron to their blades, which allowed them to dig deeper and increase productivity, and iron horseshoes also protected the hooves of horses

Cutting-Edge Farming Techniques in Europe, 1300–1340 At first glance, the two men working the land may seem to be using traditional farming techniques. In fact, though, this detail from a manuscript illustrates two of the most important innovations in the cerealization of Europe: horse-drawn plowing equipment and the use of iron tools. The horse is pulling a harrow, a large rakelike tool with many teeth that broke up lumps of earth after the soil had been plowed. (© British Library Board/Robana/Art Resource, NY)

pulling the plows. By 1200, many villages had their own blacksmiths who repaired horseshoes and plow blades.

The final innovation left the deepest imprint on the landscape. As early as 500, but particularly after 1000, farmers began to harness the water in flowing rivers to operate mills. Water mills were first used to grind grain and then were adapted to other uses, such as beating wool to make it thicker ("fulling" cloth), sawing wood, and sharpening or polishing iron. By 1100, records show that at least 5,600 water mills existed throughout England, or one mill for every thirty-five families.

● **CONTEXT&CONNECTIONS** Even more powerful than water mills were those powered by wind. The world's first windmills were built in Iran around 700; positioned on a vertical axis, the blades drove pumps that moved water from one irrigation channel to another. They came into use in coastal Europe in Normandy, France, and across the channel in England, just before 1200. However, the sails of European windmills were mounted on a horizontal, not vertical, axis. It seems that travelers to West Asia returned to Europe with the idea and then developed a new technology for capturing wind power. ●

Each farming family performed a wide variety of tasks. Women tended to do the jobs closer to the home, like raising children, cooking, tending the garden, milking cows, and caring for livestock. Men did the plowing and sowed seed, but both sexes helped to bring in the harvest. Many households hired temporary help, both male and female, at busy times of year to assist with tasks like shearing sheep, picking hops for beer, and mowing hay.

Population Growth and Urbanization

The clear result of Europe's cerealization was the marked population growth that occurred between 1000 and 1340, during which time Europe's population nearly doubled, from less than 40 million to around 75 million. Even more significant was the geographic pattern of population growth. The number of people living in southern and eastern Europe—in Italy, Spain, and the Balkans—increased by 50 percent. But the population of northern Europe shot up by a factor of three, with the result that nearly half of Europe's people lived in northern Europe by 1340.

● **CONTEXT&CONNECTIONS** This shift northward occurred in the same centuries that China's population shifted southward from the Yellow River Valley to the Yangzi River Valley (see Chapter 12). And just as market growth in China freed many farmers from having to work full-time on the land, the process of cerealization allowed large numbers of Europeans to pursue other occupations or to produce goods for market. ●

Individual households began to produce products such as butter and cheese or textiles and soap to sell at local markets. At first, people went to periodic markets to trade for the goods they needed. Around 1000, when rulers minted the first coins since the fall of the Western Roman Empire, many periodic markets gradually evolved into permanent markets that opened daily. Inside the walls of most European market towns were the marketplace, the lord's castle, and several churches.

These market towns arose first on the coasts of the Mediterranean, the English Channel, and the Baltic or along inland rivers like the Rhine. During the 1000s and 1100s, more and more people traveled from one market to another, sometimes going overland on new roads, to attend the fairs that occurred with increasing frequency.

Before 1000, only a handful of cities, all the sites of castles or church centers, existed north of the Alps. After 1000, this number increased sharply. European cities between 1000 and 1348 were not large.

• **CONTEXT&CONNECTIONS** One of the largest cities in Europe, Paris, had a population of 80,000 in 1200, compared with 450,000 people in Islamic Córdoba, in today's Spain, and 1 million in the Chinese city of Hangzhou. •

Still, like urban dwellers around the world, the people who lived in Europe's cities had crossed an important divide: because they had stopped working the land, they depended on the city's markets for their food supply. Many urban artisans worked either in food preparation, like butchers and bakers, or in the field of apparel, like tailors and shoemakers. Because one-third to one-half of these artisans worked with no assistants, they depended on their wives and children to sell their goods. Some merchants specialized in transporting goods from one place to another; for example, a German woman in 1420 bought and sold *"crossbows, saddle bags, bridles, harnesses, halters, spurs, and stirrups, as well as . . . arrow quivers, soap, parchment, wax, paper, and spices."* *

The people who lived in cities were intensely aware that they differed from those who worked the land and those who owned it. Most importantly, changing lengths of day and seasons dictated their work lives. Tradesmen who worked in the same occupations and merchants who dealt in similar goods formed **guilds** that regulated prices and working hours; they decided who could enter the guild and who could not; only those who belonged to the guild could engage in the business the guild regulated. After 1000, urban residents frequently petitioned their rulers for the right to pass regulations concerning trade and to mint coins. Local rulers often granted these rights in the hope that the guilds would support them against their rivals.

guilds
Associations formed by members of the same trade or merchant group that regulated prices and working hours.

One visible sign of the guilds' influence was the cathedrals they financed throughout Europe, sometimes with contributions from others. Starting around 1150, people throughout Europe built cathedrals in the Gothic style. A cathedral was both a religious and an economic center. Pilgrims flocked to the Cathedral of Notre Dame at Chartres, France, for example, to worship Mary, the Virgin Mother of Jesus, and her robe, which they believed survived inside the cathedral. The pilgrims hoped that Mary would heal their illnesses and grant their prayers. Wealthy worshipers could afford to buy copies of her robe made for tourists, while others could purchase cheaper, lead figurines to pray to at home. Cathedrals were often the site of periodic markets where people purchased and sold food stuffs and various goods, sometimes from distant places. (See the feature "Visual Evidence in Primary Sources: The Gothic Cathedral at Chartres.")

---

*Claudia Opitz, "Life in the Late Middle Ages," in *A History of Women in the West*, vol. 2: *Silence of the Middle Ages*, ed. Chistiane Klapisch-Zuber (Cambridge, Mass.: Belknap Press of Harvard University Press, 1992), p. 296.

The Gothic Cathedral at Chartres

The Cathedral of Notre Dame at Chartres, France, is one of the best examples of the Gothic cathedral. It has an unusual front because the south tower (on the left) was built in 1160, while the much more opulent north tower was added in 1513 after a fire destroyed the original.

High, arched ceilings inspired awe in those who entered cathedrals, but medieval builders faced a major engineering challenge. Arches built in the traditional manner required thick walls to support them. Two innovations allowed stoneworkers to deflect the pressure away from the walls and build taller structures: vaults with ribs inside the church and flying buttresses outside the walls. With the help of these supports, the ceiling of Chartres rises a glorious 121 feet (37 m) above the ground.

Since the walls did not bear the weight of the ceiling, they could be cut away to hold glass windows. The cathedral's dark shadowy corridors suddenly opened up into illuminated areas where beams of light poured through the stained glass, symbolizing the power of God to illuminate the imperfect world.

Unlike many other cathedrals, Chartres preserves much of its original stained glass, which was made

The north tower, completed in 1507, is so heavily decorated that architectural historians call its style "flamboyant style." It contrasts sharply with the original Gothic style of the south tower. ***Which economic activities does the Cathedral at Chartres portray, and how did it contribute to the local economy in the 1100s?***

Half arches connect these flying buttresses outside to the cathedral wall, which they support, making it possible to build a high interior roof.

Sandro Vannini/Corbis

in multiple steps using state-of-the-art technology. The first step was to make a drawing with different colors marked. Using minerals to color the glass, glassmakers produced flat panes that could be cut to fit the outline of the original drawing. An artist painted metallic oxide onto the cut glass and then heated it in an annealing oven to fix the design. Then a metalworker used a soldering iron to melt lead strips that held together the different pieces of glass to form the window, which was then raised and inserted into the wall.

The window shown here was dedicated to Saint Lubin, the bishop of Chartres in 558, whose devotees believed that he performed miracles, including curing the afflicted. Wine merchants and local innkeepers paid for the window, which was completed in 1210.

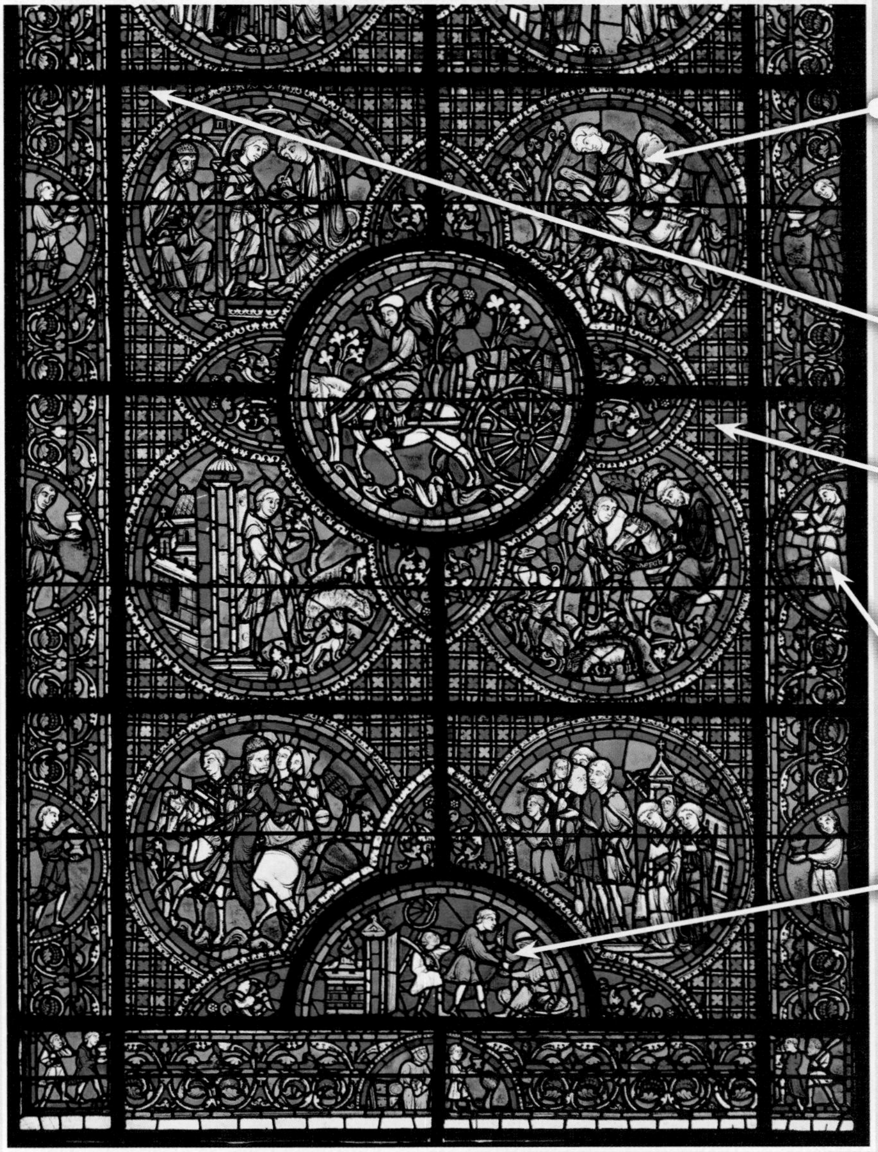

The young Lubin studies his alphabet while behind him his companion quaffs a glass of wine. All the round background windows portray scenes from the life of Saint Lubin.

This smooth side of the window faced the church interior, while the backside, subject to severe weathering, shows the effects of corrosion and deep pitting.

The colors of deep blue, green, red, and white were all achieved by mixing metallic oxides into hot, blown glass.

Artists painted these details with silver nitrite that turned yellow as it was absorbed into the glass. Yellow is the only color stained onto—and not baked into—the glass.

A wine seller gives a goblet of wine to a seated traveler, while the young boy behind him announces that a new barrel of wine has been opened. Above his head is a barrel hoop, the sign of a tavern.

Erich Lessing/Art Resource, NY

AP® THEMES

How did the changes in agriculture contribute to changes in social hierarchy and labor systems in Europe?

Land Use and Social Change, 1000–1350

The sharp increases in productivity brought dramatic changes throughout society. These changes did not occur everywhere at the same time, and in some areas they did not occur at all, but they definitely took place in northern France between 1000 and 1200.

One change was that slavery all but disappeared, while serfs did most of the work for those who owned land. Although their landlords did not own them, and they were not slaves, a series of obligations tied serfs to the land. Each year, their most important duty was to give their lord a fixed share of the crop and of their herds. Serfs also owed labor to their lords, for example, to build roads. After 1000, a majority of those working the land became serfs.

Many serfs lived in settlements built around the castles of their lords or churches, which were protected by the lord's knights. Some use the term **feudal** for such a society. Yet historians today often avoid the term because no one alive between 1000 and 1350 used such a word. The term came into use only after 1600 as a legal concept.

feudal
A term that came into use after 1600 as a legal concept and refers to the legal and social system in Europe from 1000 to 1400, in which serfs worked the land and subordinates performed military service for their lords in return for protection.

The prominent French historian Georges Duby has described the social order of the eleventh and twelfth centuries in the following way. After 1000, the powerful comprised clearly defined social orders—lords, knights, clergy—who held specific rights over the serfs below them. Many lords also commanded the service of a group of warriors, or knights, who offered them military service in exchange for military protection from others.

Knights began their training as children. At the age of fourteen, knights-in-training accompanied a mature knight into battle. They usually wore tunics made of metal loops, or chain mail, as well as headgear that could repel arrows. Their main weapons were iron and steel swords and crossbows that shot metal projectiles called bolts.

One characteristic of the age was weak centralized rule. Although many countries, like England and France, continued to have monarchs, their power was severely limited because their armies were no stronger than those of the nobles who ranked below them. They controlled the lands immediately under them but little else. The king of France, for example, ruled the region in the immediate vicinity of Paris, but other nobles had authority over the rest of France.

In the eleventh and twelfth centuries, landowners frequently gave large tracts of land to various monasteries (discussed later in this chapter), which did not pay any taxes on this land, and no one dared to encroach on church-owned land for fear of the consequences from God. By the end of the twelfth century, the church owned one-third of the land in northern France and one-sixth of all the land in France and Italy combined.

One of the most unusual changes was the rise of primogeniture in northern France, England, Belgium, and the Netherlands, unusual because it arose in no other part of the world. Before 1000, when the head of the family died, aristocratic families divided their property among their sons, and sometimes even granted their daughters a share of the estate. After 1000, they kept their estates intact by passing the property on to only one son. As Peter Abelard explained, as the first-born son, he was entitled to his father's lands but chose to give up his inheritance to pursue his studies.

He was an exception. Much more often, first-born sons kept their family estates, and their brothers pursued other careers, whether as bureaucrats, churchmen, or knights in someone else's service. In many cases, they attended schools and universities before embarking on their chosen careers. (See the feature "World History in Today's World: Debating the *Downton Abbey* Law.")

Debating the *Downton Abbey* Law

The television series *Downton Abbey* has captured a huge viewership on both sides of the Atlantic because of its riveting portrayal of life on a large British estate in the early twentieth century. Although it portrays a bygone world, some of the plot elements persist even today, particularly those relating to the British laws stipulating primogeniture. The patriarch of the family portrayed on *Downton Abbey* is the character Robert Crawley, Earl of Grantham, father to three beautiful daughters of marriageable age. In the first episode of *Downton Abbey*, Robert Crawley's first cousin once removed and heir to his title, Patrick Crawley, dies on the *Titanic*. None of Robert's three daughters is entitled to inherit Downton Abbey and its land. Ultimately, the property goes to another male cousin, who fortuitously marries one of the daughters.

Why could none of the daughters inherit their father's estate or title? Even today British law holds that titles and property held by the aristocracy can pass only to a single male heir, the eldest son, and if there are no sons, then to a male descendant. No matter how distant the tie, the male heir's claim to the property is stronger than that of any of his female kin, even if he is a distant cousin and they are daughters, as was the case in the first season of *Downton Abbey*.

Britain has passed standard legislation banning discrimination on the basis of gender, and it is also subject to the laws of the European Economic Union, which similarly forbid gender discrimination. But this legislation does not apply to Britain's aristocracy, to those who hold titles such as "duke" or "earl" and often inherit lands and property.

At the top of the aristocracy stands the British royal family, who have been rethinking the traditional preference for sons. Unlike other aristocrats, a royal daughter may succeed her father as monarch in the absence of any sons or grandsons. The universally admired Queen Elizabeth II has been on the throne for over sixty years. Her son, Prince Charles, is in line to succeed her, followed by his older son, William, who recently fathered a son. A new law stipulates that the first-born child, boy or girl, will inherit the British throne. And a proposed law, universally known as the Downton Law, would extend this change to all British peers, including dukes and earls.

Even as the British reconfigure primogeniture to make it gender-blind, no one is proposing the division of estates into equal shares among all children. Because British law maintains primogeniture even as the other countries of Europe have shifted to equal shares, the British landscape is dotted with picturesque, intact estates. The ongoing debate over British inheritance law and the limited changes considered show how powerful the rationale for primogeniture continues to be.

Sources: Sarah Lyall, "Son and Heir: In Britain, Daughters Cry No Fair," *New York Times*, June 23, 2013; Geordie Greig, "The Earl with the 35 Million Pound Downton Dilemma," *The Daily Mail*, January 18, 2014.

The Rise of the European Universities, 1100–1400

Although schools had existed in Europe at least since the time of the Roman Empire, literacy rates remained low. Starting around 1100, groups of teachers gathered in two major centers—Paris, France, and Bologna, Italy—and began to attract large numbers of male students, many of them financed by their family's surplus wealth, the product of cerealization. In this early period, the universities were unregulated and free, as Peter Abelard experienced himself. Soon, however, the curriculum became more standardized. In a crucial development, cities, kings, and popes granted the universities a certain amount of self-rule and the right to grant degrees, rights that allowed universities to develop into independent centers of learning.

AP® THEMES

What was the relationship between European governments and learning institutions from 1100 to 1400?

Education in Europe Before the Universities, ca. 1100

Latin remained the language of all educated people, the church, and administrative documents, and students had to learn to read and write Latin before they could advance to other subjects. The most basic schools also taught the simple mathematics needed by peddlers. Before 1100, most people who learned to read and write did so in local schools or at home with tutors or their parents. Some of these schools admitted girls, whether in separate classrooms or together with boys. Many schools were headed by a married couple so that the husband could teach the boys and the wife the girls. Often the schools were located close to the cathedrals that administered them.

While young, Heloise studied at a convent outside Paris. Many years later, the abbot Peter the Venerable recorded what he had heard about her when she was a school girl: *"I used to hear at that time of the woman who although still caught up in the obligations of the world, devoted all her application to knowledge of letters, something which is very rare, and to the pursuit of secular learning."** Few women equaled Heloise in her learning: thoroughly grounded in Latin, she also knew some Greek and Hebrew.

Peter Abelard has little to say about his early education except that he loved learning and that his favorite subject was "dialectic," by which he meant the study of logic. Dialectic was one of three subjects, along with grammar and rhetoric, that formed the trivium, a curriculum with roots in ancient Greece and Rome: one studied the structure of language in grammar, expression in rhetoric, and meaning in dialectic, the most advanced subject of the three. Then one advanced to the quadrivium, which included arithmetic, astronomy, geometry, and music theory. The trivium and quadrivium formed the basic core of the curriculum and together were known as the **liberal arts**. The highest-level subjects, beyond the trivium and the quadrivium, were theology, church law, and medicine.

liberal arts

Basic core of the curriculum in Europe between 500 and 1500 that consisted of the trivium (logic, grammar, and rhetoric) and the quadrivium (arithmetic, astronomy, geometry, and music theory).

Abelard wrote a treatise called *Sic et Non* (Yes and No) whose prologue explained his method of instruction:

> *to gather together the various sayings of the holy Fathers which have occurred to me as being surrounded by some degree of uncertainty because of their seeming incompatibility. These may encourage inexperienced readers to engage in that most important exercise, enquiry into truth. . . . For by doubting we come to inquiry, and by inquiry we perceive the truth.*†

Sic et Non poses a series of questions and then provides citations from classical sources and the Bible on 156 different topics without directly providing any solutions. If one posed the question correctly and considered the proper authorities, one could draw on the powers of reasoning to arrive at the correct answer, Abelard and his contemporaries believed. This approach, called **scholasticism**, was the prevailing method of instruction in Europe between 1100 and 1500.

scholasticism

Prevailing method of instruction in Europe between 1100 and 1500 that held students could arrive at a correct answer if they used their powers of reasoning and consulted the appropriate sources.

In 1114, Abelard was named to his first teaching position in Paris as master of the cathedral school at Notre Dame. He became a canon, that is, a member of the small group of salaried clerics living close to the cathedral. In the following year,

---

*From *The Letters of Abelard and Heloise*, translated and introduced by Betty Radice (Penguin Classics, 1974), p. 217. Copyright © Betty Radice, 1974. Reproduced by permission of Penguin Books Ltd.

†A. J. Minnis and A. B. Scott, *Medieval Literary Theory and Criticism, c. 1100–c. 1375* (Oxford: Clarendon Press, 1988), p. 99.

in his mid-thirties, he met Heloise, who was in her teens or twenties (the exact year of her birth is unknown). Writing his *Story* fifteen years later, he explains:

> *There was in Paris at the time a young girl named Heloise, the niece of Fulbert, one of the canons, . . . and so much loved by him that he had done everything in his power to advance her education in letters. In looks she did not rank lowest, while in the extent of her learning she stood supreme. A gift for letters is so rare in women that it added greatly to her charm and had made her most renowned throughout the realm.**

Fulbert hired Abelard to be Heloise's tutor, and the two fell in love almost immediately, as the *Story* continues: "*Need I say more? We were united, first under one roof, then in heart; and so with our lessons as a pretext we abandoned ourselves entirely to love. . . . My hands strayed oftener to her bosom than to the pages; love drew our eyes to look on each other more than reading kept them on our texts.*"* Sometime in 1118, Heloise became pregnant.

Writing in 1131, Abelard claimed that he was willing to marry Heloise in secret. As a canon, he was allowed to marry, but in the 1100s more and more churchmen were celibate, especially high-ranking churchmen, and marriage would have lessened his chances for promotion. Both Heloise and Abelard saw marriage as a sacrament that joined the property of two families together, not as an expression of love. It is unclear whether Abelard actually proposed, but he was certainly secretive: he smuggled the pregnant Heloise out of Paris in nun's clothing even though she was not a nun.

Heloise's uncle, Fulbert, had no way of knowing about the marriage—if it ever took place—but he found out about the pregnancy. The *Story* explains what happened next: Fulbert's men found Abelard and "*punished me with a most cruel and shameful vengeance of such appalling barbarity as to shock the whole world; they cut off the parts of my body whereby I had committed the wrong of which they complained.*"* The couple then separated permanently. Leaving their child Astrolabe (born in 1118, year of death unknown) with Abelard's sister, Heloise entered the same nunnery at Argenteuil where she had studied as a child.

When the news of Abelard's affair broke, he left Paris and returned only in the 1130s, when he resumed teaching. In 1136, John of Salisbury arrived from England to study with Abelard, and he reported that Abelard "*was so eminent in logic that he alone [of those teaching] was thought to converse with Aristotle.*"† Paris had become the most important center of learning in Europe because more people taught there than anywhere else.

Also during the early 1100s, the university at Bologna in Italy became a center for the study of law. Legal study flourished as people realized that law could be used to resolve the disputes that occurred constantly between kings and subjects, churches and nobles, and merchants and customers. All kinds of groups, whether in monasteries, guilds, or universities, began to write down previously unwritten

---

*From *The Letters of Abelard and Heloise*, translated and introduced by Betty Radice (Penguin Classics, 1974), pp. 17, 217, 9–11. Copyright © Betty Radice, 1974. Reproduced by permission of Penguin Books Ltd.

†Constant Mews, *Abelard and Heloise* (New York: Oxford University Press, 2005), pp. 11–12.

laws. The Magna Carta, which formalized the relationships between the English king and his barons in 1215, is a good example.

The Import of Learning and Technology from the Islamic World, 1150–1250

From about 1150 to 1250, scholars recovered hundreds of Greek texts that had disappeared from Europe along with the Western Roman Empire in 476 (see Chapter 10). Arabic versions of these texts had been preserved in the Islamic world, and their recovery fueled a period of great intellectual growth. Between 1160 and 1200, all of Aristotle's works were translated from Arabic into Latin.

- **CONTEXT&CONNECTIONS** Many highly educated European men, including Peter Abelard, did not know more than a few words of Greek, so the translation of Greek texts into Latin had a direct impact on Europe's intellectual life, just as the translation and annotation of those texts from Greek into Arabic had transformed scholarly inquiry in *Abbasid* times (key term in Chapter 9). ●

After 1100 multiple texts about Muslim learning came to circulate in Europe. Some praised the learning of the Islamic world and held that Christians could learn from it. Others took the opposite stance: one text presented multiple passages from the Quran and then refuted them one by one to demonstrate the superiority of Christianity. Even if readers accepted this author's argument, familiarity with the text increased the reader's knowledge of Islam to a much higher level than prevailed before 1100.

AP® THEMES
How did the introduction of Muslim texts transform Europeans' knowledge of math, science, and medicine?

- **CONTEXT&CONNECTIONS** The reintroduction of the classic texts particularly transformed mathematics. Adelard of Bath (ca. 1080–ca. 1152) translated Euclid's geometry into Latin from an Arabic translation of the original Greek text from 300 B.C.E. (see Chapter 6). Adelard did not know Arabic himself. Instead, he translated with the help of a native speaker who read aloud the original text and explicated it on the spot; Adelard then wrote down the Latin. This was precisely the technique that the early Chinese Buddhists had used to translate texts from *Sanskrit* (Chapter 3). Adelard also introduced the use of the abacus, a Chinese mechanical calculator that uses beads, to the treasury officials of the English king Henry I. ●

Building on Adelard's translation of Euclid, Fibonacci (ca. 1170–ca. 1240), a native of Pisa in Italy, wrote a textbook that revolutionized European mathematics and whose impact we still feel today. His textbook introduced Arabic numerals (which he called "Indian") as a replacement for the cumbersome Roman numerals still in use throughout Europe. (See the feature "Movement of Ideas Through Primary Sources: Fibonacci's New System for Writing Numbers.")

- **CONTEXT&CONNECTIONS** Along with the new numbering system, other innovations from the Islamic world, such as magnifying glasses, eyeglasses, and the *astrolabe* navigational instrument (Chapter 9), entered Europe in the late 1200s. Europeans profited, too, from Islamic knowledge of medicine, which was much more advanced than European knowledge. Paper, which the Chinese had first invented and which was transmitted to the Islamic world in the eighth century, won wide use in Europe only between 1250 and 1350. In the era before printing, booksellers formed workshops in which literate craftsmen copied texts at maximum speed. The ship's compass and the adjustable rudder also originated in China and came to Europe via the Islamic world. ●

Some European scholars clearly admired Islamic learning. Among them were Peter Abelard and Heloise, who named their son Astrolabe. Others, however, remained suspicious of the Islamic world because it was not Christian.

The Universities Come of Age, 1150–1250

As contact with the Islamic world began to invigorate learning, the universities at Paris and Bologna gained significant independence in the century after Abelard's death in the 1140s. As trade guilds regulated their own membership, so too did students and instructors decide who could join the university.

Modern degrees have their origins in the different steps to full membership in the guild of university teachers. Starting students, like apprentices, paid fees, while more advanced bachelors, like journeymen, helped to instruct the starting students. Those who attained the level of masters were the equivalent of full members of the guild. In the 1170s, the masters of Paris gained the right to determine the composition of the assigned reading, the content of examinations, and the recipients for each degree, creating a more formalized structure than existed during Abelard's lifetime.

Most students came from well-off families and had ample spending money; therefore, they formed a large body of consumers whose business was crucial to local shopkeepers. Whenever students had a dispute with local authorities, whether with the city government or the church, they boycotted all local merchants.

The most dramatic conflicts occurred in Paris. In 1229, during the Mardi Gras season, a disturbance broke out, and the authorities killed several students in the confusion. The masters of the university demanded that city officials be punished and left the city for two years until the monarch gave in and agreed.

By 1200, with Paris and Bologna firmly established, other universities formed in England, France, and Italy and later in Germany and eastern Europe. Universities offered their home cities many advantages, all linked to the buying power of a large group of wealthy consumer-students.

● **CONTEXT&CONNECTIONS** As in both the Islamic world and *Song Dynasty* China (Chapter 12), young men came to study to prepare for careers in government, law, religious institutions, or education. However, unlike either Islamic schools or Song schools, European universities had the power to grant degrees independently. University studies, even short of a degree, prepared young men for careers in the church or in government administration, as did the civil service examinations in Song China. ●

Most students did not study long enough to get their first degree, which was the equivalent of a modern master's degree. Instead, many concentrated on improving their command of Latin, which remained the language of educated people and the church throughout Europe before 1500. Learning to take notes in Latin during a lecture greatly enhanced the ability to draft a Latin document quickly. Some knowledge of mathematics was also useful.

With such skills, many young men received employment as literate bureaucrats working for a noble or for members of the clergy, often near their hometown. Over time, as more and more families sent their sons to university, it became the norm for officials and clergy to be literate, and the proportion of students finishing their degrees consistently increased over time.

Fibonacci's New System for Writing Numbers

Fibonacci's name should be familiar from Fibonacci numbers: the sequence 2, 3, 5, 8, 13, and so on, derived from adding two numbers together to produce the third, a series that occurs frequently in nature, as for example, in the number of petals on a flower. But Fibonacci's most important contribution to European mathematics lies in the replacement of Roman numerals with Arabic numbers, which are so much easier to use for doing any calculation, even addition and subtraction.

The paragraph below from the preface to *Liber Abaci (Book of Calculation)*, about his education in Bugia, constitutes almost everything that is known about Fibonacci. His father was consul in the North African coastal town where many merchants of Pisa lived and conducted business. After Fibonacci completed his studies, he travelled around the Mediterranean. His book was pathbreaking not only in its use of Arabic numbers but also in its rigorous use of proof, which Fibonacci adopted directly from the Greek mathematician Euclid (see Chapter 6).

Fibonacci's book explains step-by-step the use of decimal places to readers who clearly have never seen a number system this simple to use. He uses the word *zephirum*, from the Arabic *zephir*, for zero, rather than the Latin *nihil*, to emphasize its Arabic roots; indeed, the English word *zero* is derived from the Arabic. Both the Maya and the Indians had discovered zero independently; it traveled from India to the Islamic world, from where Fibonacci brought it to Europe (see Chapters 5 and 8).

Fibonacci's verbal explanation of the place system is too long to include here; his explanation for the difference between 209 and 290 gives a good sense of his rigorous reasoning. His chart says it all: each of his nine examples is written with just four Arabic numbers but from two to ten Roman numerals. Just for the fun of it, try adding MMMMcccxxi to Mccxxxiv. (The answer is $\overline{\text{V}}$DLV or 5,555.)

Doing so will give you a sense of how much easier Fibonacci's new numbering system was to use. Entering Europe in the 1200s, Arabic numbers have remained state of the art for eight hundred years: even if computers calculate using only 0 and 1, everyone in the entire world uses Fibonacci's numbers on a daily basis.

Historical Thinking Skill:

CAUSATION **What were the long-term effects of switching from Roman numerals to Arabic numerals?**

Historical Thinking Skill:

PATTERNS OF CONTINUITY AND CHANGE OVER TIME **What other innovation developed by the Phoenicians of the ancient world is still used today?**

Source: L. E. Sigler, *Fibonacci's Liber Abaci: A Translation into Modern English of Leonardo Pisano's Book of Calculation* (New York: Springer, 2002), pp. 15–18.

[From the preface to *Book of Calculation Composed by Leonardo Pisano*, Family Bonaci, in the Year 1202]

As my father was a public official away from our homeland in the Bugia customshouse established for the Pisan merchants who frequently gathered there, he had me in my youth brought to him, looking to find for me a useful and comfortable future; there he wanted me to be in the study of mathematics and to be taught for some days. There from a marvelous instruction in the art of the nine Indian figures, the introduction and knowledge of the art pleased me so much above all else, and I learnt from them, whoever was learned in it, from nearby Egypt, Syria, Greece, Sicily and Provence, (France), and their various methods, to which locations of business I traveled considerably afterwards for much study, and I learnt from the assembled disputations.

But this, on the whole, the algorithm and even the Pythagorean arcs I still reckoned almost an error compared to the Indian method. Therefore strictly embracing the Indian method, and attentive to the study of it, from mine own sense adding some, and some more still from the subtle Euclidean geometric art, applying the sum that I was able to perceive to this book, I worked to put it together in xv distinct chapters, showing certain proof for almost everything that I put in, so that further, this method perfected about the rest, this science is instructed to the eager, and to the Italian people above all others....

[From the First Chapter]

The nine Indian figures are:
9 8 7 6 5 4 3 2 1.

With these nine figures, and with the sign 0 which the Arabs call zephir any number whatsoever is written, as is demonstrated below. A number is a sum of units, or a collection of units, and through the addition of them the numbers increase by steps without end. First, one composes from units those numbers which are from one to ten. Second, from the tens are made those numbers which are from ten up to one hundred. Third, from the hundreds are made those numbers which are from one hundred up to one thousand. Fourth, from the thousands are made those numbers from one thousand up to ten thousand, and thus by an unending sequence of steps, any number whatsoever is constructed by the joining of the preceding numbers. The first place in the writing of the numbers begins at the right. The second truly follows the first to the left. The third follows the second. The fourth, the third, and the fifth, the fourth, and thus ever to the left, place follows place. And therefore the figure that is found in the first place represents itself; that is, if in the first place will be the figure of the unit, it represents one; if the figure two, it represents two; if the figure three, three and thus in order those that follow up to the figure nine; and indeed the nine figures that will be in the second place will represent as many tens as in the first place units; that is, if the unit figure occupies the second place, it denotes ten; if the figure two, twenty; if the figure three, thirty; if the figure nine, ninety.

And the figure that is in the third place denotes the number of hundreds, as that in the second place tens, or in the first units; . . . the figure which is in the fourth place denotes as many thousands . . .; and thus ever changing place, the number increases by joining. And as this principle is clearly revealed, it is shown with figures.

For example, if in the first place is the zephir, and in the second the figure nine, and in the third the figure two, then 290 will be denoted. If indeed you will wish to write hundreds with units and without tens, you put in the second place, namely in the place of the tens, the zephir, and in the first the number of units that you will wish, and in the third, the figure two, 209; and thus according to the above demonstrated principle you write with three figures whatever number you will wish from one hundred up to one thousand. And with four, from one thousand up to ten thousand, and the numbers noted above are shown with figures in the following.

Mi	MMxxiii	MMMxxii	MMMxx	MMMMMdc
1001	2023	3022	3020	5600

MMM	Mcxi	Mccxxxiiii	MMMMcccxxi
3000	1111	1234	4321

And thus it is continued with the remaining numbers.

A Medieval University Classroom This colored manuscript page, illustrated by Laurentius de Voltolina, dates to the 1350s and shows a heavily bearded lecturer seated at a podium reading aloud. In the foreground an assistant, most likely an advanced bachelor who served as his assistant, stands before a small class, very few of whom are paying any attention at all, suggesting that this may be a humorous depiction. Although the artist shows the presence of women (such as the veiled figure sitting in the middle of the front row), girls did not attend European university lectures until the late nineteenth century.

The Movement for Church Reform, 1000–1300

Although historians often speak of the church when talking about medieval Europe, Peter Abelard and Heloise's experiences make it clear that no single, unified entity called the church existed. The pope in Rome presided over many different local churches and monasteries, but he was not consistently able to enforce decisions. Many churches and monasteries throughout Europe possessed their own lands and directly benefited from the greater yields of cerealization. They also received donations of money from devotees. As a result, monastic leaders had sufficient income to act independently, whether or not they had higher approval.

Starting in 1000, different reformers tried to streamline the church and reform the clergy. Yet reform from within did not always succeed. The new begging orders founded in the thirteenth century, like the Franciscans and the Dominicans, explicitly rejected what they saw as lavish spending.

The Structure of the Church

By 1000, the European countryside was completely blanketed with churches, each one the center of a parish in which the clergy lived together with laypeople. Some churches were small shrines that had little land of their own, while others were magnificent cathedrals. The laity were expected to pay a tithe, or 10 percent, of their income to their local parish priest, and he in turn performed the sacraments for each individual: baptism at birth, confirmation and marriage at young adulthood, and a funeral at death. The parish priest also gave communion to his congregation. By the year 1000, this system had become so well established in western Europe that no one questioned it, much as we agree to the obligation of all citizens to pay taxes.

The clergy fell into two categories: the secular clergy and the regular clergy. The secular clergy, like Abelard, worked with the laity as local priests or schoolmasters. Regular clergy lived in monasteries by the rule, or *regula* in Latin, of the church or monastic order.

Reform from Above

In 1046, one of three different Italian candidates vying for the position of pope had bought the position from an earlier pope who decided that he wanted to marry. Such **simony** was universally considered a sin. The ruler of Germany, Henry III (1039–1056), intervened in the dispute and named Leo IX pope (in office 1049–1056). Leo launched a reform campaign with the main goals of ending simony and enforcing celibacy.

simony The sale of church office, considered a sin in Europe.

But from the very start, celibacy for clergymen prompted intense controversy. Some Europeans believed in continence—that male clergy could remain married but not engage in sexual relations with their wives. They cited the precedent of Jewish priests at the Temple in Jerusalem, who refrained from sex during the Holy Days, such as Yom Kippur, but cohabited with their wives for most of the year. In the 1000s, when the debate about celibacy raged, many priests' wives came from locally prominent families who felt strongly that their female kin had done nothing wrong in marrying a clergyman. Moreover, the church did not permit divorce, so that option was not open to the women who were already married to clergymen.

Those who called for clerical celibacy interpreted the Jewish precedent differently. Since Christian priests performed the Eucharist, giving wine and unleavened bread to congregants, every Sunday, they had to be in a state of ritual cleanliness year round, which is why they could not be married. Pope Gregory VII powerfully summarized this argument in a letter to an archbishop in 1075: "*those guilty of the crime of fornication should not celebrate masses.*"* Those who supported celibacy believed that childless clergy would have no incentive to divert church property toward their own family, and their view eventually prevailed in the Roman church, but never in the Eastern Orthodox Church based in Constantinople.

---

*Helen Parish, *Clerical Celibacy in the West: c. 1100–1700* (Burlington, Vt.: Ashgate Publishing Company, 2010), p. 100.

● **CONTEXT&CONNECTIONS** Religious teachings took diverging approaches to the issue of celibacy, and religions classed as similar often disagreed on whether sexual abstinence brought ritual purity. Jewish and Muslim teachers abstained from sex only temporarily during certain festivals (see Chapter 9). Buddhists and Manichaeans required celibacy of all clergy, while the *Zoroastrians* (Chapter 6) encouraged their priests to have many children so that their teachings could survive until Judgment Day. ●

Pope Gregory VII also sought to reform the papacy by drafting twenty-seven papal declarations asserting the independence of the church from secular powers. In his efforts to strengthen the papacy, he even claimed *"that the Roman Church has never erred, nor will it ever err, as the scripture testifies."** However, the separation of church and state did not occur until several hundred years later.

Reform Within the Established Monastic Orders

heresy The offense of believing in teachings that the Roman Catholic Church condemned as incorrect.

Abelard was condemned twice, once after his affair with Heloise and again near the end of his life, for **heresy**, a grave charge. Historians may never fully understand the charges against Abelard because many of the original documents are lost. Though he was found guilty, powerful patrons protected him. In 1140, Peter the Venerable (abbot from 1122 to 1156) invited him to Cluny (CLUE-nee), the largest monastery in Europe, and refused to give him up. Peter's invitation quite possibly saved Abelard's life.

Cluny's holdings in land and money were greater than those of the church in Rome, and the abbot there was more powerful than anyone in the church except for the pope. Founded in 910, the monastery at Cluny followed the rules of Saint Benedict (see Chapter 10). Three hundred monks, many from the most prominent families in France, lived at Cluny itself, and one thousand monasteries, home to twenty thousand monks, were associated with Cluny.

Since the abbot did not visit most of these monasteries, monastic discipline suffered. In 1098, several monks broke away from Cluny and began the Cistercian Order, which called for a return to the original rules of Saint Benedict. Unlike the Cluniac monasteries, each Cistercian monastery had its own abbot, and no one was admitted until he was over fifteen and had served a full year as a novice. All Cistercian abbots convened at regular intervals to ensure that everyone followed the same regulations. The Cistercians lived more austerely than the monks at Cluny, wearing simple clothes of undyed wool, eating only vegetarian food, and building undecorated churches. The Cistercian monasteries proved enormously popular, as did other movements for monastic reform.

About half of the Cistercian monasteries were nunneries for women. After 1000, as Europe's population surged, many more women joined nunneries. But because their contemporaries did not think it appropriate for them to do the work monks did, a nunnery needed male staff to run its estates, farm the land, and perform religious services. The resulting chronic lack of revenue made the nunneries vulnerable to outside intervention, as Heloise's experience at Argenteuil shows.

In the years after she entered the nunnery, Heloise rose to the rank of prioress, the second in command at the convent. When the king abruptly ordered the nuns to move elsewhere because he wanted their land, Heloise received a letter from Abelard for the first time since they had parted. He offered to her his own church,

*Joseph H. Lynch, *The Medieval Church: A Brief History* (London: Longman, 1992), p. 146.

named the Paraclete, which had its own lands given by supporters. She accepted Abelard's invitation and served as abbess until her death in the 1160s. They were both buried in the graveyard at the Paraclete.

Reform Outside the Established Orders

Although the Cistercians certainly thought of themselves as reformers, they still accepted the need for groups of men or women to live on landed monasteries or nunneries. But as the drive to reform continued, some asked members of religious orders to live exactly as Jesus and his followers had, not in monasteries with their own incomes but as beggars dependent on ordinary people for contributions. Between 1100 and 1200, reformers established at least nine different begging orders, the most important of which was the Franciscans founded by Saint Francis of Assisi (ca. 1181–1226). Members of these orders were called **friars**.

friars
Members of the begging orders established in Europe between 1100 and 1200, of which the Franciscans were the best known.

Francis was born to the well-off Italian family of a textile merchant, but while in his twenties he abandoned his family and began to live as a beggar. He attracted a small group of followers, and in 1209 the pope granted the Franciscans the right to preach on simple topics like the correct conduct of a Christian, but not to speak on complex theological issues.

The Franciscan movement grew rapidly even though Francis allowed none of his followers to keep any money, books, or extra clothes, or to live in a permanent dwelling. In 1217, Francis had 5,000 followers; by 1326, some 28,000 Franciscans were active. Francis also created the order of Saint Clare for women, who lived in austere nunneries where they were not allowed to accumulate any property of their own.

In 1215, Saint Dominic (ca. 1170–1221) founded the order of Friars Preachers in Spain. Unlike Francis, he stressed education and sent some of his brightest followers to the new universities. **Thomas Aquinas** (1224/25–1274), one of the most famous scholastic thinkers, belonged to the Dominican order. Aquinas wrote *Summa Theologiae* (Summary of Theology), a book juxtaposing the teachings of various church authorities on a range of difficult questions, just as Abelard had; but where Abelard had trusted each reader to determine the correct interpretation, Aquinas wrote detailed explanations that remained definitive for centuries.

Thomas Aquinas
(1224/25–1274) One of the most famous scholastic thinkers and a member of the Dominican order; author of *Summa Theologiae*, which interpreted difficult theological questions.

The Crusades, 1095–1291

The founding of the Franciscans and the Dominicans was only one aspect of a broader movement to spread Christianity that included Crusades. Some Crusades within Europe targeted Jews, Muslims, and members of other non-Christian groups. In addition, the economic surplus resulting from cerealization and urban growth financed a series of expeditions to Muslim-governed Jerusalem (the symbolic and pilgrimage center of the Christian world because Jesus had preached and died there) to make it Christian again (see Map 13.1).

The Crusaders succeeded in conquering Jerusalem but held it for only eighty-eight years. During these years the Europeans who traveled to West Asia encountered new ideas and commodities that they introduced to Europe on their return home. The Crusades marked the first time since the Roman Empire that European armies ventured beyond Europe. Although unsuccessful in the long term, the Crusades established an important precedent for Europeans to establish colonies in distant foreign lands.

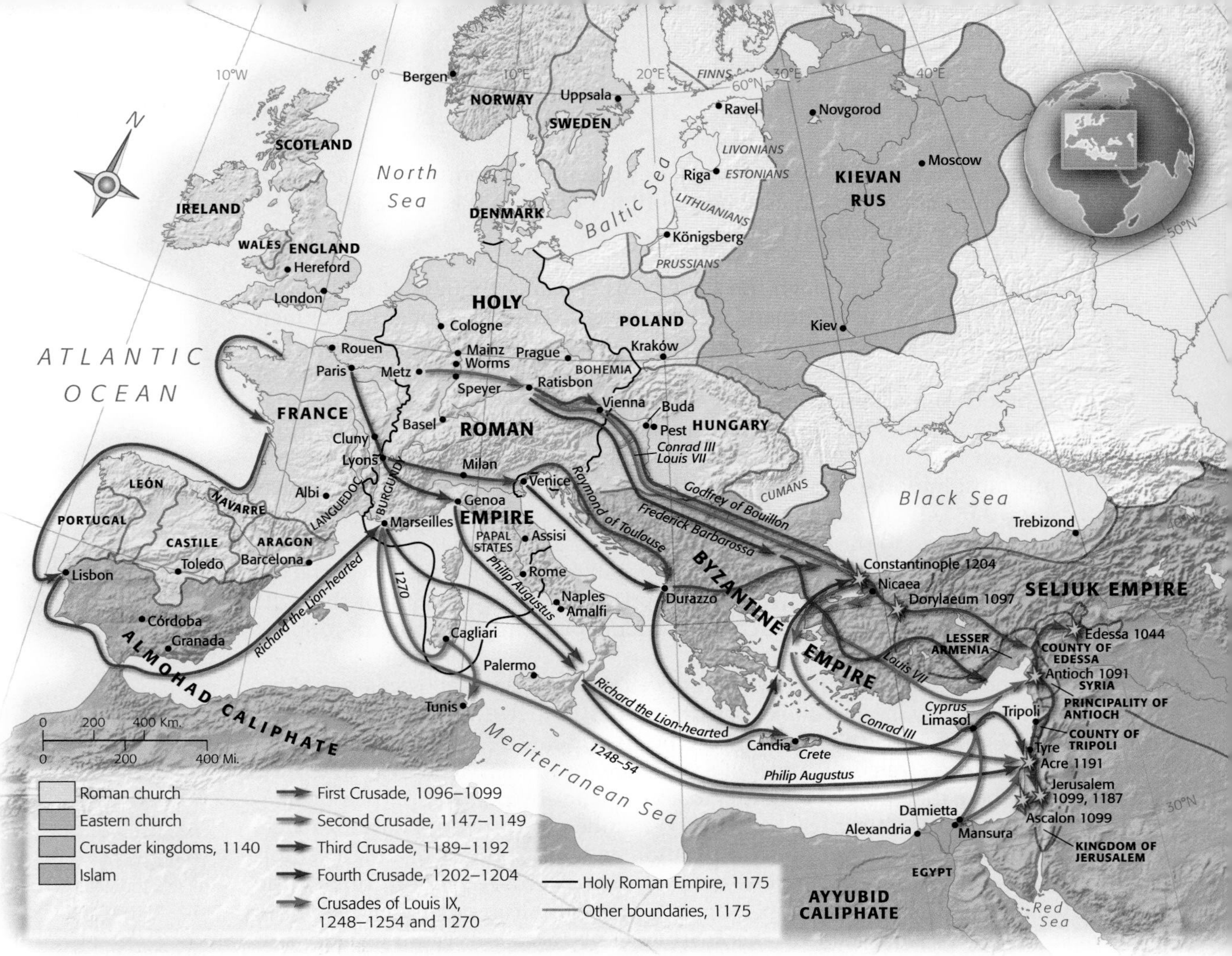

Map 13.1 The Crusades In response to the pope's request, thousands of Europeans walked more than 2,000 miles (3,200 km) overland through the Byzantine empire to reach Jerusalem, which the Europeans governed from 1099 to 1187. Others traveled to the Holy Land by sea. The Europeans who lived in Jerusalem for nearly a century developed their own hybrid culture that combined French, German, and Italian elements with the indigenous practices of the eastern Mediterranean.

The Crusades to the Holy Land

> ***Crusader***
> Term that indicated anyone who attached a cross to his or her clothes as a sign of belonging to a large, volunteer force against Muslims between 1095 and 1291.

Historians use the term *Crusades* to refer to military efforts in the name of Christianity between 1095, when the pope first called for Europeans to take back Jerusalem, and 1291, when the last European possession in Syria was lost. The word ***Crusader*** referred to anyone belonging to a large, volunteer force against Muslims, as indicated by a cross on Crusaders' clothing. In 1095, Pope Urban II (1088–1099) addressed a large meeting of church leaders, telling them that the Byzantine emperor requested help against the Seljuq Turks (see Chapters 9 and 10). He urged those assembled to recover Jerusalem:

This royal city, therefore, situated at the center of the world, is now held captive by . . . those who do not know God. . . . She [Jerusalem] seeks therefore and desires *to be liberated, and does not cease to implore you to come to her aid. . . . Accordingly undertake this journey for the remission of your sins, with the assurance of the imperishable glory of the kingdom of heaven.**

If Crusaders died en route, the pope promised, they could be certain that God would forgive their sins because God forgave all pilgrims' sins. His audience cried, "*It is the will of God*" in response. This marked the beginning of the First Crusade.

An estimated 50,000 combatants responded to the pope's plea in 1095; of these, only 10,000 reached Jerusalem. Of those 10,000, some 1,500 were knights, the only fighters properly equipped for siege warfare. The Crusader forces consisted of self-financed individuals who, unlike soldiers in an army, did not receive pay and had no line of command. The problems of disorganization extended to the top ranks, which included some of France's and England's most prominent nobles. Rarely agreeing with each other about military strategy, they often could not even decide on their main commander. Nevertheless, the Crusaders succeeded in taking Jerusalem in 1099 from the rulers of Egypt, who controlled it at the time. After Jerusalem fell, the out-of-control troops massacred people still in the city.

Reflecting Jerusalem's profound significance for Christians, European mapmakers often placed it in the exact center of world maps that we now call **T-O maps** because they located Afro-Eurasia inside a circle (the "O") divided by a T symbolizing rivers and the Mediterranean. Most often Asia occupied the top half of the circle, with Africa on the lower right and Europe on the lower left. T-O maps were stylized: European geographers realized that Jerusalem did not lie at the midpoint of the world. They knew, too, that the earth was sphere-shaped. The two-dimensional T-O maps depicted only the Northern Hemisphere because geographers believed a torrid zone, too hot for human habitation, separated the Northern and Southern Hemispheres (see Chapter 15). As the Crusaders reported what they saw of the Islamic world and what they learned from Islamic geographers about the world beyond (including Africa), T-O maps showed more and more places.

T-O maps
Stylized European maps of the world that showed Asia, Africa, and Europe with Jerusalem at the center.

The Crusaders ruled Jerusalem as a kingdom for eighty-eight years, long enough that the first generation of Europeans died and were succeeded by generations who saw themselves as residents of Outremer (OU-truh-mare), the term the Crusaders used for the eastern edge of the Mediterranean. Even though Jerusalem was also a holy site for both Jews and Muslims, the Crusaders were convinced that the city belonged to them. The Muslim ruler Saladin, however, disagreed. In 1169, Saladin overthrew the reigning Egyptian dynasty and in 1171 founded the Ayyubid dynasty (see Chapter 9). His biographer explained the extent of Saladin's commitment to jihad, or holy war against the Crusaders:

The Holy War and the suffering involved in it weighed heavily on his heart and his whole being in every limb: he spoke of nothing else, thought only about equipment for the fight, was interested only in those who had taken up arms.†

*Robert the Monk's account, James Harvey Robinson, ed., *Readings in European History: Vol. I* (Boston: Ginn and Co., 1904), 313.

†Francesco Gabrieli, *Arab Historians of the Crusades*, trans. E. J. Costello (London: Routledge and Kegan Paul, 1969), p. 100.

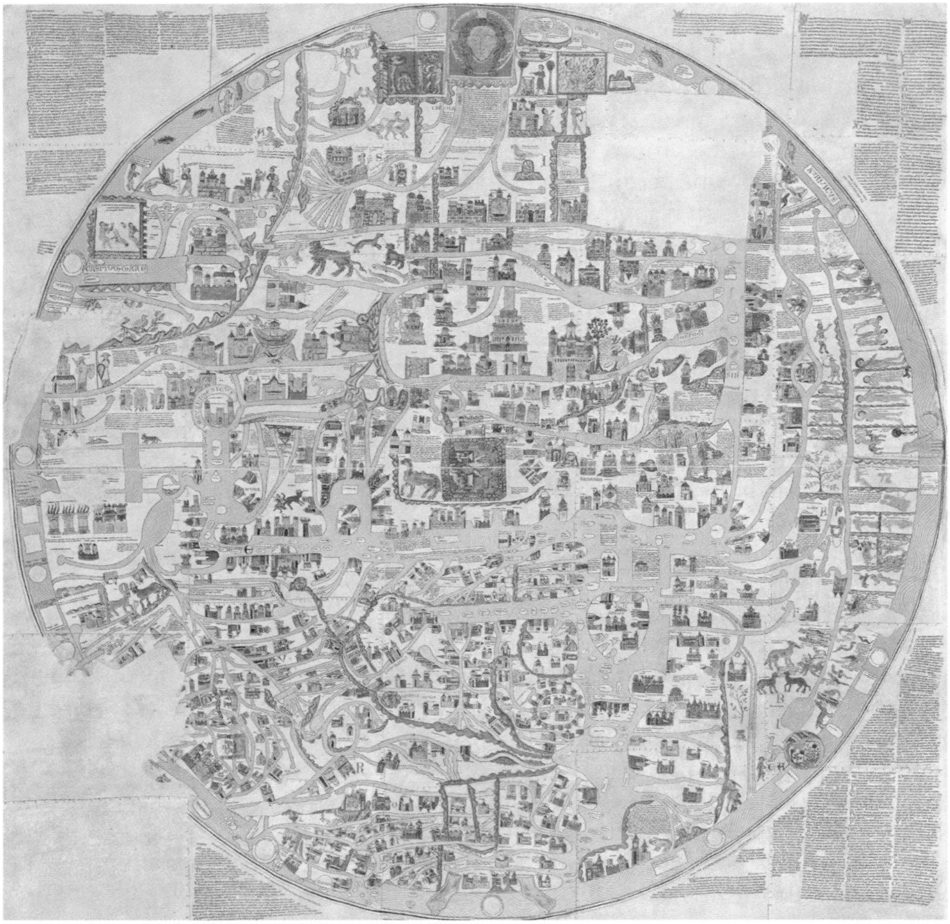

bpk, Berlin / (name of museum) /(name of photographer)/Art Resource, NY

T-O Maps, Both Geographic and Symbolic The Ebstorf Map, made in the 1200s, shows the world known to the cartographer, who combines knowledge of Afro-Eurasian geography with religious symbolism. Because the world is the body of Jesus, his head appears at the top of the map (the east, where Paradise is located), his feet at the bottom, and his hands on both sides. The walled city of Jerusalem, thought by all Christians to be the center of the world, appears at his navel with several large buildings inside it. The map follows the standard T-O format of Asia at the top, Europe at the lower left, and Africa to the lower right.

In 1176, Saladin married the widow of the Seljuq ruler of Central Asia, effectively allying the two great powers of the Islamic world. With this combined power, he devoted himself to raising an army strong enough to repulse the Crusaders.

After completing the hajj, on his way back to Spain in 1185, Ibn Jubayr (see Chapter 9) traveled through Saladin's realm on his way to the Crusader-controlled port city of Acre, where he was able to go even though Saladin was at war with the Crusaders. Ibn Jubayr saw hundreds of Christian prisoners taken captive by Saladin. Like all speakers of Arabic, he called the Crusaders *"Franks,"* although they came from all over Europe, because there was no word *"crusader"* in Arabic. The incongruity of the situation struck him: *"One of the strangest things in the world is that Muslim caravans go forth to Frankish lands, while Frankish captives enter Muslim lands."**

By 1187, Saladin had gathered an army of thirty thousand men on horseback carrying lances and swords like knights but without chain-mail armor. Half of his army consisted of light cavalry who could maneuver much more quickly than the twenty thousand Crusaders they faced. Saladin laid a trap for the Crusaders in an extinct Syrian volcano called the Horns of Hattin. The Crusader forces had no way to replenish their water supply, but the Muslim armies made sure that each camp had storage tanks supplied by camels carrying goat skins filled with water. On the day of the battle, Saladin's well-rested forces easily defeated the parched and exhausted Crusaders, baiting them by pouring fresh water out on the ground instead of giving it to them to drink.

When Saladin's victorious troops took Jerusalem back, they restored the mosques as houses of worship and removed the crosses from all Christian churches, although they did allow Christians to visit the city. Subsequent Crusades failed to recapture Jerusalem, but in 1201, the Europeans decided to make a further attempt in the Fourth Crusade. Because they did not have enough ships, they promised to pay the Venetian navy to transport them to the Holy Land. In June 1203, the Crusaders reached Constantinople and were astounded by its size: the ten biggest cities in Europe could easily fit within its imposing walls, and its population surpassed 1 million (see Table 13.1). One awe-struck soldier wrote home, *"If anyone should recount to you the hundredth part of the richness and the beauty and the nobility that was found in the abbeys and in the churches and the palaces and . . . in the city, it would seem like a lie and you would not believe it."*†

Table 13.1 **The World's Largest Cities in the Year 1300**

City	Modern Location	Population
Hangzhou	China	1,000,000
Cairo	Egypt	400,000
Beijing	China	400,000
Paris	France	230,000
Constantinople	Turkey	100,000
London	United Kingdom	45,000
Baghdad	Iraq	40,000
Córdoba	Spain	40,000

All figures for premodern populations are only rough approximations based on uncertain data; their actual populations may have been half or double the figures given here.

Sources: Tertius Chandler, *Four Thousand Years of Urban Growth: A Historical Census* (Lewiston, N.Y.: Edwin Mellen Press, 1987); George Modelski, *World Cities, -3000 to 2000* (Washington, D.C.: Faros, 2000, 2003).

**The Travels of Ibn Jubayr*, trans. R. J. C. Broadhurst (London: Jonathan Cape, 1952), p. 313.

†Thomas F. Madden, ed., *The Crusades: The Essential Readings* (Oxford: Blackwell, 2002), p. 109, n4; citing Robert of Clari, *The Conquest of Constantinople*, trans. Edgar Holmes McNeal (New York: Columbia University Press, 1936), p. 112.

When Byzantine leaders refused to help pay their transport costs as they had promised, Crusade leaders commanded their troops to attack and plunder the city. One of the most infamous atrocities in world history resulted: the Crusaders rampaged throughout the beautiful city, killing all who opposed them and raping thousands of women. They treated the Eastern Orthodox Christians of Constantinople precisely as if they were the Muslim enemy. As a result the diplomatic dispute between the two churches, which had begun in 1054 (see Chapter 10), became a genuine and lasting schism between Roman Catholics and Eastern Orthodox adherents. After the devastation of the Fourth Crusade, Constantinople and its population declined dramatically.

● **CONTEXT&CONNECTIONS** Europeans did not regain control of Jerusalem, but Cyprus remained in European hands until 1570. The Crusades provided an important precedent for the view that the conquest and colonization of foreign territory for Christianity was acceptable. Europeans would follow this precedent when they went to new lands in Africa and the Americas (see Chapter 15). ●

The Crusades Within Europe

European Christians, convinced that they were right about the superiority of Christianity, also attacked perceived enemies within Europe, sometimes on their own, sometimes in direct response to the pope's command.

Many European Christians looked down on Jews, who were banned from many occupations, could not marry Christians, and often lived in separate parts of cities, called *ghettos*. They also resented Jewish moneylenders (a profession that these different restrictions pushed Jews to do). But before 1095, Christians had largely respected the right of Jews to practice their own religion. This fragile coexistence fell apart in 1096, as the out-of-control crowds traveling through on the First Crusade attacked the Jews living in the German towns of Mainz, Worms, and Speyer and killed all who did not convert to Christianity. Thousands died in the violence. Anti-Jewish prejudice worsened over the next two centuries; England expelled the Jews in 1290 and France in 1306.

These spontaneous attacks on Jews differed from two campaigns launched by the pope against enemies of the church. For example, in 1208, Pope Innocent III launched a crusade against the Cathars, a group of Christian heretics who lived in the Languedoc region of southern France. In the crusade to Languedoc, the pope's forces gradually killed many of the lords and bishops who supported Catharism.

● **CONTEXT&CONNECTIONS** Like the Zoroastrians of Iran, the Cathars believed that the forces of good in the spiritual world and of evil in the material world were engaged in a perpetual fight for dominance. ●

inquisition
Special court established by the pope to hear charges against those accused of heresy.

In the early thirteenth century the pope established a special court, called the **inquisition**, to hear charges against accused heretics. Unlike other church courts, which operated according to established legal norms, the inquisition used anonymous informants, forced interrogations, and torture to identify heretics. One inquisitor in south France, active between 1308 and 1323, sentenced 633 offenders, many to life imprisonment. The inquisition remained active in the region of the Cathars until 1330, and later popes established inquisition courts whenever they felt it necessary.

In 1212, the pope approved a crusade against non-Christians in Spain. Historians use the Spanish word *Reconquista* ("Reconquest") to refer to these and other military campaigns by Christians against the Muslims of Spain and Portugal. Before 1200, various Christian rulers had recovered isolated cities, such as Toledo, Spain, and Lisbon, Portugal, and the Crusader army won a decisive victory in 1212 and captured Córdoba and Seville in the following decades. After 1249, only the kingdom of Granada, on the southern tip of Spain, remained Muslim.

Disaster and Recovery, 1300–1400

The three centuries of prosperity and growth caused by cerealization and urbanization came to a sudden halt in the early 1300s, when first a series of food shortages and then the Black Death, which Ibn Battuta had observed in Damascus (see Chapter 11), rocked Europe. The fighting of the Hundred Years' War (1337–1453) between England and France caused additional deaths. In the long run, however, the economy and population recovered. The structure of European society also changed, and European kings, especially in France and England, emerged from this difficult century with more extensive powers than their predecessors.

Continuing Expansion of Trade Outside Europe

The Crusaders who returned from the Holy Land were one source of information for those seeking to learn about the world beyond Europe. Europeans gained access to other sources of information as trade networks linking Europe with Asia expanded. During the 1300s, merchants, usually from the Italian city-states of Venice or Genoa, traveled to West Asia, and sometimes to East Asia, to pursue trading opportunities (see Map 13.2).

AP® THEMES

What were the long-term effects of the Crusades on networks of exchange in the Mediterranean?

In the twelfth and thirteenth centuries, Europeans consumed huge quantities of the new spices—such as pepper, cinnamon, ginger, cloves, and nutmeg—that entered Europe from Southeast Asia. Europeans used spices to enhance flavor and as medicines, not to preserve meat, as is often said. (Unpreserved meat spoiled and could not be salvaged; the wealthy ate freshly killed meat.) Surprisingly large quantities of spices went into a single meal: in 1319, the pope presided at a dinner for six guests in which he served lamb, pork, chicken, and partridges seasoned with 1 pound each of ginger and cloves. To obtain spices, European merchants often traveled to Constantinople, the Black Sea, or Iran, where they established small commercial colonies with warehouses and homes.

• **CONTEXT&CONNECTIONS** During the 1330s and 1340s, a small group of merchants lived in the Mongols' capital at Beijing, China (see Chapter 14), where a bishop served the Christian congregation. The tombstone of a Venetian merchant's daughter who died in 1342 was found in the city of Yangzhou, near the mouth of the Yangzi River. No surviving documents mention her or her family, but her tombstone, made by a Chinese artist and illustrated with scenes from the life of her namesake saint, offers incontrovertible evidence of a European community in the Chinese port city. It also suggests that similar communities existed in other Chinese ports as well. •

During these years, European readers avidly devoured books about distant foreign places, especially those that purported to describe the actual travels of their authors. Marco Polo (1254–1324), a Venetian merchant who traveled to Asia, portrayed the wonders of the known world and painted China as especially wealthy. Even more popular was *The Travels of Sir John Mandeville*, published in the 1350s, which described a legendary Christian king named Prester John who ruled over a realm distant from Europe. Polo combined some firsthand knowledge with hearsay; Mandeville's writing was based on pure hearsay. Even so, both books created an optimistic impression of Asian wealth that inspired later explorers like Columbus to found overseas colonies (see Chapter 15).

Map 13.2 Trade Routes and Movement of the Plague The complex network of trade routes linking Europe with Asia and Africa facilitated the movement of goods, like Asian spices, but also of disease, like the Black Death. Small communities of Europeans lived in the nodes of the network: in Constantinople, Kaffa, Khara Khorum, and the Chinese capital of Beijing.

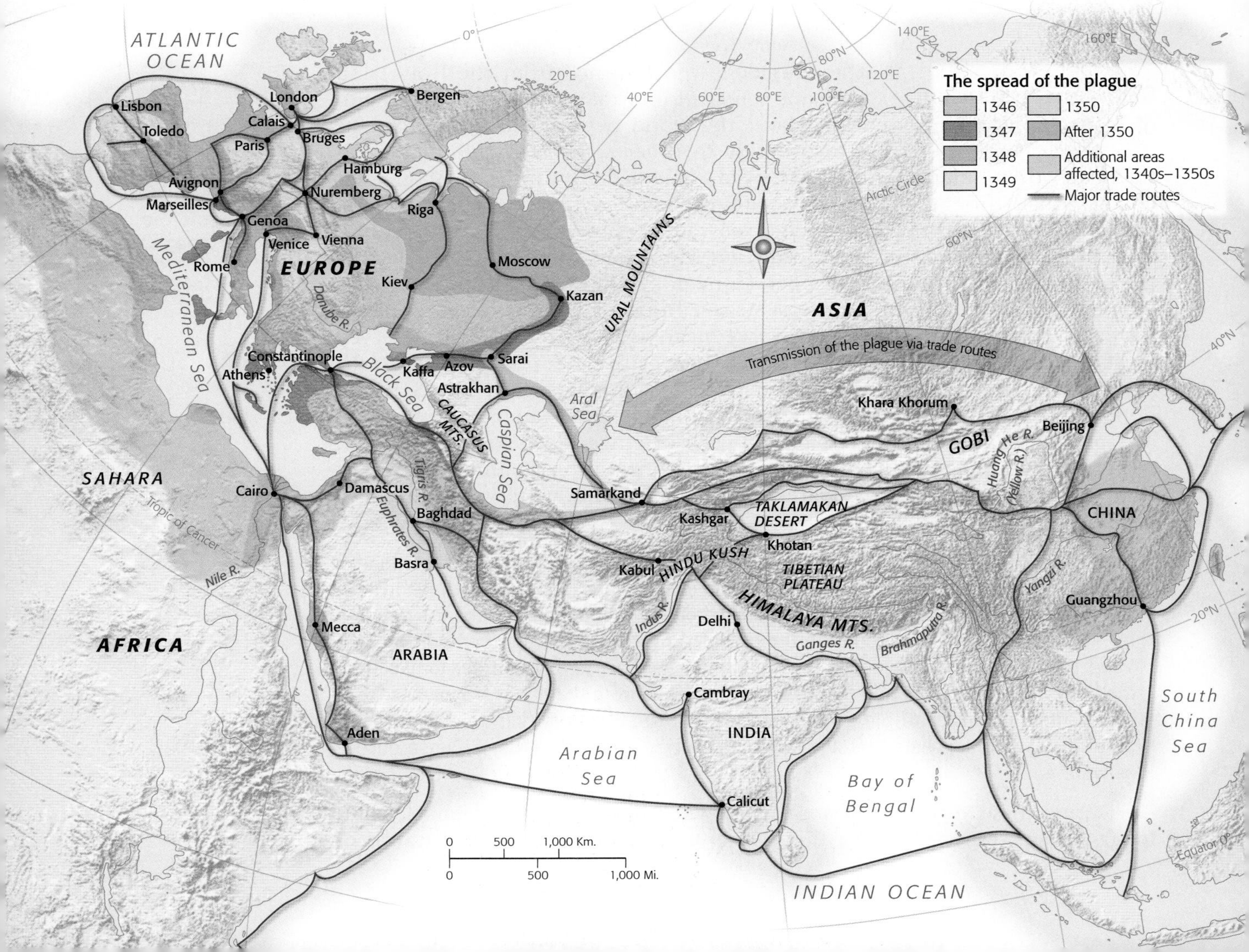

Portraying the Black Death This painting, made more than a century after the Black Death struck Europe between 1346 and 1348, shows Saint Sebastian praying for those who have fallen ill with the plague (top). The artist depicts a plague victim wrapped in a white shroud, presumably because the black swellings on the bodies were too grisly to include in a painting displayed in a church.

Rural Famines and the Black Death

The first signs that three centuries of growth had come to an end were internal. The Great Famine of 1315–1322 affected all of northern Europe, and it was the first of repeated food shortages. Many starved to death, and thousands fled the barren countryside to beg in the cities.

These difficult times caused financial strains that, in turn, led to changes in rural society as rulers and lords struggled to increase their tax revenues. Rulers found that they needed more money than they could obtain from the traditional obligations tying peasants to their lords. In 1315, therefore, the French king freed all the serfs on royal land so that he could charge them new and higher taxes. Landlords in other places, like England and Germany, adopted short-term leases that replaced the lists of customary obligations and fixed rents at higher rates. These changes marked the end of the system of obligations to one's lord, sometimes called feudalism, that characterized western Europe before 1300.

During these difficult decades, the Black Death came first to Europe's ports from somewhere in Asia, possibly north China (see Map 13.2). In 1346, the rats infected

AP® THEMES

What were the short- and long-term social and economic effects of the Black Death in Europe?

with the Black Death traveled by ship to the Genoese colony of Kaffa on the Black Sea. In 1348, the plague struck Italy, and then France and Germany one year later. Like the plague in sixth-century Byzantium, it had two phases: bubonic plague and pneumonic plague, which was almost always fatal (see Chapter 10). Historians reserve the term *Black Death* for the outbreak of the 1300s.

The Black Death reduced Europe's population from about 75 to about 55 million, and it only returned to pre-plague levels after 1500. Since nearly six hundred years had passed since the most recent outbreak of 767, Europeans had lost whatever immunity they had developed, and the losses of the first outbreak were greatest. One doctor in Avignon, France, reported that, in 1349, two-thirds of the city's population fell ill, and almost all died. By the fourth outbreak, in 1382, only one-twentieth of the population was afflicted, and almost everyone survived.*

The Hundred Years' War and Monarchy in England and France

Hundred Years' War (1337–1453) War between the English and French fought entirely on French soil; it enhanced the powers of the kings of England and France to tax and to maintain a standing army.

During this difficult century, the rulers of England and France engaged in a long series of battles now known as the **Hundred Years' War** (1337–1453). In 1337, Edward III of England (1327–1377) was next in line to the French throne, but the French nobles selected his cousin as king instead. Asserting his claim, Edward sent an army to France and launched a conflict that took more than a century to resolve.

France, with a population of some 15 million, was far richer than England, which had only around 4 million. The war took place entirely on French soil, and the opportunity for plunder provided a strong incentive for the English troops.

The long conflict saw the end of battles fought by mounted knights, whose services were provided by the lords under the monarchs. Knights had donned heavier armor to protect themselves, but they could not protect their horses. Moreover, the armor was so heavy that a knight who fell off his horse could not get up to fight an assailant on foot. Early in the war, the English won significant victories because they used a new type of longbow 6 feet (1.8 m) tall that shot metal-tipped arrows farther and more accurately than the crossbows then in use.

By the final years of the war, both sides had turned to gunpowder, a Chinese invention that came to Europe in the 1200s, to shoot stones or cannonballs. Although difficult to aim accurately, these new weapons could destroy the walls surrounding a castle or town under siege and make it possible to take the city. The monarchs could not, though, depend on their subordinates to provide ballistics experts and siege warfare specialists; they had to pay them directly, and the kings instituted new taxes on the lords. Over time, the kings gained the right to tax the lords of their country. The French defeated the English in 1453, when the French and the English signed a treaty marking the end of the war. The Hundred Years' War significantly changed the political structure of France and England: at the beginning of the war, the two kingdoms consisted of patchworks of territory ruled by a king who shared power with his nobles. By the end of the war, the two countries had become centralized monarchies governed by kings with considerably more power.

In England, the king had summoned groups of advisers since the 1200s; contemporaries called these meetings "Parliament," which literally means "to talk."

---

*Samuel K. Cohn, Jr., "The Black Death: End of a Paradigm," *American Historical Review* 107, no. 3 (June 2002): 703–738; p. 727 (Avignon death statistics).

Parliament (PAR-la-ment) consisted of different groups, some nobles and some well-off city dwellers. It met whenever the English king convened his most powerful subordinates to explain why he needed new taxes. Most European rulers convened bodies similar to Parliament; the French equivalent, weaker than Parliament, was called the Estates General and included the nobles, clergy, and townsfolk.

The monarchies that evolved in France and England differed from earlier political structures. France and England were smaller than the earlier Roman and Byzantine empires, and their rulers consulted with their subordinates more often, through newly established bodies like Parliament and the Estates General. Consultation helped them gain the allegiance of their subjects, and once Europe had recovered from the losses of the Black Death, the new monarchies proved to be extremely effective.

Parliament
(literally "to talk") Name for the different councils that advised the English kings and approved their requests for taxation.

CONTEXT AND CONNECTIONS

The World of Europe's Commercial Revolution

Heloise and Abelard, the direct contemporaries of Li Qingzhao and Zhao Mingcheng (see Chapter 12), also experienced great prosperity, but on the western edge of Eurasia. As the shift to rice cultivation underpinned Chinese economic growth, cerealization sustained Europe's. Rotating crops and the use of horses and iron horseshoes, iron plow blades, and windmills allowed Europeans, particularly those living in France and England, to bring more land under cultivation. Between 1000 and 1340, Europe's population almost doubled to reach 75 million, making it the world region with the second-largest population, after China's 100 million. As the population boomed, Europe's cities grew dramatically, too.

As a young man Abelard started lecturing in Paris in 1114, when the cathedral there was in the early stages of becoming a university, and returned several times over the following decades. In Abelard's day Paris did not grant degrees, but by the 1170s instructors determined readings, the content of examinations, and degree recipients. The independent granting of degrees distinguished

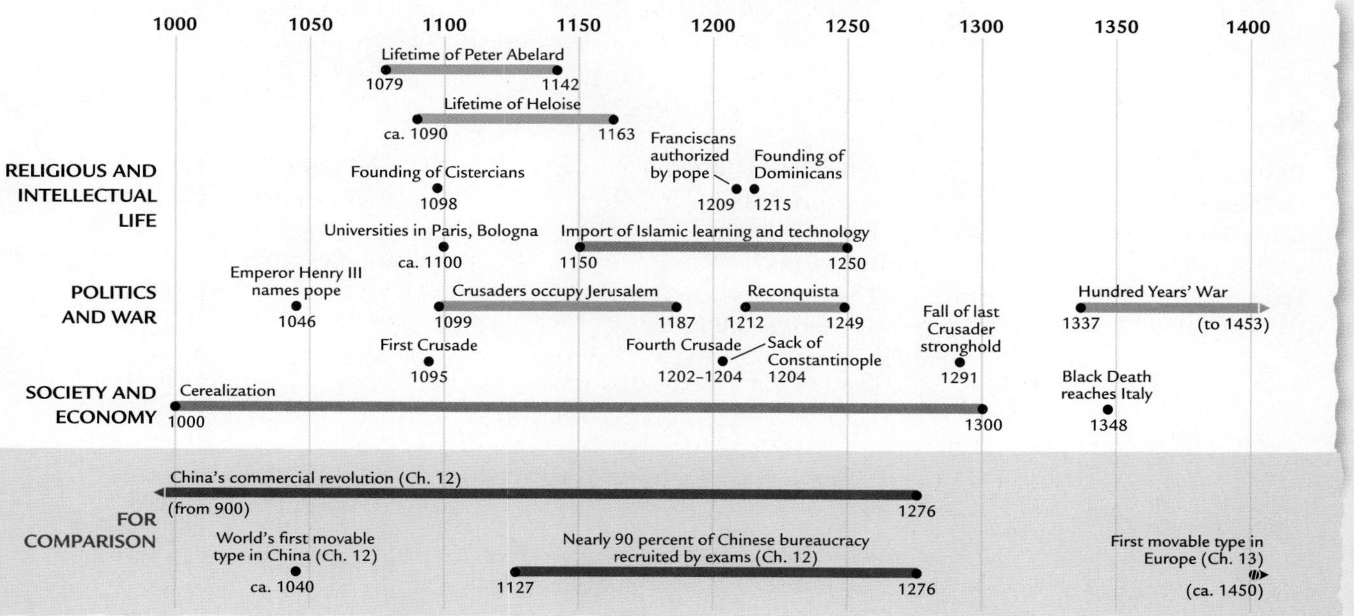

European universities from Islamic madrasas, which did not grant degrees (see Chapters 9 and 11), and Chinese academies, which also did not grant them but prepared students for civil service examinations that could lead to a degree, such as advanced scholar, conferred by the central government on the top performers (see Chapter 12).

Like Li Qingzhao, Heloise, the niece of a canon, had received an excellent education. She could read Latin and some Greek and Hebrew, and like Zhao Mingcheng and Li Qingzhao, Heloise and Abelard delighted in learned conversation. Heloise's education made her unusual for her time, but many girls managed to attend village schools for at least a few years. Some also, like Heloise, joined Christian nunneries, which offered women an alternative to marriage, just as Buddhist nunneries did in Asia.

The church was one of the most important institutions in Europe, although its titular heads, popes, continuously vied with monarchs to control church property, to choose bishops and other high-ranking clerics, and to decide legal disputes involving the church. In the late 1000s, Pope Gregory VII asserted the complete independence of the church; the actual separation of church and state was attained only several centuries later. This church-state division was not as sharp in the Islamic world or in China, where rulers often patronized religious institutions.

In 1095, Pope Urban II called for Christians to recover Jerusalem from the Muslims. We should not overestimate the impact of the Crusades: far more young men traveled within Europe to pursue their studies than joined the Crusades, and many fewer actually made it all the way to Jerusalem. Still, disorganized as they were, the Crusaders managed to gain control of Jerusalem for eighty-eight years.

The Crusades left a more important legacy: for the first time since the Roman empire, Europeans established colonies beyond Europe (Cyprus remained under European control until 1570). Some Crusaders found much to admire and copy in the Islamic world. Even the Europeans who stayed home were affected by imports from Muslim regions: Latin translations via Arabic of Greek texts, eyeglasses, new medical ideas, and an entirely new and much more flexible numbering system. Other imports to Europe that originated in China also came via the Islamic world: the adjustable rudder, the steel-needle compass, and most influential of all, paper, which displaced parchment by 1350. The increasing complexity of T-O maps reflected the growing European curiosity about and knowledge of the outside world.

As European markets continued to expand, demand rose for different commodities, particularly those imported from Asia. The European appetite for spices was enormous. As we will learn in the next chapter, the most detailed account of the Mongol Empire that survives today was written by a Franciscan friar sent by a French king, a clear indication of European interest in the world beyond Europe.

Key Terms

Peter Abelard (370)
Heloise (370)
cerealization (370)
guilds (373)
feudal (376)
liberal arts (378)
scholasticism (378)
simony (385)
heresy (386)
friars (387)
Thomas Aquinas (387)
Crusader (388)
T-O map (389)
inquisition (392)
Hundred Years' War (396)
Parliament (397)

For Further Reference

Baldwin, John W. *The Scholastic Culture of the Middle Ages, 1000–1300*. Prospect Heights, Ill.: Waveland Press, 1997.

Cipolla, Carlo M. *Before the Industrial Revolution: European Society and Economy, 1000–1700*. New York: W. W. Norton, 1994.

Clanchy, M. T. *Abelard: A Medieval Life*. Malden, Mass.: Blackwell, 1997.

Hoffman, Richard C. *An Environmental History of Medieval Europe*. New York: Cambridge University Press, 2014.

Lynch, Joseph H. *Early Christianity: A Brief History*. New York: Oxford University Press, 2010.

Madden, Thomas F. *The New Concise History of the Crusades*. 3d ed. New York: Rowman and Littlefield, 2014.

Mews, Constant. *Abelard and Heloise*. New York: Oxford University Press, 2005.

Moore, R. I. *The First European Revolution, c. 970–1215*. Malden, Mass.: Blackwell, 2000.

Opitz, Claudia. "Life in the Late Middle Ages." In *Silence of the Middle Ages*, ed. Chistiane Klapisch-Zuber, vol. 2 of *A History of Women in the West*. Cambridge, Mass.: Belknap Press of Harvard University Press, 1992, pp. 259–317.

Parish, Helen. *Clerical Celibacy in the West: c. 1100–1700*. Burlington, Vt.: Ashgate Publishing Company, 2010.

Rosenwein, Barbara. *A Short History of the Middle Ages*. 4th ed. Toronto: University of Toronto Press, 2014.

Spufford, Peter. *Power and Profit: The Merchant in Medieval Europe*. New York: Thames and Hudson, 2002.

AP® Review Questions for Chapter 13

Multiple-Choice Questions

QUESTIONS 1–3 REFER TO THE FOLLOWING IMAGE.

1. In the Postclassical era, the above image reflects which of the following trends?
   (A) Innovations in labor management
   (B) Improvements in technology that led to an increase in agricultural and commodity production
   (C) Decline in agricultural productivity that led to the decline of cities in some regions
   (D) Increasing diversification in labor that led to the development of guilds

2. The trend portrayed in this image resulted in which of the following?
   (A) A further expansion and intensification of interregional trade in luxury commodities
   (B) Peasant revolts because of increasing taxation and diminishing land rights
   (C) A demographic upswing in some regions of Europe
   (D) A reorganization of class structures in both urban and rural regions

3. The effectiveness of the technology in the image enabled which resulting trend?
   (A) New forms of coercive labor were a common occurrence during this time period.
   (B) The new technology was so effective that the majority of the population moved to urban areas.
   (C) The technology was exported to colonized regions.
   (D) Interregional trade was relied on to fulfill food needs of the population.

QUESTIONS 4–6 REFER TO THE FOLLOWING PASSAGE.

I used to hear at that time of the woman (Heloise) who although still caught up in the obligations of the world, devoted all her application to knowledge of letters, something which is very rare, and to the pursuit of secular learning. . . . In looks she did not rank lowest, while in the extent of her learning she stood supreme. A gift for letters is so rare in women that it added greatly to her charm and had made her most renowned throughout the realm.

—Peter Abelard, *The Story of His Misfortunes*, 1132

4. The passage above most clearly demonstrates which of the following about the Postclassical era?
   (A) Universities developed in both Christian and Muslim regions.
   (B) Divorce was a right that was exercised by both men and women.
   (C) Religious institutions dominated every aspect of learning in most regions.
   (D) Patriarchy continued to deny rights and opportunities to most women.

5. The expansion of learning, mentioned by Abelard, was possible in this time period because
   (A) many regions were experiencing an urban revival.
   (B) a severe drop in agricultural production led to demographic declines.
   (C) the influence of religious institutions declined.
   (D) feudal structures transferred from rural to urban areas.

6. Which of the following would be an argument opposing Abelard's belief that women were rarely educated?
   (A) Women were not allowed to attend cathedral schools in Europe.
   (B) Nuns in convents frequently had access to books.
   (C) Women were not allowed to inherit property.
   (D) Women frequently handled the running of the household.

QUESTIONS 7–10 REFER TO THE FOLLOWING PASSAGE.

This royal city, therefore, situated at the center of the world, is now held captive by . . . those who do not know God. . . . She [Jerusalem] seeks therefore and desires to be liberated, and does not cease to implore you to come to her aid. . . . Accordingly undertake this journey for the remission of your sins, with the assurance of the imperishable glory of the kingdom of heaven.

—Pope Urban II, sermon given in a field outside the cathedral in Clermont after a church council, 1095

7. Pope Urban II gave this sermon because he was hoping to accomplish which of the following?
   (A) Reunite the Roman empire by invading Byzantium
   (B) Take Jerusalem from Islam and reestablish Christian control
   (C) Reestablish direct contact with the remnants of the Abbasid Caliphate
   (D) Curtail Viking activity in the Mediterranean region

8. Which of the following was a long-term effect of Pope Urban's actions?
   (A) Permanent control of the eastern Mediterranean by Europeans
   (B) Loss of a predominately Christian culture in much of Europe
   (C) A permanent Muslim majority in Iberia
   (D) Sustained European contact with Asian trading centers

9. In what way were Pope Urban's actions common for the time period?
   (A) States were actively separating secular and religious authority.
   (B) Religious elites dominated all of the civilizations during the time period.
   (C) Religious and political power was often combined in single leader.
   (D) Most religious elites existed only to serve the political elites.

10. Which of the following was the cause of Pope Urban II's sermon?
   (A) The reclamation of Jerusalem by the Jews
   (B) Jerusalem surrendering to Muslim armies
   (C) Persian Zoroastrians pushing into traditional Christian territory
   (D) The purging of the eastern Mediterranean of Nestorian Christianity

Short-Answer Questions

1. Answer parts A and B.
   A. Explain ONE cause for the rise of universities in Europe.
   B. Explain TWO effects of universities on European society.

2. Answer parts A, B, and C.
   A. Briefly explain ONE cause for the reestablishment of trade between Europe and Asia.
   B. Briefly explain ONE way in which the renewal of trade affected the European economy.
   C. Briefly explain ONE unintended consequence of trade on Europe.

14 The Mongols and Their Successors, 1200–1500

William of Rubruck

INTERFOTO/Alamy

In 1255, after his return from Mongolia, **William of Rubruck** (ca. 1215–ca. 1295) wrote a confidential report about his attempt to convert the Mongols to Christianity. He addressed it to his sponsor, the pious French king Louis IX (1214–1270). William's letter runs nearly three hundred pages long in translation and contains the most detailed, accurate, and penetrating description of the Mongols and their empire that exists today. In 1206, the Mongols exploded out of their homeland just north of China and conquered most of Eurasia by 1242. For the first time in world history, it became possible for individual travelers, like William, to move easily across a united Eurasia. Such movement prompted an unprecedented exchange of ideas, goods, and technologies. (The highly decorated capital letter below from a medieval manuscript shows two scenes from William's travels.) William's report is just one example of the different cultural exchanges that resulted and whose effects persisted long after different successor states replaced the Mongol Empire. His account opens as follows:

So we set off on our journey about June 1st with our own four covered carts and with two others I had received from them in which was carried bedding for sleeping on at night. They gave us five horses to ride on, for we were five in number, myself, my companion Friar Bartholomew of Cremona, Gosset the bearer of this letter, Abdullah the interpreter, and a boy, Nicholas, whom I had bought at Constantinople out of the alms you gave me. They also gave us two men who drove the carts and looked after the oxen and horses. . . .

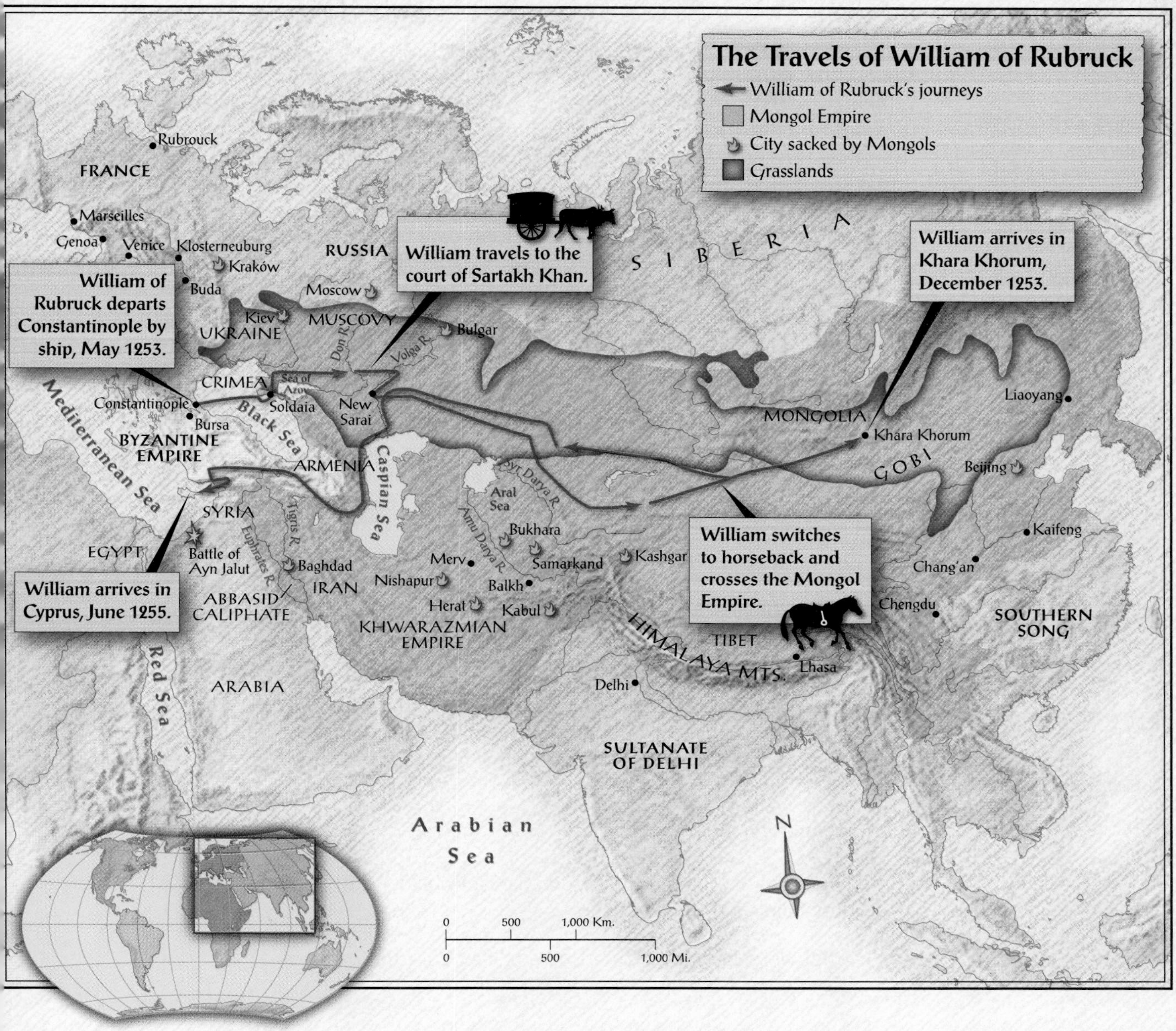

*And so on the third day after leaving Soldaia we came across the Tartars; when I came among them it seemed indeed to me as if I were stepping into some other world, the life and customs of which I will describe for you as well as I can.**

---

*Christopher Dawson, ed., *The Mongol Mission: Narratives and Letters of the Franciscan Missionaries in Mongolia and China in the Thirteenth and Fourteenth Centuries* (London and New York: Sheed and Ward, 1955), pp. 92–93.

William of Rubruck
(ca. 1215–ca. 1295) Franciscan monk from France who visited the court of the Mongol khan Möngke in 1253–1254 and sent back one of the most detailed surviving sources about the Mongols.

In December 1253, after nine months of traveling—first by cart, then on horseback—through modern-day Turkey, Russia, the Ukraine, Siberia, and Mongolia, William arrived at the court of the Mongol leader Möngke (MUNG-keh) (d. 1259), the grandson of Chinggis Khan (the Mongolian spelling; Genghis Khan in Persian). His route through the grasslands ran several hundred miles north of the traditional Silk Routes linking China and Iran (see Chapter 8).

Called William of Rubruck because he was born sometime around 1215 in the village of Rubrouck, France, William was educated in Paris. A Franciscan friar, he went to Syria, then under the control of the Crusaders (see Chapter 13), in 1248 and from there departed for Mongolia.

As an outsider, William writes about the appearance of Mongol men and women, their process for making fermented horse's milk, and their worship of household spirits. No comparably detailed account by a Mongol survives. William visited the Mongols at the height of their power, during the years after Chinggis Khan had united the empire and before it broke apart.

William's gripping description allows us to understand how the Mongols created the largest contiguous land empire in world history, stretching from Hungary to the Pacific. Once they conquered a region or the local rulers surrendered, the Mongols placed a governor in charge and granted him considerable autonomy. Their loosely structured empire allowed many people, including William, to cross Eurasia and resulted in the interaction of societies and cultures that had been previously isolated. This chapter will also examine the states that succeeded the Mongols: the principality of Muscovy (Moscow) in Russia, the Ottomans in Turkey, the Yuan and Ming Dynasties in China, and the successor states of Korea, Japan, and Vietnam.

KEY CONCEPT QUESTIONS

- How did the Mongols and other pastoralists succeed in conquering so many sedentary populations? **(Key Concept 3.1)**
- What techniques did the Mongols use to govern their vast and diverse empire? **(Key Concept 3.2)**
- What techniques did the Ottomans use to expand their empire? **(Key Concept 4.3)**
- What were the long-term effects of Mongol rule for Eurasia? **(Key Concept 3.3)**

From Nomads to World Conquerors, 1200–1227

Chinggis Khan
(ca. 1167–1227) Founder of the Mongol Empire who united the different peoples living in modern-day Mongolia in 1206, when he took the title Chinggis Khan.

Founded by **Chinggis Khan** (ca. 1167–1227), the Mongol Empire came into being between 1200 and 1250. At the time of Chinggis's birth around 1167, the Mongols lived as nomads in modern-day Mongolia with their herds of sheep, cattle, and horses, trading with their sedentary neighbors primarily for grain, tea, textiles, and metal goods. After conquering the different peoples in Mongolia, Chinggis forged them into a fearsome fighting force that conquered gigantic sections of Europe, Central Asia, and China. The Mongols' skill with horses and systematic use of terror brought them unprecedented military success.

The Mongols' Nomadic Way of Life Before 1200

Nomadic peoples lived in the Mongolian grasslands even before the Mongols moved into Central Asia around 1000. The Mongols spoke Mongolian and different Turkic languages that are the basis of modern Turkish. The only source in Mongolian about the Mongols' early history is *The Origin of Chinggis Khan*, an anonymous oral epic that took shape in 1228 and was committed to writing a century or more later. (Many English translations are entitled *The Secret History of the Mongols*.) In 1206, Chinggis Khan ordered a Central Asian prisoner of war to record something he said in Mongolian. The prisoner wrote in his native Uighur, a Central Asian language spoken in Central Asia and in modern-day Xinjiang in west China. After this incident, the Mongols used the Uighur script to write the Mongolian language.

AP® THEMES
How did the geography of the steppe region contribute to the development of the Mongols' pastoral society?

The Origin of Chinggis Khan gives a vivid sense of how the Mongols lived before they were unified. The Mongols' traditional homeland occupies much of the modern-day Mongolian People's Republic as well as the Inner Mongolian autonomous region just northwest of Beijing. This steppe region consists largely of grasslands, watered by a few rivers. Few trees grow there. While the soil and limited rainfall could not support a sedentary, farming population, the extensive grasslands perfectly suited pastoral nomads grazing their herds.

Religious Practices of the Mongols

The Mongols worshiped a variety of nature spirits. Each of the Mongols' tents, William noticed, contained several felt figurines representing protective spirits. The supreme deities of the Mongols were the sky-god Tengri and his counterpart, the earth-goddess Itügen. Certain people, called **shamans**, specialized in interceding with these gods, sometimes traveling to high mountains where the gods were thought to live. On other occasions, shamans burned bones and interpreted the cracks as indicators of the gods' will, much like Shang Dynasty diviners in ancient China (see Chapter 4).

shamans
Mongol religious specialists who contacted deities by burning bones and interpreting the cracks to determine the gods' wills.

The Mongols in central and western Mongolia had some contact with Christian missionaries from the Church of the East, which was based in Syria. These missionaries, the Christians most active in Central Asia, spoke the Turkic language Uighur when they preached among the Mongols. William called them Nestorians after Nestorius, a Syrian patriarch in Constantinople in 428, but in fact the Church of the East did not accept the teachings of Nestorius, whom successive church councils had declared a heretic. William came to realize that the Mongols saw no contradiction between worshiping their traditional deities and praying to the Christian God.

Mongol Society

Mongol society had two basic levels: ordinary Mongols and the families of the chiefs. The chief's sons and grandsons formed a privileged group from which all future rulers were chosen. Differences in wealth certainly existed, with some men having larger herds or better clothes than others, but no rigid social divisions or inherited ranks separated ordinary Mongols. Below them in rank, however, were slaves, who had often been captured in battle. The chiefs periodically collected a 1 percent tax simply by taking one of every hundred animals. Unlike sedentary peoples, who collected taxes once a year (usually in the fall after the harvest was in), Mongol chiefs imposed the tax whenever they chose.

AP® THEMES
How did the organization of the Mongol economy help shape and define the Mongol social hierarchy?

The Mongols lived in felt tents that could be put up and dismantled rapidly. While the men led their herds to new grazing areas, the women packed up their households and pitched tents at the new campsite. William described the Mongols' traditional division of labor:

> *It is the duty of the women to drive the carts, to load the houses on to them and to unload them, to milk the cows, to make the butter and khumis, to dress the skins and to sew them. . . . They never wash their clothes, for they say that that makes God angry and that it would thunder if they hung them out to dry. . . .*
>
> *The men make bows and arrows, manufacture stirrups and bits and make saddles; they build the houses and carts, they look after the horses and milk the mares. . . . Both sexes look after the sheep and goats, and sometimes the men, sometimes the women, milk them.**

Because Mongol women ran their households when their menfolk were away and often sat at their husbands' side during meetings, they had much more decision-making power than women in sedentary societies, William realized. Living in close proximity to their herds, the Mongols used the products from them: they made their tents from felt, wore clothes of skins and wool, ate meat and cheese, and drank fermented horse's milk, or khumis. William describes his first reaction to this drink with unusual frankness: *"as I drank it I sweated all over from fright and the novelty of it, for I had never before drunk of it. However it struck me as being very tasty, as in truth it is."**

The Mongols, however, could not obtain everything they needed from their herds and depended on their agricultural neighbors to provide grain, which they valued as a supplement to their monotonous meat-based diet. The Mongols also relied on settled peoples to obtain silks and cottons that were so much softer and lighter than the Mongols' rough wool and felt. Although they could make do, if necessary, without grain, tea, or textiles, they required metal trade items like knives, daggers, and spears.

Before 1200, an uneasy peace prevailed among the Mongols and their neighbors. Individual Mongol groups might occasionally plunder a farming community, but they never expanded outside their traditional homelands. Under the powerful leadership of Chinggis Khan, all that changed.

The Rise of Chinggis Khan

Sometime around 1167, *The Origin of Chinggis Khan* reports, a chieftain of a small Mongol tribe and his wife gave birth to a son they named Temüjin, the future Chinggis Khan. When he was nine, a rival poisoned his father, and his widowed mother and her children were able to eke out a living only by grazing a small herd of nine horses and eating wild plants.

---

*Christopher Dawson, ed., *The Mongol Mission: Narratives and Letters of the Franciscan Missionaries in Mongolia and China in the Thirteenth and Fourteenth Centuries* (London and New York: Sheed and Ward, 1955), pp. 103, 108.

Soon, though only a teenager, Temüjin skillfully forged alliances with other leaders and began defeating other tribes (a term Mongols use themselves). He eventually formed a confederation of all the peoples in the grasslands of modern Mongolia. In 1206, the Mongols awarded the thirty-nine-year-old Temüjin the title of universal ruler: Chinggis (literally "oceanic") Khan ("ruler").

The Mongols used a political process called **tanistry** to choose a new leader. "Put briefly, the principle of tanistry held that the tribe should be led by the best qualified member of the chiefly house," explains one prominent historian of the Mongols.* In practice, each time a chief died or was killed by a challenger, all contenders for power fought to defeat their rivals in battle. When one warrior emerged victorious, the Mongols gathered at an assembly, or **khuriltai**, to acclaim the new leader. When this leader died, the destabilizing and bloody selection process began again.

tanistry
Process the Mongols used to choose a new leader. Under tanistry, all contenders for power had to prove their ability to lead by defeating their rivals in battle.

khuriltai
Name of the Mongols' assembly that gathered to acclaim the new leader after he had defeated his rivals. Not an electoral body.

Conquests Under Chinggis

Once he had united the Mongols, Chinggis weakened their group loyalties by dividing all his soldiers into units that crossed group lines. Each soldier belonged to four units: a unit of ten was part of a unit of one hundred, within a larger unit of one thousand, which finally belonged to one of ten thousand men. All able-bodied men between the ages of fifteen and seventy fought in the army, and women did so if necessary. Scholars estimate the total population of the Mongols at 1 million, far less than the populations of the lands they conquered and governed. Numbering only one hundred thousand in 1206, the Mongol forces reached several hundred thousand at the height of Chinggis's power in the 1220s.

The Mongols started with only one significant advantage over the European and Asian powers they conquered: horses. Their grassy homeland provided them with an unending supply of horses, and, because Mongol children were raised on horseback, they matured into highly skilled riders who could shoot from horseback with their compound bows of wood, horn, and sinew. The Mongols had so many horses that they could change their mounts three times a day, and they frequently put dummies on riderless horses to make their army look larger.

The overriding goal of the Mongol armies was to conquer territory as quickly as possible. It was much cheaper and faster, the Mongols realized, to take a city whose occupants surrendered without a fight than to lay siege to a walled, medieval settlement that could take months to fall. To encourage surrender, the Mongols placed captives on their front lines to be killed by their own countrymen. If the enemy submitted voluntarily, the Mongols promised not to destroy their homes.

AP® THEMES
How did the relationship between the Mongols and their settled neighbors change during the thirteenth century?

Mongol traditions held that Chinggis Khan could command the total obedience of his warriors in wartime but not in peacetime. Accordingly, he had good reason to keep conquering new territory. In war, the Mongols viewed all plunder as their due, but they limited their plunder to one-tenth of all the enemy's movable property if the enemy submitted voluntarily. Because the

*Joseph Fletcher, "The Mongols: Ecological and Social Perspectives." *Harvard Journal of Asiatic Studies* 46, no. 1 (1986): 1–56, explanation of tanistry on 17.

A Mongol Archer in Italian Eyes This Mongol warrior's skull-like face stares menacingly at the viewer. He clasps a compound bow in his left hand, an arrow in his right. Ordinary bows were too big for a mounted warrior to shoot, but the compound bow was short enough for use on horseback. When the Mongols laid siege to cities, row after row of mounted archers shot showers of arrows with devastating effect.

ruler shared the spoils with his men whenever he conquered a city, his followers had a strong incentive to follow him, and the ruler had no reason to stop fighting. Under Chinggis's leadership, the Mongols built one of the most effective fighting forces the world had ever seen.

At first Chinggis led his troops into north China, which was under the rule of the Jin Dynasty (see Chapter 12), and conquered the important city of Beijing in 1215. In 1219, Chinggis turned his attention to Transoxiana, the region between the Amu Darya and Syr Darya Rivers, then under the rule of the Islamic Khwarazmian empire. In rapid succession the Mongols conquered the region's glorious cities (see the map on page 401). The Persian historian Juvaini (1226–1283) quotes an eyewitness: *"They came, they sapped, they burnt, they slew, they plundered, and they departed."**

Mongol Governance

After conquering Bukhara, Chinggis appointed one man, usually a Mongol, to be governor, or **darughachi** (dah-roo-GAH-chee), of a conquered region. The darughachi's main responsibility was to collect the required taxes. The darughachi were free to try different types of taxes in the various parts of the empire, as long as they produced sufficient revenue. The Mongols continued to levy irregular taxes, like their traditional 1 percent tax on herds, in addition to taxes on agriculture, and in many locations they also instituted a 5 percent tax on commercial transactions.

● **CONTEXT&CONNECTIONS** Since the Mongols allowed the local governments to rule as they had before the conquest, the darughachi more closely resembled the *satraps* of the Persian empire (key term in Chapter 6) than either Roman or Chinese governors (see Chapters 7 and 12). ●

*Ata-Malik Juvaini, *Genghis Khan: The History of the World Conqueror*, trans. J. A. Boyle (Seattle: University of Washington Press, 1958), p. 107.

The Mongols reserved the highest positions in the occupying government, such as the darughachi, for Mongols. Above the darughachi were the khan and his kin, who did not hold official titles but made all the major decisions affecting the empire. Conquered peoples staffed the lower branches of government and were permitted to continue their own religious practices. Religious institutions did not have to pay taxes.

darughachi
Regional governor appointed by the Mongols to administer a newly conquered region and to collect taxes.

The Mongols' willingness to leave much of the local government and customs intact meant that they could conquer enormous swaths of territory quickly without having to leave behind a large occupying force to rule the conquered lands, which allowed them to move on quickly.

The United Mongol Empire After Chinggis, 1229–1260

When Chinggis Khan died in 1227, no one knew whether his empire would survive him. From 1229 to 1260, the Mongols remained united but were led by different rulers (see the chart "Mongol Rulers, 1206–1260"). They continued their conquests and took eastern Europe and northern China. During this time, they also introduced important innovations, such as the postal relay system, and began work on the Mongol capital at Khara Khorum. The postal relay system, the requirements for receiving envoys, and the court-financed merchant networks were the only institutions holding the different parts of the far-flung Mongol Empire together, as William of Rubruck discovered when he traveled to Khara Khorum in the 1250s. His trip exemplifies the ease of movement across Eurasia and the cultural exchanges that resulted from the Mongol conquest.

The Reign of Ögödei, 1229–1241

Before he died, Chinggis had divided his entire realm into four sections, each for one of his sons. Instead of following the traditional prolonged process of choosing the new ruler, a khuriltai held two years after Chinggis's death acquiesced to his request that his third son, Ögödei (r. 1229–1241), govern all four sections of the Mongols' realm.

In the 1230s, the Mongols attacked Russia repeatedly and subdued the Russian principalities (see Chapter 10). With nothing now standing between the Mongols and Europe, western European rulers belatedly realized how vulnerable they were to Mongol attack. Until then, they had been preoccupied with taking back Jerusalem (see Chapter 13). Ignorantly assuming that any enemy of Islam had to be Christian and so a natural ally of theirs, the Europeans tried to enlist the Mongols in the Crusades. The Mongols responded by demanding that the Europeans submit to them and give up one-tenth of all their wealth. The Europeans refused. In 1241–1242, the Mongols attacked Poland and crossed the Danube, advancing to within a few miles of Vienna, Austria.

There, on the brink of overrunning western Europe, the Mongols suddenly halted. News of Ögödei's death had reached the troops, and according to custom, all the warriors returned home to attend the khuriltai. Unable to choose a new leader quickly from among the brothers, sons, and nephews of Chinggis Khan, the Mongols never returned to eastern Europe. The western European powers were spared invasion.

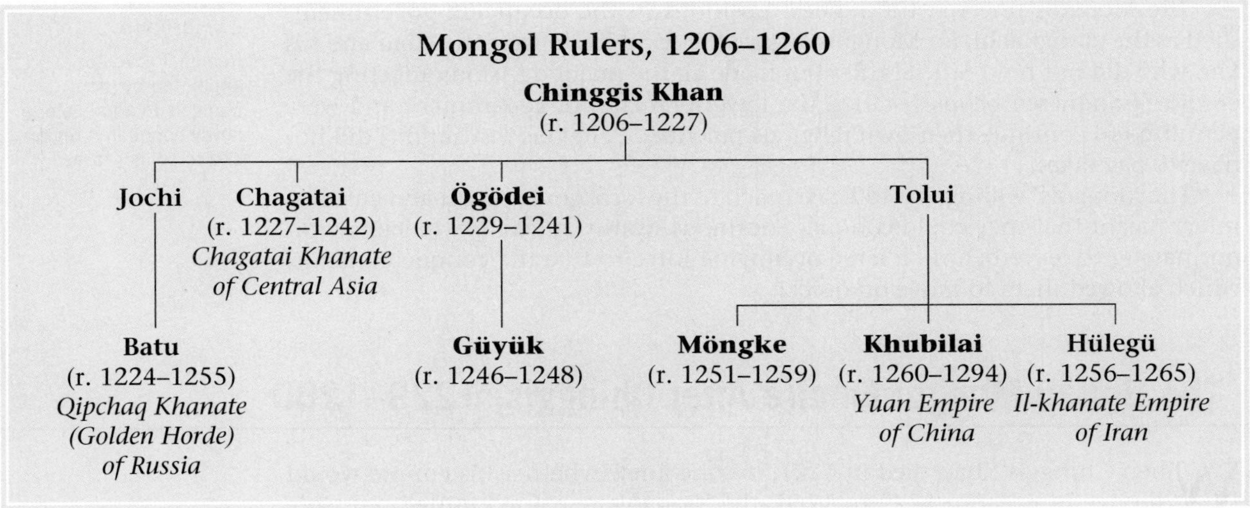

postal relay system
Mongol institution of fixed routes with regular stops where messengers could eat and get fresh mounts, which functioned as the central nervous system of the sprawling empire.

The Postal Relay System

The warriors in Europe learned of Ögödei's death fairly quickly because of the **postal relay system**, which took shape during his reign and allowed the ruler to communicate with officials in the furthest regions of the Mongol Empire. The Mongols established fixed routes, with regular stops every 30 or so miles (50 km) at which messengers could eat and get fresh mounts. Official messengers carried a silver or bronze tablet of authority that entitled them to food and fresh horses. Because the riders could cover some 60 miles (100 km) a day, the relay system functioned as the central nervous system of the sprawling empire. The Mongols also used the postal relay stations to provide visiting envoys with escorts, food, and shelter and, most important, to guarantee their safe return.

● **CONTEXT&CONNECTIONS** Because so few Europeans traveled to Mongolia at the time, and almost all were envoys sent by the pope and European rulers hoping to form an alliance against the Muslims in the Crusades, the Mongols assumed that William of Rubruck was a diplomat. Yet William was a missionary who wore a brown robe and went barefoot because he was a Franciscan *friar* (Chapter 13). The Franciscan order, founded by Saint Francis in the early 1200s, did not allow its friars to carry money, possess extra clothing, or own books. These rules imposed strict discipline on friars living in Europe, and they made William's trip to Mongolia especially arduous. ●

William began his journey in 1253, two years after the Mongols had finally settled on Möngke, one of Chinggis Khan's grandsons, as Ögödei's successor. As a friar-missionary, William wanted to meet those Mongols who were Christians and encourage others to convert to Christianity. Just before he entered Mongol territory, however, he learned that if he denied he was an envoy, he might lose his safe-conduct guarantee and the right to provisions and travel assistance. William decided to accept the privileges granted to envoys while continuing to wear his Franciscan clothing and to go barefoot.

The system for receiving envoys functioned well but not flawlessly, as William discovered. When he crossed the Don River, local people refused to help. To his dismay William found that the money he brought from Europe was useless: in one village, no one would sell him food or animals. After three difficult days, William's party once again received the mounts to which they were entitled. For two months, William reported, he and his compatriots *"never slept in a house or tent but always under the open sky or under our carts."**

On July 31, 1253, they arrived at the court of Sartakh, a great-grandson of Chinggis. Earlier envoys had reported that Sartakh was an observant Christian, and William hoped that Sartakh would permit him to stay. In his quest to obtain permission to preach, William personally experienced the decision-making structure of the Mongol government. Sartakh said that, to preach, William needed the approval of Sartakh's father, Batu, a grandson of Chinggis Khan who ruled the western section of the empire. When William asked Batu, Batu in turn decided that William needed the approval of the highest ruler of all, Möngke, before he could preach among the Mongols. Rather than write and ask permission, each ruler chose to send William in person to see his superior, a sign of how decentralized the empire was.

William and his companion Bartholomew departed for Khara Khorum with a Mongol escort, who provided them each with a sheepskin coat, trousers, felt boots, and fur hoods. At last, taking advantage of the postal relay system, William began to travel at the pace of a Mongol warrior, covering some 60 miles (100 km) each day: *"For sometimes we changed horses twice or three times in a day. . . . Of the twenty or thirty horses we always had the worst since we were foreigners, for they took the better horses before us; me they always provided with a strong horse, as I was very heavy.** William's reference to his bulk provides a rare personal detail. The Mongols ate solid food only in the evening and breakfasted on either broth or millet soup. They had no lunch. Although William and Bartholomew found the conditions extremely trying, the speed at which they traveled illustrates the postal relay system's crucial role in sending messages to officials and orders to the armies throughout the Mongol Empire.

The Mongols did not view William's mission as urgent so he travelled fairly slowly. The postal relay stations allowed riders on urgent missions to cover enormous distances quite rapidly. One of Chinggis Khan's generals went from the northern coast of the Caspian Sea almost all the way to Samarkand—a distance of 1,200 miles (2,000 km)—in little over a week. After consulting with Chinggis, he returned just as quickly. In the era before machines, this was breathtakingly fast. (See the feature "World History in Today's World: The World's Longest Horse Race.")

On December 27, 1253, William and Bartholomew arrived at the winter court of Möngke on the River Ongin in modern Mongolia, where the ruler and his retinue pitched their tents and where their herds stayed with them. On January 4, 1254, the two Franciscans entered Möngke's tent, whose interior was covered with gold cloth. Möngke *"was sitting on a couch wearing a speckled and shiny fur like sealskin. He is a flat-nosed man of medium height, about forty-five years old."** William

*Christopher Dawson, ed., *The Mongol Mission: Narratives and Letters of the Franciscan Missionaries in Mongolia and China in the Thirteenth and Fourteenth Centuries* (London and New York: Sheed and Ward, 1955), pp. 107, 132, 154, and Chapter XXVIII: Mangu's Court and the First Audience.

WORLD HISTORY IN TODAY'S WORLD

The World's Longest Horse Race

In 2009 the Adventurists Tour Company organized the first Mongol Derby, a race designed for extreme athletes, and the race has been held annually since. Starting from Khara Khorum, racers on horseback complete a circular course of 600 miles (1000 km), all within the borders of modern Mongolia, in the space of a week.

Because the race is modeled on the postal system created by the Mongols, the thirty participants, almost all non-Mongols who pay around $10,000 each, ride one mount for about 25 miles (40 km) until reaching the next station, where they are given a fresh horse. The full race has twenty-eight stations total, and eighteen riders finished in 2013. How did the organizers determine the length of each leg? They based the length on Marco Polo's description of the postal system (see Chapter 13). However, not everything follows Polo, who often exaggerated and reported that the postal system employed an unbelievable 300,000 horses. The race organizers have prepared a more realistic 800 horses. (Horses outnumber people in Mongolia by about seven to one, with the country's human population around 3 million.)

Unlike the postal system of the 1200s, the race organizers make full use of modern technology. After giving each participant a special map designed for the race, they provide each with GPS coordinates for water holes and postal stations. Each rider also receives a satellite-tracking device, in case anyone gets lost or has an accident.

Look at clips of the race on the web (for example, http://abcnews.go.com/Nightline/video/mongol-derby-worlds-longest-toughest-horse-race-20513269). The riders face real dangers: menacing thunderstorms that arise out of nowhere and drench everyone; horses that toss their riders to the ground or simply refuse to go forward; colds and more severe diseases like rabies; and thieves who steal the riders' possessions and sometimes even their horses.

Watching the race gives the viewer genuine appreciation of the difficulties that William of Rubruck and his Mongol escorts faced. How do you think they survived such a long trip in such difficult conditions?

asked Möngke for permission to preach in his territory. When his interpreter began to explain the khan's reply, William *"could not grasp a single complete sentence."** To his dismay, he realized that both Möngke and the interpreter were drunk.

His interpreter later informed him that he had been granted permission to stay two months, and William ended up staying three months at Möngke's court and another three at the capital of Khara Khorum, where he arrived in the spring of 1254. Khara Khorum was home to a small but genuinely international group of foreigners, who introduced important innovations from their home societies to the Mongols. There, William met a French goldsmith named William. Captured in Hungary and technically a slave who was not free to return to his home, the goldsmith worked for Möngke, who paid him a large amount for each project he completed. The goldsmith made an elaborate drinking fountain that dispensed khumis, honey wine, grape wine, and rice ale. This fountain illustrates the many cultural exchanges of the time: the technology was French, while the drinks were both European and Mongol. Although they had originally come as captives, such Europeans possessed valuable skills and enjoyed a much higher standard of living than the typical Mongol warrior.

---

*Christopher Dawson, ed., *The Mongol Mission: Narratives and Letters of the Franciscan Missionaries in Mongolia and China in the Thirteenth and Fourteenth Centuries* (London and New York: Sheed and Ward, 1955), p. 154.

Whenever the Mongols conquered a new city, they first identified all the skilled workers and divided them into two groups: siege-warfare engineers and skilled craftsmen. The engineers made catapults to propel large stones that cracked holes in city walls, and Chinese and Jurchen experts taught the Mongols how to use gunpowder (see Chapter 12). Mongol commanders sent all the other skilled craftsmen to help build Khara Khorum. The Mongols' willingness to learn from their captives prompted extensive cultural exchange.

Some historians have coined the term *Pax Mongolica* (literally "Mongolian peace") for the period of Mongol unity; they are consciously invoking the precedent of Pax Romana, the peaceful first two centuries of the Roman Principate when travel throughout the Mediterranean facilitated the spread of Christianity (see Chapter 7). The period of Mongol unity differed in an important way, though. As the American historian of the Mongols, Thomas Allsen, has so aptly put it, "The peoples of the steppe were not a premodern equivalent of the United Parcel Service, disinterestedly conveying wares hither and yon between the centers of civilization."* Ideas, goods, and people did not flow freely across the grasslands: playing a crucial role as a filter, the Mongols determined what moved across the Eurasian steppe.

Since the Mongols needed the help of siege engineers and metallurgists, they brought captives with those skills to their capital. Among the foreign captives Rubruck met at Khara Khorum, he encountered astronomers who could predict eclipses of the moon and sun, a particularly valuable skill since the Mongols retreated indoors until an eclipse had ended. The Mongols also collected maps and geographic works about any of the places they conquered, because knowledge of local geography allowed them to obtain control faster.

The Mongol rulers designated a group of Central Asian merchants as their commercial agents, who would convert the Mongols' plunder into money and then travel caravan routes and buy goods the rulers desired. As a nomadic people, the Mongols particularly valued textiles because they could be transported easily. Instead of a fixed salary, rulers gave their followers suits of clothes at regular intervals. The Mongols' tents could be very large, holding as many as a thousand people, and the largest were lined with thousands of yards of lavishly patterned silks.

AP® THEMES

What strategies did the Mongols use to support the economy of their empire?

Illustrating the Mongols' tolerance for and interest in other religious beliefs, Möngke invited William to debate with Eastern Christian, Muslim, and Buddhist representatives at court. The French goldsmith generously offered his bilingual son as a replacement for William's incompetent interpreter. William accepted the invitation, and so participated in a rare documented encounter among clergy of different faiths. Yet on the one occasion he had a competent interpreter, even William realized that he made no converts in the debate. (See the feature "Movement of Ideas Through Primary Sources: A Debate Among Christians, Buddhists, and Muslims at the Mongol Court.")

After his stay in Khara Khorum, William returned to Acre (modern Akko, Israel) in the Holy Land, the last port that the Crusaders still controlled. He then

*Thomas Allsen, *Commodity and Exchange in the Mongol Empire: A Cultural History of Islamic Textiles* (New York: Cambridge University Press, 1997), p. 106.

A Debate Among Christians, Buddhists, and Muslims at the Mongol Court

In May 1254, Möngke sent word to William that, before departing, the Christians, Muslims, and Buddhists should meet and debate religious teachings, since Möngke hoped to "*know the truth.*" William agreed to participate, and he and the Eastern Christians, whom William called Nestorians, had a practice session in which he even took the part of an imaginary Buddhist opponent. On the appointed day, Möngke sent three of his secretaries—a Christian, a Muslim, and a Buddhist—to be the judges. William reports that the Muslims said little; like the Crusaders, William refers to the Muslims as Saracens.

Since William's report is the only record that survives, historians cannot compare it with other descriptions of what happened. It is possible, for example, that he exaggerated his own role in the debate or misunderstood the arguments of his opponents.

The debate began with William arguing points with a Chinese Buddhist, whom William identifies by the Mongolian word *tuin* (TWUN).

Historical Thinking Skill:
ARGUMENTATION What argument does William use to discredit the tuins' (Chinese Buddhists') beliefs?

Historical Thinking Skill:
CONTEXTUALIZATION Why do you think rulers of diverse empires, such as Möngke Khan of the Mongol empire, would be interested in hosting a debate between religious authorities?

Source: From Christopher Dawson, ed., *The Mongol Mission: Narratives and Letters of the Franciscan Missionaries in Mongolia and China in the Thirteenth and Fourteenth Centuries* (New York: Sheed and Ward, 1955), pp. 191–194.

The Christians then placed me in the middle, telling the tuins to discuss with me. The tuins, of whom there was a great gathering there, began to murmur against Möngke Khan, saying that never before had any Chan attempted to find out about their secrets. They then chose as my opponent one who had come from Cathay and he had an interpreter with him. I had Master William's son.

He [the opponent] opened by saying to me: "Friend, if you are brought to a standstill, seek one wiser than yourself." I held my peace. Next he asked what I wanted to discuss first, how the world had been made or what happens to souls after death.

I replied: "Friend, that ought not to be the beginning of our disputation. All things are from God and He is the source and head of all things; therefore we ought first to speak of God, concerning Whom you have different beliefs from us and Möngke wishes to know whose are the best." The judges decided that this was right.

They wanted to begin with the points mentioned above, because they consider them the most important, for they are all followers of the Manichean heresy that half of creation is evil and the other half good, and that there are at least two principles; and concerning souls they believe that all migrate from one body to another.

Even the wisest priest among the Nestorians asked me if the souls of dumb animals could escape anywhere after death where they would not be compelled to work. As a proof of this false doctrine, so Master William told me, a boy was brought from Cathay, who, judging by his size, was not yet three years old, nevertheless his reasoning powers were fully developed, and he himself said that he had had three reincarnations; he knew also how to read and write.

So I said to the tuin: "We firmly believe in our hearts and profess with our lips that God exists and that there is but one God and that He is one with a perfect unity. What do you believe?"

He answered: "Fools say that there is but one God, but wise men say that there are many. In your country are there not mighty lords, and here is not the chief lord Möngke Khan? So it is with the gods; in the different regions there are different gods."

To this I gave answer: "That is a bad illustration or simile you put forward, arguing from men to God; for, according to this, any powerful man could be called a god in his own territory."

When I wanted to refute the comparison, he prevented me by inquiring, "What is your God like, of Whom you say there is but one?"

I replied: "Our God, besides Whom there is none other, is omnipotent, and therefore He has no need of anyone's help, rather do we all need His help. It is not so with men. No man can do all things, consequently there have to be many lords on the earth, for no single man can bear everything. Also He knows everything, and therefore has no need of a councillor; but rather all wisdom is from Him. Again, He is the supreme good and has no need of our goods, but in Him we live and move and have our being. Such is our God and therefore no other ought to be considered."

"It is not so," said he. "On the contrary there is one supreme god in heaven, of whose origin we are still ignorant, below him are ten, and under them is one lower. On earth there is an infinite number." When he wanted to weave other fairy tales, I questioned him about this supreme god, whether he believed he was omnipotent or dependent on another god.

He, fearing to reply, asked: "If your God is such as you say, why did He make half of creation evil?"

"It is untrue," said I, "it is not God who made evil; and all things that are, are good."

All the tuins were astonished at this saying and put it down in writing as something untrue and impossible. Then he began to ask, "That being so, where does evil come from?"

"You ask the wrong thing," I replied. "First you ought to ask what evil is, before asking where it comes from; but go back to the first question, whether you believe that any god is omnipotent, and afterwards I will answer all the questions you wish to put."

He sat for a long time unwilling to reply, so that the scribes who were listening on behalf of the Khan had to order him to give an answer. At length he said that no god was omnipotent. At that all the Saracens burst into loud laughter.

When there was silence again I said: "And so not one of your gods can save you in every danger, for a mishap may occur over which he has no power; moreover 'no man can serve two masters,' how therefore can you serve so many gods in heaven and on earth?"

The audience told him to reply, but he remained silent. When I wanted to put forward the arguments for the Unity of the divine essence and the Trinity in the hearing of all, the Nestorians belonging to the country told me I had said enough, for they wished to speak.

I then gave place to them and when they wanted to dispute with the Saracens, the latter replied: "We grant that your faith is true and that whatever is in the Gospel is true, therefore we do not wish to argue on any point with you." They admitted that in all their prayers they beseech God to grant that they may die a Christian death. . . .

Yet not one of them said, "I believe, I wish to become a Christian."

When this was finished the Nestorians and Saracens alike sang loudly while the tuins kept silence, and afterwards they all drank their fill.

proceeded to France, where, in 1257, he met Roger Bacon (ca. 1214–1294), an English Franciscan who had a deep interest in science. In 1267 Bacon wrote about gunpowder: "*No thunderclap can compare with such terrifying noises; nor lightning playing among the clouds with such terrifying flashes.*"* His vivid description, the first by a European observer, suggests that Bacon witnessed a live display of gunpowder, most likely brought back from China or Mongolia by Rubruck or another friar.

Intensely interested in Rubruck's manuscript, Roger Bacon was responsible for preserving four of the five surviving manuscripts of Rubruck's account. Since Rubruck wrote his account as a private letter to King Louis of France, it barely circulated during his lifetime, and very few people read it then or have done so since.

William's lack of success as a missionary is confirmed by one contemporary: in 1259, the king of Armenia, Hetum I (1226–1269), visited a Franciscan missionary outpost in Tripoli (in modern Libya) and reported what the Mongols had told him about William. When William "*appeared before the great king of the Tartars [Batu], he began to press on him the Christian faith, saying that the Tartar—and every infidel—would perish eternally and be condemned to everlasting fire.*"† William might have been more successful, the Mongol ruler Batu wryly commented, if he had tried to persuade the Mongols of the benefits of being a Christian, rather than threatening them with everlasting punishment.

● **CONTEXT&CONNECTIONS** The Armenian king's report provides crucial evidence confirming William's trip. It is a key report from an independent witness that William had indeed reached Khara Khorum. No comparable report in Chinese or any European language exists about Marco Polo (see Chapter 13); all that survives is his claim to have gone, which is why some scholars doubt that he ever traveled to China. ●

The Empire Comes Apart, 1259–1263

William's letter to his monarch reveals that only the postal relay stations bound the different parts of the Mongol Empire together. The Mongols granted the darughachi governors wide latitude in governing, and they never developed an empire-wide bureaucracy. Officials from one part of the empire were not transferred to other regions, and they did not implement uniform standards and policies. Because the Mongols allowed the darughachi governors to use the local language for administration and the recruitment of local officials, Chinese, Persian, and Turkish continued to be spoken throughout the empire. The Mongols did not impose Mongolian as the language of administration. During William's trip, the different sections of the empire continued to forward some taxes to the center, but the empire broke apart after Möngke's death in 1259.

---

*Joseph Needham, *Science and Civilisation*, vol. 5, part 7 (New York: Cambridge, 1987), pp. 48–50.

†From Peter Jackson, *The Mission of Friar William Rubruck* (London: The Hakluyt Society, 1990), p. 240 and Appendix V, p. 282.

• **CONTEXT&CONNECTIONS** The Mongol Empire was one of the largest and also the most loosely structured of the different empires of the past. The Mongols sought revenue from their subjects, but they had no policies that encouraged subjects to adopt Mongol ways, whether the Mongol language, religion, or lifestyle. If we arrayed the empires of the past on a continuum from most to least structured, the Chinese would be among the most structured (see Chapters 4 and 8), and the Mongols, the least. The Roman and Persian empires would fall somewhere in between (see Chapters 6 and 7). •

A year before Möngke's death, his brother Hülegü had led the Mongols on one of the bloodiest campaigns in their history, the conquest of Baghdad, in which some eight hundred thousand people died. Hülegü also ordered the execution of the caliph and so, in 1258, put a final end to the Abbasid caliphate, founded in 750 (see Chapter 9). In 1260, the Mamluk dynasty of Egypt defeated the remnants of Hülegü's army in Syria at the battle of Ain Jalut.

Arriving from Iran, the Mongols did not expect a major fight; the willingness of the Mamluks to fight for Islam surprised them. The climate also deceived them. In the winter, the plains of Israel resembled the Mongol grasslands, with great fields of grass stretching in the distance, and the soldiers were confident of finding food for their horses. But, since no rain falls at all during the Israeli summer, the grass withers to nothing. Used to fighting in the winter, the Mongols were completely unprepared for the heat.

This defeat was the first time the Mongols had lost a battle and also marked the end of a united Mongol Empire. One khuriltai named Möngke's brother Khubilai (KOO-bih-leye) (d. 1294) the rightful successor, while a rival khuriltai named his brother Arigh Boke (d. 1264) the new khan. After 1260, it was impossible to maintain any pretense of imperial unity.

Another setback occurred in 1263, when the ruler of the Qipchaq (KIP-chack) khanate in Russia actively sought an alliance with the Mamluks against his cousin Hülegü in Iran. Never before had a Mongol allied with a non-Mongol force against another Mongol leader, and the alliance provides a clear date for the end of the unified Mongol Empire.

Successor States in Western Asia, 1263–1500

After this breakup the Mongol empire divided into four sections, each ruled by a different Mongol prince (see Map 14.1). The eastern sector consisted of the Mongolian heartland and China (discussed later in this chapter). In the western sectors, in a practice contrary to the traditions of tanistry, each time a ruler died his living sons divided his territory. Accordingly, succession disputes were common. Three important realms dominated the western sector: the Il-khanate in Iran; the Qipchaq khanate or Golden Horde, north of the Black, Caspian, and Aral Seas; and the Chaghatai khanate in Central Asia. None of these khanates built an empire as large as the earlier Mongols had, and border disputes often prompted war among the three realms. The Mongol tradition of learning from other peoples continued as each of the three ruling families converted to Islam, the religion of their most educated subjects.

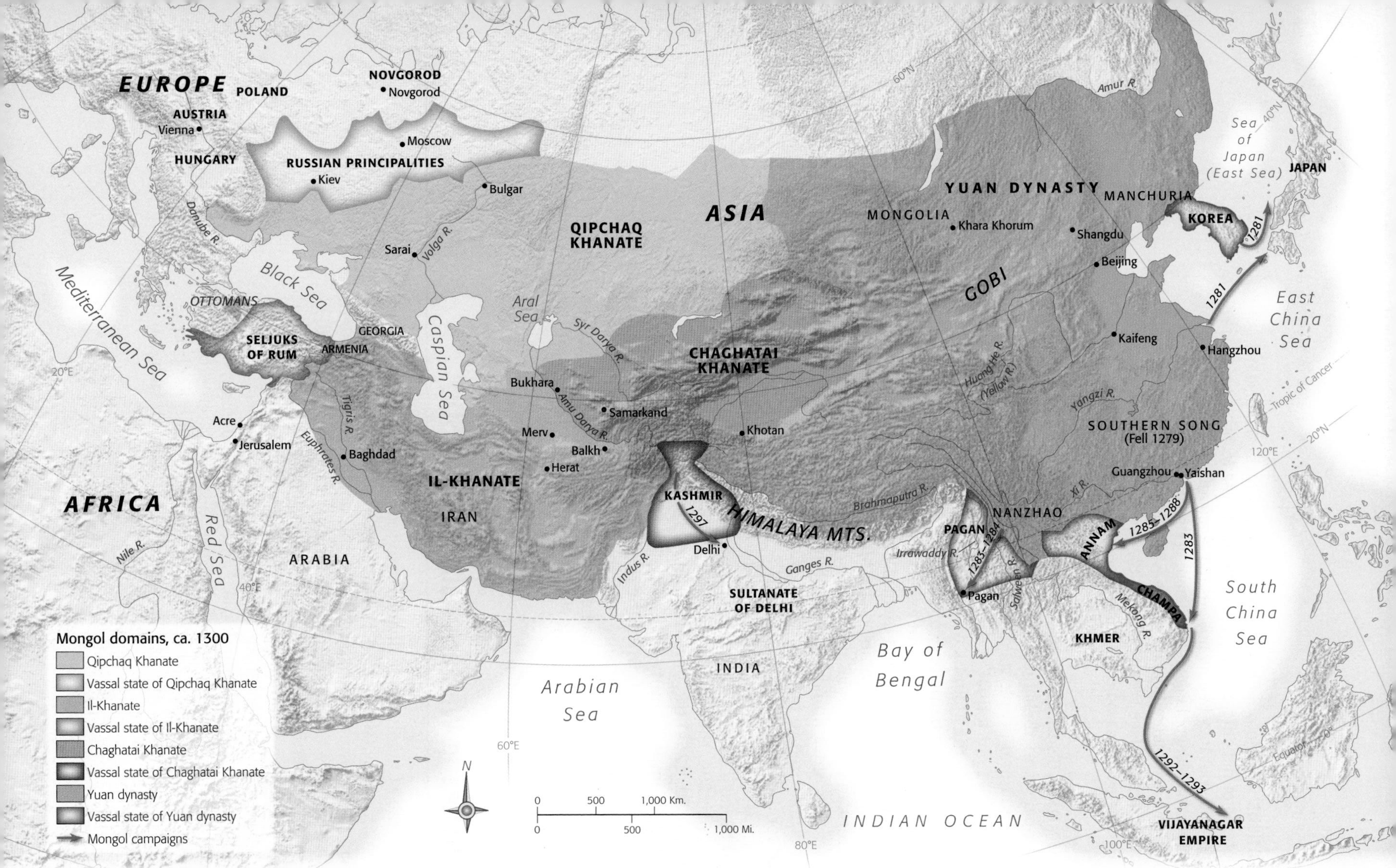

Map 14.1 The Four Quadrants of the Mongol Empire After 1263 The first three Mongol rulers had governed the largest contiguous land empire in world history. But the Mongols were unable to choose a single successor to Möngke, the grandson of Chinggis Khan, who died in 1259. The empire broke into four quadrants, each governed by a different member of the founder's family.

The Il-khanate, the Qipchaq Khanate, and the Rise of Moscow

Since the Mongols had conquered Iran in 1258, only two years before the empire broke apart in 1260, they were not well established there. Hülegü took the title *il-khan* ("subordinate khan" in Persian) to indicate that he was lower in rank than his brother Möngke; he ruled the **Il-khanate** (1256–1335). Like his brother Möngke, Hülegü was primarily a believer in shamanism. Five of Hülegü's sons and grandsons ruled Iran between 1265 and 1295. They allowed Muslims, Buddhists, and Eastern Christians to continue to worship their own belief systems. When Hülegü's great-grandson Ghazan (r. 1295–1304) took the throne in 1295, he announced his conversion to Islam, the religion of most of his subjects, and his fellow Mongols followed suit.

Il-khanate
Mongol government of the region of Iran (1256–1335), founded by Hülegü, who took the title *il-khan* ("subordinate khan" in Persian) to indicate that he was lower in rank than his brother Möngke.

The Il-khanate never found an efficient way to tax Iran. Infamous for collecting taxes twenty or more times a year, officials frequently resorted to force to get Iran's cultivators to pay. The end result was severe impoverishment of the countryside, which had already been devastated in the 1250s during the Mongol invasions. The Il-khanate had regular contact with the Yuan dynasty in China (covered later in this chapter), and in the 1290s the government introduced paper money (using the Chinese word for it). The paper money failed completely, bringing commerce to a standstill, but the experiment testifies to the Il-khanate's willingness to borrow from neighboring peoples. The Il-khanate ended in 1335 when the last of Hülegü's descendants died, and Iran broke up into many small regions.

To the north in the Qipchaq khanate, which stretched from the Carpathian Mountains to the steppes of Siberia, individual rulers converted to Islam as early as the 1250s, but Islam became the official religion only during the reign of Muhammad Özbeg (r. 1312–1341), as Ibn Battuta observed when he visited in the early 1330s on his way to Delhi (see Chapter 11). The Qipchaq ruled the lower and middle Volga River Valley, the home of the Bulgars, who had converted to Islam in the tenth century (see Chapter 10). Ibn Battuta was surprised by how well the women of the Qipchaq khanate were treated; they traveled in their own lavish carts, had large numbers of female servants, wore beautiful clothing, and drank khumis with their husbands as equals. More important, just like male princes, they ruled their own lands.

● **CONTEXT&CONNECTIONS** Many Qipchaq subjects in Russian cities to the north and west remained Eastern Orthodox Christians. One of the khan's wives was the daughter of the *Byzantine* emperor (Chapter 10), and Ibn Battuta accompanied her to Constantinople, so she could give birth in her parents' home. In the 1300s it was common for Muslims to visit the Christian city of Constantinople, which was surrounded by different Muslim countries. Ibn Battuta stayed there for over a month and saw the beautiful Hagia Sophia church without entering it (see Chapter 10). He even met the Byzantine emperor, who used an Arabic-speaking Jewish interpreter to ask Ibn Battuta about Jerusalem and the other countries he had visited. Constantinople had once been one of the largest and most beautiful Christian cities in the world, with a population of 1 million, but the Byzantines ruled only a tiny slice of territory when Ibn Battuta visited. Hit hard by the Black Death, the city's population fell to about 50,000 after 1348. ●

Before the Mongols conquered the region in the 1230s, the descendants of Prince Vladimir of Kiev had governed the various Rus principalities (see Chapter 10).

Overwhelmed by the Mongols, the different Russian princes surrendered. At the beginning of the Mongol era, Kiev had been the most important city in Russia, but the conquests devastated the city, prompting many to move to other places.

principality of Muscovy
Successor to the Qipchaq khanate in modern-day Russia.

Ivan III
(r. 1462–1505) Muscovy's most important leader, who overthrew the Qipchaq khanate in 1502.

The **principality of Muscovy** (Moscow) eventually emerged as Kiev's successor, partially because the rulers of Moscow were frequently better able to pay their share of tribute and so were favored by the Qipchaq khanate. **Ivan III** (r. 1462–1505) defeated other Russian families to become the undisputed leader of the region; in 1480 he stopped submitting tribute to the Qipchaq khanate, and in 1502 he brought the khanate to an end. Ivan III controlled large chunks of modern-day Russia: from the Black Sea in the south to Novgorod in the north and much of modern-day Poland.

The Chaghatai Khanate and Timur the Lame

Straddling the Amu Darya and Syr Darya River Valleys, the Chaghatai khanate included the eastern grasslands in what is now modern Mongolia and a western half that included the great Silk Road cities of Bukhara and Samarkand. In the grasslands to the east, the Mongols followed their traditional nomadic way of life, and different chieftains continued to rule this region after the breakup of the empire. In the early 1330s, still on his way to Delhi, Ibn Battuta visited the Chaghatai khan who had first converted to Islam and noted the devastation of Bukhara, which had not yet recovered from the Mongol conquest of the 1220s. After he arrived in Delhi, he learned that the khan's nephew had overthrown his uncle.

Timur the Lame
(ca. 1336–1405) Also known in English as Tamerlane. Successor to the Chaghatai khanate, he also conquered a large swath of Central Asia south and east of the Caspian Sea.

Starting around 1350, a Turkish-speaking leader of Mongol descent took power in Samarkand and the western section of the Chaghatai khanate. This leader, known to his Persian enemies as **Timur the Lame** (ca. 1336–1405), contracted to *Tamerlane* in English, succeeded in forming a powerful confederation and conquered much of modern-day Iran, Uzbekistan, Afghanistan, north India, and the Anatolian region of Turkey. He married a descendant of Chinggis Khan so that he could claim to be his successor, and he used terror to reduce resistance. Timur was known for setting his enemies on fire or throwing them off cliffs.

Following Mongol precedent, Timur the Lame forcibly resettled artisans and architects from among the conquered townspeople of India, Iran, and Syria. In his capital of Samarkand, these craftspeople built foreign-influenced buildings with elaborate mosaic tilework that is still visible today. Samarkand became one of the most beautiful of all Central Asian cities.

Timur died in 1405 as he was preparing to lead his troops into China. Continuing the Mongol legacy of patronizing learning, Timur's grandson Ulugh Beg (1394–1449, r. 1447–1449) built an enormous astronomical observatory and compiled a star chart based on ancient Greek and Islamic learning. Ulugh Beg ruled for only two years before his son ordered him killed and took over as ruler, in keeping with the Mongol tradition of tanistry. Timur's empire soon fragmented because the different members of the royal house, unable to decide on a successor, simply divided it among themselves.

By 1500, almost all the Mongol successor states had ceased to exist in western Asia. The region of Iran had broken into smaller states, as had the territory of the former Chaghatai khanate. Muscovy emerged as the major power in the Volga region, leaving only a small Mongol successor state in the Crimea.

The Shah-i-Zinda Burial Complex at Samarkand This burial complex, within the city walls of Samarkand, contains structures, built from the 800s to the reign of Timur the Lame in the early 1400s, that show how the use of tiles changed over time. The earliest buildings display patterns made entirely with sand-colored brick. In the next phase, builders combined colored and uncolored bricks in complex mosaics. And in the final phase, the builders used tiles of a single hue to make the brilliantly blue roofs for which Samarkand is so famous. (Ivan Vdovin/Robert Harding World Imagery)

The Ottomans, 1300–1500

In the centuries that saw the fragmentation of the khanates in the west, a new power arose that initially replicated many elements of Mongol rule but then made crucial innovations that allowed it to build an empire that outlasted all the Mongol successor states. The **Ottomans** first gained control of Anatolia, in modern Turkey, which lay between the eastern edge of the Byzantine empire and the western edge of the Il-khanate. Over time, the Ottomans shifted from an army that fought for plunder to an army that received a fixed salary. Their conquest of Constantinople in 1453 marked the end of the Byzantine empire and the establishment of a major Islamic power in western Asia. Although they had started in 1300 as nomadic warriors, by 1500 the Ottomans had become the undisputed rulers of western Asia.

Ottomans
Group of Turkic Muslim nomads who gained control of the Anatolia region in modern Turkey around 1300. Their conquest of Constantinople in 1453 marked the end of the Byzantine Empire.

The Rise of the Ottomans, 1300–1400

Even at the height of their power during the thirteenth century, the Mongols sent few troops to Anatolia, which lay on the western edge of their empire. Around 1300 a man named Osman (the origin of the name *Ottoman*) emerged as the leader of a group of nomads who successfully conquered different sections of the Anatolian peninsula.

Few documents survive from this early period, and one of the most important sources about the Ottomans' own religion is Ibn Battuta's journal. In 1331, he visited the port city of Bursa, near Constantinople. Referring to the Ottoman leader Orhan (Osman's son) as "sultan," the term he used for Muslim rulers, Ibn Battuta reported that he "*fights the infidels [Byzantium] continually and keeps them under siege.*"* This is one of the earliest reports of the Muslim beliefs of the Ottomans. The Ottomans welcomed local Christians to join them in their fight against the Byzantine empire and did not force them to convert to Islam.

In the 1300s, the Ottomans continued to conquer chunks of the weakened Byzantine empire in Greece, Bulgaria, and the Balkans, but they bypassed Constantinople. By 1400, they became the most powerful group professing loyalty to the Byzantine ruler, who controlled only the city of Constantinople and its immediate environs. The Ottomans could not stand up to the armies of Timur the Lame, but they resumed their conquests after his death in 1405.

As the Ottoman realm expanded, Ottoman rulers began to see themselves as protectors of local society, with Islamic law as their main tool. They paid mosque officials salaries and included them as part of their government bureaucracy. Agriculture thrived under their rule, and they were able to collect high revenues from their agricultural taxes, which they used to build roads for foot soldiers.

The Ottomans enjoyed unusual military success because of their innovative policies. Unlike their enemies, they paid market prices for food and did not simply steal supplies from the local people. As a result, farmers willingly sold produce to the Ottomans.

When the Ottomans captured Christian soldiers, they forced these enslaved prisoners of war to join the army. Called **Janissaries**, many eventually converted to Islam. To prevent the Janissaries from building up large private estates, the Ottomans required them to be celibate so that they would not have descendants. Even so, many local people volunteered their sons for Janissary units because the boys could rise to a much higher position than if they remained on family farms.

Janissaries
(Turkish word meaning "new soldiers") Soldiers of the Ottomans, recruited from conquered Christians and required to be celibate.

A Frenchman who traveled from Dijon, France, to the Ottoman Empire in 1432–1433 offered European readers an eyewitness description of the Ottomans' power during the reign of Murad II (r. 1421–1451). The sultan's army impressed the visitor because the soldiers ate only small amounts when traveling and rode strong horses. Their armor was lighter than the armor of the French, and their level of discipline seemed high.

*H. A. R. Gibb, trans., *The Travels of Ibn Battuta* A.D. *1325–1354*, vol. 2 (London: Hakluyt Society, 1958–1994), p. 452.

● **CONTEXT&CONNECTIONS** The salaried Janissary army was much more stable than the Mongol army, which had been propelled by the desire for plunder. Like the Mongols, Ottomans adopted new technologies from the peoples they conquered, notably the use of gunpowder weapons. ●

Although the Mongols had used some gunpowder, their most effective troops were mounted cavalry with bows and arrows. Around 1400, however, gunpowder weapons improved noticeably, and the Ottomans demonstrated their command of the new gunpowder technology in the 1453 conquest of Constantinople.

The Ottoman Conquest of Constantinople, 1453

In 1453, after the Byzantine emperor requested the doubling of an annual subsidy from the Turks, the young Ottoman emperor Mehmed II (r. 1451–1481) decided to end the fiction of Byzantine rule. Mehmed, who is known as **Mehmed the Conqueror**, constructed a large fort on the western shore of the Bosphorus, just across from Constantinople, and positioned three cannon on the fort's walls where they could hit all ships that entered the harbor to provision the Byzantine troops.

Mehmed the Conqueror
(r. 1451–1481) Leader of the Ottomans who conquered Constantinople in 1453 and patronized scholars from different countries.

To protect the city, the Byzantines connected a giant chain (not shown in the illustration "The Siege of Constantinople, 1453") across the entrance to its harbor to block the Ottoman warships, but the Ottomans simply transported their ships overland in wooden cradles along metal tracks to waters just outside the city, where they could fire on the walls. They carried a total of seventy ships. Outside the city the Ottomans arrayed a force of eighty thousand to lay siege; inside the city, a combined force of eight thousand Byzantines and their non-Byzantine allies succeeded in defending the city for fifty-three days before it fell.

Even though the Byzantine emperor had refused his offer of a chance to surrender, Mehmed the Conqueror controlled his troops and treated the Christian inhabitants of the city with restraint, taking no punitive measures against them. The behavior of the Ottomans contrasted sharply with the out-of-control looting and rampaging of the Fourth Crusade in 1204 (see Chapter 13). On the day the city fell, Mehmed II led a small group of guards and advisers to the Hagia Sophia (see page 423), the largest and most striking church in the city, and explained his plans to convert the church into a mosque. (Some Turks believe that Hagia Sophia, now a museum, should once again become a mosque, while the Patriarch of the Eastern Orthodox Church urges that it become a church instead.) Turning many churches into mosques, the Ottomans transformed Constantinople from a Christian into a Muslim city. The official name of the city was Qustantiniyya, "city of Constantine," but its residents referred to it as Istanbul, meaning simply "the city" in Greek.

Under Ottoman rule, the Greek, Slavic, and Turkic peoples living in the region moved to the city, bringing great prosperity. Mehmed commissioned scholars to copy the ancient Greek classics, to write epic poetry in Italian, and to produce scholarly works in other languages, like Arabic and Persian. Realizing that the state needed educated officials, he established Islamic schools in the different cities of the realm.

Ms Fr 9087 f.207v The Siege of Constantinople in 1453, from "Le Voyage d'Outremer" by Bertrandon de la Broquiere, c.1450–75 (vellum), French School, (15th century)/Bibliotheque Nationale, Paris, France/Bridgeman Images

The Siege of Constantinople, 1453 This illustration from a French manuscript is one of the few surviving portrayals of the fall of Constantinople. Although based on secondhand information, the painting is surprisingly accurate. The artist captures the city's vulnerability: the Ottoman forces gather on all sides, while the Byzantine troops are concentrated in the central walled triangle. The artist has even included the pontoon bridge (the lower bridge on the left) that the Ottomans used to transport their guns closer to the city's walls. One can easily grasp that the Ottoman forces arrayed outside the walls will soon conquer the city.

● **CONTEXT&CONNECTIONS** The year 1453 marked a turning point in world history, annually celebrated by the people of Turkey, but historians differ about its importance. Predictably Christian historians have seen the fall of Constantinople as a disaster, while Muslim historians have seen it as a triumph. More interesting, though, is the claim of some historians that Mehmed's policies of tolerance and support for scholarship marked the beginning of the early modern era and the end of the Middle Ages. Those historians, however, are thinking only about Europe; West Asia had been under Islamic rule for centuries before 1453, and the fall of Constantinople had no consequences for East Asia, much less Africa or the Americas. Most world historians see 1492, when Columbus arrived in the Americas, as the genuine turning point, and the beginning of the early modern era, because the events that followed directly affected the whole world (see Chapter 15). ●

Converting a Church into a Mosque The Ottomans transformed Hagia Sophia into a mosque by adding four minarets outside the original church building and by clearing a giant hall for prayer inside. They also constructed a traditional Islamic garden, complete with fountain, behind the mosque. (Steve McCurry/Magnum Photos)

East Asia During and After Mongol Rule, 1263–1500

At the time the Mongol empire broke apart in 1260, Chinggis's grandson Khubilai Khan (r. 1260–1294) controlled the traditional homeland of Mongolia as well as north China. Conquering south China, where the wet terrain proved extremely difficult for the Mongol horsemen to traverse, posed a genuine challenge. Only after building a Chinese-style navy did the Mongols succeed in taking south China, but they never conquered Japan or Southeast Asia. The Mongols ruled China for nearly one hundred years until, in 1368, a peasant uprising overthrew them. The cultural exchanges of the Mongols continued to influence Ming dynasty (1368–1644) China, most clearly in the sea voyages of the 1400s.

Khubilai Khan

(1215–1294) Grandson of Chinggis Khan who became ruler of Mongolia and north China in 1260 and who succeeded in conquering south China in 1276, but not Japan or Vietnam.

The Conquests of Khubilai Khan and Their Limits

Of the Mongol rulers who took over after 1260, **Khubilai Khan** (1215–1294) lived the longest and is the most famous. Suspicious of classical Chinese learning, Khubilai learned to speak some Chinese but not to read Chinese characters. During his administration in China, the Mongols suspended the civil service examinations (see Chapter 12); preferring to

A Mongol Hunting Party as Seen by a Chinese Artist The Chinese artist Liu Guandao rendered the hunting party of Khubilai Khan in exquisite detail. Note the different animals the Mongols, but not the Chinese, used for hunting: a greyhound dog to the right of the khan and a cheetah on the saddle of the lowermost horse. The archer (*top, left*) leans backward to shoot a bird flying above. The skills the Mongols developed while hunting were directly transferable to warfare.

appoint officials, they tried to pair a non-Chinese official, either a Mongol or a Central Asian, with each Chinese appointee, though the small number of Mongol officials available made it difficult to do so. The Mongol administration in China absorbed many local customs. For example, in 1271 Khubilai adopted a Chinese name for his dynasty, the Yuan, meaning "origin."

Khubilai Khan's most significant accomplishment was the conquest of south China, resulting in the unification of north and south China for the first time since the tenth century. Demonstrating a genuine willingness to learn from other peoples, Khubilai Khan commissioned a giant Chinese-style navy that conquered all of south China by 1276. The Mongols became the first non-Chinese people in history to conquer and unify north and south China.

Like all Mongol armies, Khubilai's generals and soldiers wanted to keep conquering to obtain even more plunder. The Mongols made forays into Korea, Japan, and Vietnam even before 1260, and they continued their attacks under Khubilai's rule.

Of these three places, Korea, under the rule of the Koryo dynasty (936–1392), was the only one to come under direct Mongol rule. In 1231, a Mongol force active in north China invaded, prompting the Korean ruler to surrender. He agreed to disband his army, made heavy payments to the Mongols, and sent five hundred young men, including the crown prince, and five hundred young women as hostages to the Mongol court. Sporadic fighting continued, and the Mongols gained firm control only in 1273. Acknowledging the Mongols as their overlords, the Koryo rulers continued on the throne, but the Mongols forced them to intermarry with Mongol princesses, and the Koreans adopted many Mongol customs.

Once they had subdued Korea and gained control of north and south China, the Mongols tried to invade Japan, then under the rule of the Kamakura (see Chapter 12), in 1274 and 1281. To this end the Mongols forced the Koreans to provide nine hundred ships as well as many soldiers and supplies. Later sources report that on each occasion a powerful wind destroyed the Mongol ships, an event described to this day by Japanese as *kamikaze* or "divine wind." In World War II, Japanese fliers who went on suicide missions were called kamikaze pilots.

Contemporary sources do not mention the weather during the Mongol invasion attempts but describe a Mongol force of no more than ten thousand turning back in both 1274 and 1281. Japan's coastal fortifications certainly played a role; so, too, did the difficulties of sending an invading fleet across the ocean to Japan. Ennin had been shipwrecked in these treacherous waters (see Chapter 8). In addition, the Japanese controlled the shoreline so they could attack any ships that landed near the coast. The Kamakura government, which had withstood the Mongol attacks, fell in 1333, and Japan began three centuries of divided political rule that ended only in 1600 when the country was reunified.

The Mongols also proved unable to conquer Vietnam, then under the rule of the Tran dynasty (1225–1400). Mongol armies sacked the capital city at Hanoi three times (in 1257, 1284, and 1287), but on each occasion an army of locals regained the city and promised to pay tribute to the Mongols, who then retreated.

● **CONTEXT&CONNECTIONS** The *Mamluks* of Egypt (Chapter 11) were the only army to defeat the Mongols in a land battle, at Ain Jalut. The Mongols failed to conquer Vietnam or Japan because their armies were overextended; the Mongols suffered no decisive defeat in either place. ●

When Khubilai Khan died in 1294, a new generation of leaders took over who had grown up in China, spoke and wrote Chinese, and knew little of life on the steppes. The fourth emperor in the Yuan dynasty, Renzong (r. 1312–1321), received a classical Chinese education and reinstated the civil service exams in 1315.

● **CONTEXT&CONNECTIONS** Under Renzong's direction, the Mongols introduced a new *Neo-Confucian* examination curriculum (Chapter 12) that tested the candidates' knowledge of Zhu Xi's commentary on *The Four Books* and remained in use until 1905. ●

After Emperor Renzong's death, the Yuan government entered several decades of decline. The 1330s and 1340s saw outbreaks of disease that caused mass deaths; a single epidemic in 1331 killed one-tenth of the people living in one province.

● **CONTEXT&CONNECTIONS** Scholars suspect the Black Death that hit Europe in 1348 may have been the same disease responsible for Chinese epidemics, but the Chinese sources do not describe the symptoms of those who died. ●

Faced with a sharp drop in population and a corresponding decline in revenue, the Yuan dynasty raised taxes, causing a series of peasant rebellions. In 1368, a peasant who had been briefly educated in a monastery led a peasant revolt that overthrew the Yuan dynasty and drove the Mongols back to their homeland, from which they continued to launch attacks on the Chinese. He named his dynasty the Ming, meaning "light" or "bright" (1368–1644).

Ming dynasty
(1368–1644) A native Chinese dynasty that overthrew the Mongols but continued many of their practices.

The First Ming Emperors, 1368–1405

The founder of the **Ming dynasty**, Ming Taizu, prided himself on founding a native Chinese dynasty but in fact continued many Mongol practices. In addition to the core areas ruled earlier by the Northern Song dynasty, the Ming realm included Manchuria, Inner Mongolia, Xinjiang in the northwest, and Tibet, which had all been conquered by the Mongols. The Ming also took over the provincial administrative districts established by the Mongols, which still define modern China.

When the Ming founder assumed office, he appointed all new officials and suspended the civil service examinations because he was suspicious of Confucian learning. In 1381, realizing how difficult it was to staff the entire central government, he reinstated the examinations with a Confucian curriculum identical to that of the Mongols. Competition for the exams intensified in succeeding centuries, and the ruling elite remained Confucian because of this decision.

Oddly, the Ming founder, the one emperor in Chinese history who was born a peasant, had a conservative vision of China's society and believed that no one could change his or her social position. On conquering China he ordered his officials to survey all the land and record how much each household owned; this was the first complete empire-wide survey since the Tang dynasty. Ming officials assigned each household a category of labor such as agriculture, military service, or salt mining and required that each household contribute a fixed number of days of that type of labor annually. In fact, many people paid others to fulfill their labor obligations.

When the Ming founder died in 1398, he hoped that his grandson would succeed him, but one of the emperor's brothers led an army to the capital and set the imperial palace on fire. The unfortunate new emperor, only twenty-one at the time, probably died in the fire, making it possible for his uncle to name himself the third emperor of the Ming dynasty, or the Yongle emperor (r. 1403–1424).

The Chinese Voyages to South and Southeast Asia and Africa, 1405–1433

Viewed as a usurper his entire life, the Yongle emperor pursued several policies to show that he was the equal of the Ming founder. For example, he ordered all written materials to be copied into a single, enormous set of books called *The Yongle Encyclopedia*. He moved the capital from Nanjing, where many remained sympathetic to the deposed emperor, to Beijing, the former capital of the Mongols. He sent five military expeditions to Mongolia in the hope of vanquishing the Mongols, but none succeeded. The Yongle emperor also launched a series of imperially sponsored voyages to demonstrate the strength of his dynasty to all of China's trading partners.

Chinese geographical knowledge of the world had grown considerably since the mid-twelfth century (see Chapter 12). No maps made under the Mongols survive today, but a Korean map copied around 1470, the Kangnido map, showing heavy Islamic influence, was based on several earlier maps that cartographers combined without paying attention to scale. (See the feature "Visual Evidence in Primary Sources: State-of-the-Art Cartography in the 1400s.")

Increasing geographic knowledge prompted the most ambitious voyages in Chinese history, which were led by the admiral named Zheng He (JUHNG huh) (1371–1433). Zheng He's ancestors were Muslims from Bukhara. He was captured at the age of ten, castrated, and forced into the Chinese military, where he rose quickly and was eventually put in charge of maritime expeditions to display the power of the Yongle emperor. The Chinese junks of the **Zheng He expeditions** visited Sumatra (soo-mah-trah), Sri Lanka, and western Indian ports, and they also crossed the Persian Gulf (see Map 14.2).

Zheng He expeditions
A fleet of Chinese junks under the leadership of the eunuch Admiral Zheng He (1371–1433) that traveled on well-established hajj routes from China to Southeast Asia, India, the Islamic world, and East Africa from 1405 to 1433.

Admiral Zheng He's fleet must have impressed everyone who saw it. Over twenty-eight thousand men staffed the full fleet of over three hundred massive

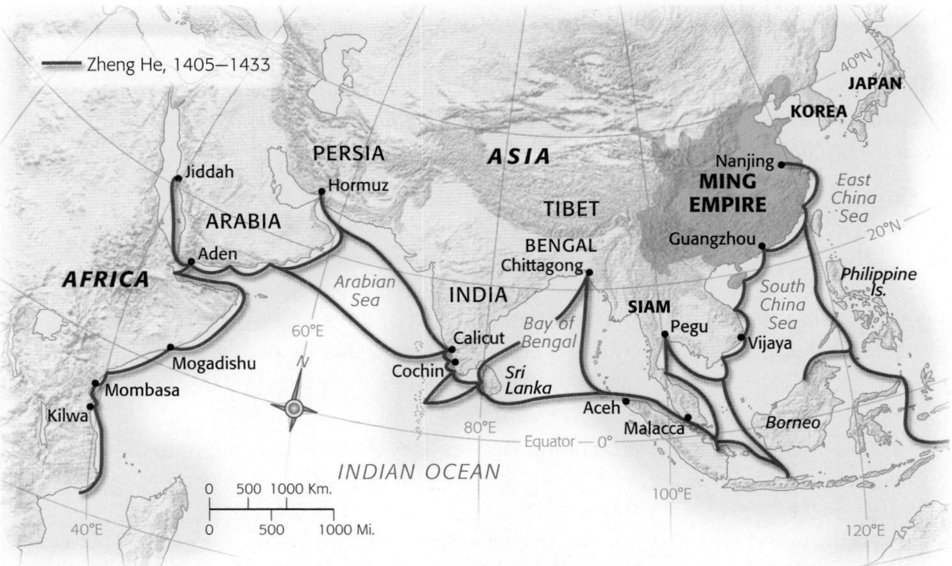

Map 14.2 Zheng He's Voyages, 1405–1433 Admiral Zheng He led a Ming dynasty fleet on seven different voyages to Southeast Asia, South Asia, the Arabian peninsula, and the East African coast. Although the voyages covered 7,000 miles (11,000 km), the sailors were not exploring but traveling on well-known hajj routes. The route from the Arabian peninsula to China was the longest sea route in regular use before Columbus crossed the Atlantic in 1492.

State-of-the-Art Cartography in the 1400s

Around the year 1400 a Korean mapmaker took on the task of making a map of the known world. Because of the extensive cultural exchanges under Mongol rule, this mapmaker had many more resources than Zhao Rugua did in 1225, when he wrote his *Description of Foreign Peoples* (see Chapter 12). Zhao was able to consult earlier Chinese maps and books and to speak with visitors to the Chinese port of Quanzhou, but by 1400 more maps, from more countries, were available, and the Kangnido mapmaker decided to use three maps. The first, based on an Arabic prototype, showed the latest information about Africa. The southern tip, what we now call the Cape of Good Hope, was surrounded by water, and the Nile had three sources, as shown on all Islamic maps. The Arabic map had the south on the top and had to be rotated 180 degrees to put the south on the bottom, as it appears on Chinese maps. The second map the mapmaker used was a historic map of China that showed both contemporary place names and earlier place names. And the third map was of Korea.

Unfortunately, these three maps did not have a scale (or maybe they did and the cartographer simply ignored it), so the cartographer simply joined the three maps together. Judged from today's standpoint, the results are far from perfect. Korea is disproportionately large, Africa is tiny, and India is missing altogether. Even so, this is one of the earliest surviving maps portraying all of Eurasia. It includes both the Islamic world and Europe, a vivid illustration of how the Mongol unification of Eurasia led to a dramatic increase in geographic knowledge.

Compare this map with the Ebstorf T-O map in Chapter 13 (page 390). How is it different? Does the mapmaker include any nongeographic information, as the Ebstorf mapmaker did?

1. The cartographer has included the Shandong peninsula.

2. This is the Korean peninsula. ***How does it differ from its actual size and orientation (as shown on the map on page 427)? What mapmaking process would have resulted in such a depiction?***

3. This island is definitely Japan, but it is difficult to decide which island is Taiwan or Hainan island.

4. Lying at the center of this map, China occupies much of the space. The cartographer has distorted the empire's overall shape, possibly so that he can fit all the labels on.

5. These three circles mark the source of the Nile, as they do on all Islamic maps.

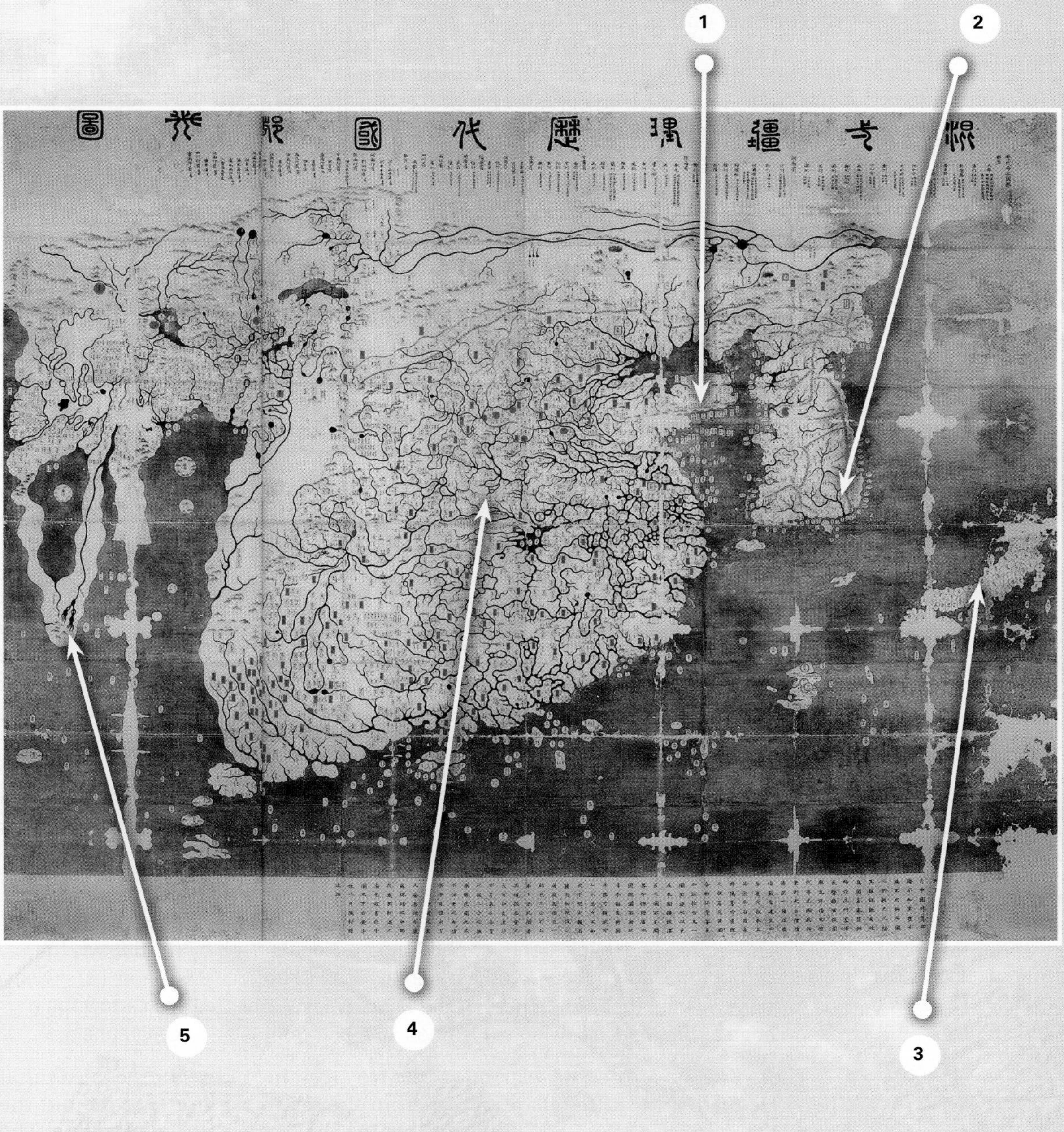

a faithful photo reproduction of the copy of the Kangnido map created by Yi Hoe and Kwon Kun, ca. 1470 wooden ships. The biggest Chinese ships—200-foot (61-m)-long "treasure ships"—were the largest ships in the world at that time. In 1341, at Calicut, Ibn Battuta had praised Chinese ships for their wooden compartments offering privacy; Zheng He's sailors filled similar compartments with fresh water and stocked them with fish for their dining pleasure.

In most cases, the ships landed at a port, gave gifts to the local ruler, and left, but they intervened in local affairs if the ruler did not obey them. In 1411, the Chinese forces took the capital city of Ceylon (modern-day Sri Lanka) and captured the ruler, replacing him with a puppet loyal to Chinese interests.

The farthest they went was more than 7,000 miles (11,000 km) to the coast of East Africa, which they visited in 1418, 1421–1422, and 1431–1433. The ships broke the long journey into smaller legs by stopping frequently at ports along the way. Although they covered enormous distances, Zheng He's ships never ventured into unknown waters. They were not exploring: their goal was to display the might of the Yongle emperor.

● **CONTEXT&CONNECTIONS** Zheng He's father and grandfather both went on the *hajj* pilgrimage to Mecca (Chapter 9), and the family was well informed about the geography of the larger Islamic world. In leading China's navy to India and Africa, Admiral Zheng He was following well-established hajj routes taken by both pilgrims and Muslim merchants. His route from China to East Africa was simply the mirror image of Ibn Battuta's from East Africa to China. ●

One of Zheng He's men, Fei Xin (1385–ca. 1436), recorded what he had been able *"to collect as true facts from the explanations"* of others about Africa. Much more detailed than Zhao Rugua's 1225 descriptions of Africa (see Chapter 12) are Fei Xin's descriptions of Mogadishu in modern-day Somalia: *"This place lies on the seashore. Piles of stones constitute the city-wall. . . . The houses are of layers of stone and four or five storeys high, the places for dwelling, cooking, easing oneself [going to the bathroom], and entertaining guests all being on the upper floors."** Fei Xin's informant describes what he saw from on board ship; the Chinese did not venture inland.

Because Zheng He's ships also engaged in trade, usually giving suits of clothing in exchange for horses, animal skins, gold, and silver, his men were well informed about local trading conditions. The commodities traded at Mogadishu included such things as *"gold and silver, colored satins, sandalwood, rice and cereals, porcelain articles, and colored thin silk."**

AP® THEMES

What contributed to the diffusion to China of knowledge about the geography of the Islamic world and Indian Ocean region?

● **CONTEXT&CONNECTIONS** Fei Xin's description of the known world ends with a description of Mecca, an indication that his account, although written in Chinese, was modeled on the Islamic genre of rihla travel accounts used by Ibn Jubayr, Ibn Fadlan, and Ibn Battuta to record their journeys (see Chapters 9, 10, and 11). This is further evidence that the Chinese of the Ming dynasty inherited the cartographic knowledge of the Mongols, who had learned so much from Islamic geographers. ●

The Ming government suspended the voyages in 1433, the year Admiral Zheng He died, and shifted its resources from the sea to the north to rebuild the Great Wall (see page 106) in the hope of keeping the Mongols from invading. The Ming dynasty stayed in power until 1644, with its attention fixed firmly on its main foreign enemy, the Mongols to the north.

---

*Fei Xin, *Xingcha Shenglan: The Overall Survey of the Star Raft*, trans. J. V. G. Mills, rev. and ed. Roderich Ptak (Wiesbaden: Harrassowitz, 1996), pp. 101–102.

The Mongol Empire and a Shrinking World

In 1253–1254, William of Rubruck traveled through the unified Mongol empire only a few years before it broke apart. Chinggis Khan and his descendants had led powerful armies fueled by the desire for plunder over huge distances. They were able to conquer so much territory because their cavalry overwhelmed the various sedentary peoples they defeated. The Mongols proved unusually willing to learn from conquered peoples and adopt their technologies. Although their empire lasted less than sixty years, the Mongols unified much of Eurasia for the first time.

The Mongols created the largest contiguous land empire in human history. Rubruck traveled from France to Khara Khorum, the Mongol capital in modern Mongolia, and when he arrived, he met a small group of Europeans who had made similarly long journeys. Unlike the earlier Persian, Roman, and Chinese empires (see Chapters 6, 7, and 8), the Mongols did not invest in roads, but they built an empire-wide system of postal stations, where riders, including William of Rubruck, could get fresh mounts and continue on their journeys.

On his trip William encountered many other Europeans who had left their homes, both voluntarily and not, to fight, to work as siege engineers, or to serve as envoys. The Mongols acted as a powerful filter for craftsmen, commodities, and ideas moving across Eurasia in an era when both China and Europe were undergoing commercial revolutions (see Chapters 12 and 13). They transmitted across great distances those items and ideas they prized, including gold, textiles, metallurgy, and geographic knowledge.

The resulting flow of people and information brought breakthroughs in multiple fields as the peoples on both sides of Eurasia learned of each other's discoveries. Gunpowder, which traveled from China west to Europe, played the determining role in the Ottoman conquest of Constantinople. Learning much from Islamic geographers (see Chapter 9), Chinese cartographers drew Europe and Africa on their maps for the first time.

Also drawing on Islamic knowledge, the Zheng He voyages to Southeast Asia, the Islamic world, and Africa

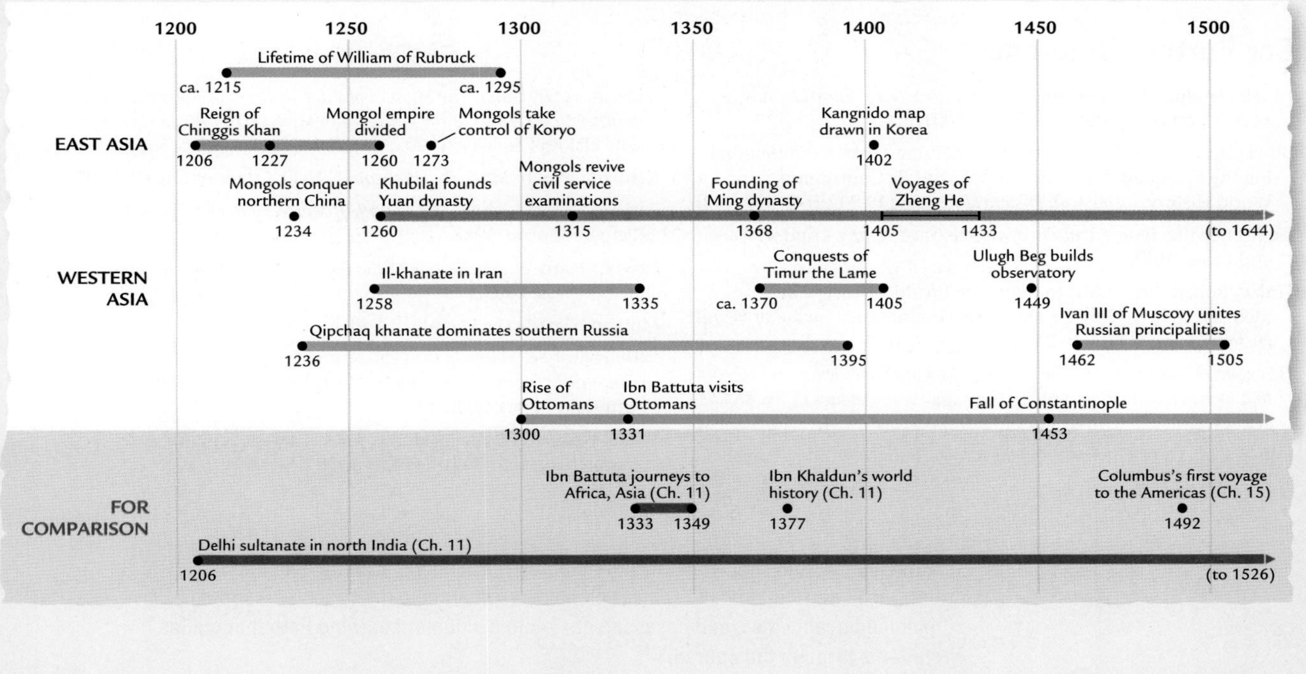

went farther than any earlier expeditions, traveling some 7,000 miles (11,000 km) from China, and were much larger in scale. When fully staffed, the fleet carried more than twenty-eight thousand men serving on over three hundred ships, some 200 feet (61 m) long (see page 456). These were not voyages of exploration: the navigators knew exactly where they were traveling on the hajj routes that linked China to Mecca and East Africa (see Chapter 11). With few exceptions, the ships stopped for only a few days before going on to the next port: the sailors who have left written records had minimal interactions with those they met, but they did record which commodities were available to trade at each port, a sign of the importance of commerce in encouraging exploration.

The primary purpose of the voyages was to awe China's neighbors and convince everyone inside and outside the empire of the Yongle emperor's legitimate claim to succeed his nephew as emperor. As the Viking voyages informed Europeans about the Americas (see Chapter 10), so too did the Zheng He voyages increase Chinese knowledge of the outside world. The voyages contributed to the shrinking of the world as distant places grew more familiar and seemed closer. Otherwise they had little effect. Some sixty years after the final Zheng He voyage in 1433, Columbus's ships had far greater historic impact even though they traveled a shorter distance. The next chapter will explain why.

Key Terms

William of Rubruck (402)
Chinggis Khan (402)
shamans (403)
tanistry (405)
khuriltai (405)
darughachi (406)
postal relay system (408)
Il-khanate (417)
principality of Muscovy (418)
Ivan III (418)
Timur the Lame (418)
Ottomans (419)
Janissaries (420)
Mehmed the Conqueror (421)
Khubilai Khan (424)
Ming dynasty (426)
Zheng He expeditions (427)

For Further Reference

Allsen, Thomas T. *Culture and Conquest in Mongol Eurasia*. New York: Cambridge University Press, 2001.

Brockett, Gavin D. "When Ottomans Became Turks: Commemorating the Conquest of Constantinople and Its Contribution to World History." *American Historical Review* 119.2 (2014): 399–433.

De Rachewiltz, Igor. *Papal Envoys to the Great Khans*. London: Faber and Faber, 1971.

Finlay, Robert. "How Not to (Re)Write World History: Gavin Menzies and the Chinese Discovery of America." *Journal of World History* 15, no. 2 (2004): 225–241.

Hodgson, Marshall G. S. *The Venture of Islam: Conscience and History in a World Civilization*, vol. 2, *The Expansion of Islam in the Middle Periods*. Chicago: University of Chicago Press, 1974.

Imber, Colin. *The Ottoman Empire, 1300–1650*. New York: Palgrave Macmillan, 2009.

Jackson, Peter, trans. *The Mission of Friar William of Rubruck: His Journey to the Court of the Great Khan Möngke 1253–1255*. London: The Hakluyt Society, 1990.

Kennedy, Hugh. *Mongols, Huns and Vikings*. London: Cassell, 2002.

Latham, Ronald, trans. *The Travels of Marco Polo*. New York: Penguin Books, 1958.

Lowry, Heath W. *The Nature of the Early Ottoman State*. Albany: SUNY Press, 2003.

Morgan, David. *The Mongols*. 2d ed. New York: Blackwell, 2007.

Park, Hyunhee. *Mapping the Chinese and Islamic Worlds: Cross-Cultural Exchange in Pre-modern Asia*. New York: Cambridge University Press, 2012.

Wade, Geoff. "The Zheng He Voyages: A Reassessment." *Asia Research Institute Working Paper Series* 31 (2004): 1–27.

AP® Review Questions for Chapter 14

Multiple-Choice Questions

QUESTIONS 1–4 REFER TO THE FOLLOWING PASSAGE.

It is the duty of the [Mongol] women to drive the carts, to load the houses on to them and to unload them, to milk the cows, to make the butter and khumis, to dress the skins and to sew them. . . .

The men make bows and arrows, manufacture stirrups and bits and make saddles; they build the houses and carts, they look after the horses and milk the mares. . . . Both sexes look after the sheep and goats, and sometimes the men, sometimes the women, milk them.

—William of Rubruck's report to King Louis IX, 1255

1. Which of the following best describes the tone of William of Rubruck toward the Mongols?
   (A) Disgust for the Mongol way of life
   (B) Envious of the Mongol way of life
   (C) Contemptuous of the way Mongol women were treated
   (D) Impressed with their division of labor

2. Compared to their sedentary counterparts, Mongol women as described in this document
   (A) had significantly fewer freedoms.
   (B) lived in a matriarchal society.
   (C) had more of an equal status.
   (D) were encouraged to remain celibate.

3. Which of the following statements most strongly refutes the author's view of Mongol gender relations?
   (A) Wives sat at their husbands' sides at council meetings.
   (B) Kidnapping women was an acceptable practice.
   (C) Women and men performed many tasks together.
   (D) Wars were fought by the men on horseback.

4. Which of the following best explains the difference in the gender roles of nomadic and sedentary peoples?
   (A) The heavy reliance on the domestication of animals for food
   (B) Women's role as primary caregiver for children
   (C) The development of writing and record keeping
   (D) Agriculture and the resulting specialization of labor

QUESTIONS 5–7 REFER TO THE FOLLOWING IMAGE.

5. The adding of minarets to the Hagia Sophia demonstrates
   (A) the conversion of much of the eastern Mediterranean region to Islam.
   (B) the continuing expansion of the Orthodox Church into the Muslim heartlands.
   (C) the religious ambiguity faced by the Ottomans after the fall of Constantinople.
   (D) the Turks' willingness to embrace both Islam and Christianity as imperial religions.

6. The Ottoman use of the Hagia Sophia as the model for other mosques, like the Blue Mosque, shows that the Turks
   (A) were committed to preserving the culture that they developed on the steppes.
   (B) held Greek culture and learning in contempt and attempted to remove it from Turkish cities.
   (C) relied on Arab learning and architecture to rebuild their capital.
   (D) were not afraid to borrow ideas and technologies from the people they conquered.

7. The use of the Hagia Sophia as a mosque by the Ottoman Turks is best explained by which of the following?
   (A) An attempt to eliminate all vestiges of Byzantine power
   (B) An attempt to eliminate Christianity from the empire
   (C) The use of architecture as a symbol of the Sultan's power and status
   (D) The continued use of Christianity to legitimize political power

QUESTIONS 8–10 REFER TO THE FOLLOWING PASSAGE.

Whenever the treasure-ships of the Central Country (Ming China) arrived there, they at once erected a line of stockading, like a city-wall.... The ships which had gone to various countries returned to this place and assembled; they marshaled the foreign goods and loaded them in ships; then waited till the south wind was perfectly favorable.... Moreover, the king of the country made a selection of local products, conducted his wife and son, brought his chiefs, boarded a ship and followed the treasure-ships; and he attended at court and presented tribute.

—Ma Huan, *The Overall Survey of The Ocean's Shores*, 1451

8. Based on this passage, which of the following is an accurate conclusion to draw about the Afro-Eurasian world of the fifteenth century?
   (A) The civilizations of the eastern hemisphere lacked the technology for extended maritime voyages.
   (B) Maritime reconnaissance was significant during the time period.
   (C) Most travel and trade from Asia to Africa and Southeast Asia was done by land.
   (D) Chinese understanding of monsoon patterns in the Indian Ocean was limited.

9. Based on the passage, what was the primary motivation for the treasure fleet voyages?
   (A) Diplomacy to demonstrate Ming superiority
   (B) Expand trade with East Africa
   (C) Provide the dynasty with a standing navy
   (D) Colonization of Southeast Asia

10. The treasure fleet having to wait for the winds to be favorable is probably a reference to which of the following?
   (A) Waiting for the typhoon season to end
   (B) The trade winds moving east to west across the Atlantic Ocean
   (C) The arrival of the monsoons on the Indian Ocean
   (D) The west-to-east trade winds of the Atlantic Ocean

Short-Answer Questions

1. Answer parts A and B.
   A. Some historians believe that many regions benefited from Mongol rule. Give TWO reasons for this argument.
   B. Give ONE reason why some historians take the opposite view.

2. Answer parts A and B.
   A. Briefly explain TWO reasons for Ming maritime activity.
   B. Briefly explain ONE effect of these voyages.

15 Maritime Expansion in the Atlantic World, 1400–1600

Bernardino de Sahagún

Clipart courtesy FCIT, from *Narrative and Critical History of America* (New York: Houghton, Mifflin, and Company, 1886):156

In 1529, at the age of thirty, **Bernardino de Sahagún** (1499–1590) landed in Veracruz, Mexico, only eight years after the Spanish army had conquered Mexico, and only thirty-seven years since Christopher Columbus had arrived in the Americas. On shipboard, Sahagún (sah-hah-GUHN) had already begun to study the local language, Nahuatl (NAH-watt). A university graduate, Sahagún was a Franciscan friar, and starting in 1547, he began to interview the local elders and collect material for a twelve-volume book, *General History of the Things of New Spain*, that he finished fifty years after he arrived in Mexico. In a note to the reader, he explained why he wrote in Nahuatl:

> *Although many have written of the Conquest of this New Spain [Mexico] in Spanish, according to the account of those who conquered it, I desired to write it in the Mexican language [Nahuatl].... Those who were conquered knew and gave an account of many things which transpired among them during the war of which those who conquered them were unaware. For these reasons, it seems to me, to have written this history, which was at a time when those who took part in the very Conquest were alive, has not been a superfluous task. And those who gave this account were principled persons of good judgment, and it is believed that they told all the truth.**

---

*Bernardino de Sahagún, *The Florentine Codex*, vol. I, trans. Arthur J. O. Anderson and Charles E. Dibble Santa Fe, N.M.: The School of American Research and the University of Utah, 1950–1982), p. 101.

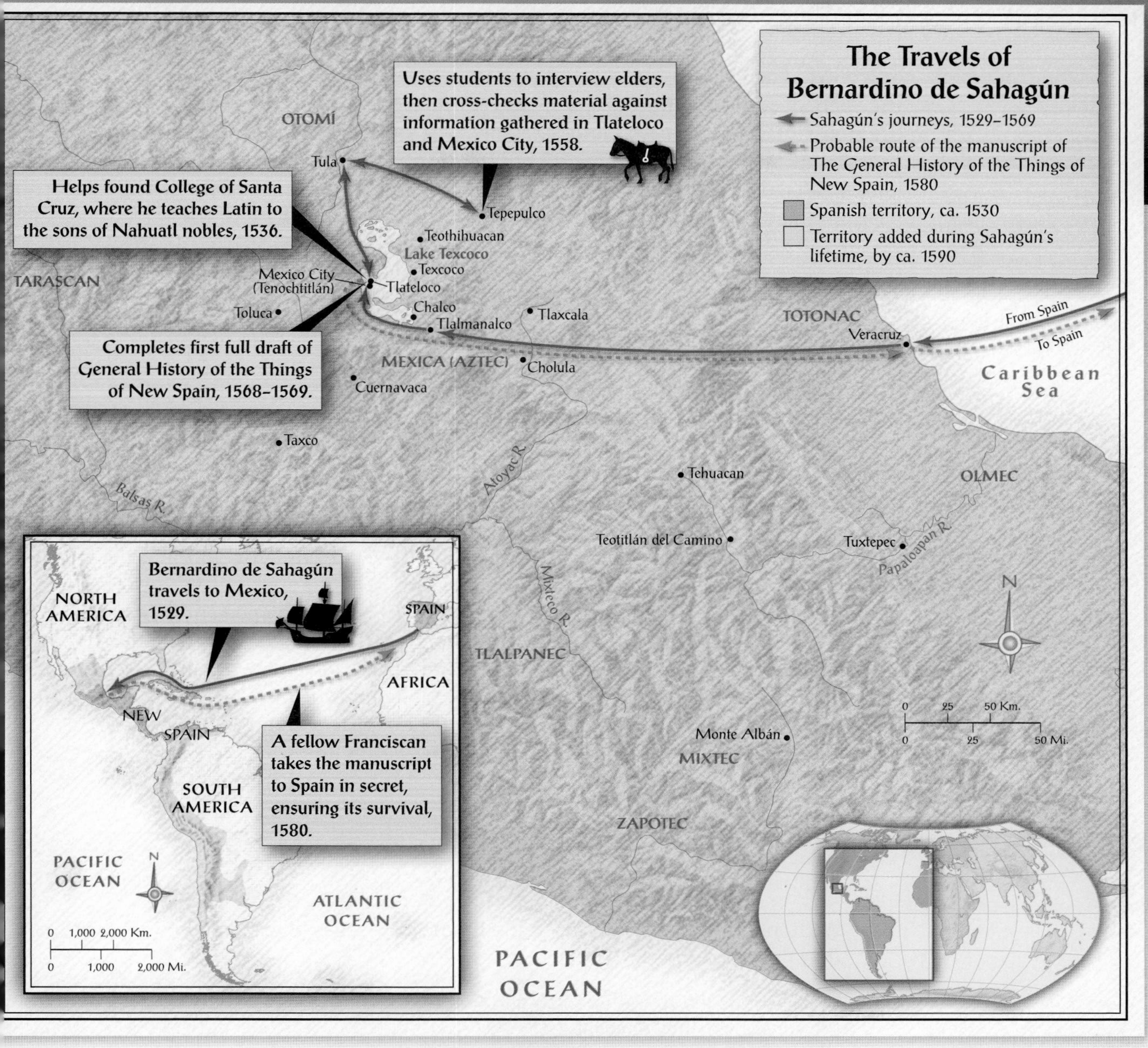

Sahagún here displays a remarkably up-to-date understanding of historical method, yet he was writing more than four hundred years ago. Because all the historical accounts of the conquest were in Spanish and reflected the view of the conquerors, Sahagún sought out the local people so that he could find out about what the Spanish had overlooked. Realizing the importance of eyewitness accounts as primary sources, he interviewed people old enough to have observed the conquest. And at a time when most of his contemporaries, even among the Franciscans, looked down on native peoples, Sahagún defended his informants as being both of good character and truthful—crucial measures of

Bernardino de Sahagún

A Franciscan friar, Sahagún (1499–1590) worked with a team of researchers to record the history of the Aztec peoples before the Spanish arrived in a long book entitled *General History of the Things of New Spain*, also known as the Florentine Codex.

reliability. The single most important source about the society in Mexico before the Spanish conquest, his *General History* narrates the arrival of Europeans from the point of view of the conquered. This type of account survives in literate societies like China (see Chapter 16) but hardly ever in illiterate societies, which makes Sahagún's *General History* of significance to anyone curious about European interactions with nonliterate indigenous peoples anywhere in the world.

In 1492, Columbus's voyage connected Europe with the Americas in a way that no previous contact had; the resulting exchange of plants, animals, people, and disease shaped our modern world. Unlike Viking voyages to Newfoundland around 1000 and Ming Chinese voyages to East Africa in the 1400s, Columbus's four voyages between 1492 and 1506 had far-reaching consequences. After 1300, while the Mexica (or Aztec) in Mexico and the Inca in Peru were creating powerful expansionist empires, on the opposite side of the Atlantic, Europeans were learning about geography as part of their humanistic studies. Spanish and Portuguese explorers traveled farther and farther, first to the islands of the Mediterranean and the Atlantic, then to the west coast of Africa, and finally to the Americas, always claiming colonies for their monarchs. The Europeans transported plants, animals, and people (often against their will) to entirely new environments on the other side of the Atlantic. Within one hundred years of Columbus's first voyage, millions of Amerindians had perished (the death toll reached 95 percent in some areas), victims of European diseases that no one understood. The Americas absorbed new populations from both Europe and Africa, and a new racially mixed society formed under Spanish colonial rule. Sahagún, who lived through two major epidemics and died in the third, saw this new society taking shape even as he observed the settlers fighting both among themselves and with the locals.

KEY CONCEPT QUESTIONS

- What were the characteristics of the imperial systems of both the Aztec and the Inca empires? **(Key Concept 3.2)**
- What innovations contributed to the European voyages of exploration? **(Key Concept 4.1)**
- What factors led to the Spanish and Portuguese acquisition of empire in the Americas? **(Key Concept 4.1)**
- How did the Columbian exchange affect both the Americas and Afro-Eurasia? **(Key Concept 4.1)**

The Aztec Empire of Mexico, 1325–1519

Because of the work of Sahagún and other Spanish missionaries, and because of archaeological discoveries, we know the history of the Aztec empire that Cortés and his forces defeated in 1521. Starting sometime around 1325, the Mexica (meh-SHE-kah), a people based in western Mexico, moved into central Mexico to

Tenochtitlan (modern-day Mexico City), which became the Aztec capital. The Mexica were one of many Nahua peoples who spoke the Nahuatl language. Like the Maya, the Nahua peoples had a complex calendrical system, built large stone monuments, and played a ritual ball game. The Mexica believed in a pantheon of gods, headed by the sun, that demanded blood sacrifices from their devotees. To sustain these gods, they continually went to war, gradually conquering many of the city-states in central Mexico to form the **Aztec empire**.

Aztec empire
An empire based in Tenochtitlan (modern-day Mexico City) that ruled over 4 to 6 million people in modern-day Mexico and Guatemala.

Sahagún's Research Method

The Nahua (NAH-wah) peoples spoke a language called Nahuatl that did not have a written form. Nahuatl texts combine pictures with rebus writing, which uses images to represent something with the same sound; in English, for example, a picture of an eye functions as a rebus for the word *I*. The Nahua's writing served as a trigger to memory; people who had been trained to tell a certain story could look at a Nahua manuscript and be reminded of the details. Because someone who did not know the story could not read it, this was not a full-fledged writing system. When the first Franciscans arrived, some five years before Sahagún, they created a new alphabet for Nahuatl and taught it to their Nahua students, mostly the sons of powerful families, who attended missionary schools and, after 1536, the Jesuit College at Santa Cruz.

The Jesuit College was successful because it unintentionally replicated the traditional Nahua schooling system. Before the Spanish arrived, boys and girls left their families at the age of fifteen to live in separate houses for boys and girls where they studied Nahua traditions. Finished at seventeen or eighteen, the girls returned to their homes to marry; the boys stayed until around twenty-one, when they took up their father's occupations. The Jesuits did not educate the girls, but the college trained boys of exactly the same age as those in the Nahua houses.

Over the course of his long life, Sahagún developed a sophisticated research method to recover the pre-Spanish past. First he made up a long outline for his *General History*. He then drew up long questionnaires detailing the topics he wanted to ask the Nahua about. For example, as he explains, when he wanted to find out in which month the new year began, he *"gathered together many elders, the most competent I could find, and together with the most able of the college students, they decided, saying that the year began on the second day of February."** In reply to Sahagún's questions, the elders drew traditional pictorial narratives on bark paper or deerskin. The young students then wrote notes in Nahuatl in the margins surrounding those drawings. To make sure that he was collecting accurate information, Sahagún conducted all his interviews in three separate cities. Sahagún combined all the information to write his *General History*.

● **CONTEXT&CONNECTIONS** Sahagún's research method was modeled on and expanded that of the Roman Pliny the Elder in his *Natural History*, completed more than one thousand years earlier between 77 and 79 C.E. After writing his long outline, Pliny consulted written sources and interviewed different scholars. He wrote entries on different topics, ranging from technological breakthroughs to the artists of his time, but he did not cross-check his information or use recorded questionnaires as Sahagún did. ●

*Luis Nicolau D'Olwer, *Fray Bernardino de Sahagún (1499-1590)*, trans. Mauricio J. Mixco (Salt Lake City: University of Utah Press, 1987), p. 108, n3.

The first versions of Sahagún's *General History*, dating to 1569, were entirely in Nahuatl (for the reasons explained in the opening of the chapter), but Sahagún later decided to add Spanish translation, so that his final product had two columns, one of Nahuatl explanation and a second one in Spanish, which was heavily illustrated with original paintings and sketches done by his informants. Nothing in Sahagún's education at the Spanish university of Salamanca prepared him for this task or introduced such a method; there he had studied the classic curriculum influenced by humanism (discussed later in this chapter). The use of a questionnaire that evolved as he interviewed more people, the conversations with multiple informants, and the cross-checking of information are all hallmarks of modern social science, and indeed Sahagún is often called the world's first anthropologist.

Sahagún was like a modern anthropologist in another way: he did not judge the Nahua. He recorded all their customs, including human sacrifice, because he wanted to understand them and to produce a complete record.

• **CONTEXT&CONNECTIONS** In this way, Sahagún was like the Greek Herodotus (ca. 485–425 B.C.E.), often called the father of history, who wrote about the Scythian practice of making handkerchiefs of human flesh in an equally dispassionate tone. Sahagún and Herodotus alike wanted to understand their subjects and did not pass judgment on their practices, however bloodthirsty they may have seemed. •

Many of his fellow Spaniards despised the Nahua as utterly uncivilized, and their objections to his work caused Sahagún many problems. His masterwork survives today only because a fellow Franciscan smuggled the full work back into Spain and told no one, including Sahagún, about it. It was preserved in the library of the Medicis in Florence, which is why scholars today refer to the *General History* as the Florentine Codex.

The Mexica Settlement of Tenochtitlan

Sahagún's informants agreed that around the 1200s various groups migrated to central Mexico. The heart of this area is the Valley of Mexico, 10,000 feet (3,000 m) above sea level and surrounded by volcanoes. The Valley of Mexico contains many shallow lakes and much fertile land. The last Nahua groups to arrive referred to themselves as "Mexica" (meh-SHE-kah), the origin of the word *Mexico*, but many historians call them by the modern word *Aztec*. Although *Aztec* is a term that no one at the time used, this text uses it to refer to the empire the Mexica built. Linguistic analysis of the Nahuatl language indicates that its speakers originated somewhere in the southwest United States or northern Mexico.

altepetl
The 450 city-states of the Aztec empire that each had its own leader and government, a palace for its ruler, a pyramid-shaped temple, and a market.

Tenochtitlan
Capital city of the Aztec empire, which the Mexica reclaimed from swampland, with a population of some two hundred thousand people.

By the 1300s, some fifty city-states, called **altepetl** (al-TEH-peh-tuhl), occupied central Mexico, each with its own leader, or "speaker," and its own government. Each altepetl had a palace for its ruler, a pyramid-shaped temple, and a market. The Mexica migrated to the region around the historic urban center of Teotihuacan, a large city with many lakes. Since this region was already home to several rival altepetl, the Mexica were forced to settle in a swampland called **Tenochtitlan** (teh-noch-TIT-lan). The Mexica gradually reclaimed large areas of the swamps and on the drier, more stable areas erected stone buildings held together with mortar. They planted flowers everywhere and walked on planks or traveled by canoe from one reclaimed area to another. Much of what they built lies under the massive cathedral of Mexico City, but even today, archaeologists use Sahagún's information to locate different temples; of the seventy-eight different temples whose existence he recorded, archaeologists have located more than forty.

Traditional accounts say the Mexica people arrived at Tenochtitlan in 1325, a date confirmed by archaeological excavation. At its height, Tenochtitlan contained sixty thousand dwellings, home to perhaps two hundred thousand people in an area of 5 square miles (13 sq km). The central marketplace offered cooked and uncooked food, slaves, tobacco products, and luxury goods made from gold, silver, and feathers. Consumers used cotton cloaks, cacao beans, and feather quills filled with gold dust as media of exchange, since the Mexica had no coins.

Nahua Religion

The Mexica believed that their patron god was Huitzilopochtli (wheat-zeel-oh-POSHT-lee), whose name meant "the hummingbird of the south." Also the warrior god of the sun, Huitzilopochtli played a key role in the Mexica origin legend. On the long migration from their original homeland in Aztlan, the Mexica arrived at a mountain where an elderly priestess guarded a temple. A ball of feathers fell from the sky, and she became pregnant with a young male fetus, the future Huitzilopochtli. Ashamed by the news of her mother's pregnancy, her daughter organized an army to kill her mother. Huitzilopochtli, still in the womb, emerged as a full-grown warrior, killed the priestess's daughter, and rolled her body parts down the hill as his army defeated the attackers.

This legend provides a rationale for the massive Mexica blood sacrifices, many of which occurred in the Great Temple in Tenochtitlan. The Nahuatl term for human blood was "precious water." The most important Nahua deity, the sun, controlled agriculture and crops, primarily the corn, beans, and peppers that were the main source of food. The sun was so important that Sahagún collected multiple sayings just about the sun. For example, if a young woman said, "*I discover my sun, I set out my sun,*"* she meant that she was married. Because of the sun's importance, eclipses terrified the Nahua, and Sahagún recorded their reactions: "*The common folk raised a cry, lifting their voices, making a great din, calling out, shrieking. There was shouting everywhere. People of light complexion were slain as sacrifices; captives were killed. All offered their blood; they drew straws through the lobes of their ears.*"*

Every 260 days, after twelve months had passed, the Nahua celebrated the festival of the sun, first by fasting for four days, and then blowing conch shells. As during eclipses, "*Straws were drawn through the flesh. And they cut the ear lobes of small children lying in cradles. Everyone drew blood. There were then no greetings. There was only the drawing of blood.*"*

Ranking just under the sun-god were the gods of rain and agriculture. The deities, the Mexica believed, needed to drink much human blood, usually of prisoners of war, so that they would keep the soil fertile, the harvest plentiful, and the succession of seasons regular; this is the kind of belief, utterly different from the Spaniards, that Sahagún hoped to understand and recorded for future generations.

While many societies engaged in human sacrifice, the Mexica apparently killed unusually high numbers of people at one time; scholars continue to debate how many. Spanish sources may have exaggerated the death toll to discredit their predecessors, but they gave much lower numbers of sacrificial victims for other

*Bernardino de Sahagún, *The Florentine Codex*, vol. I, trans. Arthur J. O. Anderson and Charles E. Dibble (Santa Fe, N.M.: The School of American Research and the University of Utah, 1950–1982), pp. 181, 2; vol. III, p. 216.

The Trustees of the British Museum

Mexica Skull-Mask Worshipers used deerskin straps to tie this skull-mask around their waists in a display of fearsomeness. The mask was made by applying small fragments of turquoise, black lignite coal, and white conch to the front half of a skull (the human teeth are original). The highly polished pyrite eyes glisten in the light, and the red mollusk shell nose inlays replicate the color of flayed human tissue. The mask vividly captures the importance of human offerings to the Mexica deities.

Amerindian peoples, suggesting that the Mexica indeed performed more sacrifices.

Nahua Society

The Nahua peoples treated certain human beings like gods. The leader of the Mexica, their Great Speaker, was carried in a feathered chair. His advisers never looked at the Great Speaker or addressed him directly: a screen always separated them from him. Sahagún's informants described his clothing, hats, and throne on different holidays in great detail. The Great Speaker was in charge of all external matters, including war, the receipt of gifts, and relations with other altepetl. A group of nobles, priests, and successful warriors chose the new Great Speaker, and although they treated him as their ritual superior, they could depose him if they did not approve of his rule. All the top officials came from the royal family and had large private estates.

Most of the Nahua were commoners, each of whom belonged to a "big house," a group who believed they were descended from a common ancestor. The lowest-ranking people in Nahua society were slaves, often the original residents of the Valley of Mexico. Ordinary people and slaves farmed the land and generated the surplus that underpinned the expansion of the Mexica altepetl. Because they had no draft animals, metal tools, or wheels, everything had to be carried and cultivated by hand.

Corn ripened in only fifty days, providing sufficient food for a family as well as a surplus. Grinding corn was exclusively women's work; for fear that they might antagonize the gods, men were forbidden to help. Ordinary people were required to pay tribute to their Mexica overlords by contributing a share of the crop, performing labor service, paying other goods, and most onerous of all, providing victims for human sacrifice.

The Military and the Conquests of the Mexica

If successful in battle, warriors could rise in Mexica society to a high position. They then received lands of their own and were not required to pay taxes on them. Conversely, the best human sacrifice one could offer to the gods, the Nahua believed, was a warrior taken captive in battle. In their system of thirteen heavens and eight underworlds, the highest heaven, the Paradise of the Sun-God, was for men who had killed the enemy in battle and for women who had died in childbirth, a type of battle in its own right. The elders told Sahagún about that heaven: it was like a desert, and the dead, armed with shields to protect them from the sun, could see the sun only through holes in their shields. After four years, the dead changed into hummingbirds and other beautiful birds who drank honey from flowers both in heaven and on earth itself.

Map 15.1 The Aztec Empire Starting from their capital at Tenochtitlan (modern Mexico City), the Mexica conquered neighboring peoples living between the Gulf of Mexico and the Pacific Ocean, who were required to pay taxes and submit tribute, but received few benefits in return. When Cortés landed on the coast of Mexico, he quickly found allies among the conquered peoples, particularly the Tlaxcalans.

The Mexica troops fitted their clubs, spears, and darts with blades made from obsidian, a volcanic glass. They protected themselves with thick cotton armor. Hand-to-hand combat was considered the most honorable form of warfare.

In 1428, the Mexica launched a series of conquests that led to the creation of an empire. By 1500, they had conquered 450 altepetl in modern Mexico, extending all the way to Guatemala, and ruled over a subject population estimated at between 4 and 6 million (see Map 15.1).

The Aztec empire, though large and with a beautiful capital, had one major weakness. Once the Mexica conquered a given people, they demanded tribute and took sacrificial victims from them, yet they did nothing to incorporate them further into their empire.

● **CONTEXT&CONNECTIONS** This Mexica policy was similar to that of the Mongols, who also conquered other peoples to get tribute and did little to foster loyalty to their new overlords. The Mexica also allowed the peoples they had conquered to speak their own language. ●

The Inca Empire, 1400–1532

The **Inca empire**, 2,500 miles (4,000 km) to the south in the Andes, differed significantly from the Aztec. Because no one like Sahagún collected information there just after the conquest, historians must weigh Spanish testimony against archaeological remains. Each time the Inca conquered a new group, they have

Inca empire
Andean empire founded in 1438 by Pachakuti (d. 1471), which ruled over a peak population of 10 to 12 million.

found, they integrated them into the empire, requiring them to perform labor and military service and resettling some groups to minimize the chances of revolt. Like the Mexica, the Inca worshiped deities that demanded human sacrifices, but never as many as in Mexico. Although the Inca successfully integrated subject peoples, they did not have an orderly system of succession, resulting in conflict each time their ruler died.

Inca Religion and Andean Society

ayllu
Andean kin groups of the Inca empire that worked the land in several adjacent ecological zones as a hedge against crop failure in any one zone.

The ordinary people of the Andes lived in kin groups called **ayllu** (aye-YOU) that worked the land in several adjacent ecological zones so they could backup yields should the crops in one zone fail.

Most ayllu were divided into smaller subgroups, and men tended to marry women from another subgroup. All the people in a given ayllu recognized one common ancestor. Ordinary people believed that, in addition to their ancestors, hundreds of spirits (*wak'a*) inhabited places in the landscape such as streams, caves, rocks, and hills.

The most important Inca deities, ranking far above these local spirits, were the Creator, the Creator's child the Sun, and the Thunder gods. By 1500, the sun-god had become the most important deity, probably because the Inca ruler, the Sapa Inca, or "Unique Inca," claimed descent from the sun-god. The priest of the sun-god was the highest-ranking priest in Inca society and the second most powerful person in the Inca empire.

AP® THEMES
How did religious beliefs shape the social hierarchy of the Inca?

Both the Sapa Inca and the sun-god priest belonged to the aristocracy, which was divided into three tiers: the close relatives of the ruler and previous rulers, more distant relatives, and then the leaders of the groups the Inca had conquered. Although most Inca traced their ancestry through their father's line, the ruler's mother's family played a central role in court politics because the ruler took his wives from his mother's family.

● **CONTEXT&CONNECTIONS** The Inca had no orderly system of succession. In a practice much like the tanistry prevalent among the Mongols, each time the Inca ruler died, all those of his male kin who hoped to succeed him launched an all-out war until a single man emerged victorious. ●

During his reign, the Sapa Inca lived as a deity among his subjects. Even so, he had to keep the support of the aristocracy, which could easily overthrow him at any time.

Like the ayllu ancestors, the ruler was believed to continue to live even after death. The Inca mummified the bodies of deceased rulers and other high-ranking family members. They placed the mummies in houses around the main square of Cuzco, their capital city high in the Andes at an elevation of 11,300 feet (3,450 m). One Spanish observer described their interaction with these mummies:

> *Most of the people of Cuzco served the dead, I have heard it said, who they daily brought out to the main square, setting them down in a ring, each one according to his age, and there the male and female attendants ate and drank. . . . The mummies toasted each other and the living, and the living toasted the dead.**

*Terence d'Altroy, *The Incas* (Malden, Mass.: Blackwell, 2002), p. 97 (citing Pedro Pizarro).

The Marvels of Incan Engineering at Machu Picchu The settlement at Machu Picchu, which stands 8,000 feet (2,400 m) above sea level, embodies the Incan talent for engineering in its even stone houses arrayed on multiple levels, connected by manmade waterways and more than one hundred stairways. Built around 1450 as a summer palace for the ruler Pachakuti, the site was abandoned after the collapse of the Inca empire and rediscovered by outsiders only in the early 1900s. Today it is one of the world's most visited sites and the most famous of all the Inca ruins. (©Kelsey Green/Shutterstock.com)

He did not explain how the living communicated with the dead, but it seems likely that priests intervened.

The Inca organized the worship of local spirits who inhabited places in the landscape, ancestors of the rulers, and deities into a complex ritual calendar specifying which one was to be worshiped on a given day. Of 332 shrines in Cuzco, 31 received human sacrifices, in many cases a young boy and a young girl, a symbolic married couple. These usually occurred in times of hardship, like an epidemic, or during unusual astronomical events, like eclipses. Occasionally, larger sacrifices occurred, such as when a ruler died, and one source gives the largest number of sacrificial victims killed at a single time as four thousand.

The Inca Expansion

As the Aztec believed their history began with their occupation of Tenochtitlan, the Incas traced their beginnings to their settlement in Cuzco. Archaeological evidence suggests that the Inca moved to Cuzco sometime around 1400.

Map 15.2 The Inca Empire In 1438, the Inca ruler Pachakuti took power in the capital at Cuzco and led his armies to conquer large chunks of territory along the Andes. Two north-south trunk routes, with subsidiary east-west routes, formed a system of over 18,000 miles (30,000 km) of roads. By 1532, the Inca ruled an empire of 1,500 square miles (4,000 sq km).

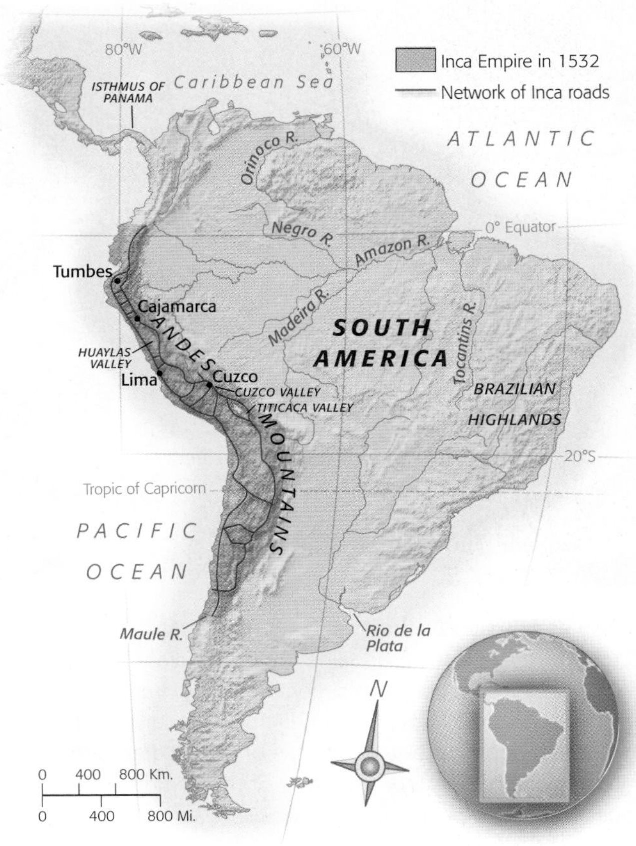

Although oral accounts conflict, most accept the date of 1438 as the year Pachakuti (patch-ah-KOO-tee) (d. 1471), the first great Inca ruler, seized the throne from his brother in a coup and launched the military campaigns outward from Cuzco. The Inca conquered neighboring lands because they desired the goods produced in each ecological zone: the herds of llamas and alpaca, crops like grain and potatoes, and the gold, feathers, shells, and minerals from the jungle lowlands and the shore.

Much of Inca warfare consisted of storming enemy forts with a large infantry, often after cutting off access to food and water. For several days enemy forces traded insults and sang hostile songs such as this: "*We will drink from the skull of the traitor, we will adorn ourselves with a necklace of his teeth,... we play the melody of the pinkullu [a musical instrument resembling a flute] with flutes made from his bones, we will beat the drum made from his skin, and thus we will dance.*"* Attackers in quilted cotton launched arrows, stones from slingshots, and stone spears, and in hand-to-hand combat used spears and clubs, some topped with stone or with bronze stars.

Like other Andean peoples, the Inca knew how to extract metallic ore from rocks and how to heat different metals to form alloys. They made bronze and copper, but they did not develop their metallurgical expertise beyond making club heads, decorative masks, and ear spools for the nobility.

At its height, the Inca army could field as many as one hundred thousand men in a single battle, most of the rank-and-file drawn from subject peoples who were required to serve in the army. The rate of Inca expansion was breathtaking. Starting from a single location, Cuzco, the Inca conquered large chunks of southern, central, and coastal Peru, Ecuador, the eastern lowlands of Peru and Bolivia, and the mountains of Argentina and Chile. By 1532, they ruled over a population estimated at 10 to 12 million (see Map 15.2).

One major legacy of the Inca empire was its magnificent road system. While some routes predated the Inca conquest and were built as early as 1000 B.C.E., the Inca linked them together into an overall system. Since the Inca did not have the wheel, most of the traffic was by foot, and llamas could carry small loads. With no surveying instruments, the Inca constructed these roads across deserts, yawning chasms, and

*Terence d'Altroy, *The Incas* (Malden, Mass.: Blackwell, 2002), pp. 226–227.

WORLD HISTORY IN TODAY'S WORLD

The Great Road Reunites Six Nations

In June 2014, the World Heritage Committee of UNESCO recognized the Incan road network, Qhapaq-Ñan (kah-pahk ni-ahn), or the Great Road, as a World Heritage site. The application was unusual for several reasons: Qhapaq-Ñan is not a single location but 273 individual temples, towers, forts, and hostels in 137 locations on a section of the road 435 miles (700 km) long. This is the World Heritage site.

Although only a fraction of the original network, the road crosses six different Latin American countries—Peru, Colombia, Ecuador, Bolivia, Chile, and Argentina—that have warred in the past and even recently over contested borders. (Peru and Ecuador fought intermittently for over 150 years before they agreed to a new border in 1995.) Attracted by the potential increase in tourists that World Heritage sites bring, the six nations came together to make a joint application some twelve years in the making. "We are all very happy," said Luis Jaime Castillo Butters, an archaeologist and a deputy culture minister in Peru, on hearing of the UNESCO approval.

A marvel of engineering, the original network's roads run up and down rain forests, deserts, and high mountains. They reached maximum use under the Inca empire in the 1400s, when the network extended across and along the full extent of the Andes Mountains. The transportation system played a key role in holding the Inca empire together, because it linked the capital at Cuzco with all outlying towns. Supplies could reach the remote site of Machu Picchu only because of the Qhapaq-Ñan road network.

Although one Inca bridge made of braided grass survives even today (a drive about four hours away from Cuzco), the road network is badly damaged in many areas. Tractor farming and cellphone towers pose the greatest threat to the existing sections of the original road. Other sections have already been paved over and converted into highways. The participating governments hope that the granting of World Heritage status will make it possible to raise the funds for necessary repairs and conservation measures.

Sources: Ralph Blumenthal, "Incas' Road Among Additions to World Heritage List," *New York Times*, June 23, 2014.

mountains over 16,000 feet (5,000 m) high. Individual messengers working in shifts could move at an estimated rate of 150 miles (240 km) per day. (See the feature "World History in Today's World: The Great Road Reunites Six Nations.")

• **CONTEXT&CONNECTIONS** These rates for the Inca messengers as recorded by the Spanish are far faster than Persian messengers' 90 miles (145 km) per day or the Mongols' 60 miles (97 km) per day, both traveling on horseback. The Inca messengers ran on excellent, but steep roads, and they must have switched off often. As fast as the Inca messengers were, the Inca armies moved much more slowly, covering perhaps 7–9 miles (12–15 km) per day. Armies throughout the ancient world traveled at a rate of 10–20 miles (16–32 km) per day. Other empires—the Persians, the Romans, and the Chinese—devoted considerable resources to building roads. But as extensive as these road systems were, they did not match the Incas in their engineering ingenuity because they used the wheel and the Inca did not. •

Inca Rule of Subject Populations

Unique among the Andean peoples, the Inca incorporated each conquered land and its occupants into their kingdom. They brought many images of subjects' ancestral deities to Cuzco, holding the images hostage so that their devotees would not rise up against their Inca overlords.

quipu
Inca system of record keeping that used knots on strings to record the population.

● **CONTEXT&CONNECTIONS** Like the Assyrians, the Inca resettled thousands of people, forcing them to move to regions far from their original homes. They also, like the Assyrians and the Mongols, encouraged different peoples to submit to them by treating those who surrendered much more gently than the peoples they had to fight in combat. ●

The Inca allowed local leaders to continue to serve but required everyone to swear loyalty to the Inca ruler, to grant him all rights to their lands, and to perform labor service as the Inca state required. Inca officials also allowed indigenous leaders a place in the central government at the lower level. Those of high birth could serve in the Inca government as long as they learned Quechua (KETCH-wah), the language of the Inca.

Keeping Records with Knots The Inca kept all their records by using knotted strings, called quipu, attaching subsidiary cords, sometimes in several tiers, to a main cord. Different types of knots represented different numeric units; skipped knots indicated a zero; the color of the string indicated the item being counted.

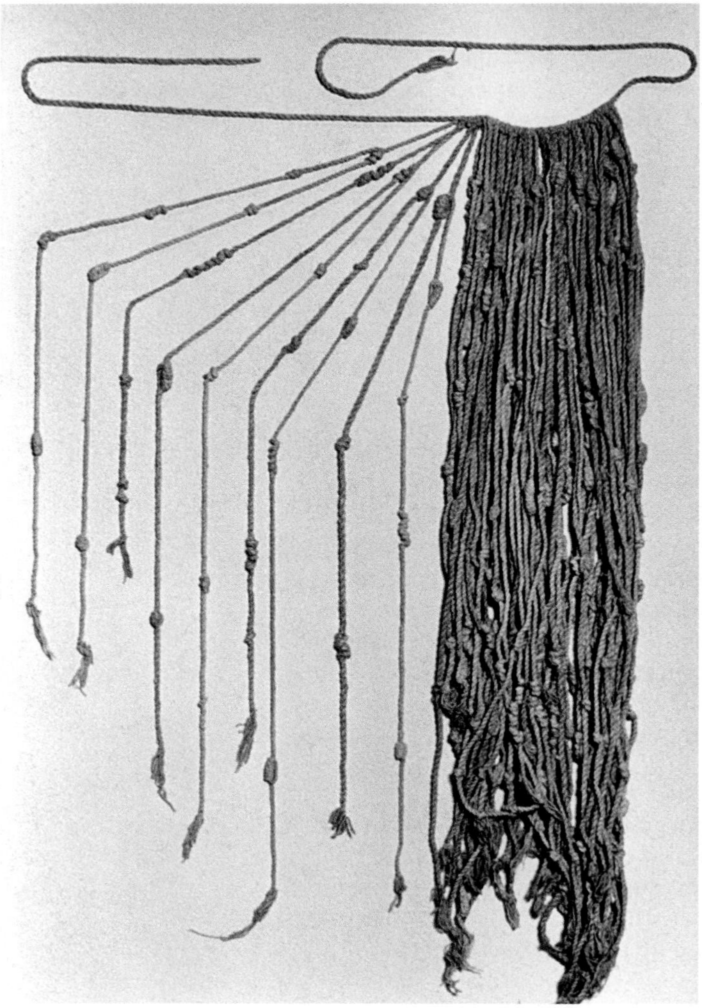

The Granger Collection, NYC

Each year Inca officials counted the population, not with a written script but by using a system of knotted strings, called **quipu** (key-POOH). Since no one can understand the quipu records, the population of the Inca empire remains unknown. Each town had a knot keeper who maintained and interpreted the knot records, which were updated annually. Some 850 examples survive today. With different knots, thicknesses, composition (of llama and alpaca fiber or cotton), and dyed hue, the strings of the quipus contain much information. Some nineteenth-century written translations of quipus have been found, but no one has managed to link a translation with a surviving example. Scholars are creating computer databases in the hope that they will provide a modern equivalent of the Rosetta Stone for understanding these still-undeciphered records.

To fulfill the Inca's main service tax, male household heads between twenty-five and fifty had to perform two to three months' labor each year. However, the Inca did not treat all subject peoples alike. From some resettled peoples they exacted extra months of labor, and many subject groups who possessed a specific skill, such as carving stones or making spears, performed that skill for the state. Others did far less. For example, many Inca looked down on a people they called Uru, literally meaning "worm," who lived on the southern edge of Lake Titicaca, because their only labor service was to catch fish, gather grasses, and weave textiles. An even more despised group was required each year to submit a single basket filled with lice, not because the Inca wanted the lice, but because they wanted to teach this group the nature of their tax obligations.

Each household also contributed certain goods, such as food, blankets, textiles, and tools, that were kept in thousands of storehouses throughout the empire. One Spaniard described a storehouse in Cuzco that particularly impressed him: *"There is a house in which are kept more than 100,000 dried birds, for from their feathers articles of clothing are made."** This storehouse system functioned so well that the corn and potatoes in the storehouses could support an army for months.

Despite its size, the Inca empire appeared stronger than it was. Many of the subject peoples resented their heavy labor obligations, and each time an Inca ruler died, the ensuing succession disputes threatened to tear the empire apart.

AP® THEMES

How did the Inca system of coercive labor compare to other systems of coercive labor, such as serfdom in Europe and Japan?

Intellectual and Geographic Exploration in Europe, 1300–1500

Between 1300 and 1500, as the Mexica and Inca were expanding their empires overland in the Americas, European scholars extended their fields of study to include many new topics. Meanwhile, new printing technology made books more available and affordable, enabling university students like Sahagún to read and compare many more books than in earlier centuries. Portuguese and Spanish ships colonized lands farther and farther away, as the pace of European exploration hastened, especially after 1450, when many different explorers, of whom Christopher Columbus is only the most famous, crossed the Atlantic.

The Rise of Humanism

Since the founding of universities in Europe around 1200, students had read Greek and Latin texts and the Bible. Instructors used an approach called scholasticism, in which the main goal was to reconcile the many differences among ancient authorities to form a logical system of thought. Often instructors taught a single book, or part of a book, over the course of a year. Around 1350, a group of Italian scholars pioneered a new intellectual movement called **humanism**. Humanists studied many of the same texts as before, but they tried to impart a more general understanding of them to their students in the hope that students would improve morally and be able to help others do the same.

humanism

Intellectual movement begun around 1350 in Italy by scholars who opposed scholasticism. Emphasized the study of the humanities, which included traditional fields like logic, grammar, arithmetic, and music and newer fields like language, history, literature, and philosophy.

One of the earliest humanist writers was the Italian poet Petrarch (1304–1374). Scholasticism, Petrarch felt, was too abstract. It did not teach people how to live and how to obtain salvation. Although he composed much poetry in Latin, he is remembered for the poetry he composed in Italian, one of several European vernacular languages that came into written use in the fourteenth and fifteenth centuries.

In 1487, a Venetian woman named Cassandra Fedele (fay-DAY-lay) (1465–1558) set out her own understanding of humanism in a public address. Having

*Terence d'Altroy, *The Incas* (Malden, Mass.: Blackwell, 2002), p. 281.

Mariotto Albertinelli (Italian, 1474–1515) Sacrifice of Isaac, ca. 1509–13 Oil on panel (oak), 9 5/16 x 6 15/16 x 3/16 in. (23.6 x 17.6 x 0.48 cm) Gift of Hannah D. and Louis M. Rabinowitz 1959.15.13b/Yale University Art Gallery

The Art of Humanism Just as Abraham is about to sacrifice the naked Isaac, the angel of God appears and stops him. The painter Mariotto Albertinelli (1474–1515) painted this scene on a thin piece of walnut wood, 10 by 7 inches (24 by 18 cm), most likely intended as decoration for a cabinet. The story of Abraham's averted sacrifice, immensely popular throughout Europe, was also the subject of a play written by Spanish missionaries in Mexico that taught the evils of human sacrifice.

studied Greek and Latin with a tutor, Fedele urged her audience to study Cicero, Plato, and Aristotle because, she maintained, while wealth and physical strength cannot last, *"those things which are produced by virtue and intelligence are useful to those who follow."* She continued: *"And how much more humane, praiseworthy and noble do those states and princes become who support and cultivate these studies! Certainly for this reason this part of philosophy has laid claim for itself to the name of 'humanity,' since those who are rough by nature become by these studies more civil and mild-mannered."** She eloquently expressed the major tenet of humanism: studying the humanities made students, whether from noble or low-born families, more refined and better people. Humanists believed that citizens should have a good grasp of rhetoric, history, and ethics and use the accounting they studied to manage their household finances. With such a citizenry, the state was bound to prosper.

Rather than treat Latin translations as flawless, the humanists checked them against texts in the original languages, including the Greek of the Bible. When they did, they found that many of the most difficult-to-understand passages were corrupted by translation errors. One product of humanist scholarship was multilingual editions of the Bible that printed the Latin, Greek, Hebrew, and Aramaic texts on the same page so that scholars could compare them. This type of book provided a prototype for Sahagún when he handwrote the manuscript of his *General History* with columns in Nahuatl and Spanish on the same page.

Historians call this period of humanist revival the **Renaissance**, which means "rebirth," to contrast it with the earlier centuries. Most historians no longer see the Renaissance as a sharp departure from earlier periods; they recognize that the intellectual advances of the twelfth and thirteenth centuries underpinned those of the humanist era.

---

*Cassandra Fedele, "Oration to the University of Padua (1487)," in *The Renaissance in Europe: An Anthology*, ed. Peter Elmer et al. New Haven: Yale University Press, in association with the Open University, 2000), pp. 52–56.

Europe's First Movable Type

The introduction of printing in Europe contributed greatly to the humanist movement because movable type made books cheaper. Johannes Gutenberg (ca. 1400–1468) printed the first European book, a Bible, using movable type sometime before 1454.

Renaissance
Literally "rebirth." Term used to refer to the period of humanist revival in Europe. Most historians now play down this term, recognizing that the intellectual advances of the twelfth and thirteenth centuries underpinned those of the humanist era.

● **CONTEXT&CONNECTIONS** This was not the first book in the world made using movable type; the Chinese knew about movable type as early as the eleventh century, and the world's earliest surviving book using movable type was made in Korea in about 1377. Moreover, Gutenberg printed most of his copies of the Bible on paper, a Chinese invention. ●

Movable type, however cumbersome for Chinese with its thousands of characters, functioned beautifully for alphabetic languages like Latin. Close analysis of Gutenberg's earliest books shows variation among individual letters, suggesting that he may have made hundreds of the same letter by hand, maybe even from wood, and did not cast them from a metal mold as is often supposed.

Within fifty years of its introduction, printing had transformed the European book. Although European readers had once prized illuminated manuscripts prepared by hand, with beautiful illustrations and exquisite lettering, now typesetters streamlined texts so that they could be printed more easily. Some of the most popular books described marvels from around the world.

● **CONTEXT&CONNECTIONS** The Latin translation of the Greek geographer Ptolemy (ca. 100–170) and the travel account of Marco Polo (1254–1324), a Venetian who traveled in Asia, were both in Christopher Columbus's personal library, and he carefully wrote long notes in the margins of the passages that interested him. ●

Early European Exploration in the Mediterranean and the Atlantic, 1350–1440

Widely read travel accounts like Marco Polo's whetted the appetite for trade and exploration. European merchants, primarily from the Italian city-states of Venice and Genoa, maintained settlements in certain locations far from Europe, such as Constantinople and the island of Cyprus (see Map 15.3). These communities had walled enclosures called *factories* that held warehouses, a place for ships to refit, and houses for short- and long-term stays. The Ottoman conquest of Constantinople in 1453 encouraged many of these merchants to go west rather than east through the Islamic world.

Starting around 1350, European navigators began to sail past the Strait of Gibraltar into the Atlantic Ocean. In 1350, two Italian explorers wrote the first book about the Canary Islands and their non-Christian inhabitants. The Europeans captured some of these Canary Islanders and sold them in the slave markets of Europe, where they were much in demand. After 1350, cartographers began to show the various Atlantic islands off the coast of Africa on their maps.

One motivation for exploring these unknown islands was religious. As the Catholic rulers of Spain and Portugal regained different Islamic cities in Iberia during the thirteenth and fourteenth centuries in a campaign called the *Reconquista*, they hoped to expand Christian territory into North Africa. At the time, Spain itself contained several distinct kingdoms. In 1415, a Portuguese prince named Henry, now known as **Henry the Navigator** (1394–1460), captured the Moroccan fortress of Ceuta (say-OO-tuh). Using the rhetoric of the Crusades and armed with an order from the pope, his goal was to convert the inhabitants to

Henry the Navigator
(1394–1460) Portuguese prince who supported Portuguese explorations in the Mediterranean, Atlantic, and along the West African coast.

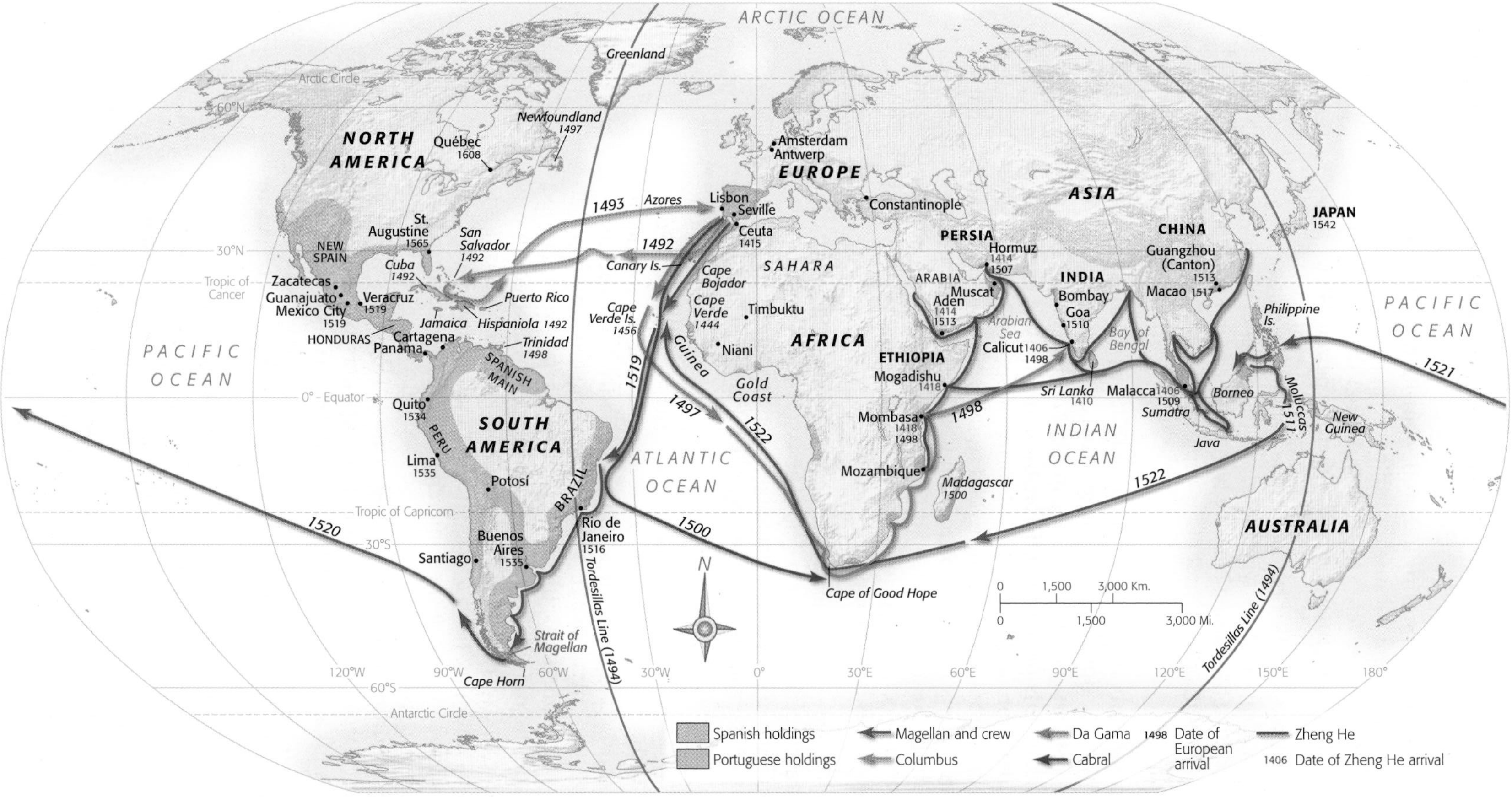

Map 15.3 The Age of Maritime Expansion, 1400–1600 Between 1400 and 1600, maritime explorers pioneered three major new routes: (1) across the Atlantic Ocean from Europe to the Americas, (2) across the Pacific from the Americas to Asia, and (3) south along the west coast of Africa to the Cape of Good Hope. Once the Portuguese explorer Vasco da Gama rounded the Cape in 1498, he connected with the well-traveled hajj route linking East Africa with China that Zheng He's ships had taken in the early 1400s (see page 456).

Christianity. Even today, Ceuta is part of Spain, and its population includes Christians, Jews, and Muslims.

Henry tried to take the Canary Islands for Christianity in 1424, but the inhabitants, armed only with stone tools, repelled the invaders; nevertheless, the Portuguese continued to capture and enslave Canary Islanders. Eventually, he Portuguese occupied the island of Madeira, and in 1454 they established plantations there, which soon exported large amounts of sugar.

• **CONTEXT&CONNECTIONS** Many navigators were afraid to venture past the Madeira Islands because of the dreaded torrid zone. Greek and Roman geographers had posited that the northern temperate zone, where people lived, was bordered by an uninhabitable frigid zone to the north and a torrid zone to the south, whose scorching heat made it impossible to cross. •

Many Europeans had assumed that Cape Bojador, in modern Morocco, marked the beginning of the impenetrable torrid zone (see Map 15.3). But in 1434 the Portuguese sailed past the cape and reported that no torrid zone existed.

The Portuguese Slave Trade After 1444

Since no torrid zone existed, Henry realized, the Portuguese could transport slaves from the west coast of Africa and sell them in Europe. Portuguese vessels had already brought back thirty-eight African slaves from West Africa. In 1444, Henry dispatched six caravels to bring back slaves from the Arguin bank, south of Cape Bojador in modern-day Mauritania. The caravel was a small sailing ship, usually about 75 feet (23 m) long, that had two or three masts with square sails.

In 1444, Henry staged a huge public reception of the slaves for his subjects. The ships' captains presented one slave each to a church and to a Franciscan convent to demonstrate their intention to convert the slaves to Christianity. An eyewitness description captures the scene: "*These people, assembled together on that open space, were an astonishing sight to behold.... Among them were some*

The Varied Lives of African Migrants to Venice Completed in the early 1490s, this painting by Vittore Carpaccio (1460–1526) shows hunters shooting birds on a lagoon. Note the presence of African gondoliers (for example, the man in the right foreground). These men, most likely skilled rowers in their homeland, continued the same profession after their arrival in Europe.

Vittore Carpaccio (Italian, about 1460 - 1526) Hunting on the Lagoon (recto); Letter Rack (verso), about 1490 - 1495, Oil on panel 75.6 x 63.8 cm (29 3/4 x 25 1/8 in.) The J. Paul Getty Museum, Los Angeles *who were quite white-skinned, handsome and of good appearance; others were less white, seeming more like brown men; others still were as black as Ethiopians.... But what heart, however hardened it might be, could not be pierced by a feeling of pity at the sight of that company?"**

This may seem to be an early critique of slavery, but in fact, the author, like many of his contemporaries, saw the trade in slaves as a Christian act: the Africans, as non-Christians, were doomed to suffer in the afterlife, but if they converted to Christianity, they could attain salvation. From its very beginnings, the European slave trade combined the profit motive with a missionary impulse.

Within ten years the Portuguese slave traders had reached agreements with two rulers in northern Senegal to trade horses for slaves each year. The price of a horse varied from nine to fourteen slaves. Horses did not live long in sub-Saharan Africa's tropical climate, but because rulers liked them as a symbol of power and a war tool, the demand never flagged. By the time of Henry's death in 1460, Portuguese ships had transported about 1,000 slaves a year, fewer than the 4,300 slaves who crossed the Sahara overland in Muslim caravans each year at the time. After 1460, the oceanic trade continued to grow. Many of the African slaves worked on sugar plantations, either in the Canary Islands or on Madeira.

The Portuguese continued their explorations along the African coast, and in 1487, a Portuguese ship commanded by Bartholomew Dias rounded the Cape of Good Hope and the southern end of Africa. The Portuguese became convinced that the quickest way to Asia and the riches of the spice trade was around Africa, as Chapter 16 will show.

The Iberian Conquest of Mexico, Peru, and Brazil, 1492–1580

Christopher Columbus's landfall in the Caribbean had immediate and long-lasting consequences. Representatives of the Spanish and Portuguese crowns conquered most of Mexico and Latin America with breathtaking speed. In 1517, the Spanish landed for the first time on the Aztec mainland; by 1540, they controlled all of Mexico, Central America, and the northern sections of South America. Portugal controlled Brazil by 1550. By 1580, Spain had subdued the peoples of the southern regions of South America. Given that the residents of the Canary Islands, armed only with stone tools, managed to repel all attempts to conquer them for 150 years, how did the Spanish and Portuguese move into the Americas and conquer two sophisticated empires so quickly?

The subject peoples of the Aztec empire, who had not been integrated into the empire, welcomed the Spanish as an ally who might help them overthrow their overlords. Moreover, the Spanish arrived in Peru just after the installation of a new Sapa Inca, from whom his opponents still hoped to wrest power. The Europeans had other advantages, like guns and horses, which the Amerindians lacked, but the newcomers were completely unaware of their most powerful weapon: the disease pools of Europe.

---

*Peter Russell, *Prince Henry "the Navigator": A Life* (New Haven: Yale University Press, 2000), pp. 242–243, n8, citing *Crónica dos Feitos na Conquista de Guiné*, II: 145–148.

Columbus's First Voyage to the Americas, 1492

In 1479, Isabella (1451–1504) ascended the throne of Castile and married Ferdinand of Aragon, unifying the two major kingdoms of Spain. Throughout the 1480s, Columbus approached both the Spanish and the Portuguese monarchs to request funds for a voyage to the Indies by sailing west from the Canary Islands.

• **CONTEXT&CONNECTIONS** Following the revival of interest in Greek and Roman geography in the twelfth century, all informed people realized, as the ancients had, that the globe was round. The American writer Washington Irving (1783–1859) invented the myth that everyone before Columbus thought the world was flat. •

In keeping with the scholastic and humanist traditions, Columbus cited several authorities in support of the new route he proposed. One passage in the Bible (II Esdras 6:42) stated that the world was six parts land, one part water. Columbus interpreted this to mean that the distance from the Iberian Peninsula to the western edge of Asia in Japan was only 2,700 miles (4,445 km). In actuality, the distance is over 6,000 miles (10,000 km), and the world is about 70 percent water and 30 percent land, but no one at the time knew this.

In rejecting his proposal, the scholars advising the Portuguese and Spanish monarchs held that the distance from Spain to Japan was far greater than Columbus realized. The men on board a ship, they reasoned, would die of starvation before reaching Asia. Although right about the distance from Iberia to Japan, these advisers did not realize that the Americas lay in between.

Several developments in 1492 prompted Isabella and Ferdinand to overturn their earlier decision. Granada, the last Muslim outpost in Spain, fell in 1492. In that same year the rulers expelled all Jews from Spain, a measure that had been enacted by France and England centuries earlier.

• **CONTEXT&CONNECTIONS** In 2014, the Spanish government offered citizenship to the descendants of the Jews expelled in 1492, but because the new law requires them to renounce their current citizenship, few are expected to apply. •

Delighted by the conquest of Granada, Ferdinand and Isabella decided to fund Columbus, primarily because they did not want the Portuguese to do so, and also because he was asking for only a small amount of money, enough to host a foreign prince for a week. The monarchs gave Columbus two titles: *admiral of the ocean sea* and *viceroy*, a new title indicating he would govern any lands to which he sailed. Columbus was entitled to one-tenth of any precious metals or spices he found, with the remaining nine-tenths going to Isabella and Ferdinand. No provision was made for his men.

Columbus departed with three ships from Granada on August 3, 1492, and on October 12 of the same year arrived in the Bahamas. He soon proceeded to Hispaniola, a Caribbean island occupied by the modern nations of Haiti and the Dominican Republic. Although Europeans knew about Islamic navigational instruments such as the astrolabe, Columbus did not use them. He sailed primarily by dead reckoning: he used a compass to stay on a westerly course. By dropping a float from the ship's bow and counting the seconds until the stern passed the float, he estimated his speed and so the approximate distance he traveled in a day. From his travels to the Canary Islands and the Azores, Columbus knew when the prevailing wind across the Atlantic blew east and when west.

On his first return trip, Columbus wrote a letter to his royal sponsors, Isabella and Ferdinand, about his impressions of the island where he had landed:

> *Hispaniola is a wonder. The mountains and hills, the plains and the meadow lands are both fertile and beautiful.... The harbors are incredibly fine and there are many great rivers with broad channels and the majority contain gold.... The inhabitants of this island, and all the rest that I discovered or heard of, go naked, as their mothers bore them, men and women alike.... I gave them a thousand pretty things that I had brought, in order to gain their love and incline them to become Christians.**

Arawak

General name for a family of languages spoken in the 1500s over a large region spanning from modern Venezuela to Florida. Also refers to speakers of these languages.

The two sides exchanged gifts and tried to make sense of each other's languages. The island's residents spoke **Arawak**. *"They are the color of Canary Islanders (neither black nor white),"** Columbus noted, an indication that he thought of the Arawak as potential slaves.

In keeping with his humanistic background, Columbus updated Ptolemy to fit with his own experience. He explained to the Spanish monarchs that *"Ptolemy and the other geographers believed that the world was spherical."* Columbus believed this until his third voyage, when he came *"to the following conclusions concerning the world: that it is not round as they describe it, but the shape of a pear,... or that it is like a round ball on part of which is something like a woman's nipple."** Columbus's eyes were troubling him, so the ocean seemed to tilt upward, and this was the only way he could explain it.

Columbus always thought that he had gone to Japan; he had no idea that he had landed on a continent unknown to the ancients. The first map to use the word *America* on a new continent (much smaller than reality) appeared in 1507; before then everyone assumed that Columbus and all the other explorers immediately after him were somewhere in the Indies.

A Comparison of Columbus's and Zheng He's Voyages

Many people have wondered why the Spanish and the Portuguese, and not the Chinese of the Ming dynasty, established the first overseas empires. The Chinese, who first set off in 1405, had almost a century's head start on the Europeans. (See the feature "Visual Evidence in Primary Sources: Comparing Zheng He's and Columbus's Ships.")

China was richer than either Spain or Portugal. It was arguably the most prosperous country in the world in the early fifteenth century, while Spain and Portugal were far smaller. Yet their small size gave both the Portuguese and the Spanish powerful motivation to seek new lands.

Unlike Europeans, the Chinese had no concept of a "colony"—nothing comparable to Madeira or the Canary Islands. The Ming emperor (r. 1403–1424) did not intend to make his huge empire bigger by using the voyages. He simply hoped

*J. M. Cohen, trans., *The Four Voyages of Christopher Columbus* (New York: Penguin, 1969), pp. 117–118, 35, 218.

Martin Waldseemüller (1470–1521) Universalis Cosmographia Secundum Ptholomaei Traditionem et Americi Vespucii Alioru[m]que Lustrationes, [St. Dié], 1507. One map on 12 sheets, made from original woodcut, Geography and Map Division, Library of Congress

The First Map to Show the Americas In 1507, a German mapmaker named Martin Waldseemüller published one hundred copies of this printed map of the world, in twelve sections, each measuring 18 by 24.5 inches (46 by 62 cm). When the Library of Congress purchased this map from a German library in 2001, it paid $10 million for it. This map depicts the Americas as a continent separate from Asia, a fact Columbus never realized. Waldseemüller named the new landmass "America," for Amerigo Vespucci, a navigator whose writings deeply influenced the mapmaker. Although difficult to see here, the word "America" appears halfway down the continent of South America, to the left of Africa.

to be acknowledged as the rightful ruler of the Chinese. Rulers of earlier Chinese dynasties had sometimes conquered other peoples, but in contiguous neighboring lands, never overseas.

The Ming government ordered an end to the voyages in 1433 because they brought no financial benefit to the Chinese. In contrast, the Spanish and Portuguese voyages brought their countries immediate returns in gold and slaves and the promise of long-term profits if settlers could establish enterprises such as sugar plantations.

● **CONTEXT&CONNECTIONS** A critical difference between Columbus's voyages and the Chinese ones was that the navigators on the Chinese treasure ships followed the best-traveled oceanic route in the world before 1500. Muslim pilgrims from East Africa traveled up the East African coast to reach their holy city of Mecca, and Chinese pilgrims sailed around Southeast Asia and India to reach the Arabian peninsula. The Zheng He voyages simply linked the two hajj routes together. In contrast, when Columbus and other European explorers set off, they were consciously exploring, looking for new places to colonize and going where no one else (or at least no one else that anyone remembered) had gone before. ●

Comparing Zheng He's and Columbus's Ships

What did Columbus's and Zheng He's ships look like? Since no drawings of any of their boats survive, nautical historians must compare multiple images of boats from the period to reconstruct what these vessels looked like. Even then, crucial information is still missing: the actual length of Columbus's main ship, the *Santa Maria*, ranged anywhere from 80–120 feet (24–37 m). A small wooden boat left as an offering in a church near Barcelona reveals the most about the construction of the *Santa Maria*. In the 1440s or 1450s, a sailor crafted it to give thanks for surviving a storm. Since he was not a shipbuilder, it may not be entirely accurate. But it has much more information about construction than do many drawings.*

We know even less about the Zheng He ships, since no contemporary models exist. Dimensions written in Chinese units survive, but scholars disagree about what they mean. Earlier studies used one value to arrive at a mind-boggling length of 400 feet (122 m), but a recent study, using a new value, has halved that to 200 feet (61 m), which naval historians agree is the longest possible length for an entirely wooden ship. Otherwise it would simply snap into pieces.

These estimates suggest that the Zheng He vessels were between 166 and 250 percent bigger than Columbus's.

The full fleet of 317 Chinese treasure ships, led by Admiral Zheng He, carried 28,000 men; the doctors on board outnumbered Columbus's entire crew. The Chinese ships were technologically more advanced, too. The ships had watertight compartments that could contain a leak. If Columbus's sailors could not plug a leak, the entire ship would fill with water and sink. The Chinese sailors feasted on fresh fish that thrived in their watertight compartments, while Columbus's men had to make do with hardtack, or dried biscuits.

Yet the size of the treasure ships was also a drawback. At 200 feet (61 m), they were simply too big to sail into unknown waters. One of Columbus's original three ships ran aground during the first voyage, and he complained that his ships were too large for successful exploration.

*Franceo Gay and Cesare Ciano, *The Ships of Christopher Columbus* (Roma: Libreria dello Stato, 1996).

Comparison of Columbus's and Zheng He's Fleets

	Distance Traveled	Length of Ships	Number of Ships	Size of Crew	Number of Voyages
Columbus's ships	4,000 miles (6,400 km)	80–120 feet (24–37 m)	3	87	4
Zheng He's ships	7,000 miles (11,000 km)	200 feet (61 m)	317	28,000	7

These sails were made with bamboo slats so that they could be shortened during storms and let out when the winds were lighter.

The rudder could be raised and lowered depending on the depth of the water. (After Bjorn Landstrom, *The Ship: An Illustrated History*)

The Chinese ships all had separate watertight compartments that significantly reduced the risk of sinking because of a single leak. ***If you were a Spanish shipbuilder, would you adopt this feature from the Chinese ships, or is some other feature more important? Why?***

The cloth sails had only one size. If it was too windy to use them, the sailors could pull some of them down.

This rudder was attached to the boat's stern and could not be moved up and down.

The base of this ship forms a single compartment. If it sprang a leak that could not be repaired, it would sink. (After Bjorn Landstrom, *The Ship: An Illustrated History*)

Spanish Exploration After Columbus's First Voyage, 1493–1517

From the beginning Columbus did not exercise tight control over his ships, the *Niña*, the *Pinta*, and the *Santa Maria*. When he first reached the Americas, the ship *Niña* set off on its own to search for gold, and Columbus had no choice but to welcome it back. The *Santa Maria* had already run aground and been dismantled to make a fort, and Columbus needed both remaining ships to return home. With only two ships, he was forced to leave thirty-nine men behind in the fort, but when he returned on his second voyage in 1493, he found that all had been killed, presumably in disputes with the Arawak over women. By then skirmishes with the Arawak regularly occurred.

Once the Spanish realized that Columbus had discovered a new landmass, they negotiated the **Treaty of Tordesillas** (tor-day-SEE-yuhs) with the Portuguese in 1494. The treaty established a dividing line: all newly discovered territory west of the line belonged to Castile, while all the lands to the east were reserved for Portugal. Lands already ruled by a Christian monarch were unaffected. Portugal gained Africa, the route to India, and eventually Brazil.

Treaty of Tordesillas
Treaty signed by the Portuguese and the Spanish in 1494 that established a dividing line: all newly discovered territory west of the line belonged to Castile, while all of the islands to the east were reserved for Portugal.

Columbus never solved the problem of how to compensate his men. When recruiting sailors in Spain he spoke of great riches, but the agreement he had signed with Ferdinand and Isabella gave his men nothing. On his first voyage, his men expected to sail with him to Asia and return, but on subsequent voyages many joined him expressly so that they could settle in the Americas, where they hoped to make fortunes. In 1497, the settlers revolted against Columbus, and he agreed to allow them to use Indians as agricultural laborers. Because Columbus was unpopular with the settlers, in 1499 the Crown replaced him with a new viceroy.

Spanish and Portuguese navigators continued to land in new places after 1503. The Spanish crossed 120 miles (193 km) from Cuba to the Yucatán Peninsula in 1508–1509 and reached Florida in 1510. In 1513, Vasco Núñez de Balboa (bal-BOH-uh) crossed through Panama to see the Pacific, and by 1522 the Portuguese navigator Magellan had circumnavigated the globe, although he died before his ship returned home.

The Conquest of Mexico, 1517–1540

One of the early Spanish **conquistadors**, Hernán Cortés (hare-NAN kor-TES; 1485–1587), who led the conquest of Mexico, came first to Hispaniola in 1506 and moved to Cuba in 1509. Like many of the other Spanish conquistadors, he came from a family of middling social influence and made his fortune in the Americas. Cortés, in Cuba, learned that the Maya peoples of the Yucatán spoke of a larger, richer empire to the north. In two weeks he recruited 530 men to launch an expedition.

conquistadors
Literally "conquerors," the term for the Spaniards who conquered Mexico, Peru, and Central America in the 1500s.

When Cortés landed on the coast of Mexico in early 1519, he immediately met a woman who helped him penetrate the Spanish-Nahuatl language barrier: a Nahua noblewoman named **Malinche** (mah-LEEN-chay) who had grown up among the Maya and could speak both Nahuatl and Mayan. Given to Cortés as a gift, Malinche learned Spanish quickly. The Spaniards called her Doña Marina. As adviser to Cortés, she played a crucial role in the Spanish conquest of Mexico, partly because she commanded the respect of the Nahua peoples.

Malinche
A Nahua noblewoman, trilingual in Spanish, Nahuatl, and Mayan, who served as translator for and adviser to Cortés.

Cortés landed on April 20, 1519, and slightly over two years later the Aztec had surrendered their capital and their empire to him (see Map 15.1). Yet this outcome was far from certain. After all, the Spanish had only 1,500 men.

Cortés's Interpreter, Malinche This image, created by a local artist, dates to the 1500s and shows what Cortés's army, a mixed force, looked like. The Spaniards, with their heavy armor and a single horse, contrast sharply with the local peoples, who use bands tied around their foreheads to bear the weight of food in containers as well as to carry a small child (*far left*). Malinche, who was Cortés's mistress and interpreter, stands at the far right, with the bearded Cortés on her left. (Snark/Art Resource, NY)

The encounter between the Nahua and the Spaniards is unusual because we have surviving sources from both sides—the European colonizers and the indigenous peoples. One of Cortés's foot soldiers, Bernal Díaz del Castillo, wrote the most detailed account from the Spanish point of view. Sahagún's *General History* is not the same as a contemporary Nahua eyewitness account, yet since Sahagún and his team systematically crosschecked what their informants reported, it is the best Nahuatl-language account we have.

Sahagún records the response of the reigning Great Speaker Moctezuma (also spelled Montezuma) to the first envoy from the Spanish:

It especially made him faint when he heard how the guns went off at the Spaniards' command, sounding like thunder.... And when it went off, something like a ball came out from inside, and fire went showering and spitting out.... And if they shot at a hill, it seemed to crumble and come apart.... Their war gear was all iron. They clothed their bodies in iron, they put iron on their heads, their swords were iron....

*And their deer that carried them were as tall as the roof.**

The Spaniards' "deer" were horses, an animal not native to the Americas, whose size greatly impressed the Mexica.

On their way to Tenochtitlan, the Spaniards fought a major battle lasting nearly three weeks with the people of Tlaxcala (tlash-CAH-lah). After their defeat, the Tlaxcalans became the Spaniards' most important allies against the hated Mexica overlords. When, in November 1519, the Spaniards first arrived at the capital city of Tenochtitlan, the Great Speaker Moctezuma allowed them to come in unharmed. The Spaniards could not believe how beautiful the city was. Bernal Díaz, described this event: "*Gazing on such wonderful sights, we did not know what to say, or whether what appeared before us was real, for on one side, on the land, there were great cities, and in the lake ever so many more, and the lake itself was crowded with canoes, and in the Causeway were many bridges at intervals....*"*

For one week the Spaniards and the Mexica coexisted uneasily, until the Spanish placed Moctezuma under house arrest. Then, in the spring of 1520, while Cortés was away, one of his subordinates ordered his men to massacre the city's inhabitants, and prolonged battles resulted. The Spaniards killed Moctezuma and, after suffering hundreds of casualties, retreated to Tlaxcala, the city of their allies. At this point, it seemed that the Mexica would win.

But by then smallpox had reached the Americas. The native peoples of America had little or no resistance to European smallpox, measles, malaria, sexually transmitted diseases, or even the common cold. Beginning in December 1518, disease ravaged Hispaniola and then Puerto Rico, Jamaica, and Cuba, and in the spring of 1520, smallpox crossed into the Yucatán and arrived in Tenochtitlan. Moctezuma's successor died of smallpox in early December, and the mass deaths threw the entire city into disarray.

AP® THEMES

How did alliances help the Spanish conquer the Aztec empire?

Even so, the Spaniards had great difficulty conquering the Aztec empire. It took eighty days of sustained fighting before Tenochtitlan surrendered in August of 1521. Spanish guns and cannon were not decisive. Some one hundred thousand troops and a portable fleet of boats supplied by the Tlaxcalans enabled the Spaniards to win.

In 1524, the first Franciscan friars arrived in Mexico. The Franciscans became the most important missionary order among the Nahuatl speakers. They searched for parallels between native beliefs and Christian teachings; at the same time they suppressed practices, like human sacrifice and polygamy, that they saw as un-Christian. (See the feature "Movement of Ideas Through Primary Sources: *The Sacrifice of Isaac*: A Sixteenth-Century Nahuatl Play.") The Spanish gradually imposed a more regular administration over Mexico under the governance of a viceroy.

The Spanish Conquest of Peru, 1532–1550

The order of events in the Spanish conquest of Peru differed from that in Mexico, where Cortés had arrived before smallpox. In a smallpox epidemic in 1528 many Inca, including the Sapa Inca, died. War among the contenders to the throne broke out. In November 1532 the Spanish forces arrived, led by Francisco Pizarro (pih-ZAHR-oh) (1475–1541), at the moment of greatest

*Stuart B. Schwartz, *Victors and Vanquished: Spanish and Nahua Views of the Conquest of Mexico* (New York: Bedford/St. Martin's, 2000), pp. 97, 133.

instability in the Inca kingdom: when the newly enthroned Sapa Inca had not yet completely subdued his main rival. Atahualpa (ah-tuh-WAHL-puh; also spelled Atawallpa) had become ruler only after defeating his older half-brother, whom he still held in captivity. Atahualpa had taken severe countermeasures against his brother's supporters, many who sided immediately with the Spaniards.

When Pizarro and his 168 men arrived at the important city where Atahualpa was living, Atahualpa initially received the Spanish peacefully. Then, on their second day in the city, the Spanish attacked unexpectedly. Their guns, armor, and horses gave them an initial advantage. An estimated seven thousand Inca, yet not a single Spaniard, died in the carnage.

Pizarro himself captured Atahualpa, who offered to pay an enormous ransom for his release: the Inca filled a room 2,600 cubic feet (74 cubic m) half with gold and half with silver, which the Spaniards melted down and divided among Pizarro's troops. Those with horses received 90 pounds (41 kg), equivalent today to perhaps $500,000, and those on foot half that amount. Then the Spanish reneged on their agreement and killed Atahualpa.

It took twenty more years for the Spanish to gain control of Peru. In 1551, they named the first viceroy for Peru and gradually established a more stable administration. The first Spanish census, taken in the 1570s, showed that half the population had died from European disease, with the toll in some places reaching as high as 95 percent. The Amerindians who lived at high altitudes suffered much fewer losses than those living on the coast.

The Portuguese Settlement of Brazil, 1500–1580

In 1500, Pedro Álvares Cabral (kah-BRAHL) (1467/68–1520) landed in Brazil. Although the Portuguese claimed Brazil following Cabral's voyage, few of them came to this resource-poor country. Most Portuguese sought their wealth in Asia, as discussed in the next chapter. In 1533 the Portuguese monarch John III (r. 1521–1557) made a systematic effort to encourage the settlement of Brazil by dividing it into fifteen slices, each occupying 160 miles (260 km) of the coastline and extending inland indefinitely. He granted these territories to Portuguese nobles, many of them his courtiers.

John III also authorized the Jesuits, or Society of Jesus, a new order of Catholic priests founded in 1540, to preach in Brazil. Many Jesuits traveled to the interior, converted the indigenous peoples, and then resettled them in villages. (The Jesuits were also active and influential in Asia, as Chapter 16 explains.) The settlers searched for gold throughout the sixteenth century but never found significant amounts.

Instead, the Portuguese began to build sugar plantations, with the guidance of technicians brought from the Canary Islands. Since so many of the indigenous Amerindians had died, the plantation owners imported slaves from Africa.

The Structure of Empire and the Encomienda System

In 1580 Philip II succeeded to the throne of both Spain and Portugal, and the two countries remained under a single king until 1640. The Portuguese and Spanish empires had evolved parallel structures independently. The highest colonial official, the viceroy, presided over a royal colony and governed in concert with an advisory council who could appeal any decisions to the king.

Both empires had the **encomienda system**, first established by the Spanish in 1503. Life under the Aztec and the Inca empires had accustomed the peoples of

encomienda system (Literally "entrusted") System established in 1503 by the Spanish in the hope of clarifying arrangements with the colonists and of ending the abuse of indigenous peoples of the Americas.

The Sacrifice of Isaac: A Sixteenth-Century Nahuatl Play

The members of the Catholic orders who lived in Mexico used different approaches to teach the Nahua peoples about Christianity. In addition to printing bilingual catechisms in Spanish and Nahuatl, they sponsored the composition of plays in Nahuatl on religious themes. Since these plays were not published but only circulated in handwritten manuscripts, very few survive. The short play *The Sacrifice of Isaac* recounts the story from the Hebrew Bible of Abraham and Isaac, which addresses a topic of great interest to the Nahua peoples: human sacrifice. The playwright chose the most important story in the Hebrew Bible. The ancient Hebrews believed that God tested Abraham, the chosen leader of their people. This story was also important to Muslims, who believed that Abraham almost sacrificed a different son, Ishmael (who makes an appearance in the play as an evil character). The lively quality of the Nahuatl language suggests that it was written sometime after the Spanish conquest, probably by a native speaker who converted to Christianity, and not by a Spanish missionary who learned Nahuatl as a second language.

As in the Bible, God the Father appears in the play to ask Abraham to sacrifice his son Isaac, but he later sends an angel to instruct Abraham to offer a lamb instead. Abraham, his first wife, and Isaac all embody obedience, a virtue prized both by the ancient Hebrews and the Nahua peoples. Abraham's slave Hagar and her son Ishmael urge Isaac to disobey his father, and both still worship the sun (not God), two sure clues to the audience that they are evil. Corresponding faithfully to the version in the Hebrew Bible, the play shows an obedient Isaac offering himself for sacrifice until the moment the angel intervenes.

Historical Thinking Skill:
CONTEXTUALIZATION Why would the Spanish missionaries choose to teach about Christianity through plays, such as The Sacrifice of Isaac?

Source: *The Sacrifice of Isaac*, translated by Barry D. Sell, with the assistance of Louise M. Burkhart, in *Nahuatl Theater, Volume 1, Death and Life in Colonial Nahua Mexico*, ed. Barry D. Sell and Louise M. Burkhart, with the assistance of Gregory Spira (Norman: University of Oklahoma Press, 2004), pp. 149–153, 159–161.

The Devil, Ishmael, and Hagar Trick Isaac

(Demon enters dressed as an angel or an old man.)

Demon: O young man, what are you doing? You appear to me to have very great cares.

Ishmael: Yes, there is much that worries me. But how do you know if I have some cares? Who told you?

Demon: Do you not see that I am a resident of heaven? I was sent here from there in order to tell you what you are to do here on earth.

Ishmael: Let me hear your commands.

Demon: Listen, here is what has you so occupied today. It concerns the high-born noble Isaac, who is of such good life. He always gives credence to the commands of his father. But you have been thinking that you want him to no longer obey his father and his mother. I will tell you how to do it.

Ishmael: How very content I am to hear your words. Let me enjoy your help since you are a resident of heaven and you are a helper of people.

Demon: Take right to heart my commands. Look. Today his father and his mother have invited people to a banquet. There will be great contentment and enjoyment. But you are to oblige him to abandon his father and his mother by you and him going somewhere to play. And if he so ruinously obeys you they will despise their child for it even though they greatly love him.

Ishmael: I will carry out your command in that fashion.

Demon: As for me, I am going into heaven for I came to console you and to tell you what you are to do. . . .

(Hagar the slave enters along with her child Ishmael.)

Hagar: Today the great ruler Abraham has yet again invited people to a banquet because of the great esteem he has for his child. But as for us, since we are lowly servants, we are held in no regard. And as for you, my child, you are doubly luckless. Would that I could find relief in you, that you could give relief to all my earthly torments, for in truth your birth and your lot are eternal weeping.

(At that point she and her child weep together.)

Ishmael: You, sun, who are very high up, warm us with your very great radiance everywhere in the world, with which you are able to please all the people of the earth. But as for us, the two of us are suffering. We are doubly luckless. But now know, O my mother, what I will do today when all are eating. Perhaps I can sneak [Isaac] out so that we will go play somewhere. Thus he will violate the orders of his father so that he will no longer love him with his heart.

Hagar: What you are thinking is very good. Do it so.

Abraham and Isaac on the Mountain

Abraham: Now listen, O my beloved child. The All-powerful, God, has strictly ordered me to [make sure] that his precious sacred commands are realized so that he will see if we people of the earth love him and if we carry out his sacred commands, for he is the ruler of the living and the dead. Now receive death with great humility, for he speaks thusly: I will be able to raise the dead for I am eternal life everywhere in the world. May his will be done.

(At that point Abraham weeps and the Misericordia is played on wind instruments.)

Isaac: Do not cry, O my beloved honored father, for it is with very great happiness that I receive death. May the precious sacred commands of God be done as he has ordered you [to do them]. . . .

Angel: Abraham! Abraham!

(He seizes his hand.)

Abraham: Who are you that calls me?

Angel: Now listen up! By the power of God and by his orders, he has thus seen how you love him and carry out his sacred commands so that you do not violate them. For today you brought your beloved child, whom you greatly love, to the top of the mountain here in order to make an offering of him to the All-powerful, God the Father. Now it is by his precious will that I have come to tell you to leave him alone so that your beloved child, Isaac, will not die.

Abraham: May his precious commands be done as is his will. Come, O my beloved child, for you have now been saved from the hands of death.

(At that point he loosens the cloth with which the eyes are wrapped and he undoes the rope with which the hands are bound.)

Angel: Now know that the substitute for your beloved child will be a little lamb you are to make ready. Such is the will of God. Let us be on our way, for I am going to leave you at your home.

Mexico and Peru to shipping large quantities of goods, especially precious metals, to their rulers, and the encomienda system continued to collect resources and send them on to the center. Under this system, the monarchs "entrusted" (the literal meaning of *encomienda*) a specified number of Amerindians to a settler, who gained the right to extract labor, gold, or other goods from them in exchange for teaching them about Christianity. The monarchs took as their model the governmental structure used to administer lands newly recovered from Muslim kingdoms in the Reconquista.

AP® THEMES

To what extent did the Spanish and Portuguese settlement of Brazil, Mexico, and Peru alter the existing social hierarchy in these conquered areas?

At first the Spaniards who received encomienda grants had much more power than the immigrants who had not, but over time their advantage lessened. The encomienda recipients had easy access to unskilled labor and could collect tribute from the locals, but ordinary Spaniards could obtain a land grant and hire labor to build estates of their own. Although designed to protect the indigenous peoples, the encomienda system often resulted in even greater exploitation.

The social structure in the colonies was basically the same throughout Latin America. At the top of society were those born in Europe, who served as military leaders, royal officials, or high church figures. Below them were creoles, those with two European parents but born in the Americas. Those of mixed descent (mestizos in Spanish-speaking regions, memlucos in Brazil) ranked even lower, with only Amerindians and African slaves below them. By 1600, one hundred thousand Africans lived in Brazil, many working in the hundreds of sugar mills all over the colony.

The Columbian Exchange

At the same time that European diseases like smallpox devastated the peoples living in America, European animals like the horse, cow, and sheep came to the Americas and flourished. In the other direction came plant foods indigenous to the Americas like tomatoes, potatoes, peanuts, and chili peppers. This transfer is referred to as the **Columbian exchange**.

Columbian exchange
All the plants, animals, goods, and diseases that crossed the Atlantic, and sometimes the Pacific, after 1492.

Of all the European imports, smallpox had the most devastating effect on the Americas. Only someone suffering an outbreak can transmit smallpox, which is contagious for about a month: after two weeks of incubation, fever and vomiting strike; the ill person's skin then breaks out with the pox, small pustules that dry up after about ten days. Either the victim dies during those ten days or survives, typically with a pock-marked face and body.

One Nahuatl description captures the extent of the suffering:

> *Sores erupted on our faces, our breasts, our bellies.... The sick were so utterly helpless that they could only lie on their beds like corpses, unable to move their limbs or even their heads.... If they did move their bodies, they screamed with pain.**

Although no plants or animals had an effect as immediate as smallpox, the long-term effects of the Columbian exchange in plants and animals indelibly altered the landscape, diets, and population histories of both the Americas and Afro-Eurasia. When Columbus landed on Hispaniola, he immediately realized how different the plants were: "*All the trees were as different from ours as day from*

*Michael Wood, *Conquistadors* (Berkeley: University of California Press, 2000), p. 81, citing the *Florentine Codex*.

night, and so the fruits, the herbage, the rocks, and all things." He also remarked on the absence of livestock: *"I saw neither sheep nor goats nor any other beast."**

On his second voyage in 1493, Columbus carried cuttings of European plants, including wheat, melons, sugar cane, and other fruits and vegetables. He also brought pigs, horses, sheep, goats, and cattle. More like wild boars than modern hogs, pigs were the first to adapt to the Americas, eating wild grasses, reproducing in large numbers, and moving into many areas emptied of humans by the depredations of smallpox.

While smallpox traveled from Europe to the Americas, there is evidence that syphilis traveled in the other direction. The first well-documented outbreaks of syphilis in Europe occurred around 1495, and one physician claimed that Columbus's men brought it to Madrid soon after 1492. No European skeletons with signs of syphilis before 1500 have been found, but an Amerindian skeleton with syphilis has, suggesting that the disease did indeed move from the Americas to Europe. Causing severe pain, syphilis could be passed to the next generation and was fatal for about one-quarter of those who contracted it, but it did not cause mass deaths.

Assessing the loss of Amerindian life from smallpox and the other European diseases has caused much debate among historians because no population statistics exist for the Americas before 1492. Different historians have come up with estimates for the regions with the heaviest populations—Mexico, between 4 and 6 million, and Peru, between 10 and 12 million—but even these numbers are controversial. Figures for the precontact population can be little more than guesswork. The first reliable figures for Amerindian populations came with Spanish colonization. In 1568, Spanish authorities counted 970,000 non-Spanish living in Mexico and 1.2 million living in Peru. For the entire period of European colonization in all parts of the Americas, guesses at the total death toll from European diseases, based on controversial estimates of precontact populations, range from a low of 10 million to a high of over 100 million.

By 1600, two extremely successful agricultural enterprises had spread through the Americas. One was sugar, and the other was cattle raising, which took advantage of huge expanses of grasslands in Venezuela and Colombia, from Mexico north to Canada, and in Argentina and Uruguay. In each case the Spaniards began on the coastal edge of a grassland and followed their rapidly multiplying herds of cattle to the interior.

As European food crops transformed the diet of those living in the Americas, so too did American food crops transform the eating habits of people in Afro-Eurasia. American food crops moved into West Africa, particularly modern Nigeria, where even today people eat corn, peanuts, squash, manioc (cassava), and sweet potatoes.

AP® THEMES

What were the demographic effects of the Columbian exchange for Europe, the Americas, Africa, and Asia?

● **CONTEXT&CONNECTIONS** Two crops in particular played an important role throughout Afro-Eurasia: corn (maize) and potatoes (including sweet potatoes). Both produced higher yields than wheat and grew in less desirable fields, such as on the slopes of hills. Although few people anywhere in the world preferred corn or potatoes to their original wheat-based or rice-based diet, hungry people gratefully ate the American transplants when their primary crop failed. By the eighteenth century corn and potatoes had reached as far as India and China, and the population in both places increased markedly. ●

*Alfred W. Crosby, *The Columbian Exchange: Biological and Cultural Consequences of 1492* (Westport, Conn.: Greenwood Press, 1972), p. 4, n2, citing Christopher Columbus, *Journals and Other Documents on the Life and Voyages of Christopher Columbus,* trans. Samuel Eliot Morison (New York: The Heritage Press, 1963), pp. 72–73, 84.

1492: The Break Between the Premodern and Modern Worlds

History departments offer many yearlong survey classes, and individual instructors often choose midway points for their classes. Not so for world history, which almost always breaks at 1500 (or 1492).

Christopher Columbus's landing on the island of Hispaniola changed the world permanently, and we know as much as we do about precolonial Mexico because of the work of Sahagún, his informants among the Nahua elders, and his young trilingual research assistants.

Many claims have been made about voyagers who reached the Americas before Columbus. Some of these voyages have left convincing evidence, like the Viking settlement at L'Anse aux Meadows on Canada's Atlantic coast in about 1000 or the chicken bones showing contact between Polynesia and the west coast of South America in the 1350s. Some of the claims are utterly baseless: absolutely no evidence suggests that Zheng He's ships reached the Americas, as has been proposed. Some theories are possible without being certain: English fishing boats that sailed from Bristol to Iceland in 1480 and 1481 to seek new fishing grounds for cod might have made it all the way to the Americas, but they left no traces there. Whatever the credibility of these claims—and new evidence is emerging all the time—none of these voyages did more than touch down in the Americas, and they had no lasting impact. Columbus's voyages were utterly different.

After Columbus's landfall in 1492, the pace of events accelerated. Spain conquered Mexico in 1521 and Peru in 1551. The once-powerful Aztec and Inca empires collapsed quickly. They both had internal weaknesses; the many subject peoples of the Mexica resented their overlords, and the Inca were right in the middle of a protracted succession struggle.

The Europeans also had superior weapons made from metal. The Mexica and the Inca knew how to work different metals, including gold and silver, but they could not work iron, and they had no metal weapons. Theirs were

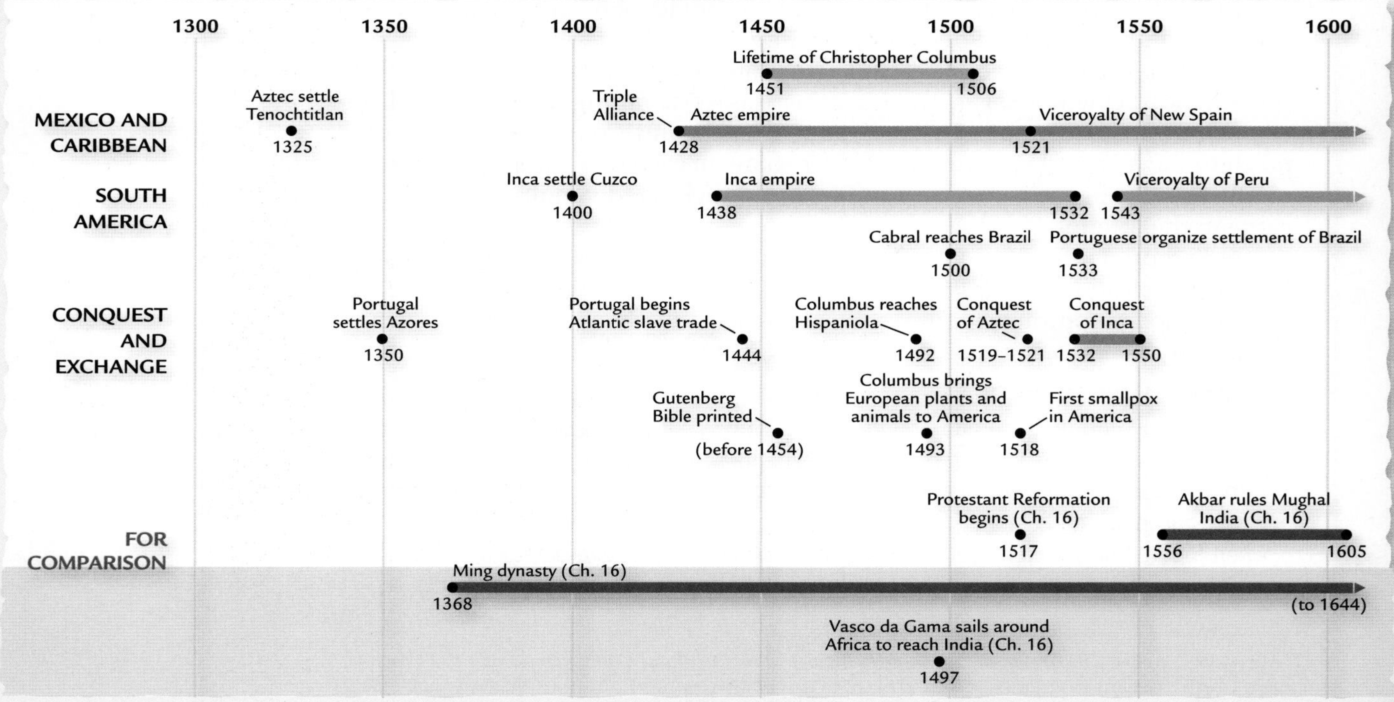

all made from stone and wood. Recall the eyewitness description from the *General History*, or Florentine Codex, of the Spanish army: their guns produced "thunder," they were clothed head to toe in iron, and their "deer" (read: horses) "were as tall as the roof."

European horses were only one example of the unfamiliar plants and animals that flowed from Europe to the Americas and from the Americas to Africa and Eurasia in the Columbian exchange. Cows, sheep, and pigs came to the Americas and altered the American landscape; tomatoes, potatoes, corn, and chili peppers traveled the other way, transforming first the European and then the African and Asian diets.

As discussed in Chapter 16, silver from Spanish mines in the Americas had an equally dramatic effect on the European economy. After 1550, when the Spanish mastered the technique of using mercury to separate silver from ore, they began to ship large quantities of silver home via the Philippines. The silver brought great prosperity to the Spanish empire and financed European purchases in Asia.

The diseases that came to the Americas from Europe devastated native peoples: smallpox progressed on its deadly route from Hispaniola to Puerto Rico, Jamaica, and Cuba and then on to Mexico and Peru. Because no population figures predate Columbus, it is impossible to know how many perished, but estimates range between 10 and 100 million. In 1568, the Spanish counted 2,170,000 non-Spanish survivors in Mexico and Peru, the two areas with the heaviest indigenous populations. Everyone else had died.

The mass deaths of the Amerindians preceded the large-scale movement of Europeans and Africans to the Americas. The migrations in the first hundred years after Columbus's arrival in Hispaniola produced the mixed population of the Americas today.

Before 1492 world history often concerns individual regions and the intermittent contacts among them. After 1492, Europe, the Americas, and Africa were so tightly connected that events in one place always affected the others. In the next chapter we will learn what happened when Europeans traveled to Asia.

Key Terms

Bernardino de Sahagún (436)
Aztec empire (437)
altepetl (438)
Tenochtitlan (438)
Inca empire (442)
ayllu (442)
quipu (446)
humanism (447)
Renaissance (449)
Henry the Navigator (449)
Arawak (454)
Treaty of Tordesillas (458)
conquistadors (458)
Malinche (458)
encomienda system (461)
Columbian exchange (464)

For Further Reference

Coe, Michael, and Rex Koontz. *Mexico: From Olmecs to the Aztecs*. London: Thames and Hudson, 2013.

Cook, David Noble. *Demographic Collapse: Indian Peru, 1520–1620*. Cambridge: Cambridge University Press, 1981.

D'Altroy, Terence. *The Incas*. Malden, Mass.: Blackwell Publishing, 2002.

D'Olwer, Luis Nicolau. *Fray Bernardino de Sahagún (1499–1590)*, trans. Mauricio J. Mixco. Salt Lake City: University of Utah Press, 1987.

Flint, Valerie I. J. *The Imaginative Landscape of Christopher Columbus*. Princeton: Princeton University Press, 1992.

Grafton, Anthony, et al. *New Worlds, Ancient Texts: The Power of Tradition and the Shock of Discovery*. Cambridge, Mass.: The Belknap Press of Harvard University Press, 1992.

Lockhart, James. *The Nahuas After the Conquest: A Social and Cultural History of the Indians of Central Mexico, Sixteenth Through Eighteenth Centuries*. Stanford: Stanford University Press, 1992.

McEwan, Colin, and Leonardo López Luján. *Moctezuma Aztec Ruler*. London: British Museum Press, 2009.

Quinn, David B. "Columbus and the North: England, Iceland, and Ireland." *William and Mary Quarterly*, 3d series, 49, no. 2 (1992): 278–297.

Schwartz, Stuart B. *The Iberian Mediterranean and Atlantic Traditions in the Formation of Columbus as a Colonizer*. Minneapolis: The Associates of the James Ford Bell Library, University of Minnesota, 1986.

Smith, Michael E. *The Aztecs*. Malden, Mass.: Blackwell Publishing, 2003.

AP® Review Questions for Chapter 15

Multiple-Choice Questions

QUESTIONS 1–2 REFER TO THE FOLLOWING PASSAGE.

Most of the people of Cuzco served the dead, I have heard it said, who they daily brought out to the main square, setting them down in a ring, each one according to his age, and there the male and female attendants ate and drank. . . . The mummies toasted each other and the living, and the living toasted the dead.

—Pedro Pizarro, a Spaniard observing Incan rituals between 1531 and 1555

1. The ritual described in this passage is an example of which of the following?
   (A) Blood sacrifice
   (B) Marriage service and contract
   (C) Ancestor worship
   (D) Harvest festival

2. Based on this passage, the Incan belief system was most similar to which of the following belief systems?
   (A) Christianity
   (B) Islam
   (C) Jainism
   (D) Confucianism

QUESTIONS 3–4 REFER TO THE FOLLOWING PASSAGE.

It especially made him faint when he heard how the guns went off at the Spaniards' command, sounding like thunder. . . . And when it went off, something like a ball came out from inside, and fire went showering and spitting out. . . . And if they shot at a hill, it seemed to crumble and come apart. . . . Their war gear was all iron. They clothed their bodies in iron, they put iron on their heads, their swords were iron. . . .

And their deer that carried them were as tall as the roof.

—Sahagún recording Moctezuma's (Montezuma's) response to the first envoy from the Spanish in 1519

3. The event described in this passage occurred for which of the following reasons?
   (A) Religious wars in Europe
   (B) European maritime reconnaissance of the Atlantic
   (C) Chinese maritime reconnaissance of the Indian and Pacific Oceans
   (D) Extension of land routes in Central Asia

4. Moctezuma's description of the Spaniards' horses can best be explained by which of the following?
   (A) There were no large domesticated animals in the Americas.
   (B) Mesoamerican horses were significantly smaller than their Asian counterparts.
   (C) Horses were used only as draft animals in the Americas and not for transportation.
   (D) Europeans had little to no experience controlling large domesticated animals.

QUESTIONS 5–8 REFER TO THE FOLLOWING MAP.

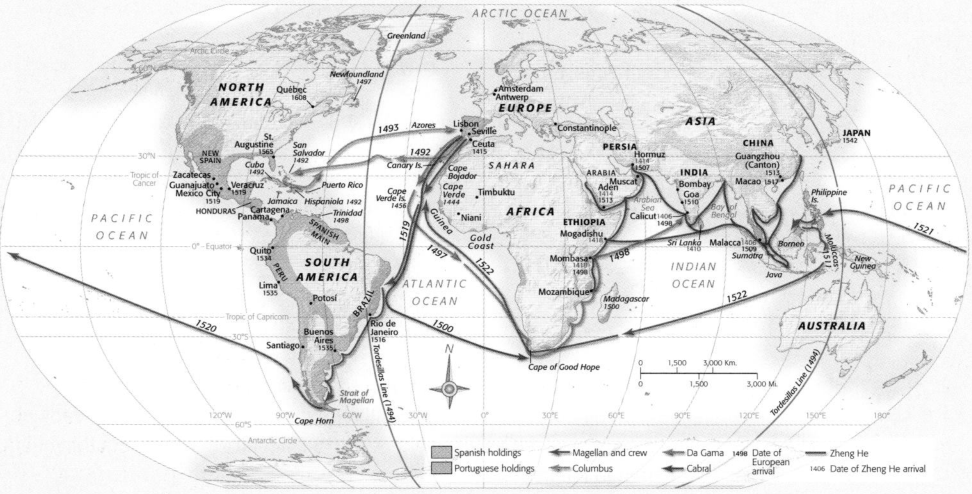

5. This map portrays which major change from the previous time period?
   (A) European interaction with Asian empires
   (B) European Christian control of the eastern Mediterranean
   (C) Direct interaction between the Eastern and Western Hemispheres
   (D) Trade between Europe and North Africa

6. Which of the following explains why the activities portrayed in the map occurred?
   (A) European knowledge retained from ancient Greece and Rome
   (B) European states hiring Muslim sailors and ships to conduct trade
   (C) European sailors' training on Chinese and Arab ships
   (D) European adoption of Chinese and Arab maritime technologies

7. Which of the following was an outcome of the activities portrayed in the map?
   (A) Europeans focused solely on the Atlantic trade system.
   (B) European states focused more on African trade than on trade with the Americas.
   (C) Europeans participated in globalized trade with Afro-Eurasia and the Americas.
   (D) European states became economically subordinate to their American colonies.

8. The motivation for the Ming treasure fleet voyages differed from the motivation for Columbus because the Ming treasure fleet wanted to
   (A) develop strong interregional trade relationships.
   (B) make a show of strength and receive tribute from foreign leaders.
   (C) control the pilgrim routes in the Indian Ocean trade for greater profits.
   (D) look for alternative routes to the Americas.

QUESTIONS 9–10 REFER TO THE FOLLOWING PASSAGE.

Hispaniola is a wonder. The mountains and hills, the plains and the meadow lands are both fertile and beautiful.... The harbors are incredibly fine and there are many great rivers with broad channels and the majority contain gold.... The inhabitants of this island, and all the rest that I discovered or heard of, go naked, as their mothers bore them, men and women alike.... I gave them a thousand pretty things that I had brought, in order to gain their love and incline them to become Christians.

—Christopher Columbus, on his first return trip to Hispaniola, 1493

9. Why does Columbus emphasize the presence of gold in his letter to the Spanish monarchs?
   (A) Columbus was hoping that Spain would fund future expeditions.
   (B) Gold was, in fact, present in great quantities in the Caribbean region.
   (C) Columbus wanted to mislead rivals about where the gold was truly located.
   (D) Columbus wanted to demonstrate what he believed was the innocent nature of the inhabitants.

10. Based on the passage, which of the following is a motivation for Columbus's travels?
   (A) To enslave the inhabitants
   (B) To gain access to tobacco and sugar growing in the region
   (C) To convert the inhabitants to Christianity and make them subjects of the crown
   (D) To encourage Spaniards to settle in the region in large numbers

Short-Answer Questions

Sores erupted on our faces, our breasts, our bellies.... The sick were so utterly helpless that they could only lie on their beds like corpses, unable to move their limbs or even their heads.... If they did move their bodies, they screamed with pain.

—Description by a Nahuatl, recorded by Sahagún between 1547 and 1572

1. Use the passage above to answer parts A and B.
   A. Explain ONE reason for the event described in the passage.
   B. Identify and explain TWO long-term effects that occurred because of the event described in the passage.

2. Answer parts A, B, and C.
   A. Briefly explain ONE impact of one American crop transferred to Eurasia.
   B. Briefly explain ONE impact of one Eurasian crop transferred to the Americas.
   C. Briefly explain ONE impact of the Columbian exchange on human populations.

16 Maritime Expansion in Afro-Eurasia, 1500–1700

Matteo Ricci

The Italian priest **Matteo Ricci** (1552–1610) knew as much about China as any European of his time. Though frustrated by the small number of converts he made to Christianity during his two decades as a missionary, Ricci (REE-chee) described Chinese political and social life in positive terms. In reading the passage below, we should be aware of the implicit criticism that Ricci, as an intellectual, makes of his own society, where men of war, he thought, had too much power and influence. Still, Ricci was correct in his assessment that China was more populous, more prosperous, and more stable than Europe in the first decade of the seventeenth century:

It seems to be quite remarkable... that in a kingdom of almost limitless expanse and innumerable population, and abounding in copious supplies of every description, though they have a well-equipped army and navy that could easily conquer the neighboring nations, neither the King nor his people ever think of waging a war of aggression.... In this respect they are much different from the people of Europe, who are frequently discontent with their own governments and covetous of what others enjoy.... Another remarkable fact and... marking a difference from the West, is that the entire kingdom is administered by... Philosophers. The responsibility for orderly management of the entire realm is wholly and completely committed to their charge and care.... Fighting and

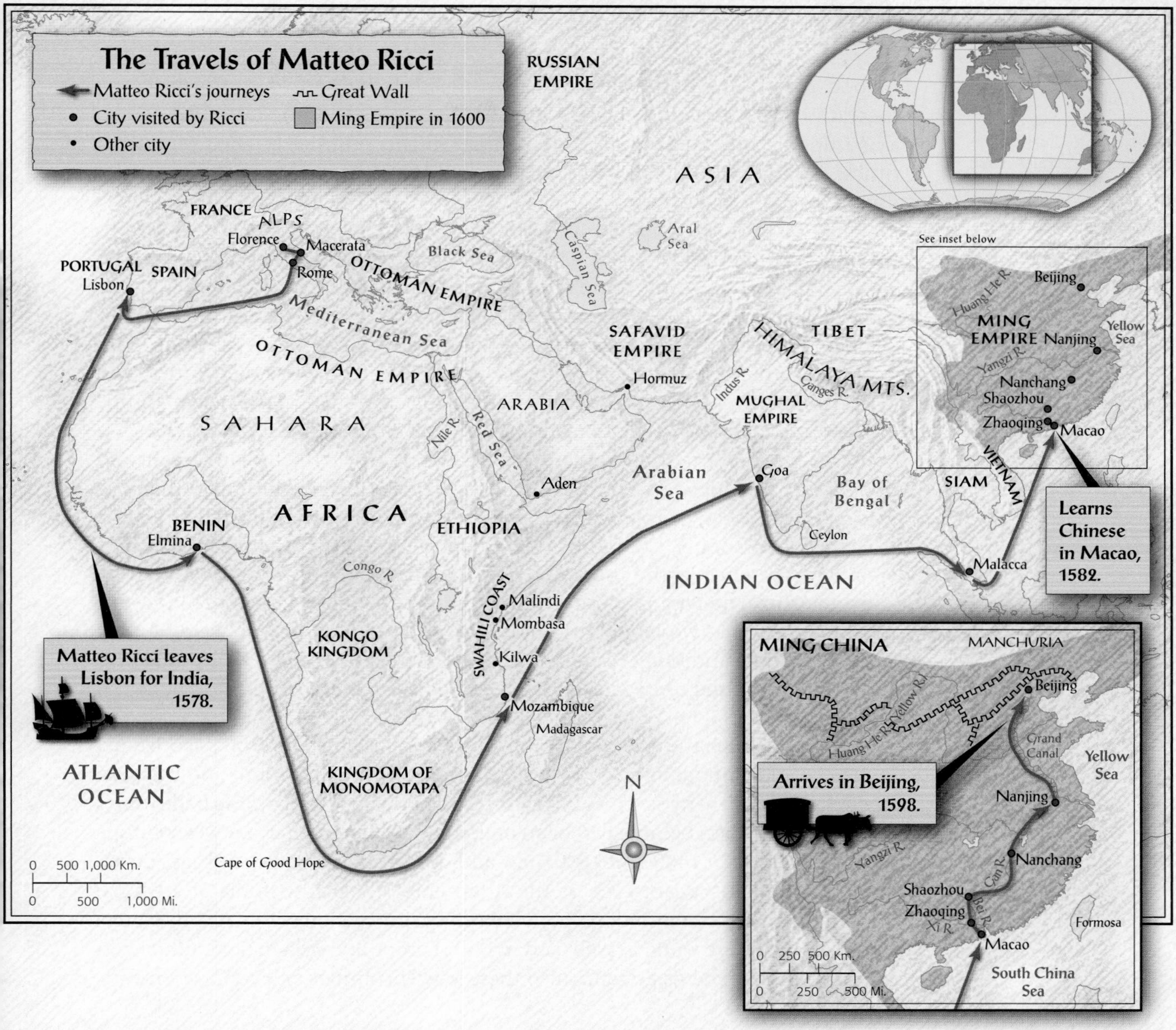

*violence among the people are practically unheard of.... On the contrary, one who will not fight and restrains himself from returning a blow is praised for his prudence and bravery.**

---

*"The Diary of Matthew Ricci," in *Matthew Ricci, China in the Sixteenth Century*, trans. Louis Gallagher (New York: Random House, 1942, 1970), pp. 54–55.

Matteo Ricci

(1552–1610) Italian Jesuit missionary who traveled to China in the sixteenth century. Tried unsuccessfully to reconcile Christianity with Confucianism and convert Ming scholar-officials.

From Ricci's point of view, all that China lacked was religious truth. He understood that to communicate his Christian ideas he had to conform to the expectations of the *"Philosophers,"* the scholar-officials who staffed the enormous imperial bureaucracy of Ming China. To this end, he learned Mandarin Chinese, studied Confucian texts, and dressed in silk garments to show a social status *"equal of a Magistrate."*

Italian by birth, Ricci joined the Jesuits, a Catholic religious order dedicated to "conversion of the Infidels" (see Chapter 15). Because it was the Portuguese who pioneered the direct oceanic route from Europe to Asia, Ricci traveled from Rome to Lisbon to learn Portuguese and prepare for his mission. He then spent four years in India before traveling to China, where he lived from 1582 until his death in 1610. Meanwhile, other Jesuits were traveling to Japan, Brazil, Quebec, West Africa, and the Mississippi River Valley. The Jesuits were taking advantage of the new maritime connections established in the sixteenth century by pioneering navigators.

In fact, the new maritime routes from Europe to Africa, the Indian Ocean, and East Asia first developed by Portuguese sailors were far less revolutionary than the connections between Europe, Africa, and the Americas that followed from the voyages of Christopher Columbus (see Chapter 15). While European mariners were a new presence in the Indian Ocean, they traveled on routes long used by Asian and African merchants, connecting the diverse peoples of the Indian Ocean's coastal regions. The two largest and most powerful empires of Asia were Mughal (MOO-gahl) India and Ming China. As Matteo Ricci's story shows, Europeans who traveled the maritime routes initially operated on the margins of these powerful Asian empires.

At the same time, the creation of more direct and sustained networks accelerated commercial and cultural interaction among Europe, Africa, and South and East Asia in the sixteenth and early seventeenth centuries. Following the maritime trade routes to China, Matteo Ricci became part of an ongoing "great encounter" between Europe and China.* Between 1400 and 1600, new and deepening economic linkages developed in the Indian Ocean, even as the Asian empires, such as India and China, became larger and more ambitious. Increased global interaction stimulated new ways of thinking about the world as well, and in both Europe and Asia major cultural and intellectual developments accompanied these new encounters and connections.

KEY CONCEPT QUESTIONS

- What were the causes and effects of European entry into the Indian Ocean region? **(Key Concept 4.1)**
- How did the global circulation of goods influence the political development of South Asian and East Asian states? **(Key Concept 4.1)**
- How did the increased interactions within Eurasia affect the religious, political, and intellectual traditions of each region? **(Key Concept 4.1)**

*E. Mungello, *The Great Encounter of China and the West, 1500–1800*, 2d ed. (Lanham, Md.: Rowman and Littlefield, 2005).

Maritime Trade Connections: Europe, the Indian Ocean, and Africa, 1500–1660

Unlike the Atlantic, the Indian Ocean had long served to connect rather than divide, facilitating trade among East Africa, the Persian Gulf, India, Southeast Asia, and China along maritime routes complementing the Silk Road that had long bridged eastern and western Eurasia by land. The Portuguese added a new element to these networks in the early 1500s. Though their intention was to create an empire like that being constructed by Spain in the Americas, their political and military ambitions went largely unmet. The Dutch followed the Portuguese and had a greater economic impact, bringing with them innovations in naval technology and business organization that stimulated older oceanic trade networks while also building new ones.

Africa was connected to both the Atlantic and Indian Ocean systems. In East Africa, the Portuguese encountered an existing commercial network. In West Africa, however, an entirely new oceanic trade began: the Atlantic slave trade.

Portugal's Entry into the Indian Ocean, 1498–1600

Henry the Navigator's exploration of the Atlantic Ocean culminated in 1488 when Bartholomew Dias and his crew rounded the southern tip of Africa at the Cape of Good Hope (see Map 15.3, page 450). The Portuguese journeys had both economic and religious motives: in seeking an oceanic trade link with Asia, the Portuguese sought to outflank Muslim intermediaries who controlled the land routes through western Asia and North Africa. They were also keenly aware of the West African gold that was enriching their Muslim enemies in Morocco, and by sailing south they hoped to divert those riches to their own treasuries.

In 1497 the Portuguese explorer **Vasco da Gama** (1460–1524) sailed for India. Arriving in East Africa after rounding the Cape of Good Hope, da Gama hired a local pilot who used Arabic-language charts and navigational guides to lead the Portuguese from Africa to western India. One of these books boasted of the superiority of Arab knowledge: *"We possess scientific books that give stellar altitudes.... [Europeans] have no science and no books, only the compass.... They admit we have a better knowledge of the sea and navigation and the wisdom of the stars."** The Portuguese were sailing into the same well-charted waters visited by Zheng He one hundred years earlier (see Chapter 15).

Vasco da Gama (1460–1524) Portuguese explorer who in 1497–1498 led the first European naval expedition to reach India by sailing around the Cape of Good Hope, laying the foundation for the Portuguese presence in the Indian Ocean in the sixteenth century.

When they reached India, the Portuguese anchored their ships in cosmopolitan ports that were part of the world's most extensive maritime trading system. In the western Indian Ocean, merchants transported East African gold, ivory, slaves, and timber to markets in southern Arabia, the Persian Gulf, and western India. Among the many goods exported from India along the same routes was highly valuable cotton cloth, often dyed by Indian craftsmen specifically to appeal to customers in distant markets across the ocean. On the east coast of India, another set of maritime networks connected the Bay of Bengal and the markets of Southeast Asia with Ming China. Here silk and sugar joined the long list of traded commodities. Cinnamon from the fabled "spice islands" was particularly precious.

---

*Ahmad ibn Majid, *Book of Useful Information on the Principles and Rules of Navigation*, cited in *Saudi Aramco World*, July/August 2005, p. 46.

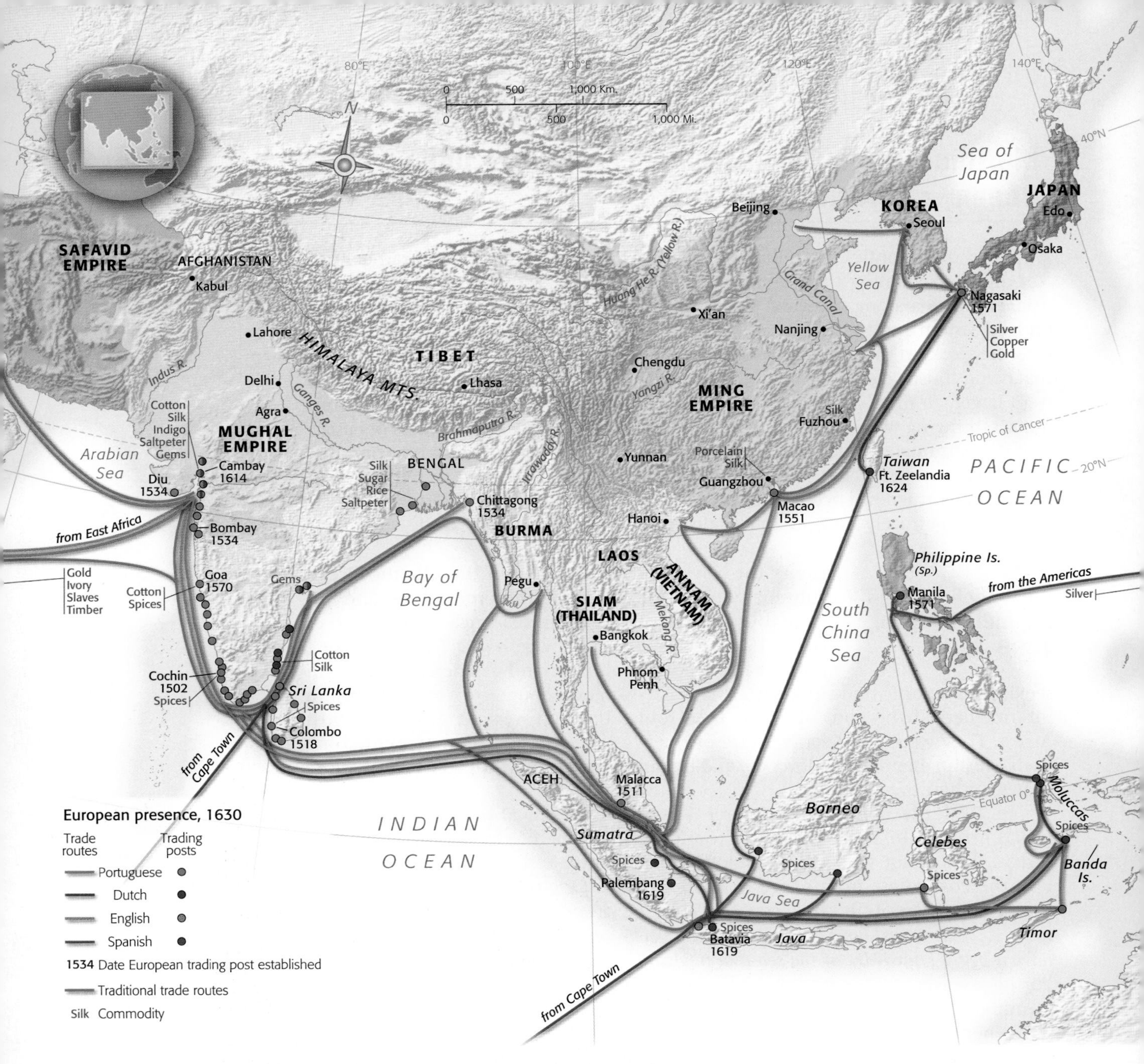

Map 16.1 Maritime Trade in the Eastern Indian Ocean and East Asia By 1630, the Dutch had overtaken the Portuguese in Indian Ocean trade, the French and English were becoming more active, and Spanish silver from American mines was stimulating trade across South, Southeast, and East Asia. Dutch ships passed through Cape Town in South Africa bearing Asian and African cargo for European markets. Still, the dominant powers in Asia remained land-based empires such as the Mughal empire in India and the Ming empire in China. Traditional trade routes controlled by local sailors and merchants were also growing in volume in the seventeenth century.

Europeans had long coveted Asian goods; the legendary "wealth of the orient" had motivated the voyages of both Columbus and da Gama. Even though the Portuguese now had direct access to these markets, they still faced a significant problem: European economies produced almost nothing that Asians valued. In fact, the first Indian king with whom da Gama negotiated ridiculed the poor quality of his gifts.

Nevertheless, the Portuguese could profit from their superior military technology. A prime example was Malacca, which they captured in 1511. Previously ruled by Muslims, the city was home to over fifteen thousand traders from all over the Indian Ocean world. Now the Portuguese controlled the narrow straits separating Sumatra from the Malay Peninsula, through which spices flowed on their way to India, Iran, and the Mediterranean (see Map 16.1). They profited handsomely. Using their cannon to seize trading centers all the way from East Africa to the South China Sea, the Portuguese earned a reputation as rough, greedy, and uncivilized.

AP® THEMES

How did the arrival of the Portuguese change existing trade networks in the Indian Ocean?

In some cases the Portuguese redirected trade away from existing channels and toward their own coastal fortifications. In East Africa, for example, the gold trade into the Indian Ocean had been dominated for centuries by Swahili (swah-HEE-lee) merchants, coastal African Muslims who lived in cities built of coral stone and sailed to the Persian Gulf and beyond. The Swahili town of Kilwa was ideally situated, close to the gold deposits of the interior and also one of the furthest points south to which mariners from India, Persia, and Arabia could make a safe round trip in the same year harnessing the monsoon winds. Then the Portuguese used their cannon to destroy the sea walls of Kilwa and diverted the gold southward through their settlement in Mozambique (see map on page 469). That they did so while flying militant Crusader crosses on their sails did not endear them to local Muslim merchants and rulers.

But the degree of disruption the Portuguese caused at Kilwa was exceptional. More often, they simply inserted themselves into existing commercial networks and used military force to extort payments from Asian and African rulers and traders. "What they set up was not an empire," argues one historian, "but a vast protection racket."* Portuguese officials required that all ships trading in the ocean purchase a license, and if an Indian Ocean captain was found trading without one he risked Portuguese cannon fire. In effect, "the Portuguese were selling protection from violence which they themselves had created."*

When it came to promoting their religion, there was a large gap between Portuguese ambition and achievement. Initially, they had hoped to ally with "Prester John," a mythical Christian African ruler. Though Prester John was just a legend, the Portuguese *did* form an alliance in Eastern Africa with the Christian kingdom of Ethiopia. In fact, in 1542 Cristovão da Gama, son of the navigator, died while leading Portuguese forces against a Muslim enemy of the Ethiopian king. But the Ethiopians, Christians for over a millennium before the Portuguese arrived, had their own unique liturgy and orthodox beliefs and resented Jesuits attempts to convert them to Roman Catholicism. The alliance did not last, and in eastern Africa and all across the Indian Ocean world, it was Islam rather than Christianity that proved most attractive to new converts.

By the early seventeenth century, other European and Asian powers were adopting ship-based cannon and challenging Portuguese dominance. In 1622, a

---

*Michael Pearson, *The Indian Ocean* (London: Routledge, 2003), p. 121.

Burning of Churches by Muslims and the Death of Cristobal de Gama and the Fall and Death of Ahmed ibn Ibrahim al-Ghazi (1506–43) Shot by a Portuguese Musketeer, c.1900 (oil on canvas), Kegneketa Jemlieri Hailu of Gondar (fl.1900)/Horniman Museum, London, UK/Bridgeman Images

The Ethiopian-Adal War In 1542–1543, Ahmad ibn Ibrahim al-Ghazi led Somali invaders from Adal in an attack on Ethiopia. Military alliances based on religion gave the conflict a wider regional impact, with Portuguese Catholics aiding Christian Ethiopia, and Ottoman Sunnis supporting Muslim Adal. The Somalis captured Cristóvão da Gama, son of the Portuguese mariner, and executed him after he refused to convert to Islam. In the top frame of this painting (by a later Ethiopian), Ahmad ibn Ibrahim al-Ghazi kills a priest, while his soldiers burn Christian churches. At the bottom, the Christians have their revenge: al-Ghazi falls from his horse, shot by a Portuguese soldier.

British-Iranian alliance drove the Portuguese from the strategic port of Hormuz, at the mouth of the Persian Gulf (see map on page 469). In 1698, an Arab siege drove the Portuguese from Fort Jesus, their principle fortress on the East African coast. But the most potent challenge to Portuguese commercial profit came from Dutch merchants, who were, by the early seventeenth century, developing both more efficient business systems and more advanced shipping technologies.

The Dutch East India Company, 1600–1660

Early Dutch trading ventures in Europe and the Atlantic were often very profitable, but merchants could be financially ruined if violent storms sank their ships or pirates stole their cargo. To spread the risk, they developed **joint-stock companies**, a new form of business enterprise based on the sale of shares to multiple owners. The joint-stock system allowed men and women of small means to buy a few shares and potentially reap a modest profit with little risk, since investors shared losses as well as profits.

joint-stock companies
Business organizations in which shares are sold to multiple stockholders to raise funds for trading ventures, while spreading both risk and profit; often backed by government charters granting monopolies of trade in particular goods or with specific regions.

These joint-stock companies put the Dutch at the forefront of early modern commercial capitalism. The development of financial institutions such as banks, stock exchanges, and insurance companies increased the efficiency with which capital could be accumulated and invested. Rather than seeking a single big windfall, investors now looked for more modest but regular gain through shrewd reinvestment of their profits. This dynamic was at the core of the new capitalist ethos associated with the **bourgeoisie**, the rising social group in Amsterdam and other urban areas of western Europe in the seventeenth century. The bourgeoisie based their social and economic power, and their political ambitions, on ownership of property rather than inherited titles.

bourgeoisie
The French term for urban middle-class society—people with education and property but without aristocratic titles.

- **CONTEXT&CONNECTIONS** In some places, trading was a low-status activity, beneath the dignity of elite families. Wishing to acquire higher status, successful merchants in cultures as diverse as China and Spain would educate their sons to be "gentlemen" (in Spain) or "scholars" (in China). But in northern Europe, and especially in Holland, commerce came to be seen as a noble calling, a cultural reorientation that accompanied the birth of modern capitalism. •

The greatest of the joint-stock companies, and the largest commercial enterprise of the seventeenth century, was the **Dutch East India Company**, founded in 1602. The government of the Netherlands granted a charter to the company giving it a monopoly on Dutch trade with Asia, overseen from company headquarters in Batavia in what became the Dutch East Indies (today's Indonesia). In the coming centuries, other European powers would copy the Dutch model and use chartered companies to extend their own national interests.

Dutch East India Company
Founded in 1602 in Amsterdam, a merchant company chartered to exercise a monopoly on all Dutch trade in Asia. The company was the effective ruler of Dutch colonial possessions in the East Indies.

Though a forerunner of modern corporate capitalism, the Dutch East India Company was a heavily armed corporate entity that paid little heed to free-market principles, often obtaining its profits through force. *"Trade cannot be maintained without war,"* said one governor of the East India Company, *"nor war without trade."** The Dutch thus repeated the Portuguese pattern of using military force in the Indian Ocean to secure commercial profit, while at the same time introducing modern, more efficient business and administrative techniques. In addition to their commercial innovations, the Dutch had made major advances in ship design and construction.

In 1641, they seized Malacca and its profitable straits from the Portuguese. After 1658, the Dutch East India Company commanded Indian Ocean sea lanes from the island of Ceylon (today's Sri Lanka), a central point from which to connect the trade routes of the eastern and western halves of the ocean (see Map 16.1). To facilitate the long journeys from Batavia, Malacca, or Ceylon back to Holland, in 1652 the Company established a fort at Cape Town, at the southernmost tip of Africa. Cape Town became a "refreshment station" where ships could take on fresh water, perhaps some beef, and most importantly some fruit, without which sailors would suffer from scurvy. The Dutch East India Company administered Cape Town not from Amsterdam but from Batavia.

AP® THEMES
What were the commercial advantages of controlling the straits of Malacca?

- **CONTEXT&CONNECTIONS** The environs of the Dutch settlement at Cape Town were the only place in sub-Saharan Africa where Europeans could live permanently without being decimated by malaria and other tropical diseases. Soon, a growing community of Dutch-descended settlers, later known as "Boers" ("farmers"), was competing with indigenous peoples for land and resources. Their descendants would dominate South African politics under apartheid and they remain an integral part of the nation today. •

---

*James D. Tracy, *The Political Economy of Merchant Empires* (New York: Cambridge University Press, 1991), p. 1.

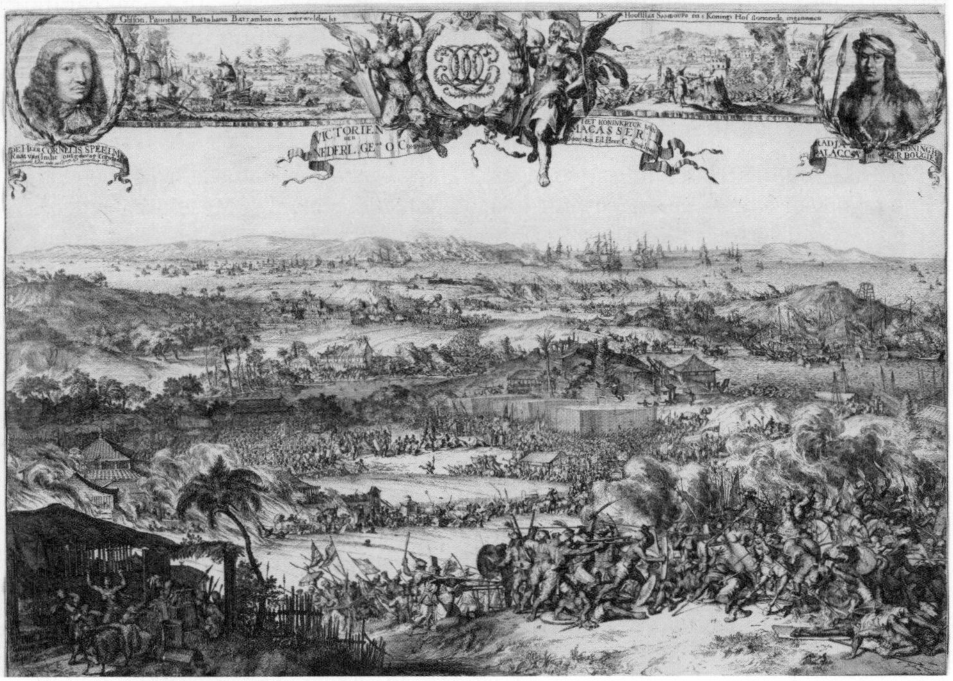

Romeyn de Hooghe (attributed to) Joost van den Vondel

The Battle of Makassar In the region that today comprises Malaysia and Indonesia, the efforts of the Dutch East India Company to control strategic trade routes brought conflict with political and religious authorities. In 1693, they had arrested an influential Muslim preacher, Sheikh Yusuf al-Makassar, and sent him into exile in Cape Town (thus introducing Islam into South Africa). Then in 1699, the Company launched a full-scale war and successfully added Makassar to their Southeast Asian empire.

Apart from carrying spices and other goods back to Europe, the Dutch made substantial profits by plugging into existing Afro-Asian trade routes. For example, they sold Indian cottons in Africa and Southeast Asia, and transported spices from the Moluccas to India and the Persian Gulf. This inter-Asian trade was a partial answer to the old question of what the Europeans might offer to trade in Asian markets. However, the main solution to that problem was silver.

The Dutch were lucky that at this time the entire Indian Ocean economy was being stimulated by large quantities of silver mined by the Spanish in South America and shipped across the Pacific. In the seventeenth century, increased access to silver finally gave European traders bargaining power in Asia. The Spanish city of Manila in the Philippines became the destination for the Manila Galleons, an annual shipment of silver from Mexico, with additional supplies flowing eastward from Europe through the Mediterranean. Thus, the flow of silver between the Americas and Asia was helping to lay the foundation of a global economy connecting the Atlantic and Pacific economies with that of the Indian Ocean. The Dutch were perfectly positioned to benefit.

The Dutch East India Company made huge profits, especially from the spice trade. To do so, they sometimes violently intervened in local affairs to increase production. On the Bandas Islands, the Dutch were unhappy with the low level of nutmeg production. Their answer was to kill or exile the local farmers, turn their lands into nutmeg plantations, and replace the local population with slaves drawn from East Africa, Japan, and India.

Dutch investors were delighted with a rate of profit that ranged from several hundred to several thousand percent, as were European consumers who, thanks to the efficiency of Dutch methods, could now enjoy Asian spices at much cheaper prices. According to one historian, seventeenth-century Holland was so prosperous the country enjoyed an "embarrassment of riches."*

Africa and the Atlantic Ocean, 1483–1660

While the East African coast had oceanic links connecting the Swahili city-states with India, the Persian Gulf, and the wider world, West Africa's international networks were traditionally land-based, across the Sahara. When the Portuguese sailed down the West African coast in the fifteenth century, therefore, these were the first significant coastal contacts that West Africans had experienced. (See the feature "Visual Evidence in Primary Sources: An Ivory Mask from Benin, West Africa.")

Portugal's initial goals were the discovery of gold and transit to the East, as well as trade in commodities such as pepper and ivory. A new source of profit developed after they settled Madeira in 1454 and began growing sugar, already part of the Mediterranean economy, on Atlantic islands (see Chapter 15).

• **CONTEXT&CONNECTIONS** Sugar and slaves were fundamental to the Atlantic plantation system (covered in Chapter 19 of Volume 2). Cane sugar, originally from India, spread to the Mediterranean, where enslaved Europeans ("Slavs") worked on Arab plantations. The Portuguese brought this system to islands in the Atlantic, then to coastal Brazil. In the seventeenth century, sugar production, and demand for slaves, boomed when the Dutch, British, and French established plantations in Brazil and the Caribbean, which by the eighteenth century accounted for the vast majority of African slave imports in the Americas. •

The **Kongo kingdom** (see map on page 469) was one of the earliest African societies to be destabilized by the new Atlantic slave trade. When the Portuguese arrived at the capital city of Mbanza Kongo in 1483, they found a prosperous, well-organized kingdom with extensive markets in domestically produced cloth and iron goods. King Afonso Mvemba a Nzinga (uh-fahn-so mm-VEM-bah ah nn-ZING-ah) (r. 1506–1543) converted to Christianity, renamed his capital San Salvador, sent his son Enrique to study in Lisbon, and exchanged diplomatic envoys with both Portugal and the Vatican.

Kongo kingdom
West-central African kingdom whose king converted to Christianity in the early sixteenth century and established diplomatic relations with the Portuguese. Became an early source of slaves for the new Atlantic slave trade.

Aided by the Portuguese, Afonso undertook wars of conquest that added territory to the Kongo kingdom. In West Africa, as in many parts of the world, captives taken during war might simply be killed, but more often they were exchanged, redeemed for a ransom, or kept as dependent workers. Slaves were a byproduct of the fighting, not its purpose. Now, into this traditional system came the new labor demands of the Atlantic plantation system. Portuguese merchants were anxious to purchase war captives, and Afonoso's battles had the side effect of further stimulating the market for slaves. As demand for slaves increased, tragically so did the supply.

*Simon Schama, *An Embarrassment of Riches: An Interpretation of Dutch Culture in the Golden Age* (New York: Vintage, 1997).

An Ivory Mask from Benin, West Africa

The kingdom of Benin (see map on page 469) already had a long history of political and cultural achievement before the arrival of the first Europeans in the sixteenth century. Believed to be descendants of Oduduwa (oh-doo-doo-wah), ancestor of all Yoruba kings, Benin's rulers, the *obas*, were associated with great spiritual powers. Starting in the fourteenth century, Beninese artists, organized into a guild by the king, began producing magnificent brass sculptures of royalty. Using a sophisticated "lost-wax" technique, they made a beeswax model, covered it with clay, fired the sculpture to melt the wax inside, poured molten bronze into the clay form, and then broke off the outer clay layer. Their achievement was not only technical but also artistic. The Benin bronzes are known for their naturalism, a quality that made them highly attractive to European collectors. In fact, in 1897, the British colonial government looted over a thousand of these invaluable pieces, and the fight to return them to West Africa continues.

The bronze used in these sculptures, however, was imported from the Mediterranean and was therefore extremely expensive. Beninese artists more often carved masks and wall decorations directly from wood and ivory, sometimes incorporating cowrie shells imported from the Indian Ocean. This ivory mask, made around 1520, depicts Idia (ee-DEE-ah), the Queen Mother of Oba Esigie (eh-see-GEE-ay). Like the Benin bronzes, it conveys a powerful sense of the individuality of its subject. The Portuguese were present in West Africa by this time and had allied with King Esigie and helped him fight off an enemy invasion. Their role in West African politics was still quite marginal, however, as indicated by the minor representation of European figures at the top.

A century and a half after this mask was made, a Dutch visitor in 1688 was impressed with the capital city:

> *The houses in this town stand in good order, one close and evenly placed with its neighbor, just as the houses in Holland stand.... The king's court is very great. It is built around many square-shaped yards. These yards have surrounding galleries where guards are always placed. I myself went into the court far enough to pass through four great yards like this, and yet wherever I looked I could still see gate after gate which opened into other yards.**

Though pepper was the main item of trade with Europeans when Oba Esigie ruled, by the time this Dutch observer described Benin, the market in slaves had become dominant. Here, as elsewhere in West Africa, a painful era had begun.

---

*Olfert Dapper, *Description of Benin* (Madison: University of Wisconsin Press, 1998), p. 40.

In Benin, as in many African societies, the Queen Mother was a pivotal figure in the king's council, and he often relied on her to gain a consensus of opinion among clan leaders.

The Queen Mother had a special role in representing the interests and opinions of women.

The oba of Benin, King Esigie, is said to have worn this mask on his hip at a commemoration ceremony for Queen Idia.

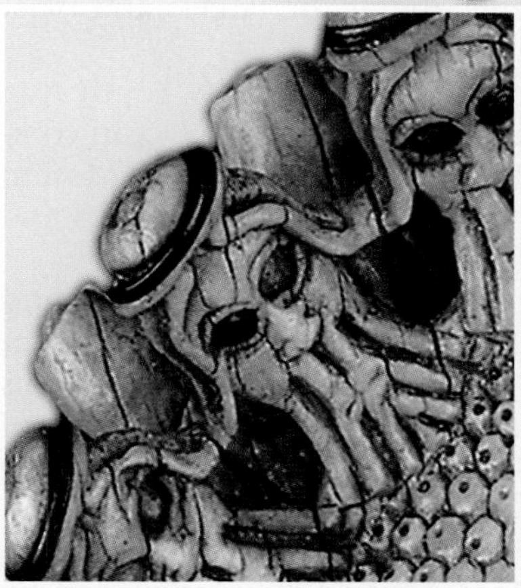

The figures on top represent the Portuguese who allied with King Esigie and helped him thwart an enemy invasion. These Portuguese figures resemble the mudfish often found in Beninese sculptures. Like mudfish, the Portuguese could travel both in the water and on land. ***From the way they are represented on this mask, what might we infer about the extent of Portuguese influence on life in Benin?***

AP® THEMES

How did commercial contacts with Europeans shape the development of African states?

Alarmed at the escalating market for slaves driven by Portuguese demand, King Afonso complained to his *"brother king"* in Portugal: *"Many of our people, keenly desirous as they are of the wares and things of your Kingdoms, . . . seize many of our people, freed and exempt men. . . . That is why we beg of your Highness to help and assist us in this matter . . . because it is our will that in these Kingdoms there should not be any trade of slaves nor outlet for them."** Foreign goods and foreign traders had distorted the traditional market in slaves, which had previously been an incidental byproduct of warfare, into an economic activity in its own right. Afonso's alliance with the Portuguese had led to rising violence, but his complaint fell on deaf ears.

As other European nations became involved in slave trading and sugar production, the demand for slaves increased decade by decade. At first, only those African societies closest to the western coasts were affected, yet by the eighteenth century the rise of the Atlantic slave trade would fundamentally alter the terms of Africans' interactions with the wider world.

Empires of Southern and Eastern Asia, 1500–1660

In the course of Matteo Ricci's long journey, he came in contact with a great variety of peoples, cultures, and political systems. By far the largest and most powerful of these societies were Mughal India and Ming China.

Mughal India was a young and rising state in sixteenth-century South Asia with an economy stimulated by internal trade and expanding Indian Ocean commerce. Keeping the vast Mughal realms at peace, however, required India's Muslim rulers to maintain a stable political structure in the midst of great religious and ethnic diversity.

In the sixteenth century, Ming China was the most populous and most productive society in the world. We have seen that Matteo Ricci was impressed with its order and good governance. But even while the Ming dynasty earned Ricci's admiration, it was beginning a downward spiral that would end in a change of dynasty in 1644.

Mughal dynasty (1526–1857) Mughal emperors who controlled most of the Indian subcontinent from their capital at Delhi during the height of their power in the sixteenth and seventeenth centuries.

Since political leaders in the neighboring East Asian states of Vietnam and Korea had long emulated Chinese systems and philosophies of statecraft, Ming officials recognized these states as "civilized." Japan, while also influenced by China in many ways, was by Ming standards disordered and militaristic in this period, though it did achieve a more stable political system in the seventeenth century. While Japanese rulers excluded European merchants and missionaries in the seventeenth century, the kingdom of Siam in Southeast Asia was far more influenced by rising maritime trade and the increasing European presence.

Emperor Akbar (r. 1556–1605) The most powerful of the Mughal emperors, who pursued a policy of toleration toward the Hindu majority and presided over a cosmopolitan court.

The Rise of Mughal India, 1526–1627

During Matteo Ricci's four-year stay in western India, the **Mughal dynasty**, the dominant power in South Asia, was at the height of its glory under its greatest leader, **Emperor Akbar** (r. 1556–1605), whose armies controlled most of the Indian subcontinent. Ruling 100 million subjects from his northern capital of Delhi, the "Great Mughal" was one of the most powerful men in the world.

*Cited in John Reader, *Africa: A Biography of the Continent* (New York: Vintage, 1999), pp. 374–375.

The Mughal state was well positioned to take advantage of expanding Indian Ocean trade. It licensed imperial mints that struck hundreds of millions of gold, silver, and copper coins. Dyed cotton textiles were a major export, along with sugar, pepper, diamonds, and other luxury goods.

State investment in roads helped traders move goods to market. The Mughals also supported movement of populations into previously underutilized lands by granting tax-exempt status to new settlements. Such settlements transformed the eastern half of Bengal (today's Bangladesh) from tropical forest land into a densely populated rice-producing region.

Agriculture was the ultimate basis of Mughal wealth and power, providing 90 percent of the tax income that paid for Mughal armies and the ceremonial pomp of the court at Delhi. The Mughals sent tax clerks out to the provinces, who surveyed the lands and diverted much of the revenue to Delhi. In those parts of India where a pre-Mughal aristocracy was used to collecting and retaining these taxes, the Mughals confirmed the old rulers' rights to 10 percent of the local revenue, and thus ensured their loyalty. This revenue system, controlled from the top but recognizing the prerogatives of local rulers, was part of a broader Mughal attempt to integrate existing Indian authorities into their government.

A principal political challenge the Mughal rulers faced was that their Islamic faith differed from the Hindu beliefs of most of their subjects. Though people may be conquered by the sword, more stable forms of administration are needed to turn conquest into long-term rule. Akbar's policy was one of toleration and inclusion. He canceled the special tax that Islamic law allows Muslim rulers to collect from nonbelievers and granted Hindu communities the right to follow their own social and legal customs. Hindu *maharajahs* and rural aristocrats were incorporated into the Mughal administrative system. Since Hindus were accustomed to a social system in which people paid little attention to matters outside their group, they could view the ruling Muslims as simply another caste with their own rituals and beliefs. Thus, the Mughals achieved a stable social order.

Akbar's policy of religious tolerance was continued by his successor Jahangir (r. 1605–1627) and his remarkable wife **Nur Jahan** (1577–1645). Jahangir himself was a weak ruler, addicted as he was to opium and alcohol. When faced with regional rebellions, therefore, it was Nur Jahan (noor ja-HAN), an intelligent and skilled politician, who took charge and kept Mughal power intact. Since women were secluded in the *zezana*, or women's quarters, she could not appear at court in person. Instead she issued government decrees through trusted family members. Taking a special interest in women's affairs, she donated land and dowries for orphan girls. From an Iranian family, Nur Jahan also patronized Persian-influenced art and architecture, building many of the most beautiful mosques and gardens in north India. So great was his admiration of Nur Jahan that Jahangir had coins struck with her image, a privilege usually reserved for the emperor himself.

Nur Jahan
(1577–1645) Mughal empress who dominated politics during the reign of her husband Jahangir and had a lasting cultural influence on north India.

Nur Jahan was also interested in commerce and owned a fleet of ships that took religious pilgrims and trade goods to Mecca. Even more than Akbar's, her policies facilitated both domestic and foreign trade and had a strong influence on the wider world. Indian merchants, sailors, bankers, and shipbuilders were important participants in Indian Ocean markets, and the cosmopolitan ports of Mughal India teemed with visitors from Europe, Africa, Arabia, and Southeast Asia (see Map 16.1). But there was little Chinese presence, and no attempt to follow up the fifteenth-century voyages of Zheng He (see Chapter 15). Unlike the Mughal rulers of India, the leaders of Ming China saw maritime trade more as a threat than as an opportunity.

Ming dynasty
(1368–1644) Chinese imperial dynasty in power during the travels of Matteo Ricci. It was at its height during the fifteenth century, but by 1610 the Ming dynasty was showing signs of the troubles that would lead to its overthrow.

The Apogee and Decline of Ming China, 1500–1644

By 1500, the **Ming dynasty** in China was at the height of its power and prestige. In 1368, the Ming had replaced the Mongol Yuan dynasty, and the early Ming rulers were highly conscious of the need to restore Confucian virtue after years of what they saw as "barbarian" rule. Like earlier Chinese dynasties, the Ming defined their country as the "Middle Kingdom" and called the emperor the "Son of Heaven." China was at the center of the world, and the emperor ruled with the "Mandate of Heaven."

The emperor's residence in the Forbidden City in Beijing (bay-JING), constructed during the early Ming period and still standing today, was at the center of a Confucian social order based on strict hierarchical relationships. The emperor stood at the top of a social hierarchy in which everyone owed him unquestioning obedience, while the emperor was expected to emulate the benevolent behavior of the greatest Confucian sages, seeking the best interests of those below him. Likewise, junior officials owed obeisance to senior ones, younger brothers to older ones, wives to husbands, and children to parents. Only men of similar age and status were "equal."

AP® THEMES
Why did the social hierarchy of China remain largely unchanged from the Han dynasty through the Ming dynasty?

Hierarchy governed foreign relations as well. Ming officials respected those societies that had most successfully emulated Chinese models, such as Korea and Vietnam. Japan and the societies of Inner Asia were usually thought of as "inner barbarians," peoples touched by Chinese civilization but still uncouth. All the rest of the world's peoples were regarded as "outer barbarians." From a Ming standpoint, the only proper relationship between any of these other kingdoms and China was a tributary one. Foreign kings were expected to send annual missions bearing tribute in acknowledgment of China's preeminent position.

Confucians believed that if such stable hierarchies of obeisance and benevolence were maintained, then the people would prosper. And in the early sixteenth century, peace and prosperity were indeed the norm in Ming China. The networks of canals and irrigation works on which so much of the empire's trade and agriculture depended were refurbished and extended. Most important for trade and governance was the Grand Canal, connecting the political and military capital Beijing with the productive Yangzi River Valley and fertile rice-producing regions further south. Public granaries were maintained as a hedge against famine. At the height of the Ming, the roads were kept safe and ordinary people could find justice in the courts. New food crops, including maize, peanuts, and potatoes from the Americas, helped improve nutrition. The Columbian exchange, therefore, contributed to significant population growth in Ming China.

examination system
Chinese system for choosing officials for positions in the Ming imperial bureaucracy. Candidates needed to pass one or more examinations that increased in difficulty for higher positions.

The **examination system**, based on the Confucian classics and requiring years of study, helped ensure that the extensive Ming bureaucracy was staffed by competent officials at the local, county, and imperial levels. With a hierarchy of well-educated officials supervised by dynamic emperors, the early Ming efficiently carried out essential tasks of government.

The elaborate and expensive Ming bureaucracy required an efficient system of tax collection. For that purpose, in 1571 Ming officials decided that all tax payments must be made in silver, generating a surge in global demand. Some silver came from Japan, but the rising demand in China was largely met by silver from the Spanish Americas. In East Asia, as in the Indian Ocean, American silver was facilitating both domestic and interregional commerce.

● **CONTEXT&CONNECTIONS** The great global demand for silver would have negative consequences for some Amerindian communities. In South America, for example, the great silver mines of Potosí relied on the heavy toil of Amerindian workers, who often died as they labored to extract the valuable metal. Some of the silver arriving in south China came from Acapulco via the Spanish Philippines, a trans-Pacific axis of early modern international trade. ●

Despite the importance of silver imports, Ming officials strongly distrusted those who engaged in seaborne trade. They saw the ocean as an unpredictable realm, where uncontrollable Japanese pirates (or Chinese pirates disguising themselves as Japanese) had now been joined by European warrior-merchants. In addition, there were real economic trade-offs from the silver-tax system. Inflation accompanied economic growth: rising prices were particularly distressing for the less well-off. And fiscal reliance on silver made the Chinese economy vulnerable to distant economic shocks, as when global silver supplies took a sharp drop after 1620. By that date, economic contraction was contributing to an accelerating crisis in Ming governance.

The decline of the Ming is associated with the **Wanli Emperor** (r. 1573–1620). As a young ruler, he had displayed great energy in turning back an invasion from Japan. As he aged, however, the Wanli Emperor developed an apathetic attitude toward his duties, allowing personalities and petty jealousies to influence the imperial court. Uneducated eunuchs, whose traditional role was limited to caring for the imperial household, rose in influence at the expense of scholar-officials. Without imperial oversight, corruption increased: gifts could determine the outcome of court cases, grain intended for famine relief was sold on the market, and irrigation works went untended. Bandits vexed merchants on the roads, and local peasant uprisings became more common. When Matteo Ricci was finally granted permission to enter the Forbidden City and performed the ritual *kowtow*, prostrating himself with his forehead on the ground, he did so before a vacant Dragon Throne. The Wanli Emperor was inaccessible, remaining deep in the recesses of the Forbidden City.

Wanli Emperor
(r. 1573–1620) Ming emperor at the time of Matteo Ricci's mission to China. Vain and extravagant, he hastened the decline of the Ming dynasty through lack of attention to policy and the promotion of incompetent officials.

Matteo Ricci, in his tribute to Ming governance cited in the chapter opening, failed to notice the decay that was setting in below the impressive façade of the Wanli Emperor's court. In 1644, northern invaders from Manchuria, taking advantage of the unrest caused by Chinese peasant rebellions, breached the walls of Beijing and drove the Ming from power.

Tradition and Innovation: Korea, Vietnam, Japan, and Siam, 1500–1650

The societies most strongly connected to Chinese civilization in the early modern period were Korea, Vietnam, and, more loosely, Japan. The Choson (choh-SAN) dynasty of Korea, which closely followed the Ming imperial model, established one of the world's most stable political systems, ruling the Korean peninsula from 1392 until the early twentieth century. The capital at Seoul (sole) was home to a Confucian academy where young men trained for examinations that led to social prominence and political power.

Early modern Korea benefitted from a remarkable series of innovations undertaken by the **Emperor Sejong** (r. 1418–1450). Earlier, learning to read and write had required years of training in Chinese script. Then in 1446, Sejong (SAY-jung) brought together a group of scholars to devise a new phonetic script based on the Korean language. This distinctive han'gul (HAHN-goor) writing system, still in use today, greatly expanded literacy. Emperor Sejong then supported projects to write

Emperor Sejong
(r. 1418–1450) Korean emperor of the Choson dynasty, credited with the creation of the han'gul script for the Korean language.

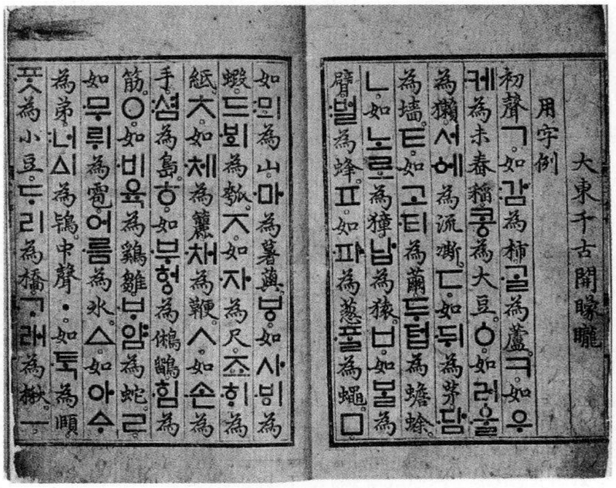

Dr. Yushin Yoo/Visual Connection Archive

Prisma/SuperStock

King Sejong and the Korean Alphabet *Hunminjeongeum* ("The Correct Sounds for the Instruction of the People") was a project sponsored by King Sejong to extend literacy by creating an alphabet based on spoken Korean. The text shown here (along with Sejong's statue in Seoul) is from 1446. Written in a mixture of Chinese and han'gul characters, it was used as a primer by those who could already read Chinese characters to learn the new phonetic script.

the history of the country in the new Korean script and to translate key Buddhist texts, using woodblock printing as well as moveable type to produce less expensive books. Korea became one of the world's most literate societies.

Vietnamese leaders copied Chinese imperial models while at the same time jealously guarding their independence. After the Ming had invaded and occupied northern Vietnam, a decade of sustained resistance led to their defeat and the creation, in 1428, of the new **Lê dynasty**. Legend tells us that General Lê (lee) sent a gift of cattle to his retreating Ming counterpart, as if to say that the invasion would not stop Vietnam from pursuing positive relations with China. Indeed, Confucian scholar-officials, literate in Chinese, gained greater influence in this period at the Vietnamese court. Military expeditions expanded the size and strength of the imperial state, and agrarian reforms led to greater equality in landholding and greater productivity in agriculture.

Lê dynasty
(1428–1788) The longest-ruling Vietnamese dynasty. Drawing on Confucian principles, its rulers increased the size and strength of the Vietnamese state and promoted agricultural productivity.

Japan lay further outside the orbit of Chinese civilization than either Korea or Vietnam. Political power was decentralized during Japan's Ashikaga (ah-shee-KAH-gah) shogunate (1336–1568), and the Japanese emperor, unlike his Chinese, Korean, and Vietnamese counterparts, was a ritual figure with no real authority. The greatest political power was the *shogun*, a supreme military ruler who acted independently of the imperial court. But the Ashikaga shoguns themselves had little control over the *daimyo* (DIE-mee-oh), lords who ruled their own rural domains. As each daimyo had an army of *samurai* (SAH-moo-rye) military retainers, incessant warfare spread chaos through the islands.

Ashikaga Japan was a land of contrasts. While the daimyo lords engaged in violent competition for land and power, they also acted as benefactors of Buddhist monasteries that promoted spiritual reflection. The samurai warriors, with their strict *bushido* code of honor and loyalty, were also practitioners of the Zen school of Buddhism, with its emphasis on mental discipline and acute awareness. (Zen practitioners are less interested in scriptural study and ritual observance than in inward contemplation, focusing on *being in the moment*.) Flower arranging and the intricate tea ceremony were peaceful counterpoints to the ceaseless war making.

Himeji Castle Incessant warfare during the Ashikaga period led the Japanese daimyo lords to build well-fortified stone castles. The introduction of cannon in the sixteenth century made the need for such fortifications even greater. Himeji Castle was begun in 1346; Toyotomi Hideyoshi greatly expanded and beautified it in the late sixteenth century. Now a UNESCO World Cultural and Heritage Site, Himeji is the best-preserved castle in all of Japan. (Jon Arnold Images Ltd/Alamy)

In the late sixteenth century, several Japanese lords aspired to replace the Ashikaga family; the most ambitious was **Toyotomi Hideyoshi** (r. 1585–1598), whose plans included not only the consolidation of power on the Japanese islands but also conquest of the Ming empire. In 1592, as Matteo Ricci was journeying in southern China, Hideyoshi's forces attacked the Korean peninsula with an army of two hundred thousand soldiers. A statue of Admiral Yi in central Seoul still commemorates his use of heavily fortified "turtle ships," armed with multiple cannon and with wooden planks shielding their decks, to defend Korea against the Japanese attack.

Toyotomi Hideyoshi

(r. 1585–1598) A daimyo (lord) who aspired to unify Japan under his own rule. His attempts to conquer Korea and China failed.

• **CONTEXT&CONNECTIONS** The East Asian balance of power would later be radically altered when industrialization empowered the Japanese empire after 1868. While Hideyoshi's earlier dream of conquering Ming China may have been a pipe dream, from 1894 to 1895 the Japanese navy did indeed crush the Chinese fleet in the Sino-Japanese War. In the 1930s, the Japanese military began its assault on China on the road to the Second World War. •

Tokugawa shogunate

(1603–1868) The dynasty of shoguns, paramount military leaders of Japan. From their capital at Edo (now Tokyo), Tokugawa rulers brought political stability by restraining the power of the daimyo lords.

In a power struggle following Hideyoshi's death, the Tokugawa (TOH-koo-GAH-wah) clan emerged victorious. After 1603, the **Tokugawa shogunate** centralized power by restraining the independence of the daimyo, forcing them to spend half the year in the shogun's new capital of Edo (today's Tokyo). Compared with the highly centralized imperial model of Korea, political power in Japan was more diffuse, with many daimyo still controlling their own domains. But the Tokugawa system brought a long-term stability that made possible economic and demographic growth. With peace came economic growth, and in the seventeenth century, as market exchanges became central to the Japanese economy, Japanese cities such as Osaka and Nagasaki emerged as vibrant commercial centers.

When the Tokugawa attempted to tame the power of the daimyo, some sought to protect their independence by forming diplomatic and trade alliances with Jesuit missionaries. Unlike in China, the Jesuits attracted many Japanese converts, but that only increased the shoguns' antagonism to the imported faith. After 1614, Tokugawa edicts outlawed Christianity. Hundreds of Japanese Christians were killed, some by crucifixion, when they refused to recant their beliefs. Apart from an annual Dutch trade mission confined to an island in the port of Nagasaki, no Europeans were allowed to enter the country. Japanese trade with China and Korea, however, continued to flourish.

In contrast to Vietnam, Korea, and Japan, the Southeast Asian kingdom of Siam (overlapping with today's Thailand) was influenced as much or more by Indian Ocean connections as by contact with China. Its Buddhist rulers welcomed merchants from all lands and sent emissaries and splendid gifts, including elephants, to the rulers of Iran, Mughal India, and Ming China. Then in the 1500s, with their rising kingdom struggling to establish independence from Burma, Siamese kings cultivated an alliance with the Portuguese, whose cannon and superior style of military fortification helped the Siamese extend their domains. Later, Siamese leaders also welcomed the Dutch, French, and British, although Asian traders still outnumbered European ones. Buddhism, Islam, and Hinduism were all more common than Christianity.

Siamese officials were usually careful to balance their relationships with the different, often competing, foreign communities. That balance was temporarily broken in the 1680s when one king sided too strongly with the French, much to the irritation of the Iranians and the English. (See the feature "Movement of Ideas Through Primary Sources: Iranians and Europeans at the Court of Siam"). In the longer term, however, Siam's diplomatic strategy was successful: the kingdom has maintained its independence ever since, its culture a rich amalgam of Southeast Asian, Indian, Chinese, Muslim, and European influences.

Eurasian Intellectual and Religious Encounters, 1500–1620

Early modern Eurasian intellectual ferment was often associated with new religious ideas. In western Europe, the Protestant Reformation divided Christians over basic matters of faith. Matteo Ricci himself was a representative of the Catholic Reformation, which sought to re-energize Roman Catholicism. In Mughal India, many people converted to Islam, and the new faith of Sikhism was founded. In China, Matteo Ricci attempted to convince Ming scholar-officials that Christianity was compatible with the oldest and purest versions of Confucianism.

Challenges to Catholicism, 1517–1620

While Renaissance humanism had led to significant artistic and intellectual achievement in western Europe (see Chapter 15), it coincided with increasing corruption in the Catholic Church. Popes and bishops raised money for prestigious building projects, such as the magnificent Saint Peter's Basilica in Rome, by selling "indulgences," which church authorities said could bring forgiveness of sins and entrance into heaven. Thus the cultural richness of the Roman church was underwritten by practices that some European Christians viewed as corrupt and worldly.

An infuriated cleric named **Martin Luther** (1483–1546) argued that salvation could not be purchased; only God could determine the spiritual condition of a human soul. With the availability of new printed versions of the Bible in vernacular languages (Luther himself translated the Bible into German), western European Christians no longer needed priests fluent in Latin to interpret God's will for them: the individual could find God's meaning in his own Gospel reading. Such ideas could be seen as a direct assault on the authority of priests, bishops, and the papacy itself. When Luther refused to recant, he was excommunicated. He then began to lead his own religious services, initiating the Protestant Reformation.

Martin Luther
(1483–1546) German theologian who in 1517 launched the Protestant Reformation in reaction to corruption in the Catholic Church. His followers, called Lutherans, rejected the priestly hierarchy of Catholicism, emphasizing that believers should themselves look for truth in the Bible.

● **CONTEXT&CONNECTIONS** The Protestant Reformation was not the first great rift among Christians. In the eleventh century the "Great Schism" had divided the Eastern Orthodox and Roman Catholic branches of Christendom. Catholics recognized the authority of the pope in Rome and used Latin as the official church language. Orthodox communities, many with Greek as their liturgical language, recognized instead regional patriarchs owing nominal obeisance to the patriarch of Constantinople (even after the city was captured by Muslim Turkish invaders in 1453). ●

Not all the western Europeans who left Catholicism became "Lutherans"; others developed a variety of alternative church structures, rituals, and beliefs. In the seventeenth century, the number of Protestant churches multiplied. With European kings and princes choosing sides, these divisions between Christians would lead to terrible violence (as those reading Volume 2 will learn in the next chapter).

Still, much of Europe, like Matteo Ricci's hometown in central Italy, remained securely Catholic. But the Protestant Reformation shook the Catholic Church out of its complacency, leading to a response known as the **Catholic Reformation**. A major focus of the Catholic Reformation was more rigorous training of priests to avoid the abuses that had left the church open to Protestant criticism. As a member of the Jesuit order, or Society of Jesus, Ricci was especially trained in the debating skills needed to fend off Protestant theological challenges. The Jesuits were one of several new Catholic orders developed to confront the Protestant challenge and to take advantage of the new maritime routes to spread the Catholic faith around the world, thus globalizing the Catholic Reformation. The debating skills Ricci learned to counter Protestant arguments would come in handy when he later tried to convince Chinese thinkers of the validity of his Christian faith.

Catholic Reformation
Reform movement in the Catholic Church, also called the Counter-Reformation, that developed in response to the Protestant Reformation. The church clarified church doctrines and instituted a program for better training of priests.

Another challenge to Catholic belief that developed during Ricci's lifetime was the "new science" associated with his fellow Italian **Galileo Galilei** (1564–1642). Catholic theologians had reconciled faith and reason by incorporating classical Greek thinkers, especially Aristotle, into church teachings. Galileo (gal-uh-LAY-oh) struck at the heart of that intellectual system by challenging both the authority of Aristotle and Catholic assumptions about the natural world. He contradicted

Galileo Galilei
(1564–1642) Italian scientist who provided evidence to support the heliocentric theory, challenging church doctrine and the authority of Aristotle. He was forced to recant his position by the inquisition, but his theories were vindicated during the scientific revolution.

Iranians and Europeans at the Court of Siam

The following description of foreign intrigue at the court of Siam is taken from the account of a diplomatic mission sent by the shah of Iran to the king of Siam in 1686. Written in Farsi (or Persian) by the Iranian envoy's secretary, *The Ship of Sulaimān* details both the longstanding influence of the Iranian merchant community, which had provided Siamese kings with key ministers and advisors, and the more recent favor shown to a French ("Frankish") advisor.

The author, Muhammad Rabī ibn Muhammad Ibrāhīm, emphasizes the cosmopolitan nature of the Siamese court and the extent of King Phra Narai's diplomacy across the Indian Ocean and around the world to Europe. By this time, Portuguese, Dutch, French, and British traders had been added to the existing mix of Indian, Malay, Chinese, and Iranian merchant communities in Siam.

As is so often the case, our source for this history is hardly an objective one: we should consider where and how ibn Muhammad Ibrāhīm brings a specifically Iranian point of view to his narrative. Still, much of what he tells us confirms what other accounts of the time tell us, such as the tendency of the Siamese to absorb diverse cultural influences and merge them into a distinctive blend (a process that continues in Thailand today).

Apart from giving us an inside view of Siamese politics, *The Ship of Sulaimān* also reveals a broader pattern typical of the early modern Indian Ocean: the ways in which Europeans inserted themselves into established Asian patterns of trade and diplomacy.

› Historical Thinking Skill:

PATTERNS OF CONTINUITY AND CHANGE OVER TIME **According to 'ibn Muhammad Ibrāhīm, how have the relationships between Siam and other nations present in Indian Ocean commerce changed?**

› Historical Thinking Skill:

CAUSATION **Based on this source, why do you think the French became involved in politics in the Indian Ocean, as they were in Siam, in the seventeenth century?**

Source: Muhammad Rabī ibn Muhammad Ibrāhīm, *The Ship of Sulaimān*, translated by John O'Kane (New York: Columbia University Press, 1972), pp. 94, 99–100, 103–104, 109–111.

From *The Ship of Sulaimān*

Since Siam is close to the ports of India and is situated on the sea route to China and Japan, merchants have always been attracted to settle there.... Perhaps the best of these peoples is a group of Hindus who make it a point to refrain from all forms of violence and oppression.... They refuse to kill any form of life and abstain from eating meat.... But the Siamese themselves... do not adhere to any fixed doctrine but will admit into their creed whatever is convenient.

From the time [Iranian] merchants first arrived... each was honored with the utmost respect, presented with a house, and given a specific position in the Siamese king's administration....

[T]he king of Siam sincerely was interested... to learn about the other kings of the inhabited world... and sent everywhere for pictures depicting the modes of living and the courts of foreign kings [and] grasped the clear fact that perfect kingship, glory and higher forms of government are the exclusive privilege of Iran. Thus... he abandoned his former style of clothing and started to wear Iranian clothes, our kind of long embroidered tunic, trousers, shorts and shoes and socks....

Since the king first broadened his horizons with education until this present day, he has been secretly devoted to Iran and has cherished hopes of effecting friendly contacts with our royal court.... [He has also] often sent gifts to the governor of Hyderabad and different rulers of India, as well as to kings of various other regions....

[After the death of an Iranian who served as prime minister at the Siamese court, Ibrahim tells us, the Iranian community in Siam became divided into two factions, causing a leadership vacuum.]

The group of Iranians which was left was neither worthy nor capable of assuming higher rank....

Two or three persons who were actually offered responsible positions by the king would not accept, fearing the jealousy of their Iranian peers.... Everyone whom the king entrusted with tasks and sent abroad fell into debauchery and never came back to Siam. Soon the situation reached a point of urgency.... The king was not able to find an Iranian to act as prime minister and since the Siamese are not capable of handling the affairs of state, the king never used them in the past and was not prepared to use them now. The only candidate who remained was that one Frank [Frenchman] who had originally worked as a sailor....

Since he is in fact an extremely clever man and full of shrewd tricks, from the beginning he took pains to acquire the appearance of a good character.... [In Siam] the important factor... is to know the language well and to be versed in their protocol. Thus the Frank applied himself to learn the local speech, the laws and customs of the land and he had the luck to be in a position where there were no capable rivals to oppose him.... After a short time he rose to the post of prime minister and he has held that office for three or four years now.

The Frank minister has succeeded in penetrating into the king's affections to such an extent... that there is never a moment in public or in private when he is not at the king's side. To the world at large this Christian minister displays a record of service, integrity, thrift and sincerity and makes every effort to increase the state revenues and cut down expenses. However, it is a fact that every year he sends huge sums of money from the king's treasury abroad to the Frank kingdoms, supposedly for business purposes. Up until now there have been absolutely no visible returns from that money.

In accord with the spirit of hatred which exists between Islam and the infidels, the Christian minister is ever competing with Muslims for the upper hand, and... the Frank has tried to drive the Iranians out. By way of harming their reputation he is always on the lookout to expose their improper deeds and find some sign of their disloyalty to the king....

Despite the fact that the Iranians have long taken the trouble to help the king of Siam and have displayed their generosity and fairness by instructing him about the outside world, that illegitimate-born Frank, that Christian... has caused the king to alter his attitudes and now the king's inner thoughts wander on the path of error. Outwardly as well the king appears beguiled.

The Frank minister exercises a great influence on state policy and is continually provoking the king to injustice by saying, "How long will you continue to squander your benevolence on merchants and travelers who appear from every land and especially from Hyderabad and the states of India?... If you were wise you would hire a group of Franks, build several ships and proceed to capture the merchants and travelers of those parts.... Confiscate all their cargo and supplies. That will give the foreign kings cause to take note of your rank and position...."

The result of this calamity is that lately fewer and fewer travelers and merchants have been coming to Siam. The prime minister's behavior has even caused the English king to open the doors of war and it is a standing order amongst the English to capture Siamese ships wherever they appear. The English king also gave the order that no Englishman was to remain in Siam. If this [French] Christian stays in favor and continues along the same path, the Siamese king's power and kingdom will soon go into serious decline.

Aristotle by showing that a body in motion would stay in motion unless acted upon by an external force, an insight that would later prove essential to new understandings of planetary motion. Pointing his telescope toward the heavens, Galileo discovered spots on the sun, craters on the moon, and other indications that the heavens were not a place of absolute, unchanging perfection as the church had said.

Galileo also affirmed the heliocentric theory, first proposed in 1543 by the Polish astronomer Nicolaus Copernicus, which placed the sun, rather than the earth, at the center of the solar system. Church authorities argued that the heliocentric theory contradicted the book of Genesis by displacing the earth from its central place in God's creation. The inquisition, a church bureaucracy devoted to the suppression of heresy, tried Galileo and forced him to recant his support for the heliocentric theory. But the "scientific revolution" that Galileo had helped to launch could not be so easily suppressed (as those who read Chapter 21 will learn).

The ferment of the new ideas arising from the Protestant Reformation and the "new science" helped sharpen Matteo Ricci's intellectual training and prepare him for his travels. In India he took part in lively religious and philosophical debates that were valuable preparation for his missionary work in China.

Islam, Sikhism, and Akbar's "Divine Faith," 1500–1605

In the Mughal capital of Delhi, Akbar, in addition to bringing Hindus and Muslims together, attracted to his court scholars, artists, and officials from Iran, Afghanistan, and Central Asia. Mughal India proved a fertile environment for artistic growth as Persian, Turkish, and Indian influences flowed together. The best-known example of Persian architectural influence on India is the Taj Mahal, a "love poem in marble" built by Akbar's grief-stricken grandson as a memorial to his wife.

Akbar was keenly interested in religion, and he routinely invited leaders from various religious traditions to debate at his court. In 1579, the year after Ricci arrived at Goa, an embassy arrived from the Great Mughal requesting that Catholic missionaries come to Delhi. *"We hope for nothing less than the conversion of all India,"** wrote Ricci. Two missionaries went to Delhi, bringing a richly produced, lavishly illustrated, and very costly Bible as a gift for the emperor. Although the emperor did not convert, his interest in the Jesuit mission characterized his open-mindedness.

During this time, Sufism was also attracting new converts. In addition to obeying the Muslim laws of submission, Sufis were mystics who used special prayers and rituals, such as rhythmic motion and repetitive chanting of the ninety-nine names of God, to bring them closer to the Divine. They showed great devotion to the spiritual leaders who guided them in these practices, later venerating these teachers' tombs and often treating them as places of pilgrimage. Some Muslim scholars, especially those who stressed the more legalistic aspects of Islam, looked with suspicion on the emotional Sufi forms of religious devotion. Anxious to hear both sides, Akbar brought both the legal scholars and the Sufi mystics to his court and listened intently to their debates. Akbar also brought Jews, Hindus, and representatives of other faiths, such as Sikhs (sicks), to Delhi. Sikhism was a new faith whose monotheistic followers rejected the caste system while striving to reconcile Islamic and Hindu beliefs. Akbar extended to the Sikhs the same tolerance he had

---

*"The Diary of Matthew Ricci," in *Matthew Ricci, China in the Sixteenth Century*, trans. Louis Gallagher (New York: Random House, 1942, 1970), p. 114.

granted more established religions (though a later emperor would reverse that policy).

Having encountered so many different spiritual traditions, Akbar announced his own adherence to a "Divine Faith" that he said both included and transcended them all:

> *O God, in every temple I see people that seek Thee; in every language I hear spoken, people praise Thee; if it be a mosque, people murmur in prayer; if it be a Christian church they ring the bell for love of Thee... it is Thou whom I seek from temple to temple.**

Akbar's "Divine Faith" never spread beyond the Mughal court and disappeared after his own death.

● **CONTEXT&CONNECTIONS** Centuries later, a Hindu reformer paid tribute to Akbar's open-mindedness, contrasting him with later, more orthodox Mughal sultans. Still "*celebrated for his clemency, for his encouragement of learning, and for granting civil and religious liberty to his subjects,*" he said, Akbar "*reigned happy, extended his power and his dominions, and his memory is still adored.*"† ●

Meanwhile, Hinduism itself was undergoing important changes and reforms. The epic story of the *Ramayana*, formerly read only by priests trained in the ancient Sanskrit language, was retold in 1575 by a prominent poet using the commonly spoken Hindi language, making this story of the ancient king, a manifestation of the god Vishnu, more accessible. This development reflected new forms of Hindu devotion that de-emphasized the role of Brahmin priests. Like the translation of the Bible into vernacular languages and the new availability of Buddhist texts in the Korean han'gul script, the Hindi *Ramayana* promoted religious inquiry at all levels of society, not just among kings, priests, and philosophers.

Ricci in China: Catholicism Meets Neo-Confucianism, 1582–1610

Ming China was less religiously diverse than Mughal India, with Buddhism as the empire's majority faith. In fact, when Ricci first arrived there, he adopted the beard, flowing robes, and shaved head of a Buddhist priest.

Private Collection/De Agostini Picture Library/Bridgeman Images

Akbar with Representatives of Various Religions at His Court For years, the Mughal emperor Akbar hosted weekly conversations among scholars and priests of numerous religions, including the Jesuits seen here on the left. Akbar sponsored the translation of varied religious texts, including the Christian Bible, into Farsi (the Persian language) even though he himself was illiterate. When criticized by some Muslim scholars for his patronage of Hindu arts and his openness to other religious traditions, including the Jewish faith, Akbar is said to have replied, "*God loves beauty.*"

---

*Steven Warshaw and C. David Bromwell with A. J. Tudisco, *India Emerges* (Berkeley: Diablo Press, 1974), p. 60.

†Raja Rammohun Roy, *The English Works*, vol. 1, ed. Jogendra Chunder Ghose (Calcutta: Srikanta Roy, 1901), p. 307.

He soon learned, however, that the Confucian scholar-officials mocked the poorly educated Buddhist clergy. Ricci subsequently changed his appearance to appeal to this more prestigious class of individuals. His plan was to convert China from the top down.

Confucian scholars emphasized education as the main route to self-cultivation. While most of the emperor's subjects remained illiterate peasant cultivators, boys from more privileged households were taught to read from a young age. After they had mastered the basics, they had to memorize the classic texts of Confucianism, collections of poems, and histories of past times that usually focused on the virtues of ancient sages.

In theory, any young man could take the annual examinations and, if successful, become an imperial official. In reality, only the elite could afford the private tutors needed for success. Still, the Ming system was based on merit: wealth and status could not purchase high office, and even the privileged had to undergo years of intensive study.

● **CONTEXT&CONNECTIONS** In the nineteenth century, Chinese reformers hoped to strengthen the empire's position in an industrializing world by balancing tradition with modernization, for example, by adjusting the imperial examinations to include natural sciences, mathematics, and modern languages. Conservatives resisted those changes, and China fell behind its rivals. Even today, though Confucianism is no longer the topic, aspiring university students in China (and Korea and Japan) study intensively for brutally difficult examinations to earn a place at a top university and thus a secure government job. ●

AP® THEMES

How did the teachings and practice of Confucianism influence gender roles and family structures in China?

Although women were barred from taking the examinations, the Ming emphasis on education did contribute to the spread of female literacy. Foreign observers noted how many girls were able to read and write. However, while boys read histories of sages and virtuous officials, girls usually read stories about women who submitted to their parents when they were young, obeyed their husbands once they were married, and listened to their sons when they became widowed. Singled out for special praise were widows who demonstrated eternal loyalty to their husbands by declining to be remarried. Chinese girls were thereby indoctrinated into the Confucian ideal of strict gender hierarchy.

Matteo Ricci paid careful attention to debates between advocates of various schools of Confucianism as he built up an argument for the compatibility of Confucianism and Christianity. At this time the Neo-Confucian philosophy of Wang Yangming (1472–1529) was especially influential. While other Confucians had emphasized close observation of the external world, Wang stressed self-reflection, arguing that everyone possesses innate knowledge. Ricci accused Wang's Neo-Confucian followers of distorting Confucianism, arguing that the original ethos of Confucianism was both more pure and more compatible with Christianity. By returning to the original works of the sages, Ricci said, the Chinese literati would discover that one could convert to Christianity while retaining their ancient ethical and philosophical traditions.

Once his language skills were sufficiently developed, Ricci took advantage of a favorite Ming pastime to share his views. Scholar-officials would often invite interesting speakers to a banquet and, after dinner, hold philosophical debates. For many in the audience Ricci's well-known ability to instantly memorize and repeat long lists of information, and even repeat them backward, would have been of greater interest than his views on Confucian philosophy and Christian theology. It was a highly relevant skill in a society where difficult exams were the main path to power and status. While his hosts might have been entertained by his arguments, few were persuaded by them.

Ricci also impressed his hosts with examples of European art and technology, especially printed books, paintings, clocks, and maps. Some Chinese artists experimented with European techniques of landscape painting, and Ming astronomers were impressed by European telescopes and the precision with which the Jesuits could predict such events as eclipses. Late-sixteenth-century European clocks, while not very reliable by later standards, were much more accurate than the water clocks used by the Chinese. Ricci's world map, locating the "western barbarians" for the first time in relation to the "Middle Kingdom," was such a success that Chinese artisans were employed to print reproductions.

For Ricci, however, mnemonic tricks, maps, and clocks were only a means to convert his audience to Christianity. Criticizing both Buddhism and Neo-Confucianism, Ricci emphasized those aspects of the Western tradition that appealed most to Confucian intellectuals: its moral and ethical dimensions rather than its character as a revealed religion. For example, after learning that Chinese scholars were disturbed by accounts of the suffering and death of Jesus, he largely avoided that central aspect of Christianity. (See the feature "World History in Today's World: Christianity in China.")

The most influential work published in Chinese under Ricci's name was *The True Meaning of the Lord of Heaven*. Composed together with Chinese Christian converts, who provided key insights on Confucian thinking and guidance with difficult translation issues, it is a dialogue between a "Chinese Scholar" and a "Western Scholar." In the following passage the text criticizes Buddhism and argues for the compatibility of Confucianism and Christianity:

CHINESE SCHOLAR: *The Buddha taught that the visible world emerges from "voidness" and made "voidness" the end of all effort. The Confucians say: "In the processes of Yi there exists the Supreme Ultimate" and therefore make "existence" the basic principle [of all things] and "sincerity" the subject of the study of self-cultivation. I wonder who, in your revered view, is correct?*

WESTERN SCHOLAR: *The "voidness" taught by the Buddha [is] totally at variance with the doctrine concerning the Lord of Heaven [i.e., Christianity], and it is therefore abundantly clear that [it does] not merit esteem. When it comes to the "existence" and "sincerity" of the Confucians, however... they would seem to be close to the truth.**

---

*Matteo Ricci, *The True Meaning of the Lord of Heaven*, trans. Douglas Lancashire and Peter Hu Kuo-chen, S.J. (Paris: Institut Ricci-Centre d'études chinoises, 1985), p. 99.

Christianity in China

Marxist ideology predicts that religion will fade away as an educated society develops a more scientific outlook. But even after six decades of official atheism, the number of practicing Chinese Christians in the People's Republic of China has increased dramatically.

Exact numbers are difficult to obtain because most Chinese Christians practice their faith outside of the official religious "Patriotic Associations" recognized by the government. Thus, although there are about 12 million Roman Catholics, at least half are members of unregistered congregations, unrecognized (and therefore not counted) by the government. When the communist government set up the National Catholic Patriotic Association in the 1950s, it took over from the Vatican the power to appoint bishops, a role central to church tradition and to papal authority. Many Catholics, still loyal to the papacy, worship with "underground" priests and bishops. Though there has been some diplomacy aimed at reconciliation, tensions between the Vatican and the communist government over appointment of bishops continues, and Chinese Catholics were prevented from traveling to South Korea when Pope Francis I visited Seoul in 2014.

Meanwhile, Protestant growth in China has been even more spectacular, from less than 1 million in 1949 to perhaps 60 million today, with the vast majority practicing in unregistered churches. In the 1950s, the government amalgamated all the different Protestant denominations into one bland, mainstream organization: the National Protestant Patriotic Association. But the official church was never intended to promote or accept the kind of rapid growth we see today, nor are most communist officials tolerant of the more emotional, evangelical forms of worship that now appeal to so many.

"Contain religion" is official policy, and local party bosses often prevent the prominent display of crosses. Occasionally, there are signs of conciliation; perhaps some communist authorities recognize that churches help people to cope with the destabilizing social changes brought on by rapid economic growth. Still, arbitrary oppression can reappear at a moment's notice. In early 2014, for example, officials in Wenzhou ordered the destruction of a large and prominent church they had earlier approved, citing "zoning" violations. "People are stunned," said one local Christian. "They have completely lost faith in the local religious authorities."

Will at least limited government tolerance toward Christianity continue? Perhaps, so longe as unregistered churches lay low and avoid national or international links that challenge communist party supremacy.

Source: "Church-State Clash in China Coalesces Around a Toppled Spire," Ian Johnson, *New York Times*, May 29, 2014.

Such arguments did not convince many, but at least in China Ming authorities accepted Catholicism as a legitimate school of philosophy (as in Mughal India, and in sharp contrast to the repression faced by Christians in seventeenth-century Japan).

Some European Catholics felt that Ricci's attempt to reconcile Christianity and Confucianism went too far. For example, Ricci argued that veneration of ancestors was compatible with Christianity and the biblical command to "honor your father and your mother." Less flexible church authorities felt that Chinese ancestor rites were pagan and should be rejected. Ricci knew that such a rigid interpretation of cultural practice would limit the appeal of Christianity among potential converts, who would be ostracized by family and friends if they abandoned their household shrines. In fact, after an eighteenth-century pope later declared that ancestor worship was idolatrous, Catholicism lost its status as a legitimate faith in China. Nevertheless, by debating these issues, Ricci had helped to lay the foundation of what became an ongoing "great encounter" between Europe and China.

Empires of Land and Sea

When Christopher Columbus sailed west to reach the "Indies," he greatly underestimated the circumference of the globe. The better-informed Portuguese, whose route Matteo Ricci followed to China, succeeded where Columbus failed by establishing a direct oceanic link to the riches of the Indian Ocean and South China Sea. Nevertheless, the biologic, demographic, political, and economic consequences of Columbus's journeys were more dramatic. The "Columbian encounter," which brought the Eastern and Western Hemispheres into systematic contact for the first time, was in many ways the starting point of modern world history.

Prior to 1500 the Indian Ocean, in contrast to the Atlantic, was already interconnected, although those connections were commercial and cultural rather than political or military, and largely remained so. Ming emperors had proven uninterested in pursuing political dominance across the ocean at the time of Zheng He in the fifteenth century (see Chapter 15), while the Portuguese and other European powers tried but failed. The story of maritime expansion in Asia is therefore as much one of continuity as of change. Massive land-based empires, especially the Mughal dynasty in India and the Ming dynasty in China, remained the dominant powers. Inter-Asian trade remained the key to commercial profit, even as the Portuguese and later the Dutch inserted themselves into these markets. In Africa, the Atlantic slave trade was new and an ominous sign for the future, but at first it affected only a few coastal West African societies; East African city-states continued their traditional orientation toward commerce with India and the Persian Gulf.

However, there were also important changes in the Indian Ocean world in the sixteenth and seventeenth centuries. The destructive power of ship-based cannon allowed the Portuguese to seize crucial transit points such as Malacca, setting an example that would later be followed by the Dutch, British, and French. The innovative ship designs and commercial practices of the Dutch further stimulated trade and made the competition between European chartered companies a new feature of Asian politics. The influx of American silver was

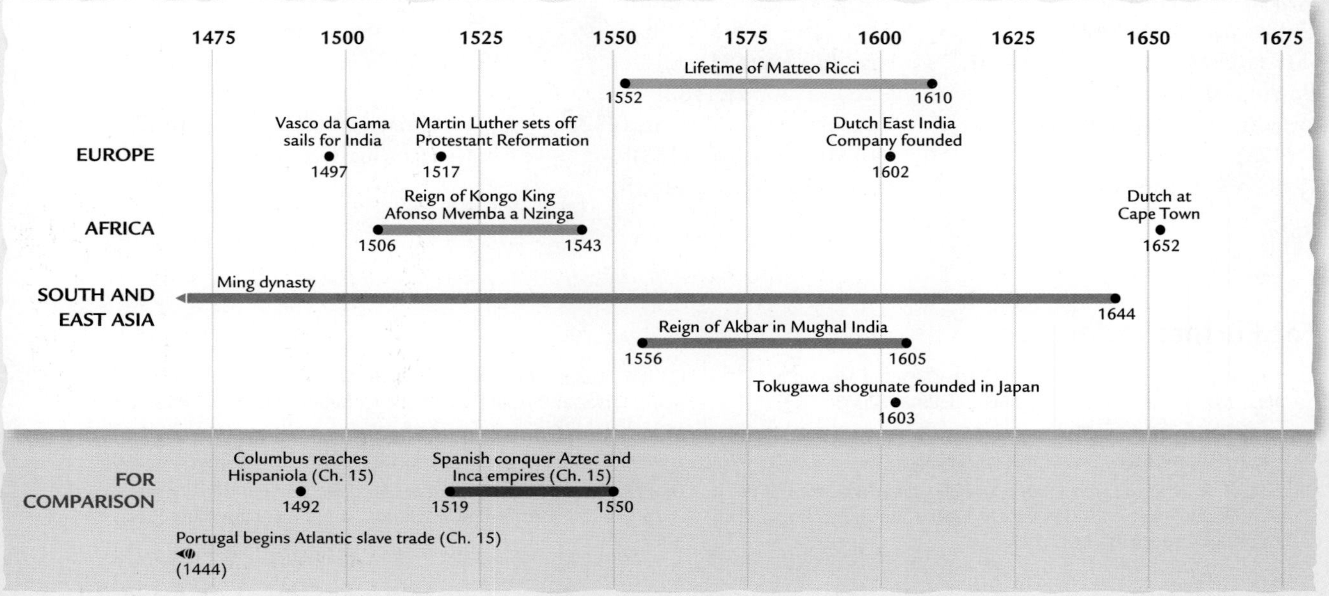

crucial. Increased availability of silver coins facilitated trade and gave European merchants the wherewithal to compete more effectively in Asian markets. The implications were not yet clear to Asian rulers, but the foundations had been laid for a new global market controlled from Europe.

Christian missionaries like Matteo Ricci played only a small part during this time of intellectual ferment across Afro-Eurasia. Whereas in some areas of the Americas, such as the Andes and Mesoamerica, conversions to Catholicism quickly followed Spanish conquest, in Africa and Asia it was Islam that expanded during this period. While the Protestant Reformation played a role in propelling the Jesuits and other Catholic orders out into the world to expand the pope's religious domain, and while "new science" forced the Catholic Church to respond to new intellectual challenges, neither European science nor religious reform had a significant impact in Asia before the end of the seventeenth century. Instead, existing religious and intellectual modes of discourse—between Muslims and Hindus in India, and between Buddhists and Confucians in China—remained the norm. In some places Christian missionaries contributed to the debate, but only in rare cases did they have a significant influence; in this regard, Japan and Kongo were exceptional.

Meanwhile, religious divisions were deepening in western Eurasia, where in both Christian and Muslim lands religion and politics formed a combustible mixture in the seventeenth and eighteenth centuries. The struggle for religious ascendency in western Europe divided the continent between warring Catholic and Protestant powers, while the old rivalry between the Sunni and Shi'ite branches of Islam magnified the struggle between the Iranian Safavid and Turkish Ottoman empires for regional predominance. In the new age of gunpowder weapons, the stakes of such conflicts would prove higher than ever before.

Key Terms

Matteo Ricci (470)
Vasco da Gama (471)
joint-stock companies (474)
bourgeoisie (475)
Dutch East India Company (475)
Kongo kingdom (477)
Mughal dynasty (480)
Emperor Akbar (480)
Nur Jahan (481)
Ming dynasty (482)
examination system (482)
Wanli Emperor (483)
Emperor Sejong (483)
Lê dynasty (484)
Toyotomi Hideyoshi (485)
Tokugawa shogunate (485)
Martin Luther (487)
Catholic Reformation (487)
Galileo Galilei (487)

For Further Reference

Brocky, Liam Matthew. *Journey to the East: The Jesuit Mission to China, 1579–1724*. Cambridge, Mass.: Belknap, 2008.

Brook, Timothy. *The Troubled Empire: China in the Yuan and Ming Dynasties*. Cambridge, Mass.: Belknap, 2010.

Chaudhuri, K. N. *Asia Before Europe: Economy and Civilization of the Indian Ocean from the Rise of Islam to 1750*. Cambridge, England: Cambridge University Press, 1990.

Clulow, Adam. *The Company and the Shogun: The Dutch Encounter with Tokugawa Japan*. New York: Columbia University Press, 2014.

Cook, Harold J. *Matters of Exchange: Commerce, Medicine, and Science in the Dutch Golden Age*. New Haven: Yale University Press, 2008.

Dale, Stephen Frederick. *Indian Merchants and Eurasian Trade, 1600–1750*. Cambridge, England: Cambridge University Press, 1994.

Findly, Ellison Banks. *Nur Jahan: Empress of Mughal India*. New York: Oxford University Press, 1993.

Green, Toby. *The Rise of the Trans-Atlantic Slave Trade in Western Africa, 1300–1589*. New York: Cambridge University Press, 2011.

Laven, Mary. *Mission to China: Matteo Ricci and the Jesuit Encounter with the East*. London: Faber & Faber, 2011.

Pearson, Michael. *The Indian Ocean*. New York: Routledge, 2007.

Sherif, Abdul. *Dhow Cultures and the Indian Ocean: Cosmopolitanism, Commerce, and Islam*. New York: Columbia University Press, 2010.

Spence, Jonathan. *The Memory Palace of Matteo Ricci*. New York: Viking Penguin, 1984.

Subrahmanyam, Sanjay. *The Portuguese Empire in Asia, 1500–1700*. 2d ed. London: Wiley-Blackwell, 2012.

Swope, Kenneth M. *A Dragon's Head and a Serpent's Tail: Ming China and the First Great East Asian War, 1592-1598*. Norman: University of Oklahoma Press, 2012.

AP® Review Questions for Chapter 16

Multiple-Choice Questions

QUESTIONS 1–4 REFER TO THE FOLLOWING PASSAGE.

It seems to be quite remarkable . . . that in a kingdom of almost limitless expanse and innumerable population, and abounding in copious supplies of every description, though they have a well-equipped army and navy that could easily conquer the neighboring nations, neither the King nor his people ever think of waging a war of aggression. . . . In this respect they are much different from the people of Europe, who are frequently discontent with their own governments and covetous of what others enjoy. . . . Another remarkable fact and . . . marking a difference from the West, is that the entire kingdom is administered by . . . Philosophers. The responsibility for orderly management of the entire realm is wholly and completely committed to their charge and care. . . . Fighting and violence among the people are practically unheard of. . . . On the contrary, one who will not fight and restrains himself from returning a blow is praised for his prudence and bravery.

—Matteo Ricci on China, ca. 1600–1610

1. Matteo Ricci writes that the entire country is administered by philosophers; this is most likely a reference to which of the following?
   (A) The importance of Buddhist monks and teachers in the imperial court
   (B) The growing influence of Christianity in the empire
   (C) The Confucian elites running the civil service
   (D) The experts in Daoism working with medicine and searching for immortality

2. Ricci's admiration for the moral character of the Chinese is a reference to which of the following?
   (A) The Daoist concept of balance and harmony in life
   (B) The Confucian belief in filial piety and deference to superiors
   (C) The Buddhist emphasis on compassion and monastic life
   (D) The Legalist use of fear of harsh punishments and rewards

3. The presence of Matteo Ricci in China was the result of which of the following?
   (A) The environmental degradation of European farmland
   (B) Expansion of European kingdoms into Central Asia
   (C) Greater presence of European merchants on the Silk Road
   (D) Increased interaction because of intensified European maritime activity

4. Which would best explain Matteo Ricci's claim that the Chinese were happy with their government?
   (A) The government constantly feared peasant revolts.
   (B) The merchant classes ran most aspects of the government and promoted trade.
   (C) Filial piety meant showing respect to one's superiors.
   (D) Daoism taught that the best government is no government.

QUESTIONS 5–7 REFER TO THE FOLLOWING PASSAGE.

Brother king: Many of our people, keenly desirous as they are of the wares and things of your Kingdoms . . . seize many of our people, freed and exempt men. . . . That is why we beg of your Highness to help and assist us in this matter . . . because it is our will that in these Kingdoms there should not be any trade of slaves nor outlet for them.

—Letter of King Afonso of the Kongo to the king of Portugal, early sixteenth century

5. The communication between these two kings was the result of which of the following?
   (A) The creation of the Atlantic trade system
   (B) Greater presence of Europeans in the trans-Saharan trade
   (C) European imperialism in the African interior
   (D) The discovery of Christian kingdoms in southern Africa

6. The taking of Africans by the Europeans is best understood by which of the following?
   (A) Increased trade between European states and the Aztec empire
   (B) Interaction between the Western and Eastern Hemispheres
   (C) Intensification of the Indian Ocean trade
   (D) The centralized nature of most states during this time period

7. Why does Afonso I consider the king of Portugal to be his brother?
   (A) Afonso I had adopted Christianity
   (B) Shared cultural heritage
   (C) Significant intermarrying between the two kingdoms
   (D) A mutual hatred for the English

QUESTIONS 8–10 REFER TO THE FOLLOWING IMAGE.

8. Interactions like the one in the painting led to which of the following?
   (A) Stricter adherence to religious traditions
   (B) The separation of state and religious institutions
   (C) Intensified religious exchanges
   (D) The eclipse of state institutions by religious elites

9. Akbar's weekly meetings with religious scholars are evidence of which claim?
   (A) Increased interactions led to syncretic beliefs and religious reform.
   (B) Increased religious interactions led leaders to take tough stands against foreign faiths.
   (C) Increased interregional and global trade networks facilitated the spread of religion.
   (D) Increased trade led to the growing status of merchants in many regions.

10. Based on the painting, Akbar, like other leaders of the time period, needed to address which of the following?
   (A) Lack of cultural creativity because of religious prohibitions
   (B) The needs of a multireligious population
   (C) Eliminating all rival religions in the region
   (D) Promoting religious authority and weakening the merchant classes

Short-Answer Questions

1. Chapter 16 describes how, in the sixteenth and early seventeenth centuries, more direct and sustained networks accelerated commercial and cultural interaction among Europe, Africa, and South and East Asia. Answer parts A and B.
   A. Identify and explain ONE reason for this change or development.
   B. Identify and explain TWO effects of this change or development.

2. Answer parts A and B.
   A. Identify and analyze TWO examples of religious interaction from the time period of 1500–1700.
   B. Identify and analyze ONE effect of this interaction on the region.

17 Religion, Politics, and the Balance of Power in Western Eurasia, 1500–1750

Evliya Çelebi

The adventures of **Evliya Çelebi** (ev-lee-yah che-LEH-bee; 1610–1683) began with a dream. Son of the chief goldsmith to the powerful sultan of the Ottoman empire, at eighteen years old Çelebi was already highly gifted in the art of religious recitation (he would recite the entire Quran over one thousand times in his lifetime). In 1628, he dreamt of a visit from the Prophet Muhammad himself, who told him, *"You will be a world traveler and unique among men."** This nocturnal blessing was welcome, since Çelebi already had a great curiosity about the world around him. *"I longed,"* he wrote, *"to set out for the Holy Land, towards Baghdad and Mecca and Medina and Cairo and Damascus."** Visiting those places and many more, he became the greatest of all Ottoman voyagers: even today in the Turkish language, you say of someone who feels a constant urge to travel: "Evliya Çelebi gibi," "He is like Evliya Çelebi."

As recorded in his *Book of Travels*, Çelebi ventured from his birthplace of Constantinople (today's Istanbul) across the vast Ottoman empire. His most memorable journey came when he performed the hajj, visiting the holy sites of Mecca, Medina, and Jerusalem, before settling in Cairo, the great commercial and intellectual center of early modern Islam. He also went beyond the empire, to Europe and Iran. In Europe, he witnessed and participated in the wars fought between the sultan's forces and those of the Holy Roman empire, while in Iran he described the tense relations between its Safavid dynasty and his own Ottoman rulers.

Though both the Ottomans and Safavids were Muslim societies, religious differences amplified their political and military competition. The Ottomans, controlling the most holy sites of Islam in Arabia, were defenders of the dominant Sunni (SOO-nee) branch of Islam, while the Safavids promoted the competing Shi'ite (SHEE-ite) interpretation. Çelebi encapsulated the competition between them in an account where, with characteristic

---

*Robert Dankoff and Sooyong Kim, translation and commentary, *An Ottoman Traveller: Selections from the* Book of Travels *of Evliya Çelebi* (London: Eland Publishing, 2010), pp. 7, 36. Reprinted by permission.

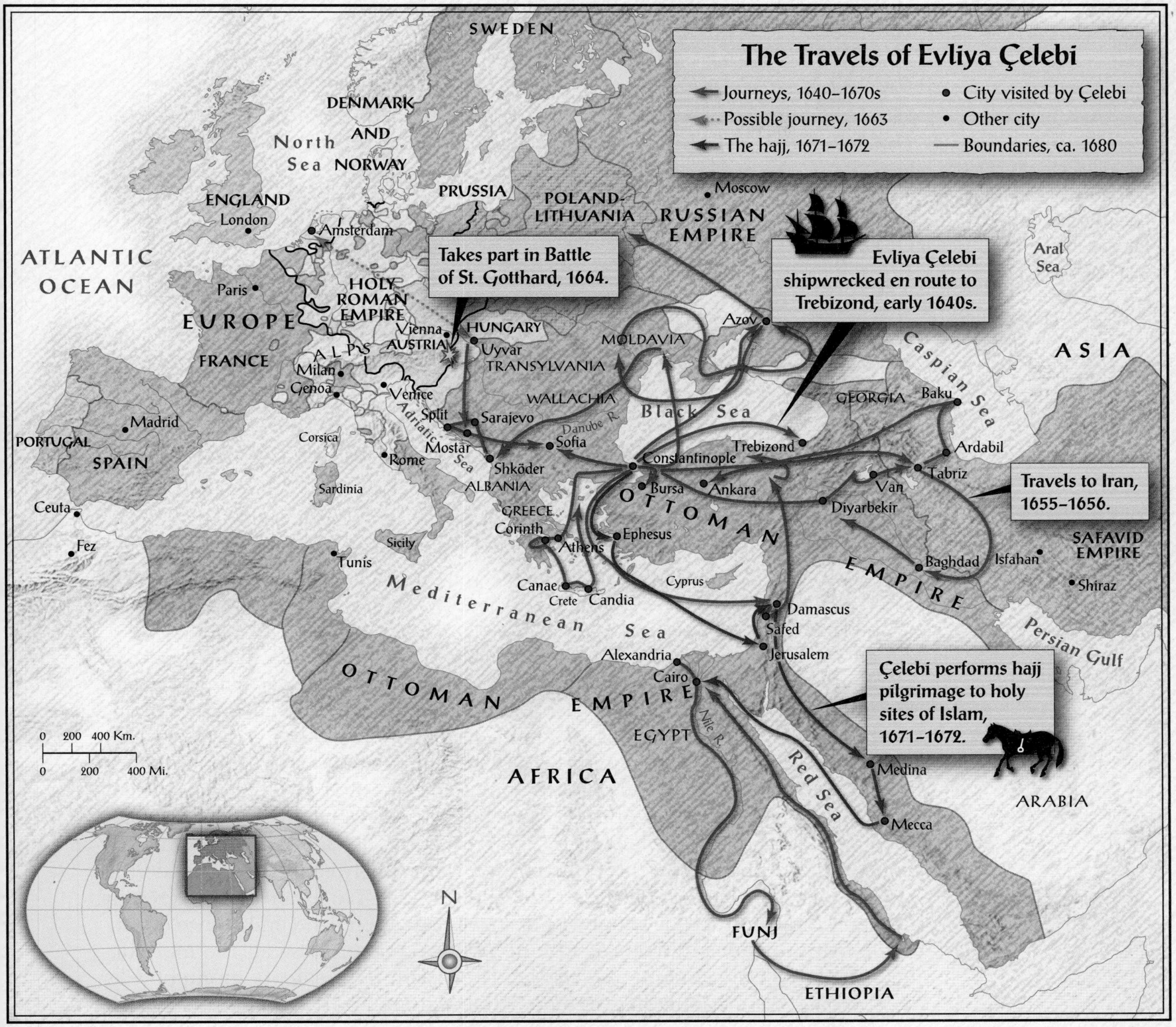

humor, he described how a sixteenth-century Ottoman ruler rejected a gift from the Shi'ite Safavid shah while building the extraordinary Sûleymaniye Mosque:

> *The minaret on the left with the three galleries is called the Jewel Minaret.... The reason is that, in order for the foundation to settle, Sûleyman Khan had the building of this mosque stop for a year.... Shah Thamasp, the King of Persia [Iran] when he heard of the halt*

Evliya Çelebi

(1610–1683) The most famous of Ottoman travelers; his writings contain rich portraits of his own society as well as those he visited in Europe, Iran, Arabia, and North Africa.

*to construction, dispatched a great embassy with 1000 purses of money and a box of all kinds of valuable jewels. In his letter he wrote, "I heard that you did not have enough money to complete the mosque.... I have sent you this amount of money from the treasury and these jewels. Sell them and spend the money, and take pains to finish the mosque. Let us have a share in your pious works...." Sûleyman Khan was incensed by the letter. In the presence of the [Safavid] emissary he distributed the 1000 purses of money to the Jews in Constantinople ... then he gave the architect Sinan the box of jewels while the emissary was still present and said to him: "The so-called precious stones he sent are worthless beside the stones of my mosque. So put them with the rest and use them in the construction." When the emissary understood the situation, he was dumbstruck.... Meanwhile, the chief architect used the jewels to decorate the grooves of that minaret with artistry of all sorts ... that is why it is called the "Jewel Minaret."**

When Çelebi reported this legendary exchange of insults a century later, the struggle between the Ottoman and Safavid empires for the geographic heart of the Islamic world continued.

In seventeenth-century Europe as well, religious divisions helped fuel the competition of ambitious men and women for wealth and power. The Protestant Reformation was opposed by the Habsburg dynasty, which, with its rich capital at Madrid funded by the wealth of the Americas, took up the Catholic cause. Çelebi's travels took him to the Habsburg-ruled city of Vienna, from which Catholic emperors struggled not only to fend off Ottoman offensives into central Europe—Çelebi himself participated in one of these campaigns in 1664—but also to suppress the theological and political challenge of the Protestant Reformation. From the early sixteenth until the late seventeenth century, warfare between Catholics and Protestants was a constant of European life, and Catholic–Protestant rivalry strongly influenced the political development of states such as England and France. Meanwhile, with religious differences making political compromise all the more difficult in both Christendom and the lands of Islam, refinements in gunpowder technologies were leading to ever more lethal warfare.

Straddling Europe and Asia, the Russian empire drew on the political and cultural traditions of both. Though its rural economy was relatively backward, its rulers amassed great wealth and power, commanding a huge standing army. As it expanded, the Russian empire became home to a wide diversity of peoples, including Jews, Armenians, and Muslims.

Since the interconnected societies of western Eurasia, from England in the northwest to Iran in the southeast, were at the center of emerging world systems of trade and empire, the competition among them had a lasting influence on the global balance of power. By the mid-eighteenth century, the Safavid empire had

---

*Robert Dankoff and Sooyong Kim, translation and commentary, *An Ottoman Traveller: Selections from the* Book of Travels *of Evliya Çelebi* (London: Eland Publishing, 2010), pp. 13–14. Reprinted by permission.

collapsed and Iran would no longer be a major political player. The Ottoman empire, while still a significant presence, had lost the initiative to rising European states, including a newly expansive Russian empire and Prussia, the strongest of numerous German kingdoms. The balance of power in western Eurasia now favored France, Britain, Austria, Prussia, and Russia, and by 1750 national competition had largely replaced religious rivalries. The building blocks for a European-dominated global order were in place.

KEY CONCEPT QUESTIONS

- › How did religious division intensify the Ottoman-Safavid state rivalry? **(Key Concept 4.3)**
- › How did the Protestant Reformation influence the power of existing political and economic elites? **(Key Concept 4.2)**
- › How did the increase in interactions between Europe and Asia affect transcontinental groups such as Russians, Armenians, and Jews? **(Key Concept 4.1)**
- › How did the balance of power in western Eurasia shift from 1450 to 1750? **(Key Concept 4.3)**

Ottoman Power and Safavid Challenge

Their seizure of Constantinople in 1453 had magnified the Ottoman empire's Great Power status and facilitated their further expansion into southeastern Europe. The Ottomans were the most successful of the Turkic-speaking peoples who had migrated westward from the central Eurasian steppes to conquer sedentary agricultural societies. Similarly, the Safavids were also Turkic-speaking and nomadic in origin, but they assimilated into Persian culture as they established their capital at the great city of Isfahan (is-fah-HAHN), a cosmopolitan center of trade and culture. Both societies were Islamic, although the Sunni Ottomans and the Shi'ite (SHEE-ite) Safavids embraced conflicting interpretations of their common faith.

Shi'ites believe that when Muhammad died, religious and political authority should have passed through his son-in-law Ali to Ali's son Hussein. Sunni Muslims, in contrast, argue that the Prophet's successors (the *caliphs*) could be chosen freely from among Muhammad's close companions. In the seventh century, the two sides came to blows. First, Ali was killed, and then his son Hussein fell in battle. Shi'ites still visit the tomb of Hussein in Karbala (in today's Iraq), and every year an elaborate festival of mourning is held to commemorate his death.

Educated men and women in both empires learned Arabic for prayer and religious study, but for everyday purposes the Ottomans spoke Turkish and the Safavids spoke Farsi (also known as Persian). In both empires, Sufi brotherhoods developed complex rituals designed to bring their members closer to God.

Ultimately, the Ottoman system of government proved more enduring. Although assaults on Vienna were turned back in both 1529 and 1683, the

Ottomans remained a major power in Europe as well as North Africa and the Arab lands southeast of Anatolia. While the Safavids collapsed in the early eighteenth century, they bequeathed a large swath of Shi'ite population as a permanent legacy of their rule.

The Ottoman Empire, 1500–1650

The splendor of the Sublime Porte, center of Ottoman power in Constantinople, was legendary. The sultan's palace defined the city as a center of political power, while other monumental buildings expressed its religious focus—for example, the Hagia Sophia, an ancient Christian church converted into a mosque after the Ottoman capture of the city, and the sixteenth-century Sûleymaniye Mosque. European visitors of the time were awestruck by the Ottoman capital. Çelebi describes one such group of *"Frankish [European] infidels": "Wherever they looked, they put finger to mouth and bit it in astonishment.... They threw off their Frankish hats and cried out in awe, 'Maria, Maria!'"**

The people of Constantinople fully mirrored the ethnic and religious diversity of the empire. In the neighborhood of Galata, for example, Çelebi found *"eighteen Muslim quarters, seventy quarters of Greek infidels, three of cranky Franks, one of Jews, and two of Armenians."* Çelebi noted that one neighborhood was full of *"grief-stricken* Mudejars *[Muslims] who came from Spain, driven out by the infidels"** after the Christian reconquest of Iberia was completed in 1492 (see Chapter 15). Although this diverse population was residentially segregated, and each community was substantially responsible for its own internal affairs, they shared common public spaces such as markets, gardens, and public baths. Constantinople was one of the world's most cosmopolitan cities, *"famous,"* Çelebi wrote, *"among travelers in Arabia and Persia, India and Yemen and Ethiopia."**

The glories of their capital reflected the successes of Ottoman governments and military elites in effectively administering and taxing the peasants, craftsmen, and merchants of their sprawling and productive domains. From their Anatolian heartland, where Turkish peasants predominated, the Ottomans added Palestine, Syria, Arabia, Iraq, and much of Hungary to the sultan's domains in the sixteenth century.

Though cavalry warfare was the origin and heart of the Ottoman military, after the conquest of Constantinople, with outlets to both the Black Sea and the Mediterranean, a great navy was constructed as well. By the sixteenth century, the Ottoman fleet had become dominant in the Black Sea and on the eastern and southern shores of the Mediterranean, and the Ottoman navy defeated Christian fleets in the Red Sea, Persian Gulf, and Indian Ocean. From southeastern Europe, Ottoman armies marched into the German-speaking lands of central Europe. The Ottomans also ruled Greece and conquered all of the Mediterranean coast of North Africa except Morocco, which remained the only significant Arab-ruled kingdom. In Egypt, Arabia, and Syria, Arabs were ruled by Turkish-speaking Ottoman administrators. Meanwhile, the increasing scale of Ottoman military operations on land and sea and the organization necessary to use gunpowder weapons, such as muskets and cannons, led to greater military professionalism.

---

*Robert Dankoff and Sooyong Kim, translation and commentary, *An Ottoman Traveller: Selections from the* Book of Travels *of Evliya Çelebi* (London: Eland Publishing, 2010), pp. 16, 18–19, 21. Reprinted by permission.

During this period, slaves became more important in the Ottoman military and in the central administration of the empire (after a winning battle in southeastern Europe, Evliya Çelebi casually described his "*share of the booty*" as "*one girl, one boy, and seven horses*"*). Indeed, to help meet their ever-increasing military manpower needs, the Ottomans had begun to rely on enslaved soldiers from conquered Christian lands, the **Janissaries**. Janissaries trained year-round and became skilled at using gunpowder weapons. As the need for such soldiers increased, the Ottomans regularly enslaved Christian youth in the Balkan and Caucasus Mountains to meet the demand, leaving a simmering sense of grievance among the communities that were forced to give up their children.

Janissaries Taken from Christian villages as boys, converted to Islam, and rigorously trained in the military arts, for centuries Janissaries formed the elite corps of the Ottoman military. They are shown here in 1683 during their siege of the Habsburg capital of Vienna. Notwithstanding their elaborate headgear, colorful uniforms, and curved swords, the muskets at their shoulders indicate the centrality of gunpowder weapons to seventeenth-century warfare in western Eurasia.

The concept of "elite slaves" may sound strange, but reliance on slaves as soldiers and administrators was an old tradition. A sultan might not be able to trust his own brothers or sons because they were vying for power of their own, but the loyalty of a slave general was absolute. If he disobeyed he could simply be killed: he had no family ties to protect him. By the sixteenth century, Janissaries played a central role in administration as well as in the military. Even the sultan's chief minister was a slave.

After conquering Arabia and Palestine, the Ottomans controlled Mecca, Medina, and Jerusalem, the three holiest cities for Muslims. Mecca was the Prophet's home city and the focal point of the Muslim *hajj*, or pilgrimage; Medina is an Arabian town that gave Muhammad shelter and rallied to his side when the people of Mecca at first rejected his message; Jerusalem is the city from which he is reported to have ascended into heaven after his death.

Janissaries

An elite corps of slaves trained as professional soldiers in the Ottoman military. Janissary soldiers were Christian youths from the Balkans who were pressed into service and forced to convert to Islam.

Since these were the holy pilgrimage sites to which all Muslims aspired to travel, their supervision was a great responsibility. Ottoman sultans therefore emphasized their role as guardians of Islam and claimed to be *caliphs*, successors to the earthly power of the Prophet.

While basing their legitimacy on Islam, however, Ottoman rulers needed to stabilize their rule over dozens of different communities with diverse religious

*Robert Dankoff and Sooyong Kim, translation and commentary, *An Ottoman Traveller: Selections from the* Book of Travels *of Evliya Çelebi* (London: Eland Publishing, 2010), p. 190. Reprinted by permission.

Süleyman
(r. 1520–1566) Credited with the development of literature, art, architecture, and law and for inclusive policies toward religious minorities, Süleyman extended the Ottoman empire while maintaining economic and political stability.

and legal traditions. The master strategist was Sultan **Süleyman** (r. 1520–1566). A strong military leader who greatly expanded the empire, Süleyman (soo-lay-MAHN) also devised an administrative system that reconciled central authority with local autonomy. His court reflected the ethnic diversity of his empire. Turkish was the language of administration and military command, Arabic the language of theology and philosophy, and Persian the language of poetry and the arts. Europeans called him "Süleyman the Magnificent" for the dazzling opulence and splendor of his court. But within the empire he became known as "Süleyman the Lawgiver" for bringing peace and stability to the realm. The sultan's officials gained power through merit rather than family lineage. As an Austrian ambassador reported, *"Those who are dishonest, lazy and slothful never attain to distinction, but remain in obscurity and contempt. That is why they succeed in all they attempt ... and daily extend the bounds of their rule."* *

Süleyman centralized religious authority and sponsored the building of mosques and religious schools, partly to combat the intermixture of pagan practices with Islam. He sent religious experts to rural Anatolia to promote Islamic orthodoxy among peasants who still embraced folk beliefs, deities, and rituals. Nevertheless, the Ottomans did not impose a single legal system on existing cultural and religious traditions. Instead, they allowed local Christian and Jewish populations, for example, to govern their own affairs and maintain their own courts as long as they remained loyal to the sultan and paid their taxes promptly.

● **CONTEXT&CONNECTIONS** Süleyman's achievement in reconciling central authority with the ethnic, linguistic, and religious diversity of his subjects anticipated by half a century *Emperor Akbar's* ability to consolidate *Mughal* power over the equally vast and diverse Indian subcontinent (key terms in Chapter 16). Both were Muslim rulers who waived the *jizya* tax that Islamic law allowed them to impose on nonbelievers. Their legacies of tolerance were not sustained, however. In the late seventeenth century one of Akbar's successors alienated his Hindu subjects by ruling more stringently in the name of Islam (see Chapter 20), while during the First World War the collapsing Ottoman empire undertook brutal suppression of minorities, most clearly in the Armenian Genocide (see Chapter 27). ●

In foreign affairs, Süleyman was aggressively expansionistic, in Europe as well as in northern Africa and western Asia. In 1534, his armies captured the strategic city of Baghdad from their Safavid rivals, restoring Sunni authority over the Arab society of the region. (As a result, since that time, Arabs of that region have been divided into Sunni and Shi'ite communities.) The Ottomans dominated the Red Sea and thus access to Islam's holy pilgrimage sites; swept across North Africa, tapping into the riches of the Nile River; charged across the Balkans to take command of the Hungarian plain; and dominated the rich commerce of the Black Sea (see map on page 499). Within this vast world, Evliya Çelebi could securely travel under his sultan's writ.

The prospect for even greater expansion into Europe was present both in Süleyman's time and a century later when Çelebi traveled to Christian lands. Ottoman assaults threatened the Habsburg empire in central Europe and the Venetian republic in Italy and the Adriatic, but Vienna's defenders turned back the Ottoman siege of the city in 1529, and in the Mediterranean a combined European fleet

---

**The Turkish Letters of Ogier Ghiselin de Busbecq, Imperial Ambassador at Constantinople, 1554–1562*, trans. Edward S. Foster (New York: Oxford University Press), p. 66.

under Spanish command defeated the Ottoman navy in 1571. Still, the Ottomans stayed on the offensive in southeastern Europe into the later seventeenth century, and in 1683 were once again at the gates of Vienna.

Çelebi was an eyewitness to many of those later campaigns, but his description of an invasion of Muslim Tatar horsemen plundering and pillaging all the way to Amsterdam was pure fantasy (reminding us that we need to assess primary sources critically and seek independent confirmation when possible). Quite realistic, however, was his description of a Habsburg victory over Ottoman forces in Austria in 1664: "*On this side was our bloodthirsty army of Islam. . . . They were tired and weak. For twenty days they had suffered from nonstop rain. Men and horses were sapped of their strength, hungry and starving.... What good were they against the infidel army on the opposite side ... covering the ground like a black cloud?*"* Thus Çelebi paid grudging tribute to the coalition of western armies that had combined their forces to hold off the Ottoman advance.

Still, even as Çelebi joined a diplomatic delegation to Vienna the next year, the Ottomans had great bargaining power. They held firm control over the Balkans, Greece, and much of Hungary. With their large and well-equipped army, the Ottomans were a major player in the European balance of power.

European diplomats thus sought an ally against the persistent Ottoman threat in the shah of Safavid Iran (referred to at the time as Persia). As the Austrian ambassador noted:

> *On [the Ottoman] side are the resources of a mighty empire, strength unimpaired, experience and practice in fighting . . . endurance of toil, unity, discipline, frugality and watchfulness. . . . [W]orst of all, the enemy is accustomed to victory, and we to defeat. . . . Persia alone interposes in our favor; for the enemy, as he hastens to attack, must keep an eye on this menace to his rear.*†

The Habsburgs and the Safavids found that mutual antipathy to the Ottomans gave them a starting point for cooperation.

The Shi'ite Challenge: Foundations of Safavid Iran, 1500–1629

Iran is a rich and productive land with a long history of influence in western and southern Asia. With Mesopotamia and the Mediterranean to the west and the Indus Valley and India to the south and east, the land called Persia benefited from contacts with other civilizations. Its agricultural wealth and its location as a commercial crossroads also attracted invaders. In the early sixteenth century, some of these invaders founded the **Safavid dynasty** (1501–1722) and challenged the power of the Ottoman empire.

Safavid dynasty
(1501–1722) Dynasty that established Shi'ite Islam as the state religion in Iran and challenged the powerful Ottoman empire. The Safavids fell to invaders from Central Asia in the early eighteenth century.

Known as *kizilbash* ("redheads") because of the color of their turbans, the Safavid invaders were members of an unorthodox Islamic sect led by a man named Ismail (r. 1501–1524). The "redheads" swept down from Azerbaijan,

*Robert Dankoff and Sooyong Kim, translation and commentary, *An Ottoman Traveller: Selections from the* Book of Travels *of Evliya Çelebi* (London: Eland Publishing, 2010), p. 225. Reprinted by permission.

†*The Turkish Letters of Ogier Ghiselin de Busbecq, Imperial Ambassador at Constantinople, 1554–1562*, trans. Edward S. Foster (New York: Oxford University Press), p. 66.

conquered the Persian-speaking lands, and drove west, capturing the important cities of Baghdad and Basra. Ismail then adopted mainstream Shi'ite beliefs and imposed them on his conquered subjects, including both Sunni Muslims and followers of Persia's ancient Zoroastrian faith. Though the Ottomans retook Baghdad, the Shi'ites, long a suppressed minority, now controlled a major Islamic state.

To ensure the religious and political loyalty of their subjects, the Safavids decreed that the names of the early Sunni caliphs should be publicly cursed. That was a problem for Evliya Çelebi: when, on a diplomatic mission, he first heard the public cursing of a leader that he, as a Sunni, venerated, he recounted, *"I nearly went out of my mind. . . . I could easily have killed that accursed curser; because when Ottoman envoys come to Persia they have the liberty of killing up to four Kizilbash cursers for the sake of the Four Companions of the Prophet."** Since he was on a diplomatic mission, he resisted the temptation, and the Safavid governor decreed that there was to be no public cursing of Sunni caliphs, upon pain of death, while the Ottoman officials were present. As they did with the Habsburgs, with the Safavids the Ottomans alternated between warfare and diplomacy.

Although the shift toward Shi'ism in Iran was permanent, over time the religious passions that drove initial Safavid policies died down. The greatest Safavid ruler, Shah **Abbas I** (r. 1587–1629), built the capital at Isfahan, which was a city of half a million residents when a European visitor commented on *"the great number of magnificent palaces, the agreeable and pleasant houses . . . the really fine bazaars, the water channels and the streets of which the sides were covered with tall plane trees."*† The gardens of Isfahan were legendary. (See the feature "Movement of Ideas Through Primary Sources: A French View of the Iranians.")

Abbas I
(r. 1587–1629) Safavid ruler who created a long and stable reign, beautified the capital city of Isfahan, promoted foreign trade, and repelled Ottoman invaders.

● **CONTEXT&CONNECTIONS** During the reign of Shah Abbas and his successors, Iranian culture spread both east and west. Persian verse was widely admired, influencing Swahili poets in East Africa (see Chapter 16) as well as Urdu poets in India, who used Arabic script to write lyrical poetry in a Persian-inflected variation of the local Hindi language. Isfahan, a showcase for Persian architecture and engineering, influenced the graceful silhouette of the Taj Mahal in India. In addition to creating beautiful abstract patterns on rich carpets, Persian artists were famous for miniature paintings depicting scenes from everyday life, art forms that influenced artisans and painters from Delhi to Constantinople. ●

AP® THEMES
What contributed to the prosperity of the Safavid economy?

The economy also blossomed under Abbas's long and stable rule, with new irrigation works supporting agriculture, extensive markets for handicrafts, and a pilgrim trade servicing visitors to the holy sites of Shi'ite Islam. Iranian silks, carpets, and ceramics were traded overland and by sea to the east and west and also into Indian Ocean circuits, most especially by minority communities of Armenian Christians (see page 525).

In addition, Shah Abbas invited other European merchants and diplomatic representatives to Isfahan. Abbas was anxious to acquire guns and cannon and training for professional soldiers. The antagonism of many Iranian leaders to all things Christian and European was offset by the Safavid need to cultivate European

---

*Robert Dankoff and Sooyong Kim, translation and commentary, *An Ottoman Traveller: Selections from the* Book of Travels *of Evliya Çelebi* (London: Eland Publishing, 2010), p. 56. Reprinted by permission.

†Cited in Ronald W. Ferrier, *A Journey to Persia: Jean Chardin's Portrait of a Seventeenth Century Empire* (London: I. B. Tauris, 1996), p. 44.

Safavid Court This painting shows the court of Shah Süleyman II in the late seventeenth century. The shah is entertained by musicians, while his retainers prepare for an evening hunt, with a European visitor looking on. The style is Iranian, although European influence can be seen in the use of perspective to create a pastoral background. Süleyman II was an ineffective ruler who enjoyed these luxuries as his empire declined in power. (Ms E-14 f.98a Shah Suleyman II (1641–91) and his courtiers (gouache on paper), Persian School, (17th century)/Institute of Oriental Studies, St. Petersburg, Russia/ The Bridgeman Art Library)

allies in their struggle with the Ottomans. The Safavid rulers abided by the old adage that "*the enemy of my enemy is my friend*" in seeking European alliances against Constantinople.

After the death of Shah Abbas in 1629, however, the quality of Iranian leadership declined. Over the next century, with their economy and military weakening, the Safavids became vulnerable to just the sort of invasion from the steppes that had brought them to Iran in the first place.

Safavid Collapse and Ottoman Persistence, 1650–1750

Shah Abbas had neglected to groom a competent successor. The next shah, pampered in the seclusion of the royal harem his whole life, set an example of debauchery and corruption that spread throughout his court. Shi'ite clerics, who had been principal supporters of the Safavid dynasty, were appalled, especially by the monarch's continual drunkenness.

A French View of the Iranians

Jean de Chardin (1643–1713) was a Frenchman who travelled twice to the Safavid empire in Iran (then called Persia), learning the language and forming strong opinions about the inhabitants. His *Travels in Persia* is a valuable primary source on European-Iranian relations in the late seventeenth century.

Still, as with all such travel accounts, we must be cautious about accepting his portrait at face value. It is important to consider the author's own point of view. For one thing, Chardin was a jeweler frustrated by what he saw as Iranian "deceits" and "tricks" in his business dealings, experiences that may have colored his perspective.

Also important to remember is that Chardin was a Protestant member of the bourgeoisie, the emerging French middle class, which stressed ethics based on plain speaking, hard work, foresight, and thrift. Therefore, as much as the following document is a comment on Iranians, it also reveals Chardin's own worldview through the contrasts he draws between his own society and that of his hosts.

❯ **Historical Thinking Skill:**
COMPARISON What were the differences Chardin noted between French society and Persian society?

❯ **Historical Thinking Skill:**
ARGUMENTATION Chardin claims that the Persians were "ignorant of the present state" of foreign places. What evidence does he cite to support this claim?

Source: Sir John Chardin, *Travels in Persia, 1673–1677*, an abridged English version of *Voyages du chevalier Chardin en Perse, et autres lieux de l'Orient* (London: Argonaut Press, 1927), p. 70. Spelling and usage have been modernized.

From *Travels in Persia*

They [Iranians] are true philosophers on the account of [their] . . . hope and fear of a future state; they are little guilty of covetousness, and are only desirous of getting, that they may spend it; they love to enjoy the present, and deny themselves nothing that they are able to procure, taking no thought for the morrow, and relying wholly on providence, and their own fate; they firmly believe it to be sure and unalterable . . . so when any misfortune happens to them, they are not cast down, as most men are, they only say quietly [so] it is ordained. . . .

The most commendable property of the manners of the Persians, is their kindness to strangers; the reception and protection they afford them, and their universal hospitality, and toleration, in regard to religion, except the clergy of the country, who, as in all other places, hate to a furious degree, all those that differ from their opinions. The Persians are very civil, and very honest in matters of religion; so far that they allow those who have embraced theirs, to recant, and resume their former opinion. . . . They believe that all men's prayers are good and prevalent; therefore, in their illnesses, and in other wants, they admit of, and even desire the prayers of different religions. . . . This is not to be imputed to their religious principles . . . but I impute it to the sweet temper of that nation, who are naturally averse to contest and cruelty. . . .

Two opposite customs are commonly practiced by the Persians; that of praising God continually, and talking of his attributes, and that of uttering curses, and obscene talk. Whether you see them at home, or meet them in the streets, going about business or walking; you still hear them uttering some blessing or prayer. . . . The least thing they set their hand to do, they say, "In the Name of God"; and they never speak of doing anything, without adding, "If it pleases God. . . ." [At] the same time, come out of the same men's mouths a thousand obscene expressions. All ranks of men are infected with this odious vice. Their bawdy talk is taken from Arse, and C——t, which modesty forbids one to name. . . . [W]hen they have spent their Stock of bawdy names, they begin to call one another Atheists, Idolaters, Jews, Christians; and to say to one another, "The Christians Dogs are better than thou. . . ."

The Eastern People are not near so restless, and so uneasy as we; they sit gravely and soberly, make no motion with their body . . . for they don't believe that a man that is in his wits, can be so full of action as we are . . . I'll repeat it once more: The Persians are the most kind people in the world; they have the most moving and the most engaging ways, the most complying tempers, the smoothest and the most flattering tongues, avoiding in their conversation, relations or expressions which may occasion melancholy thoughts. . . .

As civil as that nation is, they never act out of generosity. . . . They do nothing but out of a principle of interest, that is to say, out of hope or fear: And they cannot conceive that there should be such a country where people will do their duty from a motive of virtue only, without any other recompense. It is quite the contrary with them; they are paid for everything, and beforehand too. One can ask nothing of them, but with a present in one's hand. . . . The poorest and most miserable people never appear before a great man, or one from whom they would ask some favor, but at the same time they offer a present, which is never refused, even by the greatest lords of the kingdom. . . .

As for what relates to travelling, those journeys that are made out of pure curiosity are . . . inconceivable to the Persians. . . . They have no taste of the pleasure we enjoy in seeing different manners from ours, and hearing of a language which we do not understand. . . . They asked me if it was possible that there should be such people amongst us, who would travel two or three thousand leagues with so much danger, and inconveniency, only to see how they were made, and what they did in Persia, and upon no other design. These people are of the opinion, as I have observed, that one cannot better attain to virtue, nor have a fuller taste of pleasure than by resting and dwelling at home, and that it is not good to travel, but to acquire riches. . . . It is from this spirit of theirs no doubt, that the Persians are so grossly ignorant of the present state of other nations of the world, and that they do not so much as understand geography, and have no maps; which comes from this, that having no curiosity to see other countries. . . . The Ministers of State generally speaking, know no more what passes in Europe, than in the world of the moon. The greatest part, even have but a confused idea of Europe, which they look upon to be some little island in the North Seas, where there is nothing to be found that is either good or handsome; from whence it comes, say they, that the Europeans go all over the world, in search of fine things, and of those which are necessary, as being destitute of them.

The last Safavid shah attempted to reverse these trends and regain the support of the clergy by imposing harsh conditions of public morality. He banned music, coffee, and public entertainments, restricted women to the home, and even destroyed the imperial wine cellar. People soon tired of such heavy-handed moral impositions, however, and public support for the Safavids slipped even further. The Safavid empire was therefore easy pickings for the Afghan invaders who descended on Isfahan in 1722 and left it in ruins. The deepest and longest-lasting legacy of the Safavid dynasty was the predominance of Shi'ite Islam in Iran and its borderlands.

The Ottomans, in contrast, persisted as a significant political and military power into the mid-eighteenth century without any radical change to their political order and with an empire that still included much of southeastern Europe (see Map 17.2, page 526). Unlike Safavid Iran, where the quality of the shah's character was such a determining factor, Ottoman administrative reforms had created stronger and more reliable institutions for both civilian and military affairs. A clear example came in the year 1648, when both the Ottoman court and the people of Constantinople grew disaffected with a sultan who spent lavishly on luxuries while ignoring matters of state. But his subsequent assassination did not lead to disorder; instead, the smooth transition to more effective leadership showed the underlying strength of Ottoman institutions.

As a sign of continuing vigor on the international scene, Ottoman armies laid siege to Vienna once again in 1683, and as late as 1739 Ottoman forces defeated the Austrians, who ceded Balkan territory to Constantinople. In general, however, the Ottomans' place in the Great Power balance was now defensive rather than expansionistic, with eighteenth-century military leaders defending the empire's borders against rising powers, especially Russia.

As the "gunpowder revolution" continued to make warfare more deadly, it also made defending an empire with expansive frontiers more expensive. While Ottoman agricultural and commercial production was still substantial, economic expansion was no longer keeping up with population growth, making it difficult to find the revenue for further military investment. Despite such longer-term problems, however, the Ottomans persisted, and in the eighteenth century their realm remained large and prosperous.

The Mystical Path: Sufism in Early Modern Islam

The diversity of Muslims should now be clear, considering differences between Sunnis and Shi'ites, as well as the cultural and linguistic diversity of Arabs, Turks, Iranians, Mughal Indians, and many others. We can understand that complexity even further by looking at the mystical **Sufi** forms of Islamic worship.

Sufi
A mystical form of Islam in which adherents follow a set of specified practices, often involving meditation and rhythmic movement, in an attempt to become closer to God. Sufis pay great respect to the leaders of their brotherhoods even after death, often erecting shrines, which they visit as saints' tombs.

Although Sufis adhere to a number of different schools, and may be either Sunni or Shi'ite, the core of their faith is to approach divine truth and love by seeking intimate communion with God. While all Muslims hope that living virtuous lives will gain them entry into heaven, Sufis believe that through certain ritual practices they can achieve a mystical union with the divine even in the here and now. Like all Muslims they practice the five "pillars" of the faith: professing that "*there is no God but God and Muhammad is His Prophet*"; praying five times daily; fasting during the month of Ramadan; supporting the poor through charity; and, if possible, making the pilgrimage to Mecca and Medina. To these mandates members of Sufi brotherhoods add additional prayers and rituals, such as the repeated recitation of the ninety-nine names of God.

Evliya Çelebi himself seems to have been a member of a Sufi order, and in his *Book of Travels*, he sometimes refers to himself as a "dervish." In its original meaning, a dervish was a wandering holy man, an ascetic who had given up all material possessions to devote himself to God (like the wandering monks of medieval Europe or the holy men of India). While Çelebi certainly was a wanderer, he was definitely not an ascetic. During Ottoman times, however, the term dervish came to be applied to whole Sufi communities, most famously to the Mevlevi Order of "whirling dervishes." Through complex rotational dances to music of intensifying rhythm, they sought to become vessels into which God might enter.

Sufism played an exceptionally important role in the spread of Islam beyond its original Arab heartland, facilitating converts' incorporation of local shrines and beliefs into their newly adopted universal religion. For example, Sufis often placed special emphasis on the spiritual power of their teachers and continued to venerate them after death. The tomb of a saintly Sufi teacher, whose *baraka*, or divine grace, continued to aid his disciples, then became a place of veneration and pilgrimage, giving those for whom a pilgrimage to Mecca and Medina was impossible a local point of ritual importance. Emotive Sufi practices, incorporating local music and dance rhythms, were more attractive to rural peoples than more staid and legalistic Islamic practices.

● **CONTEXT&CONNECTIONS** Sufism spread widely in Africa, the Middle East, and across the Indian Ocean world. Sufi brotherhoods encouraged conversions by blending local leadership and cultural practices with Islamic forms, a process known as religious *syncretism* (Chapter 18). For that very reason, Sufis were, and still are today, often looked down upon and even attacked by Muslims who have viewed Sufi practices as impure or even heretical. ●

Religion and Politics in Western Europe

The sixteenth century and the first half of the seventeenth century were a time of turmoil in western Europe. As religious strife became entangled with the ambitions of emperors, kings, and princes, warfare became more common. Urbanization and commercialization heightened social tensions, and attempts to expand royal power often met resistance.

The Habsburgs were the most powerful family in Europe at the beginning of this period. Originally from central Europe, the **Habsburg dynasty** aspired to create a pan-European Catholic empire. Conflict with the Ottomans was one check on Habsburg ambitions. Another was the rise of Protestant England and competition from the Catholic kings of France. By the mid-seventeenth century the reach of Habsburg dominance had contracted to a central European empire ruled from Vienna, still a great European power, but no longer a global one.

Habsburg dynasty
Powerful ruling house that expanded from Austria to Spain, the Netherlands, and the Spanish empire, as well as throughout the German-speaking world when Charles V (r. 1516–1556) was elected Holy Roman emperor.

By the early eighteenth century the religious wars were over and European stability had returned. Catholic France and Protestant England had established stable constitutional orders that allowed their leaders to focus on international expansion. Apart from Habsburg Austria, the strongest military power in central Europe was Prussia, the rising power in the politically fractured German-speaking lands. By 1750 England, France, Austria, and Prussia, along with Russia, were the dominant European powers.

WORLD HISTORY IN TODAY'S WORLD

Pope Francis, Europe, and the World

Catholics believe that the papacy traces its lineage through 265 previous popes in an unbroken line back to Saint Peter, a disciple of Jesus Christ. By the sixteenth century, in breaking from that lineage, Protestants pointed to the Church's corruption, its focus on worldly matters of wealth and power.

Again in 2013, scandals were rocking the Catholic Church. Jorge Mario Bergoglio was elected to serve as Pope Francis I and, with his emphasis on personal simplicity, pledged broad reforms. Priorities included cleaning up the corrupt Vatican Bank, cooperating with civil authorities in identifying and prosecuting pedophile priests, and bringing greater overall transparency to church affairs.

It is significant that Pope Francis, from the South American nation of Argentina, is the first non-European pope chosen in over 1200 years. From late Roman times through the twentieth century, western Europe was the demographic and cultural center of Roman Catholicism. Today, however, all the growth in Catholic numbers, like growth in Christianity generally, is taking place in Africa, Asia, and Latin America. Pope Francis has acknowledged that trend by appointing more diverse church leaders.

In 1900, 65 percent of the world's 291 million Catholics lived in Europe. Today, just 24 percent of the world's 1.1 billion Catholics are European (and among those are many who no longer practice as faithfully as their great-grandparents did). The percentage of the world's Catholics in North America has stayed relatively flat, going from 5 percent to 8 percent in that same period.

In contrast, in 1910, only 24 percent of Catholics lived in Latin America or the Caribbean; today that percentage is 39 percent. The Asian-Pacific percentage of Catholics, although relatively small, has still more than doubled in that period, from 5 percent to 12 percent. By far the greatest growth of the church has taken place in sub-Saharan Africa, which was home to less than 1 percent of Catholics in 1900 but over 16 percent today.

Although the Catholic Church is notoriously slow to change, it seems inevitable that the worldwide growth in membership outside of Europe will have cultural implications and maybe even theological ones. At a minimum, it seems to be just a matter of time before an African pope joins the long list of successors to Saint Peter.

Source: Pew Research, Religion and Public Life Project, "The Global Catholic Population," February 13, 2013, http://www.pewforum.org/2013/02/13/the-global-catholic-population/.

The Habsburgs: Imperial Ambitions and Political Realities, 1519–1648

The greatest of the Habsburg monarchs was Charles I, who from 1516 to 1556 ruled Spain and the Habsburg domains in central Europe. Charles's Spanish possessions included all the wealth of the Americas, and the Netherlands, rich in trade, was part of his family inheritance, which also made him king of Naples, controlling the southern part of Italy. The central European territories dominated from Vienna were crucial in the European military balance.

In 1520, the pope crowned Charles as Holy Roman Emperor, after he had been elected to that position by seven of the many archbishops and princes who ruled over German-speaking lands. Charles thus became the principal defender of the Catholic faith. (See the feature "World History in Today's World: Pope Francis, Europe, and the World.")

With extensive territorial possessions in Europe and all the wealth of the Americas at their disposal, it seemed that the Habsburgs might be able to create a political unity in western Europe. But the French were a powerful a rival in the west, while the Ottoman Turks challenged Habsburg supremacy in eastern Europe and the Mediterranean. Equally significant were the violent repercussions from the Protestant Reformation that began to appear in the mid-sixteenth century (see Map 17.1).

Map 17.1 The Protestant Reformation By the middle of the sixteenth century, Protestant churches were dominant in England, Scotland, the Netherlands, Switzerland, and Scandinavia. German principalities were divided between Protestants and Catholics. Catholicism remained dominant across most of southern Europe, though Protestants formed a significant minority in France. The religious landscape was especially complex in southeastern Europe where, under Ottoman authority, there were substantial communities of Catholics, Protestants, Orthodox Christians, and Muslims.

Martin Luther preaching, c.1517 (engraving), German School, (16th century)/ Private Collection/The Stapleton Collection/Bridgeman Images

Martin Luther Preaching Martin Luther was known as a powerful preacher, as seen in this contemporary depiction. The rapid spread of his Protestant ideas, however, resulted from the printing press as well. Korean craftsmen had first invented metal moveable type in the fourteenth century, then in 1455 that achievement was repeated by a German goldsmith. The lower cost of books made possible by the printing press then allowed Martin Luther's influence to spread far and wide.

Charles V became Holy Roman emperor just as Martin Luther was challenging church authority (see Chapter 16). When the emperor presided over a meeting to bring Luther back under papal authority, Luther refused to back down and was declared an outlaw. The German princes then chose sides, some declaring themselves "Lutherans," others remaining loyal to the pope and Holy Roman emperor. Decades of inconclusive warfare followed, and religious division became a permanent part of the western European scene.

Finally, in 1555, Charles gave up his attempt to impose Catholicism through military means, and agreed to a peace recognizing the principle that princes could impose either Catholicism or Lutheranism within their own territories. Exhausted, he abdicated his throne, retired to a monastery, and split his inheritance between his brother Ferdinand, who took control of the Habsburgs' central European domains, and his son Philip, who became king of Spain. The Habsburgs had failed to hold Europe together.

Philip II (r. 1556–1598) ruled over a magnificent court at Madrid, the Spanish empire in the Americas, and the new southeast Asian colony of the Philippines. However, even with the vast riches of New Spain, wars severely strained the treasury, and increased taxes led to unrest. Philip's militancy in attempting to impose Catholic orthodoxy on his subjects made religious divisions even more acute. One example is the rebellion in 1568 of the Spanish *moriscos* (mohr-EES-kos), Arabic-speaking Iberians who stayed in Spain after 1492. Though forced to convert to Christianity, many morisco families continued to practice their original faith in private (as did many Spanish Jews, who had also been forcibly converted to Catholicism). When the church moved to impose strict Roman Catholicism, the moriscos rebelled. It took two years for Philip's forces to crush the uprising; the king then ordered the expulsion of all those left alive. (Among their descendants were the Spanish Muslims Çelebi encountered in Constantinople.)

Religion also inflamed Philip's war on the Calvinists in his Dutch provinces. **John Calvin** was a Protestant theologian whose Reformed Church emphasized the absolute power of God over weak and sinful humanity. The possibility of salvation for human souls lay entirely with God, Calvin argued: *"eternal life is foreordained for some, eternal damnation for others."*

Philip regarded Calvinists as heretics, and when he tried to seize their property they armed themselves in self-defense. Attempts to put down the rebellion only stiffened Dutch resistance. The struggle was never resolved in Philip's lifetime, but

Philip II

(r. 1556–1598) Son of Charles V and king of Spain. Considering himself a defender of Catholicism, Philip launched attacks on Protestants in England and the Netherlands.

The Hanging Tree This French engraving from 1633 shows the awful violence that ravaged Europe during the Thirty Years' War. The victims, says the text, *"hang from the tree like unfortunate fruit."* (Erich Lessing/Art Resource, NY)

in 1609 a treaty was signed that led to the effective independence of the Dutch United Provinces. It was in this political context that the Dutch East India Company emerged as a powerful trading enterprise (see Chapter 16).

John Calvin
(1509–1564) A Protestant leader whose followers emphasized individual scriptural study and the absolute sovereignty of God.

Protestant England was another constant source of concern to Philip. Its rulers harassed the Spanish at every turn, for example by supporting the privateers who plundered Spanish treasure ships in the Caribbean. In 1588, Philip sent a great naval armada to invade England, but poor weather combined with clever English strategy to defeat the attempt. The English took the defeat of the Spanish Armada as a sign that God was indeed on their side.

By the early seventeenth century, the Spanish Habsburgs were reeling from the expense of fighting on so many fronts, even as silver imports from the New World began to decline. Like the rulers of Ming China, another great empire for which expanding supplies of silver were a necessity (see Chapter 16), the Spanish Habsburgs found themselves in a difficult financial position. In addition, the peace of 1555 had broken down, and warfare continued to rock central Europe.

Unrest between Catholic and Lutheran rulers finally led to the catastrophic **Thirty Years' War** (1618–1648). As armies rampaged through the countryside, up to 30 percent of the rural population died from famine and disease. Finally, the Peace of Westphalia (1648) recognized a permanent division between Catholic and Protestant Germany. The ideal of a single overarching imperial structure was gone, replaced by the concept of separate national states that recognized one another's sovereignty and agreed to abide by rules governing war and diplomacy. After 1648, the era of Habsburg dominance and of religiously inspired warfare came to an end.

Thirty Years' War
(1618–1648) Series of wars fought by various European powers on German-speaking lands. Began as a competition between Catholic and Lutheran rulers and was complicated by the dynastic and strategic interests of Europe's major powers.

Still, Vienna remained an impressive cosmopolitan capital, drawing on the cultural riches of central Europe. Evliya Çelebi noted the prolific use of religious statues and paintings in Vienna's Catholic churches, which as a Sunni Muslim, he (like many Protestants) viewed as idolatrous. But fair-minded as usual, he goes on to relay to his Ottoman audience the Catholic explanation: "*When the priests harangue the people, just as your sheikhs do, they have difficulty conveying their message with fine words alone. So we convey the message through images of the prophets and saints and paradise, depictions of divine glory.... But we do not worship them in any way.*"* Çelebi was especially impressed by European painting: "*When one sees the depiction of paradise,*" he wrote of one painting, "*one wishes to die and go to heaven. . . . Truly, when it comes to painting, the Franks prevail over the Indians and Persians.*"*

He also acknowledged the skills of Vienna's men of learning, comparing Austrian doctors and scholars favorably to ancient Greek and medieval Muslim models. "*In the city of Vienna,*" he wrote, "*there are perfect masters of surgery ... and scholars of such wisdom and skill the equal of Ibn Sinā and Pythagoras together.*"† He was equally impressed by their libraries, complaining that Muslims did far less to preserve their ancient texts. Vienna's commercial life, too, brought praise from Çelebi. Of the numerous shops, he wrote, "*so prosperous and well stocked are they that each shop is worth an Egyptian treasure.*"*

On the other hand, he also found fault with Habsburg society, as during a diplomatic mission to Vienna in 1665, where he wondered at the free mixing of men and women in the city: "*The women sit together with us Ottomans, drinking and chatting, and their husbands do not say a word.... The reason is that throughout Christendom women are in charge, and they have behaved in this disreputable fashion ever since the time of the Virgin Mary.** Of course, he exaggerated Austrian women's equality, knowing that his Ottoman readers would be fascinated by reports of the Europeans' transgression of strict social segregation by gender.

• **CONTEXT&CONNECTIONS** Evliya Çelebi's comments on Christian women repeat a stereotype that circulated widely in the Muslim world. In fact, Austrian and Ottoman societies were equally patriarchal; that is, men defined women's lives legally and socially. Muslim societies, though, had adopted the ancient eastern Mediterranean practice of sharply segregating the sexes and veiling women in public. This practice was initially limited to elites, but as with footbinding in China (see Chapter 20), elite practice became popular custom. While European women enjoyed relatively greater liberty of social interaction, fathers and husbands controlled their educations, marriages, property, and housing—their bodies if not their minds—just as in Constantinople. •

As we might expect given that the Ottomans and Austrians had recently fought a bitter war, Çelebi was particularly critical of Habsburg military affairs. He contrasted the Austrians unfavorably to the Hungarians: "*The Austrians ... have no stomach for a fight and are not swordsmen and horsemen. Their infantry musketeers, to*

---

*Robert Dankoff and Sooyong Kim, translation and commentary, *An Ottoman Traveller: Selections from the* Book of Travels *of Evliya Çelebi* (London: Eland Publishing, 2010), pp. 240–241, 230–232. Reprinted by permission.

†J. W. Livingstone, "Evliya Çelebi on Surgical Procedures in Vienna," *Al-Abath* 23 (1970): 232.

*be sure, are real fire-shooters; but ... they can't shoot from the shoulder as Ottoman soldiers do. Also, they shut their eyes and fire at random."** Like the Persians, he said, the Austrians were guilty of excessively brutal forms of torture, and for this and other reasons he had a better opinion of the Hungarians, who "*though they have lost their power, still have fine tables, are hospitable to guests, and are . . . true warriors. . . . They do not torture their prisoners as the Austrians do. . . . In short, though both of them are unbelievers without faith, the Hungarians are the more honorable and cleaner infidels.*"*

Çelebi's visit came during a break in the fighting, as the military balance between Austrians and Ottomans in southeastern Europe seesawed back and forth. Though horsemanship, as Çelebi indicated, still had strong cultural and military value in the seventeenth century, it was the effective use of gunpowder weapons that was fast becoming crucial to success. Mastering that technology, the Habsburgs, though now limited to central Europe, managed to hold their own and remain one of the Great Powers of western Eurasia.

Religious Conflict and Political Control in France and England, 1500–1715

In France and England, ambitious kings claimed ever greater power, though in both countries their plans were complicated by religious differences as well as conflicts with noblemen who resented losing some of their own authority to the king's men. In the end both countries found paths to political stability but followed very different formulas: absolute monarchy in France, and a constitutional balance of power between king and parliament in England.

AP® THEMES
How did the emergence of Protestantism affect political policies in France and England?

French Protestants, largely Calvinists known as Huguenots (HEW-guh-noh), were a relatively small but prosperous minority (see Map 17.1). Catholic persecution reached a crescendo in 1572. The Saint Bartholomew's Day massacre began as an anti-Protestant conspiracy led by the mother of the French king, the assassination of Huguenot leaders followed by riotous assaults on Protestants beginning in Paris and spreading across the country. Tens of thousands of Huguenots were butchered, and the Saint Bartholomew's Day massacre permanently crippled the Protestant communities of France. After a change in dynasty, however, compromise followed. In 1598 the Edict of Nantes granted limited toleration of Protestant worship within a specified group of cities.

The dominant French political figure of the age was Cardinal Richelieu (1585–1642). Though Richelieu was a high-ranking Catholic Church official, he formulated his policies wholly in the interests of the French monarchy. For example, to position France as the leading defender of the Catholic faith, he was willing to ally France with German Protestants against Spain's Catholic monarch. But tensions came with Richelieu's attempt to amass greater power for the king and his ministers, which alienated the French nobility, while the common people resented increased taxes to pay for military campaigns.

Louis XIV
(r. 1643–1715) Known as the "Sun King," Louis epitomized royal absolutism and established firm control over the French state. Aggressively pursued military domination of Europe while patronizing French arts from his court at Versailles.

Revolts broke out soon after Cardinal Richelieu died, with the child-king **Louis XIV** (r. 1643–1715) having just come to the throne. From 1648 to 1653, France was wracked by civil war. But the French monarchy survived the crisis, and Louis XIV came of age to become a monarch of legendary power. His court and Versailles Palace rivaled Constantinople's Sublime Porte in splendor and luxury.

---

*Robert Dankoff and Sooyong Kim, translation and commentary, *An Ottoman Traveller: Selections from the* Book of Travels *of Evliya Çelebi* (London: Eland Publishing, 2010), pp. 230–231. Reprinted by permission.

Louis XIV All French politics orbited around the "Sun King." Louis cultivated the support of the nobility by hosting lush entertainment at his palace of Versailles. Here the setting is urban, as he is honored at a banquet hosted by the leaders of the municipal government of Paris.

AP® THEMES

In what ways were Louis XIV's efforts to consolidate power different from the efforts of earlier rulers?

When Louis XIV became king, the nobility still dominated the countryside, and they remained jealous of their prerogatives. Both lords and peasants lived in a world where local affiliations and obligations were more important than national ones. As during medieval times, peasants labored on their lords' estates and were subject to manorial courts.

Following Richelieu's example, Louis increased the number of royal officials sent to the countryside and provincial cities, men who depended on royal patronage and owed their loyalty to the king. These officials enforced royal edicts that cut into the power of the landed nobility. By now the nobles had given up the fight; there were benefits to staying on the king's good side. The nobles sought their own royal patronage as they gravitated toward Louis' lavish court at Versailles, enjoying its extravagant banquets, first-rate theater and music, and scandalous gossip.

Louis XIV's motto—*"One King, One Law, One Faith"*—emphasized the Catholic nature of his kingdom. After he revoked the Edict of Nantes in 1685, hundreds of thousands of French Protestants fled to England, Switzerland, the Netherlands, and Cape Town in South Africa. Like Richelieu before him, Louis was determined to weaken Spain and Austria and position France as the world's dominant Catholic power, poised to challenge England in a global competition for empire.

Louis XIV's form of government has been termed "royal absolutism." *"I am the state,"* he said, implying that all of public life should be directed by his own will. The French "Sun King" was the envy of all who aspired to absolute power, including contemporary English monarchs. However, in England the outcome would be entirely different, with parliamentary checks on royal power.

Under Queen Elizabeth, English society had entered the seventeenth century in relative tranquility and with increasing national confidence. In religious matters, Elizabeth followed the Anglican Church of England tradition established by her father, King Henry VIII. Although Catholicism was made illegal, Henry actually retained many Catholic rites and traditions, including a hierarchy of powerful bishops.

Many English Protestants wanted further reform to purge Catholic influences. Among them were the English Calvinists, Protestant reformers known as **Puritans**, who grew discontented with the Stuart kings who came to power after Elizabeth. They scorned the opulence of court life and Anglican bishops' culture of luxury and what they saw as continuing "Roman" elements in Anglican rituals and church organization.

Puritans
Seventeenth-century reformers of the Church of England who attempted to purge the church of all Catholic influences. They were Calvinists who emphasized Bible reading, simplicity and modesty, and the rejection of priestly authority and elaborate rituals.

Under the Stuart king Charles I (r. 1625–1649), tensions exploded. Charles pursued war with Spain and supported Huguenot rebels in France, but he could not raise taxes to finance his wars without the approval of Parliament. In 1628, when Parliament presented a petition of protest against the king, he disbanded it for eleven years. By then, Charles was so desperate for money that he had no choice but to reconvene Parliament. Reformers in Parliament tried to use the occasion to compel the abolition of the Anglican ecclesiastical hierarchy. When Charles arrested several parliamentary leaders on charges of treason, the people of London reacted with violence. The king fled London, and the English Civil War (1642–1649) began.

Puritan leader Oliver Cromwell (1599–1658) organized the opposition to the king's forces. Puritan soldiers showed their disdain for residual Catholic influences on the Church of England by stabling their horses inside Anglican cathedrals, smashing statues, and knocking out stained-glass windows. After seven years of fighting, Cromwell prevailed. The king was captured and, in 1649, beheaded. Cromwell became Lord Protector of the English Commonwealth and instituted a series of radical reforms. But the Commonwealth was held together by little other than his own will and his control of the army, and some of his policies were highly unpopular. Puritan suppression of the theaters, for example, while in keeping with strict Calvinist ideals, was resented by many Londoners (just as imposed morality had provoked unrest in late Safavid Iran.)

After Cromwell died, Parliament invited Charles's son home from exile to reestablish the monarchy. But Anglicans saw the last two Stuart kings as too tolerant of Catholicism. So powerful was their prejudice that they even blamed Catholics for the Great Fire that swept through London in 1666, inscribing on the monument commemorating the tragedy: *"But Popish frenzy, which wrought such horrors, is not yet quenched"* (an accusation that was scratched out only in 1831).

In the so-called Glorious Revolution of 1688, Parliament took charge to assure that the English monarch, head of the Church of England, would always be staunchly Protestant. They drove the last Stuart king from the throne and invited a reliably Protestant princess, together with her Dutch husband, to take his place. The accession of Queen Mary and King William made permanent the Protestant character of the English monarchy.

Bill of Rights
In 1689, King William and Queen Mary of England recognized a Bill of Rights that protected their subjects against arbitrary seizure of person or property and that required annual meetings of Parliament.

As a result of the Glorious Revolution, William and Mary were required to accept the principle of annual parliamentary meetings. In 1689, they also approved a **Bill of Rights**. While restrictions on individual liberty remained, including substantial disabilities for English Catholics, and while most people had no voice in governance, the Bill of Rights established important precedents—freedom of speech in Parliament, for example, and the right to trial by jury—for England and for the world (see Chapter 22).

By the eighteenth century, the balance between king and Parliament gave a stable foundation to England and to the wider British society that came after union with Scotland in 1707. Commerce thrived both domestically and internationally, where the British navy "ruled the waves." The French and the British, with their very different political cultures and religious foundations, would soon be engaged in a global contest that would bring war to Europe, the Americas, and South Asia (see Chapter 19).

Between East and West: Russians, Jews, and Armenians

The geographic distinction between Europe and Asia is conventional but somewhat misleading. As we have seen, the Ottoman empire had its roots in Central Asia and Anatolia but was a significant European power as well. Likewise, Russia looked both west and east in its early development and its imperial expansion. *"In Europe we are Asiatics,"* a later Russian author commented, *"whereas in Asia we are Europeans."** By the mid-seventeenth century, under the Romanov dynasty, the Russian empire was moving westward toward Sweden and Poland, eastward into Siberia, and southward toward the edges of Ottoman and Safavid power. The influence of the Russian Orthodox Church spread along with the empire.

The Russians and Ottomans were not the only people who straddled both Asia and Europe. Jews and Armenians are two important examples of peoples who lived all across western Eurasia, as well as in North Africa and the Indian Ocean world. Their experiences bring to the fore world history's emphasis on the movement and interaction of peoples.

The Rise of the Russian Empire, 1500–1725

Before the sixteenth century, the Slavic-speaking Russian people had been deeply influenced by Greek-speaking Byzantium. Medieval Russian princes and merchants cultivated relations with Constantinople, and the monastic tradition of Orthodox Christianity took deep root. Thus Russian rulers took the title tsar ("Caesar"), asserting continuity with the Byzantine emperors who, until they lost Constantinople to the Ottomans, had been the standard bearers of the Orthodox faith.

Tsar Ivan IV (r. 1533–1584) centralized power in his own hands while extending Russia's frontiers. His strategy of maintaining a large territorial buffer around the core Russian lands to protect them from invasion would become a perennial element of Russian imperial policy. Ivan's accomplishments, however, came with a price. He earned the nickname "Ivan the Terrible" for the random cruelty of his later years. Following Ivan's death came a "time of troubles" with no

*Fyodor Dostoevsky, cited in Tony Judt, *Post-War: A History of Europe since 1945* (New York: Penguin, 2005), p. 749.

clear successor to the title of tsar. Then in 1613 the Russian nobles offered royal power to Mikhail Romanov. The Romanov dynasty (1613–1917) continued Russia's imperial expansion.

• **CONTEXT&CONNECTIONS** The Russian and Ottoman empires endured straight into the twentieth century. The Romanov dynasty came to an end when the Bolsheviks under *Vladimir Lenin* (Chapter 27) seized power in 1917 and brought communism to Russia; the Ottoman empire collapsed in the wake of World War I, its core territories forming the modern Republic of Turkey (see Chapter 28). •

Profit lured Russian traders to the east, where the quest for animal furs led them across the Ural Mountains to frigid Siberia; state power followed later. Already in the seventeenth century, Russians were trading furs on a substantial scale, meeting demand from England to Iran. In fact, Evliya Çelebi described a specialized Ottoman guild of furriers whose goods included *"furs of sable, ermin, Russian silver fox"* and *"outlandish bearskin caps."**

AP® THEMES
What were the environmental advantages and disadvantages of Russian expansion into Siberia?

Agricultural surpluses, however, were the main sources of revenue for the tsars and the Russian nobility. Distinctive about Russia was the long persistence of serfdom. Russian peasants were tightly bound to their villages, and the tsars and aristocracy increasingly saw these "souls," as they called them, as property that could be bought and sold. The oppressive conditions of serfdom in Russia contrasted with developments in western Europe, where serfdom had either disappeared altogether or where peasant obligations were becoming less burdensome. Serfdom would long remain a marker of Russian backwardness (see Chapter 23).

Still, a major reorientation toward the west began under Tsar **Peter the Great** (r. 1685–1725). Peter visited western Europe as a young monarch, and came back urgently aware that his country had fallen behind in technology and science. As tsar, he was determined to put Russia on par with the rising states to his west. To enable rapid transformation, he accumulated greater power for himself by bringing the nobles more tightly under control. In a move that symbolized both Peter's desire to bring the country in line with Western models and his mastery over the nobles, he ordered Russian aristocrats to shave off their luxurious beards, and his courtiers were required to dress in the latest Western fashion. Any Russian man who wanted to keep his old-fashioned Orthodox beard would now have to pay a "beard tax" and carry a metal receipt marked with the motto: *"the beard is a superfluous burden."* As with the imposition of the *queue* hairstyle by the Manchu in China (see Chapter 20), men's heads instantly showed who was in charge. Change in Russia would flow in just one direction: from the top down.

Peter the Great
(r. 1685–1725) Powerful Romanov tsar who built a new Russian capital at St. Petersburg, emulated Western advances in military technology, and extended the Russian empire further into Asia.

With great expense and immense manpower Peter built the new city of St. Petersburg, situated on the Baltic Sea, to serve as Russia's "window on the West." Its elegant baroque buildings, emulating those of Rome and Vienna, stood in contrast to the churches and palaces of Moscow, which reflected Central Asian architecture. Henceforth, Russia would be a power in both Europe and in Asia. (See the feature "Visual Evidence in Primary Sources: European and Asian Influences in Russian Architecture.")

---

*Robert Dankoff and Sooyong Kim, translation and commentary, *An Ottoman Traveller: Selections from the* Book of Travels *of Evliya Çelebi* (London: Eland Publishing, 2010), p. 27. Reprinted by permission.

European and Asian Influences in Russian Architecture

Architecture reflects the diverse cultural influences on a people who straddle the geography of Europe and Asia. Russia's cultural exceptionality within the history of European Christianity traces back to the tenth century, when Prince Vladimir chose to affiliate the Principality of Kiev with the Greek-speaking Byzantine Church, headquartered in Constantinople, rather than with the Latin-speaking Catholic Church centered in Rome (or with the Muslims of the Volga River). Apart from strong Byzantine influence in religion, art, and architecture, early Russians also had long-term cultural exchanges with the nomadic peoples of the Eurasian steppe, a cultural factor that was greatly enhanced when Russia was absorbed into the Mongol empire in the fourteenth century. In the early modern period, as the Russian empire expanded south and east, interactions with Iranian and Turkish peoples also left their cultural mark.

Russia's cultural orientation shifted westward, however, under Peter the Great and his successors. As a young monarch, Peter traveled west to France and the Netherlands hoping, among other goals, to find allies for his wars with the Ottoman empire. In the process he became aware of the great advances

St. Basil's Cathedral was built by Ivan the Terrible in the 1550s to commemorate his conquest of the khanate of Kazan centered on the Volga River, whose rulers were Muslim descendants of Mongolian conquerors. The church's bright colors were added later, in the seventeenth and eighteenth centuries.

Some scholars theorize that the "onion dome" architecture was inspired by the central mosque at Kazan (destroyed by Ivan's army), combined with Greek Byzantine influences and Renaissance styles from Italy.

The official name of the church is the "Cathedral of the Protection of Most Holy Theotokos on the Moat." Theotokos is a Greek title ("God-bearer") for Mary, the mother of Jesus.

The close proximity of St. Basil's to Red Square in Moscow, near the Kremlin, the heart of Russia's political establishment, shows the traditionally close connection between tsarist rule and Russia's Orthodox Christian Church.

Image Source/Superstock

In 1929, under the officially atheistic communist government of the Soviet Union, the church was secularized and turned into a museum. Currently, one church service a year is held at St. Basil's, which has been a UNESCO World Heritage Site since 1990.

taking place in Western shipbuilding and resolved to create a Baltic fleet along modern lines. Similarly, he built the city of St. Petersburg in emulation of the latest architectural styles and employing Western construction techniques. From the eighteenth century onward, then, Russia's cultural legacy has included a broad range of European and Asian features in music, religious life, dance, and architecture. Examples can be found in the images here, with striking architectural and aesthetic differences between St. Basil's Church in Moscow and the Winter Palace in St. Petersburg.

The Winter Palace building was originally planned as the main residence of the Romanov family and as the focal point for the new city of St. Petersburg, begun in 1703 after Peter the Great returned from his tour of western Europe. It took hundreds of thousands of conscripted laborers more than two decades to complete the city.

Later Romanovs moved the capital back to Moscow, though they returned to the milder climate of St. Petersburg during the winter; hence the name "Winter Palace." Continual additions eventually led to a palace with over fifteen hundred rooms.

The palace complex was greatly expanded and thoroughly redecorated in the elaborate Baroque style during the reign of Empress Catherine the Great (r. 1762–1796; see Chapter 20) under a French architect. ***What are the main differences in architectural form between St. Basil's Church and the Winter Palace, and what varying cultural influences do they show?***

Peter Christopher/Masterfile

Catherine began the art collection that today forms the core of the Hermitage Museum, one of the world's great art galleries. Today, the Hermitage Museum attracts over 3 million visitors each year.

The Winter Palace played a central role in later Russian history. In 1905, revolution erupted when the tsar's guard massacred protesters in its courtyard (see Chapter 27). In 1917, after the abdication of the last tsar, the building was temporarily the seat of the Russian government once again, until the communists moved the capital back to the Kremlin in Moscow.

Peter's ultimate goal was clear when he created a regular standing army larger than any in Europe, bringing in the latest military technology from the West while working toward Russian self-sufficiency in guns and cannon. He also sponsored a new educational system to train more efficient civilian and military bureaucrats. But the situation of the serfs was worse than ever. It was their heavy taxes that paid for the grandeur of St. Petersburg and the power of the Russian military, and it was their sons who fought in Peter's armies, extending Russia's frontiers in wars against Sweden and Poland, and laying the groundwork for later conquests of Muslim steppe societies. For all the elegance of Peter's new capital, the top-down tsarist command structure and the expansionist thrust of his imperial strategy had not changed very much since the days of Ivan the Terrible.

The Jewish and Armenian Diasporas

In his *Book of Travels*, Evliya Çelebi was careful to describe the customs and languages of the many different peoples he met. When describing the "Jewish" language, he started with the numbers "un, dos, tire, korta," describing not Hebrew but Ladino, the language based on medieval Spanish spoken by the Iberian Jews known as the Sephardim. Driven into exile from Catholic Spain in 1492, many Sephardim found refuge in the Ottoman empire, both in North Africa and in Çelebi's own Constantinople.

In Ottoman lands, as in Europe, Jews faced persistent popular prejudice. Çelebi himself referred to them as *"an ancient and accursed people."** Still, the Koran defines Jews as "People of the Book," a status that gives them autonomy from Islamic law and the right to adjudicate their own affairs. As long as they paid their taxes, Ottoman Jews were free to regulate their community following their own laws and customs. As they had in medieval Spain, Ladino-speaking Jews made significant contributions to the intellectual and commercial life of the Ottoman empire, for example by serving as medical doctors. Sephardic Jews could also be found in largely Arab cities like Baghdad and in Iranian Isfahan as well. Some even settled in Jerusalem, from which their ancient Hebrew ancestors had been forcibly expelled in the days of the Roman empire.

The larger branch of the Jewish *diaspora*—from a Greek word meaning "dispersal"—were the **Ashkenazim**, Jews who had settled in central and eastern Europe and spoke Yiddish, a German-derived language mixed with Hebrew and, in the east, with words from Slavic languages. The Ashkenazim were broadly scattered: many were peasant villagers within the Russian empire; further west they were more likely to live in cities and engage in commerce. Partly by their own preference and partly because of their exclusion by Christians, Ashkenazim usually lived not just as religious outsiders but as a community apart, following their own legal traditions and usually marrying within their own group. Thus, while they both contributed to and borrowed from majority communities over a very long period, the European Jews remained culturally distinctive in their music, cuisine, and folktales, as well as in their Yiddish language.

Ashkenazim
The largest group in the Jewish diaspora, speaking the German-derived language of Yiddish and living in central and eastern Europe.

AP® THEMES
How did the Jewish diaspora affect social structures in eastern Europe?

In this setting, the Ashkenazim were vulnerable and insecure, facing deep prejudice, and sometimes theft of property or even violent attacks, from their Christian neighbors. Çelebi witnessed a chilling ceremony in the Balkans during which Christians had marched through the town at night with statues of Jesus and his mother, Mary. They explained to Çelebi that they had been commemorating an

*Robert Dankoff and Sooyong Kim, translation and commentary, *An Ottoman Traveller: Selections from the* Book of Travels *of Evliya Çelebi* (London: Eland Publishing, 2010), pp. 93–94. Reprinted by permission.

episode in which, they claimed, Jews had once kidnapped Jesus and Mary. When their forebears supposedly found out about this, Çelebi was told, they *"armed themselves, and began to search for Jesus in the Jews' houses ... with a great hue and cry, just like last evening. Then they found Jesus and Mary in a Jew's house and massacred all the Jews."** All across Europe, Jewish communities faced this kind of terrifying intimidation, often based on similar historical distortions casting their ancestors as killers of the Christian messiah.

The Armenians, followers of an ancient orthodox Christian church, lived across an even wider Eurasian arc, including Russian and Ottoman lands, with distinct Armenian neighborhoods in Constantinople, Jerusalem, and other cities. Their mountainous homeland was dangerous territory, on the borderlands between the Ottoman and Safavid empires. In fact, Shah Abbas I resettled as many as 150,000 Armenians in a separate quarter of Isfahan in a move intended both to secure his border with the Ottomans and to make use of Armenian skills in handicrafts and commerce. Though the move was involuntary, the Armenians of Isfahan were allowed to build churches and look after their own community's affairs. By the seventeenth century, Iranian Armenians were at the center of a commercial network stretching across the Indian Ocean, with business interests all the way from the Mediterranean to the South China Sea.

When Evliya Çelebi visited the Adriatic port of Dubrovnik (in today's Republic of Croatia), he found a city with *"numerous Armenians, Greeks, Jews, Persians, and Franks . . . a place of security and a safe haven of Christendom, a very prosperous entrepôt."** In fact, the city's largely Christian government had sought Ottoman protection against the expanding Venetian republic. Here it seems that safety of travel, security of property, and the right to practice your own religion and regulate your own community made the Ottoman empire a place where diverse peoples might thrive. While it may have been cold comfort to Christian families whose children were taken away for service in the Janissary corps, in Çelebi's time it still seemed possible for diverse Ottoman subjects to live together in relative peace and prosperity.

The Shifting Balance of Power in Western Eurasia by 1750

By the mid-eighteenth century the center of Eurasian power was shifting north and west (see Map 17.2). Britain, France, Austria, and Prussia were ascendant, with the rulers of imperial Russia, whose armies penetrated deeper into Asia, looking west for models of military innovation. This was not yet global hegemony: most African and Asian rulers continued to mind their own affairs with little reference to Europeans; Ottoman sultans remained lords over vast and rich territories; and the great Qing and Mughal dynasties in China and India were still wealthier and more populous than any single European state. But in hindsight, we see the foundations of a Europe-centered world being laid.

Having solved its constitutional crisis, British society took the lead in creating more refined and efficient business methods, building on early Dutch innovations.

---

*Robert Dankoff and Sooyong Kim, translation and commentary, *An Ottoman Traveller: Selections from the* Book of Travels *of Evliya Çelebi* (London: Eland Publishing, 2010), pp. 209, 207. Reprinted by permission.

Map 17.2 Western Eurasia in the Early Eighteenth Century By the early eighteenth century the Habsburg attempt to unify western Europe had failed, and the continent was permanently divided between Catholic and Protestant powers. In 1715 the dominant powers in the west were France, Britain, Austria, and Prussia. The Russian and Ottoman empires to the east were formidable military powers, but the golden age of Spain had ended.

In 1694, for example, the founding of the Bank of England made it much easier for the government to raise funds at modest interest rates for the building of infrastructure, especially for naval expansion. Trade was Britain's life blood, its navy essential for global commercial success. The slave-based sugar plantations of the West Indies brought misery to Africans but vast fortunes to Englishmen, providing them with capital that could be used for investment in new techniques of industrial manufacture (see Chapters 19 and 23). Meanwhile, by 1750 Britain had become by far the world's greatest sea power.

The English and French monarchies had been great rivals since the middle ages. By 1750 their competition was going global, with competing colonial and trade interests in North America, the West Indies, and South Asia.

As Paris became Europe's most important center of philosophy (see Chapter 21), King Louis XV built on his father's accomplishments, investing in both a large army and a naval force strong enough to challenge the British. French success at maintaining its central role on the European continent while challenging the British across the oceans was limited, however, by the great expense of having to maintain military forces decade after decade on both land and sea (while their enemy could focus on its navy).

● **CONTEXT&CONNECTIONS** After a series of early-eighteenth-century wars proved inconclusive, the *Seven Years' War* (1756–1763; Chapter 19) swung the imperial balancer of power in favor of Great Britain. Sometimes referred to by historians the first truly "world" war, it was fought simultaneously in the West Indies, North America, India, and continental Europe. British control of India (see Chapter 20) and Canada (see Chapter 25) were important outcomes. ●

In Protestant-dominated northern Germany, **Prussia** was the rising power in the aftermath of the Thirty Years' War. Although the German-speaking lands were still divided into numerous territories, Prussia, from its capital at Berlin, emerged as the strongest German state. King Frederick William I (r. 1713–1740) made his country a pioneer in military technology and organization, using the latest cannon and muskets and developing a professional standing army of well-trained and disciplined troops. Precision marching and constant drilling were the hallmarks of the Prussian military. The middle class had little political influence. Instead, the traditional rural aristocracy, accepting and benefiting from the Prussian kings' innovations, was the bedrock of royal absolutism. Their cooperation in taxing and controlling the peasants gave Frederick William and his successors resources to expand the military and make Prussia a force to be reckoned with.

Prussia
With its capital at Berlin, Prussia was the rising German power of the eighteenth century. Its military prowess set it in competition with Habsburg Austria for influence over the many German-speaking kingdoms and principalities.

Austria, with its traditional leading role among German states, was threatened by Prussia's rise, leading to complex diplomacy and sometimes war. When Habsburg Austria sought to bolster its position through an alliance with France, the Prussians allied themselves with Britain, a tangle of alliances that by the mid-eighteenth century was turning local conflicts into international ones. Similar alliances and entanglements would mark European power politics straight into the twentieth century, when the First World War saw French, Britain, and Russia allied against Germany, Austria, and the Ottoman empire (see Chapter 27).

Evliya Çelebi wrote in a confident, sometimes even arrogant, tone of superiority about the varied Christian and Muslim lands he visited. Indeed, from his mid-seventeenth-century perspective the Ottoman empire was something to boast about: even as he enjoyed his peaceful retirement in Cairo, Ottoman armies were preparing once again to lay siege to Vienna. But the balance of power was changing. Çelebi did not see it coming, but the winds of history were shifting, and the direction of that change was from the west.

CONTEXT AND CONNECTIONS

Climate Change and the Seventeenth Century

We are apt to read the historical time lines below from left to right, perhaps seeing events like the English Civil War (1642–1649) and the collapse of the Ming dynasty in China (1644) as entirely disconnected. But what happens if we scan our regional time lines vertically, looking for connections between global, regional, and national histories?

A long-standing approach has been to emphasize interactions of large states and empires. As this chapter shows, important lessons can be learned for both northern Europe and western Asia by charting the dynamics of state-building in a period when gunpowder technology raised the stakes of military victory and defeat and when religious conflict fueled imperial competition.

Another obvious global link in early modern times is the increase in maritime networks. Indeed, the previous two chapters have shown the transformative power of new oceanic interchange, though we need to be cautious not to overemphasize European impacts. While the effects of Christopher Columbus's voyages were indeed revolutionary, Matteo Ricci's story indicates that Europeans of his time were relatively marginal to the histories of powerful societies like Mughal India and Ming China.

In the past few decades, quite different sorts of connections across regional histories have been developed by environmental historians exploring the dynamics of the Columbian exchange (see Chapter 15). They have shown the profound effects of multidirectional biological exchanges—flows of plants, animals, seeds, and germs—across the oceans and around the world following the integration of the Eastern and Western Hemispheres. Among other implications of the Columbian exchange, we are now well aware of its impact on the size and distribution of human populations.

Most recently, the study of climate change has offered a radically new approach to integrating early modern global history, as seen in Geoffrey Parker's *Global Crisis: War, Climate Change and Catastrophe in the Seventeenth Century* (2013). European historians have long noted a conjunction between the "little ice age" of the seventeenth century and the century's political crises, religious conflicts, societal mayhem, and violence. Professor Parker has now extrapolated that story and made it global.

Parker argues that in the 1600s "an intense episode of global cooling coincided with an unparalleled spate of revolutions and state breakdowns around the world.... Throughout the Northern Hemisphere, war became the norm for resolving both domestic and international problems."* If participants in the political struggles of western Eurasia used religion to explain their motives and behavior, climate

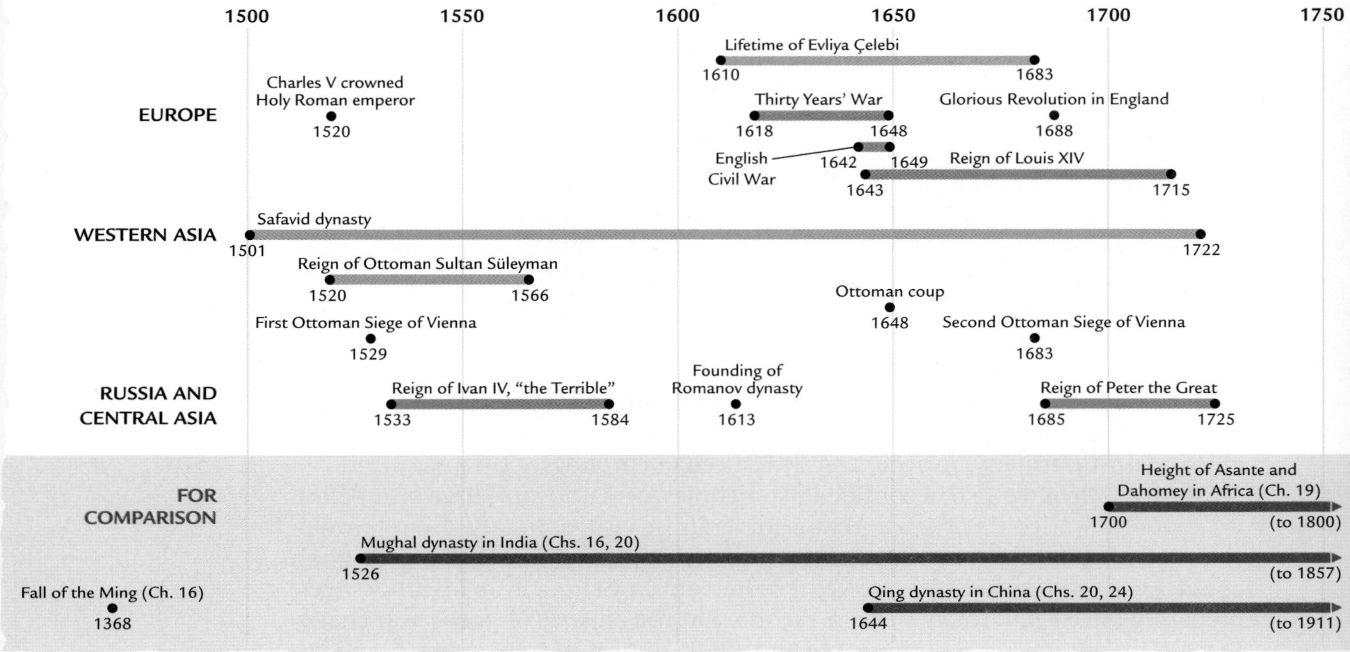

historians looking at the miserable harvests of the 1640s might point to a more basic cause of conflict: hunger.

During the 1640s, we find on our time lines civil wars in England and France; the destruction of the Ming dynasty in China; and rebellion in the Ottoman palace. Amazingly, the suicide of the last Ming emperor, the beheading of the English king, and the assassination of the Ottoman sultan all took place within the space of just five years, between 1644 and 1649. Was that just a coincidence? Of course, a detailed understanding of each of these events requires close attention to particular actors and their specific circumstances. But there was a common context, says Professor Parker. Cooler temperatures caused poor harvests and lower tax revenues in England, France, China, and the Ottoman empire, weakening their rulers, inspiring revolts, and bringing decades of war and violence.

Fortunately, the 1680s brought greater stability. The English had their Glorious Revolution (1688), bringing balance to relations between king and Parliament; Louis XIV asserted royal authority in France (the Versailles Palace was built at this time); and the Ottomans were once again strong enough to lay siege to Vienna (1683). The return of stability, Parker notes, coincided with warmer weather and better harvests.

If the conjunction of climate change and global crisis in the seventeenth century has a message for us today, it is not a reassuring one. If contemporary global warming is more than a short-term weather cycle, and if large climate swings do correlate with widespread outbursts of violence, then we could be in for difficult times.

---

*Geoffrey Parker, *Global Crisis: War, Climate Change and Catastrophe in the Seventeenth Century* (New Haven: Yale University Press, 2013), pp. xvi–xvii.

Key Terms

Evliya Çelebi (500)
Janissaries (503)
Süleyman (504)
Safavid dynasty (505)
Abbas I (506)
Sufi (510)
Habsburg dynasty (511)
Philip II (514)
John Calvin (515)
Thirty Years' War (515)
Louis XIV (517)
Puritans (519)
Bill of Rights (519)
Peter the Great (521)
Ashkenazim (524)
Prussia (527)

For Further Reference

Beik, William. *Louis XIV and Absolutism: A Brief Study with Documents*. New York: Bedford/St. Martin's, 2000.

Bergin, Joseph. *The Seventeenth Century: Europe 1598–1715*. New York: Oxford University Press, 2001.

Braudel, Fernand. *The Mediterranean and the Mediterranean World in the Age of Philip II*. Sian Reynolds, trans. New York: Harper and Row, 1972.

Casale, Giancarlo. *The Ottoman Age of Exploration*. New York: Oxford University Press, 2011.

Chardin, Jean de. *A Journey to Persia: Jean Chardin's Portrait of a Seventeenth Century Empire*. Ronald W. Ferrier, trans. and ed. London: I. B. Tauris, 1996.

Clot, Andre. *Suleiman the Magnificent*. London: Saqi Books, 2004.

Cressy, David, and Lori Anne Farrell, eds. *Religion and Society in Early Modern England: A Sourcebook*. New York: Routledge, 2005.

Dankoff, Robert, and Sooyong Kim. *An Ottoman Traveler: Selections from the* Book of Travels *of Evliya Çelebi*. London: Eland Publishing, 2010.

Fichtner, Paula Sutter. *Terror and Toleration: The Habsburg Empire Confronts Islam, 1526–1850*. New York: Reaktion Books, 2008.

Friedrich, Karin. *Brandenburg-Prussia, 1466-1806: The Rise of a Composite State*. New York: Palgrave Macmillan, 2011.

Hughes, Lindsay. *Russia in the Age of Peter the Great*. New Haven: Yale University Press, 2000.

Isom-Verhaaren, Christine. *Allies with the Infidel: The Ottoman and French Alliance in the Sixteenth Century*. London: I.B. Tauris, 2013.

Ruderman, David B. *Early Modern Jewry: A New Cultural History*. Princeton: Princeton University Press, 2011.

Şahin, Kaya. *Empire and Power in the Reign of Suleyman*. Cambridge: Cambridge University Press, 2013.

Savory, Roger. *Iran Under the Safavids*. New York: Cambridge University Press, 2007.

Tezcan, Baki. *The Second Ottoman Empire: Political and Social Transformation in the Early Modern World*. New York: Cambridge University Press, 2010.

AP® Review Questions for Chapter 17

Multiple-Choice Questions

QUESTIONS 1–3 REFER TO THE FOLLOWING PASSAGE.

On [the Ottoman] side are the resources of a mighty empire, strength unimpaired, experience and practice in fighting. . . endurance of toil, unity, discipline, frugality and watchfulness. . . . [W]orst of all, the enemy is accustomed to victory, and we to defeat. . . . Persia alone interposes in our favor; for the enemy, as he hastens to attack, must keep an eye on this menace to his rear.

—Austrian ambassador on the Ottoman empire, ca. 1665

1. Which of the following best describes the ambassador's attitude toward the Ottoman empire?
   (A) Indifferent because the Ottoman empire was weak
   (B) Impressed by their cultural achievements
   (C) Fear that they may defeat the Austrians
   (D) Contempt toward their arrogance

2. Which of the following best explains why the Ottoman empire was so powerful?
   (A) The Ottomans were able to reunite the Islamic world under one state.
   (B) The population of the Ottoman empire was larger than that of Christian Europe.
   (C) A large number of Arab mercenaries were hired by the Ottoman sultan.
   (D) The Ottomans used their vast wealth from trade to build a large military.

3. Why does the Austrian ambassador believe the Persians might be a possible ally?
   (A) The Persians held the Arabs ruling the Ottoman empire in contempt.
   (B) The Persians were rivals of the Ottomans and forced the Ottomans to attend to this additional threat.
   (C) The Persians and the Ottomans were competing for control of the Islamic holy cities of Mecca and Medina.
   (D) The Persians were inciting Christian minorities in the Ottoman empire to rebel.

QUESTIONS 4–7 REFER TO THE FOLLOWING MAP.

4. Which of the following is an accurate statement concerning the Protestant movement in Europe?
   (A) The reformers were united under a single religious authority.
   (B) Several different Protestant sects emerged from the Reformation movement.
   (C) Most Protestant sects still acknowledged the authority of the pope.
   (D) The Reformation was strongest in the southern regions of Europe.

5. According to the map, which of the following is true of Scandinavia?
   (A) Scandinavia remained loyal to the Catholic Church even though its neighbors were Protestant.
   (B) Sweden and Norway were heavily influenced by the Orthodox Church.
   (C) Like much of Brandenburg and Saxony, Scandinavia was predominately Lutheran.
   (D) Calvinism was the state church in Denmark.

6. The Huguenots identified on the map can best be described as?
   (A) Supporters of the Jesuits
   (B) French Calvinists
   (C) Finnish Lutherans
   (D) Muslim converts

7. The religious division of Europe is symptomatic of what larger challenge during this time period?
   (A) Rulers finding ways to absorb and empower religious and ethnic minorities
   (B) Likelihood of rulers converting to a new religion to appease their subjects
   (C) Rulers attempting to limit the power and influence of ethnic and religious minorities
   (D) Rulers attempting to increase the participation of religious minorities in the ruling process

QUESTIONS 8–10 REFER TO THE FOLLOWING PASSAGE.

. . . that Kings are absolute seigneurs, and from their nature have full and free disposal of all property both secular and ecclesiastical, to use it as wise dispensers, that is to say, in accordance with the requirements of their State.

—Louis XIV, king of France, letter to the crown prince of France, ca. 1661–1666

8. The passage from Louis XIV demonstrates that in this time period European monarchs
   (A) were weaker than their medieval counterparts.
   (B) had increased their power compared with medieval monarchs.
   (C) were significantly weaker than Muslim sultans.
   (D) relied on foreign advisors to run their bureaucracies.

9. How were Louis XIV's attitudes similar to those of other state leaders during this time period?
   (A) Leaders around the world found their power being eclipsed by religious elites.
   (B) Leaders created a separation between state and religious authority
   (C) State leaders were consolidating power under their personal authority.
   (D) State leaders were ceding power to legislative bodies.

10. According to the passage, one way European monarchs legitimized their rule was by
   (A) claiming both political and religious authority.
   (B) acknowledging the superiority of religious institutions over state institutions.
   (C) suppressing opposition by using torture.
   (D) encouraging trade and supporting merchant activity.

Short-Answer Questions

One King, One Law, One Faith

—Louis XIV, king of France, 1643–1715

1. Use the passage above to answer parts A and B.
   A. Identify and explain ONE reason for Louis XIV wanting "One Faith."
   B. Identify and explain TWO ways Louis XIV implemented his motto in France.

2. Answer parts A and B.
   A. Briefly explain ONE cause of the Thirty Years' War in Europe.
   B. Briefly explain TWO effects of the Thirty Years' War on Europe.

18 Empires, Colonies, and Peoples of the Americas, 1600–1750

Catalina de Erauso

Hulton Archive/Getty Images

By the early 1600s, the Spanish had conquered the once-mighty Aztec and Inca and secured an American empire. But in some areas that they had not effectively occupied, Amerindian peoples held on to their independence. A battle-hardened young soldier, **Catalina de Erauso** (1585–1650), described an encounter with one such group in South America:

*On the third day we discovered a village of Indians who immediately took up arms. We went in and, feeling the [muskets] they scattered leaving some dead.... [A soldier] weary of his helmet, took it off to wipe off the sweat. A demon of a boy about twelve years old, who was blocking our exit up in a tree, fired an arrow which knocked him over. He was so badly hurt, unfortunately, that he died the next day. We cut the boy into ten thousand pieces.... The Indians, meanwhile, were returning to the village, about ten thousand of them. We attacked them with such fury and wreaked such havoc among them that a gutter of blood like a river flowed down through the place.... [I]n the houses of the village more than seventy thousand pesos in gold dust were found. Along the edge of the river, much more was found, and they filled their hats with it.**

---

*Early Americas Digital Archive, *The Autobiography of Doña Catalina de Erauso,* an electronic edition. http://mith.umd.edu/eada/html/display.php?docs=erauso_autobiography.xml&action=show%2522. Original Source: Ferrer, Joaquín María de. *Historia de la Monja Alférez (Doña catalina de Erauso)*. Madrid: Tipo Renovación, 1918. Translation and annotations by Dan Harvey Pedrick. Copyright 2007. This text is freely available provided the text is distributed with the header information provided.

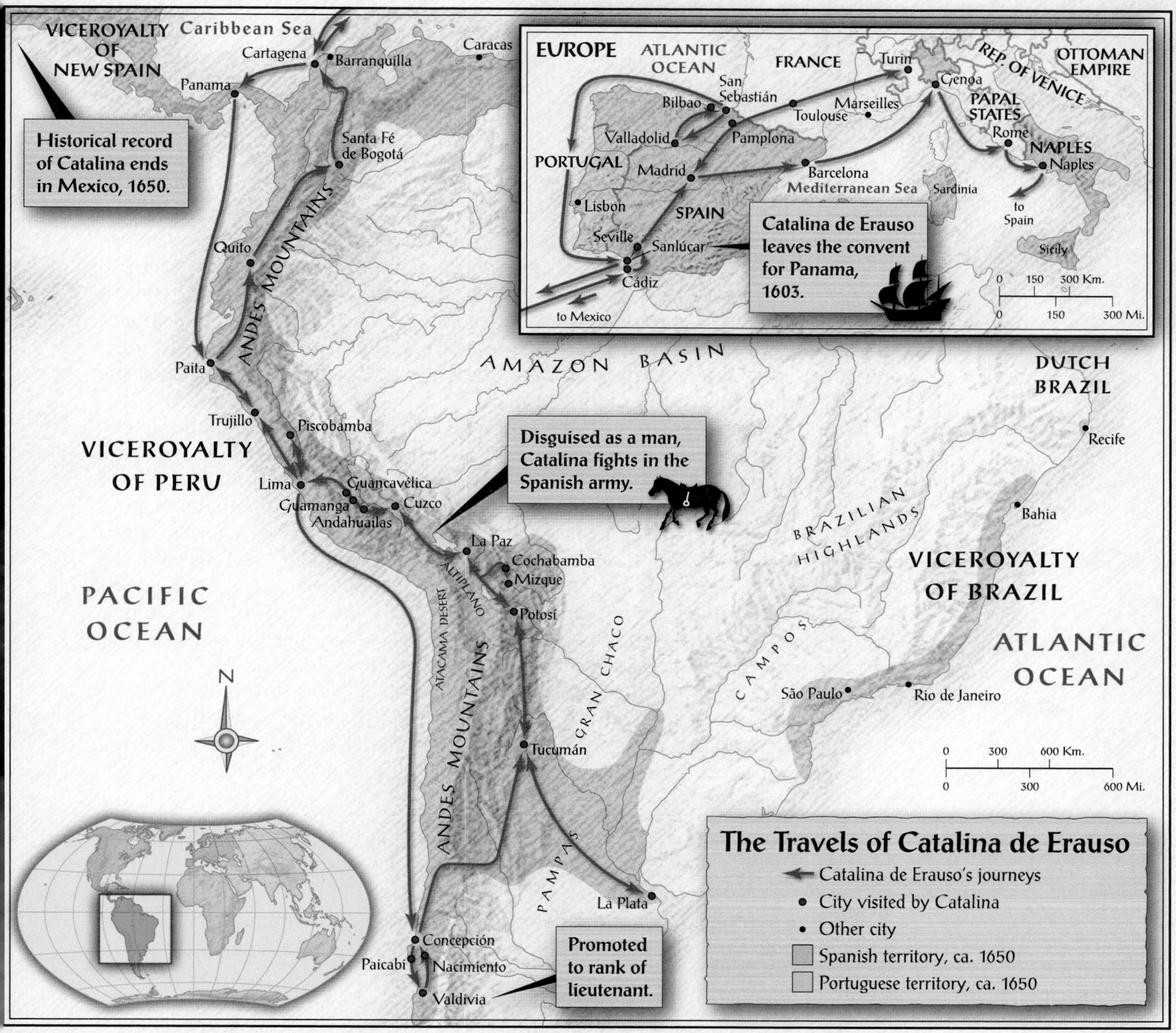

Surprisingly, it was a woman who painted this matter-of-fact picture of slaughter. Catalina de Erauso (kat-ah-LEE-nah day eh-rah-OO-so) was born in northeastern Spain and was placed in a convent by her family at age four. At age fifteen, when she was about to take the permanent vows that would confine her for a lifetime, she stole the keys and escaped:

> *I went out into the street (which I had never seen before) not knowing which way to turn or where to go.... I made myself a pair of trousers from a skirt of*

Catalina de Erauso
(1585–1650) Female Basque/Spanish explorer who, dressed as a man, lived the life of a soldier and adventurer in the Spanish colonial Americas.

*blue cloth that I had, and a shirt and leggings from the green shift that I wore underneath. Not knowing what to make of the rest of my [nun's] habit, I left it there. I cut off my hair and threw it away.**

Disguised as a boy, Erauso found employment as a personal assistant for a local nobleman, but she left when he "*insisted to the point of laying his hands on me.*" Afraid of being found out by her father, she stole some money, boarded a ship for Panama, and joined the Spanish army. For the next twenty years, Erauso traveled in the Spanish Americas, disguised as a man. A member of Spain's ethnically distinct Basque (bask) community, Erauso often teamed up with fellow Basques as she soldiered her way across Panama, Peru, Chile, Bolivia, and Argentina. According to her own story, her violent streak kept getting her into trouble. Card games often ended with insults and drawn swords, and more than once she had to run from the law after killing a man.

Erauso's exceptional story has become part of Latin American folklore, where she is known as *la monja alférez* (la mon-ha al-FAIR-ez), "the lieutenant nun." Her deception was made easier by frontier conditions, as new arrivals from Europe and Africa increased decade by decade, interacting with indigenous inhabitants in a fluidly changing cultural landscape. It was literally a "new world"—new for European officials, settlers, and adventurers; new for African slaves who did much to build the new American societies; and new for America's indigenous peoples, who saw their ways of life undermined as they came under the control of Spain, Portugal, France, and England. The interaction of peoples from Europe, Africa, and the Americas was the foundation upon which colonial American societies would be built.

This chapter examines the political, economic, social, and cultural life of colonial America in the seventeenth and early eighteenth centuries, focusing especially on gender and race relations, the role of the Americas in the global economy, and the differences between the various European colonial ventures.

KEY CONCEPT QUESTIONS

- What innovations were implemented in the Spanish Americas to meet the growing need for raw materials from the New World? **(Key Concept 4.2)**
- What were the results of the demographic and cultural interactions caused by the migration of Europeans and Africans to the Americas? **(Key Concept 4.1)**
- What were the similarities and differences among the various European colonies in the Americas? **(Key Concept 4.3)**

The Americas in Global Context: The Spanish Empire, 1600–1700

The Spanish laid waste to the Aztec and Inca empires in a remarkably short time (see Chapter 15). To rule their vast new territories, they immediately set up a highly centralized government that relied on close cooperation between crown

*Early Americas Digital Archive, *The Autobiography of Doña Catalina de Erauso,* an electronic edition. Original Source: Ferrer, Joaquín María de. *Historia de la Monja Alférez (Doña catalina de Erauso).* Madrid: Tipo Renovación, 1918. Translation and annotations by Dan Harvey Pedrick. Copyright 2007.

and church. It was a strictly hierarchical power structure, with officials from Spain and locally born Spaniards at the top, the increasing number of people of mixed descent in the middle, and Indians and African slaves at the bottom. As Erauso's story shows, however, the farther one went from centers of authority the more fluid relations of gender and race became, giving at least some people with modest backgrounds new possibilities in life.

From Conquest to Control

When Erauso arrived in Panama in 1603, the Spanish empire was the most powerful European colonial venture in the Americas and a rising maritime force, having established a base of power at Manila in the Philippines. True, a Spanish armada had been repulsed by England in 1588, and the Dutch, still under Spanish rule, were laying the foundations for their own global enterprise. But Philip II of Spain could count on American silver as a foundation for power (see Chapter 17) while the Spanish continued to advance their imperial frontier.

During the sixteenth century, the Spanish Habsburgs asserted increasing authority through a centralized bureaucracy headed by the Council of the Indies. In 1535, they sent the first viceroy to Mexico City, and in 1542 a second was dispatched to Lima. From that time forward, the emperor in Madrid sent officials to America as representatives of royal power. Four **viceroyalties** were eventually created: New Spain (with a capital at Mexico City), Peru (Lima), New Granada (Bogotá), and La Plata (Buenos Aires; see Map 18.1). Below the viceroys were an array of subordinate officials, such as governors and municipal authorities.

viceroyalties
Seats of power of the Spanish officials representing the king in the new world.

● **CONTEXT&CONNECTIONS** Spain's colonial structure was quite centralized compared to other imperial systems in world history. In the Ottoman empire, for example, the sultan's officials were more likely to work through intermediaries representing subject peoples such as Greeks or Armenians (see Chapter 17). In Spanish America, conquered Amerindians had very limited opportunity to secure official representation. ●

The other great institution of Spanish rule was the Catholic Church. The pope granted the Spanish crown the right to exercise power over the church in the Americas in all but purely spiritual affairs. Civil authorities appointed and dismissed bishops, while church leaders often served as top government officials. In the early colonial period, bishops sent directly from Spain occupied the higher church positions. In frontier areas, missionaries brought both Catholicism and Spanish rule.

At the same time that their missionary work extended the zone of Spanish control, some priests criticized the appalling conditions that ensued. Many representatives of Catholic religious orders positioned themselves as protectors of indigenous peoples against more rapacious Spanish settlers. The most prominent of these was the Dominican friar **Bartolomé de las Casas**, who argued for humane treatment of Amerindians as he criticized *"the outrageous acts of violence and the bloody tyranny"* of Spaniards who had *"lost all fear of God, all love of their sovereign, and all sense of self-respect."**

Bartolomé de las Casas
(ca. 1484–1566) A Spanish Dominican friar who argued for the humanity of Amerindians and criticized Spanish mistreatment of them.

As more Iberians crossed the ocean, American-born Spaniards grew in number. Known as *criollos* (kree-OY-os) ("creoles" in English), by the seventeenth century they were participating in government. Although officials from Spain continued to hold the top positions, criollos became a social and economic elite,

---

*Bartolomé de las Casas, *A Short Account of the Destruction of the Indies*, trans. Nigel Griffin (London: Penguin, 2004), p. 42.

Map 18.1 The Spanish Empire in the Americas This map of the early-eighteenth-century Americas shows the territorial dominance of the Spanish empire and its four viceroyalties. Though Portuguese Brazil was also large and rich, English and French colonial possessions were small and poor in resources by comparison. We should remember that this map shows European *claims* to territory. Some Amerindian societies remained autonomous and unconquered, especially in more remote regions of mountains, forests, and deserts.

often by seizing Amerindian land and exploiting Amerindian labor. Over time, they would become dissatisfied with the dominance of *peninsulares*, civic and religious officials sent directly from Spain (see Chapter 22).

Although lust for gold had been a principal motive of the early conquistadors, it was silver that filled the Spanish treasury and transformed the world economy. In 1545, the Spanish found a whole mountain of silver high in the Andes at **Potosí** (poh-toh-SEE), the greatest silver discovery in world history. Andean silver enabled European trade with Asia, and much of the silver extracted from Potosí ended up in China, stimulating the development of a more integrated early modern world economy (see Chapter 16).

Potosí
Location high in the Andes in modern Bolivia where the Spanish found huge quantities of silver. Silver exports from Potosí and other American mines helped finance development of the early modern world economy.

Silver mining generated huge profits, but not for the workers who dug open the mountain. Conditions were so brutal that force was needed to get workers for the mines. Though the crown had placed restrictions on *encomienda* (in-coh-mee-EN-dah) holders (see Chapter 15), a new legal system called the *repartimiento* (reh-par-TEE-me-en-toh) gave Spaniards the right to coerce Amerindian labor for specific tasks. Although the intent of reforming the encomienda system had been to limit abuses, most Spaniards still casually assumed they retained a right to enslave Amerindians. Erauso, for example, commented that during one of her trading ventures a civic leader *"put me in charge of ten thousand llamas to pack with and about one hundred or so Indian drivers."** Apparently, the Amerindians had no say in the matter.

AP® THEMES
What economic strategies did the Spanish use in their American colonies?

Although the Spanish called their Andean labor system *mita* (mee-tah)—the same name used by the Inca for their system of labor tribute—the Spanish mita differed greatly from the Inca one. Under the Inca, mita required every household to contribute labor for tasks such as military service, road construction, and the maintenance of irrigation works. Exemptions were granted for families in difficult circumstances, and workers were fed, clothed, and well treated. In contrast, the Spanish paid scant attention to the well-being of local communities or individual laborers. Under the Spanish mita system, every adult male had to spend one full year out of every seven working in the mines at wages that were not sufficient for his own support, let alone for his family.

After 1554, both Spanish profits and Amerindian suffering multiplied with the discovery of the **mercury amalgamation process**, which increased the efficiency of silver extraction from ore but also led to illness and death for many miners. Meanwhile, women, children, and the elderly back in their villages had to work harder to compensate for the absence of adult males. The silver economy predicated the wealth of some on the suffering of many: that was to be a recurring theme in Latin American history.

mercury amalgamation process
A process used to increase the efficiency with which silver could be extracted from ore. The use of mercury was highly toxic and led to the death of many Amerindian mine workers.

By 1600, Potosí was a major market, with a population over one hundred thousand when Erauso set off with her llamas and one hundred Indians: *"[The official] gave me a large amount of money to go to the plains of Cochabamba, buy wheat and mill it, and take it to Potosí where it was scarce and valuable."** The llamas were indigenous, but the wheat grew from European seed, an example of the ongoing Columbian exchange (see Chapter 15).

Expanding markets accompanied the growth of administrative centers such as Mexico City, Lima, and Buenos Aires, which stimulated local and regional trade in foodstuffs. In colonial Latin America, market-based agriculture took place on large

---

*Early Americas Digital Archive, *The Autobiography of Doña Catalina de Erauso,* an electronic edition. Original Source: Ferrer, Joaquín María de. *Historia de la Monja Alférez (Doña catalina de Erauso).* Madrid: Tipo Renovación, 1918. Translation and annotations by Dan Harvey Pedrick. Copyright 2007.

haciendas
Large estates characteristic of colonial agriculture in Latin America.

estates known as **haciendas** (ha-cee-EN-das). While many Amerindian communities remained largely self-sufficient by farming small village plots, the Spanish hacienda owners focused on meeting the rising demand for agricultural produce. In addition to growing crops for sale, many grazed vast herds of cattle.

Within the boundaries of their own large estates, hacienda owners had almost total control, governing their lands and the people who lived on them without reference to outside authority. They used debt peonage as a means of control, making loans to "their" Indians that were to be repaid in labor. But wages were never enough to repay the debt. Often, descendants of the original borrowers inherited these obligations and became permanently bound to a single estate, unable to seek higher wages or better working conditions elsewhere.

The Silver Mine at Potosí The silver mines of Spanish America, of which Potosí was the greatest, enriched the Spanish treasury and facilitated the expansion of global trade. As this engraving from 1590 shows, however, it was the heavy toil of Amerindian workers on Potosí's mountain of silver that made it all possible. Spanish mine operators used the mercury amalgamation process to increase the yield of silver from ore, resulting in the frequently lethal mercury poisoning of workers such as those seen here. (The Granger Collection, NYC)

• **CONTEXT&CONNECTIONS** The hacienda system would long persist in Latin America, and the inequalities associated with large agricultural estates actually increased after the colonial period, when nineteenth century hacienda owners began to focus on production of commercial crops for international markets. Many previously autonomous villagers in Central America, to give one example, were forced onto plantations to cultivate bananas and other commodities for rock-bottom wages (see Chapter 25). •

African labor supplemented that of Amerindians in some parts of Spain's American empire, most notably in Peru and Mexico. In the early conquest period, African slaves played a variety of roles, including fighting alongside the Spanish conquerors of the Andes and engaging in skilled crafts they brought with them from Africa, such as goldsmithing. As the mixed Spanish/Amerindian population grew, however, Afro-Peruvians began to lose their status as intermediaries between the Spanish and Amerindians, and by the eighteenth century they had become a despised subclass of manual laborers. Still, Afro-Peruvians made important cultural contributions to colonial society. (In coastal Peru, as in the Mexican coastal state of Guerrero where Africans also lived in large numbers, African musical instruments and rhythms are still found today.)

Spain's main goal was to extract minerals and other raw materials from America. Although it imported from the Americas such goods as dyes, cotton, and livestock hides for the manufacture of leather, no product came close in value to the tons of silver bullion sent in the annual armadas both directly to Spain and via the Manila galleons from Mexico to the Spanish Philippines (see Chapter 16).

Taking much from its American empire but investing little, Spain failed to lay the foundations for long-term economic growth. While other European nations were developing innovative commercial organizations (see Chapter 16), the Spanish crown and nobility were overly reliant on mineral wealth. As a consequence, the Dutch, English, and French effectively challenged stagnant Spain for American preeminence during the seventeenth and eighteenth centuries.

• **CONTEXT&CONNECTIONS** The Spanish crown and Spanish nobility remained largely aloof from commercial life, unlike in the Netherlands, where merchant capitalists dominated (see Chapter 16), or in England, where traders and trading companies were to be patronized by the crown and by the landed gentry (see Chapter 21). •

Colonial Society: Gender and Race on the Margins of Empire

The basic patterns of life in Spanish-speaking America were set by 1750, and the subjugation of indigenous societies was well advanced. Large-scale haciendas and mining operations were the foundation of commercial economies based on exploitation of the labor of Amerindians and African slaves. Officials from Spain dominated the upper ranks of both church and state, while criollos became local officials, hacienda landowners, and merchants. On the further frontiers, away from vice-regal centers like Mexico City and Lima, the Spanish presence was weaker, often with only a few hacienda owners or missionaries extending colonial networks to otherwise autonomous indigenous communities. (See the feature "World History in Today's World: Indigenous Studies and Indigenous Languages.")

Between the small Spanish elite at the top of the social hierarchy and the Amerindians who continued to practice ancient cultural traditions at the bottom, a complex mix of peoples and cultures emerged. Ingredients of this mix included European immigration, the forced migration of African slaves, and indigenous

WORLD HISTORY IN TODAY'S WORLD

Indigenous Studies and Indigenous Languages

In recent years, the world's indigenous peoples have become a focal point of scholarly research. Scholars of Indigenous Studies have focused on issues of persistent poverty: only 5 percent of the world's people are classified as "indigenous," but they make up nearly 15 percent of the global poor. Culture is another major concern. Just as scientists worry that rapid species extinction decreases the planet's biodiversity, so linguists argue that whenever an indigenous language disappears, cultural diversity suffers. When a language is lost, so is all the knowledge embedded within it.

In South America, although many indigenous American languages have faded away in the centuries since conquest, over 600 survive today. The Quechua (KETCH-wah) language is the most prolific, still spoken by over 10 million people in the Andes Mountains (see Chapter 15). The Spanish banned Quechua for official purposes in colonial times and restricted education and religious worship to Spanish and Latin. Nevertheless, Quechua survived and is now recognized as an official national language in Bolivia, Ecuador, and Peru. That cultural persistence has not brought economic benefit, however: Quechua speakers are among the poorest people in the Americas.

In North America as well, some indigenous tongues are spoken by substantial numbers: there are over 1 million speakers of Nahuatl, the language of the Aztecs, in Mexico, nearly 200,000 Navajo speakers in the United States, and about 140,000 people able to communicate in one of the Algonquian languages in Canada. But in some areas, like California and the Pacific Northwest, the situation is dire. California once had ninety indigenous languages. Only fifty survive, and half of those are spoken only by a small number of elders. In a race against time, linguists, cultural anthropologists, and tribal educators are developing programs to help indigenous speakers pass their knowledge on to a new generation.

The issue is also global: *National Geographic* researchers have identified five regions where indigenous languages are in the greatest danger of extinction: eastern Siberia, northern Australia, central South America (including Amazonia), Oklahoma, and the Pacific coastal regions of Canada and the United States. Without accelerated intervention, they predict that "by 2100, more than half of the more than 7,000 languages spoken on Earth—many of them not yet recorded—may disappear, taking with them a wealth of knowledge about history, culture, the natural environment, and the human brain."

Source: National Geographic, "Disappearing Languages," http://travel.nationalgeographic.com/travel/enduring-voices/.

populations that, though weakened by disease and deprivation, began a demographic recovery by the later seventeenth century.

The Spanish elite brought an outlook concerned with enforcing strict hierarchies of caste, gender, and religious and ethnic identity. Men were guided by a code of family honor, responsible for the virginity of their daughters and the fidelity of their wives. At the same time, they did not hold themselves to the same standards, often boasting of their multiple sexual conquests.

● **CONTEXT&CONNECTIONS** The fixation of the Spanish elite with *limpieza de sangre*—"purity of blood"—went back to the period of the Reconquista, when the Spanish reconquered Iberia from Muslim rulers (see Chapter 15). At that time, reserving public office for men of pure Spanish descent was instituted to keep converted Jews and Muslims out of positions of power. This policy was transferred to the Americas: those of non-Spanish and non-Catholic origin were expected to defer to their social superiors. ●

Maintaining elitist hierarchies in the courts, schools, and urban spaces of Mexico City, Lima, and other bastions of Spanish authority was easy enough. Outside the cities, however, conditions were more fluid. Spanish men rarely brought their wives and families to the Americas, and liaisons between Spanish men and indigenous women made "purity of blood" impossible to maintain. In Mexico by the seventeenth century, for example, a distinct **mestizo** (mes-TEE-zoh), or mixed Spanish/Amerindian, category had emerged.

mestizo
Offspring of an Amerindian and Spanish union. Cultural and biologic blending became characteristic of Mexican society.

Under frontier conditions, the Catholic Church also had difficulty imposing religious orthodoxy. In Spain itself, the inquisition (the Catholic bureaucracy devoted to suppressing heresy) strictly monitored the beliefs and behavior of the population. Families of *conversos* and *moriscos* (mohr-EES-koz), who had been forcibly converted from Judaism and Islam, were subjected to special scrutiny. On the colonial frontier, however, such groups were sometimes able to retain elements of their old faith, such as by incorporating Jewish rituals into their family traditions.

Converted Amerindians were the largest group of Catholics deviating from church doctrine, especially in Mexico and Peru, where missionaries had baptized many descendants of the Aztec and Inca. Many Amerindians embraced the church as a way to adapt to their new world, perhaps feeling that their old gods had abandoned them. At the same time, these converts adapted Christianity to maintain their own spiritual, ritual, and aesthetic traditions. Unlike in China, where Matteo Ricci had adapted Christianity to the traditions of his intended converts (see Chapter 16), in Spanish America it was not the missionaries but the colonized peoples themselves who blended their cosmologies and ritual traditions into Catholicism.

While some church leaders campaigned against the continuation of "idol worship" among baptized Amerindians, more often Spanish missionaries tolerated such practices. Amerindian populations gradually stabilized after the great losses of the sixteenth century, and where they formed a majority, as in the Andes, missionaries had little choice but to work through indigenous cultures. The result was a blend of existing and imported ideas known to historians as religious **syncretism**.

syncretism
The fusion of cultural elements from more than one tradition. In colonial Latin America religious syncretism was common, with both Amerindians and Africans blending their existing beliefs and rituals with Catholicism.

Unlike the Aztec (and Maya) pantheon of gods, the Christian God was resolutely male. Still, veneration of Mary as the Virgin Mother allowed Catholic Aztecs to retain the female presence in their religious worship previously represented by the fertility goddess Tonantzin. The centrality of the female principle in Mexican worship crystallized in the cult of the **Virgin of Guadalupe**.

In 1531, a peasant named Juan Diego reported to a Spanish bishop that the Virgin Mary had appeared to him. The bishop was initially doubtful but was unwilling to suppress the great popularity of the new cult. Though apparitions of the Virgin Mary were relatively common in Spain, the Virgin of Guadalupe had a special appeal in Mesoamerica, helping to fill the gap left as worship of goddesses like Tonantzin declined. In fact, the seventeenth-century Basilica of Our Lady of Guadalupe was built at the foot of a hill where Tonantzin herself had earlier been worshipped. Represented as dark in complexion, like most of her devotees, the Virgin of Guadalupe remains a symbol of Mexican identity and an embodiment of religious syncretism.

Virgin of Guadalupe
An apparition of the Virgin Mary, with a dark complexion, said to have appeared to a Mexican farmer in 1531. The cult of the Virgin of Guadalupe exerted a powerful attraction to Mesoamerica's surviving Amerindians. She remains a symbol of Mexican identity.

● **CONTEXT&CONNECTIONS** World historians have written about religious syncretism in a wide variety of global contexts, such as the Africanization of Islam and the cultural adaptation of Buddhism in China. The history of Christianity has repeatedly demonstrated how converts to the faith have blended new beliefs with older ones. Indeed, a thousand years before the appearance of the Virgin of Guadalupe, northern European converts to Christianity had adapted many of their pagan rituals to the new faith, as when German converts continued the old custom of bringing evergreen boughs into their homes to mark the winter solstice: today's "Christmas trees" are a legacy of that Germanic Christian syncretism. ●

AP® THEMES

How did Catholic beliefs and practices in the New World compare to Catholic beliefs and practices in Europe?

In Catalina de Erauso's story, the Catholic Church plays a more practical role. Once, after she had stabbed a man in a fight, she sought refuge in a church, where the civil authorities could not pursue her without the bishop's permission. In tough spots such as these she also relied on fellow members of the Basque-speaking minority for protection. Facing discrimination in Iberia, many Basques joined the Spanish army in the Americas. Erauso was exceptionally proud of her Basque heritage, but when dealing with Italians or Portuguese she was always quick to identify herself with Spain and assert Spanish superiority. Her multiple identities are another example of the fluidity of frontier life.

Erauso's autobiography also gives us fascinating insights into race and gender in frontier Spanish America (though we should bear in mind that she may have been more concerned with dramatic storytelling than the absolute truth). Once in Peru, she tells us, she deserted the army and wandered alone into the mountains, where she nearly died but was rescued by two men who took her to their mistress's ranch:

> *The lady was a half-breed, the daughter of a Spaniard and an Indian. She was [a] widow and a good woman who, upon seeing me and hearing of my plight and helplessness, pitied me and kindly took me in. She put me in a reasonable bed, fed me well, and allowed me to rest and sleep, with which I restored myself.... Seeing that I was totally lacking, she gave me a decent woolen suit, and went on treating me very well and generously. She was comfortably well-off and had many pack animals and cattle. Few Spaniards passed through there and it seems she wanted me as a spouse for her daughter.**

Erauso never intended to marry the girl: "*The daughter was very dark, and ugly as the devil, very contrary to my taste, which was always the pretty faces.*"* Still, she pretended to go along with the plan while accepting the widow's gifts. Meanwhile, she simultaneously became engaged to the niece of a Spanish official and, once again, accepted gifts from her potential in-law. "*Then came the part where I mounted the horse and disappeared,*"* she writes, never learning whatever became of the two young women she had courted.

casta system

The system of racial categorization in the Spanish Americas. Dozens of different "casta" terms were developed for various mixtures of European, African, and Amerindian descent. Though a flexible system that allowed movement "up" or "down" the racial hierarchy, markers of Spanish descent always carried the highest status.

What might explain Erauso's success at wooing young women in the guise of a man? Even allowing for embellishments, this incident suggests that Iberian men (as Erauso presented herself to be) were highly desirable marriage partners for families wishing to sustain or improve their social status. Marriage to a Spaniard could "improve" the family blood line, but outside the main cities, Spanish men were in such short supply that Erauso could easily, by her own account, contract multiple engagements. Of course, Spanish women were even less available as marriage partners. Most Spanish men could not afford to "import" wives from Iberia, so they made the best unions they could, usually fathering mixed-race children.

Erauso's narrative shows the complexities of the **casta system** of racial hierarchy, with dozens of terms for various racial mixtures and skin tones. She describes

*Early Americas Digital Archive, *The Autobiography of Doña Catalina de Erauso,* an electronic edition. Original Source: Ferrer, Joaquín María de. *Historia de la Monja Alférez (Doña catalina de Erauso).* Madrid: Tipo Renovación, 1918. Translation and annotations by Dan Harvey Pedrick. Copyright 2007.

Mexican Casta Painting A popular artistic tradition in colonial New Spain was the depiction of family groups of mixed heritage. This work by Miguel Cabrera is labeled, "From a Mestizo and an Indian, Coyote." Dozens of combinations are shown in other paintings, for example: *castizo*—one Spanish parent and one *mestizo* parent; *morisco*—one Spanish parent and one *mulatto* parent; *zambo*—one mulatto parent and one Indian parent; and *lobo*—one African parent and one Indian parent. Wealth and social status are clearly linked to racial background in casta paintings, but often, as here, poorer families are depicted quite sympathetically.

Elisabeth Waldo-Dentzel

the widow as a "half-breed" who is "good" and "well-off," trying to interest a Spaniard in marrying her "black" and "ugly" daughter. Here we see two fundamental racial realities. On the one hand, racial mixing was accepted as a part of life. On the other hand, whiteness always conferred status. So even in the many places where mestizos or mulattos (of mixed Spanish/African descent) formed the majority, social conventions and racial prejudices reinforced the superiority of Spanish descent, even among those of mixed race. Perhaps the widow thought marriage to a white soldier like Erauso could improve the color and status of her "ugly" daughter's children.

Gender relations and the social roles of women varied by social class. As in many societies, including the North African ones that had strongly influenced medieval Iberia, Spanish men demonstrated their wealth and status by keeping women away from the public realm. Elite parents, preoccupied with protecting the family honor, arranged unions for adolescent daughters who would, upon marriage, lead restricted lives. Those for whom no acceptable marriage could be found were sent to convents. Poorer families in which women played vital economic roles as farmers and artisans could not imitate such behavior; darker skin and ruddy complexions resulting from outdoor work marked their lowly status.

At the same time, elite women sometimes had access to education, and those in convents might rise to positions of authority within their all-female communities. **Sor Juana Inés de la Cruz** (1648–1695) was the most famous of such women. Born into a modest family, she was a child prodigy who learned to read Latin before the age of ten. She became a lady-in-waiting for the viceroy's wife in

Sor Juana Inés de la Cruz

One of the great literary figures of colonial New Spain. Wrote poetry, prose, and philosophy despite having been denied a university education. Best known for her defense of the intellectual equality of men and women.

Mexico City and a popular figure at court. But after her application to the University of Mexico was denied, she entered the convent. In contrast to Catalina de Erauso, who saw the convent as a prison, for Sor Juana life in an all-female community allowed her to develop her remarkable literary and intellectual skills.

Sor Juana's writings cover many topics, and her poetry is still taught to Mexican schoolchildren. She is best known for her passionate defense of the spiritual and intellectual equality of women with men: "*There is no obstacle to love / in gender or in absence, / for souls, as you are well aware, / transcend both sex and distance.*"* After years of correspondence and debate with church leaders who denounced her work, however, she saw the futility of trying to change their minds and stopped publishing altogether. In 1694, church officials forced her to sell her library of four thousand books, and the next year she died of plague.

Sor Juana's story illustrates the degree to which New Spain duplicated the Spanish social order. But Erauso's narrative reminds us that the "new world" could also mean new possibilities. In frontier conditions, the watchfulness of church and state was not as strong as it was in Europe or in Mexico City, giving Erauso a chance to carve out a life appropriate for her personality and ambition.

Brazil, the Dutch, New France, and England's Mainland Colonies

Throughout the sixteenth century and into the seventeenth, Spain remained the dominant imperial force in the Americas. Portugal, though more focused on Asia, did control Brazil, with its vast economic potential. Then, by the mid-seventeenth century, Spain was losing its global lead to up-and-coming Protestant powers, especially England and the Netherlands, and to the competing Catholic monarchy of France (see Chapter 17). Latecomers France and England started their settlements in North America well after the Spanish had created their great empire to the south. In French and British North America as well, the interactions of Europeans, Africans, and indigenous peoples created diverse cultural patterns, and again, the farther one moved toward the frontier, the more fluid those interactions were.

AP® THEMES

How did Portuguese colonization of Brazil contribute to new conceptions of racial ideologies?

The Portuguese and Brazil

In the sixteenth century, Portugal's overseas efforts focused on the Indian Ocean (see Chapter 16). Brazil, discovered by accident and acquired by treaty, was an afterthought, with no large cities to conquer and no empires to plunder. Portuguese settlement was initially limited to the coast, and apart from a lucrative trade in precious types of wood, Brazil initially offered little promise.

This situation changed dramatically in the later sixteenth century with the expansion of sugar plantations in northeastern Brazil. By the end of the seventeenth century, 150,000 African slaves made up about half of the colony's population. Meanwhile, Portuguese adventurers pushed into the interior seeking slaves, gold, and exotic goods such as brightly colored feathers from the Amazon. In 1695, gold was discovered in the southern interior. European prospectors brought African slaves to exploit the gold deposits, displacing the local Amerindians in the process.

Missionaries were powerful players in Brazil. Jesuits operated large cattle ranches and sugar mills to raise funds for church construction and missions to the interior.

*Quoted in Octavio Paz, *Sor Juana, trans*. Margaret Sayers Peden (Cambridge: Harvard University Press, 1988), p. 219.

As in the Spanish and French empires, Catholic missionaries often did their best to protect Indians from more brutal forms of colonial exploitation, but in the process they unwittingly introduced epidemic diseases that devastated the very people they had come to "save." Religious orders thus inevitably extended colonial control to the frontier, undercutting indigenous life. Thus, by the early eighteenth century, profits from sugar and gold had turned Brazil into Portugal's most important overseas colony.

As soon as the sugar plantation economy took hold in northeastern Brazil, slaves began to run away into the interior. Some of the runaways assimilated into Amerindian groups (see Chapter 19). Others formed their own runaway communities known as *quilombos* (key-LOM-boz). Since the members of quilombos were born and raised in different African societies, their political and religious practices combined various African traditions and gods.

The quilombo community of **Palmares** (pal-MAHR-es) was founded in the early seventeenth century, where slave runaways adapted the Central African institution of *kilombo*, a merit-based league of warriors that cut across family ties, ruled by their elected *Ganga Zumba* (Great Lord). Their syncretic religious life combined traditions of the Kongo kingdom (see Chapter 16) with other African traditions and Catholicism. With tens of thousands of residents, Palmares defended itself against decades of Portuguese military assaults until it was finally defeated in 1694. However, the adaptation of African religion and culture to the American environment continued long afterward.

Palmares
The largest and most powerful maroon community (1630–1694) established by escaped slaves in the colonial Americas. Using military and diplomatic means, their leaders retained autonomy from Portuguese Brazil for over half a century.

By 1750, Brazil had an exceptionally diverse culture. The Brazilian elite remained white, dominating laborers who were primarily African. As in Spanish

Africans in Colonial Brazil This watercolor from 1775 depicts a "royal parade" in which African cultural influence is unmistakable. While the "king" seems to wear a European-style crown, the umbrella is a characteristically West African symbol of kingship. The Brazilian penchant for parading in elaborate costumes began in colonial times and still culminates each year in Carnival celebrations infused with African cultural legacies

DEA/G. DAGLI ORTI/Getty Images

America, a large mixed-race group emerged, along with a similarly complex hierarchy. Catholicism served to unite Brazilian society while manifesting its diversity. While membership in religious brotherhoods devoted to specific saints or to the Virgin Mary was common across all social groups, for example, each brotherhood was organized by men from similar social backgrounds as determined by a combination of wealth, color, and place of origin. Across that spectrum, regardless of background, Brazilian Catholicism showed the infusion of African beliefs and rituals, although syncretism was, of course, strongest among the most recent African arrivals.

Though many were condemned to work in the brutal conditions of the sugar cane fields, Africans in colonial Brazil actually played many different roles, some even serving as soldiers. Indeed, the quality of African artisans' work frustrated some Portuguese immigrants who found it difficult to compete, and free blacks, facing no legal restrictions, were sometimes quite successful. A former slave named Cardoso, for example, bought his own freedom, made a fortune in trade, and left his money to his Catholic brotherhood.

As in the Spanish Americas, Brazil's social and racial hierarchy was flexible enough that individuals or families might try to improve their standing. Dress, speech, education, marriage, and above all, economic success were means by which Brazilians of mixed descent might gain higher status. Still, the basic polarities remained: white at the top of society, black at the bottom.

The Dutch in the Americas

Like the Portuguese, the Dutch were initially focused on Indian Ocean trade. However, from 1630 to 1654, they seized control of the northeastern coast of Brazil as part of their larger global offensive against the Catholic empires of Spain and Portugal. After an extremely violent conflict, in 1619 the Protestant Dutch had won their independence from Catholic Spain, which at that time also ruled over Portugal and therefore Brazil. Following the model of the successful Dutch East India Company, a group of merchants formed the Dutch West India Company in 1621 to penetrate markets and challenge the Spanish in the Americas. They sought advantage through aggressive capitalism, constantly reinvesting their profits in faster ships and larger ventures. In Brazil, the most important of these were the sugar plantations, to which the Dutch brought more capital investment and a larger supply of slaves.

Ousted from Brazil by the Portuguese in 1654, some Dutch planters transferred their business techniques and more advanced sugar-processing technology to the Caribbean. The resulting explosion of sugar production transformed Spanish-ruled islands like Cuba and Puerto Rico, as well as English ones like Jamaica and Barbados and French ones like Martinique and Saint-Domingue, and had dramatic consequences for Africa and the world economy (see Chapter 19).

Farther north, the Dutch West India Company founded the colony of New Netherland in 1624 and traded up the Hudson River Valley, allying with the powerful Iroquois Confederacy to tap into the lucrative fur trade. A small number of Dutch immigrants came as settlers to farm these rich and well-watered lands. But overall, Dutch commercial goals were still focused on Southeast Asia. In 1664, the Dutch surrendered New Netherland to the English without a fight. Their largest outpost, New Amsterdam, was renamed New York, and henceforth only the French and English would compete for dominance in North America.

New France, 1608–1754

Since the days of Columbus, European navigators had sought a western route to Asia. In the second half of the sixteenth century, French mariners sailed up the St. Lawrence River looking for a "northwest passage" to Chinese markets. What they found instead was the world's largest concentration of freshwater lakes and a land teeming with wildlife. In 1608, Samuel de Champlain founded the colony of New France with its capital at **Québec** (keh-BEC). In the later seventeenth century, French expeditions on the Mississippi and Ohio Rivers added vast territories, although here there were fewer Europeans and less immediate economic impact. The abundance of valuable furs in today's Canada was what most attracted French attention. Their indigenous trading partners did the actual work of trapping beavers and bringing the pelts to French trading posts. The yields of Amerindian trappers increased with the use of iron tools from Europe, driving the quest for fur ever deeper into the interior.

Québec
(est. 1608) Founded by Samuel de Champlain as the capital of New France (in modern Canada); became a hub for the French fur trade and the center from which French settlement in the Americas first began to expand.

● **CONTEXT&CONNECTIONS** Just like the Russians, who were expanding fur gathering into Siberia, French fur traders went far beyond the frontiers of formal colonial control, driven by lucrative European, Ottoman, and *Safavid* markets (Chapter 17). North American and Siberian peoples benefited little from the fur trade, however, and were also vulnerable to newly imported diseases. From a merchant's standpoint, Northern furs were akin to Southeast Asian spices (see Chapter 16): with great value relative to weight, both were cheap to transport and fetched exceptionally high prices. ●

Living far from other Europeans, French fur traders adapted to the customs of the First Nations peoples (as they are called in Canada). For example, tobacco smoking was an important ritual that cemented trade and diplomatic alliances. Sometimes traders assimilated deeply into First Nations communities, and their children were Amerindian in language and culture. More often French trappers and traders visited only seasonally; their mixed-race children, known in French as ***métis*** (may-TEE), learned both French and indigenous languages such as Cree and served as cultural and commercial intermediaries between First Nations and European societies.

métis
In colonial New France, the offspring of a European and Amerindian union.

Museum of Fine Arts, Boston/Laurie Platt Winfrey/The Art Archive

French Fur Trader French traders ventured far beyond the borders of European colonial society in their quest for valuable furs such as beaver pelts. They frequently adopted the technologies, languages, and customs of Amerindian peoples, and sometimes married into Amerindian societies. At the same time, on the other side of the world, the global fur market was also driving Russian traders deep into the forests of Siberia.

The fur trade had complex environmental and political effects. Once their traditional hunting grounds were exhausted, Amerindians had to venture farther to lay their traps. Bands came into conflict as they competed for beaver pelts, while guns for which they traded furs made skirmishes more lethal. New technologies and the desire for new commodities (iron tools and alcohol, as well as firearms) affected indigenous life well beyond the areas of European colonial control. On the Great Plains, for example, the introduction of firearms from New France and horses from New Spain enabled a new and more efficient style of buffalo hunting and mobile warfare among groups like the Lakota Sioux (see Chapter 25).

Huron
A matriarchal, Iroquoian-speaking Amerindian group in the St. Lawrence region that was devastated by the smallpox brought by French fur traders and missionaries in the mid-seventeenth century.

In the St. Lawrence region, the French were allied with the **Huron** people, who were receptive to the Jesuit missionaries who came up the river. French traders established residence in Huron country and negotiated with local chiefs to supply them with furs. Division of labor by gender facilitated the process. Since Huron men worked in agriculture only when clearing fields in early spring, they were available for hunting and trading parties during the rest of the year, while the women stayed behind to tend the fields. The political power and economic resources that came from the fur trade therefore went mainly to men, a development that undercut the traditional power of Huron women: male chiefs became more powerful at the expense of the matriarchs chosen by their clans to represent them on the Huron confederacy council.

AP® THEMES

How did the natural resources available to Europeans influence European settlement patterns in North America?

While some Huron chiefs and hunters benefited from fur trading, the overall effects of contact with the French were disastrous. By 1641, half of the Huron population had been killed by disease. Many Huron sought baptism, praying that the priests' holy water would save them from the smallpox that the missionaries themselves had unknowingly introduced.

Meanwhile, French settlers were attracted to the farmlands surrounding the city of Québec, where some fifty thousand French men and women lived by 1750. These farmers, and the small urban population they supported, represented the beginnings of quite a different European presence in what would later become Canada. While the fur traders and missionaries sought to integrate into indigenous societies in their search for pelts to buy or souls to save, French settlers were driven by the search for cheap land and higher wages. In later years, as their numbers swelled and the frontier advanced, such settlers would increasingly displace First Nations peoples (see Chapter 25).

In the first half of the eighteenth century, however, the most valuable French possessions in the Americas were not vast North American territories but relatively small Caribbean islands. Using African slave labor, French plantations in the West Indies made huge profits producing sugar for European markets. The same was true for England.

Mainland English Colonies in North America

For the English, as for the French, the Caribbean islands and sugar were the economic focal points of their American venture (see Chapter 19). Also like the French, the English were relative newcomers to mainland America in the first half of the seventeenth century, settling initially in Virginia and Massachusetts. Jamestown, founded in 1607 and the first permanent English settlement in **Virginia**, was nearly wiped out in its early years, but by the 1630s the colony was thriving after the colonists discovered a lucrative Atlantic market for tobacco. Long used by Amerindian peoples for social and ritual purposes, tobacco became the foundation of Virginia's prosperity and generated a strong demand for labor.

Virginia
(est. 1607) English colony in North America with an export economy based on tobacco production. The use of European indentured servants gave way to dependence on slave labor.

In colonial North America, Amerindians formed a miniscule part of the labor force. Unlike the Spanish, who used Amerindians as miners and as farm labor, the English often drove Amerindians off the land with the goal of replacing them with "civilized" English farmers. Not only were the indigenous peoples weakened by disease, there were also cultural barriers. In eastern North America's woodland societies, women were the principle farmers, while men focused more on hunting. English colonists therefore had little success in recruiting the local men as dependent workers.

● **CONTEXT&CONNECTIONS** Patterns of European global settlement were determined largely by disease environments. In New England, in the southwestern corner of Africa at Cape Town (see Chapter 16), and in Australia (see Chapter 21), Afro-Eurasian diseases like smallpox proved fatal to indigenous peoples, clearing the way for colonies of European settlement. Across most of Africa and Asia, however, it was Europeans who were more vulnerable to local disease. There, Europeans would never constitute more than a tiny percentage of the total population, even following their nineteenth-century conquests (see Chapters 24 and 26). ●

North America's English farmers were in direct competition with indigenous peoples for the land, water, and hunting opportunities they needed to survive. Sir Walter Raleigh, a major investor in Virginia settlement, had set a precedent when, after putting down a late-sixteenth-century Irish rebellion, he created settlements where the *"savage Irish"* were to be replaced by more dependable English farmers. In Virginia, the "savages" were Amerindian rather than Irish, but Raleigh's strategy remained the same. Throughout the English colonies, European settlers generally drove indigenous peoples toward the margins of colonial settlement. (See the feature "Movement of Ideas Through Primary Sources: Prospero and Caliban.")

However, plantations in England's southern colonies required more work than free settlers could provide. One solution was indentured labor. In this system, employers paid for the transportation costs of poor English and Irish peasants in return for four to seven years of work, after which they received either a return passage or a small plot of land. Cheap as this labor was, tobacco planters needed a labor force even cheaper and more servile. In 1619, when the first shipment of captive Africans arrived at Jamestown, they were treated as indentured servants. By the 1650s, however, a racial distinction between white servants and African slaves had become the rule. By the late seventeenth century, planters were buying larger numbers of African slaves in Virginia markets.

Colonial authorities worried about contact between Europeans and Africans; as early as 1630, one Hugh Davis was whipped *"for abusing himself to the dishonor of God and the shame of Christians, by defiling his body in lying with a Negro."** By the later seventeenth century, Virginia law prohibited all interracial unions. Though such liaisons continued, of course, the principle that would later be known as the "one drop" rule was being established: any sign of African descent became a badge of inferiority, with both mixed-race Virginians and the small number of free blacks suffering persistent discrimination. Such racial absolutism in the English colonies stood in contrast to the more flexible hierarchies of color and status common in Brazil and the Spanish Americas.

---

*Quoted in George Fredrickson, *White Supremacy: A Comparative Study in American and South African History* (New York: Oxford University Press, 1981), p. 100.

Prospero and Caliban

When Catalina de Erauso arrived in New Spain, William Shakespeare was the leading playwright in the English-speaking world. Shakespeare's imagination, like that of many Europeans in the early seventeenth century, was stimulated by tales of exotic adventure in what one of Shakespeare's characters referred to as "this brave new world." That line comes from *The Tempest* (1611), a drama that reflects European fascination with new discoveries in the Americas. Shakespeare used reports from Virginia settlers who had survived a shipwreck to weave a fantastic tale of magic, revenge, and the triumph of justice.

A great magician named Prospero and his daughter, Miranda, are stranded on an island. In the scene below, Prospero speaks with a misshapen monster named Caliban, the only native inhabitant of the island. From Prospero's perspective, Caliban deserves harsh treatment. In spite of the kindness shown by the magician, the monster attempted to rape Miranda. Things look very different from Caliban's viewpoint. The powers he inherited from his mother, Sycorax, cannot counter Prospero's magic, and he has no choice but to serve as the magician's slave while plotting his vengeance. Their unequal positions are even reflected in their names, which might be translated as "Prosperity" and "Cannibal." Though Shakespeare presents Prospero as having justice on his side, we should look for places where he also allows Caliban to voice his complaints as an abused native imprisoned by a colonial master.

› **Historical Thinking Skill:**
COMPARISON What similarities do you find between Prospero's treatment of Caliban and the treatment of conquered Amerindian peoples?

› **Historical Thinking Skill:**
SYNTHESIS How did works of literature, such as Shakespeare's *The Tempest*, help shape people's understanding of foreign societies in the time of exploration and early settlement of the New World?

Source: Excerpt from William Shakespeare, *Tempest.* http://the-tech.mit.edu/Shakespeare/tempest/index.html. The glossary is original.

The Tempest, Act I, Scene 2

Prospero: Thou poisonous slave, got• by the devil himself
Upon thy wicked dam,• come forth!

Caliban: As wicked dew as e'er my mother brush'd
With raven's feather from unwholesome fen
Drop on you! a south-west blow on ye
And blister you all o'er!

Prospero: For this, be sure, tonight thou shalt have cramps,
Side-stitches that shall pen thy breath up; urchins•
Shall, for that vast of night that they may work,
All exercise on thee;• thou shalt be pinch'd
As thick as honeycomb, each pinch more stinging
Than bees that made 'em.

Caliban: This island's mine, by Sycorax my mother,
Which thou takest from me. When thou camest first,
Thou strokedst me and madest much of me, wouldst give me
Water with berries in't, and teach me how
To name the bigger light, and how the less,
That burn by day and night:• and then I loved thee
And show'd thee all the qualities o' the isle,
The fresh springs, brine-pits, barren place and fertile:
Cursed be I that did so! All the charms
Of Sycorax, toads, beetles, bats, light on you!
For I am all the subjects that you have,

•**got** Begotten.
•**dam** Mother.
•**urchins** Goblins.
•**exercise on thee** Torment you.
•**day and night** The sun and moon.

Which first was mine own king: and here you sty• me
In this hard rock, whiles you do keep from me
The rest o' the island.

Prospero: Thou most lying slave,
Whom stripes• may move, not kindness! I have used• thee,
Filth as thou art, with human care, and lodged thee
In mine own cell, till thou didst seek to violate
The honour of my child.

Caliban: O ho, O ho! would't had been done!
Thou didst prevent me; I had peopled else•
This isle with Calibans.

Prospero: Abhorred slave,
Which any print of goodness wilt not take,
Being capable of all ill! I pitied thee,
Took pains to make thee speak, taught thee each hour
One thing or other: when thou didst not, savage,
Know thine own meaning, but wouldst gabble like
A thing most brutish, I endow'd thy purposes
With words that made them known. But thy vile race,
Though thou didst learn, had that in't which good natures
Could not abide to be with; therefore wast thou
Deservedly confined into this rock,
Who hadst deserved more than a prison.

Caliban: You taught me language; and my profit on't
Is, I know how to curse. The red plague rid you
For learning me your language!

Prospero: Hag-seed,• hence!
Fetch us in fuel; and be quick, thou'rt best,
To answer other business. Shrug'st thou, malice?
If thou neglect'st or dost unwillingly
What I command, I'll rack thee with old cramps,
Fill all thy bones with aches, make thee roar
That beasts shall tremble at thy din.

Caliban: No, pray thee.
Aside
I must obey: his art is of such power,
It would control my dam's god, Setebos, and make a vassal of him.

Prospero:
So, slave; hence!

•**sty** Imprison.
•**stripes** Whippings.
•**used** Treated.
•**else** Otherwise.
•**hag-seed** Child of a witch.

• **CONTEXT&CONNECTIONS** The "one drop" rule in the United States has historically meant that even individuals with one black parent and one white parent have been classified as "black." The term *mulatto* exists, but one would hardly refer to a U.S. president as "mulatto." In South Africa, in contrast, people of mixed race call themselves "coloured," a positive label affirming a distinctive social and racial identity. In contrast to both the United States and South Africa, in Brazil and much of Latin America, numerous racial classification are arranged along a scale from white to black, and an individual's placement on that scale may be influenced by markers of wealth, education, and other social factors beyond mere skin color. •

Even as slave bondage increased, Virginia evolved a system of governance in which free, propertied white men had a voice, and they took more and more matters into their own hands during England's long constitutional crisis in the seventeenth century (see Chapter 17). By the 1660s, Virginia's assembly, the House of Burgesses, was acting as an independent deliberative body. By the eighteenth century, Virginia's ruling class of planters were accustomed to running their own affairs and jealous of any signs of English interference (see Chapter 22).

Slavery was less important in the middle colonies, where New York City and Philadelphia emerged as vibrant political and economic centers. Twenty thousand German settlers had arrived in Pennsylvania by 1700, but the European immigrant population was still primarily English and Scottish. (After 1707, with the union of England and Scotland, we may refer to the two groups together as "British.")

New England
Colony that began with the arrival of English Calvinists in 1620s, and characterized by homogeneous, self-sufficient farming communities.

The settlement of **New England** began with the arrival in the 1620s and 1630s of religious dissenters dissatisfied with the established Church of England. More English settlers soon came for economic reasons: land was cheap, and wages were relatively high. As in French Québec, entire families migrated to New England intending to recreate the best features of the rural life they knew in England and combine them with American economic opportunity. Whereas elsewhere European men outnumbered European immigrant women, in New England their numbers were equally balanced, making cultural and racial mixing much less common. Since families did their own farm work, there was little call for slave labor.

In the seventeenth and early eighteenth centuries, then, England's mainland colonies were of limited economic and strategic importance. The silver of New Spain and the sugar of the West Indies generated profits on a much greater scale. With a hostile alliance of French and Indian societies to the north and west, the potential for expansion beyond the Atlantic seaboard seemed uncertain. However, by 1750, England and France were poised to battle for control of such diverse colonial territories as the Ohio River Valley, plantation colonies in the Caribbean, and trade settlements in South Asia (see Chapters 19 and 20). By that time the significance of Britain's mainland American colonies had grown substantially, and by the eighteenth century they had achieved a degree of self-governance. Not willing to give up the voice in public affairs to which they had become accustomed, colonists would increasingly resist attempts by the English monarchy to impose more central control (see Chapter 22).

Comparisons Across the Colonial Americas

By 1750, Europe's impact on the Americas was profound. While different geographical conditions led to diverse economic and demographic outcomes, the various political, religious, and cultural traditions of the European colonial powers also left deep marks.

● **CONTEXT&CONNECTIONS** Throughout the Americas, one common feature was the continuing effects of the *Columbian exchange* (Chapter 15). First introduced by the Spanish, horses and cattle flourished on wide-open American grasslands. Other domesticated imports, especially sheep and pigs, added to livestock supplies. European grains like wheat and barley were planted along with American crops like maize, potatoes, squash, and tomatoes, creating a richer and more varied diet than was common in Europe. ●

However, few Amerindians shared in the bounty. Contagious disease continued to cause high mortality, even beyond the formal boundaries of European empires. The decimation of Amerindian populations transformed the landscape. In Mexico, Amerindian farmlands were converted to grazing for European livestock; in the Chesapeake area, tobacco plantations replaced the more varied Amerindian agricultural and hunting landscapes.

All European powers harnessed American profits to augment the wealth and power of their monarchs and to advance their place among the contending Great Powers (see Chapter 17). Although they all tried to strictly regulate their colonial economies—for example, by restricting colonial trade to ships bound for the mother country—actual imperial control of commerce was never as great in practice as it was in theory. In the seventeenth century, smuggling and piracy were common, and colonists were frequently able to evade laws that required them to trade only with their home countries. Later in the eighteenth century, when European states attempted to regulate trade more closely, tensions with colonists resulted (see Chapter 22).

AP® THEMES

How did policies promoting mercantilism facilitate the European state formation and expansion?

Within the various colonies, quite different economic regimes took hold. Some enterprises were merely extractive: mines in Spanish America or furs in New France, for instance. Here indigenous people formed the workforce (usually by compulsion in New Spain and often voluntarily in Canada). In New Spain, large mining operations and expanding urban centers offered growing markets for hacienda owners, exceptionally powerful men whose large estates commanded the labor and obedience of dependent workers, usually Amerindians or mixed-race mestizos.

Lacking minerals to exploit, the economies of the English colonies all relied on agriculture (and, in New England, fishing), though their agricultural regimes and settlement patterns differed. In temperate New England, independent farmers worked small but productive plots, largely with family labor. In contrast, large plantations were the characteristic form of landholding in colonial Carolina, where the coastal settlement resembled the West Indian pattern, exploiting massed African slave labor to produce great quantities of high-value commodities for export. In Virginia, slave labor was central to the economy, but the plantations were smaller than in Carolina, and European settlers generally used relatively fewer slaves to supplement family and indentured labor.

Religious traditions shaped the development of all of the colonial American cultures. Not surprisingly, the religious rivalries of the Reformation were exported to the Americas. The politics of the Reformation magnified territorial and commercial competition between the Catholic Spanish and Protestant English, as well as between the Catholic Portuguese and Protestant Dutch. These politics also affected French settlement. After 1627 the French monarchy, doubtful of Huguenot loyalty, banned Protestant emigration to New France. Among the English colonies, Rhode Island and Pennsylvania were the only colonies that guaranteed freedom of religious worship, accommodating Catholic settlers who were not welcome in New England or Virginia. (See the feature "Visual Evidence in Primary Sources: Catholic and Protestant Churches in the Americas.")

Catholic and Protestant Churches in the Americas

The great diversity of Christian religious beliefs and rituals is clearly demonstrated by church architecture. There is a sharp contrast between the interior of the Spanish colonial church of Santa Maria Tonantzintla (*left*) in Puebla, Mexico, and that of the Old Whaling Church (*right*) in Sag Harbor, New York. The Spanish church embodies the Catholic preference for richly embellished church interiors associated with elaborate rituals, while the colonial English church reflects the asceticism and simplicity of the Calvinist tradition.

The name of the church, *Tonantzintla*, means "place of our little mother" in the Nahuatl (NAH-watt) language. Tonantzintla was the name of the Aztec earth goddess who converts then identified with the Virgin Mary, mother of Jesus.

One architectural commentator has written of this church: "The fruits, flowers, children, faces, masks, birds, figures of saints and more, together form an extraordinary mosaic—a frank '*horror vacui*,' or fear of empty spaces—that is so typical of the Baroque style and here is interpreted in an indigenous fashion."*

The term "indigenous baroque" has been used to describe this elaborately decorated form of church architecture. "Indigenous" refers to the use of Amerindian design elements, while "baroque" refers to the florid, expressive style of ornamentation then popular in southern Europe.

akg-images/Gilles Mermet/Newscom

The Catholic mass at that time was held in Latin. Preparing for communion, the priest performed the Eucharistic rite, in which bread is transformed into the body of Christ, facing the altar, which was designed to move the congregation's focus forward and upward, toward the heavens. ***How does the function of this church differ from that of the Old Whaling Church?***

*Ignacio Cabral, *Religious Architecture in San Andrés Cholula, Puebla.* http://www.puebla-mexico.com/tag/santa-maria-tonantzintla/

The name "Old Whaling Church" commemorates the sea captains who sponsored its construction. From colonial times into the nineteenth century, the whaling industry provided income and employment for many New Englanders.

The church was built in the "Greek Revival" style, emphasizing clean, classical lines and an overall emphasis on order and harmony. The parishioners were entirely of European ancestry: there is no trace of Amerindian or African influence.

David Lyons/Alamy

Old Whaling is a Presbyterian church, a branch of Protestantism strongly influenced by the teachings of John Calvin (see Chapter 17). Members of such "reformed" churches emphasized Bible reading, quiet contemplation, hard work, strict discipline, and the avoidance of all forms of excess. ***How are those values reflected in this Presbyterian church's architecture?***

The democratic structure of the Presbyterian Church contrasts sharply with the Roman Catholic Church hierarchy. While Catholic bishops are appointed from Rome, Presbyterian "elders" are elected by their own congregations.

Presbyterianism was the dominant faith of seventeenth-century Scotland, and it was largely Scottish immigrants who brought the faith to British North America.

As part of colonial competition and the tensions following the Protestant Reformation, the English developed a strongly negative view of the Spanish and their empire. Associating Spain with religious intolerance and violent treatment of native peoples, the "black legend" of Spanish barbarism and cruelty infused English literature and philosophy. In the twentieth century, the Mexican poet Octavio Paz turned the "black legend" on its head, arguing that it was actually the English who were most harsh, by excluding Amerindians from colonial life altogether. Paz argued that the Spanish church at least allowed indigenous people *"to form a part of one social order and one religion."* That chance to be an accepted part of colonial society, *"even if it was at the bottom of the social pyramid,"* Paz wrote, *"was cruelly denied to the Indians by the Protestants of New England."**

Perhaps Paz underestimated the missionary impulse among Protestants, some of whom did make a strong effort toward converting Amerindians. He was correct, however, in pointing out the difference between the more fluid racial hierarchy of the Spanish empire and the more rigid forms of racial discrimination that developed in English North America. The Spanish system (and the Portuguese one in Brazil), though based on hierarchy and inequality and emphasizing Amerindian and African inferiority, was flexible, allowing for gradations of identification and classification among people of mixed European, African, and Amerindian backgrounds. The English system of racial classification was more sharply segregated. Though substantial intermixing occurred among the main population groups in the early colonial period, English authorities made little accommodation for mixed-race identities.

Gender identities were strongly fixed in every colonial society. However, as we have seen, social realities could be more fluid on the frontier, as when French fur traders interacted with matrilineal First Nations peoples and adopted their customary respect for female authority.

Catalina de Erauso was, of course, most exceptional. Badly wounded in a fight, and thinking she had better confess her sins before she died, Erauso told a priest about her deception. He did not believe her, but the nuns sent to discover the truth confirmed that she was actually a woman. After she recovered, Erauso went to Spain to seek a pension from the king for her service as a soldier, and to Rome to meet the pope. News of her strange story spread across Europe, and as she journeyed by horseback across France on her way to Italy, people came out to the road to see the famous woman warrior in a man's uniform. During her papal audience at the Vatican, the pope chastised Erauso for her violent behavior, but then granted her formal permission to dress as a man for the rest of her life.

While in Rome, Erauso narrated her story to an unknown scribe, ending with the following anecdote:

> *While strolling along the wharf in Naples one day, I perceived the loud laughter of two girls who were chatting with a couple of boys. We stared at each other and one said to me, "Where to, Lady Catalina?" I answered, 'To give*

*Octavio Paz, *The Labyrinth of Solitude* (New York: Grove Press, 1961), pp. 101–102.

*you a hundred whacks on the head, my lady whores, and a hundred slashes to whoever may wish to defend you!' They shut up and slipped away.**

How did Erauso see herself? Did she resent having to act as a man to live her own life as she pleased? Or was her cross-dressing more than a masquerade? History provides no additional evidence.

It seems that Erauso preferred the life of the colonial frontier. According to legend, she returned to Mexico, disappeared into the mountains with a pack of burros, and was never heard from again. She was one of many European immigrants for whom the Americas represented new possibilities.

---

*Early Americas Digital Archive, *The Autobiography of Doña Catalina de Erauso,* an electronic edition. Original Source: Ferrer, Joaquín María de. *Historia de la Monja Alférez (Doña catalina de Erauso).* Madrid: Tipo Renovación, 1918. Translation and annotations by Dan Harvey Pedrick. Copyright 2007.

CONTEXT AND CONNECTIONS

Spain, the Americas, and the World

That the Habsburg dynasty won the sixteenth-century silver and gold lottery was significant for world history (see Chapter 17). American mineral wealth, combined with extensive Habsburg territorial control in Europe, elevated the court of Madrid to the top rank in an interconnected world where European dynastic rivalries had gone global. The political and military impulses of the *reconquista* (the Christian reconquest of Iberia, completed in 1492) were then transferred to the international stage, as Catalina de Erauso's narrative shows. The Spanish emphasis on "purity of blood" once directed at Jews and Muslims was one such continuity (even as, ironically, racial mixture was common in the Spanish Americas); the admixture of militarism and Catholicism was another.

Spain's leading role would not long endure, however: even the fabulous riches flowing from Potosí and other American mines were not sufficient to enable the Spanish to turn back the challenge of the Protestant Reformation or to maintain their lead in imperial affairs (see Chapter 17). Following the Spanish head start, the English, French, and Dutch were left to vie for what seemed less desirable territories to the north. Though initially less well endowed with resources and population, the colonial economies of the northern Europeans were more dynamic.

The Dutch were pioneers in the development of the tools of merchant capitalism, including joint-stock companies and chartered monopolies to develop new markets (see Chapter 16). The English, who had begun their American venture as little more than pirates, built on and further developed these tools of mercantile capitalism to become the greatest naval force in the world by the eighteenth century, further expanding their empire in both Asia and the Americas. By then, with Spain reduced to a minor power, it was the British and the French who would compete for European supremacy on the global stage (see Chapters 19 and 20).

We should not, however, repeat the common error of overstating the global role of the West in the period from 1500 to 1750. The Americas were unique in the degree to which the Western impact transformed society environmentally, politically, and culturally. Even here, though, some indigenous societies long remained outside the orbit of colonial empires, and through cultural mixing and merging, indigenous traditions continued.

In Afro-Eurasia, European ascendency was less assured in the early eighteenth century. Land-based empires still remained more important in Asia than maritime ones. As we shall see in upcoming chapters,

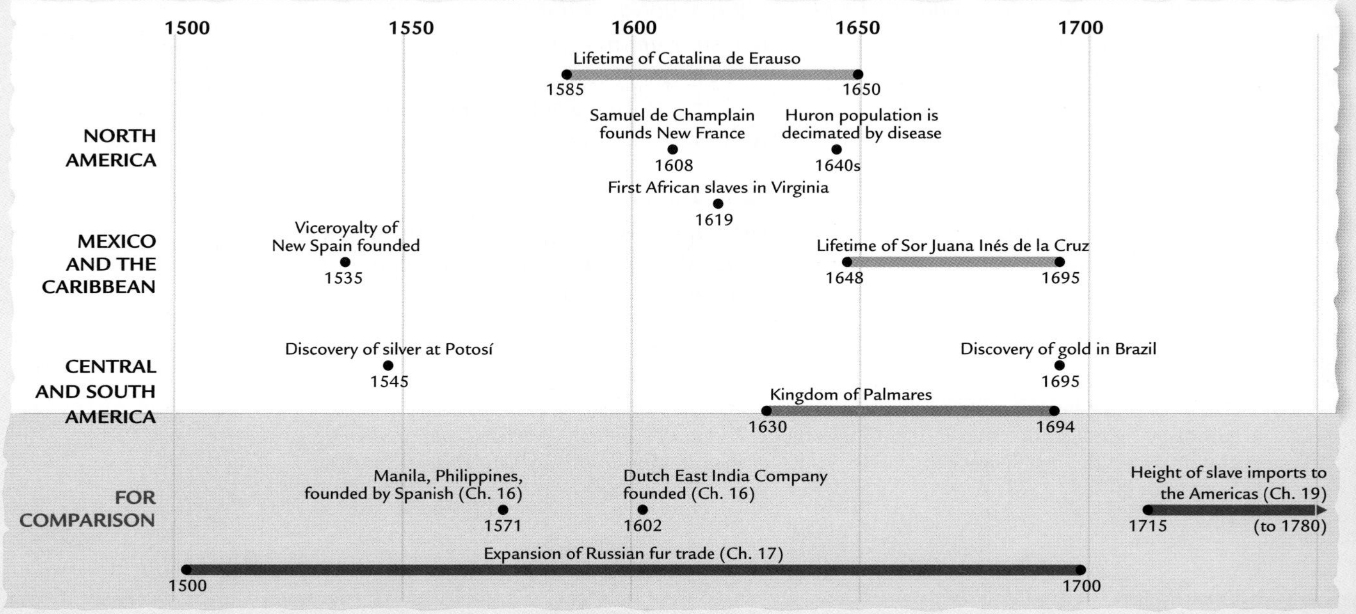

European global dominance was not fully secured until the nineteenth century, in the wake of the Industrial Revolution.

Although Europeans had only a tiny footprint on the African continent by 1750, millions of African lives had been utterly transformed by the Atlantic slave trade. Their experiences in the Americas varied, with some finding opportunities in the new world, much like Catalina de Erauso. The most common new world story for Africans, however, was the hardship of brutal plantation work. On the sugar islands of the West Indies, Africans slaved to harvest the sugar and other crops that enriched and empowered their European masters. The trade in slaves brought untold misery to both those Africans forced into exile and to the continent of Africa itself, as we will see in the next chapter.

Key Terms

Catalina de Erauso (532)
viceroyalties (533)
Bartolomé de las Casas (533)
Potosí (535)
mercury amalgamation process (535)
haciendas (536)
mestizo (539)
syncretism (539)
Virgin of Guadalupe (539)
casta system (540)
Sor Juana Inés de la Cruz (541)
Palmares (543)
Québec (545)
métis (545)
Huron (546)
Virginia (546)
New England (550)

For Further Reference

Benton, Lauren A. *Law and Colonial Cultures: Legal Regimes in World History, 1400–1900*. New York: Cambridge University Press, 2002.

Burns, Kathryn. *Colonial Habits: Convents and the Spiritual Economy of Cuzco, Peru*. Durham: Duke University Press, 1999.

Eccles, William J. *The French in North America, 1500–1783*. Rev. ed. Lansing: Michigan State University Press, 1998.

Fernandez-Armesto, Felipe. *The Americas: The History of a Hemisphere*. London: George Weidenfeld and Nicholson, 2003.

Kamen, Henry. *Empire: How Spain Became a World Power, 1492–1763*. New York: HarperCollins, 2003.

Lavrin, Asunción. *Sexuality and Marriage in Colonial Latin America*. Lincoln: University of Nebraska Press, 1992.

Nash, Gary. *Red, White and Black: The Peoples of Early North America*. 6th ed. New York: Prentice Hall, 2009.

Nellis, Eric. *An Empire of Regions: A Brief History of British Colonial America*. Toronto: University of Toronto Press, 2010.

Paz, Octavio. *Sor Juana*. Margaret Sayers Peden, trans. Cambridge, Mass.: Harvard University Press, 1988.

Restall, Matthew. *Latin America in Colonial Times*. Cambridge: Cambridge University Press, 2011.

Sweet, James H. *Recreating Africa: Culture, Kinship, and Religion in the African-Portuguese World, 1441–1770*. Durham: University of North Carolina Press, 2006.

Taylor, William. *Magistrates of the Sacred: Priests and Parishioners in Eighteenth Century Mexico*. Stanford: Stanford University Press, 1996.

AP® Review Questions for Chapter 18

Multiple-Choice Questions

QUESTIONS 1–3 REFER TO THE FOLLOWING IMAGES.

Santa Maria Tonantzintla
(Catholic)

Old Whaling Church
(Protestant)

1. Which of the following statements best explains the design of the Catholic church Santa Maria Tonantzintla?
   (A) The Catholic Church's rejection of indigenous beliefs and images
   (B) The subordination of European beliefs and designs to Native American designs
   (C) The willingness of the Catholic Church to incorporate indigenous designs and rituals
   (D) The Catholic Church's forcing of various racial groups to worship in separate parishes

2. Which of the following statements best explains the design of the Old Whaling Church?
   (A) Protestant churches were less willing to incorporate Native American designs or iconography.
   (B) Protestant churches contained a great deal of Native American images.
   (C) Protestant churches banned images to avoid disagreements between the racial groups.
   (D) Protestant congregations suppressed indigenous images but allowed Native Americans to hold leadership positions.

3. Which of the following statements is supported by both images?
   (A) Both Spanish and British colonies adopted Native American religions.
   (B) Both Spanish and British colonies outlawed missionary activity in the Americas.
   (C) Both Spanish and British colonies denied indigenous peoples church membership.
   (D) Both Spanish and British colonies transplanted Christianity into their colonies.

QUESTIONS 4–7 REFER TO THE FOLLOWING PASSAGE.

Prospero: Thou most lying slave,
Whom stripes [whippings] may move, not kindness! I have used [treated] thee,
Filth as thou art, with human care, and lodged thee
In mine own cell, till thou didst seek to violate
The honour of my child.
. . . I pitied thee,
Took pains to make thee speak, taught thee each hour
. . . I endow'd thy purposes
With words that made [thine own meaning] known. But thy vile race,
Though thou didst learn, had that in't which good natures
Could not abide to be with
Caliban: You taught me language; and my profit on't
Is, I know how to curse. The red plague rid you
For learning me your language!

—William Shakespeare, *The Tempest*, 1611

4. The speech by Prospero is meant to justify which of the following?
   (A) The attitude that Native Americans should be treated as equals with Europeans
   (B) The belief that concepts of race and social hierarchy should be rejected
   (C) The abuse and enslavement of Native Americans by Europeans
   (D) The belief that religion should be used to raise the status of the Native Americans

5. Prospero's actions toward Caliban are meant to justify which of the following beliefs?
   (A) Native Americans and other non-European groups are immoral and untrustworthy.
   (B) Europeans need to learn moral lessons from the people they encounter overseas.
   (C) Native Americans and Europeans could learn from each other.
   (D) All value systems from all cultures are equally valid.

6. Based on Caliban's response, what was the reaction of many Native Americans to the arrival of Europeans in the Americas?
   (A) The abuses suffered at the hand of the Europeans were made up for in the new technologies they brought with them.
   (B) The "civilizing" process of the Europeans was really an excuse to abuse the Native Americans.
   (C) Native Americans preferred not to share their technology with the Europeans.
   (D) The Native Americans made distinctions between Spanish and English.

7. Caliban having to learn Prospero's language is a reference to which of the following?
   (A) Attempts by European powers to incorporate colonized peoples into their empires
   (B) Attempts by European powers to allow indigenous people to retain their cultures
   (C) Attempts by European powers to merge all the cultures in their empires
   (D) Attempts by European powers to develop a multilingual bureaucracy

QUESTIONS 8–10 REFER TO THE FOLLOWING PASSAGE.

. . . the Mita Indians go up every Monday morning to the locality of Guanyna Potosi which is at the foot of the range. . . . After each has eaten his ration, they climb up the hill, each to his mine, and go in, staying there from that hour until Saturday evening without coming out of the mine; their wives bring them food, but they stay constantly underground, excavating and carrying out the ore from which they get the silver.

—Antonio Vazquez de Espinosa, *Compendium and Description of the West Indies*, ca. 1620s

8. This passage supports which of the following statements?
   (A) By the sixteenth century, Europeans were present only in North America.
   (B) The Spaniards had abolished Native American coercive labor systems.
   (C) The Native Americans were a source of labor for the Spanish colonies.
   (D) North American colonies were more profitable than South American colonies.

9. According to the passage, why was the Mita system especially cruel?
   (A) Native Americans spent significant amounts of time away from home and could not leave the mines.
   (B) The native population was forced to sell their wives into slavery.
   (C) The mines were excavated primarily by children.
   (D) The Europeans forced women to carry the ore out of the mines.

10. Which of the following inferences accurately explains the importance of mines like those at Potosi?
   (A) The silver from the mines was used primarily for jewelry in Europe.
   (B) Silver from the Spanish colonies in the Americas was used by Europeans to buy commodities in Asia.
   (C) The Spanish crown used the silver to pay debts owed to Dutch bankers.
   (D) American silver stayed in the Americas and was used to build infrastructure.

Short-Answer Questions

1. Using your knowledge of world history, answer parts A and B.
   A. Explain how TWO of the following aspects of life were affected by the casta system.
      - Religion
      - Family life
      - Labor
   B. Briefly explain the ONE difference between the casta system and the treatment of Native Americans in British colonies.

2. Answer parts A and B.
   A. Briefly explain how the economy of the French colonies in North America differed from that of the British colonies in North America.
   B. Briefly explain TWO similarities between the British and Spanish colonies in the Americas.

19 The Atlantic System: Africa, the Americas, and Europe, 1550–1807

Olaudah Equiano

In 1789, members of England's growing abolitionist movement, campaigning against the slave trade, provided an eager audience for a new publication, *The Interesting Narrative of the Life of Olaudah Equiano, or Gustavus Vassa, the African.* For many, it was the first time they heard an African voice narrate the horrors of slavery. The story of **Olaudah Equiano** (ca. 1745–1797) shows how he suffered as a slave, but also how he beat the odds. Equiano's readers learned of the horrors of the infamous Middle Passage across the Atlantic:

*The first object which saluted my eyes when I arrived on the coast was the sea, and a slave-ship.... These filled me with astonishment, which was soon converted into terror.... [T]hey made ready with many fearful noises, and we were all put under deck ... now that the whole ship's cargo was confined together [the stench of the hold] was absolutely pestilential. The closeness of the place, and the heat of the climate, added to the number in the ship, which was so crowded that each had scarcely room to turn himself, almost suffocated us.... This wretched situation was again aggravated by the galling of the chains, now become insupportable; and the filth of the [latrines], into which the children often fell, and were almost suffocated. The shrieks of the women, and the groans of the dying, rendered the whole a scene of horror almost inconceivable.**

---

*Olaudah Equiano, *The Interesting Narrative of the Life of Olaudah Equiano, or Gustavus Vassa, the African*, ed. Vincent Carretta, 2d ed. (New York: Penguin, 2003), p. 55.

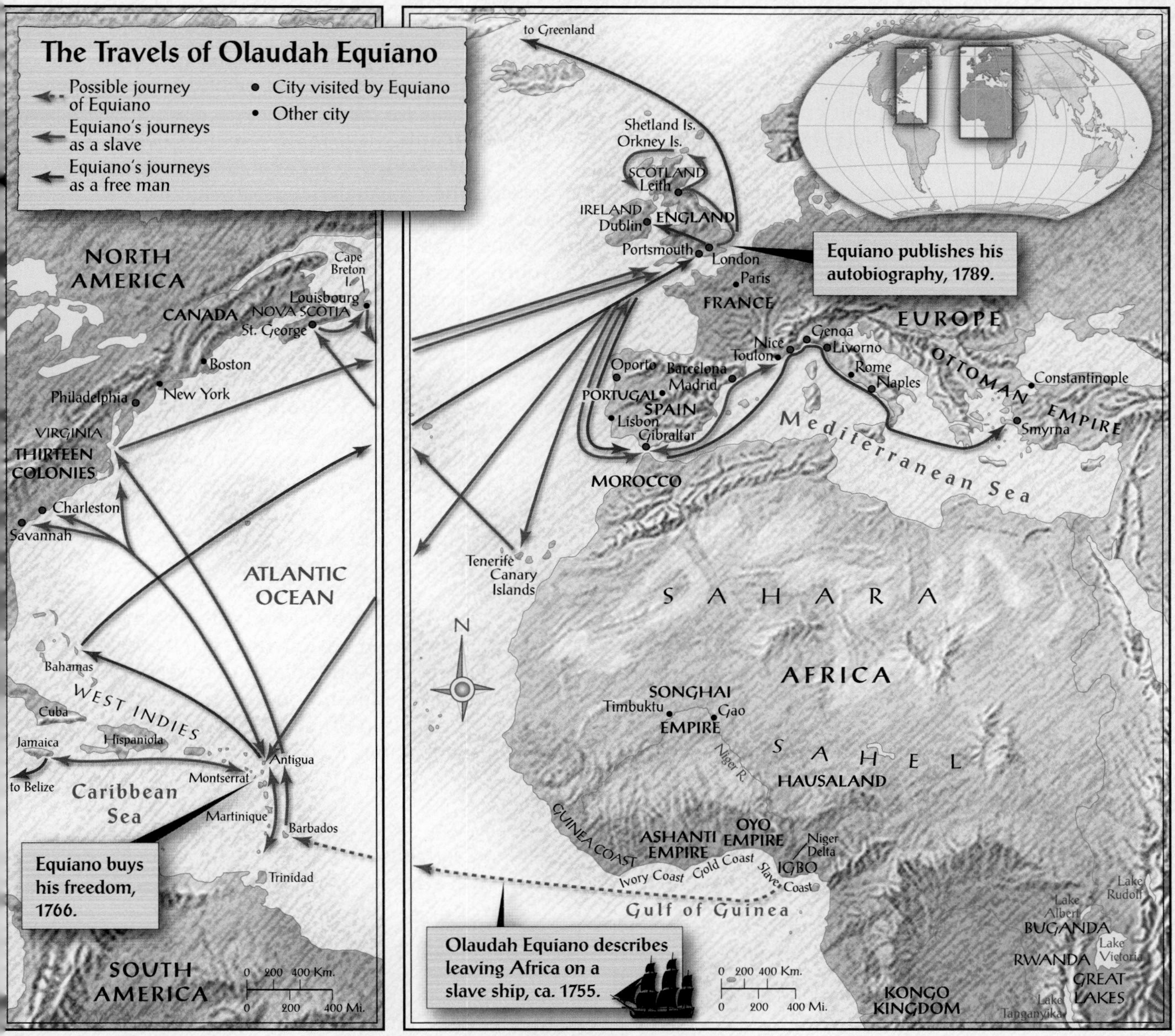

At least 12 million Africans had similar experiences between the sixteenth and nineteenth centuries, and an unknown number perished even before they reached the slave ports on the West African coast.

The historical importance of Equiano's *Interesting Narrative* has been established and his adult activities well-documented, though some scholars question the authenticity of its earliest passages. (Some evidence, albeit inconclusive, suggests that the author was born in the Americas and created his account of Africa and the voyage across the Atlantic by retelling other slaves' stories, reminding us to be cautious when using memoirs as history.) Still, whether Olaudah Equiano (oh-lah-OO-dah ek-wee-AHN-oh) personally experienced the terror he reports in

Olaudah Equiano
(1745–1797) Afro-British author and abolitionist who told of his enslavement as a child in Africa, his purchase of his own freedom in the West Indies, his move to England, and his wide travels as a sailor.

the passage above or based the story on other accounts, few other sources bring us closer to the reality faced by millions of Africans in this period or offer a more eloquent critique of slavery.

By 1745, when Equiano's life began, the Atlantic slave trade was at its height. Hundreds of thousands of Africans crossed the Atlantic every year. They lived in diverse environments—the Brazilian tropics, the temperate lands of Virginia, the rocky shores of Nova Scotia—and performed a great variety of tasks. Most, however, were destined for the sugar plantations of the West Indies. Sugar was the foundation of the Atlantic economy, a source of immense profit and great suffering.

Complex interconnections between Africa, America, and Europe characterized the Atlantic system. The so-called triangular trade sent Africans to the Americas as slaves; sugar, tobacco, and natural resources from the Americas to Europe; and manufactured goods from Europe to both Africa and the Americas. Africans labored on American plantations whose profits enriched Europe, stimulating its economic growth, while in much of Africa life became less secure.

The Atlantic system fostered political competition. Warfare among West Africans increased, while European powers vied for Atlantic supremacy; Equiano himself participated in naval clashes between the French and British. The slave trade also had cultural repercussions. Africans arrived not merely as slaves but also as carriers of traditions that were to profoundly influence the development of American societies (see also Chapter 18).

Finally, the abolition of slavery was itself a complex process involving actors from different parts of the Atlantic, including plantation slaves who resisted bondage and Europeans who grew uncomfortable with the contradiction between the inhumanity of plantation slavery and Christianity's admonition to treat others as you would be treated yourself. It was to his readership of fellow Christians that Olaudah Equiano especially appealed with his *Interesting Narrative*.

KEY CONCEPT QUESTIONS

- How did the development of plantation agriculture in the Americas influence West African economic and political systems? **(Key Concept 4.2)**
- What were the economic, social, and environmental effects of coercive labor systems on the Americas? **(Key Concept 4.2)**
- What were the economic, demographic, and environmental effects of the plantation complex in the Americas on Europe? **(Key Concept 4.1)**
- Why did the British end the Atlantic slave trade in the early nineteenth century? **(Key Concept 5.3)**

African History and Afro-Eurasian Connections, 1550–1700

Judging the impact of the Atlantic slave trade on African history requires understanding Africa's cultural and geographic context. Contrary to common assumptions, Africa had not been an isolated continent: it had ancient connections to Europe and Asia across the Mediterranean, the Red Sea, and the Indian Ocean.

Africa's diverse deserts, grasslands, and rainforests produced a variety of political systems. Some Africans lived in small bands of hunter-gatherers, while others were subjects of powerful monarchs. Equiano described the Igbo-speaking villages in the Niger Delta region of West Africa as productive communities where yam-based agriculture supported a dense population. Other nearby societies had more centralized and hierarchical political structures, but in Igbo (ee-BWOH) society, men and women accumulated titles and authority on the basis of achievements rather than birth. As was nearly universal in Africa, clan elders played a crucial role in negotiating the consensus needed for community decisions. Even when owing tribute or obeisance to a more distant chief or king, African villages retained their own mechanisms for keeping peace and administering justice.

Much of the cultural and economic energy of the continent came from interaction among African peoples themselves. For example, in the **Great Lakes region** of east-central Africa, migration led to fruitful encounters between Africans of different linguistic and cultural backgrounds. Bantu-speaking migrants from the west brought knowledge of grain agriculture, and invented sophisticated iron technologies. In return, these farmers gained access to cattle from their pastoralist neighbors, descendants of migrants from the upper Nile River Valley. In the societies that resulted, farming provided the bulk of calories and was the focus of work, while cattle represented wealth and prestige. No proper marriage contract could be negotiated unless the groom's family gave cattle to the family of his intended. Agriculture in the Great Lakes region was also stimulated by the introduction of plantains (bananas), a Southeast Asian fruit that traveled across the Indian Ocean with Indonesian voyagers to the island of Madagascar. Supported by agricultural surpluses and dominated by clans wealthy in cattle, a number of powerful kingdoms such as Rwanda and Buganda emerged in the seventeenth-century Great Lakes region.

Great Lakes region
A temperate highland region in and around the Great Rift Valley in east-central Africa, characterized by agriculture and cattle pastoralism, a substantial iron industry, and dense populations.

Many other African societies had formative contacts with external political systems, commercial markets, and religious traditions. For example, Ethiopia, Kongo, and South Africa all had connections to the wider Christian world. The Ethiopian Coptic Church, connected to the Orthodox branch of the faith and with a strong monastic tradition, was already over a thousand years old when the Portuguese attempted a military alliance in the sixteenth century, in the same period when the royal court of Kongo was converting to Roman Catholicism (see Chapter 16).

In the Kongo kingdom, civil war and invasion by outside forces had led to disintegration of the monarchy and the abandonment of the Kongo capital of San Salvador in the seventeenth century. Into this political vacuum stepped **Kimpa Vita** (ca. 1680–1706). In a powerful example of religious syncretism (see Chapter 18), Kimpa Vita declared that she had been visited by Saint Anthony and conversed with God, who told her that the people of Kongo must unite under a new king. She taught that Christ and the apostles were black men who had lived and died in Kongo. Her doctrine was popular, and her followers repopulated the old capital city. But Portuguese missionaries regarded her beliefs as heresy. She was captured by rivals, tried for witchcraft, and burned at the stake. But the Kongo tradition of depicting Jesus as an African endured.

Kimpa Vita
(ca. 1680–1706) Christian reformer in the Kongo kingdom, also known as Dona Beatriz. She preached that Jesus Christ was an African, blending Kongo beliefs with Catholic ones, before being executed as a heretic by a leader vying for the Kongo throne.

- **CONTEXT&CONNECTIONS** Kimpa Vita's role as a prophetess was in keeping with Kongo traditions of female spiritual leadership. Across Africa, in fact, it was often women who were touched with the gift of communicating with unseen forces, as the story of the *Xhosa Cattle Killing* in South Africa in response to nineteenth-century European intrusions also shows (key term in Chapter 26). In Mesoamerica, the identification of the Aztec fertility goddess Tonantzintla with the Catholic *Virgin of Guadalupe* was yet another example of converts to Christianity retaining a female principle through religious *syncretism* (Chapter 18). ●

AP® THEMES

What was the impact of expanding networks of exchange on the development of religious beliefs and practices in Africa?

Utterly different from both the mysticism of Ethiopia's Coptic faith and the syncretism in the Kongo was the Protestant Christianity brought to seventeenth-century South Africa by Dutch Calvinists and French Huguenots (see Chapter 17) as they expanded at the expense of the indigenous Khoisan (KOI-sahn)-speaking peoples, who lacked both metal weapons and resistance to diseases such as smallpox. It would be another two centuries, however, before significant numbers of southern Africans converted to Christianity (see Chapter 26).

The *Dar-al-Islam*—the domain of Islam—gave Africans an even more significant avenue for early modern global interconnections. From the Indian Ocean coast, Muslim Swahili merchants and sailors had long plied maritime trade routes connecting East Africa with India and the Persian Gulf (see Chapter 16). After the Arab sultans of Oman (oh-MAAN) wrested control of Fort Jesus in Mombasa from the Portuguese in 1696, Swahili princes and aristocrats generally acknowledged their authority while continuing to regulate the affairs of their own city-states. Traditional Swahili arts and crafts—poetry, jewelry, and elaborately carved wooden doors for wealthy houses—continued through such political transitions, combining Islamic and African motifs.

Sahel
Arid region south of the Sahara Desert that played an important historic role as a West African center of trade and urbanization. Islam traveled with the caravans across the Sahara, making the Sahel a diffusion point for Islam in West Africa.

The other center of African Islam was the **Sahel**, the arid region south of the Sahara where Islam had come across the desert with Arab traders from the north. That caravan trade in salt, gold, and slaves had further stimulated an existing African urban civilization based on trade among grain farmers, cattle pastoralists, and producers in the rainforest further south. Kola nuts from the forest, for example, were a mild stimulant highly appreciated by Muslim consumers in the Sahel (and later by "cola" drinkers worldwide).

The great Niger River was an essential concourse for West Africans. Flowing from the mountains of the west, through the savanna to the desert's edge, and on through the rainforests of the coastal Niger Delta—where Equiano placed his childhood home—the river was a highway of trade, with West Africa's most important cities clustered on its banks. Fisherman drew on its natural bounty, and the river's great inland delta, far north at the edge of the Sahara desert, was a highly productive agricultural region.

The cities along the Niger River connected West Africa with Mediterranean economies through the trans-Saharan trade. Cities like Timbuktu were southern destinations for camel caravans from North Africa. (The term "Sahel" shares the same Arabic root as the word "Swahili," both referring to a sea shore. Since crossing the Sahara was like traversing an ocean, to an Arab merchant Timbuktu seemed like a port.)

Songhai empire
(1464–1591) Important Islamic empire with prosperity based on both interregional and trans-Saharan trade. Stretched from the Atlantic into present-day Nigeria, reaching its height in the sixteenth century before being invaded by Morocco.

The **Songhai empire**, with its capital at Gao along the Niger River, arose from a thousand-year-old tradition of large-scale states in this region (see Map 19.1). In addition to leading armies of conquest, the *askias* (emperors) of Songhai (song-GAH-ee) were patrons of Islamic arts and sciences. The Sankore Mosque in Timbuktu, with its impressive library, became a center of intellectual debate, drawing scholars from far and wide. Timbuktu was famous for its gold trade as well as its book market, where Arab and African Muslim scholars eagerly sought finely bound editions. When rulers, traders, and intellectuals from Songhai went on the hajj (pilgrimage) to Arabia, they amplified the empire's connections with the broader world.

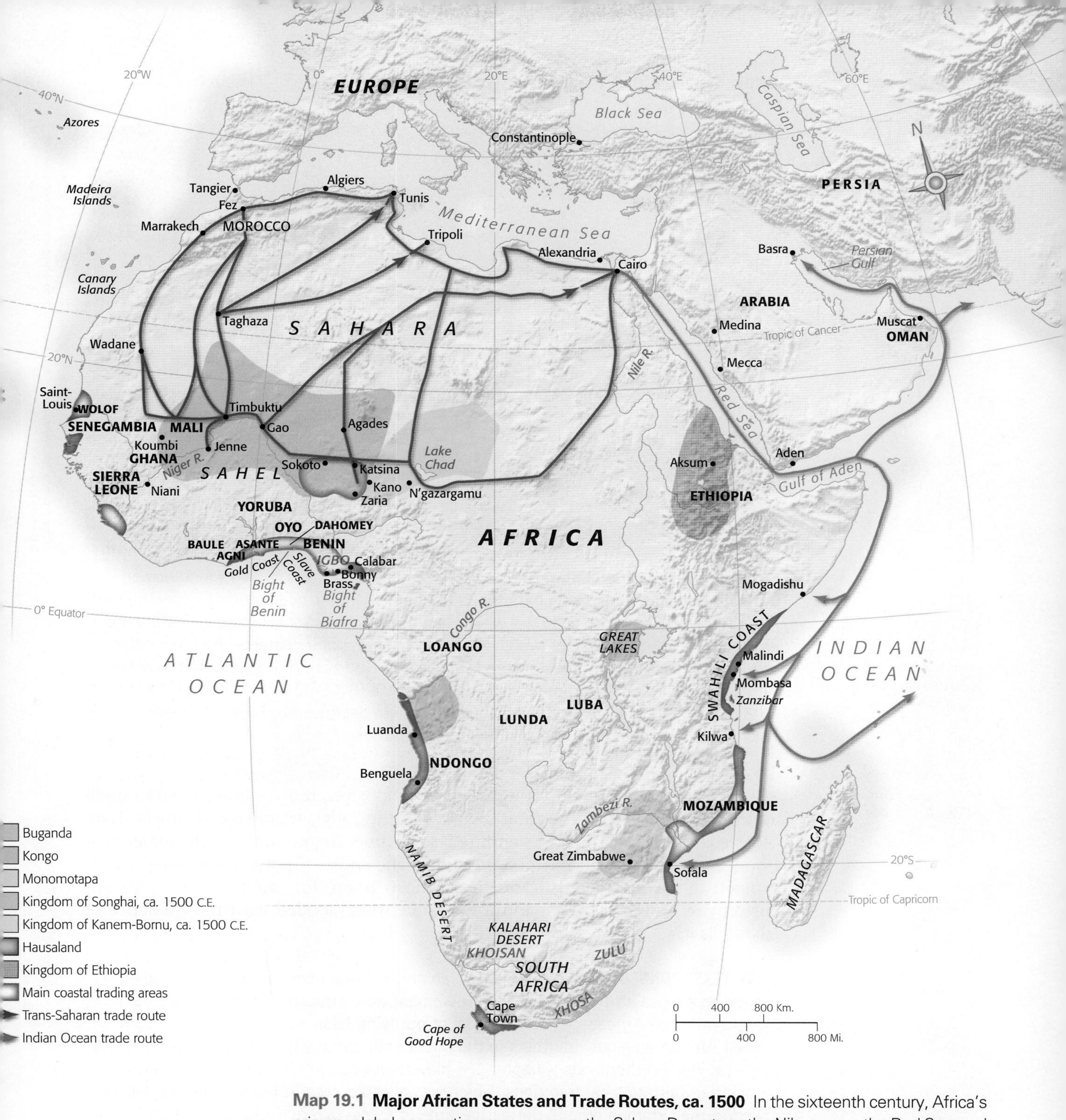

Map 19.1 Major African States and Trade Routes, ca. 1500 In the sixteenth century, Africa's primary global connections were across the Sahara Desert, up the Nile, across the Red Sea, and into the Indian Ocean. Large kingdoms and empires such as those of Songhai in the west and Ethiopia in the northeast benefited from participation in world trade, as did the Swahili city-states in the east. The arrival of Europeans added a new set of interconnections along the West African coast, but only in South Africa did Europeans come as settlers. Large states were the exception in Africa; smaller societies populated vast regions of the continent.

Caravan Approaching Timbuktu The city of Timbuktu was an important terminus of the trans-Saharan trade dating back to the thirteenth century, its strategic location on the Niger River making it central to the wealth and power of the Songhai empire. Under the patronage of Songhai's rulers, Timbuktu became an important center of Islamic scholarship as well: the library at the Sankore Mosque attracted both African and Arab scholars. Although the site is today protected by its status as a UNESCO World Heritage Site, in 2013 some of Timbuktu's precious manuscripts were destroyed by Muslim extremists who hoped to wipe out records of Afro-Islamic synthesis.

Even within the mighty Songhai empire, however, most Africans lived in small agricultural villages. In the rural societies of the Sahel, Islam spread slowly. Here older gods and ritual practices endured, sometimes incorporated with elements of Islam. Even in cities like Timbuktu and at the court of powerful Songhai kings, syncretism was characteristic of West African Islam, for example, when African customs regarding marriage and inheritance were blended with the influence of Islamic law.

● **CONTEXT&CONNECTIONS** Enduring African cultural practices in the Islamic Sahel, such as a loose attitude toward veiling women, were criticized by Arab visitors and more orthodox African clerics. The goal of purifying Islamic practice would inspire West African religious reformers in the nineteenth century (see Chapter 26). In West Africa, *Sufi* brotherhoods (Chapter 17) played an important role in adapting the imported faith to local traditions, which was also the case in India under the *Mughals* and in the Ottoman empire during the time of *Evliya Çelebi* (Chapters 16 and 17). ●

The success of the askias (AH-skee-as) attracted military as well as commercial attention from Songhai's Moroccan neighbors to the north. Morocco's leaders had remained independent of the Ottoman empire and had successfully driven off the Portuguese. The Moroccan sultan envied Songhai's gold and salt mines, and in 1591 the army he sent out from Marrakesh conquered Songhai, shattering it into smaller kingdoms, chiefdoms, and sultanates. Never again would a large-scale African state rise to such dominance in the Sahel.

Meanwhile, when Songhai was at its height in the sixteenth century, Europeans were constructing fortifications along the West African coast. Though the major centers of population and prosperity still lay in the interior regions of the Sahel, connected to the wider world across the Sahara, European merchants were now striving to redirect West African trade to the coast. Gold was always of interest, but they came over time to focus on another commodity: slaves. By the eighteenth century, African Muslims whose ancestors may have crossed the Sahara to Morocco by camel might instead be enslaved and sent by ship to Jamaica. While connections to the Islamic world across the Sahara Desert and the Indian Ocean continued, by the eighteenth century Africa's international connection was turning toward the Atlantic Ocean and beyond, to the Americas.

Africa and the Americas: The Plantation Complex

European occupation of the Americas, the continuing decline of Amerindian populations, and new trade links with West Africa set the stage for the rise of the **Atlantic plantation system**. The enslavement and forced emigration of millions of Africans to the Americas reaped huge fortunes for the British, French, Dutch, Spanish, and Portuguese who controlled the system. On the islands of the Caribbean, where the plantation complex was centered, landscapes changed dramatically as imported plants and animals replaced indigenous ones and Africans became the predominant population. Sugar planters exploited their slave labor to supply expanding global markets for sugar and related products like molasses and rum.

Atlantic plantation system
The focal point in the new set of interchanges among Africa, Europe, and the Americas that peaked in the eighteenth century. Utilized African slave labor to produce large quantities of agricultural products, particularly sugar, for international markets.

As Equiano's story illustrates, Africans were more than passive victims of the Atlantic slave trade and plantation system. Many resisted. And though mortality rates among slaves were high and survivors were often deprived of the use of their own languages, many managed to retain much of their culture and contributed it to the new American societies (see also Chapter 18). Meanwhile, in West Africa, integration into the Atlantic system disrupted many indigenous societies.

The Economics of Plantation Production

From the very beginning, Africans played a variety of roles in the conquest and settlement of the European New World empires (see Chapter 18). As we saw with the settlement of Brazil, for example, Africans worked as artisans, traders, and soldiers, as well as plantation slaves. The skills that Africans brought with them to the Americas included metalworking, weaving, and agricultural knowledge that contributed to the introduction and spread of crops like rice. In the Spanish empire as well, Africans played multiple roles and were part of evolving patterns of racial and cultural intermixture. Still, in the Caribbean and British North America, the words "black" and "slave" had become nearly synonymous by the eighteenth century.

AP® THEMES
What were the effects of diseases on the development of labor systems and social hierarchies in the Americas?

When the Spanish first conquered the islands of the Caribbean, they were unable to effectively exploit the labor of the indigenous Amerindian inhabitants, who could stand neither the strain of European rule nor the deadly effects of diseases for which they had no immunity. Europeans later imported indentured

WORLD HISTORY IN TODAY'S WORLD

Twenty-One Million Slaves

According to the International Labor Organization (an agency of the United Nations), 21 million people in the world were living in slavery in 2012, with the biggest number in central and southeastern Europe, followed by Africa, the Middle East, Asia/Pacific, Latin America, and the Caribbean.

After Great Britain abolished slavery in its empire in 1834, the country began an international campaign to suppress the institution. With the abolition of slavery in Brazil in 1888, three hundred years of slave importation into the Americas finally came to an end. Subsequent national and international laws and treaties banned slavery globally.

Nevertheless, people have used a number of different strategies to enslave their fellow human beings. Some involve the continuation of traditional systems. In Mauritania, for example, descent-based slavery, where some children still inherit their parents' slave status, bonds individuals to particular families for life without compensation or freedom of movement.

Debt peonage (long present in Latin America; see Chapter 18) is another old practice that continues: a desperate man takes a loan on terms that guarantee it can never be repaid and then has to do his creditor's bidding without pay for the rest of his life. His children may even inherit the unpaid debt and find themselves enslaved as well.

Even today, slave owners anxious for profit use confinement as well as physical and emotional abuse to prevent complaints or attempts at escape. Women from India or the Philippines, for example, might sign contracts to work as domestic servants in Persian Gulf countries, only to find that they are trapped within the household, their passports seized and their voices silenced. Some have accused construction companies in Qatar of abusing slaves, mainly from South Asia, in the buildup to the 2022 World Cup.

Perhaps the most horrible crimes in our world take place at the intersection of child slavery, human trafficking, and the global sex trade. The U.S. Department of State has estimated that as many as a million underage kids are exploited sexually for profit every year, often illegally transported across national borders by organized crime syndicates, who also control "sex tourism" in countries like Thailand. The campaign to bring freedom to those crushed by slavery, begun by Olaudah Equiano and other eighteenth-century abolitionists, is still not complete.

Source: International Labor Organization, "21 Million People Are Now Victims of Forced Labour," http://www.ilo.org/global/about-the-ilo/newsroom/news/WCMS_181961/lang–it/index.htm.

servants, but they were vulnerable to the tropical diseases such as yellow fever and malaria that had come from Africa. By 1680, when sugar had become virtually the sole focus of West Indian agriculture, neither Europeans nor Amerindians could provide sufficient labor.

Enslaved Africans filled the void. They were expensive, but from a sugar planter's perspective they were worth the investment because they could survive the harsh Caribbean disease environment. West Africans had long been exposed to the same Afro-Eurasian diseases as Europeans; unlike Amerindians, they were therefore resistant to diseases like smallpox. In addition, through genetic adaptation and childhood exposure, Africans were also more likely to survive malaria and yellow fever, which were deadly to Europeans. Tragically, their ability to survive in difficult disease environments, enhanced their value as slaves. (See the feature "World History in Today's World: Twenty-One Million Slaves.")

Slavery had been common before, but the scale and commercial orientation of the sugar industry were something new. Many societies allowed for slavery, but most were "societies with slaves" where slavery existed but was not the main driver of production, and not "slave societies" where slaveholding is at the heart of social and economic life. "Societies with slaves" were common in the Islamic world and in Africa itself. Equiano described a mild form of servitude in the Niger Delta region, where the slaves had a lower place in society but retained legal rights. Genuine "slave societies," in contrast, developed in northeastern Brazil and the Caribbean, where 80 percent of enslaved Africans were sent and where slavery was central to every facet of social and economic life.

• **CONTEXT&CONNECTIONS** As we have seen in Chapter 17, slavery was common in the Ottoman empire. However, that was a "society with slaves" rather than a genuine "slave society." Under the Ottomans, while slaves played a wide variety of roles, including military and administrative leadership, the bulk of production came from free artisans and peasant farmers. Such "societies with slaves" have been fairly common in world history; there are fewer examples of societies, like those of the Roman empire or the early modern Caribbean, fundamentally based on the deployment of massed slave labor in agriculture. •

Purchasing and provisioning a sugar plantation, and buying the slaves needed to work it, took substantial capital. Sugar planters were men of property, often middle-class businessmen striving to improve their finances and elevate their social standing by, for example, using sugar profits to build impressive country houses, including some of the finest estates and chateaux of eighteenth-century France and Britain. More broadly, the need to provision the sugar islands with food, clothing, and manufactured goods stimulated economic development in eighteenth-century North America and western Europe, providing many Europeans with jobs and markets for their goods.

Absentee ownership of Caribbean plantations became more common, and the work of overseeing slave labor usually went to lower-status European immigrants, legendary for their harshness, or to men of mixed race. Lighter skin did not automatically confer higher status, however: Equiano told of a French sugar planter on Martinique with *"many mulattoes working in the fields [who] were all the produce of his own loins!"**

Slaves performed all the backbreaking work of planting, weeding, harvesting, and processing. Because raw sugar is bulky, the juice had to be squeezed out of the cane and boiled down for shipment. Sugar production was thus an agro-industrial enterprise, organized like a factory where profitable operation requires that the assembly line is always rolling, with raw materials ready at hand. Sugarcane was processed year round, with full-time use of the crushing machinery and the large copper boiling kettles. The entire process was physically strenuous, and the kettles sometimes exploded, maiming or killing African laborers.

The brutal work lives of slaves on Caribbean sugar plantations thus had much in common with the harshest forms of later factory labor, governed by the relentless grinding of machines rather than by more gentle rhythms of nature. Only Sunday was a day of rest, and even then slaves usually needed to work on their small food plots.

Under such conditions, overseers frequently worked Africans to death. Barbados is representative. In 1680, fifty thousand African slaves toiled on the island. Over the

---

*Olaudah Equiano, *The Interesting Narrative of the Life of Olaudah Equiano, or Gustavus Vassa, the African*, ed. Vincent Carretta, 2d ed. (New York: Penguin, 2003), pp. 105–109.

Caribbean Sugar Mill Sugar production was an industrial as well as agricultural enterprise. Here wind power is used to crush the sugarcane; the rising smoke indicates the intense heat of the furnaces used to boil down the juice. The slaves' work was hard, dangerous, and unceasing: such machinery was usually operated six days a week, year-round.

next forty years, planters imported another fifty thousand slaves, but the total black population actually *dropped* to forty-five thousand because the harsh conditions and poor diet led to high mortality and low birth rates. As Equiano noted, the overseers, "*human butchers, ... pay no regard to the situation of pregnant women. The neglect certainly conspires with many others to cause a decrease in the births, as well as in the lives of the grown negroes.*"* Equiano calculated that Barbados, not the worst island in terms of African mortality, required a thousand fresh imports annually just to maintain a level population (see Table 19.1). One historian has put it with chilling simplicity: "Most of the slaves died early and without progeny."†

Equiano himself escaped the harsh fate of working on a Caribbean sugar plantation. While still a boy he was sold to a British naval officer; he spent much of his early life aboard ships and developed a lifelong fondness for London. He was then sold to a Philadelphia merchant with business interests in the West Indies. Aboard ship, Equiano had learned to read and had developed a good head for numbers. He enjoyed good treatment and significant freedom while tending to his master's business, which sometimes included trading in slaves. Of course, he witnessed many cruelties:

> *It was very common in several of the islands, particularly in St. Kitt's, for the slaves to be branded with the initial letters of their master's name, and a load*

---

*Olaudah Equiano, *The Interesting Narrative of the Life of Olaudah Equiano, or Gustavus Vassa, the African*, ed. Vincent Carretta, 2d ed. (New York: Penguin, 2003), pp. 105–109.

†Patrick Manning, "Migrations of Africans to the Americas: The Impact on Africans, Africa, and the World," *The History Teacher*, 26 (May, 1993): 295.

Table 19.1 Importation and Black Population Statistics for the British West Indies

Year	Barbados: Slave Imports	Barbados: Total Black Population	Jamaica: Slave Imports	Jamaica: Total Black Population	Leeward Islands: Slave Imports	Leeward Islands: Total Black Population
1640–1650	18,700		?		3,000	
1670		30,000		7,000		3,000
1651–1675	51,100		8,000		10,100	
1680		50,000		15,000		9,000
1676–1700	64,700		77,100		32,000	
1713		45,000		55,000		30,000

Note: The British Leeward Islands consisted of Antigua, Barbuda, Anguilla, the British Virgin Islands, Montserrat, and St. Kitts–Nevis.
Source: From Richard Dunn, *Sugar and Slaves: The Rise of the Plantar Class in the English West Indies, 1624–1713* (New York: Norton, 1972), pp. 230, 312.

*of heavy iron hooks hung around their necks.... I have seen a negro beaten till some of his bones were broken, for only letting a pot boil over. It is not uncommon, after a flogging, to make slaves go on their knees and thank their owners and ... say "God Bless You."**

While distressed by his own bondage, Equiano was keenly aware of the even worse fate he could have faced as a field slave.

Sugar was not the only slave-produced plantation crop in the Americas. Slaves also labored on the tobacco plantations of Virginia and the rice and indigo plantations of Carolina (see Chapter 18). But in British North America, slave mortality was lower, and a better diet and more equal gender balance led to higher fertility. Unlike in the Caribbean, the slave populations of the British colonies were self-reproducing by 1720, although planters continued to import slaves.

• **CONTEXT&CONNECTIONS** In the United States, slavery is associated with cotton production in the Deep South, which became a genuine "slave society." The extension of cotton, however, was a later, nineteenth-century development. Only in the wake of the *Industrial Revolution* (Chapter 23) did mass production of cotton begin in the Americas. •

African Culture and Resistance to Slavery

African resistance to slavery was endemic. Slaves everywhere looked for ways to escape their bondage and, failing that, to resist their captivity in large or small ways. Slave traders, owners, and overseers were ever vigilant, and exacted gruesome penalties for open insubordination. Equiano tells of a slave trader who had once cut off the leg of a slave for running away. When Equiano asked how the man could square such an action with his Christian conscience, the trader simply said *"that his scheme had the desired effect—it cured that man and some others of running away."**

*Olaudah Equiano, *The Interesting Narrative of the Life of Olaudah Equiano, or Gustavus Vassa, the African*, ed. Vincent Carretta, 2d ed. (New York: Penguin, 2003), pp. 105–109, 59.

Slaves often found safer, more subtle ways to assert their humanity and express their defiance. Songs and stories derived from African cultural traditions might be used to ridicule a master using coded language he could not understand. Religious rites—African, Christian, or a synthesis of multiple belief systems and rituals—might serve as assertions of dignity and spiritual resilience. Music played an important role in maintaining cultural independence, and slaves' songs often ridiculed their masters. Knowing that Africans often use drums to communicate, slave owners banned them from the slave quarters. Still Africans were inventive in using whatever they could find to keep the beat; if all they had was their own bodies, then complex rhythmic clapping and slapping was enough.

Resistance to slavery sometimes began even before the slave ships arrived in America. Equiano describes the nets that were used to keep Africans from jumping overboard and relates that *"one day ... two of my wearied countrymen, who were chained together ... preferring death to such a life of misery, somehow made through the nettings and jumped into the sea."** Insurrections aboard slave ships were also common, as this dramatic description from 1673 attests:

> *A master of a ship ... did not, as the manner is, shackle [the slaves] one to another ... and they being double the number of those in the ship found their advantages, got weapons in their hands, and fell upon the sailors, knocking them on the heads, and cutting their throats so fast as the master found they were all lost ... and so went down into the hold and blew up all with himself.**

Even after landing, some Africans managed to escape. Yet if an individual or a small group got away, where would they go, and how would they live? Options for escaped slaves included joining pirate groups in the Caribbean, settling among Amerindian populations, or forming their own autonomous communities.

maroon communities
Self-governing communities of escaped slaves common in the early modern Caribbean and in coastal areas of Central and South America.

Already in the sixteenth century, escaped slaves were banding together to form **maroon communities**. Perhaps the best known were the *quilombos* of Brazil, of which Palmares was the largest and best known (see Chapter 18). Palmares was unique in scale, but significant maroon communities also took root in the interior regions of Venezuela, Guyana, and Florida. In some places, runaway slaves assimilated into indigenous societies, occasionally resulting in larger-scale cooperation with Amerindians. In Florida, for example, Africans who escaped from slavery in Carolina and Georgia formed an alliance with Creek Indians, and the cultural interaction between the two groups led the "Black Seminoles" to adopt many elements of Creek culture.

Some Caribbean sugar islands were too small for maroons to escape and avoid recapture, but the interior mountains of Jamaica were perfect for that purpose. When the Spanish fled Jamaica in 1655 during a British attack, they left behind hundreds of African slaves who headed for the hills. Now free, these maroons farmed, fished, and occasionally pillaged British sugar plantations on the coasts. Their threat to the British came not so much from raiding but from the sanctuary they could provide to other escaped slaves. In the early eighteenth century, the British and maroons fought to a stalemate, leading to a treaty that allowed the

---

*Richard Ligon, *A True and Exact History of the Island of Barbadoes* (London: Parker and Guy, 1673), p. 47.

maroons autonomy in exchange for the promise that they would hunt, capture, and return future runaways.

Even when Africans had to resign themselves to their fate as plantation slaves, covert resistance was possible. Slowing down and subverting the work process was common, even where the risk of the whip was ever present.

Religion is perhaps the area where Africans could best resist the psychological and spiritual torments of enslavement without risking flight or outright rebellion. Where Africans were greatest in number, their religious practices showed the strongest continuity. In both Brazil and Cuba, for example, Africans (like the Amerindians of Mesoamerica) merged their existing beliefs with Christianity. In both colonies the *orisas* (or-EE-shahs), gods of the Yoruba (yaw-roo-bah) people (of present-day western Nigeria), were transformed into Catholic saints. The illustration on this page shows Xàngó (CHAN-go) the Yoruba deity of fire, thunder, and lightning, who was especially venerated. The illustration also shows Naná Buruku (supreme creator and mother of the spirits of the sun and moon) and Oxala Oxalufan (a wizened elder representing peace and tranquility).

In areas where Africans were a smaller percentage of the population, as in most of British North America, European cultural influences were more dominant. But religion allowed self-assertion here as well. While white Christians preached obedience now and rewards in the afterlife, slaves sung hymns of liberation and focused on biblical stories relevant to their plight, such as that of Moses leading his enslaved people to freedom.

Equiano's life story shows us an unusual strategy of escape from slavery: working within the system. His freedom came about through a combination of good fortune and business acumen. He was fortunate that his final owner was a

African Gods in the Americas West African gods still worshiped in the Americas include Naná Buruku, Oxala Oxalufan, and Xàngó invoked for his physical power and bravery. These West African *orisas* appear as *santos*, or saints, in the hybrid Christian-African religions of *Santeria* (from Cuba) and *Candomblé* (originating in Brazil). Santeria and Candomblé follow the African tradition of recognizing the special spiritual qualities of women. Their priestesses are especially attuned to possession by divine spirits and serve as conduits of communication with them.

Gil Abelha

Gil Abelha

Gil Abelha

member of the Society of Friends, called Quakers, who had strong doubts about whether Christians should own slaves. This master agreed that if he could repay the money of his purchase, Equiano would have his freedom, and he allowed Equiano to trade on his own account in his spare time to make that possible. In 1767, having surprised his master by saving the required amount, Equiano returned to England, which he regarded as his home. Still, he frequently went back to sea, even joining an unsuccessful voyage to the North Pole. He worked as a hairdresser for the London elite and learned to play the French horn. When they had the chance, free blacks like Equiano explored the many possibilities of the interconnected Atlantic world.

manumission
The voluntary freeing of slaves by their masters.

In some places, the freeing of slaves, or **manumission**, was encouraged as an act of Christian charity. Of course, those most likely to be freed were women, children, and the elderly, though in in colonial Latin America the church did encourage manumission. Moreover, in the Spanish Americas all persons were assumed to be free unless proven otherwise, so black men who escaped their masters and moved far enough away had a good chance of "passing" as free men.

In British North America, in contrast, manumission was rare and legal codes made little distinction between free blacks and slaves. Here the equation between skin color and slave status was so strong that free blacks were in a very uncomfortable situation, as Equiano's story of his arrest in Georgia shows:

> *After our arrival we went up to the town of Savannah; and the same evening I went to a friend's house ... a black man. We were very happy at meeting each other .... [A]fter supper ... the watch or patrol came by, and, discerning a light in the house ... came in and sat down, and drank some punch with us.... A little after this they told me I must go to the watch-house with them; this surprised me a good deal after our kindness to them, and I asked them "Why so?" They said, that all Negroes who had a light in their houses after nine o'clock were to be taken into custody, and either pay some dollars or be flogged.**

This was not an isolated incident: on other occasions Equiano's trade goods were confiscated for no reason other than his vulnerability as a black man, and several times he was nearly re-enslaved in spite of the document he always carried with him attesting to his freedom. Thereafter, Equiano avoided Georgia and Carolina altogether.

Effects of the Atlantic Slave Trade on West Africa

As early as the sixteenth century, the Atlantic slave trade had brought conflict to some West African societies, such as the Kongo kingdom (see Chapter 16). Over the next two centuries, as the Caribbean sugar industry dramatically increased the demand for African slaves, the transformative consequences of the Atlantic plantation system became greater and greater for West African social, economic, and military institutions.

*Olaudah Equiano, *The Interesting Narrative of the Life of Olaudah Equiano, or Gustavus Vassa, the African*, ed. Vincent Carretta, 2d ed. (New York: Penguin, 2003), p. 158.

Whether African leaders embraced the slave trade as a means of increasing their own wealth and power or sought only to shield their people from its ravages, few escaped its impact.

One society whose leaders participated in the Atlantic slave trade was the rising **Asante kingdom**. Asante was an expanding power in the forest region of eighteenth-century West Africa, and as its rulers pursued their ambitions, their armies took many prisoners. Before the rise of the Atlantic trade, these war captives would have been sent home through prisoner exchanges, redeemed for ransom, or kept as household servants and farm workers. (Only rarely would they be killed; labor was scarce relative to land in most of Africa, so both the productive and reproductive power of men and women were highly prized.) But where war captives had once been a mere byproduct of wars fought for other purposes, now some African leaders, as in Asante, had an added motive for military expansion, including access to valuable imported goods. British slave traders sailed to Cape Coast Castle, one of many coastal fortifications built to facilitate the slave trade, to pay with currency, rum, cloth, and guns for these unfortunate captives.

Asante kingdom
(ca. 1700–1896) A rising state in eighteenth-century West Africa in the rainforest region of what is now Ghana. Asante's wars of expansion produced prisoners who were often sold into the Atlantic slave circuit.

The kings of **Dahomey** (dah-HOH-mee) were even more aggressive in using the slave trade to advance state interests, trading slaves for guns to build a military advantage over their neighbors. As the prices for slaves rose during the eighteenth century, more and more guns were imported into West Africa. Faced with aggressive neighbors like Dahomey, other African rulers found they too needed to enter the slaves-for-guns trade for their own self-defense. Thus, protecting your own people could leave little choice other than selling people from neighboring societies.

Dahomey
(ca. 1650–1894) African kingdom in present-day southern Benin, reaching its height of influence in the eighteenth century. Its leaders sought regional power by raiding for slaves in other kingdoms and selling them for firearms and European goods.

It was a vicious cycle reinforced by differing European and African gender preferences. Europeans preferred to buy young males, since they were destined for hard physical labor. Males therefore fetched the highest prices on the Atlantic market. West African societies, however, preferred female slaves, valuing both their contribution as agricultural and domestic workers and the added fertility they brought to a village or clan: Africans tended to count their wealth in people. Thus leaders of societies like Asante and Dahomey could doubly benefit from the slave trade, exchanging imprisoned men for imported commodities while using captive women for their own social and economic benefit.

The Atlantic slave trade transformed indigenous African slavery in myriad ways. Before the Atlantic system developed, for example, an African parent in desperate circumstances might "pawn" a child to someone with sufficient resources to keep him or her alive. It was a desperate move, but sometimes necessary; no one viewed a pawned child as mere property of his or her master. Rather, the chances were good that the child would be incorporated into the new master's village society.

This common process of incorporating dependent outsiders often took the form of "fictive kinship." Over time, descendants of pawned children or war captives would come to be identified with local lineages and recognized as members of the community. The patrilineal nature of most African societies, where a child inherits the lineage status of his or her father, helped that process along. It meant that a child born from a slave mother and a man of full lineage status would become a member of the father's lineage, and thus would be accepted as a full member of the community. Such African practices stood in contrast to the situation in the Americas, where European masters seldom acknowledged responsibility for their own slave-borne offspring.

Armed Women with the King at their Head, plate II from "The History of Dahomey" by Archibald Dalzel, engraved by Francis Chesham (1749–1806) pub. 1793 (engraving), Norris, Robert (d.1791) (after)/Private Collection/The Stapleton Collection/The Bridgeman Art Library

Armed Dahomey Female Warriors Dahomey was a rising West African power in the eighteenth century, infamous for its militarism and systematic use of the slave trade to secure the weapons needed to expand its power. Dahomey was also known for its battalion of fierce and well-trained women soldiers, called *Mino* ("our mothers") in the Fon language, and "Amazons" by Europeans. The *Mino* were accorded high status. Led by female officers, they took on some of the social attributes of men and were not allowed to marry or bear children during their term of service.

African slave raiders profited from the complementary preference of African masters for female slaves and European plantation owners for male ones. Male slaves could be exported, while female captives were more likely to be sold within West Africa's own slave markets. In each case, the fates of their children were likely to be quite different. In Africa, the women's offspring would often be assimilated into the host community; in the Americas assimilation into European society was hardly an option.

● **CONTEXT&CONNECTIONS** Arab societies, like most African ones, are patrilineal, meaning that a child inherits the clan status of his or her father. Children of Arab fathers and slave mothers would thus usually be considered Arabs and full members of the community, a sharp contrast with colonial North American practices. For this reason it is exceptional to find segregated "black" communities in contemporary Arab lands, even though the slave trade between Africa and Arab lands began much earlier than the Atlantic one. ●

As an antislavery activist, Equiano perhaps had an interest in downplaying the negative aspects of indigenous slavery. But he addresses the issue of slavery in Africa in a forthright way, whether the account is based on his own childhood memories or on accounts he had heard from other slaves:

> *Each master of a family has a large square of ground.... Within this are his houses to accommodate his family and slaves; which, if numerous, frequently cause these tenements to present the appearance of a village.**

In such a village, where there was so little physical distance between master and slave, where conditions of housing and diet were relatively equal, and where the ability to exploit the labor of slaves carried with it a responsibility to protect them, there was little chance that the type of chattel slavery characteristic of the American plantation could ever develop. But the transformation of West African systems of slavery under the impact of the Atlantic trade is suggested by a passage from the *Interesting Narrative* where Equiano, being taken to the coast, is purchased by an African master, a wealthy widow whose "*house and premises were the finest I ever saw in Africa.*" Equiano sketches the traditional practice of incorporating outsiders:

> *When mealtime came, I was led into the presence of my mistress, and ate and drank before her with her son. That filled me with astonishment; and I could scarcely avoid expressing my surprise that the young gentleman should suffer me, who was bound, to eat with him who was free.... Indeed everything here, and their treatment of me, made me forget that I was a slave. The language of these people resembled ours so nearly, that we understood each other perfectly. They had also the very same customs as we.... In this resemblance to my former happy state, I passed about two months; and now I began to think I was to be adopted into the family....**

As in times past, his new mistress could have kept the young man, and by marriage he and his descendants would likely have become integrated into that society. However, by this time traditional systems had been transformed under the influence of the Atlantic trade. His new mistress now had the option of selling him for cash; in Equiano's account, she sold him back into the slave export channel that led to the coast.

As warfare increased, the resulting climate of insecurity often enabled warrior chieftains to gather followers, with sharper political hierarchies reflecting greater inequality. African merchants and political leaders who traded in slaves thus gained power and status. Traditional institutions could be corrupted as a result, as when judges near Equiano's home region were corrupted by the slave trade, abusing their authority to banish wrongdoers in order to benefit from the slave trade. In such ways, on scales large and small, the Atlantic market transformed traditional institutions.

---

*Olaudah Equiano, *The Interesting Narrative of the Life of Olaudah Equiano, or Gustavus Vassa, the African*, ed. Vincent Carretta, 2d ed. (New York: Penguin, 2003), pp. 36, 52–53.

By the later eighteenth century, as more African states came to rely on slaves not just as commodities for export but also as soldiers and laborers, some African "societies with slaves" started to become "slave societies" where slavery became essential to the functioning of state and society. While this intensification of slavery under the influence of the Atlantic trade enhanced the power of some Africans, by far the biggest political and economic advantages went to European slave traders and plantation owners.

● **CONTEXT&CONNECTIONS** Ironically, abolitionism was one of the main arguments used by Europeans to justify their partition of Africa during the *New Imperialism* (Chapter 26) of the late nineteenth century. In their "scramble for Africa," European societies might justify their military invasions and often brutal colonial occupations by claiming the need to eliminate conditions of slavery, conditions that their own nations had originally helped to create. ●

AP® THEMES
How were the social structures of Africa altered as a result of the forced migration of Africans destined for slavery in the Americas?

Some historians have warned that we should not exaggerate the impact of the Atlantic slave trade on continental Africa. It is true that some African societies were still part of trans-Saharan and Red Sea commercial networks with slave markets of long standing (see Map 19.2). It is also true that many African societies had no connection at all with external slave markets. Despite the Atlantic slave trade, farming and herding remained the principal economic activities in Africa.

However, on a continent where land was plentiful but people were scarce, the loss of population through the export of slaves harmed economic growth. Europe and Asia experienced surges in population during the eighteenth century, due in large part to the introduction of productive new food crops from the Americas. While such crops were introduced in Africa as well, the total population of the African continent remained stagnant, strongly suggesting that the large-scale export of slaves had a deeply damaging effect on Africa's overall economic productivity.

Europe and the Atlantic World, 1650–1807

By the eighteenth century, the Atlantic Ocean was awash with people, goods, plants, animals, diseases, religious and political ideas, and cultural forms such as music and storytelling traditions, all circulating freely among Europe, Africa, and the Americas. The Atlantic world emerged as a transcultural zone where enterprising adventurers, even former slaves like Olaudah Equiano, sought their fortunes. Meanwhile, Britain and France—now surpassing the Spanish, Portuguese, and Dutch as the world's dominant naval powers—were locked in nearly constant conflict.

triangular trade
The network of interchange among Europe, Africa, and the colonial Americas. Consisted of raw materials and agricultural produce sent from the Americas to Europe; manufactures sent to Africa and used for the purchase of slaves; and slaves exported from Africa to the Americas.

Economic and Military Competition in the Atlantic Ocean, 1650–1763

The economic exchange among Europe, Africa, and the Americas is often called the **triangular trade**, which refers to the movement of manufactured goods from Europe to Africa, of African humanity to the Americas, and of colonial products such as sugar, tobacco, and timber back to Europe (see Map 19.2).

The image of a triangular trade is convenient, but it simplifies the global dimensions of world trade in this period. For example, Indian Ocean trade

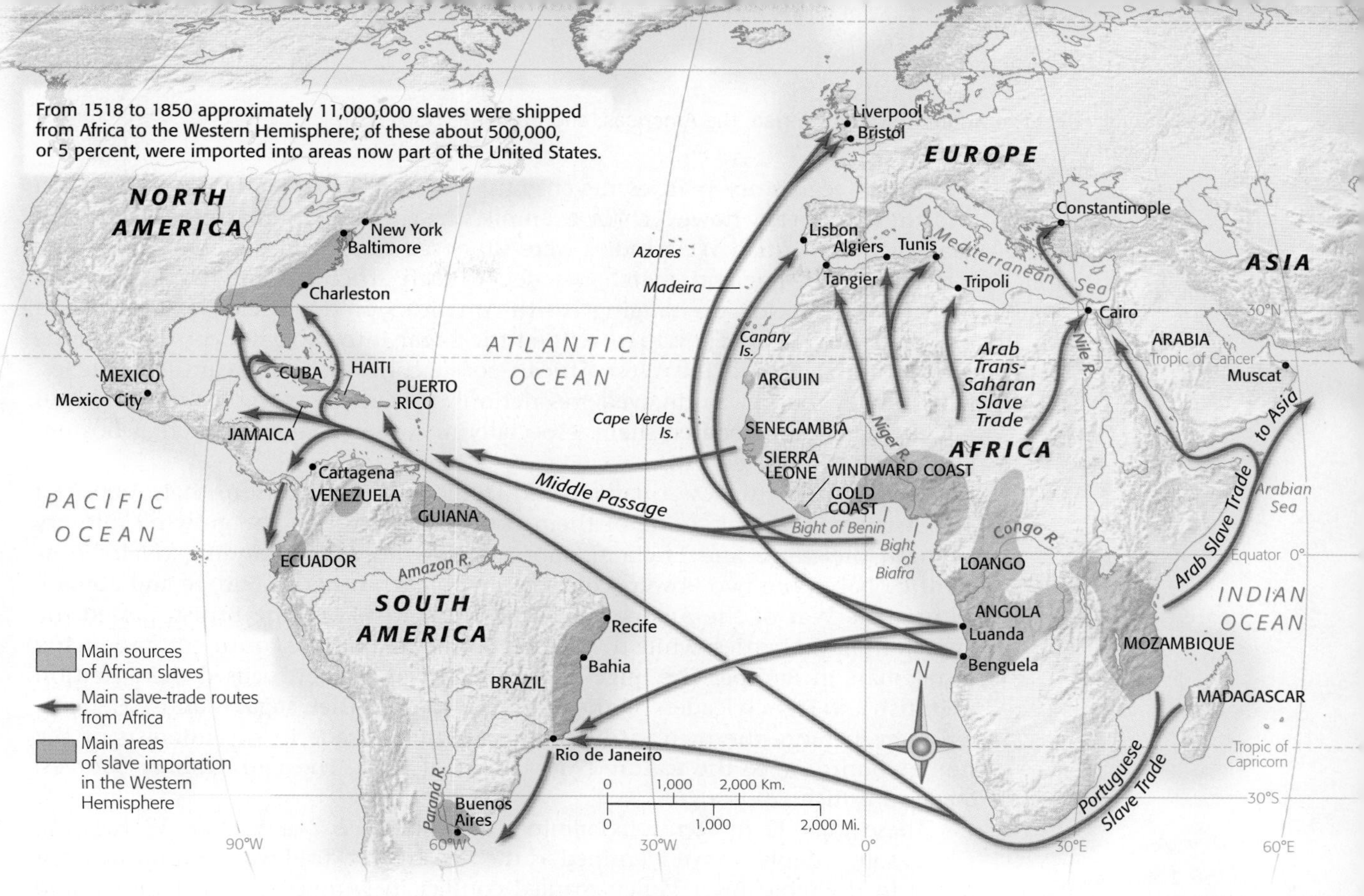

Map 19.2 The Atlantic Slave Trade The Middle Passage from Africa to the Americas was the greatest forced migration in human history. The vast majority of the Africans who lived through it were put to work on Caribbean islands or coastal plantations. The Arab trade in African slaves, across the Sahara Desert and the Indian Ocean, was much older, but at no time matched the scale of the Atlantic trade.

networks connected to Atlantic networks whenever Indian cotton textiles, paid for in American silver, were exported to Africa, Europe, and the Americas. In West Africa, the use of cowrie shells from the Indian Ocean as currency (imported in enormous quantities and frequently used in African sculpture as well) also shows that trade links were not simply triangular but interoceanic. The Atlantic system was part of an emerging global economy.

Competition for commercial ascendency inevitably led to military conflict in an age when the concept of international free trade had not yet developed. Instead of believing that everyone could benefit from open markets, Europeans saw economic exchange as a zero sum game, one where enriching your own nation meant beggaring your neighbor. That is why all the major trading nations followed policies of economic **mercantilism**, regulating colonial trade by restricting colonial producers, merchants, and shippers as much as possible to the home country's own markets. Thus, for instance, New England merchants were officially prohibited from trading in the French West Indies, even if they saw good market opportunities.

mercantilism

Dominant economic theory in seventeenth- and eighteenth-century Europe that emphasized the role of international economics in interstate competition. Under mercantilism, restrictive tariffs were placed on imports to raise their prices, maximize the country's exports, and build up supplies of gold and silver bullion for military investment

British regulatory policies never entirely controlled trade in North America and the Caribbean, however. For example, the sugar and molasses produced on islands in the British West Indies were supposed to be sent directly to England. However, New England merchants defied such strictures and traded directly with the Caribbean, exchanging North American products such as timber and foodstuffs for sugar. They then refined the sugar into molasses or rum to trade directly for slaves on the West African coast, contrary to mercantilist policies. Even as they found ways to evade restrictions on trade, however, North American merchants deeply resented them, especially in commercial cities such as Boston, Philadelphia, and New York.

While the Portuguese, Spanish, and Dutch still profited from their American and Asian possessions, none of them could keep up with the growing military strength of France and England, monarchies whose longstanding rivalry now went global as the two powers competed with each other in Europe and abroad. During the War of the Austrian Succession (1740–1748), the British bested the French in naval battles, while the French dominated on the continent, producing a stalemate in Europe. The huge costs of that war further focused the attention of British and French leaders on the economic value of their sugar islands, strengthening even more the mercantilist urge to regulate trade in the interests of the home country. (See the feature "Movement of Ideas Through Primary Sources: Sugar in British Politics.")

Seven Years' War
(1756–1763) Fought simultaneously in Europe, the West Indies, North America, and South Asia, this war shifted the balance of power between Britain and France in favor of the British, making their influence paramount in India and Canada.

These Anglo-French tensions culminated in the **Seven Years' War** (1756–1763), which some scholars have identified as the first truly "world war." Skirmishes that began in the Ohio River Valley sparked conflict in Europe, the West Indies, and South Asia as well, resulting in a tri-continental contest for supremacy between the British and the French that involved alliances with societies as disparate and widely scattered as the Iroquois, Prussians, and Bengalis.

A major turning point in North America was the successful British siege of Louisburg at the mouth of the St. Lawrence River, gateway to New France. Thirteen year-old Olaudah Equiano, still the property of a Royal Navy officer, was there:

> *The engagement now commenced with great fury on both sides: [the French ship] immediately returned our fire and we continued engaged with each other for some time; during which I was frequently stunned with the thundering of the great guns, whose dreadful contents burned many of my companions into eternity.**

AP® THEMES

How did conflicts among European states alter the balance of power not only between European states but also between European states and non-European states?

British victory in this engagement soon led to the conquest of Québec and all of New France, giving Britain a dominant position in North America. At the same time, victories in India were positioning the British for eventual mastery over South Asia (see Chapter 20).

Meanwhile, the Seven Years' War added to tensions between the British crown and American colonists. Having spent a huge sum to defend the colonies from France, the British thought Americans should now help pay for their own defense. But new taxes and restrictions on trade soon prompted the colonists to seek independence (see Chapter 22).

---

*Olaudah Equiano, *The Interesting Narrative of the Life of Olaudah Equiano, or Gustavus Vassa, the African*, ed. Vincent Carretta, 2d ed. (New York: Penguin, 2003), p. 83.

• **CONTEXT&CONNECTIONS** In the wake of the Seven Years' War, the British lost one empire and gained another. Just when the movement was stirring for independence in the American colonies, the British were displacing the *Mughals* (Chapters 16 and 20) as the dominant power in India. Historians thus refer to a "second British empire" to mark the transition from North America to South Asia as the center of late-eighteenth-century British imperial activity. By the nineteenth century, India was the "jewel in the crown" of the British empire, the most expansive the world had ever seen (see Chapter 24). •

Life on the Eighteenth-Century Atlantic Ocean

Rimming the Atlantic, and manning the ships that transported goods and people around it, were a multitude of uprooted people. Olaudah Equiano, who spent almost half his life aboard ship, was familiar with the turbulent mass of humanity that made its living from the sea: slave traders, cod fishermen, pirates, and officers and crew fighting for king and country. Violence was common. Some were desperate enough to volunteer for life at sea; others were forced into it. Press gangs stalked the English coast looking for a chance to seize the able-bodied and force them onto British ships chronically short of sailors, a situation that Equiano and many others saw as akin to slavery.

Life aboard ship was rough. Sailors had no privacy, and discipline was tight. Captains had to be alert or they might lose control of their crews and face a mutiny. *"A ship is worse than a jail,"* stated one writer. *"There is, in a jail, better air, better company, better convenience of every kind; and a ship has the additional disadvantage of being in danger."*

Nevertheless, Equiano, *"being still of a roving disposition"* after he gained his liberty, never stayed for more than a few years on dry land. Life at sea offered opportunity for an ambitious soul from a poor background. Military prowess, acumen in trade, and seamanship all required competence, and life at sea rewarded ability, in contrast to most of British life, where ancestry and social class held sway. Even as a young slave, Equiano was able to earn a promotion to the rank of "able seaman" for his service during the Seven Years' War, making him eligible for a payment from the crown at war's end. Equiano equated that promotion with status as a freeman, so he was exceptionally bitter when his owner, who was also his commanding officer, not only pocketed his pension but also sold him to a new master. Still, life at sea gave Equiano his greatest opportunities.

• **CONTEXT&CONNECTIONS** One strength of the British navy was its relative openness to promotion based on merit rather than (as in the army) on social standing or aristocratic background. During Equiano's lifetime, for example, Captain *James Cook* (1728–1779) (Chapter 21) was becoming one of the nation's most capable naval officers. The son of a farmer, Cook rose through the ranks on the basis of his leadership abilities and navigational expertise to become one of the empire's most famous men. •

The Atlantic Ocean also represented opportunities for fishermen, who pulled enormous hauls of cod from the **Grand Banks** off the coast of Newfoundland. Basque fisherman first discovered this area in medieval times, and salted cod had become a staple of the Mediterranean diet. By the eighteenth century, ships from many nations were exploiting this rich source of protein, which once cured was easily stored and transported.

Grand Banks
Fishing area located south and southeast of present-day Newfoundland, Canada. Noted for its immense quantities of cod, a source of protein for the residents in and around the Atlantic and of large profits for British colonial traders.

Sugar in British Politics

In the mid-eighteenth century, West Indian sugar was the most profitable resource in the British empire, with small islands like Jamaica and Barbados generating huge revenues. Plantation owners were not the only beneficiaries, as we see in this *Letter to a Member of Parliament* from 1745. The question had to do with how much the British government should tax sugar at the point of its arrival in England, that is, how high the "duty" should be. The huge profits that the sugar industry generated made a tempting target for a government trying to raise revenue to fight its increasingly expensive wars with France. The letter was published anonymously, meaning that the publisher was most likely trying to influence public opinion against a rise in the sugar tax, which the author warns would do more harm than good.

> **Historical Thinking Skill:**
> **ARGUMENTATION What evidence does the author present to argue against the increase in the tax on sugar?**

> **Historical Thinking Skill:**
> **ANALYZING EVIDENCE What characteristics of the transatlantic trade network of the eighteenth century do we see in this source?**

Source: A Letter to a Member of Parliament, Concerning the Importance of our Sugar-Colonies to Great Britain, by a Gentleman, who resided many Years in the Island of Jamaica (London: J. Taylor, 1745). Spelling modernized.

From *A Letter to a Member of Parliament, Concerning the Importance of our Sugar-Colonies*

In the first place, I will endeavour to convince you, that whatever additional duty shall be laid on sugar, it will be at the cost of the sugar planter....

Secondly, I shall show, that such an additional duty will be an oppression and discouragement and an unequal load upon our sugar colonies at this juncture especially, and will render abortive the very scheme itself which is intended by it, of advancing the revenue. And,

Thirdly, I shall set forth the great advantages that this nation receives from the sugar colonies, and especially from the island of Jamaica, and the great advantages that it will continue to receive, if due encouragement be given to the sugar planter....

Now the case of the sugar planter is, that he is at a prodigious distance from the market ... and being already in debt, as the greatest number of the sugar planters are, and having already established his sugar works ... he must be ruined if those are not kept employed....

We have no foreign market worth notice, but Holland and Hamburg, and ... the Dutch will buy the French sugar, at the French colonies at a low price, and carry it securely to Holland in their own ships. And it is well known that the French at their colonies can and do sell their sugar much cheaper than we can in our colonies, because they have better sugar land in their islands, and nearer the seaside than we have....

[T]he sugar planter is [now] at a vast deal greater expense to make sugar.... His Negro slaves ... were sold at Jamaica at £35 per head [but now cost] £50 per head.... The sugar planter pays double the freight for his sugar home than he did before ... and double the freight out for all his utensils for making sugar, and all his furniture for his house use and family, and slaves....

[U]nless the price of sugar here at market do advance very considerably, the sugar planter can't go on, but will be ruined. If the planter, to all his other advanced charges, hath a further duty laid upon his commodity, he will be disabled from purchasing every year a fresh supply of Negroes, mules, and cattle; and as his present stock drops off, he will disabled from making the quantity of sugar he does at present ... by which means the scheme for raising more money upon that commodity, by advancing the duty, will be rendered abortive....

The principal charge which the sugar planter is at, to raise and carry on his work, is Negroes; and those are purchased in Africa by the English merchants, chiefly with the produce and manufactures of this nation, such as woolen goods.... At the same time that they are purchasing the Negroes on the coast of Africa, with those cargoes of British manufactures, they purchase also a great deal of gold, elephants' teeth, and some very valuable dying woods....

For strength to carry on his sugar work, next to the negroes, the planter must be furnished with mules, cattle, horses, etc. Of cattle the most part are raised in the colonies; some horses are raised in the colonies and some are supplied from North America.... [His equipment] ... will cost him at least 500 pounds. Add to this, the great quantity of nails, locks, hinges, bolts, and other sorts of iron ware; and lead that he must have for his buildings. And for his field work he must have great quantities of bills, hoes, axes, iron chains; also gear for his mill and his cattle ... and all this of English manufacture....

Besides this extraordinary expense ... he must have a house to live in, and furniture, and clothes, and other necessaries for himself and family, servants and slaves. To build his house he must have materials from England ... and his furniture and clothing entirely from England....

And for their food, they have a great deal, as cheese, bacon, pickles, some flour and biscuits, when cheap, and beer, ale and cider, in great quantities from England; salted beef and butter from Ireland; and salted fish, flour, biscuits and sundry other kinds of provisions for their negroes from North America.

There are in the island of Jamaica only, a hundred thousand negroes, a few more or less; every one of these ... do make use of the value of twenty shillings a year, in goods from England. In clothing they make use of a vast quantity of Manchester goods ... and many other implements, all of British manufacture. I believe ... it amounts to a hundred thousand pounds a year in British manufactures, consumed by the negroes in Jamaica only.

And now, Sir, if you'll be pleased to take a view of the whole process of the sugar manufacture, from the beginning to the time of delivering the commodity into the hands of the consumer; that is to say, from purchasing the negroes on the coast of Africa, and transporting them to the West Indies ... I am sure that you will be amazed to consider, what a prodigious number of ships, of sailors, of merchants, of tradesmen, manufacturers, mechanics, and laborers, are continually employed, and reap a profit thereby....

And should the sugar colonies be so much discouraged, by the laying on of an additional duty ... you see plainly how very much our trade and navigation, and how many of our manufactures would be affected by it, and that would not be the worst of it [because] in proportion as our sugar colonies should decline, those of our neighbours, our enemies and rivals in trade and navigation would advance.

In New England, fishing became a symbol of proud independence and prosperity, symbolized by the "Sacred Cod," a wooden cod effigy still hanging in the Massachusetts State House. Men with little property but a strong work ethic could make a good living working the Grand Banks or specializing in the abundant oysters and lobsters closer to shore. New England's fishing profits, however, were connected to slavery. Merchants often bought molasses in the Caribbean with the lowest quality salted cod, used as a cheap source of protein. Thus, while cod fishing might instill an independent spirit in New England, it also provided plantation owners with a cheap way to feed captives in the West Indies and helped finance the slave trade. In the Atlantic world, slavery and freedom were two sides of the same coin.

Abolition of the British Slave Trade, 1772–1807

In 1775, now a free man, Olaudah Equiano worked as a plantation supervisor on the Central American coast. Equiano did not seem to mind, and when the job was over he even congratulated himself on a job well done: *"All my poor countrymen, the slaves, when they heard of my leaving them were very sorry, as I had always treated them with care and affection, and did everything I could to comfort the poor creatures."**

Equiano seemed to imply that slavery could be made humane. Over the next decade, however, he came to believe that slavery was inherently evil and needed to be abolished. His change in thinking was partly an outcome of deepening religious conviction. After surviving a shipwreck, Equiano joined the Methodist movement, whose founder had argued that slavery was incompatible with Christian morality. *"O, ye nominal Christians!"* Equiano wrote, *"Might not an African ask you, 'learned you this from your God, who says unto you, Do unto all men as you would men should do unto you?'"** Throughout the 1780s, more and more British Christians raised their voices in opposition to slavery. Though the slave owners and slave traders formed a powerful lobby in the British Parliament, public opinion was turning against them. (See the feature "Visual Evidence in Primary Sources: The Horrors of the Middle Passage.")

abolitionist
A man or woman who advocated an end to the practice of slavery. In the late eighteenth century, a powerful abolitionist movement grew in England.

Apart from Christian conscience, other factors aided the antislavery **abolitionist** cause. In 1772, a judge had ruled that no slave, once he or she reached England, could be compelled to return to a colony where slavery was practiced. Essentially, this meant that the condition of slavery had no legal basis in British law, reflecting the pride that Britons felt in their tradition of "liberty," constitutionally guaranteed by the Bill of Rights of 1689 (see Chapter 17). But the British constitution also protected property rights. The crux of the debate was which rights should take precedence: those of a slave owner to property for which he had paid, or those of the slave to his own person?

To make the case for the superior claim of liberty over property, British abolitionists invoked public opinion. One way to make the issue more tangible for people in England was to focus on the link between their own sugar consumption, by far the highest in the world, and the evils of slavery. In his poem "Poor Africans," William Cowper wrote:

I pity them greatly, but I must be mum,
For how could we do without sugar and rum?
Especially sugar, so needful we see,
What, give up our desserts, our coffee and tea?

Abolitionist boycotts helped win the debate at the breakfast table, as more Britons came to see slavery not as something distant and abstract, but as an evil in which they personally participated by consuming slave-grown sugar.

Equiano intended his *Interesting Narrative* to be part of this accelerating abolitionist campaign. Like many authors at this time, he advertised for

*Olaudah Equiano, *The Interesting Narrative of the Life of Olaudah Equiano, or Gustavus Vassa, the African*, ed. Vincent Carretta, 2d ed. (New York: Penguin, 2003), pp. 211, 61.

subscribers who would pay in advance and receive their copies once the book was written and printed. Subscriptions were a way for people to support causes they believed in. The subscribers to Equiano's book included major antislavery campaigners such as Thomas Clarkson, who wrote a university essay on the theme "Is enslaving others against their will ever justified?" and devoted himself to the abolitionist cause; Josiah Wedgwood, the highly successful ceramics entrepreneur (see Chapter 23) who designed a best-selling plate featuring the image of an African in chains saying *"Am I Not a Man and a Brother?"*; and William Wilberforce, the member of Parliament who took the abolitionist cause to the House of Commons.

AP® THEMES

What were the causes and effects of the movement to abolish slavery?

After the publication of the *Interesting Narrative* in 1789, Equiano spent three years touring England, Scotland, and Ireland speaking at antislavery meetings. He was hugely successful in advancing the cause of abolitionism while doing well for himself financially. Book royalties made him the wealthiest black man in England, and when he married an English wife in 1792 her family income moderately increased his property. Proud of his new status as a married man, he announced the marriage in the new edition of his *Interesting Narrative*.

As he began an English family, Equiano remained politically active. Wilberforce had decided to press for abolition only of the slave trade, not of the condition of slavery itself. This more limited agenda had a better chance in Parliament, since many members thought it was permissible to stop slaves from being seized and transported but not for the government to strip slave owners of their property, even when that property consisted of human beings.

The British abolitionist cause, while largely religiously inspired, was also stimulated by eighteenth-century Enlightenment philosophies stressing rational thought and the quest for human liberty (see Chapter 22). The Scottish free-market economist Adam Smith, for example, argued that slavery, by preventing the negotiation of free labor contracts, distorted economies and undermined growth. And it was French thinkers who were most influential in developing the concept of *"liberty, equality, and fraternity"* as a universally applicable ideal (see Chapters 21 and 22). However, the extreme radicalism of the French Revolution, including the execution of the French king, led the British government to look on political reform with deep suspicion. Equiano even removed the names of some of his more radical subscribers from the *Interesting Narrative* to avoid guilt by association.

The abolition of the slave trade thus took much longer than its proponents had hoped. Sadly, Equiano was still waiting when he passed away prematurely at the age fifty-two (leaving behind his wife Susanna and daughter Joanna, who inherited his substantial estate).

Finally, in 1807 Parliament passed the **Act for the Abolition of the Slave Trade**, ending the trade in slaves among British subjects. Another whole generation of Africans had to wait before slavery itself was abolished in the British empire, an advance that still did not help slaves in non-British territories such as Cuba, Brazil, and the southern United States. Meanwhile, the British government, with the full backing of public opinion, pursued a global campaign to eliminate slave markets. That was a significant turnabout, considering Britain had benefited more than any other nation from four centuries of the Atlantic slave trade. Meanwhile, millions of Africans had been violently uprooted, while many of those who remained behind suffered from the Atlantic slave trade's legacy of insecurity, warfare, and population decline.

Act for the Abolition of the Slave Trade

Law passed in 1807 by the British Parliament ending the trade in slaves among British subjects. The British government then used the Royal Navy to suppress the slave trade internationally.

The Horrors of the Middle Passage

British abolitionists were well aware of the power of visual images to advance their cause, anticipating that a shocked public would pressure Parliament to end the trade in slaves. Political cartoons were one way to both express and influence public opinion. The cartoon below refers to the case of a slave trader, Captain John Kimber, who was accused in 1792 of torturing a fifteen-year-old African girl to death when she refused to "dance" for him. ("Dancing" was a required physical activity for slaves when they were

Library of Congress Prints and Photographs Division

Captain Kimber is clearly depicted as being responsible for the abuse of the African girl. He seems to be enjoying himself.

For his portrayal of the victim the artist chose to use dark ink, obscuring her features. What effect does this technique have on the viewer?

The sailor pulling the rope says: "Damn me if I like it I have a good mind to let go." The other two sailors say: "My Eyes Jack our Girls at Wapping are never flogged for their modesty," and "By G-d that's too bad if he had taken her to bed to him it would be well enough. Split me, I'm almost sick of this Black Business."

brought up to the ship's deck for exercise; slave captains routinely enforced that rule with the lash.) Kimber was acquitted, and the sailors who gave evidence against him were convicted of perjury. Abolitionists were outraged and their opponents encouraged by this legal ruling. The title of the illustration reads: "The Abolition of the Slave Trade, or the inhumanity of the dealers in human flesh exemplified in Captn Kimbers treatment of a Young Negro Girl of 15 for her virgin modesty."

The image below, the slave ship *Brooks*, was widely circulated by abolitionists to show (in the words of a modern historian) "that the slaver itself was a place of barbarity, indeed a huge, complex technologically sophisticated instrument of torture."* First circulated by the Society for Effecting the Abolition of the Slave Trade in 1788, this engraving was widely known across Britain and the United States. Its depiction of a "close packed" slave ship made *"an instantaneous impression of horror upon all who saw it"* according to Thomas Clarkson, the prominent abolitionist who wrote the text that accompanied this image. Clarkson interviewed British sailors in slave ports like Bristol and Liverpool, who told him bloodcurdling stories of inhumanity on ships like the *Brooks*, where, another abolitionist wrote, *"human creatures [were] reduced nearly to the state of being buried alive."* The *Brooks* made ten voyages to Africa between 1781 and 1804, its captains purchasing 5,163 slaves, of whom 4,559 survived the Atlantic crossing. This image of the *Brooks* undoubtedly contributed to the abolition of the British slave trade in 1807.

*Marcus Rediker, *The Slave Ship: A Human History* (New York: Viking, 2007), p. 309.

How might these two images have affected viewers differently? Which might have had the greater impact on the abolitionist movement, and why?

Each adult African man aboard the *Brooks* was allocated a plank 6 feet by 16 inches with no more than 2 feet 6 inches of vertical space, too little to allow him to sit up. Not shown are the tubs of excrement that fouled the air in the slave hold.

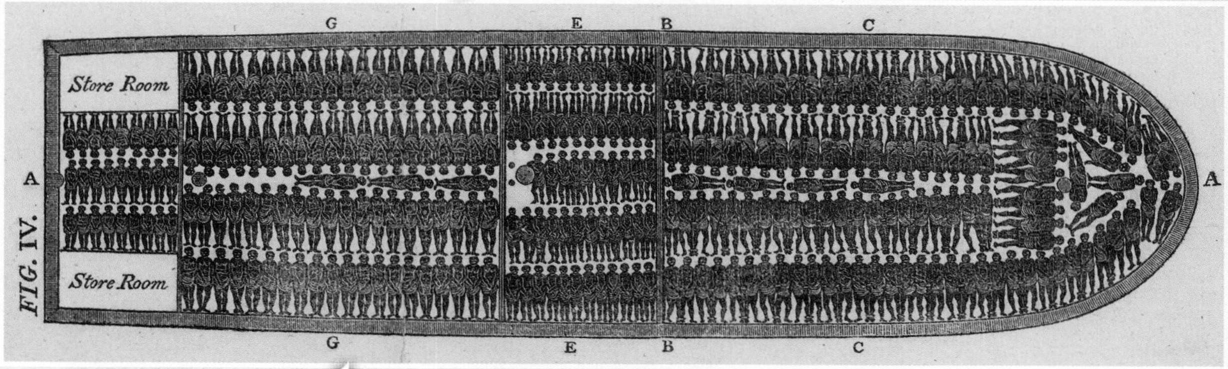

The artist who produced this engraving carefully drew every individual African on board, showing each wearing only a loincloth. Shown here are 482 slaves. On an earlier voyage, before a 1788 law that regulated the slave trade, one *Brooks* captain had crammed 609 Africans in this same space: 351 men, 127 women, 90 boys, and 41 girls.

CONTEXT AND CONNECTIONS

Atlantic Slavery and the Plantation Complex in World History

The use of massed slave labor on agricultural plantations was part of world history from ancient empires through the final abolition of slavery in Brazil in 1888. Still, the type of slavery Olaudah Equiano experienced, witnessed, and fought against was exceptional in scale: the largest, most intensive, and most profitable plantation slave system ever.

Not all societies treated slaves simply as brute labor. In the Ottoman empire, slaves could rise to positions of significant power even as they suffered constraints on their freedom of movement or endeavor (see Chapter 17). In Africa, as Equiano described it, slaves were often incorporated into the communities of which they became a part, and they tended to lose their disabilities over time. Such "societies with slaves" were quite different from the "slave societies" associated with sugar.

Sugar plantations had relied on massed slave labor even before the rise of the Atlantic slave trade. From ninth-century Arab origins, the plantation complex moved westward into the Mediterranean, fed by slave-trading circuits that extended south into Africa and east toward the Black Sea. The Portuguese then transferred the sugar plantation system to islands offshore of western Africa and across the Atlantic to Brazil, from which it moved into what became the world's most intensive center of production, the West Indies (see Chapter 16).

It was ironic that Europeans were the ones who created the harsher forms of modern slavery associated with brutal plantation work in the Americas. After the fall of the Roman empire, a true "slave society," slavery had virtually disappeared from Europe. The upsurge in Christian religious conviction following the Reformation was making it more difficult to reconcile faith with slavery (see Chapter 17). And it was during the height of the Atlantic slave trade, in the eighteenth century, when Enlightenment ideas of rationality, freedom, and liberty were being developed (see Chapter 21).

Of course, the vast profits to be made by cheaply producing commodities like sugar provided individuals and nations with powerful motives for involvement in the plantation system. From the seventeenth century on, increasingly sophisticated financial mechanisms and maritime technologies had made possible the concentration of resources and the development of global markets necessary for such

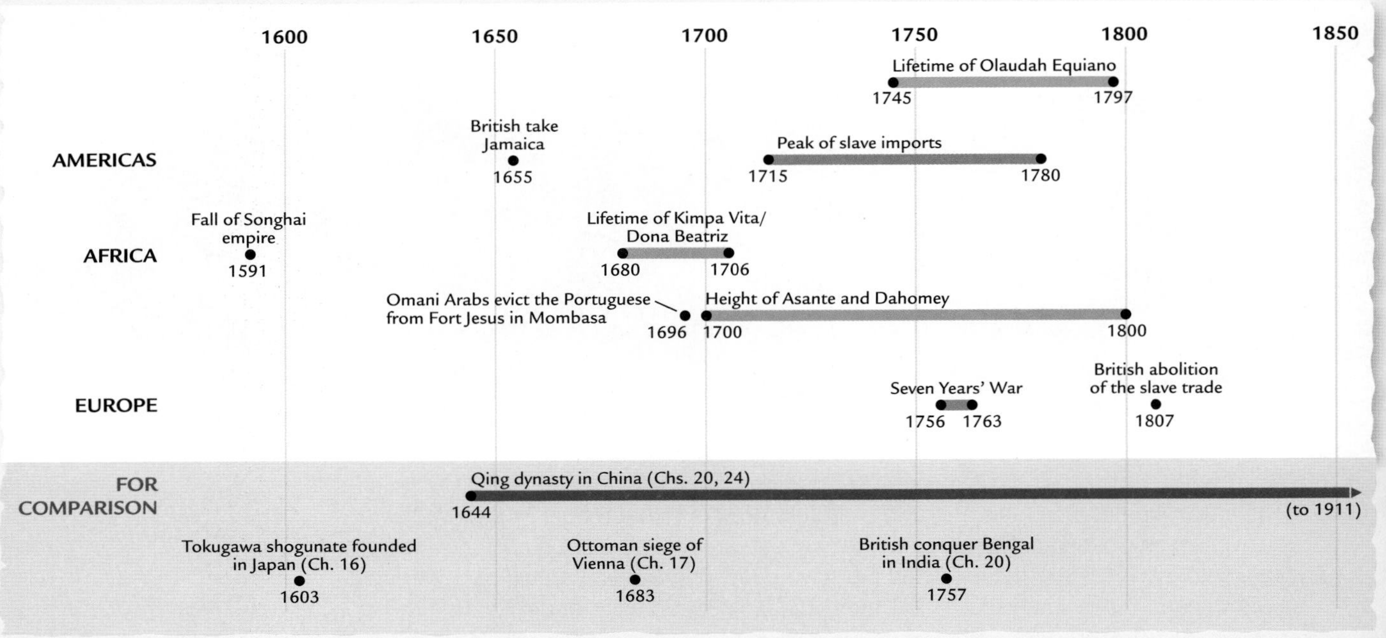

large-scale agro-industrial business operations. At the same time, competition between European states, especially France and Britain, made sustaining plantation profits a matter of great national interest (see Chapter 17).

Then, in the late eighteenth century, the beginnings of the Industrial Revolution, the independence of the United States, and a shift in British priorities toward India all lessened the importance of West Indian sugar (see Chapters 20, 22, and 23). The British, after ending the slave trade in 1807 and outlawing slavery within the British empire in 1834, became global abolitionist campaigners. In some parts of the world, slavery has continued into the twentieth-first century, but by the 1800s the slave-based plantation complex had come to an end. Brazilian and Caribbean industries declined and new centers of sugar production, such as Hawai'i and Fiji, relied on indentured contract laborers rather than slaves.

For Africa, however, the story was not over, for those who had remained behind had suffered as well. In the short run, African life had become more dangerous and insecure, and in the long run the continent suffered from the lost vitality and productivity of millions of its sons and daughters.

Key Terms

Olaudah Equiano (560)
Great Lakes region (561)
Kimpa Vita (561)
Sahel (562)
Songhai empire (562)
Atlantic plantation system (565)
maroon communities (570)
manumission (572)
Asante kingdom (573)
Dahomey (573)
triangular trade (576)
mercantilism (577)
Seven Years' War (578)
Grand Banks (579)
abolitionist (582)
Act for the Abolition of the Slave Trade (583)

For Further Reference

Anstey, Roger. *The Atlantic Slave Trade and British Abolition, 1760–1810.* New York: Macmillan, 1975.

Blackburn, Robin. *The Making of New World Slavery: From the Baroque to the Modern, 1492–1800.* 2d ed. London: Verso, 2010.

Carretta, Vincent. *Equiano, the African: Biography of a Self-Made Man.* New York: Penguin Books, 2007.

Curtin, Philip. *The Rise and Fall of the Plantation Complex: Essays in Atlantic History.* 2d ed. New York: Cambridge University Press, 1998.

Davis, David Brion. *Inhuman Bondage: The Rise and Fall of Slavery in the New World.* New York: Oxford University Press, 2008.

Eltis, David. *Economic Growth and the Ending of the Trans-Atlantic Slave Trade.* New York: Oxford University Press, 1987.

Klein, Herbert S., and Francisco Vidal Luna. *Slavery in Brazil.* Cambridge: Cambridge University Press, 2009.

Lovejoy, Paul. *Transformations in Slavery: A History of Slavery in Africa.* 3d ed. New York: Cambridge University Press, 2011.

Mintz, Sidney. *Sweetness and Power: The Place of Sugar in Modern History.* New York: Penguin Books, 1985.

Northrup, David. *Africa's Discovery of Europe, 1450–1850.* New York: Oxford University Press, 2002.

Patterson, Orlando. *Slavery and Social Death: A Comparative Study.* Cambridge, Mass.: Harvard University Press, 1985.

Rediker, Marcus. *The Slave Ship: A Human History.* New York: Viking, 2007.

Thornton, John. *A Cultural History of the Atlantic World, 1250–1820.* Cambridge: Cambridge University Press, 2012.

AP® Review Questions for Chapter 19

Multiple-Choice Questions

QUESTIONS 1–3 REFER TO THE FOLLOWING MAP.

1. The trade network identified in the map was responsible for which of the following?
   (A) The rise of powerful new trading cities
   (B) A decline in urban life
   (C) A lack of luxury goods in many of the world's regions
   (D) Halting the spread of universal religions

2. The extent of the reach of the trade networks in the map could be used to explain which of the following?
   (A) The extensive use of gunpowder by the kingdoms of sub-Saharan Africa
   (B) The spread of commodities across West Africa
   (C) The expansion of silk production in the Swahili city-states
   (D) The importing of slaves from India to eastern Africa

3. Which of the following occurrences significantly altered the trade network depicted in the map after 1450?
   (A) The expansion of the Silk Road and related land routes
   (B) The beginning of the Crusades
   (C) The development of the Atlantic system
   (D) The adoption of Christianity by the kings of Mali

QUESTIONS 4–7 REFER TO THE FOLLOWING PASSAGE.

The first object which saluted my eyes when I arrived on the coast was the sea, and a slave-ship.... These filled me with astonishment, which was soon converted into terror.... [T]hey made ready with many fearful noises, and we were all put under deck... now that the whole ship's cargo was confined together [the stench of the hold] was absolutely pestilential. The closeness of the place, and the heat of the climate, added to the number in the ship, which was so crowded that each had scarcely room to turn himself, almost suffocated us.... This wretched situation was again aggravated by the galling of the chains, now become insupportable; and the filth of the [latrines], into which the children often fell, and were almost suffocated. The shrieks of the women, and the groans of the dying, rendered the whole a scene of horror almost inconceivable.

—Olaudah Equiano, *The Interesting Narrative of the Life of Olaudah Equiano*, 1789

4. Based on the passage above, which is a valid inference?
   (A) The importing of slaves to the Caribbean increased during this time period.
   (B) Levels of slave imports essentially remained unchanged.
   (C) The importing of slaves dropped at a consistent rate.
   (D) After an initial rise in the slave trade, the numbers dropped off significantly.

5. Which of the following statements best explains the presence of slave ships in the Americas?
   (A) The spread of religiously based antislavery beliefs
   (B) The expansion of tobacco plantations in South America
   (C) The exposure of slaves to American diseases
   (D) The expansion of sugar production to the Americas

6. Which of the following explains the effect of the Atlantic system described in the passage?
   (A) The start of slave trading in all African regions
   (B) The intensification and partial redirection of the slave trade to the Americas
   (C) The role of Europeans in capturing slaves in the African interior
   (D) The demise of the slave trade and the expansion of the ivory trade

7. Which of the following best explains the rise of the slave trade during this time period?
   (A) European powers transporting slaves to Asia for profit
   (B) An attempt by South Asian kingdoms to import more laborers
   (C) The rise of plantation economies in the Americas
   (D) Importing Africans to Europe to rebuild the population after the Plague

QUESTIONS 8–10 REFER TO THE FOLLOWING PASSAGE.

Each master of a family has a large square of ground.... Within this are his houses to accommodate his family and slaves; which, if numerous, frequently cause these tenements to present the appearance of a village. In the middle stands the principal building, appropriated to the sole use of the master.... On each side are the apartments of his wives.... The habituations of the slaves and the rest of his family are distributed throughout the rest of the enclosure.

—Olaudah Equiano, *The Interesting Narrative of the Life of Olaudah Equiano*, 1789

8. This passage supports which of the following statements?
   (A) The capturing of slaves in Africa was done by Europeans.
   (B) Slavery in Africa predates the arrival of the Europeans.
   (C) The capturing of slaves was done by both Africans and Europeans.
   (D) Slaves were taken from primarily one tribe in the West African region.

9. The passage is evidence of which of the following concerning the status of women in West Africa?
   (A) Gender roles were not strictly followed in West Africa during this time period.
   (B) Polygamy was practiced in West Africa.
   (C) Most regions had developed into egalitarian societies by the end of this time period.
   (D) Women were forced to perform tasks and jobs that men found demeaning.

10. Which statement accurately compares the slavery in Africa and in the Americas?
   (A) Master–slave relationships were essentially the same on both sides of the Atlantic.
   (B) Slaves were seen as part of the household in the Americas but not in Africa.
   (C) Slaves were seen as part of the household in Africa but not the Americas.
   (D) Slavery in Africa was harsher than in the Americas.

Short-Answer Questions

1. Answer parts A, B, and C.
   A. Identify ONE way that Europe was involved in the Atlantic system.
   B. Identify ONE way the Americas were involved in the Atlantic system.
   C. Identify ONE way Africa was involved in the Atlantic system.

2. Answer parts A and B.
   A. Briefly explain TWO arguments used to justify the institution of slavery.
   B. Briefly explain ONE argument used against slavery.

20 Empires in Early Modern Asia, 1650–1837

Rammohun Roy

During the lifetime of **Rammohun Roy** (1772–1833), South Asia was in transition from Mughal to British rule, and Roy's repertoire of languages reflected the cultural and religious diversity of his environment. His father, though a Hindu, was from a long line of officials serving Muslim rulers in northeastern India; thus, when still a child, Rammohun Roy (rahm-MOH-hoon ROY) added to his native Bengali by studying the court languages of Persian and Arabic. His mother's family included Hindu religious scholars, and since he was a Brahmin—a member of the highest, priestly caste—Roy also learned Sanskrit, the language of their ancient scriptures. As a teenager, he traveled across north India on a quest for knowledge and even, legend has it, debated with Buddhist lamas in Tibet. At age twenty-four he began to learn English, now essential to Bengal's politics and commerce, and found employment with the British East India Company.

Navigating such diversity, Rammohun Roy became a leading figure of the Bengal Renaissance, a rich intellectual encounter between varied spiritual and cultural traditions. As an adult, Roy embraced them all: the graceful Sufi verse of Iranian poets, the complex *Vedanta* literature at the root of Hinduism, and the message of love and forgiveness at the heart of Christianity's New Testament.

Roy was a powerful advocate for a reformed Hinduism. The faith of his ancestors, Roy believed, had degraded through the centuries. Superstition had replaced learning, and barbaric practices, such as burning widows on their husbands' funeral pyres, were thought of as religious rites. In fact, Roy's sister-in-law had been burned alive after the death of his own elder brother. Campaigning to end *suti*, the practice of widow burning, Roy wrote of his opponents:

You, however, consider women devoted to their passions and consequently incapable of acquiring divine knowledge. . . . [T]hey . . . are not allowed to marry again after the death of their

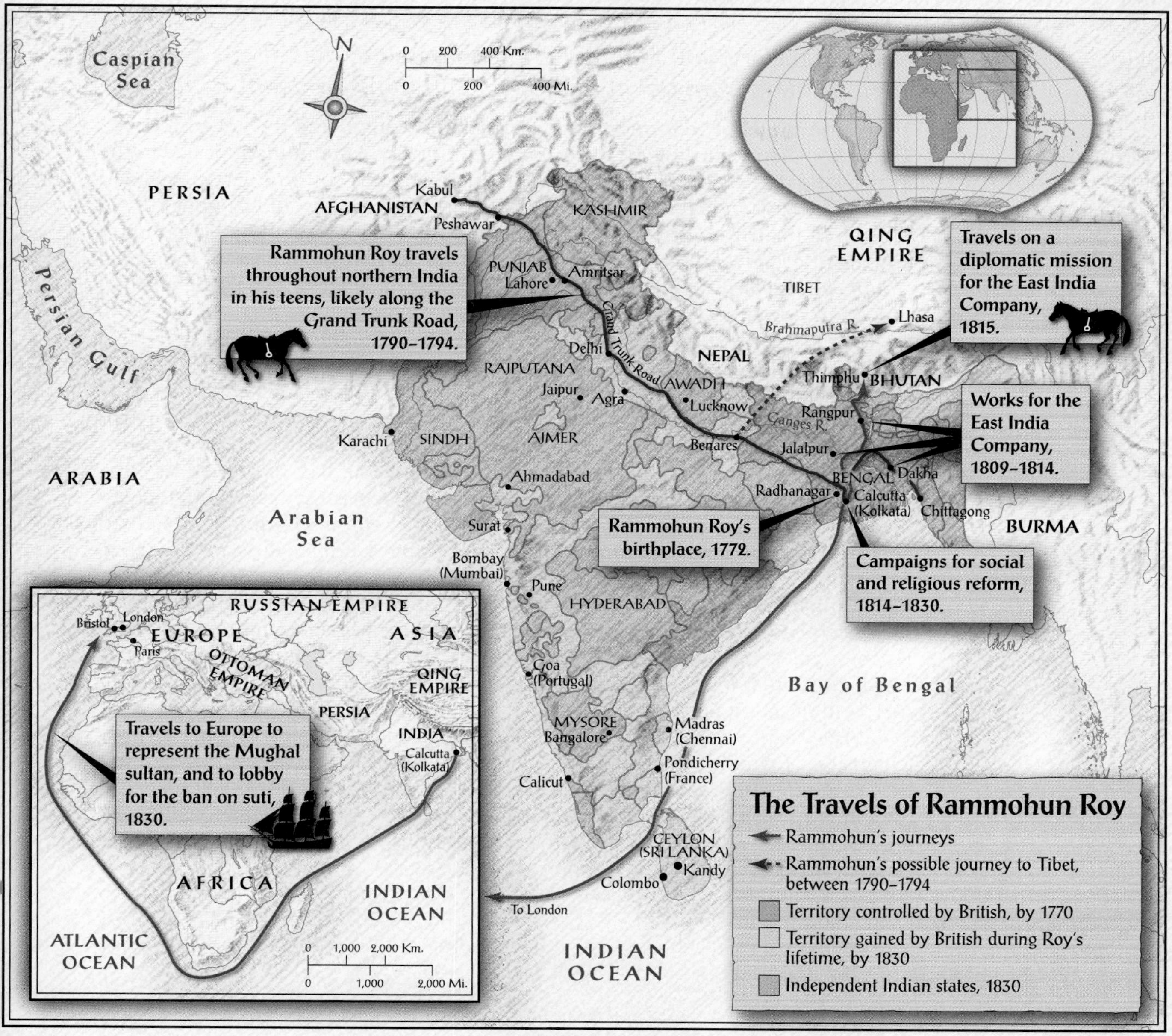

husbands, and consequently despair at once of all worldly pleasure; hence it is evident that death to these widows is preferable to existence. . . . [Still] to remove every chance of their trying to escape from the blazing fire, in burning them [you] first tie them down to the pile. . . . [But] the faults which you have imputed to women are not implanted in their constitution by nature; it would, therefore, be grossly criminal to sentence them to death. . . . What I lament is, that, seeing the women . . . dependent and exposed

Rammohun Roy
(1772–1833) A leader of the Bengal Renaissance in India who studied the religious texts of Islam, Christianity, and Hinduism for both religious truth and social reform. Roy argued that Hindus should return to their ancient texts, reject polytheism and superstition, and eliminate backward practices such as *suti*, or widow burning.

*to every misery, you feel them no compassion, that might even exempt them from being tied down and burnt to death.**

Roy and his fellow reformers were successful in convincing the government to outlaw widow burning; however, when conservative Brahmins appealed to the British king that such a ban would violate their religious customs, Roy traveled to London in 1830 to make sure that the reformist legislation would be upheld.

Before his trip to Britain, the Mughal emperor in Delhi had bestowed upon Roy the title *Raja* ("prince") and asked him to *"bring before the authorities in England certain encroachments on his rights by the East India Company."*† The Mughals had slipped in power and dignity since the days of Akbar (see Chapter 16): by 1830, the Mughal emperor had to beg the king of England for favors.

In a broader Asian context, the displacement of the Mughals by the British in India was part of a larger pattern of invading forces building larger and more powerful empires. In China, to give another example, Manchu invaders from the north unseated the Ming dynasty to create the Qing (ching) empire, whose emperors controlled not just China but also extensive Central Eurasian territories. As Qing generals and diplomats extended their emperor's influence, they came into increasing contact with emissaries of the expanding Russian empire. Central Eurasia then became the borderland between three powerful empires: British, Russian, and Qing.

Taken together, the expansion of the British and Russian empires showed the increasing influence of Europe in Asian affairs, though Qing China long remained unconcerned with European expansion. The Japanese were even more indifferent. Japanese rulers resisted the eighteenth-century trend toward imperial aggrandizement, consolidating power on their own islands rather than seeking further territory, and rejecting European influence as a matter of state policy.

While taking account of the Japanese exception, this chapter focuses on the expansion of empires from the late seventeenth to the early nineteenth centuries in East, South, and Central Asia. In the process, we will see how imperial leaders had to contend with factors such as changing military technologies, commercial growth, increasing social and religious interactions, expanding population, and ecological change, all of which might affect the success or failure of their policies.

KEY CONCEPT QUESTIONS

- What policies did the Manchu (Qing dynasty) implement to solidify their control of China? **(Key Concept 4.3)**
- What factors motivated Russia to expand in the eighteenth century? **(Key Concept 4.3)**
- What were the causes and effects of the decline of the Mughal empire in South Asia? **(Key Concept 4.3)**
- What factors facilitated Japan's rapid rise to an imperial power? **(Key Concept 5.2)**

*Raja Rammohun Roy, *The English Works*, vol. 2, ed. Jogendra Chunder Ghose (Calcutta: Srikanta Roy, 1901), pp. 164, 176, 180.

†Raja Rammohun Roy, *The English Works*, vol. 1, ed. Jogendra Chunder Ghose (Calcutta: Srikanta Roy, 1901), p. 319.

The Power of the Qing Dynasty, 1644–1796

By the early seventeenth century, underlying weaknesses had made the Ming dynasty in China vulnerable to invasion and conquest (see Chapter 16). In 1644, armies from Manchuria overran Beijing, deposed the Ming dynasty, and established the Qing dynasty. From 1683 to 1796, just three long-reigning emperors ruled Qing China. It was a time of remarkable political stability, explosive population growth, economic expansion, and intellectual and artistic dynamism. The territory ruled from Beijing expanded to its greatest extent, encompassing parts of Central Asia, Tibet, and the island of Taiwan. Qing emperors ruled China until 1911.

Establishment of Qing Rule, 1636–1661

The Manchu had been nomads who lived on the steppe to the northeast of China beyond the Great Wall (see Map 20.1). By the sixteenth century, under Chinese influence, some Manchu had taken up agriculture; literacy and Confucian philosophy were influencing Manchu society as well.

Ming officials, following a time-honored strategy for maintaining peace along the borders, had earlier bestowed favors on Manchu leaders, such as the right to wear elaborate dragon-patterned robes of silk. The Manchu in turn emulated Chinese-style governance, while maintaining their own language and nomadic traditions such as fighting on horseback and a love of hunting. Then in the 1590s, when the Ming called on Manchu forces to help resist a Japanese invasion, the Manchu armies united under a ruler who declared himself leader of a new **Qing dynasty** and organized his fighters into eight "banners," named for the color of the flags that the different regiments carried in battle. Fifty years later, with Ming authority in sharp decline, some Mongol and Chinese generals switched their allegiance to the Qing, incorporating their units under separate regimental banners. Thus, the banner system allowed Manchu warriors to maintain their separate identity and command structure even while absorbing Chinese and Mongol forces into their armies.

Qing dynasty (1644–1911) Sometimes called the Manchu dynasty after the Manchurian origins of its rulers. The Qing (meaning "brilliant") extended their rule from Beijing as far as Mongolia and Tibet.

In 1644, after one of China's own rebel armies stormed the capital and the last Ming emperor committed suicide, the Manchu established their power over Beijing and the north. However, Ming holdouts waged fierce battles against Qing forces for decades in the south. The Qing used diplomacy as well as force in dealing with this resistance: adversaries who surrendered were well treated and were incorporated into the banner system. Thus, the Manchu, earlier regarded by the Chinese as "barbarians," became masters of China itself.

AP® THEMES

How did Qing rulers use Confucianism to support their rule and assert Manchu superiority?

To legitimize the new dynasty, Qing rulers maintained Confucianism as the official state ideology. They also retained the examination system and the Chinese system of ministries, assigning one Chinese and one Manchu official to each. The Chinese scholar-officials had the requisite knowledge and experience, but the Manchu officials, thought to be more loyal, were there to supervise the work. In their quest for legitimacy, Qing emperors stressed the continuities between their own rule and great empires of the past.

Carefully guarding their Manchu language and identity, however, the Manchu never fully assimilated into Chinese culture. Intermarriage between Manchu and Han Chinese was forbidden. (The term *Han Chinese*, which derives from an early Chinese dynasty, is used to differentiate Chinese people from other ethnic groups in China.) Qing emperors spent their summers at the great palace of Chengde (chungh-deh), beyond the Great Wall, where horsemanship, hunting, and camping were reminders of nomadic life. And the Manchu continued to practice the distinctive Tibetan form of Buddhism, which aligned them more fully with their Central Eurasian subjects than with their Chinese ones.

At the same time, the Manchu made few efforts to impose their culture on Chinese subjects. One exception was a decree that all men had to cut their hair in the distinctive Manchu style, called a *queue* (kyoo), with a shaved forehead and a single long braid in back. Chinese men reluctantly complied with the Manchu order: *"Keep your head, lose your hair. Keep your hair, lose your head."*

Map 20.1 The Qing Empire, 1644–1783 Beginning from their homeland in the north, the Manchu rulers of the Qing dynasty not only conquered China but also built an empire stretching far into Central Asia, matching the contemporary expansion of the Russian empire. The Qing empire grew to more than twice the size of its Ming predecessor. Tibetans, Mongols, and other subject peoples were ruled indirectly through local authorities allied to the Qing emperors. China's contemporary rulers use this map to reject calls for autonomy by western peoples such as Tibetans and Uighurs.

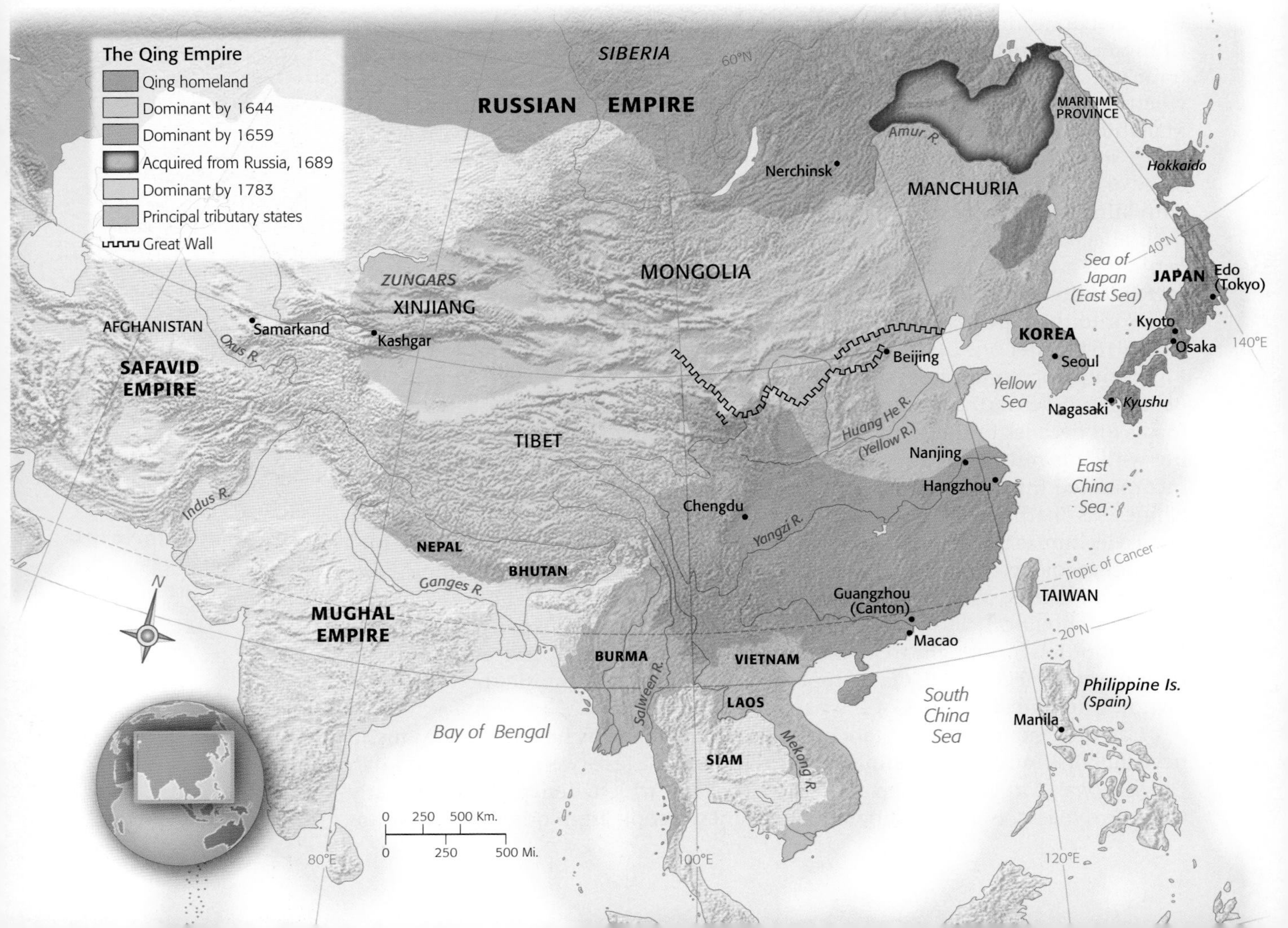

The Age of Three Emperors, 1661–1796

The success of the Qing emperors in retaining their own culture while earning the cooperation and loyalty of Han Chinese subjects found expression in the social, economic, and intellectual achievements of the late seventeenth and eighteenth centuries. When **Emperor Kangxi** (r. 1662–1722) ascended the Dragon Throne in 1662, the fate of the Qing was still in doubt. However, by 1683, he had successfully suppressed Ming resistance and annexed their last redoubt, the island of Taiwan. To military affairs, Kangxi brought knowledge of making cannons and the mathematics necessary for their effective deployment, which he learned from Jesuit tutors as a young man. Six decades of Kangxi's rule established the Qing as masters of one of the greatest empires the world had ever known. His successors Yongzheng (r. 1723–1735) and Qianlong (r. 1736–1796) consolidated that achievement. Together, these three emperors ruled for more than 130 years.

Emperor Kangxi (r. 1662–1722) One of the most powerful and long-ruling emperors in Chinese imperial history, who extended the Qing empire, expanded the economy, and cultivated an image as a Confucian scholar and sage.

Though Kangxi retained his ancestral culture and spoke Manchu with his family and close confidantes, he studied the Chinese classics deeply and presented himself as a sage Confucian ruler. At the pinnacle of the imperial bureaucracy, he oversaw tremendous economic expansion. Confucians believed that land and agriculture are the source of wealth and that a large population is a sign of prosperity. Farmers improved agricultural productivity by planting American crops like peanuts, potatoes, and maize in previously marginal areas. China's population boomed, surging past 400 million by 1800, another important outcome of the Columbian exchange (see Chapter 15). Meanwhile, American ingredients like chili peppers transformed Chinese cuisine, and tobacco became a daily ritual for many.

Kangxi's successor, the Yongzheng (YOHNG-jung) emperor, promoted an empirical form of Confucianism based on critical examination of sources. Yongzheng then encouraged scholars to gather data in minute detail from across the empire, and compiled an 800,000-page encyclopedia, by far the largest such reference work in the world. By ordering a thorough census of landholdings and basing rural taxation on updated land registers, Yongzheng both increased state revenue through more efficient tax collection and spread the tax burden more equitably between commoners and gentry.

During the long reign of the **Qianlong** (r. 1736–1796) emperor, the power of Qing China reached its height. Coming to the throne as a young man, Qianlong (chee-YEN-loong) ruled for sixty years before abdicating: true to Confucian ideals of filial piety, he did not want his reign to exceed that of his grandfather, Kangxi. During these six decades the commercial economy became even more dynamic. Mainstays of production were luxury goods for export, especially silk and porcelain. Vast quantities of silver from Japan and Spanish America continued to flow into Qing China, financing public works as well as private investment. For some farmers, tobacco became a profitable addition to their fields. Artisans and small-scale entrepreneurs expanded the glass-making, brewing, and coal-mining industries. Thus, eighteenth-century China retained its long-established position as the largest industrial economy in the world.

Qianlong (r. 1736–1796) Qing emperor who ruled during the empire's greatest territorial expansion and prosperity. Late in his reign, corruption began to infect the state bureaucracy. Rejected an English attempt to establish diplomatic relations.

The World of Women in Qing China

Cotton textile production emerged as a major commercial industry around the city of Nanjing in the lower **Yangzi River Valley**. Unlike silk, cotton cloth was affordable for all but the poorest Chinese consumers

Yangzi River Valley Agriculturally productive region with the important urban center of Nanjing. The Yangzi River Delta was the site of strong industrial and commercial growth in the eighteenth century.

China: The 4th Qing Emperor Kangxi (1654–1722) at his writing desk. His temple name was Shengzu. He is considered one of China's greatest emperors./Pictures From History/Bridgeman Images

Kangxi: Emperor and Scholar The Emperor Kangxi was careful to model his image on that of China's Confucian "sage rulers" to secure the loyalty of Han Chinese scholar-officials. Kangxi was in fact a dedicated scholar with deep knowledge of the Confucian classics. At the same time, however, he emphasized his fealty to the Tibetan form of Buddhism to secure the loyalty of his Central Eurasian subjects.

and had the advantages of being comfortable, durable, and easy to clean. Traditionally, women produced textiles in China; the expansion of the cotton industry reinforced those traditions.

All Chinese women were expected to work with their hands. Wealthy women, not expected to contribute to the household income, often produced beautiful embroideries. For rural women, tending silkworms and spinning silk thread were admired accomplishments that had the additional virtue of providing income. A traditional adage summed up the division of labor: *"Men plow, women weave."** Spinning and weaving cotton within the household meshed neatly with traditions, and in commercialized regions such as the Yangzi (yang-zuh) delta, these activities drove economic growth.

Chinese women did not receive much benefit from this work. Upon marriage young women left their own families to join their husband's household, where they were subject to their husband's authority and often at the mercy of demanding mothers-in-law. Chinese widows, especially those without sons, were especially vulnerable to neglect and abuse (though their plight was perhaps not as extreme as that of the widows Rammohun Roy sought to protect in India).

Their role in textile production may in fact have made women's situation worse, since more time working at home may have increased the practice of footbinding. Originally bound feet were a distinction signifying wealth and leisure, but the fashion spread throughout the Han Chinese population. Young girls' feet were broken and compressed into 3-inch balls by binding the four smaller toes under the sole of the foot and forcing the big toe and heel together. Women with bound feet suffered constant pain, limited mobility, and frequent infections. However, the old practice of female infanticide did decline during this period, perhaps because the improved financial prospects of women in textile production softened the attitude that boys were a blessing while girls were a burden.

The Manchu had never bound their own daughters' feet; indeed, they found the practice repulsive. The cultural traditions they brought from the grasslands required that women be able to ride horses and perform other strenuous physical tasks. But footbinding was so well established among the Han Chinese that Qing officials decided not to try to abolish it.

While most Chinese women lived lives of constant toil, elite women had opportunities for education and artistic expression. Unlike the sons of elite households, who were prepared by tutors for the state examinations, girls were educated to be refined, sensitive, and cultured to bring honor to their husbands and their

---

*Susan Mann, *Precious Records: Women in China's Long Eighteenth Century* (Stanford: Stanford University Press, 1997), p. 149.

"The Weaving of Flower'd Silks," Two Women at Work, China, late 18th century (woodcut), Chinese School (18th century)/Private Collection/The Stapleton Collection/Bridgeman Images

Silk Weaving Silk weaving was a highly profitable enterprise in eighteenth-century China. Women played a central role in all stages of silk production, operating large and complex looms such as the one pictured here. The spinning of cotton thread and weaving of cotton cloth were also increasingly important at this time, and women dominated production in the cotton industry as well.

household. These women wrote many of the greatest poems from Qing times. Often they expressed deep emotional attachment to the other women in their lives, as in these lines from Wang Duan in tribute to the aunt who had mentored her:

Holding my hand, you lead me to the west garden
Where, I still remember, I used to read.
*With deep emotion I recall your kindness in educating and cultivating me. . .**

The Qing Empire and Its Borderlands

Territorial expansion, by both force and diplomacy, was one of the greatest Qing achievements. The Qing complemented the advances of the "gunpowder revolution" (see Chapter 17) by using the banner system to successfully incorporate frontier peoples into the imperial armies, extending Qing power far to the west.

*Wang Duan, "Xinwei chunri fanzhao Wulin fucheng Chusheng yimu ji yong ci ti Minghu yinjian tu yuanyun," trans. Haihong Yang, "'Hoisting one's own banner': Self-inscription in lyric poetry by three women writers of late imperial China," 2010, http://ir.uiowa.edu/etd/766, p. 219.

During the century after the Manchu secured southern China and Taiwan, the Qing empire doubled in size. The Manchu then had to deal with the age-old Chinese problem of bringing stability to their unsettled western and northern frontiers. That meant asserting their control over Mongolian nomads and Turkic-speaking Muslim peoples to their west, stationing soldiers as far away as Tibet.

As in the past, the main threat came from steppe nomads, of which the most formidable were the Zunghars (ZUN-gahrs), Central Eurasian Mongols devoted to Tibetan Buddhism. The spiritual leader of both Tibetans and Zunghars was the Dalai Lama (DAH-lie LAH-mah). The Manchu used both force and subterfuge against the Zunghars, sending an army to Tibet but also supporting one of the rival contenders for the title of Dalai Lama, correctly assuming that their support would win his loyalty. Tibet began paying tribute to Beijing, which weakened the Zunghars.

Finally in 1757, Qianlong ordered that "*they must all be captured and executed.*"* Zunghar men were slaughtered; women and children were enslaved; and the lands were repopulated with sedentary peoples, such as the Muslim Uighurs (who still live in the western Xinjiang (shin-jyahng) province). Chinese territory was never again threatened by steppe nomads.

Elsewhere, Qing officials relied on diplomacy, much as the Ming had exacted tribute from societies outside their direct control. Annual tribute missions to Beijing symbolized the fealty even of powerful leaders, such as the emperors of Korea and Vietnam, who preserved their own political autonomy through ritual recognition of the Qing as overlords. Tribute was also sent by non-Han peoples living on the margins of Chinese society in the hills, jungles, and steppes.

Though the western regions of Tibet and Xinjiang had been brought under Qing rule, these areas were not, like Chinese provinces, administered directly by scholar-officials. Rather, local political authorities were allowed to continue under Manchu supervision as long as taxes were paid, order was maintained, and loyalty to Qing authorities was assured. The Qing appointed an official to report on Tibetan affairs, for example, but otherwise did nothing to supplant the power and influence of local Buddhist monks.

The Manchu often received Tibetan and Mongol emissaries outside the Great Wall at Chengde, the Manchu summer palace, rather than in the Forbidden City in Beijing. In fact, Qianlong had a replica of the Dalai Lama's Tibetan palace built at Chengde, an act of respect but also one implying the Dalai Lama's dependence on Manchu authority. As one historian observes, Manchu devotion to the Dalai Lama "contained always an element of menace."†

Unlike the Ming, however, the Qing were not interested in asserting cultural superiority over tributary societies. They viewed China as one part of a wider Manchu empire. Rather than imposing a single language on their empire, for example, Qing documents could be produced in five quite different scripts: Chinese, Manchu, Mongolian, Tibetan, or Arabic. Thus eighteenth-century Qing maps had Chinese labels for Chinese provinces and Manchu labels for non-Chinese areas, illustrating how Qianlong saw himself as a Chinese emperor when ruling lands conquered from the Ming, but as a Manchu emperor when dealing with peoples to the west. (See the feature "World History in Today's World: The Train to Tibet.")

---

*Peter C. Perdue, *China Marches West* (Cambridge, Mass.: Belknap, 2010), p. 284.

†Matthew Kapstein, *The Tibetans* (New York: Wiley Blackwell, 2008), p. 148.

WORLD HISTORY IN TODAY'S WORLD

The Train to Tibet

The $4.2 billion railway to Tibet takes passengers from Beijing to Lhasa, the Tibetan capital, skirting magnificent Himalayan peaks while climbing to an elevation above 16,000 feet (4,900 m). Passengers are given supplementary oxygen for altitude sickness, and a complex engineering system keeps the tracks level as they cross long stretches of permafrost, where the ground alternately melts and freezes. The train to Tibet is part of the Chinese government's agenda to better exploit the resources of the far interior by moving people to Tibet and other western regions from the crowded eastern and southern parts of the country.

The project has its critics. Some argue that intensive resource extraction will upset the delicate environmental balance of the Tibetan plateau. Human rights observers have focused on cultural and political issues, worrying that Han Chinese immigrants are a threat to traditional Tibetan language, culture, and religion. Tibetans themselves fear becoming second-class citizens in their own land.

The controversy exploded into violence early in 2008, when protestors took to the streets, replacing Chinese flags with Tibetan ones and, in some cases, attacking Han Chinese residents. That uprising was easily suppressed, but since 2009 over 130 self-immolations by Tibetan Buddhist monks to protest Chinese policies have deeply embarrassed the government in Beijing.

Supporters of Tibetan autonomy argue that there was never any direct imperial control of Tibetan affairs until China's People's Liberation Army invaded in 1950 and then forced the Dalai Lama, Tibet's spiritual leader, into exile in India. The Dalai Lama's advocacy of substantial Tibetan autonomy within the context of the Chinese state is thus consistent with earlier Qing imperial practice. The Chinese government, however, insists on central control.

Whatever political compromises might be made, the train to Tibet remains a symbol of the demographic changes that seem all but unstoppable as more Han Chinese move west looking for economic opportunity.

Source: Pankaj Mishra, "The Train to Tibet: What will the greatest rail journey on earth do to its destination?" *The New Yorker*, April 16, 2007.

Qing Trade and Foreign Relations

Not all of the Qing empire's external relations took place within the tributary system. The Qing treated the Russians, a growing presence, on equal terms. But they were reluctant to grant diplomatic equality to other European powers, even in the nineteenth century, when the British were completing their conquest of India.

As the Russian empire expanded eastward, Kangxi worried the Russians might ally with the steppe nomads. After some skirmishes, the Russians and the Chinese agreed to the **Treaty of Nerchinsk** in 1689, according to which the Qing recognized Russian claims west of Mongolia, while the Russians agreed to disband settlements to the east. Yongzheng and Qianlong continued this policy of avoiding conflict through treaties that fixed the boundary between the two empires.

Treaty of Nerchinsk
1689 treaty between Romanov Russia and Qing China that fixed their Central Asian border.

While the Russians came overland, other Europeans came by sea. European trade focused on south China, especially Guangzhou (called Canton by the Europeans). Manchu rulers associated Guangzhou with "greedy" traders rather than sober scholar-officials, and with adventurous sailors rather than dependable village-bound farmers. Accordingly, the Qing restricted European trade to this single port and required European traders to deal only with state-approved firms known as *cohongs*. Since cohong merchants had a monopoly on trade with Europeans, they found it easy to fix prices and amass huge profits.

The structure of the China trade frustrated the British in particular. Having little to exchange for Chinese goods but silver, they saw the continued outflow of bullion toward Asia as a fiscal problem. Britain, the greatest maritime commercial power of the time, rankled at its lack of open access to the vast Chinese market.

As a result, the British government sought to establish formal diplomatic relations. In 1792, King George III sent the **Macartney Mission** to negotiate an exchange of ambassadors. Qing officials allowed Lord Macartney and his party to travel from Guangzhou to Beijing but expected this representative of a "barbarian" king to recognize the superiority of the Qianlong emperor. However, Macartney refused to perform the ritual *kowtow* of full prostration before the emperor, consenting only to drop to one knee, as he would before his own king. Macartney asked that more ports be opened to foreign trade and that restrictions on trade be removed.

Macartney Mission
The 1792–1793 mission in which Lord Macartney was sent by King George III of England to establish permanent diplomatic relations with the Qing empire. Because he could not accept the British king as his equal, the Qianlong emperor politely refused.

Qianlong's response to King George III was unequivocal: "*We have never valued ingenious articles, nor do we have the slightest need of your country's manufactures. Therefore, O King, as regards your request to send someone to remain at the capital, while it is not in harmony with the regulations of the Celestial empire we also feel very much that it is of no advantage to your country.*"* Qianlong saw China as the center of the civilized world, and he insisted that the British should appear before him only if bearing tribute in recognition of his superior position.

Qianlong's attitude was understandable. The Qing controlled the largest and wealthiest empire on earth and had no need to look beyond their borders for resources. But all was not well. As in late Ming times, inefficiency and corruption were creeping into the system. As Qianlong grew old, the power of eunuchs once again increased, their petty rivalries at court distracting from vigorous public administration. The absence of technological improvements in farming put pressure on the food supply. As more marginal lands were cleared for cultivation, deforestation led to the silting up of rivers, and floods resulted. As the situation worsened, some Chinese peasants rebelled, dreaming of restoring the Ming dynasty while viewing the non-Chinese Manchu as illegitimate, lacking the "Mandate of Heaven" (see Chapter 16).

● **CONTEXT&CONNECTIONS** Peasant rebellion was a recurring theme in Chinese imperial history. Peasants have repeatedly risen up, angered by high taxes, drought, and plague. From early times, peasants sought moral renewal as well as political change, often inspired by Buddhist visions for social reform. Though the Manchu had benefited from rural unrest in unseating the Ming, they themselves later faced religiously inspired rebels. The greatest and most destructive of all the Chinese peasant uprisings was the *Taiping Rebellion* (1850–1864; key term in Chapter 24). ●

When Qianlong abdicated in 1796, the gravity of these internal challenges was not yet clear. And while Qianlong was fascinated by a British gift of a miniature steamship with 110 tiny mounted cannon, he did not foresee how powerful the British would be in fifty years, when they returned to impose their demands by force (see Chapter 24). As the nineteenth century began, Qing officials still believed that the old ways sufficed to meet current challenges. But the threat to imperial China no longer came by land, and as the nineteenth century unfolded no Great Wall could keep out new invaders from the sea.

*J. L. Cranmer-Byng, ed., *An Embassy to China: Lord Macartney's Journal, 1793–1794* (Hamden, Conn.: Archon Books, 1963), p. 340.

The Russian Empire, 1725–1800

Though they themselves were a settled agrarian people, the Russians, like the Chinese, had long experience with steppe nomads. The Russian state had been founded as part of the dissolution of the Mongol empire, and Russian leaders viewed control of the steppes as necessary for the security of their heartland. Subsequent expansion to the south and east would make Russia a Great Power in Asia. After Peter the Great pushed Russia's borders further west, Russia became a major European power as well (see Chapter 17). Yet for all the splendor of the Romanov court, conditions for the majority of Russians, serfs living in rural villages, remained grim.

Russian Imperial Expansion, 1725–1800

To the west, Russia dominated the Baltic Sea region after Peter's army decisively defeated the Swedes in 1721. When the Polish kingdom collapsed after the 1770s, Russia, along with Prussia and Austria, shared in its partition. Russian power thrust to the south as well, largely at the expense of the Ottoman empire. The great prize was the Crimean peninsula, a major trade emporium on the Black Sea since ancient times. Annexed in 1783, the Crimea brought both strategic and economic benefits. Russia made its first inroads into the difficult terrain of the Caucasus Mountains at this time as well (see Map 20.2).

In the Caucasus, Russian penetration was not carried out by imperial forces but by mercenary soldiers called **Cossacks** (from the Turkish word *kazakh*, meaning "free man"). The Cossacks originated as fiercely independent horsemen, Slavic-speakers who had assimilated the ways of their nomadic Mongol and Turkish neighbors on the steppes. The Cossack code of honor was based on marksmanship, horsemanship, and group spirit.

Cossacks
Horsemen of the steppes who helped Russian rulers protect and extend their frontier into Central Asia and Siberia.

As Russia expanded to the east across Siberia, Cossacks were at first hired by private traders who were extending the lucrative fur-trapping frontier (see Chapter 17). Though trappers and soldiers might profit from the fur trade, Russian merchants and the Russian treasury reaped the lion's share. Once the fur-bearing animals of a given area had been slaughtered to clothe the fashionable in Moscow, Paris, or Constantinople, trappers moved on to virgin terrain.

AP® THEMES
In what ways did Cossack migration into Siberia change existing social structures?

As in New France at the same time (see Chapter 18), the fur trade in Siberia exploited the expertise and labor of indigenous peoples, who the Russians called the "small people of the north." These people were vulnerable to the military technology and diseases brought from the west. If a community did not deliver its quota of furs, Cossacks might attack, carrying women and children off into slavery.

Russian soldiers and administrators subsequently followed fur traders and Cossacks into Siberia, taking formal control to make sure the tsars got their share. Thus the eastern frontier of the Russian empire extended to Alaska, which the Bering Expedition claimed for the tsar in 1741 (see Map 20.2).

The Russian empire also established influence over parts of Asia south of Siberia. In hopes of creating direct trade links with India, Peter the Great maintained armed control over the steppes on Russia's borders while pursuing a diplomatic strategy on the Central Eurasian frontier. Meanwhile, as we have seen, on the Qing frontier, skirmishes between Russian and Manchu soldiers led to the Treaty of Nerchinsk.

Map 20.2 The Expansion of Russia, 1500–1800 By the end of the eighteenth century, the Russian empire extended westward into Europe, southward toward the Black Sea and Caspian Sea, and most dramatically, eastward into Central Asia, Siberia, and the Americas.

- **CONTEXT&CONNECTIONS** In the nineteenth century, Russian imperialism in Central Eurasia would become more highly militarized, a legacy of forceful intervention inherited by the Communist regime led by *Vladimir Lenin* (Chapter 28) after the Russian Revolution of 1917. The old boundary between the Qing and Romanov dynasties continued to cause tensions straight into the 1960s, when the Soviet Union and the People's Republic of China exchanged fire along their long frontier. ●

Erich Lessing/Art Resource, NY

Catherine the Great Equestrian portraits of monarchs on white horses were common in eighteenth-century Europe, though rarely were women represented this way. Catherine, a German princess who married into the Russian royal family, removed her husband from the throne in 1762 in a bloodless coup. Tough and brilliant, she ruled under her own authority for over three decades.

Reform and Repression, 1750–1796

During her reign, **Catherine the Great** (r. 1762–1796) consolidated control over these vast imperial frontiers. A German princess who married into the Romanov family, Catherine accumulated ever more personal power to become one of the dominating figures of eighteenth-century Eurasian politics. The Russian nobility benefited from Catherine's authoritarianism. In return for their loyalty and service in the bureaucracy and the military, Catherine gave the nobles more power over the serfs who farmed their estates. At the same time, the profitable market for grain in western Europe gave them incentive to make increasingly harsh demands on their serfs. In their elegant townhouses and country estates, the Russian aristocracy saw Western luxuries as essential to their lifestyle, and most thought little of those who toiled for them like slaves.

- **CONTEXT&CONNECTIONS** Catherine brought cultural and intellectual influences from western Europe to the tsarist court at St. Petersburg at a time when the *Enlightenment* (Chapter 21) and its exciting new ideas were energizing reform and revolution in the West (see Chapter 22). However, while Catherine brought the latest trends in art, architecture, fashion, and even philosophy to Russia, she adamantly ruled out political reform. ●

As the serfs' situation deteriorated, unrest led to rebellion. In the 1770s, a Cossack chieftain named Yemelyan Pugachev gained a huge following after claiming that he was the legitimate tsar. Pugachev promised the abolition of serfdom and an end to taxation and military conscription. After several years of rebellion, Pugachev was captured, brought back to Moscow, and sliced to pieces in a public square. Catherine became even less tolerant of talk of reform.

Catherine the Great (r. 1762–1796) German princess who married into the Romanov family and became empress of Russia. Brought western European cultural and intellectual influences to the Russian elite. Her troops crushed a major peasant uprising.

Catherine's imperial policies were pragmatic, as when she restrained the Orthodox Church from converting non-Russian peoples. In the case of Siberia, the reason was financial: converts to Orthodoxy had tax protections that indigenous people lacked. In the cases of the steppes and the Central Asian frontier, Catherine saw that working with local Muslim leaders was the best way to maintain stability. In the Crimea, for example, she protected the rights of the local Tatar Muslim nobility, declaring, *"It is Our desire that without regard to his nationality or faith, each [nobleman] shall have the personal right to these lands."* Thus while conditions for Russian serfs deteriorated and force prevailed on the Siberian frontier, Catherine, like the Qing emperors, brought people of the Central Asian steppes within the Russian imperial orbit without requiring cultural assimilation. (See the feature "Movement of Ideas Through Primary Sources: Petitioning Catherine the Great.")

Petitioning Catherine the Great

One of Catherine the Great's innovations was to invite petitions from her subjects. Often people felt that oppression resulted from the misuse of power by local and provincial officials: if only the tsarina herself knew of these abuses, they thought, surely she would correct them. Catherine the Great encouraged this attitude and invited her subjects (other than the serfs, who had no right to address her) to submit petitions. Such a flood of petitions flowed to St. Petersburg, however, that it is unlikely that she even saw most of them, and once the French Revolution showed the dangers of stirring up public opinion (see Chapter 22), the freedom to petition the tsarina was revoked.

The first of the two petitions below was submitted by a group of Tartar nobles, that is, by the Muslim, Turkic-speaking elite of an area incorporated into the Russian empire. The Kazan Tartars had ruled the Volga River region in the fourteenth century, but in the fifteenth century this region was conquered by the Russian tsar Ivan the Terrible. Ivan slaughtered much of the Muslim population and forcibly converted many of the survivors to Orthodox Christianity. Not until the reign of Catherine did the tsars allow new mosques to be built again in Kazan.

The second petition to Catherine was submitted by a group of Jewish leaders in Belarus. The majority of the population of Belarus (meaning "white Russia") consisted of Slavic speakers closely related to Russians in language and culture. Belarus was ruled from Poland/Lithuania until the eighteenth century, after which it was incorporated into the Russian empire. The Jews of this region were known as *Ashkenazim* (see Chapter 17). Their liturgical language was Hebrew, but their everyday language was Yiddish, a dialect of German infused with Hebrew vocabulary, unintelligible to Russian speakers. To the greatest extent possible, the Ashkenazim took care of their own community affairs.

Historical Thinking Skill:

PATTERNS OF CONTINUITY AND CHANGE OVER TIME By the eighteenth century, there were numerous examples of rulers governing diverse empires in world history. To what extent does the legal treatment of ethnic and religious minorities in the 1700s represent a continuity in strategies leaders used to unite diverse peoples into one empire?

Source: David G. Rowley, *Exploring Russia's Past: Narratives, Sources, Images*, vol. I, To 1850 (New York: Pearson, 2006), pp. 208–209.

Petition from Tartar Nobles in Kazan Province, 1767

12. We the under-signed believe that nothing is more offensive to a person, regardless of his faith and rank, than to suffer disrespect and insults toward his religion. This makes one extremely agitated and provokes unnecessary words of abuse. But it often happens that people of various ranks say extremely contemptuous things about our religion and our Prophet . . . and this is a great affront for us. Therefore we request a law that anyone who curses our religion be held legally accountable. . . . [We further ask that] we Tartars and nobles not be forced to convert to Orthodoxy. . .

15. If any of our people are voluntarily baptized into the faith of the Greek confession [i.e., into the Orthodox Church] they should be ordered to move to settlements with Russians the very same year in which the conversion takes place. . . . We ask that, under no circumstances, are converts to be permitted to sell their houses, garden plots, and pastures to Russians or people of other ranks, but are to sell only to us Tartars; they must sell either to unconverted kinsmen or other Tartars. . . . Also, without a special personal order from Her Imperial Majesty, no churches should be built in our localities. . . .

Petition from Belarussian Jews, 1784

1. Some [Belarussian Jews] who live in towns engage in trade and, especially, in the distillation of spirits, beer and mead [honey beer], which they sell wholesale and retail. This privilege was

extended to them when Belarus joined the Russian empire. Hence everyone active in this business used all their resources to construct buildings suitable for distillation. . . . After the Belarussian region joined the Russian empire, the Jews in some towns constructed more of these in the same fashion and at great expense. The imperial monarchical decree [on Jews] emboldens them to request tearfully some monarchical mercy.

2. According to an ancient custom, when the squires built a new village, they summoned the Jews to reside there and gave them certain privileges for several years and the permanent liberty to distill spirits, brew beer and mead, and sell these drinks. On this basis the Jews built houses and distillation plants at considerable expense. . . . But a decree of the governor-general of Belarus has now forbidden the squires to farm out distillation in their villages to Jews, even if the squires want to do this. As a result [these] poor Jews [have been left] completely impoverished. . . . They therefore request an imperial decree authorizing the squire, if he wishes, to farm out distillation to Jews in rural areas.

3. . . . Jews have no one to defend them in courts and find themselves in a desperate situation—given their fear, and ignorance of Russian—in case of misfortune, even if innocent. . . . To consummate all the good already bestowed, Jews dare to petition that . . . in matters involving Jews and non-Jews . . . a representative from the Jewish community . . . be present to accompany Jews in court and attend the interrogation of Jews. But cases involving only Jews . . . should be handled solely in Jewish courts, because Jews assume obligations among themselves, make agreements and conclude all kinds of deals in the Jewish language and in accordance with Jewish rites and law (which are not known to others). Moreover, those who transgress their laws and order should be judged in Jewish courts. Similarly, preserve intact all their customs and holidays in the spirit of their faith, as is mercifully assured in the imperial manifesto. . . .

India: From Mughal Empire to British Rule, 1650–1833

Mughal India was the first of the old land-based Asian empires to be overtaken by European imperialism, a transition that was taking place during Rammohun Roy's own lifetime. None could have foreseen the coming of British domination in the seventeenth century, when the Mughal empire reached its territorial zenith under the emperor **Aurangzeb** (ow-rang-ZEB), who extended his power across India and took the title *Alamgir*, "World Seizer."

Aurangzeb
(r. 1658–1707) Mughal emperor who used military force to extend his power but whose constant campaigns drained the treasury and whose policy of favoring Islam at the expense of India's other religions generated social and political tensions.

However, even during Aurangzeb's long rule (1658–1707), ambitious regional leaders had begun to resist the central power of Delhi, and after his death the empire began to fragment, leading to invasions from Iran and Afghanistan and to the emergence of autonomous regional states. As in the past history of India and other land-based empires in Eurasia, the wealth of empire attracted invaders from the mountains and steppes who were strong enough to destabilize the existing order, but not to replace it. Arriving by sea, however, the British represented something entirely new. Starting from their base in Bengal, they would fill the power vacuum left by Mughal decline.

Aurangzeb and the Decline of Mughal Authority, 1658–1757

Aurangzeb was an energetic, capable, and determined ruler who presided over a stable and prosperous realm. The wealth he controlled was staggering. Some came from territorial conquests, but agriculture, trade, and industry were the true foundations of India's prosperity. Mughal officials encouraged the commercial farming of sugarcane, indigo, and cotton to enhance the tax base, and many peasants benefited from the focus on marketable produce. American crops like maize and tobacco were another stimulus to growth. The population did not increase as rapidly as China's in the same period: disease and periodic famine kept mortality rates high. Still, the population of India rose from about 150 million in 1600 to about 200 million in 1800. As in other land-based empires, taxes on peasant agriculture were the principal source of government revenue.

AP® THEMES
How did Mughal rule in India affect Indian Ocean networks of commercial exchange?

The stability of the Mughal heartland in north India was good for trade and industry. Participation in the expanding Indian Ocean economy brought in gold and silver. Silk and opium were produced for Southeast Asian markets, but the principal source of prosperity was textiles. Exports now expanded beyond established African, Persian, and Southeast Asian markets to northern Europe, where consumers found Indian cotton cloth cheaper, more comfortable, and easier to wash than domestic woolens or linens. South Asians were among the most powerful commercial agents in the world, using the silver that flowed in through Indian Ocean trade to pay cash advances to weavers, who then contracted lower-caste women to spin cotton yarn.

For Mughal rulers, commercial wealth was a mixed blessing, however. Prosperity afforded provincial leaders the cash and incentive to build up their own military forces. Aurangzeb's constant military campaigns were largely driven by the need to assert central control over restive provinces.

In the process, Aurangzeb reversed Akbar's earlier policy of religious tolerance (see Chapter 16). Whereas Akbar had courted allies among Hindus and other communities, Aurangzeb stressed the Islamic nature of his state. His imposition of a special tax on nonbelievers caused great resentment.

Historical memories of Aurangzeb were mixed. Many Indian Muslims would later look back on the power and glory of Aurangzeb's reign with nostalgia. Hindu writers like Rammohun Roy (see Chapter 20) generally had harsher memories. Writing a century after Aurangzeb's death, Roy emphasized the emperor's *"cruelty and intolerance."* Contrasting him with Akbar, whose *"memory is still adored,"* Roy judged that Aurangzeb, *"met with many reverses and misfortunes during his life time, and his name is now held in abhorrence."**

The Sikhs likewise had an ill memory of Aurangzeb. Sikhism was a new religion that emphasized equality before God, rejecting the caste system and polytheism of Hinduism while incorporating other elements of Hindu belief and ritual (see Chapter 16). Their leader Guru Tegh Bahadur (1621–1675) defended the rights not only of Sikhs but of Hindus to follow their own forms of worship. In response, Aurangzeb had him captured, brought to Delhi in an iron cage, tortured after he resisted conversion to Islam, and, finally, beheaded. Sikhism, formerly pacifistic, then became more militant. To this day, ceremonial knives are part of the daily attire of Sikh men.

---

*Raja Rammohun Roy, *The English Works*, vol. 2, ed. Jogendra Chunder Ghose (Calcutta: Srikanta Roy, 1901), p. 307.

V&A Images, London/Art Resource, NY

V&A Images, London/Art Resource, NY

Mughals at War Mughal control of South Asia was based on military supremacy, from early-sixteenth-century conquest through the reign of Aurangzeb. As this Mughal painting (in the Persian style) shows, cavalry played a central role, but the use of gunpowder weapons was also crucial to Mughal strategy.

In other regions, Aurangzeb's religious intolerance was probably less critical as a cause of rebellion than the opportunities afforded to ambitious provincial leaders by the increasing value of Indian Ocean commerce, which allowed them to amass greater wealth and arms, and thus to challenge Mughal rule. The Hindu rebellions in the western **Maratha kingdoms**, for example, were incited as much by leaders' desire for political and economic autonomy as by religious resentment.

Maratha kingdoms Loosely bound, west-central Indian confederacy that established its autonomy from Mughal rule in the eighteenth century and challenged the invading British in the nineteenth.

While Aurangzeb had fairly easily subdued other regions, Maratha leaders used guerilla tactics, well suited to the region's tough terrain, to keep the Mughal armies at bay. From 1695 to 1700, Aurangzeb left Delhi to live in military encampments, spending vast sums on his campaigns. As military affairs preoccupied the emperor, corruption and incompetence crept into the government. By the time of his death in 1707, Aurangzeb was full of despair. From his deathbed, he wrote his son: *"I have not done well to the country or to the people, and of the future there is no hope."* A prolonged succession struggle ensued, tax collectors withheld government funds, and the empire became even more vulnerable to regional uprisings and foreign invasions.

Nader Shah

(1688–1747) Iranian ruler who invaded India from the north in 1739, defeating the Mughal army and capturing the Mughal emperor, who handed over the keys to his treasury before Nader Shah agreed to withdraw. Mughal power went into permanent decline.

The initial threat came from Iran. Taking advantage of Safavid weakness (see Chapter 17), a brilliant general, **Nader Shah** (1688–1747), took the title shah for himself, establishing a new Iranian dynasty while expelling Russian and Ottoman forces. In 1739, his armies stormed into northern India. Begging for mercy, the Mughal emperor handed over the keys to his treasury, and even the fabled Peacock Throne, before Nader Shah agreed to withdraw.

This humiliating sack and plunder sounded the death knell of Mughal authority. After the Iranians withdrew, a Maratha army marched on Delhi but was defeated by Afghani invaders. If neither Iranians, nor Afghanis, nor Marathis were strong enough to rule India, it seemed likely that the Mughal empire would break into pieces, with provincial rulers ascendant. Instead it was the British who inherited Mughal imperial power.

Foundations of British Rule, 1739–1818

The seaborne European empires in Asia were originally geared toward commercial profit rather than territorial control. Mughal rulers paid little attention to the Dutch, British, and French East India Companies, which controlled only their own "factories," fortified outposts where they lived and kept their trade goods, and perhaps a bit of adjacent territory (see Chapter 15).

Calcutta (today's Kolkata), Rammohun Roy's city of residence, had its origins as one such "factory," founded in 1690 when the *nawab* (ruler) of Bengal granted a license to the English East India Company to settle and trade. After 1717, by Mughal command, the Company was permitted to trade duty-free, giving it a great advantage over both Indian and European competitors. Cotton cloth was a major trade item at Calcutta, as were opium (first destined for Indonesian markets and later for China), raw silk (exported to both Europe and Japan), pepper, sugar, and saltpeter, a key ingredient in gunpowder. To the south, a similar English "factory" at Madras (today's Chennai) competed for trade with the French East India Company settlement at Pondicherry (today's Puducherry).

With the decline of Mughal authority after the Iranian invasion of 1739, some European agents, like many provincial Indian rulers, seized the opportunity to expand their enterprises and retain more of their profits. Indeed, it was Company men acting on their own initiative, rather than policymakers in distant European capitals, who laid the foundations for further European expansion. One of the first and most brilliant of these "men on the spot" was the French Company's commander **Joseph Francois Dupleix** (1697–1764).

Joseph Francois Dupleix

(1697–1764) Governor-general in charge of all French establishments in India. Dupleix used diplomacy to forge alliances with local rulers and with their help defeated a much larger British force in the 1740s.

During the War of the Austrian Succession between France and Britain in the 1740s (see Chapter 18), Dupleix (doo-PLAY) took the British factory at Madras, only to be attacked in turn by a local Indian prince. Badly outnumbered, Dupleix commanded just 230 European soldiers plus some 700 *sepoys* (SEE-poyz), Indian soldiers the Europeans had employed and trained. Nevertheless, superior French firepower and organization enabled him to defeat an invading Indian force of nearly ten thousand and to establish himself as master of Madras. But for diplomatic reasons, the French ordered Dupleix to surrender those gains back to the British, who would soon follow his example with more lasting effect.

A decade later, threatened by French advances in South Asia during the Seven Years' War (1756–1763; see Chapter 19), the British fortified their trading post at Calcutta. The young nawab of Bengal, Siraj ud-Daulah (suh-RAJ uhd-duh-OO-lah), saw these new British fortifications as a provocation. He withdrew authorization for the Company settlement and then attacked and captured Calcutta.

However, Robert Clive, a British soldier of fortune, outmaneuvered Siraj ud-Daulah. Clive had allied the East India Company with the region's Hindu commercial and banking interests, and also with Siraj's own uncle, himself an aspiring nawab. In 1757 at the **Battle of Plassey**, Bengal's leader faced only eight hundred British soldiers and some two thousand sepoys. But many of Siraj ud-Daulah's fifty thousand soldiers (secretly paid off by Clive's moneylender friends) fled the battlefield; others (allied with his ambitious uncle) betrayed him and fought with his enemy.

Battle of Plassey
1757 battle that gave the British East India Company control of the rich eastern Mughal province of Bengal. Sir Robert Clive used alliances with Indian rulers to defeat the larger forces of Siraj ud-Daulah, the nawab of Bengal.

After the British victory, Siraj's uncle was duly installed as nawab, but that office profited him little after Company officials plundered the treasury. The chests full of silver they sent back home finally reversed the earlier outward flow of European silver into South Asia, loot that financed the construction of many a fine English country house.

Once in control of Bengal, the British could perhaps have marched on Delhi and ended the Mughal era once and for all. But Clive decided on a more subtle policy of recognizing the weakened Mughal emperor while insinuating the Company into existing Mughal institutions. The East India Company became the official revenue collector of India's rich northeastern provinces. Clive used the threat of military force to divide and conquer, extorting alliances from various nawabs, maharajahs, and sultans by offering them "protection." (See the feature "Visual Evidence Through Primary Sources: Colonel Mordaunt's Cock Fight.")

When a terrible famine in 1769 killed one-third of Bengal's population, some in Parliament blamed the East India Company, which fed its own employees and soldiers but did nothing for starving Bengalis, while insisting that they continue to pay their taxes. One member of Parliament complained: "*We have outdone the Spaniards in Peru. They were at least butchers on a religious principle. . . .We have murdered, deposed, plundered, usurped—nay, what think you of the famine in Bengal being caused by a monopoly of the servants of the East India Company?*"*

The India Act in 1784 attempted to redress such abuses. **Lord Charles Cornwallis** was dispatched as governor-general and commander of British forces in India. Unlike Clive, Cornwallis was an aristocrat and a member of the British establishment. His assignment was to draw a strict line between administration and trade by implementing a policy whereby Company employees might serve as either officials or traders, but not as both. Cornwallis believed that British colonial rule could be fair and just. As his successor declared: "*No greater benefit can be bestowed on the inhabitants of India than the extension of British authority.*"† That justification for colonial rule would long endure.

Lord Charles Cornwallis
(1738–1795) British general who surrendered to American forces at Yorktown and later served as governor-general of India and Ireland.

British influence in India spread through force, but also through diplomacy when provincial rulers looked to the British as patrons and protectors in the insecure conditions that accompanied Mughal decline. The British also absorbed Indian influences, learning Indian languages and adopting Mughal styles of dress and behavior. Because there were no English women in India, Company employees frequently consorted with local women and even took Indian wives, who provided a cultural and linguistic bridge to Indian society.

---

*Horace Walpole, speech quoted in *Cambridge History of India*, vol. 5 (Cambridge: Cambridge University Press, 1929), p. 187.

†Quoted in Francis Watson, *A Concise History of India* (London: Thames and Hudson, 1979), p. 131.

Colonel Mordaunt's Cockfight

This 1784 painting by Johann Zoffany was commissioned by Warren Hastings, the governor-general of the British East India Company, who had it sent back to Britain as a memento. The image is based on an actual cockfight arranged between John Mordaunt and Asaf-ud-Daula, nawab of Awadh, in the latter's capital city of Lucknow. Mordaunt had been hired by the nawab to command his personal bodyguard and to arrange such amusements.

Though the British and the Indians are here portrayed as getting along well, tensions existed. Warren Hastings, later tried for wanton corruption before a court in London, was accused of having stolen the fortune of Asaf-ud-Daula's grandmother. Later, in 1857, the city of Lucknow became the epicenter of a massive revolt against British authority after the East India Company ignored local traditions of inheritance in staking its claim over all of Awadh (see Chapter 24).

This image can be analyzed as an exemplar of *orientalism*, a concept developed by the late Palestinian-American scholar Edward Said. Said argued that Westerners' self-image in this period developed in opposition to their concept of the "Orient" as an exotic, sensual, irrational space of "otherness."

The liveliness and dynamism of the Indians on the left and in the background seem to contrast with the more formally posed British figures. ***What differences are there in the depiction of the Europeans and Indians in this portrait? How might this painting be interpreted as an example of Western artistic "orientalism," of the rendering of Indians as exoticized "others"?***

Tate, London/Art Resource, NY

The Europeans are more stiffly posed but are painted with greater attention to their individual characteristics than the surrounding Indians. They are also elevated *above* the cockfight, symbolically distanced from both Mordaunt, a man of lower class, and Asaf-ud-Daula, a foreigner and an "oriental." As a group they pay little attention to the main event: cockfighting is beneath them.

1 Mordaunt stands tall near the center of the action, separated from the other European figures on the right. Cockfighting was not a “gentlemanly” sport, but then Mordaunt was both illiterate and illegitimate, and, needing to make his own way in the world, he had headed for India. His distance from the other Europeans marks his status as servant of the nawab rather than as an officer of the Company.

2 The rulers of Awadh were Shi’ite Muslims who built many mosques and fostered religious learning. Asaf-ud-Daula did so as well, but he was also famous for warm hospitality, ribald humor, and sensuality. Some have seen Asaf-ud-Daula’s posture in this painting as indicating sexual arousal; an intimation of homosexuality can be seen in the background just over his left shoulder. The nawab had many adopted children, but despite having a wife and access to hundreds of concubines, it was said he had no children of his own.

3 We can identify most of the European figures in the painting, including John Wombell, the chief accountant for the East India Company in Lucknow, and, seated to his left, the artist himself, Johann Zoffany. Seated in the front of the European group, holding a cock, is Lieutenant Golding of the Company’s Corps of Engineers.

4 Claude Martin, shown here in dress uniform, was an infamous French adventurer. A self-made man, he had a commission with the British East India Company while serving simultaneously as Asaf-ud-Daula’s Superintendent of the Arsenal. He accumulated a fortune, which he used to support a number of much younger Indian mistresses, to patronage Mughal artists, and to pursue eccentric passions: in 1785, he organized a hot-air balloon ascent over Lucknow.

In the field of law, we see one example of the complex intercultural processes that developed. A visiting Chinese sailor witnessed a Company court proceeding at Calcutta in the 1780s; in his memoirs, he provided a snapshot:

> *The head judge sits, and ten guest judges [the jury] sit on his side. The head guest judge is the elder of the guest merchants. . . . On the day they consider the suit and then decide the outcome, if one of the guest judges does not agree they must hear the case again. Even if this happens two or three times, no one views this as inconvenient.**

The Chinese visitor was struck by the elaborate procedures of a jury trial. But while the Company men used British-style jurisprudence among themselves, they did not try to replace South Asian legal traditions with their own. Instead, a situation of legal pluralism developed, in which Indian litigants could pursue their

---

*Xie Qinggao, *Hailu jiaoyi*, ed. An Jing (Beijing: Shangwu yingshugan, 2002), translation by Valerie Hansen.

AP® THEMES

What challenges did Mughal rule face internally from the Maratha kingdoms and externally from the British?

cases in either local courts or in British ones. The British East India Company hence employed both Muslim and Hindu legal advisers to guide them in implementing a multilayered judicial system.

The expansion of British power in India was not a planned exercise in imperialism. In fact, one Company official had declared in the 1770s: *"The dominion of all India is what I never wish to see."* But the vacuum left by declining Mughal power combined with the greed and ambition of "men on the spot" to push British frontiers forward. In the west, when Maratha armies threatened the British East India Company's factory at Bombay (today's Mumbai), the British engaged in a series of alliances and interventions in that region. Finally, in 1818 they defeated the Marathas, and from thence moved toward control of all South Asia. Without central planning or foresight, the British had gone from maritime prowess to mastery over one of the world's most populous and productive regions.

Rammohun Roy: Liberal Imperialism and the Bengali Renaissance

Rammohun Roy's early life corresponded to the period when the British East India Company was accumulating more and more South Asian territory and affecting Indian economic and social life ever more deeply. In those early years, he tells us, *"I proceeded on my travels, and passed through different countries, chiefly within, but some beyond, the bounds of Hindustan, with a feeling of great aversion to the establishment of the British power in India."**

However, after he returned in 1814 to live in Calcutta Roy developed friendships with some of its British residents and changed his mind. *"Though it is impossible for a thinking man not to feel the evils of political subjection and dependence on foreign people,"* he wrote, *"yet when we reflect on the advantages which we have derived and may hope to derive from our connection with Great Britain, we may be reconciled to the present state of things which promises permanent benefits to our posterity."*†

● **CONTEXT&CONNECTIONS** Later Indian nationalists disagreed about Rammohun Roy's legacy. *Mohandas K. Gandhi* (Chapter 28) criticized him for an elitist, pro-British attitude. Rabindranath Tagore, winner of the Nobel Prize for Literature (1913), saw Roy's legacy differently: *"[Roy] knew that the ideal of human civilization does not lie in the isolation of independence, but in the brotherhood of interdependence of individuals as well as of nations. . . . [He] devoted himself to . . . rescuing from the debris of India's decadence the true products of its civilization, and to make our people build on them as the basis . . . of an international culture."*‡ ●

Roy thus vigorously supported the development of an English-language college for Calcutta. When some British scholars argued that the Company should endow a Sanskrit-language school, Roy rejected the idea: *"the pupils will there acquire what was known two thousand years ago with the addition of vain and empty*

---

*Raja Rammohun Roy, *The English Works*, vol. 1, ed. Jogendra Chunder Ghose (Calcutta: Srikanta Roy, 1901), p. 318.

†"A Letter on Grant's Jury Bill," *India Gazette*, January 22, 1833; cited in Amiya P. Sen, *Rammohun Roy: A Critical Biography* (New York: Penguin, 2012).

‡Rabindranath Tagore, "Rammohun Roy, the Path Maker and Luminous Star in Our Hour of Decadence," an address delivered by Rabindranath Tagore as President of the Preliminary Meeting of the Rammohun Roy Centenary held at the Senate House, Calcutta, on February 18, 1933. http://www.thebrahmosamaj.net/articles/rammohun_pathmaker.html.

*subtleties."** The English language, which he associated with science, inquiry, and liberty, would liberate young Bengalis from the passivity that had come from centuries of Mughal rule and from the clouds of superstition then darkening Hindu civilization.

Some British officials also supported English-language schooling for Indian boys, but differed sharply with Roy on the *purpose* of that education. One such Englishman argued that the goal of schooling should be *"to create a class of persons, Indian in blood and color, but English in taste, in opinions, in morals, and in intellect."*† For Roy, progress would come not through such wholesale assimilation, but rather through the creative intertwining of multiple influences. The Bengal Renaissance looked to reform, not to displace, local languages, cultures, and religious traditions.

Critical reasoning always guided Roy's assessments of religion, whether Hindu, Jain, Muslim, or Christian. Even as a teenager, his criticism of contemporary Hindu practices caused a deep rift with his father and separation from his family. After studying the ancient philosophy of the Jains, whose doctrine of *ahimsa* required absolute nonviolence toward all living things, he rejected it as impractical. From Islam, he took a profound and insistent belief in the unity of God. He rejected, however, the concept of prophetic revelation and criticized what he saw as Muslims' intolerance, which, he thought, stemmed from their doctrinaire tendencies.

Christianity was a relatively new influence in Roy's adult years, when larger numbers of missionaries came to Bengal. Studying their texts, Roy came away with a deep appreciation of the moral quality of the teachings of Jesus Christ and applauded the Christian humanism he saw practiced by some members of Calcutta's British community. On the other hand, he rejected the idea of the Holy Trinity, insisting on the unity of God, drawing the ire of some missionaries, Other European Christians, however, shared his philosophical viewpoint. The *Brahmo Sabha* religious community that Roy founded in Calcutta in 1828 became aligned with the Unitarian Church in England, which he visited when in London. Both *Brahmo Sabha* in India and Unitarianism in Britain and the United States avoided complex rituals and theologies, stressed quiet contemplation of the unity of Godhood, and affirmed a humanistic emphasis on good works.

Thus, Roy's intellectual and spiritual path led him to emphasize the compatibility of reformed Hinduism with British Christianity. He was indeed deeply grateful for British officials' support in his campaign against *suti*, bringing a petition before the British House of Commons celebrating *"that this barbarous and inhuman practice has been happily abolished."*‡ As the first prominent Indian to visit England, he was well-received by political and cultural leaders and, after his early death, was respectfully buried in English soil.

However, history would frustrate Roy's vision of social improvement through the fusion of Indian, Islamic, and European beliefs. As the economic changes that came with British rule cut more deeply into Indian society, more Hindus began to resent official patronage of a foreign religion; some saw the abolition of suti as an intrusion of Christian beliefs on their own religion and culture. Many Muslim Indians also came to regard Christianity as a threat to their traditions.

---

*Raja Rammohun Roy, *The English Works*, vol. 2, ed. Jogendra Chunder Ghose (Calcutta: Srikanta Roy, 1901), p. 325.

†T. B. Macauley, "Minute on Education," 1835, http://www.columbia.edu/itc/mealac/pritchett/00generallinks/macaulay/txt_minute_education_1835.html.

‡Raja Rammohun Roy, *The English Works*, vol. 2, ed. Jogendra Chunder Ghose (Calcutta: Srikanta Roy, 1901), p. 333.

• **CONTEXT&CONNECTIONS** Not long after Roy's death, a huge uprising against British authority and Christian influence, the *Indian Revolt of 1857* (Chapter 24) would create serious obstacles along his favored path of Anglo-Indian accommodation. •

Meanwhile, as the fates of Britain and India became entwined in the early nineteenth century, Tokugawa Japan stood on the other end of the continuum of Asian-European interaction. At the same time that Rammohun Roy was sailing to England, the Japanese shogun reaffirmed the total ban on European entry into his domains.

Tokugawa Japan, 1630–1837

After Hideyoshi's failed invasion of China (see Chapter 16), early modern Japan remained largely aloof from empires and empire building. Unlike Korea and Vietnam, Japan did not pay tribute to the Chinese emperor. It was subject to no foreign power and followed its own distinctive political, economic, and cultural dynamic. The Tokugawa (toe-koo-GAH-wah) shoguns and daimyo lords ruled over a rapidly growing society with a flourishing economy and major accomplishments in fields such as poetry, theater, and architecture.

The story of early modern Japan divides roughly into three periods. From 1630 to 1710, the Tokugawa system was at its height. But from 1710 to 1790, financial and environmental problems stymied the Tokugawa. Population growth stalled, and a widening gap between rich and poor led to social tension. After 1790, increased foreign interactions tested the Tokugawa commitment to isolationism.

Stability and Prosperity in Early Tokugawa Japan, 1630–1710

While the Japanese emperor remained a shadowy figure secluded in the ritual center of Kyoto, real political power rested with the Tokugawa shoguns in the political capital at Edo (Tokyo). The shoguns, literally "commanders of force," successfully brought peace and stability to the Japanese islands, even while the provincial lords, the daimyo, retained substantial authority within their own domains (see Chapter 16). Seventeenth-century Japan reaped the fruits of peace.

The nation brought back into production valuable resources that had been neglected during the violence and insecurity of the sixteenth century. Farmers improved irrigation, replacing dry field agriculture with rice paddies, and cleared forests and terraced hillsides to bring more fields into production. Fishermen increased harvests from the surrounding seas.

The shoguns and daimyo tapped into this productive wealth through an efficient tax system based on precise surveys of land and population. Farmers, no longer subject to arbitrary taxes, boosted production. At the same time, Chinese demand for silver and copper stimulated mining. Some of the new wealth went toward the improvement of roads and irrigation works, further stimulating economic growth. An increase in coinage and a great expansion of internal trade marked the shift from local and regional self-sufficiency to a truly national economy. This economic dynamism led to the expansion of Japanese cities. Many castle towns, originally civil war strongholds, now developed into cultural and commercial centers. The most spectacular example was the capital Edo (ED-doe), which grew from a small village to a city of more than a million people by 1720.

A pressing social issue was to define a peacetime role for the samurai warriors. Samurai were expected to give absolute loyalty to their lords and to display courage and valor in battle. However, the samurai code—or *bushido* ("the way of the warrior")—instructed them to cultivate civil as well as military arts, and in times of peace to emphasize the former: *"Within his heart [the samurai] keeps to the ways of peace, but . . . keeps his weapons ready for use. The . . . common people make him their teacher and respect him."** In the more peaceful Tokugawa atmosphere, some samurai positioned themselves as intellectual and cultural leaders, establishing schools, writing Confucian treatises, and patronizing the arts. Still, they maintained absolute allegiance to their daimyo lords, for whom they were ever ready to die.

The dynamism of the times tested boundaries. Regulations requiring peasant villages to be self-sufficient were widely ignored as farm families increasingly geared their production toward urban markets. In gender relations, some activities contradicted the Tokugawa theory of strict Confucian hierarchy. Elite women made prominent literary contributions, and women of other social classes claimed some mobility and economic opportunity. While women in samurai households were most subject to tight patriarchal control, urban merchant and artisan families were less restrictive. Thus, women participated as performers as well as audience members in some of the new forms of dance and theater.

New artistic forms arose in Japan's burgeoning cities. Poets experimented with a simple new form called *haiku*, and urban audiences patronized the new *kabuki* (ka-BOO-ki) theater, more realistic and emotive than previous forms of Japanese drama. These artistic trends marked the social fluidity of urban life, a worry to Tokugawa leaders who wanted everyone to keep to his or her place. Constant edicts ordering people to dress in clothes and live in houses appropriate to their social status are a good indication that many were *not* doing so.

● **CONTEXT&CONNECTIONS** Japan was certainly not unique in its imposition of sumptuary laws regulating how people should dress based on gender and social status. In medieval Europe purple was the color of royalty; in Ming China, it was the five-clawed dragon that was restricted to imperial display. Merchants in both Europe and Japan, meanwhile, defied aristocratic restrictions by wearing silk: the rising *bourgeoisie* (Chapter 16) would not be prevented from flaunting its wealth. Regulation of women's dress was even more common. ●

Tokugawa artists expressed the social fluidity of their urban milieu in works expressing *ukiyoe*, a "floating world" of languid pleasures: *"living only for the moment, turning our full attention to the pleasures of the moon, the snow, the cherry blossoms . . . diverting ourselves in just floating, floating; caring not a whit for the pauperism staring us in the face."*† The works of *ukiyoe* artists, though often exquisite, betray a sense of complacency in the face of the mounting challenges eighteenth century Japanese society was experiencing.

AP® THEMES
How did environmental factors contribute to the decline of Tokugawa rule?

Challenges, Reform, and Decline, 1710–1790

In 1710, Japan was rich, populous, and united. But the eighteenth century brought new challenges. One problem was ecological. During the seventeenth century the population of Japan had doubled to over 30 million people.

---

*Quoted in Ryusaku Tsunoda et al., *Sources of the Japanese Tradition* (New York: Columbia University Press, 1958), pp. 399–400.

†Quoted in Richard Lane, *Images from the Floating World* (New York: Putnam, 1978), p. 11.

The Art of the Floating World This 1745 work by Utagawa Toyoharu captures the spirit of *ukiyoe* in Tokugawa Japan. Ukiyoe artists often depicted courtesans and their patrons, and their conversations and pleasant pastimes, in a languid and sensual manner. Here reflections-within-reflections and deep three-point perspective pull the viewer into a world unconcerned with the hustle and bustle of life outside.

Farms became smaller and smaller, and without improvements in technology or sources of energy, Japan had nearly reached its limit in food production. As in China, irrigation had led to silting up of rivers and increased flooding. In addition, economic growth and urban construction had depleted Japan's timber resources. Wood became more expensive, and excessive logging led to soil erosion.

Yoshimune
(1738–1795) Eighth Tokugawa ruler to hold the title of shogun. A conservative but capable leader under whose rule Japan saw advances in agricultural productivity.

Yoshimune (r. 1716–1745), one of the greatest Tokugawa shoguns, issued edicts emphasizing frugality and curtailment of unnecessary consumption. True to the Confucian tradition, Yoshimune interpreted social problems as resulting from moral lapses. But his edicts could not change people's behavior.

Nevertheless, Yoshimune did sponsor some successful reforms. Most importantly, he reformed tax collections to eliminate local corruption, and he set strict limits on interest rates to relieve indebted farmers. He also sponsored the cultivation of sugar and ginseng to replace imports from Korea and Southeast Asia and promoted planting sweet potatoes on marginal land to increase the food supply. Support for fishing resulted in greater supplies of seafood and also of fertilizer needed to refresh the exhausted soil.

Yoshimune sought to bring merchants under greater control. Increased government involvement in commerce especially suited larger trading houses that were anxious to secure government-backed monopolies. But these policies tended to undermine entrepreneurialism, and they gradually made Japanese business more regulated and monopolistic and less dynamic and inventive.

For all his effort and energy, Yoshimune's reforms mainly amounted to "struggling to stand still."* Japan's social problems arising from the ecological and economic crises continued to escalate, as incidents of rural unrest nearly doubled in

*Conrad Totman, *Early Modern Japan* (Berkeley: University of California Press, 1993).

the later eighteenth century. Hundreds of thousands perished during the famine of the 1780s. It was becoming clear that the Tokugawa shoguns' conservative domestic policies were as inadequate as their continued attempts to seclude themselves from the outside world.

Tokugawa Japan and the Outside World, 1790–1837

The shoguns' conservative policies were most evident in foreign affairs. In the seventeenth century, alarmed by the early success of Christian missionaries, Tokugawa leaders had outlawed the faith (see Chapter 16), and they promulgated a series of **Seclusion Edicts** that strictly limited contact with Europeans, forbidding Japanese even to risk exposure through travel overseas. Those policies continued into the nineteenth century.

Seclusion Edicts
Series of edicts issued by the Tokugawa shoguns that, beginning in the 1630s, outlawed Christianity and strictly limited Japanese contact with Europeans. Only a single annual Dutch trading mission was allowed, with the stipulation that no Bibles or other Christian texts were to enter the country.

However, pragmatism did sometimes temper the policies of isolation. For one thing, Japanese seclusion applied only to Europeans. Trade with Chinese and Korean merchants grew, and overall Japanese foreign trade thereby increased. While contact with Europeans was limited, the scientific and philosophical books that reached Japan through the annual Dutch trade mission found an eager audience, especially among samurai. For centuries the Japanese called Western knowledge **Dutch learning**, and the ability to read Dutch became a sign of worldly sophistication. Nevertheless, for most Japanese aspiring to cultural sophistication it was still China, long the predominant external influence, which provided the templates for science and philosophy.

Dutch learning
Traditional Japanese title for Western knowledge. Knowledge of Dutch in Tokugawa Japan was a sign of worldliness and sophistication.

However, some Tokugawa thinkers, many of them samurai, downplayed even China's influence. They exalted Japan's indigenous Shinto religion and its emphasis on the spiritual forces of the natural and ancestral worlds. In rejecting foreign influences such as Buddhism, Confucianism and Dutch learning, advocates of Shinto reinforced the Tokugawa trend toward nativism and isolationism.

In contrast to the Qing, Russians, and British, Tokugawa Japan simply opted out of empire building. Its only territorial expansion was to lightly populated northern islands, especially Hokkaido (ho-KIE-do), where the indigenous Ainu people lived by hunting, gathering, and fishing and were no match for Japanese weapons. Even as external pressures increased in the late eighteenth century, the Tokugawa focus on self-sufficiency remained.

● **CONTEXT&CONNECTIONS** Japanese attitudes toward empire would change dramatically in the later nineteenth century, when Japan's naval defeat of China led to the acquisition of Taiwan and Korea (see Chapter 24). Japanese imperialism became even more aggressive in the first half of the twentieth century. Before and during the Second World War, the country conquered much of East and Southeast Asia (see Chapter 29). ●

In 1791, the first American ship landed in Japan, and the next year a Russian delegation sent by Catherine the Great arrived to establish trade relations. Although these events tested the shoguns' commitment to their isolationist policies, their response was unequivocal: the shogun reaffirmed the full force of the Seclusion Edict of 1639. The Japanese attacked foreign whaling vessels and fired on an 1837 American expedition, forcing it to flee.

This Japanese response was even less accommodating than that of the Qianlong Emperor in China, who at least allowed regulated trade with the British to continue even as he turned aside the Macartney Mission. Russia and the Western powers were, however, persistent. Soon Japan's leaders, like those in China, would face an ultimatum: open your doors to foreign trade, or advanced industrial weapons will blow them down (see Chapter 24).

CONTEXT AND CONNECTIONS

World Economies and the Great Divergence

As our own times change, often our views of the past change as well. The recent economic successes of China and India have led some historians to reconsider Asia's place in the development of the modern world economy (see Chapters 31 and 32).

In the late seventeenth century, Mughal India was one of the world's most prosperous empires; Tokugawa Japan was urbanizing and commercializing; and the rulers of Qing China were cultivating the continuing expansion of the world's largest economy. By the early nineteenth century, however, the Industrial Revolution in Europe was rapidly shifting the global balance of economic power westward (see Chapter 23), ensuring the military and technological supremacy of Europe. The relationship between Britain and China shows just how suddenly and dramatically the change occurred. In 1793, the emperor Qianlong easily rebuffed British emissaries seeking stronger commercial and diplomatic ties; in 1839, ironclad British steamships destroyed China's coastal defenses and imposed their own terms of trade on humiliated Qing rulers (see Chapter 24).

In the past, many historians assumed that an exceptional bundle of European characteristics paved the way for industrial modernity. These factors included an early lead in scientific inquiry (see Chapter 21); the development of commercial capitalism and the relatively high status of merchants; competition between nations for economic and military advantage; and higher labor costs leading to increased innovation in manufacturing (see Chapters 16 and 17). In this view, Europe's early modern commercial empires translated smoothly into global economic dominance in the industrial age. Those assumptions have now been critiqued by historians who insist on a more global perspective, arguing that, prior to 1800, Europe's industrial potential was not unique.

That is the argument of historian Kenneth Pomeranz in his comparative study of what he calls the "great divergence" between the economies of Great Britain

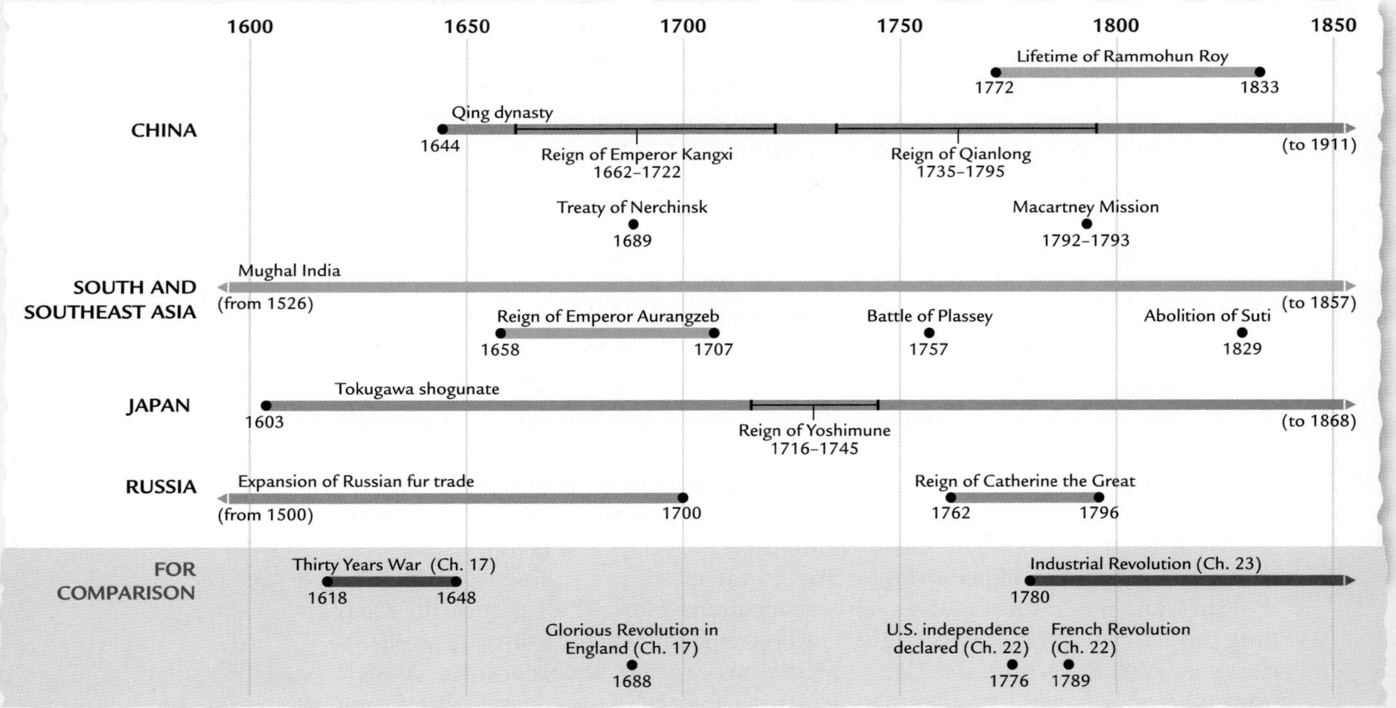

and China's Yangzi River Delta in the early nineteenth century.* According to Pomeranz, contingencies and accidents, not deep historical or cultural differences, explain Britain's early lead in industrial development. For example, Britain's coal deposits were much more easily accessible than China's. Access to the resources of the Americas was another key factor (see Chapters 18 and 19): American sugar plantations contributed greatly to the capital and organizational expertise that would later propel industry, and access to American timber and other natural resources freed the British from the ecological constraints of their own small island. In addition, Britain's maritime focus gave it a compelling interest in steam power that did not exist in Qing China, where security interests focused on Central Asia, not on the sea coast.

*Kenneth Pomeranz, *The Great Divergence: China, Europe, and the Making of the Modern World Economy* (Princeton: Princeton University Press, 2000).

It was also simple good fortune that monopoly trading companies like the British East India Company were in the right place at the right time to shift their priorities to providing raw materials for European industry and cultivating global markets for the products of European factories. Rammohun Roy was perhaps naïve to think that the Company's commercial activities would help elevate the Indian economy. In fact, political control would allow the Company to manipulate tariffs and markets to their own advantage, and at the expense of Indian manufacturers (see Chapter 23).

Though the debate among historians continues, a growing consensus emphasizes that vigorous economic growth in contemporary China and India marks a return to an earlier status quo when Asian economies were at the global forefront. Their relative poverty for the past two hundred years now looks to have been an aberration, and their current ascent a return to historical norms.

Key Terms

Rammohun Roy (590)
Qing dynasty (591)
Emperor Kangxi (593)
Qianlong (593)
Yangzi River Valley (593)
Treaty of Nerchinsk (597)
Macartney Mission (598)
Cossacks (599)
Catherine the Great (601)
Aurangzeb (603)
Maratha kingdoms (605)
Nader Shah (606)
Joseph Francois Dupleix (606)
Battle of Plassey (607)
Lord Charles Cornwallis (607)
Yoshimune (614)
Seclusion Edicts (615)
Dutch learning (615)

For Further Reference

Bayly, C. A. *Indian Society and the Making of the British Empire*. New York: Cambridge University Press, 1990.

Brower, Daniel R., and Edward J. Lazzarini. *Russia's Orient: Imperial Borderlands and Peoples, 1700–1917*. Bloomington: Indiana University Press, 1997.

Crossley, Pamela. *The Manchus*. Oxford, England: Blackwell Publishers, 2002.

Dalrymple, William. *White Mughals: Love and Betrayal in Eighteenth Century India*. New York: Penguin, 2004.

Dasgupta, Subrata. *Awakening: The Story of the Bengal Renaissance*. Delhi: Random House, 2011.

Kappeler, Andreas. *The Russian Empire: A Multiethnic History*. Harlow, England: Longman, 2001.

Keay, John. *The Honourable Company: A History of the English East India Company*. London: HarperCollins, 1991.

Matsunosuke, Nishiyama. *Edo Culture: Daily Life and Diversions in Urban Japan, 1600–1868*. Honolulu: University of Hawai'i Press, 1997.

Perdue, Peter C. *China Marches West: The Qing Conquest of Central Eurasia*. Cambridge, Mass.: Harvard University Press, 2005.

Richards, John. *The Mughal Empire*. New York: Cambridge University Press, 1996.

Totman, Conrad. *Early Modern Japan*. Berkeley: University of California Press, 1993

AP® Review Questions for Chapter 20

Multiple-Choice Questions

QUESTIONS 1–4 REFER TO THE FOLLOWING PASSAGES.

The Treaty of Nerchinsk [between the Russian empire and Qing China] laid down a frontier rather than a boundary, that is, a separation of sovereignties that was zonal rather than linear, using for delineation major geographical features such as mountain ranges rather than the precisely defined lines on maps and on the ground that modern states require. . . . The treaty provided for the destruction of the Russian forts and settlements in the Amur Basin, and its overall effect was to preserve imperial China's territory from Russian encroachment for a century and a half.

—Journalist Neville Maxwell, "How the Sino-Russian Boundary Conflict Was Finally Settled," 2007

For much of the Qing dynasty, for example, the "Sino-centric worldview" dominated diplomatic policy. Under its auspices, Qing rulers were in no doubt as to their world status. It was expressed in the principle: "I am a superior authority, therefore all lands are subject to me." The emperor was the self-acclaimed Son of Heaven who, as long as he held the Mandate of Heaven, ruled supreme over all mankind. . . . Between the years 1655 and 1793 CE, a total of 17 Western diplomatic missions arrived in China, for reasons of self-interest. All, with the exception of the English mission, performed the kowtow ceremony before the emperor, which affirmed the Qing's sense of superiority.

—Zhang Xiaomin and Xu Chungfeng, "The Late Qing Dynasty Diplomatic Transformation," 2007

1. Which of the following best explains the series of treaties between the Qing and the Russians?
   (A) Qing indifference to Russian expansion
   (B) Contraction of land-based empires, which was common during this time period
   (C) Contempt and arrogance by the Russians toward Qing claims
   (D) Increased competition between states over territory and trade routes

2. Although they were a foreign power in China, based on the passages above, the Qing continued which Confucian policy?
   (A) Preferring merchants over farmers and scholars
   (B) Asserting political domination over its neighbors
   (C) Encouraging farming over trade as the primary occupation basis for the economy
   (D) Claiming male superiority over women

3. Which of the following best explains Qing policies toward the western Europeans in the passages?
   (A) The development of vast land-based empires by the Europeans
   (B) The establishment of European trading-post empires around the world
   (C) The European push into the central regions of Africa, Asia, and the Americas
   (D) The ability of land-based empires in Asia and Africa to resist European encroachment

4. Based on the second passage, which of the following is an accurate statement about the global economy in the Early Modern Era?
   (A) The Europeans had grown powerful enough to dictate terms of trade in both Africa and Asia.
   (B) The Asian powers were significantly stronger than the European states and could ignore their presence in East Asia.
   (C) East Asian and European states competed for economic control of Africa.
   (D) Although growing in influence, the European powers had to deal with strong Asian states when negotiating trade.

QUESTIONS 5–7 REFER TO THE FOLLOWING IMAGE.

The Weaving of Flower'd Silks, two Women at Work.

5. Based on this image, which of the following statements is true concerning women during the Qing dynasty?
   (A) Women were excluded from all aspects of economic life.
   (B) Women were only allowed to perform tasks that dealt with the daily running of the household.
   (C) Women were involved in some parts of the larger economy.
   (D) Women were denied the opportunity to learn artisan skills.

6. The extensive weaving enterprise portrayed in the image confirms which of the following?
   (A) East Asian commodities were no longer in high demand on the world market.
   (B) East Asian merchants and artisans needed to find new commodities to sell on the world market during this time period.
   (C) East Asian commodities were sold exclusively in domestic markets.
   (D) Traditional East Asian commodities were still in high demand in the Early Modern Era.

7. Which of the following would account for the growing importance of cotton weaving during this time period?
   (A) Growing demand for cotton in goods in Europe and the Americas
   (B) Confucian civil servants replacing silk with cotton as a sign of status
   (C) The rise of industrialized cotton mills in South Asia
   (D) A decline in cotton weaving in Europe

QUESTIONS 8–10 REFER TO THE FOLLOWING PASSAGE.

The head judge sits, and ten guest judges [the jury] sit on his side. The head guest judge is the elder of the guest merchants. . . . On the day they consider the suit and then decide the outcome, if one of the guest judges does not agree they must hear the case again. Even if this happens two or three times, no one views this as inconvenient.

—Visiting Chinese sailor in British Calcutta, 1780s

8. The passage most directly reflects which of the following policies used by Britain in its colonies?
   (A) Allow all cases to be heard by local courts.
   (B) Cases involving British citizens and interests were heard in British courts.
   (C) Both the British and the colonials shared the same court.
   (D) British courts imitated Chinese legal practices.

9. The passage reveals that
   (A) most of the British in India were there for business.
   (B) the military made up most of the British population in India.
   (C) the British had penetrated deep into the Indian subcontinent.
   (D) the British were primarily involved in missionary activity.

10. We can infer from the presence of a Chinese sailor in British Calcutta which of the following?
   (A) The British kept their ports open to foreign merchants.
   (B) In an attempt to dominate trade, the British closed their ports to all foreign merchants.
   (C) The British were forced to deal exclusively with the Chinese.
   (D) British forms of justice often conflicted with local sensibilities.

Short-Answer Questions

1. Answer parts A and B.
   A. Explain how Sikhism is BOTH an example of a religious reform AND a syncretic belief system.
   B. Briefly explain how ONE religion from a different region played a role similar to Sikhism.

2. Answer parts A and B.
   A. Briefly explain the TWO roles of the Samurai in Tokugawa Japan.
   B. Briefly explain how elites in ONE other region played a similar role.

21 European Science and the Foundations of Modern Imperialism, 1600–1820

Joseph Banks

Sir Joseph Banks (1743–1820), 1771–72 (oil on canvas), Reynolds, Sir Joshua (1723–92)/Private Collection/Photo © Agnew's, London/Bridgeman Images

When the young botanist **Joseph Banks** (1743–1820) sailed aboard the *Endeavour* as part of a British expedition across the Pacific Ocean, his interest went beyond flora and fauna to include the people he encountered on the voyage. From the Amerindians of Tierra del Fuego (the southern tip of South America), to the Polynesians of the Pacific, to the Aboriginal peoples of Australia, Banks kept careful notes of his interactions with peoples of whom Europeans had little previous knowledge. His concern with these cultures went beyond mere curiosity. He was interested in understanding the relationships *between* societies. For example, when Banks learned that Tahitians understood the speech of the Maori (MAO-ree) of New Zealand, he recognized that there was a family connection between the two peoples. Banks was a pioneer of *ethnography*, the study of the linguistic and cultural relationships between peoples. However, he was mystified by the behavior of the Polynesian people he and his shipmates met when they stepped ashore on the island of Tahiti:

Though at first they hardly dared approach us, after a little time they became very familiar. The first who approached us came crawling almost on his hands and knees and gave us a green bough. . . . This we received and immediately each of us gathered a green bough and carried it in our hands. They marched with us about 1/2 a mile and then made a general stop and, scraping the ground clean . . . every one of them threw his bough down upon the bare place and made signs that we should do the same. . . . Each of us dropped a

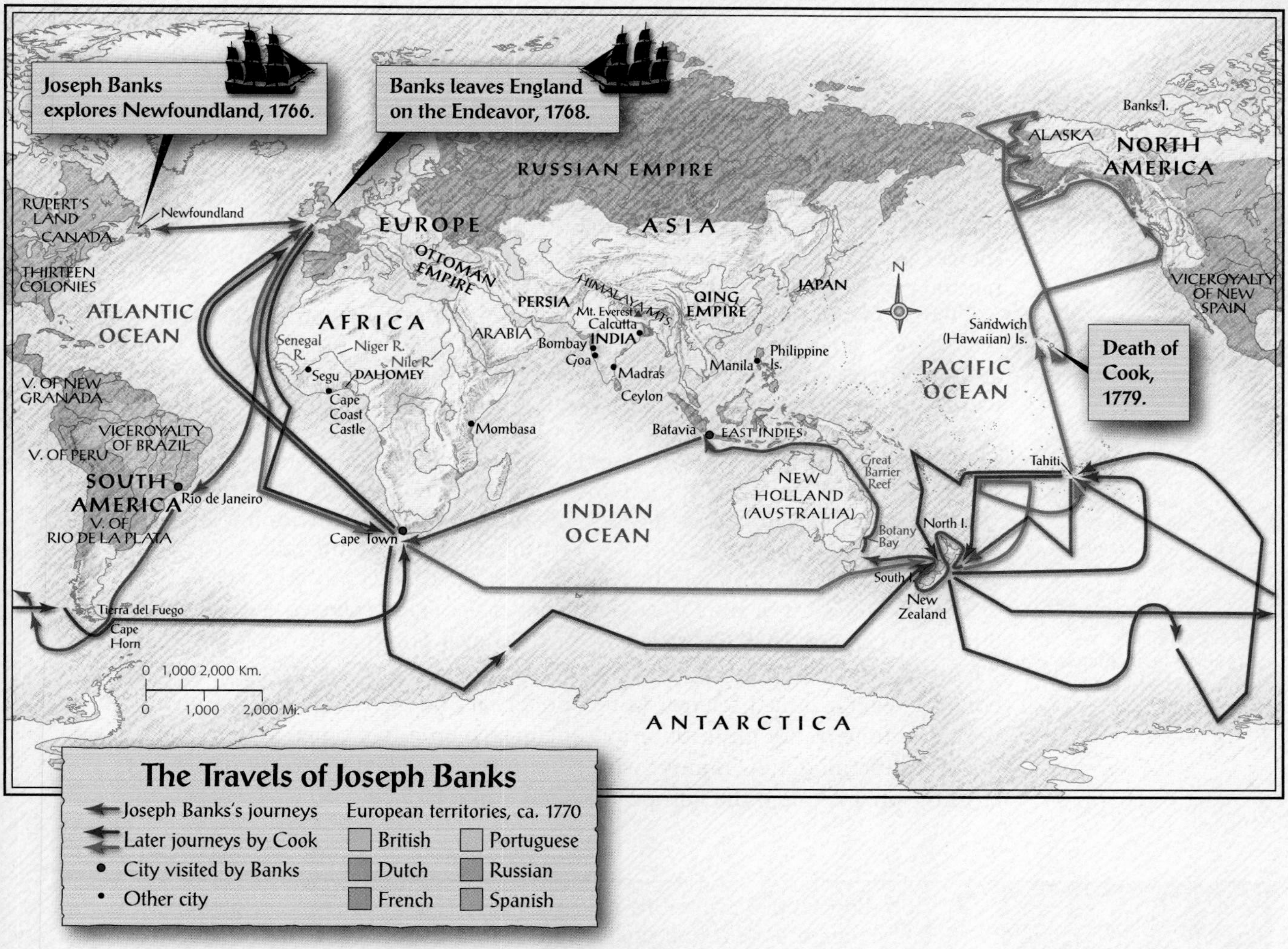

*bough upon those that the Indians had laid down, we all followed their example and thus peace was concluded.**

Such ceremonies became a bit less mysterious to Banks after he began to learn the Tahitian language and made friends with a high priest who helped him understand Polynesian customs. Still, even after years of contact, the cultural gulf between the Tahitians and the Englishmen remained.

Banks returned to England in 1771 after a three-year journey. The crewmen who had survived the *Endeavour*'s three years at sea were among the few at that time who had sailed around the world. Their captain, **James Cook** (1728–1779), became an instant celebrity. He had accomplished his mission of charting the Pacific Ocean,

---

*J. C. Beaglehole, ed., *The Endeavour Journal of Joseph Banks*, 2d ed., vol. 1 (Sydney: Halsted Press, 1962), p. 252. Here as elsewhere, some revisions of Banks's punctuation and usage have been made.

Joseph Banks
(1743–1820) English botanist on Captain James Cook's first voyage in the Pacific, who categorized different species of plants and brought them back to England. Also established the Royal Botanic Gardens at Kew.

James Cook
(1728–1779) British sea captain whose three voyages to the Pacific Ocean greatly expanded European knowledge of the region. Regarded as a great national hero by the British public, he was killed in an altercation with Hawai'ian islanders in 1779.

thus facilitating future European voyages to such places as Hawai'i, New Zealand, and Australia. He had also carried out important astronomical observations.

In fact, scientific inquiry was central to the *Endeavour*'s mission. The drawings and specimens of plant and animal life Banks brought back greatly expanded European knowledge of the natural world. He was interested not merely in collecting exotic flora and fauna but also in systematically classifying and cataloging his findings. While Cook was using his mathematical and navigational skills to chart the oceans, Banks was helping to develop a system for naming and describing natural phenomena to clarify familial relationships in nature.

Banks's work on the *Endeavour* produced no immediate, tangible benefit. But science now enjoyed considerable social and political support. Especially in Britain and France, leaders understood the connection between science and empire. Banks's reconnaissance of the natural world, like that of the physical world undertaken by Cook, was a prelude to the more assertive European imperialism of the nineteenth century. While Polynesians were struggling to understand what they saw as the strange behavior of their British visitors, Cook was claiming their islands *"for the use of his Brittanick majesty."* Banks came home dreaming of *"future dominions,"* an influential advocate of British settlement in Australia.* Science and empire would remain companions throughout the nineteenth century.

After the return of the *Endeavour*, Banks never again traveled outside Europe. But from 1778 to 1820, as president of the Royal Society, the most prestigious scientific establishment of the day, he focused on fields such as "economic botany," which linked science to technological and economic development. At the same time, more philosophically inclined men and women were extending the scientific model of inquiry, with its emphasis on reason, to human society, creating what is called the European Enlightenment.

KEY CONCEPT QUESTIONS

- How did European scientific advancements affect overseas exploration and increase agricultural production? **(Key Concepts 4.1 & 4.2)**
- How did technology affect European imperialism? **(Key Concept 4.3)**
- How do the effects of European contact with the Americas compare with the effects of European contact with Oceania and Australia? **(Key Concept 4.1)**
- How did Enlightenment philosophers such as Voltaire, Montesquieu, Locke, and Rousseau fundamentally alter European society? **(Key Concept 5.3)**

From Scientific Revolution to Practical Science, 1600–1800

Joseph Banks was heir to a tradition that stretched back to the sixteenth century, when Nicolaus Copernicus first published his theory of a heliocentric solar system and Galileo Galilei upset church authorities by providing strong

*Quoted in Patrick O'Brien, *Joseph Banks: A Life* (Chicago: University of Chicago Press, 1987), pp. 105, 264.

evidence that the earth rotates around the sun (see Chapter 16). For most Europeans in the eighteenth century, the Christian faith, whether Catholic or Protestant, still held most of the answers to basic questions about relationships between God, humanity, and the natural world. By then, however, especially among the elites of northern Europe, men and women who embraced rational inquiry were becoming increasingly prominent. Aided by royal and aristocratic patronage, they began to pursue the "new science."

The development of science was important not only from a purely intellectual standpoint. Western science became "revolutionary" in global terms as its practical applications increased the political and military power of Europeans on the world stage. As president of the Royal Society and in his own research, Joseph Banks contributed to developments linking scientific inquiry to real-world applications and economic purposes on his own English estate, in Britain more generally, and across the expanding British empire.

The Development of the Scientific Method

In seventeenth-century western Europe an intellectual debate divided thinkers into two camps: the "ancients" and the "moderns." The "ancients," who carried forward the scholarly traditions of the humanists (see Chapter 15), emphasized the authority of Aristotle and other classical authors as the foundation on which knowledge in fields such as medicine, mathematics, and astronomy should be built. The "moderns" had a bolder idea.

AP® THEMES
How did innovations in scientific inquiry affect the beliefs and practices of European Christians?

Rejecting the infallibility of classical authority as well as Christian theology, the "moderns" argued that human reason provided the key to knowledge. It was an optimistic viewpoint that contradicted the traditional Christian conception of humanity as "fallen" from God's grace, tainted by original sin, and capable of salvation only through divine mercy. The "moderns" believed instead that humankind was endowed by God with reason and through that reason could apprehend and accurately describe God's creation. *"All our knowledge begins with the senses, proceeds then to the understanding, and ends with reason. There is nothing higher than reason,"* wrote the German philosopher Immanuel Kant (1724–1804).*

● **CONTEXT&CONNECTIONS** In imperial China, Confucian scholars also had long debated the reliability of input from the senses. Doubt characterized the late *Ming dynasty* period, when the Neo-Confucianism of Wang Yangming focused on the priority of inward contemplation (key term in Chapter 16). The eighteenth century, however, saw a reemphasis on the more empirical tradition of Confucianism during the reign of the Yongzheng emperor, when "evidential learning" led to the compilation of what was then the world's largest encyclopedia (see Chapter 20). For most Hindus and Buddhists, on the other hand, the issue was hardly debatable: the material world is illusory, and our senses are distractions from the truth, not guides toward it. ●

One seventeenth-century thinker who applied reason using a *deductive* approach—arguing from general principles to specific truths—was the Frenchman **René Descartes** (1596–1650). Descartes (DAY-cart) argued that the axioms of true philosophy had to be firmly grounded in the human capacity to reason. He associated rationality with mathematics and thought that logic could result in a

René Descartes
(1596–1650) French scientist, mathematician, and philosopher who developed the deductive method of reasoning (moving from general principles to particular facts).

*Immanuel Kant, *Critique of Pure Reason*, ed. and trans. Wolgang Schwarz (Berlin: Scientia Verlag Aalen, 1982), p. 217.

Robin Treadwell/Science Source

Elisabeth and Johannes Hevelius The German-Polish astronomer Johannes Hevelius was an innovator in celestial observation and data collection, using telescopes of his own design to study lunar topography. A member of London's Royal Society, Hevelius is shown here with his second wife, Elisabeth, who came to him begging for instruction when she was just a teenager. They married and collaborated from that point on. After Johannes died, Elisabeth Hevelius achieved independent recognition for her continued work.

unified system of truth. Emphasizing systematic doubt as a key to knowledge, he questioned even his own existence. His famous solution, *"I think, therefore I am,"* demonstrated that his ability to reason was the proof of his existence. Descartes also believed he had to doubt the existence of God before proving to himself that God did, in fact, exist. For Descartes, proof of God's existence came from rational thought rather than inherited wisdom or sacred texts.

While Descartes' philosophy was based on introspection, others were laying the foundations for modern science based on experimentation and observation of the natural world. The Englishman **Sir Francis Bacon** (1561–1626) was one of the main proponents of an *inductive* approach to science: working from modest, carefully controlled observations toward larger truths. Like Descartes, Bacon believed that doubt produced knowledge. *"If a man will begin with certainties,"* he wrote, *"he shall end in doubts; but if he will be content to begin with doubts he shall end in certainties."** (See the feature "Movement of Ideas Through Primary Sources: A Japanese View of European Science.")

Sir Francis Bacon
(1561–1626) English politician, essayist, and philosopher who argued for inductive reasoning—working from observation of natural phenomena to larger truths.

As Copernicus and Galileo had demonstrated (see Chapter 16), astronomy was a prime example of how empirical scientists used systematic observation and the application of mathematics to unlock the secrets of a rationally ordered cosmos. Tycho Brahe (1546–1601), a Danish nobleman, also contributed to this effort. Using observations made with only the naked eye, in 1573 Brahe challenged the Aristotelian concept of an eternally unchanging celestial sphere by demonstrating that a bright supernova had emerged beyond the earth's atmosphere.

One of Brahe's assistants, the younger German mathematician Johannes Kepler (1571–1630), then applied Brahe's data to an analysis of the orbit of the planet Mars, using a Copernican framework placing the sun at the center of the solar system. Kepler's calculations, published in 1609, showed that planetary motion could be most simply explained by plotting the planets' orbits along elliptical rather than circular paths. But both Aristotle and Christian teaching insisted that all celestial motion was circular, the perfect form of movement for a perfect heavenly domain. Kepler thus reinforced Galileo's challenge to the traditional Christian idea that the "perfect" heavens

*Sir Francis Bacon, *Advancement of Learning*, with a preface by Thomas Case (London: Oxford University Press, 1906), p. 35.

above are governed by different physical laws than the "sinful" earth below. This was a real breakthrough for science: the notion that identical laws of nature prevail throughout the entire universe, and that those laws can be elegantly described through mathematics.

At first, such radical new ideas caused discomfort, as when an English poet of the early seventeenth century expressed his feeling of disorientation in a Copernican universe: *"The sun is lost, and the earth, and no man's wit / Can well direct him where to look for it . . . / 'Tis all in pieces, all coherence gone."** Tensions between "faith" and "reason," whether religion or science offered the surest path to truth, would continue far into the future (see Chapter 23). A century later, however, the prestige of science was on the rise. More Europeans became comfortable with the idea that it is our God-given ability to reason and to use our senses to observe nature that gives us the means to comprehend the brilliance of creation, and to strive toward truth on the basis of science.

The achievements of the Englishman **Isaac Newton** (1642–1727) confirmed that increasingly confident and optimistic worldview. Newton followed Descartes' lead in using reasoned, deductive thinking to establish general principles that tied together his own findings and those of other scientists. He was also a brilliant observer of the natural world, following Bacon's inductive approach to experimental science. Newton described a predictable natural world in which all matter exerts gravitational attraction in inverse proportion to mass and distance: the universal law of gravitation. To achieve the mathematical rigor necessary to describe the acceleration and deceleration of bodies in motion, Newton became one of the inventors of differential calculus.

Isaac Newton
(1642–1727) Skilled theoretical and experimental scientist who did more than anyone to create a new, systematic architecture for science by stating the universal law of gravitation. Also one of the inventors of differential calculus, he undertook extensive experiments with optics that led to much more powerful telescopes.

Now, by the early eighteenth century, an English poet could write: *"Nature and Nature's laws lay hid in night; God said Let Newton Be! and all was light."*† The association between God and Newton in this poem shows that the tension between science and faith was beginning to ease. Newton himself was a devout Christian, and while many continued to believe that God actively intervened in nature, those who adopted Newton's outlook tended to see the universe as a self-functioning outcome of God's perfect act of creation. God was like a master clock maker who, having set his elegant machine in motion, did not need to further interfere.

● **CONTEXT&CONNECTIONS** Deists like Newton embraced the ethics of the New Testament and retained their belief in God, while rejecting the idea of His active intervention in the natural world or human affairs. Others with a similar viewpoint included *Rammohun Roy* (Chapter 20) and Thomas Jefferson. Jefferson and many other deists were also Freemasons, members of lodges that used secret rites and rituals to promote reason, charity, and brotherly love (see Chapter 22). ●

Newton confidently declared that he could use mathematics to *"demonstrate the frame of the system of the world."* Joseph Banks inherited not only Newton's optimism but also his position as president of the Royal Society. Starting with Newton and continuing with Banks, this assembly of leading thinkers served as a nerve center for European science.

---

*John Donne, "An Anatomy of the World," The Poetry Foundation, http://www.poetryfoundation.org/poem/173348

†Alexander Pope, "Epitaph Intended for Sir Isaac Newton," in *Pope: Selected Works*, ed. Herbert Davis (London: Oxford University Press, 1966), p. 651.

A Japanese View of European Science

In the history of modern science, a common pattern has been repeated around the world. Those who generated new ideas, such as Galileo, were often attacked for their assault on tradition, but later their innovations were absorbed into the status quo. When Europeans then took the new science to other continents, once again these ideas and approaches challenged established tradition. Here we have an example from anatomy, with a Japanese observation of the dissection of a human corpse.

For medieval Europeans, the main authority in anatomy was the ancient Greek physician Galen who, though he dissected many birds and animals, had theories about the inner workings of the human body that were based largely on speculation. Then, in 1543, a Belgian physician published a new scheme of human anatomy based on actual dissection of human cadavers. Adherents of Galen's view were upset, as were those many Christians who saw the violation of dead bodies as sacrilegious. Over the next two hundred years, however, dissection became a routine process.

In the eighteenth century, the Tokugawa shoguns had severely limited Japanese contacts with Europeans. But through the annual Dutch trade mission to Nagasaki, a few books entered the country, and some curious Japanese scholars learned Dutch so they could read them (see Chapter 20). Below, a physician named Sugita Gempaku (1733–1817) describes how, having looked at a Dutch anatomy text, he was astonished to see how accurate it was when he witnessed the dissection of a human body.

Historical Thinking Skill:

COMPARISON **How do the explanations of human anatomy in the Dutch textbook compare to the explanations of human anatomy that Japanese physicians traditionally studied?**

Historical Thinking Skill:

INTERPRETATION **How does Gempaku's account of this human dissection indicate that witnessing the dissection of a corpse was not a common practice in Japanese society?**

Source: Japan: A Documentary History, ed. David J. Lu (Armonk, N.Y.: M. E. Sharpe, 1997), pp. 264–267. Used with permission of M. E. Sharpe, Inc.

A Dutch Lesson in Anatomy

Somehow, miraculously I obtained a [Dutch] book on anatomy. [Then] I received a letter from . . . the Town Commissioner: "A post-mortem examination of the body of a condemned criminal by a resident physician will be held tomorrow. . . . You are welcome to witness it if you so desire."

The next day, when we arrived at the location . . . Ryotaku reached under his kimono to produce a Dutch book and showed it to us. "This is a Dutch book of anatomy called *Tabulae Anatomicae*. I bought this a few years ago when I went to Nagasaki, and kept it." As I examined it, it was the same book I had and was of the same edition. We held each other's hands and exclaimed: "What a coincidence!" Ryotaku continued by saying, "When I went to Nagasaki, I learned and heard," and opened this book. "These are called *long* in Dutch, they are the lungs," he taught us. "This is *hart*, or the heart." . . . However, they did not look like the heart given in the Chinese medical books, and none of us were sure until we could actually see the dissection.

Thereafter we went together to the place that was especially set aside [for] us to observe the dissection. . . . That day, the butcher pointed to this and that organ. After the heart, liver, gall bladder and stomach were identified, he pointed to other parts for which there were no names. "I don't know their names. But I have dissected quite a few bodies from my youthful days. . . . Every time I had a dissection, I pointed out to those physicians many of these parts, but not a single one of them questioned 'What was this,' or 'What was that?'" We compared the body as dissected against the charts both Ryotaku and I had, and could not find a single variance from the charts. The Chinese *Book of Medicine* says that the lungs are like the eight petals of the lotus flower, with three petals hanging in front, three in back, and two petals forming like two ears. . . . There were no such divisions, and the position and shapes of intestines and gastric organs were all different from those taught by the old theories. The official physicians . . . had witnessed dissection seven or eight times. Whenever they witnessed the dissection, they found that the old theories contradicted reality. Each time they were perplexed and could not resolve their doubts. Every time they wrote down what they thought was strange. They wrote in their books, "The more we think of it, there must be fundamental differences in the bodies of Chinese and of the eastern barbarians." I could see why they wrote this way. . . .

We decided that we should also examine the shape of the skeletons left exposed on the execution ground. We collected the bones, and examined a number of them. Again, we were struck by the fact that they all differed from the old theories while conforming to the Dutch charts. . . .

On the way home we spoke to each other and felt the same way. "How marvelous was our actual experience today. It is a shame that we were ignorant of these things until now. As physicians . . . we performed our duties in complete ignorance of the true form of the human body." . . . Then I spoke to my companion, "Somehow if we can translate anew this book called *Tabulae Anatomicae*, we can get a clear notion of the human body inside out. It will have great benefit in the treatment of our patients. Let us do our best to read it and understand it without the help of translators." . . .

The next day, we assembled at the house of Ryotaku and recalled the happenings of the previous day. When we faced the *Tabulae Anatomicae* we felt as if we were setting sail on a great ocean in a ship without oars or a rudder. With the magnitude of the work before us, we were dumbfounded by our own ignorance. . . . At that time I did not know the twenty-five letters of the Dutch alphabet. I decided to study the language with firm determination, but I had to acquaint myself with letters and words gradually.

Practical Science: Economic Botany, Agriculture, and Empire

Reliant on the natural world for medicine as well as food, people have always studied plant life. It was only with the rise of modern botany, however, that scientists began to systematically collect and organize a catalogue of the world's flora.

Carl Linnaeus
(1707–1778) Swedish founder of the modern systems of botany and zoology. The basics of his classification systems are still in use.

Carl Linnaeus (1707–1778) was the pioneering figure in this area. As a medical student, Linnaeus first studied plants for their medicinal properties, but as his enthusiasm for plant collecting grew, he enlarged his focus. He traveled across Sweden gathering plant specimens, restored the botanical gardens at his university, and eventually sent nineteen of his students on voyages around the world to gather specimens for study. Two of Linnaeus's students were aboard the *Endeavour* with Joseph Banks.

Like Newton, Linnaeus combined close scientific observation with theoretical system building. In 1735, he published his classification of living things, *Systema Naturae*. The Linnaean system orders species into hierarchical categories still in use today—genus/order/class/kingdom—in which any new plant from anywhere in the world can be classified. To Linnaeus, this orderly relationship among living things was another demonstration of the harmony of God's creation.

Linnaeus also developed the binomial ("two name") system of Latin names for organisms, with the first name indicating the genus and the second the species. Though the world's plants already had names used by the people who were familiar with them, those local names fit no consistent network of classification. Now, as Linnaeus's students brought more and more specimens back to Europe, they received new names that made them, for the first time, part of a single knowledge system.

Though Joseph Banks was perhaps a less original botanical thinker than Carl Linnaeus, he was exceptionally adept at deriving practical economic lessons from his work. Banks was a leading figure in the drive for "improvement." In agriculture, "improvement" meant using scientific methods to increase the productivity of existing land and to bring new land under cultivation. Both Banks and King George III (r. 1760–1820), sometimes called "the farmer king," eagerly supported the effort to bring to agriculture the insights gained from natural science. Since the seventeenth century, English farmers had learned to improve the soil by sowing clover and turnips in fields that had previously been left fallow. They also practiced selective breeding of livestock to boost the production of wool, meat, and milk.

Joseph Banks was among the wealthy "gentleman farmers" in England who could afford to invest in water engineering technology pioneered by the Dutch, reclaiming low-lying land by using windmills to pump water from diked marshes. Banks's estate exemplified all the other measures that were improving agricultural productivity in eighteenth-century England, including experimenting with crop rotations and crossbreeding farm animals. The outcome of this "agricultural revolution" was more arable land for planting and greater efficiency in production. The timing was significant, since increased food supplies would support urbanization during the Industrial Revolution (see Chapter 23).

- **CONTEXT&CONNECTIONS** The use of canals, dikes, and irrigation ditches to control water for agricultural production is as old as civilization itself. In Chinese history, imperial states actively sponsored and controlled large-scale water projects, building canals, irrigation channels, and dams (see Chapters 16 and 20). Grain agriculture in northwestern Europe, in contrast, was less dependent on irrigation, and here royal support for labor-intensive water control projects was far less common. Some historians argue that long-term differences in the roles of Chinese and European states can be explained through such differences in water management. ●

This agricultural revolution led to greater inequality, however. Previously, English village society, like peasant societies elsewhere, was oriented toward stability and security. Farm families all shared common access to pastures and woodlands. But in the seventeenth and eighteenth centuries, members of the English gentry, like the Banks family, accumulated larger landholdings under new laws allowing them to "enclose" common lands as private property. Collective food security in the countryside now mattered less than productivity and profitable crop sales.

AP® THEMES

How did changes in agricultural practices transform social hierarchies in England?

Having lost access to the commons, many rural families could no longer sustain themselves. Those who could not find work serving the gentry drifted to cities or coal mines looking for employment. One person's "improvement," therefore, could be another's ticket to unemployment. Banks himself received numerous protests from displaced farmers, and his London house was once stormed by protesters of a trade law that benefited landholders like Banks while raising the price of bread for the urban poor. Hunger also resulted in rural areas when new laws barred the poor from hunting wild game, a traditional way to supplement their diets: "poaching" royal and aristocratic game became a hanging offense. Notwithstanding popular resistance to enclosure and hunting restrictions, the law was on the side of the upper class: the interests of "gentlemen" were well represented in Parliament and in the courts; those of the poor were not.

Joseph Banks was also an advocate for "improvement" on the imperial stage, playing a pivotal role in globalizing the practical application of science through his advocacy of "economic botany." To this end, he developed a pioneering experimental facility at Kew Gardens, *"a great botanical exchange house for the empire."** Scientists brought new plant specimens from around the world to Kew to be examined, catalogued, and cultivated, and the benefits of this "economic botany" could then be disseminated in Britain and its colonies.

Throughout the expanding British empire, in such places as the West Indies, South Africa, and India, British governors and commercial concerns established botanical gardens as part of the effort to achieve "improvement" on a global scale. Unlike the haphazard Columbian exchange, this was biological diffusion aided by science. For example, when the British Navy needed secure supplies of timber from tall trees for ship construction, English botanists identified South Asian mahogany as a possible supplement to British and North American oak and shipped seeds from India to botanical gardens in the British West Indies for study. Another famous example is the story of breadfruit, a nutritious plant food first encountered by Joseph Banks on the island of Tahiti. Banks saw the potential for transferring breadfruit from Polynesia to the West Indies as inexpensive food for slaves, and through his influence the Royal Navy sent the *Bounty* in 1787 to bring specimens to Kew Gardens. (The *Bounty* failed at its task when the crew mutinied against their captain; however, subsequent attempts to diffuse tropical crops like breadfruit across the British empire succeeded.)

The emphasis on science and "improvement" also served to justify the dominance of the British elite at home and abroad. Advocates of enclosure argued that those who were thrust aside would ultimately benefit from scientifically rational

---

*Quoted in Richard Drayton, *Nature's Government: Science, Imperial Britain, and the 'Improvement' of the World* (New Haven: Yale University Press, 2000), p. 108.

Botany and Art Most scientific expeditions, starting with Banks's own journey to the Pacific and Australia, employed artists to catalog in fine detail the new flora they encountered. This exquisite rendering of a Corypha Elata plant, native to northern Australia, was produced by an anonymous Indian artist employed by the British.

agriculture. The same attitude applied across the empire. Francis Bacon had earlier applied this idea to British colonization in Ireland: "*We shall reclaim them from their barbarous manners . . . populate, plant and make civil all the provinces of that kingdom.*"* If "barbarous" peoples like the Irish were not using the land efficiently, the argument went, it could be legally seized from them by those who would make it "civil."

Banks regarded Australia as "empty" land, because its aboriginal inhabitants had not "improved" it. Aboriginal Australians might not understand the necessity of fencing off vast land holdings for sheep—thus barring them from their ancestral hunting and gathering lands—but no one, the "improvers" would say, should stand in the way of progress.

The British would long justify their empire by claiming that it created the best possible life for the local inhabitants. Banks shared in that view. Economic botany, he once wrote, "*would help to banish famine in India and win the love of the Asiatics for their British conquerors.*"*

---

*Quoted in Richard Drayton, *Nature's Government: Science, Imperial Britain, and the 'Improvement' of the World* (New Haven: Yale University Press, 2000), pp. 55, 118.

Museums, Science, and Empire

The work of museums in the collection, analysis, classification, and preservation of natural and cultural phenomena can be traced back to the foundation of the British Museum in 1759. Today, museums must often contend with legacies of imperialism marking their collections, such as demands for repatriation of prized items.

From the sixteenth century, the inquisitive thrust of the new science had an acquisitive dimension as well. Gentlemen and aristocrats competed to assemble "cabinets of curiosities"—shelves full of interesting and exotic specimens—both for their own amusement and to provoke their visitors' envy and astonishment.

Then the eighteenth century brought a new seriousness of purpose, the rise of a more rigorous culture of evidence and classification. Sir Hans Sloane (1660–1753) pioneered this more focused approach. Sloane was a member of the Royal Society who traveled to Jamaica, collecting not only flora and fauna, but also cultural artifacts characteristic of its largely African population (see Chapter 19). As Sloane's acquisitions and reputation grew, others sent him samples from their own collections, forming the basis of the donation that would found the British Museum. Joseph Banks contributed ethnographic material from his Polynesian voyage.

Modern museums descended from this tradition are not, however, without their controversies. One is determining the proper ownership of artifacts. The British Museum's Elgin Marbles, for example, were taken from Athens by a British ambassador to the Ottoman empire two centuries ago and then sold to the British government. The government of Greece has long demanded their return, seeing the marbles as a cornerstone of their national culture. Similarly, some of the most exquisite examples of bronze statuary from the West African kingdom of Benin (see Chapter 16) are on display at the British Museum, having been looted during the British sack of the royal palace in 1897. Like the Greek government, the royal family of Benin has demanded the repatriation of their cultural patrimony.

Museums are an example of the longstanding entanglement of science and empire. While we all have a great deal to learn from visiting the world's great museums, we should keep in mind the question of how those objects arrived in their current settings and ask whether descendants of the original owners might still have a legitimate claim upon them.

Measuring and Mapping: Exploration and Imperialism in Africa, India, and the Americas, 1763–1820

In an age of expanding European empires, the scientific quest for classification and quantification had global implications. In the late eighteenth and early nineteenth centuries, increased sophistication in the measurement of time and the mapping of space firmly linked science and empire.

Europeans' acquisition of more detailed information on world geography was an essential step toward global control. As European expeditions gathered geographical information across the globe, proliferating scientific societies communicated that knowledge internationally. Expeditions also brought back cultural artifacts from around the world, stimulating interest in the scientific study of culture. (See the feature "World History in Today's World: Museums, Science, and Empire.")

Practical Science: The Royal Society and the Quest for Longitude

As a natural scientist, Banks was most competent in the field of living organisms and their interconnections. Within the Royal Society, over which he presided from 1778 to 1820, many saw mathematics and astronomy as the superior sciences. All scientists, however, were interested in practical applications of their theories. For a nation whose rising global power depended on its maritime prowess, the most important applications of mathematics and astronomy concerned navigation. The **problem of longitude**—how to determine a ship's position on an east-west axis—occupied some of the best minds of the time.

problem of longitude

The lack of an accurate way to determine a ship's position on an east-west axis. English cabinetmaker John Harrison's invention of an accurate shipboard chronometer solved the problem.

It was a riddle that had puzzled mariners for much of human history. The best way to describe the location of any given point is with a set of imaginary intersecting lines that we know as latitude and longitude. For centuries, mariners had been able to determine their latitude, or north-south position, using Arab technologies such as the quadrant and astrolabe (AS-truh-labe) and, later, the more accurate sextant. Longitude was another matter. East-west distance traveled could be measured only if the time at any two points could be accurately compared. Until the late eighteenth century, ships' captains had no better solution than using a log and a measured rope to roughly calculate the speed and distance traveled. By this system, captains often miscalculated their position by hundreds of miles, looking in vain for land they expected to find or crashing onto rocky shores they did not. A heavy toll resulted, in shipwrecks, destroyed cargo, and lost lives, whether from drowning or dehydration.

The regular, clocklike cosmos described by scientists from Galileo to Newton offered hope. Longitude could be accurately fixed if a captain knew exactly what time it was at his current position relative to any other fixed location on earth. Observing that the motion of the heavens could be described mathematically, European scientists set out to find a way to translate celestial time into local time on board a ship. But into the eighteenth century, they had not worked out a practical solution.

● **CONTEXT&CONNECTIONS** In the early fifteenth century, Zheng He, commander of Ming China's "precious ships," determined his latitude by using the compass and innovative "star boards" that gave extremely accurate determinations of the height of various celestial objects. But Zheng He did not have any better means of determining longitude than Christopher Columbus or other European mariners. The problem of longitude was probably less critical in this case, however, since the Chinese ships spent less time crossing open seas as they navigated the coasts of Southeast Asia, India, the Persian Gulf, and Africa (see Chapter 15). ●

To an ambitious maritime power like England, the "problem of longitude" was a matter of public policy. In 1714, the British Parliament offered a cash prize to anyone who could solve it, but for decades no proposals were worthy of serious consideration. In popular speech, "discovering the longitude" came to mean "attempting the impossible."

But the astronomers in the Royal Society were persistent. The key to the problem, Isaac Newton believed, was to determine the "lunar distance" by finding a way to accurately measure the position of the moon relative to the sun by day, and to the stars by night. Doing so would require sky charts by which the future locations of these heavenly bodies could be accurately predicted. Further complicating the problem, a separate star chart would be needed for the entirely different night sky of the Southern Hemisphere.

By the 1760s, having spent hundreds of thousands of hours working on these charts, the astronomers and mathematicians of the Royal Society believed they were close to a solution. The role of the *Endeavour*, which set out in 1769, was to observe the movement of Venus across the face of the sun, an event that occurred every eight years. By using identical observations made in a wide variety of geographic locations, of which Cook's was by far the farthest from the Royal Observatory at Greenwich, astronomers would be able to predict much more accurately the future path of Venus. The solar, lunar, and stellar charts available to Cook on this journey were already much better than any other captain had ever used in the Pacific.

Meanwhile, another, potentially simpler solution would be to use a clock that accurately showed the current time at the point of departure. A captain could use stellar readings to easily calculate the time at his present location and compare that with the time at his starting point, as kept by the timepiece. Eighteenth-century clocks, however, were not accurate enough. Relying on a shipboard clock that was gaining or losing fifteen seconds a day could send a ship hundreds of miles off course.

English carpenter and clockmaker John Harrison took on the challenge of perfecting a timepiece that would be reliable enough to maintain its accuracy at sea despite the constant motion from the waves, excessive humidity, and changes in temperature. Harrison began work on his first "chronometer," as these timepieces came to be known, in 1727. It became his life's work: the last of his four versions was not finished until 1763, when he completed a compact chronometer that was accurate in oceanic conditions within one second per day.

Harrison's challenges were not only technical. Many astronomers in the Royal Society were highly status conscious and looked down on a mere "cabinetmaker" like Harrison, and they were unwilling to give his prototypes the kind of trials that might lead to the prize. They believed that only mathematics could provide a solution.

As it turned out, both Harrison and the astronomers were on the right track. On Cook's first voyage, he used the latest astronomical charts with great success. On his second voyage, Cook also took a chronometer and was very impressed, reporting that *"it exceeded the expectations of its most zealous advocate and . . . has been our faithful guide through all vicissitudes of climate."** By the early nineteenth century, Harrison's chronometer was standard equipment on British naval vessels.

Mariners needed a fixed point from which the 360 degrees of longitude could be established. That "prime meridian" was set at Greenwich, the site of the Royal Observatory. Even the French, who first used Paris as the zero point, eventually accepted the British standard. Greenwich had become the "center of the world," the starting point for global lines of longitude and the reference point for the world's clocks. (Today, Universal Coordinated Time [UTC] still derives from "Greenwich Mean Time.")

Just up the Thames River from Greenwich, meanwhile, Joseph Banks had developed Kew Gardens as the world's leading center of botany. In both astronomy and botany, therefore, "practical science," the ability to apply the scientific outlook to real-world applications, propelled the rising power of Britain, and of Europe, across the globe.

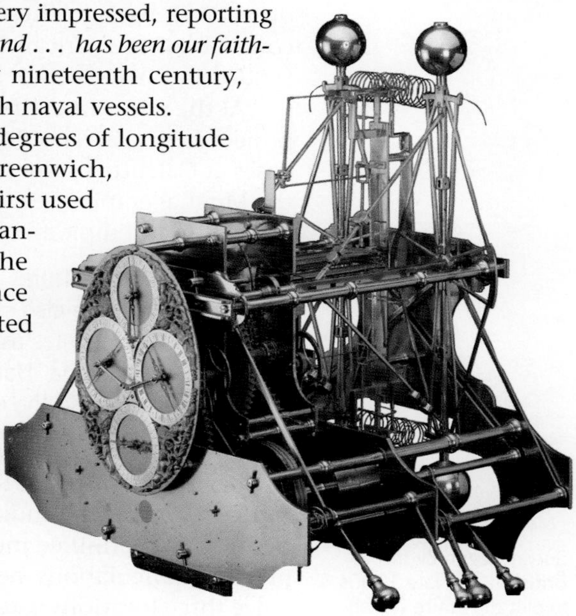

Harrison's Chronometer John Harrison solved the "problem of longitude," greatly increasing the safety and efficiency of oceanic navigation, when he perfected his chronometer in 1763. An elegant piece of craftsmanship, Harrison's chronometer was a sophisticated and durable timepiece that kept accurate time even on rough seas and in high humidity, exemplifying the British tradition of "practical science." (National Maritime Museum, London/The Image Works)

*Quoted in Dava Sorbel and William J. H. Andrews, *The Illustrated Longitude: The True Story of a Lone Genius Who Solved the Greatest Scientific Problem of His Time* (New York: Walker and Co., 1998), p. 176.

Mapping Africa, Central Asia, India, and the Americas

African Association
Society founded in 1788 by Joseph Banks to sponsor geographical expeditions into Africa and chart the course of the Niger River, a feat partially achieved by Mungo Park.

Under the leadership of Joseph Banks, geographic exploration became a priority for the Royal Society, part of a larger European effort to map the world. As part of that focus, Banks and the Royal Society founded and funded the **African Association**, primarily in response to French competition. Until this time, Europeans in Africa had restricted themselves to small coastal settlements connected with the Atlantic slave trade (see Chapter 19). But the French seemed positioned to expand inland from their long-established outpost at the mouth of the Senegal River, a gateway to the rich and populous lands of the predominantly Muslim Sahel.

The founders of the African Association guessed that the key to the West African interior was the Niger River. The Niger was indeed the region's major thoroughfare, but they knew little of its origins and path. Exploring the course of the Niger would add to geographic, botanical, and ethnographic knowledge and might also promote British imperial expansion. Recruiting a young Scottish doctor named Mungo Park, whom Banks had earlier recommended as surgeon on a ship bound for Southeast Asia, the African Association sponsored a voyage of exploration to West Africa in 1795.

Park's voyage was difficult. The West African interior had been destabilized by the Atlantic slave trade, and his mission depended on the hospitality of Africans he met en route. He made it safely to Segu on the upper reaches of the Niger, an important political and economic center ever since the empire of Songhai (see Chapter 16). There his African hosts gave him an accurate picture of how people and goods moved along the river and into the wider Islamic world through North Africa and Egypt, while confirming that the Niger flowed west to east. But illness drove Park back to the coast before he could complete his mission; the precise contours of the African interior would remain obscure to European geographers for decades (see Chapter 26).

At the same time, the British were pursuing an even more elaborate geographic project in India. The British East India Company ruled rich territories from its bases at Calcutta in the northeast and Madras in the south as it began to supplant the Mughal empire (see Chapter 20). British rule in India was established not only with guns and diplomacy, but also with maps.

• **CONTEXT&CONNECTIONS** In the eighteenth century, officials in *Qing dynasty* China (Chapter 20) were also systematically compiling maps and ethnographic information about subject peoples as their empire expanded to include not only China but also parts of Central Asia. But Qing maps dealt only with a single empire, while European maps encompassed the entire globe, as Western explorers from various nations contributed to a single, expanding network of knowledge. •

Great Trigonometrical Survey
Survey begun by the British in the late 1790s to plot the entire Indian subcontinent on a mathematically precise grid. The survey was a prelude to the expansion of Britain's Indian empire.

Beginning in the 1790s, the British undertook the **Great Trigonometrical Survey** to map the Indian subcontinent in a mathematical grid. From an astronomically determined meridian of longitude in the south of India, surveyors made precise triangulations between two other points and the first known location. Once three locations could be precisely defined in terms of longitude and latitude, the survey could proceed with further triangular measurements. Eventually the Great Trigonometrical Survey drove straight through India to the Himalayas. The highest mountain peak in the world, called Chomolungma, "Mother of the Universe," by the Tibetans, was renamed by the British "Mount Everest" after George Everest, the British surveyor-general. Such renaming occurred all over the world.

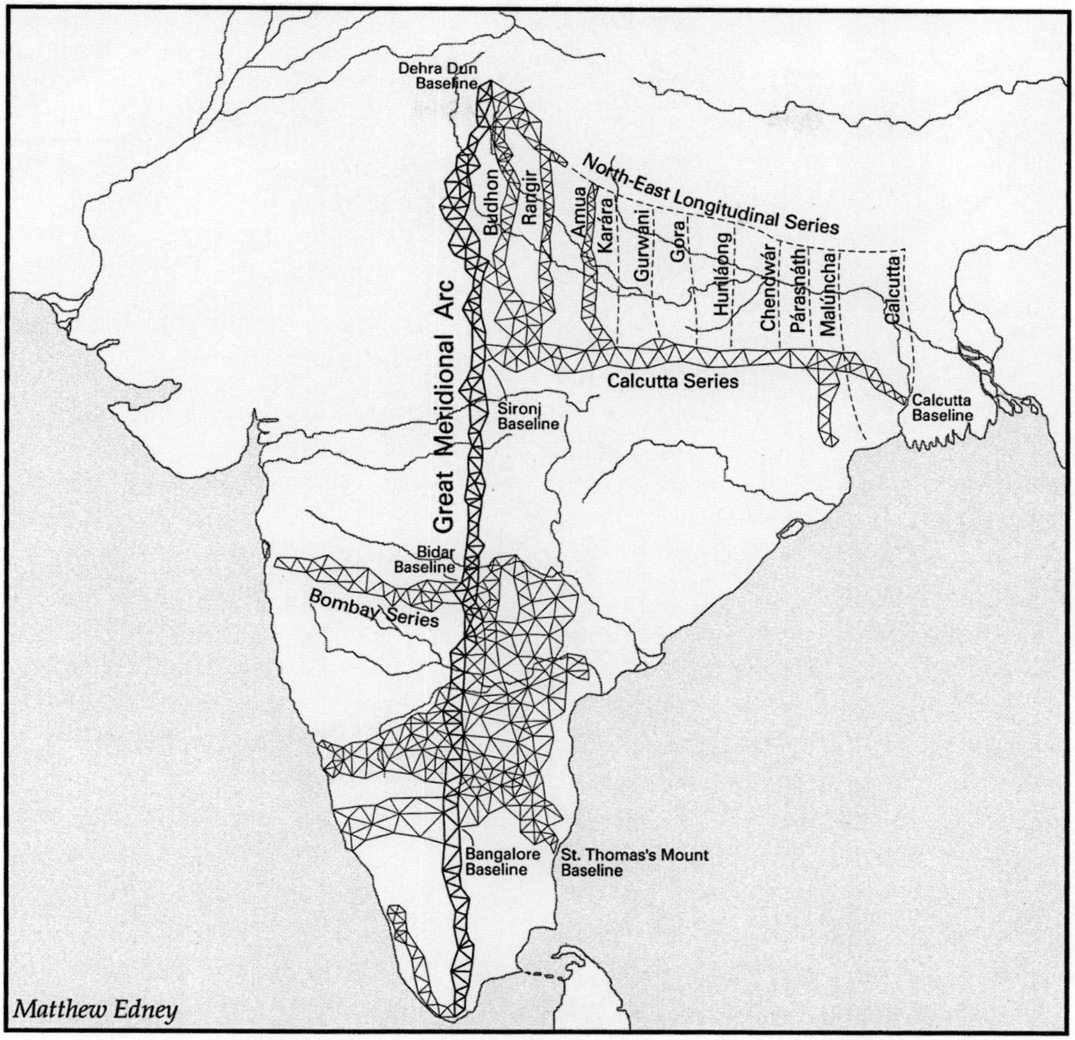

Matthew H. Edney, *Mapping an Empire*, University of Chicago Press, 1997, p. 20

The Great Trigonometrical Survey Beginning in southern India in the 1790s, British surveyors undertook a painstaking mapping project using a triangulation technique to map vast territories. By 1843, the survey had reached the Himalayas. Accurate maps were a key source of British imperial power.

The purposes of the Great Trigonometrical Survey were in keeping with Newtonian principles of rationality, harmony, and order. Previously, Europeans had seen the Mughal empire as an exotic and mystical land. The survey transformed the strange and unknowable "Hindustan" of earlier maps into a precisely ordered "India," a coherent world region. The process of mapping expressed imperial control, even over areas that had not yet been conquered. The Great Trigonometrical Survey created the skeletal structure onto which the bones, muscle, and skin of British India would be grafted.

AP® THEMES

How were networks of exchange affected by technological developments?

Similar surveys were also being conducted elsewhere, including the Americas. Captain Cook's Pacific journeys helped determine the size of North America

Map 21.1 The Exploration of Western North America While Captain George Vancouver followed James Cook's Pacific expeditions and traced the Pacific coastline of North America, in the 1790s Alexander Mackenzie traced routes into the frigid interior. A decade later, Meriwether Lewis and William Clark investigated a route from St. Louis to the Oregon coast, while David Thompson traced the course of the Columbia River. U.S. Army captain Zebulon Pike led expeditions up the Mississippi River and explored the southern and western regions of the Louisiana Purchase, turning south from the Colorado Mountains into New Spain. Geographic exploration went hand in hand with expanding state frontiers across North America, as in the wider world.

(see map on page 619); then in the 1790s Captain George Vancouver and his crew charted its western coasts as far north as Alaska. At the same time, the explorer Alexander Mackenzie traveled a difficult passage from the Arctic Ocean, through what is now northern Canada, to the Pacific coast, relying on the latest technology from London (a sophisticated compass, sextant, chronometer, and telescope) as well as the knowledge of indigenous guides (see Map 21.1).

The new United States (see Chapter 22) became involved in western exploration with the **Lewis and Clark Expedition** from the Mississippi River to the Pacific coast (1804–1806), an effort, as in India, to bring what the British and Americans considered "exotic" lands into "rationality." One of President Thomas Jefferson's motivations in sponsoring the expedition was to assess the potential for an American outlet to the Pacific Ocean to facilitate trade with Asia, but the reports also made clear the huge size and vast economic potential of the American interior itself.

Lewis and Clark Expedition
(1804–1806) Government-sponsored team led by Meriwether Lewis and William Clark to explore a route through Native American territory to the Pacific. The expedition also documented plants and animals.

Like Banks and his protégés, Meriwether Lewis and William Clark carefully noted the flora and fauna on their journey, bringing the natural world of the American West into the orbit of scientific knowledge. Also like Banks, they noted the customs of indigenous peoples, speculating on their possible origins and the linguistic and cultural relationships between them. They carried surveying equipment, creating maps that settlers would later use to help them occupy the land. In the subsequent transformation of indigenous landscapes into the American West, we see another example of the intimate relationship between science and empire.

In every case, whether it was a new plant species, the height of a mountain, or the location of a harbor, Europeans added any new fact to a central bank of data, where it could be related to a centralized system of classification organized along hierarchical and mathematical lines. Control of such knowledge would radically increase the global power of Europe in the nineteenth century.

Oceania and Australia, 1770–1820

The three journeys of Captain James Cook consolidated the role of science in advancing the expansion of the British empire. Extending the reach of his first expedition, accompanied by Joseph Banks aboard the *Endeavour*, on his second and third journeys, Cook sailed near the coast of Antarctica and north to the Arctic Ocean; he also added the Hawai'ian Islands to Europe's map of the Pacific. Joseph Banks did not accompany Cook's later journeys. But from England he played a major role in the settlement of Australia, a British colony on a continent that had been virtually unknown to Europeans before Cook's voyage.

Captain Cook in Polynesia, 1769–1779

On the first voyage, Cook and Banks were aided by a Tahitian high priest named **Tupaia** (ca. 1725–1770). Tupaia (too-PUH-ee-uh) knew several Polynesian languages and, coming from a family of navigators, was able to supplement Cook's instruments and charts with a local understanding of winds and currents. He also helped Banks understand Polynesian cultural practices, such as the meaning of the peace ritual that had so mystified the Englishman when he first set foot on the island.

Tupaia
(ca. 1725–1770) A Polynesian high priest who contributed his expert navigational skills to Captain James Cook's first Pacific voyage.

In spite of Tupaia's help, miscommunications persisted. In his journals, Banks noted with frustration *"how much these people are given to thieving." "All are of the opinion,"* he writes, *"that if they can once get possession of anything it immediately becomes their own."** It was usually small items that went missing, but when some of their important astronomical devices disappeared, Cook was worried. Banks, with his developing knowledge of Tahitian laws and customs, was able to get the equipment back.

Theft among the British was a problem as well. Sailors kept stealing nails from the ship to trade with the islanders, for whom iron was new and valuable. However, one day when a Tahitian woman refused to sell her stone axe for an iron nail, a sailor took it anyway, and Cook decided to make an example of him. He ordered a flogging for the man and invited some Tahitian chiefs to witness the punishment. Banks describes the scene:

> *[The chiefs] stood quietly and saw him stripped and fastened to the rigging, but as soon as the first blow was given they interfered with many tears, begging the punishment might cease, a request which the Captain would not comply with.**

The Tahitians' views of property and punishment were quite different from those of the English; they were much less focused on exclusive ownership of material goods and would never use corporal punishment in a simple case of theft. Unlike Banks, who made a genuine attempt to understand the people of the island and to mediate such disputes, Cook had a strictly utilitarian attitude: he wanted to make his astronomical and navigational observations, get fresh supplies of food and water, and move on.

When Cook and his men had first arrived, they received a joyous and generous reception. Nevertheless, there were tensions. His men were exhausted from a futile trip to the Arctic in search of a "northwest passage" linking Asia and Europe, and they resented Cook's attempts to stop them from their usual practice of trading iron nails for sex. Cook was trying to protect the Hawai'ians from the venereal diseases rampant on his ship. Still, the Hawai'ians treated Cook, in particular, with great respect.

Cook departed on good terms with the islanders, but then had to return after a storm damaged his ship's mast. The mood was now much darker, and tension greeted the British as soon as they stepped ashore. Before long an argument escalated into violence, and an islander stabbed Cook to death. (See the feature "Visual Evidence in Primary Sources: The Death of Captain Cook.")

Notwithstanding the power of predictability afforded by modern science, the death of Captain Cook shows the limitations of reason in governing human interactions. No chronometers, astronomical sightings, surveys, or charts could help safely navigate the waters of cross-cultural communication.

Polynesians suffered and died in great numbers in the coming decades, killed by Afro-European diseases for which they had no immunity. Tupaia, who had aided Cook with navigation and Banks with language and culture, died of dysentery within two years of his first encounter with them. Meanwhile,

---

*Quoted in Patrick O'Brien, *Joseph Banks: A Life* (Chicago: University of Chicago Press, 1987), pp. 94, 95.

changing economies, new technologies, and imported Christianity undermined the existing order of island societies drawn into the European-dominated global system.

• **CONTEXT&CONNECTIONS** Hawai'ian history shows the increasing potency of nineteenth century imperialism. The eight main islands of Hawai'i were united in 1818 under King Kamehameha the Great, and his successors struggled to maintain their independence. After the abolition of slavery in the British empire led to a drop in Caribbean production (see Chapter 19), Hawai'ian lands were bought up by foreigners and planted with sugar cane. In the 1890s, American sugar planters spearheaded the removal of the Hawai'ian royal family from power and annexation of the islands by the United States (see Chapter 25). •

Joseph Banks and the Settlement of Australia

The impact of Joseph Banks on the history of Australia is inscribed on one of its most famous geographic features, Botany Bay, where Banks undertook an intensive reconnaissance of eastern Australia's unique plant life. He is sometimes called "the Father of Australia" for the role he played in the foundation of the colony of New South Wales in 1788 with its capital at Sydney.

New South Wales began as a penal colony, its overwhelmingly male population consisting of prisoners, many of them Irish, who had little to lose from taking a chance on resettlement halfway around the world. The colony got off to a rocky start. Few of the convicts knew how to survive in this foreign terrain. Nor could they rely on help from the aboriginal population, which initially kept its distance and then launched a series of attacks.

> **AP® THEMES**
> What was the role of the imported sheep in the migration and settlement of the British colonies in Australia?

The colonial economy of New South Wales strengthened with the introduction of merino sheep in 1805, descendants of the same sheep that Joseph Banks had imported from Spain to Kew Gardens. The grasslands of New South Wales proved to be ideal grazing grounds, and wool exports financed the development of colonial society. By the early nineteenth century, most settlers were free immigrants rather than convicts, the cities of Sydney and Melbourne were on paths to prosperity, and new British colonies were founded across the continent. After 1817, the name *Australia* was used to refer to this collection of colonies.

Joseph Banks regarded those developments as "improvement," another successful outcome of the application of practical science. But British settlement had a devastating impact on the original inhabitants of the continent. Aboriginal Australians had rich and complex religious and artistic traditions, as well as keen knowledge of the local environment from which, as hunter-gatherers, they derived all the necessities of life. But they had no metal tools, no hierarchical political organization, and like the Polynesians, no immunity to Afro-Eurasian diseases like smallpox. As in the Americas in previous centuries, the Aborigines experienced the European territorial advance as a plague: more than half died in the nineteenth century. The survivors fled to remote deserts and mountains, worked for Europeans on their commercial ranches, or moved to cities, a disenfranchised subclass. However, the perspectives of those displaced by "progress" (whether Australian aborigines, English peasants, or Tahitian mariners) were of little interest to Joseph Banks and others who benefited from the application of science to the extension of empire.

The Death of Captain Cook

James Cook had been sent off in royal fashion when his ships departed the Hawai'ian islands in the summer of 1779. When they returned to mend a broken mast, however, the Hawai'ians seemed disappointed and confused at their return. Tensions ran high, especially after a high chief was flogged for stealing a pair of iron tongs. Cook's crew noticed that some men were piling stones on the beach, as if getting ready for an attack. Cook invited one of the chiefs with whom he had been

The Death of Cook, 1779, Webber, John (1750–93)/© Dixson Galleries, State Library of New South Wales/The Bridgeman Art Library

The anger of the Hawai'ians that led to this incident, Obeyesekere argues, came from Cook's unwillingness to help them in their war with Maui and his increasingly belligerent demands for food and supplies.

Obeyesekere notes that as soon as news of Cook's death reached England, his status as a Hawai'ian god became a subject of music, art, and theater. Cook's godlike status, he argues, came about not from Hawai'ian beliefs but from European myths of "conquest, imperialism, and civilization."*

---

*Gananath Obeyesekere, *The Apotheosis of Captain Cook: European Mythmaking in the Pacific* (Princeton: Princeton University Press, 1997), p. 3.

friends to come aboard his ship, but the *kahuna* (kah-HOO-nuh) was prevented by his own people from doing so. A warrior then threatened Cook with an iron dagger. Cook shot at him, and a melee broke out. On that morning, July 14, 1779, on a beach at Kealakekua Bay, Captain James Cook was stabbed to death. That fact is certain. But the cause and context of Cook's death are controversial. The engraving reproduced here, made by John Webber, the officially appointed artist of the expedition, provides some evidence but does not resolve scholarly differences in the interpretation of Cook's death.

Anthropologist Marshall Sahlins argues that Cook had first arrived during the Makahiki (ma-kah-HEE-kee) festival dedicated to the fertility god Lono. His appearance at that precise time, and his landing near the god's main temple, caused the Hawai'ians to identify him with Lono. When Cook later returned to repair a broken mast, however, the Makahiki cycle had ended. Now it was time for Lono to be symbolically defeated, Sahlins explains, and replaced by the war god Ku. In conformity with the ritual cycle, Lono-Cook was killed.

Nonsense, says Gananath Obeyesekere, who maintains that Sahlins is guilty of typical European arrogance in saying that the Hawai'ians saw Cook as a god. In fact, Obeyesekere argues, the Hawai'ians were guided by "practical rationality," a universal common sense that would make it impossible for them to mistake a man for a god. Sahlins responds that he is the one interpreting events from within the logic of traditional Hawai'ian beliefs, while it is actually Obeyesekere who is imposing foreign beliefs on the Hawai'ians by ignoring their own cosmology and value structures. In Hawai'ian belief, he notes, there was a strong equation between status as a powerful chief and affiliation with a god like Lono.

There is no clear conclusion to this debate, as Sahlins and Obeyesekere offer differing interpretations of this image.

Area of detail

Sahlins claims that he can identify the actual killer of Cook in this image: Nuha, a powerful warrior who was "an ideal champion for the aging king in the ritualistic murder of Lono-Cook."*

Accepting the overall accuracy of this image, Sahlins even claims to be able to identify the murder weapon: "an iron spike manufactured at [a] factory in Birmingham, requisitioned by Cook 'to be distributed to them as presents toward obtaining their friendship.'"† ***Though John Webber was at the scene, he could not possibly have had the perspective on events that is shown in this drawing. Does the change in perspective from what he actually saw to how he represented the event diminish the reliability of the image as a historical source?***

*Dan Lynch, "Gananath Obyesekere v. Marshall Sahlins: Did Hawaiians Consider Captain Cook as a God?" Unpublished paper, California State University Long Beach, 2006.

†Marshall Sahlins, *Islands of History* (Chicago: University of Chicago Press, 1985), p. 131.

The European Enlightenment, 1700–1800

Enlightenment
European philosophical movement of the late seventeenth and eighteenth centuries that stressed the use of reason, rather than the authority of ancient philosophers or religious leaders, in descriptions of society and the natural world.

The optimism characteristic of the new science also influenced European views on society. During the eighteenth century, **Enlightenment** thinkers argued that just as the inner workings of nature could be understood by human reason, so reason offered the means to understand and improve society. By the late eighteenth century, progress in human affairs seemed to some not only possible, but inevitable. Many thought that the lofty ideals of the Enlightenment would be realized through the efforts of those at the top of society. The new philosophical emphasis on reason did indeed impress Europe's kings, queens, and aristocracies. But there were limits to how far "enlightened" rulers would follow through on reform; few were willing to risk the traditions that gave them authority.

"Enlightened" Ideas: Politics, Economics, and Society

The contrast between two English political philosophers of different generations, Thomas Hobbes (1588–1679) and John Locke (1632–1704), shows the growing optimism of the Enlightenment. A friend of René Descartes, Hobbes applied deductive reasoning to the question of how best to sustain political order in society. In the state of nature, he pessimistically argued, anarchy prevails, and life is *"nasty, brutish, and short."** Social and political order become possible, Hobbes argued, only when individuals relinquish their autonomy to a despotic ruler. However, Hobbes rejected the traditional "divine right of kings," the idea that God bestowed royal authority, and instead based his advocacy for absolute monarchy on reasoned arguments.

John Locke
(1632–1704) Philosopher who applied Bacon's inductive reasoning to the study of politics and argued that a stable social order is based on a contract between rulers and ruled and requires the safeguarding of "life, liberty and property."

The younger and more optimistic philosopher **John Locke** (1632–1704), a medical doctor who preferred Bacon's inductive approach, starting with experience and observation, argued in his *Essay Concerning Human Understanding* (1690) that political order derives from a contract in which individuals receive protection of basic rights, *"life, liberty and property,"* while voluntarily giving up some of their autonomy to the state. This was a contract that balanced the needs of public authority with the rights of individual subjects. What Locke described was not a democracy: in his view only propertied males were capable of participating in government. Still, everyone's basic rights would be protected.

Differences in personal experience may have helped shape the differing worldviews of these two philosophers. Hobbes had lived through the English Civil War, witnessing the anarchy and bloodshed that followed the execution of the king (see Chapter 17). Locke, on the other hand, grew up amid the peace, prosperity, and cultural achievements of the later seventeenth century, and played an important role as an adviser to King William and Queen Mary following the Glorious Revolution. The balance between the powers of king and Parliament, and the protection of individual liberties through a Bill of Rights, were real-world applications of Locke's more expansive and optimistic theories.

English constitutional thought influenced the French thinker Montesquieu (1689–1755), who traveled to England to observe its very different constitutional system. His book *The Spirit of the Laws* (1748) argues for limitations on the power of government and a rational distribution of power between social classes. Montesquieu (maw-tuh-SKYOO) believed that as societies became more advanced, their political

*Thomas Hobbes, *The Leviathan*, 1651.

systems would become more liberal and their people more free. John Locke had advocated separate and balanced executive and legislative powers; now Montesquieu added that judicial functions should also be protected from executive interference.

The most original economic thinker of the Enlightenment was Adam Smith. His *Wealth of Nations* (1776) emphasized the self-regulating power of markets, arguing for unfettered economic interchange within and between nations. The French term ***laissez faire*** (lay-say FAIR; "leave it alone") has often been applied to Smith's vision of free-market capitalism unhindered by excessive regulation.

laissez faire
(French, "leave it alone") Economic philosophy attributed to Scottish Enlightenment thinker Adam Smith, who argued that businesses and nations benefit from a free market where each party seeks to maximize its comparative economic advantage.

Smith argued that economic productivity increased with a more complex division of labor. For example, an individual performing all the processes necessary to make a pin would be hard pressed to produce a single one in a day. But thousands could be produced if the work process were subdivided, each worker specializing in one part of the process.

Smith applied his concept of division of labor to international trade as well. If each nation specializes in the production of what it is best fit to produce, and trades with other nations specializing in products best fitted to their economic potential, everyone gains. For Smith, the "*invisible hand*" of the market functioned like Isaac Newton's laws of gravitational attraction, maintaining balance and harmony in economic affairs. Like Locke, he believed that protection of private property was a core function of government. Smith was also opposed to slavery because he thought that labor contracts negotiated in a free market lead to more efficient production than coerced labor obtained through force.

Like other Enlightenment thinkers, Smith was using reason to challenge received assumptions, as when his argument for competition in free markets contradicted existing economic policies based on monopoly and mercantilism (see Chapter 19). Whereas the trade restrictions of mercantilism were based on a zero-sum view of economics, in which one nation could advance only at another's expense, Smith believed that freer international trade would lead to more wealth for all. Like John Locke, Adam Smith had an optimistic view of human potential.

While philosophers across Europe aspired to the title "enlightened," it was through Paris that the intellectual currents of the Western world flowed. Indeed, we still use the French word for philosophers—***philosophes*** (fill-uh-SOHF)—to describe these intellectuals today. The most important of them was **Voltaire** (1694–1778). Voltaire (vawl-TARE) was most famous as a satirist who used his reason like a searchlight to illuminate all the superstitions, prejudices, and follies of eighteenth-century European society. In his great novel *Candide* (1759), Voltaire mocked the corruption and injustice of the world around him. He believed that reason makes all phenomena and situations intelligible to the human intellect. He also thought that relativism, the ability to see yourself and your own social circumstances in a wider context, is a necessary component of enlightened thinking, since tolerance toward and understanding of others is a precondition for self-knowledge. Voltaire incurred the displeasure of religious authorities by arguing that organized religion is always and everywhere a hindrance to free and rational inquiry.

philosophes
French intellectuals who promoted Enlightenment principles.

Voltaire
(1694–1778) The pen name of François-Marie Arouet, one of the most prominent Enlightenment writers, who used satire to critique the irrationality of French society.

French women of means and education frequently hosted events in their *salons* (drawing rooms) at which elegantly dressed Parisians passionately debated the latest Enlightenment contributions to science, philosophy, and art. Voltaire and other notable thinkers were highly sought-after guests. But even as women organized and participated in these gatherings, few Enlightenment thinkers were

RMN-Grand Palais/Art Resource, NY

A Parisian Salon Mid-eighteenth-century Paris was the center of European intellectual life. Salons were gatherings at private homes that combined entertainment with intellectual edification, including poetry readings and discussion of the latest Enlightenment philosophies. Wealthy women often hosted these lively events, competing to attract prestigious guests and distinguished authors.

willing to recognize that restrictions on the role of women in society did not reflect reason, but were merely a traditional prejudice.

Some women protested their exclusion. At the same time that Sor Juana's writings were meeting resistance from church authorities in New Spain (see Chapter 18), a seventeenth-century English scientist, Margaret Cavendish, noted that restrictions on women's roles resulted from nothing more than *"the over-weening conceit men have of themselves."** Another Englishwoman, Mary Astell, challenged John Locke's idea that absolute authority, while unacceptable in the state, was appropriate within the family. Late in the eighteenth century, **Mary Wollstonecraft** went even further in her *Vindication of the Rights of Women* (1792), asking: *"How many women waste life away . . . who might have*

Mary Wollstonecraft (1759–1797) An English author and reformer who advocated equality of rights for women.

*Quoted in Moira Ferguson, ed., *First Feminists: British Women Writers, 1578–1799* (Bloomington: Indiana University Press, 1985), p. 86.

*practiced as physicians, regulated a farm, managed a shop, and stood erect, supported by their own industry?"** Equal access to education, full citizenship, and financial autonomy, Wollstonecraft said, would be necessary before women's full potential as individuals and as wives and mothers could be achieved.

Of all the French social classes, such daring Enlightenment ideas had the greatest impact on the bourgeoisie, or middle class. For the elite who attended salons, philosophical arguments were more a matter of fashion than of passion: members of the aristocracy had plenty of time for discussion, but little incentive to actually change social rules from which they benefited so extravagantly. On the other side of the social divide, Enlightenment ideas were of little concern to tradesmen and farmers, people who Voltaire and most other philosophes considered irrational and tradition-bound.

The French bourgeoisie, on the other hand, though economically successful, lacked the social status and political weight of aristocrats. Skepticism toward authority thus came naturally to them. Expanding literacy meant that even those who did not travel in refined circles, and who might never be invited to a salon, nevertheless had access to Enlightenment ideas.

● **CONTEXT&CONNECTIONS** In the nineteenth century, the German socialist thinker *Karl Marx* (Chapter 23) would place a strong emphasis on the historical role of the *bourgeoisie* (Chapter 16). At first they played a progressive role, he argued. Their fight against the aristocracy and its vestiges of feudal privilege were an important step toward the liberation of humankind. After the French Revolution, however (see Chapter 22), it was the bourgeoisie itself that stood in the way of further social and political progress, Marx argued, and the industrial working class created by the factory system would rise to overthrow them: bourgeois capitalism would then be replaced by a more advanced socialist system. ●

The most important publishing project of the Enlightenment was the **Encyclopedia**, or *Rational Dictionary of the Arts, Sciences and Crafts*, compiled in Paris between 1751 and 1776. More than any other work, this encyclopedia made the case for a new form of universal knowledge based on reason and critical thinking. The growth in printing and publishing facilitated the dissemination of the *Encyclopedia*, and translation into English, Spanish, and German gave it international impact.

Encyclopedia
(1751–1776) A collection of the works of all the great Enlightenment thinkers that promoted a new form of universal knowledge based on reason and the critical use of human intellect.

According to the German philosopher Immanuel Kant, it was simple cowardice that stood in the way of personal and social enlightenment. It is unquestioned tradition and blind faith, *"man's inability to make use of his understanding without direction from another,"* that hinder our progress. *"Have courage to use your own reason,"* Kant concluded; *"that is the motto of enlightenment."*† But translating that motto into political reality meant confronting powerful vested interests, with radical, and ultimately revolutionary, implications.

Most eighteenth-century philosophes thought that if society were to become enlightened, the change would have to come from above. The mass of ill-educated and uncultured humanity, they thought, could never be expected to follow the path of reason.

---

*Mary Wollstonecraft, *A Vindication of the Rights of Women* (Boston: Peter Edes, 1792; New York: Bartleby.com, 1999), chapter 9.

†Immanuel Kant, *What Is Enlightenment?* ed. and trans. Lewis White Beck (Indianapolis: Bobs-Merrill, 1959), p. 85.

Enlightenment and Reform

enlightened despots Eighteenth-century European rulers who sought to systematically apply Enlightenment ideals to the administration of government.

The idea that men of reason could reform society from above provided some eighteenth-century monarchs, so-called "**enlightened despots**," with a new rationale for absolute power. Rather than simply claiming their traditional "divine right" to rule, they could portray themselves as bringing order, harmony, and reason to their domains. Earlier, Louis XIV of France is supposed to have said, *"I am the state."* Now, the Prussian ruler Frederick the Great (r. 1740–1786) defined himself as *"first servant of the state."* Frederick implied that the kingdom was greater than the king, who needed to demonstrate his competence in action.

Frederick was perhaps the most "enlightened" of the great monarchs of the eighteenth century. As a young man he studied music and literature and became a first-rate flute player. Under his patronage Berlin, previously known mainly for its military exploits, became a center for the arts, and the Prussian Academy of Sciences developed as a major seat of learning. Like Joseph Banks, Frederick paid close attention to practical applications of science, draining marshlands to extend Prussian agriculture and encouraging the planting of new crops, especially potatoes, to improve local diets.

AP® THEMES

How did the Enlightenment influence existing functions and institutions of government?

Frederick absorbed French literature and the ideas of the philosophes. After meeting in 1750, he and Voltaire maintained a correspondence, trading philosophical ideas. Frederick reformed the Prussian legal system to emphasize reason and justice over tradition, advocated freedom of conscience, and allowed some freedom of the press. However, Prussia's firm military ethic still made it a tightly regimented society, its territory doubling in size as Frederick's army became one of the strongest in Europe.

Enlightenment thinking also influenced two powerful women rulers, Empress Maria Theresa of Austria and Catherine the Great of Russia. Maria Theresa (r. 1740–1780) put strict limits on landlords' power and was also the first European monarch to call for compulsory public education, moving Austria in the direction of what she called a *"God pleasing equality."* Maria Theresa's successors later carried her reforms forward, abolishing serfdom and liberalizing restrictions on the press and religion across the Habsburg lands.

● **CONTEXT&CONNECTIONS** The great Tokugawa shogun *Yoshimune* (Chapter 20), whose reign overlapped that of Empress Maria Theresa of Austria, was also an active agricultural reformer. He took a characteristically conservative course, however, in issuing repeated edicts reminding the Japanese to follow Confucian precepts and keep to their place in society. While the Japanese lords (the *daimyo*) retained tight control over their retainers, in eighteenth-century Austria (as in England) such feudal legacies as the requirement that peasants provide free labor for their lords were fading. ●

In Russia, Catherine the Great also took a lively interest in Enlightenment philosophy, and like Frederick the Great, she avidly corresponded with Voltaire. For Catherine, however, Enlightenment ideals, while enticing in theory, proved inapplicable to Russia. Under her rule, the monarchy and the Russian aristocracy became more authoritarian than ever as the conditions faced by Russia's multitude of serfs grew even more miserable. The Russian middle class, meanwhile, was too weak and dependent on the monarchy to effectively lobby for more liberal Enlightenment reforms (see Chapter 20).

In England, the balance struck between the monarchs and Parliament in 1689 forestalled any thought of despotism there, "enlightened" or otherwise (see

Chapter 17). Throughout, this period, the English constitution continued to evolve, albeit slowly and without any master plan. The Scottish and English thrones were peacefully united to form Great Britain in 1707, and over the next few decades parliamentary factions developed into organized political parties that alternated in forming governments. In 1714, a reliably Protestant German prince, crowned King George I, accepted the powers of Parliament and hence the limitations on his own authority. True, restrictions on the civil rights of British Catholics remained, and attempts to reform the House of Commons to increase the representation of merchants and professionals initially failed. Nevertheless, as the century progressed, the British parliamentary system managed social and political change without revolutionary strife.

Elsewhere in Europe, however, the eventual failure of "enlightened despots" to substantially reform their societies would lead to revolution. Ironically, as we will see in the next two chapters, the struggle to implement lofty Enlightenment ideals of reason and harmony would unleash conflicts of deep passion and dark violence.

CONTEXT AND CONNECTIONS

Science, Technology, and Revolution in World History

Initially, Europe's scientific revolution had only limited global effects. While many Asian and African producers and consumers felt the impact of Europe's involvement in the expanding early modern economy of the sixteenth and seventeenth centuries, they largely retained their own cultural and intellectual traditions. True, "Dutch learning" had entered Japan, European cartography had influenced the Qing empire (see Chapter 20), and some Iranian and Chinese artists had borrowed Western artistic techniques. However, in most of Asia and Africa (unlike

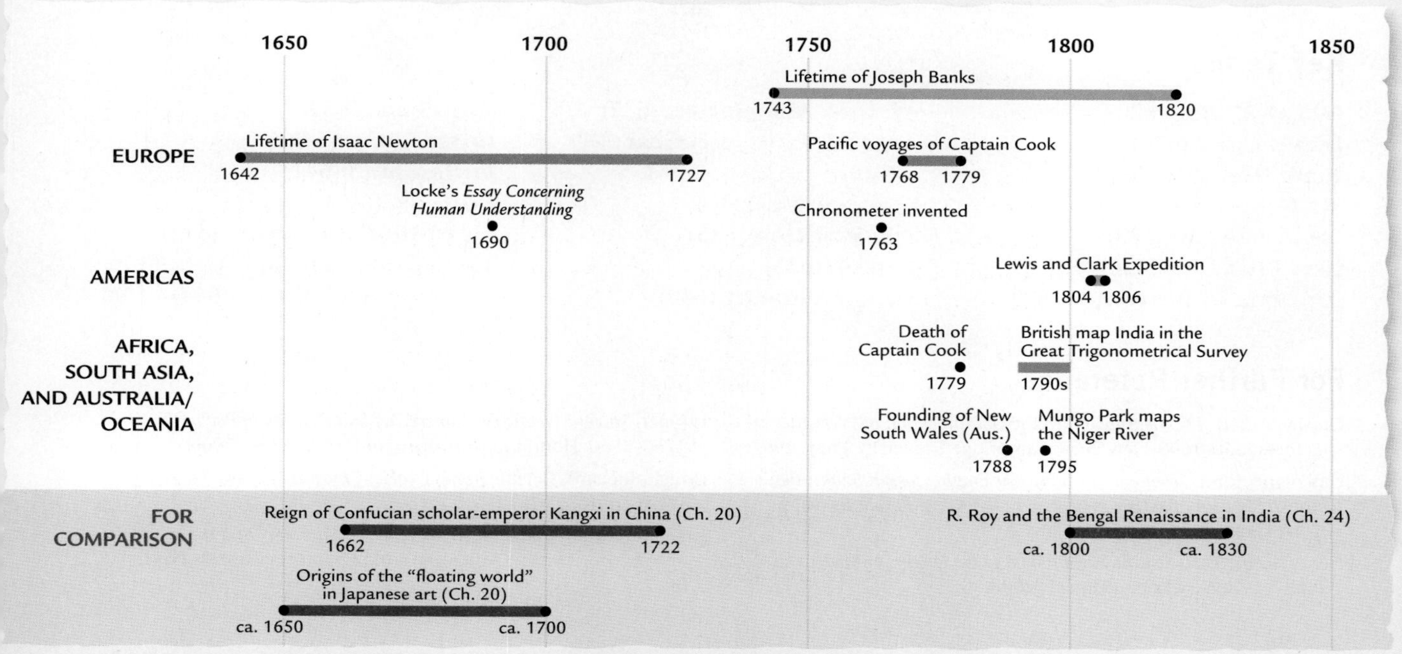

the colonial Americas), European ideas, both religious and scientific, were only marginal, if present at all.

The "practical science" advocated by Joseph Banks helped bring more and more of the world under European sway, if not always direct control, and the Industrial Revolution would magnify Europe's cultural and intellectual influence even further (see Chapter 23). Already during Banks's lifetime new technologies like the steam engine and new forms of factory organization were revolutionizing the British economy. By the late nineteenth century a flood of new technologies—railroads, steamships, telegraph lines—were boosting the productivity of industrial societies and propelling change around the world (see Chapters 24–26).

When confronted with the overwhelming material outcomes of European science and technology, people across the world would be forced to call their own beliefs and traditions into question. Should they adopt the new ideas as superior to their own, like Sugita Gempaku? Should they resist them as undermining their own way of life, as conservatives in the Russian, Ottoman, and Qing empires would advocate during the nineteenth century? Or maybe, like Japanese society, seek out a middle ground, synthesizing their own traditions with Western science and the insights of the Enlightenment (see Chapters 23 and 24)?

Many peoples across the world would have to struggle to find the freedom even to be able to make their own choices about how to adapt. In colonial Africa, for example, Western conquest was so rapid and comprehensive in the decades before 1900 that people had little time to adjust (see Chapter 26). Here, as in Polynesia and Oceania, Joseph Banks's idea that progress need take no account of indigenous interests would long prevail. Ideas of European racial superiority increasingly reinforced such attitudes.

Within Europe, science had challenged the intellectual monopoly of religious authorities, a tension that would continue into modern times with the development of evolutionary biology (see Chapter 23). Enlightenment philosophy, while it attracted the interest of kings, queens, and aristocrats, would also prove problematic for the status quo once members of the middle class began to push for reform—and revolution when necessary—in support of ideas that undercut traditional authority. The "age of reason" promised a better future, while challenging much that people had long held to be tried and true. Both the promise of progress and the unsettling consequences—such as questioning the relationship between rulers and ruled, between faith and science, between individuals and communities—would become an intrinsic part of the human condition over the next two centuries. First, Westerners had to deal with such issues themselves, as they did in revolutions in the United States, France, and Latin America, the topic of the next chapter.

Key Terms

Joseph Banks (620)
James Cook (620)
René Descartes (621)
Sir Francis Bacon (622)
Isaac Newton (623)
Carl Linnaeus (626)
problem of longitude (630)
African Association (632)
Great Trigonometrical Survey (632)
Lewis and Clark Expedition (635)
Tupaia (635)
Enlightenment (640)
John Locke (640)
laissez faire (641)
philosophes (641)
Voltaire (641)
Mary Wollstonecraft (642)
Encyclopedia (643)
enlightened despots (644)

For Further Reference

Crosby, Alfred. *The Measure of Reality: Quantification in Western Europe, 1250–1600*. New York: Cambridge University Press, 1997.

Gascoigne, John. *Science in the Service of Empire: Joseph Banks, the British State and the Uses of Science in the Age of Revolution* New York: Cambridge University Press 2011.

Henry, John. *The Scientific Revolution and the Origins of Modern Science*. 3d ed. New York: Palgrave, 2008.

Hooper, Steven. *Pacific Encounters: Art and Divinity in Polynesia, 1760–1860*. Honolulu: University of Hawai'i Press, 2006.

Hough, Richard. *Captain James Cooke: A Biography*. New York: W.W. Norton, 2013.

Israel, Jonathan. *Radical Enlightenment: Philosophy and the Making of Modernity, 1650–1750*. New York: Oxford University Press, 2002.

Jacob, Margaret. *The Scientific Revolution: A Brief History with Documents*. New York: Bedford St. Martin's, 2009.

Pagden, Anthony. *The Enlightenment: And Why It Still Matters*. New York: Random House, 2013.

Principe, Lawrence. *Scientific Revolution: A Very Short Introduction*. New York: Oxford University Press, 2011.

Salmond, Anne. *The Trial of the Cannibal Dog: The Remarkable Story of Captain Cook's Encounter in the South Seas*. New Haven: Yale University Press, 2003.

Slack, Paul. *The Invention of Improvement: Information and Material Progress in Seventeenth Century England*. New York: Oxford University Press, 2015.

Veth, Peter, ed. *Strangers on the Shore: Early Coastal Contact in Australia*. Canberra: National Museum of Australia Press, 2008.

AP® Review Questions for Chapter 21

Multiple-Choice Questions

QUESTIONS 1–4 REFER TO THE FOLLOWING PASSAGE.

Like the refinement of the arts of navigation, the Scientific Revolution in general required the combination of a political landscape that gave protected space to thinkers and broader circumstances that favored the long-distance flow of ideas and information. . . . Hence, Europeans alone developed a culture of scientific inquiry that after 1500 provided immense practical knowledge. Navigation and astronomy came first. Physics and ballistics—useful in artillery—followed, as, more slowly, did systematic sciences of medicine, botany, and chemistry, among others. Slowly, these sciences yielded practical advantages in military affairs, agriculture, mining, metallurgy, and elsewhere. These, particularly the military sciences of fortification, artillery ballistics, and mathematically precise organization of men and supplies, made even small European states increasingly formidable from the late sixteenth century. By the mid-nineteenth century, science in Europe (and the United States) systematically informed technology, generating a self-sustaining process of technological change to which no end is in sight.

—J. R. McNeill & William H. McNeill, historians, *The Human Web: A Bird's-Eye View of World History*, 2003

1. Which of the following would best explain the authors' conclusion that "Europeans alone developed a culture of scientific inquiry"?
   (A) Europeans explored secular knowledge that was originally developed in the classical, Islamic, and Asian worlds.
   (B) As literacy expanded, Europeans became less curious about the natural world.
   (C) With the introduction of American crops to Europe, scientific interest expanded in order to develop the best cultivation practices.
   (D) The Islamic conquest of the Iberian Peninsula had demonstrated the limits of European knowledge, which spurred a Scientific Revolution.

2. Based on your knowledge of world history, which of the following contributed LEAST to the European technological developments in the period from 1450 to 1750?
   (A) Increased literacy
   (B) The Columbian exchange
   (C) Maritime and navigational development
   (D) Improved understanding of global winds and currents

3. Which of the following is the most likely political outcome of the social process described in the passage above?
   (A) Expansion of suffrage to working classes
   (B) Newly imagined national communities based on ethnicity
   (C) Decline of divine right and a new focus on rights-based discourses
   (D) Mass migrations from regions where religion still held sway

4. Which of the following most affected the development of Christianity from 1450 to 1750?
   (A) European technological developments contributed to a rise in conservative orthodoxy in Europe.
   (B) The discovery of the Americas prompted a radical reformation of traditional Christian beliefs.
   (C) Christianity became increasingly diversified by diffusion and the Reformation.
   (D) The political rivalry between England and France intensified the split between Protestantism and Catholicism.

QUESTIONS 5–7 REFER TO THE FOLLOWING IMAGE.

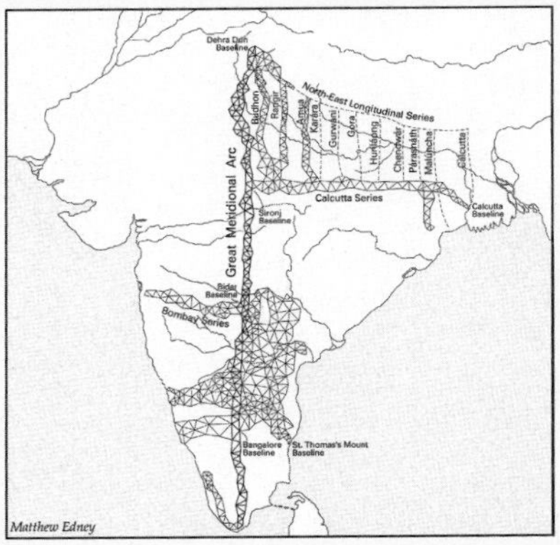

5. The development of the map above is best understood in the context of which of the following?
   (A) English advances in cartography that were used to further consolidate their empire
   (B) The diffusion of Arab and Chinese navigational tools to Europe
   (C) The decreased need for raw materials in the industrialized regions of the West
   (D) The establishment of a settler colony in India

6. The Great Trigonometrical Survey is best seen as evidence of which of the following in Western society from 1750 to 1900?

(A) Using Social Darwinism to justify imperialism
(B) State-sponsored vision of industrialization
(C) Large-scale British migration to India
(D) The application of Enlightenment principles of observation

7. Maps served several purposes but would have been most useful as a means of
   (A) implementing techniques of economic imperialism, such as the opium trade to China.
   (B) facilitating the development of nationalism in regions divided by cultural differences.
   (C) enhancing the efficiency of the global silver trade from the Americas to Asia.
   (D) strengthening control of transoceanic empires by implementing European systems of land division.

QUESTIONS 8–10 REFER TO THE FOLLOWING PASSAGES.

The Chinese *Book of Medicine* says that the lungs are like the eight petals of the lotus flower, with three petals hanging in front, three in back, and two petals forming like two ears.... There were no such divisions, and the position and shapes of intestines and gastric organs were all different from those taught by the old theories. They [official physicians] wrote in their books, "The more we think of it, there must be fundamental differences in the bodies of Chinese and of the eastern barbarians."

—Sugita Gempaku (1733–1817), Japanese physician comparing a dissection with Chinese medical practice

Another error... is, that men have used to infect their meditations, opinions, and doctrines, with some conceits which they have most admired, or some sciences which they have most applied; and given all things else a tincture according to them utterly untrue and unproper. So hath Plato intermingled his philosophy with theology, and Aristotle with logic.... For these were the arts which had a kind of primogeniture with them severally.

—Sir Francis Bacon, English philosopher and advocate of inductive reasoning, *Advancement of Learning*, 1605

8. The tone of the *second* passage reflects which of the following developments during the Enlightenment?
   (A) The Enlightenment was predicated on the diffusion of classical knowledge from the Arab world.
   (B) Enlightenment thinkers questioned established traditions in all areas of life.
   (C) The increase in interactions between East and West led to a rejection of Greek philosophy.
   (D) Northern Europeans viewed southern Europeans as less developed.

9. The views expressed in the *first* passage are best seen as evidence of which of the following in Tokugawa Japan?
   (A) The decline of the Qing dynasty allowed Japan to break off its tributary relationship with China.
   (B) Japanese physicians had adopted Social Darwinist ideas.
   (C) Even before the Meiji Restoration, some Japanese intellectuals were questioning tradition.
   (D) American influence in Japan sparked a movement to restructure all aspects of Japanese society.

10. The *second* passage is evidence of an important continuity in Western civilization because
    (A) Enlightenment Europeans used philosophy to reinforce existing social structures.
    (B) as in earlier eras, Europeans restructured racial and gender hierarchies during the Enlightenment.
    (C) tradition, as a basis for knowledge, continued to be held as superior to observation.
    (D) Enlightenment thinkers emphasized logic and empirical observation just as the Greeks and Romans did.

Short-Answer Questions

1. Answer parts A and B.

   Many historians argue that the Enlightenment fundamentally altered European society.

   A. Identify and explain TWO pieces of evidence that *support* this argument.

   B. Identify and explain ONE piece of evidence that *undermines* this argument.

2. Answer parts A, B, and C.

   A. Explain ONE cause of the European maritime technological developments.

   B. Explain ONE economic effect of the European maritime technological developments.

   C. Explain ONE social effect of the European maritime technological developments.

22 Revolutions in the West, 1750–1830

In the summer of 1805, young **Simón Bolívar** (1783–1830) traveled to Madrid, Rome, and Paris in the company of his tutor, a Venezuelan exile who had followed the allure of revolution to Europe. His teacher had required Bolívar to study the great texts of the Enlightenment (see Chapter 21), and now he was there to witness firsthand the excitement and the fear caused by the rising empire of Napoleon Bonaparte in the aftermath of the French Revolution.

Simón Bolívar

One day, they climbed one of the famous hills of Rome to gain a panoramic view of the "eternal city." Bolívar was awestruck by the echoes of the city's great imperial past, which, he thought, summed up all that was truly great and all that was most tragic in history. But he saw the destiny of the Americas as greater still, and he pledged to play his part to liberate South America from the Spanish empire and thus advance the cause of liberty for all mankind:

Here every manner of grandeur has had its type, all miseries their cradle. . . .

[Rome] has examples for everything, except the cause of humanity: . . . heroic warriors, rapacious consuls . . . golden virtues, and sordid crimes; but for the emancipation of the spirit . . . the exaltation of man, and the final perfectibility of reason, little or nothing. . . . The resolution of the great problem of man set free seems to have been something . . . that would only be made clear in the New World. . . . I swear before you, I swear by the God of my fathers, I swear on their graves, I swear by my Country that I

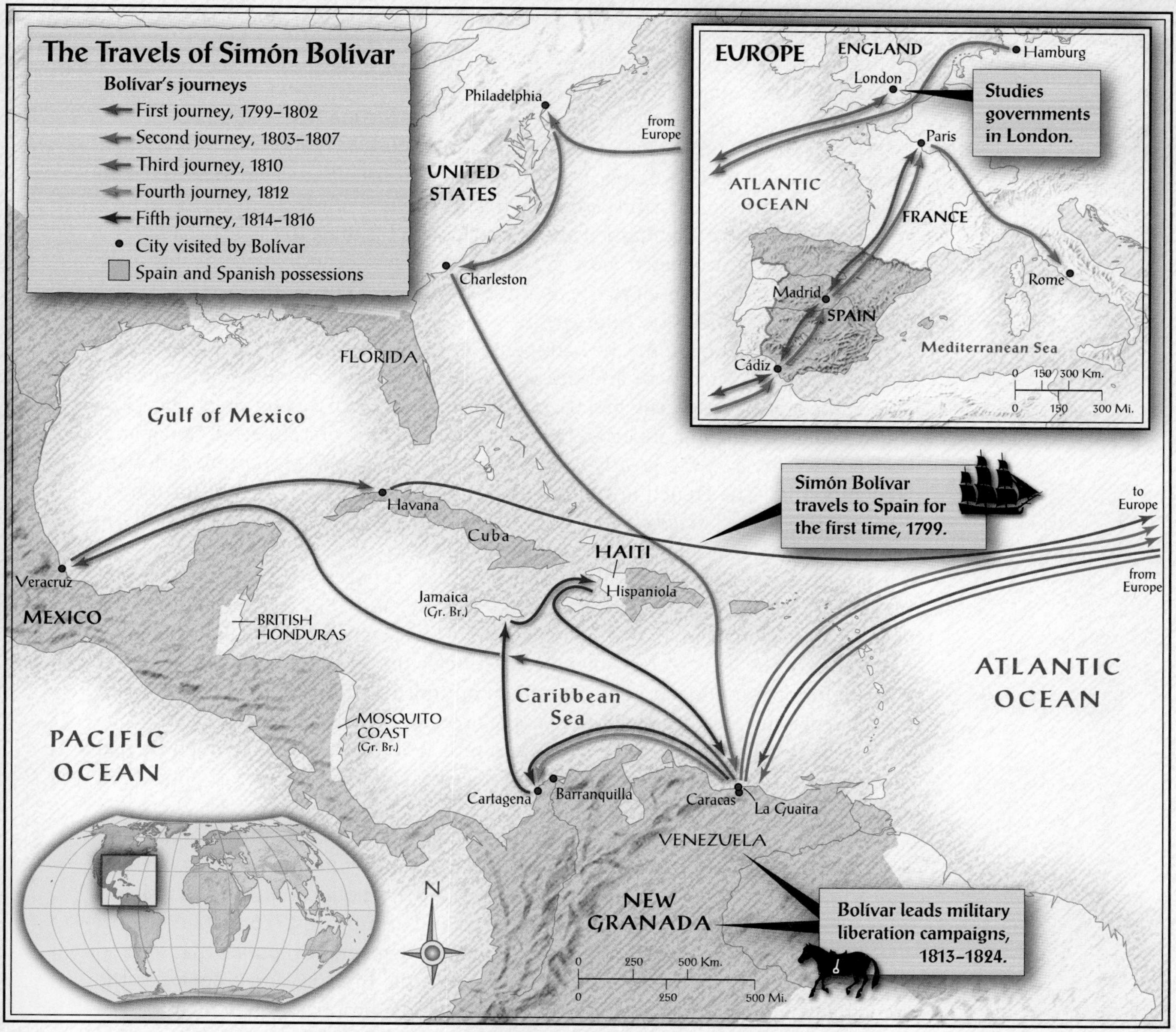

*will not rest body or soul until I have broken the chains binding us to the will of Spanish might!**

---

*Excerpt from Simón Bolívar, "Oath Taken at Rome, 15 August 1805," trans. Frederick H. Fornoff, in *El Libertador: Writings of Simón Bolívar*, ed. David Bushnell (New York: Oxford University Press, 2003), pp. 113–144.

Simón Bolívar
(1783–1830) Revolutionary who was born in Venezuela and led military forces throughout present-day Ecuador, Colombia, Bolivia, and Peru, becoming the most important military leader in the struggle for independence in South America.

Simón Bolívar's (see-MOAN bow-LEE-var) oath changed not only his own life but also the course of Latin American history. Over the next two decades, he led the drive for the independence of Spain's South American colonies.

Having grown up in one of the richest households in Venezuela, Bolívar first went to Europe in 1799, when he was only sixteen, to visit an uncle in Madrid. There he spent his money freely while enjoying the life of the Spanish court. He fell in love and, in spite of his youth, married and returned with his bride to Caracas. Sadly, she died just eight months later. Now, returning from his second voyage in his early twenties, he devoted himself to the political and military pursuit that would occupy the rest of his life: liberation from Spain.

Apart from visiting Rome, he had spent most of this trip in Paris, the intellectual center of the Enlightenment and the political center of revolution. In the previous decade the French monarchy had been overthrown and replaced by a republic. Now the republic was being superseded by the dictatorship of Napoleon Bonaparte. Bolívar's worldview was greatly affected by his experience of postrevolutionary French politics. The French Revolution, like ancient Rome, had brought forth both *"golden virtues"* and *"sordid crimes."* Only in the Americas, thought Bolívar, could the full liberation of the human spirit be achieved.

Bolívar proved himself a brilliant military leader. Between 1813, when he entered his native Caracas at the head of a liberation army, and 1824, when he drove the Spanish army from Peru, he fulfilled the oath he had taken in Rome. Like other revolutionaries of the late eighteenth and early nineteenth centuries, Bolívar started out with high hopes founded in Enlightenment optimism. Turning independence from Spanish rule into true liberty for the people of South America proved difficult, however. Bolívar never achieved the stable and united South America of which he had dreamed, making his story, as one biographer has emphasized, one of "liberation and disappointment."*

Elsewhere in Latin America and the Caribbean, and in North America and France, other revolutionaries also believed that prejudice and tradition would give way to rationality and enlightenment, and that new political and social systems would both guarantee liberty and provide order and security. In 1776, Britain's North American colonists had broken free and founded a democratic republic that seemed to combine liberty with moderation. A more volatile historical precedent was the French Revolution, which swung violently from constitutional monarchy to radical republic to military dictatorship. In the Caribbean, the Republic of Haiti was created following one of the largest slave uprisings in world history.

The issue of slavery was very much on Bolívar's mind. Like his North American counterpart George Washington, Bolívar was a slave owner. Could the dream of liberty be compatible with the reality of slavery? Such discrepancies between dreams and harsher realities were, in fact, a central theme of the age. Reconciling the twin mandates of liberty and equality, and securing both within a stable and well-ordered state, was a tremendous challenge for revolutionaries across North and South America, the Caribbean, and France.

---

*David Bushnell, *Simón Bolívar: Liberation and Disappointment* (New York: Pearson Longman, 2004).

KEY CONCEPT **QUESTIONS**

- How are the American Declaration of Independence, the French Declaration of the Rights of Man and the Citizen, and Bolívar's Jamaica Letter similar and different? **(Key Concept 5.3)**
- What were the causes and consequences of revolutions in Latin America and the Caribbean? **(Key Concept 5.3)**
- What effect did revolutions in Europe and the Americas have in expanding suffrage, abolishing slavery, and ending serfdom? **(Key Concept 5.3)**

Rebellion and Independence in America, 1763–1797

On April 19, 1775, after British soldiers marched on the town of Concord to seize and destroy arms secretly stockpiled there by the Massachusetts militia, the two sides exchanged gunfire. Surprised and confused by the colonials' irregular tactics, the British beat a retreat back to Boston, harassed along their flanks all the way.

This skirmish in a small corner of the British empire set in motion events that would have a powerful global impact. The rebels' Declaration of Independence (1776) is one of the most influential political statements in world history, and the founding of the United States was a powerful testament to the principles of Enlightenment. Nevertheless, compromises made during the nation-building process, especially about slavery, undermined the Enlightenment's highest aspirations of universal liberty and equality.

Rebellion and War, 1763–1783

A key turning point in the relations between Britain and the colonists was the British victory in the French and Indian War, the name in North America for the Seven Years' War (1756–1763) that pitted Britain against France around the world (see Chapter 19). To Britain's North American colonists, victory opened possibilities for expansion into the Ohio River Valley and other areas west of the Appalachian Mountains. But British leaders were cautious. No sooner had they defeated the French than they faced a Native American uprising. European settlements on the frontier would generate more conflict, inevitably requiring more British troops and resources. Britain's Proclamation of 1763 fixed a westward limit to colonial expansion, much to the disgust of colonists.

The British then imposed new taxes so that the colonies would help bear the cost of their own defense. Colonists bitterly resented these new taxes, such as the Stamp Act of 1765, as well as tighter restrictions on their trade with the West Indies. Resistance took the form of illegal smuggling, embargoes on British goods, and various kinds of public protests, sometimes leading to violence or destruction of property. Concluding that British policies assailed their rights as freeborn British subjects, some colonists started to call themselves "Americans," rallying to the slogan *"No taxation without representation!"* When they formed militias to assert their rights, the stage was set for the confrontation at Concord.

George Washington
(1732–1799) Commander of the Continental Army in the American War of Independence from Britain; also the first president of the United States of America.

Declaration of Independence
(1776) Document written by Thomas Jefferson justifying the separation of Britain's North American colonies, declaring them free and independent states.

● **CONTEXT&CONNECTIONS** Tea from South Asia played an economic role in the history of British North America and affected the political symbolism of the rebellion. At the famous "Tea Party" of May 1773, colonists threw Indian tea into Boston harbor, protesting a new British policy intended to oblige them to buy tea directly from the East India Company (see Chapter 20). The Tea Act angered local merchants who had been smuggling tea into Massachusetts, as well as consumers who anticipated that an East India Company monopoly would eventually lead to higher prices. By then, the combination of Asian tea and sugar from the West Indies (see Chapter 19) had become an expected part of their daily routine. ●

After the skirmish in Massachusetts, a Continental Congress convened, bringing together representatives from each of the thirteen colonies. **George Washington** (1732–1799) was appointed commander of its army. Washington, a Virginian, had served as an officer during British military campaigns in the Ohio River Valley. Then on July 4, 1776, Congress approved Thomas Jefferson's **Declaration of Independence**, which not only detailed the colonists' grievances but also made a stirring announcement of universal political values:

> *We hold these truths to be self-evident, that all men are created equal, that they are endowed by their Creator with certain inalienable Rights, that among these are Life, Liberty and the pursuit of Happiness. —That to secure these rights, Governments are instituted among Men, deriving their just powers from the consent of the governed.*

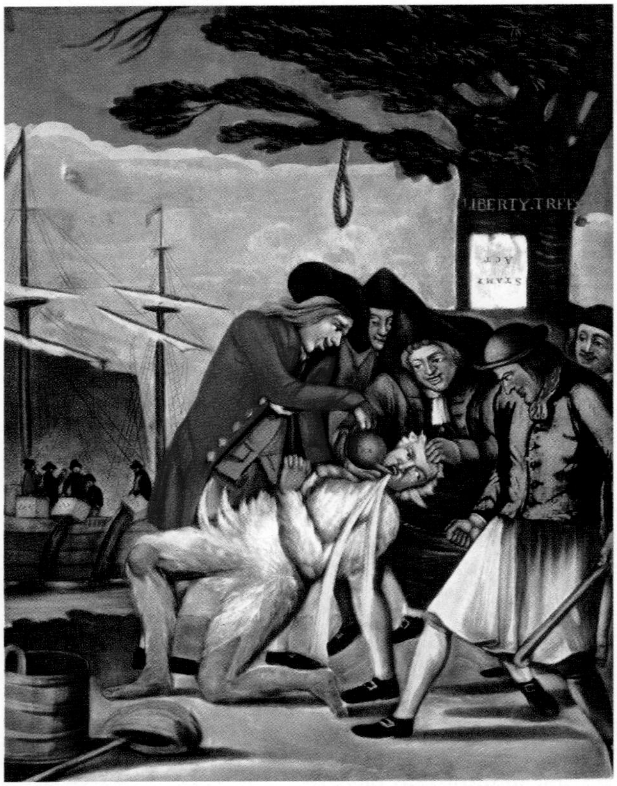

GL Archive/Alamy

Protesting Taxation Needing additional resources to control its expanded American frontier after victory in the Seven Years' War, the British Parliament imposed new taxes on the North American colonies. In this engraving, angry colonists have tarred and feathered one of the king's officials beneath a "Liberty Tree." Tarring and feathering, which often left the victim permanently disfigured, was an exceptionally violent form of vigilante justice.

The phrase "consent of the governed" built on John Locke's theory of government as based on a contract in which individuals receive protection of their basic rights by voluntarily submitting to a legitimate government (see Chapter 21). Without that consent, Jefferson argued, rebellion was justified.

The British had some advantages in the war that began in 1776. The tens of thousands of "redcoat" soldiers in North America were well equipped and well trained. Moreover, many Loyalists in the colonies argued against rebellion. Inventor, diplomat, and continental congressman Benjamin Franklin only reluctantly exchanged his British identity for an American one, and his son William, the royally appointed governor of New Jersey, refused to do so. Many free blacks, aware that slavery had been eliminated in Britain and knowing that prominent leaders of the rebellion included slave owners like Washington and Jefferson, were Loyalist as well.

• **CONTEXT&CONNECTIONS** Amerindians were divided in their response to the American war for independence. Though other Iroquois elders argued for neutrality, Joseph Brant (Thayendanegea) allied his Mohawk people with the British. After the war, Brant's descendants, exiled to Canada, remained loyal to the empire. Brant's grandson, Smoke Johnson (Sakayengwaraton), led Mohawk forces against the United States in the War of 1812, and his great-great-granddaughter, *Pauline Johnson-Tekahionwake*, achieved fame as a Canadian poet (key term in Chapter 25). •

The French saw support for the revolutionaries as another way to inflict damage on their perennial British nemesis; their aid proved essential for rebel success. A Franco-American treaty provided for arms supplies and French harassment of British ships in the Atlantic and Caribbean. Apart from the French alliance, the rebellious colonists had several advantages. The rural population supported the Continental Army with supplies, information on British movements, and knowledge of the local terrain. Women played a notable role. They did extra work, including blacksmithing and other "male" jobs, in the absence of their soldier-husbands, and they produced shoes, clothes, and munitions for the Continental Army. Also, since British soldiers were reluctant to search them, women made excellent spies and couriers.

Another advantage was the leadership of General Washington, who managed to maintain the morale of his troops through harsh winters, especially at Valley Forge in 1777–1778. In 1781, after Washington's army surrounded the British under Lord Cornwallis at Yorktown, French ships cut off Cornwallis's route of retreat, forcing him to surrender his army. In the Treaty of Paris (1783), the British government acknowledged the independence of the new United States of America.

• **CONTEXT&CONNECTIONS** After his surrender at Yorktown, *Lord Cornwallis* (Chapter 20) retained his high political standing and was appointed governor-general of British India. Subsequent British expansion in South Asia laid the foundation for what historians call "the second British empire" (see Chapter 20). •

Creating a Nation, 1783–1797

An early motto of the new republic was *Novus Ordo Secolorum*: "A New Order of the Ages." The founders saw the birth of their nation as an event that would usher in a new era, *"an epoch,"* as Washington put it, *"when the rights of mankind were better understood and more clearly defined, than at any former period."* Nevertheless, in the new nation social continuities accompanied political change.

Under British rule, each of the thirteen colonies had developed a distinct political culture, and representatives of the individual states proved reluctant to sacrifice local sovereignty to create a more unified nation. The first constitution, the Articles of Confederation, allowed the federal government no tax-raising power and required it to request funds from the individual states. Under the Articles, the states were responsible for debts remaining from the war, and they levied taxes to meet those obligations. These taxes forced poorer farmers, who lived primarily through barter, to sell land to raise the necessary cash. Such farmers also stood to lose their right to vote, which was accorded only to property owners. In Massachusetts, incensed war veterans rose up in an armed rebellion, strengthening arguments for a stronger federal government with powers of taxation. Debates over the degree to which a central government should have license to tax and borrow would continue far into the future.

Mercy Otis Warren, one of the most prolific writers of her time, put it this way: *"On the one hand we are in need of a strong federal government founded on principles that will support the prosperity and union of the colonies. On the other we have struggled for liberty...[and will not relinquish] the rights of man for the dignity of government."** At the Constitutional Convention in 1787, central issues facing delegates were how to balance the powers of government with the rights of individuals and the power of the federal government with that of the states.

Constitution of the United States of America

(1787) Agreement that created a more unified national structure for the United States, providing for a bicameral national legislature and independent executive and judicial authority, and incorporating a Bill of Rights.

Compromise was the hallmark of the new **Constitution of the United States of America** (1787). While granting to the federal government powers of taxation, judicial oversight, international diplomacy, and national defense, specific powers, such as determining the voting franchise, were left to the states. A system of checks and balances, as earlier proposed by the French philosophe Montesquieu (see Chapter 21), ensured the separation of executive, legislative, and judicial authority. The convention struck a balance between the interests of large and small states by creating a two-house legislature, with representation in the House of Representatives based on population and that in the Senate equal at two senators for each state.

Congress amended the Constitution in 1791 with a Bill of Rights that guaranteed specific civil liberties, such as freedom of religion, of the press, of assembly, and other fundamental freedoms. However, most states restricted the vote to property-owning men. No political agency was given to women, Native Americans, slaves, or even most free blacks.

AP® THEMES

How did Enlightenment ideas shape the formation of the political institutions of the United States of America?

George Washington was the unanimous choice of the state electors as president. Washington, like Simón Bolívar on his European sojourn, looked to ancient Rome for inspiration. His model was the general Cincinnatus who, after leading Roman armies to victory, left the political stage to live as a simple citizen. In 1797, after two terms as president, Washington refused a third term and retired to his plantation. Washington's example of voluntarily leaving office when he felt his public service was completed powerfully reinforced constitutional limitations on executive power. (Like many subsequent world leaders, Napoleon Bonaparte did not follow Washington's example; see the feature "Visual Evidence in Primary Sources: Portraits of Power: George Washington and Napoleon Bonaparte.") Washington's Farewell Address, warning against any *"permanent alliances with any portion of the foreign world,"* would have a lasting influence on United States foreign policy.

Neither Washington nor the other leaders of the Constitutional Convention could resolve the fundamental dichotomy between liberty and slavery. Southern delegates had no intention of applying the principle that *"all men are created equal"* to the 40 percent of Southerners who were slaves. Though the abolitionist movement was gaining momentum (see Chapter 19), plantation owners prevailed. The Constitution cynically defined each slave as three-fifths of a person in calculating the size of congressional delegations, and allowed the states to define slaves as nonpersons for all other purposes.

Here was a conundrum. To bring perfect rationality and harmony to society, in line with Enlightenment ideals, one would need to start with a "blank slate" free from inherited prejudice and exploitation. The issue of slavery shows that this was not possible for the new United States. Both before and after 1776, Northern

---

*Mercy Otis Warren, Letter of September 17, 1787, to Catherine Macauley, Gilder Lehrman Collection, GLC 1800.3, pp. 1–2. http://www.digitalhistory.uh.edu/exhibits/dearmadam/letter4.html.

merchants and Southern slaveholders dominated the social and economic order. For this reason, historians continue to debate whether the war for independence should really be considered a "revolution," signified by a significant rearrangement of social and economic power. For the French Revolution, in contrast, there is no such debate.

The French Revolution, 1789–1815

The French Revolution quickly moved through three distinct stages. At first, the focus was on the relatively moderate goal of constitutional monarchy. When that proved impossible, radical republicans then led the second phase of the Revolution, seeking to fundamentally transform French society. Their rule soon degenerated into a bloody Reign of Terror.

The attempt by French revolutionaries to turn the noblest words of the Enlightenment into action was strongly opposed by the monarchy, the nobility, the church, and neighboring kingdoms, as well as by many French themselves who thought the revolutionaries were going too far. Significant numbers in the provinces resented the primacy of Paris as the revolutionary center. In the resulting disorder compromise proved impossible.

Finally, amid the turmoil emerged a military genius, Napoleon Bonaparte, who not only restored order but also extended French power across Europe. Thus, as in ancient Rome, but all in the course of one dizzying decade, monarchy was replaced by a republic, and then the republic by a new empire.

Louis XVI and the Early Revolution, 1789–1792

The complex causes of the French Revolution are still debated by historians. The heightened ambitions of the French middle class certainly must be taken into account: many members of the bourgeoisie detested the inherited privileges of the king and nobility. Though most of them were still committed to the idea of monarchy, a minority, aware of the example of the new United States, argued that the people themselves should be sovereign. These lawyers, doctors, teachers, merchants—with property and education but no titles—drew from Enlightenment ideas to promote reform and, failing that, revolution.

The vast majority of French men and women were farmers whose resentment over the feudal obligations they still owed their aristocratic overlords intensified when bad harvests in the 1780s caused hunger and hardship. Many fled to the cities, especially Paris, where overcrowding and unemployment added fuel to the revolutionary fire. Ruling over 24 million subjects from his fabulous palace at Versailles, **Louis XVI** (r. 1774–1793) was one of the wealthiest and most powerful people in the world, but he proved incapable of uniting his deeply divided people.

Louis XVI
(r. 1774–1793) King of France whose inability to adequately reform the French fiscal system laid the foundation for the French Revolution. After showing reluctance to rule as a constitutional monarch, Louis was arrested and beheaded by republican revolutionaries.

The most immediate cause of the revolt of 1789 was the precarious state of French finances. When Louis XVI took the throne, the French treasury was nearly empty. The loss of the Seven Years' War (1756–1763) left a pile of debt made higher by the expense of backing the American rebels. The common people were crushed by taxes, while the nobility, lavishly entertained at Versailles, paid none at all.

The economic crisis led to a political one when Louis and his ministers decided in 1789 that they had no choice but to convene an Estates-General in Paris, to which each of the three Orders of French society would send representatives.

Portraits of Power: George Washington and Napoleon Bonaparte

During the eighteenth and nineteenth centuries in Europe and the Americas, political leaders commissioned paintings of themselves to project images of power. Portraits such as those reproduced here could inform people not merely of the fact of power but also of the particular type of power leaders were associated with. President George Washington of the United States (in office 1789–1797) and

The stormy sky in the background might illustrate the difficult times that Washington and his comrades passed through, while the rainbow just above his upper arm might symbolize their ultimate victory.

The inkstand on the table and the books below show his importance in crafting the nation's foundational documents.

Washington wears no signs of military rank, holds a sheathed sword with its point down, and offers his open hand. The impression is one of peace.

Gérard Blot/Hervé Lewandowski

Emperor Napoleon Bonaparte of France (r. 1799–1814) were keenly aware of classical Greek and Roman models in projecting images of power, as were their portraitists Gilbert Stuart (1796) and Jean-Auguste-Dominique Ingres (1806). Washington identified himself with the democratic tradition of Athens and the republican period of Rome; Napoleon, in contrast, emphasized the imperial Roman tradition. Simón Bolívar, whose portrait at the beginning of the chapter can be compared with those here, was also keenly aware of both the republican and imperial traditions of ancient Rome.

Napoleon holds a scepter topped by a figure of Charlemagne, the early medieval king whose empire was one of his models.

Unlike Washington's open right hand, Napoleon's right fist is clenched high on his scepter, adding to the contrast between the two portraits. ***In these portraits, what do such differences tell us about how the artist wished to represent each man's character, his nature as a leader, and his vision for his nation? Compare each of these portraits with that of Simón Bolívar at the beginning of the chapter, with the same question in mind.***

At his coronation in 1804, Napoleon wore two different crowns, first a laurel crown like the one shown here and then a bejeweled reproduction of Charlemagne's crown. New rulers often seek legitimacy by associating themselves with older symbols of power.

What different reactions might Napoleon's supporters and detractors have had in viewing this portrait? Napoleon did not commission this painting, and we do not know what he himself thought of it.

Erich Lessing/Art Resource, NY

The First Estate consisted of the Catholic Church, the Second Estate consisted of the nobility, and the Third Estate comprised everyone else, that is, the vast majority of French men and women. It was an extreme measure: there had been no meeting of the French Estates-General since 1614.

Third Estate
Before the French Revolution, the order of French society that included the common people (the First Estate was the clergy, the Second the aristocracy, and the Third everyone else).

In the provinces, elections were held for **Third Estate** delegates, many of whom were middle-class professionals. Inspired by the American Revolution, they demanded fundamental reforms, such as the creation of a representative legislative body. They collected notebooks of grievances in the French provinces to bring to Paris as a catalogue of complaints and ideas for change.

Many bishops representing the First Estate were from noble families, and the Catholic Church, by far the biggest landowner in France, was, like the aristocrats of the Second Estate, exempt from direct taxation. Since each estate had only one vote, Louis anticipated that the privileged members of the First and Second Estates would vote together, canceling out radical proposals from the Third Estate.

National Assembly
(1789) Assembly that launched the French Revolution, formed by members of the Third Estate after the failure of the Estates-General. They agreed on the "Declaration of the Rights of Man and of the Citizen," forcing the king to sign the assembly's constitution.

Delegates from the Third Estate, however, took matters into their own hands. When Louis had them locked out of the assembly hall where they planned to meet, the furious delegates met on a tennis court, declared themselves to be a **National Assembly**, and took an oath not to disband until a constitutional monarchy had been established. Reacting with fear, Louis XVI summoned eighteen thousand troops to defend his palace at Versailles, 12 miles (19.3 km) outside Paris. The French Revolution had begun.

Thus far, the contest was between the men of power—the king and his nobles—and the relatively wealthy and well-educated delegates of the Third Estate, men who *aspired* to power and influence. But the actions of the common people pushed events in a new direction. Parisians stormed the Bastille (bass-TEEL), a building that served as both a jail and an armory. They freed prisoners, armed themselves from the arsenal's stockpile, and killed the mayor.

After the Bastille uprising, Louis decided he had better compromise with the Third Estate after all. He recognized the National Assembly, which promptly declared the principle of equality before the law, eliminated the special prerogatives of the nobility, and abolished serfdom and all the remaining feudal obligations of the peasantry. In the "Declaration of the Rights of Man and the Citizen," the National Assembly declared that *"men are born and remain free and equal in rights,"* that *"the natural and inalienable rights of man"* are *"liberty, property, security, and resistance to oppression,"* that all citizens are eligible for government positions *"without other distinctions than that of virtues and talents,"* and that necessary taxation *"must be assessed equally on all citizens in proportion to their means."* Freedom of thought and religion were established, and mandatory payments to the Catholic Church were eliminated. The assembly thus articulated the ideas of the philosophes as political principles.

In one way, the National Assembly was quite traditional: this all-male body would not consider extending equality to women. They ignored the lobbying of middle-class Parisian women's groups and the arguments of author Olympe de Gouges (oh-limp duh GOOJ), who in her *Declaration of the Rights of Women*, protested: *"The exercise of the natural rights of women has only been limited by the perpetual tyranny that man opposes to them; these limits should be reformed by the laws of nature and reason."**

*Olympe de Gouges, *Écrits politiques, 1788–1791*, trans. Tracey Rizzo (Paris: Côtes Femmes, 1993), p. 209. Reprinted in Tracy Rizzo and Laura Mason, eds., *The French Revolution: A Document Collection* (Boston: Houghton Mifflin, 1999), p. 111.

Parisian Women March to Versailles Women played a distinctive role in the French Revolution. Elite women sponsored the gatherings that spread Enlightenment and revolutionary ideals in their *salons*, while the common women engaged in direct action, as here in 1789, where they are shown marching to Versailles to force the king to return to Paris. (The Granger Collection, NYC)

Within the National Assembly, revolutionary zeal was secondary to cooperating with Louis XVI in establishing a new constitutional monarchy. But neither the king nor the assembly could control events. In the fall of 1789, the poor again took direct action. Angered by the high price of bread and distrusting the king's intentions, twenty thousand Parisians, mostly women, marched to Versailles. This "March of the Women" forced the king and his family to leave Versailles and return to his palace in Paris where the people could keep a closer eye on him.

Despite the centrality of Paris, the vast majority of French men and women were village-based peasants. Their "justice" came from courts presided over by their lord. They had to donate free labor cultivating his estates and were often forced to grind their wheat into flour at the lord's mill, where he could charge whatever he liked. While the National Assembly calmly deliberated the elimination of such feudal practices, French farmers rose up and stormed their lords' estates, sometimes content to burn the manorial rolls that listed their feudal obligations, sometimes burning magnificent country houses to the ground. Panicked aristocrats began to flee the country, seeking refuge with their relatives across Europe.

In this tense atmosphere, the National Assembly organized a Legislative Assembly to draft a new set of basic laws, following the United States's example of a written constitution and the British example of sharing power between the king and representatives of the people. But in the summer of 1791, Louis tried to escape from France, hoping to rally support from other European monarchs for his return as an absolute ruler. Instead, he was captured and held a virtual prisoner in his palace.

Meanwhile, French nobles who had fled abroad were doing their best to convince Europe's kings and aristocrats to help overthrow the revolution. The defeat of French forces by Habsburg regiments in the Netherlands in 1792 led supporters of the revolution to fear an Austrian invasion of France itself. At the same time, a poor harvest and severe grain shortage further increased tensions. In Paris, the people staged anti-monarchical demonstrations and attacked the royal palace. Hundreds of citizens and soldiers died.

The window for compromise was now closed. Some in the Legislative Assembly were happy that the experiment in constitutional monarchy had not worked. They were *republicans*, who believed that any form of monarchy undermined liberty. The next phase of the French Revolution would belong to them.

The Jacobins and the Reign of Terror, 1793–1795

Under pressure from the people of Paris, the Legislative Assembly declared a republic and instituted universal manhood suffrage. The National Assembly dissolved itself in favor of a National Convention, which immediately declared the end of the monarchy and began writing a republican constitution. They found Louis XVI guilty of treason and beheaded him in January 1793.

Jacobins

The most radical republican faction in the National Convention. They organized a military force that saved the republic, but their leader Maximilien Robespierre, head of the Committee of Public Safety, ruled by decree and set in motion the Reign of Terror.

Under the **Jacobins**, the radical republican faction led by Maximilien Robespierre (ROBES-pee-air), the French Revolution passed through its most idealistic and most violent phase. Robespierre had been deeply influenced by the philosophy of Jean-Jacques Rousseau, who had argued that the only legitimate state was one that expressed the "general will" of the people. Rousseau envisioned a form of direct democracy practiced by enlightened citizens, but he rejected the checks on government power proposed by Montesquieu and implemented in the Constitution of the United States. Instead Rousseau had talked of constructing a "Republic of Virtue."

Perfect equality was part of the Jacobin plan to wipe the slate clean and transform society from bottom to top. The republic confiscated lands belonging to the church and to the nobility and abolished slavery in the French empire. In the name of "*liberty, equality, and fraternity*" everyone, rich and poor alike, was to be addressed as "*Citizen*." The year 1793 would be "*Year One*" of a new calendar, marking the victory of reason over the old Christian faith. Time itself would have a revolutionary new beginning.

But no fresh start was really possible; the past could not be so easily erased. Devout Catholics, especially in the provinces, deeply resented the Jacobins' moves against the Catholic Church. Meanwhile the seizure of private property by the Jacobins, fighting to save the Revolution, deeply shocked the bourgeoisie. Many who had initially supported the Third Estate and plans for constitutional monarchy now recoiled from the revolutionary excess of Robespierre and his followers. (See the feature "Movement of Ideas Through Primary Sources: Edmund Burke's Reflections on the French Revolution.")

Robespierre then imposed an even harsher dictatorship after the kings of Prussia and Austria declared counterrevolutionary war on France. Not for the last time in world history, a revolutionary leader declared that to save the revolution, its most cherished principle—liberty—would have to be sacrificed. A dictatorial Committee of Public Safety replaced the fledgling democratic institutions of the republic. The committee quashed its enemies with a so-called Reign of Terror in which forty thousand people were beheaded.

The symbol of the Revolution now became the guillotine (gee-yuh-TEEN), in which the condemned had their heads removed by the quick fall of a sharp, heavy blade. That the guillotine became a symbol of revolutionary violence is ironic. The philosophes were horrified by grisly public executions, where the executioner often needed several swings of his heavy axe to fully decapitate the condemned. Dr. Joseph Guillotin had intended his invention as an enlightened means of execution, clean and swift. Now his attempt at humane reform had been transformed into an efficient instrument of terror.

Though their methods were harsh, the Jacobins were successful in securing the republic against Austrian and Prussian invaders. They fielded an enormous army of conscripts who first stemmed the tide of invasion and then went on the offensive. Mass conscription had cultural and political ramifications as well. Most of the soldiers were peasants who had never before traveled far from home, where they practiced local customs and spoke distinct regional dialects. Once trained for defense of the republic, many developed a stronger sense of national identity, transformed, in one historian's words, "from peasants into Frenchmen."

Reduced foreign threats, however, emboldened the Jacobins' domestic enemies. People in the provinces were angry at the radicalism they associated with Paris, and most members of the middle class favored a more moderate republic. Many Jacobins themselves now lost their heads, including Robespierre himself. *"Revolutions,"* a French journalist commented, *"devour their children."*

The Age of Napoleon, 1795–1815

The National Convention reasserted power and created a new constitution with a more limited electorate and a separation of powers. From 1795 to 1799, however, the country remained sharply divided. The Directory, which formed the executive branch of the new government, faced conspiracies by both the Jacobins and by monarchists. Meanwhile, French armies continued to gain victories as a young general named **Napoleon Bonaparte** (1769–1821) took northern Italy from the Austrians. In 1799 two members of the Directory plotted with Napoleon to launch a coup d'état and form a new government.

Napoleon Bonaparte
(1769–1821) Military commander who gained control of France after the French Revolution. He declared himself emperor in 1804 and attempted to expand French territory, but failed to defeat Great Britain and abdicated in 1814. He died in exile after a brief return to power in 1815.

Like George Washington, Napoleon looked to ancient Rome for inspiration. But unlike the American general, Napoleon followed Rome's imperial example, transforming the republic into an empire (see Map 22.1, page 664). In a series of referendums the French people voted their approval of Napoleon's enhanced power, tired of chaos and bickering politicians, and proud of his armies' successes. Napoleon neutralized political opposition by bringing all but the most fervent monarchists into his administration. In 1801, he reached a compromise restoring papal authority, gaining the allegiance of Catholics who had felt oppressed by the

Edmund Burke's Reflections on the French Revolution

British parliamentarian Edmund Burke (1729–1797) has been called "the father of conservatism," a reputation that came mostly from his denunciation of the excesses of the French Revolution in a letter he wrote to a French aristocrat, published as *Essays on the French Revolution*. In fact, Burke's politics were generally liberal: he upheld the rights of Parliament and limitations on those of the king; supported the American Revolution, Catholic rights in his native Ireland, and the abolition of the slave trade; and spoke strongly against the corruption of the British East India Company (see Chapter 20).

In the *Essays*—written in 1790 before the execution of Louis XVI, the bloodshed of the Reign of Terror, and the dictatorship of the Jacobins—Burke argued that the French had been mistaken in basing their case for liberty on abstract ideals such as "the rights of man." Instead, he explained how liberty was better protected with a constitution grounded on inherited cultural and political institutions. Using abstract ideas to overrule custom and tradition pushed the revolutionaries, he said, toward corruption and dictatorship. Critics of Burke, defenders of Enlightenment thinking such as Thomas Paine (*The Rights of Man*) and Mary Wollstonecraft (*A Vindication of the Rights of Women*), rejected his arguments, though it was not long before the violence unleashed by the Jacobins and the tyranny imposed by Napoleon seemed to vindicate Burke's position.

Historical Thinking Skill:
ARGUMENTATION **What evidence does Burke use to support his argument against the French Revolution?**

Historical Thinking Skill:
INTERPRETATION **Based on Burke's commentary on the people he observed leading the French Revolution, what characteristics of the new lawmakers does Burke believe would prevent them from legislating effectively?**

Source: Edmund Burke, *Works* (London: 1867).

From Essays *on the French Revolution*

The question of dethroning [a king] will always be, as it has always been, an extraordinary question of state. . . . As it was not made for common abuses, so it is not to be agitated by common minds. The speculative line of demarcation, where obedience ought to end, and resistance must begin, is faint, obscure, and not easily definable. It is not a single act, or a single event, which determines it. Governments must be abused and deranged indeed, before it can be thought of; and the prospect of the future must be as bad as the experience of the past. . . . The wise will determine from the gravity of the case . . . but, with or without right, a revolution will be the very last resource of the thinking and the good. . . .

The [British] parliament says to the king, "Your subjects have inherited this freedom," claiming their franchises not on abstract principles "as the rights of men," but as the rights of Englishmen, and as a patrimony derived from their forefathers. You will observe that from Magna Carta [onward] it has been the uniform policy of our constitution to claim and assert our liberties as an entailed inheritance derived to us from our forefathers, and to be transmitted to our posterity . . . without any reference whatever to any other more general or prior right. . . . Thus . . . in what we improve, we are never wholly new; in what we retain, we are never wholly obsolete. . . .

You [in France] chose to act as if you . . . had everything to begin anew. You began ill, because you began by despising everything that belonged to you. . . . Respecting your forefathers, you would have been taught to respect yourselves. You would not have chosen to consider the French as a . . . nation of low-born servile wretches until the emancipating year of 1789. . . . You would not have been content to be... a gang of Maroon slaves, suddenly broke loose from the house of bondage, and therefore to be pardoned for your abuse of the liberty to which you were not accustomed....

Compute your gains: see what is got by those extravagant and presumptuous speculations which have taught your leaders to despise all their predecessors, and all their contemporaries, and even to despise themselves, until the moment in which they became truly despicable.... France, when she let loose the reins of regal authority, doubled the license of a ferocious dissoluteness in manners, and of an insolent irreligion in opinions and practices; and has extended through all ranks of life, as if she were communicating some privilege, or laying open some secluded benefit, all the unhappy corruptions that usually were the disease of wealth and power. This is one of the new principles of equality in France....

Remember that your parliament of Paris told your king, that, in calling the states together, he had nothing to fear.... It is right that these men should [now] hide their heads.... They have seen the French rebel against a mild and lawful monarch, with more fury, outrage, and insult, than ever any people has been known to rise against the most illegal usurper, or the most [bloody] tyrant. Their resistance was made to concession; their revolt was from protection; their blow was aimed at a hand holding out graces, favors, and immunities....

They have found their punishment in their success. Laws overturned; tribunals subverted; industry without vigor; commerce expiring, the revenue unpaid, yet the people impoverished; a church pillaged, and a state not relieved; civil and military anarchy made the constitution of the kingdom; everything human and divine sacrificed to the idol of public credit, and national bankruptcy the consequence.... The principle of property, whose creatures and representatives they are, was systematically subverted....

After I have read over the list of the persons and descriptions elected into the Third Estate, nothing which they afterwards did could appear astonishing. Among them, indeed, I saw some of known rank; some of shining talents; but of any practical experience in the state, not one man was to be found. The best were only men of theory.... Nothing can secure a steady and moderate conduct in such assemblies, but that the body of them should be respectably composed, in point of condition in life, of permanent property, of education, and of such habits as enlarge and liberalize the understanding....

Judge, Sir, of my surprise, when I found that a very great proportion of the assembly (a majority, I believe) was composed of practitioners in the law. It was composed, not of distinguished magistrates... but... of obscure provincial advocates... the fomenters and conductors of the petty war of village vexation.... To these were joined men of other descriptions, from whom as little knowledge of, or attention to, the interests of a great state was to be expected, and as little regard to the stability of any institution; men formed to be instruments, not controls. Such in general was the composition of the Third Estate in the National Assembly; in which was scarcely to be perceived the slightest traces of what we call the natural landed interest of the country.

Map 22.1 Napoleonic Europe in 1810 Although the enlargement of France by 1810 was only temporary, Napoleon's campaigns had lasting effects on the map of Europe. By consolidating territory in German- and Italian-speaking areas, challenging the power of traditional aristocracies, and exemplifying the power of nationalism, Napoleon helped lay the foundations for the later emergence of new nation-states (see Chapter 23).

Jacobins. Then, in 1804, he crowned himself Emperor Napoleon I, though only after securing the approval of the legislature and ratifying the move through a national plebiscite.

By the orderliness and rationality of his administration, Napoleon seemed an "enlightened despot," fulfilling the hopes of the eighteenth-century philosophes. He sponsored the creation of the Bank of France to stabilize finances, enforced use of the metric system of weights and measures to rationalize trade and accounting, and initiated a new system of laws, the Napoleonic Code, recognizing the legal equality of all French citizens. To create it, eminent jurists used the deductive Cartesian approach (see Chapter 21). Starting from general principles (rather than inherited custom), they constructed a reasoned system of civil law.

● **CONTEXT&CONNECTIONS** The Napoleonic Code became highly influential across Europe and, exported with the French overseas empire, worldwide. However, the French long refused to treat conquered Africans as citizens to whom the Code applied, ruling instead through administrative fiat. Then in the 1950s and 1960s, when African nationalists successfully organized for reforms and independence, the Napoleonic Code formed the template for new legal systems in nations such as Mali, Senegal, and Côte d'Ivoire (see Chapters 26 and 30). ●

Historians have also seen in Napoleon's campaigns the origins of modern **nationalism**, the belief that individuals are bound together by ties of language, culture, and history. National identity was not entirely new, but in France in the wake of the Revolution and Napoleonic campaigns, national feeling became much stronger. Earlier, members of the nobility were tied by marriage to aristocracies in other countries and had only limited feelings of "French" identity. Peasants, meanwhile, were tied more strongly to their local communities and provincial cultures than to the French state in Paris. But when conscripts returned to their villages, full of pride as soldiers for France, they now saw themselves as citizens of a nation rather than subjects of a king. Napoleon cultivated that sense of patriotism and national pride, promising them not liberty but glory.

nationalism
The defining ideology of the nation-state, emphasizing the rights and responsibilities of citizens toward the nation as superior to those based on regional, religious, familial, or other identities. Nationalism often asserts a common ethnic and linguistic heritage in legitimizing state power.

French nationalism grew in parallel with Napoleon's military achievements. Though the emperor abandoned his planned invasion of England after the British defeated his navy in 1805, Napoleon's forces seemed unstoppable on the continent of Europe. French armies, commanded by the greatest general of the age and by military officers chosen for their talent rather than their aristocratic connections, swept through Iberia and Italy; asserted control over the Netherlands, Poland, and the western half of Germany; and inflicted embarrassing losses on the Austrians and Prussians. Simón Bolívar, living in Paris after his visit to Rome, was disappointed by Napoleon's imperial pretensions, but like many, he admired Bonaparte's political and military skills.

● **CONTEXT&CONNECTIONS** Nation-states, what one historian has called "imagined communities," where "peoples" form "governments" within "nations," became common only in modern times. Earlier, great empires always included diverse peoples; multiethnicity was as characteristic of ancient Rome as of the later Ming, Mughal, Ottoman, Austrian, and Russian empires (see Chapters 16-17). In Holland, France, and England in the seventeenth century, however, national solidarity began emerging when people started to think of themselves as belonging to "Dutch" or "French" or "English" nations which transcended loyalty to any particular leader or dynasty. Nineteenth-century Europeans more clearly articulated the concept of "nationhood" (see Chapter 23) and through their empires exported the idea across the globe. Now "national" thinking is nearly universal, though still problematic: there have been many nations (like Nigeria) without coherent "peoples," and many peoples (like the Kurds) without their own nations (see Chapter 27). ●

In reaction to French invasion, feelings of nationalism intensified across Europe. When the French had first crossed the Rhine River, many Germans greeted them as bearers of Enlightenment, of liberty and equality. After Napoleon and his troops behaved more like occupiers than liberators, however, many Germans were bitterly disappointed. Likewise, on the Italian peninsula, French invasion caused the subjects of disparate monarchies to assert a common "Italian" identity in rallying against the intruders (see Chapter 23).

AP® THEMES

What impact did the French Revolution and Napoleonic Wars have on the process of state-building in Europe?

In the end, it was Napoleon's ambition that caused his own downfall. In 1812 he mounted a massive attack on Russia. The Russian army could in no way prevent this assault, but they used their vast landscape to military advantage. When Napoleon reached Moscow, he found that the city had been abandoned and largely burned to the ground by its own people. Retreat through the harsh Russian winter decimated the French army. Of the 700,000 troops that had invaded Russia, fewer than 100,000 returned.

A broad coalition of anti-French forces now went on the offensive, invaded France, forced Napoleon to abdicate, and restored the Bourbon monarchy by placing Louis XVIII (r. 1814–1824) on the throne. Dramatically, Napoleon escaped his exile, returned to Paris, and re-formed his army before finally being defeated by British and Prussian forces at the Battle of Waterloo in 1815. By this roundabout route, France finally became a constitutional monarchy. Napoleon died in exile on a remote South Atlantic island.

Napoleon's impact beyond France itself was substantial. His amalgamation of small western German states into the Confederation of the Rhine set the stage for the development first of nationalism among Germans, who were bound together by language and culture but politically fragmented, and later of a centralized German nation-state. Similarly, on the Italian peninsula after Napoleon's

Battle of the Pyramids The Napoleonic Wars came to North Africa with the French invasion of 1798 and their defeat of the Mamluk army. Subsequently, the British victory over Napoleon's Mediterranean fleet forced him to abandon Egypt. Muhammad Ali, an Ottoman general, soon filled the power vacuum created by the French invasion (see Chapter 23).

conquest, modern Italian nationalism and the quest for a unified Italian nation began. As far away as Egypt, Napoleon's invasion in 1798 destroyed the status quo, stimulating Egyptians' national consciousness and setting the stage for the emergence of a more powerful Egyptian state (see Chapter 23).

For Simón Bolívar, Napoleon's most relevant impact occurred in Spain where, by overthrowing the monarchy, Napoleon gave an opening to the forces of South American liberation. Within France's own overseas empire, the most dramatic developments took place on the Caribbean island of Saint-Domingue (san-doe-MANG).

The Haitian Revolution, 1791–1804

The colony of Saint-Domingue was by far France's richest overseas possession. Occupying the western half of the island of Hispaniola, Saint-Domingue accounted for as much as a third of French foreign trade. Half a million African slaves toiled on the colony's plantations under conditions so harsh that the planters had to constantly import more Africans to keep enough slaves working in the fields (see Chapter 19).

As the reverberations of 1789 reached Saint-Domingue, revolution in Haiti also moved through several stages. Initially, the central conflict was between the whites who dominated the plantation economy and the *gens de couleur* (zhahn deh koo-LUHR), free men and women of mixed race, who about equaled the whites in number. Artisans and small farmers, some gens de couleur were even prosperous enough to own a few slaves themselves. Many were literate, and having followed the events of the American and French Revolutions, they demanded liberty and equality for themselves. By 1791, civil war broke out between the planters and the gens de couleur.

While neither group wanted to end slavery, civil war between them created an opening for a vast slave uprising organized by a *Voudun* (voh-doon) priest called Boukman (because he was literate). Voudun beliefs and rituals derived from West and Central Africa, and as a religious leader Boukman had great authority among African slaves, while his position as his master's coach driver gave him the mobility to organize thousands of slaves to rise up at his signal. When they did so, in the summer of 1791, the rebels were spontaneously joined by tens of thousands of other slaves from across the island, as well as by maroons, runaway slaves who lived in the mountains (see Chapter 19).

Just as French peasants had burned the manor houses of their aristocratic overlords, now Boukman's slave army attacked the planters' estates in Saint-Domingue. Forty thousand marched on the city of Le Cap, where whites and gens de couleur had taken refuge. The slaughter lasted for weeks, until planter forces finally captured and executed the rebel leader; they fixed his head to a pole with a sign that read: *"This is the head of Boukman, chief of the rebels."*

● **CONTEXT&CONNECTIONS** Ironically, the Haitian Revolution played a role in delaying the abolition of the slave trade in the British empire. In 1791, planters in the British West Indies, and their allies in Britain, used fear of revolt to lobby effectively against *abolitionist* legislation, a delay that pushed back the end of the British slave trade until 1808, much to the disappointment of *Olaudah Equiano* (Chapter 19). ●

Portrait of Toussaint Louverture (1743–1803) on horseback, early 19th century (colour engraving), French School (19th century)/Bibliotheque Nationale, Paris, France/Archives Charmet/Bridgeman Images

Toussaint L'Ouverture This contemporary engraving shows the Haitian revolutionary leader Toussaint L'Ouverture in an equestrian pose associated with civil and military power. Toussaint brought Enlightenment ideals to the elemental struggle of Haiti's slaves for liberation. His leadership was sorely missed in Haiti after he was tricked into negotiations with France and died in a French prison.

In 1792, the French government sent an army to restore order. But then a new commander emerged. François-Dominique Toussaint was born a slave but had been educated by a priest and had worked in his master's house rather than in the fields. The name by which he is remembered, **Toussaint L'Ouverture** (1744–1803), reflects his military skill: *L'Ouverture* refers to the "opening" he would make in the enemy lines. But Toussaint's political, intellectual, and diplomatic strengths were equally important in turning Haiti into an independent nation freed from the savage inequalities of slavery.

Like Olaudah Equiano (see Chapter 19), Toussaint L'Ouverture (too-SAN loo-ver-CHUR) had diverse experiences that allowed him to bridge the worlds of slave and master. He could organize the slaves to fight while forging alliances with whites, gens de couleur, and the foreign forces that intervened in the conflict. By 1801, his army controlled most of the island. Toussaint supported a new constitution that granted equality to all and declared him governor-general for life.

Initially, some radical French revolutionaries supported the rebels, but Napoleon had other ideas, and in 1802 he sent an expedition to crush Toussaint's army. Toussaint was open to compromise as long as slavery would not be restored and freely agreed to meet with French officers to discuss the matter. They betrayed him: sent to France and harshly treated, Toussaint died in prison.

Toussaint L'Ouverture
(1744–1803) Leader of the Haitian revolution. Under his military and political leadership, Haiti gained independence and abolished slavery, becoming the first black-ruled republic in the Americas. He died in exile in France.

Meanwhile, many of the soldiers sent by Napoleon to Haiti, lacking immunity to tropical diseases, succumbed to malaria and yellow fever. In Haiti, it was mosquitos more than firepower that drove away the French, just as it was frostbite more than cannon that later ejected them from Russia.

• **CONTEXT&CONNECTIONS** Historians now recognize the role of disease in the Atlantic revolutions. Africans had often arrived in the Americas with disease immunity, which European settlers also developed from childhood exposure. Troops fresh from Europe, in contrast, were extremely vulnerable. Toussaint and other rebels could use differential immunity to their advantage, for example by luring European troops into swampy, malaria-infested areas. •

The subsequent independence of Haiti terrified slave owners in the United States. Some plantations stepped up security measures, while the U.S. government refused to grant Haiti diplomatic recognition. Venezuela was even more directly affected. In 1795, a Venezuelan who returned from Haiti, a free *zombo* (of mixed African-Amerindian ancestry), led a rebellion of slaves and free persons of color, sending the elite of Caracas into a panic. Simón Bolívar was just twelve at that time, but later he would seek the support of the Haitian government and would argue for the abolition of slavery.

AP® THEMES

What was the impact of the Haitian Revolution on coercive labor systems in the Americas?

The Latin American Wars of Independence, 1800–1824

Simón Bolívar and other Latin American revolutionaries looked to the ideals of the Enlightenment and the examples of the United States, France, and Haiti in charting their own wars of independence. Also shaping the course of revolution here were relations between *criollos* (American-born Spaniards) and people of African, Amerindian, or mixed descent (see Chapter 18). Beyond widespread agreement on the need to expel the Spanish, the divergent interests of these groups made it difficult to establish common political ground.

Francisco Miranda, Simón Bolívar, and South American Independence

His Venezuelan predecessor, Francisco Miranda (1750–1816), anticipated Simón Bolívar's path. While Bolívar came of age only during the French Revolution, Miranda had earlier traveled to the United States where, in 1783, he met with George Washington and Thomas Jefferson, seeking their inspiration and support for a parallel uprising against Spain. He then toured Europe, escaping Spanish attempts to capture him, and participated in the French Revolution. In Paris, the Jacobins jailed and nearly executed him for denouncing their dictatorship. When he finally returned to South America in 1806, Miranda's goal was to inflame continental revolution against Spain and to forge a unified Gran Colombian state. (See the feature "World History in Today's World: Competing Visions of South American Cooperation.")

Miranda was a living embodiment of the Atlantic Ocean as a transmission zone for revolution. While in Paris, he had been inducted into the society of the Freemasons, a transnational group whose members' belief in Enlightenment rationality took the form of secret rites and rituals emphasizing honesty, integrity, charity, and brotherly love. Though they met in secret, masons were among the most influential intellectual and political actors of the eighteenth century. Members included Benjamin Franklin, Voltaire, George Washington, and the Austrian composer Wolfgang Amadeus Mozart. In 1803, while in Europe, Simón Bolívar was himself inducted into a masonic lodge in Cádiz, Spain.

By the time Bolívar went back to Venezuela in 1807, finding that Francisco Miranda had returned as well, conditions were ripening for Latin American independence. In 1808 Napoleon put his own brother on the Spanish throne, forcing the Spanish king to abdicate. Rejecting the Napoleonic regime as illegitimate, South American elites created *juntas* (ruling groups) to assert temporary local rule.

Loyalists thought these juntas (HUN-tahs) should be disbanded as soon as the legitimate king returned to power. But republicans like Miranda, Bolívar, and

Competing Visions of South American Cooperation

For two centuries, South American unity has been an elusive goal. Francisco Miranda's vision of Gran Colombia was only partly realized by Simón Bolívar and did not last beyond 1830. Still, any discussion of South American unity is sure to invoke the names Miranda and Bolívar.

Since 1991, the Common Market of the South, or Mercosur, has promoted interregional collaboration under the leadership of Venezuela, Brazil, and Argentina. In 2012, however, a competing organization, the Pacific Alliance, was established by Chile, Mexico, Colombia, and Peru.

Apart from the geographic split, the two organizations are also divided by political philosophy and economic policy. The Mercosur governments have mostly been controlled by populist political parties emphasizing a central role for the state. The Pacific Alliance, on the other hand, was created by more conservative political leaders who stress neoliberal, free-market policies. The Pacific Alliance member states are also much friendlier to the United States than those of Mercosur, where traditional suspicions of U.S. intervention and economic domination run deep.

For now, the Pacific Alliance seems to have greater potential. Chile, Mexico, Colombia, and Peru have already eliminated 90 percent of trade tariffs as well as visa requirements. Their plan is for a common market, as they pursue negotiations toward trade pacts with both the United States and the European Union.

The governments of Brazil, Argentina, and Venezuela reacted to the rise of the upstart Pacific Alliance as a threat to their longer term goal of fuller integration, eventually with a common currency and a South American legislature. That agenda has stalled for a number of reasons. Economic disputes between booming Brazil and debt-plagued Argentina have made cooperation over trade issues difficult, and the death of Venezuelan leader Hugo Chávez removed the most charismatic proponent of socialist defiance of the United States.

There have been calls for cooperation between the competing blocs. In 2013, the government of Uruguay proposed that Mercosur embrace a "multiplicity of memberships" to allow its members to work more closely with the Pacific Alliance, and Chilean President Michelle Bachelet organized meetings to identify points of collaboration. Still, as in the days of Miranda and Bolívar, South American unity remains a far-off dream.

AP® THEMES

How did independence efforts in Spanish America challenge racial ideologies?

their Argentinean counterpart José de San Martín (1778–1850) saw the chance to win complete independence. This division of opinion meant that to win independence, South American republicans would have to fight against powerful local loyalists as well as Spanish troops.

A principal grievance for men of Bolívar's background was that *peninsulares*, the direct representatives of royal authority in Spanish America, dominated the affairs of church and state. Ambitious criollos felt that the existing system was an impediment to their rightful place as leading members of their communities. Criollo merchants, for example, were continually frustrated by restrictions on trade imposed by the peninsulares.

But the struggle involved more than just imperial representatives and local elites. In most places, building a popular base of support for independence required appealing to Indians, Africans, mestizos, and other people of mixed descent, who together made up the majority of the population.

For example, Bolívar's home city of Caracas, facing the sea, was culturally and economically connected to the Caribbean. Slave plantations were an important part of its economy, and Bolívar spent part of his childhood on such a plantation. In addition, Caracas had a large community of *pardos*, free men and women of mixed African-Spanish-Native American ancestry. As in Haiti, unity across these deep divides of class and race was hard to achieve.

In the Venezuelan interior, Bolívar would need the cooperation of *llaneros* (yah-NEYR-ohs), tough frontier cowboys of mixed Spanish-Amerindian descent (like the *gauchos* of Argentina and the *vaqueros* of Mexico). Farther south, Bolívar's armies eventually entered the Viceroyalty of Peru, where the main social divide was between the Spanish-speaking colonists of the coastal areas and the still considerable Amerindian population of the Andes. Simón Bolívar (unlike George Washington) constantly faced the challenge of forging alliances between disparate racial and ethnic groups.

Meanwhile, local elites had taken power in Caracas. Their conservative junta saw local control as temporary, and sent the well-traveled Bolívar on diplomatic missions to London and Washington in 1810. But Bolívar betrayed them by lobbying the British to support his own plan for independence. Upon his return, Bolívar attended the first Congress of Venezuela, which on July 3, 1811, following the passionate advocacy of Francisco Miranda, became the first body in Latin America to declare independence from Spain.

However, racial, ethnic, and regional divisions inhibited any strong sense of "Venezuelan" identity upon which a new nation could be founded. The constitution restricted voting rights to a small minority of criollo property owners and did nothing to abolish slavery. In addition, the llaneros of the interior felt threatened by a constitutional provision that extended private property ownership to the previously uncharted plains. If wealthy ranchers fenced off the lands where they herded wild cattle, the cowboys might lose their livelihood and their independence.

Taking advantage of these divisions, forces loyal to Spain were soon on the offensive. A massive earthquake in the spring of 1812 compounded a sense of foreboding as support for the republic wavered. Miranda began negotiations with Spanish officials for an armistice. Bolívar regarded Miranda's actions as treasonous and had him arrested, a harsh turn against his older colleague that caused some to view Bolívar with suspicion. Amid such acrimony, the young republic collapsed.

Bolívar then set out on the military path he would pursue for the next twelve years, proclaiming a *"war to the death."* Captured Spaniards would be executed, he declared, while American-born Spanish loyalists would be given a chance to mend their ways. In the summer of 1813, Bolívar's army was strong enough to enter Caracas, but again divisions within Venezuelan society worked against him. To broaden his movement's appeal, Bolívar had forged alliances with groups that had been excluded from the first congress and constitution, including llaneros and slaves. Many criollos, however, distrusted Bolívar's army, regarding his black and cowboy soldiers as mere bandits and outlaws.

In addition to such internal dissension, the cause of independence suffered a setback in 1815 after Napoleon's defeat at Waterloo and the restoration of the Spanish monarchy. The Madrid government then reasserted its political and economic control over its American dominions. Seeking greater efficiency through administrative reform, the new Spanish king reinforced the preference for peninsulares in positions of colonial command, while dispatching fifty ships and over ten thousand soldiers to restore imperial authority.

Put on the defensive, Bolívar retreated to the island of Jamaica, where he once again sought British help. He also traveled to Haiti, pursuing support from its government with a pledge to seek "*the absolute liberty of the slaves who have groaned beneath the Spanish yoke in the past three centuries.*"* Most importantly from a military standpoint, he recruited battle-hardened British mercenaries to serve as his elite force.

Returning once more to Venezuela in 1817, Bolívar established himself in the interior and was recognized as the supreme commander of the various patriotic forces. He offered freedom to slaves who joined his army, and he revived his alliance with the llaneros of the plains. Bolívar's toughness in battle and his willingness to share the privations of his men—once spending a whole night immersed in a lake to avoid Spanish forces—won him their loyalty.

Congress of Angostura
(1819) Congress that declared Venezuelan independence after Simón Bolívar gave an opening address arguing for a strong central government with effective executive powers.

In 1819, even while the Spanish still held Caracas, delegates to the **Congress of Angostura** planned for the resuscitation of independent Venezuela. Bolívar argued for a strong central government with effective executive powers, fearing that a federal system with a strong legislature would lead to division and instability. Rather than stay to see these plans carried out, however, he went south and west to confront imperial forces in the Spanish stronghold of Bogotá. Seeking a broader foundation for Latin American liberty, he began his fight for *Gran Colombia*, a proposed constitutional union encompassing today's Venezuela, Colombia, Panama, Ecuador, and Peru (see Map 22.2).

Bolívar and his troops suffered greatly on their trek into the frigid Andes, but their morale remained high. The Spanish forces, on the other hand, became demoralized. Led by generals who could not match Bolívar's strategic brilliance, they quickly gave way, first in Bogotá and then in Ecuador. Meanwhile, further south, other liberators were scoring equivalent successes. José de San Martín (hoe-SAY deh san mar-TEEN) took the region of Rio de la Plata (today's Argentina), while Chile's successful republican forces were led by Bernardo O'Higgins (the Spanish-speaking son of an Irish immigrant). Together San Martín and O'Higgins had occupied the coastal regions of Peru, leaving only its Andean region in loyalist hands.

Tupac Amaru II
(1741–1781) José Gabriel Condorcanqui Noguera, a descendant of the last Inca ruler; called himself Tupac Amaru II while leading a large-scale rebellion in the Andes against Spanish rule. He was defeated and executed.

The situation in the Andes had been tense since an Amerindian uprising in 1780 led by **Tupac Amaru II** (1741–1781), a descendant of the last Inca ruler. Tupac Amaru (TOO-pack ah-MAR-oo) had been baptized and educated by Jesuit priests and for a time served the Spanish government. But the poverty, illiteracy, and oppression faced by his people caused him first to petition for reform and then, when his pleas were ignored, to raise an Andean rebellion.

Spanish authorities savagely suppressed Tupac Amaru's revolt, forcing him to witness the torture and death of his own wife and family before his own execution. The coastal criollo elite of Peru in and around Lima supported this repression of Andean rebellion, fearing a race war in which they might be victims. The Spanish tried to enforce cultural assimilation by banning indigenous cloth and the use of the indigenous Quechua (KETCH-wah) language. But the Amerindians of the mountains avoided the ban, and as much contact with Spanish officials as possible. Though these highland Amerindians were potential allies of Bolívar, they remained aloof, more concerned with the autonomy of their own communities than the independence of nations.

---

*Excerpt from Simón Bolívar, "Oath Taken at Rome, 15 August 1805," trans. Frederick H. Fornoff, in *El Libertador: Writings of Simón Bolívar*, ed. David Bushnell (New York: Oxford University Press, 2003), p. 77.

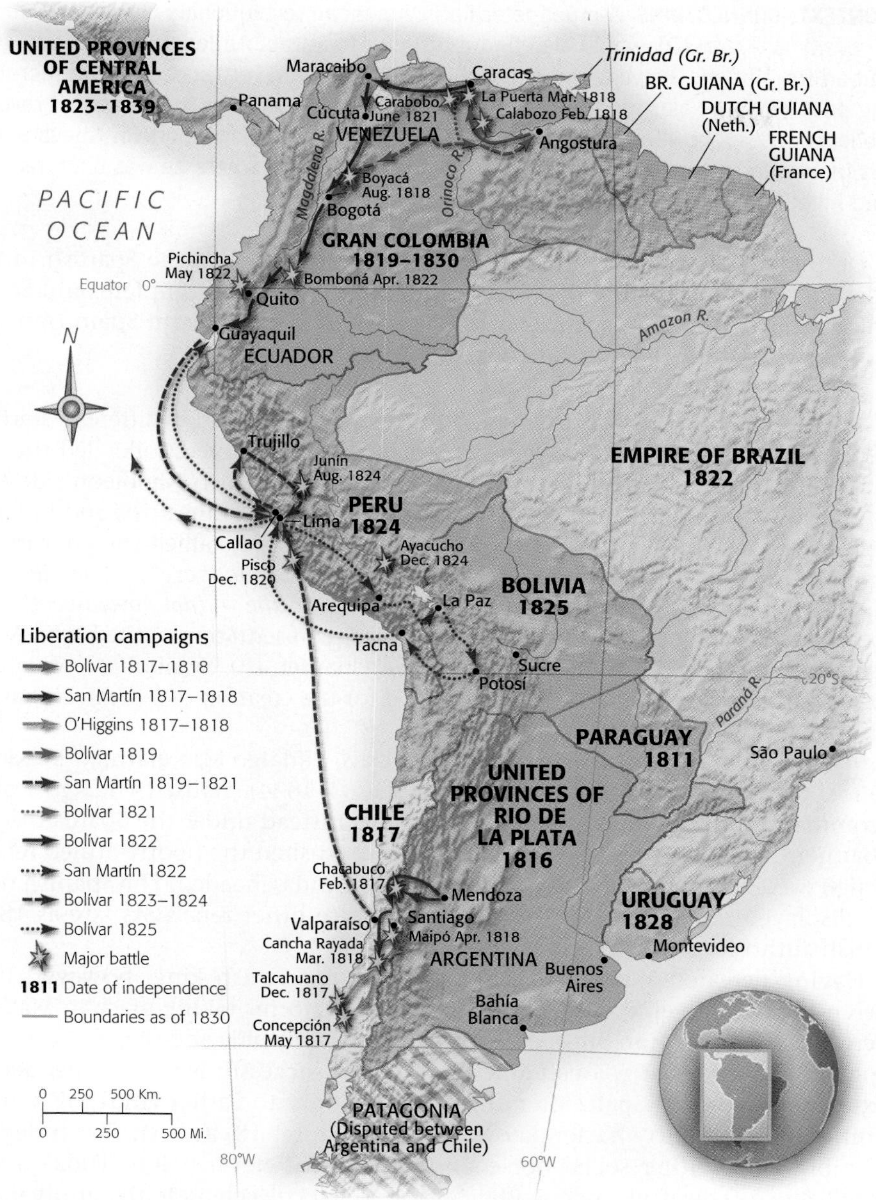

Map 22.2 Independence in Latin America Paraguay led the way toward Latin American independence in 1811. The United Provinces of Rio de la Plata (the core of today's Argentina) followed in 1816. The next year, José de San Martín and Bernardo O'Higgins secured Chilean independence. By 1819, Simón Bolívar had secured the independence of Venezuela and Ecuador, uniting them into the independent state of *Gran Colombia*. Combined Chilean and Colombian forces defeated the Spanish at Ayacucho in 1824, finalizing the independence of Spanish Latin America.

● **CONTEXT&CONNECTIONS** A much later Latin American revolutionary, *Ernesto "Che" Guevara* (Chapter 30), would also find it difficult to attract Andean allies. During the Cuban Revolution, Guevara and his compatriots had been very successful in recruiting poor peasants as supporters. When he went to Bolivia to try to repeat that revolutionary success, however, the local Amerindians remained unsupportive. Guevara and his men found themselves isolated in the cold mountains, where he was captured and killed. ●

Despite Amerindian disinterest, Bolívar's troops engaged the Spanish in the Andes in 1824 at the Battle of Ayacucho. Their victory was complete, and South America was free from Spanish control. But would freedom from Spain translate into liberty for diverse South American peoples?

Mexico, 1810–1821

Mexico's path to independence had a different starting point. Whereas socially conservative criollos led the initial struggle in Venezuela, in Mexico Napoleon's deposition of the Spanish king quickly led to a popular uprising of mestizos and Indians. Parish priest **Miguel de Hidalgo y Costilla** (1753–1811) rallied the poor in the name of justice for the oppressed, issuing his famous *Grito* ("cry"): *"Long live Our Lady of Guadalupe! Long live the Americas and death to the corrupt government!"* His appeal to the Virgin of Guadalupe, a dark-skinned representation of the Virgin Mary as she had appeared to a lowly peasant (see Chapter 18), symbolized Hidalgo's appeal to Indians and mestizos. Hidalgo called for the creation of a Mexican nation with the words *"¡Mexicanos, Viva México!"*

Miguel de Hidalgo y Costilla
(1753–1811) Mexican priest who launched the first stage of the Mexican war for independence. Hidalgo appealed to Indians and mestizos and was thus viewed with suspicion by Mexican criollos. In 1811, he was captured and executed.

While this was shocking to Spanish officials, Hidalgo also alarmed Mexico's criollos. One of them, Agustín de Iturbide (1783–1824), refused Hidalgo's offer to command the rebel army, leading his troops instead under the Spanish loyalist banner. Iturbide's well-trained soldiers easily crushed the poorly armed rebels: Hidalgo was excommunicated and then captured and beheaded. The Spanish publicly displayed his mutilated head as a warning to other rebels. As late as 1820, Spanish authority seemed secure.

Having defeated Hidalgo in the name of the Spanish king, however, Iturbide and the criollo elite were alarmed by liberal reforms taking place in Madrid, where a new constitution limited royal power. Now Iturbide and the Mexican elite turned on their former Spanish allies and fought successfully for independence. Mexico was free from Spain after 1821, but contrary to Father Hildago's vision, domination by wealthy hacienda owners (see Chapter 18) assured that independence brought neither social nor economic reform. Nevertheless, Hidalgo still symbolizes the country's independence, and Mexicans celebrate the anniversary of the *Grito de Dolores*, September 16, as Mexico's national day.

● **CONTEXT&CONNECTIONS** The social divisions left unaddressed at the time of Mexican independence in 1821 festered until the outbreak of the Mexican Revolution in 1910, when mestizos and Indians organized by *Emiliano Zapata* (Chapter 25) rose again to challenge the large landowners and big ranchers. ●

Brazil and the Caribbean, 1808–1835

The age of Atlantic revolutions played out much differently in Brazil, which became an empire under the former Portuguese ruling family, and in the Caribbean, where rule from Europe and, as in

Gale Beery/Getty Images

Father Hidalgo In 1810, Father Hidalgo rallied the common people of Mexico, especially mestizos and Indians, under the banner of the Virgin of Guadalupe for independence from Spain. Mexican elites opposed him, however, and cooperated with Spanish authorities to crush the uprising. Hidalgo was executed.

Brazil, slave plantation economies continued. (Independent Haiti was the exception.)

Brazil had followed its own distinct path toward independence. In 1808, the Portuguese royal family fled Napoleon's invasion, seeking refuge in Brazil. In 1821, the king returned to Portugal, leaving his son Pedro behind as his representative. Pedro, however, declared himself sympathetic to the cause of independence, and in 1824 Pedro I (r. 1824–1831) became the constitutional monarch of an independent Brazil.

Brazil's independence was therefore managed by its social and economic elites and was a deeply conservative affair. Like the United States, Brazil became independent with its merchant and slave-owning elites intact. Encountering less political and economic disruption than the Spanish-speaking Americas, Brazil was poised to attract immigrants and capital investment, and to deepen penetration of its vast interior.

Nevertheless, deeper social fissures were exposed during the constitutional transition, leading to the largest *urban* slave uprising in the history of the Americas, the Malê Revolt, or Muslim Uprising, of 1835. The population of the northeastern city of Salvador de Bahia, where the uprising took place, was not only majority African, but primarily Yoruba (from what is now western Nigeria). Muslim scholars led the revolt, and even used Arabic in their correspondence to avoid detection. The response of the authorities was harsh. The Muslim clerics who led the uprising were quickly executed. Both sides were well aware of the Haitian example. As in Brazil, slavery endured late into the nineteenth century in Cuba and other Spanish possessions in the Caribbean.

• **CONTEXT&CONNECTIONS** Yoruba religious life in Brazil was a complex mix of Christianity, Islam, and belief in the power of the traditional *orisas*, the Yoruba gods (see Chapter 19). As in today's Nigeria, followers of all three traditions were found in nineteenth-century Brazil, though even more common was a blending of monotheistic and traditional beliefs and practices. The *syncretism* (Chapter 18) of the Malê rebels, for example, included the use of African amulets as protective devices, though sometimes incorporating Koranic passages. •

Meanwhile, in the Caribbean, Jamaica was the scene of another significant slave uprising in 1831–1832, the Christmas Rebellion, under the leadership of a Baptist preacher. Inspired by the British abolitionist movement and the peaceful outlawing of the slave trade, the rebels demanded that they be paid for their labor and free to leave their plantations in search of better opportunity. As always, the plantation owners ferociously repressed the rebellion. But that was their last hurrah. Just two years later, in 1834, Parliament freed all slaves in the empire, with compensation due to former slave owners. In Jamaica and elsewhere, blacks swiftly abandoned the sugar fields. Abolition thus came to the British Caribbean without either revolution, as in Haiti, or national independence, as in the Spanish Americas.

Revolutionary Outcomes and Comparisons to 1830

The circulation of revolutionary ideas and revolutionary experiences connected the Atlantic world in the late eighteenth and early nineteenth centuries: Simón Bolívar's goals and achievements grew directly from earlier struggles in the United States, France, and Haiti to transform politics in the name of liberty and equality. By 1830, however, the outcomes of revolution in Europe and across the Americas were quite different.

In Europe, the excesses of French politics led to a strong counterreaction of conservatism in defense of tradition over change. Europe's revolutionary flame was extinguished when princes, priests, and aristocrats used the defeat of Napoleon to suppress reform (even, after all that had happened, placing yet another "Louis" on the throne of France!). Leading this attempt by European conservatives

Map 22.3 Europe in 1815 After the disruptions in the political map of Europe caused by the French Revolution and the expansion of Napoleon's empire (see Map 22.1), in 1815 European diplomats restored earlier boundaries and established a conservative status quo at the Congress of Vienna. One important change was the appearance of a larger Prussian kingdom, now including Rhineland territories in the west of Germany, a territorial expansion that would later form the foundation for German unification (see Chapter 23). Austria competed with Prussia for influence, founding a German Confederation centered in Vienna.

to turn back the clock was Prince Metternich of Austria, who orchestrated the **Congress of Vienna** (1815), which restored the balance of power among Britain, France, Austria, Prussia, and Russia (see Map 22.3). Aristocrats once again flaunted their wealth in the capitals of Europe, no longer afraid of revolutionary violence.

However, the spread of nationalism and the association of that idea with progressive reform proved a constant challenge to European rulers. When Greek nationalists won their independence from the Ottoman empire in 1829, the event did not at first appear to threaten the European status quo. But it was not long before ethnic minorities in the Austrian and Russian empires also began organizing

Congress of Vienna
(1815) Conference at which the balance of power among European states was restored after the defeat of Napoleon Bonaparte.

along national lines, while the idea of a single, powerful German nation began to spread as well. Other ideals of the French Revolution also remained alive, such as the idea that equality could only be achieved through a more equitable distribution of wealth. Before long a rising generation of revolutionaries would try once again to overturn Europe's status quo (see Chapter 23).

AP® THEMES

What similar challenges did the rulers of newly independent nations in the Americas face in establishing stable governments?

The United States of America, following George Washington's farewell advice, stayed largely aloof from European affairs. In the first half of the nineteenth century the new country focused on expansion, with relatively high wages and cheap land attracting swelling numbers of European immigrants. In 1803, anxious for funds to fight on other fronts, Napoleon agreed to the Louisiana Purchase. Vast new territories were thus added to the United States, and soon Lewis and Clark's expedition was pointing the way west (see Chapter 21). These lands were not, however, unoccupied. Over the course of the nineteenth century, violence and dislocation would mark U.S. westward expansion. And since the issue of slavery remained unresolved, regional tensions increased, ultimately exploding in a violent civil war (see Chapter 25). Conversations, and disagreements, about the true meaning of "liberty" would continue in the United States far into the future.

In Haiti, the transition from slave colony to free republic proved exceedingly difficult. Freed slaves fled the plantations to establish their own farms on small plots of land, and a massive decline in overall production followed. The sharp decline in plantation exports robbed the new government of its tax base. The political transition to independence proved equally problematic. The personal ambitions of early Haitian rulers, fueled by tensions between the mixed-race gens de couleur and Haitians of African/slave descent, created political divisions and a long-standing culture of corruption and dictatorship. Centuries of an economic and social system based almost solely on sugar and slavery had left Haitians ill-prepared to achieve either democracy or prosperity.

In Latin America, Simón Bolívar's attempt to create a state of *Gran Colombia* fell apart. The great liberator ended his life in disappointment, as all across the region military commanders seized power in a patchwork of often squabbling new republics. Lacking strong traditions of local governance, these new republics were easily dominated by military dictators who allied with wealthy landowners and church officials. Concentrated wealth, a legacy of the colonial era, provided a poor foundation on which to build democracy. And before long, as Bolívar foresaw, the fragmentation of *Gran Colombia* left South America vulnerable to external powers such as Great Britain and the United States.

caudillos
Latin American military men who gained power through violence during and after the early nineteenth century.

By 1830, those ruling in much of Latin America were ***caudillos*** (cow-DEE-yos), strong-arm rulers who looked after their own interests and those of the military above all else, usually with the support of the dominant landowners and the Catholic Church. In Venezuela, for example, one of Bolívar's top commanders, José Antonio Páez, separated the country from *Gran Colombia* while establishing an authoritarian style. In Mexico, it was one of Iturbide's commanders at the time of independence, General Antonio López de Santa Anna (1794–1875), who came to typify the venality and weakness of caudillo rule, serving as president nine different times starting in 1833, and eventually losing half of Mexico to the United States (see Chapter 25). Soon, reformers across Latin America were striving to create liberal constitutional orders to replace the caudillos.

Although Africans, Amerindians, and people of mixed descent played important roles in the Latin American wars of independence, their efforts were not to be rewarded with power or privilege, even where slavery was abolished. Benefiting most from independence were the criollos who had consolidated their political and economic dominance by assuming positions of authority vacated by departing peninsulares. As for the church, while individual priests might side with the downtrodden, the Catholic hierarchy still allied itself with the wealthy and powerful.

Nowhere were the goals of liberty, equality, and fraternity decreed by French revolutionaries fully realized. But Enlightenment concepts were now a permanent part of the political conversation around the Atlantic and, as the nineteenth century progressed, across the world.

CONTEXT AND CONNECTIONS

The Global Legacies of Revolution

To go through a "complete revolution" means to experience a bottom-to-top transformation, a thorough reordering of society. Of the cases considered in this chapter, only the brief period of extreme republicanism in France under the Jacobins and the Haitian revolution approach that definition. In the other cases—in the United States, in France under the National Assembly and Napoleon, across Latin America—in spite of significant political change, notable continuities with prerevolutionary societies remained.

Enlightenment philosophers were, of course, the ones who suggested that custom and tradition should be tossed aside if and when they stood in the way of a rationally ordered society. They were more conservative on the question of how to achieve that end, however, generally trusting that sophisticated, cosmopolitan elites

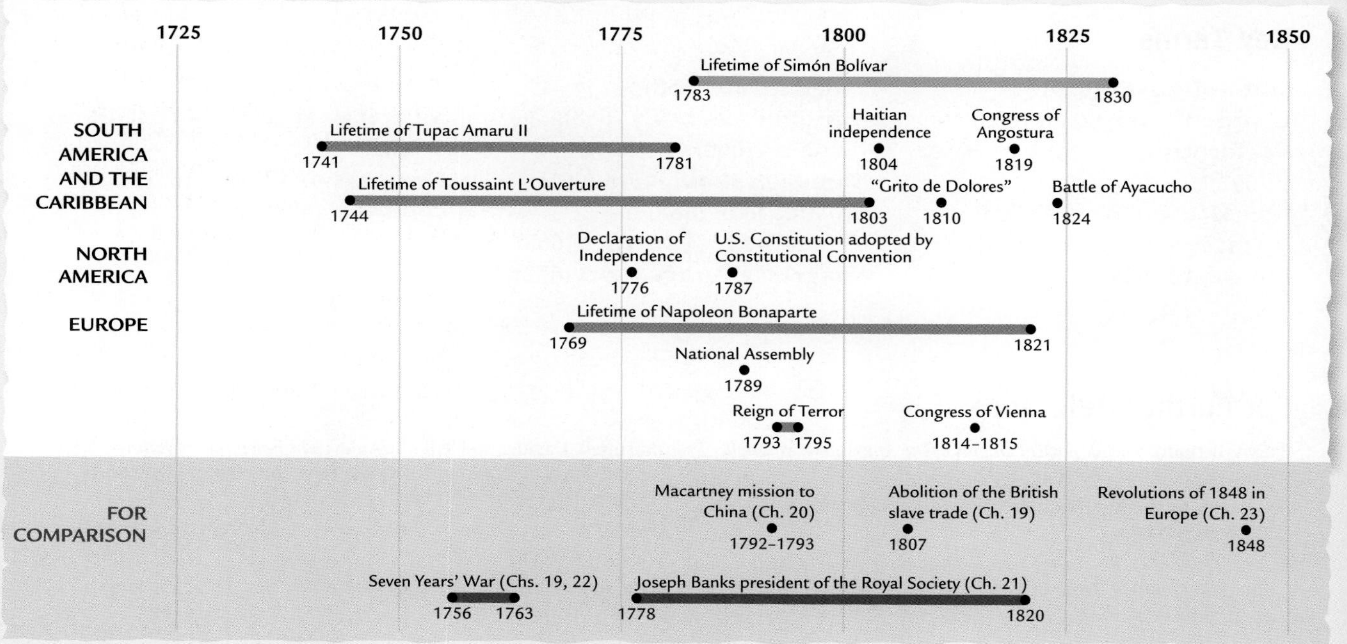

would lead the way. In Britain's North American colonies, it was indeed the more privileged and well educated who led the war of independence and the creation of the new republic. Even so, the doctrine of popular sovereignty required them to look beyond their own self-interest as planters, merchants, and professionals and take seriously the aspirations of the broader society (if not of blacks, Amerindians, or women).

In every other case, however, the old order's resistance to change required revolutionaries to mobilize excluded members of society to generate the power they needed, as when Simón Bolívar assembled his coalition of criollos, cowboys, and slaves to throw off Spanish rule. Even if, as in France and Haiti, revolutionaries did not originally plan it that way, those at the bottom usually rose up demanding to be heard (peasants burning manor houses in France, Parisians seizing the Bastille, Haitian slaves attacking sugar plantations and their owners, mestizos and Indians rallying to the banner of Father Hidalgo in Mexico).

Once the genie of mass agitation was out of the bottle, middle-class revolutionaries were generally anxious to put it back: to define liberty in a way that protected property, and to limit voting rights to those "responsible" enough to use them wisely. That was the path advocated by philosopher John Locke and reflected in the British constitution. In contrast, the more radical restructuring of society in France led to the Jacobin dictatorship and ultimately to Napoleon's empire, precedents that both historians and aspiring revolutionaries would closely investigate for centuries to come.

As we will see, the eighteenth-century revolutions left enduring global legacies. Later revolutionary leaders in Russia and China found inspiration in the events of 1789 (see Chapters 23 and 27), while anticolonial nationalists in Asia and Africa would look to the history of North and South American liberation to inspire their own quest for independence from European empires (see Chapter 30). The French and Haitian examples were especially inspiring to revolutionaries mobilizing masses of people to achieve wholesale change. For conservatives, on the other hand, the dangers of mass mobilization outweighed the benefits: they recalled Edmund Burke's warning that radical revolution leads to dictatorship.

Key Terms

Simón Bolívar (650)
George Washington (652)
Declaration of Independence (652)
Constitution of the United States of America (654)
Louis XVI (655)
Third Estate (658)
National Assembly (658)
Jacobins (660)
Napoleon Bonaparte (661)
nationalism (665)
Toussaint L'Ouverture (668)
Congress of Angostura (672)
Tupac Amaru II (672)
Miguel de Hidalgo y Costilla (674)
Congress of Vienna (677)
caudillos (678)

For Further Reference

Bailyn, Bernard. *The Ideological Origins of the American Revolution*. Cambridge, Mass.: Belknap, 1992.

Bell, Madison Smartt. *Toussaint Louverture: A Biography*. New York: Pantheon, 2007.

Brown, Howard G. *Ending the French Revolution: Violence, Justice, and Repression from the Terror to Napoleon*. Charlottesville: University of Virginia Press, 2007.

Bushnell, David, and Neill MacAuley. *The Emergence of Latin America in the Nineteenth Century*. New York: Oxford University Press, 1994.

Doyle, William. *Origins of the French Revolution*. New York: Oxford University Press, 1999.

Englund, Steven. *Napoleon: A Political Life*. New York: Scribner's, 2004.

Geggus, David P. *The Impact of the Haitian Revolution in the Atlantic World*. Columbia: University of South Carolina Press, 2002.

McNeill, J. R. *Mosquito Empires: Ecology and War in the Greater Caribbean, 1620–1914*. New York: Cambridge University Press, 2010.

Reis, João José. *Slave Rebellion in Brazil: The Muslim Uprising of 1835 in Bahia*. Baltimore: Johns Hopkins University Press, 1993.

Van Young, Eric. *The Other Rebellion: Popular Violence, Ideology, and the Mexican Struggle for Independence, 1810–1821*. Stanford: Stanford University Press, 2001.

Wood, Gordon S. *The American Revolution*. New York: Modern Library, 2002.

AP® Review Questions for Chapter 22

Multiple-Choice Questions

QUESTIONS 1–3 REFER TO THE FOLLOWING PASSAGES.

We hold these truths to be self-evident, that all men are created equal, that they are endowed by their Creator with certain inalienable Rights, that among these are Life, Liberty and the pursuit of Happiness—That to secure these rights, Governments are instituted among Men, deriving their just powers from the consent of the governed.

—U.S. Declaration of Independence, 1776

Our situation is truly delicate and critical. On the one hand we are in need of a strong federal government founded on principles that will support the prosperity and union of the colonies. On the other hand we have struggled for liberty and made lofty sacrifices at her shrine: and there are still many among us who revere her name too much to relinquish (beyond a certain medium) the rights of man for the dignity of government.

—Mercy Otis Warren, a political writer and propagandist, in a letter to Catherine Macauley, September 1787

1. Both passages are best understood in the context of which of the following?
   (A) Nationalism was an important factor in the American Revolution.
   (B) Religion played a prominent role in Enlightenment-inspired rebellions.
   (C) Women's rights were a central issue in Enlightenment thought.
   (D) Enlightenment ideas contributed to the expansion of rights.

2. The tone of the *first* passage best reflects which of the following developments in the eighteenth century?
   (A) The abolition of slavery was a fundamental principle for the early United States.
   (B) Individual rights were essentially vague and undefined by Enlightenment philosophers.
   (C) Protecting individual rights was the government's function.
   (D) The American Revolution guaranteed freedom for all citizens.

3. The two passages best support which of the following Enlightenment political notions?
   (A) The social contract
   (B) Separation of powers
   (C) Property rights
   (D) Freedom of religion

QUESTIONS 4–6 REFER TO THE FOLLOWING PASSAGE.

We are not Europeans; we are not Indians; we are but a mixed species of aborigines and Spaniards. Americans by birth and Europeans by law, we find ourselves engaged in a dual conflict: we are disputing with the natives for titles of ownership, and at the same time we are struggling to maintain ourselves in the country that gave us birth against the opposition of the invaders. Subject to the threefold yoke of ignorance, tyranny, and vice, the American people have been unable to acquire knowledge, power, or [civic] virtue. The lessons we received and the models we studied, as pupils of such pernicious teachers, were most destructive. We have been ruled more by deceit than by force, and we have been degraded more by vice than by superstition. Venezuela had, has, and should have a republican government. Its principles should be the sovereignty of the people, division of powers, civil liberty, proscription of liberty, and the abolition of monarchy and privileges.

—Simón Bolivar, Latin American revolutionary leader, *Advice to the Congress of Angostura*, 1819

4. Which of the following conclusions about Latin America during the period from 1750 to 1900 is most directly supported by the passage?
   (A) Growing nationalism led to anticolonial movements.
   (B) Enlightenment ideas influenced many people to challenge existing notions of social relations.
   (C) Demands for women's suffrage led to challenges to political and gender hierarchies.
   (D) Slave resistance challenged existing authorities in the Americas.

5. The tone of the passage best reflects which of the following developments in early-nineteenth-century Latin America?
   (A) Religion played an important role in Bolívar's revolutionary thought.
   (B) Economic imperialism was a primary cause of Latin American revolutions.
   (C) Bolívar was attempting to appeal to a new sense of commonality based on social customs and territory.
   (D) The industrial working class in Latin America was Bolívar's primary target for support.

6. In the early nineteenth century, which of the following contributed most directly to Latin American revolutions?
   (A) Demands for women's suffrage
   (B) Socialism and Marxism
   (C) Anti-immigrant prejudice
   (D) The American Revolution

QUESTIONS 7–10 REFER TO MAP 22.1 *NAPOLEONIC EUROPE IN 1810* ON PAGE 664 AND MAP 22.3 *EUROPE IN 1815* ON PAGE 677.

7. Which of the following was a *direct* cause of the political border shifts indicated in the *first* map?
   (A) The French Revolution
   (B) Economic imperialism
   (C) John Stuart Mills's classical liberalism
   (D) Anarchism

8. The two maps best support which of the following conclusions about the time period from 1750 to 1900?
   (A) Principles of nationalism led to the Napoleonic conquest of much of Europe.
   (B) The application of Enlightenment ideas led to a new sense of commonality based on language and customs in some regions.
   (C) Enlightenment ideals developed into new transitional movements such as Marxism.
   (D) The Industrial Revolution united the economic and political sectors of Europe.

9. The inclusion of the boundary of the German Confederation in map 22.3, Europe in 1815, is a consequence of which of the following?
   (A) Revolutionary movements
   (B) Diverse religious ideas
   (C) Discontent with monarchist rule
   (D) Growing German nationalism

10. Nationalist rivalries that saw their origins in the period from 1750 to 1900 led to which of the following developments in the nineteenth and twentieth centuries?
   (A) The scramble for Africa
   (B) Opium Wars
   (C) World War I
   (D) Transnational corporations

Short-Answer Questions

QUESTION 1 REFERS TO THE FOLLOWING PASSAGE.

The rational character of the seventeenth century's political philosophy becomes even clearer if, instead of analyzing its first principles, we look at its general method. As to the question of the principles of the social order we find a sharp opposition between the systems of absolutism...and the defenders of popular rights and of the sovereignty of the people. But both parties, however combating each other, agree in one point. They try to prove their point by going back to the same fundamental hypothesis. The doctrine of the state-contract becomes in the seventeenth century a self-evident axiom of political thought....[I]f we reduce the legal and social order to free individual acts, to a voluntary contractual submission of the governed, all mystery is gone. There is nothing less mysterious than a contract. A contract must be made in full awareness of its meaning and consequences; it presupposes the free consent of all the parties concerned.

—Ernst Cassirer, philosopher, *The Myth of the State*, 1946

1. Answer parts A and B.
   A. Identify and explain ONE change or development instituted by Western revolutions that would sup-port the author's assertion in the passage above.
   B. Identify and explain TWO changes or developments instituted by Western revolutions that would challenge the author's assertion in the passage above.

QUESTION 2 REFERS TO THE FOLLOWING IMAGE.

2. Answer parts A and B.
   A. Identify and explain TWO nationalistic aspects of Hidalgo's rebellion that can be supported based on the image.
   B. Identify ONE limitation of the image as a source of information about nationalistic aspects of Hidalgo's rebellion.

23 The Industrial Revolution and European Politics, 1765–1880

In the summer of 1848, Russian émigré **Mikhail Bakunin** (1814–1876) rushed to Paris as revolution once again engulfed the French capital. The fire of revolt quickly spread to Berlin, Vienna, Budapest, Rome, Milan, and all across Europe. History was on the revolutionaries' side, Bakunin thought. Freedom was coming: kings, princes, and popes would be tossed aside.

Mikhail Bakunin

Mikhail Alexandrovitch Bakounine, c.1865 (photogravure), Nadar, (Gaspard Felix Tournachon) (1820–1910)/Private Collection/The Stapleton Collection/ Bridgeman Images

Those were distant memories by the summer of 1851, as Bakunin sat in solitary confinement in the imposing Peter and Paul Fortress in the Russian capital. He had been taking part in a rebellion in Prague when Austrian forces captured him, sentenced him to death, and then turned him over to Russian authorities, who gave him the chance to write a "confession" to the tsar. "*There was in my character,*" he wrote, "*a radical defect: Love for the fantastic, for out-of-the-way, unheard of adventures, for undertakings which open up an infinite horizon and whose end no man can foresee.*"*

Though Bakunin was dispirited and in poor health, with little chance of ever seeing his family or the light of day again, his message to Tsar Nicholas still conjured up the heady days of 1848:

Now what shall I say to you, Sire, of the impression produced on me by Paris! This huge city, the center of European enlightenment, had suddenly been turned into the wild Caucasus: on every street, almost everywhere, barricades had been piled up like mountains. . . . NOBLE WORKERS in rejoicing, exulting crowds, with red banners and patriotic songs [were] reveling in their victory! And in the midst of this unlimited freedom, this mad rapture, all were

*Cited in E. H. Carr, *Mikhail Bakunin* (New York: Vintage, 1937), p. 1.

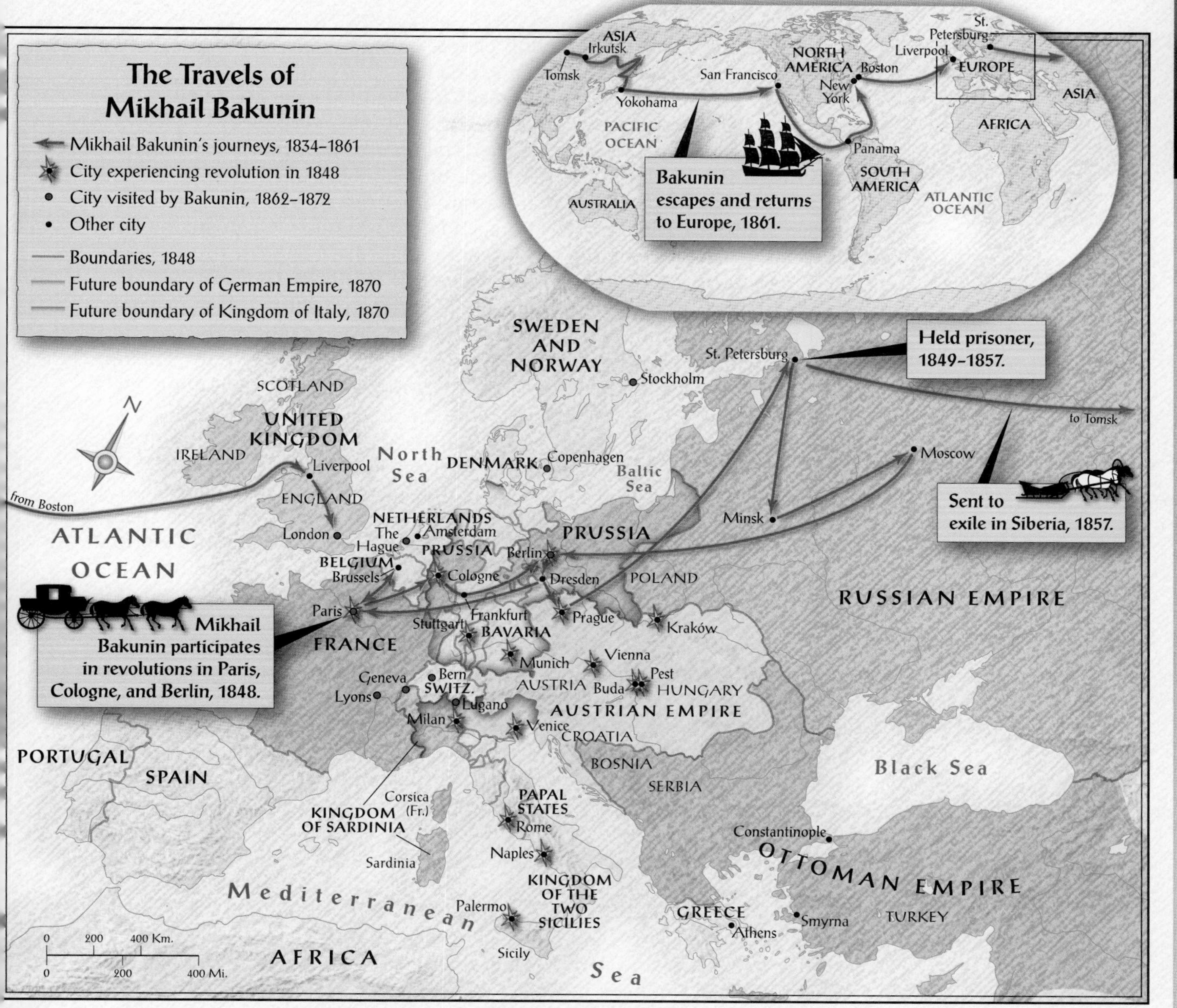

so forgiving, sympathetic, loving of their fellow man. . . . [N]owhere have I found so much noble selflessness, so much truly touching integrity . . . with such heroism as I found in these simple, uneducated people, who always were and always will be a thousand times better than their leaders! . . . It seemed that the whole world had been turned upside down.*

**The Confession of Mikhail Bakunin*, trans. Robert C. Howes (Ithaca: Cornell University Press, 1977), pp. 54–55.

Mikhail Bakunin (1814–1876) A Russian anarchist and revolutionary imprisoned for his role in the revolutions of 1848. He escaped from Siberian exile, circled the world, and returned to Europe to continue his campaign for liberty.

Bakunin's celebration of the common people did not move the tsar to forgive him. He was stripped of the aristocratic title inherited from his father and sent on a long journey by sleigh over frozen roads to exile in Siberia. Meanwhile, conservative rulers had re-established order in all the European capitals.

Undeterred, Bakunin planned another *"unheard of adventure."* In 1861, he escaped, crossed the vast expanses of Siberia by steamboat to the Pacific Ocean, avoided a Russian naval patrol by boarding an American ship to Japan, and then sailed to San Francisco, Panama, New York, and finally London. On board, he sang Russian songs, discussed religion with a young English clergyman (from whom he managed to borrow 250 dollars), and spread the words *freedom* and *revolution* wherever he traveled. Bakunin circled the world to return to Europe, the epicenter, he thought, of humankind's quest to overthrow the dead weight of the past and build a truly democratic future. He traveled restlessly, to France, Italy, Poland, Germany, Switzerland, and Sweden, his fame growing as one of the leading revolutionaries of Europe's industrial age.

Mikhail Bakunin's tumultuous life encompassed one of history's most eventful periods: the Industrial Revolution. Coal-driven steam engines unleashed the power of fossil fuels in the industrializing economies of western Europe and the United States, driving the machinery of new factories and propelling steamships and locomotives. More efficient transportation bound the entire world's people more tightly in networks of trade and communication. Bakunin's own early travels were by cart, sleigh, and sailing ships, his later ones by railroad and steamship.

As more people moved to cities, often living in squalid conditions, rapid social change further stimulated debates among European reformers and revolutionaries, for example, between liberals, who emphasized individual rights, and socialists, who stressed the collective good. Reformers in other parts of the world would take inspiration from these ideals of 1848, and also from the emotive power of nationalism surging across Europe. Mikhail Bakunin's anarchism—his belief that states are inherently oppressive—stood in contrast with the communism of his archrival, Karl Marx, whom he accused of attempting to replace one form of government oppression with another. Marx was ultimately more influential. His writings, along with the very different ones of the English evolutionary biologist Charles Darwin, contributed to the widespread belief that the industrial age was a time of progress.

Societies across Asia and Africa would be forced to cope with myriad consequences of European progress; indeed, western Europe's rapid economic growth and technological empowerment posed immediate challenges to its Eurasian neighbors, the Russian and Ottoman empires. Political elites in these old land-based states were torn between policies of reform involving adaptation of Western models of law and governance and conservative policies that stressed continuity over change.

The Industrial Revolution tremendously empowered western European nations relative to other societies. Therefore, it is essential to understand Europe's nineteenth-century economic, political, and ideological developments, models that would be exported around the world.

KEY CONCEPT QUESTIONS

- What were the economic, social, and political effects of the Industrial Revolution? **(Key Concept 5.1)**
- How did political and economic theories affect the revolutions of 1848? **(Key Concept 5.1)**
- How were the effects of Karl Marx's ideas similar to and different from the effects of Charles Darwin's ideas? **(Key Concept 5.1)**
- How did nineteenth-century reforms in Russia compare to reforms in the Ottoman empire **(Key Concept 5.1)**

The Industrial Revolution: Origins and Global Consequences, 1765–1870

It would be difficult to exaggerate the consequences of the **Industrial Revolution**. The productive capacity of human societies had not received such a boost since the emergence of agriculture eleven thousand years earlier. With the unlocking of fossil fuels as the key source of energy, total global output of manufacturing rose over 400 percent between 1750 and 1900. The same period also saw a massive shift of production from east to west: India and China accounted for over half of the world's manufacturing production in 1750, but Europe and the United States accounted for nearly three-quarters by 1900 (see Table 23.1). Global population doubled in the same period.

Innovations—new forms of energy, new technologies, new ways of organizing human labor—were the foundation of the Industrial Revolution. By burning

Industrial Revolution
Changes that began in late-eighteenth-century Britain and transformed the global economy by creating new markets for raw materials and finished goods; accompanied by technological changes that revolutionized production processes, living and working conditions, and the environment.

Table 23.1 Manufacturing Production of Selected Countries, 1750–1900, as Percentage of Global Total

	1750	1800	1830	1860	1880	1900
China	33.1	33.3	29.9	19.5	12.5	6.3
India/Pakistan	24.4	19.7	17.9	8.4	2.8	1.7
Russia	4.7	5.4	5.4	7.1	7.8	8.9
France	3.9	4.1	5.4	8.0	7.8	6.8
Japan	3.9	3.4	2.7	2.7	2.5	2.4
Germany	3.2	3.4	3.8	4.9	8.4	13.1
Italy	2.4	2.7	2.2	2.7	2.5	2.6
Great Britain	1.6	4.1	9.8	19.9	22.8	18.5
United States	—	0.7	2.7	7.1	14.7	23.7
World	100	100	100	100	100	100

Adapted with permission from David Christian, *Maps of Time: An Introduction to Big History* (Berkeley: University of California Press, 2004), p. 404, Table 13.1.

coal to drive steam engines, applying those steam engines to power machinery, and organizing mechanical processes in factories to centralize and rationalize the division of labor, industrial societies achieved unprecedented economic growth. Britain took the lead, soon followed by continental Europe and the United States. By the middle of the nineteenth century, industrialized societies were poised to translate economic power into military and political predominance on the world stage.

The Industrial Revolution was a global process. Improvements in transportation and communications—the steamship, railroad, and telegraph—created a worldwide market for raw materials. At the same time, as industrial production outstripped domestic demand, industrialists sought world markets to expand production even further.

Origins of the Industrial Revolution, 1765–1850

The British empire stimulated Britain's early modern economy. Timber and furs from Canada, sugar from the Caribbean, cotton textiles from India, and tea from China were part of a global trade network dominated by British shipping. Trade profits generated investment capital for industrial production, and Britain's trade and communications infrastructure supported British merchants seeking to expand global markets and sources of raw materials.

• **CONTEXT&CONNECTIONS** Apart from Britain's lead in global commerce and the easy availability of its coal deposits, the nation's social and cultural norms may also have spurred industrial innovation. Elsewhere in Europe the titled nobility remained aloof from commerce. In Britain less rigid lines divided aristocrats, members of the gentry like *Joseph Banks* (key term in Chapter 21), and merchant families. •

James Watt
(1736–1819) Scottish inventor who developed the world's first powerful and cost-effective steam engine; one of the most important contributors to Britain's Industrial Revolution.

In 1765, **James Watt** (1736–1819) helped launch "the age of steam and iron" when he unveiled the first workable steam engine. Building on earlier experiments with vacuum pumps, Watt's steam engine was fired by coal, a cheap and abundant source of energy in the English midlands, where coal production increased tenfold between 1750 and 1850. Now the working power of human muscles, wind and water, and horses and oxen would be supplemented, and even replaced, by the ignition of fossil fuels—first coal, then later petroleum—an energy revolution that would eventually alter the balance between human beings and the biosphere. (See the feature "World History in Today's World: The Anthropocene: A New Geological Epoch?")

AP® THEMES
How did the environment of Britain facilitate the development of the Industrial Revolution?

Equally important were improvements in iron production. Iron smelters worldwide had long used wood charcoal to fuel their furnaces, but doing so limited production to small batches. Meanwhile, much British coal was too impure to burn at the high temperatures necessary for iron production. Then inventors devised a way of purifying coal to make a more concentrated product called coke, and by the 1760s coal could be used to make low-cost, high-quality iron in plentiful amounts.

Meanwhile, other entrepreneurs were focusing on the social organization of production. In his *Wealth of Nations*, Adam Smith had argued that division of labor was a key to increased productivity (see Chapter 21). A shoemaker could make a fine pair of shoes, for example, but not as efficiently as a group of workers who each focused on a single step in the process. Smith's insight paved the way for the factory system of production.

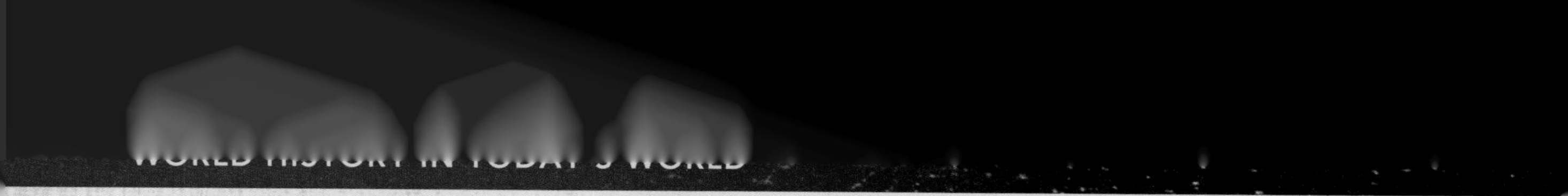

WORLD HISTORY IN TODAY'S WORLD

The Anthropocene: A New Geological Epoch?

Geologists employ much larger time frames than historians. In fact, 31 of the 32 chapters in *Voyages in World History* are entirely encompassed by a single geological epoch: the Holocene, marking the 11,700 years since the end of the last ice age.

Now some geologists think it is time to insert a new benchmark: the *Anthropocene* ("human epoch"). They argue that the planet's physical features have been so strongly affected by the human species since 1800 that this new designation better describes earth systems in the very recent past. According to this view, the Anthropocene began about two centuries ago with the intensive use of fossil fuels during the Industrial Revolution.

According to an article published by the Royal Swedish Academy of Sciences, using atmospheric carbon dioxide measurements to track fossil fuel impacts, the preindustrial level of 270–275 parts per million (ppm) had been elevated to 310 ppm by 1950. In 2014, carbon dioxide peaked at over 400 ppm. This "Great Acceleration," as the authors call it, "is reaching criticality. Whatever unfolds, the next few decades will surely be a tipping point in the evolution of the Anthropocene."* That tipping point could mean a catastrophic and irreversible regimen of global warming.

The International Union of Geological Sciences is currently considering a proposal that the Holocene be formally declared to have ended in the year 1800, and that the current epoch should be named the Anthropocene. That term, they state, "has emerged as a popular scientific term used by scientists, the scientifically engaged public and the media to designate the period of Earth's history during which humans have had a decisive influence on the state, dynamics and future of the Earth system."†

Historians have long recognized that the Industrial Revolution was also an energy revolution. Now geologists are affirming that the global effects of those changes were even more revolutionary than previously thought.

*Will Steffen, Paul J. Crutzen, and John R. McNeill, "The Anthropocene: Are Humans Now Overwhelming the Great Forces of Nature?" *Ambio*, vol. 36, no. 8 (December 2007): 1. http://www.ambio.kva.se.

†Working Group on the Anthropocene, http://quaternary.stratigraphy.org/workinggroups/anthropocene/.

In the 1760s, entrepreneur and abolitionist **Josiah Wedgwood** began to experiment with a more complex division of labor in his ceramics factory. By breaking the production process down into specialized tasks, his factory produced greater quantities of uniform dinnerware at less expense. Wedgwood advanced the factory system of production even further when, in 1782, he was the first to install a steam engine, combining Smith's division of labor and Watt's steam power. The age of mass production had begun: the days when a master potter and a few apprentices painstakingly produced pottery by hand were ending.

Josiah Wedgwood (1730–1795) English ceramics manufacturer who combined the use of steam power with factory organization to greatly increase the output and lower the cost of his products. He was a prominent supporter of the abolition of slavery.

Wedgwood modeled his designs on those found on imported Chinese porcelain, the finest in the world and avidly collected by the British elite. Once Wedgwood brought the price down, even the less affluent could afford a few pieces of "china" for their cupboard. Middle-class consumers (then and now) played a key role in the expansion of industrial markets.

• **CONTEXT&CONNECTIONS** Josiah Wedgwood was also an advocate of the abolition of slavery and a subscriber to *Olaudah Equiano's Interesting Narrative* (Chapter 19). Wedgewood mass-produced plates showing an African in shackles declaiming "*Am I not a man and a brother?*" •

It was in the textile industry, however, where division of labor and steam power combined to full potential. Traditionally, India had been by far the world's largest producer of cotton textiles, and Indian calico cloth flooded the British market. Unhappy with such competition, British wool producers convinced Parliament to impose high tariffs on Indian calicoes, making them less affordable.

However, the tariffs did not apply to imports of raw cotton, which surged as British entrepreneurs developed a decentralized "putting-out" system to produce cotton cloth domestically. They would provide raw materials to a rural family, and in a traditional gender division of labor, the women spun the cotton into thread that the men then wove into cloth. Since spinning took more time than weaving, men frequently had to wait for the women to catch up.

These old methods of spinning and weaving held back production, giving industrialists an incentive to mechanize the process. British inventors first mechanized spinning and then developed steam-driven power looms. By the 1830s, the manufacture of cloth had been fully mechanized and consolidated into factories.

Of course, inexpensive labor was needed to make the factories profitable, and Britain's agricultural revolution helped create such a workforce (see Chapter 21). Driven off the land by "improving farmers," many desperate English peasants moved to the mines and emerging factory towns. Their lives were no longer governed by the seasons and the constraints of muscle power; instead, harsh whistles herded them down mine shafts or through factory gates with relentless regimentation.

Artisans were displaced as well. In its efficiency, the factory system led to a deskilling of labor and a depression of wages for skilled craftsmen, many of whom actively resisted. In the early years of the nineteenth century, some organized secret societies to assault the machinery that was depriving them of their traditional livelihoods. (Those machine smashers were called "Luddites," a term that even today may be used for those who resist technological change.) In response to such incidents, Parliament made industrial sabotage a capital crime, and sent the army to protect property and restore order. No one would be allowed to stand in the way of "improvement," even if the costs and benefits of industrial progress were unequally shared.

The energy revolution of coal and steam, together with the more efficient social organization of the factory system, transformed virtually every field of manufacture. Britain's early lead in industrialization combined with its strength in international commerce to make it the dominant global power. Following Britain's lead, coal-rich Belgium also developed a substantial network of steam-fired factories, followed by France, Germany, and northern areas of the United States.

Global Dimensions of the Industrial Revolution, 1820–1880

AP® THEMES
How did technology and new economic ideas help shape the process of industrialization both within and outside of Europe?

From its inception, the Industrial Revolution was a global process. Improvements in transportation and communications dramatically increased the pace of global interactions. Industrial economics bound people around the world ever more tightly as producers and consumers. Militarily, the nineteenth century brought constantly increasing mobility of soldiers and their ever more sophisticated weaponry. Culturally and intellectually, European tastes and ideas achieved unprecedented status among global elites. By century's end, most of humankind was participating in the global commodity markets of industrial capitalism.

- **CONTEXT&CONNECTIONS** *Globalization* is the term we use to refer to the contemporary shrinking of the world—what some have called the "annihilation of time and space"—by rapid transport and communications (see Chapter 31). In fact, world historians see a precedent in the nineteenth century for the more recent wave of globalization. In the first industrial era, railroads, steamships, and telegraphs were also making the world a much smaller place, and economists point out that then, as now, relatively free markets played a pivotal role in boosting global trade. ●

Water transport, via coastal shipping, rivers, and canals, had always been more efficient than transport by land, but as the price of iron dropped, railroads became a viable alternative. By midcentury a dense network of railroads covered western Europe, increasing both urbanization and mobility (see Map 23.1). In North America, transcontinental railroads crossed the United States and Canada. If Mikhail Bakunin had arrived in San Francisco just ten years later on his round-the-world voyage, in 1871 rather than 1861, he would likely have used the transcontinental railroad to cross from the Pacific to the Atlantic, instead of going by ship. By 1880, railroad construction had also begun in Russia, British India, and Mexico.

By 1850, steamships also had improved transportation in industrial nations, especially in the United States, where large waterways like the Mississippi River conveyed people and goods over great distances. With steamships and railroads supporting access to markets, the availability of inexpensive iron plows made possible the agricultural settlement of the Great Plains and the east-to-west integration of North America (see Chapter 25).

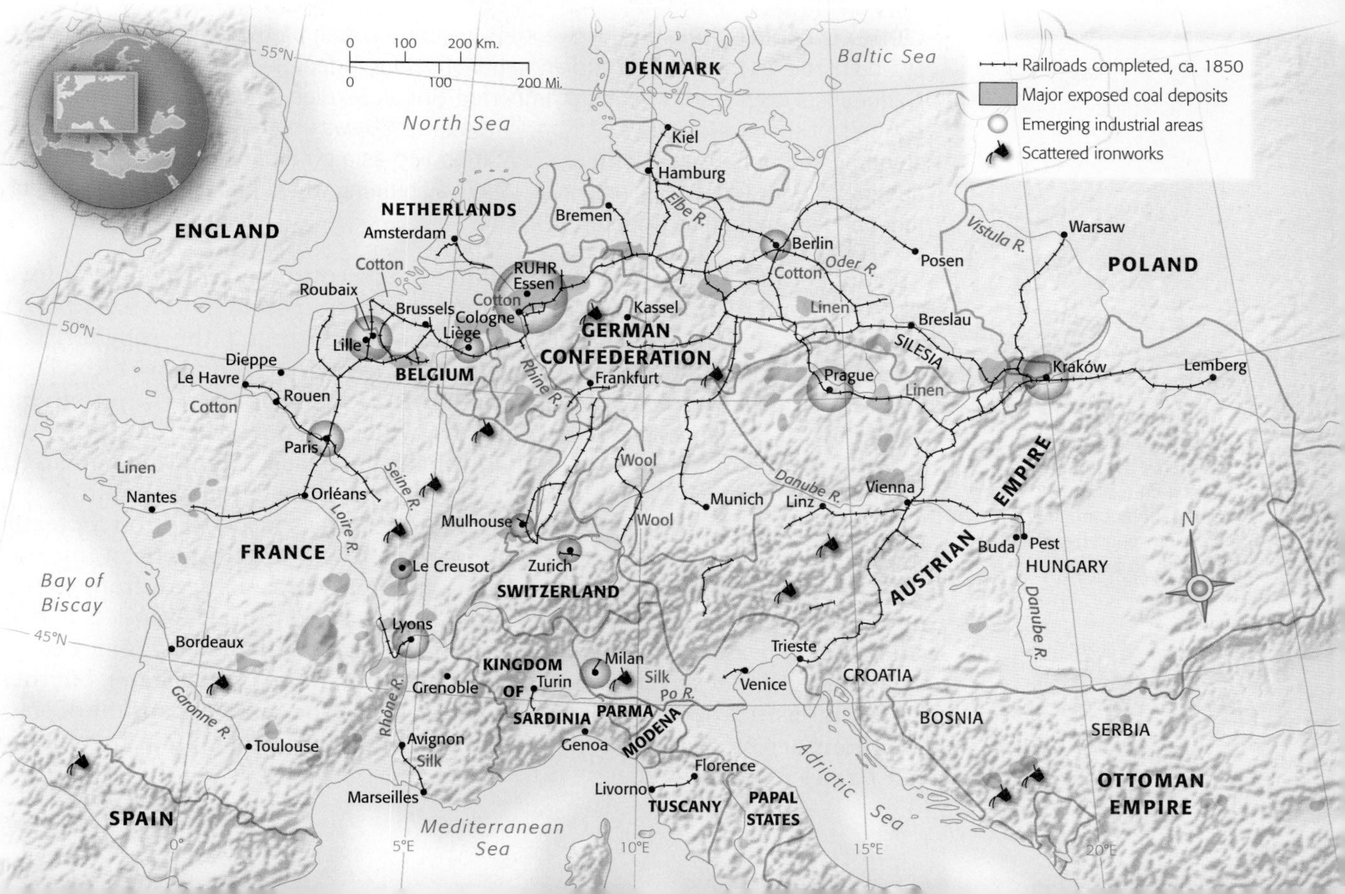

Map 23.1 Continental Industrialization, ca. 1850 Ease of access to iron and coal spurred industrialization in parts of Europe, such as northeastern France, Belgium, and northwestern regions of the German Confederation. Railroads supplemented rivers and canals as efficient transport by 1850 and by the end of the century tightly integrated the nations in Europe.

The international influence of steamships was just as revolutionary. The first steam-powered crossing of the Atlantic took place in 1838 and of the Pacific in 1853. Though sailing ships remained common, by the 1870s steamships were dramatically reducing transportation times and shipping costs and enhancing the military advantage of Western nations around the world. With the completion of the Suez Canal in 1869 (linking the Mediterranean and Red Seas) steamships cut transportation time from Europe to South Asia from months to weeks. Such advances enabled the expansion of European imperialism in Africa and Southeast Asia and the tightening of control over existing colonies, like British India (see Chapters 24 and 26).

With the newly invented telegraph, information moved even more quickly than people and goods. The first long-range telegraph message was sent in 1844. In 1869, a submarine cable was laid beneath the Atlantic Ocean. Telegraphs allowed traders to accurately compare prices instantaneously across continents. Shipping companies used the telegraph to lower their costs and increase global trade. Military officers with telegraphic information had a powerful tactical advantage.

Industrialization expanded the need for raw materials, especially cotton. After the British gained control (see Chapter 20), the export of raw Indian cotton replaced the export of finished cloth, partly because of the lower cost of factory-made textiles, and partly because of the tariffs aiding British industry. Unemployed Indian spinners, weavers, and dyers then fled to the countryside. Such were the complex and uneven outcomes of industrialization: British villagers were forced off the land and into cities, while at the very same time Indian artisans had no choice but to leave their towns for the villages.

• **CONTEXT&CONNECTIONS** In the twentieth century, cotton cloth would play a large symbolic role in the quest of Indian nationalists for independence from Britain. Nationalists organized boycotts of imported British textiles, and sometimes made bonfires of them. *Mohandas K. Gandhi* (Chapter 28) was noted for sitting and spinning cotton both as a form of meditation and as a symbolic rejection of British domination; for those reasons, since 1947, a spinning wheel has adorned the flag of independent India (see Chapter 30). •

Egypt became another important source of raw cotton. After Napoleon's invasion (see Chapter 22), an ambitious Ottoman military commander seized power. **Muhammad Ali** (r. 1808–1848) had witnessed firsthand the superiority of European weaponry and knew that his regime needed to keep up with the latest advances. Muhammad Ali (moo-HAH-muhd AH-lee) encouraged cotton production to pay for railroads, factories, and guns, while sending science and engineering students to study in France. Defying the sultans' authority, Muhammad Ali reoriented Egypt toward the West, further weakening the Ottoman empire.

Muhammad Ali
(r. 1808–1848) Egyptian ruler who attempted to modernize his country's economy by promoting cotton cultivation and textile manufacturing and by sending young Egyptians to study in Europe.

The Deep South of the United States was the largest source of cotton for textile manufacturers, with its production surging after 1793, when American inventor Eli Whitney created the cotton gin to more efficiently separate seeds from cotton. Undoubtedly, slaves picking cotton in the American South saw even less benefit than Egyptian peasants from supplying cotton to industrial markets. Some observers had thought that slavery would gradually die out in the United States, but then the new industrial demand for cheap cotton led to the rapid expansion of slave plantations across regions newly conquered from their Amerindian inhabitants (see Chapter 25).

The web of industry drew in commodities from around the world. Palm oil from West Africa helped lubricate industrial machinery. Cattle hides from the *pampas* (PAHM-pahs) grasslands of Argentina spurred a proliferation of leather goods. Mexican plantations exported sisal for making rope. These examples all show how Africans and Latin Americans participated in the Industrial Revolution primarily as suppliers of raw materials.

As we will see in the following three chapters, the Industrial Revolution challenged ways of life in the Americas, Africa, Asia, and the Pacific. In fact, similar challenges faced the peoples of Europe. In the machine age, artisans lost customary control over their crafts, some began to view traditional political and religious institutions as anachronistic, and millions of new city dwellers traded longstanding bonds of community for urban anonymity. Pessimists saw the rapid social and cultural changes of industrial society as markers of moral decay and social disorder. But for many Europeans, Mikhail Bakunin among them, the new industrial age represented fresh possibilities for the liberation of the human spirit.

Reform and Revolution in Nineteenth-Century Europe, 1815–1880

In 1815, the great powers of Europe had banded together to quell the fires of the French Revolution and its aftermath (see Chapter 22). Their success did not last long. Monarchy and aristocratic prerogative no longer sat well with Europe's rising bourgeoisie and new industrial working class. Proponents of change embraced the ideals of the Enlightenment and the example of the French Revolution while debating the political ideals of liberalism, socialism, and anarchism.

Tensions rising from industrial change reached a crescendo in 1848, when revolutions across Europe seemed ready to sweep the old order away. Shock and disappointment befell revolutionaries like Mikhail Bakunin when conservative, authoritarian leaders re-established control. Still, Bakunin, like many others, kept alive the hopes and high ideals of 1848.

Nineteenth-Century Ideologies: Liberalism, Socialism, Romanticism, Anarchism, and Nationalism

Mikhail Bakunin embodied the new sensibilities of his time. His writings show the influence of the five different, sometimes contradictory ideologies emerging from industrializing Europe: liberalism, socialism, romanticism, anarchism, and nationalism.

Liberalism, most strongly associated with urban middle classes and most strongly developed in Britain, implied open-mindedness and the need for social and political reform, a trend resisted by many continental monarchs and their supporters, especially in the military. Liberals favored freedom of conscience, freedom of trade, the protection of property rights, and limitations on the political power of religious authorities. They emphasized constitutional government and further extension of voting rights (at least to men with sufficient property and education).

Socialism was better developed in France and Germany, where its advocates debated whether workers' rights would be better advanced through the overthrow of the state or by working within existing institutions. In the later nineteenth century, when workers gained the vote in Britain, France, and Germany, the trend was toward *evolutionary* socialism, with parliamentary parties dedicated to workers' rights and fuller social equality. Where workers had no vote, as in Russia, it was the revolutionary strand of socialism that predominated.

Romanticism was less of a political program than a cultural style, one that prioritized emotional intensity and authenticity as a backlash against Enlightenment rationalism. Romantic painters evoked forests, mountains, and moonlight, as a counterpoint to the gritty, crowded conditions of cities and factories. German composers developed highly influential musical romanticism, culminating in the long, complex, and powerful operas of Richard Wagner (1813–1883). Landscape architecture in Europe moved from parks and gardens of classical linearity to a wilder, less cultivated look.

Romanticism was strongly connected to *nationalism*, the most powerful political ideology of the industrial age. While liberals emphasized the rights of individuals, and socialists largely focused on the interests of workers, nationalists believed in the destiny of peoples. While liberalism and socialism had universal application, nationalists often restricted their vision to "their own" people, often with a romanticized appeal to their nation's destiny for greatness. For peoples (like the Germans) who did not yet have nation-states to represent them, nationalists (like Wagner) sought to develop cultural and historical pedigrees. The revolutionary potential of the national idea was most clear where nationalists sought to separate their group from multinational empires, such as the Poles from Russia, the Greeks from the Ottomans, and the Hungarians from Austria.

Mikhail Bakunin debated adherents of each of these ideologies while promoting his own brand of *anarchism*. Liberals, he thought, were on the right track in their advocacy of individual freedom. However, he sharply criticized them for favoring such rights only for the middle class, saying "*when the masses are restless, even the most enthusiastic liberals immediately reverse themselves and become the most fanatical champions of the State.*"* In this critique of liberalism, Bakunin agreed with the socialists, who also saw the liberal defense of property rights as a way for the middle class to protect its interests against working people.

Where Bakunin differed with the socialists was in his belief that governments are by nature repressive: the leaders of a socialist state, he predicted, would look after their own interests, not those of the masses. "*The free human society may arise at last,*" he wrote, "*no longer organized ... from the top down ... but rather starting from the free individual and the free association and autonomous commune, from the bottom up.*"*

Though Bakunin was a romantic figure himself—passionate, fearless, and unconventional—he warned that romanticized nationalism was being used by conservative leaders to gain the patriotic support of the very workers who should, he thought, oppose them. Only if workers saw through such tricks would their revolutionary actions achieve "*what they really want, the free self-organization and administration of their own affairs from the bottom upward, without any interference or violence from above.*"* Instead of seizing the state, Bakunin thought revolutionaries should destroy it.

---

*Mikhail Bakunin, "God and the State," "The Program of the Brotherhood, 1865," "Some Preconditions for a Social Revolution," in *Bakunin on Anarchy*, ed. Sam Dolgoff (New York: Dover, 1972), pp. 234, 134, 338.

● **CONTEXT&CONNECTIONS** Except in small utopian communities organized along communal lines, Bakunin's anarchist vision has never been effectively put into practice. But his influence remained great among twentieth-century radicals like *Emma Goldman* (Chapter 27), and the 1960s witnessed a resurgence of interest in the life and thought of Mikhail Bakunin among some student rebels. ●

Victorian Britain, 1815–1867

In 1815, Britain was dominated by those who associated change with the excesses of the French Revolution. The landed classes still dominated in Parliament and imposed stiff tariffs on imported grain, raising the price of bread. Meanwhile, unemployment was high among soldiers returning from the wars against Napoleon, while the enclosure movement and the new factory system were driving many out of villages and into urban slums.

Conditions in cities were appalling. Wages were low, and many employers preferred children, especially girls, as factory workers because they were nimble, could fit into tight spaces, and were easy to control. Industrial cities were unhealthy places, as German socialist leader Friedrich Engels observed during a visit to Manchester in 1844:

> *Right and left a multitude of covered passages lead from the main street into numerous courts, and he who turns in thither gets into a filth and disgusting grime.... Inhabitants can pass into and out of the court only by passing through foul pools of stagnant urine and excrement. At the bottom flows, or rather stagnates, the Irk, a narrow, coal-black, foul-smelling stream, full of debris and refuse, which it deposits on the shallower right bank. In dry weather, a long string of the most disgusting, blackish-green, slime pools are left standing on this bank.**

Disease spread rapidly in such neighborhoods, becoming even more deadly after increased contact with India brought cholera to England. In London, thousands died from infected water supplies.

Better-off families moved to pleasant suburbs, isolated from filth, disease, and the pollution spewed by what poet William Blake called England's "*dark, satanic mills.*" The prevailing view of the upper class was that the poor were responsible for their own fate, an attitude satirized by novelist Charles Dickens in *A Christmas Carol*, when Ebenezer Scrooge says that if people are so poor that they are likely to die, "*they should do so and decrease the surplus population.*"

Heritage Image Partnership Ltd/Alamy

Mining Coal Apart from employing adult male labor, Britain's mine owners also relied on adolescent boys and "pit ponies" to extract coal from ever-deeper shafts and to transport it to the surface. Mining was dangerous work, and even those who survived the frequent accidents were likely to die early from lung disease. The "pit ponies" were often stabled underground, seeing the light of day perhaps only once a year, during an annual shutdown holiday.

*Excerpt from *The Marx-Engels Reader*, Second Edition, edited by Robert C. Tucker. Used by permission of W. W. Norton & Company, Inc.

Before 1832, the British middle and lower classes had no right to vote and thus no direct means of influencing policy. Attempts by industrial workers to form unions were outlawed by Parliament. Factory workers might find solidarity in churches: Methodism's egalitarian ethos allowed workers to assert spiritual, if not social and political, equality. Others sought solace in gin and opium.

By the time of Queen Victoria (r. 1837–1901), however, a reform impulse animated British politics. Charitable organizations grew in size, their leaders arguing that the poor could improve their lot if only they would adopt middle-class values like thrift and sobriety. Many saw that the government also had a role to play, especially in improving health and sanitation.

In the tradition of British "practical science" (see Chapter 21), the government sponsored scientific studies to improve urban planning, water supplies, and hygiene. Early Victorian reform drew on a philosophy called *utilitarianism*, which brought the enlightenment belief in rationality to issues of social reform. For example, utilitarians successfully lobbied for reform of Britain's appalling prisons, bringing in air and light, and a new emphasis on rehabilitation. Similarly, investigations of child labor led to public outcry and legislation that regulated abhorrent labor conditions. Restrictions on the activities of Catholics were finally lifted. And by the 1850s wages had increased: even less-skilled workers were beginning to benefit from British pre-eminence in industry and trade.

The conservatism of the post-Napoleonic period was giving way to a more open political environment. Parliament responded to the frustrations of the growing but still disenfranchised urban middle class by passing the **Reform Bill of 1832**. The bill brought Parliament into closer accord with the social changes brought on by industrialization. First, seats in Parliament were redistributed to take account of the growth of cities. Second, the bill lowered the property requirements for voting so that better-off members of the middle class, such as male shopkeepers, could vote. This new Parliament better reflected urban interests, as when it slashed tariffs on imported grain, lowering bread prices for workers at the expense of profits for the rural gentry.

Reform Bill of 1832
Bill that significantly reformed the British House of Commons by lowering property qualifications for the vote. Still, only wealthier middle-class men were enfranchised.

● **CONTEXT&CONNECTIONS** One interested foreign observer of the parliamentary debate over the Reform Bill in 1832 was *Rammohun Roy* (Chapter 20), who had traveled to London in support of legislation abolishing widow burning in India. Meeting with leaders of the utilitarian movement, Roy stressed their commonality of purpose with the social reforms of the Bengal Renaissance. ●

John Stuart Mill (1806–1873), who Mikhail Bakunin admiringly called an "*apostle of idealism,*"* was a powerful voice of British liberalism. In his book *On Liberty* (1859), Mill argued that liberty involved freedom not only from arbitrary government interference but also from "*the tendency of society to impose … its own ideas and practices as rules of conduct on those who dissent from them.*"† His emphasis on freedom from both political oppression and social conformity led Mill to conclusions that were radical for the time: he thought the vote should be extended not only to working men but also to women.

John Stuart Mill
(1806–1873) English philosopher and economist who argued for the paramount importance of individual liberty and supported greater rights for women.

By the 1860s, further social change again necessitated political reform. The Reform Bill of 1867 nearly doubled the number of voters, and at the end of the 1880s

---

*Paul McLaughlin, *Mikhail Bakunin: The Philosophical Basis of His Theory of Anarchism* (New York: Algora Publishing, 2002), p. 113.

†John Stuart Mill, *On Liberty* (London: Longman, Roberts and Green, 1869), p. 5.

another reform bill gave nearly all British men the vote. Through these gradual steps toward greater electoral inclusion, Britain was becoming a democracy. (Women, however, were not fully enfranchised until as late as 1928.) Meanwhile, the easing of restrictions on trade unions increased the bargaining power of the working class.

AP® THEMES

How did new ideologies shape the development of the British government in the nineteenth century?

The combination of economic success and relatively peaceful political reform made many mid-Victorians supremely confident of their nation and optimistic about its future. (See the feature "Visual Evidence in Primary Sources: The Great Exhibition and the Crystal Palace.") The British constitution was evolving to suit new circumstances, just as Edmund Burke had predicted (see Chapter 22). On the European continent, in contrast, many societies were rocked by revolution and unsettled by changing national borders.

France: Revolution, Republic, and Empire

In 1815, diplomats at the Congress of Vienna restored the Bourbon dynasty to power in France (see Chapter 22). After the revolutionary and Napoleonic years, however, it was impossible to return to the past, and in 1830 a popular uprising overthrew the Bourbon monarch.

Some of those who organized street protests against the king clamored for a return to republican government. Many middle-class liberals, however, feared that a republic would favor working-class interests at the expense of private property. Their leaders advocated a constitutional monarchy and invited Louis Philippe, a nobleman more interested in business than in royal protocol, to take the throne. King Louis Philippe, the "bourgeois king," certainly maintained a more open regime than that of the Bourbons, though voting was restricted to a small minority of property-owning men. Republicans despised him.

In early 1848, police in Paris fired on a crowd of demonstrators, and 1,500 republican barricades went up around the city. Louis Philippe abdicated and fled the country. *"No sooner had I learned that they were fighting in Paris,"* Bakunin wrote in his confession to the tsar, *"than . . . I set out again for France."** Suddenly, for the first time in fifty years, France was a republic in which the people themselves were sovereign. The change was so dramatic that men met in a newspaper office to plan the country's future, divided on how to proceed.

An influential socialist, Louis Blanc (loo-EE blawnk), argued that private ownership of industry was inefficient and unfair, leaving many unemployed and giving workers no say in how the factories were run. He called for cooperative workshops to be set up by the government and run by the workers. Employment would be guaranteed for all. Bakunin strongly disagreed with Blanc's government-centered approach, which *"advised the people to rely in all things upon the State."*† Instead, he thought, workers should seize the factories and run them cooperatively without interference from either bourgeois owners or state functionaries.

Blanc's socialist ideas were also opposed by middle-class defenders of property rights, and under their influence the republic implemented only a weakened version of his plan. The state funded some public works projects, such as planting trees, and guaranteed those who could not find work enough money to live on. Almost all this money was spent in Paris, a fact resented by the rural majority.

**The Confession of Mikhail Bakunin*, trans. Robert C. Howes (Ithaca: Cornell University Press, 1977), p. 56.

†Mikhail Bakunin, "Socialism," in *Bakunin on Anarchy*, ed. Sam Dolgoff (New York: Knopf, 1972), p. 121.

The Great Exhibition and the Crystal Palace

London's Hyde Park was the site of mid-Victorian Britain's monument to industrial, technological, and commercial progress: the Great Exhibition of the Works of Industry of All Nations. Queen Victoria herself opened the Exhibition to great public acclaim in 1851. Her husband, Prince Albert, one of the principal planners, was at her side. The Great Exhibition received over 6 million visitors, some traveling from continental Europe and the United States, and raised enough money through admission fees to endow the great Victoria and Albert Museum and the Natural History Museum, both of which still stand near Hyde Park today. The Crystal Palace, an imposing glass and iron structure built to enclose the Exhibition and protect attendees from the weather, was itself a wonder of industrial technology.

Over half the exhibit space was devoted to the tools and products of British manufacturers, and

The Crystal Palace, completed in time for the opening of the Great Exhibition in 1851, was 1,851 feet (564 m) long, with an interior height of 128 feet (39 m). It used more than a million square feet of glass, more than any other building up to that time.

Recent innovations in glass manufacturing provided the architects with the large panes necessary to give the building the "crystal" effect of clear walls and ceilings. Queen Victoria bestowed a knighthood on creator Joseph Paxton, who designed the building in just ten days, for his achievement.

Another innovation was the provision of public toilets, first just for men and later for women as well. Visitors paid a penny to use the facilities, hence the term "to spend a penny" in British English for making a lavatory trip.

SSPL/The Image Works

The huge central transept was the site of concerts, circuses, and tightrope walking; music was provided by the world's largest organ.

When the Great Exhibition ended, the Crystal Palace was taken apart and re-erected in a South London suburb. The Crystal Palace Football Club is a reminder of the role the surrounding grounds then played in sporting life, even after the building was destroyed by fire in 1936.

great attention was paid to colonial contributions to the country's wealth and power. Collecting Indian artifacts and containing them within the exhibition hall, for example, was an implicit assertion of the legitimacy of Britain's imperial claim over South Asia and another expression of the ongoing relationship between science and empire (see Chapter 21).

The Great Exhibition had an enduring global influence. Later, other nations would also erect monumental buildings and put their achievements on display, inviting all nations to participate in "world's fairs" such as those held in Paris (1878), Chicago (1893), and, more recently, Shanghai, at China's World Expo (2010).

Visitors to the Great Exhibition passed through a series of courts focused on the history of art and architecture (from ancient Egypt through the Renaissance) and natural wonders of the world. The main attractions, however, were exhibits of the latest industrial technology: *"every conceivable invention,"* as Queen Victoria noted in her diary.

Visitors gasped in amazement at the Koh-I-Noor diamond, the largest cut diamond in the world at that time; took their first ever look at photographs at the display of the recently invented daguerreotype; witnessed the powerful and fast-loading revolving pistol of Samuel Colt; and wondered at the latest ingenuities of industrial machinery and design. ***How would the wonders of technology displayed in London in 1851 compare with those that might be assembled for a similar "Great Exhibition" today?***

Some one hundred thousand objects were spread over 10 miles (16 km) of viewing space.

Prince Albert emphasized that the Great Exhibition demonstrated the orderly progress of British society. *"We have no fear here either of an uprising or an assassination,"* he bragged to his cousin, King William of Prussia, who had survived a revolutionary uprising just three years earlier, in 1848.

V&A Images, London/Art Resource, NY

The largest exhibit was a huge hydraulic press used for bridge building, with a series of metal tubes, each weighing well over 1,000 tons.

An even more popular display was a simple statue of a female Greek slave, demurely hidden in a small red tent and wearing only a simple chain. Exoticism and sexual allure, it seems, were just as interesting to the Victorians as mechanical might.

Even in Paris, the tide was turning away from republicanism in the summer of 1848. One of Bakunin's fellow Russian exiles heard a commotion outside his window, and saw a group of *"clumsy, rascally fellows, half peasants, half shopkeepers, somewhat drunk"* as they *"moved rapidly but in disorder, with shouts of 'Vive Louis-Napoleon!'"* In response, the Russian socialist shouted *"'Vive la République!'"* But *"those who were near the windows shook their fists at me,"* he remembered, *"and an officer muttered some abuse, threatening me with his sword."**

Louis Napoleon
(1808–1873) Conservative nephew of Napoleon Bonaparte who was elected president of the Second Republic before winning a plebiscite making him Emperor Napoleon III in 1852. Was forced to abdicate in 1870 after losing the Franco-Prussian War.

With the rise of **Louis Napoleon** (1808–1873), revolutionary dreams were crumbling. Louis Napoleon represented, in his own words, *"order, authority, religion, popular welfare at home, national dignity abroad."* He was popular with liberals fearful of socialism, peasants resentful of Parisian domination, and everyone who recalled with pleasure the glorious days of his uncle, Napoleon Bonaparte. After being elected president, Louis Napoleon organized and won a plebiscite making him Napoleon III, emperor of France.

● **CONTEXT&CONNECTIONS** As in the 1790s, France went swiftly from constitutional monarchy to republic to empire (see Chapter 22). Karl Marx was among those who noted the parallels between the aftermaths of the French revolutions of 1789 and 1848. *"All great world-historic facts and personages appear twice,"* Marx commented bitterly, on what he saw as a second-rate version of the original Napoleon, *"the first time as tragedy, the second time as farce."*† ●

Napoleon III presided over the Second empire (1852–1870), a period of stability, prosperity, government investment in infrastructure and support for industry, and expanding French power. As president, Louis Napoleon eliminated Blanc's socialist program, seeking instead to stimulate the economy by selling government bonds to finance railway construction and by backing semipublic financial institutions to provide capital for commerce and industry. Although Napoleon III was authoritarian, he respected the rule of law and basic civil liberties. Like Napoleon Bonaparte, he gained support by appealing to French nationalism and by expanding the overseas French empire (see Chapter 26).

The Habsburg Monarchy, 1848–1870

News of the 1848 uprising in Paris spread like wildfire across Europe. The dominant power in central Europe was the Austrian empire, still ruled by the Habsburg family. Protestors, university students prominent among them, took to the streets of Vienna in early 1848 demanding new rights. The befuddled emperor reportedly asked, *"Are they allowed to do that?"* Prince Metternich, the conservative architect of the Congress of Vienna, resigned his position as chancellor and fled to England.

While nationalism held nations like France together, it had the potential to tear multiethnic empires like Austria apart, when Italian, Hungarian, Czech, Croatian, and other Habsburg subjects agitated for national rights. In Budapest, a Hungarian assembly created a new constitution ratifying religious freedom, equality before the law, and an end to the privileges of the old feudal nobility.

*Alexander Herzen, *My Pasty and Thoughts*, trans. Constance Garnett (Berkeley: University of California Press, 1982), pp. 333–334.

†Karl Marx, *The Eighteenth Brumaire of Louis Napoleon*, Part VII, 1852, https://www.marxists.org/archive/marx/works/1852/18th-brumaire/ch01.htm.

Revolution also swept Milan, the chief city of Austria's northern Italian possessions, and Prague, where Bakunin was captured by Austrian forces.

As in France, peasants were shocked by the radicalism in the cities, and their support helped Habsburg authorities under the young Emperor Franz Joseph II (r. 1848–1916) re-establish control within their German-speaking territories. But by 1859 Italian rebels won independence from Austria, and in 1866 Prussian forces defeated the Habsburg army. The discontent of subject nationalities continued.

With crises looming, the emperor proclaimed a Dual Monarchy in 1867 under which he would be simultaneously emperor of Austria and king of Hungary, allowing each state its own separate institutions. Through this compromise Austria retained its Great Power status and settled the long struggle between German rulers and Hungarian subjects, though many other ethnic and national grievances in the empire remained unresolved.

● **CONTEXT&CONNECTIONS** Religious differences compounded ethnic divisions in Central Europe (see Chapter 17). The Austrians themselves were Catholic, as were the emperor's Croatian and Italian subjects; Hungary was divided between Catholics and Protestants; Serbs were Orthodox Christians, while Bosnians were Muslims, a legacy of Ottoman influence in the Balkans. Tensions between them helped spark world war in the next century (see Chapter 27). ●

The Unification of Italy, 1848–1870

In 1848, Italian liberals dreamt of a new political order based on ties of language, culture, and history. But they would have to overcome significant regional differences and the long-standing division of the Italian peninsula into numerous states. The north, much of it under Austrian rule, was subject to the same forces of industrialization and urbanization as western Europe, while the south was still largely peasant and traditional in its Catholicism. Differences in dialect made it difficult for Italians to understand one another. Such divisions had enabled conservatives to stifle liberal reforms and attempts at unification.

Like other Italian idealists of the time, **Giuseppe Garibaldi** (jew-SEP-pay gar-uh-BAWL-dee) (1807–1882) believed in the need for a *risorgimento*, a political and cultural renewal of Italy that would restore its historic greatness. After being condemned to death for leading an uprising in Genoa, Garibaldi, with romantic swagger, fled to South America and then took part in a Brazilian rebellion.

Giuseppe Garibaldi (1807–1882) Italian nationalist revolutionary who unified Italy in 1860 by conquering Sicily and Naples. Though he advocated an Italian Republic, the new country became a constitutional monarchy instead.

The revolution of 1848 called Garibaldi back to Italy. Rebels on the streets of Turin demanded liberal reforms; protestors in Milan forced Austrian authorities onto the defensive; and in Rome rebels declared a new Roman republic and chased the pope, ruler of vast central Italian domains, out of the city. Garibaldi headed to Rome to resist French forces dispatched by Louis Napoleon to restore papal rule. Garibaldi's defeat ended the short-lived Roman republic, another victory for the "forces of order" that had sent Bakunin to his lonely prison cell.

Another chance for Italian unification came in 1860 after a rebellion broke out in southern Italy. With the kingdom of Naples tottering, Garibaldi landed on the island of Sicily, overthrew its corrupt ruler, and crossed to the mainland. His army marched north, bringing Naples and Sicily into a new, united Italy in 1861. Garibaldi's exploits stirred Mikhail Bakunin, and when the two finally met in 1864, their warm embrace was cheered by an enthusiastic crowd. Inspired by the spontaneous mass support for Garibaldi's campaign, Bakunin felt the hopefulness of 1848 returning.

Yet once Garibaldi and the revolutionaries had paved the way, more conservative leaders commandeered the process and founded Italy as a constitutional monarchy

Battle of Palestrina, May 9, 1849, Second Roman Republic, Italy, 19th century/De Agostini Picture Library/A. de Gregorio/Bridgeman Images

Defense of the Roman Republic In 1848, Giuseppe Garibaldi and his followers declared a Roman Republic. Here we see their successful defense of the republic against invaders from the kingdom of Naples in 1849. Later, however, French forces laid siege to Rome and restored the pope to power. Finally, in 1871 Rome became the capital of a unified Italy.

with a limited electorate and a relatively weak legislature. Still, while this outcome dashed the hopes of more radical republicans, it did put unified Italy on the list of European great powers, especially after 1870, when the French garrison protecting the pope withdrew, bringing the city of Rome into the new Italy as its capital.

Sharp divisions remained, however. For many, the concept of being "Italian" was something entirely new. Especially in the south, church and family retained their traditional importance, and local customs predominated over the much newer national ideals. Many in the north felt more comfortable with European culture than with the Mediterranean lifestyle of their new countrymen. In contrast to France, where revolution and empire had helped give the French people a shared sense of national solidarity, Italians had a longer road ahead in forging their common identity.

AP® THEMES

What are the similarities in the ways that nationalism promoted the formation of the new nations of Italy and Germany?

Germany: Nationalism and Unification, 1848–1871

From the standpoint of world history, the most important European political development of the nineteenth century was the creation, in 1871, of a unified Germany. Almost immediately, Germany became a significant force in world affairs.

After 1815, the Congress of Vienna (see Chapter 22) had recognized a tapestry of forty-two separate polities, only loosely affiliated within a German Confederation. Prussia, with its capital in Berlin, was the most powerful member, though its ambitions to dominate the Confederation were strongly resented by Habsburg Austria. As a result of this rivalry, when Prussia sponsored the expansion of a German customs union from the 1820s onward to increase inter-German trade, it excluded Austria.

A potent legacy of the Napoleonic era was the very *idea* of German nationhood. France had demonstrated the power of national unity, and now more

Germans aspired to go beyond confederation to nationhood of their own. But would the process of nation building be controlled by liberals, strongest in the west, or by monarchical conservatives, represented by Prussia? That was the key question when the revolutionary flame of 1848 swept across the German states.

Having left Paris, Bakunin found himself in Dresden, the capital of the kingdom of Saxony, when an insurrection broke out. He helped lead the democratic forces until Prussian soldiers came to the rescue of the Saxon army. As Bakunin fled to Prague, it was clear that the Prussian government would oppose unification based on a popular uprising.

Indeed, Friedrich Wilhelm IV of Prussia (r. 1840–1857) took a hard line, using military force to crush demonstrators who stormed an arsenal and seized a royal palace in Berlin. Although the king did grant Prussia a constitution with a representative assembly elected through universal manhood suffrage, he and his ministers remained free to ignore it and rule as they liked. Friedrich Wilhelm saw the Prussian constitution as an expression of royal beneficence, not as a matter of rights.

Elsewhere, however, there was significant support for a unified Germany under a liberal constitution. A committee of prominent liberals organized an election, and in 1848 delegates at the **Frankfurt Assembly** drafted a constitution that embodied progressive principles, such as freedom of assembly and freedom of the press. Seeking a symbol of unity, they offered the crown to the Prussian king as constitutional monarch of a democratic German state. But Friedrich Wilhelm refused to accept what he called *"a crown from the gutter,"* rejecting the very principle of popular sovereignty upon which the proposed constitution was based.

Frankfurt Assembly Assembly held in 1848 to create a constitution for a united German Confederation; elected Friedrich Wilhelm IV as constitutional monarch, but Wilhelm refused the offer on the principle that people did not have the right to choose their own king.

Friedrich Wilhelm's refusal killed any hope of unifying Germany under a liberal constitution. But the forces of industrialization, the building of railroads, and rapid urbanization were creating conditions in which a unified Germany seemed more desirable than ever. In the 1860s, under the initiative of Prussian chancellor **Otto von Bismarck** (1815–1898), Prussia supervised the creation of a new German nation. "Germany" became a reality in 1871 when a coalition of armies led by Prussia defeated those of Napoleon III, forcing the emperor to abdicate. The victors then crowned Prussian king Kaiser Wilhelm II emperor of Germany in the grand Versailles Palace, a tremendous blow to French national pride, and a signal that militarism would be the foundation stone of the new German state.

Otto von Bismarck (1815–1898) Unified Germany in 1871 and became its first chancellor. Previously, as chancellor of Prussia, he led his state to victories against Austria and France.

Bismarck had told a committee of the German Confederation in 1862: *"Not through speeches and majority decisions are the great questions of the day decided—that was the mistake of 1848—but by iron and blood."** Bismarck's victories over Denmark, Austria, and most especially France sparked German national pride, inspiring many with a romantic vision of a grand German state fulfilling the people's destiny as a great world power. From Bakunin's perspective, Bismarck was *"an out-and-out aristocrat . . . with a militarist and bigoted bugbear of an emperor as chief."*†

Inspired by Prussian victories, many Germans now envisioned a grand German state fulfilling the people's destiny as a great world power. German manufacturing boomed, and the gross national product doubled between 1870 and 1890. But the German achievement had unsettling implications for the other great powers, which now faced an invigorated competitor for markets and empire.

*Quoted in Otto Pflanze, *Bismarck and the Development of Germany*, vol. 1 (Princeton: Princeton University Press, 1990), p. 184.

†Mikhail Bakunin, "Critique of Economic Determinism and Historical Materialism," in *Bakunin on Anarchy*, ed. Sam Dolgoff (New York: Knopf, 1972), p. 315.

New Paradigms of the Industrial Age: Marx and Darwin

Of the many scientists and social theorists of Europe's industrial age, Karl Marx and Charles Darwin stand out for their global influence. Marx, in his dissection of capitalism and explanation of the inevitability of socialist revolution, developed a systematic framework for the analysis of human history. Darwin, in describing how natural selection drives the process of evolution, developed an original framework for understanding natural history. Both created new ways of ordering knowledge that substantially altered previous modes of thought.

Karl Marx, Socialism, and Communism

Karl Marx
(1818–1883) German author and philosopher who founded the Marxist branch of socialism; wrote *The Manifesto of the Communist Party* (1848) and *Das Kapital* (1867).

The Manifesto of the Communist Party, published during the revolutionary year of 1848 by **Karl Marx** (1818–1883) and Friedrich Engels, directly challenged the status quo:

> *The Communists ... openly declare that their ends can only be attained by the forceful overthrow of all existing social conditions. Let the ruling classes tremble at a Communistic revolution. The proletarians have nothing to lose but their chains. They have a world to win. WORKING MEN OF ALL COUNTRIES UNITE!* *

Even though conservatives reasserted control after 1849, Marx believed that socialist revolution in Europe was not only possible, but inevitable.

Marx was a brilliant student who had earned a doctoral degree in philosophy while absorbing much from the works of the prominent German philosopher G. W. F. Hegel. Hegel had described a process in which a dominant idea, called a thesis, generates a contending idea, called an antithesis. These two ideas come into conflict until they generate a new, superior idea called a synthesis. He used the term *dialectic* for this process, proposing that each new intellectual synthesis was a step toward perfect knowledge.

Marx accepted Hegel's dialectical theory but interpreted it in terms of material relations rather than abstract ideas. To greatly simplify Marx's concept of scientific materialism, he held that economic forces—the way things are produced—generate the social, political, and ideological characteristics of a given society. Changing "modes of production" produce antagonistic social classes, which then come into conflict in the political arena, generating ideologies that match their class interests. To Marxists, the mainspring of history is the struggle of class against class.

As Marx analyzed the original French Revolution, for example, he explained that the rise of capitalism challenged the old feudal system of production, leading to the rise of the bourgeoisie (the propertied middle class that stood between the aristocracy and the mass of French society) and its overthrow of the monarchy and aristocracy. Whereas the aristocracy had promoted an ideology of power that emphasized family lineage, the bourgeoisie emphasized rights of property. Soon, however, the now-dominant bourgeoisie created their own antithesis: the propertyless urban proletariat. For Marx, the stage was now set for the next revolutionary cycle, the beginnings of which he saw in the uprisings of 1848.

---

*Excerpt from *The Marx-Engels Reader*, Second Edition, edited by Robert C. Tucker. Used by permission of W. W. Norton & Company, Inc.

Marx recognized that the bourgeoisie, *"during its rule of scarce one hundred years, has created more massive and more colossal productive forces than have all preceding generations together."** But he argued that capitalism contains a fatal flaw. The very efficiency of capitalism causes recurrent crises when more goods are produced than the market can absorb. Wages are slashed and factories are closed. Then the economy recovers, but each crash increases the division between the men of capital and the working class proletariat. *"Society as a whole,"* Marx wrote, *"is more and more splitting up into two great hostile camps, into two classes directly facing each other: Bourgeoisie and Proletariat."** In the struggle between these two classes, the victory of the working class, Marx argued, would lead to the realization of socialism. The full establishment of socialism, though it might take a long time, would be the final stage in human progress, after which there would be no further class conflict.

The life work of Karl Marx was his analysis of capitalism; he spent little time describing what a socialist future might look like. In fact, Marx and Engels distinguished their own *"scientific socialism"* from what they called the *"utopian socialism"* of other thinkers. Among the latter was the Frenchman Charles Fourier, who thought that perfectly balanced human communities could be forged, combining both agriculture and industry, based on collective work and shared proceeds. (The key, Fourier thought, was to bring together people with complementary talents and inclinations so that everyone could do the job they most enjoyed!) Marx disdained such utopian schemes, insisting that class conflict was the driving force of history, and that revolution was the mechanism that propelled history forward.

• **CONTEXT&CONNECTIONS** From a global perspective, Marx explained the link between industrial capitalism and European imperialism: *"The need of a constantly expanding market for its products chases the bourgeoisie over the whole surface of the globe.... In place of the old local and national seclusion and self-sufficiency, we have intercourse in every direction, universal inter-dependence of nations."** Later socialists and anti-imperialists would expand on Marx's insight, including the Russian leader *Vladimir Lenin* (Chapter 27). Lenin argued that profits from the "super-exploitation" of African and Asian colonies might delay the collapse of capitalism, but could not prevent it. Anticolonial uprisings, Lenin predicted, would further sharpen capitalism's contradictions and help to usher in the socialist future. •

Marx's internationalist philosophy challenged the idea of nationalism. Nationalists argued that bonds of culture and history unified a people across lines of social class. To them, a German was a German, whether she was a princess or a chambermaid, whether he lived in Hamburg or Vienna. To Marx, such romanticized notions merely distracted proletarians from recognizing that their true interests lay not with the rich and powerful who spoke the same language, but with workers across the world. The Socialist International, which Marx helped to organize, worked to foster such working-class solidarity. But despite Marx's arguments, nationalism exerted an increasingly powerful influence among all social classes.

Conservatives hated and feared Marx, but even many fellow socialists disagreed with his approach. Some "evolutionary socialists" believed that liberalism and socialism were compatible, that individual rights, workers' rights, and the common good should be pursued all at once. Through the extension of voting

---

*Excerpts from *The Marx-Engels Reader*, Second Edition, edited by Robert C. Tucker. Used by permission of W. W. Norton & Company, Inc.

rights to working people, they thought, socialism could develop through democratic rather than revolutionary means.

Bakunin, while he agreed with Marx that revolution would be necessary, saw dangerous seeds of dictatorship in his German competitor's philosophy. A government founded on Marxist principles, Bakunin warned, *"will not content itself with ... governing the masses politically ... it will also administer the masses economically, concentrating in the State the production and division of wealth.... It will be the reign of scientific intelligence, the most aristocratic, despotic, arrogant, and elitist of regimes."**

Though by the time of Marx's death in 1883 there had been no socialist revolutions, his ideas were spreading and his followers increasing. And, as we will see when examining communist regimes of the twentieth century (Chapters 27–30), Bakunin's prophecy proved perfectly accurate.

Charles Darwin, Evolution, and Social Darwinism

Charles Darwin
(1809–1882) English natural historian, geologist, and proponent of the theory of evolution.

Prior to publishing his groundbreaking book *On the Origin of Species by Means of Natural Selection* in 1859, the British scientist **Charles Darwin** (1809–1882) had spent many years gathering evidence. Geologists had already determined that the earth was millions of years old and that its surface features had changed greatly over time. Darwin believed that long-term biologic change, or evolution, also characterized natural history. His search was for the mechanism of the evolutionary process.

In the Galápagos Islands off the coast of South America, Darwin observed that finches and turtles differed from those on the mainland and even in other areas of the islands. He theorized that the variations resulted from the adaptation of species to different environments. His principal contribution was the idea that natural selection drove this process.

Darwin explained that the origins of all life on earth resulted from the imperative of survival. Organisms with traits that gave them a better chance of survival passed those traits along to their offspring. Over time, random genetic mutations lead to the accumulation of diverse traits and, when beneficial genetic variations are passed through generations, to the increased success of some species and the appearance of new ones. Failure to adapt to changing conditions, meanwhile, could lead to extinction. Like Newton's theory of gravitation, Darwin's evolutionary theory was elegant, universally applicable, and a substantial advance in understanding.

In *The Descent of Man* (1871), Darwin made it clear that human beings had also undergone natural selection in their evolution as a species, contradicting Biblical accounts of human creation. In Europe, but even more strongly in the United States and the Islamic world, many religious leaders denounced his work.

Religious ideas themselves were not standing still. In western Europe and North America, evangelical Protestantism, with an emphasis on a more personal and emotionally intense relationship with the divine, was inspiring many to seek out converts in the slums or to become missionaries abroad. In the Islamic world, an important nineteenth-century development was the emergence of the Wahhabis, who emphasized a return to the purity of early Islam. Across religions, critics of industrial modernity complained of a shift from spiritual life to a new obsession with the production and consumption of material goods. In offering a purely materialist explanation for the origin of our species, Darwin offended those who believed that

*Mikhail Bakunin, "Critique of Economic Determinism and Historical Materialism," in *Bakunin on Anarchy*, Sam Dolgoff ed. (New York: Knopf, 1972), p. 319.

faith, not science, was the key to knowledge. (See the feature "Movement of Ideas Through Primary Sources: Religious Leaders Comment on Science and Progress.")

Yet Darwin's insights were quickly accepted by virtually all natural scientists, and his ideas resonated with broader intellectual trends. The intense competitiveness of industrial capitalism, after all, was bringing on more complex and productive economic enterprises, leading to a belief in progress bolstered by popular views of evolution as "improvement." Even Karl Marx saw Darwin's theory of evolution as reinforcing his own view that human history proceeds through stages (feudalism, capitalism, socialism) on a progressive path forward.

AP® THEMES

How did people use Darwin's ideas to reinforce the racial ideologies of the nineteenth and twentieth centuries?

Some, however, applied Darwin's concept of adaptation and survival in the natural world directly to human society, with dangerous implications. *Social Darwinism* was the idea that differences in wealth and power could be explained by the superiority of some and the inferiority of others. Analogies from nature were thus used to justify social inequality. Social Darwinism was also used to explain Europe's increasing global dominance: European imperialism was an inevitable natural process—the "survival of the fittest"—in which "inferior peoples" would be displaced. Darwin himself did not draw such social and political corollaries from his work, but Social Darwinism became deeply entrenched in European thought as racists looked increasingly to science to justify their prejudices.

Challenges to Reform in the Russian and Ottoman Empires, 1825–1881

The Russian and Ottoman empires seemed to be on different trajectories in the nineteenth century. Russia, one of the great powers of Europe, had the world's largest army and a vast Eurasian empire. The Ottomans, in contrast, were contracting, having lost territories across their domain. Sensing Ottoman weakness, the Russians went on the offensive in the **Crimean War**, anxious to gain warm water Black Sea ports and access to the Mediterranean. Had Britain and France not intervened on the Ottomans' side (fearing a too powerful Russian neighbor), the tsars may well have succeeded.

Crimean War (1853–1856) War fought in the Crimean peninsula between the Russian and Ottoman empires. France and Britain sent troops to aid the Ottomans and prevent Russian expansion.

Yet the Crimean War highlighted a crucial similarity between the Russian and Ottoman empires. Both had already been put on notice by Napoleon Bonaparte's invasions (see Chapter 22) that burgeoning power lay to their west. Half a century later, that western advantage had grown much greater not only in armaments, but also in finance, logistics, medical science, engineering, and myriad other fields. When the war finished in a deadlock, elites in both Istanbul and St. Petersburg needed to take stock of how to remain competitive in this new environment. Should they emulate the reforms of western Europe through more liberal policies, or follow the advice of conservatives to reject foreign influences and remain true to their own traditions?

Emancipation and Reaction in Russia

Mikhail Bakunin was from a generation of educated Russians inspired by the revolutionary changes to the west and anxious to transform their homeland. "*Russia figures as a synonym for brutal repression,*" he said; "*thanks to the execrable [policies] of our sovereigns, the name 'Russian' . . . stands for 'slave and executioner.'*"*

*Mikhail Bakunin, "On the 17th Anniversary of the Polish Insurrection," in *Bakunin on Anarchy*, ed. Sam Dolgoff (New York: Knopf, 1972), p. 59.

Religious Leaders Comment on Science and Progress

While the nineteenth century saw the rise of secular ideologies such as liberalism, socialism, and nationalism, religion continued to shape the views of most people around the world. The excerpts below illustrate the implications of modern industrial ideologies for religious faith as interpreted by a Sunni Muslim scholar and a Roman Catholic pope.

The first selection comes from Sayyid Jamāl ad-dīn al-Afghani (1838–1897). He was educated in Islamic schools in Afghanistan and Iran and then spent twenty years in British-ruled India, also traveling to western Europe and the Ottoman empire. Al-Afghani saw pan-Islamic unity as necessary for effective resistance to European dominance and worked to heal divisions between the Sunni and Shi'ite Muslim communities. His efforts did not go unchallenged. Sufi mystics and Wahhabi purists, for example, had little use for his attempt to reconcile Islam with Western science.

The second passage is by Pope Pius IX (r. 1846–1878), who became a staunch conservative after republican revolutionaries forced him to temporarily flee Rome in 1848. Pius IX greatly increased papal authority when he proclaimed the doctrine of papal infallibility, which stated that the pope's statements on central issues of faith were to be regarded as coming directly from God and could not be challenged. His criticism of the loss of spiritual focus in the face of materialism has been a consistent theme of the Roman Catholic Church ever since.

Historical Thinking Skill:

COMPARISON **What were the differences in the views of Pius IX and al-Afghani toward religion and faith in the age of industry?**

Historical Thinking Skill:

PATTERNS OF CONTINUITY AND CHANGE OVER TIME **What elements of Pius IX's and al-Afghani's arguments have remained a part of debates about faith and science into the twenty-first century?**

Sources: Excerpt cited and translated in Nikki Keddie, *Sayyid Jamāl ad-dīn "al-Afghani": A Political Biography* (Berkeley: University of California Press, 1972), pp. 161, 186. Reprinted by permission; excerpt, Pope Pius IX, *Quanta Cura (Condemning Current Errors)*, from www.ewtn.com.

Sayyid Jamāl ad-dīn al-Afghani

1. "Lecture on Teaching and Learning" (1882)

If someone looks deeply into the question, he will see that science rules the world. There was, is, and will be no other ruler in the world but science.... In reality, sovereignty has never left the abode of science. However, this true ruler, which is science, is continually changing capitals. Sometimes it has moved from East to West, and other times from West to East.... The acquisitions of men for themselves and their governments are proportional to their science. Thus, every government for its own benefit must strive to lay the foundation of the sciences and to disseminate knowledge....

The strangest thing of all is that our *ulama* [scholarly community] these days have divided science into two parts. One they call Muslim science, and one European science. Because of this they forbid others to teach some of the useful sciences. They have not understood that science is that noble thing that has no connection with any nation, and is not distinguished by anything but itself. Rather, everything that is known is known by science, and every nation that becomes renowned becomes renowned through science....

How very strange it is that the Muslims study those sciences that are ascribed to Aristotle with the greatest delight, as if Aristotle were one of the pillars of the Muslims. However, if the discussion relates to Galileo, Newton and Kepler, they consider them infidels. The father and mother of science is proof, and proof is neither Aristotle nor Galileo. The truth is where there is proof, and those who forbid science and knowledge in the belief that they are safeguarding the Islamic religion are really enemies of that religion. The Islamic religion is the closest of religions to science and knowledge, and there is no incompatibility between science and knowledge and the foundation of the Islamic faith....

2. "Answer of Jamāl ad-dīn to Renan" (1883)

All religions are intolerant, each one in its way. The Christian religion, I mean the society that follows its inspirations and its teachings ... seems to advance rapidly on the road of progress and science, whereas Muslim society has not yet freed itself from the tutelage of religion.... I cannot keep from hoping that Muslim society will succeed someday in breaking its bonds and marching resolutely in the path of civilization after the manner of Western society.... No I cannot admit that this hope be denied to Islam.

Pope Pius IX

Quanta Cura (Condemning Current Errors), 1864

For well you know, my brothers, that at this time there are many men who applying to civil society the impious and absurd principle of "naturalism," dare to teach that "the best constitution of public society ... requires that human society be conducted and governed without regard being had to religion any more than if it did not exist; or, at least, without any distinction between true religion and false one." From which false idea ... they foster the erroneous opinion ... that "liberty of conscience and worship is each man's personal right, which ought to be legally proclaimed and asserted in every rightly constituted society; and that a right resides in the citizens to an absolute liberty, which should be restrained by no authority whether ecclesiastical or civil, whereby they may be able openly and publicly to manifest and declare any of their ideas whatever, either by word of mouth, by the press, or in any other way." Whereas we know, from the very teaching of our Lord Jesus Christ, how carefully Christian faith and wisdom should avoid this most injurious babbling.

And, since where religion has been removed from civil society, and the doctrine and authority of divine revelation repudiated, the genuine notion itself of justice and human right is darkened and lost, and the place of true justice and legitimate right is supplied by material force ... [then] human society, when set loose from the bonds of religion and true justice, can have, in truth, no other end than the purpose of obtaining and amassing wealth, and ... follows no other law ... except ... ministering to its own pleasure and interests.

Amidst, therefore, such great perversity of depraved opinions ... and (solicitous also) for the welfare of human society itself, [we] have thought it right again to raise up our Apostolic voice.

Yet Bakunin still held high hopes for Russia. The history of peasant uprisings in Russia, such as Pugachev's rebellion (see Chapter 20), assured him that Russians would not *"patiently resign themselves to their misery"* forever. He saw the Russian *mir*, or village, with its collective decision making and community ownership of land, as a foundation on which an anarchist future could be built. In the short term, however, revolutionary prospects in Russia were bleak, as the tsar's secret police sent Mikhail Bakunin and hundreds of other dissenters into exile

● **CONTEXT&CONNECTIONS** While Karl Marx disparaged peasants, comparing them to a "*sack of potatoes,*" Mikhail Bakunin idolized them. He believed that with their traditions of community decision making, peasants could form the foundation of a liberated Russia. In the end, it was the communist dictator Joseph Stalin who settled the issue, brutally resettling millions of rural Russians and Ukrainians on state-run farms during the *collectivization* of the 1930s (Chapter 28). ●

Russia was still overwhelmingly rural. It had a powerful aristocracy but a weak middle class and almost no modern industry. Russian society was divided between a landowning nobility and serfs so poor, illiterate, and lacking in rights that aristocrats could win or lose these "souls" (as they called their serfs) in a game of cards. The nobility profited from this system, as did the government, which depended on serf conscripts for the huge army. Yet the Crimean War had shown that modern wars could not be won without an industrial foundation. Russia's social structure, lacking both a self-confidant property-owning class to build factories and a proletariat to work in them, was inadequate to the task.

Tsar Alexander II (r. 1855–1881), who came to the throne near the end of the Crimean War, understood the need for change. In 1861 he issued his **Emancipation Edict** freeing the serfs. However, to avoid antagonizing the nobility, the edict required that serfs pay for their own emancipation, even though the amount of land they were allocated was insufficient.

Emancipation Edict
1861 edict by Tsar Alexander II that freed the Russian serfs. However, serfs had to pay their former owners for their freedom, and the land they were allocated was often insufficient to produce the money needed to meet that cost for freedom.

At the same time, the tsar's government began taking action in support of industrialization. During the 1870s government support led to a boom in railroad construction, stimulating the coal and iron industries. High tariffs on foreign goods promoted the development of Russian factories, although growth continued to lag well behind western Europe's. While by 1880 British, French, and German workers were enjoying some benefits of increased productivity, such as better clothing and housing, Russian workers still suffered the dangerous and squalid conditions that had marked the first phase of industrialization.

Another challenge for Alexander's government was the question of nationalities. In Germany, nationalism helped overcome regional and class differences to unify the young nation. The use of nationalism by conservative elites was impossible in the Russian empire, however, where over half the people were not Russian. As in multiethnic Austria, here nationalism was a divisive force. The tsarist state harshly suppressed ethnic minorities, as during an 1863 rebellion in Poland.

By that time, Bakunin's generation was losing influence to a younger group of Russian revolutionaries with little patience for philosophical debate. The secret police were everywhere, forcing dissidents underground. Russian anarchists, agreeing with Bakunin that freedom could be achieved only through the abolition of the state, its bureaucracy, and its army, despaired of doing so through a popular uprising. Some anarchists accepted the need for violence and even terrorism to achieve their ends: a bomb killed Tsar Alexander II in 1881, causing a further

Emancipated Serfs As with freed slaves in the U.S. South during the late nineteenth century, living conditions for most Russian serfs were not immediately transformed by emancipation in 1861. Most were illiterate and, like the wheat threshers shown here, had to rely on their own labor power. (Adoc-photos/Art Resource, NY)

crackdown on dissidence and establishing a link between anarchism, violence, and assassination foreign to Bakunin's thinking.

With the stifling of liberal, socialist, and even nationalist thought, Russian intellectuals and artists instead focused on the question of whether and to what degree Russia should learn from and adopt western European cultural and constitutional models. "Westernizers" answered in the affirmative, while "Slavophiles" declared that Russia should stand by her Slavic traditions, Orthodox Christianity, and tsarist state. The debate was irresolvable, but it did produce some magnificent music. Peter Ilich Tchaikovsky followed Western classical models to become Russia's best-known composer, while "Slavophiles" like Nicolai Rimsky-Korsakov emphasized Slavic and Central Eurasian themes.

Meanwhile, the assassination of Alexander II had shut the window on further reforms. Reform instigated from above can be revoked from above, and Alexander's son and successor did just that. A more conservative attitude toward nationalities is one example. While Alexander II had given considerable freedom to his Finnish subjects, his son declared that everyone in the empire should learn Russian. State support for Orthodox Christianity increased, and repression of Jews intensified. While the building of railroads and encouragement of industry continued, modest steps toward representative government, even at the local level, were shelved. The Slavophile slogan *"Orthodoxy, Autocracy, and Nationality"* guided Russian policy in the later nineteenth century.

Reform and Reaction in the Ottoman Empire

Though still large and powerful, after 1800 the Ottoman empire was under increasing pressure. The Ottomans lost control of Egypt to the independent regime of Muhammad Ali, Greece to an independence movement in 1829, and Algeria to French invaders in 1830, and they were also slipping in the Balkans, the mountainous region of southeastern Europe they had controlled since the days of Süleyman the Magnificent (see Chapter 17). Even sooner and more insistently than their Russian counterparts, Ottoman leaders recognized the need for reform.

Having modernized the military by eliminating the outmoded Janissary Corps (see Chapter 17) Ottoman rulers next laid the foundations for extensive overhaul of the empire's governmental, legal, and educational systems. The resulting **Tanzimat Reforms** (1839–1876) were an ambitious attempt at top-down modernization. In the Tanzimat (TAHNZ-ee-MAT) period, the Ottoman government established new European-style primary and secondary schools to supplement the traditional Islamic schools, introduced colleges of military science and medicine, and sponsored student study in France and Germany. The urban elite began to travel more widely and to read French, Armenian, and Turkish newspapers, and European-style buildings were erected in Istanbul to modernize the capital. The legal system was revamped so that the same civil code applied to everyone, Muslim and non-Muslim alike, with full equality before the law. Finally, to facilitate trade with the West, the Tanzimat reformers introduced a new commercial code modeled on western European rather than Islamic principles.

Tanzimat Reforms
(1839–1876) Restructuring of the Ottoman empire; control over civil law was taken away from religious authorities, while the military and government bureaucracies were reorganized to gain efficiency.

The Tanzimat Reforms led to better administrative efficiency and greater investment and economic growth. They also opened up a longstanding divide between more secular, European-oriented elites, especially in the Western-facing capital city of Istanbul, and more conservative, religiously oriented Turks in the rural interior. Like Slavophiles who stressed Orthodox Christianity as a foundation of Russian society, Muslim religious leaders worried that by borrowing so many ideas from the West the government was undercutting the traditional religious and cultural foundations of their society. They also resented their loss of control over the educational and legal systems that had been a principal source of their power and prestige. Meanwhile, even, some educated Turks (as well as minority Armenians and Greeks) were dissatisfied with the centralized and bureaucratic nature of the Tanzimat program and argued for a constitutional monarchy guided by the principles of liberalism.

Issues of nationality and ethnic identity were another significant challenge for Ottoman reformers. Traditionally, legal pluralism characterized a system where Christian Orthodox, Armenian Apostolic, or Jewish law would prevail in separate courts for the empire's diverse minority communities (see Chapter 17). But that system proved incompatible with modern nationalism, which stressed a tight identification of religion, ethnicity, and political loyalty. While Tanzimat

Turkish Factory In the global industrial processes of the nineteenth century, the role of many world regions was solely as suppliers of raw materials and consumers of finished products. Here we see that in the western Ottoman empire, factory production itself became a part of economic life. In this factory girls and women are weaving silk thread into cloth; the factory supervisor, however, is a man. In Japan as well (see Chapter 24), early textile production relied primarily on women's labor. As in England and India, skilled male artisans lost work when displaced by factories employing less skilled laborers, including young women and children. (Roger-Viollet/The Image Works)

reformers hoped that a unified "Ottoman" identity could be fostered across the empire, in reality non-Turkish subjects of the Sultan were now more likely to see themselves as separate national groups and to turn to outside powers for protection, as when Orthodox Slavs looked to Russia in defiance of Ottoman authority.

Though Ottoman reforms went deeper than Russian ones, the Tanzimat program was also subject to autocratic whim. Just as Russia had relapsed after the assassination of Tsar Alexander II, so the Tanzimat Reform agenda lost momentum with the accession of Sultan Abd al-Hamid (AHB-dahl-ha-med) II (r. 1876–1918). With the backing of conservatives, he suspended proposals for constitutional reform and ruled arbitrarily. In Istanbul, as in St. Petersburg, after 1880, reactionary policies triumphed over reformist ones, with catastrophic results: just two generations later, both of these once-great imperial states would collapse (see Chapter 27).

Global Repercussions of the Industrial Revolution

Europe's prominent place in world affairs was not, of course, something that began with the Industrial Revolution. As described in Chapters 15–18, maritime expansion and access to American resources, especially silver, had enriched European societies in the early modern period. But in the late eighteenth century, much of the world's population—most notably in China—was only marginally affected (see Chapter 20).

It was the Industrial Revolution that placed western Europe firmly at the center of world power. Economically, that meant heightened competition for the raw materials necessary for factory production, many of which (cotton and rubber, for example) were available only outside Europe. As other European states, especially Germany, caught up with Britain's early lead, competition for such resources, as well as for markets for industrial products, intensified. By the late nineteenth century, heightened economic competition would drive a "New Imperialism" that led to direct European control over hundreds of societies (see Chapters 24–26).

Militarily, the Industrial Revolution changed the global balance of power dramatically. Earlier maritime and gunpowder technologies were not a European monopoly, as their effective use by the Ottoman empire demonstrated (see Chapter 17). Now, with steam-powered battleships, more powerful field artillery, and rapidly repeating rifles, the technological and financial costs of keeping up with the rising industrial powers of the West escalated decade by decade. Not even the mighty Russian military was able to keep pace.

The global tensions that resulted from European industrial supremacy had social, cultural, and political implications as well. As we have seen, in both the Russian and Ottoman empires, nineteenth-century elites debated whether to assimilate western European cultural traits as a spur to modernization or to abide by their established cultural and religious traditions. By the late nineteenth century, such debates resonated around the world. For example, while Chinese leaders vacillated on whether and how they might meet the Western challenge by borrowing Western ideas, Japanese reformers won a decisive victory with the Meiji Restoration in 1868 (see Chapter 24). By 1880 the Japanese government had learned, like the Russians and Ottomans before them, that industry was key to success, perhaps even survival, in the harshly competitive Western-dominated world order.

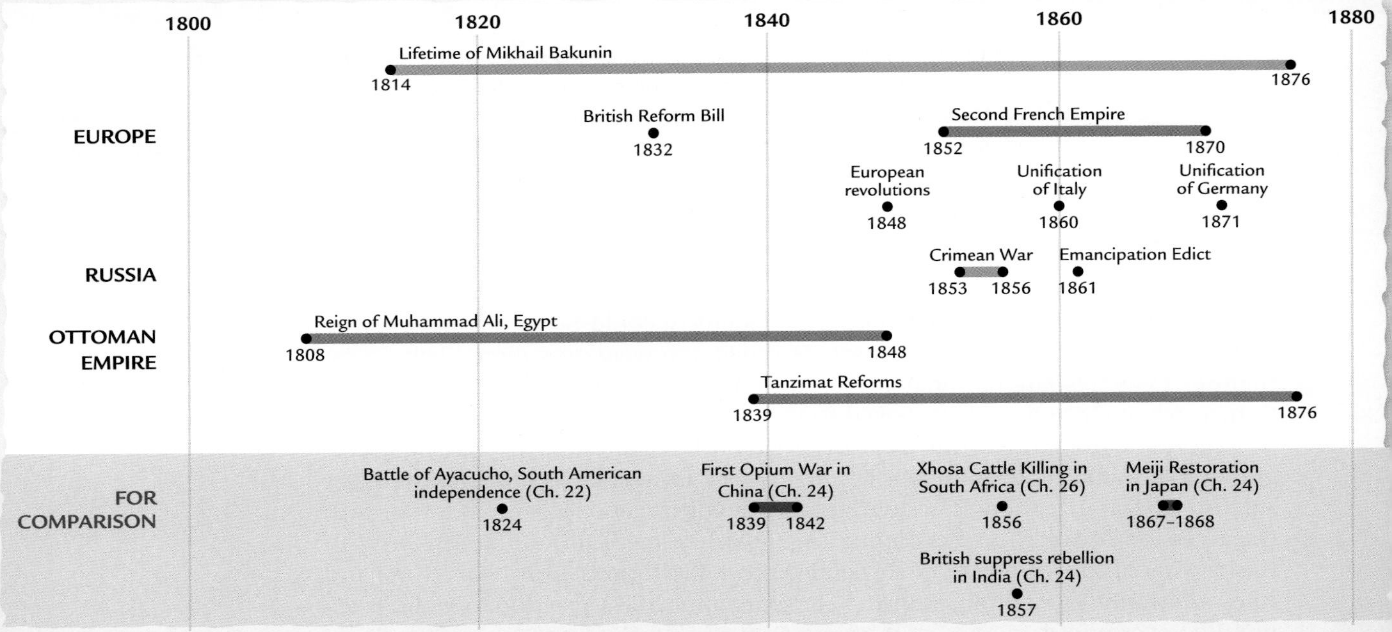

The social consequences of the Industrial Revolution, including the movement of many more people to cities, were also global. Social change led to intellectual ferment. Latin Americans, Africans, and Asians, as well as Europeans, were soon discussing the merits of the key ideas—nationalism, socialism, liberalism—that had formed the background for Mikhail Bakunin's political activism and anarchist philosophy. The revolutionaries of 1848 took aim at the traditional foundations of European social and political authority, attacking the inherited position of kings, landed aristocrats, and religious leaders. Such tensions appeared elsewhere in the world as well whenever new conditions and new ideas undermined customary authority. Faced with aggressive European expansion and a resulting social and political disequilibrium, Africans, Asians, Arabs, Amerindians, and others began to question how they might best adapt. In the industrial age, the mandate for change became insistent.

Meanwhile, within Europe, the rise of a unified Germany significantly altered the balance of power, removing Britain from its previous pinnacle of supremacy and alarming the French and the Russians as well. After 1890, Germany would become more aggressive in challenging the British empire, helping propel a scramble for colonies in Africa and Asia (see Chapter 26), and in the twentieth century the explosion of aggressive militarism present at the birth of Germany in 1871 would lead to two devastating world wars (see Chapters 27–29). Industrial progress, it seems, was a mixed blessing.

Key Terms

Mikhail Bakunin (684)
Industrial Revolution (685)
James Watt (686)
Josiah Wedgwood (687)
Muhammad Ali (690)
Reform Bill of 1832 (694)
John Stuart Mill (694)
Louis Napoleon (698)
Giuseppe Garibaldi (699)
Frankfurt Assembly (701)
Otto von Bismarck (701)
Karl Marx (702)
Charles Darwin (704)
Crimean War (705)
Emancipation Edict (708)
Tanzimat Reforms (710)

For Further Reference

Allen, Robert C. *The British Industrial Revolution in Global Perspective.* New York: Cambridge University Press, 2009.

Anderson, Benedict. *Imagined Communities: Reflections on the Origin and Spread of Nationalism.* London: Verso, 1991.

Auerbach, Jeffrey. *The Great Exhibition of 1851: A Nation on Display.* New Haven: Yale University Press, 1999.

Bakunin, Mikhail. *Bakunin on Anarchy: Selected Works by the Activist-Founder of World Anarchism.* Sam Dolgoff, ed. and trans. New York: Knopf, 1972.

Haniolgu, M. Sükrü. *A Brief History of the Late Ottoman Empire.* Princeton: Princeton University Press, 2010.

Hobsbawm, Eric. *The Age of Capital, 1848–1875.* New York: Simon and Schuster, 1975.

Mayr, Ernst. *One Long Argument: Charles Darwin and the Genesis of Modern Evolutionary Thought.* Cambridge, Mass.: Harvard University Press, 1993.

Randolph, John. *The House in the Garden: The Bakunin Family and the Romance of Russian Idealism.* Ithaca, N.Y.: Cornell University Press, 2007.

Rapport, Mike. *1848: Year of Revolution.* New York: Basic Books, 2010.

Reeves, Richard. *John Stuart Mill: Victorian Firebrand.* London: Atlantic Books, 2008.

Rosen, William. *The Most Powerful Idea in the World: A Story of Steam, Industry, and Invention.* New York: Random House, 2010.

Sperber, Jonathan. *Karl Marx: A Nineteenth Century Life.* New York: Liveright, 2013.

Stearns, Peter. *The Industrial Revolution in World History.* 4th ed. Boulder: Westview, 2012.

Tilly, Louise. *Industrialization and Gender Inequality.* Washington, D.C.: American Historical Association, 1993.

AP® Review Questions for Chapter 23

Multiple-Choice Questions

QUESTIONS 1–3 REFER TO TABLE 23.1 *MANUFACTURING PRODUCTION OF SELECTED COUNTRIES, 1750–1900 AS PERCENTAGE OF GLOBAL TRADE* ON PAGE 685.

1. Which of the following conclusions is best supported by the data in the table?
   (A) The need for specialized and limited metals led to the development of extensive mining centers in Mexico.
   (B) The rapid development of steam-powered industrial production in European countries and the United States contributed to these regions' increase in their share of global manufacturing.
   (C) The global economy of the nineteenth century expanded dramatically from the previous period as a result of increased exchanges of raw materials and finished goods.
   (D) Industrialization fundamentally changed how goods were produced in all regions of the world.

2. A historian researching the global impact of the Industrial Revolution in the period from 1750 to 1900 would most likely find the table above useful as a source of information about which of the following?
   (A) The decline of Asian countries' shares in global manufacturing
   (B) The global nature of trade and production
   (C) Major developments in transportation and communication
   (D) The impact of the capitalistic and classical liberal theories of Adam Smith and John Stuart Mill

3. The data presented in the table best support which of the following conclusions about the Industrial Revolution?
   (A) Merchants and companies based in Europe and the United States possessed a distinct economic advantage.
   (B) The "second Industrial Revolution" was less productive than the "first Industrial Revolution."
   (C) The accumulation of capital was a critical feature that led to the rise in industrial production.
   (D) Industrialization began in northwestern Europe and then spread to other parts of Europe and the United States.

QUESTIONS 4–6 REFER TO THE FOLLOWING PASSAGE.

For well you know, my brothers, that at this time there are many men who applying to civil society the impious and absurd principle of "naturalism," dare to teach "that the best constitution of public society...requires that human society be conducted and governed without regard being had to religion any more than if it did not exist...." And, since where religion has been removed from civil society, and the doctrine and authority of divine revelation repudiated, the genuine notion itself of justice and human right is darkened and lost, the place of true justice and legitimate right is supplied by material force...[then] human society, when set loose from the bonds of religion and true justice, can have, in truth, no other end than the purpose of obtaining and amassing wealth, and...follows no other law...except...ministering to its own pleasure and interests.

—Pope Pius IX, *Quanta Cura* (Condemning Current Errors), 1864

4. Which of the following conclusions about the period from 1750 to 1900 is most directly supported by the passage?
   (A) Subjects were increasingly challenging centralized imperial governments.
   (B) The development of communism was the result of discontent with monarchist rule.
   (C) Classical liberalism and capitalism had begun to challenge traditional sources of authority.
   (D) Workers were organizing in industrialized states to improve working conditions, limit hours, and gain higher wages.

5. Which of the following best explains the motive behind Pope Pius's publication of *Quanta Cura*?
   (A) To respond to the Enlightenment principles that questioned the role religion played in public life
   (B) To suppress demands for women's suffrage and the emergent feminist movement that challenged political and gender hierarchies
   (C) To insinuate the role of religion in the wave of nineteenth-century rebellions throughout Europe
   (D) To appeal to faith as a unifying force in order to develop a sense of commonality among Catholics

6. Compared to the sentiments regarding the role of religion in society expressed in the passage, European practices concerning rights in the period from 1750 to 1900 *differed* in that they
   (A) were largely the result of continued reliance on coerced and semicoerced migrant workers.
   (B) embraced liberal principles to varying degrees as a response to monarchist rule.
   (C) tended to ignore liberal principles such as the expansion of suffrage and end to serfdom.
   (D) justified violent rebellions that had been inspired by rebellions in the Americas.

QUESTIONS 7–10 REFER TO THE IMAGE ON PAGE 709, *EMANCIPATED SERFS*, AND THE IMAGE ON PAGE 711, *TURKISH FACTORY*.

7. Which of the following conclusions about the Industrial Revolution does the image on page 709 most directly refute?
   (A) Enlightenment ideas led to the end of serfdom in Russia.
   (B) Russian serfs enjoyed better conditions after emancipation than American slaves.
   (C) Marxist ideology was especially appealing to Russian serfs.
   (D) Industrialization improved agriculture productivity.

8. Which of the following conclusions is best supported by the information in the image on page 711?
   (A) The Ottoman empire attempted to maintain preindustrial forms of production.
   (B) Ottoman share in global manufacturing declined.
   (C) Ottoman gender roles changed in response to the Industrial Revolution.
   (D) Ottoman workers embraced feminist ideas.

9. Which of the following was an important aspect of the period from 1750 to 1900 demonstrated by the two images?
   (A) Political ideologies of socialism and communism never spread to Russia and the Ottoman empire.
   (B) The role of women in both regions underwent dramatic shifts as a result of migration.
   (C) Both Russia and the Ottoman empire underwent political reforms as a result of industrialization.
   (D) In some regions, preindustrial forms of production persisted.

10. The Tanzimat Reforms in the Ottoman empire and the emancipation of Russian serfs were both the result of
   (A) state-sponsored efforts to modernize within their own cultural contexts.
   (B) extensions of economic imperialism to dependent populations within their empires.
   (C) nationalist movements intended to unite their multicultural populations with a new sense of community.
   (D) both states' full endorsement of Western Enlightenment ideals.

Short-Answer Questions

1. Answer parts A and B.
   Many historians argue that Europeans during the Industrial Age believed that human society could be improved through rational inquiry.
   A. Provide TWO pieces of evidence that *support* this argument, and explain how each piece supports the argument.
   B. Provide ONE piece of evidence that *undermines* the argument, and explain how it undermines the argument.

2. Answer parts A, B, and C.
   A. Explain ONE cause of the Industrial Revolution.
   B. Explain ONE social effect of the Industrial Revolution.
   C. Explain ONE political effect of the Industrial Revolution.

24 The Challenge of Modernity in China, Japan, and India, 1800–1910

In 1859, the government of Japan sent its first delegation to visit the United States. On the crossing **Fukuzawa Yûkichi** (foo-koo-ZAH-wah yoo-KEE-chee) (1835–1901), a twenty-four-year-old samurai, studied *Webster's Dictionary*, but it did not prepare him very well for his experiences in San Francisco. *"There were many confusing and embarrassing moments,"* he later wrote, *"for we were quite ignorant of the customs of American life."**

Fukuzawa Yûkichi

Portrait of a Japanese man named Fukuzawa Yukichi, a samurai and officer on the 1862 Takenouchi mission to Europe, employed as an interpreter of Dutch and English, 1862 (albumen print), Potteau, Jacques-Philippe (1807–76)/Pitt Rivers Museum, Oxford, UK/Bridgeman Images

At his hotel, he was amazed when his hosts walked across expensive carpets with their shoes on. Fukuzawa attended a dance wearing the outfit of a samurai, with two swords and hemp sandals:

*To our dismay we could not make out what they were doing. The ladies and gentlemen seemed to be hopping around the room together. As funny as it was, we knew it would be rude to laugh, and we controlled our expressions with difficulty as the dancing went on. . . . Things social, political, and economic proved most inexplicable. . . . I asked a gentleman where the descendants of George Washington might be. . . . His answer was so very casual that it shocked me. Of course, I know that America is a republic with a new president every four years, but I could not help feeling that the family of Washington would be revered above all other families. My reasoning was based on the reverence in Japan for the founders of the great lines of rulers—like that for Ieyasu of the Tokugawa family of Shoguns.**

---

*From *The Autobiography of Yukichi Fukuzawa*, by Eiichi Kiyooka, 1960, pp. 114–116.

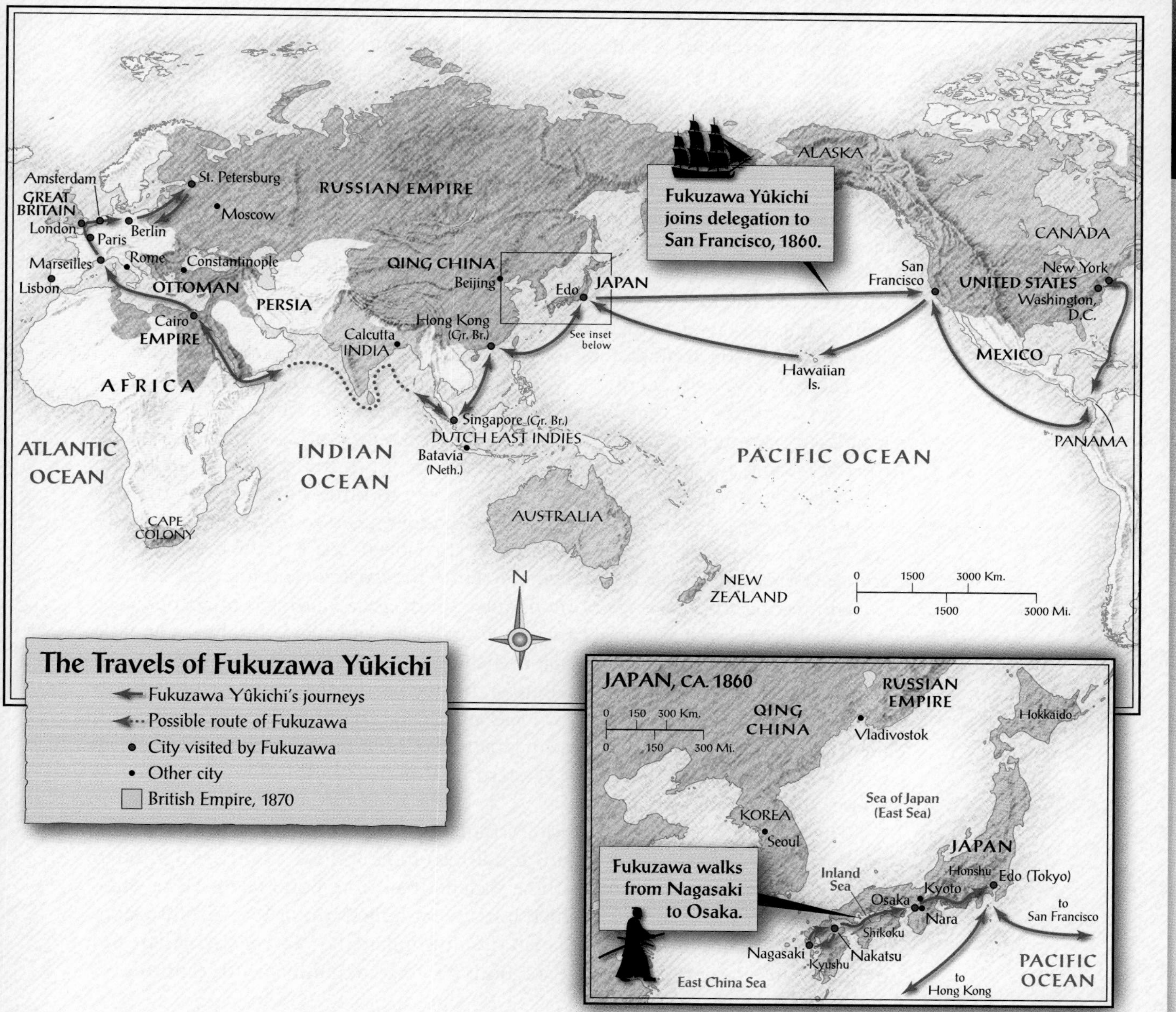

Though he was much more knowledgeable about the Western world than most Japanese, Fukuzawa said of himself and his American hosts, *"neither of us really knew much about the other at all."**

Fukuzawa had grown up in a low-ranking samurai family that was expected to give unconditional support and service to their lord, but he was an ambitious nonconformist. As a young man he dedicated himself to "Dutch learning" (see Chapter 20)

---

*From *The Autobiography of Yukichi Fukuzawa*, by Eiichi Kiyooka, 1960, p. 115.

Fukuzawa Yûkichi
(1835–1901) Japanese writer, teacher, political theorist, and founder of Keio Academy (now Keio University). His ideas about learning, government, and society greatly influenced the Meiji Restoration. Considered one of the founders of modern Japan.

and, becoming convinced of the merits of Western science, he developed a philosophy that emphasized independence over subservience and science over tradition.

Fukuzawa's lifetime was one of remarkable change. All across the world, societies struggled to adapt to the new industrial age with its advances in transportation and communications technologies, the spread of new religious and secular ideologies, and the dynamics of a changing global economy. In western Europe, rulers, reformers, and rebels all struggled for control over the direction of change, while at the same time Russian and Ottoman elites debated calls for liberal reform versus conservative appeals to tradition (see Chapter 23). Societies in East Asia were similarly divided. Japanese reformers like Fukuzawa embraced change along Western lines as a means of empowerment, but conservatives there and elsewhere in East Asia saw Europe and the United States as hostile threats to their established social, political, and economic systems.

Fukuzawa was a leader of the Westernizing faction that came to dominate Japan after the overthrow in 1868 of the Tokugawa shogunate (see Chapter 20). The new Japanese government was able to resist the Western powers and, with military victories over China and Russia, expand its own empire. In contrast, the leaders of Qing China proved incapable of reforming their society to turn aside the Western challenge. By the late nineteenth century, China had been carved into spheres of influence by outside powers. Korean leaders were also slow to adapt to the industrial age, and the Korean peninsula was incorporated into the Japanese empire.

In meeting the challenge of modernity, South Asians also had to adapt to the industrial age, as well as balance their own traditions with powerful new economic forces and cultural influences. A major rebellion in 1857 signaled how deeply many Indians resented British rule. The failure of that revolt stimulated Indian intellectuals and political leaders to develop new ideas and organizations to achieve self-government. Indian nationalists, like those in Japan and China, struggled with the question of how to deal with the power of Western models in everything from clothing to house design to political philosophy.

This chapter focuses on the various strategies of resistance and accommodation used by the peoples of China, Japan, and British India in their attempts to come to terms with the industrial age. All these societies had to respond to the rising challenges of industrial modernity, which initially took the form of Western intrusion. Fukuzawa Yûkichi's proposal that Japan should emulate the West to strengthen and modernize itself was just one of the solutions put forward in nineteenth-century East and South Asia.

KEY CONCEPT QUESTIONS

- What factors led to the collapse of the Qing dynasty? **(Key Concept 5.1)**
- How did the Meiji Restoration contribute to the rise of Japan? **(Key Concept 5.1)**
- What role did nationalism play in Indian resistance to British rule? **(Key Concept 5.3)**
- How did Chinese, Japanese, and Indian societies respond differently to the challenges of industrial modernity? **(Key Concept 5.3)**

China's World Inverted, 1800–1906

Four decades after China's emperor dismissed Britain's diplomatic advances (see Chapter 20), the British returned with firepower to forcibly open Chinese markets. Suddenly faced with Europe's industrial might, Qing officials agreed to a series of unequal treaties. Soon after, a major rebellion shook the Qing dynasty to its foundations. While some officials, humiliated by the decline in imperial prestige, entertained reform, they were outmaneuvered by conservatives who opposed adopting Western political, educational, and economic models.

The conservatives' policies were a disaster. By the end of the nineteenth century, soldiers from Britain, France, Russia, the United States, and Japan had occupied Beijing's Forbidden City, as Imperial China lost its ancient status as the "Middle Kingdom" to become a chessboard on which the great powers moved their pieces, dividing China into spheres of influence.

Fukuzawa Yûkichi, who had helped implement Western-style reform in Japan, observed in 1899: *"I am sure that it is impossible to lead [the Chinese] people to civilization so long as the old government is left to stand as it is."** Seven years later the last Manchu emperor abdicated, but by then China's long-dominant role in East Asia had been usurped by Japan.

Qing China Confronts the Industrial World, 1800–1850

In the late eighteenth century, the British East India Company faced an old problem for Western traders in China: apart from silver, they had few goods of value in Chinese markets. But in the 1770s, after they came to dominate opium-producing regions in India, the British began exchanging illicit opium for tea, silk, and other valuable commodities. The strategy was commercially brilliant, since narcotics create their own demand through the spiral of drug addiction. But it was ethically problematic and even hypocritical. Opium induces such lethargy and such a sense of hopelessness that those in its clutches neglect their own health and the care of their dependents. Even while the British sought to stamp out opium addiction at home, the East India Company was smuggling opium into China in open disregard of Chinese governmental authority. Widespread addiction undercut China's economy through lost productivity.

By 1839, Sino-British relations were in crisis. The Qing government declared that drug traders would be beheaded and sent a scholar-official named Lin Zezu (lin say-SHOE) to Guangzhou to suppress the opium trade. In a letter to Queen Victoria, Lin made his government's position clear:

> *[By] introducing opium by stealth [the British] have seduced our Chinese people, and caused every province in the land to overflow with that poison. They know merely how to advantage themselves; they care not about injuring others!...*

---

*From *The Autobiography of Yukichi Fukuzawa*, by Eiichi Kiyooka, 1960, p. 277.

*Therefore those foreigners who now import opium into the Central Land are condemned to be beheaded and strangled.**

To the British, however, the issue was not so much opium as free trade. Commercial interests were lobbying the British government for more open access to Chinese markets, which had traditionally been highly regulated. And according to an extreme interpretation of liberal economic theory, free trade is always and everywhere best for everyone. If the Chinese did not agree, then they would have to be *forced* to open their markets.

Opium War
In the first Opium War (1839–1842), Britain invaded the Qing empire to force China to open to trade. In the second Opium War (1856–1860), an Anglo-French force once again invaded to enforce the unequal treaties that resulted from the first war and extract further concessions.

The first **Opium War** (1839–1842) was a severe shock to the Qing government. The British used their iron-clad gunboats to blockade the Chinese coast and bombard coastal cities such as Guangzhou and Shanghai. Being so easily defeated by "Western barbarians," many Qing commanders committed suicide in disgrace. In 1842, as the British sailed up the Yangzi River and prepared to blast apart the walls of Nanjing, Qing officials realized that they would have to negotiate.

Treaty of Nanjing
(1842) One-sided treaty that concluded the first Opium War. Britain was allowed to trade in additional Chinese ports and took control of Hong Kong. The provision for extraterritoriality meant that Britons were subject to British rather than Chinese law.

With no bargaining power, the Qing felt compelled to agree to the humiliating terms of the **Treaty of Nanjing**, the first of a series of unequal treaties that eroded Chinese sovereignty. The agreement opened five "treaty ports" to unrestricted foreign trade and gave possession of Hong Kong, upriver from the great port of Guangzhou, to the British. The treaty's provision of extraterritoriality, making Britons subject to British rather than Chinese law at the treaty ports, was a crushing blow to Chinese pride.

The Treaty of Nanjing only whetted British and other European appetites. Using supposed Qing violations of the Nanjing treaty as a pretext, in the second Opium War of 1856 the British and French burned Qianlong's magnificent summer palace to the ground, and briefly occupied the Forbidden City. In 1860, the Qing agreed to another, even more unequal treaty that opened more ports to Western trade and allowed "international settlements" in key Chinese cities such as Shanghai and Guangzhou. These settlements, where only Europeans were allowed to live, were foreign enclaves on Chinese soil. The British also mandated that the Manchu would no longer refer to them as "barbarians" in imperial documents.

The Taiping Rebellion, 1850–1864

The Opium Wars and the unequal treaties that followed had exposed Qing weakness, leading some Chinese to conclude that the Manchu had lost the "Mandate of Heaven" (see Chapter 16). Indeed, as early as the 1790s, some peasant rebels had questioned Qing imperial legitimacy. Such challenges would cascade in the decades to come.

Behind the political chaos of nineteenth-century China was a startling fact: the population had grown by over 100 million between 1800 and 1850. Farmers brought more marginal lands into production; agricultural yields declined; villages were repeatedly flooded. People were suffering from neglect, misrule, and hunger. Although imperial governments had long been responsible for flood control and famine relief, the Qing bureaucracy, fighting foreign invaders, instead raised taxes for its military in the midst of the people's suffering.

*Mark A. Kishlansky, ed., *Sources of World History*, vol. 2 (New York: HarperCollins College Publishers, 1995), p. 268.

• **CONTEXT&CONNECTIONS** Chinese historians long used a cyclical theory to explain the rise and fall of imperial dynasties. At the beginning, strong leaders with Confucian virtue are active in administration, assuring ethical behavior by scholar-officials. Imperial decline and the consequent loss of the Mandate of Heaven would begin when emperors became distracted from day-to-day administration: courts became corrupt; canals silted up; peasants revolted; warlords defied imperial authority; and famine and calamity stalked the land. The theory of dynastic cycles seems applicable to the late *Ming dynasty* period (key term in Chapter 16) and to the Manchu as well. Of course, apart from issues of political leadership, modern historians also take account of demographic, environmental, and economic factors in charting the rise and fall of dynasties. •

In the mid-nineteenth century, further peasant revolts shook the empire, including a major Muslim uprising in the northwest. The situation was especially desperate in Guangdong province, where the **Taiping Rebellion** (1850–1864) began, and then spread throughout southern China, sending the empire into chaos. The leader of the Taiping (tie-PING) was Hong Xiuquan (hoong shee-OH-chew-an). Hong had traveled to Guangzhou for the imperial examinations where, having failed in several attempts, he then studied with Western missionaries and added a unique interpretation to their message.

Taiping Rebellion
(1850–1864) Massive rebellion against the Qing led by Hong Xiuquan, who claimed to be the younger brother of Jesus Christ come to earth to create a "Heavenly Kingdom of Great Peace." The imperial system was greatly weakened as a result of the uprising.

Hong claimed to be the younger brother of Jesus Christ, come to earth to establish a *"Heavenly Kingdom of Great Peace."* Mixing Christianity with peasant yearnings for fairness and justice, Hong attracted hundreds of thousands of followers to his vision of reform. In their Heavenly Kingdom, the Taiping proclaimed, *"inequality [will not] exist, and [everyone will] be well fed and clothed."**

• **CONTEXT&CONNECTIONS** Movements such as the Taiping are referred to as *millenarian*. Some Christians believe that after the second coming of Christ a millennium (one thousand years) of earthly peace and prosperity will follow. Another such millenarian movement occurred at the very same time in South Africa. During the tragic *Xhosa Cattle Killing* (Chapter 26), a young prophetess predicted that departed ancestors would rise from the dead to purge evil from the land, borrowing the concept of the resurrection of the dead from Christian missionaries. In both China and South Africa in the mid-1850s, religious *syncretism* (Chapter 18) followed from contact with European missionaries, influencing mass millenarian movements. •

AP® THEMES
How did the Taiping movement use Christianity in its push for political and social reform?

Many in the disciplined core of the Taiping movement were, like Hong, from the Hakka ethnic group. The Hakka were only brought under imperial control during Ming times and had never fully assimilated Confucian ideas of hierarchy. Women had relatively independent roles, and their feet were never bound. Hong's "long-haired rebels" refused to wear the long, braided ponytail (or *queue*) mandated by Manchu authorities as a sign of subservience. *"Ever since the Manchus poisoned China,"* Hong said, *"the influence of demons has distressed the empire while the Chinese with bowed heads and dejected spirits willingly became subjects and servants."*†

In late 1850 some twenty thousand Taiping rebels defeated an imperial army sent to crush them; they then went on the offensive and captured the city of

---

*Franz Michael and Chang Chung-li, *The Taiping Rebellion: History and Documents*, vol. 2 (Seattle: University of Washington Press, 1971), p. 314.

†Jen Yu-Wen, *The Taiping Revolutionary Moment* (New Haven: Yale University Press, 1973), pp. 93–94.

Nanjing, just upriver from Shanghai. Tens of thousands of Manchu were systematically slaughtered. Hong moved into a former Ming imperial palace and declared Nanjing his capital.

After 1853, however, the Taiping rebels gained no more great victories. Their rhetoric of equality alienated landowners and educated elites: influential members of the gentry organized militias to fight them. The Taiping were unable to recruit experienced administrators because their religious beliefs were at odds with the Confucian ideals of scholar-officials, and corruption seeped into the movement when some leaders abandoned the plain living advocated by Hong and indulged in expensive clothing, fine food, and elaborate rituals.

From their base at Nanjing, the Taiping threatened the rapidly developing European interests in Shanghai. So now, in the early 1860s, the British and French, who had done so much to undercut the Qing, rallied to the dynasty's defense. In 1864, Qing forces, supported by European soldiers and armaments, stormed and took Nanjing. A Manchu official reported: *"Not one of the 100,000 rebels in Nanjing surrendered themselves when the city was taken but in many cases gathered together and burned themselves and passed away without repentance."** A staggering 30 million people had been killed by the end of the Taiping Rebellion, and China's rulers were more beholden to European powers than ever before.

"Self-Strengthening" and the Boxer Rebellion, 1842–1901

In the wake of the Opium War and Taiping Rebellion, some educated Chinese began arguing that only fundamental change would enable the empire to meet the rising Western challenge, as more and more representatives of industrial capitalism arrived by steamship looking for markets and cheap labor. Some joined together in the **Self-Strengthening Movement**, with the motto *"Confucian ethics, Western science."* China, these reformers said, could acquire modern technology and the scientific knowledge underlying it while retaining the ethically superior Confucian tradition. As one of their leaders stated, *"What we have to learn from the barbarians is only one thing, solid ships and effective guns."*†

Self-Strengthening Movement
Nineteenth-century Chinese reform movement with the motto "Confucian ethics, Western science." Advocates of Self-Strengthening sought a way to reconcile Western and Chinese systems of thought.

Reformers supported the translation of Western scientific texts (the first since the days of Jesuit influence in the seventeenth century) and established new educational institutions that merged the study of Confucian classics with coursework in geography and science. And for the first time some young Manchu and Chinese men ventured to Europe and the United States to study Western achievements firsthand. They were sowing seeds of change along the same lines as Fukuzawa Yûkichi in Japan.

Conservatives, however, scoffed at the Self-Strengthening Movement. A prominent Neo-Confucian rejected education in science and engineering, sneering that no one *"could use mathematics to raise a nation from a state of decline or to strengthen it in times of weakness."*‡ Like Muslim scholars in the Ottoman empire, Chinese

---

*Franz Michael and Chang Chung-li, *The Taiping Rebellion: History and Documents*, vol. 3 (Seattle: University of Washington Press, 1971), p. 767.

†Teng Ssu-yü and John K. Fairbank, *China's Response to the West: A Documentary Survey, 1839–1923* (Cambridge, Mass.: Harvard University Press, 1954), pp. 53–54.

‡Quoted in Patricia Buckley Ebrey, *Cambridge Illustrated History of China* (London: Cambridge University Press, 1996), p. 245.

A Qing Arsenal A major focus of the Self-Strengthening Movement was military modernization. Here Qing officials survey cannon at an arsenal built in 1865, after the suppression of the Taiping Rebellion. The reformers hoped to achieve self-sufficiency in military infrastructure with the aid of foreign advisers; however, the corruption and inefficiency of the imperial bureaucracy prevented them from achieving that goal, a great contrast to Japanese achievements in military production in the following decades.

scholar-officials derived their power and prestige from training in a historically successful body of knowledge. To accept foreign principles in education would undercut their influence, and to emphasize military over scholarly pursuits would go against Confucianism. *"One does not waste good sons by making them soldiers,"* went an old saying.

• **CONTEXT&CONNECTIONS** The relatively low status of soldiers in imperial China stood in contrast to the social norms of both Japan and western Europe. The Middle Kingdom had no equivalent to the valiant knights of European lore or the steadfast *samurai* who had long been the bedrock of Japanese society. Indeed, in the sixteenth century, *Matteo Ricci* (Chapter 16) had applauded the Ming Chinese who, in contrast to rulers on his own violent continent, emphasized culture and learning over military affairs. •

Conservative attitudes coalesced at the top of the imperial hierarchy when, during the reign of two child emperors, real power lay in the hands of a conservative regent, the **Empress Ci Xi** (1835–1908), an intelligent and ambitious concubine who came to dominate the highest reaches of the Qing bureaucracy. Conservatives rallied around Ci Xi (kee SHEE). She discouraged talk of reform and diverted funds meant for modernization, such as programs to build railways and strengthen the military, to prestige projects like rebuilding the ruined summer

Empress Ci Xi (1835–1908) The "Dowager Empress" who dominated Qing politics in the late nineteenth century, ruling as regent for the emperor Guangxu. She blocked the Hundred Days' Reforms and other "Self-Strengthening" measures.

palace. Indeed, instead of building a real warship, she ordered an ornamental marble boat to decorate the palace lake.

Ci Xi resented the unequal treaties with European nations, and the arrogance of their representatives infuriated her. Despite limited beginnings of industrialization and the acquisition of some modern armaments, however, the Qing military was still no match for its rivals. In 1884, during a dispute over rights to Vietnam, French gunboats obliterated the Qing southern fleet within an hour. Southeast Asia, no longer tributary to the Qing, would now belong to France (see Chapter 26).

AP® THEMES

How were efforts to reform Chinese economic policies influenced by Confucianism?

The Japanese, pursuing a policy of rapid industrialization and militarization, were also a threat. In 1894 an uprising against Korea's imperial dynasty drew in both Japanese and Chinese military forces, resulting in the Sino-Japanese War. The Qing, having lost their southern fleet to France, now lost almost their entire northern fleet to Japan. The treaty that ended the war gave Japan possession of both Korea and the island of Taiwan.

After these military defeats, Chinese reformers finally won official support in 1898, when the young Guangxu (gwahng-SHOO) emperor issued a series of reform edicts. Guangxu was inspired by a group of young scholars who had traveled to Beijing to present a petition urging that the government found a state bank, sell bonds to support large-scale railroad building, and create a modern postal system. The most fundamental reform concerned education. Expertise in poetry and calligraphy would no longer be required. Instead, examination questions would focus on practical issues of governance and administration. Beijing College was to add a medical school, and all the Confucian academies were to add Western learning to their curricula.

Ci Xi quickly intervened to suppress Guangxu's reforms, confining him, along with his most progressive advisers, to the palace. Some advocates of Self-Strengthening were charged with conspiracy and executed; others left the country or lapsed into silence.

Meanwhile, the aggression of external powers intensified. Germans seized the port city of Qingdao (ching-DOW) and claimed mineral and railway rights on northeastern Shandong peninsula (birthplace of Confucius). The British expanded their holdings from Hong Kong, and the Russians increased their presence in Manchuria (see Map 24.1). Public anger grew, directed at the Manchu for letting the empire slip so dramatically.

Boxer Rebellion
(1898) Chinese uprising triggered by a secret society called the Society of Righteous and Harmonious Fists, a fiercely anti-Western group. Intended to drive out Westerners, it resulted instead in foreign occupation of Beijing.

Throughout the tumultuous nineteenth century, Chinese had sought security by joining secret societies. One of these, the "Society of Righteous and Harmonious Fists," also known as the Boxers because of their emphasis on martial arts, now rose to prominence. The Boxers were virulently antiforeign. In 1898 they attacked European missionaries and Chinese Christian converts, thus beginning the **Boxer Rebellion**. Empress Ci Xi decided to side with these antiforeign rebels and declared the Boxers a patriotic group: *"The foreigners have been aggressive towards us, infringed upon our territorial integrity, trampled our people under their feet. . . . They oppress our people and blaspheme our gods."** (See the feature "Visual Evidence in Primary Sources: The Boxer Rebellion: American and French Views.")

---

*Victor Purcell, *The Boxer Uprising: A Background Study* (New York: Cambridge University Press, 1963), p. 224.

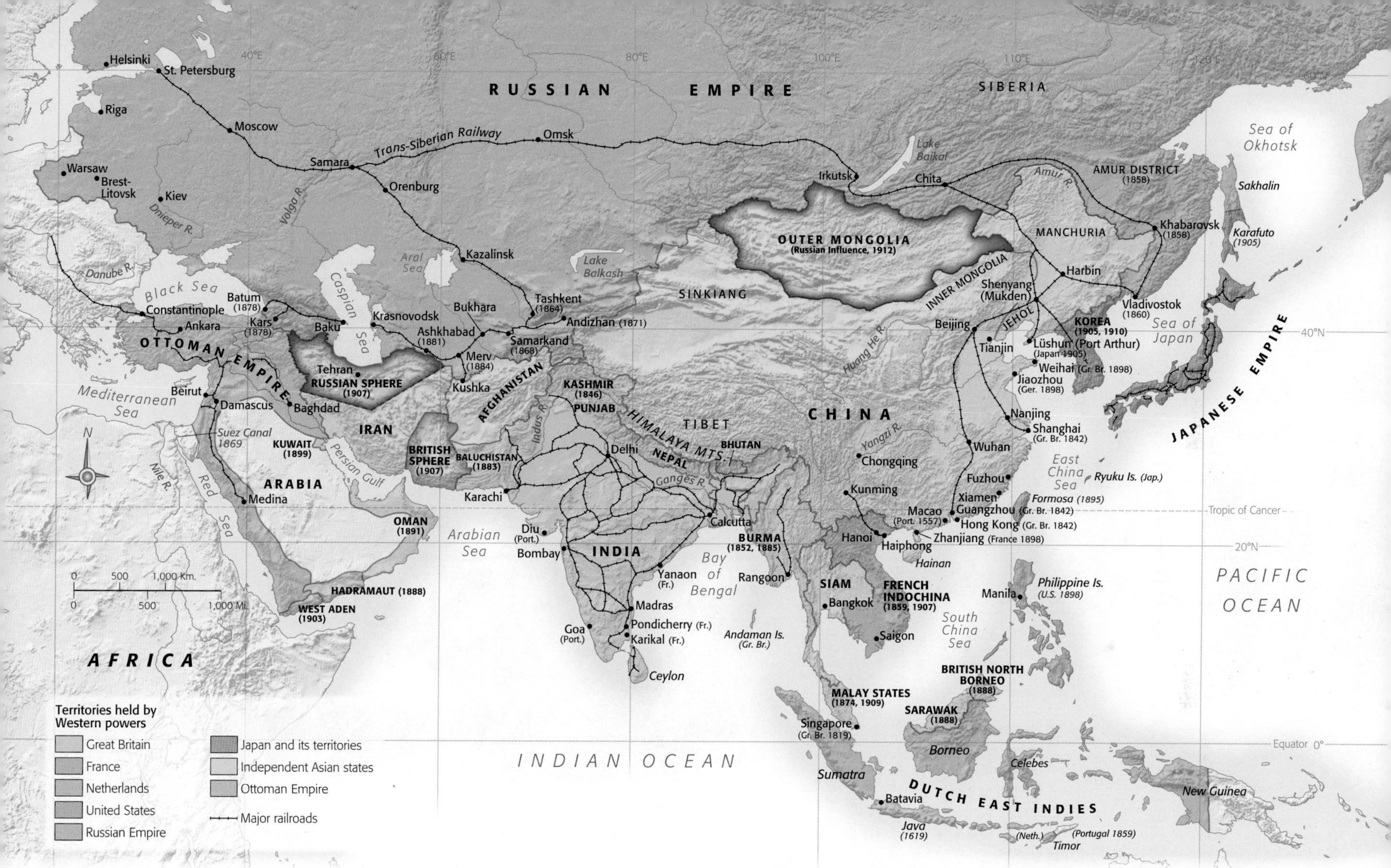

Map 24.1 Asia in 1910 By 1910, empire was the status quo across Asia. In addition to the established British, French, and Dutch possessions, the United States (Philippines) and Japan (Korea and Taiwan) were new imperial players. The Russian empire was also a powerful presence, expanding at the expense of Iran, though its defeat by Japan in 1905 showed the limits of its influence in East Asia. Qing China was still technically a sovereign state; however, important coastal regions were under de facto European colonial control.

VISUAL EVIDENCE IN PRIMARY SOURCES

The Boxer Rebellion: American and French Views

The Boxer Rebellion (1898–1901) marked the death throes of the Qing dynasty. The decision of the Dowager Empress, Ci Xi, to support the "Righteous Society of Harmonious Fists" against the "Western barbarians" was calamitous. The Qing had to pay huge reparations, and though they did finally institute real political and social reforms, it was too late. In 1912, a new Republic of China marked the final end of China's long imperial history.

One of the Boxers' principal grievances was against Christian missionaries, who came to China in increasing numbers in the second half of the nineteenth century. Unlike Matteo Ricci (see Chapter 16), who had adapted his Christian message to Confucian traditions and Chinese cultural norms, the European and American missionaries who arrived in the 1800s expected converts not only to accept Christianity, but also to conform to Western family models, styles of dress and housing, medical systems, and other cultural practices.

As with the Indian rebels of 1857 (discussed later in this chapter), who were driven in part by their belief that the British planned to use Christianity to subvert local cultures and traditions, so too the Boxers singled out missionaries as particular enemies. In the summer of 1900, 239 foreign Christians were killed by the Boxers across north China; Chinese converts and sympathizers were murdered

National Archives, Washington, D.C.

President William McKinley (in office 1897–1901) wields a sword, while the figure of Uncle Sam attacks with a bayonet at the end of his rifle. The two figures represent the five thousand American soldiers sent as part of the China Relief Operation in 1900 to break the Boxer siege of Western delegations in Beijing.

"Life, Liberty, and the Pursuit of Happiness under Treaty Rights," inscribed on the American flag, justifies their actions in defense of the unequal treaties, which, since the Treaty of Nanjing in 1842, had made it impossible for the Qing rulers of China to regulate international trade.

The Boxer rebels are shown as savages, with frenzied expressions. They march with heads on pikes, reach to stab a prostrate woman, and have murdered the child at her feet. The baby is wrapped in a tattered American flag, an image that would arouse strong emotions.

In spite of the United States's participation in the occupation of the Forbidden City, McKinley's Open Door Policy advocated free trade with China without territorial annexation.

as well. As the Boxers marched on Beijing, foreigners took refuge in a walled compound. Although the Qing commander acted to protect them, twenty thousand foreign soldiers (from Britain, France, Russia, Japan, and the United States) also arrived to occupy the capital and rescue the besieged.

Another principal grievance of the Boxers was the partition of China into Western "spheres of influence." But in the end, their uprising only led to further foreign interference. Though the United States, with its Open Door Policy, proclaimed its opposition to the further partition of China, the division of the world's oldest and most populous empire continued unabated.

The political cartoons here, one from the United States and the other from France, are both from the period of the Boxer Rebellion but demonstrate different attitudes toward the conflict. In neither case does it seem that the Chinese will have much to say about the outcome.

China leaps up in alarm, shown here in the stereotypical late-nineteenth-century Western fashion, with exceptionally long fingernails and a long flowing queue of braided hair. ***Compare the Chinese characters in the two cartoons. Both are caricatures, but what different impressions do they make on the viewer?***

Queen Victoria of Great Britain (left) seems shocked as Kaiser Wilhelm of Germany aggressively takes the first slice of the Chinese "pizza."

The United States is missing from this scene.

Tsar Nicholas of Russia eyes Wilhelm's action and seems to be ready to join in; looking over Nicholas's shoulder, France is unarmed and, while she seems interested, appears less engaged. ***Compare the Western figures in the two cartoons. What arguments for or against the Western invasion of China might the two artists be making?***

The Japanese figure on the right studies the "pizza" as if he is planning a chess move. He holds no weapon, but his menacing sword lies on the table ready for action.

Imperial support for the Boxers proved disastrous. In the summer of 1900, on the grounds that foreigners in China had to be protected, twenty thousand troops from over a dozen different nations marched on Beijing and occupied the Forbidden City. Another humiliating treaty followed. The Qing were required to pay 450 million ounces of silver (twice the country's annual revenue) to the occupying forces.

Finally, the Manchu government implemented substantial reforms, abolishing the examination system and making plans for a constitutional order with some degree of popular representation. At long last, an imperial decree abolished the cruel practice of footbinding. But it was much too late. In 1912, revolutionaries overthrew the decrepit Qing dynasty (see Chapter 27).

● **CONTEXT&CONNECTIONS** The worst of times in China have often come during a period of chaos and uncertainty between the fall of one dynasty and the consolidation of power by another. That pattern would be repeated in the first half of the twentieth century. After the fall of the Qing dynasty in 1912, decades of civil war followed. A semblance of stability returned only after the Second World War, with the end of Japanese occupation and the foundation of the People's Republic of China in 1949 under Mao Zedong (see Chapters 28 and 29). ●

The Rise of Modern Japan, 1830–1905

When Fukuzawa Yûkichi wrote that China could never move forward under Qing leadership, he was in a good position to judge. He had been instrumental in Japan's own transformation from weakness and isolation to industrialization, centralized state power, and imperialism. After the Meiji (MAY-jee) Restoration of 1868, Japan adapted to the new industrial age by looking to the West not just for its technology but also for principles of education, economic organization, and state building. Yet socially, culturally, and spiritually, the Japanese retained their ancient traditions. By borrowing foreign ideas and adapting them to Japanese culture, Japanese society actually achieved the "self-strengthening" that eluded Chinese reformers.

After the arrival of a U.S. fleet in 1853, isolation from the West was no longer possible. Having observed the devastating consequences of the Opium Wars, Fukuzawa and others advocated radical reform based on rapid acquisition of Western knowledge and technology. As elsewhere, the reform was opposed by conservative defenders of the status quo. But in Meiji Japan, reformers took charge of imperial policy, laying the foundations of military and industrial modernization, and fulfilling Fukuzawa's vision that his country would be recognized as an equal in Asian affairs by the Europeans and Americans.

Late Tokugawa Society, 1830–1867

Growing up, Fukuzawa was ashamed of the gap between his family's samurai status and its low income. Samurai were not supposed to deal with mundane affairs such as shopping and handling money. But since they could not afford servants, the Fukuzawa family had no choice but to do so. Fukuzawa remembered how they would do their shopping at night, with towels over their faces to hide their shame. Particularly acute was the scornful treatment he endured: *"Children of lower samurai families like ours were obliged to use a respectful manner of* *address in speaking to the children of high samurai families, while these children invariably used an arrogant form of address to us. Then what fun was there in playing together?"** Although Fukuzawa's father was an educated man and well versed in the Chinese classics, no achievement on his part could raise his family's status.

Even so, the Fukuzawa family had higher status than most people. Below them were the farmers, then the artisans, and then the merchants (who were seen more as economic parasites than as productive members of society). Lowest of all were the outcasts who performed such unsavory tasks as working in leather and handling the bodies of executed criminals.

As a young man, Fukuzawa tested the attitude of the peasants by addressing them first in the haughty tones of the samurai and then speaking to them in the dialect of an Osaka merchant. The peasants abased themselves with humility when Fukuzawa spoke as a samurai, but they treated him with scorn when he imitated the speech of a merchant.

The young Fukuzawa longed to escape the social strictures that limited his ambitions. Education proved the key. Fukuzawa received no formal education until he was fourteen, and then it was the traditional curriculum of Confucian classics taught in Chinese. Frustrated, he obtained his family's permission to travel to the port city of Nagasaki, which was the site of the annual Dutch trade mission and the center of "Dutch learning" (see Chapter 20). Fukuzawa's study of Western medical and scientific texts convinced him of the superiority of Western over Chinese styles of education.

In 1853, shortly after Fukuzawa had begun his Western studies, American **Commodore Matthew Perry** (1794–1858) steamed into Edo harbor, his "black ships" sending shock waves through Japanese society. Perry's mission was to impress the power of American technology on the Tokugawa government and force it to establish diplomatic relations and open Japanese ports to foreign trade. Fearing that the Americans and Europeans might unleash a destructive barrage, the Tokugawa government submitted and, in 1858, signed an unequal treaty with the United States and five European powers granting access to treaty ports and rights of extraterritoriality.

Commodore Matthew Perry
(1794–1858) American naval officer and diplomat whose 1853 visit to Japan opened that country's trade to the United States and other Western countries.

Among those who accused the shogun of having humiliated the nation by signing the 1858 treaty were some daimyo lords who hoped to use the crisis to increase their independent power. Some even acquired modern weapons to fire at passing European ships. In the early 1860s, it was not clear whether the Tokugawa government still possessed enough authority to enforce its edicts.

Seeking some breathing space, in 1862 the shogun sent a delegation to Europe hoping to delay further unequal treaties. Fukuzawa, a member of this delegation, later published his observations of European life in a widely read book called *Western Ways*. (Fukuzawa became the Japanese public's main source of information on the Western world; in fact, *all* translations of Western books were known as *Fukuzawa-bon*.)

The situation was becoming dangerous by the time of his return in 1863. Apart from rebellious daimyo, the Tokugawa government was also opposed by a militant group of *rônin* (ROH-neen). Samurai without masters, these rônin were a floating population of proud men of limited means, stridently antiforeign and

*From *The Autobiography of Yukichi Fukuzawa*, by Eiichi Kiyooka, 1960, p. 18.

Commodore Perry's Arrival in Japan This Japanese print shows the arrival of Commodore Matthew Perry's steam-powered "black ships" near Edo (modern Tokyo) in 1853. After submitting to Perry's demand that Japan be opened to Western trade, Japanese leaders in 1859 sent the Tokugawa mission to San Francisco, on which Fukuzawa Yûkichi served, as an attempt to discover more about the U.S. government and its motives in East Asia.

nostalgic for a glorious past when their military skills were highly prized. "*The whole spirit,*" Fukuzawa said, "*was one of war and worship of ancient warriors.*"* Fukuzawa, who had now learned English and was working as a government translator, was a potential target for their anger. For years he never left his home at night, fearful of being assaulted by anti-Western thugs.

The Meiji Restoration, 1867–1890

The challenge of the West required a coordinated national response, and neither the weakened Tokugawa government nor the rebellious daimyo could provide one. But another possible source of national unity was the imperial court at Kyoto. Some anti-Tokugawa rebels flocked to the banner of a new child emperor under the slogans "*Revere the Emperor!*" and "*Expel the Barbarians!*"

*From *The Autobiography of Yukichi Fukuzawa*, by Eiichi Kiyooka, 1960, p. 164.

In 1867, supporters of the emperor clashed with the shogun's forces. Fukuzawa was teaching in Edo at the Keio Academy he had founded, lecturing on economics from an American textbook while a battle raged nearby: "*Once in a while . . . my pupils would amuse themselves by bringing out a ladder and climbing up on the roof to gaze at the smoke overhanging the attack.*"* He remained neutral, for his own safety and that of his students, and feared that the imperial forces would prove to be just as antiforeign as those of the shogun.

The armies of the imperial party were successful. In 1868, the **Meiji Restoration** brought a new government to power at Edo, now renamed Tokyo. Fukuzawa was delighted to discover that reformers dominated the administration of the Meiji ("enlightened") child emperor. They began to utterly transform the closed, conservative society Fukuzawa had known as a child. Most were, like him, men from middle and lower samurai families that placed a strong emphasis on scholarship.

Meiji Restoration
(1868) A dramatic revolution in Japan that overthrew the Tokugawa, restored national authority to the emperor, and put the country on a path of political and economic reform. Meiji industrialization turned Japan into a major world power.

The Meiji reforms replaced the feudal domains of the daimyo with regional prefectures under the control of the central government. Tax collection was centralized to solidify the government's economic control. The Meiji government allowed commoners to carry arms for the first time, as it created a national conscript army equipped with the latest weapons and led by officers trained in modern military organization. All the old distinctions between samurai and commoners were erased: "*The samurai abandoned their swords,*" Fukuzawa noted, and "*non-samurai were allowed to have surnames and ride horses.*"† Fukuzawa expressed hope for the transformative power of individualism: "*It is time to make it possible for wealth, honor, and happiness to be entirely the fruits of a man's own efforts.*"‡

Fukuzawa coined two of the Meiji reform's most popular slogans: "*Civilization and Enlightenment*" and "*Rich Nation, Strong Army.*" Viewing education as the key to progress, the government set up a national system of compulsory schooling and invited Fukuzawa to head the Education Ministry, but he preferred to keep his independence by founding a newspaper.

The policy of the Meiji oligarchs was to adopt Western methods to strengthen Japan so it could resist Western intrusion and engage the world as an equal. Some Japanese remained critical of this new direction, including the forty-two thousand samurai who participated in the Satsuma Rebellion of 1877. Their leader, Saigō Takamori, ritually disemboweled himself when the battle turned against his men, and he became a hero to conservatives. But the Meiji reformers countered by creating their own cult of Saigō, using the same clever strategy by which they had used a traditionalist slogan—"*Revere the Emperor*"—to mobilize support for radical reforms.

As in Europe, the rewards of increased industrial productivity were unequally distributed in Meiji Japan. Landowners benefited the most from advances in agriculture. Rice output increased 30 percent between 1870 and 1895, but peasants often paid half their crop in land rent, and now had to pay taxes to the central government as well.

---

*From *The Autobiography of Yukichi Fukuzawa*, by Eiichi Kiyooka, 1960, p. 210.

†Fukuzawa Yûkichi, *The Speeches of Fukuzawa: A Translation and Critical Study*, ed. Wayne Oxford (Tokyo: Hokuseido House, 1973), p. 93.

‡Yûkichi Fukuzawa, *An Outline of a Theory of Civilization*, rev. trans. David A. Dilworth and G. Cameron Hurst III (New York: Columbia University Press, 2008), Kindle pp. 3000–3001.

To make ends meet, many rural families sent their daughters to work in factories the government was setting up. Poorly paid and strictly supervised, young women lived in factory dormitories, their dexterity and docility exploited for the benefit of others. Fukuzawa was critical and argued that *"the position of women must be raised at once,"* stressing education for girls as the first step toward greater gender equality.*

Kishida Toshiko

(1863–1901) An early Japanese feminist who urged that as part of the Meiji reforms, women should have equal access to modern education and be allowed to take part in public affairs.

A twenty-year-old woman named **Kishida Toshiko** (KEE-she-dah toe-she-ko) went even further, speaking eloquently for women's rights in meetings across the country. *"Equality, independence, respect, and a monogamous relationship are the hall marks of relationships between men and women in a civilized society,"* she said. *"Ah, you men of the world, you talk of reform, but not of revolution. When it comes to equality, you yearn for the old ways, and follow, unchanged, the customs of the past."*† She even leavened her criticism with a little humor: *"If it is true that men are better than women because they are stronger, why aren't our sumo wrestlers in the government?"*‡ Kishida was soon arrested, fined, and silenced. The men at the top of Meiji society chose the slogan *"Good Wife, Wise Mother"* to reinforce traditional patriarchy, defining proper women as submissive, subservient, and legally inferior.

AP® THEMES

How did industrialization affect gender roles and social hierarchy in Japan?

The gender debate exemplifies another of Fukuzawa's contributions: his encouragement of open discussions, creating a space for "public opinion" in Japanese politics. Even if he disagreed with Kishida's advocacy of full and immediate equality for women, when she traveled the country making her case she was embodying Fukuzawa's principle of *enzetsu*, "public speaking." (It was a concept so new in Japanese society that Fukuzawa had to make up a word for it.) In becoming a modern nation, Japan was also becoming a mass society where rulers had to take account of popular feelings and opinions.

Fukuzawa was particularly proud of his part in stimulating public opinion to pressure the Meiji oligarchs for a formal constitution. In 1873 he had returned from another mission to Europe particularly impressed with the newly unified Germany. Responding to the call for a constitution, Meiji oligarchs now looked not to the model of liberal Britain, but to that of imperial Germany. The Japanese constitution of 1889 was therefore based on the German one, where the emperor rather than elected representatives controlled the real levers of power.

● **CONTEXT&CONNECTIONS** Like Germany under Chancellor *Otto von Bismarck* (Chapter 23), Meiji Japan achieved unification through conservative nationalism rather than through liberalism based on individual rights. The slogan *"For the sake of the country"* urged individuals to sacrifice for the larger good. And as in Germany, militarism combined with nationalism to make Japan more aggressively imperialistic. ●

Meiji Japan went even further than Germany in giving the state control of industrial development. The government itself constructed railroads, harbors, and telegraph lines, making direct investments in industry as well. The Meiji

---

*Fukuzawa Yûkichi, *Fukuzawa Yukichi on Japanese Women: Selected Works* (Tokyo: University of Tokyo Press, 1988), p. 138.

†"The Meiji Reforms and Obstacles for Women Japan, 1878–1927," excerpts from the speeches of Kishida Toshiko, http://www.womeninworldhistory.com/WR-04.html.

‡http://womenshistory.about.com/library/qu/blqutosh.htm?pid=2765&cob=home.

ministers and the oligarchs behind them did not leave economic development to market forces, viewing economic planning as more conducive to social harmony than market competition. (When translating the word "competition" for an economics textbook, Fukuzawa used the word *kyōsō*, literally, "race-fight." A treasury official objected, however: *"I understand the idea,"* said the official, *"but that word 'fight' is not conducive to peace. I could not take the paper with that word to the chancellor."**)

Even after the government sold off its industrial assets and encouraged private capital to play a leading role in commerce and industry, a tight connection between state and private enterprise continued. After 1880, Japanese industry was dominated by **zaibatsu** (zye-BOT-soo), large industrial cartels that collaborated closely with the civil service. (Some of the nineteenth-century zaibatsu, like Mitsubishi, still exist today.) Liberal, free-trade economic notions were never as strong in Japan as in Britain and the United States.

zaibatsu
Large corporations that developed the Japanese industrial economy in close cooperation with the imperial government.

In fact, the Japanese trend, reflecting a global one, was away from liberalism and toward militarism. In 1875, Fukuzawa Yûkichi had cited Mill's *On Liberty* (see Chapter 23) when applauding liberal reforms. As Japan's military competition with her neighbors heated up, however, Fukuzawa took a more nationalistic view, de-emphasizing individual rights and women's rights, while placing a greater emphasis on Japan's collective imperial destiny.

By the 1890s, the great powers, including Japan, were coming to see global competition as a zero-sum struggle for survival. A more cynical Fukuzawa could now write, *"There are only two ways in international relations: to destroy, or to be destroyed.... A nation does not come out on top because it is in the right. It is right because it has come out on top."*†

Japanese Imperialism, 1890–1910

Japan was now in a position to be a player in an imperial game whose rules had been established by Europe and the United States. Late in life, believing Japanese national prestige required the acquisition of an empire, Fukuzawa embraced Social Darwinist concepts, promoting the idea that the Japanese were racially superior to other Asians and destined to lead the continent forward. His opinion mattered, not only because of his books and his newspaper, but also because graduates of his own Keio Academy were now rising to power in the Meiji bureaucracy.

Japan flexed its imperial muscle first in Korea, where its forces confronted those of China while both were responding to an uprising in 1894. Japanese victory in the consequent **Sino-Japanese War** (1894–1895) caused a wave of national pride. In addition to acquiring control over Korea and Taiwan, the Meiji government forced Qing China to grant access to treaty ports and rights of extraterritoriality similar to those enjoyed by European powers. At the same time, Japan renegotiated its own treaties with Europe, this time on a basis of equality. Chinese bitterness at the humiliation ran deep. (See the feature "World History in Today's World: Senkaku or Diaoyu Islands?")

Sino-Japanese War
(1894–1895) A war caused by a rivalry over the Korean peninsula; ended with a one-sided treaty that favored Japan, which obtained treaty rights in China as well as control of Korea and Taiwan.

---

*From *The Autobiography of Yukichi Fukuzawa*, by Eiichi Kiyooka, 1960, p. 190.

†Quoted in Helen M. Hopper, *Fukuzawa Yûkichi: From Samurai to Capitalist* (New York: Pearson Longman, 2005), p. 120.

WORLD HISTORY IN TODAY'S WORLD

Senkaku or Diaoyu Islands?

The eight tiny, unpopulated islands in the East China Sea seem an unlikely touchstone for international conflict. But the disputed islands, called *Senkaku* by the Japanese and *Diaoyu* by the Chinese, have sparked repeated confrontations, wars of words that analysts worry might escalate.

The stakes are higher than they may appear. The islands straddle strategic shipping lanes, and their waters may prove rich in oil and gas. Moreover, this territorial dispute brings back divisive historical memories. Japanese conservatives, tired of focusing on transgressions from World War II, are anxious to project a stronger military profile after decades of pacifism. For their part, Chinese nationalists recall with deep resentment the violence inflicted on their ancestors by the Japanese empire, such as the infamous Rape of Nanjing (see Chapter 28). Japan, they believe, has never properly apologized.

Tensions escalated in 2012 when Japanese politicians proposed having the government buy some of the islands from their private owners. "No one will ever be permitted to buy and sell China's sacred territory," responded the Chinese foreign ministry.* Anti-Japanese demonstrations broke out across China, with attacks on Japanese car dealerships and factories. Though calm was restored, both Japanese and Chinese leaders have continued to stoke the nationalist instincts of their citizens by keeping the controversy alive.

In the spring of 2014, the Chinese government took matters one step further by asserting control of the islands' airspace, backing down when U.S. bombers defied that claim. Still, the Chinese defense minister told his American counterpart: "China has indisputable sovereignty over the Diaoyu Islands" and would "make no compromise, no concession, no treaty."† Meanwhile, some Japanese, watching how easily the Russian government annexed Crimea in 2014 (see Chapter 32), worried whether the United States would indeed live up to its treaty obligations and back their claim in the case of a Chinese military offensive. Rarely has so little geography contained such grave dangers.

*"Japan Protests at Chinese Ships Near Disputed Islands," *BBC News*, July 11, 2012.

†Quoted in Helene Cooper, "Hagel Spars with Chinese over Islands and Security," *New York Times*, April 8, 2014.

Japan pressured Korea to adopt reforms. At first the Korean king allied himself with the Japanese; then in 1896 he sought protection from the Russians. For the next eight years, Korean reformers allied with Japan while the king and other conservatives promoted Russian interests. Meanwhile, Meiji rulers saw the presence of Russian troops in the Qing province of Manchuria as a direct threat to their own "sphere of influence" in northeastern Asia.

Russo-Japanese War (1904–1905) War caused by territorial disputes in Manchuria and Korea. Japan's defeat of Russia was the first victory by an Asian military power over a European one in the industrial age. (1772–1833)

The result was the **Russo-Japanese War** of 1904–1905. Just as the Japanese Navy had decimated the northern Qing fleet ten years earlier, now it scored another major victory, destroying or disabling most of Russia's Pacific fleet. While the United States brokered peace negotiations, the Japanese government posted advisers to all the important Korean ministries. In 1910, after a Korean nationalist assassinated the Japanese prime minister, the Meiji government formally annexed Korea.

Japan's victory in the Russo-Japanese War had global consequences. Russia was a traditional European great power, with the world's largest military. Its defeat meant that Japan must now be counted among the great powers of the world. And there was also the question of race. The defeat of a European power by an Asian one inspired nationalists across Asia and Africa with the thought that European superiority was not inevitable.

- **CONTEXT&CONNECTIONS** The war with Japan was unpopular in Russia, and defeat added to mounting tensions in the capital of St. Petersburg. After suppressing

Peace Negotiations This print by Kiyochika Kobayashi shows Japanese and Chinese negotiations at the end of the Sino-Japanese War. By the harsh terms of the Treaty of Shimonoseki (1895), the Qing empire ceded the island of Taiwan to Japan, recognized Japanese rights over Korea, and agreed to make substantial reparation payments. The Qing and Meiji diplomats in this portrait are clearly differentiated by their clothing, reflecting the divergent Meiji and Qing attitudes toward adoption of Western ways. (RMN-Grand Palais/Art Resource, NY)

a rebellion in 1905, Tsar Nicholas II finally approved limited reforms. However, as in Qing China after the Boxer Rebellion, they were too little and too late. The Romanov dynasty collapsed in the wake of the First World War to be replaced by the Bolsheviks led by *Vladimir Lenin* (Chapter 27). ●

As Japanese imperial ambitions grew in Asia and the Pacific, Germany, France, Britain, and the United States were also expanding their presence in the region. The world was becoming a smaller place, and the imperial aspirations of the great powers, now including Japan, would become a touchstone of conflict in the twentieth century.

British India, 1818–1905

By the early nineteenth century, the British were the "new Mughals," the dominant political force on the Indian subcontinent. Hundreds of millions of artisans and farmers felt the effects when the British used that political power to drain India of raw materials for Britain's own industrialization.

Unlike the rulers of Qing China and Tokugawa Japan, who initially retained their authority as they struggled to adapt to industrial modernity, Indian elites were subject to direct colonial control. Even so, as the story of Rammohun Roy demonstrated (see Chapter 20), South Asians carried on the same type of debate that could be heard in China and Japan: whether to adjust to the new circumstances by rejecting Western models, by embracing them, or by trying to balance them with indigenous traditions. The first of those choices inspired a major rebellion in 1857, but the British suppressed the revolt and consolidated their rule even further. Indian nationalists then began developing new ideas and organizations in response to the problem of British rule, and by the beginning of the twentieth century they had laid the foundations of modern Indian nationalism.

The Last Phase of Company Rule in India, 1835–1857

The authority of the British East India Company had spread across the subcontinent after the Battle of Plassey in 1757, though as late as the 1830s many Indians were still just beginning to feel the impact of British rule. At that time, Rammohun Roy (see Chapter 20) was one of only a handful of Indians who had learned English and begun to assimilate European ideas.

Over the next two decades, however, the implications of British rule for Indians, both peasants and elites, greatly intensified. The reasons were largely economic, stemming from the international impact of the industrial revolution. While Mughal rulers had promoted the South Asian commercial economy's connection with Indian Ocean markets, the British yoked the Indian economy to British commercial and industrial interests.

As we have seen, one result was Indian *deindustrialization*, notably in the textile manufacturing centers of the northeastern region of Bengal (see Chapter 23). By 1830, unemployment among India's textile workers was reaching a critical level, leaving India "to fall backward in time . . . losing most of its artisan manufacturing abilities, forcing millions of unemployed craftsmen to return to the soil."* In Bengal we find that the rural-to-urban migration of English industrialization was actually reversed.

AP® THEMES

How did technological advances change the patterns of migration and settlement of Europeans in Asia?

Technological and social changes caused shifts in Anglo-Indian social and cultural interactions as well. Steamships, telegraphs, and (after 1869) the Suez Canal, shortened the distance between Europe and India. Company employees who had previously spoken Indian languages, worn Indian clothing, and established relationships with Indian women were now more likely to bring British wives with them, use English both privately and in their official capacities, and hold themselves aloof from Indian society. In segregated British towns, officials now carefully followed the rituals of Victorian social life, dressing formally for dinner no matter how high the temperature and replacing local curries with tinned meats from home. Every British outpost had a "club" where British officials and merchants gathered to socialize. Indians—no matter how accomplished—were excluded, except as servants.

Such cultural distancing contributed to a tense political situation in the 1850s. Meanwhile, increasing British intrusion on Indian customs and ways of life provoked a powerful counter-reaction, especially after an increase in the number of British missionaries stoked Indian concerns that the British were seeking to overturn their cultural traditions and convert them to a foreign religion. This fear,

---

*Stanley Wolpert, *India* (Berkeley: University of California Press, 1991), p. 51.

combined with economic strains and the loss of support for the British presence from some of India's traditional elites, created a volatile situation.

The Indian Revolt of 1857 and Its Aftermath

The **Indian Revolt of 1857** began with a mutiny among the sepoys (SEE-poyz), the two hundred thousand Indian soldiers under British command. The immediate cause of the revolt was Britain's introduction of a new, faster-loading rifle. The loading procedure required soldiers to bite off the greased ends of the guns' ammunition cartridge casings. The rumor spread among Muslim troops that the cartridges had been greased with pig fat; many Hindus believed that fat from cattle had been used. Since contact with pork was forbidden to Muslims and cattle were sacred to Hindus, both groups suspected that the British were trying to pollute them as part of a plot to convert them to Christianity. (See the feature "Movement of Ideas Through Primary Sources: Religion and Rebellion: India in 1858.")

Indian Revolt of 1857
Revolt of Indian soldiers against British officers when they were required to use greased ammunition cartridges they suspected were being used to pollute them and cause them to convert to Christianity. The revolt spread across north India.

A group of soldiers killed their British officers after some soldiers were arrested for refusing to use the new cartridges. They marched to Delhi and rallied support for the restoration of the aging Mughal emperor. The revolt quickly spread across northern and western India, where the rani (queen) of Jhansi (JAN-see), one of the Maratha kingdoms, rode into battle with her troops. Violence was terrible on both sides, the rebels sometimes killing British women and children, and the British strapping rebels to cannon and blowing them to pieces. The resulting bitterness would long poison race relations in the British Raj, further accelerating the process of segregation.

British observers believed that the cause of the rebellion was simply the backwardness of the Indian people. Earlier liberal beliefs in Indian capacity were now challenged by the Social Darwinist notion that South Asians (like Africans) were naturally and permanently inferior, both culturally and genetically.

AP® THEMES
How did the British East India Company facilitate British imperial expansion in South Asia?

The Indian rebels knew what they were fighting against but were less unified about what they were fighting for. In South Asia the cultural, linguistic, and religious landscape was exceptionally diverse, making it all the more necessary to develop a sense of identity embracing all the peoples under British rule. Lack of unity and coordination among regional rebellions, however, made it easy for the British to retake control.

By 1858 the revolt was over, and the British government responded by disbanding the East India Company and abolishing the last vestiges of Mughal authority. In 1876, Queen Victoria added "Empress of India" to her titles. The British now emphasized alliances with conservative Indian elites, such as the maharajahs and sultans who were allowed to keep nominal control over "princely states," while the British retained real power for themselves, centralizing the colonial administration and enhancing its fiscal responsibilities. At the top of that system stood the Indian Civil Service, elite government officials selected on the basis of a rigorous examination. In theory, anyone who passed the examination could join the Indian Civil Service. Since the exams were only administered in England, however, Indian candidates did not have a realistic chance.

Westernized Indians, following the example of the earlier Bengal Renaissance in their quest to balance indigenous and imported cultural traditions, were dismayed when the British mocked them for trying to assimilate English culture, and were disheartened when the British turned to the remnants of the old aristocracy for allies. In 1885 they organized a new political movement called the Indian National Congress.

Religion and Rebellion: India in 1858

The following passage was written in the Urdu language in 1858 by an Indian Muslim, Maulvi Syed Kutb Shah Sahib. Maulvi Syed saw the Indian Revolt as a chance to drive the British out of India. In this letter to Hindu leaders, he urged Hindu-Muslim cooperation to accomplish that goal, arguing that the British were consciously defiling both religions in an attempt to force conversions to Christianity.

One of the grievances Maulvi Syed mentions is British laws concerning widows. Islamic law encourages the remarriage of widows, following the example of Muhammad, whose wife Khadijah was a widow. Among Hindus, however, patriarchal beliefs dictated that a wife's life was essentially over once her husband died. Thus the custom of sati encouraged widows to throw themselves on the fire when their husbands were cremated to demonstrate their devotion and to allow them to be reunited in the next life. In fact, relatively few Hindu women, usually from the highest castes, actually did so. In 1829, with the approval of the Bengali reformer Rammohun Roy, the British abolished sati and issued another order that widows should be allowed to remarry (see Chapter 20).

Another controversy to which the author refers is the "doctrine of lapse," a colonial ruling that if an Indian prince died without a male heir, direct control over his territory would go to the British, ignoring local traditions of adoption and inheritance. In 1856, the city of Lucknow and the rich province of Awadh had been taken over by the British through this device.

❯ Historical Thinking Skill:
ARGUMENTATION What evidence in this letter serves as proof that Maulvi Syed's purpose in writing the letter was to encourage cooperation between Muslims and Hindus?

❯ Historical Thinking Skill:
ANALYZING EVIDENCE Based on Maulvi Syed's letter, what can we conclude about the way the British gained political control over the people of India?

Source: Records of the Government of the Punjab and Its Dependencies, New Series, No. VII (Lahore: Punjab Printing Company, 1870), pp. 173–175.

Maulvi Syed on British Christians

The English are people who overthrow all religions. You should understand well the object of destroying the religions of Hindustan [India]; they have for a long time been causing books to be written and circulated throughout the country by the hands of their priests, and, exercising their authority, have brought out numbers of preachers to spread their own tenets. . . .

Consider, then, what systematic contrivances they have adopted to destroy our religions. For instance, first, when a woman became a widow they ordered her to make a second marriage. Secondly, the self-immolation of wives [sati] on the funeral pyres of their deceased husbands was an ancient religious custom; the English . . . enacted their own regulations prohibiting it. Thirdly, they told people it was their wish that they . . . should adopt their faith, promising that if they did so they would be respected by Government; and further required them to attend churches, and hear the tenets preached there.

Moreover, they decided and told the rajahs that such only as were born of their wives would inherit the government and property, and that adopted heirs would not be allowed to succeed, although, according to your [Hindu] Scriptures, ten different sorts of heirs are allowed to share in the inheritance. By this contrivance they will rob you of your governments and possessions, as they have already done with Nagpur and Lucknow.

Consider now another of their designing plans: they resolved on compelling prisoners, with the forcible exercise of their authority, to eat their bread. Numbers died of starvation, but did not eat it, others ate it, and sacrificed their faith. They now perceived that this expedient did not succeed well, and accordingly determined on having bones ground and mixed with flour and sugar, so that people might unsuspectingly eat them in this way. They had, moreover, bones and flesh broken small and mixed with rice, which they caused to be placed in the markets for sale, and tried, besides, every other possible plan to destroy our religions.

They accordingly now ordered the Brahmins and others of their army to bite cartridges, in the making of which fat had been used. The Muslim soldiers perceived that by this expedient the religion of the Brahmans and Hindus only was in danger, but nevertheless they also refused to bite them. On this the British resolved on ruining the faith of both, and [lashed to the cannons] all those soldiers who persisted in their refusal [and blew them to pieces]. Seeing this excessive tyranny, the soldiery now, in self-preservation, began killing the English, and slew them wherever they were found, and are now considering means for slaying the few still alive here and there. It is now my firm conviction that if these English continue in Hindustan they will kill everyone in the country, and will utterly overthrow our religions; but there are some of my countrymen who have joined the English, and are fighting on their side....

Under these circumstances, I would ask, what course have you decided on to protect your lives and faith? Were your views and mine the same we might destroy them entirely with a very little trouble; and if we do so, we shall protect our religions and save the country....

All you Hindus are hereby solemnly adjured, by your faith in Ganges; and all you Muslims, by your belief in God and the Koran, as these English are the common enemy of both, to unite in considering their slaughter extremely expedient, for by this alone will the lives and faith of both be saved....

The slaughter of cows is regarded by the Hindus as a great insult to their religion. To prevent this a solemn compact and agreement has been entered into by all the Muslim chiefs of Hindustan, binding themselves, that if the Hindus will come forward to slay the English, the Muslims will from that very day put a stop to the slaughter of cows, and those of them who will not do so will be considered to have abjured the Koran, and such of them as will eat beef will be regarded as though they had eaten pork....

The English are always deceitful. Once their ends are gained they will infringe their engagements, for deception has ever been habitual with them, and the treachery they have always practiced on the people of Hindustan is known to rich and poor. Do not therefore give heed to what they say. Be well assured you will never have such an opportunity again.

Popperfoto/Getty Images

Princely States After the Indian Revolt of 1857, the British placed a greater emphasis on cooperating with traditional Indian authorities, sometimes recognizing their nominal sovereignty over "princely states." Here a British "resident" is surrounded by maharajas and nawabs of the northwestern Punjab province in 1895. Such rulers maintained luxurious lifestyles while helping stabilize colonial rule. The same use of "native authorities" would characterize British Africa (see Chapter 26).

The Origins of Indian Nationalism, 1885–1906

After 1857, amid all the political and social tensions, the Indian economy grew. As in Europe, railroads played a major role (see Map 24.2). The British imported tracks and engines, benefiting British manufacturers and workers, while Indian taxpayers financed 50,000 miles (80,500 km) of rail construction. The primary economic purpose of the railways was to speed the export of Indian raw materials, such as cotton, in support of British industry, as well as the import of British manufactured goods, such as the iron goods and finished textiles that were displacing India's own manufactures. Fukuzawa Yûkichi was critical of these impacts: *"Have the European countries,"* he asked, *"really respected the rights and interests and integrity of the countries with which they have come into contact?... Wherever the Europeans come, the land ceases to be productive."**

*Cited in Carmen Blacker, *The Japanese Enlightenment, A Study of the Writings of Fukuzawa Yukichi* (New York: Cambridge University Press, 1969), p. 131.

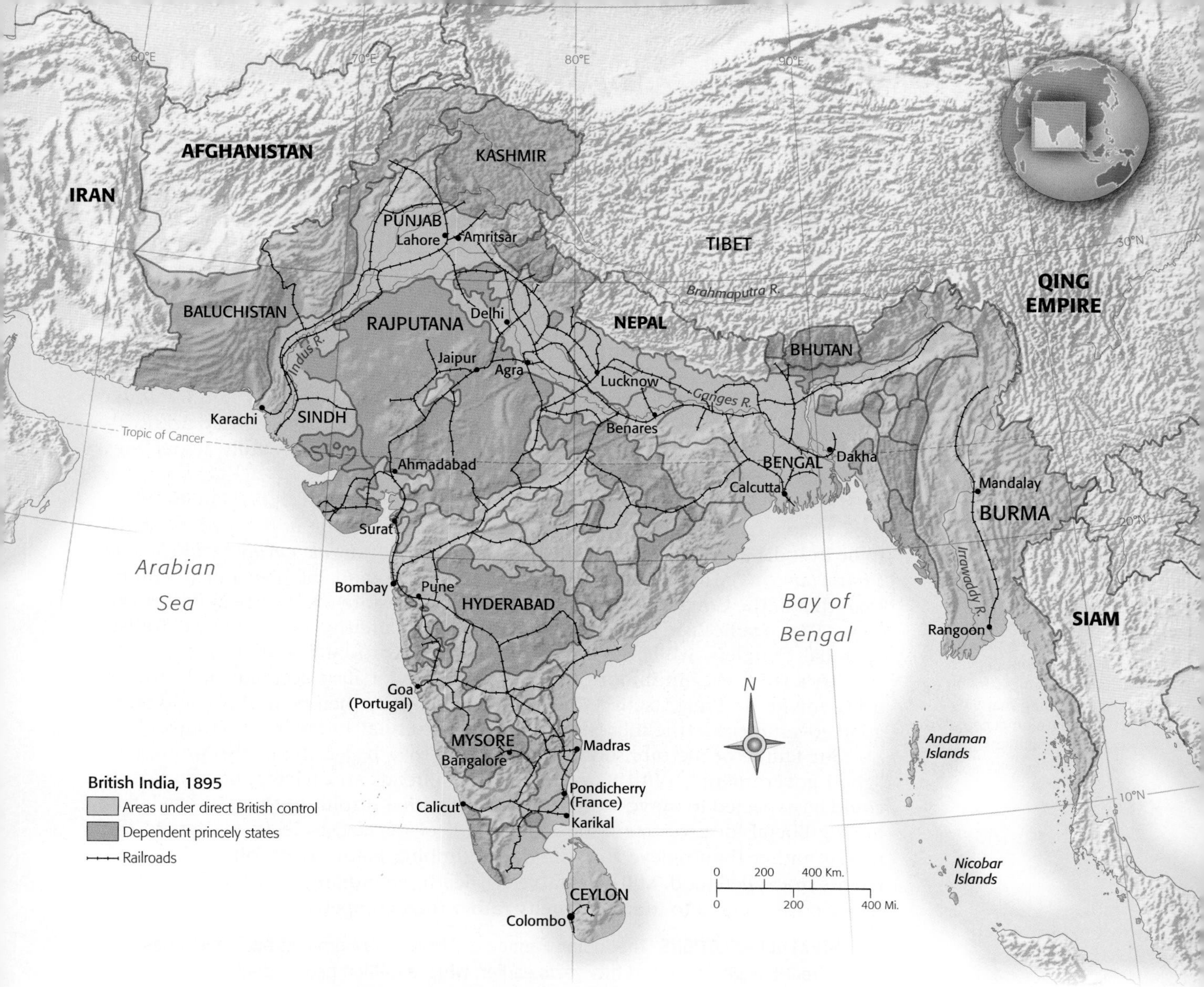

Map 24.2 Indian Railroads, 1893 After the Indian Revolt of 1857, the British stabilized their rule by allying themselves more strongly with traditional Indian rulers. Some of the "princely states" were very extensive and their rulers, such as the Nizams of Hyderabad, were quite wealthy. Even in the princely states, however, the British were clearly predominant. After 1857, the British built an extensive railroad and telegraph network to tighten their control, though improved transport and communications had the unintended consequence of helping bring Indians together from across the subcontinent, fueling the growth of Indian nationalism.

Still, developing networks of transportation and communication brought benefits to Indians. Railroads, along with telegraphs and a postal service, created a communications infrastructure that put India's diverse peoples and regions in closer contact than ever before and served as a crucial precondition for nationalist organization.

India's emerging middle class, now often educated in English following a British school curriculum, had the clearest vision of "India" as a single, unified

Indian National Congress

(1885) Formed by wealthy, Western-educated Indians to advance the cause of Indian involvement in their own governance. In the twentieth century, it would become the vehicle for India's independence under the leadership of Mohandas K. Gandhi.

Bal Gangadhar Tilak

(1856–1920) Indian nationalist who demanded immediate independence from Britain, mobilizing Hindu religious symbolism to develop a mass following and arguing that violence was an acceptable tactic for anticolonial partisans.

political space. In the beginning, however, the relatively advantaged men of the **Indian National Congress** cared most about the interests of their own social class. For example, the Congress campaigned to have the Indian Civil Service examination administered in India so that Indians would have a better opportunity to compete. They challenged their rulers to live up to the promise that Queen Victoria had made in 1858, that *"our subjects, of whatever race or creed, be freely and impartially admitted to office in our service, the duties of which they may be qualified by their education, ability, and integrity."**

At the beginning, the Indian National Congress was fighting not to change the system but to find a place within it, believing that slow reform was better than revolutionary change. They did not seek independence, but self-rule for India within the British empire. And self-rule could not be achieved, they acknowledged, until India's people learned to respect one another more fully across lines of religion, caste, and language.

Less patient Indian nationalists, notably **Bal Gangadhar Tilak** (1856–1920), took a more confrontational approach, questioning why the British had any right to be in India at all. Tilak (TIH-lak) declared: *"Swaraj ['self-rule'] is my birthright, and I must have it!"*† Tilak's appeal was more emotional, and his plan much simpler than that of the Congress: organize the masses to pressure the British, and they will leave. Tilak's radicalism challenged both the British and the more moderate Indian National Congress, while his use of Hindu symbols to rally support alarmed the country's large Muslim minority. While Indian nationalists accused the British of using "divide and rule" tactics, the British claimed only their neutrality could bring good government to the subcontinent's diverse cultural and religious groups.

The failure of the monsoon rains in 1896–1897 tested the British promise of "good government." With its command of railroads and telegraphs, the British could be expected to move food from regions with a surplus to those in need. Following liberal ideas of free trade, however, they decided to leave matters to the market rather than relieve the suffering. Climbing grain prices followed as merchants stockpiled food. Millions starved to death. To Indians, British lack of action in the crisis seemed to indicate cruelty rather than competency.

● **CONTEXT&CONNECTIONS** The Indian Famine of 1896–1897 brought back memories of the Great Hunger in Ireland fifty years earlier, when a million people died and a million more despairing exiles left the island. In both cases, the British government, convinced of the superiority of market forces over state economic intervention, refused to implement sufficiently active relief programs to save the lives of their colonial subjects. ●

The British government, meanwhile, continued to use spectacular public rituals to display its power and legitimize its rule. The most impressive was the "durbar" procession, a combination of circus, parade, and political theater held at Delhi in 1903, which featured maharajahs in ceremonial garb, hundreds of parading elephants, tens of thousands of marching soldiers, and elaborate salutes to the new King Edward VII, Emperor of India.

Grand political theater notwithstanding, conflict arose in 1905 when British bureaucrats, for no reason other than administrative expediency, decided to split

---

*Proclamation by the Queen to the Princes, Chiefs, and the People of India, November 1, 1858.

†Quoted in Stanley A. Wolpert, *Tilak and Gokhale: Revolution and Reform in the Making of Modern India* (Berkeley: University of California Press, 1991), p. 191.

in two the culturally and economically integrated northeastern province of Bengal. No Indians were consulted about the **Partition of Bengal**, which created a predominantly Muslim province in the east. Nationalists again accused the British of using communal rivalries to reinforce their power by separating Hindus from Muslims.

- **CONTEXT&CONNECTIONS** At the end of the colonial era, British India was in fact partitioned between two separate states: the Republic of India (with a Hindu majority) and Pakistan (with a Muslim majority). The partition line of 1905 is now a national border, with Bengali-speakers divided between the Indian state of West Bengal and the separate nation of Bangladesh (see Chapter 30). ●

Protesting the Partition of Bengal, the Indian National Congress organized a boycott of British goods. Bengali activists made huge bonfires of English cloth across the province. Conditions were now ripe for the development of mass nationalism, bringing together the Western-educated elite of the congress and the millions of urban and rural Indians struggling toward a better future. The new spirit was captured by Rabindranath Tagore, a Nobel Prize winning poet whose grandfather had been a close colleague of Rammohun Roy:

India: Swami Vivekananda, Jaipur, c.1895/Pictures From History/Bridgeman Images

Swami Vivekananda Since the nineteenth century, Hindu spirituality, including the practice of yoga, has had a global appeal. Swami Vivekananda (1863–1902) played an important role, developing a large following in Europe, and in the United States after he addressed an international religious gathering in Chicago at the time of the Columbian Exposition (see Chapter 25). Like members of the earlier Bengal Renaissance, Vivekananda advocated a reformed Hinduism purged of superstition and caste prejudice.

> *Where the mind is without fear and the head is held high . . .*
> *Where the world has not been broken up into fragments by narrow domestic walls . . .*
> *Where words come out from the depth of truth;*
> *Where the clear stream of reason has not lost its way into the dreary desert sand of dead habit . . .*
> *Into that heaven of freedom, my Father, let my country awake.**

Tagore's vision came a step closer to realization in 1906 when Mohandas K. Gandhi (1869–1948), then a little-known lawyer, returned home from leading South Africa's Indian community in protests against racial discrimination. Gandhi (GAHN-dee) would soon come to symbolize a new India, forging alliances between leaders and people to lead his country toward independence (see Chapter 28).

Partition of Bengal (1905) A British partition of the wealthy northeastern Indian province of Bengal for administrative expediency; became a touchpoint of anticolonial agitation.

*Rabindranath Tagore, "Chitto Jetha Bhayashunyo (Where the Mind Is Without Fear)," http://allpoetry.com/Where-The-Mind-Is-Without-Fear.

CONTEXT AND CONNECTIONS

Asia in the Modern World

Even prior to 1800, Asian societies were contending with the challenges of modernity. Commercial expansion and the growth of cities in the seventeenth and eighteenth centuries were signs of economic and social dynamism but strained the cultural traditions and political institutions in Mughal India, Qing China, and Tokugawa Japan (see Chapter 20). This was the world of Fukuzawa Yûkichi's childhood, one in which his family's samurai traditions were no longer in sync with the evolution of Japanese society.

Rapid population growth was an even greater modern challenge: China's population grew from about 110 million in 1600 to 330 million in 1800, India's from approximately 100 million to 225 million, and Japan's from 12 million to 30 million. During the eighteenth-century agricultural revolution in Britain, innovators like Joseph Banks brought greater productivity to rural areas (while displacing many farmers in the process; see Chapter 21). In contrast, the growth of food production in Asia was largely *extensive* rather than *intensive*, requiring peasant communities to bring marginal lands under cultivation to keep pace with population growth. In manufacturing as well, Asian growth was based on the abundance of cheap labor rather than on innovations leading to higher productivity per worker.

By the early nineteenth century, the Industrial Revolution in the West had greatly magnified the difference in economic productivity between western Europe and South and East Asia (see Chapter 23). By the mid-nineteenth century, industrialization and its new technologies gave European nations both the motive and the means to intervene more forcefully in Asian affairs.

India was already feeling the impact in the late eighteenth century (see Chapter 20). In gradually expanding British East India Company authority at the expense of the Mughal empire, the British took advantage of the centrifugal force of Indian regionalism. At first, the British largely accommodated themselves to Indian languages and cultures, but after 1800, and especially after the rebellion of 1857, they formed a tightly bound ruling clique. In responding to British rule, Indian reformers faced the challenge of resisting British political and cultural intrusions while at the same time absorbing British influences.

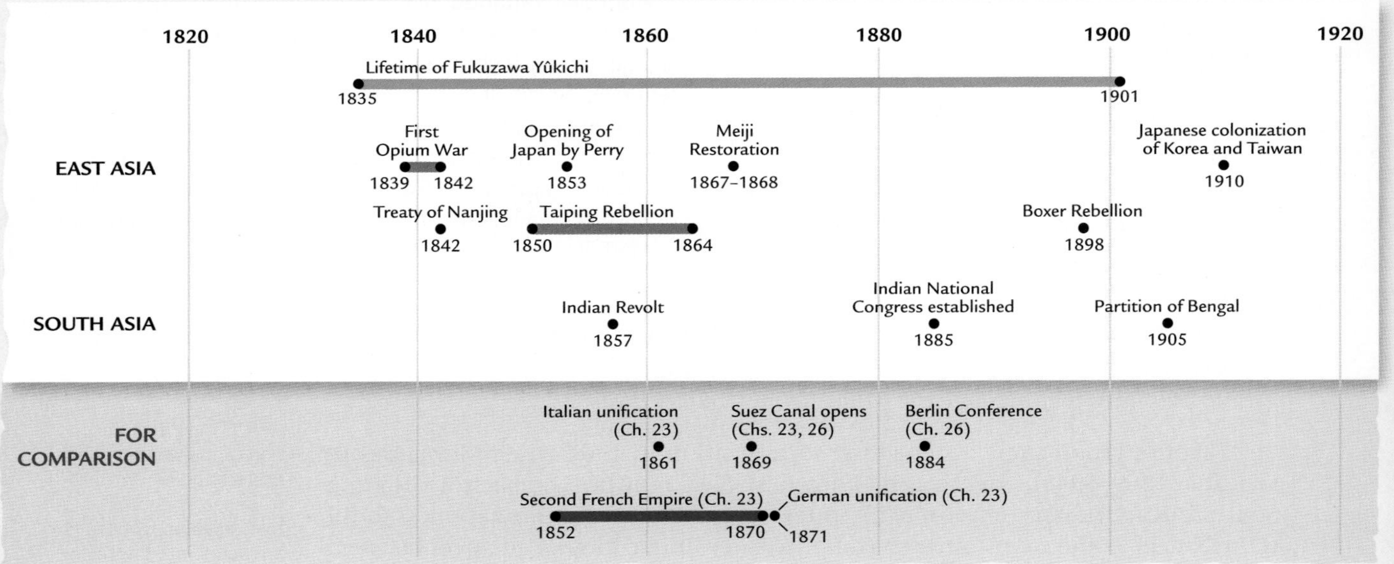

China's confrontation with the industrial West came much more suddenly. Only two generations separated the British diplomatic mission of 1793, arrogantly dismissed by the Qianlong emperor (see Chapter 20), and the humiliation of the first Opium War of 1839. The remainder of the nineteenth century saw China's Confucian elite, in the midst of foreign invasions and domestic rebellions, struggle to find a response. The changes advocated by partisans of Self-Strengthening might have been enough to propel the empire toward modernization, but the resistance of conservatives doomed all such initiatives. The occupation of the Forbidden City in 1900 by foreigners once disparaged as "barbarians" was the deepest possible humiliation, one from which twentieth-century Chinese leaders would strive to recover.

Japan also had its conservatives who resisted change, and before 1868 it was by no means clear that Fukuzawa's relentless advocacy of reform along Western lines would be successful. After the Meiji Restoration, however, Fukuzawa's plans were implemented. By 1910, the Japanese had defeated both the Chinese and the Russians, renegotiated unequal treaties, and built the infrastructure of a modern industrial state. Meiji authorities could boast that they, alone among Asian leaders, had transformed their nation from a victim into a player in the global competition for military prestige and economic growth.

It would take another century for China to return to its long-standing position as the largest economy in Asia, joining independent India as one of the world's fastest-growing countries (see Chapter 32). Even as its economy surpassed that of Japan in 2011, however, China still lagged far behind the United States, which, even back in 1900, had set the pace, simultaneously the world's largest industrial and agricultural producer.

Key Terms

Fukuzawa Yûkichi (716)
Opium Wars (718)
Treaty of Nanjing (718)
Taiping Rebellion (719)
Self-Strengthening Movement (720)
Empress Ci Xi (721)
Boxer Rebellion (722)
Commodore Matthew Perry (727)
Meiji Restoration (729)
Kishida Toshiko (730)
zaibatsu (731)
Sino-Japanese War (731)
Russo-Japanese War (732)
Indian Revolt of 1857 (735)
Indian National Congress (740)
Bal Gangadhar Tilak (740)
Partition of Bengal (741)

For Further Reference

Anderson, Marnie S. *A Place in Public: Women's Rights in Meiji Japan*. Cambridge, Mass.: Harvard University Asia Center, 2011.

Cohn, Bernard S. *Colonialism and Its Forms of Knowledge: The British in India*. Princeton: Princeton University Press, 1996.

Dalrymple, William. *The Last Mughal: The Fall of a Dynasty, Delhi 1857*. New York: Vintage, 2008.

Fogel, Joshua A., ed. *Late Qing China and Meiji Japan: Political and Cultural Aspects*. Norwalk, Conn.: Eastbridge Press, 2004.

Fukuzawa, Yûkichi. *The Autobiography of Yûkichi Fukuzawa*. Eiichi Kiyooka, trans. New York: Columbia University Press, 1960.

Hobsbawm, Eric. *The Age of Empire, 1875–1914*. New York: Vintage, 1989.

Jansen, Marius B. *The Making of Modern Japan*. Cambridge, Mass.: Harvard University Press, 2000.

Rawksi, Evelyn Sakakida. *The Last Emperors: A Social History of Qing Imperial Institutions*. Berkeley: University of California Press, 2001.

Spence, Jonathan. *God's Chinese Son: The Taiping Heavenly Kingdom of Hong Xiuquan*. New York: W. W. Norton, 1997.

Wiley, Peter Booth. *Yankees in the Land of the Gods: Commodore Perry and the Opening of Japan*. New York: Penguin, 1991.

Zachmann, Urs Matthias. *China and Japan in the Late Meiji Period: China Policy and the Japanese Discourse on National Identity, 1895–1904*. New York: Routledge, 2009.

AP® Review Questions for Chapter 24

Multiple-Choice Questions

QUESTIONS 1–3 REFER TO MAP 24.2 *INDIAN RAILROADS, 1893* ON PAGE 739.

1. Which of the following was a *direct* result of the development of railroads shown on the map?
   (A) Labor was increasingly specialized in India.
   (B) The trade in raw materials and finished goods increased dramatically.
   (C) Indian oil reserves were exploited more efficiently.
   (D) An Indian middle class and industrial working class developed.

2. Which of the following led directly to the railroad networks shown on the map?
   (A) The British creation of a settler colony in India
   (B) Religious conflicts between Hindus and Muslims
   (C) Britain's desire to strengthen its control of India
   (D) Indian resistance during the Opium Wars

3. Which of the following best explains how the railroad system contributed to the anticolonial movement in India?
   (A) The Indian Revolt of 1857 used the railroads to move sepoys quickly to the battlefields.
   (B) Indians challenged British rule by vandalizing the railroads.
   (C) Indian workers organized into labor unions to resist British industrial demands.
   (D) Railroads served to unite Indians by facilitating communication between them.

QUESTIONS 4–7 REFER TO THE FOLLOWING PASSAGE.

I have heard that the smoking of opium is very strictly forbidden by your country; that is because the harm caused by opium is clearly understood. Since it is not permitted to do harm to your own country, then even less should you let it be passed on the harm of other countries—how much less to China! Of all that China exports to foreign countries, there is not a single thing which is not beneficial to people. . . . On the other hand, articles coming from the outside of China can only be used as toys. Since they are not needed by China, what difficulty would there be if we closed the frontier and stopped the trade? . . . The goods from China carried away by your country not only supply your own consumption and use, but can also be divided up and sold to other countries, producing a triple profit.

—Lin Zezu, Qing scholar-official in a letter to Queen Victoria of England, 1839

4. Which of the following conclusions about the period from 1750 to 1900 is most directly supported by the passage?
   (A) Industrialized states practiced economic imperialism in parts of Asia.
   (B) Social Darwinism facilitated and justified imperialism.
   (C) European states used warfare and diplomacy to establish empires.
   (D) Some rebellions against colonial rule were influenced by religion.

5. The views expressed in the passage are best seen as evidence of which of the following in Qing society?
   (A) Qing officials resisted economic change and attempted to maintain earlier norms.
   (B) The Qing mitigated the negative effects of industrial capitalism by promoting reform.
   (C) Qing scholar-gentry were influenced by Enlightenment ideas regarding the expansion of rights.
   (D) The development of liberalism in Qing China was inspired by discontent with imperial rule.

6. The interactions described in the passage are best understood in the context of which of the following?
   (A) The "second Industrial Revolution" led to new methods in the production of goods.
   (B) The profits from raw materials like opium were used to purchase finished goods.
   (C) The addictive quality of opium gave European merchants a distinct economic advantage.
   (D) The global nature of trade contributed to the spread of transnational peace-keeping bodies.

7. Compared to the production of trade goods in the period from 1450 to 1750, the production of trade goods in the period from 1750 to 1900 saw
   (A) the specialization of labor and the factory system that decentralized labor in a single location.
   (B) European countries and the United States increasing their share of global manufacturing while the Asian share of manufacturing declined.

(C) Chinese advantages in geography, accumulation of capital, and access to foreign resources leading to a rise in industrial production.

(D) the Qing Self-Strengthening Movement successfully propelling China from a largely agrarian to a modern industrialist empire.

QUESTIONS 8–10 REFER TO THE FOLLOWING PASSAGE.

It was said that the Meiji Restoration was to bring about equality among the four classes of people. However, in practice, those who engaged in commerce and industry were regarded as plain townspeople as before. . . . I . . . felt that it was necessary to raise the social standing of those who engaged in commerce and industry, and by way of setting an example, I began studying and practicing the teachings of the Analects of Confucius. . . . It shows very clearly how a businessman must act in this world. Thus when I entered the business world, I engaged in commerce and industry in the way consistent with the teachings of the Analects, and practiced the doctrine of unity of knowledge and action.

—Shibizawa Eiichi, Japanese industrialist and government official, 1873

8. Which of the following was a *direct* cause of the economic reforms described in the passage?
   (A) The expansion of U.S. and European influence over Tokugawa Japan
   (B) Japanese adoption of Chinese political ideas
   (C) Establishment of compulsory education for both males and females
   (D) Acquisition of Korea and Taiwan to form a new Japanese empire

9. Compared to the description of Japanese economic reforms in the passage, Meiji practices regarding modernizing Japan's economy *differed* in that they
   (A) were followed by an expansion of suffrage to women.
   (B) rejected Confucian economic principles.
   (C) were largely the result of state-sponsored visions of industrialization.
   (D) focused on exporting raw materials.

10. Which of the following was a *direct* result of the Meiji Restoration?
   (A) Japan engaged in economic imperialism in mainland Asia.
   (B) Japanese subjects challenged the increasingly centralized imperial government.
   (C) Japan became reliant on Chinese coerced and semicoerced labor migration.
   (D) Japan established colonies in Asia.

Short-Answer Questions

QUESTION 1 REFERS TO THE FOLLOWING PASSAGE.

The Qing overhauled the customs service. Provincial governors . . . launched efforts to reform agriculture, education, and armaments production. . . . They also built shipyards and railroads. Reformers sought sufficient military technology to defend China against "barbarian" aggression, and recognized that a certain amount of industrialization was required, although they hoped not to disturb the fundamentals of an agrarian, Confucian society. But their modest initiatives aroused opposition from more tradition-minded members of the gentry. . . .

—J. R. McNeill & William H. McNeill, historians, *The Human Web: A Bird's-Eye View of World History*, 2003

1. Answer parts A, B, and C.
   A. Identify and explain ONE change or development instituted by the reformers in China that would support the authors' assertion.
   B. Identify and explain ONE reaction by the tradition-minded gentry that would support the authors' assertion.
   C. Identify and explain ONE reaction in a region other than China that would support the authors' assertion.

2. Answer parts A, B, and C.
   A. Explain ONE cause of the Indian Revolt of 1857.
   B. Explain ONE effect of the Indian Revolt of 1857 on relations between Indians and the British.
   C. Explain ONE effect of the Indian Revolt of 1857 on British colonial policy in India.

25 State Building and Social Change in the Americas, 1830–1910

Pauline Johnson-Tekahionwake (1861–1913) watched nervously as several older male poets recited their verse. It was the winter of 1892, and the hall in Toronto was packed for an "Evening with Canadian Authors." Her ambition was to be a well-known, financially independent poet, and here was her chance to make an impression. She chose to recite "A Cry from an Indian Wife," a poem that focused on her concern with Canada's First Nations, its indigenous inhabitants:

They but forget we Indians owned the land
From ocean unto ocean; that they stand
Upon a soil that centuries agone
Was our sole kingdom and our right alone.
They never think how they would feel today,
If some great nation came from far away,
Wresting their country from their hapless braves,
Giving what they gave us—but war and graves...
Go forth, nor bend to greed of white man's hands,
By right, by birth we Indians own these lands,
Though starved, crushed, plundered, lies our nation low...
*Perhaps the white man's God has willed it so.**

---

*Excerpt from *Flint and Feather: The Complete Poems of E. Pauline Johnson (Tekahionwake)*. Toronto and London: The Musson Book Co., Ltd., 1912.

Patriotic Canadians might have heard these as dissonant words; nevertheless, they gave Johnson's powerful performance loud applause.

"A Cry from an Indian Wife" reflected Johnson's own mixed ancestry. Her father's family was Mohawk, an Iroquois (IR-uh-kwoi) band that had established a close alliance with the British during the colonial period. As a child, Pauline would listen to Mohawk legends and tales of a family history that included Joseph Brant, the Mohawk leader who had fought with the British in the American War of Independence (see Chapter 22). The British family connection went deeper when Pauline's father married an Englishwoman. Their wedding photograph shows optimism toward this

Pauline Johnson-Tekahionwake
(1861–1913) Canadian poet of mixed English and Mohawk ancestry.

cultural mixture: the groom wears both British medals and an Iroquois wampum belt, while the English bride's stiff Victorian attire is offset by the ceremonial tomahawk she holds in her lap.

Pauline's father balanced two worlds, serving as both a Canadian government employee and a respected member of the Six Nations Band Council. Her mother instilled strict Victorian values in her children on the Six Nations Reserve in Ontario. Johnson-Tekahionwake (da-geh-eeon-WA-geh) would have a lifelong challenge trying to balance her Mohawk heritage with her English ancestry. Though she grew up on the Iroquois reserve, she spoke only English, and though fascinated by Mohawk tales, she was most influenced by British literature. She was a loyal and patriotic Canadian, yet she spoke out against her country's policies toward indigenous First Nations societies.

As an adult, Pauline Johnson began to use her father's Mohawk family name, Tekahionwake ("double life"), in advertisements for a new career: traveling across Canada performing her poetry. Variety shows had become a popular form of entertainment on the frontier. Pauline Johnson-Tekahionwake became one of the nation's best-known entertainers. Her performances drew attention to her dual heritage. She took the stage in a dramatic buckskin outfit to perform poems such as "A Cry from an Indian Wife," after intermission reappearing in a Victorian evening gown to recite poems of nature and love. Having found a way to earn a living through her art—a challenge for a woman of her time—Johnson-Tekahionwake crossed Canada nineteen times, often performing in the United States as well, before retiring to Vancouver on the Pacific coast, where she collected native stories.

But the late nineteenth century was a difficult time for a mixed-race person. Racial divisions were sharpening in Canada, where the white majority thought that Amerindian peoples were doomed to disappear in the face of industrial and commercial progress, symbolized by the very railroad that Johnson used to reach her audience.

Indeed, the nineteenth century was a time of relentless change across the Western Hemisphere. In 1830, much of North and South America still lay outside the control of European-derived governments. By the end of the century revolutionary changes in transportation and communications technologies, along with the arrival of many new European immigrants, had changed the situation forever. The frontiers of modern nations expanded at the expense of indigenous peoples. Industrialization, mining, and commercial forestry and agriculture became the keys to wealth and power in the Americas.

Perhaps the most striking feature of this period was the rise of the United States as both the dominant hemispheric power and a global force. Canada was also a growing economic power, where many shared in rising prosperity. In Latin America, where industrialization lagged behind, only privileged elites enjoyed the benefits of state building.

Telegraphs, steamships and railroads, massive new cities, and enormous industrial fortunes helped consolidate the power of national states, while posing challenges to many older ways of life. Social readjustments in the nineteenth-century Americas included the abolition of slavery, the arrival of new immigrants, the struggle of workers for rights and representation, changing gender relations, and as Johnson-Tekahionwake's story indicates, difficult times for indigenous peoples.

KEY CONCEPT QUESTIONS

- What features of transoceanic European imperialism are also present in the American concept of "manifest destiny"? **(Key Concept 5.3)**
- Why did socioeconomic inequities in Latin America persist after independence? **(Key Concept 5.3)**
- How did nineteenth-century developments in North and South America affect workers, indigenous peoples, ethnic and racial minorities, and women? **(Key Concept 5.1)**

Political Consolidation in Canada and the United States

Consolidation of state power was a major feature of nineteenth-century North America. Canada overcame deep regional divisions to become a nation, while the United States emerged from the Civil War with the federal government more powerful and ambitious than ever before. In both cases, governments extended their authority more deeply into society and more broadly across the continent. Through activities and acquisitions in the Caribbean and Pacific, by century's end the United States had become an imperial power as well.

Confederation in Canada

Canada was a product of slow evolution rather than revolutionary transformation. In 1830, British North America consisted of more than half a dozen disconnected colonies. Yet by 1892, when Pauline Johnson-Tekahionwake made her debut on a Toronto stage, Canadians possessed a strong national identity even while affiliating themselves with the British empire. Like many, Johnson-Tekahionwake was proud of being both Canadian and British: *"And we, the men of Canada, can face the world and brag/That we were born in Canada beneath the British flag."**

British North America contained a diversity of peoples and landscapes. Upper Canada, with its capital at Toronto on the northern shore of Lake Ontario, was the fastest-growing region, where cheap land attracted English, Irish, and Scottish immigrants. Lower Canada, the lands along the St. Lawrence River known as Québec, retained its French-speaking Catholic majority, the *Québecois* (kay-bek-KWAH). The Atlantic colonies were primarily populated by seafaring people dependent on the bounty of the Atlantic Ocean. And at the opposite end was British Columbia, its Pacific capital of Victoria more accessible to San Francisco than to Toronto.

Far from the main population centers lay trading posts that brought commercial opportunity to the frontier, but also guns, alcohol, and violence to indigenous

*Excerpt from *Flint and Feather: The Complete Poems of E. Pauline Johnson (Tekahionwake)*. Toronto and London: The Musson Book Co., Ltd., 1912.

Library and Archive of Canada, acc. 1973-84-1

A Métis Man and His Wives The métis of the Canadian frontier were culturally and biologically mixed descendants of French traders and First Nations women. Protective of their independence, many métis resisted incorporation into the Canadian confederation, often in alliance with First Nations communities. These rebellions were defeated by Canadian forces in 1869 and 1885.

communities (see Chapter 18). Several First Nations, such as the Cree, Ojibwa (oh-JIB-wuh), and Sioux (soo), still lived freely on the Great Plains. Mingled among them were communities of French-speaking *métis* (may-TEE), frontiersmen of mixed European-Amerindian descent. Farther from the main areas of European settlement and British control were the Inuit hunters of the far north.

Having learned from the American War of Independence to accommodate settlers' political ambitions, the British government offered Britons who emigrated to British North America (or to Australia, New Zealand, or South Africa) limited participation in government, while still appointing a governor from London. By 1830, however, British North Americans were calling for **responsible government**, which would give many powers of the British-appointed governor to a prime minister, leader of the dominant party in parliamentary elections. As the climate for reform increased in Britain (see Chapter 23), an official report recommended responsible government for Canada, as well as a cut in tariffs on imports to Canada that led to a boom in cross-border trade with the United States.

responsible government

Nineteenth-century constitutional arrangement in British North America that allowed colonies to achieve dominion status within the British empire and elect parliaments responsible for internal affairs. The British appointed governors as their sovereign's representative and retained control of foreign policy.

Most French-speakers also favored these changes. As far back as 1763, the British Parliament had guaranteed equal rights for French-speaking Catholics. Despite the influx of British settlers, most Québecois trusted that British constitutional models would protect their linguistic, religious, and cultural traditions.

Likewise, many First Nations peoples in Canada favored continuing association with the British empire. For the Johnson family, whose ancestors had fought alongside the British for generations, the beneficence of Britain and of Queen Victoria was unquestioned. With such consensus, and with British support, the birth and evolution of Canada took place peacefully, especially once the American Civil War (1861–1865; discussed in the next section) gave Britain an added incentive to stabilize its North American territories.

Thus in 1867, the British Parliament passed the British North America Act, creating the **Confederation of Canada** with a federal capital at Ottawa. Though only four of the current Canadian provinces were included in the original confederation, its legal framework was established. Canada was now a "dominion" within the British empire. Local affairs were in the hands of the Canadian and provincial governments. However, Queen Victoria appointed a governor-general to represent the Crown, and Britain continued to control Canada's foreign relations.

Confederation of Canada
(1867) Confederation of former British colonies united under a single federal constitution, a dominion within the British empire.

Political consolidation and economic growth went hand in hand after 1867 with the building of the **Canadian Pacific Railway** (1867–1884). The railway led to the incorporation of new provinces (Manitoba, the Northwest Territories, and British Columbia), while utterly transforming Canada's Great Plains.

Canadian Pacific Railway
(1881–1885) The railway's completion led to the transcontinental integration of Canada and opened Canada's Great Plains to European settlement.

Before the Industrial Revolution, the plains' tough grasses supported only buffalo and, later, horses and cattle. Now, with the advent of cheap steel plows and the inexpensive transport provided by the railway, grain production boomed. Canadian wheat exports rose from 10 million bushels in 1896 to 145 million bushels in 1914. Over a million farmers and their families moved out onto the prairie, taking advantage of free land and the cheap agricultural implements churned out by the new industrial plants. They were the audience for Pauline Johnson-Tekahionwake as she took her act to the town halls and opera houses springing up in farming centers and mining camps. Marking the rise of the Canadian west, Alberta and Saskatchewan (sa-SKACH-uh-won) entered the confederation in 1905 (see the map on page 745).

• **CONTEXT&CONNECTIONS** Locked up in the North American prairie was a staggering potential of calories for human consumption, but without domesticated herds or steel tools to cut through the tough grassland soil, Amerindians could extract only a limited amount, mainly by hunting buffalo. Then, with the *Columbian exchange* (key term in Chapter 15), came cattle, along with the horses needed to manage them. By the late nineteenth century, the American buffalo had been hunted nearly to extinction and its habitat overrun, first by open cattle ranges then by farmers using steel plows to turn the soil and plant imported grains like wheat, displacing native grasses. From this transformed landscape, vast supplies of grain and meat entered global markets. •

A stable and effective federal government promoted economic growth in Canada. Twenty-five years of Conservative Party dominance ended in 1896, followed by four consecutive elections won by the Liberals, with a strong centrist base. The Liberal Party emphasized "race fusion," acknowledging Canada as a bicultural land where English and French, Protestant and Catholic, could live in peace, forging a Canadian identity based on mutual tolerance. Canadians did not always live up to that ideal: Amerindians and Asian immigrants experienced sometimes brutal racism. Still, a unique nationalism accommodating Canada's affiliation with the British empire was taking shape.

AP® THEMES
How did the system of government in Canada differ from the system of government in the United States?

Sectionalism and Civil War in the United States

Unlike Canada, the United States entered the nineteenth century with a strong constitution and a lively sense of national identity. (See the feature "Movement of Ideas Through Primary Sources: Alexis de Tocqueville's *Democracy in America*.") The Louisiana Purchase of 1803 gave the young country a sense of unbounded opportunity, opening paths westward (see Map 25.1). But westward expansion also provoked crisis. As new states entered the Union, would they be slave states or free? Could balance between the North and South be maintained? Would American nationalism prove stronger than American sectionalism?

Map 25.1 U.S. Expansion, 1783–1867 The United States expanded dramatically during the decades after independence. Vast territories were purchased from France (the Louisiana Purchase) and Russia (Alaska), acquired by treaty with Great Britain (the Pacific Northwest) and Spain (Florida), and annexed from Mexico after its defeat in the Mexican-American War (the desert Southwest and California). Contemporaries in the United States regarded this transcontinental growth as the nation's "manifest destiny."

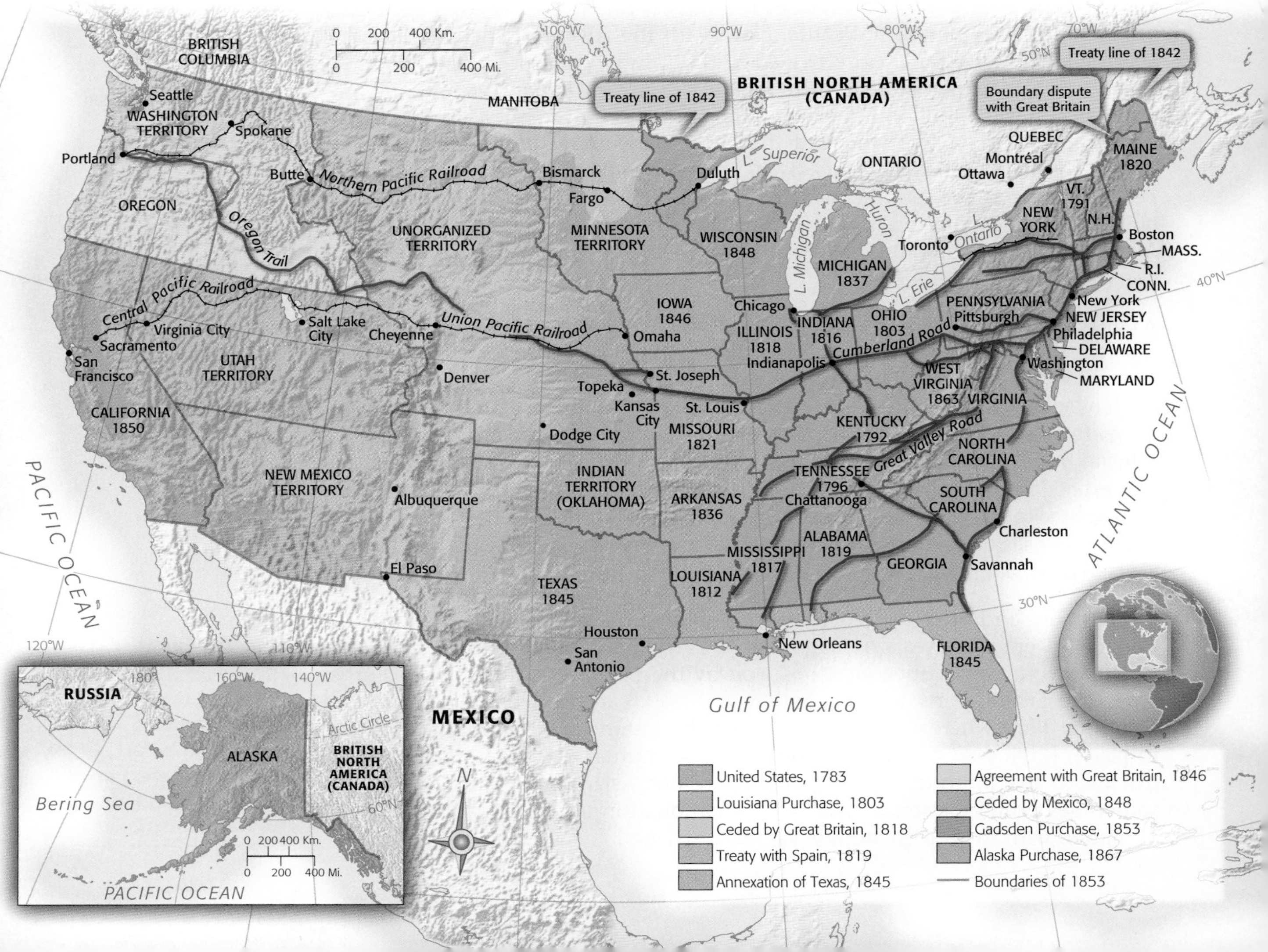

An important context for those questions was the massive economic expansion of the United States in the first half of the nineteenth century, what historians have called a "market revolution." The technological advances of the Industrial Revolution led to an economy focused on factories, cities, and market-oriented farming in the North and, in the South, on the massive expansion of cotton planting resulting from industrialized textile production (see Chapter 23).

Better roads and, especially, canals and railways linked producers with markets as never before. The completion in 1825 of the 363-mile Erie Canal, for example, connected the Great Lakes with New York City, drastically lowering the costs of transporting grain to eastern cities and across the Atlantic. The Southern economy was also booming: by 1860 cotton made up more than half the value of U.S. exports. But the economies of North and South were diverging further as a result.

Populism and expanded democracy marked the presidency of **Andrew Jackson** (in office 1829–1837). Unlike previous American presidents, Jackson, a hero of the war with Britain in 1812, presented himself as representing the common man, emphasizing his humble roots rather than his experiences as a slaveholder and plantation owner. Jackson's emphasis on populist democracy was symbolized by his inauguration party: he threw the doors of the White House open to one and all, and a near riot broke out. Indeed, the United States was becoming more democratic as new states entering the Union allowed all free men to vote and the established eastern states reduced or eliminated property qualifications. Expanded voting rights brought popular passions to political campaigns, as catchy songs, stirring advertisements, and vigorous attacks on opponents' character became the norm.

Andrew Jackson
(in office 1829–1837) The seventh president of the United States; a symbol of the expansion of voting rights and an aggressive advocate of westward expansion.

As Jackson took office, sectional tensions between North and South, between the industrializing and agricultural parts of the country, were on the rise. Most Northern congressmen favored an enhanced federal role in support of the infrastructure for economic growth, while in the South, states' rights advocates were dominant.

Meanwhile, westward expansion was exacerbating these regional tensions. Already in 1820, the question of whether the new state of Missouri would allow slavery had bitterly divided the nation. The question intensified after 1848 when the U.S. victory in the Mexican-American War (discussed later in this chapter) added California and new territories in the Southwest to the Rocky Mountains and Great Plains. Would those vast spaces be settled by free white homesteaders or by plantation owners and black slaves?

The Democratic Party, which had become identified with Southern planter interests, declared that the issue should be decided by "popular sovereignty," meaning by the voters within the new states. **Abraham Lincoln** (in office 1861–1865), a leader of the new Republican Party founded by antislavery activists in 1854, disagreed. To put the issue in the hands of territorial voters, Lincoln declared, would be little more than giving them *"the liberty of making slaves of other people."* More than most Northern politicians, Lincoln stressed the moral dimension of the question, viewing slavery as a *"monstrous injustice."* Other Republicans opposed slavery not because it was wrong but because they thought that slavery was incompatible with the spread of the free, independent farmers they saw as the bedrock of society.

Abraham Lincoln
(in office 1861–1865) Sixteenth president of the United States and the country's first Republican president. His election on an antislavery platform led eleven states to secede from the Union, plunging the country into the American Civil War.

For many white Southerners, Lincoln and the Republican Party threatened freedoms long protected by the sovereignty of the states. To them, Republicans represented a hard-edged industrialism that contrasted with Southerners' perception

Alexis de Tocqueville's *Democracy in America*

The French historian Alexis de Tocqueville first traveled to the United States in 1831 at the age of twenty-six, and at age thirty he published the original French version of *Democracy in America*. Later, as a deputy in the French National Assembly, he was a political moderate and opposed both the Socialists and Louis Napoleon (see Chapter 23). Based on extensive travels and personal observations, *Democracy in America* is still regarded as one of the most insightful analyses of the "American character" ever written.

Historical Thinking Skill:
INTERPRETATION **How might de Tocqueville's perception of American democracy have been shaped in part by his own experiences as a French citizen?**

Historical Thinking Skill:
PATTERNS OF CONTINUITY AND CHANGE OVER TIME **To what extent do de Tocqueville's observations on patriotism and the relationship between religion and democracy still describe the American people today?**

Source: Alexis de Tocqueville, *Democracy in America*, http://xroads.virginia.edu/~HYPER/DETOC/toc_indx.html.

Author's Introduction

Among the novel objects that attracted my attention during my stay in the United States, nothing struck me more forcibly than the general equality of condition among the people.... The more I advanced in the study of American society, the more I perceived that this equality of condition is the fundamental fact from which all others seem to be derived and the central point at which all my observations constantly terminated.

On Patriotism

As the American participates in all that is done in his country, he thinks himself obliged to defend whatever may be censured in it; for it is not only his country that is then attacked, it is himself.... Nothing is more embarrassing in the ordinary intercourse of life than this irritable patriotism of the Americans. A stranger may be well inclined to praise many of the institutions of their country, but he begs permission to blame some things in it, a permission that is inexorably refused.

Geography and Democracy

The chief circumstance which has favored the establishment and the maintenance of a democratic republic in the United States is the nature of the territory that the Americans inhabit. Their ancestors gave them the love of equality and of freedom; but God himself gave them the means of remaining equal and free, by placing them upon a boundless continent. General prosperity is favorable to the stability of all governments, but more particularly of a democratic one, which depends upon the will of the majority, and especially upon the will of that portion of the community which is most exposed to want.... In the United States not only is legislation democratic, but Nature herself favors the cause of the people.

In what part of human history can be found anything similar to what is passing before our eyes in North America? The celebrated communities of antiquity were all founded in the midst of hostile nations, which they were obliged to subjugate before they could flourish in their place.

Even the moderns have found, in some parts of South America, vast regions inhabited by a people of inferior civilization, who nevertheless had already occupied and cultivated the soil. To found their new states it was necessary to extirpate or subdue a numerous population. . . . But North America was inhabited only by wandering tribes, who had no thought of profiting by the natural riches of the soil; that vast country was still, properly speaking, an empty continent, a desert land awaiting its inhabitants. . . .

Three or four thousand soldiers drive before them the wandering races of the aborigines; these are followed by the pioneers, who pierce the woods, scare off the beasts of prey, explore the courses of the inland streams, and make ready the triumphal march of civilization across the desert. . . . Millions of men are marching at once towards the same horizon; their language, their religion, their manners differ; their object is the same. Fortune has been promised to them somewhere in the West, and to the West they go to find it. . . .

Religion and Democracy

The Americans combine the notions of Christianity and of liberty so intimately in their minds that it is impossible to make them conceive the one without the other. . . .

In France I had almost always seen the spirit of religion and the spirit of freedom marching in opposite directions. . . . [American Catholics] attributed the peaceful dominion of religion in their country mainly to the separation of church and state. I do not hesitate to affirm that during my stay in America I did not meet a single individual, of the clergy or the laity, who was not of the same opinion on this point. . . .

Associations and Civil Society

In no country in the world has the principle of association been more successfully used or applied to a greater multitude of objects than in America. . . . The citizen of the United States is taught from infancy to rely upon his own exertions in order to resist the evils and the difficulties of life; he looks upon the social authority with an eye of mistrust and anxiety, and he claims its assistance only when he is unable to do without it. . . . If some public pleasure is concerned, an association is formed to give more splendor and regularity to the entertainment. Societies are formed to resist evils that are exclusively of a moral nature. . . . In the United States associations are established to promote the public safety, commerce, industry, morality, and religion. There is no end which the human will despairs of attaining through the combined power of individuals united into a society.

Tyranny of the Majority

I know of no country in which there is so little independence of mind and real freedom of discussion as in America. In any constitutional state in Europe every sort of religious and political theory may be freely preached and disseminated. . . . In America the majority raises formidable barriers around the liberty of opinion; within these barriers an author may write what he pleases, but woe to him if he goes beyond them.

of their gracious way of life based on virtues like valor and honor. After all, some argued, sick or elderly slaves were cared for by their masters, while industrial workers injured on the job were thrown into the street.

After Lincoln's election in 1860, these divisions could no longer be bridged. Eleven Southern states declared their independence as the Confederate States of America, plunging the country into civil war (1861–1865). Some people, thinking the war would soon be over, brought picnics to witness the first battles. They did not account for the technological changes that made modern warfare more deadly. Increasingly precise weapons and powerful explosives, combined with tactics that threw waves of uniformed soldiers upon each other, led to mass suffering. Over six hundred thousand people died, the most in any American armed conflict.

● **CONTEXT&CONNECTIONS** Battles between Union and Confederate armies in the U.S. Civil War often featured desperate charges against well-entrenched forces supported by artillery, in which thousands of young men might be killed. That mode of fighting anticipated the brutal trench warfare in World War I (see Chapter 27). Because European politicians and generals had not learned the lessons of the U.S. Civil War, they went to war in 1914 with no inkling of the scale of slaughter they were putting in motion. ●

The North had clearly superior resources in the Civil War: railroads for moving men and material, iron foundries to produce guns and munitions, and textile factories to produce uniforms. The Confederates had less tangible advantages: superior military leadership and soldiers who were fighting to defend their homes and traditions. However, the South's export-oriented agricultural economy left the Confederacy vulnerable to a Union naval blockade since it depended on British markets for tobacco and cotton and on British factories for arms and ammunition. By 1865, the productivity of Northern farms and factories overwhelmed Southern resistance.

In 1863, Lincoln had issued the Emancipation Proclamation, making the abolition of slavery, not simply the preservation of the Union, a goal of the war. By the time of Union victory in 1865, the U.S. Senate had already passed the Thirteenth Amendment, abolishing slavery. With Union victory, the question became how the Northern victors would treat their vanquished foes. The assassination of Abraham Lincoln in 1865 meant that the most able American politician would not be there to help resolve that issue.

Federal troops occupied the South to enforce federal law as part of a process known as **Reconstruction**, which was deeply resented by most white Southerners. In spite of further constitutional amendments intended to protect the civil and voting rights of freed slaves, "Redeemers" and secret societies like the Ku Klux Klan terrorized freed men and women, while Southern politicians in the Democratic Party sought to end Reconstruction and restore race-based governance. The presidential election of 1876 was the turning point. Amid a dispute over electoral votes, the Republican candidate, Rutherford B. Hayes, secured the election when he agreed to withdraw federal troops from the former Confederacy, putting an end to Reconstruction.

Reconstruction
(1865–1877) Period immediately after the American Civil War during which the federal government took control of the former Confederate states and oversaw enforcement of constitutional provisions guaranteeing civil rights for freed slaves.

Some felt Reconstruction had unconstitutionally magnified the power of the federal government. But for Southern blacks, "states' rights" was a disaster. Vigilante violence against blacks increased dramatically, and Southern state legislatures enacted segregationist policies that came to be known as Jim Crow laws.

The American Civil War had several important global implications. First, the conflict showed how tightly interconnected the global economy was in the age of industry. When the fighting disrupted cotton exports from the American South, a surge in the price of raw cotton on global markets resulted, hitting British textile manufacturers hard, while benefiting alternative cotton producers (such as those in Egypt; see Chapter 26). Other globally relevant lessons of the American Civil War were the pivotal role of industry in determining its outcome and the degree of civilian mobilization required to keep large armies in the field for such an extended period. Not until the world wars of the twentieth century, however, would the terrible cost of industrialized conflict be fully realized.

The Gilded Age

After the Union victory, the United States experienced a spurt of population growth and productivity. As in Canada, the opening of the Great Plains brought huge economic dividends. The spread of railroads and steamships lowered transport costs and made commercial agriculture possible in more regions. Increased agricultural production led to falling grain prices in the cities, where industrial employment surged. Silver and gold booms brought a flood of investment capital to the nation's banks, while overwhelming Amerindians with invading settlers in the Black Hills of Dakota and the Sierra Nevada Mountains of California.

• **CONTEXT&CONNECTIONS** Nineteenth-century gold strikes took place across the world. In California after the Mexican-American War, the Gold Rush brought hundreds of thousands from eastern U.S. states as well as Europe, China, the Pacific Islands, and Mexico. When the California mines played out, some prospectors followed news of fresh strikes north to Canada and Alaska, or crossed the ocean to Australia. The greatest gold strikes of all were in South Africa beginning in 1884 (see Chapter 26). •

Urbanization was a key development in the United States, as the percentage of Americans living in cities rose from roughly 10 percent in 1850 to over 30 percent by 1890. Most dramatic was the growth of Chicago: the "city with broad shoulders" served as the principal hub for the processing and transport of agricultural goods from the West, growing from merely thirty thousand citizens in 1850 to over 2 million by 1900.

During the last two decades of the nineteenth century, American steel firms and railroad companies exceeded any level of economic organization the world had ever seen. Mark Twain, the great American author and humorist, called it a **Gilded Age** (gilded with gold on the outside, concealing base metal within). For beyond the fortunes of the most privileged lay deep inequalities: grinding rural poverty across the South; an urban working class crammed into filthy unsafe tenements in the industrial North; and political favors for sale to the highest bidder. By 1890, less than 1 percent of the U.S. population controlled 90 percent of the nation's wealth.

Gilded Age
Period of economic prosperity in the United States in the last two decades of the nineteenth century, when the opulence displayed by the wealthy masked the poverty, political corruption, and unsafe living and occupational conditions for the working class.

In reaction to such economic pressures and inequalities, farmers in the Plains states organized a movement against the corporate and railroad interests that controlled the storing and shipping of grain. At the same time, industrial workers began to form unions to fight for better pay and working conditions, sometimes with violent results. One notorious example occurred in Chicago. Across the country on May 1, 1886, workers peacefully demonstrated in favor of an eight-hour work day. (Thus May 1st became recognized as international workers' day nearly everywhere except, ironically, in the United States.) In Chicago, after police killed two strikers on May 3, local anarchists called a workers' rally in Haymarket Square.

Orphans of the Gilded Age Jacob Riis captured this image of street children in New York in the 1880s. Riis, a Danish-American social reformer, used such photographs to bring the middle class's attention to the distress of those left behind by surging American economic growth.

Late in the peaceful rally, police moved in and someone threw a bomb toward them; shots followed, and several policemen and workers died. Authorities arrested some German and Czech anarchists as the press stoked anti-immigrant and anti-labor fervor; historians continue to debate the guilt or innocence of the four men who were hung.

AP® THEMES
What caused the push to reform labor systems in industrial nations, such as the United States?

- **CONTEXT&CONNECTIONS** The most prominent anarchist in the United States was *Emma Goldman* (Chapter 27), an immigrant from Russia who was radicalized by the "Haymarket martyrs" and fought for workers' freedom from both governmental and corporate oppression. ●

In spite of the Haymarket affair, the labor movement in the United States gradually grew stronger and better organized. Still, few advocated socialism. When most Americans demanded equality, what they really meant was equality of opportunity. It was their deep belief in individual opportunity that inspired Americans' characteristic sense of optimism.

In 1893, the United States celebrated its self-confidence at the World's Columbian Exposition held in Chicago. The fair featured a dazzling model city, with the world's first Ferris Wheel as a response to the new Eiffel Tower of Paris. It was the first time that many spectators arriving from farms and small towns had ever seen electric lights, a telephone, or a "horseless carriage" with a diesel engine.

Like London's Great Exhibition before it (see Chapter 23), the Columbian Exposition was a monument to industrial and technological progress.

Even as crowds flocked to the Columbian Exposition, the U.S. economy suffered a great jolt, the Panic of 1893. The exuberance of Gilded Age capitalism had been founded on price speculation. In 1893, the bubble burst when a bank failure in Argentina led to a run on U.S. banks. A sharp decline in investment and employment followed. From the new "progressive" wing of the Republican Party came calls for greater government regulation of irresponsible corporate speculators.

● **CONTEXT&CONNECTIONS** The overall pattern of the late-nineteenth-century international economy was volatile, with periods of exuberant growth followed by deep downturns. Marxists at the time argued that this boom-and-bust cycle would inevitably bring capitalism crashing down (see Chapter 23). Contemporaries referred to the slump of the early 1890s as the "Great Depression," a title usurped by an even more devastating global economic collapse in 1929 (see Chapter 28). ●

The Panic of 1893 was a short-term economic setback, but that same year, at least one observer noted a more fundamental shift. In his essay "The Significance of the Frontier in American History," historian Frederick Jackson Turner argued that the availability of an open frontier underlay the democracy and lack of class enmity in American life, compared with the harsher social conflict in Europe. With that frontier "closed," how would Americans adjust? The United States was in fact no longer a youthful frontier society. In the three decades following the Civil War, it had become the world's leading industrial *and* agricultural producer, with increasingly complex global interests.

Indeed, toward the century's end, the United States was trading continental frontiers for global ones. In addition to its activities in the Pacific (see Chapter 24), the United States intervened in Latin America, occupying Cuba and Puerto Rico (as well as the Philippines) after the Spanish-American War (1898–1900). In Cuba, U.S. occupation derailed an indigenous independence movement and sponsored an oligarchy sympathetic to U.S. corporate interests. Then, in 1903, the United States, anxious to create a U.S.-controlled canal on the Isthmus of Panama, supported Panamanian aspirations for independence from Colombia (breaking the last link of Simón Bolívar's Gran Colombia; see Chapter 22). Having annexed Hawai'i and declared a U.S. protectorate over the Philippines, the United States would soon control the fastest route westward from Atlantic to Pacific. It was clear to the world's people that the United States was now playing the imperial game, both within its own hemisphere and beyond.

Reform and Reaction in Latin America

Like Canada and the United States, Latin American nations had to overcome regional and sectional differences to develop effective national institutions. But where Canada and the United States were fundamentally secure within their borders, many Latin American nations faced severe external challenges, both political and economic. In the middle of the nineteenth century, Mexico lost northern territory to the United States and then suffered a decade of French occupation. Domination by Europe and the United States skewed Latin American economic production toward foreign markets. Overreliance on exports of agricultural produce and natural resources and imports of industrial goods and technologies hindered the development of integrated national economies.

Economic Dependency in Latin America

The Industrial Revolution had profound economic consequences for Latin Americans. Already during the colonial period their economies had been geared toward high-value exports like gold and silver, exchanged for luxury goods consumed by Spanish officials and local elites, the *criollos*. The benefits of trade were very unequally shared. Except in areas with slave plantations, international trade was fairly limited and local self-sufficiency still common. That changed quickly after about 1820, with surging foreign investment directed toward increasing export production.

Latin Americans fell into an economic trap that historians have called a "dependency complex." Rather than developing their own industrial base or integrating their national and regional markets, they depended almost exclusively on exporting raw materials, typically agricultural produce or minerals, in order to import manufactured goods. Relying on lightly processed exports to obtain higher-value industrial goods reinforced the sharply drawn social inequalities inherited from colonialism. (See the feature "World History in Today's World: The Roller Coaster of Commodity Prices.")

While rough-and-ready military men often dominated national politics, it was the oligarchs at the top of the social pyramid, descendants of "good" Iberian families, who controlled economic life, using their international connections to profit as intermediaries between local producers and global markets. Meanwhile, the lack of local industry and the focus on international rather than domestic trade stunted the growth of a vigorous middle class.

Economic dependency undermined peasant communities. With the transition to labor-intensive plantation crops for export, they often lost control over their own land and labor, forced by taxes, debt peonage, and sometimes direct coercion to leave their villages to work for miserable wages in mines and on plantations (see Chapter 18). Economies were growing in ways that made many people poorer, a process that one historian has called "the poverty of progress."

• **CONTEXT&CONNECTIONS** In the 1960s, radical sociologists identified the "development of underdevelopment" as a key feature of the modern world economy, focusing on economic dependency as an exploitative framework of international capitalism, funneling resources from "third-world" societies in Latin America, Asia, and Africa, to enrich the already dominant "first world" (see Chapter 30). •

Conservatives, Liberals, and the Struggle for Stability in Mexico

After Mexico won independence from Spain in 1821, the government fell into the hands of ineffective soldier-politicians, the *caudillos* (cow-DEE-yos) (see Chapter 22). General Antonio López de Santa Ana (1794–1876), who served as president of Mexico nine different times while losing half the country to the United States, was the most notorious.

The Roller Coaster of Commodity Prices

In the twenty-first-century era of globalization, South American nations have been rising stars. Brazil's economy, for example, grew by 4.2 percent annually from 2004 to 2010 (see Chapter 32).

But has Brazil and its neighbors escaped the long-standing trap of economic dependency, overreliance on the export of a limited range of agricultural products, minerals, and energy sources? That question came into renewed focus when a sharp fall in commodity prices from 2014 into 2015 demonstrated the exceptional vulnerability of South American countries to roller-coaster fluctuations in the world economy.

A staggering drop in oil prices, for example, sent Venezuela into a state of shock. From a 2011 peak of $117 a barrel, and a mid-2014 price of $108 a barrel, the price of crude oil plunged by more than half, to less than $50 a barrel in early 2015. While the country's non-oil exports have remained flat for twenty years, crude oil has accounted for over 90 percent of export revenue. Venezuela is now paying the price for failing to translate oil wealth into a more diversified portfolio.

The Brazilian economy is not as reliant on a single commodity, but its growth estimates have also been revised downward. Soybean exports, especially to China, peaked at a price of $621 a metric ton in 2012, but then bottomed out at less than $390 a ton at the end of 2014. (In fact, slowing demand from China affected economies across Latin America.) The Brazilian government found itself with declining tax revenues even while bearing the costs of the 2014 World Cup and the 2016 Summer Olympics. Meanwhile, some farmers found it was no longer worth the cost to plant soybeans on fields they have only recently cleared from the tropical forest (although the steep environmental costs of that land clearance cannot be recovered.)

Of course, global commodity prices eventually will recover. But volatility will undoubtedly remain, and Latin America's legacy of economic dependency will continue to challenge governments and businesses far into the future.

A major problem for Mexico was its northern state of Texas. Traditionally, Mexico's wealth in people, resources, settled agriculture, and culture was in its central and southern parts. Texas, in contrast, was an untamed frontier with only a few officials and missionaries mixed in with *vaqueros* (vah-KAIR-ohs; cowboys), Amerindians such as Apache and Comanche, and the occasional American adventurer. None of them paid much attention to Mexican authorities.

In the 1820s, Mexico attempted to stabilize this distant frontier by inviting English-speaking settlers into Texas. Most were Americans who planned to use slave labor to produce cotton. But since Mexico had already abolished slavery, the importation of slaves was illegal. President Santa Ana would either have to enforce that law or allow slaveholding Texans to flout his authority.

By 1836, when Santa Ana came north with his troops, thirty thousand American settlers lived in Texas. Unhappy with Mexican rule, these settlers allied with discontented Spanish-speaking Texans to fight for independence. Despite victories at the Alamo and elsewhere, Santa Ana lost Texas. In the new Republic of Texas, a referendum prepared the way for U.S. annexation in 1845. Mexico's loss of territory to the United States continued when a U.S. administration provoked war with Mexico in 1846, sending its forces all the way to Mexico City. The Treaty of Guadalupe Hidalgo (1848) gave the United States the northern half of Mexico. Mexico's "*Norte*" had become the American Southwest.

Mexican liberals, distraught by their country's weakness and inspired by the European revolutions of 1848 (see Chapter 23), supported *La Reforma*, a movement to get rid of caudillo rule and create a more progressive nation. One of their leaders, Benito Juárez (beh-NEE-toh WAH-rez) (1806–1872) became the country's first Amerindian president.

Juárez and the liberals succeeded against conservative resistance and enshrined the principles of *La Reforma* in the Mexican Constitution of 1857. The new constitution restricted the privileges of the Catholic clergy and the military. Most liberals saw the church as restricting individualism and progress while upholding the power of the large landowners. The constitution also contained a Bill of Rights, ending the old caste system and making everyone equal before the law.

Conservatives reacted angrily to such reforms, especially limitations on the church's power and the seizure of its land. While some priests followed the example of Father Hidalgo in supporting the rights of the majority (see Chapter 22), Mexican bishops allied with the *hacendados*, the large landowners who had opposed Hidalgo's revolution in 1810 and who now rejected the liberal constitution.

Contention between liberals and conservatives created an opening for the French emperor Napoleon III (see Chapter 23) who sent troops to Mexico in 1861. His stated intention was to force payments of Mexican debt, but his real motive was to resurrect a French empire in the Americas. The liberal government fought back. In 1862, on the fifth of May (*Cinco de Mayo*), a small army of Mexicans defeated a much larger French force at the Battle of Puebla. But Mexico lost the war after conservatives helped the French invaders take Mexico City. While pressure from Europe and the United States eventually forced the French to withdraw, the struggle between Mexico's liberals and conservatives continued.

Porfirio Diáz
(1830–1915) President of Mexico from 1876–1880 and 1884–1911. While he ignored Mexican civil liberties, Diáz courted foreign investment to develop infrastructure and provided much-needed stability.

In 1876, **Porfirio Diáz** (1830–1915) came to power. Like the old caudillos, he ruled as a dictator, and during his long tenure as president (1876–1880 and 1884–1911), he ignored the ideals of *La Reforma*, such as freedom of speech and assembly. He was, however, a firm believer in free trade and foreign investment, actively courting investors from Britain and the United States. Such economic development had political implications: the power of the state expanded, for example, as improved rail transportation gave the government greater access to the entire country.

Apart from railroads and mining, most new investment was in agriculture. As was typical of Latin American economic dependency, holders of large estates responded to the expansion of markets with extensive planting of export crops like cotton, sugar, and hemp. Commercial agriculture brought great wealth to Mexico's landowners, its urban commercial class, and foreign investors. However, these groups prospered at the expense of many formerly self-sufficient peasants.

Porfirio Diáz ruled Mexico as an elected dictator, winning rigged elections from 1884 on. By the early twentieth century, however, a younger generation of middle-class Mexicans chafed at the old dictator's political monopoly. Among their leaders was Francisco Madero, who ran for the presidency in 1910 under the slogan *"Effective Suffrage and No Reelection,"* and then launched a revolution when Diáz once again claimed victory. Finally, the aged Diáz fled to Europe.

Emiliano Zapata
(1879–1919) Leader of a popular uprising during the Mexican Revolution; mobilized the poor in southern and central Mexico to demand "justice, land, and liberty."

Removing a dictator is usually easier than creating a new political order, and that proved true in Mexico from 1910 to 1928. In 1913, Madero was assassinated by a military officer, who in turn was deposed by the liberal Venustiano Carranza. Though Carranza held Mexico City and controlled the federal army, two former partners in his revolutionary coalition, **Emiliano Zapata** (1879–1919) and Pancho Villa (1878–1923), now turned against him.

Villa and Zapata This photograph from 1915 shows Pancho Villa (*center*, sitting on the presidential throne in the National Palace) with Emiliano Zapata (*right*) at his side, his trademark hat on his knee. Forces loyal to Venustiano Carranza soon chased the two revolutionaries from Mexico City, however. Both were later assassinated. (Underwood & Underwood/Historical/Corbis)

In the north, the dashing Villa came to represent for many the romance of revolution as he and his comrades, mostly cowboys and small ranchers, fought big property owners for land and water rights. In the south, Zapata galvanized support among hardscrabble southern peasants, many of them Amerindians, with the demand for "*¡Justicia, Tierra, y Libertad!*"

Although Carranza's government instituted a new constitution in 1917, trying to balance the different interests that had emerged during the revolution, chaos continued to engulf the country into the 1920s. Carranza's agents assassinated Zapata in 1919; Carranza himself fell to an assassin in 1920, and Villa in 1923. Other leaders and causes emerged, and as many as 2 million people had been killed in the revolution by 1929, when the Party of the Mexican Revolution finally restored stability (see Chapter 27).

Spanish-Speaking South America

Simón Bolívar's vision of a great confederation had failed (see Chapter 22), leaving nine separate South American nations by the 1830s. As in Mexico, their economies fell into the trap of economic dependency, exporting relatively low-value raw materials and importing higher-cost finished products. And as in Mexico, this economic system made them highly vulnerable to the price swings of global commodity markets. While plantation owners, commercial intermediaries, political elites, and foreign investors might prosper, peasants and laborers rarely did.

The story of Venezuela was fairly typical. The president, José Antonio Páez (1790–1873), had been a self-made military leader in the liberation campaigns. Páez (PAH-ays) consolidated his power in typical caudillo fashion by forging an alliance with the old criollo aristocracy, who overlooked Páez's rough manners since he was able to control the common people for them. Nevertheless, in the 1860s, after a brief civil war, Venezuelan reformers established a more liberal regime, abolishing slavery, building railroads, and expanding school facilities. Still, economic inequalities remained entrenched, with an export-oriented agricultural sector controlled by a Venezuelan oligarchy closely tied to foreign investors.

Library of Congress Prints & Photographs Division

Buenos Aires The Argentine capital of Buenos Aires was an exceptionally prosperous city in the first decade of the twentieth century. As in Paris, New York, and Berlin, automobiles were beginning to compete with horse-drawn carriages along its spacious boulevards. But Argentina's prosperity was overly dependent on volatile international commodity markets, and revenue from its exports went disproportionately to those at the very top of society.

Argentina was more economically successful. Railroads now made it easier to get Argentine cattle to market, and the development of refrigerated steamship compartments in the 1860s brought Argentine beef to European consumers. As the economy boomed, the capital, Buenos Aires, became one of the world's great cities. Cosmopolitan politicians, merchants, and lawyers enjoyed the city's elegant plazas and pleasant cafés. A growing working class, many of them recent immigrants from Italy, worked in meatpacking plants and other export-oriented industries. From their neighborhood cafés arose the sensual *tango*, Argentina's gift to musical culture.

Apart from Argentina, the most successful South American republic was Chile, another country with a largely European demographic profile. As elsewhere in Latin America, conservatives and liberals squared off, as did centralizers and believers in provincial autonomy. But in Chile a conservative consensus emerged early on, supported by the powerful Catholic Church.

Political consensus may have been easier to achieve in Chile because of its success in competing with its neighbors, Peru and Bolivia. Starting in the 1840s, the three countries greatly benefited from *guano* (GWA-noh), or bird droppings, along the Pacific coast: guano makes an excellent fertilizer and was in high global demand. Of course, shoveling guano was not pleasant: tens of thousands of Chinese laborers, escaping from the disruption of the Taiping Rebellion (see Chapter 24), were desperate enough to cross the ocean as indentured laborers to do the job.

As guano deposits declined, Peru, Bolivia, and Chile began to develop nitrate mines in the same region as an alternative source of fertilizer. The intensifying competition led to the **War of the Pacific** in 1879. Chile's victory enhanced its reputation, and Chileans developed a stronger sense of national identity. But the war was disastrous for Bolivia, which became a landlocked country and one of the poorest societies in the Americas (see Map 25.2).

War of the Pacific
(1879) War among Bolivia, Peru, and Chile over the natural resources of the Pacific coast. Chile emerged victorious, gaining international prestige, while Bolivia's loss made it a poor, landlocked country.

Still, even in Chile and Argentina, the most economically successful South American societies of the late nineteenth century, industrialization lagged far behind the pace set by the United States and Canada. Production of raw materials and importation of manufactured goods remained the norm, as did foreign investors' hold on much of the profit from growth.

From Empire to Republic in Brazil

Brazil's large size, distinct ecology and demography, and relationship to Portugal led on to a unique path. After Brazilian liberals declared the country's independence from Portugal in 1822, the heir to the Portuguese throne, already living in Brazil, agreed to serve as the new nation's constitutional monarch. Brazil therefore achieved independence more smoothly than other South American nations (see Chapter 22).

Still, Brazil's principal political tensions were quite similar to those of its republican neighbors. Brazil's progressive middle-class liberals were at odds with the country's conservatives, mostly large estate owners and military men who stressed traditional values such as the authority of the Catholic Church. The abolition of slavery, although a major liberal priority, was not achieved until 1888, later than anywhere else in the Americas.

AP® THEMES
What were the environmental implications of Brazil's role as an exporter of raw materials?

By then, coffee had replaced sugar as the primary export: in response to rising demand among newly affluent middle-class consumers in Europe and the United States, Brazil became the world's largest coffee exporter. The government took an active role in stimulating the production of rubber, now in great demand for industrial purposes, by granting gigantic land concessions in the Amazon. As a result, the Amazonian city of Manaus grew as fast as the mining towns of the western United States, its opulent opera house a symbol of the excesses that came with quick money.

Their growing export economy boosted the confidence of Brazilians as they abolished first slavery and then the monarchy, proclaiming a republic in 1889 with the motto *"Order and Progress"* proudly displayed on the country's new green and gold flag. But Brazil still found itself in the same dependency trap as other South American nations. The rubber boom collapsed when production spread to Central Africa and Southeast Asia, and coffee exports sharply declined during the global economic slump of the 1890s.

Map 25.2 Latin America, ca. 1895 By 1895, all of the nations of South and Central America were independent except for British, French, and Dutch Guyana and Honduras. Panama seceded from Colombia in 1903 with military backing from the United States, which was anxious to further its canal interests. Many Caribbean islands remained British, French, and Dutch colonies. However, Cuba was freed from Spanish rule in 1898, the same year the United States took control over Puerto Rico. Railroad networks seen in Mexico, Chile, Argentina, and southern Brazil were a sign of foreign investment in exports like minerals and livestock products.

• **CONTEXT&CONNECTIONS** The rubber industry of the late nineteenth century was notorious for labor exploitation and abuses. The most infamous case occurred in the Congo Free State, the Central African domain of *King Leopold II of Belgium* (Chapter 26), where the violence and avarice of European rubber companies left as many as 10 million Africans dead. In the Amazon as well, rubber barons and their agents expropriated Amerindian lands and subjected Amerindian workers to slave-like servitude. •

The Nineteenth-Century Americas in Perspective

All across the Americas, changes resulted from integration into global markets and consolidation of state power. Amerindian sovereignty came to an end, ever larger numbers of European immigrants altered racial demographics, and changes were taking place in gender roles. Pauline Johnson-Tekahionwake was not the only woman seeking greater autonomy in late-nineteenth-century society, when an increasingly organized women's movement was articulating a platform of voting rights and social equality.

The Fates of Indigenous Societies

The nineteenth century was decisive for America's indigenous peoples. Before the Industrial Revolution, Amerindian societies in regions as diverse as the Andes, the Arctic, Amazonia, and the Great Plains retained control over their own political, social, and cultural lives. Some, like the Johnson family and other Iroquois on the Six Nations Reserve, maintained connections with settler societies while balancing old traditions and new influences. But by the end of the century Amerindian sovereignty had disappeared.

In Mexico, for example, following independence in 1821, Mayan-speaking villagers on the Yucatán (yoo-kah-TAHN) peninsula continued to live much as before, with little reference to Spanish-speaking government officials. They grew maize, beans, and other staple crops in communities deeply rooted in the pre-Columbian past. While Christian, their Catholicism mixed local and imported beliefs. Though connected to wider networks as producers and consumers, their self-sufficiency nevertheless allowed them to choose their own terms of contact with the outside world.

That autonomy was challenged in the 1840s with a boom in plantation agriculture. At first, planters of sugar and *henequen* (a fibrous plant used for rope making) could not attract Amerindian workers at the wages they offered. Just at this time, however, Mexican tax collectors were becoming more aggressive because of the expensive wars with Texas. Forced to earn cash to pay their taxes, formerly self-sufficient peasants had to seek work on plantations. Many were then entrapped by debt peonage: never able to repay their employers, they could not leave to seek better wages elsewhere.

Meanwhile, a small group of Maya militants began a guerrilla campaign in 1847 known as the **Yucatán Rebellion**, attacking both Mexican government officials and local hacienda owners. With the Mexican army occupied against the United States, the rebels soon controlled over half of the Yucatán peninsula. Once the war in the north was over, however, Mexican forces redeployed against the Maya rebels and gradually reimposed government authority. Elite Mexicans, liberal and conservative alike, viewed the Maya rebels as primitive folk standing in the way of the "progress" of nation building and market expansion.

Yucatán Rebellion (1847) Maya uprising on Mexico's Yucatán peninsula, challenging the authority of the Mexican government and local landowners. Some Maya communities defended their sovereignty into the 1890s.

Scattered fighting continued until 1895. By then Maya resistance had been broken: the need for cash to pay their taxes had driven them to low-wage peonage on plantations producing for export. Taxes tied them to the Mexican state; their labor tied them to the global economy. The autonomy for which they had fought was gone.

In the United States, the dominant society had no use for Amerindians even as subservient laborers. Driven primarily by the discovery of gold in Georgia and insistent pressure for fresh land on which to grow slave-produced cotton, the U.S. Congress passed the **Indian Removal Act** in 1830. President Jackson supported and oversaw the forced migration of southeastern Amerindians such as the Creek and Cherokee to a designated "Indian Territory" in today's Oklahoma. Ironically, in 1827 the Cherokee had emulated the U.S. model in drafting a constitution in an attempt to protect their independence. That experiment ended tragically with a forced march west that killed over four thousand on what the Cherokee call the *Nunna daul Tsuny*, the *"Trail Where They Cried"* or the *"Trail of Tears"* (see page 798).

Indian Removal Act
(1830) Legislation leading to the dispossession of Amerindian peoples in the southeastern United States. Thousands of Cherokee died when forcibly marched to Oklahoma along the "Trail of Tears."

The life and customs of the indigenous communities of the Great Plains were quite different from those of the agricultural Maya and Cherokee. Plains Amerindians lived in mobile bands and depended on buffalo hunting for both food and goods to trade. The ancient buffalo-hunting culture of the Plains took on new impetus with the arrival of horses in the sixteenth and seventeenth centuries. Formerly semi-agricultural people, like the Cheyenne and the Lakota (luh-KOH-tuh) moved onto the Plains year-round and used horses and rifles to hunt.

Then after 1846, when Great Britain ceded Oregon to the United States, large numbers of settlers sought their fortune on the "Oregon Trail." By the time of the American Civil War, a series of forts in the Dakota Territory protected settlers-in-transit from Amerindian attacks.

For a time it seemed that negotiations between the Lakota and the U.S. government might preserve stability. An 1868 treaty, for example, forbade white settlement for all time in the Black Hills, sacred to the Lakota and other Plains societies. Four years later, however, gold was discovered, and waves of white prospectors descended on mining camps in the heart of sacred Lakota land. To leaders like **Sitting Bull** (ca. 1831–1890) treaties with the U.S. government now seemed worthless, and they prepared for war.

Sitting Bull
(ca. 1831–1890) Lakota chieftain who led Amerindian resistance to white settlement of the Black Hills. After defeating U.S. cavalry and Lieutenant Colonel George Custer at the Battle of Little Bighorn in 1876, he was killed in 1890 during conflict surrounding the Ghost Dance Movement.

In the summer of 1876, Lakota and Cheyenne warriors defeated Lieutenant Colonel George Custer and his forces at the Battle of Little Bighorn, killing Custer and over half of his men. Although Custer's demise was the outcome of a military blunder, the American press portrayed it as a heroic *"last stand"* against *"savages."* Amid calls for swift vengeance, some advocated not just the defeat of the Lakota confederation but also the total annihilation of Amerindians.

Then, just a few years later, European immigrants and American settlers began arriving in the Dakota Territory as permanent homesteaders, a dramatic change made possible by railroads. In 1890, the U.S. government abrogated its treaty with the Lakota to open lands for these settlers. Now confined to reservations, the Lakota, who had depended on open lands where buffalo grazed, found their way of life imperiled.

Some despairing Plains Amerindians were attracted to the teachings of a mystic named Wovoka (wuh-VOH-kuh), leader of the Ghost Dance Movement. Wovoka's followers believed that he was a messiah sent to liberate them and that by dancing the Ghost Dance they would hasten a new age in which the invaders would disappear from the earth and the native peoples would live in peace and prosperity.

• **CONTEXT&CONNECTIONS** Scholars have compared the Ghost Dance Movement and the *Xhosa Cattle Killing* (Chapter 26) as examples of "millenarian" spiritual movements combining indigenous and Christian beliefs and promising to bring about a new age of peace and justice. Resurrection of the dead, an idea common to both the Xhosa prophetess Nongqawuse in the 1850s and Wovoka on the Great Plains in the 1880s, was borrowed from Christian preachers and adapted to the needs of indigenous societies faced with invasion and cultural marginalization. •

The U.S. government regarded the Ghost Dance Movement as subversive and ordered the arrest of Sitting Bull in the mistaken belief that he was one of its leaders. Early in 1890, Sitting Bull died in a skirmish when tribal police tried to detain him. Two weeks later, U.S. soldiers fired into a group of Lakota captives, killing between 150 and 300 people. Nearly half of the victims of this Wounded Knee Massacre were unarmed women and children. An editorial writer at a South Dakota newspaper had this to say:

> *The Whites, by law of conquest, by justice of civilization, are masters of the American continent, and the best safety of the frontier settlements will be secured by the total annihilation of the few remaining Indians. Why not annihilation? Their glory has fled, their spirit broken, their manhood effaced; better that they die than live the miserable wretches that they are.**

The Granger Collection, NYC

Chief Joseph Chief Joseph (Hin-mah-too-yah-lat-kekt, "Thunder Rolling Down the Mountain") was a Nez Perce Amerindian leader and a famous man of peace. The discovery of gold led the U.S. government to renege on its treaty with the Nez Perce, shrinking their reservation to a tenth of its former size. In 1877, Chief Joseph led his people, pursued by U.S. cavalry, in a desperate attempt to reach Canada. He was captured and exiled to Oklahoma. Only in 1885 were Joseph and his remaining followers allowed to return to their homes in the Pacific Northwest.

Such violent racism in support of a policy of genocide was not uncommon. (The author of this editorial, L. Frank Baum, would later write the beloved children's story *The Wonderful Wizard of Oz*.)

Rather than pursuing outright annihilation, however, the federal Bureau of Indian Affairs separated Amerindian children from their parents to prevent them from learning the language, culture, and rituals of their own people—a form of cultural genocide. Amerindian armed resistance was over. The frontier wars persisted only in entertainment, courtesy of Buffalo Bill Cody's tremendously popular Wild West shows, where Americans flocked to be thrilled by stylized reenactments of the frontier wars.

Traveling across Canada in the 1890s, Pauline Johnson-Tekahionwake saw firsthand the tragedy of the Plains Amerindians in the sad spectacle of *"a sort of miniature Buffalo Bill's Wild West"*† in which Blackfoot warriors, seeking coins from travelers, caricatured their old war maneuvers. Some might have been veterans of the **Métis Rebellions**, the uprisings of mixed-race and First Nations peoples that had inspired Johnson to write "A Cry from an Indian Wife."

The métis settlement in the Red River Valley of what is now the Canadian province of Manitoba represented an older form of European-First Nations interaction.

Métis Rebellions

(1867 and 1885) Rebellions by the métis of the Red River Valley settlement in Manitoba, a group with mixed French-Amerindian ancestry that resisted incorporation into the Canadian Confederation. In 1885 their leader, Louis Riel, again led them in rebellion against Canadian authority.

*L. Frank Baum, *Aberdeen Saturday Pioneer*, December 20, 1890.

†Pauline Johnson-Tekahionwake, cited in Betty Keller, *Pauline: A Biography of Pauline Johnson* (Toronto: Douglas and Macintyre, 1981), p. 94.

During the heyday of the fur trade, mixed-race families were not uncommon and sometimes established their own communities (see Chapter 18).

The first of two Métis Rebellions came immediately after Canadian confederation in 1867. London had transferred authority over the vast territories of the Hudson's Bay Company to the Canadian government without consulting the people who lived there. The métis leader Louis Riel organized his community to resist incorporation into Canada, which they feared would lead to loss of their lands and the erosion of their French language. Riel declared an independent provisional government, but soon accepted British guarantees that Canada would protect the language and Catholic religion of his people. Negotiations led to the incorporation of the province of Manitoba into Canada in 1870.

AP® THEMES

How were the cultural practices of the First Nations peoples altered as a result of European political policies?

At the same time, Canadian policies assumed that increasingly desperate First Nations peoples of the plains would disappear as a distinct population. The buffalo were dwindling; alcohol was becoming a scourge. Amerindian hunting traditions and lack of capital made a transition to commercial farming almost impossible. In exchange for exclusive reserves and small annuities, band after band gave up claim to the lands of their forebears as the railroad brought in settlers and commerce.

The Indian Act of 1876 asserted the authority of the Canadian state over First Nations communities. As in the United States, children were separated from their families and sent to "industrial schools," given English names, and forbidden to speak their own languages. (See the feature "Visual Evidence in Primary Sources: The Residential School System for First Nations Children.")

In the Pacific Northwest, where Pauline Johnson-Tekahionwake lived out her retirement collecting tales of the Squamish (SKWAW-mish) people, Canadian officials banned traditional rituals such as the *potlatch*, where men solidified their social position by distributing their wealth as gifts. The potlatch expressed the core cultural values of the First Nations of the Pacific West, but the idea of giving away your possessions could not have stood in greater contrast to the ethos of industrial and commercial capitalism on which Canada was then being built.

Meanwhile, the flood of arriving settlers would make the métis a minority in their own land. In 1885 Louis Riel once again organized resistance, this time forging alliances with disaffected Cree, Assiniboine, and other First Nations peoples. Métis partisans attacked a government outpost as Riel's indigenous allies burned down white homesteads. But they were no match for three thousand troops sent west by rail. Riel was arrested, convicted of high treason, and hanged. When Pauline Johnson-Tekahionwake recited "A Cry from an Indian Wife" in 1892, these events were still fresh in the minds of her audience.

If we compare the Yucatán Rebellion, the struggles of the Lakota, and the Métis Rebellions, we might first be struck by this difference: whereas the Mexican government and economic oligarchy wanted to incorporate the Maya peasantry as laborers in the commercial plantation system, the United States and Canada had no use for Amerindians even as workers. But the three cases have this in common: in the Yucatán, the Black Hills, and Manitoba, people rose up to defend their long-established cultures against foreign intrusion and commercial agriculture. All three societies had creatively merged indigenous and imported ideas: Maya beliefs and Catholicism, Lakota traditions with horse-based buffalo hunting, French and First Nations cultures in the days of the fur trade. Now all these peoples lost their ability to control their interactions with the national societies being constructed around them.

Immigration, Abolition, and Race

During Pauline Johnson-Tekahionwake's lifetime, the picture of Canada's society was complicated by the arrival of new immigrants: Chinese, Italians, Russians, and others. Early in the twentieth century, half of the population on the prairies was born outside of Canada. The same was true throughout the Americas. The United States was the most favored destination, but Argentina and Brazil also attracted many European immigrants.

In Brazil and the Caribbean, the abolition of slavery was connected to immigration patterns and policies. Slavery was abolished in Haiti in 1803, on the British West Indies in 1833, and on the remaining French islands fifteen years later. Unable to keep the former slaves as poorly paid wage earners, landowners turned to indentured workers. In the English-speaking Caribbean, indentured laborers came largely from British India, part of a broader South Asian diaspora (scattering) that also took contract workers to South Africa, Malaya, and Fiji. In Cuba, where slavery was not abolished until 1878, over a hundred thousand Chinese workers came to the island as indentured workers to supplement slave labor.

● **CONTEXT&CONNECTIONS** Demand for cane sugar was still rising in the 1830s when newly freed slaves abandoned Caribbean plantations, driving down production. Entrepreneurs responded by starting new plantations wherever conditions of heat and humidity were appropriate. Instead of slavery, the new plantations relied on indentured laborers brought across the seas from impoverished lands, for example, Filipinos to Hawaii and Indians to Fiji and South Africa. ●

Like Cuba, Brazil was bringing in new migrants even before slavery was abolished, such as contract laborers from Japan to work on coffee farms. (Today the largest group of Japanese-descended persons outside Japan is found in Brazil.) Much larger and more influential in Brazilian culture, however, was the Afro-Brazilian population with its origins in the old sugar plantation system. Brazilian art, music, dance, and religious worship all show a deep African influence.

Reflecting the racism of their age, the rulers of republican Brazil were embarrassed by the country's African heritage. Their motto was *"Order and Progress,"* and in their minds black people represented neither. To "improve" the country racially, the government recruited immigrants from Europe. Incentives lured Germans, Italians, and others to the economically dynamic southern part of the country. The northeast, the base of the old plantation system, remained more African in population and culture.

Even so, Brazil retained the traditional flexibility and ambiguity in race relations inherited from the colonial period. While the elite class was predominantly white and the poorest class predominantly black, there was a vast intermediate stratum of mixed descent. Complex racial designations classified people by speech, education, style of clothing, and other factors in addition to color. Racial classification, therefore, could be a matter of negotiation rather than simple appearance: as they say in Brazil, *"Money whitens."*

Racism was also evident in immigration to the United States. For example, the Anglo-Protestant majority portrayed Irish Catholics as drunk, violent, and lazy. Demeaning stereotypes also greeted new immigrants from southern and eastern Europe, such as Italian Catholics and Russian Jews. Prejudice against Chinese and Japanese immigrants on the west coast was even more intense, and Congress banned Chinese immigration altogether in 1882. Still, in 1913, fully 15 percent of the population (more than at any time since) had been born outside the United States.

The Residential School System for First Nations Children

After the conquest of Amerindian communities, nineteenth-century governments in both the United States and Canada implemented residential school systems designed to separate Amerindian children from their families and thus from the culture of their people. Children in these often church-run schools were given new names, converted to Christianity, forced to speak only English, and punished for speaking the language of their own people. Physical and sexual abuse were common, and rates of infectious disease, especially tuberculosis, were high. In Canada, attendance by First Nations children at residential schools was compulsory until 1948.

In this photograph, "Thomas" wears long braided hair and leans against a large fur robe. He holds what appears to be a toy gun, perhaps given to him as a prop by the photographer.

Assuming the photographer posed the boy, what impression does he seem to have wanted the photograph to have on its viewers?

One writer says that this image shows "the disorder and violence of warfare and of the cross-cultural partnerships of the fur trade . . . that had dominated life in Canada since the late sixteenth century."* How does the image show that?

Saskatchewan Archives Board, Regina Industrial School

*John S. Milloy, *A National Crime: The Canadian Government and the Residential School System, 1879 to 1906* (Winnipeg: University of Manitoba Press, 1999), p. 4.

Finally, in 1998 the Canadian government formed the Aboriginal Healing Foundation to support community projects in reparation for the damage done by this attempted cultural genocide of First Nations peoples. In 2008, the Canadian prime minister made a formal statement of apology, recognizing that "the consequences of the Indian residential schools policy were profoundly negative and that this policy has had a lasting and damaging impact on aboriginal culture, heritage, and language." The statement highlighted the "tragic accounts of the emotional, physical, and sexual abuse and neglect of helpless children, and their separation from powerless families and communities."

These two photographs were taken at the Regina Industrial School in the Canadian province of Saskatchewan and published in the *Annual Report* of the Canadian Department of Indian Affairs in 1904. They record the appearance of a First Nations child identified only as "Thomas Moore" (his true name was not recorded), supposedly upon his first arrival and again a few years later.

Saskatchewan Archives Board, Regina Industrial School

Apart from his hair and clothing, what is different and meaningful about Thomas's facial expression and posture in the second photograph?

The wall against which Thomas is leaning in this photograph seems much more solid and permanent than the fur robe in the earlier picture, perhaps symbolizing the superior strength of Christian Canadian society.

The goal of the Canadian government was to replace buffalo hunting with settled agriculture, a transformation perhaps symbolized by the potted plant included in this photograph. ***Taken together, what do these two photographs tell us about the ideology behind the residential school system in turn-of-the-century Canada?***

In Australia as well, aboriginal children were taken from their parents, forced into residential schools, and denied the chance of learning their own language and culture.

Some doubted whether these new arrivals, with their unfamiliar foods, languages, and customs, could ever be assimilated.

Racism continued to drive policy toward Americans of African descent, where the "one drop rule," in contrast with Brazil's more complex race-status hierarchy, classified all individuals with any appearance of African descent as black. In 1896, the Supreme Court upheld the legality of racial segregation in the South. Those African Americans who tried to escape racism by moving to northern states or beyond to Canada were disappointed by the prejudice they still faced. For example, after a thousand black farmers fled Oklahoma to the Canadian prairies to escape disenfranchisement and segregation, the Canadian government subjected them to arbitrary and humiliating medical examinations.

Meanwhile, recent immigrants from Europe, in spite of prejudices against them, fared better than U.S. African Americans. Many Irish Americans, for example, found good work as police officers and firemen, jobs that were closed to blacks. The cruel irony was that African Americans, whose ancestors had witnessed the birth of the republic, now watched as new arrivals from Europe leaped ahead of them.

Harsh racial rhetoric and even harsher racial realities pervaded the Americas. Encounters among Amerindians, Africans, Asians, and Europeans seemed decisively to favor the latter. For all the variation among the nations of North and South America, they had one thing in common: light-skinned men were in charge.

Gender and Women's Rights

AP® THEMES

How did the Seneca Falls Convention challenge traditional perceptions of gender roles?

In 1848, the Seneca Falls Convention, sometimes seen as the beginning of the modern women's movement, was held in upstate New York. Inspired by the abolitionist movement and the revolutions of the same year in Europe (see Chapter 23), the women met to proclaim universal freedom and gender equality, declaring:

> *Now, in view of this entire disfranchisement of one-half the people of this country, their social and religious degradation... and because women do feel themselves aggrieved, oppressed, and fraudulently deprived of their most sacred rights, we insist that they have immediate admission to all the rights and privileges which belong to them as citizens of these United States.*

Such proclamations would eventually transform gender relations in the United States, Canada, and the world. In the short run, however, most women, like Pauline Johnson-Tekahionwake, had to explore their own possibilities without much external support. Just as she investigated her own complex identity through life and art, her public performances also explored her identity as a woman. The costume change she made halfway through her recitals—from buckskin to evening gown, from Tekahionwake to Pauline Johnson—transformed her from a passionate and even erotic persona to a distant and ethereal one.

For many middle-class women in the United States and Canada, the bicycle became a symbol of a new mobility and a new kind of freedom. For Pauline Johnson-Tekahionwake, the canoe played this role. Some of her nature poems, such as "The Song My Paddle Sings," were based on canoe trips she took as a young woman on the Six Nations Reserve:

> *... The river rolls in its rocky bed;*
> *My paddle is plying its way ahead...*
> *And up on the hills against the sky,*

A fir tree rocking its lullaby,
Swings, swings,
Its emerald wings,
*Swelling the song that my paddle sings.**

In her canoe poems, Johnson-Tekahionwake is always in control, even when, as is often the case, she has a male companion. The independence asserted in her poetry was reflected in her personal life as well. She had several significant relationships but no marriage, and though money was a constant worry, she was financially independent. Perhaps Johnson-Tekahionwake's autonomy arose from her mixed heritage, deriving from both the matriarchal tradition of the Mohawk and the new possibilities for women proclaimed at Seneca Falls.

The Granger Collection, NYC

Bicycle Advertisement This advertisement from 1896 associates the bicycle with the newfound mobility and independence of the "new woman." In the poems of Pauline Johnson-Tekahionwake, it was often a canoe that allowed women to "be content."

How exceptional were Pauline Johnson-Tekahionwake's attitudes and experiences? Women's progress toward equality and autonomy varied tremendously according to geographic location and class standing. Among wealthier women in major commercial cities like Toronto, Chicago, or Buenos Aires, some were politically active, seeking legal equality and the vote for women. Some organized campaigns for social improvement, working to limit abuses of child labor, to improve sanitary conditions, or to fight the evils of alcohol. Some daughters of the middle class took advantage of new educational opportunities. Female doctors, lawyers, and university professors were few, but there were many new openings for schoolteachers and nurses. The invention of the typewriter and the emergence of large corporations also created a vast new job market for female secretaries, many from the working class.

Often, young women from the working or middle classes viewed employment as temporary, lasting only until they married. According to the "cult of true womanhood" dominant at the time, woman's role was in a "separate sphere," where she would maintain a refined home as a sanctuary from the brutal and competitive "men's world" of business and industry. Even though women like Johnson-Tekahionwake might reject the "cult of true womanhood," many urban middle-class women and poorer women who aspired to be middle class embraced the idea.

Of course, American women lived diverse lives. A middle-class homemaker in Buenos Aires had greater comfort than a Swedish pioneer getting her family through the winter on the Canadian prairie. An Irish nun teaching immigrant children in Chicago would be difficult to compare with a Maya mother sending her sons off to work on a Yucatán plantation. For her part, Pauline Johnson-Tekahionwake enjoyed a life of mobility and autonomy that would have been unimaginable to her foremothers.

---

*Excerpt from *Flint and Feather: The Complete Poems of E. Pauline Johnson (Tekahionwake)*. Toronto and London: The Musson Book Co., Ltd., 1912.

CONTEXT AND CONNECTIONS

The Americas: Hemispheric and Global Connections

After growing up in a world of horses and canoes, Pauline Johnson-Tekahionwake made her career as a performer traveling by railroad and steamship, planning her trips and advertising her upcoming shows with the help of the telegraph. Mass audiences for news and entertainment were an important outcome of the increased pace of communications and transport in the late nineteenth century. Widespread access to inexpensive newspapers and common experiences of dance hall revues were part of the nation-building process, helping to create national cultures not just in the rapidly growing cities, but also across the vast frontier spaces of North America. In the early twentieth century, the invention of the radio and wider use of automobiles would magnify that trend toward mass national culture, as would cinema and, later, television.

Popular culture in North America, including the new popularity of spectator sports like baseball, ice hockey, and football, though scorned by cultural elites, marked the rising influence and spending power of the middle class and, increasingly, of industrial workers as well. At the same time, urban opportunity attracted immigrants from around the world. In 1910, almost a fourth of all Canadians and 15 percent of the U.S. population were foreign born.

The Industrial Revolution had quite different effects in Latin America. Here small elites continued to dominate culture, politics, and economics. Mexico and Central and South America all inherited colonial social systems based on the hacienda, where large landowners dominated local societies. In the nineteenth century, the commercialization of agriculture in response to new industrial markets further magnified the pattern of exceptionally concentrated landholding. Foreign investors, with little interest in tying local and regional markets together, constructed railroads to smooth the export of raw materials to Europe and North America. Likewise, foreign investment in mining and agriculture encouraged reliance on a narrow range of commodities demanded by the industrial powers.

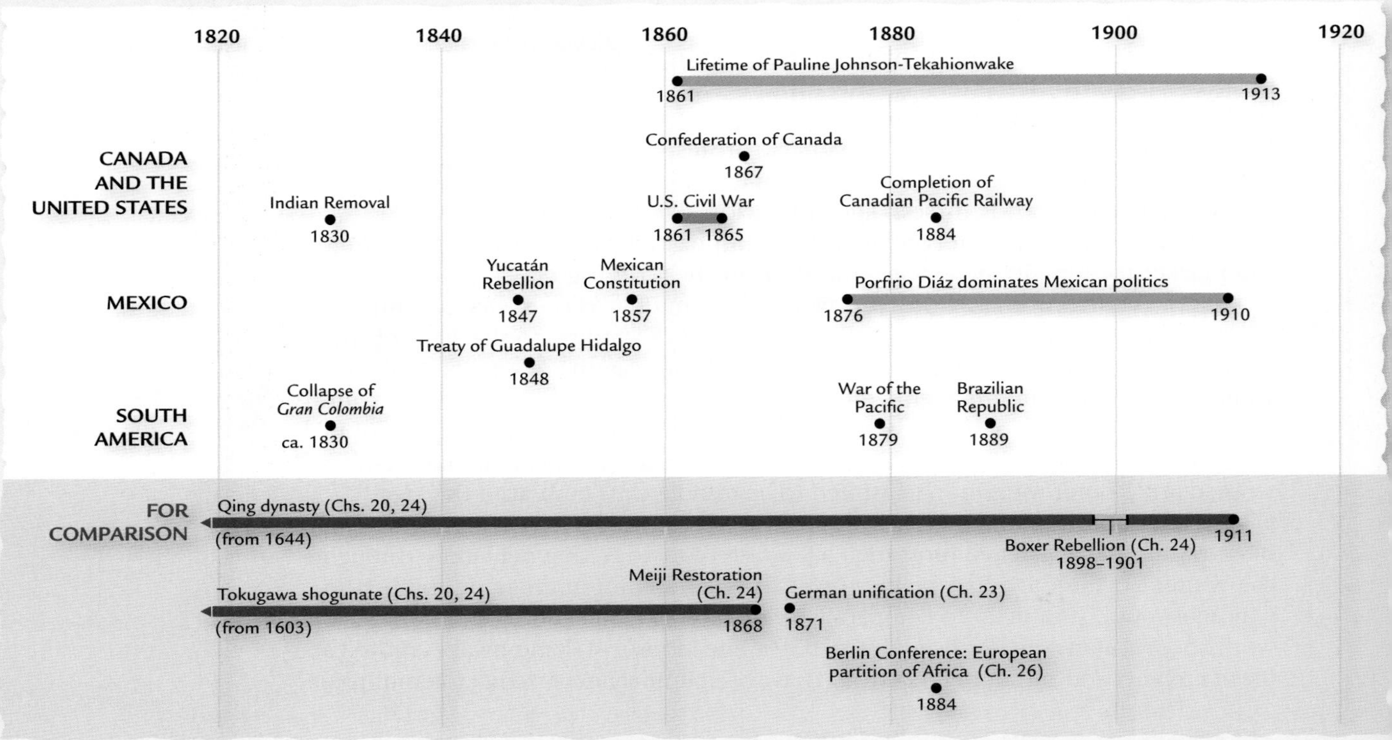

The Industrial Revolution thereby reinforced and expanded the power of Latin American elites, but the vast majority of people saw little benefit, losing land and control over their own labor as commercial plantations spread. Cities such as Buenos Aires and Mexico City grew dramatically, but they were dominated by the oligarchs who controlled export channels and access to foreign capital. Entering the twentieth century, Latin American economies had become more dependent than ever on the export of raw materials and the import of manufactured goods, often producing what they did not consume and consuming what they did not produce.

For much of the nineteenth century, the British were the dominant investors, adding the Latin American economies to their "informal empire." By the end of the century, however, the United States had overtaken Britain as the leading source of investment in Latin American economies and was asserting itself more aggressively in politics as well. In many nations, the power of local oligarchies became closely tied to American corporate interests, themselves actively supported by American political and, sometimes, military power. Such an imbalance of wealth and power in the Western Hemisphere found expression in the old complaint: "*Poor Mexico, so far from God and so close to the United States.*" Mexico's devastating territorial loss in 1848 was a preview of more aggressive U.S. imperialism to come.

At century's end, the United States projected its power not only across Latin America but across the Pacific as well, joining Europeans in a wave of empire building across the globe, the subject of the next chapter.

Key Terms

Pauline Johnson-Tekahionwake (746)
responsible government (748)
Confederation of Canada (749)
Canadian Pacific Railway (749)
Andrew Jackson (751)
Abraham Lincoln (751)
Reconstruction (754)
Gilded Age (755)
Porfirio Diáz (760)
Emiliano Zapata (760)
War of the Pacific (763)
Yucatán Rebellion (765)
Indian Removal Act (766)
Sitting Bull (766)
Métis Rebellions (767)

For Further Reference

Bender, Thomas. *A Nation Among Nations: America's Place in World History*. New York: Hill and Wang, 2006.

Bushnell, David, and Neill Macauley. *The Emergence of Latin America in the Nineteenth Century*. 2d ed. New York: Oxford University Press, 1994.

Conrad, Margaret. *A Concise History of Canada*. New York: Cambridge University Press, 2012.

Dickason, Olive Patricia. *Canada's First Nations*. 3d ed. New York: Oxford University Press, 2001.

Edwards, Rebecca. *New Spirits: America in the Gilded Age*. New York: Oxford University Press, 2005.

Fausto, Boris and Sergio Fausto. *A Concise History of Brazil*. 2d ed. New York: Cambridge University Press, 2014.

Fernández-Armesto, Felipe. *The Americas: A Hemispheric History*. New York: Modern Library, 2003.

Frazier, Donald S. *The United States and Mexico at War*. New York: Macmillan, 1998.

Gray, Charlotte. *Flint and Feather: The Life and Times of E. Pauline Johnson, Tekahionwake*. Toronto: HarperCollins, 2002.

Kolchin, Peter. *Unfree Labor: American Slavery and Russian Serfdom*. Cambridge, Mass.: Belknap, 1990.

McPherson, James. *Battle Cry of Freedom: The Civil War Era*. New York: Oxford University Press, 2003.

Wasserman, Mark. *Everyday Life and Politics in Nineteenth Century Mexico*. Albuquerque: University of New Mexico Press, 2000.

AP® Review Questions for Chapter 25

Multiple-Choice Questions

QUESTIONS 1–4 REFER TO THE FOLLOWING PASSAGE.

Capital projects always had to be financed from the outside—overwhelmingly, over the nineteenth century as a whole, from Britain, with significant inputs from the United States, Germany, and France.... Between 1870 and 1913, British investment in Latin America rose from £85 million to £757 million; this amounted to about two-thirds of the total foreign investment in the continent.... [In Mexico] Britain had been pre-empted by the United States. Mexico had been victimized by her northern neighbor through European-style business imperialism, for Yankee investments exceeded Britain's by half as much again.... From the 1890s, Yankee imperialism in Latin America would get more strident and far-reaching, with arbitration of Venezuela's border (1895), annexation of Puerto Rico and a protectorate over Cuba (1898), dismemberment of Colombia and administration of the Panama Canal Zone (1903), armed interventions in the Dominican Republic, Haiti, Mexico, and Nicaragua between 1905 and 1916, and incorporation of the Virgin Islands (1917).

—Felipe Fernández-Armesto, historian, *Millennium: A History of the Last Thousand Years*, 1995

1. Which of the following conclusions regarding European investment in Latin America is best supported by the passage?
   (A) The need for raw materials for the factories was the primary motivation for European investment.
   (B) Europeans were interested in establishing settler colonies in Latin America.
   (C) With the end of slavery, Europeans needed ready access to cheap labor.
   (D) Investment was a step to establishing trans-oceanic empires.

2. Which of the following examples most closely compares to the American conquest of Mexican territory in 1848?
   (A) The British and French expanding their influence in China through the Opium Wars
   (B) The expansion of U.S. and European influence over Tokugawa Japan
   (C) Russia expanding its land empire to the east
   (D) British colonization of Australia and New Zealand

3. Which of the following thinkers provided the best justification for American economic investment in Latin America?
   (A) Voltaire
   (B) Montesquieu
   (C) John Locke
   (D) Adam Smith

4. The passage is best understood in the context of which of the following?
   (A) Industrialized states practicing economic imperialism
   (B) European establishment of settler colonies
   (C) The decline of Spanish and Portuguese influence
   (D) State-sponsored industrialization

QUESTIONS 5–7 REFER TO THE FOLLOWING PASSAGE.

The newspapers now inform us that, in December, 1835, a treaty contracting for the exchange of all the Cherokee territory was pretended to be made by an agent on the part of the United States with some persons appearing on the part of the Cherokees; that the fact afterwards transpired that these deputies did by no means represent the will of the nation.... It now appears that the government of the United States choose to hold the Cherokees to this sham treaty, and are proceeding to execute the same. Almost the entire Cherokee Nation stand up and say, "This is not our act. Behold us. Here are we. Do not mistake that handful of deserters for us;" and the American President and the Cabinet, the Senate and the House of Representatives, neither hear these men nor see them, and are contracting to put this active nation into carts and boats, and to drag them over mountains and rivers to a wilderness at a vast distance beyond the Mississippi.

—Ralph Waldo Emerson, American author writing to President Martin Van Buren, 1836

5. The tone of the letter best reflects which of the following developments from 1750 to 1900?
   (A) American emulation of transoceanic European imperialism
   (B) Anti-imperial resistance within empires
   (C) Use of warfare and diplomacy to establish empires in Latin America
   (D) Establishment of a settler colony in the Americas

6. The argument that the Cherokee were protesting their treatment at the hands of the U.S. government is best understood in the context of
   (A) the development of an independent Cherokee state.
   (B) slave resistance challenging existing authorities in the Americas.
   (C) challenges to existing social relations influenced by Enlightenment ideas.
   (D) rebellions influenced by religious ideas.

7. Which of the following was an important continuity underlying the interactions between the United States and the Cherokee described in the passage?
   (A) Industrializing powers established transoceanic empires.
   (B) Social Darwinism facilitated and justified imperialism.
   (C) Imperialism influenced state formation, such as the acquisition of territory within the continental United States.
   (D) Increased discontent with imperial rule effected revolutionary movements.

QUESTIONS 8–10 REFER TO THE FOLLOWING PASSAGES.

The Federal Government shall foster European immigration; and may not restrict, limit or burden with any tax whatsoever, the entry into the Argentine territory of foreigners who arrive for the purpose of tilling the soil, improving industries, and introducing and teaching arts and sciences.

—Article 25, Constitution of Argentina, 1853

. . . From her beacon-hand
Glows world-wide welcome; her mild eyes command
The air-bridged harbor that twin cities frame.
"Keep ancient lands, your storied pomp!" cries she
With silent lips. "Give me your tired, your poor,
Your huddled masses yearning to breathe free,
The wretched refuse of your teeming shore.
Send these, the homeless, tempest-tost to me,
I lift my lamp beside the golden door!"

—Emma Lazarus, "The New Colossus," engraved on the pedestal of the Statue of Liberty, 1903

8. The two passages best support which of the following conclusions?
   (A) Migrants often created ethnic enclaves.
   (B) Migrants contributed to increasing global urbanization.
   (C) Migrants tended to be male.
   (D) Migrants relocated for a variety of reasons, including looking for work.

9. The first passage most directly contradicts which of the following developments of the period from 1750 to 1900?
   (A) Global capitalism relied on forced labor.
   (B) Receiving societies did not always embrace immigrants.
   (C) Many people benefitted economically from migration.
   (D) Migrants presented challenges to fostering national identities.

10. Which of the following contributed most *directly* to the migration patterns indicated in the passages?
   (A) Government reforms to lessen the effects of industrial capitalism
   (B) The development of the industrial working class
   (C) The global nature of trade and production
   (D) Major developments in transportation and communication

Short-Answer Questions

1. Answer parts A, B, and C.
   A. Explain ONE cause of nineteenth-century resistance to existing political authority in Latin America.
   B. Explain ONE political effect of nineteenth-century resistance to existing political authority in Latin America.
   C. Explain ONE social effect of nineteenth-century resistance to existing political authority in Latin America.

QUESTION 2 REFERS TO THE FOLLOWING IMAGE.

2. Answer parts A and B.
   A. Identify and explain TWO historical claims about changes to gender norms that can be supported based on the image.
   B. Identify ONE limitation of the image as a source of information about changes to gender norms.

26 The New Imperialism in Africa and Southeast Asia, 1830–1914

King Khama III

In the short space of twenty years, between 1870 and 1890, European powers drew colonial boundaries on their maps of Africa without the consent, and in most cases without even the knowledge, of those they planned to rule. In many places, Africans mounted spirited resistance, but the Europeans' technological superiority proved impossible to overcome. As the British poet Hilaire Belloc observed: "*Whatever else happens, we have got the Maxim gun, and they have not.*"*

During his lifetime, **King Khama III** (ca. 1837–1923) of the Bangwato (bahn-GWA-toe) people of southern Africa witnessed the great changes that came with the advance of the European empires. As a child, he was familiar with the occasional European hunter or missionary crossing the kingdom; as a king, he was forced to take drastic action to prevent the complete subjugation of his society:

> *At first we saw the white people pass, and we said, "They are going to hunt for elephant-tusks and ostrich-feathers, and then they will return where they came from." . . . But now when we see the white men we say "Jah! Jah!" ("Oh Dear!"). And now we think of the white people like rain, for they come down as a flood. When it rains too much, it puts a stop to us all. . . . It is not good for the black people that there should be a multitude of white men.*†

*Hilaire Belloc, *The Modern Traveler* (London: Edward Arnold, 1898), p. 41.

†King Khama of the Bangwato, quoted in Neil Parsons, *King Khama, Emperor Joe and the Great White Queen: Victorian Britain Through African Eyes* (Chicago: University of Chicago Press, 1998), p. 103.

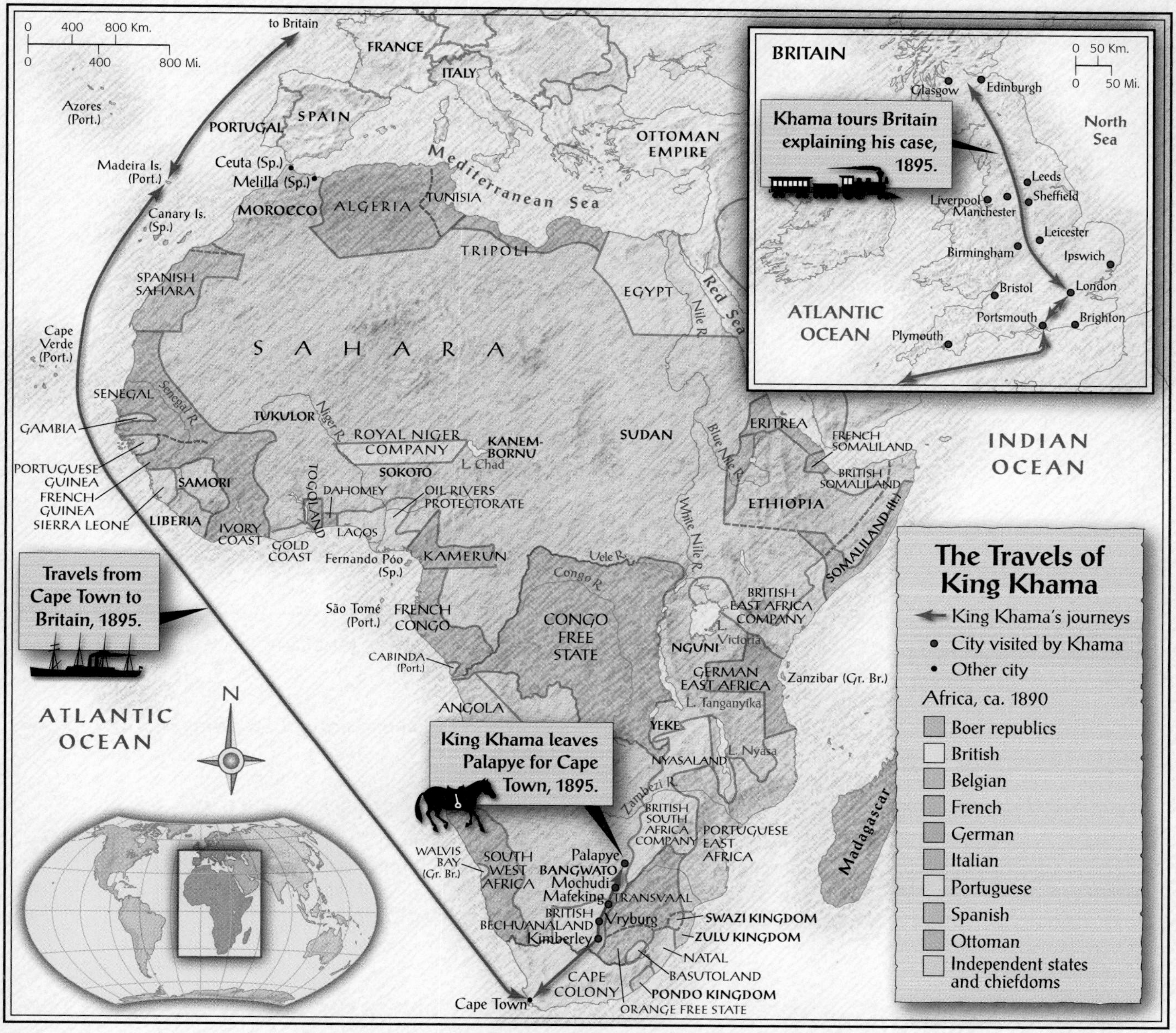

In 1895, King Khama (KAH-ma) and two neighboring kings began a long diplomatic mission, journeying by horse, railroad, and steamship from their homes in what is now Botswana, across South Africa, and all the way to London. They were in a difficult position. The frontier of white settlement already established in South Africa was moving northward, and the discovery of diamonds and gold had added further momentum to European expansion. The kings' goal was to have the British government declare a protectorate that would allow the Bangwato people to retain their farming and grazing lands and at least some control over their own affairs. The British public responded positively to their appeals, the colonial secretary argued in their favor, and they even had an audience with Queen Victoria.

King Khama III
(ca. 1837–1923) King of the Bangwato, a Tswana-speaking southern African group. His successful diplomacy helped establish the Bechuanaland protectorate, putting the Bangwato and other kingdoms under British rather than South African rule.

Thanks in great part to their effort and skill, the people of Botswana were later spared the agonies of *apartheid* ("separateness") as practiced in twentieth-century South Africa (see Chapter 30).

Still, Khama's success was only partial. Individual African societies might make better or worse deals with the forces of imperialism, but none could escape them. The late nineteenth century was the time of the New Imperialism, when powerful industrial nations vied for control of colonial territories and resources all across the globe. In Southeast Asia as well, Europeans were competing for colonies, while American, French, German, and British flags went up over scattered Polynesian islands, Meiji Japan took control over Korea and Taiwan, and the last sovereign Amerindian societies were defeated in the United States and Canada (see Chapters 24 and 25).

Applied science and industrial productivity generated the technological, military, and economic advances that powered the New Imperialism. Those societies in possession of the tools of empire—modern firearms, telegraphs, and steamships—were able to assert their power as never before. In Africa and Southeast Asia, local leaders were able to resist only by manipulating European rivalries for their own ends, though even such independent states as Siam and Ethiopia were incorporated into the unequal global system based on empire. Indigenous leaders around the world could relate to King Khama's predicament.

KEY CONCEPT QUESTIONS

- How did industrialization affect European New Imperialism? **(Key Concept 5.1)**
- How did Africans, such as the Zulu and the Xhosa, resist European imperialism? **(Key Concepts 5.2 and 5.3)**
- How did New Imperialism affect Southeast Asia? **(Key Concept 5.2)**
- How was the African experience with New Imperialism similar to and different from the Southeast Asian experience with New Imperialism? **(Key Concept 5.2)**

The New Imperialism

Europeans and Africans had interacted long before the Industrial Revolution. After the sixteenth century, especially in western Africa, their relationship increasingly focused on the slave trade, though direct European involvement was limited to coastal fortifications (see Chapter 19). Until the late nineteenth century, Europeans in Africa's interior included only a small group of settlers moving out from Cape Town and a few intrepid explorers.

The Industrial Revolution altered this pattern. By 1808, when the British Parliament abolished the slave trade, the economic needs of European economies were shifting: the slave-based West Indian sugar plantations were declining in importance, while factory owners sought inexpensive sources of raw materials and new export markets for their manufactures. In the mid-1800s, European explorers fanned out across the continent to assess its cultural and physical geography, identify its resources, and evaluate the transportation potential of its rivers. Pressed by evangelical Christians once involved in the abolitionist movement, the British government took an active role in stamping out the slave trade.

For most of the nineteenth century, African merchants and African political authorities facilitated the new trade connections as Europeans still largely remained at the coasts. Then, something dramatic happened. As King Khama noted, suddenly after 1870 Africans confronted *"a multitude of white men."* The era of **New Imperialism** had begun. Heightened competition among industrial states for African raw materials and markets was a major factor in European colonial expansion. Geopolitical rivalries, personal ambitions, and religious convictions were additional motives.

New Imperialism
An increase in European imperial activity during the late nineteenth century, caused primarily by increased competition between industrial states for raw materials and markets and by the rise of a unified Germany as a threat to the British empire.

At the same time, the "tools of empire" available to the invaders expanded beyond more accurate rifles. Steamships and telegraphs allowed quicker coordination between European centers of command and European officials on the ground. Because African rivers drop sharply from highlands to the sea, sailing ships could not travel far inland. But steam-powered ships could readily penetrate the continent's interior, and beginning in the 1890s, railroads too conveyed troops and colonial administrators. Advances in medical technology were also vital: in the 1840s it was discovered that quinine, from the bark of a South American tree, provided protection against malaria. Routes to the interior of Africa, once known as "the white man's graveyard," were now open.

Political and Economic Motives

Though the French and Portuguese had long-standing coastal enclaves, the British dominated European-African interactions for the first two-thirds of the nineteenth century. Long the world's most important maritime power, by this time the British had taken the lead in industrialization as well, aggressively pursuing new sources of raw materials and markets across the globe. Before 1870, however, the British were reluctant to add vast new holdings to their formal empire. In Latin America and in China, the British had asserted their economic dominance without the expense of direct colonial occupation, an approach supported by free-trade ideology. At first, it seemed that relations with Africa would follow that pattern of "informal empire."

- **CONTEXT&CONNECTIONS** In Latin American countries such as Argentina, national oligarchies maintained social, financial, and legal orders conducive to British capital investment, making colonial conquest unnecessary (see Chapter 25). In contrast, military invasion had been necessary to open China's doors to trade at the time of the *Opium Wars* (key term in Chapter 24), and Britain went on, with others, to divide China into "spheres of influence." Both Latin American and East Asian experiences thus differed from the direct colonial partition that affected Africans and Southeast Asians. ●

The global dynamic of European imperialism changed after 1871 with the unification of Germany, the fastest-growing industrial economy in the second half of the nineteenth century. Having defeated the French (see Chapter 23), the Germans wanted to assert their equality with the British by acquiring an empire of their own. For their part, the French wanted to restore their country's international standing after its humiliating defeat by the Germans. Imperial expansion in Africa and Southeast Asia accomplished that goal and gave legitimacy to the government of the French Third Republic.

With the United States and Japan also asserting themselves as military powers in Asia, by the 1880s the whole international system was becoming much more competitive; the liberal belief that every nation's economic needs could be met through free trade in open markets was starting to dim. European policymakers began to see secure and protected colonial markets as essential to further industrialization.

Imperial expansion in the age of the New Imperialism was closely tied to industrial capitalism, coinciding with the **Second Industrial Revolution** in the latter half of the nineteenth century. A rapid acceleration in industrial technology meant that electricity, steel, and petroleum superseded coal, steam, and iron. Large chemical and metal industries required secure access to natural resources like tin, oil, and rubber from around the world. Believing free markets were not adequate to their needs, nationalistic policymakers reintroduced mercantilist economic strategies from the early modern era (see Chapter 17).

Second Industrial Revolution
The more technologically sophisticated and capital intensive industrialism of the later nineteenth century. Electricity, steel, and petroleum superseded coal and iron, and large corporations now required secure access to natural resources from around the world.

AP® THEMES
What characterized the relationship between the state and multinational corporations during the era of New Imperialism?

Chartered companies—state-backed monopolies—were once again used to secure markets, sources of raw materials, and overseas investment opportunities. Just three decades after the British East India Company became defunct in 1858, a new charter was granted to the British South African Company. As in the eighteenth-century days of mercantilism, private corporations with their own armies and administrative personnel allowed European nations to pursue imperial expansion on the cheap.

Meanwhile, domestic politics spurred more active imperialism when politicians used patriotic appeals to cultivate popularity with newly enlarged electorates. Leaders of the French Third Republic appealed to "national honor" in extending their colonial frontiers. In Britain, the Conservative Party became the "party of empire," using appeals to pride in global dominance to win elections. German leaders believed that if the public's attention could be focused on military glory and imperial expansion, then nationalism would strengthen German unity and weaken the appeal of socialism.

Ideology and Personal Ambition

In the late nineteenth century, Europeans advanced the idea of a "civilizing mission"—that the "natives" needed European stewardship for their own "improvement"—cloaking their self-interest in humanitarian justifications. Earlier, the French and mid-Victorian Britons had approached Africa with a more liberal orientation emphasizing African potential for civilizational equality. Of course, their concept of "civilization" was ethnocentric: they sought to raise Africans and other "natives" to the "superior" European level. Still, they had placed no limit on what Africans with proper education and social circumstances might achieve. Missionaries inspired by the abolitionist movement focused on the salvation of African souls and the redemption of the continent from spiritual practices they regarded as primitive superstition, but many thought it would be Africans themselves who would ultimately uplift the continent spiritually and materially.

The career of **David Livingstone** (1813–1873), the great Scottish missionary, exemplifies this belief in Africans' intellectual and spiritual capacity. Livingstone spent the better part of his life exploring the continent and preaching Christianity to its people. His dream was to have African Christians take over positions of church leadership. In pursuit of this goal, he spent time among the Bangwato, serving as a tutor to one of the kings who accompanied Khama to London.

David Livingstone
(1813–1873) Scottish missionary and explorer idolized in Britain for his commitment to the spiritual and moral salvation of Africans.

On the other side of the continent, Samuel Ajayi Crowther, the first African bishop of the Church of England, was fulfilling Livingstone's goal. Born in what is now western Nigeria, Crowther was sold into slavery in 1821. By then the British were committed to abolition, and the Royal Navy seized the Portuguese ship on which he was held captive, dropping the twelve-year-old off at Freetown in Sierra Leone, earlier established as a home for such "re-captives." After education in Sierra Leone and England, and having served on a mission to the Niger River, Crowther was ordained as an Anglican priest. One of his enduring contributions to African Christianity was his translation of the Christian texts into his own native Yoruba and other African languages.

AP® THEMES

What were the changes and continuities in the ways Christianity was practiced as it spread among African peoples?

In 1864, Crowther became the Anglican bishop of West Africa. But some white missionaries resented his appointment and refused to follow his directives. Unlike Livingstone, they viewed blacks as permanent children, incapable of handling high office. Such racism forced Crowther into retirement, and an English bishop replaced him. In the harsher racial environment fostered by the New Imperialism, the dream of African church leadership withered.

Some African Christians responded to clerical racism by rejecting European religious authority altogether. In founding their own churches, African Protestants often looked to the ancient Ethiopian Church for inspiration, stressing the historical fact that African Christianity could flourish under African control. (See the feature "Movement of Ideas Through Primary Sources: Pan-Africanism and African Identity.") African Catholics, in contrast, did not have the option of autonomy, bound as they were to the authority of Rome. It would be many years before African priests and bishops would rise to prominence.

Bishop Crowther's story shows that by the later nineteenth century liberal optimism in African capacities was fading. By the end of the century, Social Darwinism, the idea that humanity consists of a set of clearly demarcated racial groups arranged along a hierarchy of ability, had become Europe's conventional wisdom. Now most white people saw themselves as sitting atop an unchangeable hierarchy of races, a belief that justified colonial expansion as part of the natural order of things.

● **CONTEXT&CONNECTIONS** The shock of the *Indian Revolt of 1857* (Chapter 24) had contributed to the hardening of British racial attitudes. ●

The change in later Victorian times is shown in the contrast between David Livingstone and the young journalist and explorer Henry Morton Stanley (1841–1904), who set off to find Livingstone in Central Africa when he was feared lost. Unlike Livingstone, who lived peacefully among Africans and acknowledged their help and hospitality, Stanley organized his expedition along military lines, treating Africans so harshly that the British government insisted that he stop flying the Union Jack. Stanley later traced the great Congo River from its source deep in Central Africa to its outlet on the Atlantic and, having been rebuffed by Britain, formed an alliance with the ambitious **King Leopold II of Belgium** (r. 1865–1909) to profit from his discoveries.

King Leopold II of Belgium

(r. 1865–1909) Ignited a "scramble for Africa" when he claimed the large area of Central Africa he called the Congo Free State. The ruthless exploitation of Congolese rubber by Leopold's agents led to millions of deaths.

Belgium was a small kingdom that had become independent only in 1830. Leopold envied Queen Victoria's vast empire and, convinced that great wealth could be gained in Africa, declared, *"I must have my share of this magnificent African cake!"* Against a background of intensified competition for markets and raw materials for industry and the surging nationalism of European politics, Leopold's initiative to use the Congo River as a gateway to a vast Central African empire was the spark that set off a mad rush for African territory.

Concerned that Leopold's imperialism might destabilize the balance of power in Europe, Germany's Otto von Bismarck brought together representatives of the European colonial powers at the **Berlin Conference** in 1884 to establish

Berlin Conference

(1884) Conference organized by the German chancellor Otto von Bismarck in which representatives of the major European states divided Africa among themselves.

Pan-Africanism and African Identity

Pan-Africanism stresses the shared destiny of people of African descent around the world, especially between continental Africans and people of African descent in the Americas. Among the first great Pan-African thinkers was Edward Wilmot Blyden (1832–1912). A child of free blacks from the Virgin Islands, Blyden spent many years living in West Africa.

In his early writings, Blyden focused on the potential for African uplift that would follow from a significant repatriation of American blacks back to their continent of origin. He lived in Liberia, an independent republic founded by free American blacks in 1847, and in Sierra Leone, where the British colony sent "re-captives" they had liberated from Atlantic slave ships.

Later, after European conquest and partition, Blyden, while himself a Christian, came to emphasize Islam as a more suitable pathway toward literacy and civilizational progress for Africans, adding the study of Arabic to his educational recommendations. (In Liberia, Blyden taught Arabic as well as classical Greek and Latin.)

By regarding all people of African descent as partaking of a common destiny and by emphasizing higher education as a pathway toward racial improvement, Blyden anticipated the projects of later Pan-Africanists, including the influential African American writer and activist W. E. B. Du Bois (1868–1963). Both men stressed the need for black racial solidarity to overcome the political disabilities and psychic traumas resulting from slavery, racism, and colonization.

› Historical Thinking Skill:
ARGUMENTATION What reasons does Blyden give for people of African descent to be wary of abandoning African identity?

› Historical Thinking Skill:
COMPARISON What differences does Blyden identify between the impact of the conversion of Africans to Islam and the conversion of Africans to Christianity?

Source: *Black Spokesman: Selected Published Writings of Edward Wilmot Blyden*, ed. Hollis R. Lynch (New York: Humanities Press, 1971).

Race and the African Personality

[F]or every one of us—there is a special work to be done ... a work for the Race to which we belong. It is a great Race—great in its vitality, in its powers of endurance and its prospect of perpetuity. It has passed through the fiery furnace of centuries of indigenous barbarism and foreign slavery and yet it remains unconsumed. Well, now, there is a responsibility which our personality, our membership in this Race involves. It is sad to think that there are some Africans, especially among those who have enjoyed the advantages of foreign training, who are blind enough to the radical facts of humanity as to say, "Let us do away with the sentiment of Race. Let us do away with our African personality and be lost, if possible, in another Race."

That is as wise ... as to say let us do away with gravitation, with heat and cold and sunshine and rain. Of course, the other Race in which these persons would be absorbed is the dominant Race, before which, in cringing self-surrender and ignoble self-suppression, they lie in prostrate admiration.... Your place has been assigned to you in the Universe as Africans, and there is no room for you as anything else....

Therefore, honour and love your Race. Be yourselves, as God intended you to be or he would not have made you thus.... If you are not yourself, if you surrender your personality, you have nothing left to give the world.... There is hardly anything new in a material sense, that the so-called civilized African can contribute to the world's resources, but if his individuality is preserved and developed on right or righteous lines, he will bring intellectual and spiritual contributions which Humanity will gladly welcome.

Christianity, Islam, and Africa

Having enjoyed exceptional advantages for observation and comparison in the United States, the West Indies, South America, Egypt, Syria, West and Central Africa, we are compelled, however reluctantly, to [say that] wherever the Negro is found in Christian lands, his leading trait is ... servility. He is slow and unprogressive. Individuals may be found here and there of extraordinary intelligence, enterprise and energy, but there is no Christian community of Negroes anywhere which is self-reliant and independent....

On the other hand, there are numerous Negro [Muslim] communities and states in Africa which are self-reliant, productive, independent and dominant, supporting, without the countenance or patronage of the parent country, Arabia, whence they derived them, their political, literary, and ecclesiastical institutions....

Now, what has produced this difference in the effects of the two systems upon the Negro race? [Islam] found its Negro converts at home in a state of freedom and independence.... When it was offered to them they were at liberty to choose for themselves.... [They] become Muslims from choice and conviction, and bring all the manliness of their former condition to the maintenance and support of their new creed.... [T]he Arab superstructure has been superimposed on a permanent indigenous infrastructure; so that what really took place, when the Arab met the Negro in his own home, was a healthy amalgamation, and not an absorption or an undue repression ... shaping many of its traditional customs to suit the milder and more conciliatory disposition of the Negro.

Christianity, on the other hand, came to the Negro as a slave, or at least as a subject race in a foreign land. Along with the Christian teaching, he and his children received lessons on their utter and permanent inferiority and subordination to their instructors.... The religion of Jesus was embraced by them as their only consolation in their deep disasters.... It found them down-trodden, oppressed, scorned; it soothed their sufferings [and] subdued their hearts.... These are great advantages, but ... all tendencies to independent individuality were repressed and destroyed. Their ideas and aspirations only in conformity with the views and tastes of those who held rule over them.... [N]o amount of allegiance to the Gospel relieved the Christian Negro from the degradation of wearing the chain he received with it.... Everywhere in Christian lands he plays, at the present moment, the part of the slave, ape, or puppet....

The Mohammedan Negro has felt nothing of the withering power of caste. There is nothing in his colour or race to debar him from the highest privileges, social or political, to which any other Muslim can attain. Mohammedan history abounds with examples of distinguished Negroes. The eloquent *Azan*, or "Call to Prayer" ... was first uttered by a Negro, Bilâl by name, whom Mohammed ... appointed the first Muezzin....

Now, it must be evident that Negroes trained under the influence of a [Muslim] social and literary atmosphere must have a deeper self-respect ... than those trained under the blighting influence of caste, and under the guidance of a literature in which it has been the fashion for more than two hundred years to caricature the African, to ridicule his personal peculiarities, and to impress him with a sense of perpetual and hopeless inferiority.

The sympathy ... between the Arab missionary and the African is more complete than that between European and the Negro. With every wish, no doubt, to the contrary, the European seldom or never gets over the feeling of distance, if not of repulsion, which he experiences on first seeing the Negro.... The African convert ... acquires a very low opinion of himself, learns to depreciate and deprecate his own personal characteristics, and loses that "sense of the dignity of human nature" which observant travelers have noticed in the Mohammedan Negro.

rules for the partition of Africa. No Africans were present. The European delegates declared that the boundaries of European possessions in Africa would be recognized only where the claimant established *"effective occupation."* For Africans, this meant twenty years of constant warfare and instability as European governments launched a wave of invasions to secure the effective occupation of the territories they claimed, setting off the "scramble for Africa." Millions of Africans would die.

Africa and the New Imperialism

AP® THEMES

What technological advances helped European nations establish a greater presence in Africa?

As late as 1878, Europe's colonial presence was almost entirely restricted to the African coast (see Map 26.1). The all-out scramble for control of African territory was therefore something new. In contrast to India, where British power had been expanding since the eighteenth century, most Africans confronted European power only *after* the development of industrial technology like machine guns, field cannon, telegraphs, and steamships. The suddenness of the onslaught caught Africans off guard. Should they fight back? Seek diplomatic options? Ally themselves with the intruders? African leaders tried all of these options, with little success.

Although European imperialists reduced Africa to a set of simple stereotypes, with "tribal Africa" representing the "heart of darkness," in reality it was a continent of immense cultural and geographic complexity. Africa's own historical dynamics, including the rise of Muslim states in West Africa, the creation of the Zulu empire in the far south, and the expanding nineteenth-century trade in ivory and slaves in East Africa, are an essential context for understanding Europe's partition of the continent.

Western and Eastern Africa

After the abolition of the transatlantic slave trade, European merchants shifted their business in West Africa from the purchase of human beings to the search for commodities needed to supply expanding factories at home. While Egypt became a major source of raw cotton for British industry (see Chapter 23), the most important product coming from sub-Saharan Africa was palm oil for use as an industrial lubricant. Starting in the 1820s, African farmers planted and processed oil products for the export market, and many West African merchants became wealthy in this trade. Factory-produced cloth and iron goods were becoming cheaper at the same time, as higher demand was increasing the price Europeans would pay for palm oil. At least in some regions, Africans found the terms of trade moving in their favor.

Initially, as West African economies became more integrated into world markets, political power remained with African kingdoms and chiefdoms. In an influential essay in 1868, a British-educated African surgeon named John Africanus Horton called for African kingdoms to reform themselves by incorporating Western constitutional practices, as their contemporaries were doing in Japan (see Chapter 24). Like Bishop Crowther, Dr. Horton had established his career at a time when it was thought that the future lay with European-educated Africans. Now, as the forces of conquest gathered, Horton's idea that African traditions might be merged with Western models to secure the continent's progress quickly became obsolete.

- **CONTEXT&CONNECTIONS** European-educated African Christians like John Africanus Horton, ambitious to reconcile local cultures and institutions with the progress and

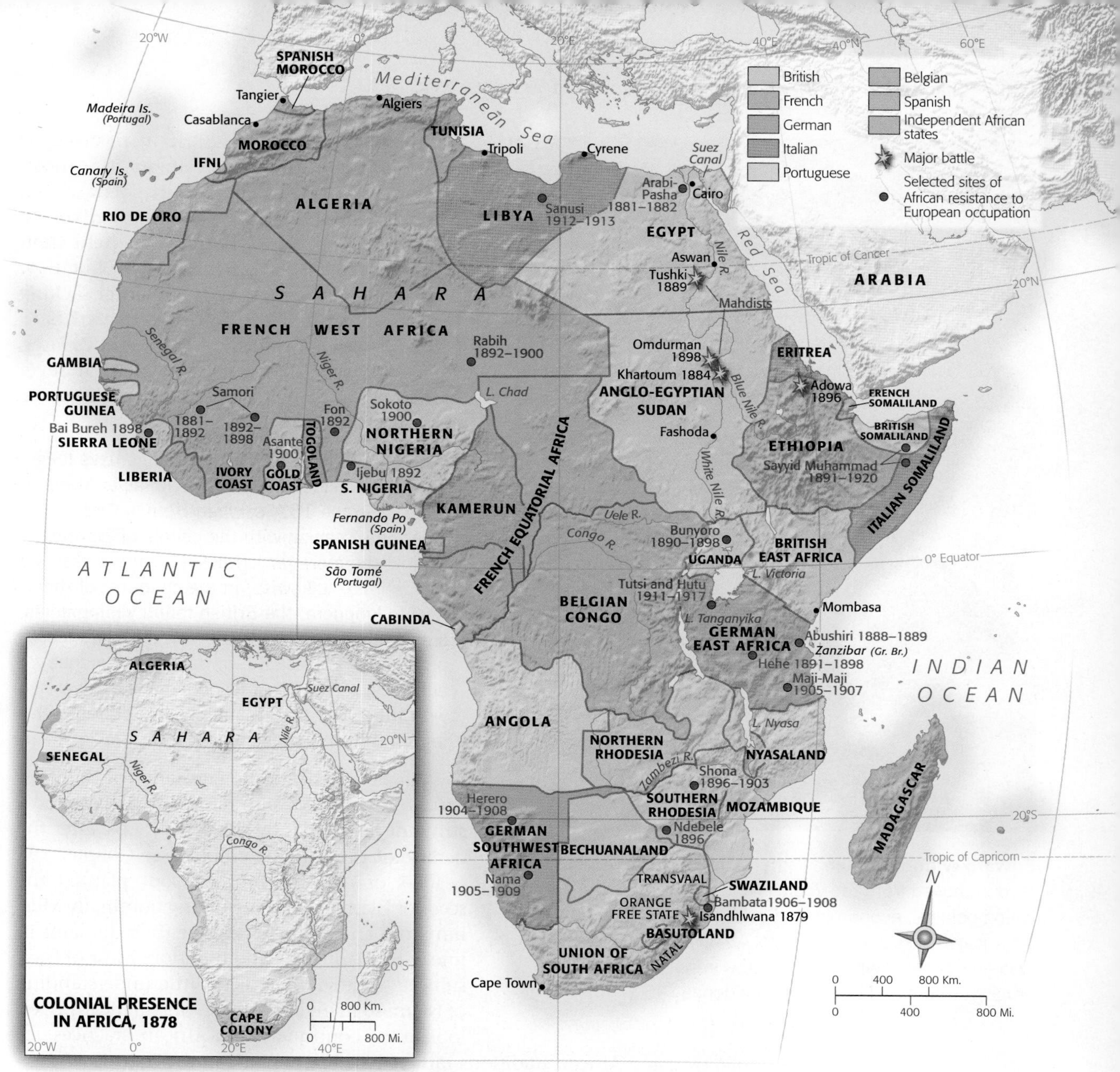

Map 26.1 Africa, 1878 and 1914 The dramatic expansion of European imperialism in Africa is seen in the comparison of maps from 1878 and 1914. Before the "scramble for Africa" the European colonial presence was largely limited to small coastal enclaves, with some movement inland only in Algeria and the Cape Colony. By 1914, Europeans dominated the entire continent, with only Liberia and Ethiopia retaining their independence. The British were the main power in eastern and southern Africa, the French in western and northern Africa, and the Belgians in Central Africa.

modernity they associated with Europe, had much in common with *Rammohun Roy* and the earlier Bengal Renaissance (Chapter 20). In India as well as Africa, these reformers' efforts were stifled by imperial officials and other whites for whom, by the end of the century, racial hierarchies had become fixed and immutable. ●

Historical/Corbis

Edward Wilmot Blyden Father of modern Pan-Africanism, Blyden moved from the Virgin Islands to West Africa, advocating political, economic, and cultural cooperation between American blacks and continental Africans. Above all, Blyden was an educator who stressed the importance of black empowerment and black self-confidence.

In 1874, for example, Britain reversed its earlier policy of noninvolvement in Africa's interior by attacking the **Asante kingdom**, the dominant power in the West African forest. In the 1820s, Asante's armies had held their own in a skirmish with the British, but now they were badly outgunned. Still, after sacking the Asante capital, the British retreated back to the coast, only returning two decades later, when the "scramble for Africa" was at fever pitch, to complete their conquest (discussed later in this section).

• **CONTEXT&CONNECTIONS** Conquerors have long used the "divide and rule" tactic, as in Mesoamerica in the 1520s, when Hernán Cortés allied the Spanish with the people of Tlaxcala against the more powerful *Aztec empire* (see Chapter 15). Likewise, in the conquest of the Asante kingdom, the British found willing allies among chiefdoms that had long resisted incorporation by the Asante. In both Mesoamerica and West Africa, local leaders made a "deal with the devil" that ultimately left them powerless in the face of alien rule. •

Further north, in the grasslands of the West African interior, Muslim reformers had created a string of new states by the early 1800s, after the demise of the Songhai empire (see Chapter 19). Leaders of religious brotherhoods planted the seeds of Islamic reform by urging nominally Muslim kings and emirs to regulate their domains in line with Islamic law and tradition. Most of their subjects were villagers with little understanding of Islam, so many leaders had pragmatically overlooked the continuation of African practices, for example, by using African traditions rather than Islamic jurisprudence in legal decision making. The origins of the jihad movements of nineteenth-century West Africa lay in reformers' criticism of such compromises with African traditions.

Asante kingdom

Dominant power in the West African forest in the eighteenth and early nineteenth centuries. The Asante capital was sacked by British forces in 1874 and again in 1896. In 1900, Yaa Asantewa's War represented a final attempt to expel the British.

One of the most important West African jihad leaders was Shehu Usuman dan Fodio (1754–1817). In what is now northern Nigeria, dan Fodio called for local emirs to put their governments in line with Islamic law. When one emir tried to assassinate him, Usuman dan Fodio (OO-soo-mahn dahn FOH-dee-oh) retreated to the desert, built a large army, conquered his enemies, and consolidated the emirates into the new Sokoto (SOH-kuh-toh) caliphate. From here the jihadist impulse spread both east and west.

Throughout the nineteenth century, West African Muslim populations became stricter in their practice, and Islam gained large numbers of new adherents. Nana Asma'u, Shehu Usuman's daughter, established an enduring reputation across the Sahel for establishing Islamic schools and advocating religious education for women. Her writings in Arabic and Hausa, especially her poems, are still widely read.

At first, the leaders of West African jihadist states were focused on reforming their own Muslim societies and paid little attention to Europeans. However, when the French began to move further up the Senegal River in the 1870s, territorial ambitions clashed and conflict followed.

The West African Muslim who organized the most sustained resistance to the French invasion was **Samori Toure** (ca. 1830–1900). From a relatively humble merchant background, Samori Toure (sam-or-REE too-RAY) built a new state on the upper Niger by training soldiers to use imported rifles. At first his ambitions were merely political, but in 1884 he declared himself to be *"commander of the faithful,"* leader of a jihad against lax Muslims and unbelievers. Even then, Samori avoided confronting the French, focusing instead on controlling trade routes in slaves, salt, and gold. But once the French had conquered his neighbors, they turned their firepower on him.

Samori Toure
(ca. 1830–1900)
Founder of a major state in West Africa who adopted the pose of a jihadist leader in competition with neighboring kingdoms. After being forced into confrontation by the French, he launched a long but unsuccessful guerrilla campaign against them.

Unable to prevail in conventional warfare, in 1891 Samori retreated to the east with his army and launched a grueling guerrilla campaign. But success at guerilla war requires support from the local population. Samori's forces had none, earning the hatred of the local people by taking whatever they needed. Cut off from access to imported ammunition and gunpowder, Samori's soldiers learned to manufacture their own from local materials but eventually succumbed. After the French captured and exiled Samori in 1893, they were masters from the Senegal to the Niger Rivers.

The French march to the east threatened British control of Egypt and the Nile Valley. British forces thus moved to achieve "effective occupation" over the savanna region still dominated by the Sokoto caliphate. After Usuman dan Fodio's death, the caliphate became decentralized into a number of separate emirates, so the British did not face the combined armies of a unified caliphate. British rifles and machine guns mowed down the emirs' cavalry charges, and British field cannon easily breached their city walls. Some emirs fought, some fled, and some surrendered, as British forces took control of what is now northern Nigeria.

In West Africa, the lack of alliances among African peoples facilitated European imperialism. Without organizational or ideological foundations for a broader unity, African leaders dealt only with the local manifestations of the scramble for Africa. Possessing a broader overview of African developments, the Europeans used their superior communications technology and geographical knowledge to great advantage.

The nineteenth century was even more violent in East Africa, where a new slave trade began even as the Atlantic trade was diminishing. Along the coast, the Swahili city-states had long focused outward, on Indian Ocean trade (see Chapter 16). In the early nineteenth century, however, interior peoples began to bring increased supplies of ivory to the coast in response to rising demand in the West for billiard balls, piano keys, combs, and other products manufactured from expensive elephant tusks. Soon well-armed caravans, often financed by Indian bankers and organized by Arab or Swahili merchants, were marching into the interior. These militarized trading ventures decimated elephant herds and, even more tragically, intensified the East African slave trade. Appeals from David Livingstone and other European observers to end the Arab-dominated trade provided a strong humanitarian argument for greater British involvement in the interior of East Africa.

By the 1880s, the British and the Germans were scrambling for East African territory, especially Lake Victoria (as the British renamed it) and the headwaters of the Nile. Already devastated by the slave trade, East Africans were unable to stop them.

Southern Africa

In southern Africa as well, the dynamics of African history intersected with European imperialism. Long before the Dutch established their settlement at Cape Town (see Chapter 16), the ancestors of King Khama and his people—Bantu-speaking farmers, herders, and ironworkers—had populated the land.

● **CONTEXT&CONNECTIONS** About four thousand years ago, the distant Bantu-speaking ancestors of peoples like Khama's Bangwato were moving outward from the region of Eastern Nigeria in a complex series of migrations. Some moved south into the Central African rain forest, and others went east to the *Great Lakes region* (Chapter 19), then southward through the eastern savannas. Bantu speakers, farming peoples with relatively dense populations, large herds of cattle, and iron tools, then displaced indigenous foraging societies as the dominant cultural force across southern Africa. ●

In the late eighteenth century, drought led small chiefdoms in southern Africa to band together to secure permanent water sources. The most successful of the new states was the Zulu empire of **Shaka** (r. 1820–1828). He formed a standing army of soldiers from different clans, emphasizing their loyalty to him and to the Zulu state rather than to their own chiefdoms, and chose his generals on the basis of merit rather than chiefly status. Young women were organized into agricultural regiments, and no one was allowed to marry without Shaka's permission.

Shaka
(r. 1820–1828) Founder and ruler of the Zulu empire. Zulu military tactics revolutionized warfare in southern Africa. Through the *mfecane*, or "crushing," Shaka violently absorbed many surrounding societies into his empire.

Shaka's conquests were known as the *mfecane* (mm-fuh-KAHN-ay), "the crushing." Many chiefdoms were violently absorbed into the Zulu empire, though some neighboring chiefs submitted voluntarily. In either case, conquered peoples were merged into Zulu society and became Zulu, as what had been a small chiefdom became a mighty nation. The mfecane set in motion a chain reaction as other leaders copied Zulu military tactics and carried the frontier of warfare a thousand miles north. The Bangwato and other societies in the interior fled, abandoning much of their land.

At the same time that the mfecane was disrupting southern African societies, descendants of earlier Dutch and French colonists, called Boers, were seeking land for further expansion. The Boers moved into territories temporarily depopulated in the wake of Zulu warfare, causing frontier conflicts that alarmed British authorities.

● **CONTEXT&CONNECTIONS** In the twentieth century, the Boers would more commonly be referred to as Afrikaners. They speak the Afrikaans language, derived from the seventeenth-century Dutch used by their ancestors when they left Cape Town to strike out on the frontier (see Chapter 16). It was Afrikaner nationalists who created the racist *apartheid* state after 1948 (Chapter 30), but who later compromised with the African National Congress and *Nelson Mandela* (Chapter 31) to build a multiracial, democratic South Africa. ●

Cecil Rhodes
(1853–1902) British entrepreneur, mining magnate, head of the British South Africa Company, and prime minister of the Cape Colony; played a major role in the expansion of British territory in southern Africa.

The British were a new factor in southern Africa in the early 1800s, having taken Cape Town from the Dutch during the Napoleonic Wars. Though their main concern was the security of Cape Town and the maritime route to India, they became embroiled on the frontier, where the Boers, searching for land and resenting British interference, came into conflict with African societies.

The Boers had never been able to subdue African resistance to their encroachment, but British firepower now overwhelmed some Xhosa (KOH-suh) chiefdoms, which lost rich grazing lands to the colonists. Neither negotiation nor military resistance could stem the European tide. Contact with colonial society also deeply divided Xhosa society. Traditionalists saw those Xhosa who converted to Christianity and grew crops for colonial markets as having abandoned their own people and traditions.

Then disaster struck. A cattle disease, inadvertently introduced by the Europeans in the 1850s, wiped out large numbers of Xhosa cattle. Facing starvation as well as invasion, some Xhosa turned to the prophecies of a young woman, Nongqawuse (nawng-ka-WOO-say) (ca. 1840–1898), who said the spirits told her that if the people slaughtered their remaining cattle, ancestral warriors would return, evil would be purged from the land, and new cattle herds would emerge from the ground. Belief in the power of ancestors, and in the power of certain women to communicate with them, was traditional to the Xhosa. But the idea that the resurrection of the dead would accompany a new era of peace was borrowed from Methodist missionaries, an example of syncretism (see Chapter 18).

Xhosa Cattle Killing (1856–1857) A large cattle die-off in Africa caused by a European disease. Some Xhosa accepted Nongqawuse's prophecies that if the people cleansed themselves and killed their cattle their ancestors would return and bring peace and prosperity. The result was famine and Xhosa subjection to the British.

Lacking other means of resistance, many Xhosa followed Nongqawuse's prophecy and killed their cattle. When the prophecy did not come true, hunger spread throughout the land. The **Xhosa Cattle Killing** of 1856–1857 ensured the success of British conquest. Over one hundred thousand African lives were lost, while the survivors were incorporated into Britain's Cape Colony.

Unlike the Xhosa, the Zulu and most other southern African societies retained their sovereignty into the 1870s. Their colonial fate was not determined until mineral discoveries—diamonds in 1868 and gold in 1884—combined with the "effective occupation" required by the Berlin Conference finally motivated the British to conquer the rest of the South African interior.

In 1879, British authorities issued an ultimatum demanding that the Zulu king Cetshwayo disband his regiments. Cetshwayo (chet-SWAY-yoh) refused to comply. Zulu warriors did defeat the British at the major Battle of Isandhlwana (ee-san-DLWAH-nah), but like the Battle of Little Bighorn (see Chapter 25), this defeat only made the invaders more determined. Zulu warriors had been trained to rush the enemy in dense regimental ranks, a successful tactic under Shaka that British cannon and machine guns rendered suicidal. Soon the British sacked the Zulu capital and sent Cetshwayo into exile.

The main figure of the New Imperialism in southern Africa was **Cecil Rhodes** (1853–1902), a mining magnate who advocated a British empire

The Granger Collection, NYC

Cecil Rhodes Victorian imperialist Cecil Rhodes dreamed of British imperial control of eastern and southern Africa "from Cape to Cairo." Combining political and economic clout, Rhodes was prime minister of the Cape Colony, owner of some of the world's richest gold and diamond mines, and head of the British South Africa Company. He later endowed the Rhodes Scholarship program to bring elite Americans of British descent to Oxford University in England so that the United States might share Britain's imperial purpose.

"from Cape to Cairo." His British South Africa Company (BSAC) was a chartered company with its own army and ambitions for conquest. It was to avoid annexation by the BSAC that Khama traveled to London.

Earlier the Boers, resentful of British intrusion and proud of their independence, had created several republics in the northern interior of South Africa. British recognition of their independence would not long endure, for in 1884 the greatest gold discovery in world history took place right in the heart of Boer territory. The clash between Boer aspirations for independence and Cecil Rhodes' drive for gold inevitably led to the South African War (1899–1902).

The British had no trouble taking control of the towns and railway lines, but the Boer combatants blended into the civilian population and launched guerrilla attacks in the countryside. To separate civilians from soldiers, the British put Boer civilians into "concentration camps" (the first use of that term). Over twenty thousand, many of them women and children, died of illness. Though the South African War was between the British and the Boers, tens of thousands of Africans were also killed.

Union of South Africa

Self-governing dominion within the British empire created in 1910 from a number of British colonies and Boer republics after the South African War. This compromise protected both British mining and Boer agriculture at the expense of African interests.

The British won the war but then compromised with their defeated foes. The **Union of South Africa** (1910) was created by joining British colonies with former Boer republics under a single constitution, creating, as in Canada, a self-governing dominion within the British empire (see Chapter 25). British and Boer leaders compromised by emphasizing what they had in common: the need for cheap African labor.

British mine owners and Boer farmers thus both embraced the Union as "an alliance of gold and maize." In 1913 the Native Land Act, passed by the new, all-white South African parliament, limited Africans to "native reserves" that included only a tiny proportion of their traditional landholdings. The goal was to strip indigenous communities of their agricultural self-sufficiency and thus drive Africans to work in mines and on white farms at the lowest possible pay, laying the economic foundations for what would later be called apartheid.

● **CONTEXT&CONNECTIONS** Two distinct types of European colonialism developed in Africa. In settler colonies like South Africa, restrictions on African landholding drove Africans onto European farms and into European mines to work for very low wages. French Algeria, British Rhodesia (today's Zimbabwe), and the "white highlands" of Kenya were other settler colonies. Elsewhere, as across West Africa, Africans retained control of their own land and labor while growing commercial crops for export and paying taxes to the colonial state. It was in settler colonies that decolonization after the Second World War would be most violent (see Chapter 30). ●

AP® THEMES

How did European imperialism in Africa reinforce European ideas about race?

Because of King Khama's negotiations with the British government, his people were not part of the Union of South Africa and were ruled instead by the British Colonial Office. The Zulu and the Xhosa, meanwhile, like other Africans incorporated into South Africa, experienced the harshest form of colonial racism. As mineworkers and low-wage laborers on settler farms, they struggled at the lowest level of the global economy.

Meanwhile, in neighboring German Southwest Africa (today's Namibia), another chilling precedent was being set for the twentieth century. In 1904, after a Herero rebellion was put down by superior European firepower, the German commander ordered that the Herero be driven into the Kalahari Desert and prevented from returning. Tens of thousands of them died in the century's first *genocide*, an attempt to destroy an entire people and their culture.

African Resistance to Conquest

Between 1880 and 1900, European powers occupied and partitioned Africa. France and Britain held the largest African empires; Portugal and Germany each had substantial territories in the east and south; Italy and Spain were relatively minor players; and King Leopold of Belgium claimed the vast Congo in the center of the continent.

In spite of European technological superiority, Africans fought back. The Nile Valley was one arena of resistance. Its strategic value increased with the construction of the **Suez Canal** between the Mediterranean and the Red Sea in 1869. Financed by French and English capital, the canal became the main shipping route between Europe and Asia.

Suez Canal
(1869) French-designed canal built between the Mediterranean and the Red Seas that greatly shortened shipping times between Europe and Asia; dominated by European economic interests.

The Egyptian *khedive* (a descendant of Muhammad Ali, see Chapter 23) thought that revenue from the canal would allow Egypt to maintain its independence. But cotton prices, and Egyptian government revenue, dropped sharply after 1865, when the end of the American Civil War brought U.S. cotton back onto the world market. Unable to pay the country's debts, the khedive was forced to sell Egypt's shares in the Suez Canal to the British and to accept European oversight of government finances. European officers were imposed on the Egyptian military, which was reorganized as an Anglo-Egyptian force.

In 1882, nationalist Egyptian military officers rebelled against the khedive and his European backers but the British quickly suppressed the uprising and then forced the khedive to accept a governor-general to oversee the Egyptian government. The British thus came to dominate Egypt, much as they dominated the "princely states" in India (see Chapter 24), taking real power into their own hands while allowing indigenous rulers their traditional titles and luxurious lifestyles.

Once in control of Egypt, the British needed to secure the Upper Nile Valley as well. Here they faced resistance from a jihadist state in Sudan, where a cleric named **Muhammad Ahmad** (1844–1885) proclaimed himself to be **the Mahdi** (MAH-dee), the "guided one" that some Muslims believe will come to announce the end of days and the final judgment of humankind. In 1881, he declared a holy war against Egypt, which also brought him into conflict with Britain. The Mahdi's forces took the strategic city of Khartoum in 1884, killing the British commander of a combined Anglo-Egyptian force. When Muhammad Ahmad died of typhus a few months later, however, his movement lost direction.

Muhammad Ahmad, the Mahdi
(1844–1885) *Mahdi* is the term some Muslims use for the "guided one" expected to appear before the end of days. Muhammad Ahmad took this title in Sudan and called for a jihad against British-dominated Egypt.

The jihadist movement regained momentum in the 1890s under the *khalifa* ("successor") to the Mahdi, as the British now sought "effective occupation" over the entire Nile Valley. The Battle of Omdurman (1898) was the bloodiest battle between European and African forces during the entire period. Though outnumbered two to one, Anglo-Egyptian forces used their Maxim guns to terrible effect. The British lost forty-seven soldiers; over ten thousand Sudanese forces were killed, some shot as they lay wounded on the field.

French conquests in the interior prompted the British to "effectively occupy" coastal territories and thus in 1896 to finally put an end to Asante independence. The Asante king reluctantly accepted a British protectorate, but his people rebelled after the new British governor demanded the "Golden Stool," the sacred symbol of the nation and its kings. (By legend, a chief priest had caused the Golden Stool to descend from the heavens; for an outsider to touch it would be a horrible desecration.)

As they prepared for war some Asante fighters, no strangers to British firepower, doubted the outcome. A queen mother, Yaa Asantewa (YAH ah-san-TAY-wuh), stood forward and spoke: *"[If] you the men of Asante will not go forward, then we ... the women will. I shall call upon my fellow women. We will fight the white men. We will fight till the last of us falls in the battlefields."** The Yaa Asantewa War of 1900 was a military defeat for the Asante, but it caused later British governors to treat the Asante royal family with greater respect and to acknowledge Asante traditions.

The British also faced stiff resistance in the southern African kingdom of the Ndebele (nn-day-BEH-lay). Descendants of a Zulu regiment that had moved northward, the Ndebele were militarily formidable, but no match for the British South Africa Company of Cecil Rhodes. Lobengula, their king, tried to protect his people by signing a treaty granting the British mineral rights while retaining his own authority on the land. Even so, Lobengula recognized that the invaders were unlikely to keep their promises. *"Did you ever see a chameleon catch a fly?"* he asked a missionary. *"The chameleon gets behind the fly and remains motionless for some time, then he advances very slowly and gently ... [then] he darts his tongue and the fly disappears. England is the chameleon and I am that fly."*† Sure enough, the Ndebele were absorbed into the British colony of Rhodesia after losing two wars of resistance in the 1890s.

● **CONTEXT&CONNECTIONS** Lobengula's quandary was very familiar to nineteenth-century Amerindian leaders. Just as *Sitting Bulll* (Chapter 25) led the Lakota into confrontation with the United States after the government broke its promise to leave the Black Hills in their hands for all time, so Lobengula rallied Ndebele warriors to defend their land and people when the British broke their treaties. ●

Coordinating resistance was even more difficult in regions where traditional political organization was less centralized. The Maji Maji (MAH-jee MAH-jee) Revolt in German East Africa was led by a religious prophet, Kinjekitile (kihn-JAY-kee-TEE-lay), who attempted to forge an alliance among numerous small chiefdoms. In the 1890s, German military conquest had met little opposition, with local leaders deciding to follow the traditional course of paying tribute in cattle to more powerful overlords while continuing to mind their own affairs. That arrangement did not suit the Germans, however, who were interested not in cattle, but in exportable commodities. By 1905, people in the region had grown angry after the Germans forced them at gun point to grow cotton. African farmers were left with little time to tend their own food crops. The payment they received was barely enough to pay colonial taxes, and cotton robbed their fields of fertility.

Maji Maji meant "powerful water," a reference to a sacred pool that attracted pilgrims from a wide area, which Kinjekitile used as a rallying point. He promised his followers that bathing in the sacred stream would make them immune to German bullets. Of course, this did not happen, and the Germans ruthlessly suppressed the uprising. But they also learned not to press their advantage too far, and they no longer enforced mandatory cotton growing. Rebellions, after all, were expensive. The Maji Maji rebellion was just one of many that showed how Africans' willingness to fight could force the Europeans to moderate their policies. While military defeat was inevitable, their resistance was not futile.

Nonetheless, the imperial powers consistently demeaned Africans, as exemplified by a new fad of displaying "natives" as a curiosity at Western expositions.

---

*Yaa Asantewa, cited in David Sweetman, *Women Leaders in African History* (London: Heinemann, 1984), pp. 34–35.
†Neil Parsons, *A New History of Southern Africa*, 2d ed. (London: Macmillan, 1993).

One wonders what King Khama and his colleagues thought when, dressed in Victorian garb, they were taken to see a "Somali village" and its "primitive" residents on display at London's Crystal Palace. The worst excess came in 1906, when a Central African named Ota Benga was displayed in a cage at the Bronx Zoo in New York. He later committed suicide. The disrespect and cruelty fostered by such racism long endured.

The New Imperialism in Southeast Asia, Austronesia, and the Pacific

As in Africa, Europeans had long competed for access to trade in Southeast Asia and had established some imperial bases, but here as well it was only in the late nineteenth century that the New Imperialism led to nearly complete Western domination. In mainland Southeast Asia, the French allied with Vietnamese emperors to extend their power over what became French Indochina. The British expanded from India into Burma and Malaya. The Dutch dominated the thousands of islands that make up insular Southeast Asia; the United States joined the imperial club when it took the Philippines from Spain (see Map 26.2). Meanwhile, the British consolidated their control over Australia and New Zealand, and Europeans, Americans, and Japanese hoisted their flags across the islands of the Pacific (see Map 26.2).

Mainland Southeast Asia

The French occupied Vietnam by displacing its imperial rulers, who had modeled themselves on the Ming dynasty (see Chapter 16). In 1802, after decades of disorder, the Nguyen (noo-WEN) family had established a new dynasty, with Catholic missionaries representing French influence at the Vietnamese court. Emperor Napoleon III (see Chapter 23) then moved the French from indirect influence to direct control when he sent an army of occupation. In 1862 the besieged Nguyen ruler ceded the commercial center of Saigon to France, opened three "treaty ports" to European trade, and gave the French free passage up the Mekong (MAY-kong) River. By 1884, the French were in control of all of Vietnam but still faced guerrilla resistance. The French army of conquest, in what French authorities called a campaign of "*pacification*," killed thousands of rebels and civilians before establishing firm control.

By then French forces had also conquered the neighboring kingdom of Cambodia and had taken Laos by agreement with the kingdom of Siam (discussed in the next section). In 1897, they combined these territories into the **Federation of Indochina**, or simply French Indochina. French colonial authorities took over vast estates on which to grow rubber and turned rice into a major export crop. The profits went almost entirely to French traders and planters, though some Chinese and Vietnamese merchants in Saigon also benefited from the increase in commerce that came with the tighter integration of Southeast Asia into global markets.

Federation of Indochina
(1897) Federation created by the French after having conquered Vietnam, Cambodia, and Laos—an administrative convenience, as the societies that made up the federation had little in common.

● **CONTEXT&CONNECTIONS** Resistance to foreign occupation is a consistent theme in Vietnamese history and has been an important part of the country's identity since the early fifteenth century, when Ming armies were driven back to China (see Chapter 16). In the twentieth century, Vietnamese armies would battle the French, Japanese, and Americans (see Chapter 30) before facing another Chinese invasion in the late 1970s. Every single time, the Vietnamese forced the withdrawal of foreign invaders. ●

Map 26.2 The New Imperialism in Southeast Asia, 1910 European nations had controlled parts of Southeast Asia, such as the Dutch East Indies and the Spanish Philippines, since the sixteenth and seventeenth centuries. The New Imperialism of the nineteenth century strengthened the European presence in those societies while bringing the entire region, with the exception of Siam (Thailand), under Western colonial rule. In remote regions, such as the highlands of central Borneo, the process of conquest was not complete until the early twentieth century.

Burma was likewise incorporated into the British empire in stages. By the 1870s, Britain controlled the south, while in the north a reformist Burmese king attempted to modernize the country under indigenous rule. British representatives had no patience for these experiments. They refused to take off their shoes in the king's presence, a terrible affront to court protocol. Finally, in 1886 British forces invaded from India and took the capital of Mandalay. While suppressing a number of regional rebellions, they brought administrators from India and began building railroads to the rich timber resources of the Burmese jungles.

The trading city of Singapore had been Britain's most valuable possession in Southeast Asia since 1819. It attracted many Chinese immigrants and became the center of the Chinese merchant diaspora in the region, while Indians arrived as

French Colonialism in Indochina Like other European colonialists, the French argued that they were developing their imperial territories for the good of their subjects through both a "civilizing" cultural mission and economic development projects such as road building. As this photograph from Southeast Asia indicates, however, it was the "natives" who did most of the work and their colonial overlords who grabbed the lion's share of profit.

clerks and office workers. Initially, the British were content to control the port and grow rich on the trade between the Indian Ocean and the South China Sea, leaving politics to the dozens of Muslim sultanates of Malaya. But after completion of the Suez Canal in 1869, British merchants became anxious to exploit the rich tin resources of the Malay Peninsula, for which the Second Industrial Revolution had dramatically increased demand.

In Malaya, as in Africa, local rivalries supported a policy of "divide and conquer." British "residents" gave local rulers "advice" on the governance of their sultanates; if a sultan refused, they would simply recognize another ambitious man as ruler and work through him. As in Egypt and the princely states of India, indigenous rulers remained in place but power was squarely in the hands of Europeans. The British prided themselves on having brought efficient administration to yet another corner of the globe. Meanwhile, they expanded plantations of commercial crops such as pepper, palm oil, and rubber.

Insular Southeast Asia, Austronesia, and the Pacific

The Dutch had been the dominant European presence in the islands of Southeast Asia since the seventeenth century (see Chapter 16). After the Dutch East India Company was disbanded in 1799, colonial authorities imposed even harsher economic conditions. In 1830, for example, Dutch authorities forced rice farmers on the island of Java to convert to sugar production. One Dutch official declared that *"they must be taught to* *work, and if they were unwilling out of ignorance, they must be ordered to work."** Through such coercion the Dutch could buy sugar at low prices and then sell it for a great profit on world markets. The Europeans demanded cash taxes, and most people could obtain colonial currency only by working for Europeans or by growing cash crops for export. Peasants thus became tied to international commodity networks as they became dependent on the sale of crops like sugar and coffee.

Dutch authorities asserted more and more formal administrative control over Java and Sumatra, where individual sultans had previously been left in charge of local affairs. At the same time, the increasing presence of other European powers motivated the Dutch to seek control of hundreds of other islands. They killed or sent into exile anyone, such as rebels on the Hindu-ruled island of Bali, who resisted. The New Imperialism thus significantly deepened Dutch power over the Indonesian archipelago.

Meanwhile, the United States had claimed a direct territorial stake in the Pacific when it annexed the Hawai'ian Islands in 1898 (see Chapter 25). The further extension of American imperialism to the Philippines came as a result of the Spanish-American War of 1898–1900. That conflict, initially centered on the Caribbean island of Cuba, spread to include the Philippines, where Spain had been in power since the foundation of Manila in 1571.

Filipino resistance to Spanish authority led, in 1896, to an independence revolt. But in 1899, the Spanish handed the islands over to the United States by secret treaty. The Filipino revolutionaries continued to struggle for independence, now against a U.S. army of occupation. Over sixteen thousand Filipino combatants died.

Some in the United States protested that waging war against people fighting for independence was contrary to American principles. The writer Mark Twain joined the Anti-Imperialist League, declaring that American motives in the Philippines were no more pure than those of European imperialists and just as driven by economics. Observing the debate in American public opinion, the British poet of empire Rudyard Kipling urged America to shoulder its imperial responsibilities:

Take up the White Man's burden—
Send forth the best ye breed—
Go bind your sons to exile
To serve your captives' need;
To wait in heavy harness,
On fluttered folk and wild—
Your new-caught, sullen peoples,
Half-devil and half-child.†

Kipling worried that the British empire was in decline and that only an imperialistic United States could save the world for "Anglo-Saxon civilization." Americans needed to *"take up the White Man's burden,"* Kipling argued, for the benefit of the *"new caught, sullen peoples"* (that is, Filipinos) themselves.

---

*Cited in D. R. SarDesai, *Southeast Asia Past and Present*, 4th ed. (Boulder: Westview, 1997), p. 92.

†Verse from "The White Man's Burden" by Rudyard Kipling, from *Rudyard Kipling's Verse Definitive Edition* by Rudyard Kipling, 1920, Doubleday.

The African American writer W. E. B. Du Bois (doo BOYZ) offered a differing view of American imperialism. Noting that the New Imperialism had led to white domination across the world, he predicted in 1903 that *"the problem of the twentieth century is the problem of the color-line."** His prophecy would prove to be as accurate for the civil rights movement in the United States as it was for twentieth-century decolonization movements in Southeast Asia, Africa, and the entire colonial world.

British motivation for expansion in Australia and New Zealand predated the New Imperialism. By the 1870s, in fact, white immigrants had already reduced Australian Aborigines to a defeated and subservient people even as the continent's economy boomed, fueled by wool exports and gold discoveries. In New Zealand, however, British settlers had faced tougher resistance from the Polynesian-speaking Maori people. Though an 1840 treaty created the framework for British-Maori coexistence, guaranteeing the Maori land rights and giving them the status of British subjects, by the 1860s warfare had broken out. British victory followed, and by 1890 indigenous Maori, like their Hawai'ian cousins, had lost nearly all of their land.

The territorial acquisitions of the New Imperialism culminated in the Pacific. Japan annexed Okinawa. French Polynesia was established. Germany took New Guinea, and Samoa was divided between Germany and the United States. By century's end, there were no more unclaimed territories on which to plant the flag of empire. (See the feature "Visual Evidence in Primary Sources: National Flags.")

Case Studies in Imperialism

Case studies from Africa and Southeast Asia demonstrate the economic and political implications of the New Imperialism. The history of rubber shows how industrial and technological developments could lead to violence and death. The story of how the rulers of Siam (Thailand) and Ethiopia retained their independence shows how these exceptions prove the rule of Western dominance.

AP® THEMES

How did industrialization change the nature of state building and expansion in the nineteenth century?

A Case Study of the New Imperialism: Rubber

During the Second Industrial Revolution, the spread of products such as waterproof clothing and factory conveyor belts, telephones, electrical lines, and bicycles generated a booming trade in rubber. At first the only source was the Brazilian Amazon, where "rubber barons" built palatial homes while indigenous Amerindian peoples suffered from the introduction of diseases to which they had no resistance (see Chapter 25). Soon, global demand for rubber outstripped the Brazilian supply, leading to the cultivation of plantation rubber in Southeast Asia by the French in Indochina, the British in Malaya, and the Dutch in their East Indies. But it would take some years for those new Asian sources of supply to come onto the market, and Central Africa was, meanwhile, the only other source of wild rubber.

Market conditions in the 1890s thus brought a frenzied search for rubber to Central Africa, leading to the infamous abuses in the Congo Free State. This was the personal domain of King Leopold II of Belgium, who now found a way to turn his vast territories into quick cash. The Belgian king leased out

*W. E. B. Du Bois, *The Souls of Black Folk* (New York: Vintage, 1990).

National Flags

Banners and flags have a long history as markers of individual and group identity. Flags took on even more important symbolic power in the nineteenth century with the rise of European nation-states and the spread of their empires. In the West, where flags had earlier been closely associated with royal families, they now became the symbols of entire nations. The imposition of a nation's flag beyond the nation's frontier became a defining symbol of imperialism.

Here are nineteenth-century flags from societies that struggled to retain their independence: Liberia (West Africa), Ethiopia (East Africa), Siam (or Thailand, Southeast Asia), the Hawai'ian kingdom, and the Cherokee nation (United States). Creating these flags and asserting the right to fly them were important expressions of resistance to colonialism.

Courtesy Rick Wyatt, www.crwflags.com

The West African Republic of Liberia was founded in 1847 by freed American slaves. An earlier version of the flag had a cross rather than a star in the upper left. When the flag was first presented, *"many eyes were suffused with tears.... Who that looked back to America and remembered what he saw and felt there, could be otherwise than agitated?"**

Courtesy Rick Wyatt, www.crwflags.com

This flag, first used in 1897, features the "Lion of Judah" as a symbol for Ethiopia. Red stands for power and faith; yellow for peace, wealth, and love; and green for land and hope. These became the colors of global African nationalism, and they can now be found on the flags of nations such as Ghana, Zimbabwe, Guyana, and Grenada. The flag has deep religious symbolism for Jamaican Rastafarians.

*Cited in Carl Patrick Burrowes, *Power and Press Freedom in Liberia, 1830–1970* (Trenton: Africa World Press, 2004), p. 60.

Courtesy Rick Wyatt, www.crwflags.com

This flag dates from 1891. One of several different flags from Siam, it was flown above the palace only when the king was present. At the center is the royal coat of arms, with a trident and golden crown above. Later, the flag of Thailand evolved to emphasize national rather than royal identity, with horizontal stripes of red, white, and blue. ***How do these flags combine indigenous and imported design elements?***

Courtesy Rick Wyatt, www.crwflags.com

This flag was commissioned by Kamehameha the Great, the first Hawai'ian to unify the islands, in 1816, and it flew until 1893. The eight bars represent the major Hawai'ian Islands, and the British Union Jack reflects the attempts of Hawai'ian monarchs to use an alliance with Britain as protection against the United States and other imperialist powers. This is the current state flag of Hawai'i.

Courtesy Rick Wyatt, www.crwflags.com

After the U.S. government forcibly moved the Cherokee people to Oklahoma (see Chapter 25), the nation adopted a constitution to mark their quest for sovereignty in their new home. The date on this flag (currently in use) commemorates that constitution. Each of the seven yellow stars represents one of the original Cherokee clans; the black star represents those who lost their lives on the "Trail of Tears."

Violence in King Leopold's Congo Here two victims of King Leopold's policies, Mola and Yoka, display their mutilated limbs. Mola's hands were eaten by gangrene after being tied too tightly by Leopold's agents. Yoka's right hand was cut off by soldiers who planned to receive a bounty at headquarters by using the hand as proof of a kill. Once the world learned about this extreme violence, humanitarian voices rose against Leopold. (Courtesy, Anti-Slavery International, London)

huge "concessions" to private companies, which ordered their agents to use whatever means necessary to maximize the harvest. The result was a reign of terror. Like the farmers forced to grow cotton in East Africa, the families of rubber collectors went hungry because they could not tend their own fields. Women were locked in cages to force their husbands to meet impossible quotas. When those rubber quotas were not met, the killing began. Belgian officers and agents paid Free State soldiers to bring back the hands of those they killed. These soldiers would sometimes chop off the hands of the living and bring them back to the Belgian trade stations for a cash reward. Eventually 10 million people died, mostly from hunger. In the West, middle-class consumers happily purchased bicycles and newfangled automobiles, unaware of the horror that produced the rubber for their tires.

Leopold brazenly claimed to be a great humanitarian, bringing "civilization" to the "dark continent," even as stories of the torture he sponsored began to reach Europe. Investigations by a suspicious shipping clerk in Brussels revealed the full horror of Leopold's crimes, and he helped form the Congo Reform Association to demand that they be ended. Finally, in 1908 King Leopold sold his African empire to the Belgian government, reaping a huge profit. A heritage of violence still affects the Congo today, while Brussels is filled with the many grand monuments that Leopold built with his bloodied fortune.

Enduring Monarchies: Ethiopia and Siam

Given the overwhelming strength of European domination in the age of the New Imperialism, it seems surprising that Ethiopia and Siam (present-day Thailand) managed to retain their independence. Factors such as competent leadership were important, but the continuing independence of these two states merely confirmed overwhelming European domination in Africa and Southeast Asia.

The ancient Christian kingdom of Ethiopia first met modern European firepower in 1868 when a British relief column was sent to rescue several British subjects held hostage by the Ethiopian king. The British easily crushed the African army they encountered. Though the Ethiopian leader had killed himself on the field of battle, leaving the kingdom defenseless, the British then withdrew. In the 1860s the "scramble for Africa" had not yet begun.

Menelik II

(r. 1889–1913) Emperor who used diplomacy and military reorganization to retain Ethiopian independence, defeating an Italian army of invasion at Adowa in 1896.

Menelik II (r. 1889–1913) was determined to strengthen his state against further assault. Ethiopia, like Tokugawa Japan, had long had a decentralized political structure in which rural lords, commanding their own armies, were as powerful as the emperor himself. Menelik (MEN-uh-lik) consolidated power at the imperial court and created his own standing army, equipped with the latest repeating rifles. He also used his credentials as a Christian to enhance his diplomatic influence in Europe, where his ambassadors played the European powers against one another to Ethiopia's advantage.

Menelik was also fortunate that the European assault on Ethiopia came from Italy, the weakest of the European imperial powers. The Battle of Adowa (1896) was an Ethiopian victory, though Italy did take the strategically important region of Eritrea on the Red Sea. Britain, by then dominant in northeastern Africa, was convinced that Menelik would maintain security on the Egyptian frontier and allow European traders free access to his kingdom. Since this was a cheaper solution than occupying the country by force, the British sponsored the development of modern infrastructure, such as banks and railroads, during Menelik's reign. The benefits, as usual, went to Ethiopian elites and European investors. The Ethiopian majority continued to scratch out a meager existence.

Simultaneously, the kings of Siam also faced the danger of absorption into European empires, with the British expanding from India in the west and the French threatening from Indochina in the east. But two long-ruling kings, Mongkut (r. 1851–1868) and Chulalongkorn (r. 1868–1910), secured the ancient kingdom's sovereignty. Both used internal reform and diplomatic engagement to deal with the threats of the New Imperialism.

As a young man, Mongkut (MANG-koot) lived in a Buddhist monastery. When he emerged to become king in 1851, his monastic experience interacting with men from all social classes helped him become a popular leader. Having learned English, mathematics, and astronomy from Western missionaries, he could interact effectively with Europeans as well.

Observing China's fate after the Opium Wars (see Chapter 24), Mongkut was determined to meet the Western challenge. Conservatives at court opposed his reforms as undermining Buddhist traditions. Nevertheless, Mongkut invited Western emissaries to his capital and installed them as advisers. Though Mongkut favored the British, he balanced their influence with French and Dutch advisers. He also opened Siam to foreign trade, giving merchants from various countries a stake in his system.

● **CONTEXT&CONNECTIONS** The Siamese tradition of welcoming foreigners to the royal court and relying on them as advisors was established well before the reign of Mongkut. In the seventeenth century, for example, Iranian and French merchants competed for influence at court (see page 488). ●

Most importantly, Mongkut chose an English tutor for his son and heir, **Chulalongkorn**. Coming to power in 1868, the same year as the Meiji Restoration in Japan, Chulalongkorn (CHOO-luh-AWHN-korn) appointed able Siamese advisers who understood that their traditions and sovereignty could be preserved only through reform. Chulalongkorn altered the legal system to protect private property, abolished slavery and debt peonage, expanded access to education, and encouraged the introduction of telegraphs and railroads. Moreover, he centralized governmental power through a streamlined bureaucracy that reached from the capital into the smallest villages.

Chulalongkorn (r. 1868–1910) King of Siam (Thailand) who modernized his country through legal and constitutional reforms. Through successful diplomacy he ensured Siam's continued independence while neighboring societies were absorbed into European empires.

Like his father, Chulalongkorn was an able diplomat who played Europeans off one another. Lacking a strong army, he gave up claims to parts of his empire, such as Laos, to protect the core of his kingdom. Not only did this appease the French and the British, but it also gave his kingdom a more ethnically Thai character. (See the feature "World History in Today's World: Political Conflict and the Thai Monarchy.")

WORLD HISTORY IN TODAY'S WORLD

Political Conflict and the Thai Monarchy

Thailand is one of forty-four nations that have retained a monarchical system of government (others include the United Kingdom, Saudi Arabia, Spain, Brunei, Swaziland, Morocco, the Netherlands, and Jordan). Like many of these states, Thailand is a constitutional monarchy where the king is expected to be above day-to-day politics. In fact, one of the general arguments in favor of monarchism is that the royal family helps unite the nation by transcending political factions.

Since coming to the throne in 1946, the world's longest-serving monarch, King Bhumibol Adulyadej (Rama IX) has indeed represented continuity and stability. The king's image is displayed, and revered, everywhere in Thailand (and across the world in the now ubiquitous Thai restaurants). Criticism of the king and his family is outlawed.

In the past few years, however, a wound has opened in Thai society that the king, now old and infirm, seems unable to heal: a disagreement between rural Thai voters, especially in the north of the country, and the urbanites in the south, especially in the capital of Bangkok. Rural voters have consistently supported members of the populist Thaksin family, whose policies of economic redistribution are strongly opposed by the military and by the urban middle class.

In 2014, the military intervened to remove Yingluck Shinawatra, Thailand's first female Prime Minister, from office, even after she had received a clear majority of votes. As a member of the Thaksin family, the military saw Shinawatra as unfit for leadership, engineering her impeachment and indictment on corruption charges.

Meanwhile, King Bhumibol seems unable to bridge the political chasm between poor and rich, north and south, canceling his annual birthday speech late in 2014 for reasons of ill health. The questions now are who will succeed the aged king after he passes away, and will his successor be able to reconcile the deep divisions in Thai society? By law, Thais are not even allowed to address the question of royal succession. It seems that the Thai military, rather than the Thai monarchy, holds the keys to the country's future.

Source: "Thai Politics: Yingluck in the Dock," *The Economist*, January 15, 2015.

Chulalongkorn was fortunate that the British and the French were anxious to avoid conflict between their Indian and Indochinese empires. Because their traders and missionaries were allowed to establish themselves in the kingdom, and because the Siamese leader was able to ensure peace and stability in his domain, the French and British agreed in 1896 to recognize the independence of the kingdom of Siam as a buffer between their empires (see Map 26.2).

As with Ethiopia, effective political leadership secured the independence of Siam through internal reform, centralization of government power, and deft diplomatic maneuvering. Nevertheless, had the British or French wished to conquer Ethiopia or Siam, they could have done so. The achievement of Menelik and Chulalongkorn in the 1890s was to position their countries to take advantage of inter-European rivalries.

In the age of the New Imperialism, African and Southeast Asian societies could retain their sovereignty only under unusual circumstances. King Khama's situation was much more common. He did his best with the diplomatic resources at his disposal, but his kingdom was too small and too poorly armed to survive as an independent state. Unlike Menelik and Chulalongkorn, most African and Southeast Asian rulers did not command sufficient resources to protect themselves from

King Chulalongkorn of Siam This photograph from 1890 shows King Chulalongkorn of Siam with his son, the Crown Prince Vajiravudh Rama, who was studying in Britain. Chulalongkorn used deft diplomacy to maintain the independence of Siam (Thailand) during the height of the European scramble for colonial territory. Father and son are dressed in European style, but the warm embrace of their hands was a Southeast Asian touch. British males rarely showed such affection in Victorian portraits.

the New Imperialism. Even in Ethiopia and Siam, the economic impact of Western industrial capitalism brought new and difficult challenges to rural peoples, who were now bound, like their counterparts in colonial empires, to a global economy to which they contributed much more than they received.

The New Imperialism in World History

In the second half of the nineteenth century many small-scale societies and kingdoms that had maintained their autonomy could no longer resist the imperial ambitions of aggressive European nation-states. The story of their often spirited resistance and ultimate defeat was a global one: from the Great Plains of Canada and the United States (see Chapter 25), to Vietnam and the Philippines, to the interior of East Africa. If even a mighty empire like Qing China succumbed (see Chapter 24) smaller states like King Khama's Bangwato could not hope to defend themselves.

When King Khama and his colleagues traveled to London in 1895, they were visiting the epicenter of global financial and military power. By then, however, the British could no longer be complacent. They had lost their early industrial lead to emerging economies in Germany and the United States, and the British empire, while still by far the world's largest, faced challenges from its newly ambitious competitors in the age of the New Imperialism.

Before 1850, European maritime prowess had only intermittently been translated into political domination, though British control over India set a precedent (see Chapter 20). It was the Industrial Revolution that provided the means and motivation for further imperial expansion (see Chapter 23). Initially, though, it seemed that the British would be content with "informal empire" rather than more direct forms of administrative domination: in China and Latin America that policy was generating great profit without the expense of conquest and control.

By the late nineteenth century, however, refinements in chemical and metallurgical processes—the Second Industrial Revolution—led to more sophisticated production techniques, much larger industrial corporations, and intensified competition for raw materials and markets. As Britain's new competitors developed newer and more efficient industrial infrastructure, such competition unleashed the rapid expansion of empires in the last quarter of the century. The "scramble for Africa" was the most dramatic example of the new global quest for imperial dominion.

By 1900, when foreign troops occupied the Forbidden City in Beijing (see Chapter 24) and the process of partition and conquest in Africa, Southeast Asia, and the Pacific neared completion, the organizing principle of a world unified by industrial markets was clear. Western Europe and the United States stood astride the globe, seemingly reinforcing the Social Darwinist claim of their

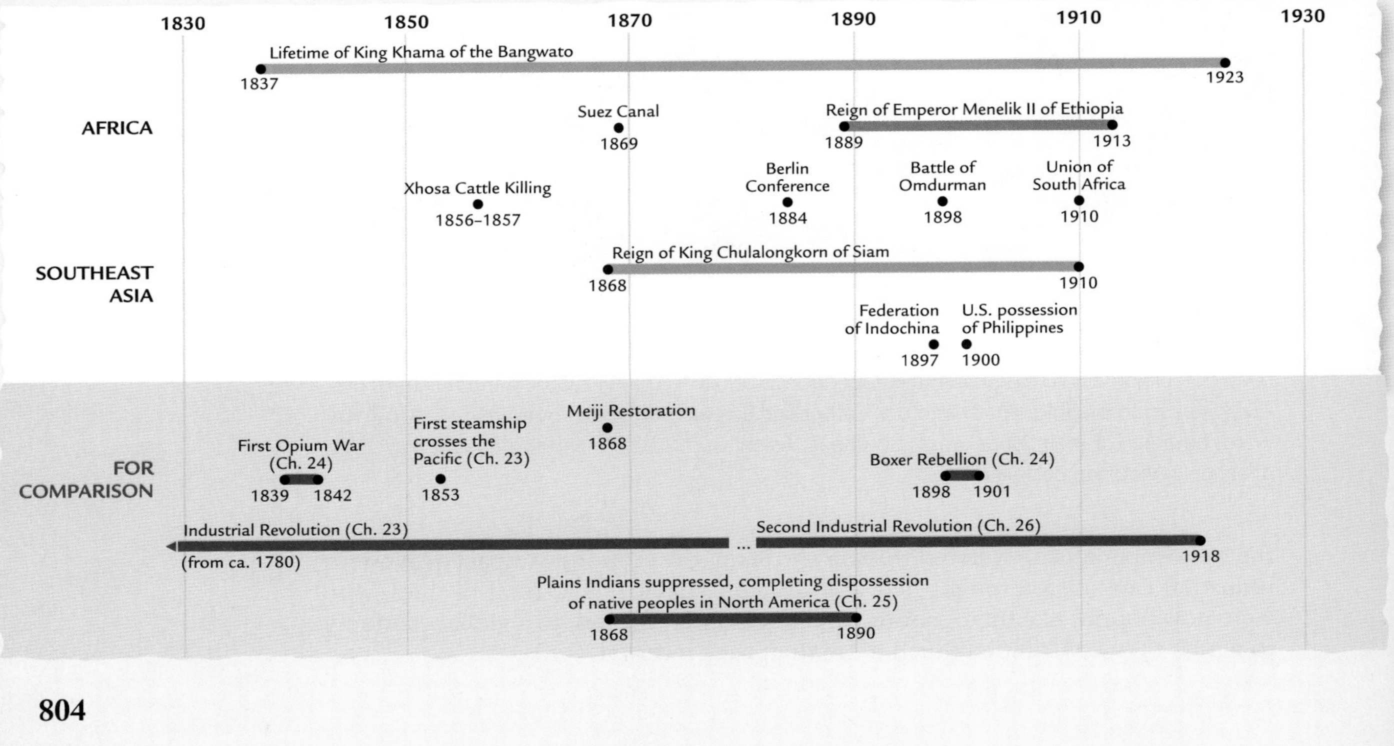

natural superiority, with only Japan offering a clear example of non-European achievement in the race to industrialized military power.

Africa, Southeast Asia, and the Pacific offered a safety valve for European and Japanese competition in the late nineteenth century, but entering the twentieth century the flags of empire crowded against each other across the world, and European conflicts would turn inward during two great world wars (see Chapters 27 and 29). The First and Second World Wars drew the world's peoples into devastating conflict arising from inter-European competition, but ultimately undercut Western domination. By mid-century, anticolonial nationalists would effectively organize themselves to campaign for national independence. Today, it seems that the West's global dominance, which had once appeared so enduring, might only have been a passing episode in world history.

Meanwhile, King Khama's mission to London had important long-term consequences. Because of his efforts, the Bangwato and the other peoples of Botswana entered the British empire as a protectorate administered by the Colonial Office and avoided incorporation into apartheid South Africa (see Chapter 31). The people of today's Botswana, a peaceful and relatively prosperous state, thereby avoided the terrible violence of twentieth-century apartheid—a small victory, perhaps, when measured against the great events of the time, but one of which Khama's descendants are justifiably proud.

Key Terms

King Khama III (778)
New Imperialism (779)
Second Industrial Revolution (780)
David Livingstone (780)
King Leopold II of Belgium (781)
Berlin Conference (781)
Asante kingdom (786)
Samori Toure (787)
Shaka (788)
Cecil Rhodes (788)
Xhosa Cattle Killing (789)
Union of South Africa (790)
Suez Canal (791)
Muhammad Ahmad, the Mahdi (791)
Federation of Indochina (793)
Menelik II (800)
Chulalongkorn (801)

For Further Reference

Baker, Chris, and Pasuk Phongaichit. *A History of Thailand.* 3d ed. New York: Cambridge University Press, 2014.

Cleall, Esme. *Missionary Discourses of Difference: Negotiating Otherness in the British Empire, 1840–1900.* New York: Palgrave Macmillan, 2012.

Headrick, Daniel. *The Tools of Empire: Technology and European Imperialism in the Nineteenth Century.* New York: Oxford University Press, 1981.

Hochschild, Adam. *King Leopold's Ghost: A Story of Greed, Terror and Heroism in Colonial Africa.* Boston: Houghton Mifflin, 1999.

Lockard, Craig. *Southeast Asia in World History.* New York: Oxford University Press, 2009.

Markus, Harold G. *The Life and Times of Menelik II: Ethiopia 1844–1913.* New York: Oxford University Press, 1975.

Martin, B. G., ed. *Muslim Brotherhoods in Nineteenth Century Africa.* New York: Cambridge University Press, 2003.

Owen, Norman G., ed. *The Emergence of Modern Southeast Asia.* Honolulu: University of Hawai'i Press, 2004.

Packenham, Thomas. *The Scramble for Africa, 1976–1912.* 2d ed. London: Longman, 1999.

Peiers, J. B. *The Dead Will Arise: Nongqawuse and the Great Xhosa Cattle Killing Movement of 1856–1857.* London: James Currey, 1989.

Reid, Richard. *A History of Modern Africa: 1800 to the Present.* 2d ed. London: Wiley-Blackwell, 2011.

AP® Review Questions for Chapter 26

Multiple-Choice Questions

QUESTIONS 1–4 REFER TO THE FOLLOWING PASSAGES.

All these men, missionaries, travelers, sportsmen, scientists, traders, in no proper sense the accredited representatives of this country, but actuated by private personal motives are at liberty to call upon the British nation to spend millions of money and thousands of lives to defend them against risks which the nation has not sanctioned. It is only right to add that unscrupulous statesmen have deliberately utilized these insidious methods of encroachment...as a pretext for a punitive expedition which results in the British flag waving over some new tract of territory.

—J. A. Hobson, English social reformer, "Imperialism," 1902

Take up the White Man's burden –
Send forth the best ye breed –
Go bind your sons to exile
To serve your captives' need;
To wait in heavy harness,
On fluttered folk and wild –
Your new-caught sullen peoples,
Half-devil and half-child.

—Rudyard Kipling, English Nobel Prize–winning writer, "The White Man's Burden," 1899

1. The interactions described in the passages are best understood in the context of which of the following?
   (A) Classical liberalism
   (B) Industrialization
   (C) New Imperialism
   (D) Nationalism

2. Which of the following conclusions about the period from 1750 to 1900 is most directly supported by the *first* passage?
   (A) Many European states used both warfare and diplomacy to establish empires.
   (B) Racial ideologies justified imperialism.
   (C) Europeans were most interested in establishing settler colonies.
   (D) Imperialism was driven by the need for raw materials.

3. The two passages differ most directly on which of the following points?
   (A) Appropriate ways to gain colonies
   (B) Legal status of empire building
   (C) The purpose of empire
   (D) Status of conquered peoples

4. Which of the following best explains why Rudyard Kipling described the "'new-caught sullen peoples" as "Half-devil and half-child"?
   (A) Pan-Africanism
   (B) Utopian socialism
   (C) Anti-Semitism
   (D) Social Darwinism

QUESTIONS 5–7 REFER TO THE FOLLOWING PASSAGE.

This is to inform you that the Europeans who are present round the White Nile with the English...intended to enter between my country and yours and to separate and divide us.... I have ordered my troops to advance towards the White Nile.... And you look to yourself, and do not let the Europeans enter between us. Be strong, lest if the Europeans enter our midst a great disaster befall us and our children have no rest. And if one of the Europeans comes to you as a traveler, do your utmost to send him away in peace; and do not listen to rumors against me. All my intention is to increase my friendship with you, and that our countries may be protected from enemies.

—Menelik II, Ethiopian emperor, in a letter to Khalifa Abdallahi of Sudan, 1897

5. Which of the following conclusions about the period from 1750 to 1900 is most directly supported by the passage?
   (A) Industrialized states practiced economic imperialism.
   (B) Discontent with imperial rule encouraged the development of political ideologies.
   (C) Africans resisted European encroachment.
   (D) Subjects accepted centralized imperial governments.

6. The views expressed in the passage are best seen as evidence of which of the following in Africa?
   (A) Ethnic and tribal conflict
   (B) Early unity among African peoples
   (C) Social Darwinism
   (D) Liberation theology

7. Which of the following socioeconomic developments was most important in creating the conditions for the conflict indicated in the passage above?
   (A) Marxist communism
   (B) Self-Strengthening Movement
   (C) European settler colonies
   (D) Second Industrial Revolution

QUESTIONS 8-10 REFER TO THE FOLLOWING IMAGE.

8. The image above most directly reflects which of the following policies employed by Siam?
   (A) Rejection of Western influences
   (B) Reform to preserve sovereignty
   (C) Cooperation with European imperialists
   (D) Nationalism as a rallying force for resistance

9. Which of the following best explains the motivation behind the king's and his son's choice of clothing in the photograph?
   (A) To counter Social Darwinist ideas about native peoples
   (B) To demonstrate cultural superiority over the West
   (C) To advertise the Siamese textile industry
   (D) To quell growing nationalism in Siam

10. European interest in colonizing Southeast Asia grew with the cultivation of
   (A) sugar.
   (B) wheat.
   (C) rubber.
   (D) tobacco.

Short-Answer Questions

1. Answer parts A, B, and C.
   A. Explain ONE cause of New Imperialism.
   B. Explain ONE effect of New Imperialism on Europe.
   C. Explain ONE effect of New Imperialism on Southeast Asia.

QUESTION 2 REFERS TO THE FOLLOWING IMAGE.

THE RHODES COLOSSUS
STRIDING FROM CAPE TOWN TO CAIRO.

2. Answer parts A and B.
   A. Identify and explain TWO historical claims about the British empire in Africa that can be supported based on the image.
   B. Identify ONE limitation of the image as a source of information about the British empire in Africa.

27 War, Revolution, and Global Uncertainty, 1905–1928

Emma Goldman

Emma Goldman (1869–1940) was one of the most provocative figures of the early twentieth century—in her native Russia, in her adopted country of the United States, and across the world. When she was a girl, her father tried to stifle her dreams. As a young immigrant in New York, she experienced grinding poverty. As a result Goldman became a tireless and outspoken campaigner for workers' and women's rights.

A notorious radical, the press dubbed "Red Emma" the "*most dangerous woman in the country.*" The U.S. government imprisoned her for her 1917 campaign against military conscription and then deported her back to Russia, which also ejected her when she became a fierce critic of Soviet totalitarianism. Later in life she had no permanent home, traveling through the United States, Canada, and Europe pleading the cause of anarchism.

Emma Goldman saw oppression in all large institutions, in governments as well as corporations, in religious institutions and political parties. She defined her anarchism as:

> *The philosophy of a new social order based on liberty unrestricted by man-made law; the theory that all forms of government rest on violence, and are therefore wrong and harmful, as well as unnecessary . . . Anarchism alone stresses the importance of the individual, his possibilities and needs in a free society. Instead of telling him that he must fall down and worship before institutions, live and die for abstractions . . . Anarchism insists that the center of gravity in society is the individual—that he must think for himself, act freely, and live fully. The aim of Anarchism is that every individual in the world shall be relieved from the*

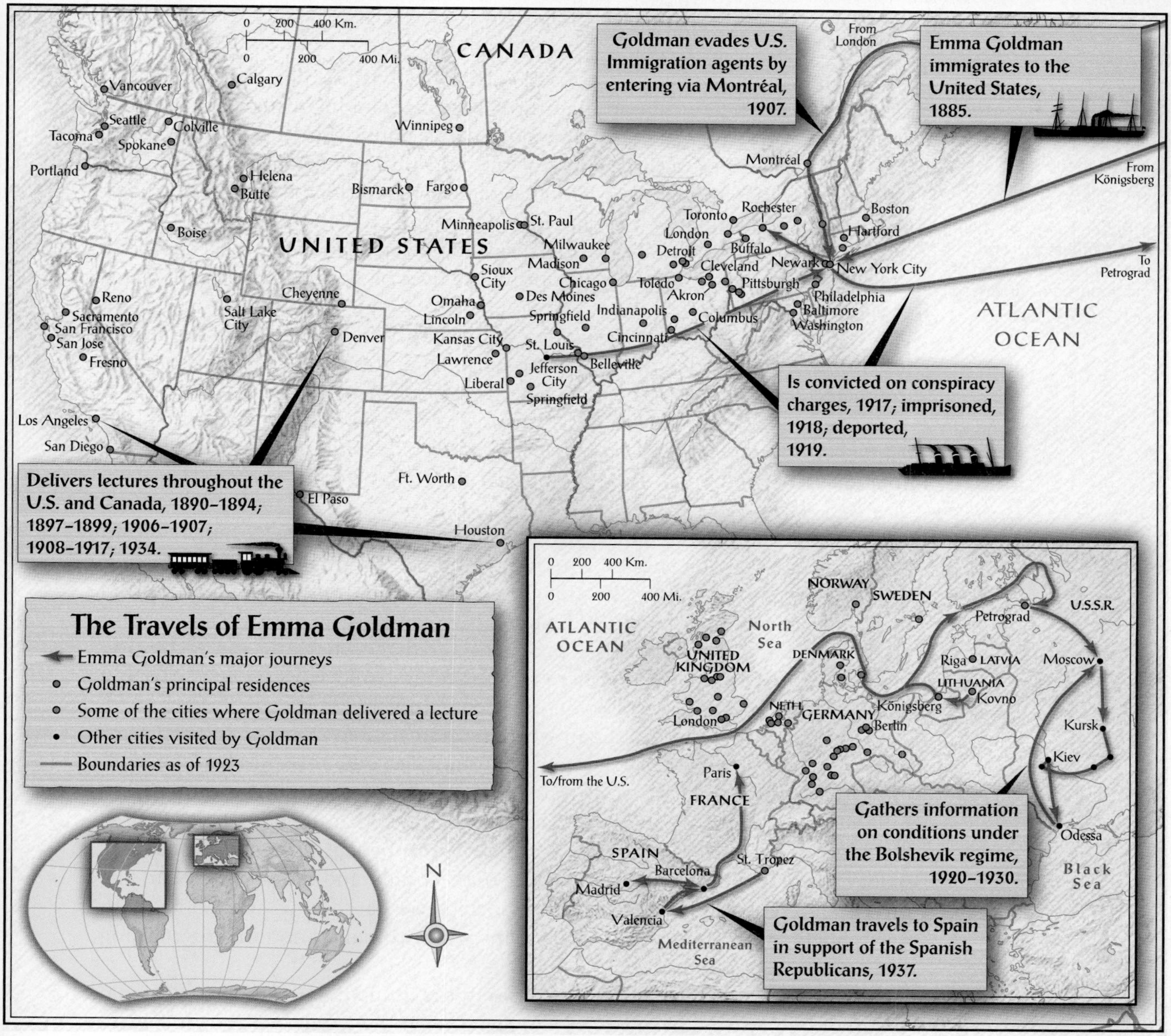

*interference and oppression of others. . . . My faith is in the individual and in the capacity of free individuals for united endeavor.**

---

*Emma Goldman, "Anarchism: What It Really Stands For," p. 64, and "Was My Life Worth Living," pp. 442–443, from *Red Emma Speaks: An Emma Goldman Reader*, comp. and ed. Alix Kates Shulman, 3d ed. (Amherst, N.Y.: Humanity Books, 1998).

Emma Goldman

(1869–1940) Russian-born anarchist who moved to the United States but was deported in 1919 for her anticonscription campaign. Militant feminist and critic both of capitalism and of communism as practiced in the Soviet Union.

At a time of triumphant patriotism, with collectivist ideologies on the rise, it seemed the tide of history had turned against Goldman's beliefs. Still, she battled on, both as a writer and as a sought-after public speaker.

It was her protest against the violence and futility of the First World War (1914–1918) that solidified Goldman's radical reputation. Industrially driven total war caused immense suffering for soldiers and civilians alike. In mobilizing their empires for the war effort, the European powers made their local conflict a genuinely global one, severely disrupting the lives of many Africans and Asians as well.

At war's end, diplomats squandered the chance to create a more stable and just international order, as competing national and imperial interests planted the seeds of conflict for the future. The shadow of the First World War loomed over the 1920s: *"The war has left a confused generation,"* Goldman wrote. *"The madness and brutality they had seen, the needless cruelty and waste which had almost wrecked the world made them doubt the values that their elders had given them."**

A true revolutionary, Goldman did not believe that gradual change within the status quo was the answer, whether for women's rights, for political justice, or for economic equality. She therefore found hope in the revolutions that rocked major world societies in Mexico, China, and Russia during the period of world war. But Goldman also recognized the dangers that war and revolution had unleashed, especially after her enforced return to Russia gave her firsthand knowledge of the brutality of Soviet-style communism.

During her lifetime, Goldman witnessed remarkable changes. In the industrialized world, telephones, electricity, automobiles, and airplanes became commonplace. In some places, women fought for and won the right to vote. African American musicians created jazz, the first significant influence of the United States on global culture. Scientific advances continued, as physicists made huge strides toward understanding nature at both cosmic and atomic levels. In the industrialized world, urbanized mass society was becoming the norm, with newspapers gaining enormous readerships and with radio and film entertaining and informing millions.

Meanwhile, urbanizing mass societies in the industrial world put traditional gender roles in flux as many more women entered the workforce and, at least in some industrial societies, won the right to vote. But Goldman's vision of female liberation went far beyond voting to embrace full emancipation, foreseeing a day when *"the road toward greater freedom [will be] cleared of every trace of centuries of submission and slavery."**

---

*Emma Goldman, "Was My Life Worth Living," p. 436, "The Tragedy of Women's Liberation," p. 159, from *Red Emma Speaks: An Emma Goldman Reader*, comp. and ed. Alix Kates Shulman, 3d ed. (Amherst, N.Y.: Humanity Books, 1998).

KEY CONCEPT QUESTIONS

- What aspects of World War I made it a "total war"? **(Key Concept 6.2)**
- How did the resolution of World War I lead to increased tension in Europe, Africa, and the Middle East? **(Key Concept 6.2)**
- How did socialism and communism influence early twentieth-century revolutions in Mexico, China, and Russia? **(Key Concept 6.2)**
- Why was Emma Goldman's challenge to traditional gender roles viewed as radical? **(Key Concept 6.3)**

World War I as Global "Total" War

World War I (1914–1918) represented a radical change in warfare. This was "total war," requiring complete mobilization of national resources and engaging masses of civilians. Governments assumed unprecedented powers to regulate social, political, and economic life, straining traditional social and political systems. Nothing would remain the same. The British called it simply the Great War.

The war was also a truly global struggle. While colonial peoples had been caught up in earlier European conflicts, the global involvement of World War I was unprecedented. Young men from the United States shipped out to Europe, Indian soldiers marched to Baghdad, Southeast Asians worked behind the lines on the western front, West Africans fought in the trenches: all had life-changing experiences.

Causes of World War I, 1890–1914

On June 28, 1914, in the Balkan city of Sarajevo, a Serbian nationalist assassinated Archduke Franz Ferdinand, heir to the Austrian throne. The Balkan region had long been an unstable zone between the Austrian and Ottoman empires (see Map 27.1). As the Ottomans declined, Austrians were asserting themselves and provoking local nationalists who did not want to escape one empire only to be dominated by another (see Chapter 23).

AP® THEMES

How did religious differences in Europe contribute to the increase in tensions between nations in the early twentieth century?

Despite their cultural similarities as Slavs and their long history of coexistence, the inhabitants of the Balkans emphasized religious differences as they developed competing nationalisms. Serbians looked to their fellow Orthodox Christians in Russia for support; Croatian nationalists allied themselves with Catholic Austria; Bosnian Muslims sided with the Ottoman empire.

These local Balkan tensions led to full-scale war because of the rising militarism, aggressive nationalism, and intense imperial competition that had preoccupied the leading industrial nations in the age of the New Imperialism (see Chapter 26). In the late nineteenth century, tensions between the great powers, now including Japan and the United States, had found an outlet in colonial rivalries outside of Europe. By 1900, however, there were no more African, Asian, or Pacific lands left to conquer. The assassination of Archduke Franz Ferdinand therefore ignited the fuse under a Europe bristling with heavily militarized national competition.

Map 27.1 World War I, 1914–1918 By the end of World War I, horrific violence along the western front in Belgium, Luxembourg, and northeastern France, and on the eastern front in the Russian empire and eastern Europe, had led to the deaths of over 8 million soldiers, with 20 million wounded. On the southern front, defeat led to the dissolution of the Ottoman empire. While these three theaters saw the fiercest fighting, the global effects of the conflict made it truly a world war.

Germany epitomized the era's militarism, especially after 1890 when **Kaiser Wilhelm II** (r. 1888–1918) dismissed Otto von Bismarck (see Chapter 23) to pursue a more aggressive foreign policy. His naval buildup caused Britain to reverse its practice of avoiding commitments on the continent. Likewise, the French and Russian governments, faced with rising German power, overcame their long-standing mutual distrust. A series of treaties produced a combination of alliances that divided Europe into two opposing blocs—the Triple Entente (ahn-TAHNT) of France, Britain, and Russia against the Triple Alliance of Germany, Austria, and Italy—leaving diplomats with no flexibility.

Kaiser Wilhelm II
(r. 1888–1918) German emperor whose foreign policy and military buildup changed the European balance of power and laid the foundation for the Triple Alliance and the Triple Entente.

Thus the Balkan crisis detonated an explosive confrontation between two hostile and heavily armed camps. The Austrian government threatened Serbia with war if it did not comply with a set of humiliating demands. The Serbs appealed to Russia, while the Germans backed up the Austrians. The Ottoman empire, fearful of Russian and British designs, allied itself with Germany. After a period of indecision, Italy joined with Britain, France, and Russia.

Public opinion compounded the war atmosphere. In urbanized, industrial societies, foreign affairs were no longer the exclusive purview of diplomatic elites. Expanding electorates had daily access to inexpensive newspapers that struck a nationalistic tone. Emma Goldman criticized *"the jingo howls of the press"* that created war fever as a way to sell newspapers, and the *"blood and thunder tirades"** of cynical politicians using patriotic appeals as a cheap way to gain votes. Indeed, declarations of war met with popular excitement and patriotic demonstrations. Only in Russia, where the tsar and his ministers ignored public opinion, did the government act without a popular mandate.

According to Emma Goldman, a fundamental cause of war was the profit-driven greed of arms manufacturers. She singled out the huge German industrial conglomerate of Krupps that *"for personal gain and profit,"* she said, had sent its emissaries all across Europe *"inciting national hatreds and antagonisms."** Goldman warned that U.S. corporations were contributing to war fever for the same reason.

Whatever the complex of causes, Europeans responded to the declarations of war with remarkable naïveté, believing it would be quick and conclusive and that their side would win. Even the German Social Democratic Party, which had long urged *"workers of the world unite!"* now supported a military mobilization that would pit German workers against French and British ones. Not having fought a general war since the defeat of Napoleon in 1815 (see Chapter 22), Europeans simply could not conceive of the horrors of modern industrialized warfare.

● **CONTEXT&CONNECTIONS** Both the *Crimean War* (key term in Chapter 23), between Russia and the Ottoman empire (1853–1856), and the U.S. Civil War (1861–1865) (see Chapter 25) had anticipated the higher mortality and logistical challenges of industrial warfare. Both conflicts took place away from western Europe, however, and the great powers did not learn those lessons. ●

Total War in Europe: The Western and Eastern Fronts

Britain had pledged to defend neutral Belgium, so when the Germans attacked Belgium en route to France war became inevitable. Unlike 1870, when the Prussians quickly took Paris, in 1914 the German advance was stopped 20 miles (32.2 km) short (see Map 27.1).

*Emma Goldman, "Preparedness: The Road to Universal Slaughter," *Mother Earth*, 10, no. 10 (December 1915).

From "Shell Shock" to Posttraumatic Stress Disorder

In 1915, "shell shock" was a new concept, invented by a British doctor to explain a disturbing phenomenon: British soldiers were returning from the front blind, deaf, or paralyzed without any apparent physical cause. Military leaders were alarmed because over 80 percent of "shell shock" victims were never able to return to service. Those who returned to civilian life were often looked down on as cowards, suffering social isolation as well as psychological trauma. Meanwhile, victims who remained at the front suffered from a variety of nervous disorders. One wartime poet described their "*dreams that drip with murder*" and their "*stammering, disconnected talk*."*

Today, we know a great deal more about the psycho-emotional difficulties resulting from intensive combat. The current term *posttraumatic stress disorder* (PTSD) originated in the 1960s, during the U.S. war in Vietnam (see Chapter 30) when U.S. soldiers faced not only incessant artillery and rifle fire, but deep uncertainty and insecurity as they moved through jungle terrain. Their enemies could be hidden in the foliage above or emerge suddenly from trapdoors below.

The Veteran's Administration (VA) hospital system in the United States thus developed expertise in dealing with PTSD. Apart from veterans of the Vietnam conflict still suffering four decades later, the VA system must now also find ways to deal with large numbers of younger PTSD sufferers from more recent wars. For example, the U.S. National Institutes of Health estimates that PTSD afflicts 20 percent of all veterans of the country's invasion and occupation of Iraq (see Chapter 32).†

Contemporary diagnoses of PTSD reach far beyond the shocks faced by soldiers in battle to include stress disorders arising from rape, torture, child abuse, accidents, natural disasters, and other traumatic events. The research of neuroscientists may lead to medications that can ameliorate the symptoms of PTSD, but to this point patients seem to benefit most from programs that include "exposure treatment," where they can talk through their original source of trauma in an emotionally secure environment. Ultimately, of course, the only sure cure for war-related PTSD is peace.

*Cited in British Broadcasting Company, "Shell Shock," *Inside Out Extra*, March 3, 2004, http://www.bbc.co.uk/insideout/southwest/series1/shell-shock.shtml.

†National Institutes of Health, "PTSD: A Growing Epidemic," *Medline Plus*, Winter 2009, http://www.nlm.nih.gov/medlineplus/magazine/issues/winter09/articles/winter09pg10-14.html.

western front
During World War I, the line separating the elaborate trenches of German and Allied positions, which soon became almost immobile. Trench warfare was characteristic of the western front.

Stalemate on this **western front** resulted in a new tactic: trench warfare. On one side, French and British soldiers fortified entrenched positions with razor wire; on the other side, Germans did the same. Miserable in the muddy trenches, soldiers were called on to charge "over the top," and try to overrun enemy positions. With machine-gunfire and bombs bursting around them, sometimes choking on poisonous mustard gas, they had little chance of survival, let alone victory. Battle lines of trenches and tunnels established early in Belgium and northern France hardly shifted.

The casualties of trench warfare were horrific. In 1916, at the Battle of Verdun more than half a million French and German troops lost their lives, and the Battle of the Somme killed nearly a million British and German soldiers. Young men from the same neighborhood, school, or village often volunteered and trained together, and then might all be killed within a few minutes. Many had married as they headed off to war; for decades afterward, war widows lived lives of regret for their lost youth, 630,000 of them in France alone.

The survivors of trench warfare lost not only their companions but also their physical and mental health. "Lost generation" was the term used to refer to the young adults who came of age during the Great War, not just those who died, but also those who lost their hopes and dreams. (See the feature "World History in Today's World: From 'Shell Shock' to Posttraumatic Stress Disorder.")

Civilians also suffered. Consumer goods became extremely scarce as domestic industries shifted toward the production of war materiel. To undermine the German war effort, the British navy blockaded Germany's seaports, and in response German submarines targeted British shipping in the Atlantic Ocean. Before 1914, Germany and Britain had been major trade partners. Now their navies crippled international trade. Since European prosperity depended on an interlinked world economy, hardship was the result.

● **CONTEXT&CONNECTIONS** The sharp decrease in international trade during World War I brought to an end the stunning growth of the world economy that had begun in the mid-nineteenth century. With the Great Depression, World War II, and the Cold War still ahead (see Chapters 28, 29, and 30), it was not until the 1990s that the momentum of international trade fully recovered, bringing a new round of economic "globalization" (see Chapter 31). ●

Protracted total war transformed European government and society. Because a nation had to tap all its energies in the interests of survival, governmental power expanded. Large corporations and the state were already in close cooperation in Germany before the war, but in Britain national economic planning represented a shift away from economic liberalism. Everywhere, the First World War began a long-term trend toward greater government involvement in economies. Anarchist notions of breaking down large companies and putting workers themselves in charge of the factories now seemed antiquated.

Indeed, government bureaucracies of all kinds expanded dramatically. Unions lost the right to strike. Traditional liberties—freedom of speech, freedom of assembly—were curtailed. The British Parliament even began to regulate the hours

Library of Congress Prints and Photographs Division [LC-USZ62-39197]

French Women and Total War With so many men away at the front, French women often took over management of family farms. Heightened authority came with a steep price, however. Here French women in the Somme region are pulling a plow, their horses and oxen having been either killed in the crossfire or requisitioned by one of the competing armies.

AP® THEMES
How did World War I affect gender roles within the nations at war?

of the nation's pubs. Less time spent drinking, it was thought, would improve industrial efficiency.

For European women, the war brought opportunities as well as costs. The nursing profession expanded, and with so many men absent, women became more important in factories. In France, many women ran family farms. Such circumstances undermined the idea that the woman's place was in the home, while men dominated the public sphere. But women paid a high price as well, toiling on extra shifts, raising children without any help, and despairing for their brothers, sons, and husbands at the front.

eastern front
The front in Russia during World War I. The German army moved quickly across eastern Europe into Russia; low morale plagued the poorly equipped Russian army in the face of superior German technology.

Nowhere were the consequences of total war greater than in eastern Europe. When the Russian army entered the Balkan conflict, warfare spread as far as Romania and Bulgaria. But the **eastern front** between German and Russian forces was the main battle line (see Map 27.1). Russia was still a primarily rural empire, a fatal weakness under conditions of industrialized total war. German invaders took hundreds of thousands of prisoners and treated them with extreme harshness.

Morale among Russian peasant conscripts was poor to begin with and deteriorated rapidly. Mutinies were common: soldiers and sailors, mostly descendants of serfs, felt little loyalty toward their aristocratic officers. Sometimes they killed their own commanders rather than head into futile battles; frequently they simply abandoned their weapons and walked home. American journalist Louise Bryant described them: *"great giants of men, mostly workers and peasants, in old, dirt-colored uniforms from which every emblem of Tsardom had been carefully removed."**

Famine stalked the Russian countryside as war disrupted food production. Factories closed when Russian industrialists lost access to Western capital. Despite deteriorating circumstances, Tsar Nicholas II refused to consider surrender. By 1917, the Russian people were demoralized and exhausted.

Total War: Global Dimensions

Total war required access to global resources. Battles were fought in Africa and the Middle East; Japan declared war on Germany to seize German concessions in China; Britain and France depended on their Asian and African empires for manpower and materiel. By the time the United States entered the war in 1917, the Great War truly was a world war.

southern front
The front in World War I caused by the Ottoman empire's decision to ally with the German army. Britain mobilized colonial forces from India, Egypt, and Australia to engage Ottoman forces at Gallipoli; British forces also occupied Mesopotamia and Palestine.

The decision by the Ottoman empire to side with Germany opened a **southern front** that extended the war to the Middle East and North Africa. During the late nineteenth century, German banks, commercial houses, and manufacturers had invested heavily in the Ottoman economy, and the Ottomans saw a German alliance as protection against the French, British, and Russians.

The most important strategic Ottoman position was the Dardanelles, a narrow strait connecting the Black Sea with the Mediterranean. In 1915, British forces, including many Australian and New Zealand Army Corps (ANZAC) troops, attacked the heavily fortified Ottoman position at Gallipoli. Ottoman forces, entrenched on higher ground, put up a tenacious defense, with great mortality on both sides. After a quarter million casualties, the British withdrew.

In the wake of Gallipoli, the British could spare neither men nor materiel from their home islands to fight on the southern front, so they mobilized regiments

---

*Quotes from Louise Bryant, *Six Red Months in Moscow* (New York: George H. Doren, 1919), p. 21.

from their African and Asian colonies. For example, black soldiers from the West Indian Regiment of the British Army, mostly from Jamaica, were deployed against the Ottomans in Palestine. Egyptian soldiers under British command were the main force there. The invasion resulted in British control over Jerusalem. Meanwhile, Indian soldiers engaged Ottoman forces in Mesopotamia.

Senegalese Sharpshooters
Mostly Muslim soldiers from French West Africa who were conscripted by the French empire in World War I and developed a reputation as fearsome fighters.

Knowing that many Arab subjects of the Ottoman empire were unhappy with Turkish rule, the British also forged an alliance with Arab leaders, with the dashing T. E. Lawrence, "Lawrence of Arabia," organizing Arab attacks on Ottoman railways and fortifications. Lawrence was an amateur archaeologist whose knowledge of Arabic and of the culture of Bedouin desert nomads proved vital to British intelligence. He was also an innovator in guerilla tactics; by dynamiting railroad bridges, he tied up the better-equipped Ottoman army.

Though the French did little fighting outside Europe, they also looked to their empire for support. When the number of volunteers from their imperial possessions did not meet wartime demand, French colonial officials pressured local African leaders to supply, by force if necessary, more conscripts for the French army. The most famous regiment of colonial recruits was the **Senegalese Sharpshooters**, many of whom died or were maimed on the western front. Soldiers from North Africa—Morocco, Tunisia, and Algeria—were also conscripted in large numbers.

Most of the Arab, Indian, and African soldiers mobilized by the British and French were Muslims, creating the potential for divided loyalty, especially since some saw the Ottoman sultan as *caliph,* successor to the political powers of the Prophet Muhammad. The British commander of the Palestinian campaign was therefore careful when entering Jerusalem—holy to Islam as well as to Christianity and Judaism—to assure his Egyptian and Indian troops, as well as the city's residents, that all their religious sites would be respected.

Battles between German East Africa and British-controlled Kenya also demonstrated the scope of total war in East Africa. On one side were African soldiers led by German officers, and on the other a largely Indian army commanded by the British. The German commander's main goal was to tie down the Anglo-Indian forces to keep them from being redeployed to the Middle East. He therefore repeatedly struck and then retreated, requisitioning local food reserves and destroying what was left to deny sustenance to his opponents. Famine and disease stalked the land; total war reached even the remote interior of East Africa.

Postcard depicting a Senegalese soldier, 1915 (coloured photo), French School (20th century)/Private Collection/Archives Charmet/Bridgeman Art Library

Franco-African Soldier Total war meant the mobilization of African and Asian colonial subjects. This young man, fighting for "the greater glory of France," is a Senegalese Sharpshooter, most likely a West African Muslim. He stands proudly, with German helmets perched atop his head.

In Southeast Asia, the French recruited young Vietnamese men for the Indochinese Labor Corps. The French assigned tedious work like digging fortifications and maintaining roads to the Vietnamese conscripts, allowing the army to concentrate more troops on the front line. At the same time, Indochinese rice and rubber were directed to support the French war effort. Chinese workers were recruited to the western front as well.

The Indians, West Africans, and Vietnamese conscripted by the British and French, as well as the civilians in colonial territories who produced coffee, rubber, tin, and other goods for imperial forces, contributed much to the war effort but received little in return. Later, anticolonial nationalists would base claims to greater self-government or independence on the sacrifices made during the war.

● **CONTEXT&CONNECTIONS** The Great War was decisive in moving the Indian nationalist *Mohandas K. Gandhi* (Chapter 28) toward mass nationalism and direct action. Gandhi urged loyalty to Britain during the war, expecting political concessions on the question of Indian self-government in return. Disappointed by the British response, during World War II Gandhi changed tactics and launched a *"Quit India"* campaign (Chapter 29), this time refusing to sanction Indian support for the British empire even during the war. ●

The End of the Great War

To achieve victory, one side would have to break the stalemate on the western front. After imposing a humiliating peace on Russia in early 1918, Germany seemed poised to do so, quickly redeploying troops westward. Just then, however, the United States entered the war to bolster French and British forces.

In 1914, the United States had only a small army, and Americans were still inclined to follow George Washington's advice that the republic should not *"entangle our peace and prosperity in the toils of European ambition."* Initially, President **Woodrow Wilson** (in office 1913–1921) kept the United States out of the war, but true neutrality proved impossible. With Germany's trade blocked by the British navy, America supplied industrial and military provisions to France and Britain. Between 1914 and 1916 American exports to these two countries grew from $824 million to $3.2 billion, bringing industrial expansion to the United States without any military cost.

Woodrow Wilson
(in office 1913–1921) President of the United States during and after World War I. Wilson's idealistic view, enshrined in his Fourteen Points, was that Allied success in the war would lead to the spread of peace and democracy.

America's entry into the war was largely in response to Germany's use of submarine warfare, itself a reaction to the British embargo on Germany. In 1915, the Germans sank the *Lusitania*, a civilian passenger ship with many Americans on board. After President Wilson protested, the Germans promised to stop attacking ships without warning. Meanwhile, business interests in the United States urged a rapid military buildup. While citing national security reasons, they also knew, as critics like Emma Goldman pointed out, that military spending was highly profitable.

Early in 1917 the Germans, aiming to stop American arms shipments to Britain, resumed submarine attacks. Proclaiming *"The world must be made safe for democracy,"* Wilson asked Congress to declare war. U.S. public opinion, inflamed by sensationalistic news reporting, was now swinging in favor of war. Goldman responded by mocking a former president—*"the blood and thunder tirades of bully Roosevelt"*—and dismissing the idealism of Wilson as *"the sentimental twaddle of our college-bred President."**

Goldman then went further by turning her antiwar message into action. Her public campaign against conscription led to her arrest, conviction, and a two-year prison sentence, with the judge recommending that she be deported upon her

*Emma Goldman, "Preparedness: The Road to Universal Slaughter," *Mother Earth*, 10, no. 10 (December 1915).

release. Goldman found that even in a liberal democracy, total war brings a grave loss of freedom.

Conscription went forward. Though the Germans were speeding troops westward from the Russian front, the arrival of a million-strong American force turned the tide in favor of the British and the French. On November 11, 1918, the Germans agreed to an armistice ending the war. The United States was now in a position to influence the peace talks that followed, taking a place alongside the major European powers. Germany was excluded from the bargaining table, as were the Asians and Africans whose fates were also to be determined.

The Postwar Settlements

As diplomats headed for France to attend the **Paris Peace Conference** in 1919, American authorities were forcing Emma Goldman and 247 other political deportees onto a ship in New York bound for the Russian capital, St. Petersburg. Meanwhile, an unprecedented outbreak of influenza was racing around the world. Between 1918 and 1920 as many as 50 million people died, far more than had lost their lives during the war itself. Wartime violence and dislocation had paved the way for an epidemic that further deepened global distress. The world seemed changed in some fundamental way, and the future was uncertain. In this atmosphere, representatives of the Allied powers—Britain, France, Italy, and the United States—gathered in Paris.

Paris Peace Conference
(1919) Conference that resulted in the Versailles treaty, which added to post–World War I tensions. A war-guilt clause and reparations payments destabilized Germany, and efforts to create stable nations from former imperial provinces in eastern Europe were problematic.

The Paris Peace Conference

The principal leaders at the Paris Peace Conference—Woodrow Wilson of the United States, Georges Clemenceau of France, and David Lloyd George of Britain—faced an enormous task. Germany had to somehow be reincorporated into Europe. The collapse of the Austrian and Ottoman empires required entirely new political systems in central Europe and western Asia (see Map 27.2). Germany would have to relinquish its colonies in Africa and the Pacific. The world's map had to be redrawn.

Wilson's high-minded "Fourteen Points," presented before the war's end, contained specific recommendations based on a few clear principles. Wilson stressed the importance of free trade, the right of peoples to national self-determination, and the creation of a permanent international assembly to provide safeguards against future wars. The British goal, on the other hand, was to safeguard its imperial interests, while the French priority was punishment of Germany.

Meanwhile, representatives from Africa, the Arab world, Southeast Asia, and other societies with deep concerns over the outcomes tried, with little effect, to influence the negotiations. Lacking a voice at the Paris Peace Conference, many of the world's people could only wait to see what the great powers would decide for them. (See the feature "Movement of Ideas Through Primary Sources: Dissenting Voices at the Paris Peace Conference.")

In the end, the Versailles treaty fell far short of Wilson's goals. The Allies did agree to Wilson's plan for a **League of Nations**. But tensions resulted from French insistence on punishment for Germany; from the failure to create coherent states in eastern Europe; from the imperial ambitions of Britain and France; and from the lack of participation in the League of Nations by both Russia, embroiled

League of Nations
Assembly of sovereign states, advocated by Woodrow Wilson, that was intended to provide a permanent diplomatic forum in the hopes of avoiding future conflict.

Dissenting Voices at the Paris Peace Conference

In 1919, delegates from the victorious nations traveled to France for the Paris Peace Conference. Concerned about the outcome of those negotiations, representatives from defeated nations like Germany, and spokesmen for societies entangled in European empires, also came to Paris. In the end, the resulting Versailles treaty left deep bitterness and future problems for central and eastern Europe, the Middle East, and the entire colonial world.

The first document is part of a letter written in May 1919 from Count von Brockdorff-Rantzau, leader of the German delegation, to French Prime Minister Georges Clemenceau, regarding a draft of the Versailles treaty. His suggestions for amendment were ignored.

The second extract is from a resolution passed by the General Syrian Congress of Damascus trying to stop the great powers from applying Section 22 of the League of Nations treaty to their country, which would allow the French to take control of Syria (and give the British control of Palestine). The Syrian resolution had no effect, and the French drove their leader, Faisal al-Hashemi, out of Syria.

The third document was drafted for submission to the Paris Peace Conference by Nguyen Ai Quoc (Nguyen the Patriot), a young Vietnamese nationalist then living and working in Paris, who would later become globally known under the name Ho Chi Minh. Nguyen's proposal was ignored by the French, who continued their colonial occupation of Indochina without any significant changes.

Another unofficial lobbying effort came from the Pan-African Congress, bringing together delegates from the United States, the West Indies, and Africa to Paris to speak for global African interests. Contrary to their pleas, European colonialism in Africa was further entrenched at Paris when the British, French, and Belgians took control of former German colonies as "mandated territories."

Historical Thinking Skill:

SYNTHESIS How were the political ideas developed during the Enlightenment echoed in each of these appeals to the European victors of World War I?

Sources: German and Syrian delegations: Cited in James H. Overfield, *Sources of Global History Since 1900*, 2d ed. (New York: Wadsworth/Cengage, 2012), pp. 99–101, 102–103. Ho Chi Minh: Peter Anthony DeCaro, *Rhetoric of Revolt: Ho Chi Minh's Discourse for Revolution* (Westport, Conn.: Greenwood, 2003), Appendix A, p. 101. Pan-African Congress: *African American Political Thought: Integration vs. Separatism, from the Colonial Period to the Present*, ed. Marcus D. Pohlmann (Oxford: Taylor & Francis, 2003), pp. 195–199.

Germany: "Leader of the German Peace Delegation to Georges Clemenceau"

I have the honour to transmit to you herewith the observations of the German delegation on the draft treaty of peace....

We were aghast when we read in documents the demands made upon us.... The more deeply we penetrate into the spirit of this treaty, the more convinced we become of the impossibility of carrying it out. The exactions of this treaty are more than the German people can bear.

With a view to the re-establishment of the Polish State we must renounce indisputably German territory [including] Danzig, which is German to the core.... The purely German district of the Saar must be detached from our empire, and the way must be paved for its subsequent annexation to France, although we owe her debts in coal only, not in men....

Germany, thus cut in pieces and weakened, must declare herself ready in principle to bear all the war expenses of her enemies, which would exceed many times over the total amount of German State and private assets.... The sum to be paid is to be fixed by our enemies unilaterally.... No limit is fixed, save the capacity of the German people for payment, determined not by their standard of life, but solely by their capacity to meet the demands of their enemies by their labor. The German people would thus be condemned to perpetual slave labor....

In other spheres also Germany's sovereignty is abolished.... Her chief waterways are subjected to international administration; she must construct in her territory such canals and such railways as her enemies wish.... The German people are excluded from the League of Nations, to which is entrusted all work of common interest to the world. Thus a whole people must sign a decree for its own ... death sentence.

From Syria: "Congress of Damascus Resolution"

We ask that the Government of this Syrian country should be a democratic civil constitutional Monarchy on broad decentralization principles, safeguarding the rights of minorities, and that the King be the Emir Faisal, who carried on a glorious struggle in the cause of our liberation....

Considering the fact that the Arabs inhabiting the Syrian area are not naturally less [capable] than other more advanced races...we protest against Article 22 of the Covenant of the League of Nations, placing us among the nations in their middle stage of development which stand in need of a mandatory power....

We do not acknowledge any right claimed by the French Government in any part whatever of our Syrian country....We oppose the pretensions of the Zionists to create a Jewish commonwealth in the southern part of Syria known as Palestine, and oppose Zionist migration to any part of our country....Our Jewish compatriots shall enjoy our common rights and assume the common responsibilities....

We also have full confidence that the Peace Conference will realize that we would not have risen against the Turks...but for their violation of our national rights, and so will grant us our desires in full...since we have shed so much blood in the cause of our liberty and independence.

From Vietnam: "Eight Points"

While waiting for the sacred right of nations to self-determination to be recognized, the people [of] Indochina, present the following demands to the governments of the Allied powers in general, and the French government in particular:

1. General amnesty for all Vietnamese political prisoners.
2. Equal rights for Vietnamese and French in Indochina, suppression of the Criminal Commissions which are instruments of terrorism aimed at Vietnamese patriots.
3. Freedom of press and of opinion.
4. Freedom of association and assembly.
5. Freedom of travel at home and abroad.
6. Freedom to study and the opening of technical and professional schools for natives of the colonies.
7. Substitute rule of law for government by decree.
8. Appointment of a Vietnamese delegation alongside that of the French government to settle questions related to Vietnamese interests.

From Africa: "Manifesto of the Second Pan-African Congress"

The absolute equality of all races, physical, political, and social, is the founding stone of World Peace and human advancement....The beginning of Wisdom in inter-racial contact is the establishment of political institutions among suppressed Peoples. The habit of democracy must be made to encircle the earth....Surely...there can be found in the civilized world enough of human altruism, learning and benevolence to develop native institutions for the native's good rather than continuing to allow the majority of mankind to be brutalized and enslaved....

The world must face two eventualities: either the complete assimilation of Africa with two or three of the great world states, with political, civil and social power and privileges absolutely equal for its black and white citizens, or the rise of a great black African State, founded in Peace and Good Will, based on popular education, natural art and industry and freedom of trade, autonomous and sovereign in its internal policy, but from the beginning a part of a great society of peoples in which it takes its place with others as co-rulers of the world.

Map 27.2 Territorial Changes in Europe After World War I The Versailles treaty altered the map of Europe dramatically through the application of Woodrow Wilson's policy of "national self-determination." New nations appeared in central and eastern Europe, carved from the former Russian, Austro-Hungarian, and Ottoman empires, though the complex ethnic composition of the region often made it impossible to draw clear lines between "peoples" and "states." The handover of the key regions of Alsace and Lorraine from Germany to France caused much bitterness among German nationalists.

in revolution, and the United States, retreating into isolationism. The First World War was not, as President Wilson had promised *"a war to end all wars,"* nor had the world been *"made safe for democracy."*

- **CONTEXT&CONNECTIONS** One of those who petitioned the peace conference to apply the principle of self-determination to his country, Vietnam, was *Ho Chi Minh* (Chapter 30). After his petition was ignored, Ho joined the French Communist Party, later traveling to Moscow. During the Second World War, he led the tenacious resistance of his Viet Minh army against Japanese invasion (see Chapter 29). Ho declared Vietnamese independence after the Japanese withdrew, but the French tried to reclaim their colonial powers. After the Viet Minh defeated the French in 1954, they faced a U.S. invasion that lasted beyond Ho's death in 1969. With victory in 1975, the communist government of newly unified Vietnam renamed Saigon as Ho Chi Minh City in his honor. ●

The Weimar Republic and Nation Building in Europe

After surrender and the kaiser's abdication, German liberals and socialists cooperated in the creation of the new **Weimar Republic**. Many years after the revolutions of 1848 (see Chapter 23), Germany finally had a liberal, democratic constitution.

Weimar Republic (1919–1933) The government of Germany created after World War I, based on a liberal democratic constitution. The new republic was immediately faced with huge war debts, political turmoil, and rising inflation.

The Weimar Republic faced enormous challenges. At war's end the German people were hungry, cold, and dispirited, and the huge reparation payments demanded by France crippled their recovery. National pride was wounded by the Versailles treaty's requirement for the complete demilitarization of the Rhineland, the German province bordering France, and severe restrictions on German rearmament.

It was in difficult circumstances that German centrists tried to foster the liberal political culture needed to sustain a free society. They faced opposition on the left from communists, who led uprisings in Berlin and Munich in 1919, and on the far right from the organizers of the Beer Hall Putsch, an attempt to seize power by angry war veterans, members of the National Socialist Party (see Chapter 28).

By 1923, the new Weimar Republic was foundering. It was unable to meet its reparation obligations, so French soldiers occupied the Ruhr Valley, Germany's industrial heartland to seize assets in lieu of cash. As the Weimar government printed more money to make up for the shortfall in its treasury, inflation spiraled out of control. People needed a wheelbarrow full of bank notes to buy a loaf of bread.

Then signs of recovery appeared. In 1925 international agreements eased Germany's reparation payments and ended the occupation of the Ruhr Valley. The German economy finally came back to prewar levels, and Berlin regained its status as a major cultural, intellectual, and artistic center. At last, Germany was offered full membership in the League of Nations. The respite was temporary, however. In just a few years another economic crisis would again drive many Germans toward the political extremes of left and right (see Chapter 28).

In the meantime, with the exception of Czechoslovakia, the new nations created by postwar diplomacy in eastern, central, and southeastern Europe proved unstable and prone to authoritarianism. A complex cultural geography meant that ethnic, linguistic, and religious groups lived scattered among each other in many places, making it impossible to use ethnic homogeneity as a simple guide for drawing new national lines on the map.

The Paris treaty recreated Poland, for example, which had been divided among Russia, Prussia, and Austria in the eighteenth century. Since the lands that became western Poland in 1920 had long been ruled from Berlin, there was a substantial German-speaking population living there, as well as a large Jewish community. Polish nationalists felt that Germans who lived in the new Poland had to either accept second-class status or move to the now reduced Germany where they "belonged." The repression of Polish Jews was even more extreme. In this tense atmosphere it proved impossible for Poland to develop a liberal, democratic political culture. In 1926, tired of the endless squabbling of politicians, conservative army officers seized power and imposed restrictions on free speech and political organization.

• **CONTEXT&CONNECTIONS** Like most Jews in the old Russian empire, including what became Poland, Emma Goldman spoke Yiddish growing up, the language of the eastern European *Ashkenazim* (Chapter 17). Also commonly spoken in New York when she arrived, Yiddish was a thriving language of poetry, philosophy, comedy, and theater. It disappeared from Poland in the 1940s, however, when nearly the entire Yiddish-speaking population, millions of people, were murdered by the Nazis as part of the *Holocaust* (Chapter 29). •

The slide toward dictatorship in eastern, central, and southern Europe arose from a contradiction that Wilson had not accounted for: nationalism is based on the rights of *groups*, while liberalism focuses on the rights of *individuals*. Nationalists, with an "us versus them" mentality, were prone to restrict the rights of minority groups rather than follow the liberal philosophy of protecting individual rights regardless of ethnic background. The problem was particularly acute for peoples with no state to protect them, such as Europe's Jews and Roma (Gypsies).

The Mandate System in Africa and the Middle East

The fate of former German colonies and Ottoman provinces was another issue to be determined at Paris. In the end, French and British colonial interests took priority, and rights of national self-determination for African and Arab peoples received only token attention. The Allies devised the **Mandate System**, whereby the great powers ruled over territories under League of Nations auspices until their peoples might be "prepared" for self-government. Race was the unspoken determinant of who was deemed capable of self-rule.

Mandate System
System by which former Ottoman provinces and German colonies were redistributed; based on the idea that some societies were not ready for national self-determination, it expanded the empires of Britain, France, Belgium, and Japan while angering African, Arab, and Chinese nationalists.

In Africa, the Mandate System allowed the French, British, Belgian, and South African governments to take over former German colonies. Britain added German East Africa (today's Tanzania) to its empire. The French expanded their West African holdings, and the Belgians enlarged their Central African empire. While the Mandate System required reports to the League of Nations showing that they were furthering "native rights," the Europeans ruled the mandated territories like colonies, doing little or nothing to prepare them for eventual self-determination.

• **CONTEXT&CONNECTIONS** With the addition of former German East Africa to its empire as Tanganyika, Britain finally achieved *Cecil Rhodes's* dream of controlling a continuous stretch "from Cape to Cairo" (Chapter 26). •

Still, the ideal of national self-determination inspired a new generation of African nationalists. In South Africa, for example, leaders of the African National Congress called for greater rights, including an extension of the right to vote to Western-educated African property owners and an end to residential segregation. In West Africa, returning war veterans brought a heightened consciousness of the continent's place in the wider world. More African students left for study in Europe and the United States and came back questioning the legitimacy of colonial rule. Thus, the seeds of African nationalism began to sprout in the wake of World War I.

In the Middle East, the collapse of Ottoman authority created a power vacuum. While the French and British wanted control of such rich and strategic areas as Turkey, Mesopotamia, Syria, and Palestine, they had to contend with well-organized forces of Turkish, Arab, and Jewish nationalism.

As the Ottoman empire collapsed, some of its subject peoples sought to liberate themselves. Hoping for an independent state, some Armenians supported Russia during the war. Ottoman officials responded by relocating millions of Armenians in a forced march west. As many as 1.5 million Armenians perished in what historians call the Armenian Genocide, an attempt by the Turkish military to destroy them as a people. The surviving Armenians did gain a state of their own in the postwar settlements, though other peoples in the region, such as the Kurdish-speaking population of the former Ottoman empire, did not. The Kurdish people were scattered across the new postwar states of Turkey, Iraq, Syria, and Iran (see Chapter 32).

The Middle East's postwar situation was complicated by three contradictory promises the British made during the war. In 1915, to gain Arab support against the Ottoman empire, the British had promised the prominent Hashemite family to *"recognize and support the independence of the Arabs"* after the war. Contradicting that agreement, the British signed a secret treaty with the French arranging to divide Ottoman provinces between them. Finally, the **Balfour Declaration** of 1917 committed the British government to support the creation of a "national home" for the Jewish people in Palestine. The British government was seeking additional support for the war effort from Zionists, Jewish nationalists who hoped to establish their own state on the site of the ancient Hebrew kingdoms.

Balfour Declaration (1917) Declaration that committed the British government to help create "a national home for the Jewish people" in Palestine. Britain made this declaration to gain support from Zionists during World War I.

Zionism had originated in the late nineteenth century among European Jews who were alarmed at persistent anti-Semitism. Zionists argued that a nation-state was necessary to represent Jewish interests in the world and give Jews a place of

Hulton Archive/Getty Images

The Syrian Delegation to the Paris Peace Conference Emir Faisal al-Hashemi led a delegation to Paris to secure the independence of a Syrian Arab kingdom. He was supported by the Englishman T.E. Lawrence ("Lawrence of Arabia") shown standing behind him, second from the right. The French drove Faisal from Syria; as a consolation prize the British made him King of Iraq.

refuge in times of crisis, and had advocated for Jewish emigration to Ottoman Palestine. Still, by 1922 well over 80 percent of the people actually living in Palestine were Muslim or Christian Arabs.

AP® THEMES

How did the Treaty of Versailles ending World War I influence the development of states in the Middle East?

After the war, the British and the French implemented their secret treaty, dividing the Middle East region between them. The French received a League of Nations mandate over Syria and Lebanon, and the British stitched together three Ottoman provinces centered on the cities of Mosul, Baghdad, and Basra into a new entity they called Iraq.

The French were not able to impose their authority on Syria without a fight. Faisal al-Hashemi had been declared king of an independent Arab state by the Syrian National Congress and had traveled to Paris as head of an Arab delegation in 1919. When the French tried to impose their authority, Faisal and his supporters resisted. Defeated by the French, Faisal then fled to Baghdad, where the British agreed to install him as king of Iraq. Lacking a local base of support in Iraq, Faisal, a Sunni Muslim, proved compliant with British authorities, who were looking for a way to balance Arab demands with their own strategic and economic interests.

Instability in Iraq could have been anticipated. An artificial creation, it was divided between a Shi'ite Arab majority in the south, a Sunni minority in the center, and a Kurdish-dominated region in the north. The choice of Faisal as king showed British favoritism toward the Sunni Arabs. Gertrude Bell, the British diplomat most responsible for the creation of modern Iraq, wrote in 1920: *"I don't for a moment doubt that the final authority must be in the hands of the Sunnis, in spite of their numerical inferiority.... Otherwise you will have a theocratic state, which is the very devil."** Shi'ite Iraqis resented Sunni political ascendancy (which would last until the American invasion of 2003; see Chapter 32).

The most complicated situation arose in Palestine. Wartime anti-Semitism had increased the appeal of Zionism among American and European Jews, and even many who had no plans to emigrate to Palestine contributed money to purchase land for those who did decide to move. Arab leaders were alarmed, fearing they would become a minority in the land where their families had lived for perhaps a thousand years.

It was impossible for the British to please both sides. When the British allowed Jewish immigration in large numbers in the early 1920s, massive Arab demonstrations erupted. When the British curtailed Jewish immigration in response, Zionist leaders were furious. The British were determined to keep Palestine because of its strategic location, but the political price was exceptionally high.

British and French leaders viewed these imperial enlargements as spoils of war and anticipated that they would retain their traditional global dominance. But the world had changed. The British had liquidated many foreign investments to fight the war and slipped from being the world's largest creditor to facing significant debts, especially to the United States. Western European economic supremacy was on the wane, while the forces of anticolonial nationalism were gathering throughout Africa and Asia.

- **CONTEXT&CONNECTIONS** Through the Mandate System, the British and the French were thus adding to their imperial commitments in Africa and Asia just when the tides of history were moving *against* European colonialism. It would have amazed the

*Gertrude Bell, "Letter to Her Father," October 3, 1920; cited in Scott Horton, "Bell on the Shi'a in Iraq," *Harpers Magazine*, March 19, 2008.

diplomats of 1919, secure in their dominant global roles, to learn that they might live to see the British and French empires all but disappear, supplanted by independent African and Asian nations (see Chapter 30). ●

Twentieth-Century Revolutions: Mexico, China, and Russia

Revolutions would spread across the world in the twentieth century, first in Mexico, China, and Russia, and later in societies across Asia, Africa, and Latin America. To the surprise of followers of Karl Marx, who had prophesied proletarian revolutions in advanced industrial societies (see Chapter 23), the revolutionary surge came from the fringes of the international system, in largely agricultural countries with peasant majorities. And while nineteenth-century European revolutionaries had struggled to balance nationalism with liberalism, now it was the mixture of nationalism and socialism that would prove more potent.

Consequences of the Mexican Revolution, 1919–1927

In 1910, Mexico had been first out of the twentieth century's gates of revolution (see Chapter 25). For Emma Goldman, Mexico provided a visceral feeling of excitement when she saw that *"the real and true proletarians, the robbed and enslaved peons, are fighting for land and liberty."** Her observation rang true for the forces gathered by Emiliano Zapata and Pancho Villa, but many other factions and interests were vying for power and influence as well.

The Mexican Constitution of 1917 resulted from the tug and pull between moderate and more radical delegates. A basic legal framework protecting property rights was offset by "social clauses" that enshrined the rights of workers, restricted the powers of the Catholic Church, and identified the mineral sector, including petroleum, as property of the nation as a whole, allowing later nationalization. The declaration that *"private property is a privilege created by the Nation"* opened up the possibility of land redistribution, a key goal of Zapata and his peasant constituency.

After his election as president in 1920, Álvaro Obregón tried to stabilize the country with cautious implementation of the "social clauses." His educational reforms, however, antagonized the Catholic Church and many of its supporters. Obregón was assassinated in 1928 by a member of the *Cristeros* movement, which opposed limits on the power and property of the Catholic Church.

Stability only came to Mexico in 1929, almost twenty years after the revolution began. The formation of the Party of the Mexican Revolution brought the debates between moderates and the more radical supporters of the "social clauses" into a single political party. Party leaders then used patronage, corruption, and backroom deals to try to reconcile the nation's contending needs and interests. Some leaders had less interest in government policy than in enhancing their own wealth, status, and power. Furthermore, by institutionalizing the revolution the party took away its energy and popular base.

---

*Emma Goldman, "Socialism Caught in the Political Trap," p. 107, from *Red Emma Speaks: An Emma Goldman Reader*, comp. and ed. Alix Kates Shulman, 3d ed. (Amherst, N.Y.: Humanity Books, 1998).

● **CONTEXT&CONNECTIONS** The Party of the Mexican Revolution, later renamed the Party of the Institutional Revolution (PRI), was the sole political party in power in Mexico for seven decades. Although progressive President Lázaro Cárdenas nationalized the oil sector and redistributed land to peasant communes in the 1930s (see Chapter 28), PRI leaders more often looked after their own wealth and power rather than the national interest. Finally, in 2000, Mexicans elected the leader of an alternative party to the presidency, breaking the PRI monopoly (see Chapter 31). ●

The Chinese Revolution

After the humiliations following the Boxer Rebellion (see Chapter 24), China entered the twentieth century in desperate need of a new government to unify its people and defend against foreign encroachment. In 1912, the last Qing emperor, a boy at the time, abdicated. Nationalists led by Sun Zhongshan, better known as **Sun Yat-sen** (1866–1925), declared a new Republic of China. Sun, head of the Guomindang (gwo-min-DAHNG), or Nationalist, Party, envisioned a modernized China, with a stable liberal legal system and a just distribution of resources, taking its rightful place among the world's great powers.

Sun Yat-sen
(1866–1925) The founding father of the Republic of China after the revolution of 1911; established the Guomindang, or Nationalist Party.

Sovfoto/Universal Images Group/Getty Images

May Fourth Movement May 4, 1919, was an important day in the development of Chinese nationalism. Hundreds of thousands of protesters gathered in Tiananmen Square in Beijing, angered by the Versailles treaty, which had given Chinese territory to Japan. Demonstrations across the country lasted for months, with students playing a large role. In this photograph, residents of Shanghai wave signs that say *"Down with the traitors who buy Japanese goods!"*

Japanese military superiority made such international standing difficult to achieve, however. Already ruling over Taiwan and controlling resource-rich Manchuria in the north, Japan received the German concession on the Shandong peninsula in acknowledgment of its wartime alliance with France and Britain. On May 4, 1919, Chinese university students demonstrated in Tiananmen Square in Beijing, appealing to the government to restore Chinese dignity in the face of Japanese aggression. Their **May Fourth Movement** led to strikes, mass meetings, and a boycott of Japanese goods. Chinese nationalism was on the rise, but the republican government was powerless to respond to the students' appeals.

May Fourth Movement

(1919) A student-led protest in Beijing's Tiananmen Square against the failure of the Versailles treaty to end Japanese occupation of Chinese territory. Such anti-Japanese protests spread across China, and focused on a boycott of Japanese goods.

• **CONTEXT&CONNECTIONS** Student activists who gathered in Tiananmen Square in 1989 commemorated the seventieth anniversary of the May Fourth Movement by organizing for democracy and liberty. In response, Communist authorities sent tanks and soldiers to clear the square, killing hundreds in the *Tiananmen Massacre* (Chapter 31). •

The domestic military situation was another challenge for Sun and the Guomindang. From 1916, regional warlords mustered private armies as the country descended into a decade of disorder. Sun retreated to Guangzhou, where the Guomindang was being rebuilt by his brother-in-law and successor Jiang Jieshi, known in the West as Chiang Kai-shek (1887–1975). By 1927, the Guomindang had defeated the warlords and re-established central authority. Under Chiang's authoritarian command, however, Sun's idealistic emphasis on reform was supplanted by a growing culture of militarism and corruption.

Meanwhile, in 1921, in the wake of the May Fourth Movement, the Chinese Communist Party was formed in Shanghai. Seeking support from the new communist government in Russia, Chiang Kai-shek made a tactical alliance with the Communists. But in 1927, when he felt more secure in power, Chiang turned against them. Guomindang soldiers and street thugs killed thousands of Communists in the coastal cities, and those remaining fled to the countryside.

Mao Zedong (1893–1976), who now came to leadership of the Chinese Communist Party, argued that there was an advantage in this forced retreat, since it would be the peasants who would lead the way to socialism. Rejecting the traditional Marxist emphasis on industrial workers, Mao wrote: *"In a very short time...several hundred million peasants will rise like a tornado...and rush forward along the road to liberation."* By allying with this elemental peasant force, Mao thought, the Communists could drive Chiang from power and bring about true revolution.

• **CONTEXT&CONNECTIONS** The Nationalists and the Communists would continue to contest power for two decades. Jiang Jieshi (Chiang Kai-shek) and his Guomindang fought on the Allied side during World War II, but were driven from the Chinese mainland in 1949 by Mao Zedong's Red Army (see Chapter 30). •

Russia's October Revolution

Even more than the Mexican and Chinese Revolutions, the Russian Revolution had a profound impact on world history. Indeed, the Bolsheviks and their leader Vladimir Lenin saw themselves as fighting not just to control one country but to change the destiny of all humanity.

Russia's first revolutionary crisis had occurred in 1905, after defeat in the Russo-Japanese War (see Chapter 24). Peaceful protesters converging on the Winter Palace in St. Petersburg to petition the tsar for reform were ridden down and murdered by mounted guards, shattering old bonds of trust.

In the ensuing crisis, Tsar Nicholas II (r. 1894–1917) conceded a series of reforms, including, for the first time, a representative assembly, called the Duma. But while property-owning men could now vote and have some voice in government, real power still lay with the tsar and his ministers and with an aristocracy that retained dominance over the military.

Nicholas had also approved a crash program of industrialization. The first phase of industrial growth only added to social instability, however. The money for industrialization came largely from higher taxes on already miserable peasants, and the new industrial workers labored under much worse conditions and at much lower pay than their Western counterparts.

While some reformers argued that the powers of the Duma should be expanded, others argued that nothing would change until the old order was entirely swept away. One of these revolutionary groups was the Social Democratic Party, communist followers of the Marxist tradition.

After 1903, the Social Democrats had split into two factions. One group, the Mensheviks, adhered to the traditional Marxist belief that a modern industrial economy would have to be built before Russia's workers would be strong enough to seize state power. The Mensheviks therefore favored an alliance with the Russian middle class that would lead to a liberal, multiparty constitutional republic.

Vladimir Lenin

(1870–1924) Born Vladimir Ilyich Ulyanov, Lenin led the Bolsheviks to power during the Russian Revolution of 1917. Leader of the Communist Party until his death in 1924.

Vladimir Lenin (1870–1924), the leader of the opposing Bolshevik faction, disagreed. Lenin's radicalism started in childhood, when his elder brother was hanged for plotting to assassinate the tsar. Lenin himself was exiled first to Siberia and then to western Europe. There he developed his theory of a "*revolutionary vanguard.*" A small, dedicated group of professional revolutionists, he argued, could seize power in the name of the working class and rule in its interests. Dictatorship rather than democracy was implicit in Lenin's concept of revolutionary leadership.

World War I offered Lenin the opportunity to implement his ideas. Faced with mutiny in the army and near anarchy across the country, Tsar Nicholas abdicated in February 1917. By the summer of 1917 the Provisional Government that had replaced him was also losing legitimacy when it decided to continue to fight Germany.

By then the Russian people were simply sick and tired of war. American journalist Louise Bryant, who befriended Emma Goldman in St. Petersburg, described the passionate appeal of one war veteran at a public meeting: "*Comrades! I come from the place where men are digging their graves and calling them trenches! I tell you the army can't fight much longer!*" "*Over and over like the beat of the surf came the cry of all starving Russia,*" Bryant wrote, "'*Peace, land and bread!*'"* The Provisional Government was unable to deliver on any of these demands.

---

*Quotes from Louise Bryant, *Six Red Months in Moscow* (New York: George H. Doren, 1919), pp. 48–49.

After the tsarist bureaucracy collapsed, a new form of social and political organization emerged: the *soviets* (Russian for "committees") of factory and railroad workers, of residents in urban neighborhoods, and even of soldiers and sailors in the military. The soviets represented a radical form of democracy where all participants had the right to speak and be represented, with decisions made through public discussion and consensus. It was exactly the model of democracy long advocated by Russian anarchists, from Mikhail Bakunin (see Chapter 23) to Emma Goldman.

As Russian society slid from dictatorship to near anarchy, Lenin returned from exile. His clear vision and organizational abilities put the Bolsheviks in a position to make a play for power. Given an interview with Lenin upon her arrival, Goldman found him to be *"a shrewd politician who . . . would stop at nothing to achieve his ends."** Her friend Louise Bryant agreed: *"He possesses all the qualities of a 'chief,' including the absolute moral indifference which is so necessary to such a part."*†

Though a sophisticated intellectual, in the summer of 1917 Lenin reduced the Bolshevik program to two simple slogans: *"Peace, Land, and Bread!"* and *"All Power to the Soviets!"* The fiery speeches and tireless organizing of another prominent Bolshevik, Leon Trotsky (1879–1940), did much to advance the communist cause that summer.

In the fall, Lenin and the Bolsheviks planned and executed a coup d'état that later communists would celebrate as the October Revolution. Hardly a shot was fired in the Provisional Government's defense. Lenin disbanded the Constituent Assembly recently elected to write a new constitution. *"A big sailor marched into the elaborate red and gold assembly chamber,"* Bryant reported, *"and announced in a loud voice: 'Go along home!'"*† Russia's brief experiment with multiparty representative democracy had ended.

Arriving in St. Petersburg in 1919, when Lenin and the Bolsheviks were fighting for the survival of their revolution, Emma Goldman at first supported their cause. *"The libertarian principle was strong in the initial days of the revolution,"* she later recalled, *"the need for free expression all-absorbing."**

Goldman was especially excited to converse with the leader of the new Women's Bureau, Alexandra Kollontai. How incredible it would have seemed during tsarist times that any woman, let alone a strong proponent of women's rights, could become a government minister! Kollontai's fierce radicalism—*"Cast off your chains! Do not be slaves to religion, to marriage, to children. Break these old ties . . . the world is your country!"*‡—was music to Emma Goldman's ears.

It did not take long for Goldman to become disillusioned, however, after she realized that the Bolsheviks really had no place for *"the libertarian principle."* She became one of the new Soviet Union's fiercest critics, earning the enmity of many socialists by claiming that *"it is not only Bolshevism that has failed, but Marxism itself."**

---

*Emma Goldman, "Afterword to *My Disillusionment with Russia*," pp. 387, 392, 398, from *Red Emma Speaks: An Emma Goldman Reader*, comp. and ed. Alix Kates Shulman, 3d ed. (Amherst, N.Y.: Humanity Books, 1998).

†Quote from Louise Bryant, *Six Red Months in Moscow* (New York: George H. Doren, 1919), pp. 138–139, 78.

‡Quoted in Louise Bryant, *Mirrors of Moscow* (Westport, Conn.: Hyperion, 1923), p. 112.

Civil War and the New Economic Policy, 1917–1924

For the Communist Party, as the Bolsheviks were now called, defending the revolution was the first order of the day. To fulfill their promise to bring peace, they signed a treaty in 1918 ceding rich Ukrainian and Belarusian lands to Germany. The Communists saw this unequal treaty as a temporary setback, certain that the German communists would soon overthrow their government and establish a true and equitable peace.

The Communists also contended with powerful counter-revolutionary forces, as aristocratic generals turned their attention from the Germans to undoing the revolution. The Russian Civil War of 1919–1921 pitted the Communist Red Army, commanded by Leon Trotsky, against the "White Armies" organized by former tsarist generals with the help of the United States and Great Britain. To eliminate a rallying point for counter-revolution, the Bolsheviks coldly murdered the tsar and his family, as Lenin organized a secret police service even more terrifying than the old tsarist one.

• **CONTEXT&CONNECTIONS** The Russian experience, where members of the displaced ruling class fomented counter-revolution in alliance with foreign powers, repeated the experience of the French Revolution and anticipated the Cuban one. Like the earlier *Jacobins* (Chapter 22) and the later Cuban revolutionaries led by *Fidel Castro* (Chapter 30), the Bolsheviks justified clamping down on freedom of speech in the name of saving the revolution from its enemies. It seems that those who would take away such rights in an emergency rarely return them. •

By 1921, when the civil war ended, Lenin was securely in control and ruling with an iron hand. The anarchic democracy of freely elected soviets was replaced by strict party discipline in all facets of life. Emma Goldman now found that the soviets, which had earlier inspired her, were being *"castrated and transformed into obedient committees."** Even within the Communist Party Central Committee, dominated by Lenin, only limited debate was permitted. Once the Communists were secure in their control of the state, all political parties and social organizations, in Goldman's words, *"were either subordinated to the needs of the new State or destroyed altogether."**

• **CONTEXT&CONNECTIONS** Goldman noted the historical continuity of Russian authoritarianism: *"Lenin takes the seat of the Romanovs, the Imperial Cabinet is rechristened the Soviet of People's Commissars."** More recently, commentators have recognized similar tendencies in *Vladimir Putin* (Chapter 32) as he consolidated personal power over Russia in the twenty-first century. •

Lenin and the Bolsheviks were able to assert their claim to power not only in Russia, but across most of the former Russian empire. Though they lost lands in the west (such as Poland, Finland, and Lithuania), they retained the rich lands of the Ukraine, the vastness of Siberia, Central Asia with its potential for agricultural development, and the strategic Caucasus Mountains in the south. These regions

---

*Emma Goldman, "Afterword to *My Disillusionment with Russia*," pp. 399, 412, 413, from *Red Emma Speaks: An Emma Goldman Reader*,, comp. and ed. Alix Kates Shulman, 3d ed. (Amherst, N.Y.: Humanity Books, 1998).

were brought together in 1922 in the Union of Soviet Socialist Republics (U.S.S.R.). Allegedly a federal republic, in reality the Soviet Union was a top-down dictatorship dominated by Moscow.

After the civil war ended, Lenin instituted the **New Economic Policy** (1921–1924). Peasants were allowed to keep the land they had recently won. Restrictions on private business were lifted for all but the largest enterprises. In Goldman's analysis, the Bolsheviks could stay in power only if they moderated their demands, especially on the peasantry. The New Economic Policy, she said, *"was introduced just in time to ward off the disaster which was slowly but surely overtaking the whole Communist edifice."** The country experienced a brief respite of relative peace and the beginnings of economic recovery. But it was also during this time that, in an ominous preview of the future, the first of the Soviet labor camps was established, with the motto *"With an Iron Hand, Mankind Will Be Driven to Happiness!"*

New Economic Policy
During the New Economic Policy (1921–1924), Vladimir Lenin's government restored some private enterprise by allowing the operation of small shops and village markets, a policy later reversed by Joseph Stalin.

Stalin and "Socialism in One Country"

The dynamic of Soviet policy changed when Joseph Stalin established dictatorial power. After Lenin died in 1924, Stalin exploited divisions within the Central Committee to position himself as a safe and neutral choice for leadership. By 1926, he had consolidated his power and established sole authority, driving Leon Trotsky, his main competitor, into exile. (See the feature "Visual Evidence in Primary Sources: History, Photography, and Power.")

AP® THEMES
How were Soviet economic policies shaped by communism?

More than personal ambition was at stake. Stalin's vision of how to move the Soviet Union forward was encapsulated by the slogan **"Socialism in One Country."** Some Communists, like Trotsky, thought socialism in Russia required the help of revolutions in advanced industrial nations and advocated a policy of fomenting proletarian uprisings in the West. Others thought that the mixed approach of the New Economic Policy, with scope for private enterprise, was necessary to nurture capital investment for further industrial development. Stalin rejected both ideas. Instead, Soviet socialism would be built through top-down government control of every aspect of life.

"Socialism in One Country"
Joseph Stalin's slogan declaring that Soviet socialism could be achieved without passing through a capitalist phase or revolutions in industrial societies. This policy led to an economy based on central planning for industrial growth and collectivization of agriculture.

In 1928, Stalin launched the first of his Five-Year Plans. The entire economy was nationalized in a crash policy of industrialization. Noting that Russia was far behind more advanced economies, Stalin said, *"We must make good this lag in ten years... or we will be crushed."* After the Soviet Union cut ties with foreign economies, there was only one way Stalin could raise the capital needed for industrialization: by squeezing it out of the Soviet people. Low wages and harsh working conditions characterized new factories built to produce steel, electricity, chemicals, tractors, and other vital foundations of industrial growth. Especially productive workers received medals rather than higher wages, while poor performance could result in exile to a Siberian labor camp.

Still, by the 1930s, the Soviet Union had the world's fastest-growing industrial economy, while the capitalist nations were dragged down by the Great Depression

---

*Emma Goldman, "Afterword to *My Disillusionment in Russia*," p. 386, from *Red Emma Speaks: An Emma Goldman Reader*, comp. and ed. Alix Kates Shulman, 3d ed. (Amherst, N.Y.: Humanity Books, 1998).

History, Photography, and Power

As Joseph Stalin consolidated his power over the Soviet Union beginning in the late 1920s, he ordered that the history of the Russian Revolution be altered to magnify his own role. Stalin's propagandists portrayed him as having been exceptionally close to Vladimir Lenin, his close confidant and handpicked successor. In fact, while Lenin appreciated Stalin's discipline and loyalty, he regarded the younger man as of limited intelligence. In the 1930s, when Stalin began purging many of Lenin's closest allies from the

Though Lenin is shown here as a passionate orator, in fact he was not a good public speaker. To stir the masses with oratory the Bolsheviks relied on Leon Trotsky, who, as described by Louise Bryant, "*swayed the assembly as a strong wind stirs the long grass.*"

http://www.newseum.org/berlinwall/commissar_vanishes/9_10.htm

During the revolution, Lev Kamenev served as editor of the communist daily newspaper *Pravda* ("Truth"). He traveled to London to explain communist policies to the British government but was deported after one week.

Although the Bolsheviks fought against Russia's deeply rooted anti-Semitism, it returned under Stalin's rule. Trotsky, born Lev Bronstein, was the most prominent of the Jewish Bolsheviks.

Communist Party and executing many of the "Old Bolsheviks" who knew Lenin personally (see Chapter 28), the historical record was "adjusted" to remove many prominent revolutionists from the story.

Stalin's propagandists altered the photographic as well as the historical record of the revolution. This picture of Lenin speaking in Moscow in 1920 (left) is an iconographic image that was reproduced around the world. From the later 1920s, when the retouched version (below) was first produced, until the 1990s, Soviet citizens saw only the altered image in which two prominent Communists, Leon Trotsky and Lev Kamenev, had been erased and replaced with a set of wooden steps.

Stalin resented the leading role that Trotsky played as commander of the Red Army during the Russian Civil War of 1919–1921, and Trotsky was airbrushed out of all photographs from that period. In 1936 Kamenev was accused of plotting against Stalin and executed. Trotsky, exiled from Russia, died in Mexico in 1940 when one of Stalin's agents plunged an ice pick into his skull. ***With today's widespread knowledge about digital editing, is it more or less likely that viewers would be fooled by such brazen alterations as seen in these photographs?***

http://www.newseum.org/berlinwall/commissar_vanishes/9_10.htm

(see Chapter 28). Some Western leftists were willing to look past Stalin's excesses to applaud Soviet achievements. But Emma Goldman pulled no punches: "*The Russian Revolution,*" she wrote, "*has demonstrated beyond all doubt that the State idea, State Socialism, and all its manifestations... is entirely bankrupt.... To call such a dictatorship, this personal autocracy more powerful than any Czar's, by the name of Communism seems to me the acme of imbecility.*"*

Among the Soviet Union's multitude of failures, in her view, was its backsliding on gender issues. True, women now had more educational opportunities and access to previously all-male professions like medicine. Still, even the most accomplished Soviet women had to bear the burdens of persistent patriarchy, such as sole responsibility for domestic drudgery. Though disillusioned by the Soviet model, Goldman remained committed to the idea that only a bottom-to-top revolution could bring gender equality and the true liberation of women's spirit.

Emma Goldman on Women's Rights

It may come as a surprise that Emma Goldman, a radical social critic and a staunch feminist, was not involved in the movement for women's suffrage. She admired the "*heroism and sturdiness of the English suffragettes,*"* who in the years before the Great War had taken direct action to advance their cause, including public demonstrations, sit-ins, and even smashing windows, but securing the vote was never Goldman's priority.

For one thing, Goldman focused on the lives of working-class women and saw the suffrage movement as "*altogether a parlor affair, absolutely detached from the economic needs of the people.*"* Her hard life as a young immigrant in New York framed her outlook. The first step, she thought, was to organize women to fight for better wages and working conditions.

Even if women were now able to leave the home and seek employment—and indeed urbanizing societies relied on masses of young female labor for office and retail work—Goldman did not see progress: "*As to the great mass of working girls and women, how much independence is gained if the narrowness and lack of freedom of the home is exchanged for the narrowness and lack of freedom of the factory, sweat-shop, department store or office?*"*

Many saw Goldman's views of marriage as scandalous, as when she mentioned marriage and prostitution in the same breath: "*Nowhere is woman treated according to the merit of her work, but rather as a sex,*" she wrote. "*It is therefore almost inevitable that she should pay for her right to exist, to keep a position in whatever line, with sex favors. Thus it is merely a question of degree whether she sells herself to one*

---

*Emma Goldman, "Afterword to My Disillusionment with Russia," pp. 393, 409, "Woman Suffrage," pp. 198, 199, "The Tragedy of Women's Liberation," p. 160, from *Red Emma Speaks: An Emma Goldman Reader*, comp. and ed. Alix Kates Shulman, 3d ed. (Amherst, N.Y.: Humanity Books, 1998).

Gaston Paris/Getty Images

Josephine Baker The most famous and wealthiest black woman in the world, Josephine Baker made her way from the slums of St. Louis to stardom in Harlem, and then in France, where she made Paris her permanent home. In the 1920s, the erotic cabaret star challenged conventional limits on women's public roles and thus joined Emma Goldman in redefining women's possibilities for the twentieth century (though from the standpoint of personal style, no two women could possibly have been more different).

*man, in or out of marriage, or to many men."** Goldman asserted that only a truly independent woman could choose marriage under conditions of equality, a very rare circumstance. Her many critics saw "Red Emma" as an unabashed promoter of "free love," a crusader against everything right and proper.

Goldman's views on contemporary motherhood were equally shocking: *"Is there anything more terrible [than] the woman, physically and mentally unfit to be a mother, yet condemned to breed: the woman, economically taxed to the very last spark of*

---

*Emma Goldman, "The Traffic in Women," p. 177, from *Red Emma Speaks: An Emma Goldman Reader*, comp. and ed. Alix Kates Shulman, 3d ed. (Amherst, N.Y.: Humanity Books, 1998).

*energy, yet forced to breed; the woman, worn and used up from the process of procreation, yet coerced to breed, more, ever more."** Goldman certainly *did* value women's role as mothers, but *not* under those kinds of circumstances.

For Goldman, therefore, girls' sex education and women's access to birth control were top priorities. Not only were these taboo subjects in "polite" society, but advocacy of birth control through the mail was a federal offense, one for which Goldman was arrested on several occasions. On the need for sex education, she was forthright: *"So long as a girl is not to know how to take care of herself, not to know the function of the most important part of her life, we need not be surprised if she becomes an easy prey to . . . a relationship which degrades her to the position of an object for mere sexual gratification."**

AP® THEMES
How do Goldman's ideas about women's rights compare to the ideas of the women's suffrage movement?

In the fight for women's access to birth control, Goldman became a friend and mentor to Margaret Sanger, a pioneering activist for women's reproductive rights and a founder of Planned Parenthood. Having worked as a nurse and a midwife on the lower East Side of Manhattan, Goldman had seen the harsh toll that serial pregnancies took on women living in poverty. At her public speeches, she courted arrest by advocating access to birth control and distributing thousands of copies of Sanger's newsletter, *The Woman Rebel*. As with marriage so with procreation, Goldman argued: only a liberated woman could properly choose the status of wife or mother. *Choice* was the sign of true independence.

Emma Goldman's definition of women's liberation was thus expansive and existential rather than narrowly political: *"True emancipation begins neither at the polls nor in the courts. It begins in woman's soul. . . . It is necessary that woman . . . realize that her freedom will reach as far as her power to achieve her freedom reaches."*† As an anarchist, Goldman did not seek freedom through state institutions, in "polls" or "courts," but through women's self-actualization. Her recipe for women's emancipation was just the same as her prescription for society as a whole: *"All I want is freedom,"* she wrote, *"perfect, unrestricted liberty for myself and others."*‡

In Goldman's later years, however, individual freedoms were being constricted from both by fascists on the political right and communists on the political left (see Chapter 28). It would not be until the student movements of the 1960s that Goldman's libertarian agenda would resurface to inspire a new generation.

● **CONTEXT&CONNECTIONS** In the 1970s, Emma Goldman's insistence that women's personal lives be consistent with their political positions was especially appealing to "second-wave" feminists (see Chapter 30). A popular tee shirt of the time featured Goldman's image and a statement attributed to her: "*If I can't dance, I don't want to be part of your revolution.*" ●

---

*Emma Goldman, "Victims of Morality," p. 173, "The Traffic in Women," p. 181, from *Red Emma Speaks: An Emma Goldman Reader*, comp. and ed. Alix Kates Shulman, 3d ed. (Amherst, N.Y.: Humanity Books, 1998).

†Cited in Alix Kates Shulman, "Emma Goldman's Feminism: A Reappraisal," p. 18, from *Red Emma Speaks: An Emma Goldman Reader*, comp. and ed. Alix Kates Shulman, 3d ed. (Amherst, N.Y.: Humanity Books, 1998).

‡Cited in Richard Drinnon, *Rebel in Paradise* (Chicago: University of Chicago, 1961), p. 102.

Entering the "Age of Extremes"

Over the past century, we have become accustomed to the drastic changes set in motion by the First World War. It is hard for us to imagine a world where Europe's political and economic domination was so thorough; where women were politically voiceless; where despite industrialization, the power of human and animal muscles was still the main energy source for farming; where centuries-old empires endured; and where a naïve belief in limitless progress was widely shared. War and revolution shattered such complacency.

The industrialized nature of total war came as a shock. Going into the war, cavalry regiments were essential to war planning. But the entire cavalry system was rendered anachronistic by the savage firepower of shells and machine guns. Hundreds of thousands of horses were killed, and the whole culture of "civilized" warfare between mounted "gentlemen" disappeared. Strafing aircraft and poison gas pointed to a more violent future when the lines between soldiers and civilians would blur even further. Just a generation later, during the Second World War, the targeting of civilian populations for aerial bombardment became common (see Chapter 29).

In cultural terms, total war accelerated the existing trend toward "mass societies" in which common people played a much larger role. Posters and newspapers were the principal media used to galvanize public

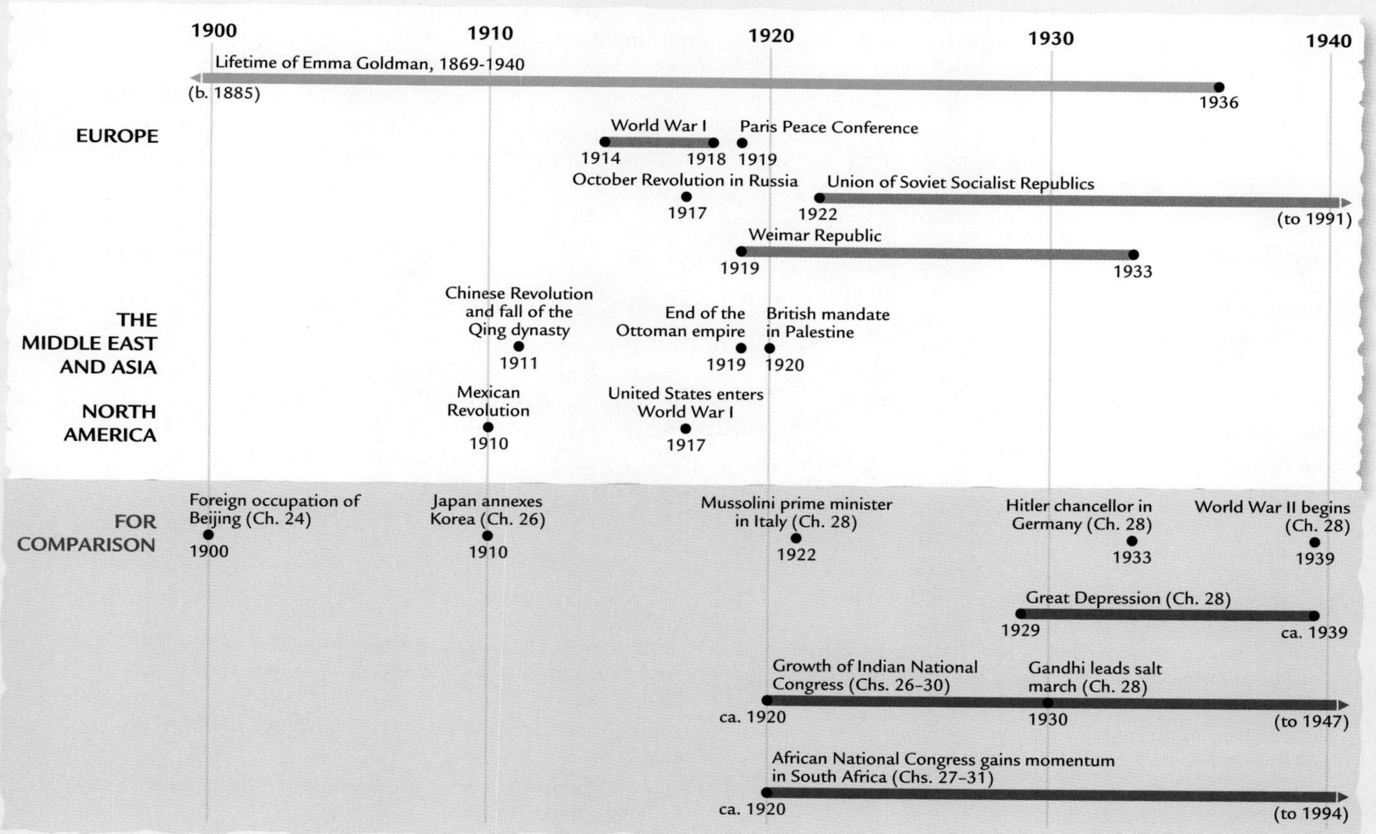

support for war, but already radio was supplementing telegraphy and new film industries had been born. By 1920, commercial radio broadcasts and the growth of cinema had created a broad platform for such dynamic cultural developments as the new African American art form of jazz music, which spread across the globe to enrich the lives of millions. Radio and film, however, also provided elites with new means to sway public opinion and could be used as mechanisms of propaganda and control, a trend that would serve authoritarian regimes in Italy and Germany in the 1920s and 1930s (see Chapter 28).

To Emma Goldman and other idealists, the revolutionary rise of the masses marked an advance toward human liberation, showing that ruling elites could no longer take the obedience of common men and women for granted. The same was true in Europe's overseas empires, where the war had caused many Africans and Asians to question the impregnability of their rulers and to aspire to nations of their own (see Chapter 30). It seemed, however, that the political activation of peasants and workers had a dark side as well, creating disordered conditions in which dictatorship could flourish, as in the absolute control established by the Communist Party in the Soviet Union under Vladimir Lenin and Joseph Stalin.

From today's perspective, communism seems to have been a historical dead end. The Soviet Union no longer exists, and the People's Republic of China, while retaining communist political control, has thrown in its lot with market economics (see Chapters 31 and 32). In the immediate postwar era, however, there were many who logically questioned whether it was liberal capitalism that might be destined for historical obsolescence. Both fascists and communists felt empowered by the uncertainty of the war's aftermath, an antiliberal trend that would be greatly magnified by the Great Depression. By the 1930s, Emma Goldman's anarchist faith in absolute individual autonomy seemed almost quaint.

As it turned out, the crisis-filled decades of the 1920s and 1930s were merely an interlude between world wars. The second would dwarf the first in intensity and global impact.

Key Terms

Emma Goldman (808)
Kaiser Wilhelm II (811)
western front (812)
eastern front (814)
southern front (814)
Senegalese Sharpshooters (815)
Woodrow Wilson (816)
Paris Peace Conference (817)
League of Nations (817)
Weimar Republic (821)
Mandate System (822)
Balfour Declaration (823)
Sun Yat-sen (826)
May Fourth Movement (827)
Vladimir Lenin (828)
New Economic Policy (831)
"Socialism in One Country" (831)

For Further Reference

Anderson, Scott. *Lawrence in Arabia: War, Deceit, Imperial Folly and the Making of the Modern Middle East*. New York: Anchor, 2013.

Chesler, Ellen. *Woman of Valor: Margaret Sanger and the Birth Control Movement in America*. New York: Simon and Schuster, 2007.

Clark, Christopher. *The Sleepwalkers: How Europe Went to War in 1914*. New York: Harper Collins, 2013.

Fitzpatrick, Sheila. *The Russian Revolution*. 3d ed. New York: Oxford University Press, 2008.

Fromkin, David. *A Peace to End All Peace: The Fall of the Ottoman Empire and the Rise of the Modern Middle East*. New York: Holt, 2001.

Goldman, Emma. *Living my Life*. Miriam Brody, ed. New York: Penguin, 2006.

Hart, John Mason. *Revolutionary Mexico*. Berkeley: University of California Press, 1997.

Keegan, John. *The First World War*. New York: Vintage, 2000.

Macmillan, Margaret. *Paris 1919: Six Months That Changed the World*. New York: Random House, 2003.

Neiberg, Michael S. *Fighting the Great War: A Global History*. New York: Cambridge University Press, 2005.

Reynolds, David. *The Long Shadow: The Legacies of the Great War in the Twentieth Century*. New York: W.W. Norton, 2014.

Schiffrin, Harold. *Sun Yat-Sen and the Origins of the Chinese Revolution*. Berkeley: University of California Press, 2010.

Service, Robert. *Spies and Commissars: The Early Years of the Russian Revolution*. New York: Public Affairs, 2013.

Strachan, Hew. *The First World War in Africa*. New York: Oxford University Press, 2004.

AP® Review Questions for Chapter 27

Multiple-Choice Questions

QUESTIONS 1–3 REFER TO THE IMAGE ON PAGE 815, *FRANCO-AFRICAN SOLDIER*.

1. The image above best illustrates which of the following conditions of World War I?
   (A) Because the war was so devastating, it was necessary to recruit younger men.
   (B) The use of government propaganda portrayed war as exciting.
   (C) Combatants drew on their colonial populations to aid in the war effort.
   (D) World War I was largely responsible for ending racial discrimination in the West.

2. A historian researching the impact of World War I outside of Europe would most likely find the image as a useful source of information about
   (A) the types of weapons issued to colonial troops.
   (B) who composed the colonial armies of European countries.
   (C) the development of color photography.
   (D) the proliferation of genocide during the war.

3. Which of the following French colonial policies occurred in the years after World War I?
   (A) France continued to exploit its colonies for economic gain despite promises made in the Treaty of Versailles.
   (B) France utilized colonial mercenaries to brutally crush nationalist movements in other colonies.
   (C) The notion of self-determination came to include Africa and Southeast Asia, and France gradually liberated its colonies.
   (D) Grateful for their participation in the war effort, France richly rewarded its colonial veterans with lifetime pensions.

QUESTIONS 4–6 REFER TO THE FOLLOWING PASSAGE.

We intend to begin on the first of February unrestricted submarine warfare. We shall endeavor in spite of this to keep the United States of America neutral. In the event of this not succeeding, we make Mexico a proposal of alliance on the following basis: make war together, make peace together, generous financial support and an understanding on our part that Mexico is to reconquer the lost territory in Texas, New Mexico, and Arizona. The settlement in detail is left to you. . . . Please call the President's [Venustiano Carranza of Mexico] attention to the fact that the ruthless employment of our submarines now offers the prospect of compelling England in a few months to make peace.

—Telegram from German Foreign Minister Zimmerman to German Minster to Mexico von Eckhardt, January 1917

4. Which of the following best explains the motivation behind the Zimmerman telegram?
   (A) Limit American involvement in World War I
   (B) Build a global antidemocratic alliance
   (C) Promote anti-imperialism in North America
   (D) Commit Germany to militarily aiding Mexico

5. The reference to lost territory is best seen as evidence of which of the following in Mexican-American relations?
   (A) Anti-imperial resistance
   (B) Mexico's imperialist ambitions
   (C) The large Mexican-American populations in those states
   (D) U.S. expansion of its land borders by conquering neighboring territories

6. Which of the following was an important continuity underlying the political interaction between Germany and Mexico in the telegram?
   (A) Population displacement resulted from redrawing old colonial boundaries.
   (B) Transnational movements sought to unite people across national boundaries.
   (C) Twentieth-century military conflicts occurred on an unprecedented global scale.
   (D) Improved military technology led to increased levels of wartime casualties.

QUESTIONS 7–10 REFER TO THE FOLLOWING PASSAGE.

To those colonies and territories which as a consequence of the late war have ceased to be under the sovereignty of the States which formerly governed them and which are inhabited by peoples not yet able to stand by themselves under the strenuous conditions of the modern world, there should be applied the principle that the well-being and development of such peoples form a sacred trust of civilisation and that securities for the performance of this trust should be embodied in this Covenant. The best method of giving practical effect to this principle is that the tutelage of such peoples should be entrusted to advanced nations who by reason of their resources, their experience or their geographical position can best undertake this responsibility, and who are willing to accept it. . . . The character of the mandate must differ according to the stage of the development of the people, the geographical situation of the territory, its economic conditions, and other similar circumstances.

—Article 22, Treaty of Versailles, 1919

7. Compared to the administration of colonies and territories described in the passage, European practices concerning colonial administration following World War I *differed* in that
   (A) many colonies were immediately granted independence because of the expense of maintaining them.
   (B) there was little real effort to promote self-governance, and Europeans often reneged on promised liberties.
   (C) European-educated indigenous peoples were placed in high-ranking administrative positions.
   (D) resource extraction was facilitated by increased technological advancement.

8. Which of the following conclusions about the Treaty of Versailles is most directly supported by the passage?
   (A) The treaty was largely successful in fostering peaceful transitions to independence in much of Africa and Asia.
   (B) Indigenous populations in Africa and Asia accepted the terms of the treaty because they acceded to them in 1919.
   (C) Germany and Turkey actually underwent an economic boom once freed from the expense of imperial administration.
   (D) Despite grand ambitions to render large-scale war obsolete, the treaty essentially reset the stage for other conflicts.

9. The views expressed in the passage are best seen as evidence of which of the following in turn-of-the-century European society?
   (A) Social Darwinism
   (B) Zionism
   (C) Imperialism
   (D) Nationalism

10. Which of the following occurred as *direct* result of the terms expressed in the passage?
   (A) Political changes were accompanied by major demographic consequences, such as population displacement and resettlement.
   (B) New military alliances were created, including NATO and the Warsaw Pact.
   (C) The Ottoman, Russian, and Qing empires collapsed.
   (D) Nonviolence was widely adopted as a way to bring about political change.

Short-Answer Questions

QUESTION 1 REFERS TO THE FOLLOWING IMAGES.

1. Answer parts A and B.
   A. Identify and explain TWO historical claims about the Soviet Union under Stalin that can be supported based on the images.
   B. Identify ONE limitation of the images as sources of information about the Soviet Union under Stalin.

2. Answer parts A and B.
   Many historians argue that women's suffrage improved their position in Western society.
   A. Provide TWO pieces of evidence that *support* this argument, and explain how each piece of evidence supports the argument.
   B. Provide ONE piece of evidence that *undermines* this argument, and explain how it undermines the argument.

28 Responses to Global Crisis, 1920–1939

Halide Edib

From *Memoirs of Halide Adviar Edib* (N.J.: Gorgias Press). Reprinted by permission of Gorgias Press.

Halide Edib (1884–1964) grew up in cosmopolitan Istanbul, the daughter of a progressive Ottoman official who made sure she learned Arabic and studied the Quran but who also had her tutored by an English governess and sent her to a Greek-run school. In 1901, fluent in Turkish, English, Greek, and Arabic, Edib was the first Muslim girl to graduate from the American College for Girls in Istanbul. As a child of privilege, she had the luxury of exploring many different ideas and forming her identity in a safe and secure environment. Following a young woman's traditional path, after graduation, Edib married and had two children: *"My life was confined within the walls of my apartment. I led the life of an old-fashioned Turkish woman."**

Before long, Edib was moving beyond traditional gender roles, publishing her first novel in 1908 and helping to found the Society for the Elevation of Women. In 1910, she left her husband after he married a second wife, in conformity with Islamic law but against her wishes. She prevailed on her husband to obtain a divorce: she had no legal grounds to demand one herself.

Then, as with so many from her generation, the First World War changed her destiny. The Ottoman government sent Halide Edib (hall-ee-DEH eh-DEEP) southeast to Damascus and Beirut to organize schools and orphanages for girls. Soon, however, the Ottoman armies were in retreat, and she returned to the capital. In May 1918, the situation for Turkey was grim. Greek forces had seized the coastal city of Smyrna (toady's Izmir); the British had landed in Istanbul itself.

British airplanes circled menacingly overhead when Halide Edib stood to address a massive crowd before Istanbul's magnificent Blue Mosque:

---

*Halide Edib, *Inside India* (London: Allen and Unwin, 1937), p. 207.

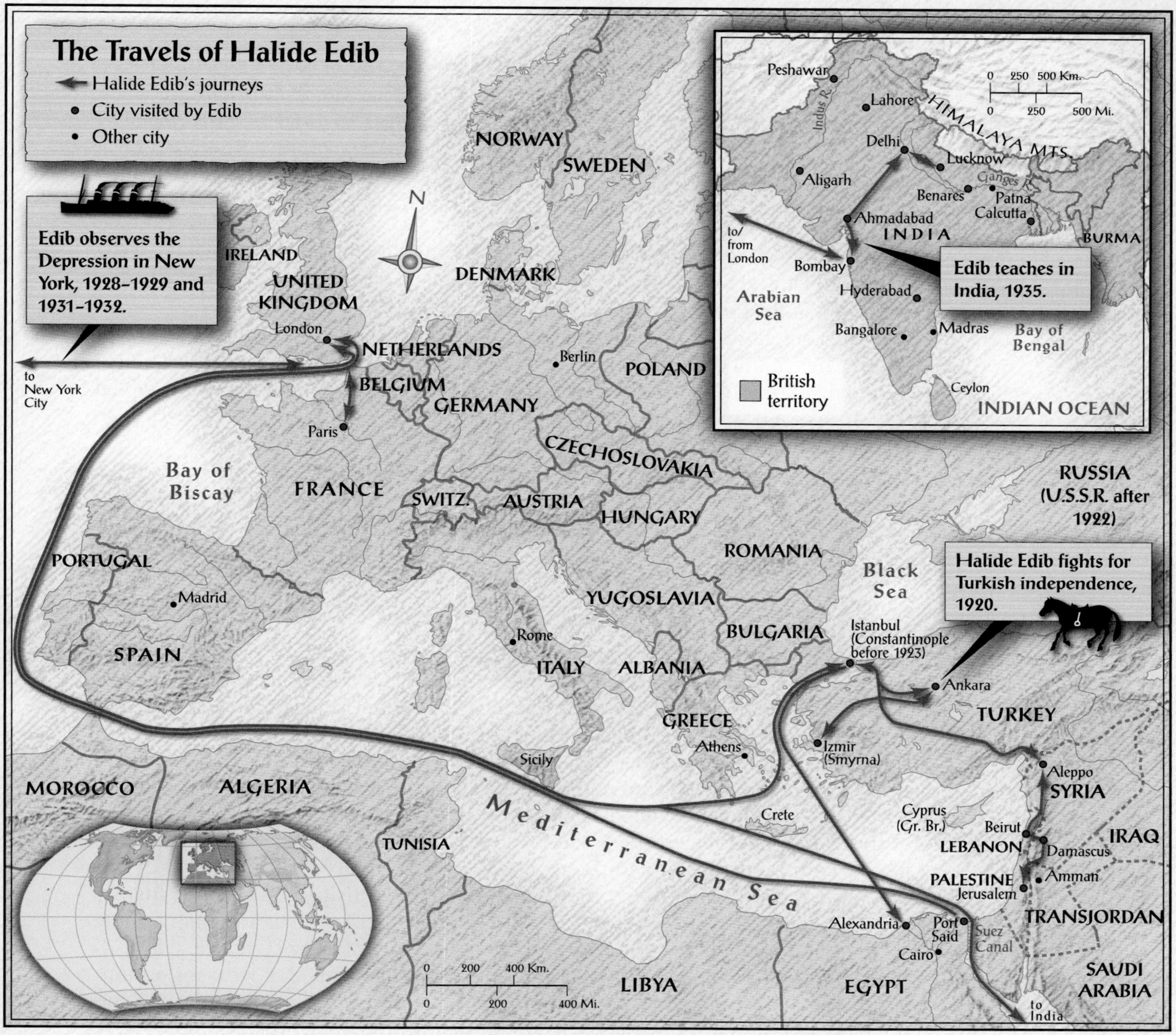

Brothers, sisters, countrymen, Muslims! When the night is darkest and seems eternal, the light of dawn is nearest.... From the tops of the minarets nigh against the heaven, seven hundred years of glory are watching.... I invoke the souls of our great [Ottoman] ancestors who had so often passed in procession through this very square.... I declare in the name of the new Turkish nation presented here, that the disarmed Turkish nation of

Halide Edib

(1884–1964) Turkish nationalist best known for her many popular works of fiction featuring female protagonists. She was part of the army that formed the Turkish nation and later served as a member of the Turkish parliament and as a professor of English literature.

*today still possesses your invincible hearts; we trust in Allah and in our rights. [The] allied powers of Europe ... have found ... an opportunity to break to pieces the last empire ruled by the crescent.... But the day will come when a greater court of justice will try those who have deprived the nations of their natural rights.**

It was a stunning performance, the first recorded instance in the history of the ancient capital of a woman addressing a public gathering. To this day, a statue of Halide Edib stands in the heart of Istanbul.

After her galvanizing speech, Edib fled east, wearing a veil and carefully concealing her manicured fingernails as she rode on horseback to join the Turkish nationalist army headquartered at Ankara. She was given official rank and served the cause as a translator and press officer to Mustafa Kemal, leader of the Turkish forces fighting for the integrity of their homeland.

They were successful in securing international recognition of the Republic of Turkey, but then she fell out of favor with the dictatorial Kemal, who forced her into exile in 1926. For the next thirteen years she traveled to France, Britain, India, and the United States, writing books and lecturing at universities. Only with Kemal's death in 1939 did she return to Turkey, winning a seat in the Turkish parliament, teaching English literature at Istanbul University, and becoming one of her country's most renowned novelists.

During Edib's years of exile, the uncertainties of the postwar world were turning into genuine global crises. When she came to New York as a visiting professor of literature at Columbia University in 1931–1932, the United States was suffering through the Great Depression. She also witnessed its global effects in Britain and France, from which she viewed the emergence of fascism with the rise to power of Benito Mussolini in Italy and Adolf Hitler in Germany. These fascist regimes represented an assault on the liberal tradition, with state power growing at the expense of individual liberties. In the Soviet Union, Joseph Stalin was further consolidating his communist dictatorship.

With the global economy in crisis and political tensions on the rise, ideologies that magnified the role of the state grew in popularity, as in Japan, where extreme nationalism heightened authoritarian control over civic life. Authoritarian tendencies gained momentum wherever liberalism was weak or absent, such as in Russia, the European colonial empires, much of Latin America, and the new nation of Turkey. Even the liberal institutions of democratic states were sorely tested by the challenges of the 1930s.

Nationalism could also be a positive force, however, providing a source of hope for many colonized Africans and Asians. The great Indian nationalist leader Mohandas K. Gandhi personified these hopes, while giving the entire world a model of peaceful political change. Like Halide Edib, Gandhi saw the fight for national independence as inseparable from the fight for justice, including equality for women, who had few rights under colonialism. Gandhi's peaceful philosophy, a source of inspiration to many, stood in sharp contrast to the renewed militarism that would soon lead to another world war.

*Halide Edib, *The Turkish Ordeal* (New York: Century, 1928), p. 24, n. 8. Edib did not keep a record of the speech, so this was her later reconstruction.

KEY CONCEPT QUESTIONS

- How did the effect of the Great Depression on the West differ from its effect on Latin America and Asia? **(Key Concept 6.3)**
- How did fascist dictators reshape their societies? **(Key Concept 6.2)**
- How did Asian and African nationalists resist colonial powers? **(Key Concept 6.2)**
- How did the international community respond to aggression from Japan, Italy, and Germany before World War II? **(Key Concept 6.2)**

The Great Depression, 1929–1939

In October 1929, prices on the New York Stock Exchange plunged; within two months, stocks lost half their value. Bank failures across Europe and the Americas brought the **Great Depression** and the global spread of economic hardship. Unemployment surged; agricultural prices plummeted. Ten years later, global markets still had not recovered.

Great Depression Economic depression beginning in 1929 with the crash of stock prices in New York followed by a series of bank failures in Europe; marked by sustained deflation, unemployment in industrial nations, and depressed crop prices.

The Great Depression in the Industrialized World

The Great Depression revealed the degree to which finance and trade integrated nearly all the world's people into a single economic system. Historians continue to debate the causes of the Great Depression, but two factors clearly stand out: the speculative excesses of the American stock market, and the international debt structure that emerged after the First World War.

By the later 1920s the global economy had recovered from postwar malaise. In the United States, financial markets reflected the frenetic pace of life during the "jazz age," with its glamorous movie stars, mass-produced automobiles, and sensational gangsters. More and more, speculators bought stock on borrowed money, trusting that markets would endlessly increase in value. When the bubble burst, ruining investors and the bankers who had lent them money, capital investment dried up, and the stock market collapse turned into a general economic crisis.

A sharp division between rich and poor magnified the problem. By 1928, only 1 percent of the U.S. population controlled 24 percent of its wealth. Since ordinary workers could no longer afford the products being churned out by American manufacturers, many plants closed. By 1932, one-fourth of workers in the United States were unemployed.

The U.S. stock market collapse soon revealed the vulnerability of the international financial system. During World War I the United States had replaced Great Britain as the world's leading creditor, and European governments were deeply in debt to American banks. The banking crisis was particularly acute in Germany, where the Weimar government was forced to borrow heavily to make huge reparations payments to France (see Chapter 27). Financiers in the United States lent Germans money, which they then paid to France, which then sent the money back to the United States as French payments on American loans. After the stock market crash, American investors called in their loans to German banks, and the system collapsed. By 1933, German factories produced only half the goods they had manufactured in 1929, and half the workforce was idle.

• **CONTEXT&CONNECTIONS** The Great Depression demonstrated the need for international institutions to stabilize the global financial system, and the lesson was learned. In 1944, even before the end of World War II, the *Bretton Woods Conference* created the International Monetary Fund and the World Bank to support national economies during economic downturns (key term in Chapter 29). •

Politicians exacerbated the crisis. In 1930, the United States imposed high tariffs to protect American manufacturing from foreign imports. Great Britain enacted a series of tariff "preferences" within its empire. Though intended to save jobs, protectionist measures caused steep declines in international trade and further loss of employment. By the early 1930s, wages and prices spiraled downward in a vicious deflationary cycle.

In these circumstances, few believed that free markets could solve the problem. The British economist John Maynard Keynes argued that the massive unemployment of the time was not just a temporary corrective, as *laissez-faire* economics would have it, but a deep structural problem stemming from a lack of demand. Governments, he proposed, should take up the slack by spending freely and expanding the money supply. Even if large-scale borrowing and risks of inflation were necessary in the short run, Keynes argued, the resulting economic revival would increase the tax revenues needed to pay off deficits.

As during World War I, and in line with the recommendations of John Maynard Keynes, governments in France, Britain, and the United States now took a much more active role in domestic economies. In the United States, President **Franklin Delano Roosevelt** (in office 1933–1945) implemented his New Deal programs. Social Security created a "safety net" for many of the nation's elderly, and the Works Progress Administration put the unemployed to work on public infrastructure. Price subsidies helped stabilize farm prices while legislation strengthened workers' rights to unionize and strike. Government protection of depositors' accounts restored faith in the banking system. However, though the New Deal was quite popular, it did not get at the root of the economic problem. In 1939, unemployment in the United States still stood at 16 percent.

Franklin Delano Roosevelt
(in office 1933–1945) President of the United States during the Great Depression and World War II. Created the New Deal, intended to stimulate the economy through government spending, financial sector reform, and a safety net for those most in need.

The same pattern of government intervention unfolded in France and Britain, while in Sweden, Norway, and Denmark, Social Democrats pledged to construct a "welfare state" that would protect their citizens through comprehensive education, health care, housing subsidies, and unemployment insurance. But while such measures reduced suffering, no merely national solution could solve the problem of depressed global markets caused by a shortage of credit.

The Great Depression in Global Perspective

Depressed agricultural prices hit farmers hard everywhere, including hundreds of millions of peasant farmers in Africa, Asia, and Latin America. In very remote areas peasants might have the option of withdrawing from market production and focusing on their own family and village subsistence. But by the 1930s the vast majority had become so enmeshed in global markets that withdrawal was not an option. In Africa, for example, small-scale family farms grew cash crops like cocoa, cotton, and coffee to buy imported goods

Destroying Brazilian Coffee By 1932 the world market price for coffee had plunged so dramatically that Brazil, the world's leading producer, destroyed tens of thousands of tons. Burning coffee and shoveling it into the sea did little to restore vigor to the international coffee market, however. Only a revival of consumer spending could achieve that.

like cloth, kerosene lamps, and bicycles and to pay the taxes demanded by European colonial governments. Parents with extra money often invested in school fees for their children, another incentive to grow commercial crops.

When coffee and cocoa prices fell by over half in early 1930, many Africans were suddenly unable to meet their tax obligations or pay their debts. Since Western manufactures had increasingly displaced indigenous industries, they had come to depend on imported goods like iron hoes and cotton clothing, which they could no longer afford. Years of hardship followed during which school attendance declined as young people were sometimes forced to leave their villages in search of work.

Conditions were equally bleak where export commodities were produced on plantations. Brazil, the world's largest coffee producer, also experienced the steep fall in coffee prices when cash-strapped North American and European consumers cut back on consumption. Exporters destroyed huge stockpiles, hoping that decreasing the supply would increase global prices. Agricultural workers left the plantations to scratch a living out of the soil or to join the destitute in the burgeoning *favelas*, or urban slums. The situation was similar in Southeast Asia, after a global decline in automobile and bicycle production caused rubber prices to crash.

In the villages of India, the drop in crop prices further squeezed farmers who already, in the words of Halide Edib, were *"at the mercy of rain, moneylender, and* *tax-gatherer."** By 1932, peasant incomes had fallen by half. To avoid losing their land, many families sold the gold jewelry they were saving for their daughters' dowries. In the 1930s, billions of rupees worth of such "distress gold" were sold, and many couples delayed or canceled marriage. At the same time, many South Asian Muslims had to cancel plans to perform the hajj, the pilgrimage to Mecca and Medina that could take a lifetime of planning (see Chapter 17).

AP® THEMES

What were the similarities in the ways various political leaders attempted to address the economic struggles resulting from the Great Depression?

Egyptian farmers were struck equally hard. As textile factories in Europe and the United States cut production or closed, cotton prices plunged. Whereas over 16,000 people a year traveled from Egypt to Arabia for the *hajj* before 1929, only about 1,700 made the pilgrimage in 1933.

In Latin America, economic nationalism was a common response to the crisis. In Mexico, for example, President Lázaro Cárdenas nationalized the country's petroleum industry, arguing that the profits should help the Mexican people rather than enrich foreign companies. To aid rural Mexicans, he redistributed large amounts of land to peasant communities, finally fulfilling the promise of the Mexican Revolution (see Chapter 27). Like other Latin American presidents, Cárdenas went even further than leaders in the United States and western Europe in asserting state economic power in response to the Great Depression.

These were also troubled times in Halide Edib's native Turkey. Mustafa Kemal was determined to build up Turkey's own industrial base by making the country less dependent on foreign imports. He pursued import-substitution policies by erecting high tariffs to shield local manufacturers from global competition. Import substitution did create some new industrial jobs. However, such policies decreased international trade, further hampering global recovery.

Fascism, Communism, and Authoritarianism

Even in the most liberal societies, where private enterprise and individual liberty were well established, the challenges of the early twentieth century brought greater government economic intervention. In Italy, Germany, and the Soviet Union, where liberalism had much shallower roots, those challenges created a climate in which explicitly antiliberal, authoritarian political ideologies—**fascism** and communism—flourished.

fascism
Authoritarian political doctrine based on extreme nationalism, elevation of the state at the expense of the individual, and replacement of independent social organizations in civil society with state organizations.

Fascists, most notably Benito Mussolini in Italy and Adolf Hitler in Germany, were contemptuous of representative government and of weak, vain, and vacillating politicians. They should be replaced by strong leaders who represented not self-interested factions but the people as a whole. Only then, they promised, could national greatness be achieved. Unity of purpose and the role of the state in organizing the collective will were more important in fascist thinking than individual rights. Fascists were extreme nationalists, and while racism was strongly present across the world—from the segregated cities and schools of the United States to the racially based empires of Britain and France—the German Nazis imposed racial policies of unprecedented severity. Jews were the principal target.

Communists likewise had no use for liberal democracy, following Karl Marx's description of representative democracy as a sham. "*The executive of the modern*

*Halide Edib, *Inside India* (London: Allen and Unwin, 1937), p. 170.

state," asserts the *Communist Manifesto, "is nothing but a committee for managing the common affairs of the whole bourgeoisie."** Unlike the fascists, however, the communists underplayed national unity while emphasizing class solidarity. In spite of evidence to the contrary, especially from World War I, many Marxists still believed that workers would unite internationally to overthrow their oppressors and create global socialism

In reality, the Soviet Union was the only existing communist society in the 1930s. As Stalin collectivized agriculture, oversaw rapid industrialization, and purged the state of his perceived enemies, the Soviet people lived in perpetual fear and deprivation. But some Western observers, their own societies wracked by economic depression, imagined that the Soviet model pointed the way toward peace, prosperity, and social justice.

Although fascists and communists hated each other passionately, they shared a common loathing for liberal democracy. Following the Great Depression, with the democratic nations struggling to restore their vitality without much success, many came to believe that either fascism or communism was the cure.

Mussolini and the Rise of Fascism

For **Benito Mussolini** (1883–1945), the state bound the people together: *"Everything for the state, nothing against the state, no one outside the state."* After World War I, Mussolini organized quasi-military groups made up largely of former soldiers, called Blackshirts, who assaulted socialists and communists in the streets. Their belligerence intimidated middle-class politicians, whose weakness, Mussolini thought, could allow Bolshevism to spread to Italy. Mussolini's supporters called him *Il Duce* (ill DOO-chey), "the leader."

Benito Mussolini (1883–1945) Prime minister of Italy and the world's first fascist leader. Also known as Il Duce, he founded the Italian Fascist Party and formed an alliance with Hitler's Germany.

It was true that disunity made the country vulnerable. After all, the Italian nation was only six decades old: for many, local dialects and cultural traditions were still more relevant than national ones. Social tensions accompanied industrialization in the north, while the south was still mired in the poverty that had driven many to emigrate to the United States and Argentina. Neither the existing constitutional monarchy nor the Catholic Church, although it dominated the lives of most Italians, seemed able to reconcile regional and class divisions. Extreme nationalism was Mussolini's answer.

Mussolini stepped in with supreme confidence and determination, offering order, discipline, and unity. His passionate speeches contrasted sharply with the bland style of most politicians. Landowners and industrialists, favoring Mussolini's call to suppress anarchism and communism, financed the fascists as the Blackshirts harassed union leaders, broke strikes, and kept potentially rebellious farm laborers and tenants in line.

In 1922, Mussolini organized disaffected war veterans in a march on Rome. Though the elected government declared a state of siege to rebuff Mussolini's play for power, the king and the military refused to enforce it. With the support of these conservative elites, Mussolini then bullied his way into the prime minister's position. As the violence of fascist thugs escalated, however, many Italians who had been attracted by Mussolini's youth and vigor began to turn against him. He responded

*Excerpt from *The Marx-Engels Reader*, ed. Robert C. Tucker, 2d ed.

by arresting opponents, assassinating socialists, and outlawing competing political parties. After 1926 Mussolini ruled as dictator.

Mussolini's definition of fascism was explicitly antiliberal: *"Liberalism denied the State in the name of the individual; Fascism reasserts the rights of the State as expressing the real essence of the individual."** One of the foundations of liberal democracy is free association, allowing people to voluntarily come together to pursue similar interests or to achieve a common objective. Mussolini instead installed a system of "corporations," in which the state itself organized all citizens involved in a common undertaking. "Corporatism" replaced independent unions with state-sanctioned ones and took over the nation's youth organizations. Even so, the fascists never actually achieved their intended degree of social control, as most Italians continued to rely on church, community, and family.

For the dull compromises of parliamentary democracy Mussolini substituted a theatrical politics that involved singing, flag waving, marching, and stirring oratory. He often invoked Rome's imperial past and promised to make it once again the center of a mighty empire. In 1935, in defiance of the League of Nations, he invaded Ethiopia to avenge Italy's humiliating defeat by King Menelik's army in 1896 (see Chapter 26). Fervent patriotism in the cause of empire proved another effective way to bind together the young Italian nation.

Some Italians were active in support of Mussolini's regime, willing to trade liberty for security and a renewed sense of national pride. Others, especially communists, paid for opposition with their lives. Most Italians probably did not care too much one way or the other and simply went on with their daily lives. As the Italian Marxist Antonio Gramsci wrote, before spending years in a fascist prison: *"Indifference is actually the mainspring of history.... What comes to pass does so not so much because a few people want it to happen, as because the mass of citizens abdicate their responsibility and let things be."*†

Hitler and National Socialism in Germany

Germany was both humiliated and financially devastated after World War I. Though the Weimar Republic had brought liberal democracy to Germany in the 1920s, the onset of the Great Depression left Germans once again desperate for solutions. With the center falling out of German politics, communists on the far left and fascists on the extreme right gained in popularity.

The German liberals and socialists who had overseen the creation of the Weimar Republic were heirs to the Enlightenment tradition that saw the use of reason as a means of achieving a just and stable social order. For many Germans, however, the war had called that belief into question. During what some historians have called an "age of anxiety" artists probed darker emotions, as with the nightmarish images painted by German expressionists.

The scientific works of the psychiatrist Sigmund Freud (1856–1939) and the astrophysicist Albert Einstein (1879–1955) were also deeply unsettling, overturning many complacent prewar assumptions. Sigmund Freud, in his quest to develop more effective interventions for neurosis, developed a view of human psychology in which unrecognized urges lay beyond the control of the conscious mind and in

---

*From *Fascism Doctrine and Institutions*, 1935, pp. 7–42. http://www.worldfuturefund.org/wffmaster/Reading/Germany/mussolini.htm.

†Antonio Gramsci, from *Avanti!, in Selections from Political Writings 1910–1920* (London: Lawrence and Wishart, 1977), p. 17.

which sexual complexes emanating from unremembered childhood experiences could dominate human behavior.

Meanwhile, in physics, scientists were challenging the "common sense" of the Newtonian framework (see Chapter 21) at both the atomic and cosmic levels. In his special theory of relativity, Einstein overthrew Newton's conception of time and space as an absolute grid, removing time as an independent variable by positing a four-dimensional space-time in which observation itself depends on the speed and location of the observer. Thus science itself, along with artistic modernism and psychotherapy, reinforced the climate of uncertainty in which the Weimar Republic had been born.

Into this anxious environment stepped **Adolf Hitler** (1889–1945) and his National Socialist Party, promising to restore greatness, confidence, and order. Modernism they decried as "degenerate art," while "Jewish science" was the term used to tar Freud, Einstein, and other brilliant minds as part of a conspiracy to demoralize the German people so that Jewish interests could prevail. In fact, restoring the vitality and historical mission of the Germans was Hitler's rallying cry.

Adolf Hitler
(1889–1945) Leader of the National Socialist Party who became chancellor of Germany and dismantled the Weimar constitution. His ultranationalist policies led to persecution of communists and Jews, and his aggressive foreign policies started World War II.

● **CONTEXT&CONNECTIONS** After 1933, when Nazi anti-Semitism became official policy, many German-Jewish artists, scientists, and thinkers were stripped of their academic and cultural positions and forced into exile. Of the many exiled scientists who contributed to later U.S. technological predominance, Albert Einstein was the most important as a public figure. Though Einstein's theoretical work laid the foundation for the atomic bomb (see Chapter 29), after World War II Einstein was a consistent advocate for peace and Cold War dialogue. ●

Hitler had a very different idea than did socialists or liberals of what was meant by "the people." For socialists it referred simply to the masses of workers. For liberals, who stressed individual autonomy, "the people" meant the sum total of those individuals. For Hitler, however, *das Volk* (das FOHLK), "the people," was a single organism bound by history, tradition, and race. Just as no cell is independent from the others in a living organism, so all Germans were connected by their racial destiny. Hitler defined Germans as an "Aryan" race superior to all others and identified race-mixing as a threat to that superiority. *"All the great civilizations of the past died out,"* Hitler proclaimed with stunning ignorance of history, *"because contamination of the blood caused them to become decadent."**

According to Nazism, Germans who did not live up to the ideal of racial pride and racial purity were like tumors that needed to be excised. Nazi targets included communists, with their internationalist doctrine; homosexuals, with their supposed rejection of traditional family values; and the physically and mentally handicapped. Proponents of the racist pseudo-science of eugenics (also popular in the United States in the 1930s) argued that selective breeding could lead to superior human beings. If the smartest "Aryan" men and women married and had children, they could produce a "master race." On the other hand, according to this racist logic, the "inferior" should be stopped from breeding: eugenic medical practices led to the sterilization of many girls from poor and ethnic minority families to stop their "genetic defects" from being passed on to another generation.

AP® THEMES
In what ways did Nazism attempt to sustain class, racial, and ethnic ideologies already present in Germany?

Looking for a scapegoat on whom to blame the country's problems, Hitler tapped into the centuries-old tradition of anti-Semitism. Although German Jews

*Cited in *Sources of Global History since 1900*, ed. James H. Overfield, 2d ed. (Boston: Wadsworth, 2013), p. 132.

Mary Evans Picture Library/The Image Works

National Socialist Propaganda The Nazi Party often used images of healthy blond children to emphasize German vitality and racial superiority and organized young people into party-based boys' and girls' clubs. This poster for the "League of German Girls" solicits donations to a fund to "Build Youth Hostels and Homes." In spite of the girl's smile and flowers, all of the money collected actually went into weapons production.

were thoroughly assimilated into national life, he identified them as the main threat: *"The personification of the devil as the symbol of all evil assumes the living shape of the Jew."* For the Nazis, the supposed racial characteristics of Jews contrasted with, and thereby illuminated, the virtues of the German *Volk*. Only by isolating the Jews, and ultimately eliminating them, could the goal of racial purity be achieved.

In the late 1920s, such ideas were on the far fringe. At that time, most National Socialists were poorly educated former soldiers and young men caught up in Hitler's emotional, patriotic appeals. But after the Great Depression, voters increasingly abandoned the parties of the center-right and the center-left for the communists and the fascists. Between 1928 and 1932, the National Socialist share of the vote jumped from 2.6 to 37.3 percent of the national total, and Hitler's deputies controlled more than a third of the seats in the Reichstag. Now some more affluent Germans voted for the National Socialists as a bulwark against communism.

Indeed, the German Communist Party had also gained strong support in the elections of 1932, alarming business leaders. Despite their distaste for Hitler, who most educated Germans saw as wild and unrefined, conservatives thought they would be able to control him from behind the scenes. Needing Hitler's support to form a governing coalition, which Hitler would join only if he was made chancellor, a reluctant President Paul von Hindenburg announced a new government with Hitler at its head in 1933.

A month after he took office, a fire broke out in the Reichstag (the German parliament). The arson was likely the work of a single individual, but Hitler accused the Communist Party of treason and had its members arrested. The remaining representatives then passed a law that suspended constitutional protections of civil liberties for four years and allowed Hitler to rule as a dictator. Dissenting from that vote, socialist deputies were then also arrested and sent to Dachau, the first of what would become a pan-European network of concentration camps.

Hitler dismantled Weimar's democratic institutions and became the *Führer* (leader) of an industrial state of huge potential power. Changes to German society were sudden and extreme. The Nazis abolished all other political parties and replaced Germany's federal structure with a centralized dictatorship emanating from Berlin. Like the fascists in Italy, they took over or replaced independent organizations in civil society such as labor unions. Hitler Youth replaced the Boy Scouts and church-sponsored youth groups as part of a plan, reinforced by a new school curriculum, to teach fascism to the next generation. Artists, architects, writers, and filmmakers who did not conform to the National Socialist vision were censored, harassed, and often driven into exile. (See the feature "Visual Evidence in Primary Sources: Angst and Order in German Cinema.") Hitler promised a Third Reich ("Third Empire") that would last a thousand years.

AP® THEMES
How did Hitler use control over artistic expression to reinforce his rule over Germany?

The Nazis also restricted the authority of German religious leaders. Protestant churches came under tight state control, and the Nazis seized Catholic Church properties and imprisoned priests brave enough to oppose them. Still, many Catholics joined the National Socialist Party, and Christian leaders of all denominations would later be criticized for not having done enough to resist Hitler.

Having already imprisoned the communists, the Führer (FYUR-ruhr) turned to the "Jewish problem." In 1935, the Nazis imposed the Nuremberg Laws, which deprived Jews of all civil rights and forbade intermarriage between Jews and other Germans. Some Jews emigrated, but many German Jews were so deeply assimilated into the country's cultural and social life that they could not imagine leaving. Then, on November 9, 1938, the Nazis launched coordinated attacks against Jews throughout Germany and Austria. After this "*Kristallnacht*" ("Crystal Night")—named for the smashing of windows in Jewish homes, synagogues, and stores—more Jews fled. The Nazis forced those who remained into segregated ghettos. After 1938, it was no longer possible to suppose that Hitler's anti-Semitic tirades were merely political rhetoric.

● **CONTEXT&CONNECTIONS** November 9 is a date of great resonance in German history, bringing to mind both great evil and great joy. On that date in 1938, *Kristallnacht* was a prelude to the *Holocaust* (Chapter 29), which included the murder of six million Jews. By coincidence, November 9 was also the date in 1989 when communist East Germany finally opened the Berlin Wall, presaging the end of the Cold War (see Chapter 31). ●

Part of Hitler's appeal was negative: at a time of fear and insecurity, the Führer pointed to "enemies" such as communists and Jews who could be blamed for the country's problems. Economic recovery also helps explain Hitler's popularity. While democracies vainly struggled to create jobs, German unemployment dropped from over 6 million people to under two hundred thousand between 1932 and 1938. It seemed that government economic intervention was key. German ministries fixed prices and allocated resources in close coordination with the country's largest corporations. Massive public works projects, such as the world's first superhighways and a large military buildup, put Germans back to work.

Hitler promised that traditional values of courage, order, and discipline would once again empower the German people. Women's highest calling was to stay in the home and nurture purebred Aryan children. The Nazis' massive rallies, with their precision marching, flag waving, and spellbinding speeches by the Führer himself, gave people a sense of being part of something much larger than themselves. Radio broadcasts and expertly made propaganda films spread the excitement throughout the land.

Of course, not everyone was taken in. But outspoken opposition to Hitler meant imprisonment or death. Most Germans were content to go about their daily lives, appreciative of the relative order and prosperity.

Stalin: Collectivization and the Great Purges

For all the ambition of Mussolini and Hitler, neither could match the total control of society achieved by Joseph Stalin (1879–1953). While Stalin's totalitarian

Angst and Order in German Cinema

Expressionism was one response to the horrific experience of war. Strongly emotive, expressionism captured the angst of a postwar generation torn from the securities of a world seemingly changed forever. Many expressionists challenged the viewer with strong colors, primitive outlines, violent emotion, rapid movement, and heightened sexual energy. It was art for an age of anxiety. In film, the most famous expressionist work is *The Cabinet of Dr. Caligari*, a 1920 horror film that plumbs the darkness of the human psyche; an advertising poster for the film is reproduced here.

Neoclassicism was a quite different response to postwar uncertainty, with the goal of restoring a sense of order by returning to the calm harmony associated with Greek art. The second image here exemplifies the neoclassical style. *Olympia*, directed by the great German film artist Leni Riefenstahl, was a tribute to the Berlin Olympics of 1936. While her technical brilliance is widely

The sets for this silent film featured jagged, canvas-painted backgrounds, with few right angles or settled spaces. The expressionistic look of the film, including sharp contrasts between light and dark, reinforced its theme of disorder and violence in the human psyche.

The film's emphasis on dark, uncontrollable urges reflected the increasing influence of Sigmund Freud, the great Austrian psychologist who emphasized the power of the unconscious mind.

Movie Poster Image Art/Getty Images

The story features the evil Dr. Caligari, who controls a sleepwalking man, Cesare. Caligari displays Cesare at carnivals, claiming he can predict the future. At night, Cesare performs murder on Caligari's behalf. Or does he?

The film leaves the viewer to doubt: who is the doctor and who is the patient? Who is sane and who is deranged? What is reality and what is fantasy? Such unsettling, unanswered questions were new to film when *Dr. Caligari* was premiered in Berlin in 1920, but in later decades they would become common in the genre of psychologically driven horror films.

acknowledged, Riefenstahl's work has also been judged by its propaganda value for the Nazi regime. Neoclassicism was the style preferred by Adolf Hitler.

The National Socialists denounced expressionism as a perverse form of modernism created by Jews and subversives to undermine the confidence and willpower of the German people. In 1937, Joseph Goebbels (Hitler's minister of propaganda) organized an exhibition of so-called "degenerate art" in Munich to rally the public against artistic modernism. Many "degenerate" painters, architects, designers, and filmmakers were driven into exile.

Germany's loss was America's gain. Hollywood benefited enormously from the influx of émigré film talent in the 1930s. Erich Pommer (the producer of *Dr. Caligari*) and Billy Wilder (one of the most productive and popular Hollywood directors) were Jewish refugees from fascism who significantly influenced film in the United States. Along with Jews from Poland, Russia, Lithuania, and elsewhere, they made enduring contributions to American culture.

The look of *Olympia* could not possibly be more different than that of *Dr. Caligari*. Here all is rational and orderly; right angles, classical harmony, and idealized depictions of the human body dominate. ***From what you know of fascism, why were the Nazis so opposed to expressionist works like Dr. Caligari and so strongly supportive of neoclassical works like Olympia? (Try to watch clips of Dr. Caligari and the opening scene of Olympia online before you answer.)***

After silently and reverently panning across the ruins of the Parthenon, Riefenstahl's camera shows a Greek statue of a discus thrower slowly fading into the statuesque figure of a modern athlete, who gracefully completes the throw. The continuity between classical and modern is immediately asserted.

As a photographer and cinematographer, director Leni Riefenstahl (1902–2003) was one of the most influential visual artists of the twentieth century. Yet the fact that her art was placed at the service of Adolf Hitler has long clouded her reputation as a pioneering female artist.

The propaganda value of *Olympia* for Nazi racism was somewhat undermined by Riefenstahl's necessary inclusion of the victories of African American athlete Jesse Owens in the 1936 Summer Olympics; his world record-setting long jump is beautifully rendered.

control predated the global depression and was independent of it, the Soviet Union also saw an escalation of state power in the 1930s.

In 1928, Stalin had launched the U.S.S.R. on a path of rapid industrialization based on centralized Five-Year Plans. Now he turned his attention to the countryside as he sought to apply "Socialism in One Country" to rural areas as well. Lenin's New Economic Policy had allowed farmers to keep their own small plots (see Chapter 27). But Stalin completely rejected private ownership. Instead, he ordered **collectivization** of the rural sector—tearing the peasants out of their villages and marching them at gunpoint onto collective farms.

collectivization
Stalin's replacement of peasant villages with large, state-run collective farms, following the idea of "Socialism in One Country." Millions died in famines and as a result of state terror campaigns.

Most Russian farming communities resisted collectivization. Stalin attributed resistance solely to *kulaks* (koo-LAHKS), more prosperous peasants who, he said, were out to exploit their fellow villagers. Stalin sent the Red Army into the countryside, supposedly to help the "masses" defeat these kulaks. In reality, the Soviet state was waging war on its own people. A resulting famine killed 2 million in 1932–1933, striking the Ukrainian people especially hard.

AP® THEMES
What was the demographic impact of collectivization agricultural techniques in the Soviet Union?

● **CONTEXT&CONNECTIONS** Stalin remembered how the Ukrainians had sought independence after World War I and took revenge during the brutal imposition of collectivization. When Ukraine finally did become an independent nation in 1991 (see Chapter 31), its leaders defined the *Holodomor* famine of 1931–1932 as genocide, an attempt to kill Ukrainians so they could be replaced by Russian immigrants. This interpretation deeply offended Russian-speaking Ukrainians, including supporters of Russia's aggressive intrusion into the Ukraine in 2014 (see Chapter 32). ●

Meanwhile, the industrial sector continued its rapid expansion. The Communist Party bureaucracy treated the non-Russian parts of the Soviet Union, especially those of Central Asia, in colonial fashion, as sources of raw materials for industrial growth in the Russian heartland. In contrast with other industrial societies, the Soviet Union allowed no unemployment. But Soviet workers' wages were kept low to generate investment for further industrial expansion, while Stalin's vast system of slave-labor camps, the gulags, also boosted industrial productivity.

In the later 1930s, Stalin, always paranoid about plots against him, stepped up his repression of the Old Bolsheviks, communists whose memories of Lenin and the revolution could be dangerous to his dictatorship (see pages 832–833). During the **Great Purges**, Stalin ordered his secret police to arrest many former colleagues of Lenin, forcing them to confess to supposed crimes before they were taken out and shot. In 1937 alone, Stalin had half of the army's officer corps imprisoned or executed. It was an irrational move with another German war on the horizon, but even as he killed and imprisoned his generals, Stalin ordered a massive military buildup.

Great Purges
The execution by Stalin in the late 1930s of many "Old Bolsheviks" he regarded as competitors for power. Public trials and forced confessions marked the Great Purges.

Soviet citizens lived in a nearly constant state of terror. "Fear by night, and a feverish effort by day to pretend enthusiasm for a system of lies," writes one historian, "was the permanent condition."* A single wrong word or glance could lead to a knock on the door and exile to Stalin's gulags, embodying Stalin's dictum: *"The easiest way to gain control of the population is to carry out acts of terror."*

*Robert Conquest, *The Great Terror: A Reassessment* (New York: Oxford University Press, 1997), p. 252.

Authoritarian Regimes in Asia and Latin America

Beyond Europe and the Soviet Union, in many other parts of the world where liberal traditions were absent or only weakly developed, uncertainty and economic crisis strengthened authoritarianism. In both Japan and Turkey, state intervention in economic and political life increased through the inter-war years. In Brazil, a quasi-fascist regime strove to reconcile the social tensions revealed by the Great Depression.

Ultranationalism in Japan

Although the Versailles treaty had rewarded Japan with territorial concessions at China's expense (see Chapter 27), nationalists remained dissatisfied:

> *We are like a great crowd of people packed into a small and narrow room, and there are only three doors through which we might escape, namely, emigration, advance into world markets, and expansion of territory. The first door has been barred to us by the anti-Japanese immigration policies of other countries. The second is being pushed shut by tariff barriers.... It is quite natural that Japan should rush upon the last remaining door ... of territorial expansion.**

The Great Depression strengthened the arguments of nationalists and militarists for a more aggressive foreign and imperial policy.

In the 1920s, the country had shown signs of heading in a more democratic direction. Japan was a constitutional monarchy, with an emperor whose role was ceremonial. Though still quite limited, voting rights were extended to more Japanese men, and the cabinet was no longer chosen by imperial advisers but by the party that gained the most votes in elections.

Other factors, however, limited liberal democracy. One was the power of civil service bureaucrats, who controlled policy together with the *zaibatsu*, Japan's large industrial conglomerates (see Chapter 24). Another was the rising influence of the military and militaristic sentiment emphasizing national glory over individual liberty. In 1926, when the new emperor Hirohito came to the throne, ultranationalists saw an opportunity to expand their influence. A new requirement stipulated that the minister of defense be an active military officer with power nearly equal to that of the prime minister. After the market collapse of 1930 led to tough times for the farm families whose sons made up most of the empire's soldiers, support for an enhanced military role in government became even greater.

Ultranationalists envisioned a new Asian economic system that would combine Japanese management and capital with the resources and cheap labor of East and Southeast Asia. The turning point came with the **invasion of Manchuria**, a province of China where the Versailles settlement had allowed the Japanese to keep soldiers in the capital. In 1931, Japanese military officers blew up some railroad tracks and then blamed Chinese nationalists as a rationale for leaving their barracks and occupying Manchuria. Since they had no orders authorizing this

invasion of Manchuria
(1931) Invasion that occurred when Japanese military officers defied the civilian government and League of Nations by occupying this northeastern Chinese province, leading to the further militarization of the Japanese government.

*Hashimoto Kingoro, "Address to Young Men," in *Sources of Japanese Tradition*, ed. William Theodore de Bary, vol. 2 (New York: Columbia University Press, 1958), p. 289.

action, the officers were brought to Tokyo for trial, where they used the courtroom to whip up public support for the army's ambitions. As imperial fever grew, elected politicians further lost control over the military.

As in Italy and Germany, militarization brought Japanese corporations lucrative government contracts. And as in the fascist countries, Japan's economic policies seemed successful. Military spending, even if it required massive government borrowing, boosted the economy, as did the occupation of Manchuria. After 1932, expanding working-class employment further solidified the ultranationalists' political support.

The Rise of Modern Turkey

Mustafa Kemal (1881–1938) Also known as Atatürk, an Ottoman officer who led the nationalist army that established the Republic of Turkey in 1923. A reformer who established the secular traditions of the modern Turkish state, he served as its leader until his death.

The new nation of Turkey emerged from the violent collapse of the Ottoman empire. Without the skillful military and political leadership of **Mustafa Kemal** (1881–1938), a former Ottoman officer, Turkey may well have been partitioned by the victorious Allies. For his role, Kemal earned the name Atatürk, "Father Turk."

With the success of Kemal's armies, by 1923 the great powers agreed to recognize a sovereign Turkish republic that retained the core territories and population of the old empire. Since the new republic was based on specifically Turkish nationalism, the new political framework proved awkward for the former empire's ethnic minorities, such as Armenians, Greeks, and the Kurds who predominated in the southeast.

Greek-Turkish relations were fraught with tension, leading to a massive population exchange that removed hundreds of thousands of Greeks westward across the Aegean to their "proper" country (one they might never have visited before) while a parallel movement of Turks went eastward to what was now their "own" nation. The scale of these dislocations showed once again the difficulty in applying the principle of "national self-determination" to organize national space along ethnic lines (see Chapter 27).

Turkish nationalism had been at the forefront since 1918, when Halide Edib had made her stirring speech. She later recalled how her heart had been *"beating in response to all Turkish hearts, I was part of this sublime national madness.... Nothing else mattered for me in life at all."** She went on to serve Mustafa Kemal as a loyal confidante during his military campaigns, admiring his steadfast leadership.

Once independence was secured, however, Halide Edib and Mustafa Kemal had a falling out. Whereas Edib favored the further expansion of liberal democracy, Atatürk intended to be the unchallenged leader of an absolutist state. When she criticized him, he scolded her: *"I want everyone to do as I wish.... I do not want any criticism or advice. I will have only my own way. All shall do as I command."* Edib responded, *"I will obey you and do as you wish as long as I believe you are serving the cause."* But Kemal ignored her and said, *"You shall obey me and do as I wish."*† Shortly thereafter he banned her political party and she went into exile.

Having forged a new country through war, Mustafa Kemal's goal was to put Turkey on an equal economic and military footing with the European powers, and he ordered rapid modernization to achieve that end. In the nineteenth century, the Ottoman empire had vacillated about adopting Western models (see Chapter 23). Kemal had no second thoughts in imposing a secular constitution with strict separation between mosque and state. His ideas would ideas would guide Turkey for decades to come.

---

*Halide Edib, http://gvcommunity.tripod.com/ladies/haide.htm.

†Halide Edib, *The Turkish Ordeal* (New York: Century, 1926), p. 128.

WORLD HISTORY IN TODAY'S WORLD

Kemalists and Islamists in the Turkish Republic

A visitor to Turkey will notice ubiquitous statues and portraits of Mustafa Kemal. Supporters of Atatürk's legacy of secular nationalism built a cult around his memory during the many years when they monopolized Turkish politics. The nation's children still learn of his exploits and memorize famous aphorisms such as: *"How happy is the one who says 'I am a Turk!'"*

But late in the twentieth century Kemalists found themselves challenged by Turks who resented having religiosity banned from public life, envisioning a greater role for religion in government. Long suppressed by the secularist military, by 2002 the expansion of Turkish democracy finally gave them a shot at governance. The Islamist Justice and Development Party (JDP) scored a definitive victory in the 2002 elections.

The JDP has dominated Turkish politics ever since, alarming Kemalists who fear that creeping Islamization will infringe on their secular lifestyles and freedoms. The use of public funds to support religious schools, for example, is strongly opposed by those who favor Atatürk's strict secularism in education. The head scarf has become symbolic of the divide between Kemalists and Islamists. Previously, women were not allowed to wear head scarves in public places, such as government offices and classrooms. In the past decade, however, they have become increasingly common.

Kemalists (and Turkish feminists) see JDP policies as rolling back Atatürk's expansion of women's rights. In 2014, President Recep Tayyip Erdoğan (see Chapter 32) publicly proclaimed that motherhood was every woman's calling, saying that women are "too delicate" for "manly" tasks. Such patriarchal pronouncements play well with the party's conservative base but arouse the ire of secularists.

Still, many daughters of the rising Turkish middle class, whose families are firm supporters of President Erdoğan, now cover their heads before going to school. Seeing them walk past a statue of Mustafa Kemal, one can easily imagine a scowl of disapproval forming on their founding father's face. Although these young women now have the freedom to express their religious convictions by wearing a head scarf, other Turks who value freedom from religion worry that religion might be imposed on them by government.

Kemal's drive to separate religion from politics included laws to improve the status of women. His policies gave girls and young women increased access to education, a move Edib strongly supported. Not surprisingly, after the emotional pain she suffered when her first husband took a second wife, she also favored the Turkish law abolishing polygamy. Edib applauded when, in 1930, Turkey became the first predominantly Muslim country in which women had the right to vote.

On the other hand, Edib critiqued the authoritarian means by which these reforms were attained. When Kemal banned women from wearing veils in all government buildings, schools, and public spaces, for example, Edib argued that while the veil should never be imposed on women, neither should it be banned by governments. *"Wherever religion is interfered with by governments, it becomes a barrier, and an unremovable one, to peace and understanding."** Education and freedom to choose were the keys to reform, she thought. Too impatient for gradual reform, Kemal simply imposed his own will on the nation. (See the feature "World History in Today's World: Kemalists and Islamists in the Turkish Republic.")

After Mustafa Kemal died in 1938, the authoritarian pattern he set in place would continue long into the nation's future, with the military playing a powerful role. But at least now Halide Edib felt secure in returning to her homeland.

*Halide Edib, *Inside India* (London: Allen and Unwin, 1937), p. 231.

Turkey's New Alphabet The Turkish leader Mustafa Kemal instituted a top-down program to modernize and westernize the new nation of Turkey. In 1928, he declared that Turkish would no longer be written in Arabic script but in Latin characters for all purposes, public and private. Here Kemal himself demonstrates the new alphabet.

Getúlio Vargas and Brazil's "New State"

Like other parts of the world with little experience of liberal governance, many Latin American nations experienced an augmentation of their authoritarian traditions during the economic crisis of the 1930s. Brazil came closest to emulating European models of fascism.

Getúlio Vargas (in office, 1930–1945, 1951–1954) came to power in 1930 and used the state as an engine of economic growth. Like Lázaro Cárdenas in Mexico, he nationalized natural resources and promoted manufacturing through import substitution. Then, in 1937, he made a bold political move by suspending the Brazilian constitution and declaring the beginning of his *Estado Novo*, or "new state."

Vargas suppressed independent civil groups by following the corporatist model of Benito Mussolini, organizing society into "corporations" that could be directly controlled by the state. The aim of the *Estado Novo*, he said, was to stimulate the moribund Brazilian economy—*"to crisscross the nation with railroads, highways, and airlines; to increase production; to provide for the laborer"*—by putting an end to regional competition and petty political bickering. His stated goal was *"to organize public opinion so that there is, body and soul, one Brazilian thought."** That "one Brazilian thought" would, of course, be his own.

Anticolonial Nationalism in Asia, Africa, and the Caribbean

Colonial governments are, by their nature, autocratic, so in the 1920s authoritarianism was already the status quo across most of South and Southeast Asia, Africa, and the Caribbean. Then the economic crisis of the Great Depression led European powers to exploit their colonies even more. Harsh policies, such as forced labor, combined with the global economic decline to spread distress throughout the colonial world. As a result, movements of anticolonial nationalism gathered strength.

Getúlio Vargas
The President of Brazil (1930–1945, 1951–1954) who implemented neo-fascist policies in his *Novo Stado* ("New State"), magnifying the role of government in many aspects of national life, including the economy.

Gandhi and the Indian National Congress

Halide Edib traveled to India in 1935: *"India seemed to me like Allah's workshop: gods, men and nature abounded in their most beautiful and most hideous; ideas and all the arts in their ancient and most modern styles lay about pell-mell.... This India must certainly have its share in shaping the future. Not*

*Getúlio Vargas, "Excerpts from Speeches and Interviews, 1937–1940," in *Sources of Global History Since 1900*, ed. James H. Overfield, 2d ed. (Boston: Wadsworth, 2013), p. 160.

*because of its immemorial age, but because of the new life throbbing in it!"** Speaking before an audience at the National Muslim University, her thoughts were on someone in the audience. Looking out at the *"fragile figure"* before her, she wrote, *"I was thinking about the quality of Mahatma Gandhi's greatness."** **Mohandas K. Gandhi** (1869–1948) had turned the Indian National Congress into the voice of India.

Mohandas K. Gandhi

(1869–1948) Indian political leader who organized mass support for the Indian National Congress against British rule. His political philosophy of nonviolent resistance had worldwide influence.

Before 1914, the Indian National Congress had been a reformist organization, seeking greater participation of Indians in their own governance but accepting the basic outlines of British rule (see Chapter 24). Given the contribution Indians had made to the British war effort, they expected to be rewarded with substantial political reform. But the British offered only modest proposals for a gradual increase in Indian participation.

Then in 1919, the **Amritsar Massacre** shocked the nation. An unarmed crowd gathered in a garden area for a religious ceremony, unaware that the British had banned public meetings. In a horrible display of the violence on which colonial authority was based, a British officer ordered his Indian troops to fire directly into the crowd, leaving 400 dead and 1,200 wounded. Cooperation turned to confrontation, and in 1920 the Indian National Congress launched its first mass public protest to gain *Hind Swaraj*, Indian self-rule.

Amritsar Massacre

(1919) A turning point in Anglo-Indian relations, when a British officer ordered his troops to fire directly into a peaceful crowd in the city of Amritsar. Following this event, in 1920 the Indian National Congress, led by Mohandas K. Gandhi, began its first mass campaign for Indian self-rule.

By then Gandhi, a Western-educated lawyer, had discarded European dress for the spare clothing of an ascetic Hindu holy man. His philosophy was in fact influenced by both traditions. Western ideals of equality informed his insistence that the so-called Untouchables, those considered outside and beneath the Hindu caste hierarchy, be given full rights and recognition as human beings. But his two main principles were from the South Asian tradition. *Ahimsa* (uh-HIM-sah), or absolute nonviolence, was at the center of Gandhi's moral philosophy. *Satyagraha* (SUHT-yuh-gruh-huh), or "soul force," was the application of that philosophy to politics. Gandhi believed that it is self-defeating to use violence to counter violence, no matter how just the cause. The moral force of his arguments earned him the title *Mahatma*, "Great Soul."

But in 1920, after the British threw Gandhi and other Congress leaders in jail, violence did accompany the first mass campaigns of civil disobedience. Deciding that the Indian people were not ready to achieve self-rule through satyagraha, Gandhi retreated to his *ashram* (AHSH-ruhm), a communal rural home, emulating the simple rural life he idealized. Meanwhile, a new generation of Congress leaders was emerging, most importantly British-educated Jawaharlal Nehru, elected as the organization's president in 1928. (See the feature "Movement of Ideas Through Primary Sources: Gandhi and Nehru on Progress and Civilization.")

● **CONTEXT&CONNECTIONS** Gandhi would spend hours sitting at a wheel spinning cotton. The gentle clicking of the wheel stimulated meditation, and also symbolized rejection of the British textiles that represented imperial economic exploitation (see Chapter 23). ●

In 1930, Gandhi re-emerged to lead another campaign of mass civil disobedience. His Salt March defied a British law against Indians making their own salt. The British responded with a combination of repression and concessions. After initially jailing Congress leaders, they then compromised with the Government of India Act of 1935, which called for elections of semi-representative regional assemblies. Congress complained that this was inadequate but decided to participate in the elections anyway, scoring huge victories across the country.

---

*Halide Edib, *Inside India* (London: Allen and Unwin, 1937), pp. 29, 81.

Gandhi and Nehru on Progress and Civilization

The two most influential Indian leaders of the twentieth century were Mohandas K. Gandhi and Jawaharlal Nehru, representing different generations in the Indian National Congress. Gandhi, born in 1869, was the inspirational force behind Indian resistance to British colonialism in the 1920s and 1930s. Nehru, twenty years younger, participated in that resistance and later led the independent Indian republic as its first prime minister, from 1947 to 1964 (see Chapter 30).

Both men were influenced by the time they spent in Great Britain. Gandhi sailed to Britain in 1888 to pursue a law degree, and while in London he was strongly influenced by cultural trends and by philosophers who called into question the relentless materialism of late Victorian society. Among them were vegetarians and Theosophists, who emphasized intuition and mysticism over rationalism and formal theology. He was also influenced by the American writer Henry David Thoreau and the Russian novelist Leo Tolstoy, both of whom celebrated the simplicity of rural life.

Nehru's British experience was quite different. His father, a famous lawyer and a man of great wealth, sent him to study at two of the world's most famous educational institutions, Harrow School and then Cambridge University. Interacting with England's elite, the young Nehru was strongly influenced by the reformist socialism fashionable with the younger generation at the start of the twentieth century. Such socialists accepted the need for the economic development that came with capitalist industrialism but argued for a more equitable distribution of its proceeds.

Gandhi and Nehru, therefore, though close friends as well as political allies, had very different visions of India's future. While many Indians have been strongly influenced by Gandhi's philosophy, Nehru's attitude has been much more evident in Indian government policy since the country achieved independence in 1947.

❯ Historical Thinking Skill:

ANALYZING EVIDENCE **What were Gandhi and Nehru trying to accomplish in writing these texts, and how does their purpose compare to that of Blyden's texts featured in Chapter 26?**

Sources: M. K. Gandhi, *Hind Swaraj* (Ahmedabad, India: Navajivan, 1938 [1908]), pp. 31–33; Jawaharlal Nehru, *An Autobiography* (New Delhi: Allied, 1942), pp. 510–511.

Mohandas K. Gandhi, *Hind Swaraj* (1909)

Let us first consider what state of things is described by the word "civilization." Its true test lies in the fact that people living in it make bodily welfare the object of life. We will take some examples. The people of Europe today live in better-built houses than they did a hundred years ago. This is considered an emblem of civilization, and this is also a matter to promote bodily happiness. Formerly, they wore skins, and used spears as their weapons. Now, they wear long trousers, and, for embellishing their bodies, they wear a variety of clothing, and, instead of spears, they carry with them revolvers containing five or more chambers. If people of a certain country, who have hitherto not been in the habit of wearing much clothing, boots, etc., adopt European clothing, they are supposed to have become civilized out of savagery. Formerly, in Europe, people ploughed their lands mainly by manual labor. Now, one man can plough a vast tract by means of steam engines and can thus amass great wealth. This is called a sign of civilization. Formerly, only a few men wrote valuable books. Now, anybody writes and prints anything he likes and poisons people's minds. Formerly, men traveled in wagons. Now, they fly through the air in trains at the rate of four hundred and more miles per day. This is considered the height of civilization.... Formerly, when people wanted to fight with one another, they measured between them their bodily strength; now it is possible to take away thousands of lives by one man working behind a gun from a hill. This is civilization. Formerly, men worked in the open air only as much as they liked. Now thousands of workmen meet together and for the sake of maintenance work in factories or mines. Their condition is worse than that of beasts. They are obliged to work, at the risk of their lives, at most dangerous occupations, for the sake of millionaires. Formerly, men were made slaves under physical compulsion. Now they are enslaved by temptation of money and of the luxuries that money can buy.... Formerly, people had two or three meals consisting of home-made bread and vegetables; now, they require something to eat every two hours so that they have hardly leisure for anything else.... This civilization takes note neither of morality nor of religion.... Civilization seeks to increase bodily comforts, and it fails miserably even in doing so.

This civilization is irreligion, and it has taken such a hold on the people in Europe that those who are in it appear to be half mad. They lack real physical strength or courage. They keep up their energy by intoxication. They can hardly be happy in solitude. Women, who should be the queens of households, wander in the streets or they slave away in factories. For the sake of a pittance, half a million women in England alone are laboring under trying circumstances in factories or similar institutions. This awful act is one of the causes of the daily growing suffragette movement.

[The English] are a shrewd nation and I therefore believe that they will cast off this evil. They are enterprising and industrious, and their mode of thought is not inherently immoral. Neither are they bad at heart. I therefore respect them. Civilization is not an incurable disease, but it should never be forgotten that the English are at present afflicted by it.

Jawaharlal Nehru, "Gandhi" (1936)

I imagine that [Gandhi] is not so vague about the objective as he sometimes appears to be.... *"India's salvation consists,"* he wrote in 1909, *"in unlearning what she has learned during the last fifty years. The railways, telegraphs, hospitals, lawyers, doctors, and suchlike all have to go...."*

All this seems to me utterly wrong and harmful doctrine, and impossible of achievement. Behind it lies Gandhi's love and praise of poverty and suffering and the ascetic life.... Personally I dislike the praise of poverty and suffering.... Nor do I appreciate in the least the idealization of the "simple peasant life." I have almost a horror of it, and instead of submitting to it myself I want to drag out even the peasantry from it.... What is there in "The Man with the Hoe" to idealize over? Crushed and exploited for innumerable generations, he is only little removed from the animals who keep him company....

The desire to get away from the mind of man to primitive conditions where mind does not count, seems to me quite incomprehensible. The very thing that is the glory and triumph of man is decried and discouraged, and a physical environment which will oppress the mind and prevent its growth is considered desirable. Present-day civilization is full of evils, but it is also full of good; and it has the capacity in it to rid itself of those evils. To destroy it root and branch is to remove that capacity from it and revert to a dull, senseless, and miserable existence. But even if that were desirable it is an impossible undertaking. We cannot stop the river of change or cut ourselves adrift from it, and psychologically we who have eaten of the apple of Eden cannot forget that taste and go back to primitiveness.

Gandhi's Salt March In 1930, Mohandas K. Gandhi galvanized his supporters and received sympathetic international press coverage when he and his followers marched 240 miles (386 km) from his ashram to the sea to make salt from ocean water. It was a perfect example of nonviolent civil disobedience, since the manufacture of salt was a legal monopoly of the British Indian government.(Dinodia Photos/Alamy)

Though Gandhi used Hindu symbols to rally mass support, he and Nehru agreed that the Indian National Congress should embrace members of all faiths. That did not mollify leaders of the new **Muslim League**, who feared that under self-rule they would be oppressed by the Hindu majority. Gandhi did his best to reassure the Muslim community, and Nehru envisioned a secular state in which religion would play no part.

Muslim League
Political party founded in British India to represent the interests of the Muslim minority. The party eventually advocated a separate nation for Indian Muslims: Pakistan.

Based on her visit to India, Halide Edib was confident that nationalist unity could transcend religious differences. Nevertheless, distrust between the two communities increased, and Muslim League leaders began to call for the creation of a separate Muslim state, Pakistan (see Chapter 30). The British insisted that their presence as a neutral arbiter between India's diverse peoples would be necessary far into the future.

Colonialism and Resistance in Africa, the Caribbean, and Southeast Asia

Nationalist movements were also developing in Africa, the Caribbean, and Southeast Asia during this period. As in India, Western-educated leaders were beginning to create political structures that could mobilize large numbers of people to challenge European authority. Nevertheless, European powers continued to rule with great confidence.

A persistent feature of empire is the need for rulers to find indigenous allies to help them control and administer their territories. While the top positions were always reserved for the ruling Europeans, members of the colonized society were educated as clerks, nurses, and primary school teachers. However, in the process of being educated, they might also learn about the French Revolution and the traditional liberties of British subjects, leading them to aspire to greater freedom for themselves and their people.

The gap between aspirations and realities was stark. The French model of assimilation, for example, held out the promise that Asians and Africans could "become" French in language and culture, and even achieve French citizenship. However, most who pursued this path—speaking perfect French and immersing themselves in French culture—found that the colonialists still saw them through a racist lens as *indigenes* (ihn-deh-JEN), "natives" who were automatically inferior. The same deeply frustrating dynamic held sway in the Dutch East Indies, where people of mixed race, educated in Dutch schools, could never be the social equals of the colonizers.

The British were the most consistent in employing what they called "indirect rule," relying to the greatest extent possible on "native authorities" to carry out day-to-day administrative tasks such as collecting taxes and keeping the peace. As a result, the British had almost no concept of assimilation.

• **CONTEXT&CONNECTIONS** The British in India, after considering assimilationist models as proposed by *Rammohun Roy* (Chapter 20), reverted to their more exclusionary attitude after the *Indian Revolt of 1857*, emphasizing a sharp and permanent cultural divide between rulers and ruled (Chapter 24). Hence the British preference for "native authorities" as subordinate intermediaries, rather than Western-educated Africans, was part of a broader pattern within the British empire. •

The European policy of relying on indigenous figureheads spurred additional resentments. In Southeast Asia, for example, the Vietnamese emperors of the Nguyen dynasty continued in office. Malaysian sultans were also given privileged positions. In Africa, "chiefs" were recognized as "native authorities," part of the supposed respect the British had for local customs. In reality, the colonialists were looking for local leaders to work at the bottom rungs of their administrations.

By the 1930s, many impatient nationalists saw the collusion of traditional elites with colonial powers as a hindrance to self-rule, as when the British divided Africans into discrete "tribes" and played their leaders against one another to secure continued control. Nigerian nationalist **Nnamdi Azikiwe** (NAHM-dee ah-zee-KEE-way) (1904–1996) deplored that policy, arguing that only when all Nigerians identified themselves with the nation as a whole, whatever their ethnic and religious backgrounds, would they be able to struggle effectively for self-rule. Having stowed away on a ship to the United States in 1925 and then graduated from the University of Pennsylvania, Azikiwe returned to West Africa in 1937 and founded the Nigerian Youth Movement while editing the *West African Pilot*, a newspaper that inspired Africans to challenge British colonial policies. Azikiwe also created a sports association focused on the increasing popularity of soccer in Nigeria to galvanize broader support for his nationalist cause.

Nnamdi Azikiwe
(1904–1996) Pioneering Nigerian nationalist who, after gaining higher education in the United States, edited a newspaper and formed cultural and political organizations to unite West Africans against British colonialism.

At the same time, sporadic popular uprisings arose in response to colonial tax, trade, and land policies. In the **Igbo Women's War** of 1929, for example, women in southeastern Nigeria rebelled against colonial intrusions into their household and village affairs. Using traditional Igbo (ee-BWOH) means of protesting male abuse of authority, the women dressed up in special costumes, gathered in large numbers,

Igbo Women's War
(1929) Rebellion led by women in colonial Nigeria who used traditional cultural practices to protest British taxation policies.

and sang songs of derision to shame the African chiefs who carried out British orders. The British modified their tax system slightly in response, but the women lacked a broader organization to connect their local efforts with a wider anticolonial struggle. A connection between broadly educated nationalists (like Azikiwe) and village-level protest would not threaten colonial rule in Africa until after 1945 (see Chapter 30).

Tensions were strongest where Europeans came not just as rulers but also as settlers, as in South Africa and Kenya. Here Africans had lost not only their sovereignty but also much of their best land. The British colony of Kenya in East Africa saw the rise of a mass protest movement in the 1920s; anticolonial feelings were strongest among Kikuyu-speaking Kenyans who lost their land to white settlers. As in the Igbo Women's War, however, local protest was not enough to gain substantial reform. Meanwhile, a young leader named Jomo Kenyatta (1895–1978) was earning a doctorate in anthropology from the London School of Economics. Only after the Second World War would Kenyatta return to lead a broad nationalist movement that connected Western-educated leaders with the mass of Kenyans, a pattern found across sub-Saharan Africa.

• **CONTEXT&CONNECTIONS** Before returning home, Jomo Kenyatta would attend the Fifth Pan-African Congress in Manchester, England, in 1946. There he met the African American activist W. E. B. Du Bois, co-organizer of the First Pan-African Congress held in Paris in 1919, as well as other Western-educated African leaders who would soon return to the continent to lead successful anticolonial revolts, among them *Kwame Nkrumah*, who would become the first prime minister of an independent Ghana in 1957 (Chapter 30). •

AP® THEMES

How did social, cultural, and economic differences contribute to tension between colonized peoples and European colonizers after World War I?

In the British West Indies, modern mass nationalism developed more rapidly. Already by the 1920s Marcus Garvey (1887–1940) had amassed a huge following in Jamaica for his United Negro Improvement Association (UNIA). Following the Pan-African tradition (see Chapter 26), Garvey's "back-to-Africa" philosophy called on everyone of African descent to band together to pursue a common destiny, specifically to promote cultural and trade connections between peoples of African descent in the Americas and on the continent itself. The UNIA message resonated not only in the Caribbean, but in the United States and South Africa as well. Though a controversial figure who was convicted in the United States on trumped-up charges of mail fraud, Garvey made lasting contributions to Pan-Africanism through his unwavering insistence on the dignity of African people and their potential for economic self-sufficiency.

Meanwhile, the Great Depression was making the already difficult conditions of colonialism even worse. Across the British West Indies, for example, falling crop prices and depressed wages from 1934–1939 led to repeated outbreaks of labor unrest among agricultural workers. Colonialists were desperate for cheap supplies from the colonies to prop up their own weakened economies. The French compelled farmers in equatorial Africa to keep planting, weeding, and harvesting cotton despite a sharp drop in market prices. The British imposed a "grow more crops" campaign in East Africa, requiring peasants to dedicate land and labor to export commodities, like coffee, that were now basically worthless. But farmers could not eat cotton or coffee, and hunger resulted from these coerced diversions from subsistence crops.

In Southeast Asia, unemployment rose in Malaya, Vietnam, and the Dutch East Indies after 1929, when the drop in automobile manufacturing depressed the world market for rubber. Even where small-scale farmers stopped growing export crops and focused on food production, colonial governments still compelled cash payment of taxes. The French penalized Vietnamese peasants who did not pay taxes with forced labor on government projects and French-owned plantations.

As in Africa, however, the peoples of French Indochina still lacked the organizational means for effective resistance.

In 1930, for example, the Vietnamese Nationalist Party was harshly suppressed after raising a failed rebellion. Earlier the group had favored moderate reform, but faced with French intransigence it opted for violent resistance. Before his execution, the group's leader stated: *"If France does not want to have increasing trouble with revolutionary movements, she should immediately modify the cruel and inhuman policy now practiced in Indochina."** In the 1950s, a revolutionary movement led by Ho Chi Minh would indeed drive the French out of Vietnam (see Chapter 30).

Africa and Southeast Asia have been called the "quiescent colonies" during this period. But in larger historical perspective, the 1930s were merely a pause in the resistance to colonial occupation that began in the late nineteenth century. Nationalist leaders during this time were laying the foundations for the large-scale movements of mass nationalism that would emerge following the new worldwide military conflict that was about to erupt.

The Road to War

World War II did not sneak up on anyone. In the 1930s numerous events in Europe, Asia, and Africa heralded a coming conflict, starting with Japanese aggression in China.

China was vulnerable because of fighting between the Guomindang government of Chiang Kai-shek and Communist revolutionaries led by Mao Zedong (see Chapter 27). Attacked in 1927 by their former Guomindang allies, the Communists had retreated to the interior. During the "Long March" of 1934–1936, the Communists walked some 7,500 miles (12,000 km) to consolidate a base in the northeast.

Meanwhile, having already defied the League of Nations with its occupation of Manchuria, the Japanese empire launched a savage attack on coastal China in 1937. Chiang and Mao then agreed to cease their hostilities and fight the common Japanese enemy, but they never combined forces or coordinated their efforts (see Map 28.1).

Convinced of their racial superiority, the Japanese invaders treated the Chinese with callous brutality. During the **Rape of Nanjing**, Japanese soldiers killed hundreds of thousands of civilians, using tactics such as gang rape and mutilation of children to spread terror among the population. Total war, with its disregard of the distinction between soldiers and civilians, was being taken to a new level.

Rape of Nanjing
Japanese occupation of the city in 1937 during which they slaughtered hundreds of thousands of Chinese civilians and used other terror tactics.

Even earlier, in 1935, international institutions had shown their inability to counter military aggression during Mussolini's invasion of Ethiopia. Here total war meant Italian pilots dropping poison gas on Ethiopian villagers. The Ethiopian emperor Hailie Selassie (1892–1975) went to Geneva to beg the League of Nations for help:

> *I ask the fifty-two nations, who have given the Ethiopian people a promise to help them in their resistance to the aggressor, what are they willing to do for Ethiopia? And the great Powers who have promised the guarantee of collective security to small States on whom weighs the threat that they may one day suffer the fate of Ethiopia, I ask what measures do you intend to take? ... What reply shall I have to take back to my people?*

---

*Nguyen Thai Hoc, "Letter to the French Chamber of Deputies, 1930," in *Sources of Global History Since 1900*, ed. James H. Overfield, 2d ed. (Boston: Wadsworth, 2013), pp. 202–203.

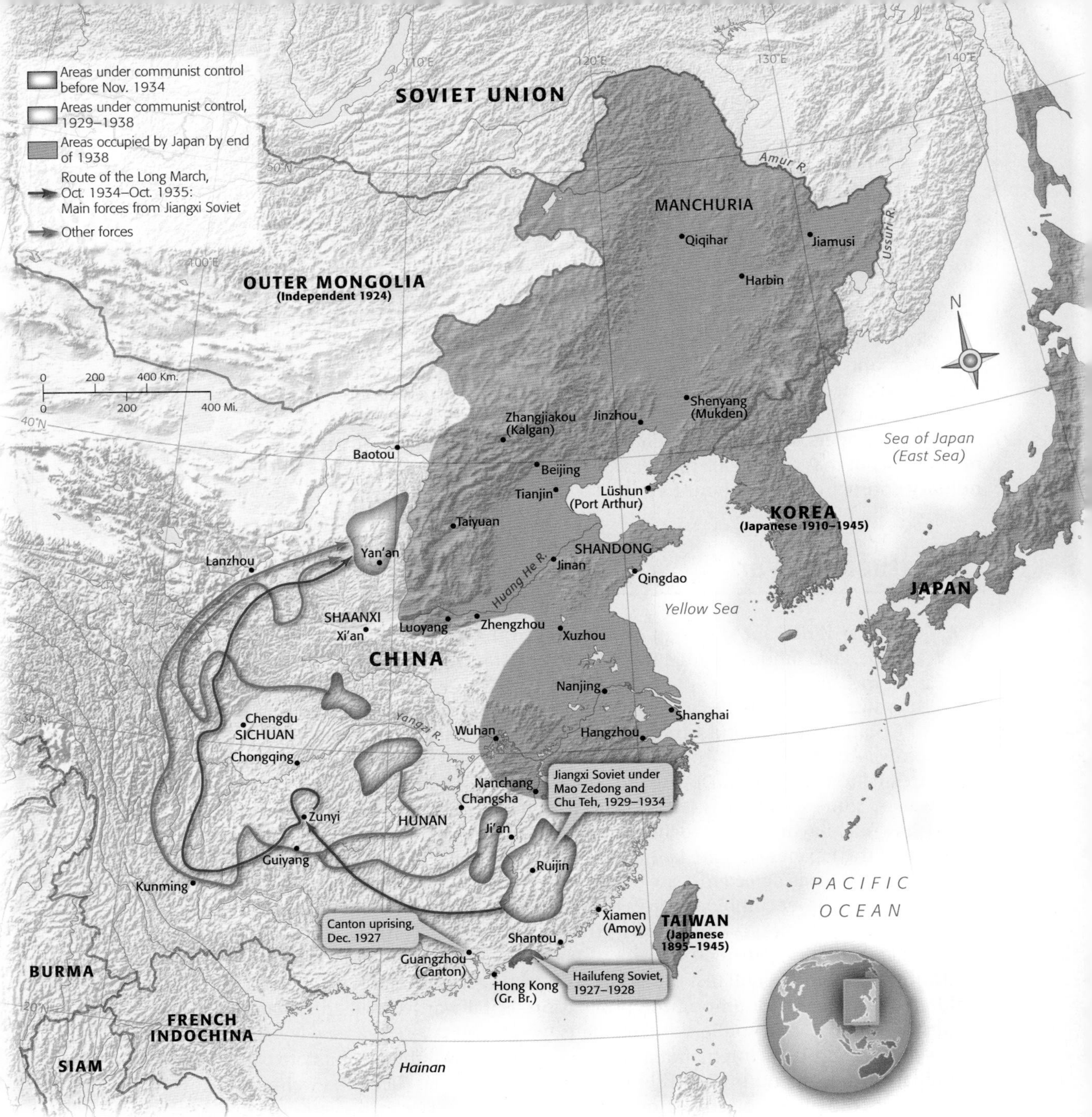

Map 28.1 The Japanese Invasion of China Six years after the invasion of Manchuria, Japanese forces began the conquest of coastal China in 1937, quickly taking Beijing, Shanghai, and other major cities. Chinese resistance, though extensive, was limited by divisions between the Guomindang government and the Communists. Expelled from coastal cities by the Guomindang after 1927, the Communists relocated first to the southern interior and then, after their dramatic "Long March," established a new base in the northeastern Shaanxi province.

The Rape of Nanjing One of the most brutal episodes during the Japanese invasion of China was the Rape of Nanjing. Here Japanese soldiers are seen using live captives for bayonet practice, with fellow soldiers and future victims looking on. Though the Chinese have long remembered such atrocities, some Japanese schoolchildren still learn nothing about them.

The emperor warned that if the international community did not take effective action, no small nation would ever be safe. The League of Nations placed economic sanctions on Mussolini but would go no further. With Italy having access to colonial resources, such as Libyan oil, and receiving aid from the German government, the sanctions had little effect.

Meanwhile, German and Italian fascists saw their movement gaining ground in Spain, where the elected government was implementing socialist policies to deal with the Great Depression. In reaction, Spanish conservatives took up arms under General Francisco Franco (1892–1975) to seize power by force. During the **Spanish Civil War** (1936–1939) Mussolini and Hitler aided Franco, while France, Britain, and the United States remained neutral. Mired in their own domestic concerns, they missed this chance to support democracy against fascism.

Spanish Civil War (1936–1939) Conflict between conservative nationalist forces, led by General Francisco Franco and backed by Germany, and Republican forces, backed by the Soviet Union. The Spanish Civil War was seen by many as a prelude to renewed world war.

The Western democracies were equally tepid in response to Hitler's heightened aggression. In 1936, German military forces moved into the Rhineland region bordering France, in clear violation of the Versailles treaty. The lack of any sustained response emboldened Hitler.

Hitler had long declared that the Germans needed *lebensraum* (LEY-buhns-rowm), "living space," in which to pursue their racial destiny, and that the ethnic Germans scattered in countries to the east needed to be reunited with

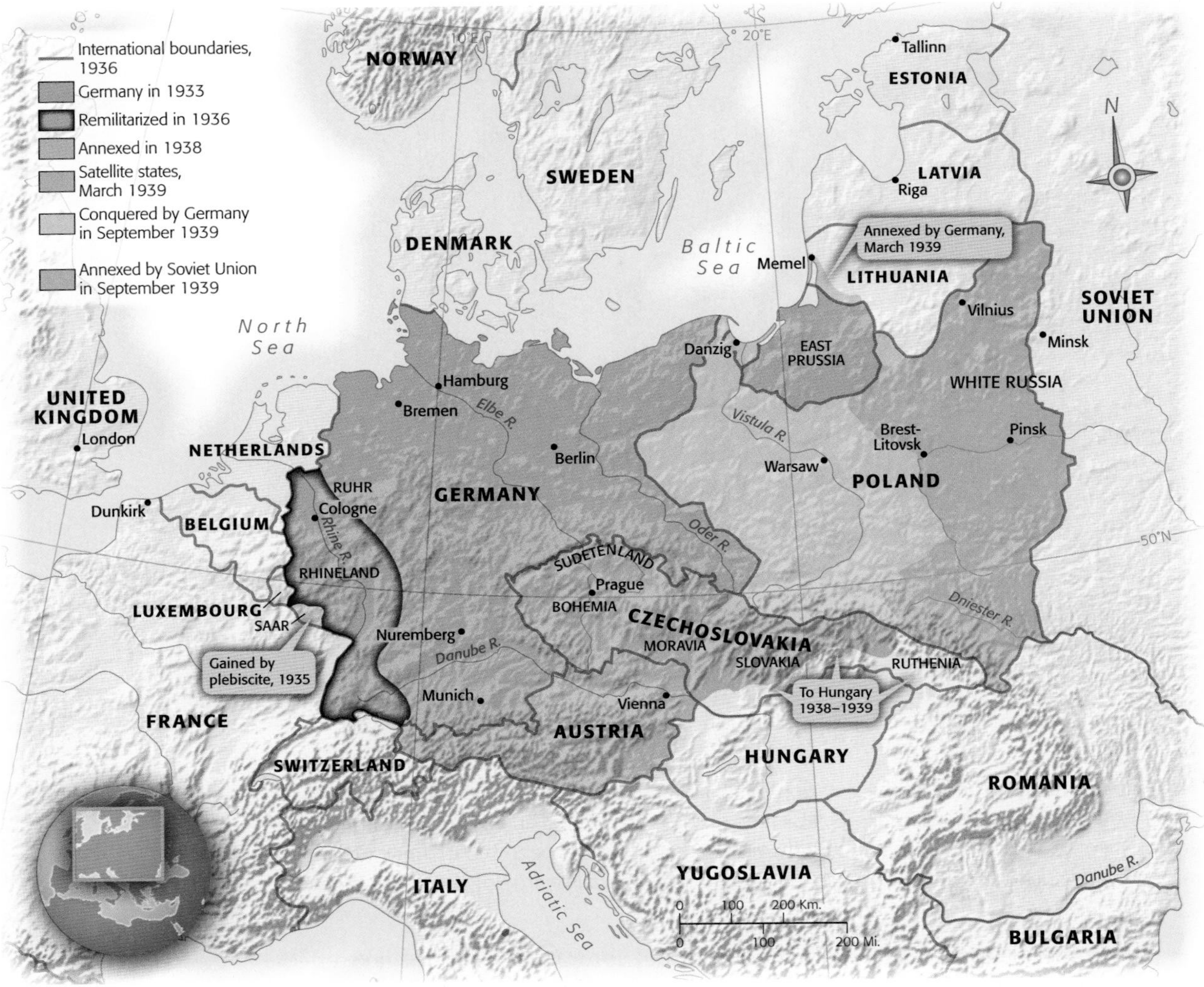

Map 28.2 The Growth of Nazi Germany, 1933–1939 The major turning point in the expansion of Nazi Germany was the annexation of the Sudetenland from Czechoslovakia in 1938. Joseph Stalin interpreted British diplomatic efforts to avoid renewed world war with alarm, and he agreed to a secret treaty to divide Poland between Hitler's Germany and his own Soviet Union. The German invasion of Poland from the west in 1939 therefore triggered the annexation of eastern Poland by the Soviet Union.

the homeland. Taking the Social Darwinist idea of a racial "struggle for existence" to the extreme, he imagined vast eastern spaces cleared of Jews, with racially inferior Slavic peoples remaining to provide slave labor under German command. While Stalin took this threat seriously, most Western leaders thought that Hitler could be contained. In fact, some Westerners sympathized with Hitler's anti-Semitism and anticommunism.

Hitler thus asserted his right to annex the Sudetenland, a province of Czechoslovakia where, he claimed, the German minority was facing discrimination (see Map 28.2). One member of the British Parliament, Winston Churchill, recommended an Anglo-French initiative to head off Hitler's expansionism. But Churchill, who would be Britain's great wartime leader (see Chapter 29), was unable to convince the British public to take a firm stand and thus risk war.

Instead, British Prime Minister Neville Chamberlain flew to Munich in 1937 to negotiate. Chamberlain's policy of *"active appeasement"* was based on the premise that Hitler would be content with minor concessions and that diplomacy could prevent a major European war. The British public, still scarred by the trauma of the Great War, largely supported Chamberlain's quest for *"peace in our time."* Germany occupied the Sudetenland unchecked, and the next year Hitler annexed Austria as well. Ever since, the term *appeasement* has meant the failure to stop an aggressor in time.

Such lack of Western resolve, shown in Ethiopia, Spain, and Czechoslovakia alike, alarmed Joseph Stalin. Stalin feared that without Western support his own army would be unable to withstand a German invasion (a problem partly of his own creation given the many officers killed during the Great Purges). Much as they hated and mistrusted each other, in the summer of 1939 Hitler and Stalin signed a nonaggression pact, secretly dividing Poland between them. Hitler was merely delaying his planned attack on Russia, while Stalin was playing for time to ready his country for war.

When Hitler invaded Poland on September 1, 1939, Britain and France immediately declared war on Germany but took no active military steps to confront the German army. Meanwhile, in the United States public opinion was largely opposed to another intervention in European politics. Soon, however, peoples across Europe, Africa, Asia, and the Americas would be embroiled in a total war the likes of which humanity had never seen.

CONTEXT AND CONNECTIONS

Suspended Between Two World Wars

After the trauma of 1914–1918, the world's people barely had a chance to catch their breath before confronting another total war, even more global and more violent. By the summer of 1940, German, Italian, and Japanese aggression and the death of democracy in Spain had sounded a warning bell that tolled across the world. Like France and Britain before, the United States was slow to take heed, avoiding involvement in the Spanish Civil War and remaining neutral even as the Germans overran France and began an aerial bombardment of Britain. By then the catastrophe of another world war was inevitable.

It is understandable that the interwar generation valued peace so highly. For those who had experienced the ravages of the Great War two decades earlier, the thought of another total war was terrible indeed. Yet even before the Great Depression, global tensions ran high, aggravated by the long list of national grievances that remained after the Paris Peace Conference (see Chapter 27). As the 1930s progressed, international institutions such as the League of Nations proved ineffective in dealing with national aggression. The emergence of Halide Edib's own Turkey through military mobilization showed that national rights were best secured not with talk, but with action.

With the Great Depression, liberal democracy and free-market capitalism lost much of their allure. Responses from the far right and the far left—fascism, communism, and ultranationalism—offered alternatives that, whatever their cruelties, reinvigorated the Italian, German, and Soviet economies and emboldened Japan. Across the world, in nations as diverse as Brazil and Turkey, authoritarian leaders magnified the role of the state in social and economic affairs, suppressing the more democratic programs of dissidents like Halide Edib.

It seemed that the French and British had come out of the Paris Peace Conference with their status strengthened. They not only retained their global empires, but with

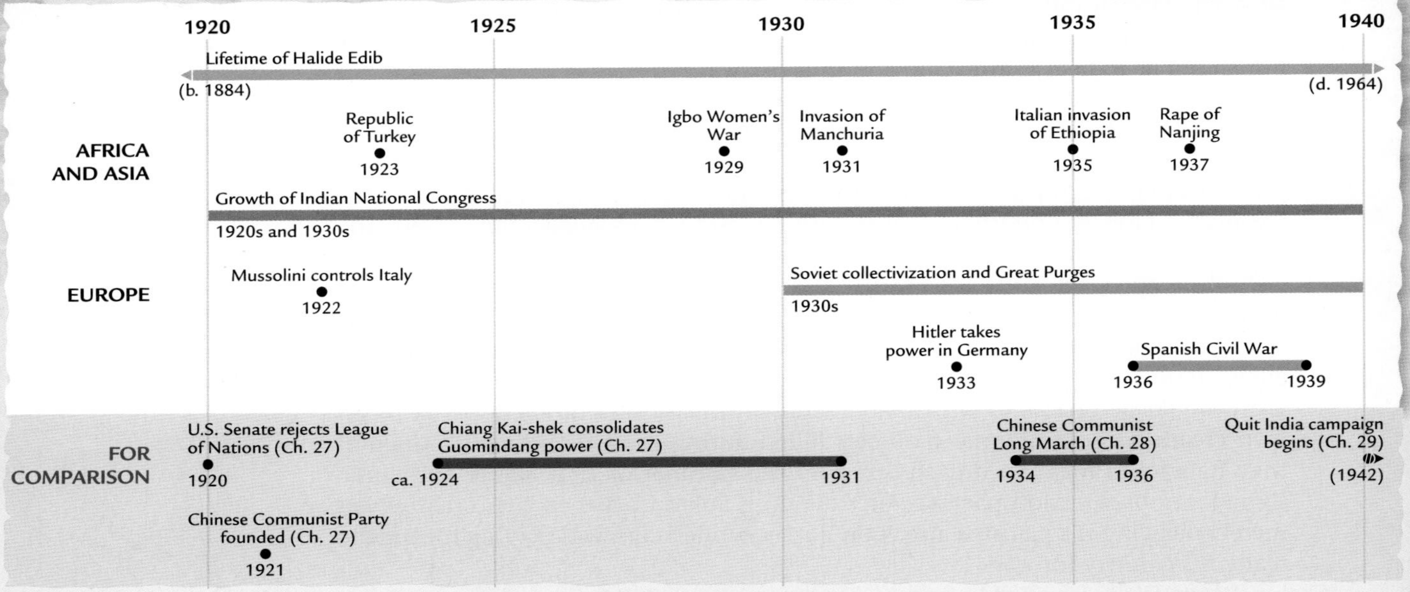

the addition of former German colonies and Ottoman provinces, expanded them. Under the exigencies of total war, however, they had expended vast sums. The British, the dominant source of global capital investment before the war, were now in debt to American financial institutions (see Chapter 27). How could they sustain a world-embracing empire when their relative global financial standing had slipped? Only after the Second World War did the British and French discover that the costs of empire exceeded the benefits, when decolonization led to a cascade of new Asian and African nations (see Chapter 30).

Meanwhile, the United States and the new Soviet Union stood on the sidelines. The Americans, having put a toe in the cold waters of international engagement during World War I, pulled back, demilitarized, and with the U.S. Senate's failure to ratify the League of Nations treaty, minded their own business. The Soviet Union, industrializing under Stalin's brutal dictatorship, was cut off from global economic and cultural developments. But as the French traveler Alexis de Tocqueville had predicted as early as the 1830s (see Chapter 25), the huge populations and vast resources of Russia and the United States were bound to put these two nations at the forefront of global affairs. When, in the aftermath of the Second World War, the global order based on European colonialism shattered, the United States and the Soviet Union would come to dominate the Cold War world (see Chapters 29–31). Fascism would be defeated by 1945, but the communist challenge to capitalism and liberal democracy would endure.

Key Terms

Halide Edib (842)
Great Depression (843)
Franklin Delano Roosevelt (844)
fascism (846)
Benito Mussolini (847)
Adolf Hitler (849)
collectivization (854)
Great Purges (854)
invasion of Manchuria (855)
Mustafa Kemal (856)
Getúlio Vargas (858)
Mohandas K. Gandhi (859)
Amritsar Massacre (859)
Muslim League (862)
Nnamdi Azikiwe (863)
Igbo Women's War (863)
Rape of Nanjing (865)
Spanish Civil War (867)

For Further Reference

Chang, Iris. *The Rape of Nanjing: The Forgotten Holocaust of World War II*. New York: Basic Books, 2012.

Chadha, Yodesh. *Gandhi: A Life*. New York: Wiley, 2008.

Crozier, Andrew. *The Causes of the Second World War*. Malden, Mass.: Wiley-Blackwell, 1997.

Edib, Halide. *House with Wisteria: Memoirs of Halide Edib*. Charlottesville, Va.: Leopolis Press, 2003.

Fitzpatrick, Sheila. *Stalin's Peasants: Resistance and Survival in the Russian Village After Collectivization*. New York: Oxford University Press, 1996.

Gellner, Ernest. *Nations and Nationalism*. Malden, Mass.: Wiley-Blackwell, 2006.

Griffin, Roger. *Modernism and Fascism: The Sense of Beginning Under Mussolini and Hitler*. New York: Palgrave Macmillan, 2010.

Hobsbawm, Eric. *The Age of Extremes: A History of the World, 1914–1991*. New York: Vintage, 1996.

Mango, Andrew. *Atatürk: The Biography of the Founder of Modern Turkey*. New York: Overlook, 2002.

Paxton, Robert. *The Anatomy of Fascism*. New York: Vintage, 2005.

Payne, Stanley. *Civil War in Europe, 1905–1949*. New York: Cambridge University Press, 2011.

Rothermund, Dietmar. *The Global Impact of the Great Depression, 1929–1939*. New York: Routledge, 1996.

Snyder, Timothy. *Bloodlands: Europe Between Hitler and Stalin*. New York: Basic Books, 2010.

AP® Review Questions for Chapter 28

Multiple-Choice Questions

QUESTIONS 1–2 REFER TO THE IMAGE ON PAGE 853.

1. Leni Riefenstahl's 1938 film *Olympia* is commonly regarded as a work of fascist artistic propaganda. Which of the following statements most strongly supports that assertion?
   (A) *Olympia* is fascist propaganda because of the consistent use of swastikas throughout.
   (B) Riefenstahl's film, shot in the neoclassical style, focused on the perfectibility of the human form and the value of motion and activity over rest and reflection.
   (C) Because motion pictures were still relatively new, the film sets up fascism as an acceptable choice for national success.
   (D) The neoclassical sets led the viewer to conclude that Nazi imagery was as old as Western civilization.

2. In his book *Mein Kampf*, Hitler wrote, "A man of little education but physically healthy . . . is more valuable to the national community than a clever weakling." Which of the following best explains how the athlete above fits that belief?
   (A) The individual and pose demonstrate that physical perfection is superior to intellectual activity.
   (B) In order to participate in the Olympic Games, an athlete must commit to studying the sport.
   (C) Hitler meant that the German army would be composed of the finest athletes in the world.
   (D) Both sources indicate that the ideal person was one who was both physically fit and highly intelligent.

QUESTIONS 3–5 REFER TO THE FOLLOWING PASSAGES.

Now thousands of workmen meet together and for the sake of maintenance work in factories or mines. Their condition is worse than that of beasts. They are obliged to work, at the risk of their lives, at most dangerous occupations, for the sake of millionaires.

—Mohandas K. Gandhi, *Hind Swaraj*, 1909

What is there in "The Man with the Hoe" to idealize over? Crushed and exploited for innumerable generations, he is only removed from the animals who keep him company.

—Jawaharlal Nehru, "Gandhi," 1936

3. The analogy of humans to animals in both passages is best understood in the context of which of the following?
   (A) The exploitation of lower classes for the economic gain of upper classes
   (B) The industrialization of India
   (C) The global flow of silver from the Americas
   (D) The decolonization movements following World War I

4. The tone of the *first* passage best reflects which of the following ideologies developed during the Industrial Revolution?
   (A) Anarchism
   (B) Nationalism
   (C) Communism
   (D) Conservatism

5. Based on the information in the two passages and your knowledge of world history, which of the following statements most accurately reflects Gandhi's and Nehru's positions?
   (A) Indian resistance to British rule had a firm foundation in Hindu values.
   (B) Both Gandhi and Nehru supported rapid Indian industrialization.
   (C) Gandhi wished for an independent and traditional India while Nehru wished for a modernized independent India.
   (D) Gandhi wished for a modernized independent India while Nehru wished for an independent and traditional India.

QUESTIONS 6–8 REFER TO THE FOLLOWING PASSAGE.

The elite are the carriers of civilization and the people are the holders of culture. Therefore, the elite's approach to the people should only have the following two purposes: to receive a training in culture from the people and then carry civilization to them. Yes, it is only with these two purposes that the elite should go to the people. The elite will find culture only there and nowhere else.

—Ziya Gokalp, Turkish nationalist and political philosopher, "On Turkism," 1923

6. Gokalp's argument is best understood in the context of which of the following developments in the twentieth century?
   (A) The reinstitution of sharia law after the failure of the early Turkish state
   (B) The Mandate System established after World War I

(C) Punitive provisions levied on Turkey by the Treaty of Versailles
(D) The collapse of the Ottoman empire and the formation of Turkey

7. Which of the following best supports the author's notion that both the elites and the people have a vital role for Turkey's development?
   (A) The path of development was to be set by the elites, and the people were to obey their directions.
   (B) Education was the domain of the elites, while the people would maintain the culture.
   (C) Turkey did not need any advancements from the West because traditional culture was sufficient to meet the needs of the day.
   (D) The role of every person was to strive for elite status so more could contribute to the marketplace of ideas.

8. Which of the following would best support the author's general notion of a paternalistic attitude of the elites toward the people?
   (A) Economic and political liberalization became increasingly common in the twentieth century.
   (B) Old assumptions about class and gender were increasingly challenged during the twentieth century.
   (C) Rights-based discourses became the standard form of state organization.
   (D) The general trend of governments was to take an active role in its citizens' lives after World War I

QUESTIONS 9–10 REFER TO THE FOLLOWING PASSAGE.

The advanced class, the class most oppressed by capitalism, is entitled to use compulsion, because it is doing so in the interests of the working and exploited people, and because it possesses means of compulsion and persuasion such as no former classes ever possessed, although they had incomparably greater material facilities for propaganda and agitation than we have.

—Vladimir Ilych Ulyanov (Lenin), "Modernizing Russia," 1920

9. Which of the following is the best example of what Lenin meant by "advanced class?"
   (A) Capitalists
   (B) Nobility
   (C) Workers
   (D) Clergy

10. Which of the following Soviet policies most closely matched Lenin's philosophy?
   (A) Newly formed international defensive alliances
   (B) Partial privatization of industry
   (C) Rapid industrialization focused on heavy machinery
   (D) Consolidation of individual farms and property into collective farms

Short-Answer Questions

1. Answer parts A and B.
   The Nazi invasion of Poland in September 1939 is commonly regarded as the beginning of World War II. However, some historians argue that the war actually began in July 1937 with the Japanese invasion of China.
   A. Provide TWO pieces of evidence that *support* this argument and explain how each piece supports the argument.
   B. Provide ONE piece of evidence that *undermines* this argument, and explain how it undermines the argument.

QUESTION 2 REFERS TO THE FOLLOWING PASSAGE.

Indeed, thanks to economic, educational, and cultural accomplishments, a growing class of Africans were able to exert pressure for change on colonial administrations from within.... Some have seen these individuals and the organizations that they founded as "collaborators."... Other observers, however, see these individuals as the first African "Nationalists."

—Erik Gilbert and Jonathan T. Reynolds, historians, *Africa in World History*, 2004

2. Answer parts A, B, and C.
   A. Identify and explain ONE example that supports the assertion that the individuals described in the passage were collaborators.
   B. Identify and explain ONE example that supports the assertion that the individuals described in the passage were nationalists.
   C. Identify ONE specific example from a region other than Africa of a similar process during imperialism.

29 The Second World War and the Origins of the Cold War, 1939–1949

By the spring of 1944, Nazi Germany had occupied France for nearly four years. In preparation for a British and American invasion at the Normandy coast, underground resistance fighters were being parachuted into the French countryside. **Nancy Wake** (1912–2011), a young Australian, was the only woman in her group. War can produce unlikely heroes, and Nancy Wake was one. While she had traveled to Paris in the 1930s looking for adventure, fun, and romance, now she was risking her life in the fight against Nazi Germany:

Nancy Wake

Epa/Australia War Museum /Landov

*As the Liberator bomber circled over the dropping zone in France I could see lights flashing and huge bonfires burning. I hoped the field was manned by the Resistance and not by German ambushers. Huddled in the belly of the bomber, airsick and vomiting, I was hardly Hollywood's idea of a glamorous spy. I probably looked grotesque. Over civilian clothes, silk-stockinged and high-heeled, I wore overalls, [and] carried revolvers in the pockets.... Even more incongruous was the matronly handbag, full of cash and secret instructions for D-Day.... But I'd spent years in France working as an escape courier ... and I was desperate to return to France and continue working against Hitler. Neither airsickness nor looking like a clumsily wrapped parcel was going to deter me.**

---

*Excerpt from Nancy Wake, *The Autobiography of the Woman the Gestapo Called the White Mouse*, © 1985 Pan Publishing.

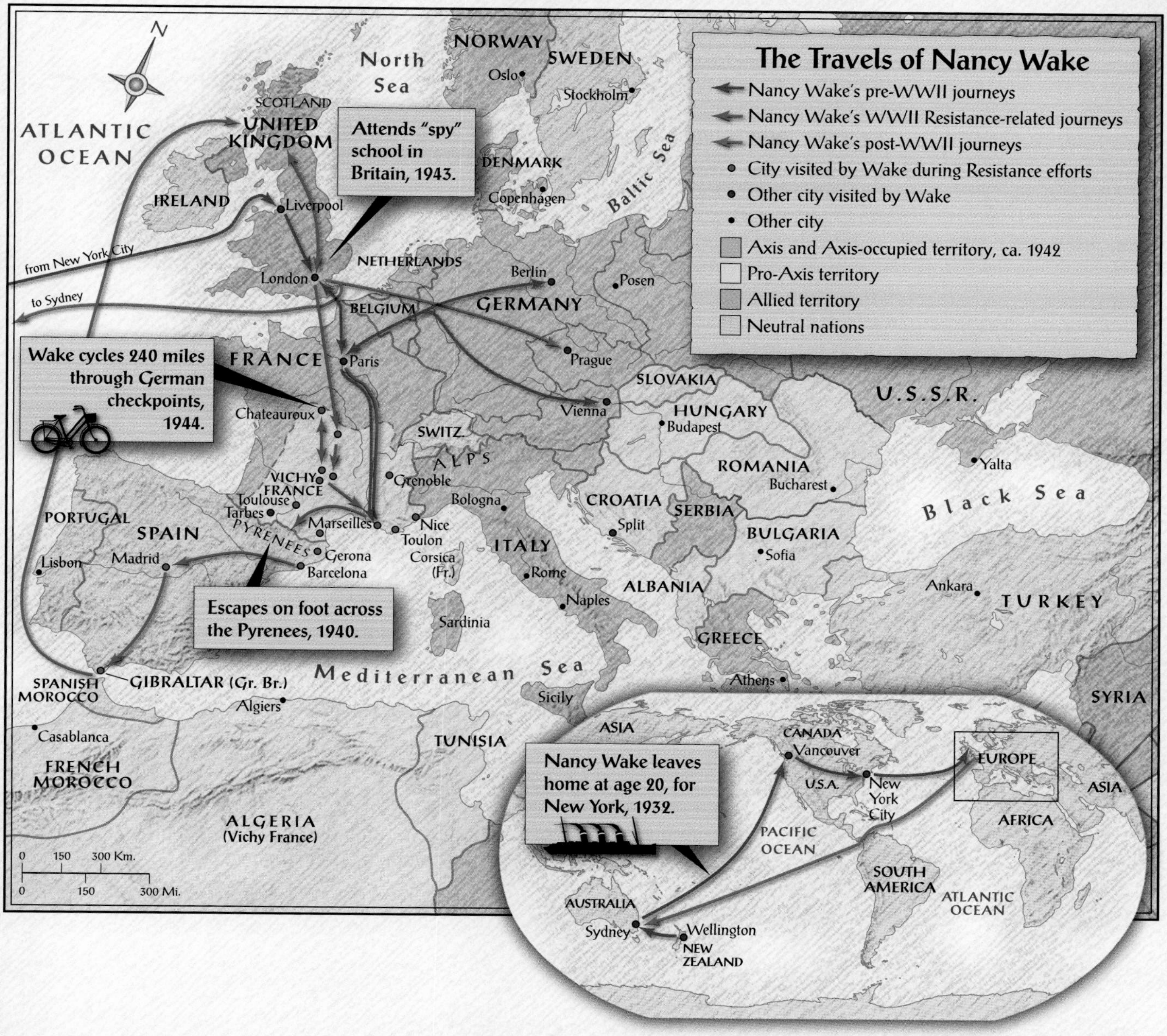

The German secret police, the Gestapo, called her "the White Mouse" and put her at the top of their "most wanted" list. But Wake evaded capture and went on to become the most highly decorated female veteran of the war.

Born in a family that was originally from New Zealand, Wake had both English and Polynesian ancestry. Even as a child she "*dreamt of seeing the world,*" and at the age of twenty she sailed from Australia to Canada and traveled by train to

Nancy Wake
(1912–2011) Highly decorated Australian veteran of the Second World War. After serving as a courier for the French underground resistance early in the war, she traveled to England for training and parachuted into central France in 1944 during the Allied reoccupation.

New York; in 1934 she settled in Paris. At that time, Wake was more interested in parties than in politics, but she had an awakening when she traveled to Vienna, where she witnessed Jews being publicly humiliated: "*The Nazis had the Jews on a big wheel going around ... maybe a dozen of them, and they were whipping them.*"* Later she wrote, "*I resolved then and there that if I ever had the chance I would do anything, however big or small, stupid or dangerous, to try and make things more difficult for their rotten party.*"†

Wake became engaged to a wealthy French industrialist and lived an exciting life, with a wide circle of Parisian friends and frequent vacations to the Alps. But there was an undercurrent of tension. "*In common with many others I feared war was inevitable and then where would we all be? When would laughter end and the tears begin?*"†

After Hitler attacked Poland in 1939, there was an ominous pause before Germany opened a western front against France. After that invasion came in 1940, Wake served as a courier for the underground resistance, passing messages and helping the *maquis* (mah-KEE)—antifascist resistance fighters—escape from both the Gestapo and collaborating French authorities. Soon there was too much heat on the "White Mouse"; she hiked to Spain over difficult and dangerous mountain passes, and from there went to England. After training in Britain, she parachuted into central France, rejoined the maquis, and witnessed the liberation of Paris.

Wake's story puts a human face on the concept of total war. The military mobilization, civilian involvement, and global reach of this conflict were even greater than during the First World War and had unprecedented effects on the world's peoples. With the war's end came the rise of the United States and the Soviet Union as global superpowers and the beginning of their Cold War rivalry.

KEY CONCEPT QUESTIONS

- What technologies allowed Japan and Germany to be so successful at the beginning of World War II? **(Key Concept 6.1)**
- How did government policies of combatant nations during World War II affect citizens at home and in European colonies? **(Key Concept 6.2)**
- Why did World War II lead to the Cold War? **(Key Concept 6.2)**

The Second World War: Battlefields, 1939–1945

The effects of the Second World War (1939–1945) reached into every corner of the globe. Japan's expansion into China made Asia and the Pacific a full-scale theater of war (see Chapter 28). As during the First World War, Africans fought for the Allies (see Chapter 27). Arab societies were disrupted by desert war in North Africa, Polynesian ones by warfare in the Pacific. But control of Europe remained

*This is found online in multiple sources, including http://www.abc.net.au/schoolstv/australians/wake.htm.

†Excerpt from Nancy Wake, *The Autobiography of the Woman the Gestapo Called the White Mouse*, pp. 7, 42. 1985 Pan Publishing.

central, with Britain and the Soviet Union allied against Germany (see Map 29.1). As during World War I, the United States made a delayed but decisive commitment to the war, this time fighting in both Asia and Europe.

After the German invasion of Poland in 1939, the Second World War proceeded in two phases. From 1940 to 1942, initiative and success lay with the **Axis powers**: Germany, Italy, and Japan. While the Germans and Italians advanced across continental Europe and the Mediterranean, Japanese armies were on the offensive in East and Southeast Asia. But after Germany invaded the Soviet Union in June 1941 and Japan attacked the United States in December of that same year, the momentum shifted as the Soviet Union and the United States mobilized their considerable resources. By 1944, aided by resistance movements in France, Vietnam, the Philippines, and elsewhere, the Allies were on the offensive.

Axis powers
Alliance of Germany, Italy, and Japan during the Second World War.

German *Blitzkrieg* and the Rising Sun of Japan, 1939–1942

When the German army invaded Poland, it unleashed a new form of warfare: the *blitzkrieg* (BLITS-kreeg) or "lightning war," which combined the rapid mobility of tanks and mechanized infantry with massive air power. As western Poland was quickly overrun, Stalin made use of his secret agreement with Hitler to occupy the eastern part of the country. In the German zone, true to Hitler's racial policies, the process of segregating Polish Jews began immediately, while ethnic Poles were forced into labor camps to serve German war industries. On the Soviet side, Stalin ordered the execution of the Polish officer corps, most notoriously carried out at the Massacre at Katyn Forest in 1940, where tens of thousands of Poles were killed.

While Hitler and Stalin crushed Poland, France and Britain declared war on Germany but took no military steps. Instead, during the so-called Phony War of 1939–1940, they shored up their own defenses. Nancy Wake and her fiancé moved south from Paris to Marseilles (mahr-SEY), trying to distance themselves from the anticipated German invasion.

In the spring of 1940, the Germans invaded Denmark and Norway and soon controlled Belgium and the Netherlands. They then bypassed France's Maginot Line, a series of defensive bulwarks rendered obsolete by blitzkrieg tactics. Moving swiftly through Belgium, the Germans soon occupied Paris. As British forces hastily retreated from France, the *Luftwaffe* (German Air Force) began to pummel Britain in preparation for a seaborne invasion.

• **CONTEXT&CONNECTIONS** The German drive toward Paris in 1940 was the third in seventy years. During the Franco-Prussian War of 1870–1871, Prussian-led armies occupied Paris and proclaimed the birth of a new German empire in the Hall of Mirrors at Versailles (see Chapter 23). In 1914, in contrast, the German army bogged down just 20 miles (32.2 km) outside of Paris, leading to the trench warfare of the *western front* (key term in Chapter 27). Thus a very elderly Parisian of the 1940s would have experienced three separate German assaults on her city. •

Though unable to destroy Britain's air defenses, the Germans continually bombarded London to terrorize its citizens and sap their morale. During this "blitz," when Londoners crowded into underground train stations to escape the bombing, Britain held together under the firm leadership of Prime Minister **Winston Churchill** (1874–1965), who exhorted Britons to *"brace ourselves to our duties, and*

Winston Churchill
(1874–1965) British prime minister during the Second World War who rallied his people to stand firm during the war's dark early days. A staunch anticommunist, he coined the term *iron curtain* after the war to describe Stalin's domination of eastern Europe.

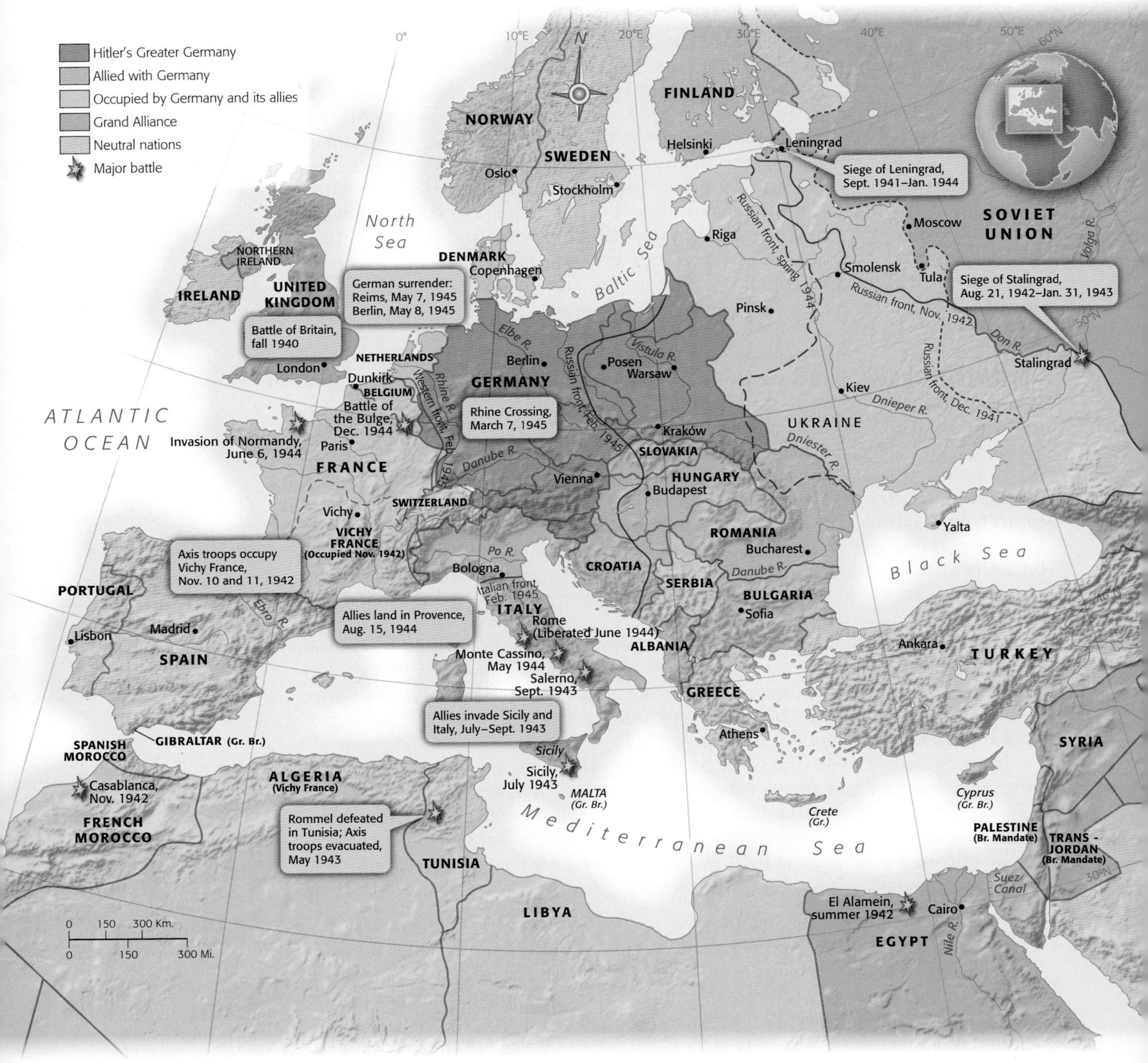

Map 29.1 World War II in Europe and North Africa Through the summer of 1941 the Axis powers, led by fascist Germany and Italy, held the momentum in the European theater of war, with Paris occupied, Britain isolated, the Soviet Union invaded, and eastern Europe and the Balkans under German domination. An important Allied triumph came with British victory at El Alamein in Egypt in 1942, but the real turning point was Soviet success in turning back the Germans at Stalingrad. After the United States entered the war, Allied invasions of Italy (1943) and of occupied France at Normandy (1944) complemented Soviet advances.

so bear ourselves that, if the British Empire and its Commonwealth last for a thousand years, men will still say, 'This was their finest hour.'" Londoners took heart that the massive Cathedral of St. Paul's in the heart of their city, though surrounded by burning rubble, stood unscathed.

German officials often found local collaborators. In both the Netherlands and Norway, for example, local fascists facilitated German conquest. As a result, collaborators with Nazism everywhere came to be called *quislings*, after the Norwegian fascist Vidkun Quisling. Meanwhile, in the Balkans, the Germans received assistance from the extreme Croatian nationalists of the Ustaše, Catholic fascists who used their German alliance to gain the upper hand over their Orthodox Serbian rivals in Yugoslavia.

The French Vichy regime was a notorious case of collaboration. After the German invaders took direct control over Paris and the north they tolerated the formation of a French-run puppet regime in the south. Some Vichy officials were motivated simply by greed or ambition, but others shared both the anticommunism and the anti-Semitism of the Nazis, later cooperating in the deportation and murder of French Jews. Vichy officials in the French colonial service extended fascist influence over parts of Africa and Asia.

Fascist Collaborators German invasions were facilitated by fascist collaborators. "*Dutchmen! For your honour and conscience! The Waffen SS summons you to fight Bolshevism!*" The Waffen-SS was the elite armed wing of the Nazi Party, a multi-national military force separate from the regular German army. After the war, the victorious Allies treated the *Schutzstaffel* as a criminal organization.

At the same time, underground opposition to the Axis was found everywhere. Men and women in France, Norway, Ethiopia, Italy, Yugoslavia, Vietnam, the Philippines, and elsewhere organized covert resistance cells to defeat fascist invaders and their local allies. Polish leaders gathered in London and formed a government-in-exile. The French partisans for whom Nancy Wake worked as a courier were loyal to a maverick general, **Charles de Gaulle** (SHARL du GAWHL) (1890–1970), who formed a Free French government-in-exile in London and began to recruit an army of liberation.

Charles de Gaulle (1890–1970) French general and statesman who led the Free French Army in resistance to German occupation. Later elected president of France.

War came to North Africa and southeast Europe when unsuccessful Italian invasions led to German intervention. Early in 1941, after the Italians failed to take Egypt in an offensive launched from Libya, German forces arrived to back them up, bringing tank warfare across the North African desert. Similarly, Mussolini's designs on the Balkans were undercut by his failure to conquer Greece. Again, the German high command had to divert troops to reinforce the Italian position, bringing most of Hungary, Yugoslavia, Romania, and Greece under Axis control.

Though the American president, Franklin Delano Roosevelt, privately agreed with Churchill about how much was at stake in the war, American public opinion balked at committing troops to Europe. Instead, Roosevelt declared that the United States would become the "arsenal of democracy" by negotiating a "lend lease" arrangement to supply American arms to Britain without need for immediate payment. In the summer of 1941, Churchill and Roosevelt met aboard a ship off the coast of Newfoundland and jointly issued the **Atlantic Charter**, reaffirming the Wilsonian principle of national self-determination: "*[We] respect the right of all peoples to choose the form of government under which they will live; and ... wish to see sovereign rights and self government restored to those who have been forcibly deprived of them.*" But America's moral and material support did no more than help the British to hold on.

Atlantic Charter
(1941) Agreement between Winston Churchill and Franklin D. Roosevelt before the entry of the United States into the war; reaffirmed the Wilsonian principle of national self-determination.

Matters looked just as bleak in East Asia. Japan had allied with Germany, and in 1940 the Vichy government of France, complying with Japanese demands, handed over much of mainland Southeast Asia. Through naval assaults Japan also controlled southern Burma, threatening British India.

Meanwhile, as tensions grew, the United States beefed up its Pacific command in the Philippines, put a freeze on Japanese assets in the United States, and most important, cut off exports of steel and the U.S. oil on which Japan depended. The empire's military and industrial planners needed to find another source of supply and focused on acquiring the oil reserves of the Dutch East Indies, which would require taking the Philippines from the United States.

Gauging that conflict was now inevitable, the Japan high command decided to launch a preemptive surprise attack on the U.S. naval outpost of **Pearl Harbor** in Hawai'i on December 7, 1941—"*a date,*" President Roosevelt said, "*which will live in infamy.*" The U.S. Pacific fleet was crippled. A few days after Pearl Harbor, the German and Italian governments also declared war on the United States. Finally, American reluctance to join the fray was overcome. Once attacked, the American people rallied to an intensive mobilization to meet Axis forces on both sides of Eurasia.

Pearl Harbor
The attack on the U.S. naval base in Hawai'i by Japanese fighter planes on December 7, 1941, bringing the United States into the Second World War.

While U.S. mobilization was taking place, Japanese momentum continued, as they occupied British Hong Kong, took the Philippines, and attacked the Dutch East Indies. With victory at the supposedly impregnable British base at Singapore the Japanese captured what had been the Allies' best naval facility in East Asia, taking 80,000 (mostly Indian) British prisoners.

• **CONTEXT&CONNECTIONS** The Philippines had been ruled from Madrid for over three centuries (see Chapter 17) before being transferred to the United States as a result of the Spanish-American War of 1898–1900 (see Chapter 26). Thus between the 1890s and the 1940s Filipino partisans had fought for independence from Spain, then from the United States, and finally from Japan, before securing independence in 1946. •

To justify expansionism in the 1930s, Japanese propagandists had touted a Greater East Asian Co-Prosperity Sphere that would supposedly free Asian peoples from Western imperialism under Japanese leadership. But the brutality the Japanese had shown in China during the Rape of Nanjing (see Chapter 28) was soon repeated elsewhere. In the spring of 1942, for example, thousands of Filipinos and hundreds of American prisoners of war died on a forced march across the Bataan (buh-TAHN) peninsula in the Japanese-occupied Philippines. Despite rhetoric about shared prosperity, it was the quest for empire that lay at the heart of Japan's war plans.

The Allies on the Offensive, 1942–1945

No one was shocked when, in June 1941, Hitler reneged on his secret pact with Stalin and invaded the Soviet Union. After the Japanese attack on Pearl

Harbor six months later, the Axis powers had brought both the United States and the Soviet Union into the war on the side of Britain. In 1943, these **Allied powers** began their effort to roll back previous Axis advances, and Nancy Wake, having escaped Vichy France by hiking across the Pyrenees, was in England, training for the Allied counteroffensive.

Allied powers
Alliance of Britain, the United States, and the Soviet Union during the Second World War.

Hitler's eastward thrust had been successful at first, and the Germans were soon assaulting the crucial city of Leningrad (as the historic capital of St. Petersburg was then called). The three-year **Siege of Leningrad** was gruesome. Residents were reduced to hunting rats for food, and many starved. Escape was possible only during winter, in convoys of trucks across a frozen lake north of the city. While some escaped, others drowned in the icy waters as German aircraft strafed and bombed them. Of a population of 3 million, one-third perished.

Siege of Leningrad
(1941–1944) German siege of this Soviet city that left the city without food or fuel, resulting in over a million deaths.

Then, as the German tanks became mired in the mud that came with spring rains, and as their supply lines stretched thin, the German advance slowed. Soviet resistance stiffened, unmatched in its toughness and resiliency. Stalin's propagandists emphasized heroic stands against earlier invaders and rallied the Soviet peoples behind the "Great Patriotic Homeland War."

Sovfoto/Getty Images

Siege of Leningrad As long as the German siege lasted, death was an everyday occurrence for the people of Leningrad (today's St. Petersburg) as a constant artillery barrage kept residents scrambling for cover. (In defiance, the great "Leningrad Symphony" by Russian composer Dmitri Shostakovich was performed in the beleaguered city in the summer of 1942. The weakened musicians received extra rations to enable them to practice, and loudspeakers broadcast the performance to the citizens of Leningrad, and to the German troops beyond.)

AP® THEMES
How did the geography and environment of Russia affect foreign military strategies and efforts to invade Russia?

• **CONTEXT&CONNECTIONS** Like *Napoleon Bonaparte* (Chapter 22), Hitler had opened a second front in Russia while Britain remained unconquered and, like Napoleon, he paid a heavy price. As with the French army of 1812, the Germans found their supply lines stretched dangerously thin, and Soviet generals, like tsarist ones, were able to use the vastness of their country and its harsh climate to their advantage. Napoleon lost more than half a million troops before abandoning his campaign; during World War II, Germans suffered over 80 percent of all their casualties in the east. •

With the United States and the Soviet Union fully mobilized, momentum shifted toward the Allies. Though this alliance between liberal democratic and communist states was an unlikely one, made possible only by their common fascist enemies, one reason for the Allied advantage in the war after 1943 was the superior coordination of the British, American, and Soviet forces. On the Axis side, in contrast, poor coordination meant that Hitler's forces had to rush in when Mussolini's faltered. The same Allied advantage held in the Pacific, where Britain and the United States collaborated closely while Japan fought alone.

The first decisive military reversal for the Axis came in North Africa, where the British finally gained the upper hand. Victory at the Battle of El Alamein in Egypt (1942) not only protected Britain's control of the Suez Canal but also secured a base for a counterattack against Italy across the Mediterranean. By 1943, British and American forces were driving northward up the Italian peninsula, aided by both Italian partisans and Free French forces, including Arab soldiers recruited from the now-liberated French colonies of Morocco and Algeria.

Faced with the Allied invasion from North Africa, Mussolini's army collapsed. Though Germany propped him up in a northern Italian enclave until 1945, he was eventually captured by the Italian resistance. To express their contempt, Mussolini's executioners hung his body by the heels from a public balcony.

In the Pacific, the Allies also gained momentum in 1942. In early summer, American aircraft sunk four of Japan's six largest aircraft carriers at the Battle of Midway. Then the United States took the offensive at Guadalcanal, the beginning of an "island-hopping" campaign to drive back the Japanese. The fighting was tough, but the huge U.S. economy was now fully geared toward military production, and new ships and airplanes rolled off assembly lines at a staggering rate, ensuring American naval dominance in the Pacific. By 1943, Allied forces were driving the Japanese back toward their home islands, as local resistance in China, Vietnam, the Philippines, and the Dutch East Indies complemented British, Australian, Canadian, and American efforts.

• **CONTEXT&CONNECTIONS** Prior to 1943, the Japanese navy had a remarkable record of success going back to the *Sino-Japanese* and *Russo-Japanese Wars* of 1894–1895 and 1904–1905 (Chapter 24). After World War II and the acceptance of a pacifist constitution imposed by the United States, Japan ceased building or deploying ships with offensive military capacity, though recent tensions with China have caused a reconsideration of that policy (see page 732). •

Battle of Stalingrad (1942–1943) One of the major turning points of World War II, when the Soviet army halted the German advance and annihilated the German Sixth Army. After victory at Stalingrad, the Soviets went on the offensive, driving the Germans out of Soviet territory.

Perhaps the most important turning point of the war was the **Battle of Stalingrad**. Unable to take Moscow, in late 1942 the Germans swung south toward the Soviet Union's strategic oil fields. House-by-house fighting in Stalingrad gave the Red Army time to organize a counteroffensive, and in 1943 they surrounded and annihilated the German Sixth Army. Galvanized by their victory, the Soviets launched a series of punishing attacks, and in the spring of 1944 Stalin's forces drove Hitler's army out of Soviet territory. Meanwhile, British and American bombing was starting to take a terrible toll: in the summer of 1943, the port city of Hamburg in Germany was obliterated in a firestorm that killed tens of thousands of civilians.

In late 1943 when Churchill and Roosevelt met with Stalin in Teheran (Iran), the Allies had taken North Africa, invaded Italy, and were preparing a counter-invasion of France on the coast of Normandy. Meanwhile, Soviet forces had driven the German army all the way back to the Polish border.

In anticipation of the Normandy invasion, Nancy Wake and her group parachuted into central France behind German lines. It was difficult and dangerous work. Once when her group lost their radio, and therefore contact with London, Wake bicycled more than a hundred miles over mountainous terrain to re-establish their communications: *"Every kilometer I pedaled was sheer agony. I knew if I ever got off the bike, I could never get on it again.... I couldn't stand up, I couldn't sit down, I couldn't walk and I couldn't sleep for days."**

After assisting in the Allied invasion of Normandy on D-Day, June 6, 1944, Wake reached Paris just as Allied forces drove the German army from the city she had once called home: *"Paris was liberated on 25 August, 1944, and the whole country rejoiced.... The aggressors were now the hunted.... The collaborators seemed to have vanished into thin air and the crowds in the street went wild with joy."** But there was still hard fighting to do. In the winter of 1944 a final German offensive in Belgium led to significant American casualties in the Battle of the Bulge before Allied forces regained the initiative. And Nancy Wake's happiness was tempered by personal loss: the Nazis had executed her husband and killed many of her friends.

The European war ended in a final fury. As the Red Army moved into eastern Germany, Soviet troops took their vengeance by raping, looting, and executing German civilians. When British and American aircraft firebombed Dresden, civilians who fled to underground shelters suffocated as the firestorm above them sucked the oxygen from the air. Over one hundred thousand died. With Soviet troops storming Berlin, Hitler killed himself in a bunker beneath the city. The nightmare of German fascism was over. On May 8, 1945—V-E Day—Germany surrendered.

In the Pacific, once the United States retook the Philippines late in 1944, the path toward invasion lay open (see Map 29.2). American submarines blockaded Japan, starving its military of supplies, while U.S. aircraft dropped incendiary bombs on Tokyo and other cities, reducing them to ashes. Still, most Americans thought that it would require a massive landing of troops, with tremendous casualties, to force a Japanese surrender.

Harry S. Truman (in office 1945–1953) had become president in April after the death of Roosevelt, and he made the decision to seek a quick end to the war with Japan by using a terrible new weapon. Atomic blasts at **Hiroshima and Nagasaki** killed hundreds of thousands. Some died instantly, others more gradually from radiation poisoning. (See the feature "Visual Evidence in Primary Sources: Hiroshima and Nagasaki.")

Hiroshima and Nagasaki

(1945) Two Japanese cities devastated by atomic bombs dropped by the United States in an attempt to end the Second World War. Hundreds of thousands were killed, many by slow radiation poisoning.

*Excerpt from Nancy Wake, *The Autobiography of the Woman the Gestapo Called the White Mouse*, pp. 225–226, 255. 1985 Pan Publishing.

Hiroshima and Nagasaki

In August 1939, President Franklin Delano Roosevelt received a letter from famed theoretical physicist Albert Einstein, a German Jew who had fled National Socialism to take up a position at Princeton's Institute for Advanced Study (see Chapter 28). Einstein informed Roosevelt that *"the element uranium may be turned into a new and important source of energy in the immediate future.... Extremely powerful bombs of a new type might thus be constructed."** Einstein warned that the German government had already begun research into the feasibility of such weapons.

Nagasaki was a major port city, in earlier times the center of Japanese trade with Europeans. After the Tokugawa seclusion edicts (see Chapter 20), Nagasaki was the site of the annual Dutch trade mission and the center of "Dutch learning."

Nagasaki Before the Atomic Bomb.

Bad weather caused the United States to change its original plan and order the "Fat Man" bomb to be dropped on the secondary target of Nagasaki.

Nagasaki after the Atomic Bomb.

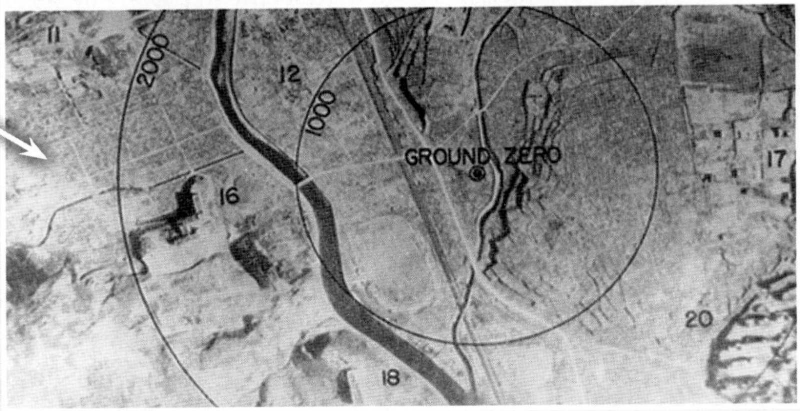

Pictorial Press Ltd/Alamy

In the heart of Nagasaki stood the largest Roman Catholic Cathedral in all of Asia, Urakami Cathedral. Its ruins are still found in the memorial park marking Ground Zero. Conservative estimates put the death toll for Nagasaki at 77,000, about 30 percent of the population.

Some of Harry S. Truman's advisors had urged the president to drop the atomic bombs on uninhabited islands as a warning that might force Japanese surrender. With only a few operational weapons, and no guarantee that they would explode as planned, Truman went ahead with the attacks on populated areas. ***The American decision to use atomic bombs on Japan in 1945 is a point of historical controversy. What are the main arguments for and against Truman's decision?***

---

*Franklin D. Roosevelt Presidential Library and Museum, http://www.fdrlibrary.marist.edu/archives/pdfs/docsworldwar.pdf.

The result was the top-secret Manhattan Project, headquartered at Los Alamos, New Mexico. Its mandate was to create an explosive device based on nuclear fission, with the greatest possible speed and without the benefit of field tests. The Manhattan Project was so secret that while serving as vice president Harry S. Truman was unaware of it, being informed only following Roosevelt's death.

In May 1945, a month after Roosevelt's death, Germany surrendered, but war in the Pacific continued, and both the United States and the Soviet Union began to redeploy forces toward Japan. Many believed that the Japanese would fight to the death in defense of their home islands and their emperor, and that perhaps a million more U.S. soldiers might die in an invasion. There was also concern in the United States that Stalin could use a protracted conflict in northeast Asia to his own benefit. Such were the circumstances under which Truman had to decide whether to deploy the new weapons.

By the end of 1945, about 140,000 people had died in Hiroshima, either from the immediate impact of the bomb or from radiation poisoning. Of those, more than one in ten were Koreans who had been forced into the service of the Japanese empire.

Fifty years later, a controversy erupted in 1995 when the Smithsonian Institution organized an exhibition on the *Enola Gay*, which dropped the bomb "Little Boy" on Hiroshima. Protestors, including veterans groups, derided the Smithsonian exhibit for asking overly critical questions about U.S. actions and for focusing too narrowly on Japanese civilian suffering.

Hibakusha ("explosion-affected people") is the Japanese term for atomic bomb survivors. Although they have played an important historical role by keeping memories alive, *hibakusha* have also faced discrimination, with some of their neighbors falsely believing that contagious genetic defects resulted from the bombings.

Victims of Hiroshima/Alinari/The Bridgeman Art Library

A survivor of Hiroshima remembered: *"We met some people from Hell. They were naked and their skin, burned and bloody, was like red rust and their bodies were bloated up like balloons.... From the burned shreds of their sailor uniforms I knew they were schoolgirls, but they had no hair left and ... they no longer appeared human."**

*Iwao Nakamura, "Recollections," in *Sources of Global History since 1900*, ed. James H. Overfield, 2d ed. (Boston: Wadsworth, 2013), p. 238.

Meanwhile, the Soviet Union occupied Manchuria and northern Korea, raising Japanese fears of a Soviet invasion. Immediate submission to the United States now seemed the only option to Japanese leaders. As his subjects tuned in their radios on August 14, it was Emperor Hirohito's own voice, which they had never heard before, announcing the empire's unconditional surrender. "*The enemy has begun to employ a new and most cruel bomb, the power of which to do damage is, indeed, incalculable, taking the toll of many innocent lives,*" Hirohito said. "*Should we continue to fight, not only would it result in an ultimate collapse and obliteration of the Japanese nation, but also it would lead to the total extinction of human civilization.*" Official surrender took place on September 2, 1945—V-J Day. Finally, the Second World War was over.

Map 29.2 World War II in Asia and the Pacific The Japanese empire, like the Axis powers in Europe, dominated the early stages of the war. By 1943, however, with the United States fully mobilized to fight the Pacific war, momentum shifted to the Allies. The war ended in the summer of 1945 when President Harry Truman ordered atomic weapons dropped on Hiroshima and Nagasaki.

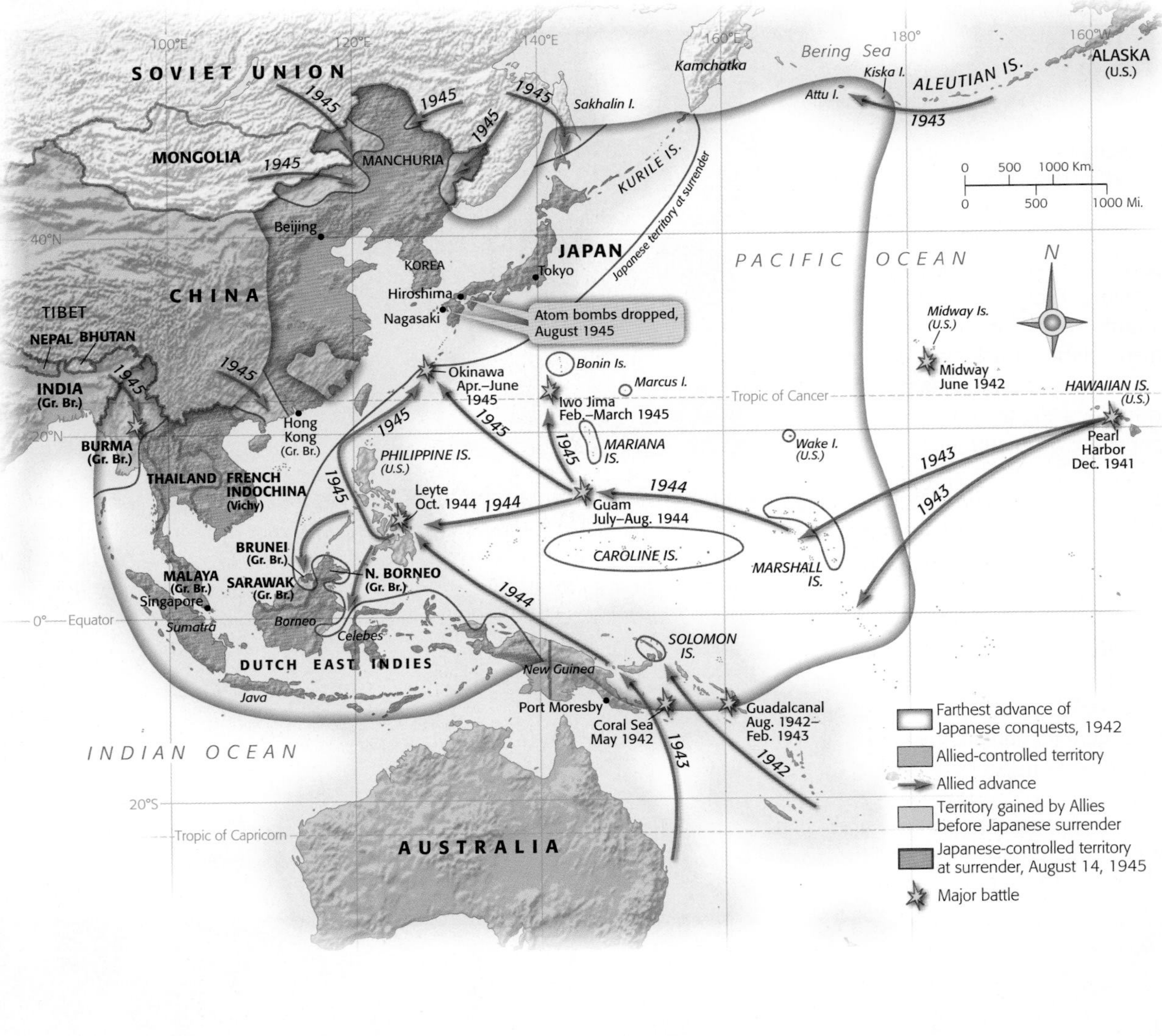

Total War and Civilian Life

Even more than during the First World War, the Second disrupted the life plans of tens of millions of ordinary people. In that sense, Nancy Wake's experience was not atypical.

In addition to witnessing the horrors of war, civilian populations were affected in myriad other ways. Consumer goods disappeared as production converted to military needs. Total war again meant intensification of government power: even the few remaining democratic societies curtailed freedom of speech and freedom of assembly. Newspapers, radio, and film were censored and often incorporated state-sponsored misinformation and propaganda.

Once again, the disruptions of total war reached civilians across the planet. Residents of remote island atolls in the Pacific found themselves trapped between U.S. and Japanese armies. Colonized Africans and Asians served as soldiers or had their labor forcibly harnessed for wartime production, their destinies hinging on the successes and failures of Allied and Axis armies. Many suffered tragic losses. Worldwide, over 50 million people were killed, including at least 25 million Soviet citizens, nearly half the total.

During the genocide known as the **Holocaust**, the Nazis murdered 6 million Jews in labor and death camps. The victims were usually starved and tortured before being killed. Of the entire European Jewish population, over 60 percent perished, including over 90 percent of Poland's Jews. The slaughter extended to millions more people as well—homosexuals, Roma (Gypsies), disabled persons, Jehovah's Witnesses, and others deemed enemies of Aryan racial supremacy.

Holocaust
The genocide in which the Nazis murdered 6 million Jews, known in Hebrew as the *Shoah* ("catastrophe"). The Nazis also killed hundreds of thousands of Roma (gypsies), homosexuals, Jehovah's Witnesses and others they saw as deviant.

Civilians and Total War in the United States and Europe

In the United States, families were disrupted as sons and husbands went to war and factories were converted from consumer to military production. But almost none of the fighting occurred on American soil, and the war actually benefited American society in a number of ways. Massive state spending on munitions put the country back to work, effectively ending the Great Depression.

For Americans who had long been at the bottom of the job ladder, especially women and African Americans, mobilization brought new opportunities. "Rosie the Riveter" became the symbol of women laboring on industrial production lines to produce the boots, bullets, and bombers needed by the military. Segregated African American military units, such as the famous "Tuskegee Airmen," distinguished themselves in combat, while other American blacks gained access to good industrial

Keystone Features/Getty Images

British War Production Total war required the complete mobilization of civilian populations behind a nation's military. As in the United States and the Soviet Union, traditional gender roles in Britain were transformed as female factory workers replaced departed servicemen. Here a British worker finalizes assembly of the nose cone of an Avro Lancaster bomber in 1943.

WORLD HISTORY IN TODAY'S WORLD

From Cryptography to Computer Science

Given the high stakes of total war, it is not surprising that both the Allied and Axis powers made heavy investments in applied scientific research attempting to get an upper hand. Today, we experience the legacy of those efforts whenever we use lightweight plastics, fly in a jet airplane guided by radar, or use electricity from a nuclear power plant. Modern computer science was also propelled forward by World War II.

For the British, a major challenge was Enigma, Germany's "unbreakable" coding machine. Secure in the secrecy of messages sent between the high command and ships, submarines, and aircraft, the Germans had a strong tactical advantage. To try to break Enigma the British established a secure decryption center in the suburban villa of Bletchley Park and recruited personnel highly skilled in advanced mathematics and computational theory.

Bletchley Park was a team effort, but its ultimate success stemmed from the contributions of Dr. Alan Turing, the Cambridge mathematician many see as the father of modern computer science. Some of the mathematicians at Bletchley Park eschewed mechanical solutions (like the astronomers who had rejected Harrison's chronometer as a solution to the "problem of longitude"; see Chapter 21), but Turing realized that human computing speeds were simply too slow to crack Enigma. Unaided, even the best minds could decode no more than a tiny number of German messages.

Turing's solution was a cylinder-driven computational device, and his "Turing Machine" is a direct ancestor of modern computers. Of course, since then, progress in miniaturization has been staggering, starting with the transistor technology that was also developed during World War II. It is safe to say that the computing device in your pocket is many times more powerful than Turing's room-filling, energy-devouring machine.

The decoding of the Enigma machine saved an incalculable number of Allied lives and shortened the war, perhaps by as much as two years. Unfortunately, that happy ending did not extend to Turing's own life. He was hounded for his homosexuality, convicted of "gross indecency," and subjected to chemical castration. Alan Turing committed suicide in 1954. Finally, in 2014 Queen Elizabeth II granted Dr. Alan Turing a royal pardon. His work endures.

employment for the first time. The nation's diversity, seen by Hitler as a source of weakness, proved a strength, as when U.S. military intelligence recruited Navajo "code talkers" to use their indigenous language to encrypt messages in the Pacific theater. The Japanese never cracked the Navajo code. (See the feature "World History in Today's World: From Cryptography to Computer Science.") More broadly, the camaraderie and discipline of both military and civilian life, dedicated to a successful fight against a great evil, gave an entire generation of Americans a shared sense of purpose.

AP® THEMES

How did the events of World War II change the way people experienced and expressed nationalism

The people of the Soviet Union also experienced the "Great Patriotic Homeland War" as a powerful collective endeavor; however, their suffering and sacrifice was much greater. Even before the German invasion, workers dismantled factories and moved them to interior regions. Millions of people were likewise uprooted and put to work on farms in safer interior areas. Soviet women bore a special burden, caring for children and the elderly while taking on dangerous jobs in mines and factories. Many Soviet women also served with distinction in the armed forces. By the end of the war, tens of millions of people had been killed or uprooted, the country's agricultural and industrial infrastructure destroyed. Wartime suffering left the Soviet people with a deep determination never again to allow an invasion from the West.

Throughout western Europe civilians also witnessed the horrors of war at their very doorsteps. In every nation, families were evacuated from cities under bombardment to safer rural areas, where farming families took them in. In countries under occupation by the Nazis, the slightest sign of anti-German feeling, or any display of sympathy for the Jews, could result in imprisonment, torture, and death. After sustained bombardment, by war's end much of urban Europe lay in ruins. At least for the British, there was something positive to take away from the terrible suffering: many would later recall the feeling of mutual purpose and national solidarity of the war years with nostalgia.

Total war came to the German people only in the last stages of the conflict, but then it did so with a vengeance. Early in the war, the civilian population of Germany had experienced a lower level of mobilization. For example, since National Socialist ideology idealized German women as wives and mothers—breeders of the Aryan master race—they were not asked to contribute much to the war effort. Instead, the Nazis would enslave subject peoples to meet their labor needs. At war's end, however, German civilians paid a heavy price for their support of the Nazis. As bombs pummeled German cities, and German soldiers and civilians fell back toward Berlin, Adolf Hitler called up children and old men to reinforce his disintegrating army. In a sense, he involved the whole country in his own suicide.

The civilian experience of total war had long-term effects on Western political culture. In Europe, bitterness remained between those who resisted and those who collaborated with the Axis powers. Meanwhile, the Soviets sought to establish a zone of buffer states to insulate them from future invasion. And the people of the United States were, for the first time, fully willing to engage themselves as a great power in world affairs.

Civilians and Total War in Asia and the Colonial World

At war, the Japanese state commanded all aspects of civilian life, regulating industry and commerce, while severely restricting speech and assembly. Even so, like the Germans, most Japanese did not experience the violence of war firsthand until 1944–1945. Then Allied air assaults, and ultimately nuclear annihilation, exacted a terrible price for their nation's imperialist adventures.

Elsewhere in the Asian theater of war, European colonies were caught in the crossfire between the Allied powers and Japan. Early in the war, Japanese forces seized the colonial territories of the British, French, Dutch, and Americans. European powers were intent on liberating "their" Asian possessions, such as French Indochina and the Dutch East Indies, only to restore colonial rule. Local nationalists in places like Vietnam and Indonesia, however, saw the fight against the Japanese as the first stage of their struggle to overthrow foreign rule forever. Once the war against the Axis was over, multiple conflicts would arise between the European powers and local nationalists fighting for self-determination (see Chapter 30).

As in Europe, civilians in Asia suffered a war fought on their own soil. The Japanese regarded exploitation of Southeast Asia's natural resources as essential to their imperial mission. They treated local populations like slaves, for example by forcing Filipino men into back-breaking labor building roads and bridges. Many of them, like the Allied prisoners of war forced into similar gang labor, died from mistreatment and disease.

> **AP® THEMES**
> How did Japanese policies during World War II sustain gender roles and patriarchal practices?

Sexual slavery also accompanied Japanese conquests. Rape and war, constant companions, were now put on a bureaucratic footing as officials responsible for the recreational needs of imperial troops set up brothels where teenagers and young women from the Philippines, Korea, Burma, and elsewhere were forced into service. Apart from their immediate trauma, these "comfort women" faced decades of emotional stress and social isolation. Elderly survivors are still pressing a recalcitrant Japanese government to finally admit to the historical truth.

Hunger and hardship was also the lot of Chinese civilians. Those under Japanese occupation especially suffered, but even those living in zones controlled by Chiang Kai-shek's Guomindang Army faced shortages of food and medicine. Malnutrition was common.

• **CONTEXT&CONNECTIONS** The lack of coordination between Chiang's Guomindang and Mao's rival Red Army hampered Chinese resistance to Japanese occupation (see Chapter 28), and the uneasy truce between them dissolved as soon as the Japanese withdrew. Mao Zedong's Red Army quickly went on the offensive, driving Chiang Kai-shek and the Guomindang to Taiwan. In 1949, Mao declared the foundation of the People's Republic of China (see Chapter 30). •

Communists dominated resistance in neighboring Vietnam, where partisans led by Ho Chi Minh harassed Japanese occupation forces in cooperation with the British and Americans. In Southeast Asia the principal Allied concern was the Burma Road, by which they supplied Chiang Kai-shek's Guomindang Army. Bitterly contested jungle warfare in Burma, engaging African and Australian troops supported by Allied bombing, caught many peasant villagers in its crossfire. Late in the war, forced replacement of food crops with industrial ones, Japanese hoarding of food, and American bombing of rail and road lines contributed to the starvation of 2 million Vietnamese.

In India, the British were astonished and appalled when Mohandas K. Gandhi refused to back the British empire in the war and launched a **"Quit India"** campaign. During World War I, Gandhi and the Indian National Congress had supported the British, hoping to be rewarded with concrete steps toward Indian self-government. But Congress leaders were frustrated when the British-controlled Government of India declared war on Germany and Japan without even consulting them. While the British viewed the Congress Party as incredibly naïve for not recognizing the priority of turning back Axis assaults on freedom everywhere, Gandhi made it a matter of principle that only Indians could decide the country's course, no matter what the circumstances.

"Quit India"
Campaign by Mohandas K. Gandhi and the Indian National Congress during World War II to demand independence. They refused to support the British war effort and instead launched a campaign of civil disobedience demanding that the British "quit India" immediately.

Even as British authorities once again threw Gandhi and other nationalist leaders into jail, the Indian army remained the bulwark of British defense in Asia, while Indian civilians continued to contribute labor and economic resources to the Allied war effort. As in China and Vietnam, however, wartime economic policies led to great hardship. In 1943, over 2 million people died in a famine in the northeastern province of Bengal.

British war strategies also provoked a nationalist backlash in Arab lands. Many Egyptians were outraged when the British mobilized their forces without seeking permission from the nominally independent government. As a result, Britain had to quell demonstrations in Cairo, even as it prepared for desert war with Italy. Arab nationalists had also been upset when the British allowed increased Jewish immigration to Palestine. The Grand Mufti of Jerusalem, leader of Palestinian Muslims, took a strongly anti-Zionist stand and, on the principle of "the enemy of my enemy is my friend," he urged collaboration with the Nazis. Likewise in Iraq, the government sided with Germany, leading the British to invade and occupy Baghdad in the spring of 1941.

Britain's African subjects, perhaps surprisingly, showed greater loyalty to the empire. The British mustered patriotic recruits for the **King's African Rifles** from colonies such as Nigeria and Kenya; many of these soldiers went on to serve in the tough jungle warfare in Burma. Here was another example of total war on an international scale, with African soldiers fighting in Burmese jungles to protect British India from Japanese invasion. Many of these Africans had never before traveled more than a few days' distance from home. Those who returned brought an expanded view of the world and of Africa's place in it. For many Africans, and people of African descent elsewhere, the Allied liberation of Ethiopia and restoration of Hailie Selassie as emperor in 1941 became symbolic of African dignity.

King's African Rifles
African regiment recruited by Britain during the Second World War; saw action in Burma, fighting against the Japanese to save India for Britain.

Africans from the French empire also helped defeat fascism. While most colonial officials supported the Vichy collaborators, the governor of French Equatorial

Africa, Félix Éboué (1884–1944), stood with Charles de Gaulle. Éboué, from French Guiana in South America and a descendant of slaves, had attained French citizenship through educational achievement. Under his leadership, the colonial city of Brazzaville became a staging ground for Free French recruitment of African soldiers. Franco-African forces then played a decisive role in driving the Germans from southern France before linking up with U.S. and British forces to clear the way for the liberation of Paris.

- **CONTEXT&CONNECTIONS** Some of the African and Arab soldiers who served in the Free French armies in World War II, helping to liberate the country from German occupation, were the sons of men who had fought under the French flag in 1914–1918, as in the famous regiment of *Senegalese Sharpshooters* (Chapter 27). Memories of African contributions to French freedom are still common in Francophone West Africa. •

Many Africans supported the Allies in the name of ideals enshrined in the Atlantic Charter: freedom and national self-determination. In South Africa, members of the African National Congress (ANC), including a young Nelson Mandela, invoked the Charter signed by Roosevelt and Churchill in their call to end racial segregation and discrimination. However, it would take another fifty years of struggle and bloodshed for democratic freedoms to become a reality for black South Africans (see Chapter 31).

The Holocaust

In the midst of war, few grasped the magnitude of Hitler's assault on Europe's Jews. Only when the death camps were liberated by Allied forces in 1945 did the scale of the horror known as the Holocaust become clear. Six million Jews had been systematically murdered in the *Shoah* (Hebrew for "catastrophe").

AP® THEMES

How did the targeting of certain groups, particularly ethnic groups, shape the expansion of Hitler's Third Reich?

In Hitler's manic racial scheme, most "inferior races" at least had a place as labor to support his Reich. For example, the Nazis regarded the Slavic peoples of eastern Europe as an inferior "race" destined to work under their "Aryan" superiors. (In fact, if the Germans had treated the Ukrainian and other Slavic peoples well, they might have found allies among those who had suffered under Stalin; instead Hitler's racial mania provoked stiff resistance.)

There were two "races" that Hitler claimed could play no useful role. One was the Roma, or Gypsies, a people whose ancestors had come originally from India. Across central Europe, their peripatetic lifestyle, traveling from season to season in search of work, and their clannish social behavior and resistance to cultural assimilation had long made the Roma subject to prejudice and discrimination. Now the Nazis turned informal prejudice into state oppression and murder.

Of course, Hitler's unquenchable obsession was with the Jews. As the Nuremburg Laws and the *Kristallnacht* had shown (see Chapter 28), thorough assimilation into German culture and society had given the country's Jews no protection from the Nazis. No mercy could then be expected for the Jews of Poland and the Soviet Union, exposed to the Nazi horror after the invasions of 1939 and 1941.

Early in 1942, Nazi officials met to devise a "final solution" to the "Jewish problem." According to the minutes of the Wannsee Conference, a bureaucracy would be set up to *"cleanse the German living space of Jews in a legal manner."* Jews *"capable of work"* would be sent to camps in Poland, *"whereby a large part will undoubtedly disappear through natural diminution."* Those who were not worked to death *"will have to be appropriately dealt with,"* meaning systematically murdered in "death camps." (See the feature "Movement of Ideas Through Primary Sources: Primo Levi's Memories of Auschwitz.")

Primo Levi's Memories of Auschwitz

Primo Levi (1919–1987) was an Italian Jew who joined the underground resistance to fascism in his home country. Like millions of other European Jews, he was sent to a Nazi concentration camp, but he survived and became one of the world's most renowned writers. The extract below is taken from an interview that appeared on Italian television in 1983. The interview took place as Levi was returning for the first time to Auschwitz on a Polish train. Primo Levi took his own life in 1987.

❯ Historical Thinking Skill:

CAUSATION What would Levi identify as the short- and long-term effects on the humanity of a person who experienced Nazi concentration camps?

❯ Historical Thinking Skill:

SYNTHESIS Levi describes the Holocaust as being "planned by the state." Since the Holocaust, what other examples of state-sponsored violence against one or more ethnic group(s) can you identify?

Source: Interview with Daniel Toaff, *Sorgenti di Vita (Springs of Life)*, a program on the *Unione Comunita Israelitiche Italiane, Radiotelevisione Italiana [RAI]*. From the transcript of a 1983 Italian radio broadcast, http://www.inch.com/~ari/levi1.html. The English translation is by Mirto Stone, modified for clarity. Reprinted by permission of the translator.

Return to Auschwitz

INTERVIEWER: Did you know where you were going [on the train to Auschwitz]?

PRIMO LEVI: We didn't know anything. We had seen on the cars at the station the writing "Auschwitz" but in those times, I don't think even the most informed people knew where Auschwitz was....

INTERVIEWER: What was your first [experience of] Auschwitz?

LEVI: It was night time, after a disastrous journey during which some of the people in the car had died, and arriving in a place where we didn't understand the language, the purpose.... It was really an alienating experience. It seemed we had abandoned the ability to reason, we didn't reason.

INTERVIEWER: And how was the journey, those five days?

LEVI: There were forty-five of us in a very small car. We could barely sit, but there wasn't enough room to lie down. And there was a young mother breast-feeding a baby. They had told us to bring food. Foolishly we hadn't brought water. No one had told us, and we suffered from a terrifying thirst even though it was winter. This was our first, tormenting pain, for five days. The temperature was below zero and our breath would freeze on the bolts and we would compete, scraping off the frost, full of mist as it was, to have a few drops with which to wet our lips. And the baby cried from morning to night because his mother had no milk left.

INTERVIEWER: What happened to the children and their mothers when [you arrived at Auschwitz]?

LEVI: Ah well, they were killed right away: out of the 650 of us on the train, 400–500 died the same evening we arrived or the next. They were immediately sorted out into the gas chambers, in these grim night scenes, with people screaming and yelling. They were yelling like I never heard before. They were yelling orders we didn't understand.... There was an officer ... who would ask each one of us, "Can you walk or not?" I consulted with the man next to me, a friend, from Padua. He was older than me and also in poor health. I told him I'll say I can work, and he answered, "You do as you please. For me, everything is the same." He had already abandoned any hope. In fact he said he couldn't work and didn't come into the camp. I never saw him again....

INTERVIEWER: And the food, how was it there?

LEVI: They gave us a minimal ration equivalent to about 1600–1700 calories a day, but ... there were thefts and we would always get less.... Now, as you know, a man who doesn't weigh much can live on 1600 calories without working, but just laying down. But we had to work, and in the cold, and at hard labor. Thus this ration of 1600 calories was a slow death by starvation. Later I read some research done by the Germans which said that a man could last, living off his own reserves and that diet, from two to three months.

Interviewer: But in the concentration camps one would adapt to anything?

Levi: Eh, the question is a curious one. The ones who adapted to everything are those who survived, but the majority did not adapt to everything, and died. They died because they were unable to adapt even to things which seem trivial to us. For example, they would throw a pair of mismatched shoes at you.... One was too tight, the other too big ... and those who were sensitive to infections would die. Die of shoes—of infected wounds which never healed. The feet would swell, rub up against the shoes and one had to go to the hospital. But at the hospital swollen feet were not considered a disease. They were too common so those who had swollen feet would be sent to the gas chambers....

Interviewer: For the Italians, there was the language problem....

Levi: Understanding one another is very important. Between the man who makes himself understood and that one who doesn't there is an abysmal difference: the first saves himself.... The majority of Italians deported with me died in the first few days for being unable to understand. They didn't understand the orders, but there was no tolerance for those who didn't understand. An order was given once, yelled, and that was it. Afterwards there were beatings....

Interviewer: We are about to return to our hotel in Kracow. In your opinion, what did the holocaust represent for the Jewish people?

Levi: It represented a turning point.... [It] was perhaps the first time in which anti-Semitism had been planned by the state, not only condoned or allowed as in the Russia of the Czars. And there was no escape: all of Europe had become a huge trap. It entailed a turning point, not only for European Jews, but also for American Jews, for the Jews of the entire world.

Interviewer: In your opinion, another Auschwitz, another massacre like the one which took place forty years ago, could it happen again?

Levi: Not in Europe, for reasons of immunity. Some kind of immunization must exist. It is [possible] that in fifty or a hundred years Nazism may be reborn in Germany; or Fascism in Italy.... But the world is much bigger than Europe. I also think that there are countries in which there would be the desire, but not the means. The idea is not dead. Nothing ever dies. Everything arises renewed.

Interviewer: Is it possible to abolish man's humanity?

Levi: Unfortunately, yes. Unfortunately, yes. And that is really the characteristic of the Nazi camps.... It is to abolish man's personality, inside and outside: not only of the prisoner, but also of the jailer. He too lost his personality in the concentration camp.... Thus it happened to all, a profound modification in their personality.... The memory of family had fallen into second place in face of urgent needs, of hunger, of the necessity to protect oneself against cold, beatings, fatigue ... all of this brought about some reactions which we could call animal-like. We were like work animals.

Interviewer: Do you think that people today want to forget Auschwitz as soon as possible?

Levi: Signs do exist that this is taking place: forgetting or even denying. This is meaningful. Those who deny Auschwitz would be ready to remake it.

Huw Jones/Getty Images

Auschwitz The Auschwitz Concentration Camp was a network of facilities in southern Poland built by the Nazis and included both slave labor camps and death camps. Over one million people were murdered here between 1941 and 1945, either worked to death, killed by torture and abuse, or exterminated with poison gas. The vast majority were Jews. New arrivals were mocked by the line above the gate: *Arbeit macht Frei*, "*Work makes you free.*"

The Nazi extermination of the Jews was methodical and cold-blooded. When a death camp administrator observed that people died faster if they were already short of breath when they entered the "shower rooms" that were actually gas chambers, he applied "the industrialist's logic," and forced Jewish captives to run to the showers in a panic, saving gas as well as time. Thus, thousands could be killed in a day. Scientific rationality and industrial progress were perverted to the most horrible of ends.

Warsaw Ghetto Uprising
(1943) Unsuccessful revolt of Polish Jews confined to the Warsaw ghetto, who rose up to resist being sent to the Treblinka death camp.

Not all Jews went meekly. The most militant resistance was the **Warsaw Ghetto Uprising**. Shortly after occupying Warsaw, the Nazis forced the city's Jews into a fenced-off ghetto where they found no work and very little food. In 1943, as the Nazis began to transport residents to the Treblinka death camp, the sixty thousand in the Warsaw ghetto rose up in armed revolt. Ten thousand paid with their lives, and the Nazis killed nearly all the rest at Treblinka.

Those Jews who somehow managed to escape were not assured of refuge. For decades the United States had imposed racial immigration quotas, limiting Jewish access even as refugees. In fact, in 1939, over nine hundred Jewish refugees seeking sanctuary from fascism were turned away at American ports and returned to Europe. (Many of them later died in the Holocaust.)

The government of the United Kingdom also restricted Jewish immigration, both to Britain and to its mandated territory of Palestine (see Chapter 27). In these desperate circumstances, the Zionist call for a secure Jewish sanctuary drew support from Jews and those sympathetic to their plight, though the British government, fearing an Arab uprising, continued to limit the number of refugees it would accept. Some Zionists, desperate to find a safe refuge for Europe's Jews, developed a guerrilla underground to aid illegal Jewish immigration to Palestine.

After 1939, however, it was almost impossible for Jews under Nazi rule to escape. Those who did so were helped by people such as Raoul Wallenberg, a Swedish diplomat who helped save thousands of Hungarian Jews from the death camps, and others like him who hid Jewish families or adopted Jewish children, putting their own lives and livelihoods at risk. But neither resistance nor the heroism of people who tried to aid their Jewish neighbors was enough to prevent Hitler from carrying out his plans.

In 1933, there had been 9.5 million Jews in Europe; by 1950, there were only 3.3 million left. In Poland and the western regions of the Soviet Union (Lithuania, Belorussia, and Ukraine), the Holocaust silenced the vibrant culture of the Ashkenazim (see Chapter 17). In what had been the largest concentration of Jews in the world, virtually none were left.

Along with 6 million Jews, the Nazis also slaughtered hundreds of thousands from other targeted groups. Viewing homosexuals as traitors to the master race, they imprisoned over one hundred thousand of them, and many died in concentration camps. Jehovah's Witnesses, who respect the primacy of their God by refusing to salute flags and other symbols of state authority, were also targeted. Nearly 80 percent of Europe's Roma were killed. The mentally and physically challenged of all ethnic groups were frequently sterilized and subjected to cruel medical experiments.

The Nazi death machine continued even after it became clear that the Allies would win the war. The mass graves in the camps sickened the Allied soldiers who liberated the emaciated survivors. Many Holocaust survivors found that their entire families had been killed. Sometimes, however, after scattering to different parts of the world after the war, survivors were lucky enough to find relatives who were still alive.

How could the Holocaust have happened? How could Hitler have attracted so many followers? The system certainly could not have worked without at least passive acquiescence from the German people. Moreover, anti-Semitism was strong all across Europe, and Nazi collaborators from France, Italy, Hungary, Poland, and elsewhere helped send Jews to the camps. Debates continue today about whether others could have done more to prevent the slaughter. For example, could religious leaders have played a greater role in fighting back against fascism? For her part Nancy Wake, appalled by the treatment of Jews in Austria before the war, did everything in her power to fight Nazi ideas. Too many people simply looked the other way.

Origins of the Cold War, 1945–1949

At the end of the European war, Soviet and American troops met each other joyfully at the Elbe River in Germany. Roosevelt envisioned that Allied cooperation would continue after the war in the new United Nations. Instead, the unlikely wartime partnership of liberal democracy and communism quickly dissolved, and the world divided into two hostile camps (see Map 30.2, page 909).

United Nations (UN)
Organization established near the end of the Second World War to guarantee international peace and security through permanent diplomacy. A Security Council of five members, each with veto power, was created to enhance UN authority.

The New United Nations and Postwar Challenges, 1945–1947

At the Yalta Conference on the Black Sea, held in early 1945, the most important priority for ailing Roosevelt was to secure Joseph Stalin's cooperation in the founding of the **United Nations (UN)**. The UN included a General Assembly of sovereign nations and a Security Council of the major war allies:

Britain, France, China, the Soviet Union, and the United States. Since each member of the council had veto power, its decisions could only be reached through consensus. It was hoped that the Security Council's special powers would make the UN more effective than the League of Nations.

The spirit of Allied cooperation that helped build the United Nations did not last. Roosevelt was realistic enough to know that he could not compel Stalin to give up the Red Army's control over eastern Europe, and Churchill was cynical about Stalin's assent to elections in Poland. The British and Americans had promised the Polish government-in-exile elections after the war. Stalin, however, knew that any Polish government chosen through free elections would be hostile to the Soviet Union and insisted that Poland must have a "friendly government." As soon as the war was over, it became clear that Stalin intended to assure that outcome by keeping his Red Army in occupation of Poland and installing a communist government to do his bidding.

By the summer of 1945, when Allied leaders met at Potsdam, the Soviet Red Army had occupied all of eastern Europe, and Roosevelt had died and been replaced by Truman. The Allies agreed on the plans for punishment of Germany, including a reduction in its size. But to American insistence that the peoples of Europe had the right to free elections, Stalin responded pragmatically, *"Everyone imposes his own system as far as his army can reach."* Europe was dividing into two opposing camps.

In 1946 Winston Churchill, now out of office, gave a speech in the United States in which he coined the term *iron curtain* to describe the imposition of communism in the Soviet sphere of influence:

> *From Stettin in the Baltic to Trieste in the Adriatic an iron curtain has descended across the Continent. Behind that line lie all the capitals of the ancient states of Central and Eastern Europe ... and the populations around them ... are subject, in one form or another, not only to Soviet influence but to a very high and in some cases increasing measure of control from Moscow.*

Ironically, in many of these countries local communists were actually a strong political force after the war, having played important roles in the antifascist resistance. But Stalin was not interested in working with them. He wanted control from the top down through men of unquestioned loyalty to Moscow, backed up by the continued presence of the Soviet army.

Nancy Wake witnessed one of the most tragic examples of Soviet domination when she traveled to Prague in 1947. Before the war, Czechoslovakia had been a prosperous society with a strong middle class and an emerging democratic tradition. But when Wake arrived to work at the British consulate, she found uneasiness: *"Although the Russians were not visible, the majority of Czechs I met used to walk around looking over their shoulders in case someone was listening to their conversation."**

Czechs saw themselves as a bridge between East and West. Local communists fared well in a free election held in 1946 and were part of a coalition government. But Stalin wanted firmer control. In 1948, Czech communists loyal to Moscow seized power and ended their country's brief postwar experiment with democracy. *"Yes, the Germans had gone,"* Wake commented, *"but who would liberate the country from the liberators?"**

---

*Excerpt from Nancy Wake, *The Autobiography of the Woman the Gestapo Called the White Mouse*, pp. 280, 285. 1985 Pan Publishing.

Sovfoto/Getty Images

Berlin, 1945 In April 1945, the Soviet army advanced on the German capital, supported by American and British aerial bombardment. While Adolf Hitler committed suicide in his subterranean bunker, Soviet soldiers hoisted the communist flag over the ruined city. The Red Army remained in occupation of most of eastern Europe after the war.

• **CONTEXT&CONNECTIONS** Czechoslovakia had been born through negotiations at the *Paris Peace Conference* that merged territories formerly within the German, Austrian, and Russian empires (Chapter 27). After German occupation during World War II and Soviet overrule from 1948 to 1989, Czechoslovakia finally emerged as a democratic country (see Chapter 31). Then the Czech and Slovak peoples decided to go their separate ways. In 1993, the country peacefully split into the Czech Republic and Slovakia, both of which have since become members of the European Union. •

The United States, the Soviet Union, and the Origins of a Bipolar World

The United States and the Soviet Union were now bitter enemies, two potent "superpowers" dividing the globe in a bipolar struggle between Washington and Moscow. But full-scale war between them never developed. This was a "cold" war, often fought by proxies (smaller nations on either side) but never by the main adversaries (see Chapter 30). The deployment of nuclear weapons, first by the United States in 1945 and then by the Soviet Union in 1949, raised the stakes of total war beyond what any leader was willing to wager.

While Soviet ideology proclaimed the desirability and inevitability of socialist revolution on a global scale, Stalin was most concerned about protecting the Russian core of the Soviet Union. With large, exposed land frontiers, Soviet Russia needed buffer states along its vulnerable European and Asian frontiers. Having been invaded twice in two generations, the Soviets would not leave themselves open to another attack.

● **CONTEXT&CONNECTIONS** The Russian empire had a long history of "defensive expansion" to protect its extensive land frontiers. Both *Peter the Great* (Chapter 17) and *Catherine the Great* (Chapter 20) built territorial buffers around core Russian territories. Joseph Stalin followed the same strategy in eastern Europe, as would *Vladimir Putin* (Chapter 32) in his aggressive policies toward Georgia and Ukraine, and his efforts to build a Moscow-centered alliance for economic and strategic cooperation as an alternative to the European Union. ●

AP® THEMES

How did American economic philosophy and policies differ from Soviet economic philosophies and policies in the post–World War II era?

The U.S. outlook was quite different. After the war, Americans retained their characteristic optimism and idealism and stood ready to project their ideals—personal liberty, democracy, technological progress, and market-driven economic efficiency—onto the world stage. Some thought it was the beginning of an "American century," a belief reinforced by economic dominance in a world where the country's major industrial competitors had all suffered huge losses. But as Americans engaged the postwar world, they found impediments to this global vision: not everyone seemed to share American ideals. Moreover, cynical observers saw such idealism as a smokescreen for the self-interested expansion of American capitalism and American imperialism.

American policy was strongly influenced by the "Long Telegram" sent to Washington in 1946 by a U.S. diplomat in Moscow who advocated a policy of "containment." *"At the bottom of [the] Kremlin's neurotic view of world affairs,"* he wrote, *"is [the] traditional and instinctive Russian sense of insecurity."** If the Western powers held firm and maintained their unity, the author argued, Soviet expansionism could be contained.

Truman Doctrine
(1947) Declaration by President Harry S. Truman that the United States would aid all peoples threatened by communism. In reality, his doctrine of "containment" meant that the United States did not try to dislodge the Soviets from their sphere of influence.

The **Truman Doctrine** of 1947 embodied the concept of containment. The context was a civil war in Greece. Communist partisans who had fought German occupiers continued their fight for socialism at the war's end. The royalist Greek government and army were unable to put down this rebellion, and in 1947 Truman promised American aid to suppress the "terrorist activities" of the Greek communists, also promising aid to Greece's neighbor and traditional enemy Turkey and to any nation struggling for freedom: *"I believe that it must be the policy of the United States to support free peoples who are resisting attempted subjugation by armed minorities or by outside pressures."* Despite the implications of Truman's strong language, in fact Stalin conceded that Greece would be under Western control. For its part the United States took no direct action in response to the Soviet takeover of Czechoslovakia, implicitly acknowledging that Stalin would control *"wherever his army could reach."*

The Cold War stalemate was most apparent in Germany, where the Soviets occupied the eastern part of the country and the British, Americans, and French occupied the west. The capital city of Berlin, which lay within the zone of Soviet occupation, was itself divided into four sectors. With the breakdown of wartime collaboration, the Soviet Union and the Western powers never concluded an agreement on Germany's future. Instead, border tensions escalated in 1948 when the Soviets cut off access to Berlin by land and the United States responded by sending supplies to West Berlin by air. The Berlin Airlift was successful, but the crisis led, in 1949, to the creation of two separate states, the Federal Republic of Germany (or West Germany) and the German Democratic Republic (or East Germany). Each side blamed the other for preventing the reunification of Germany, but in reality neither France nor the Soviet Union was unhappy with the outcome, given that German aggression had twice in a generation posed a grave threat to their peace and security. As long as the Cold War lasted, the division of Germany was its symbolic battle line.

*George Kennan, the "Long Telegram," Moscow, 1946.

Meanwhile, the United States took an active role in rebuilding war-ravaged western Europe, most famously through the **Marshall Plan**. Although some Americans wanted the United States to withdraw from European affairs, Truman saw that the reconstruction of western European economies was essential. First, a revival of global trade, in which Europe would play a central role, was necessary for postwar American economic progress. Second, the communist parties of Italy and France were still quite strong, and continued economic difficulties might increase their popularity. In early 1948, the United States announced that $12 billion would be made available for European reconstruction.

Marshall Plan
U.S. effort to rebuild war-ravaged Europe, named after the American secretary of state, George C. Marshall.

In 1944, even before the war was over, the American-sponsored **Bretton Woods Conference** had formed a plan to prevent a repeat of the economic catastrophe that followed World War I. It created the World Bank to loan money to nations in need of a jumpstart, and the International Monetary Fund to provide emergency loans to nations in danger of insolvency. The Marshall Plan and the Bretton Woods institutions were designed to enhance the stability of a free-market international economic order. Critics pointed out that the U.S. government was creating international institutions that favored American-style capitalism.

Bretton Woods Conference
(1944) Conference that led to creation of the World Bank and the International Monetary Fund, designed to secure international capitalism by preventing global economic catastrophes.

The Soviet Union and its eastern European satellites were invited to join the Marshall Plan, but Stalin refused, aware that the socialist economic system could not bear integration with the market-based system of the West. Thus, after 1948 the Cold War division of Europe would be economic as well as political and military. While the U.S. sphere of influence consisted of market-based, industrialized economies, in the Soviet sphere, centralized planning shielded socialist economies from international market forces. To the weakest, least industrialized areas—Asian and African colonies, weak and dependent Latin American countries—the United States would promise development assistance, while the Soviet Union would advocate prosperity through socialist revolution.

Having undergone enormous industrial expansion during the war, the United States was in a much better position to aid its allies. The Soviet Union was itself in need of reconstruction. So while the United States offered the Marshall Plan, the Soviets exploited their eastern European satellites economically. Entire factories were dismantled and moved from eastern Germany to the Soviet Union. While the United States could use a combination of military strength, diplomacy, and economic aid to gain allies during the Cold War, the Soviet Union more often relied on direct military control.

Both sides also expanded their intelligence operations. The Soviet spy agency, known by the initials KGB, worked through local proxies, such as the East German *Stasi*, to maintain tight control over its satellites while trying to infiltrate Western political, military, and intelligence communities. The United States formed the Central Intelligence Agency (CIA) out of its wartime intelligence service, the first time a U.S. government agency was dedicated to collecting foreign intelligence. The CIA's first secret operation was to pay Italian journalists to write negative stories about communist parliamentary candidates.

• **CONTEXT&CONNECTIONS** The *Central Intelligence Agency (CIA)* (Chapter 30) would greatly expand the scope of its covert operations during the 1950s, acting to counter perceived Soviet influence in the postcolonial, developing world. Thus the CIA was involved in the overthrow of elected leaders in Guatemala (1953), Iran (1954), and the Democratic Republic of the Congo (1961). •

As we will see in the next two chapters, the Cold War divided the globe. Outside Europe, communist regimes took power in the People's Republic of China, the

Democratic People's Republic of Korea, the Democratic Republic of Vietnam, and the Republic of Cuba. As the British and French empires declined in Asia and Africa, emerging new nations were often caught in the tension between the communist East and capitalist West. Some nations, such as India, were able to steer a middle course. But others, like Vietnam, Angola, Afghanistan, and Nicaragua, would be torn apart by Cold War rivalries. Two generations of humanity lived in the shadow of the Cold War, with the terrible knowledge that it could one day lead to a nuclear doomsday.

CONTEXT AND CONNECTIONS

Total War in World History

"The Second World War was the single most globalizing experience in human history." Hyperbole, perhaps, but it is difficult to think of any other series of events that have affected more people more deeply. The scale of death was unprecedented: more than 50 million all told. The number of lives sent onto entirely new trajectories in the first half of the 1940s is impossible to count. For Nancy Wake and many others who fought and survived, it was the defining period of their lives.

As the war years recede—Nancy Wake died in 2011, just weeks shy of her one-hundredth birthday—we are beginning to see the two world wars of the twentieth century as a single war during which hostilities were merely suspended. Total war was the unifying theme. Both the earlier and later conflicts mobilized civilian populations as never before and hinged on the ability to sustain industrial production. In both, imperial rulers brought colonized peoples into the war. And in both, an alliance including Britain, France, the United States, and Russia battled a German-led coalition, including the Ottoman empire in the first war and Japan in the second.

The contrasts were in enlargement of scale, such as the development of a full-fledged theater of battle in East Asia during the second war. Technological developments were another contrast, with the rapidly moving fronts of the second war a marked difference from the static battle lines of the first, and aerial bombardment now a key to success rather than a marginal tactic. Partly for that reason, civilians were much more likely to be in the direct line of fire in World War II. From China, Spain, and Ethiopia, through the London blitz, the firebombing of Dresden, and the nuclear nightmare of Hiroshima and Nagasaki, the intensity and terror of civilian bombardment increased year by year.

The Holocaust was a benchmark of evil, though it was not altogether unique. Hitler's "final solution" followed

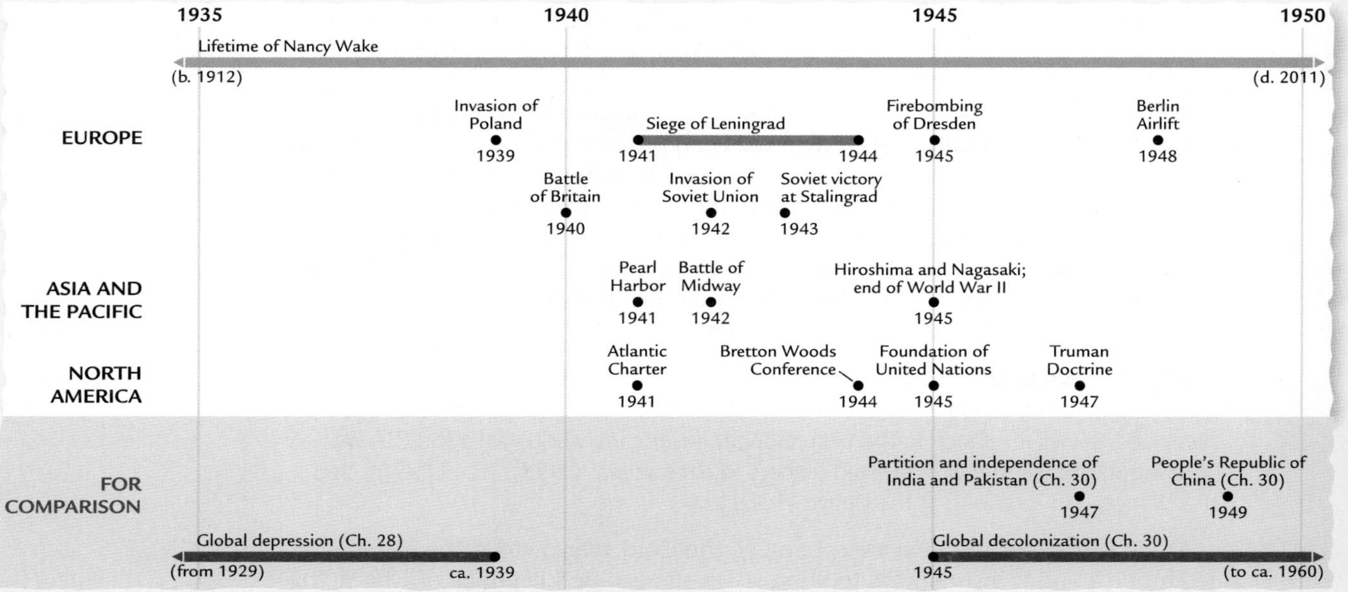

earlier twentieth-century genocides targeting the peoples of Southwest Africa and Armenians in the Ottoman empire (see Chapters 26 and 27), and it would not be the last attempt to annihilate a group of people, as later tragedies in Serbia and Rwanda would show (see Chapter 31). But the Nazis' ruthlessly methodical machinery of slaughter was unprecedented, a nightmare execution of the racist logic of Social Darwinism and the purported "struggle for existence" that had for generations infected the world (see Chapters 23 and 26). The Holocaust did not, of course, cure the world of racism. But Hitler's madness was a wake-up call for humanity: at a terrible cost, racism had lost much of its respectability.

Through both world wars, the international system had, in fact, been ordered around racial principles, with western Europeans in control of global empires that systematically denied rights of self-determination to colonized peoples in Africa and Asia. After 1945, that would quickly change. India, long the "jewel in the crown" of the British empire, became independent in 1947. In 1960, seventeen new African countries left the British and French empires to join the United Nations as sovereign states (see Chapter 30).

But for many of the world's people the road to freedom was complicated by the Cold War. The United States and the Soviet Union were unwilling to confront each other directly, since the prospect of nuclear annihilation was very real. Instead, the two sides sponsored proxy conflicts in Africa, Latin America, and Asia, undermining for decades the quest of the world's poorest and most disenfranchised for a better future. Still, however harsh the Cold War climate, the world's worst fears were never realized. Somehow, our species avoided nuclear self-destruction.

Key Terms

Nancy Wake (874)
Axis powers (875)
Winston Churchill (875)
Charles de Gaulle (877)
Atlantic Charter (878)
Pearl Harbor (878)
Allied powers (879)
Siege of Leningrad (879)
Battle of Stalingrad (880)
Hiroshima and Nagasaki (881)
Holocaust (885)
"Quit India" (888)
King's African Rifles (888)
Warsaw Ghetto Uprising (892)
United Nations (UN) (893)
Truman Doctrine (896)
Marshall Plan (897)
Bretton Woods Conference (897)

For Further Reference

Burleigh, Michael. *Third Reich: A New History*. New York: Hill and Wang, 2001.

Chang, Iris. *The Rape of Nanking*. New York: Basic Books, 2012.

Dower, John. *War Without Mercy: Race and Power in the Pacific War*. New York: Pantheon, 1987.

Dwork, Deborah, and Robert Jan Van Pelt. *Holocaust: A History*. New York: W. W. Norton, 2003.

Hopf, Ted. *Reconstructing the Cold War: The Early Years, 1945–1958*. New York: Oxford University Press, 2012.

Higgonet, Margaret, ed. *Behind the Lines: Gender and the Two World Wars*. New Haven: Yale University Press, 1989.

Iriye, Akira. *Power and Culture: The Japanese-American War, 1941–1945*. 2d ed. Cambridge, Mass.: Harvard University Press, 2004.

Keegan, John. *The Second World War*. New York: Penguin, 2005.

Larson, Erik. *In the Garden of Beasts*. New York: Crown, 2012.

Mercatante, Stephen. *Why Germany Nearly Won: A New History of the Second World War in Europe*. Westport, Conn.: Praeger, 2012.

Morgan, Philip. *The Fall of Mussolini: Italy, the Italians, and the Second World War*. New York: Oxford University Press, 2007.

Osborne, Richard. *World War II in Colonial Africa: The Death Knell of Colonialism*. Indianapolis: Riebel-Roque, 2011.

Thurston, Robert W., and Bernd Bonwetsch, eds. *The People's War: Responses to World War II in the Soviet Union*. Champaign: University of Illinois Press, 2000.

Wake, Nancy. *The White Mouse*. Melbourne: Macmillan, 1986.

Yahil, Leni. *The Holocaust: The Fate of European Jewry*. New York: Schocken, 1987.

AP® Review Questions for Chapter 29

Multiple-Choice Questions

QUESTIONS 1–3 REFER TO THE FOLLOWING PASSAGE.

65 years ago, they survived the unimaginable: the atomic bombings of Hiroshima and Nagasaki. They are called the Hibakusha. They are a unique group which hopes their dramatic stories will convey the need to eliminate the scourge that nearly killed them during two days that changed the world. . . . According to recent statistics by the Japanese Ministry of Health there are around 227,000 Hibakusha left. They include not only the survivors of the bombs, but also the fetuses that were being carried by their mothers at the time. Many who survived the bomb, died later because of a lack of medical infrastructure and assistance from the Japanese government, which was struggling to recover from the attacks. Radiation sickness was not understood in the years immediately following the bombings, and many of the Hibakusha found themselves ostracized from society.

—Seni Tienabeso, journalist reporting about survivors of Hiroshima and Nagasaki, 2010

1. Which of the following conclusions about the twentieth century is most directly supported by the passage?
   (A) The use of nuclear power ended World War II.
   (B) Nuclear technology led to a revolution in energy production.
   (C) Military technological advances led to increased levels of wartime casualties.
   (D) The fallout from an atomic strike is devastating but temporary.

2. The Hibakusha's message most clearly supports which of the following ideologies?
   (A) Antinuclear movement
   (B) Non-Aligned Movement
   (C) Anti-Apartheid movement
   (D) Environmental movement

3. The use of atomic weapons detailed in the passage above led most directly to which of the following events of the twentieth century?
   (A) The Korean War
   (B) The Berlin Airlift
   (C) The Soviet-Afghan War
   (D) The Cold War

QUESTIONS 4–6 REFER TO THE FOLLOWING PASSAGE.

The war with fascist Germany cannot be considered an ordinary war. It is not only a war between two armies, it is also a great war of the entire Soviet people against the German-fascist armies. The aim of this national patriotic war in defense of our country against the fascist oppressors is not only to eliminate the danger hanging over our country, but also to aid all the European peoples groaning under the yoke of German fascism. In this war of liberation we shall not be alone. In this great war we shall have true allies in the peoples of Europe and America, including the German people which is enslaved by the Hitlerite misrulers.

—Josef Stalin, radio broadcast after the German invasion of the Soviet Union, July 1941

4. Which of the following World War II principles does Stalin's speech most support?
   (A) Transnational unity based on political or cultural ties
   (B) Government mobilization of all of a nation's resources known as "total war"
   (C) A rededication to the policy of Russian imperial expansion
   (D) The formation of permanent defensive alliances in eastern Europe

5. The views expressed in the passage are best seen as evidence of which of the following in Soviet society?
   (A) Multinationalism
   (B) Ethnic homogeneity
   (C) Socioeconomic barriers
   (D) Depopulation

6. Which of the following changes to Stalin's diplomatic policy occurred after World War II?
   (A) The Soviet Union became a leader in the global environmental movement.
   (B) Stalin began a series of economic reforms known as the New Deal.
   (C) The wartime alliance with the United States ended and the Cold War began.
   (D) Stalin urged global use of nonviolence as a means to achieving political goals.

QUESTIONS 7–10 REFER TO THE FOLLOWING PASSAGE.

Thus, from that date [1940], our people were subjected to the double yoke of the French and the Japanese. Their sufferings and miseries increased. The result was that towards the end of last year and the beginning of this year . . . more than two million of our fellow citizens died from starvation. On the 9th of March this year, the French troops were disarmed by the Japanese. The French colonialists either fled or surrendered, showing that not only were they incapable of "protecting" us, but that, in a period of five years, they had twice sold our country to the Japanese.

—Ho Chi Minh, "Declaration of Independence of the Democratic Republic of Vietnam," 1945

7. The French behavior described in the passage above most directly mirrors which of the following?
   (A) The collaboration of some French politicians with the Nazis
   (B) The French refusal to surrender their colonies during the war
   (C) Churchill's call to the British to remain steadfast
   (D) Mao Zedong's continued opposition to both the Nationalists and the Japanese

8. Which of the following statements most strongly supports Ho Chi Minh's statement about the "double yoke of the French and the Japanese"?
   (A) The French and the Japanese both claimed portions of Vietnam as colonies.
   (B) Both the French and the Japanese treated the Vietnamese as slaves.
   (C) Japanese occupation continued the French tradition of exploiting the Vietnamese.
   (D) French imperial ambitions were only reinforced by World War II.

9. Which of the following most closely represents Ho Chi Minh's views toward resistance?
   (A) Vietnamese resistance had the goal of uniting with the Allied war effort.
   (B) Resisting both the French and the Japanese was ordered by Stalin.
   (C) The United States, as an ideological ally, would eventually provide aid.
   (D) The goal of resistance was Vietnamese independence.

10. The passage is best understood in the context of what twentieth-century development?
    (A) Decolonization
    (B) Imperialism
    (C) Global communism
    (D) Nationalism

Short-Answer Questions

QUESTION 1 REFERS TO THE IMAGE ON PAGE 885, *BRITISH WAR PRODUCTION*.

1. Answer parts A, B, and C.
   Many historians argue that World War II offered new job opportunities for women and minorities in western Europe and the United States.
   A. Identify and explain ONE piece of evidence that *supports* this argument.
   B. Identify and explain ONE piece of evidence that *undermines* this argument.
   C. Identify and explain ONE long-term effect of World War II on job opportunities for women and minorities in western Europe and/or the United States.

QUESTION 2 REFERS TO THE TIMELINE ON PAGE 898.

2. Answer parts A, B, and C.
   A. Identify and explain ONE reason why the Great Depression led to World War II.
   B. Identify and explain ONE reason why World War II led to the Cold War.
   C. Identify and explain ONE reason why World War II led to decolonization.

30 The Cold War and Decolonization, 1949–1975

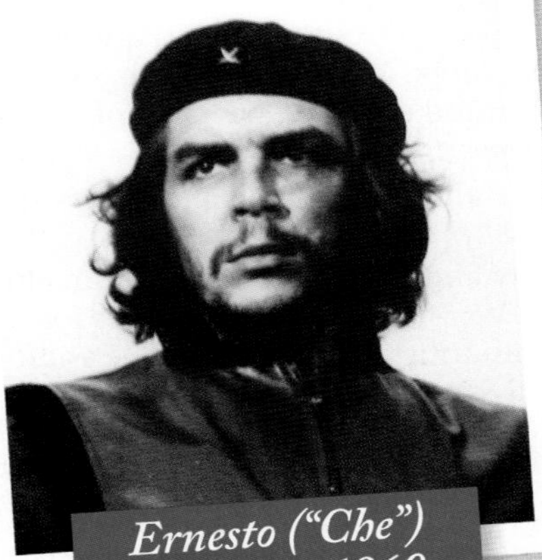

Stefano Rellandini/Reuters/Corbis

Ernesto ("Che") Guevara, 1960

In 1952, Alberto Granado and **Ernesto Guevara** (1928–1967), two Argentine students with promising futures in medicine, decided to take an ambitious road trip across South America on an aging motorcycle. At first, their motive was fun and adventure, *"not setting down roots in any land or staying long enough to see the substratum of things; the outer surface would suffice."* Soon, however, their encounters with Indians, peasants, and miners changed the nature of Guevara's quest:

*We made friends with a [Chilean] couple. . . . In his simple, expressive language he recounted his three months in prison . . . his fruitless pilgrimage in search of work and his compañeros, mysteriously disappeared and said to be somewhere at the bottom of the sea. The couple, numb with cold, huddling against each other in the desert night, was a living representation of the proletariat in any part of the world. They had not one single miserable blanket to cover themselves with, so we gave them one of ours and Alberto and I wrapped the other around us as best we could. . . . The communism gnawing at [their] entrails was no more than a natural longing for something better, a protest against persistent hunger transformed into a love for this strange doctrine, whose essence they could never grasp but whose translation, "bread for the poor," was something which they understood and, more importantly, filled them with hope.**

*Ernesto Guevara, *The Motorcycle Diaries: Notes on a Latin American Journey*, ed. and trans. Alexandra Keeble (Melbourne: Ocean Press, 2003), pp. 75–78.

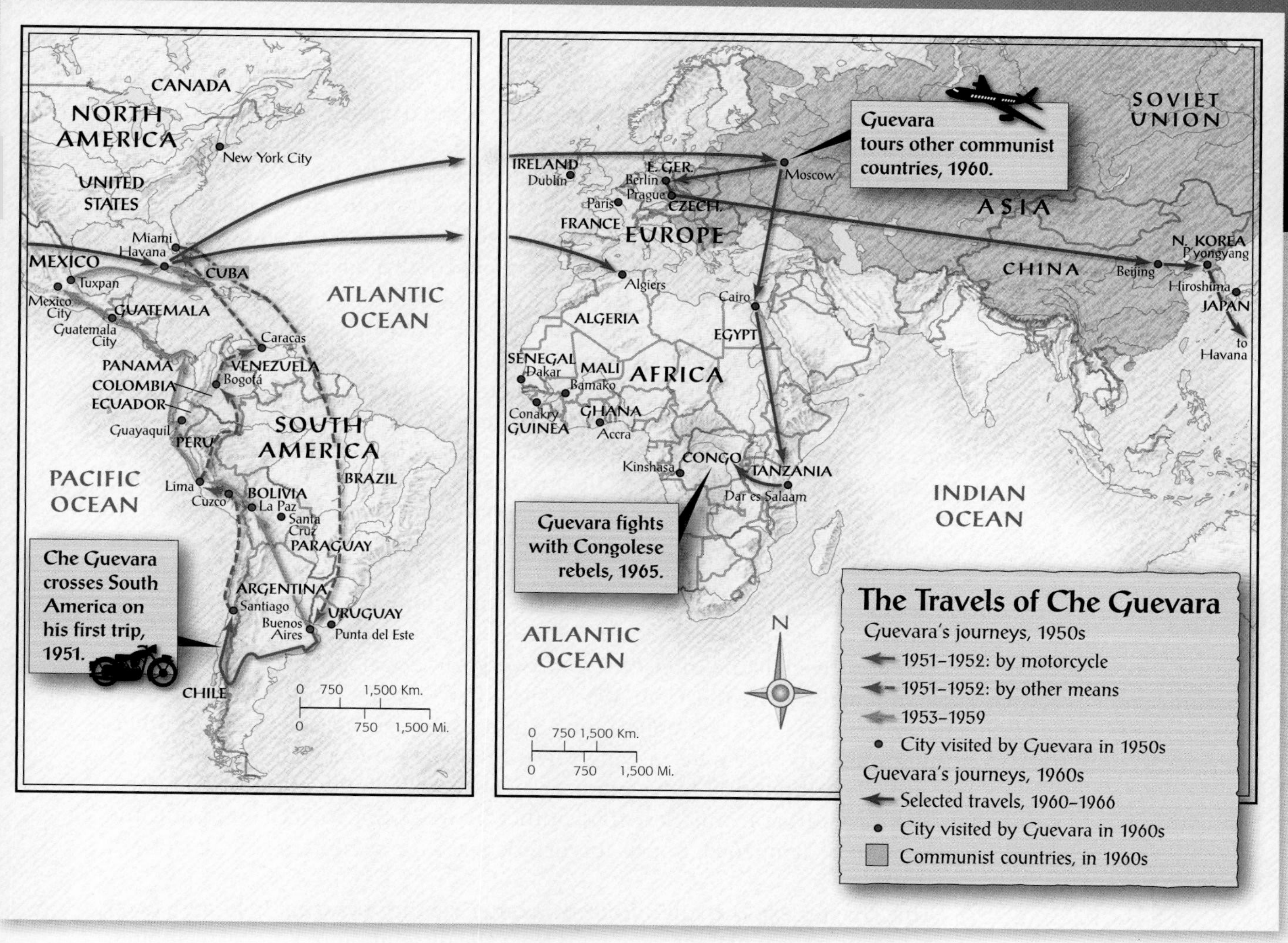

By the time Ernesto returned to Buenos Aires, he was a different man and on the path to becoming "Che," the most charismatic of twentieth-century revolutionaries.

It took one more trip to change Guevara's path from that of an Argentine doctor to that of a professional revolutionary. After completing his degree, he set out on another road trip, this time with heightened political consciousness. While in Guatemala in 1954, he witnessed the overthrow of its democratically elected socialist government by a right-wing rebel army organized and financed by the United States. Fearing arrest, Guevara fled to Mexico, where he met a group of Cuban exiles determined to overthrow their own dictator. Che joined them as a soldier and military commander, using guerrilla tactics such as quick raids and surprise ambushes to defeat the Cuban army. After the success of the Cuban Revolution in 1959, Che's fame spread around the world.

Ernesto Guevara
(1928–1967) Argentinean socialist and revolutionary, called "Che," who played a crucial role in the Cuban Revolution. After serving as a Cuban government minister, he left to organize guerrilla campaigns in the Congo and Bolivia. He was executed in 1967 by the Bolivian army.

Guevara identified completely with the downtrodden, especially those in the "Third World." In 1952, a French journalist had pointed out the tripartite division of the postwar world. The capitalist United States and its allies constituted the wealthy First World, and the socialist Soviet Union and its allies were the Second World. The Third World, lacking in industry and with little voice in world affairs, made up two-thirds of the world's population. Guevara chose to speak and act on behalf of this disempowered majority, the people Frantz Fanon, another advocate of Third World revolution, called *"the wretched of the earth."*

Rather than settling down in socialist Cuba, Guevara pursued his dream of revolution in Africa and South America. In 1965, he traveled to the Congo and in 1967 to Bolivia, in both cases organizing guerrilla armies in the name of socialist revolution. But there were to be no more glorious victories: in 1967, Bolivian troops captured Che and executed him. Yet in death he became even more powerful and influential than in life. When his remains were discovered in 1998, they were sent to Cuba, where Che received a hero's burial. By then he had long been an icon of youth culture. The familiar image of "Che," reproduced on endless T-shirts and posters, became emblematic of the social and political idealism of the 1960s. As a symbol, Che was loved and admired, or hated and feared, by millions.

Guevara lived at the intersection of two great global struggles. One was the East-West division of the Cold War. The other was the North-South division between the global haves and have-nots. This was the age of decolonization, when many former colonies were moving toward national independence. Across Asia and Africa, mass political movements brought the possibility of positive change. But there, as in Latin America, the conflict between the Soviet Union and the United States dampened hopes for democracy and reinforced trends toward dictatorship.

This chapter explores the turbulent quarter century between 1949 and 1974, when dozens of new nations were born from the dissolution of European empires; when communist revolutionaries took power in mainland China; when the United States and the Soviet Union, the new "superpowers" of the Cold War era, faced off across a deep nuclear chasm; when antidemocratic political forces in strategic parts of the world found sponsorship from the American and Soviet governments; and when young people dreamed of transforming the world. For many, Che Guevara symbolized their dreams and their disappointments.

KEY CONCEPT QUESTIONS

- How did the revolutions in China and Cuba contribute to the Cold War? **(Key Concept 6.2)**
- How did the Cold War affect decolonization movements in Africa, South Asia, and Southeast Asia? **(Key Concept 6.2)**
- What aspects of the economic, social, and political order did youth protest from the mid-1960s to the mid-1970s? **(Key Concept 6.2)**

The Cold War and Revolution, 1949–1962

By the 1950s, the United States and Soviet Union were amassing nuclear weapons many times more powerful than those dropped on Hiroshima and Nagasaki. Since any direct conflict between them threatened mutual annihilation, both sides were cautious not to push the other too far. Official U.S. policy remained one of "containment," of preventing an expansion of the Soviet sphere of influence but not intervening within it. Insults, propaganda, and espionage characterized U.S.-Soviet relations.

While the Cold War in Europe was a standoff, communist revolutions elsewhere increased the potential sphere of Soviet influence. In 1959, ten years after Mao Zedong had declared the foundation of the People's Republic of China, Fidel Castro and Che Guevara led a rebel army into Havana and founded a socialist government in Cuba, an island just 90 miles (145 km) from Florida. From the perspective of anticommunists in the United States and elsewhere, the "Soviet menace" was increasing.

The People's Republic of China, 1949–1962

Almost immediately after Japan's defeat, the competition between Chiang Kai-shek's Guomindang and Mao Zedong's Chinese Communist Party for control of China resumed (see Chapter 28). By the time war ended in 1949, the Communists controlled the People's Republic of China on the mainland, and Chiang Kai-shek and his Nationalist followers fled to the island of Taiwan, where they established the Republic of China (see Map 30.1).

The Communists succeeded even though the Nationalists started with a larger army, a stockpile of weapons supplied by the Allies during World War II, and control of China's largest cities. Mao's tough, disciplined army had cultivated support among the Chinese peasantry while fighting Japanese invaders. Mao used this popular base to advantage, telling his soldiers to *"swim like fishes in the sea"* of rural China, camouflaging their activities amid the routines of village life. Since the People's Liberation Army treated Chinese peasants with greater respect than Chiang's Guomindang, they rode mass support to success.

Once in power, the Communists revolutionized China from the bottom up. They organized peasants into agricultural cooperatives, expanded educational opportunities, indoctrinated young people in youth organizations guided by the party, and enrolled workers in state-sponsored trade unions. Within the unions, the army, and other mass organizations, mandatory "thought reform" sessions focused on the study of "Mao Zedong Thought." Those accused of deviation from socialist thought were shamed and forced to publicly confess their "errors."

The Korean War (1950–1953) put the new People's Republic of China into direct conflict with the United States. After North Korea attacked South Korea, the United States rushed to defend its ally. The mainland Chinese government, fearing that the United States intended to attack them as well, threw its massive forces into battle to reinforce the north. In the end, the south fended off invasion, but stalemate ensued along the demilitarized zone that separated the communist regime in North Korea, which allowed no freedom at all, from the stern authoritarian regime in South Korea, which allowed very little.

Map 30.1 China and Taiwan After World War II, the Communist forces of Mao Zedong took the offensive against the Guomindang, or Nationalist army, of Chiang Kai-shek. They drove the Nationalists off the mainland to the island of Taiwan, and Mao created the People's Republic of China on October 1, 1949. The Communists and Nationalists agreed that there was only "one China," and their continuing animosity became another zone of conflict in the global Cold War. Far to the west, tensions have arisen from border disputes between China and India.

• **CONTEXT&CONNECTIONS** South Korean and North Korean societies diverged sharply over time. South Korea, a very poor country in 1960, became a "First World" consumer society after decades of export-led economic development (see Chapter 31). After liberal reforms and free elections in 1987, South Korea became a democratic society as well. North Korea, in contrast, became more isolated after the end of the Cold War, the paranoid Kim family dynasty refusing even modest market reforms while rigidly rejecting political liberalization (see Chapter 32). •

Initially, the People's Republic of China followed Soviet-style economic policies of state-run heavy industry and collective farming. In 1953, the Chinese adopted a Five-Year Plan and sent engineers and state planners to Russia for training. But the results were disappointing. Not only was the growth of production slower than Mao expected, but the dull, bureaucratic socialism of the U.S.S.R. did little to inspire him. Mao felt that the fire was going out of the revolution.

In 1956, Mao launched a public call for new ideas, using the phrase *"Let a hundred flowers bloom."* China's intellectuals responded by openly criticizing the Communist Party, and even Mao himself. Either the criticism was more than Mao had expected, or perhaps he had intended all along to trick opponents into the open, but during the savage repression of 1957, intellectuals were arrested, imprisoned, and exiled. Independent thinking was now a "rightist" deviation.

Having purged such "rightists," Mao still saw the Communist Party as divided into two factions, which he labeled "red" and "expert." The "experts" managing collectivization and industrial development were becoming an elite cut off from the masses. It was the "red" leadership, emphasizing socialist willpower rather than technical ability, that would rapidly bring about socialist prosperity by unleashing the true revolutionary potential of China's peasants and workers. The people, in Mao's thinking, could move mountains.

In 1958, Mao launched the **Great Leap Forward** decreeing that the agricultural collectives should be harnessed for industrial development. Rather than relying on large steel factories, revolutionaries would set up small furnaces all across the country. The "masses" were directed to pour all their energy and enthusiasm into communal production. Meanwhile, property rights were restricted, and peasants lost access to the small plots they had relied on to feed their families.

Great Leap Forward (1958) Mao Zedong's attempt to harness the revolutionary zeal of the Chinese masses for rapid industrialization. The result was a massive economic collapse and millions of deaths from famine.

The Great Leap Forward was disastrous. The steel produced in small communal furnaces was virtually useless, and food production suffered as farm workers wasted their energies on Mao's inefficient scheme. As many as 30 million people died in the resulting famine. By 1961, the failure of the Great Leap Forward led the more pragmatic "experts" in the Communist Party to reduce Mao's authority behind the scenes (still publicly acknowledging his leadership) while reinstating rationality to economic planning.

Still, Mao's belief in the power of revolutionary enthusiasm would inspire a younger generation of revolutionaries. Che Guevara was among those attracted to the Chinese model as an alternative to both capitalism and the stodgy Soviet model of technocratic socialism.

AP® THEMES

How did Chinese economic strategies compare to Soviet economic strategies in the twentieth century?

The Cuban Revolution and the Cuban Missile Crisis

In the 1950s, Cuba was an island of contrasts. Its capital, Havana, was famous for its beaches and nightclubs, where musicians fused African and Latin traditions. But Cuba's vibrant culture obscured a darker underside. The American Mafia controlled Havana's casinos, prostitution flourished, and the Cuban dictator Fulgencio Batista, supported by American business interests, allowed no democratic freedoms. Most Cubans, the poorest of them descendants of slaves, had no access to good employment, health care, or education.

• **CONTEXT&CONNECTIONS** Cuba did not abolish slavery until 1878 (see Chapter 25) and Afro-Cubans, while making enduring cultural contributions, were still at the bottom of Cuban society. For many of them, socialism brought access for the first time to education and health care. •

Fidel Castro (b. 1926) Cuban prime minister from 1959 to 1976 and president from 1976 to 2008. Led the successful Cuban Revolution in 1959, after which his nationalization policies led to deteriorating relations with the United States and increasing dependence on Soviet support.

Central Intelligence Agency (CIA) U.S. federal agency created in 1947 whose responsibilities include coordinating intelligence activities abroad as well as conducting covert operations—for example, against the Soviet Union and its allies during the Cold War.

Cuban Missile Crisis Tense 1962 confrontation between the United States and the Soviet Union over placement of nuclear missiles in Cuba. A compromise led to withdrawal of Soviet missiles from Cuba and of American missiles from Turkey.

Fidel Castro (b. 1926), like Ernesto Guevara, was an idealistic young man who renounced middle-class privilege in the name of revolution. Imprisoned in 1953 for leading an attack on an army barracks, he went into exile in Mexico City after his release in 1955. There he formed a deep friendship with Che Guevara, newly arrived from Guatemala, where the overthrow of the democratically elected government had been coordinated by the U.S. **Central Intelligence Agency (CIA)**. Che joined Castro's small rebel band for military training.

In 1956, Castro and Guevara left Mexico by boat for Cuba, finding sanctuary in the island's Sierra Maestra Mountains. Gradually they stockpiled ammunition by attacking police stations and military barracks while attracting recruits from the local population, whose assistance enabled them to outmaneuver their government pursuers. During two years of hard fighting, Che's medical background proved useful in tending wounded colleagues, but his most important role was as commander and tactician. Conditions were ruthless, and Guevara had no second thoughts about executing suspected government agents without trial or legal defense. Guevara himself often pulled the trigger. By 1958, the rebels were poised to attack Havana, and on New Year's Day 1959 Batista fled when Castro's forces marched triumphantly into the capital.

The new Cuban leader toured Washington and New York, seeking both public and official support. But relations with the United States deteriorated after Cuba's Agrarian Reform Law nationalized land owned by American corporations. Both corporate lobbyists and Cold War hawks soon portrayed Castro as a Soviet threat on America's doorstep, as the pro-Batista forces that had fled to the United States lobbied for an American-backed invasion. Faced with counter-revolution, Castro's government focused on "defense of the revolution" rather than protection of civil liberties. While neither Castro nor Guevara had ever joined the Cuban Communist Party, preferring a more populist approach over rigid Marxist orthodoxy, conflict with the United States gave them little option but to seek Soviet protection. As tensions increased, the Eisenhower administration in the United States drew up plans for invasion.

In the spring of 1961, a U.S.-sponsored group of Cuban exiles stormed ashore at the island's Bay of Pigs. The new American president, John F. Kennedy (in office 1961–1963), having had strong doubts about their prospects, had given only lukewarm support. Their invasion was a debacle and validated Castro's distrust of U.S. intentions. Meanwhile, the United States had placed an economic embargo on Cuba, making diplomacy and compromise all but impossible.

In the fall of 1962, tensions climaxed during the **Cuban Missile Crisis**. Convinced that the United States would never let his socialist experiment proceed in peace, Castro developed ever-closer ties with the Soviet Union. Nikita Khrushchev (KHROOS-chev), Soviet premier and First Secretary of the Communist Party (in office 1953–1964), took advantage of the situation to secretly ship nuclear missiles to Cuba. Khrushchev departed dangerously from the Soviets' usual policy of focusing on the security of their own borders and avoiding provocations within the American sphere of influence. When American surveillance aircraft detected the missiles, Kennedy presented an ultimatum: withdraw the missiles or court annihilation. On the brink of nuclear conflict, both sides blinked: Khrushchev agreed to remove Soviet missiles from Cuba, Kennedy quietly agreed to remove U.S. missiles from Turkey, and the world's people breathed a sigh of relief.

To help Cuba withstand the American trade embargo, the Soviets agreed to buy the island's entire sugar output at above-market prices and to subsidize the socialist transformation of the island with cheap fuel and agricultural machinery. By the mid-1960s, Cubans were better fed and better housed than they had been before the revolution; they also had free access to basic health care and were more likely to be able to read and write.

But underlying economic problems remained. As was common in Latin America since colonial times, Cuba had been subject to economic dependency (see Chapter 25), exporting agricultural produce (mostly sugar and tobacco) while importing higher-valued industrial goods. With the Soviet Union as an economic patron, Cuba's reliance on agricultural exports was as strong as ever. Economic development was further hampered by Cuba's Soviet-style command economy, characterized by bureaucratic inefficiency and low worker morale.

When Cuban workers agitated for higher wages, Che Guevara, as minister for industry, told them to be content with knowing that their hard work supported the glorious cause of socialism. Himself willing to work long hours for no personal gain, Guevara thought that others should do the same. But without material rewards for workers or incentives to inspire creativity and entrepreneurship, the Cuban economy settled into lethargy. Fidel Castro's verbose four-hour speeches exhorting Cubans to rally around the revolution did nothing to help workers facing shortages of basic goods.

In Cuba, as earlier in France and Russia, leaders faced with counter-revolution set aside early promises of democratic liberties and equated dissent with treason. Castro's government viewed all opposition to its policies as emanating from the United States and the hostile community of Cuban émigrés in Florida. Authorities on the island executed hundreds and sent thousands to prison labor camps based on the Soviet model. Guevara regarded such repression as the justifiable cost of war against capitalism and American imperialism.

Still, Guevara was bored by the endless meetings and plodding pace of government. A romantic revolutionary idealist, he left for Africa in 1965 to pursue his dreams on a global stage.

Spheres of Influence: Old Empires and New Superpowers

The Cuban Missile Crisis illustrated the dangers of one superpower intervening in the other's sphere of influence. Usually such interventions took place within a superpower's own strategic domain, as when the United States sponsored the overthrow of the Guatemalan government in 1954 or Soviet tanks crushed a prodemocracy uprising in Hungary in 1956.

But much of the world lay outside either sphere. In Asia and Africa, decolonization movements were supplanting European empires. Where former imperial powers like Britain and France managed to negotiate relatively smooth transitions, especially in Africa, they often maintained strong neocolonial influence even after independence. Elsewhere, however, in the power vacuum created by the decline of European empires, new African and Asian nations left the European orbit only to become ensnared in Cold War tensions. Some, like the Congo and Vietnam, were pulled apart in the process.

Recognizing that danger, in 1955 a group of African and Asian leaders met to discuss ways to defend their sovereignty. Their goal in founding the Non-Aligned Movement was both to avoid neocolonial influence from Europe and, by refusing to undertake formal alliances with either the Soviet Union or the United States, to sidestep superpower intervention in their affairs. It was not a simple goal to achieve, as U.S. entry into the former French zone of warfare in Vietnam would show.

Superpower Interventions, 1953–1956

During the Cold War, the United States allied with the European democracies and Turkey in the North Atlantic Treaty Organization (NATO), and the Soviet Union countered with the Warsaw Pact allying eastern European nations under its sway. Both superpowers presented themselves as champions of freedom. The Soviets, identifying colonialism and imperialism as the main barriers to liberation, supported nationalists and socialists in the Third World who were fighting to throw off European or American domination. But Moscow would not tolerate similar liberation movements within its own sphere, where the Soviets brutally crushed movements toward self-determination and freedom of speech, association, or religion (see Map 30.2).

AP® THEMES

In what ways did the development of political alliances, such as NATO and the Warsaw Pact, influence international relationships during the Cold War?

In eastern Europe, secret police networks kept people from openly expressing anticommunist or anti-Soviet views. In East Germany, for example, the *Stasi* planted informers at all levels of society and encouraged neighbors to spy on neighbors. Hopes for reform came after the death of Stalin in 1953 and Nikita Khrushchev's denunciation of Stalinism's excesses at a Communist Party congress. Still, though Khrushchev preached limited reform, he would not tolerate popular movements for change.

In 1953, when demonstrators in East Berlin demanded better wages and working conditions, the communist authorities cracked down, plainly showing that communist rule was based more on Soviet coercion than popular legitimacy. Over the next eight years, thousands of East Berliners fled to the West. Finally, in 1961, East Germany constructed the Berlin Wall to stem the flow of skilled laborers, doctors, and engineers to West Germany, where livings standards were much higher. The Wall symbolized Cold War confrontation for the next 28 years.

The predominantly Catholic people of Poland detested the pro-Moscow government imposed on them by Stalin, especially the official atheism of the communist state. In 1956, a religious gathering attended by a million Poles turned into an antigovernment demonstration. Here the Soviet government compromised, allowing reforms such as an end to the collectivization of agriculture and some religious freedom. But it was clear that attempts to further weaken Poland's ties to the Soviet Union would not be tolerated.

Hungarian Uprising
(1956) Popular revolt against the Soviet-controlled government of Hungary, leading to a Soviet invasion and reimposition of communist authority.

The **Hungarian Uprising** tragically confirmed Soviet intolerance for real change. In 1956 Hungarian students, factory workers, and middle-class professionals rose up to protest the Soviet-imposed communist dictatorship. The Hungarian government collapsed, and though leaders of the new provisional government feared a Soviet invasion, they expected support from the Western democracies.

Map 30.2 **Cold War Confrontations** Two military alliances, the North Atlantic Treaty Organization (NATO) led by the United States, and the Warsaw Pact dominated by the Soviet Union, were the principal antagonists in the Cold War. Fearful of mutual nuclear annihilation, however, they never engaged in direct combat. Instead, the Cold War turned hot in proxy struggles around the world.

Laszlo Almasi/Reuters/Landov

The Hungarian Uprising A rebellion against their communist regime brought thousands of Hungarians onto the streets of Budapest in 1956, provoking a Soviet invasion. The Hungarians showed great courage in confronting Soviet tanks and troops, but they were bitterly disappointed when the United States and NATO provided no military support for their freedom struggle.

Despite Voice of America broadcasts encouraging rebellion, however, the United States failed to intervene, considering the danger of nuclear confrontation with the Soviets to be too great. Soviet tanks rolled in and crushed the Hungarian revolt with mass arrests and executions.

Americans were quick to point out the obvious contradiction between Soviet rhetoric, which equated socialism with democracy, and the Soviet practice of suppressing freedom. But U.S. practices also contradicted American ideals. By the early 1950s, Cold War tensions were leading many Americans to develop an almost paranoid fear of the Soviet Union, an attitude stoked by Senator Joseph McCarthy with his accusations of communist infiltration into the country's government. Since communism was evil, many thought, anyone who opposed Marxism-Leninism must be on the side of "freedom." The reality was that the anticommunist regimes backed by the United States were frequently authoritarian dictatorships.

The CIA often covertly assisted authoritarian leaders who were willing to support American interests. Iran was one example. In the early 1950s, Shah Muhammad Reza Pahlavi (pahl-AH-vee), a constitutional monarch, aspired to greater power. He was checked by the Iranian parliament, led by a popular prime minister, Muhammad Mossadegh (MOH-sah-DEHK). Pahlavi, an ardent anticommunist, cultivated a close alliance with the Eisenhower administration, which was concerned that the Soviet Union still had designs on the oil-rich lands of northern Iran it had occupied during World War II.

With Britain's Anglo-Iranian Oil Company reaping the lion's share of oil profits, Mossadegh and his parliamentary allies tried to renegotiate Iran's contracts with the multinational petroleum companies. When negotiations failed, Mossadegh threatened in 1953 to nationalize the entire oil sector. In response the Iranian military, with the covert support of the CIA, arrested Mossadegh, expanding the shah's authority and ending prospects for a more democratic Iranian future. Many Iranians now saw their king as an American puppet.

The next year, the United States similarly undermined democracy in Guatemala. Long ruled by authoritarian dictators, Guatemala had a typically dependent export economy, dominated by the United Fruit Company, which owned vast banana plantations, the only railroad, the only port, and the country's telephone system. A small Guatemalan elite benefited, but the country was a study in inequality: 72 percent of the land was owned by 2 percent of the population.

During World War II, reformist army officers had seized control and organized elections. In 1946, the new democratic government planned for land and labor reform. After another free election in 1950, the new president, **Jacobo Arbenz** (1913–1971), reaffirmed those reformist policies, arguing that democracy could not be built on the foundation of such stark social and economic inequality. The Eisenhower administration, believing the Arbenz government had been penetrated by Soviet agents, invoked the "domino theory," claiming that the "loss" of Guatemala would lead to communist victories elsewhere in the Americas. United Fruit used high-level government connections to lobby for action, and the CIA organized and financed a rebel movement, which overthrew Arbenz in 1954. Guatemala's brief experiment with democracy was over, as the country reverted to a dictatorship in the caudillo style (see Chapter 22). That was when Ernesto Guevara, an eyewitness to the U.S.-sponsored overthrow, had dedicated himself to revolution.

Jacobo Arbenz
(1913–1971) President of Guatemala from 1951 to 1954. A moderate socialist, Arbenz enacted comprehensive land reforms that angered Guatemalan elites and U.S. corporations. He was deposed by rebel forces backed by the United States.

Decolonization and Neocolonialism in Africa, 1945–1964

During World War II, Africans had become more aware of the wider world and increasingly dissatisfied with their colonial status. The French, British, and Belgians underestimated African sentiments; entering the 1950s, colonial officials still thought they were in Africa to stay.

Europeans' refusal to recognize the power of African nationalism was strongest in the settler colonies, especially South Africa, where after 1948 the Afrikaner-dominated National Party instituted **apartheid**, or "separateness." Already deeply entrenched, racial segregation now became more systematic and more centrally dictated than ever before. Over the next four decades, apartheid institutions would control where black South Africans could live and work, what they could (and could not) study, who they could love and marry, and even whether they should even be counted as "South Africans."

Elsewhere, however, by 1960 nationalist movements had freed most of the continent from colonial rule and created many new African nations (see Map 30.3). The Swahili word *uhuru* (oo-HOO-roo), "freedom," was heard around the world, and **Kwame Nkrumah** (1909–1972), the first president of independent Ghana after 1957, became an international symbol of African aspirations and Pan-Africanism.

The economic structures of colonialism remained, however, making true independence difficult. Economic development required capital and expertise, and both had to be imported. This situation created ideal conditions for neocolonialism: the continuation of European dominance even after independence had been attained.

apartheid
"Separateness" in the Afrikaner language, starting in 1948 this was the official policy of the white government of South Africa, enforcing strict racial segregation in all spheres of life, including work, education, and place of residence. Strongly opposed by the African National Congress, apartheid ended when democratic, non-racial elections were held in 1994.

Kwame Nkrumah
(1909–1972) One of the most prominent postwar African nationalists, he emphasized Pan-African unity while leading Ghana to independence in 1957.

• **CONTEXT&CONNECTIONS** As a Pan-Africanist, Kwame Nkrumah believed that only continental unity, a "United States of Africa," could empower Africans to resist the neocolonial control of Europe and the United States. Similarly, in a different era, the South American liberator *Simón Bolívar* (key term in Chapter 22) had sponsored the creation of Gran Colombia to assure true independence. Neither leader was successful in promoting broader territorial unity as protection against outside intrusion. •

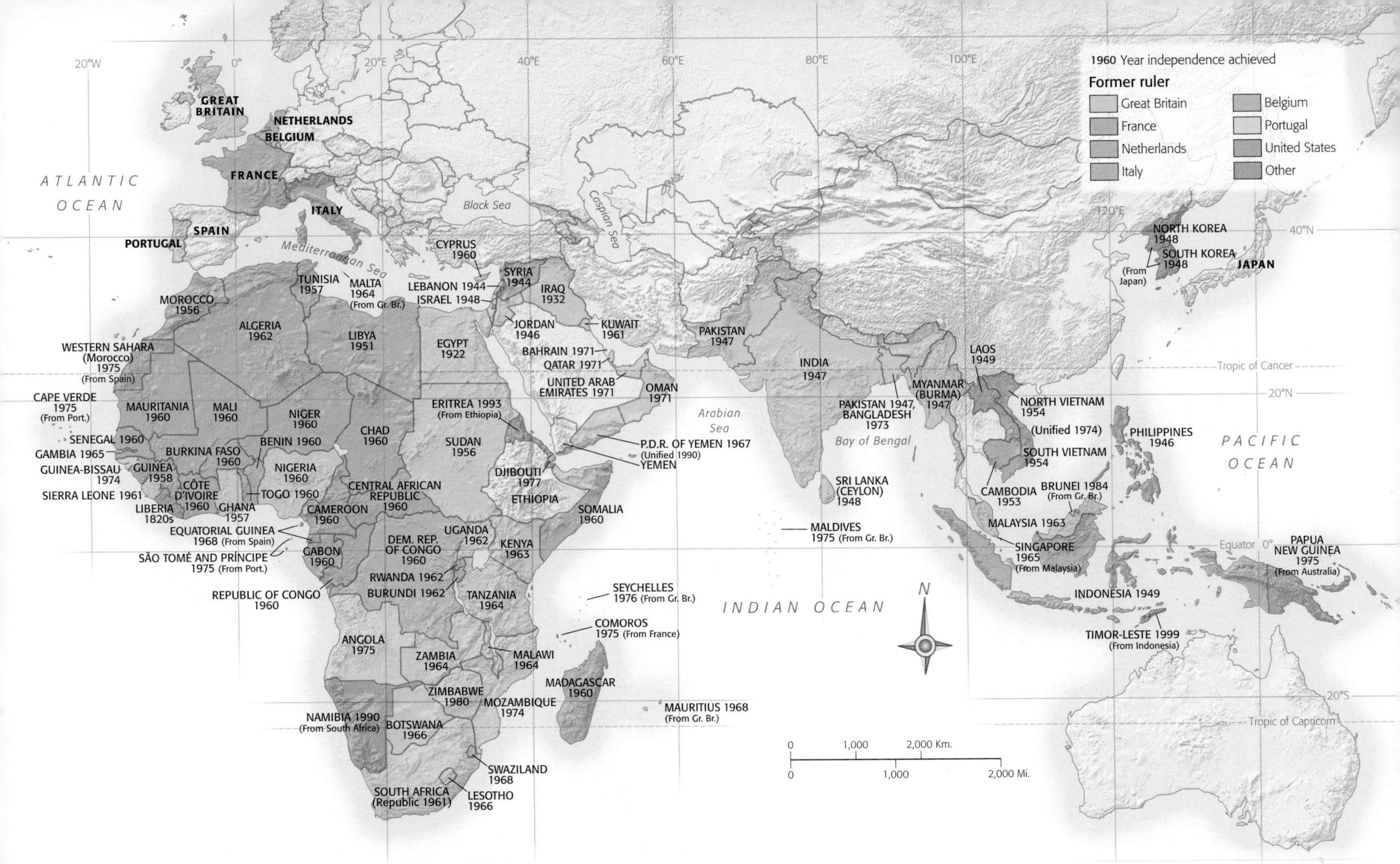

Map 30.3 Decolonization In the three decades following Indian independence in 1947, the European colonial empires in Asia and Africa unraveled, adding many new "Third World" representatives to the United Nations. Their aspirations toward dignity and development were frequently thwarted, however, by Cold War politics, continued Western economic domination, poor leadership, and ethnic and religious rivalries. In the twenty-first century, stronger economic growth has come to some of these nations of the Global South.

Even before independence, the French had laid the foundations for neocolonial control of their former African colonies. Colonial policies of "assimilation" held out the promise of French citizenship for educated Africans, creating an African elite that identified strongly with French culture. Appealing to their sentiments, in 1958 President Charles de Gaulle announced a referendum to be held across French Africa. A "yes" vote meant that the former French colonies would receive control over their own internal affairs but would remain part of a larger French "community". The French government would retain control over economic policy, foreign affairs, and the military. A "no" vote meant complete and immediate independence, severing all ties to France.

All but one of the colonies voted to become members of the French community. The exception was Guinea, where a radical trade union leader, Sekou Toure (SEY-koo TOO-rey), campaigned for complete independence. The French government responded to Guinea's "no" vote by withdrawing their administrators overnight, stopping economic aid, and even ripping telephones from the walls as they vacated their offices. The French message was clear, and other African leaders learned the lesson and cooperated with France. With their currencies pegged to the value of the French franc, new nations such as the Ivory Coast, Senegal, and Mali had little control over their own economic policies.

Elsewhere, Africans had to take up arms to liberate themselves, especially where Europeans had come not just as rulers but also as settlers. For instance, over a million Europeans lived in Algeria. After the Second World War, Algerian nationalists, some of whom had fought for de Gaulle's Free French Army, demanded rights equal to those of the white settlers and a voice in their own governance. Harshly repressed, these nationalists formed the National Liberation Front (FLN—the French acronym) and, in 1954, began their armed struggle.

It was a brutal war, with the FLN sometimes launching terrorist attacks on French civilians and the French military systematically torturing Algerian resistance fighters. Over time, French public opinion soured on the violence, and in 1962 an agreement recognizing Algerian independence was finally negotiated. (See the feature "Movement of Ideas Through Primary Sources: *The Wretched of the Earth*.")

Kenya, in East Africa, also had a large settler population. There, the main nationalist leader, **Jomo Kenyatta** (JOH-moh ken-YAH-tuh), had met with other African nationalist leaders, including Kwame Nkrumah, at the Fifth Pan-African Congress before returning home from studies in England in 1946 (see Chapter 28), and he hoped to develop a mass organization to force the British into negotiations. But an impatient group of Kenyan rebels took a more militant stand, forming a secret society, stealing arms from police stations, assassinating a collaborationist chief, and naming themselves the Land and Freedom Army. The British called them the Mau Mau and depicted them as "savages" who had returned to a "primitive" state of irrationality. Hopelessly outgunned by colonial forces, the rebels used their knowledge of the forest and the support of the local population to carry on their fight.

Jomo Kenyatta
(1891-1978) The British-educated leader of Kenya's nationalist movement after World War II, Kenyatta spent years in prison before becoming the first democratically elected leader of an independent Kenya in 1963.

Superior British firepower was overwhelming, though, and the government moved the rural population into fortified villages to cut them off from the rebels. By the late 1950s the rebellion was contained. Embarrassed by revelations of military abuse of African civilians, however, the British government now favored compromise with more moderate African nationalists. In 1963, Jomo Kenyatta became the prime minister of an independent Kenya.

The Wretched of the Earth

Frantz Fanon (1925–1961) was an advocate of Third World revolution, guerrilla warfare, and socialism. Born on the Caribbean island of Martinique in the French West Indies, Fanon volunteered for service in the Free French Army and was wounded during the liberation of France in 1944. After training in Paris as a psychiatrist, he was stationed in North Africa. During the Algerian war Fanon's medical practice included psychiatric treatment of both French practitioners and Arab and Berber victims of torture. From this experience he concluded that colonialism was intrinsically violent and could only be removed by violence. He joined the Algerian National Liberation Front and became a prominent spokesman for their cause. Fanon was dying of leukemia in 1961 while writing *The Wretched of the Earth*, his bitter indictment of colonialism.

❯ **Historical Thinking Skill:**
COMPARISON **What similarities do you find between Fanon's description of European culture and attitudes and Gandhi's description in Chapter 28?**

❯ **Historical Thinking Skill:**
CONTEXTUALIZATION **What experiences with European treatment of colonized people would have shaped Fanon's opinion about how to proceed through the decolonization process?**

Sources: From Frantz Fanon, *The Wretched of the Earth* (New York: Grove, 1963), pp. 36, 39–41, 43, 45, 59, 61, 312, 315–316. Reprinted by permission; David Macy, *Frantz Fanon* (New York: Picador, 2000), p. 483.

Decolonization is the meeting of two forces, opposed to each other by their very nature.... Their first encounter was marked by violence and their existence together—that is to say the exploitation of the native by the settler—was carried on by dint of a great array of bayonets and cannons....

The naked truth of decolonization evokes for us the searing bullets and bloodstained knives which emanate from it. For if the last shall be first, this will only come to pass after a murderous and decisive struggle between the two protagonists....

The settlers' town is a strongly built town, all made of stone and steel. It is a brightly lit town; the streets are all covered with asphalt, and the garbage cans swallow all the leavings, unseen, unknown, and hardly thought about.... The settlers' town is a town of white people, of foreigners....

The native town is a hungry town, starved for bread, of meat, of shoes, of coal, of light. The native town is a crouching village, a town on its knees, a town wallowing in the mire.... The look that the native turns on the settlers' town is a look of lust, a look of envy; it expresses his dreams of possession—all manner of possession: to sit at the settler's table, to sleep in the settler's bed, with his wife if possible. The colonized man is an envious man....

The violence which has ruled over the ordering of the colonial world, which has ceaselessly drummed the rhythm for the destruction of native social forms and broken up without reserve the systems of reference of the economy... that same violence will be claimed and taken over by the native at the moment when, deciding to embody history in his own person, he surges into the forbidden quarters....

As if to show the totalitarian character of colonial exploitation the settler paints the native as the quintessence of evil. Native society is not simply described as a society lacking in values.... The native is declared insensible to ethics; he represents not only the absence of values, but the negation of values... and in this sense he is the absolute evil....

The violence with which the supremacy of white values is affirmed and the aggressiveness which has permeated the victory of these values over the ways of life and thought of the native mean that, in revenge, the native laughs in mockery when Western values are mentioned in front of him.... In the period of decolonization, the colonized masses mock at these very values, insult them, and vomit them up....

[When the urban militants] get into the habit of talking to the peasants they discover that the rural masses have never ceased to pose the problem of their

liberation in terms of violence, of taking back the land from the foreigners, in terms of a national struggle. Everything is simple.... They discover a generous people prepared to make sacrifices, willing to give of itself, impatient and with a stony pride. One can understand that the encounter between militants who are being hunted by the police and these impatient masses, who are instinctually rebellious, can produce an explosive mixture of unexpected power....

Come, then, comrades, the European game has finally ended; we must find something different. We today can do everything so long as we do not imitate Europe, so long as we are not obsessed with desire to catch up with Europe.... European achievements, European techniques, and European style ought to no longer tempt us and to throw us off our balance.

When I search for Man in the technique and style of Europe, I see only a succession of negations of man, and an avalanche of murders.... It is a question of the Third World starting a new history of Man, a history which will have regard to the sometimes prodigious theses Europe has put forward, but which will also not forget Europe's crimes.... For Europe, for ourselves, for humanity, comrades, we must turn over a new leaf, we must work out new concepts, and try to set afoot a new man.

● **CONTEXT&CONNECTIONS** Kenyan nationalism had been stimulated immediately after the First World War when European settlers had taken over much of the best Kenyan land. In the interwar period, however, Africans found it difficult to connect such local grievances to broader organizational frameworks (see Chapter 28). Jomo Kenyatta's return in 1946, and the merging of popular demands with educated leadership, were thus part of a broader maturation in African nationalism after World War II. ●

In southern Africa, apartheid made compromise between white settlers and African nationalists impossible. Because South African leaders were adamantly anticommunist, governments in London and Washington usually overlooked their repressive policies. In response, the African National Congress, led by Nelson Mandela (see Chapter 31), organized a "defiance campaign" based on Gandhian tactics of non-violent resistance, and when that failed turned to a sabotage campaign. When Mandela was arrested and sentenced to life in prison in 1964, hopes for transforming South Africa were at an all-time low.

Still, absent the settler factor, once the British and French realized that the "winds of change" were blowing in the direction of African independence (as noted by the British prime minister in 1960), they managed the process of negotiating a handover of power peacefully, avoiding superpower intervention. Tragically, Belgium did not. The new Democratic Republic of the Congo descended into anarchy and became the site of a proxy war between the United States and the Soviet Union.

After King Leopold's brutal reign (see Chapter 26), the Belgian government had created a tightly centralized colonial administration. They did little to prepare Africans for independence: after eighty years of Belgian rule, only sixteen Africans in the entire Congo had university degrees. Still, with the Congo caught up in the nationalist excitement spreading across the continent, in 1960 the Belgians made hasty plans for independence, believing that a weak Congolese government would be susceptible to neocolonial control.

Patrice Lumumba A fiery nationalist, Lumumba faced insurmountable hurdles as prime minister of the Democratic Republic of the Congo, including political intrigues by the Belgian government and mining interests. The United States CIA cooperated in Lumumba's capture and brutal execution.

The Congolese National Movement won the election, and a government was formed by Prime Minister **Patrice Lumumba** (loo-MOOM-buh) (1925–1961). At the independence ceremony in 1960 the Belgian king made a patronizing speech praising his country's "civilizing mission" in Africa. Lumumba responded with a catalogue of Belgian crimes against Africans. *"Our wounds,"* he said, *"are still too fresh and painful for us to be able to erase them from our memories."* The speech made Lumumba a hero to African nationalists, but he was now regarded as a dangerous radical in Brussels and Washington.

Lumumba faced immediate challenges. African soldiers mutinied against their Belgian officers, and the mineral-rich province of Katanga seceded. When the United Nations sent in peacekeeping forces, Lumumba suspected their real purpose was to defend Western mining interests. After turning to the Soviet Union for military aid, Lumumba was branded a "communist," and—with the complicity of the CIA—he was arrested, beaten, and murdered by rivals. Rebel armies arose in several provinces. Finally Joseph Mobutu (mo-BOO-too), an army officer long on the CIA payroll, seized dictatorial power.

Che Guevara was among those who regarded Lumumba as a fallen hero and Mobutu as an American puppet. In 1965, Che joined up with Congolese rebels in the eastern part of the country. But he was to be disappointed at the rebels' lack of discipline and ideological commitment, later writing, *"I felt entirely alone in a way that I had never experienced before, neither in Cuba nor anywhere else, throughout my long pilgrimage across the world."** When Che returned to Cuba in 1966, the Congo was firmly under Joseph Mobutu's authoritarian control. The United States was the main power broker in Central Africa, allied with Mobutu to secure the mineral riches of the Congo, some of which were vital to defense and aerospace industries.

Patrice Lumumba (1925–1961) The first prime minister of the Democratic Republic of the Congo in 1960. He was deposed and assassinated by political rivals in 1961.

The Bandung Generation, 1955–1965

In 1955, the leaders of former colonial states met in Bandung (bahn-DOONG), Indonesia, for the first Asia-Africa conference, strategizing to avoid both neocolonialism and superpower intervention. The careers of the Indonesian, Indian, and Egyptian representatives at the Bandung Conference illustrate how difficult it was to remain nonaligned with either the United States or the Soviet Union.

*Quoted in David Sandison, *Che Guevara* (New York: St. Martin's Griffin, 1997), pp. 105, 108.

In 1945, Indonesian nationalist **Ahmed Sukarno** (1901–1970) and his party declared Indonesia free of both the Dutch and the Japanese, but it was not until 1950 and the defeat of Dutch reoccupation forces an independent nation was created from hundreds of islands scattered across thousands of miles. Sukarno sponsored the development of an Indonesian language with a simplified grammar as a way to unify Indonesia's great diversity of peoples. (Indonesia is the world's fourth largest nation and its largest Muslim-majority country.)

Ahmed Sukarno
(1901–1970) Leader in the struggle for Indonesian independence from the Netherlands, achieved in 1949. Indonesian military leaders, backed by the United States, thought Sukarno incapable of battling communism and removed him from power.

Sukarno was widely popular at first, but he had had no experience running a country and became erratic after declaring himself "president for life" in 1963. As his popularity waned, he faced a potent communist insurgency. Suspecting that Sukarno was either sympathetic to the communists or too weak to stave them off, the Indonesian military launched a murderous crackdown in 1964.

In 1967, General Suharto, a military commander backed by the United States, ousted Sukarno, suspended the constitution, and took power. The United States was glad, as in Mobutu's Congo, to have another dependable ally in the struggle against communism, especially in a nation whose strategic importance increased with the escalation of war in neighboring Vietnam. And as with Mobutu, the United States turned a blind eye to Suharto's corruption and authoritarianism.

India's prime minister, **Jawaharlal Nehru** (juh-wah-HER-lahl NAY-roo) (1889–1964), was more successful in securing his country's nonalignment. Like other leaders of newly independent nations, Nehru faced tremendous problems. As the Muslim League had urged (see Chapter 28), in 1947 the British had partitioned their Indian colony into two separate independent states: India and Pakistan. However, a substantial Hindu minority resided in Pakistan, and an even larger Muslim minority remained in the new state of India. In a climate of fear and uncertainty, millions of people tried desperately to cross to the country where they "belonged." In the intercommunal violence that followed, as many as 10 million people were dislocated, perhaps seventy-five thousand women were raped or abducted, and more than 1 million people lost their lives.

Jawaharlal Nehru
(1889–1964) Statesman who helped negotiate the end of British colonial rule in India and served as independent India's first prime minister from 1947 to 1964. Nehru was an influential advocate of the Non-Aligned Movement, refusing to choose sides in the Cold War.

Despite its violent birth and the enduring challenges of poverty and illiteracy, India emerged as the world's largest democracy. And while military tensions emerged on India's borders with Pakistan and China, Nehru kept his country nonaligned by purchasing military hardware from both the United States and the Soviet Union.

Next door in Pakistan, however, corruption and misrule led to a military seizure of power. A longstanding alliance began in 1958 when Pakistan's government entered into a defense agreement with the United States, which was concerned about India's military ties with the Soviet Union and anxious to have a reliably anticommunist ally in this strategic region. Despite India's nonalignment, therefore, the Cold War deeply affected South Asian politics.

Another prominent figure at Bandung was **Gamal Abdel Nasser** (1918–1970). Nasser, who came to power in a military coup in 1952, argued that Arabs should unite to fight both European neocolonialism and American imperialism. He embraced secular Arab nationalism, rejecting religion as a basis for politics, banning the Muslim Brotherhood, and elevating the military as a political force.

Gamal Abdel Nasser
(1918–1970) Prime minister of Egypt from 1954 to 1956 and president from 1956 to 1970. The nationalization of the Suez Canal in 1956 made Nasser a Pan-Arab hero, though the loss of the Six-Day War to Israel in 1967 badly damaged that reputation.

In 1954, Nasser successfully negotiated the withdrawal of British troops from the Suez Canal Zone (see Chapter 26). He also began plans for building the giant Aswan Dam on the Nile River to provide electricity for industrialization. He approached Britain and the United States for aid but, sticking to his nonaligned principles, refused to join an anti-Soviet alliance as a precondition. In 1956, after they refused further assistance, Nasser proclaimed the nationalization of the Suez Canal to finance the dam, outraging the British government.

The Nonaligned Movement After the Bandung Conference of 1955, leaders of the Nonaligned Movement continued annual summit meetings. In Belgrade in 1960 we see Jawaharlal Nehru (India), Kwame Nkrumah (Ghana), Gamal Abdel Nasser (Egypt), Ahmed Sukarno (Indonesia), and Marshall Tito (Yugoslavia). While the others were most concerned with maintaining distance from former colonial powers and the United States, Tito's goal was to avoid Soviet domination of his socialist regime.

The Suez Crisis of 1956 deepened when the British, French, and Israelis, after clandestine negotiations, sent troops to the Canal Zone. However, the intervention lacked American support, and the British and Israelis withdrew when confronted with Egyptian opposition and international criticism. A triumphant Nasser became a hero across the Arab world for standing his ground, and the Aswan Dam was later completed with Soviet aid.

Nasser's reputation in the Arab world was grounded in his support of the Palestinian cause and belligerence toward Israel. After the British relinquished their control in 1947 a United Nations plan would have partitioned Palestine into separate Arab and Jewish states. In 1948, when neighboring Arab states refused to accept that UN plan, Zionist leaders declared the independence of Israel. Egypt, Lebanon, Syria, Jordan, and Iraq immediately attacked. Nasser himself fought in the Pan-Arab army.

• **CONTEXT&CONNECTIONS** The British had taken over the Ottoman province of Palestine following World War I under the *Mandate System* (see Chapter 27). In the interwar years the British struggled to keep the peace, especially after the rise of *Adolph Hitler* in Germany increased the pressure to allow greater Jewish immigration from Europe (Chapter 28). In 1947, still recovering from war, the British handed over responsibility for Palestine to the new *United Nations* (Chapter 29). •

As Arab refugees fled the fighting, some driven from their homes by Israeli soldiers, the Israelis routed the Arab armies, and the Israeli government expanded its borders beyond what the UN planners had envisioned. Shocked and humiliated, many Arabs thereafter looked to Nasser as their best hope to destroy Israel and return Palestinian refugees to their native land.

Nasser's reputation, however, was severely damaged after he made a series of threatening moves that prompted a preemptive Israeli attack. In the Six-Day War of 1967, Israeli forces occupied Egypt's Sinai Desert, Syria's Golan Heights, and the West Bank of the Jordan River. Israeli occupation of predominantly Arab East Jerusalem was particularly galling. U.S. support had helped make Israeli victory possible, a cause of resentment across the Muslim world. The Soviet Union gave rhetorical support to the Palestinians, but little material and military aid.

All those who participated at the Bandung meeting were aware that Cold War entanglements would compromise their ability to move their nations forward. They had different levels of success in achieving the nonalignment to which they had dedicated themselves at Bandung. Sukarno was the least successful, supplanted by a military dictatorship allied with the United States. Nehru was by far the most successful, maintaining India's status as a genuinely nonaligned democracy, though his friendship with the Soviets led the United States to arm neighboring Pakistan. In Egypt, Nasser chose to ally more closely with the Soviet Union after the Suez Crisis, but only because the Soviets were enemies of the United States, Israel's main ally. The Cold War created a difficult balancing act for Third World leaders who subscribed to the principles of nonalignment.

Vietnam: The Cold War in Southeast Asia, 1956–1974

As in Indonesia, Vietnamese nationalists had to fight colonial reoccupation forces to win their independence. After helping drive the Japanese from his country during World War II, **Ho Chi Minh** had declared an independent Democratic Republic of Vietnam in 1945, explicitly referring to the American Declaration of Independence in asserting the right of the Vietnamese people to be free from foreign rule. Ignoring Ho's declaration, France sent forces to re-establish colonial control, only to be defeated by the Viet Minh at Dien Bien Phu (dyen byen FOO) in 1954. French military officers told their government that they could not wage two counterinsurgencies—in Algeria and Vietnam—simultaneously. Since Algeria was home to a million French citizens, it was the greater priority, and the French finally withdrew from Indochina.

Ho Chi Minh
(1890–1969) Vietnamese revolutionary and Marxist who led military campaigns against Japanese invaders, French colonialists, and American and South Vietnamese forces.

At the multination Geneva Conference, Vietnam was temporarily partitioned into northern and southern regions, pending national elections. Fearing that Ho Chi Minh's Communists would win those elections, the United States supported the formation of a separate South Vietnamese regime. Conflict between the two Vietnams intensified as the United States supplied the south with weapons and military training, while North Vietnam sponsored a southern-based rebel army, the National Front for the Liberation of South Vietnam (or the Vietcong).

In 1964, President Lyndon Johnson (in office 1963–1969) began full-scale war against the communist regime in Hanoi, and by the next year two hundred thousand American combatants were in Southeast Asia. The policy of the United States hinged on success in creating a legitimate nationalist government in South Vietnam, a goal that was never achieved. Leaders in the southern capital of Saigon never came close to replicating the leadership that Ho Chi Minh had achieved in the north through years of fighting the Japanese and French.

Despite massive bombing attacks on North Vietnam, the Vietcong grew in strength. American soldiers were often unable to distinguish guerrilla soldiers from civilians. At home, Americans were incredulous when their troops brutally

Vietnamese Protest On June 11, 1963, Thich Quang Duc, a Vietnamese Buddhist monk, burned himself to death on a Saigon street. His self-immolation was a protest of the policies of the U.S.-backed South Vietnamese government, which many Buddhists thought favored the Catholic minority.

slaughtered the villagers of My Lai (mee lie) in 1969 and spread poisonous clouds of defoliating chemicals across the Vietnamese countryside. Images of burning children fleeing napalm bomb blasts sickened global audiences. In this first "televised war," images of death and destruction were transmitted around the world.

In 1968, the Vietcong took the fight straight to the South Vietnamese capital of Saigon during the Tet Offensive. In 1969, as antiwar protests spread across American college campuses and anti-American feelings rose in much of Europe, Asia, Africa, and Latin America, the new administration of President Richard Nixon (in office 1969–1974) promised "peace with honor" through even more intensive bombing of North Vietnam and the replacement of American ground forces with South Vietnamese ones. Demoralized and corrupt, the South Vietnamese government and military were not up to the task. On April 30, 1975, after the United States withdrew its ground troops, Communist forces entered Saigon, renamed it Ho Chi Minh City, and reunified the country under their dictatorship.

• **CONTEXT&CONNECTIONS** Entering the Vietnam War, Americans were inclined to think that any fight against communism was necessarily a fight for freedom. But while the Viet Minh were dedicated Marxist-Leninist revolutionaries, their movement had its roots in Vietnam's long history of resistance to foreign intrusion: China in ancient times, Japan and France more recently, and now the United States (see Chapters 16, 26, and 29). Nationalism was thus key to Viet Minh success. •

Meanwhile, the war in Southeast Asia had global reverberations as it galvanized opposition to U.S. military actions, especially among college students on the political left. For some antiwar protestors, the war was simply wrong and should be ended right away. As a member of the Vietnam Veterans Against the War put it in 1971: "*How do you ask a man to be the last man to die for a mistake?**"

A more radical view of Vietnam critiqued the conflict not as a "mistake" but as the logical outcome of U.S. imperialism in defense of international capital, with the heroic Viet Minh unmasking the American threat to peace and progress.

---

*John Kerry, Statement to the Senate Committee on Foreign Relations, April 23, 1971. http://www2.iath.virginia.edu/sixties/HTML_docs/Resources/Primary/Manifestos/VVAW_Kerry_Senate.html.

Che Guevara, as he traveled the Third World promoting the cause of revolution on the Cuban model, made this point insistently: *"Create Two, Three, or Many Vietnams!"* Guevara declared. *"And let us develop a true proletarian internationalism."** Guevara's call resonated with some young activists who rejected both the exploitative model of U.S. capitalism and the dreary state-dominated socialism of the U.S.S.R. They looked instead to the more scintillating revolutionary models of the Third World, and by 1968 dorm rooms around the world featured posters of Che Guevara and Mao Zedong. Glorification of Third World revolution became just one of the many strands of political and cultural upheaval that came to define "the Sixties."

A Time of Upheaval, 1966–1974

People who grew up during "the Sixties" remember it as a time of political, social, and cultural turmoil. The Civil Rights Movement in the United States, under the leadership of figures like Dr. Martin Luther King, Jr., paralleled other liberation movements taking place around the world. Young people took center stage, proclaiming that the world could, and should, be made a place of peace, love, and justice. In 1963, the poet-musician Bob Dylan captured the spirit of the time:

Come mothers and fathers throughout the land
And don't criticize what you can't understand
Your sons and your daughters are beyond your command
Your old road is rapidly aging
Please get out of the new one if you can't lend your hand
For the times they are a-changing.†

This global trend toward greater youth involvement in politics and society arose among students who had come of age after the Second World War, their dissatisfaction with the status quo peaking in 1968, a "year of revolution" that saw battles between protestors and authorities in cities as diverse as Paris, Chicago, Mexico City, and Prague.

Meanwhile, across Latin America a vast gulf separated opposing camps. On the political right, traditional economic oligarchies, foreign interests, military officers, and Catholic bishops confronted an increasingly radicalized left of students, academics, parish priests, labor leaders, and professional revolutionaries inspired by Che Guevara. The peasant-based revolutionary approach of Mao Zedong also drew the interest of Latin American revolutionaries, even as Mao's own Great Proletarian Cultural Revolution (1966–1970) spread chaos and hardship across the world's largest nation.

In most of the world, existing authorities had re-established control by the 1970s, though the Sixties spirit of idealism endured in the environmental movement, feminism, and educational reform. At the same time, diplomats stabilized the international order with a new emphasis on arms reductions and a multilateral spirit of "understanding," or *détente*.

---

*Ernesto Guevara, "Create Two, Three, or Many Vietnams," cited in *Sources of Global History since 1900*, ed. James H. Overfield, 2d ed. (Boston: Wadsworth, 2013), pp. 342–345.

†Bob Dylan, "The Times They Are A-Changing." Copyright © 1963, 1964 by Warner Bros. Inc.; renewed 1991, 1992 by Special Rider Music. Reprinted courtesy of Special Rider Music.

The Sixties: The Rising Expectations of Surging Youth

"The Sixties" refers more to an attitude than a strict chronology, with massive social, political, and cultural changes appearing in some places as early as the 1950s (among "beat" poets in New York, for example) but not until the early 1970s (or never at all) elsewhere. But the common denominator was generational: it was the children growing up in the wake of the Second World War who prompted the upheavals of the time. The "baby boom" phenomenon was a global one: by the mid-1960s children born at the end of the war were turning twenty and making their mark on the world.

Their agitation stemmed from their desire for so much more than their parents, who had come of age during the Great Depression and the Second World War, were willing to accept. College students were at the forefront of this trend. As college enrollments surged around the world, parents were astonished by the rebellion of their children, thinking that they should be grateful for all the work and sacrifice that had made their advanced study possible. The generation gap widened when the kids responded "*never trust anyone over thirty*."

In the industrialized world, rising expectations accompanied the grand leaps of productivity that came with postwar recovery, the period from 1945 to 1975 that the French call *Les Trente Glorieuses* ("The Glorious Thirty"). And while economies were growing, social inequalities were declining, meaning that even working-class people were able to afford an extended range of consumer goods, educate their children, own property, and save for retirement. For those who had experienced the privations of the first half of the twentieth century, it was a golden time. Teenagers who previously would have been working at age sixteen to help support their families could now delay adulthood and devote time to "finding themselves," often going far beyond the cultural legacies of their forebears.

An emphasis on cultural authenticity led many young people to reject corporate commercialism and embrace "roots" music from around the world, to return to a more natural diet and vegetarianism, to join the burgeoning new environmental movement, and to reject the "rat race" of consumerism for a simpler, sometimes communal living style. The "hippie" movement of the late 1960s was awash with these and many other exploratory trends, including smoking marijuana and using psychedelic drugs to open consciousness, to "*tune in, turn on, and drop out*."

Intense interest in international influences was part of that quest, whether it meant identifying with political revolutionaries like Che Guevara or with spiritual practices of foreign cultures. Eastern religions achieved renewed popularity. (See the feature "Visual Evidence in Primary Sources: *Sgt. Pepper's Lonely Hearts Club Band*.")

The youth movement was also, fundamentally, a sexual revolution, especially after 1960, when the "pill" went on the market. Though contraceptives were opposed by religious authorities and banned in some places, their availability in a cheap, convenient form under women's control facilitated sexual experimentation.

AP® THEMES

What led to the changes in expectations for gender roles in the 1960s?

● **CONTEXT&CONNECTIONS** In the 1950s the now elderly Margaret Sanger, a "first wave" feminist and a proponent of birth control, raised funds for research into oral contraception. Meanwhile feminists revived the ideals of her friend *Emma Goldman* (Chapter 27), supporting Goldman's position that women must have freedom of choice in partners, in employment, and in child rearing. In fact, Goldman's ideas appealed strongly to the counterculture at large, with her insistence that individuals be free from both government intrusion *and* corporate exploitation. ●

At the same time, new thinking about gender roles transformed women's rights. Even though women had achieved legal equality in much of the world, their opportunities remained sharply limited; the common expectation was that young women need not advance in their careers because they would quickly marry and devote themselves to motherhood. In the 1960s, however, "second wave" feminists demanded full equality of social and economic rights.

1968: A Year of Revolution

In the industrial world, countercultural exploration was intertwined with postwar affluence. Poorer children, of course, might not have much opportunity for self-exploration before realities like military service, the need for employment, or parenthood intervened. The same was true for less affluent parts of the world—the Soviet-dominated Second World and the teeming and diverse Third World. But even here the Sixties brought rising expectations. The global nature of youthful rebellion in the Sixties is perhaps best demonstrated by the simultaneous outbreak in 1968 of large-scale student protests in nations as diverse as the United States, France, Czechoslovakia, and Mexico.

In the "summer of love" in 1967, psychedelic art and music and slogans such as *"make love, not war"* emanated from U.S. college campuses. But harsher realities soon tempered the hopes of feminists, civil rights advocates, and student leaders. Drug use ruined lives, peace marches turned violent, and demonstrations resulted in mass arrests. In 1968 two voices for peace and moderation—civil rights leader Martin Luther King, Jr. and Democratic presidential candidate Robert F. Kennedy—were assassinated. Violence spread through American cities.

During the 1968 Democratic National Convention, American television viewers watched in horror as Chicago police bludgeoned youthful protesters; a few months later, Republican Richard Nixon won the presidency. To those Americans appalled by the ferment of the Sixties, Nixon was an experienced, thoughtful anticommunist who would restore order. To those who dreamt of a new age of peace and justice, Nixon represented everything that was wrong with "the establishment." The nation became even more bitterly divided after Ohio Army National Guardsmen shot four student protesters to death at Kent State University in the spring of 1970.

In Europe, Paris was a major center of student unrest. As in the United States, the number of university students had risen sharply in the post-1945 period. After three college students were arrested for occupying a dean's office, students all over France rose to their defense. In May 1968, student marchers, assaulted by riot police, built barricades of overturned cars and garbage cans.

Whereas in the United States most working Americans, including most union members, tended to side with the forces of "law and order," in France the major trade unions joined the protests. Two million French workers went on strike, some taking over factories and proclaiming that their bosses were unnecessary. Art students expressed this anarchistic spirit on posters they plastered around Paris, with slogans such as *"Be realistic, ask for the impossible!"* and *"It is forbidden to forbid!"*

In response, French president Charles de Gaulle appeared on television to proclaim: *"The whole French people . . . are being prevented from living a normal existence by . . . Reds and Anarchists . . . preventing students from studying, workers from working."* But he also offered concessions: an increase in the minimum wage and new elections. De Gaulle's re-election in late 1968, like the election of U.S. conservative Richard Nixon, made it clear that most voters wanted a return to "normal existence." After workers were appeased with new contracts, and French students left campus for the summer, the forces of "law and order" reasserted themselves.

In eastern Europe, students also played a prominent role in the **Prague Spring** of 1968. By the mid-1960s, discontent with the stifling conditions of

Prague Spring
(1968) An attempt by political reformers in Czechoslovakia to reform the communist government and create "socialism with a human face." The Soviet Union invaded Czechoslovakia, ending this attempt at reform and reimposing communist orthodoxy.

Sgt. Pepper's Lonely Hearts Club Band

Listen and compare two songs by the British group the Beatles, "I Want to Hold Your Hand" (1963) and "A Day in the Life" (1967), to get an idea of the depth and rapidity of cultural change in the mid-1960s. In a mere four years, John Lennon, Paul McCartney, George Harrison, and Ringo Starr went from pop stars adored by screaming adolescent girls to artists whose words, music, and rapidly evolving public images made them globally influential figures.

Tribute is paid to the Rolling Stones, the Beatles' main rival on the rock music scene, and Bob Dylan, a strong influence on their musical development. ***Given your knowledge of 1960s popular culture, what ideas and emotions would this image have evoked at the time of its first release?***

Michael Ochs Archives/Getty Images

John Lennon's suggestion that Jesus, Gandhi, and Hitler all be included was vetoed. Lennon had been criticized the previous year for declaring that the Beatles were "*more popular than Jesus,*" and the inclusion of Hitler would have been even more offensive. An image of Gandhi was included at the photo shoot but was later removed at the request of the record company.

Millions anxiously anticipated the release of their new album, *Sgt. Pepper's Lonely Hearts Club Band*, on June 1, 1967. Their albums had become more complex in musical structure and more ambitious in lyrical content, influenced by the highly conceptual songwriting of Bob Dylan, an opening of the imagination commonly attributed to marijuana and psychedelic drugs, and the brilliance of their producer/engineer George Martin, with his strong background in classical music. While recording *Sgt. Pepper*, the group traveled to India for training in transcendental meditation, a journey eagerly covered by the global media and one that provided further artistic stimulation.

The album lived up to expectations. No one had ever heard anything like it before. But the album was more than just a collection of songs. Eager fans sought symbolic meanings not only in the sometimes obscure lyrics but also in the visual images that adorned the large gatefold cover of the album. The Beatles were clearly playing with ideas of celebrity and shifting identity, for example, by creating the persona of "Billy Shears" as front man of the mythical Sgt. Pepper's Band, and by posing for the album cover next to wax models of themselves circa 1964. The resulting image was studied for meaning by millions of young people around the world.

1

Michael Ochs Archives/Getty Images

The inclusion of figurines of the Beatles (*a*) from Madame Tussauds wax museum highlights the transformation of the group's visual self-representation between 1964 and 1967.

Scattered among the historical figures and film stars are three Indian spiritual leaders (*b*), included at the suggestion of George Harrison. The influence of both Indian instrumentation and Hindu philosophy on Harrison can be heard on the album track "Within You Without You."

2

Michael Ochs Archives/Getty Images

3

Michael Ochs Archives/Getty Images

Famous historical figures include Karl Marx (*c*), T. E. Lawrence ("Lawrence of Arabia") (*d*), and writers Edgar Allan Poe (*e*), Lewis Carroll (*f*), and Oscar Wilde (*g*). Actors include Marlon Brando (*h*), Marilyn Monroe (*i*), and Stan Laurel (*j*).

Soviet-imposed communism was growing. Early in 1968 workers' strikes and students' protests forced the resignation of the hardline communist leadership.

The new head of the Czechoslovak Communist Party, Alexander Dubcek (DOOB-chek), promised *"socialism with a human face,"* including freedom of speech and association as well as more liberal, market-oriented economic policies. The Czech public rallied to Dubcek's cause, and students and teachers took advantage of the new atmosphere to discussed how economic justice and democratic freedoms could be achieved within a socialist framework.

Fearing that the movement toward liberalization would spread, the Soviet leadership ordered a half-million Soviet and Warsaw Pact troops into Czechoslovakia. They replaced Dubcek with a more compliant Czech communist leader. Reformers in Czechoslovakia, as well as in Poland, Hungary, and the Soviet Union itself, were put on notice: no changes to the status quo would be allowed.

• **CONTEXT&CONNECTIONS** Twenty years after the Prague Spring, *Mikhail Gorbachev* (Chapter 31) would pursue similar reforms in the Soviet Union; his efforts were unsuccessful and the U.S.S.R. slid into oblivion. At that same time, former activists from the Prague Spring were leading anti-Soviet protests, including Vaclav Havel, the first democratically-elected president of Czechoslovakia. •

Mexico was another country where a large school-age population showed discontent. But while Mexican society was changing rapidly, Mexican politics were not. The Party of Institutional Revolution (PRI) was the elitist, bureaucratic, and corrupt descendant of the old National Revolutionary Party (see Chapter 27). Since the PRI did not allow free elections, Mexican advocates of political change had no choice but to go to the streets.

The tensions of 1968 began when riot police used force to break up a fight between two student groups. Over a hundred thousand students, with support from many of their teachers and parents, went on strike, marching through the city shouting *"¡Mexico, Libertad!"* ("Mexico, Liberty!"). The timing of the protests was particularly awkward. The Summer Olympic Games were to be held in Mexico City in October. Desperate to project a positive image to the worldwide television audience, the government decided to crack down.

Tlatelolco Massacre (1968) Massacre that occurred when ten thousand university students, faculty, and other supporters gathered in Tlatelolco Plaza in Mexico City to protest the closing of the Mexican National University; government forces opened fire and killed three hundred people.

The result was the **Tlatelolco Massacre**, in which shooting broke out as thousands of people protested the closing of the National University. The government said the protesters fired first, a contention contradicted by many eyewitnesses watching from apartments lining the square. Hundreds were killed, but the Olympic Games went on as planned, and most of the world heard nothing about the bloodshed at Tlatelolco (tlah-tel-OHL-koh).

Although student protesters in the United States, France, Czechoslovakia, and Mexico were unable to radically change the status quo, in the longer view of history the impact of this generation seems unmistakable. The spirit of the 1960s informed social movements in the decades to come, bringing idealism and activism to music and the arts, educational reform, environmental sustainability, and gender equality. The cause of civil rights had been greatly advanced, with traditionally marginalized groups organizing to secure their rights, as when gays and lesbians came out to demand decriminalization as well as social and political equality. Of course, conservative counter-reactions to such trends continued, as in Latin America, where military governments targeted student activists for arrest, torture, and murder.

AP® THEMES

What kinds of political reforms were student protestors calling for in the United States, France, and Mexico in the 1960s?

Death and Dictatorship in Latin America, 1967–1975

After his failed sojourn to Central Africa, Che Guevara was still looking for a place where a dedicated band of rebels could provide the spark for revolution. In 1967, he headed for Bolivia, convinced that its corrupt government would fall swiftly once the oppressed indigenous population rose against it. But long-exploited Andeans were wary of Spanish-speaking outsiders who claimed to be fighting on their behalf. Short on rations, Che's rebel band wandered in the frigid mountains. In September 1967, Guevara was captured by Bolivian soldiers and executed as a CIA agent stood by.

Guevara's death occurred as dictatorships arose throughout Latin America, with authoritarian governments justifying repression in the name of anticommunism. One example is the overthrow of Chile's democratic government after an alliance of left-wing parties led by the Marxist **Salvador Allende** (uh-YEN-day) (1908–1973) won a bitterly contested election in 1970. Chilean businessmen and landowners strongly opposed Allende's effort to build a socialist economy, and his nationalization of the copper mines alarmed American economic interests. In the fall of 1973, with the backing of the United States, the military staged a coup. Allende committed suicide as a force commanded by General Augusto Pinochet (ah-GOOS-toh pin-oh-CHET) stormed the Presidential Palace in Santiago.

Salvador Allende
(1908–1973) Socialist leader, elected president of Chile in 1970. His government was overthrown in a U.S.-backed military coup in 1973, during which Allende took his own life.

Pinochet hired American advisors to institute free-market economic policies and welcomed foreign investment, while at the same time dismantling the institutions of Chilean democracy. Thousands of students and union leaders, like the couple Che had once met on the open road, were tortured and killed. (See the feature "World History in Today's World: Michelle Bachelet and Dilma Rousseff: From Protest to Leadership in South America.")

By the mid-1970s military governments prevailed across South America. In Argentina, thousands of students vanished as the soldiers took control. For years, desperate mothers would hold silent vigils in central Buenos Aires, holding pictures of their children, the *desaparecidos* (DEH-say-pah-re-SEE-dohs) ("disappeared ones"). Many of their sons and daughters had been killed, some drugged and pushed out of airplanes over the open sea. Successive administrations in Washington supported murderous regimes like those of Chile and Argentina, ever fearful that communism might gain advantage in "America's own backyard."

The Great Proletarian Cultural Revolution, 1965–1974

After 1965, China's version of the "youth revolution" took a bizarre and dangerous direction when Mao began organizing young people into **Red Guard** units, who were taught that Mao himself was the source of all wisdom. His thoughts were collected in a "little red book" that became the bible of the Red Guard movement, waved enthusiastically in the air by millions of students when paying homage to the "Great Helmsman."

Red Guard
Young people who rallied to the cause of Maoism during the Great Proletarian Cultural Revolution. As their enthusiasm got out of control, the Red Guards spread anarchy across the People's Republic of China.

Mao used the Red Guards to attack his enemies within the Communist Party, the "rightists" and "experts" who had resisted him during the Great Leap Forward. An atmosphere of anarchy soon prevailed, as Red Guards attacked party offices, publicly humiliated their teachers, destroyed cultural artifacts that linked China to its past, and harassed anyone they thought needed "re-education." Educated Chinese were sent to farms and factories to humble themselves and absorb the authentic revolutionary spirit of the masses. Many died.

By 1968, this Cultural Revolution had reduced the country to chaos, its economy at a standstill. Pragmatic Communist leaders finally convinced Mao to allow

Michelle Bachelet and Dilma Rousseff: From Protest to Leadership in South America

Since the 1980s, Chile and Brazil have both fully emerged from the darkness of military authoritarianism as vibrant democracies. In Chile, Michelle Bachelet (in office 2006–2010 and 2014–2018) and, in Brazil, Dilma Rousseff (in office 2011–2018) took unusual paths to leadership, as both had earlier been imprisoned for political reasons.

Michelle Bachelet had a privileged upbringing, since her father was a brigadier general in the Chilean Air Force. When Alberto Bachelet opposed his colleague Augusto Pinochet's coup in 1973, however, he was arrested and tortured, and he died soon after. His wife and his daughter, Michelle, were also detained and abused, but were lucky when a sympathetic commander arranged for their exile. The communist German Democratic Republic accepted them and gave Michelle Bachelet a medical education. By the 1980s she had returned home, working in health care while connecting with the nascent prodemocracy movement.

Brazilian President Dilma Rousseff was politically active even as a teenager, opposing the military government that had taken power in 1964. In the late 1960s, she was a part of a revolutionary movement that allied itself with Cuba and took up arms against the dictatorship before being captured, imprisoned, and tortured. After her release and the return of Brazilian democracy, she was mentored by the hugely popular President Luiz Inácio Lula da Silva (in office 2003–2011). During that period, she served as his chief of staff and as chair of Petrobas, Brazil's state oil company (a role for which she was later implicated in a huge corruption scandal) before succeeding Lula as the Workers' Party candidate for president.

Though Bachelet and Rousseff both started from the far left of the political spectrum, and while both suffered from conservative military authoritarianism, they have followed pragmatic, neoliberal policies recognizing the central role of private capital in economic growth (see Chapter 31), even while tailoring their policies toward alleviation of poverty and reduction of economic inequality. Even today, that is a difficult balancing act. Thirty years ago, one could hardly have imagined socialists in Chile and Brazil sitting down with bankers to work out solutions to the country's problems, with the generals sitting on the sidelines obeying the rule of law!

the People's Liberation Army to restore governmental authority. Now, Red Guards themselves faced "downward transfer" to remote villages and labor camps. But while authorities curbed the worst excesses of the Cultural Revolution, a bitter power struggle took place behind the scenes. A radical faction called the "Gang of Four," led by Mao's wife, Jiang Qing (jyahng CHING), schemed to restore the Cultural Revolution. On the other side were pragmatists like Deng Xiaoping (DUNG shee-yao-PING), an "expert" who was struggling to regain his influence. With an aging Mao no longer in complete command, Deng and the "expert" faction reasserted themselves.

AP® THEMES

What was the impact of Mao's Cultural Revolution on Chinese society and politics?

The pragmatists scored a victory in 1972 when the American president Richard Nixon came to Beijing. Relations between the two countries had long been severed. But the Chinese were worried about their long border with the Soviet Union, where armed confrontations had recently taken place. Although a die-hard anticommunist, Nixon judged that better relations with communist China would increase his own bargaining power with the U.S.S.R. and might help the United States extricate itself from Vietnam.

While the shadow of the Cultural Revolution still hung over China at the time of Mao's death in 1976, the eventual victory of Deng Xiaoping's pragmatic faction over the Gang of Four sent the People's Republic of China in an entirely new, market-oriented direction (see Chapter 31). But the people of China had paid a terrible price for Mao's political adventures: the Great Leap Forward and the Great Proletarian Cultural Revolution had killed tens of millions.

Everett Collection Historical/Alamy

Cultural Revolution Poster Propaganda posters featuring Mao's image and references to the "little red book" were ubiquitous during the Cultural Revolution. This one depicts a soldier sacrificing himself to save a comrade while crossing a river. The slogan reads: "*Establish a new standard of merit for the people: just as the heroic 4th platoon comrade Li Wenzhong worked to defeat selfishness and promote the common good, we should convert Chairman Mao's most recent directive into action!*"

Détente and Challenges to Bipolarity

The strained relations between the United States and the Soviet Union play out in images from the early 1960s—Soviet premier Nikita Khrushchev banging his shoe on a table at the United Nations while angrily denouncing American imperialism, and President John F. Kennedy pledging to put American astronauts on the moon before the end of the decade. In 1957, the Soviets had launched *Sputnik* (SPUHT-nick), the first artificial satellite to orbit the earth. In response, America developed the Apollo space program, accomplishing the first manned mission to the moon in 1969. Indeed, the Cold War propelled continuous technological innovation, as each side poured huge resources into applied scientific research.

By the mid-1960s, a state of reluctant coexistence between the superpowers was becoming the norm. Both nations faced increasing challenges, domestic and foreign. While the United States was dealing with social discord related to the Civil Rights Movement and the Vietnam War, the Soviet Union wrestled with poor living standards. The Soviet people had guaranteed employment, universal education, and health care, but they faced persistent shortages of consumer goods, and those available were often shoddy. Moscow was looking for some breathing space in which to develop its domestic economy.

In theory, the division between East and West, between capitalism and communism, was absolute. In reality, both the United States and the U.S.S.R. were having increasing difficulty controlling their respective blocs. It was the strained relations between Moscow and Beijing after 1960 that gave Richard Nixon an opening with the People's Republic of China. Meanwhile, in 1957 the Treaty of Rome laid the foundation for what would become the European Economic Community, as western European leaders began to emerge from under the economic and political umbrella of the United States.

Although the Cold War divisions appeared likely to remain for the foreseeable future, the two superpowers began to soften their rhetoric and seek ways to live together in a spirit of ***détente*** (DAY-tahnt). The greatest achievement was the U.S.-U.S.S.R. Strategic Arms Limitation Treaty (SALT) of 1972, which froze the number of ballistic missiles in the possession of each nation. The specter of nuclear war never disappeared, but in the mid-1970s it began to recede.

détente The easing of hostility between nations, specifically the movement in the 1970s to negotiate arms limitations treaties to reduce tensions between the Eastern and Western blocs during the Cold War.

Idealism Amid Cold War Constraints

Painful as it was, the Second World War had opened new vistas for humanity by upending the status quo across much of the world. Hope for liberation from confining traditions became a global theme. Idealism took many forms in the post-war world, even as the Cold War and the threat of nuclear annihilation cast heavy shadows over the quest for a better future.

In the Soviet sphere, after Stalin's death in 1953 repeated uprisings in the U.S.S.R.'s captive states, even in the face of harsh reprisals, showed an intense longing for more prosperous and open societies. Those idealistic visions of a better future were consistently crushed, however, as during the Hungarian Uprising of 1956 and the Prague Spring of 1968. In the world's largest communist state, the People's Republic of China, Mao Zedong's Great Leap Forward and the Great Proletarian Cultural Revolution could themselves be viewed as versions of idealism, distorted in their enthusiasm and risking anarchy in the name of revolution. In this case, the pragmatism of Deng Xiaoping (see Chapter 31) seemed a safer alternative.

In the United States, the idealism of the "Sixties" had splintered into numerous social movements by the next decade, with traditionally marginalized groups organizing for greater equality. Advocates of Black Power, second wave feminists, Chicano and Native American rights activists, and leaders of the nascent gay rights movement all demanded recognition. Though the environmental movement offered the prospect of unity around a compelling common interest, the political left remained fractured even as conservative critics of "diversity" initiatives regained momentum with the election of President Ronald Reagan in 1980 (see Chapter 31).

A similar fracturing of social movements was evident in Western Europe, though here idealism had a more mainstream outlet: the building of a "new Europe" in the context of the European Economic Community (EEC). The path from the EEC to the European Union (see Chapter 31) was thought of in terms of economic prosperity, but also in terms of peace. With the exception of Margaret Thatcher's United Kingdom, by the 1980s the states of Europe were strongly supportive of diplomatic *détente*

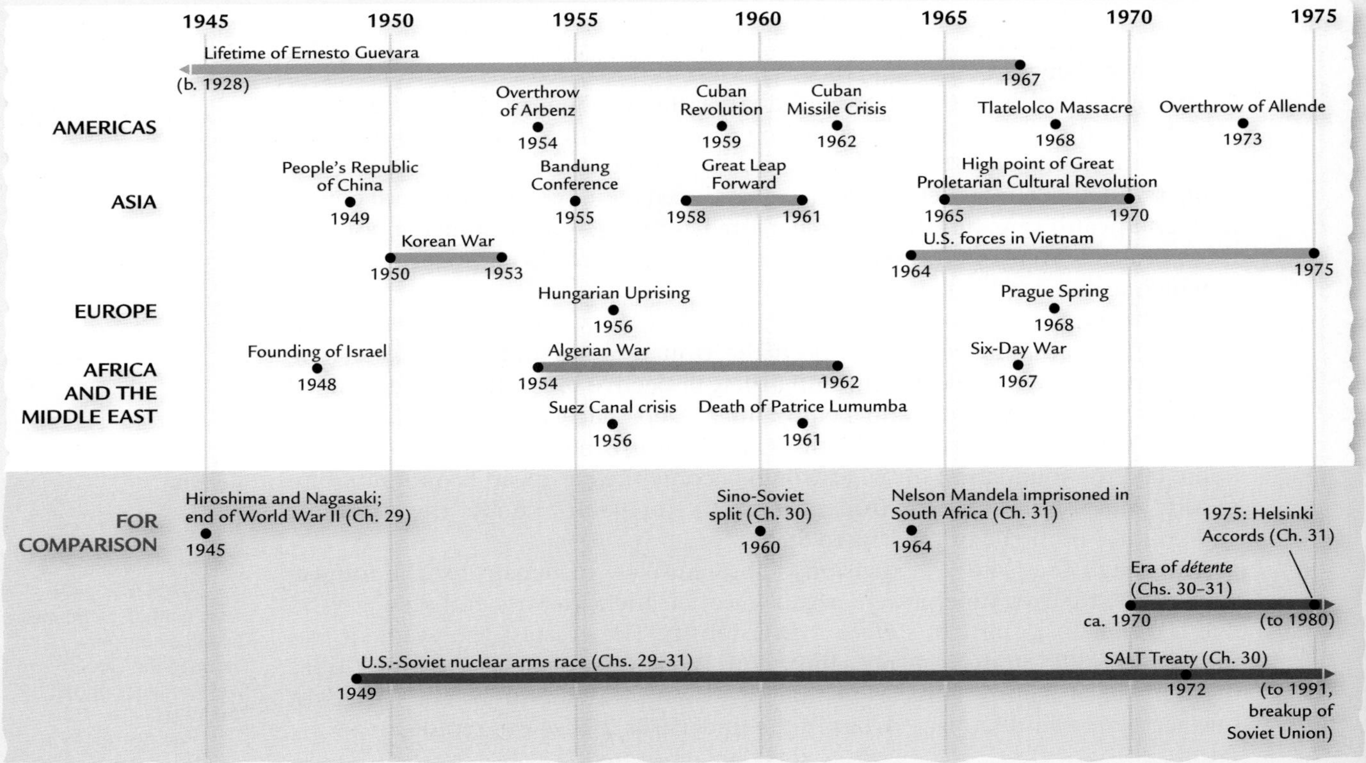

and arms reductions treaties, what the Germans called an *Ostpolitik* ("eastern politics") intended to defuse Cold War tensions. Thus in Western Europe the peace agenda of the Sixties endured.

In the Third World, dreams of revolutionary transformation persisted throughout the 1970s and 1980s, for example, in Latin America, where armed uprising might seem the only way to displace vicious military regimes, or in South Africa, where the racist apartheid regime was well-entrenched and heavily armed. It was here that young idealists might find in Che Guevara a lodestar for the new world they hoped to create. Then the Soviet Union fell, and with the onset of globalization the whole ideological context in which Guevara lived his life was gone.

In 1997, after lying for two decades in an unmarked Bolivian grave, Ernesto Guevara's body was returned to Havana, receiving a hero's welcome and full state honors. After the fall of communism in the Soviet Union, and its transformation in China into a form of market socialism, was Guevara's legacy still relevant? The inequalities and injustices that drove him to a life of revolutionary combat still exist wherever the life chances of the world's poor and their children are stunted by the greed of the powerful. But Che's solution no longer attracts many followers or sympathizers. The idea that the salvation of the "wretched of the earth" will come through mass uprisings sparked by single-minded revolutionaries now seems naïve, after a century in which all such attempts—under Lenin, Mao, Castro, and others—led to cruel and stifling dictatorships.

To young people raised after 1990, the post-war world, with its scrum of ideological conflicts feeding into the churning turmoil of the Sixties, might seem like a very distant past. Still, they might ponder their own connections to that seemingly distant world by remembering the words of American novelist William Faulkner: "*The past is never dead. It isn't even past.*"

Key Terms

Ernesto Guevara (902)
Great Leap Forward (905)
Fidel Castro (906)
Central Intelligence Agency (CIA) (906)
Cuban Missile Crisis (906)
Hungarian Uprising (908)
Jacobo Arbenz (911)
apartheid (911)
Kwame Nkrumah (911)
Jomo Kenyatta (913)
Patrice Lumumba (916)
Ahmed Sukarno (917)
Jawaharlal Nehru (917)
Gamal Abdel Nasser (917)
Ho Chi Minh (919)
Prague Spring (923)
Tlatelolco Massacre (926)
Salvador Allende (927)
Red Guards (927)
détente (929)

For Further Reference

Guevara, Ernesto. *The Motorcycle Diaries: Notes on a Latin American Journey*. Alexandra Keeble, ed. and trans. Melbourne: Ocean Press, 2003.

Hunt, Michael. *The World Transformed: 1945 to the Present*. New York: Bedford/St. Martin's, 2004.

Jeffrey, Robin, ed. *Asia: The Winning of Independence*. London: Macmillan, 1981.

Judge, Edward H., and John W. Langdon. *The Cold War: A Global History with Documents*. 2d ed. New York: Prentice Hall, 2012.

Kurlansky, Mark. *1968: The Year That Rocked the World*. New York: Random House, 2005.

Lee, Christopher J., ed. *Making a World After Empire: The Bandung Moment and Its Political Afterlives*. Athens: Ohio University Press, 2008.

Prashad, Vijay. *The Darker Nations: A People's History of the Third World*. New York: New Press, 2007.

Spence, Jonathan. *Mao Zedong*. New York: Viking Penguin, 1999.

Stark, Steven. *Meet the Beatles: A Cultural History of the Band That Shook Youth, Gender, and the World*. New York: William Morrow, 2006.

Westad, Odd Arne. *The Global Cold War: Third World Interventions and the Making of Our Times*. New York: Cambridge University Press, 2007.

Wiener, Tim. *Legacy of Ashes: The History of the CIA*. New York: Anchor, 2008.

Zubok, Vladislav. *A Failed Empire: The Soviet Union in the Cold War from Stalin to Gorbachev*. Charlotte: University of North Carolina Press, 2008.

AP® Review Questions for Chapter 30

Multiple-Choice Questions

QUESTIONS 1–3 REFER TO THE FOLLOWING PASSAGES.

You are under serious misapprehension in regard to events in Cuba. For months there has been evident and growing resistance to the Castro dictatorship. More than 100,000 refugees have recently fled from Cuba into neighboring countries. . . . These are unmistakable signs that Cubans find intolerable the denial of democratic liberties and the subversion of the 26th of July Movement by an alien-dominant regime.

—John F. Kennedy, U.S. President, letter to Nikita Khrushchev, Soviet Premiere, April 18, 1961

In the present case, apparently, the United States Government is seeking to restore to Cuba that "freedom" under which Cuba would dance to the tune of her more powerful neighbor and foreign monopolies would again be able to plunder the country's national wealth, to wax rich on the sweat and blood of the Cuban people.

—Nikita Khrushchev, reply to Kennedy's letter, April 22, 1961

1. The interaction between Kennedy and Khrushchev is best understood in the context of which of the following?
   (A) The normalization of relations between the United States and the Soviet Union during *glasnost*
   (B) The ideological struggle between the United States and the Soviet Union during the Cold War
   (C) The redrawing of old colonial boundaries after World War II
   (D) Imperialism as a source of global conflict in the twentieth century

2. The tone of the *second* letter best reflects which of the following developments during the twentieth century?
   (A) Nationalism in Cuba
   (B) The role of the United Nations
   (C) Communism as a transnational movement
   (D) Ethnic struggle against colonial power

3. A historian researching the U.S. role in the Caribbean during the twentieth century would most likely find the passages useful as sources of information about which of the following?
   (A) Intensification of military conflict between the United States and the Soviet Union
   (B) The role of the United Nations in mitigating international conflict
   (C) Proxy wars between the United States and the Soviet Union in Latin America
   (D) The increasing economic interdependence between states in the later Cold War

QUESTIONS 4–6 REFER TO THE FOLLOWING PASSAGE.

These classes, led by the working class and the Communist Party, unite to form their own state and elect their own government; they enforce their dictatorship over the running dogs of imperialism—the landlord class and the bureaucrat-bourgeoisie, as well as the representatives of those classes, the Kuomintang reactionaries and their accomplices. . . . The peasant economy is scattered, and the socialization of agriculture, judging by the Soviet Union's experience, will require a long time and painstaking work. Without socialization of agriculture, there can be no complete, consolidated socialism. The steps to socialize agriculture must be coordinated with the development of a powerful industry having state enterprise as its backbone.

—Mao Zedong, from a speech, 1949

4. The speech by Mao Zedong is most clearly an example of which of the following?
   (A) The increased privatization of the Chinese economy
   (B) The increased role of China in global trade
   (C) State control of agriculture and industry
   (D) The political fragmentation of China during the Civil War

5. Which of the following was an important continuity underlying the relationship between capitalist states and communist states described in the passage?
   (A) Capitalist and communist states used violence to achieve political aims.
   (B) Capitalist and communist states formed military alliances and engaged in open conflict with one another.
   (C) Capitalist and communist states both used proxy wars to spread their ideologies.
   (D) Capitalist and communist states engaged in ideological struggles throughout the globe.

6. Which of the following changes to Chinese economic policy occurred under Mao's successor, Deng Xiaoping?
   (A) China began to encourage free-market policies and promoted economic liberalization.
   (B) China took on an even greater role in directing the national economy.
   (C) China protested the formation of global economic institutions as a capitalist plot.

(D) China closed its borders and forbade multinational corporations from doing business there.

QUESTIONS 7–8 REFER TO MAP 30.3 *DECOLONIZATION* ON PAGE 912.

7. Which of the following was a *direct* cause of the decolonization patterns indicated in the map?
   (A) World War I
   (B) World War II
   (C) The Great Depression
   (D) The Cold War

8. Which of the following was a *direct* demographic and social consequence of the decolonization process?
   (A) Ethnic and religious conflict in the newly formed states
   (B) Rapid industrialization across much of the old colonial world
   (C) A global reorganization along Soviet or American loyalties
   (D) The emergence of new diseases, such as AIDS

QUESTIONS 9–10 REFER TO THE FOLLOWING PASSAGE.

You asked about the extent to which the Cuban Communists or other foreign groups were involved in the Mexican riots this week. The CIA...concludes that the student demonstrations were sparked by domestic politics, not masterminded by Cubans or Soviets.... There is no hard evidence that either the Cuban or Soviet embassies in Mexico City masterminded the current disturbances despite repeated allegations to the effect by the Mexican government.

1. Despite the participation of many Communist groups in the disorders, [redacted] has no firm evidence that the Communists instigated the present crisis. As in other countries, the extremists have capitalized on the disorders and members of the Mexican Communist Party (PCM), the Communist Youth (JCM), the Communist-oriented National Democratic Students' Central (CNED), and the Trotskyist and Castroite groups have all participated in varying ways.

—CIA memorandum to President Lyndon Johnson on student demonstrations in Mexico, October 5, 1968

9. Which of the following conclusions about the period from 1949 to 1975 is most directly supported by the passage?
   (A) The Soviet Union was responsible for instigating student uprisings throughout the world.
   (B) Student demonstrations had little short-term success but caused long-term social changes.
   (C) The United States viewed the Soviet Union as the cause of unrest in Latin America.
   (D) Revolutionary zeal spread throughout the globe during the Cold War.

10. Based on the CIA's analysis, the Mexican student demonstrations of 1968 were an example of which of the following?
   (A) The increasing globalization of popular culture
   (B) Large demonstrations protesting environmental degradation
   (C) The liberalization of political systems in Latin America
   (D) The increased role of university students in political discourse

Short-Answer Questions

QUESTION 1 REFERS TO THE IMAGE ON PAGE 929, *CULTURAL REVOLUTION POSTER.*

1. Answer parts A and B.
   A. Identify and explain TWO historical claims about the Chinese Communist Party that can be supported based on the image.
   B. Identify ONE limitation of the image as a source of information about the Chinese Communist Party.

QUESTION 2 REFERS TO THE FOLLOWING PASSAGE.

By the time the Chinese, the Americans, and their respective Korean allies at last managed to agree on an armistice, in July, 1953, the war had left the peninsula devastated, with no clear victory for either side: the boundary between the two Koreas had hardly shifted from where it was in 1950. The only decisive outcome of the war was the precedent it set: that there could be a bloody and protracted conflict involving nations armed with nuclear weapons—and that they could choose not to use them.

—John Lewis Gaddis, historian, *The Cold War: A New History*, 2005

2. Answer parts A, B, and C.
   A. Identify and explain ONE reason that supports the assertion that the Korean War was a proxy war.
   B. Identify and explain ONE reason that denies the assertion that the Korean War was a proxy war.
   C. Identify and explain ONE continuity that the Korean War established for the Cold War overall.

31 Toward a New World Order, 1975–2000

Nelson Mandela

David Turnley/Historical Premium/Corbis

Throughout the 1950s, **Nelson Mandela** (1918–2013) had campaigned for racial justice and democracy as a member of the African National Congress (ANC). Forced underground in 1961 when the South African government banned the ANC, Mandela then traveled across Africa seeking support for the creation of a guerrilla army. After returning to South Africa, he was captured and, in 1964, tried for treason and sentenced to life in prison.

Finally, in early 1990, after decades of repression and violence, South Africa's white leaders responded to international calls for Mandela's release. A few hours after he walked through the prison gates, he spoke before a large crowd in Cape Town and before a global television audience:

Today, the majority of South Africans, black and white, recognize that apartheid has no future. . . . Negotiations on the dismantling of apartheid will have to address the overwhelming demand of our people for a democratic, nonracial, and unitary South Africa. There must be an end to white monopoly on political power and a fundamental restructuring of our political and economic systems to ensure that the inequalities of apartheid are addressed and our society thoroughly democratized. . . . I wish to quote my own words during my trial in 1964. They are as true today as they were then: "I have fought against white domination and I have fought against black domination. I have cherished the ideal of a democratic and free society in which all persons live together in harmony and with equal opportunities.

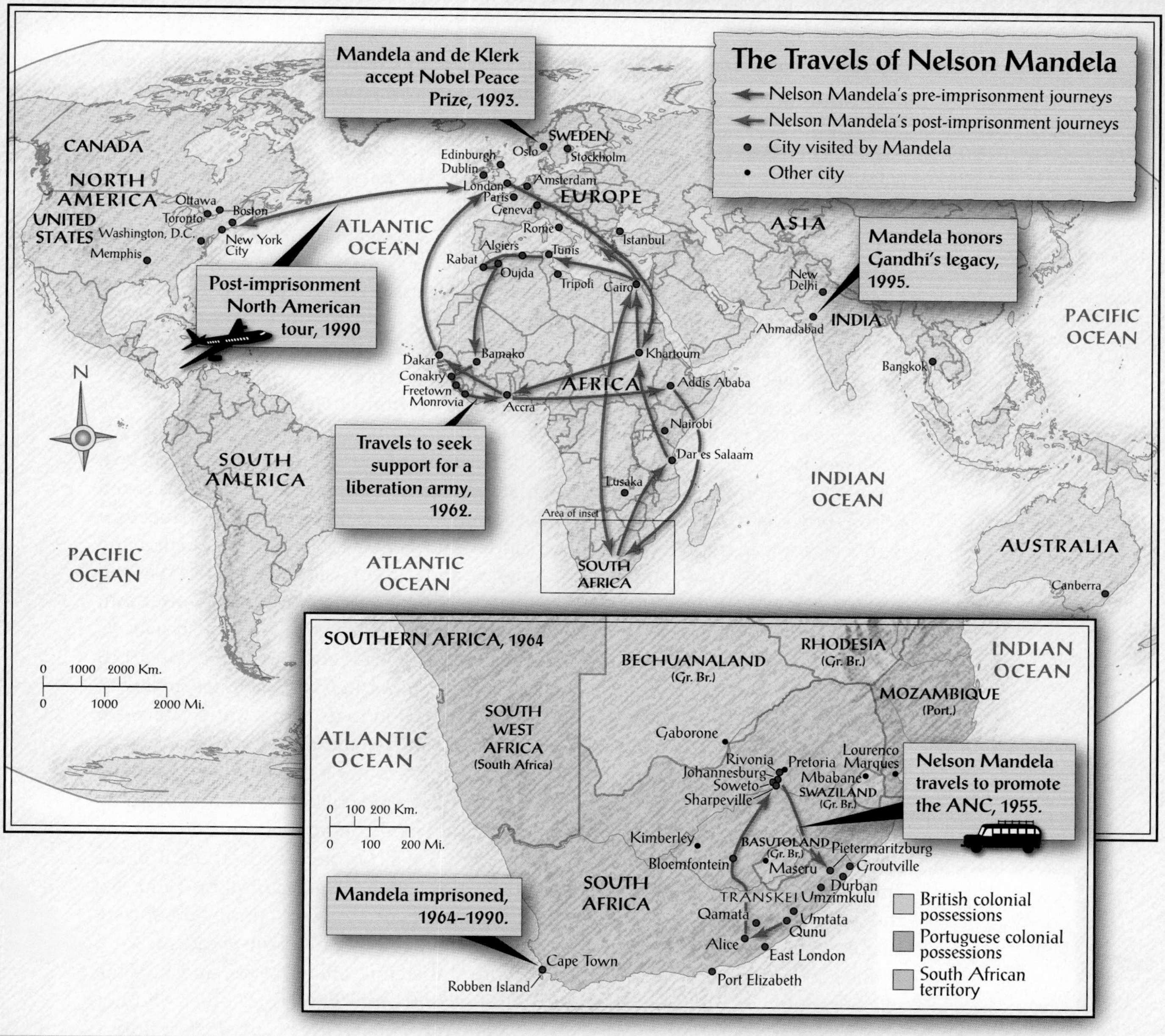

*It is an ideal which I hope to live for and to achieve. But if needs be, it is an ideal for which I am prepared to die."**

None of Mandela's many journeys before and after his imprisonment were as significant as his short walk through those prison gates.

---

*Nelson Mandela, *Nelson Mandela in His Own Words*, ed. Kader Asmal, David Chidester, and Wilmot James (New York: Little, Brown, 2003), pp. 46–47.

Nelson Mandela
(1918–2013) South African leader of the African National Congress and opponent of apartheid. Sentenced to life in prison in 1964; released in 1990. After winning the Nobel Peace Prize in 1993, he became the country's first democratically elected president in 1994.

As a youth, Mandela received an education in the history of his own Tembu people and in the protocols of the chief's court while also attending an English-language primary school. There a teacher assigned him the "proper" English name of Nelson; before that, he was called Rolihlahla ("pulling the branch of a tree," or "troublemaker"). He lived up to his African name at the all-black Methodist college he attended when he became embroiled in student politics and was expelled after leading a protest. In 1941, he fled to Johannesburg to avoid an arranged marriage, completed his B.A. degree, and became one of the country's few black lawyers.

Mandela combined his practice of law with a passion for politics, taking a leadership role in the African National Congress, the party that had, since 1912, worked for racial equality in South Africa (see Chapters 27 and 29). When their nonviolent campaign was met with police brutality and escalating repression, Mandela was set on the path that led to his imprisonment and his later triumph. In 1994, he became the country's first democratically elected president.

The world changed dramatically in the period of Mandela's confinement. In 1964, Cold War tensions had dominated international affairs. By the time of his release from prison, however, the collapse of the Soviet Union brought new possibilities. Hopes for democracy spread not only across Russia and the former Soviet sphere but also in many other parts of the world—Africa, Latin America, and parts of Asia—where Cold War alliances had empowered authoritarian regimes (see Chapter 30). Capturing the optimism of the time, President George H. W. Bush of the United States spoke of a *"new world order."* With the stalemate of the Cold War broken the path lay open, he said in 1991, to *"a world in which freedom and respect for human rights find a home among all nations."*

Still, myriad challenges remained. Russia's transition to democracy and capitalism was difficult, peace in the Middle East remained elusive, and democratic elections in South Africa did not instantly or automatically remove the inequalities of apartheid. The liberal association between free trade and democratic politics was contradicted by the People's Republic of China, where market-driven economic reforms created the world's fastest-growing economy under the control of a communist government. Some critics of the United States equated "globalization" with "Americanization" and saw the "new world order" as a means of expanding American power. Among them were Islamist activists who joined the struggle against what they saw as the decadent West. While the last decade of the twentieth century therefore offered hope, and in some places genuine progress toward freedom and security, the "new world order" did not offer a clear and agreed-upon road map as humanity entered the twenty-first century.

KEY CONCEPT QUESTIONS

- How did economic and political shifts lead to the collapse of the Soviet Union? **(Key Concept 6.3)**
- How did increased economic liberalization contribute to stability and democracy in Latin America? **(Key Concept 6.3)**
- How did the redrawing of old colonial boundaries in the Middle East lead to increased conflict? **(Key Concept 6.2)**
- What was the influence of organizations such as the International Monetary Fund, the World Bank, and the World Trade Organization on global economics? **(Key Concept 6.3)**

The Late Cold War and the Collapse of the Soviet Union, 1975–1991

Abandoning Vietnam in 1975, the United States was divided and weary of war. Sensing an American lack of resolve, Soviet leaders expanded their military and their support for rebel movements. In 1981, however, a reassertive United States confronted the Soviet regime with the need to increase its military spending or fall behind in a renewed arms race. Meanwhile, in eastern Europe simmering discontent was threatening outright rebellion. After 1985 a new Soviet leader, Mikhail Gorbachev, initiated reforms, but it was too little, too late. In 1989, the Berlin Wall fell, and in 1991 the Soviet Union dissolved.

After Soviet communism's collapse, Germany reunified, while Poland, the Czech Republic, and other formerly communist states became stable democracies. But in Russia and some other nations that emerged from the U.S.S.R.'s breakup, establishing democratic institutions proved difficult. Where authoritarian traditions persisted, sharp inequalities attended the introduction of capitalist markets.

The United States in the Post-Vietnam Era, 1975–1990

Misadventure in Vietnam, and the resignation in 1974 of President Nixon as a result of the Watergate scandal, left U.S. society in disarray. At the same time, a steep rise in oil prices engineered by the Organization of Petroleum Exporting Countries (OPEC) shocked Americans, as did the combination of slow growth and inflation that was to afflict the U.S. economy throughout the 1970s.

When Iranian revolutionaries seized American hostages in late 1979 and a rescue attempt the following spring failed to free them, Americans felt powerless and angry. In the 1980 presidential campaign, Republican **Ronald Reagan** (in office 1981–1989) promised to restore American power and confidence. His sweeping victory brought a brash, nationalistic, and sternly anticommunist tone to American foreign policy and sharp increases in military spending. The "Reagan Revolution" was a backlash among conservatives against what they considered the liberal excesses of the 1960s and 1970s. This modern American conservative movement hoped to turn back the stronger role the government had taken for five decades in areas such as civil rights, social welfare, regulation of financial institutions, and environmental protection.

Ronald Reagan (1911–2004) Fortieth president of the United States. A staunchly anticommunist Republican, he used harsh rhetoric toward the Soviet Union and increased American military spending but compromised when negotiating arms limitations agreements.

Reagan found a strong British ally in Conservative Prime Minister Margaret Thatcher, who was equally committed to rolling back the scope of government at home and to confronting the Soviet Union more forcefully abroad. However, many in Europe, as well as in the United States, were alarmed by Reagan's refusal to use the diplomatic language of détente. Europeans rallied for peace, and their leaders rejected Reagan's description of the Soviet Union as an "evil empire," preferring instead to continue the language of "peaceful coexistence." Still, when Reagan traveled to Germany in 1987 he stood before the Berlin Wall and demanded, *"Mr. Gorbachev, tear down this wall!"* Few guessed just how soon the wall would indeed come down.

From Leonid Brezhnev to Mikhail Gorbachev

The period from 1964 to 1982, when Leonid Brezhnev led the Soviet Union, was a time of relative stability for many Soviet citizens. While their standard of living was low, employment, education, and health care were guaranteed. Soviet citizens might never own a car, but they could take an annual vacation. While they had no freedom of speech, religion, or assembly, they did have secure old-age pensions. Perhaps for those who had lived through the ravages of Stalinism and the Second World War, basic security was enough. But for the younger Soviet generation, aware of the higher standard of living in the West, dissatisfaction with the dull status quo was growing.

Some Russian and eastern European dissidents were emboldened to assert their views after détente with the United States led to the **Helsinki Accords**, signed in 1975. This agreement committed western Europe and the United States to recognize the borders of the communist bloc countries in return for a Soviet pledge to respect basic human rights. Among those brave enough to speak out was Russian physicist Andrei Sakharov (1921–1989), the man most responsible for the development of the Soviet hydrogen bomb.

Helsinki Accords
A 1975 agreement made during the Cold War that gave recognition to the borders of communist bloc countries in eastern Europe in return for a Soviet promise, never fulfilled, to respect basic human rights.

Sakharov argued that Soviet society could advance only through greater freedom of information: "*We are infinitely outstripped in computer technology,*" Sakharov and dissident colleagues wrote as early as 1970 to the Soviet leadership, "*crucial because the introduction of electronic computers into the economy is a phenomenon of decisive importance.*"* While Soviet computer scientists and mathematicians were world class, the centralized system they worked in denied them the avenues to creativity open to their American counterparts. There could be no Soviet equivalent to the Apple Corporation, which starting in 1977 pioneered the individual use of computers, democratizing access to this increasingly powerful technology. The idea that computing would be accessible to individuals apart from state control was inconceivable in Brezhnev's Soviet Union. "*We simply live in another age,*"* Sakharov concluded.

Though he was awarded the Nobel Prize in 1975, Brezhnev prevented Sakharov from traveling to receive his award and cut him off from communications with the outside world. Soviet promises to respect human rights meant nothing in practice.

A large gap separated the Soviet Union's global ambitions from the resources generated by its inefficient economy. Huge food imports were financed by energy exports, but better and more abundant consumer options never materialized as promised. Brezhnev worsened the economic problem by making major new military commitments in the wake of the American withdrawal from Vietnam. When the Reagan administration subsequently stepped up American military spending in the 1980s, an already overstretched Soviet Union could not keep pace.

War in Afghanistan took an especially heavy toll on Brezhnev's regime. After Afghan communists seized power in Kabul in 1978 with the help of Soviet Special Forces, a Soviet occupation faced tough resistance from Islamic guerrilla fighters known as *mujahaddin* (moo-jah-ha-DEEN). The mujahaddin, aided by the United States and Pakistan, used their familiarity with the land and the populace to counter superior Soviet technology. As death tolls increased, the Soviet people grew weary of the war in Afghanistan, just as Americans had with Vietnam.

---

*Andrei Sakharov, Roy Medvedev, and Valentine Turchin, "Letter to Comrades Brezhnev, Kosygin, and Podgorny," in *Sources of Global History since 1900*, ed. James H. Overfield, 2d ed. (Boston: Wadsworth, 2013), p. 300.

• **CONTEXT&CONNECTIONS** Afghanistan was already known as the "graveyard of empire," after local fighters repeatedly repelled British invaders in the nineteenth century. After expelling Soviet forces, many mujahaddin would turn on their former American patrons, as discussed later in this chapter. •

When Brezhnev died in 1982, he left a difficult situation to the aging party functionaries who replaced him. Then in 1985 came a startling change when **Mikhail Gorbachev** (b. 1931) consolidated power. Believing that real reform would be necessary to save the Soviet system, and sensing the impatience of Russia's younger generation, Gorbachev denounced what he called *"the era of stagnation"* under Brezhnev. He withdrew from Afghanistan, reached out to President Reagan in pursuit of further arms limitations, and introduced policies of *perestroika* ("restructuring") and *glasnost* ("openness"). Perestroika brought an end to massive economic centralization. While the state would still dominate, industry would now use market incentives rather than bureaucratic command to manage production. Glasnost allowed formerly taboo subjects to be discussed.

Mikhail Gorbachev
(b. 1931) Leader of the Soviet Union from 1985 to 1991 who introduced "openness" to Soviet politics and "restructuring" to the Soviet economy. Unable to control calls for even greater changes, Gorbachev presided over the collapse of the Soviet Union.

Gorbachev's new policy was tested in 1986, when officials tried to cover up the Chernobyl disaster, the worst nuclear accident in history to that time, enraging both the Soviet people and their European neighbors. Gorbachev promised that the old pattern of Soviet lies would be replaced by honesty and openness.

Glasnost was effective. For the first time since the earliest days of the revolution, Russians were free to speak their minds and publish their opinions. However, the economic progress promised by perestroika failed to materialize. The Russian people still faced their dreary daily routine of standing in long lines for basics like milk, bread, and eggs. The only difference from the Brezhnev era was that they were now free to complain about it. By the end of the 1980s, Gorbachev's popularity was plummeting.

AP® THEMES
How did Gorbachev's policies represent a change in Soviet economic, social, and cultural life?

Glasnost also contributed to the unraveling of the Soviet Union. When members of disaffected ethnic groups gained a public voice for their grievances with Russian rule, the forces of repressed nationalism exploded in various republics, such as Georgia in the Caucasus Mountains and the Baltic states of Latvia, Lithuania, and Estonia. The Soviet Union began to break apart as Gorbachev agreed to a treaty giving the republics of the U.S.S.R. their de facto independence as part of a commonwealth led from Moscow (see Map 31.1).

This political fragmentation was too much for hard-line conservatives in the Communist Party who, in the summer of 1991, attempted a coup d'état. But huge crowds rallied to protect the newly elected government of the Russian Republic, which then outlawed the Communist Party of the Soviet Union. Gorbachev had failed to find a middle ground between reform and revolution. His combination of Marxism-Leninism with market reforms and political transparency was a halfway measure, doomed to failure.

Revolution in Eastern Europe

As the Hungarian uprising in 1956 and the Prague Spring in 1968 had shown, force had been necessary to keep eastern Europe in Moscow's orbit (see Chapter 30). By the mid-1980s, however, the Soviet Union was no longer willing to intervene to retain control. In Poland, for example, Catholicism was a touchstone of Polish nationalism and a historical connection with the West. The surprise announcement in 1978 that the Polish cardinal Karol Wojtyla would become Pope John Paul II powerfully affirmed that national feeling.

Map 31.1 The Dissolution of the Soviet Union In the 1990s, the collapse of the Soviet Union led to the creation of new states across eastern Europe, the Caucasus Mountains, and Central Asia, regions that in the nineteenth century had been part of the Russian empire. The Baltic states of Estonia, Latvia, and Lithuania emerged as thriving democracies. Conflict was endemic in the Caucasus, however, where Russia battled separatists in Chechnya and Armenia and Azerbaijan fought for control of territory. The new nations of formerly Soviet Central Asia were dominated by strong-armed dictators.

Solidarity
Polish trade union created in 1980 that organized opposition to Communist rule. In 1989, Solidarity leader Lech Walesa was elected president of Poland as the Communists lost their hold on power.

In 1980, discontent with the communist regime reached a turning point with the formation of **Solidarity**, the first independent trade union in the Soviet bloc. In a direct challenge to the authority of the Communist Party, nearly a third of Poland's population joined Solidarity. Faced with increasing unrest, the government agreed to an election in 1989. The result was a massive victory for Solidarity and the election of its leader Lech Walesa to the position of president. The "iron curtain" was starting to crumble.

In Czechoslovakia, the young rebels of the Prague Spring of 1968 were now adults and began pushing for a new constitution. They had an additional grievance: the terrible pollution and environmental degradation caused by communism's industrial policies. Unaccountable to public opinion, the communists had not matched western European progress in protecting their nation's air, water, and forests. The police cracked down on democratic protesters, but they were unable to control events: this time no Soviet forces arrived to save them.

Communism's fall went so smoothly in Czechoslovakia that it has been called the "Velvet Revolution."

The new presidents of Poland and Czechoslovakia could not have come from more different backgrounds: Lech Walesa was a shipyard worker and labor organizer, while the Czechoslovak leader, Václav Havel, was a dramatist and intellectual. When they met as leaders of truly independent and democratic states, their complementarity was obvious, showing that for all their differences, industrial workers and artists had both been straitjacketed by communism. Now, no longer would Polish and Czech workers have to settle for the phony trade unions imposed on them by Communist Party officials, and no longer would eastern European artists have to conform to the dictates of cultural commissars.

Communism fell more suddenly and violently in Romania, where Nicolae Ceausescu (chow-SHES-koo) had ruled with an iron fist, building sumptuous palaces while his people went hungry. Isolated in his palace, Ceausescu did not realize the depth of public anger. Then, at a large public rally, Ceausescu stepped forward to receive the accolades of the crowd; instead, he was loudly jeered. Television showed Ceausescu's confusion as he heard, for the first time, his people's true opinion. His own security officials turned on him, and he and his wife were summarily executed by firing squad—the end of a brutal and vain dictator who died despised by the people he had long abused.

● **CONTEXT&CONNECTIONS** The humiliating end of Nicolae Ceausescu, with the video of his execution shown on Romanian television, was reminiscent of the ignoble treatment of the Italian fascist *Benito Mussolini*, his corpse hung by his heels from a balcony (key term in Chapter 29). Other dictators whose brutality caught up with them include Saddam Hussein of Iraq and Muammar Qaddafi of Libya (see Chapter 32). ●

The most evocative image of the fall of communism in eastern Europe was the destruction of the Berlin Wall, symbol of the Cold War since 1961. In the summer of 1989 pressure was increasing on East German authorities to allow freer transit to the West after Hungary opened its border with Austria. As huge crowds gathered at the Wall, a single gate was unexpectedly opened and a flood of East Berliners streamed across. Soon after, euphoric Berliners demolished the Wall in a festival of constructive mayhem.

If, in retrospect, the fall of communism in Europe seems to have been inevitable, it certainly did not seem so to people at the time. In East Germany, Bulgaria, Romania, and across eastern Europe, soldiers under the command of communist officials faced the awful prospect of being ordered to fire on crowds of protesters. When they did not do so, the people's sense of relief was palpable, and their feeling of joy in victory all the more intense.

Post-Soviet Struggles for Democracy and Prosperity

The failure of the communist coup in 1991 and the fall of Mikhail Gorbachev put Russian President **Boris Yeltsin** (1931–2007) in charge of defining a new path for the country. (See the feature "Visual Evidence in Primary Sources: Tanks and Protests in Moscow and Beijing.") Advised by American economists that free markets would bring prosperity, Yeltsin instituted bold economic reforms. The immediate results, however, were disappointing. A few "new oligarchs" of the post-Soviet economic elite grew

Boris Yeltsin
(1931–2007) First president of the Russian Federation, from 1991 to 1999. He rallied the people of Moscow to defend their elected government during the attempted communist coup of 1991, but his presidency was marred by financial scandals and war in Chechnya.

Tanks and Protests in Moscow and Beijing

Among the many striking images associated with the late Cold War period are these very different representations of the role that tanks played in political protests in Beijing in 1989 and Moscow in 1991. The Chinese image shows the repression of democracy, the Russian one its triumph.

As China opened up to the world in the 1980s, it was undertaking a much more successful economic restructuring than Mikhail Gorbachev's perestroika, but its leaders had done virtually nothing to emulate his program of glasnost, or "openness." By 1989, some Chinese, especially students in the capital city of Beijing, thought it was time for a change. They were inspired by a visit from Gorbachev but also by ideals of democracy they associated with the United States.

From April to August 1989, large crowds assembled in Beijing's Tiananmen Square to protest corruption and to advocate democracy. Under the giant banner of Chairman Mao that dominates the square, students erected a facsimile of the Statue of Liberty. Some Communist officials were sympathetic to the protests and urged dialogue. Chairman Deng Xiaoping rejected their advice and sent in the People's Army to dislodge the protesters. Estimates on the number of those killed range from the hundreds to the thousands.

AP Images/Jeff Widener

Taken with a long-range lens from a Beijing hotel room, this photograph of a lone individual trying to stop a line of surging tanks (which eventually went around him) summed up both the heroism and futility of the Tiananmen protests. He has never been identified. In 1989, *Time* magazine declared the "Unknown Rebel" to be one of the one hundred most influential people of the twentieth century.

By this time, it was becoming clear that fundamental changes were likely to occur in the Soviet Union. Gorbachev was in danger of losing central control as nationalists began discussing separation from the U.S.S.R. After first resisting that trend, he then agreed to a compromise that would enhance the power of the individual republics, reversing the old domination from Moscow. In the summer of 1991, a group of Communist Party officials and army officers, understanding that the Soviet Union stood on the brink of dissolution, launched the August Coup to restore central authority.

How does the manner in which the photographer has framed each of the shots affect the viewer's reactions?

Boris Yeltsin, elected president of the Russian Republic, stands on top of a tank, rallying the people of Moscow in defense of their new democratic institutions. The commander of the tank brigade had declared his loyalty to the Russian Republic and had refused to join Soviet forces against it. Contrary to the wishes of the coup plotters, this image was shown on state television and became a rallying point for further defense of democracy.

In the background is the Russian "white house," the parliament of the Russian Republic. The authority of this elected body was part of the shift away from centralized Soviet control toward newly empowered governmental institutions within the republic. After declaring a state of emergency, the coup leaders had the building shelled.

AP Images

The coup plotters were unable to muster enough military strength to overcome this resistance, which would have required a level of violence and death that was intolerable to most military commanders. Gorbachev regained his authority and declared the orders of the coup leaders null and void. It was not much of a victory, however, as the Soviet state quickly unraveled around him.

very wealthy very suddenly when state assets were auctioned off. But they often behaved more like gangsters than corporate executives, using government ties to enrich themselves and suppress competition.

Many Russians suffered when the old sureties of the Soviet system—free education and health care, guaranteed employment, old-age pensions—disappeared: the market system did not instantly make up for their loss. Even as imported consumer products became widely available, few had the means to purchase them. By the end of the 1990s, life expectancy and fertility rates were in decline, and too many Russians were hungry and cold.

Yeltsin's problems were compounded by unrest in the southern Caucasus region, where Muslim guerrillas organized a separatist movement in Chechnya (CHECH-nee-yah). Though Yeltsin used massive military force against them, he was unable to suppress the uprising. In 1999 an ailing Yeltsin handed power to a former intelligence officer, Vladimir Putin.

Putin was elected to his office in 2000 by Russian voters anxious to embrace an authority figure who promised order. Putin reined in capitalism by restoring state authority over the economy and the media, using control of oil revenues and television as bases of power. He crushed the Chechnya rebellion, stood up to the United States in global forums, and restored order to the Russian Republic. Stability was achieved, but at the expense of democracy and civil rights.

● **CONTEXT&CONNECTIONS** The stakes of *Vladimir Putin's* (Chapter 32) gambit to restore Russian dignity and power in global forums increased significantly in 2014. His invasion and annexation of the Crimean peninsula and support for rebels in eastern Ukraine brought Western economic sanctions, and the plummeting price of oil revealed underlying weaknesses in a Russian economy overly dependent on energy exports. ●

The former Central Asian republics of the U.S.S.R. faced equally difficult transitions. Located on the borderlands between China, Russia, and the Muslim world, these newly independent nations had plentiful natural resources, especially oil and gas. The potential for democracy, however, was limited because, unlike in eastern Europe, regime change came from the top down rather than through popular mobilization. Kazakhstan and Uzbekistan were typical, with independence overseen by former communist officials who paid lip service to democracy while keeping a tight rein on power and resources.

In general, the transition to liberal governance and market economics was smoother in eastern Europe. Estonia, the Czech Republic, and Poland all experienced political and economic progress in the 1990s, with a blossoming of the free associations that characterize civil society.

The reunification of Germany was more difficult. East Germans were much poorer than West Germans and usually lacked competitive job skills. The first decade after the fall of the Berlin Wall brought freedom and opportunity to eastern Germany, but also unemployment and insecurity. Still, reunification magnified Germany's diplomatic and economic centrality to Europe and its place as a global leader in science, technology, and manufacturing.

The fall of the Soviet Union was clearly a momentous turning point in modern history. It marked not only the failure of the world's longest experiment with communism but also the breakup of the formerly great Russian empire.

The Late Cold War in Latin America and Africa: Crisis and Opportunity

During the late stages of the Cold War (1975–1990), political crises afflicted many parts of Africa and Latin America. Then the collapse of the Soviet Union brought opportunities to heal political divisions and bring greater democracy. In Central America, violence between leftist insurgents and military regimes aligned with Washington gave way in the 1990s to elections and new hope for democracy and stability. Likewise in southern Africa, elections superceded warfare. But civil war and genocide in Central Africa demonstrated the destructive legacies of colonialism and superpower intervention.

From Dictatorship to Democracy in Central America

In the 1980s, a principle battleground between leftist rebels and military forces backed by the United States was Central America. Through its controversial School of the Americas, the U.S. military had trained the officer corps of many Latin American nations, a number of whom either directly intervened in politics (as in Chile and Argentina, see Chapter 30) or supported corrupt dictatorships. Latin American leftists ascribed the cruelty and corruption of such regimes to American imperialism.

Nicaragua, for example, had long been ruled by the Somoza family, dictators aligned with American economic interests. Resistance to the Somoza dictatorship was organized by the rebel Sandinista National Liberation Front. Following a major earthquake in 1972, the Somoza family stole millions of dollars of relief aid, pushing many Nicaraguans toward sympathy with the rebels. In 1979, the Sandinistas ousted the Somoza regime and formed a new government.

After Ronald Reagan took office in 1981, his administration threw its support behind anti-Sandinista insurgents known as *Contras*, illegally evading congressional oversight to get funds for the Contras by selling arms to the Iranian regime. To protect the revolution, the Sandinistas then clamped down on civil liberties, following Fidel Castro's earlier example and relying on Cuban support.

Then Soviet decline brought new possibilities for a negotiated settlement. Since Cuba's economy was undercut as Gorbachev phased out Soviet subsidies, Cuba could no longer aid the Sandinistas, and U.S. leaders no longer saw the Contras as necessary allies. Free elections were held in Nicaragua in 1989. The defeated Sandinistas respected the election results by peacefully handing over power, a major step forward for Nicaraguan democracy.

Violence also marred Guatemalan society in the 1980s. Paramilitary death squads connected with Guatemala's right-wing leaders targeted villagers, mostly indigenous Maya people, suspected of collusion with rebel armies. The killers themselves were often boys who had been kidnapped by the army and forced into service. As many as a million refugees fled from the mountains to the cities or across the border into Mexico.

● **CONTEXT&CONNECTIONS** After 1954, when *Che Guevara* (Chapter 30) had witnessed the U.S.-backed overthrow of the reformist Arbenz regime, Guatemala's leftists took up arms. In the 1980s, with violence wracking the countryside, the situation of the nation's poor was worse than ever. ●

Jean Louis Atlan/Sygma/Corbis

Sandinistas Nicaragua's Sandinistas were victorious in 1979 but U.S.-backed Contra rebels challenged their control. The Sandinistas modeled themselves on Cuban revolutionary heroes; the soldier on the right wears a red-starred beret like that of Che Guevara (see Chapter 30).

After the Cold War, the United States pressured the Guatemalan government and military to work toward a solution. A peace deal was finally brokered in 1996, when the rebels agreed to lay down their arms in exchange for land. For the first time since 1952 Guatemalans went to the polls to vote in free elections, and a government panel was soon set up to investigate paramilitary atrocities.

The relationship of the Roman Catholic Church with the politics of repression and democratization in Latin American was especially complex. During the 1970s many parish priests, influenced by 1960s radicalism, subscribed to "liberation theology" with its "preferential option for the poor." Members of the higher Church hierarchy, on the other hand, tended to maintain traditional ties to ruling oligarchs and their military allies. That division within the Catholic Church deepened after the accession of the strongly anticommunist Pope John Paul II, who quickly reined in the liberation theologians.

An especially dark chapter was the murder in 1980 of three nuns and a lay missionary from the United States by El Salvador's National Guard and the assassination that same year of the relatively moderate Archbishop Óscar Romero, who had spoken out publicly against government abuses.

But by the 1990s, the trend in El Salvador, as in Latin America as a whole, was toward democracy. In Argentina, change had come in 1982 after defeat in the Falklands War against Great Britain showed the incompetence of Argentine generals and brought about irresistible calls for change. Elections swept the military from power in Brazil as well. Even in Chile, where the Pinochet regime was deeply entrenched (see Chapter 30), pressures mounted for a free election, and in 1988 Chilean voters turned down his continued dictatorship.

Thus the democratization of Latin American nations paralleled the liberation of eastern Europe. But where countries like Poland had escaped from Soviet domination, those like Chile had freed themselves from dictatorships allied with the United States.

In Mexico, however, the problem was neither military governments nor Cold War alignments, but rather the political monopoly of the Party of Institutional Revolution (PRI), which constrained Mexican freedoms while binding the country to incompetence and corruption (see Chapter 30). Finally, in 1989, a conservative opposition party made inroads in the state of Baja California, ushering in more open electoral competition at the national level. In 2000, the election of an opposition candidate as president finally ended the PRI monopoly on Mexico's national politics.

South African Liberation

During Nelson Mandela's many years in prison, South African apartheid became more and more extreme. The government oversaw a "Bantu education" system that prepared blacks only for menial jobs. Strictly enforced residential segregation made it illegal for blacks to be in "white" areas unless they could prove they were there for employment. Meanwhile, white South Africans enjoyed a First World standard of living.

To complete racial separation, the South African government developed the system of **Bantustans**, based on the idea that Tswana, Zulu, Xhosa, and other African peoples did not belong to a common South Africa but to "tribal" enclaves where they should seek their rights. According to apartheid, these impoverished and scattered territories would form the basis for independent "nations," one for each of South Africa's "tribes." In reality, the Bantustans were simply a device to exclude blacks from South African citizenship and deprive them of any hope for rights in a unified South Africa.

Bantustans
Term used by apartheid planners for "tribal regions" in which Africans, denied citizenship in a common South Africa, were expected to live when not working for whites. They were not internationally recognized and were later reabsorbed into democratic South Africa.

• **CONTEXT&CONNECTIONS** The boundaries of the Bantustans of the 1970s derived from the Native Land Act of 1913, originally designed to turn Africans into low-cost workers (see Chapter 26). From that time, inadequate land and overcrowding had forced blacks to seek work for low wages at white-controlled mines, cities, and farms. •

With Nelson Mandela and other African National Congress (ANC) leaders languishing in jail or in exile, in the 1970s a new generation of leaders emerged. The Black Consciousness Movement was led by Steve Biko, who argued that black South Africans faced not only the external challenge of apartheid but also an inner challenge to surmount the psychological damage it caused. The first step toward liberation, Biko said, was for blacks to eliminate their own sense of inferiority.

• **CONTEXT&CONNECTIONS** In emphasizing the need for colonized blacks to liberate themselves from an internalized sense of inferiority, Steve Biko echoed the message of Frantz Fanon in *The Wretched of the Earth* (see Chapter 30). •

In 1976, black South African youths who heeded Biko's call were at the forefront of the **Soweto Uprising**, protesting the dismal quality of their education. When marchers refused an order to disband, police fired into the crowd, killing dozens of children. As protests spread across the country, authorities responded with their usual brutality. But Black Consciousness stayed alive in the Soweto generation even after 1977, when Steve Biko's jailers beat him to death.

Soweto Uprising
(1976) Youth demonstrations in South Africa that were met with police violence. The Soweto Uprising brought a new generation of activists, inspired by Steve Biko's Black Consciousness Movement, to the forefront of resistance to apartheid.

Soweto Uprising In 1976, schoolchildren in South Africa protested the compulsory teaching of the Dutch-based Afrikaans language in their schools. When police fired into the crowd, made up mostly of teenagers, hundreds were killed and thousands injured. The Soweto generation played a central role in bringing down apartheid over the next fifteen years. (Bettman/Corbis)

By 1983, black trade unions, church groups, and student organizations had formed a nationwide United Democratic Front. Schoolchildren boycotted apartheid schools. Resistance on the streets became violent. Sometimes African militants cruelly executed those accused of collaboration with apartheid by putting tires around their necks and setting them ablaze. In 1986, the government declared a state of emergency and sent the army into the black townships to restore order.

Meanwhile, critics outside South Africa argued that economic sanctions could help force meaningful change. In 1986, the U.S. Congress passed a comprehensive bill limiting trade with and investment in South Africa, overriding the veto of President Reagan, who saw the white government as a staunch ally and viewed Mandela and the ANC as communist sympathizers.

Feeling the pressure from domestic resistance and from sanctions, the South African government offered to release Mandela if he renounced the ANC.

His daughter Zindzi read his response at a packed soccer stadium: *"I will remain a member of the African National Congress until the day I die.... Your freedom and mine cannot be separated. I will return."** Finally, as the decline of the Soviet Union undercut the government's claim that Mandela and the ANC represented a front for Soviet-backed communism, and as sanctions undermined an already weak economy, South African President F. W. de Klerk granted Mandela an unconditional release in 1990. Despite ongoing violence, elections were held in 1994. Mandela was easily elected president, and the ANC became the dominant political force in the new South Africa.

True to the words he had spoken at his trial in 1964, Mandela emphasized inclusiveness in his government. South Africa, christened the "rainbow nation," had a new flag, a new sense of self-identity, a multiracial Olympic team, and one of the world's most democratic constitutions. A Truth and Reconciliation Commission was instituted to uncover the abuses of apartheid, while offering amnesty to those who publicly acknowledged their crimes.

Immense challenges faced Mandela as he took up his presidency. The deeply rooted inequalities of apartheid would not disappear overnight, and HIV/AIDS was beginning to take a heavy toll. At first President Mandela paid little attention to HIV/AIDS, a mistake he later acknowledged and corrected, revealing that his own son had died of the disease and urging South Africans toward a frank discussion of sexuality and sexual health. In this crisis, as in the many others he faced, Mandela's deep ethical integrity marked him as a leader of rare ability. Without Nelson Mandela, it is doubtful whether South Africa could have navigated the end of apartheid as safely and successfully as it did.

AP® THEMES
What were the lasting effects of the emergence of the HIV/AIDS epidemic?

South Africa's successful first democratic, nonracial election on April 24, 1994, was one of the greatest and least expected outcomes of the post–Cold War period. But just a few weeks earlier, two thousand miles to the north in Rwanda, a genocidal slaughter had begun.

The Rwandan Genocide and Congolese Conflict

The Rwandan genocide of 1994 is often presented as having "tribal" or "ethnic" roots, but Rwandans, Hutu as well as Tutsi, speak the same language, participate in the same culture, and mostly share a common Roman Catholic faith. As colonial rulers, however, the Belgians had sharply differentiated the two groups, favoring the Tutsi as local allies and giving Tutsi children preferred access to European education. Consequent resentments surfaced upon independence in 1960, when the previously disenfranchised Hutu took power and expelled many Tutsi. By the 1980s, these Tutsi exiles had organized a rebel army in neighboring Uganda.

In 1994, Hutu death squads went on a rampage when the plane carrying the Rwandan president was shot from the sky, and within a few months nearly a million people had been slaughtered, many cut with machetes. Extremist Hutu radio announcers urged young men to grab weapons and exterminate the Tutsi "cockroaches" and any moderate Hutu who tried to protect them. Since there were high rates of intermarriage, and since Hutu and Tutsi lived together in the same villages, the murderers might even kill their own neighbors and family members.

---

*Nelson Mandela, *Nelson Mandela in His Own Words*, ed. Kader Asmal, David Chidester, and Wilmot James (New York: Little, Brown, 2003), pp. 59–62.

Smartphones and "Conflict Minerals"

Internet-enabled smartphones have become ubiquitous, with the total number of users likely to surpass 2 billion in 2016. It is impossible to predict the long-term cultural and economic impacts of this global telecommunications revolution.

Engineers are constantly trying to find smaller and more efficient components for these devices, and the mineral tantalum, derived from coltan, is essential to their plans. Tantalum is irreplaceable as a material for building highly efficient, miniaturized capacitors for mobile electronics. And the quest for coltan leads directly to the Democratic Republic of the Congo, where 80 percent of the world's supply is found in the north and east of the country. Unfortunately, this is the same region deeply affected by the aftershocks of the Rwandan genocide, including foreign incursions and the depredations of murderous warlords. The smartphones on which we increasingly rely connect us, whether we know it or not, to the central African trade in "conflict minerals."

Ironically, given its high-technology applications, coltan is mined in the most primitive conditions, in places with poor roads and telecommunications, where men and boys literally scrape mud out of stream beds to locate it. The real profits come not in mining coltan, however, but in its transport and sale. This is where the warlords and smugglers get involved, and the human rights tragedy begins. Warlords are apt to recruit small boys as soldiers and to force girls into dependent domestic and sexual relationships. In addition to these human costs, the illicit and unregulated coltan trade, and the high-powered arms introduced along with it, is further threatening the endangered lowland gorilla population of the eastern Congo.

Meanwhile, profits from the coltan in our handheld devices, which might have helped Congo build its infrastructure for development, have instead gone to warlords, foreign invaders, and arms merchants. In a globalized world, the distance from the smartphones in our pockets to the war zones of eastern Congo is not great at all.

Source: "Where Apple Gets the Tantalum for Your iPhone," Lynnley Browning, *Newsweek*, February 4, 2015.

AP® THEMES

How did imperialism and foreign intervention in Rwanda contribute to the violence between the Hutu and Tutsi?

Another million Rwandans fled to neighboring countries, as United Nations peacekeepers stood by, unwilling to intervene. The conflict then spread west to further destabilize the already tottering Democratic Republic of the Congo.

The huge Congo nation, with its staggering mineral wealth, had been the great Cold War prize of the United States (see Chapter 30). Mobutu Sese Seko was the compliant dictator looking after American strategic and economic interests while stealing aid and resources so brazenly that analysts referred to his regime as a *kleptocracy*.

But with the fall of the Soviet Union and the release of Nelson Mandela, the U.S. affiliation with Mobutu Sese Seko became an embarrassment, and in 1990 Congress cut off direct aid and supported democratization efforts. Those efforts failed for two reasons. First, the political opponents of Mobutu were themselves bitterly divided; as in the early days of the Congo, most politicians represented regions and ethnic groups rather than ideas or policies. Second, the region was destabilized by the shock of genocide in Rwanda.

As a Tutsi army re-entered Rwanda to establish a new government, Hutu extremists who had perpetrated the horrible violence fled to refugee camps in neighboring Congo. When Mobutu Sese Seko sickened and died, his authoritarian rule was replaced not by freedom but by near anarchy, the country divided between multiple militias. Neighboring African countries compounded problems by sending in armies to back the various factions and vie for Congo's mineral wealth. (See the feature "World History in Today's World: Smartphones and 'Conflict Minerals.'")

Although the "new world order" of democracy and civil rights did not arrive in the Democratic Republic of the Congo, after 1995 Rwanda did make strides toward restoring peace and civility. And while a few African dictators of the old school refused to step off the stage and yield power to a new generation, signs of hope appeared in more and more places. In fact, enough progress was made toward rule of law, multiparty democracy, and economic reinvigoration on the continent that the phrase "African Renaissance" came to be used to indicate a renewed Afro-optimism as the twenty-first century approached. Democratic South Africa was just one of the now brighter lights to which those optimists might point.

Enduring Challenges in the Middle East

Throughout the twentieth century, the Middle East had been a politically unsettled region, where ethnic and religious rivalries created divisions magnified by the involvement of external powers. By the 1970s, the strategic importance of the Middle East as a source of petroleum had raised the stakes of conflict even higher.

Tension between Israel and its Arab neighbors intensified after 1973, when a brief war led Arab representatives of the **Organization of Petroleum Exporting Countries (OPEC)** to declare a boycott on oil exports to the United States in retribution for its military aid to the Jewish state. Greatly increased energy prices and the global economic slowdown that followed showed that the Arab-Israeli conflict could not be quarantined.

Organization of Petroleum Exporting Countries (OPEC) An international organization of oil-producing nations created to set production quotas in an attempt to influence prices. OPEC's policies led to a steep rise in oil prices in the early 1970s.

Meanwhile, after the Iranian Revolution of 1979, for the first time in the post-colonial era a state would be ruled under a constitution derived explicitly from Islamic law. In the 1980s, both Sunnis and Shi'ites were increasingly open to the appeals of **Islamists** who promised to restore dignity, ethical behavior, and prosperity by returning to core religious values. Islamism threatened regimes founded on the principles of secular Arab nationalism, such as Egypt, Syria, Iraq, and Jordan, while inspiring revolutionaries in Afghanistan. Meanwhile, the Israeli-Palestinian conflict endured. In spite of occasional signs of compromise, no resolution was forthcoming, although it seemed impossible that any meaningful "new world order" could ever be constructed without one.

Islamists Muslims who believe that laws and constitutions should be guided by Islamic principles and that religious authorities should be directly involved in governance.

Iran and Iraq

In the 1950s, American intervention had magnified the power of the shah of Iran while suppressing radical secular nationalism (see Chapter 30). For the next twenty years, Shah Pahlavi used oil money to modernize the country while his secret police repressed political dissidents, including conservative religious leaders who accused him of promoting decadent Western values and serving as a tool of U.S. power. On the other hand, these *mullahs* were no more sympathetic to the atheistic Soviet Union. Iranians shared their northern border with the U.S.S.R., which had occupied the north of the country in World War II and which they still regarded as a threat.

With riots and demonstrations spreading, the shah fled to the United States early in 1979. Returning from exile in Paris at the same time was **Ayatollah Khomeini** (1902–1989), whose authority was recognized by the ninety-thousand-member *ulama* (oo-leh-MAH), or community of Shi'ite religious scholars. Khomeini envisioned a tight connection between religious and governmental authority.

Ayatollah Khomeini (1902–1989) Shi'ite cleric who led the Islamic Revolution in Iran in 1979 and became Supreme Leader of the Islamic Republic of Iran.

The path toward a just society, Islamists argued, was not through absorption of Western influences and modernity but through a return to the guiding precepts of their religion. Their argument was an explicit rejection of the secular ideologies that had dominated nineteenth- and twentieth-century global political discourse. Though the radicals who seized the American embassy and hostages in Teheran were motivated more by nationalism than by religion, they responded to Khomeini's assessment of the United States as *"the great Satan."*

After Iraq invaded Iran, a surge of nationalism further consolidated support for Khomeini's government. During eight years of brutal fighting (1980–1988), over a million people were killed. Iranian civilians and soldiers suffered terribly when the Iraqi army used chemical weapons in violation of international law. That the U.S. administration of President Ronald Reagan aided the Iraqi military only furthered tensions between Washington and Teheran.

• **CONTEXT&CONNECTIONS** The battle lines of the Iran-Iraq War of the 1980s overlapped with both earlier and later ones. The armies of the Iranian *Safavid dynasty* and the Ottoman empire struggled over the same ground in the sixteenth century (Chapter 17) as did ISIS invaders and Iraqi forces beginning in 2014 (see Chapter 32). In every case, these armies struggled for control of the religious frontier between Sunni and Shi'ite majorities along the cultural frontier between Arab and Iranian populations. •

Iranian Revolution Iranian nationalists, suspicious of both the United States and the Soviet Union, flocked to the banner of Ayatollah Khomeini to establish an Islamic Republic in 1979. Khomeini returned from exile in France as their spiritual and political leader, denouncing the United States as the "great Satan" for its longstanding support of the deposed shah. (AFP/Getty Images)

After reaching a stalemate with Iran, Iraqi President Saddam Hussein turned his expansionist ambitions toward Kuwait, a small, oil-rich state on the Persian Gulf. Hussein considered Kuwait part of Iraq's rightful patrimony, taken away from Baghdad's control during Britain's redrawing of former Ottoman boundaries in 1919 (see Chapter 27). Miscalculating that the United States, which had supported him in his war with Iran, would not oppose him now, Hussein invaded Kuwait in the summer of 1990 (see Map 31.2).

President George H. W. Bush reacted to Hussein's move by forging an international coalition against him. In the past, Hussein might have tried to counterbalance the United States by seeking an alliance with the Soviet Union, but that option no longer existed. Early in 1991, the **Persian Gulf War** began with the devastating U.S. bombing of Baghdad, after which the coalition swiftly liberated Kuwait. Hussein's army melted away, but while the path to Baghdad was open, the Bush administration calculated that removing Hussein would upset the delicate Middle Eastern balance of power. As Americans withdrew, Hussein brutally crushed a rebellion in the largely Shi'ite south.

Persian Gulf War
(1991) War that occurred when an international coalition led by the United States expelled Iraqi forces from Kuwait. Coalition forces then evacuated Iraq, and Saddam Hussein remained in power.

Afghanistan and Al-Qaeda

In 1993, the administration of new U.S. President William Jefferson (Bill) Clinton became increasingly concerned about Afghanistan. In the aftermath of the Soviet withdrawal, Afghanistan came under the control of the Taliban, Sunni Islamists advocating a severe form of fundamentalism. Women especially suffered; education for girls was eliminated completely. Mujahaddin from around the world had joined the fight against the Soviets in the 1980s, inspired by the call to holy war. After the Soviet withdrawal, some returned home to places like Egypt and Saudi Arabia determined to bring Islamic revolution to their own societies. Others found refuge in Afghanistan under the Taliban.

The most notorious was **Osama bin Laden** (1957–2011), son of a wealthy builder in Saudi Arabia. Though formerly allied with the United States against the Soviets, bin Laden despised the way America and the West propped up Israel and what he saw as illegitimate and corrupt Middle Eastern regimes, and he decried the presence of American soldiers on Saudi Arabian soil. Bin Laden and his followers in al-Qaeda (el-ka-AYE-dah) carried out truck bomb attacks on American embassies in Kenya and Tanzania in 1998. In retaliation, the Clinton administration bombed southeastern Afghanistan in an unsuccessful attempt to kill bin Laden and destroy al-Qaeda's base of operations.

Osama bin Laden
(1957–2011) Saudi Arabian leader of the Islamist group al-Qaeda, whose goal is to replace existing governments of Muslim countries with a purified caliphate; killed by U.S. commandos in 2011.

The Israeli-Palestinian Conflict

The unresolved Israeli-Palestinian conflict fueled Arab and Muslim resentments. A vicious cycle of violence rocked Israel and the occupied Palestinian territories in the 1970s and 1980s. Israel retained the territories it had occupied during the Six-Day War of 1967 (see Chapter 30), arguing that continued control of the West Bank and Gaza ensured Israeli security. But some Zionists believed that these lands, as part of the ancient Hebrew kingdom, should be permanently annexed. Thus the conservative Likud (lih-KOOD) Party, which ruled Israel for much of the period after 1977, sponsored the construction of Jewish settlements on the West Bank, violating international laws prohibiting lands taken in war from being resettled with citizens of the conquering nation. Return of the territory to its Arab inhabitants was becoming more and more difficult as Israeli settlements multiplied (see Map 31.2).

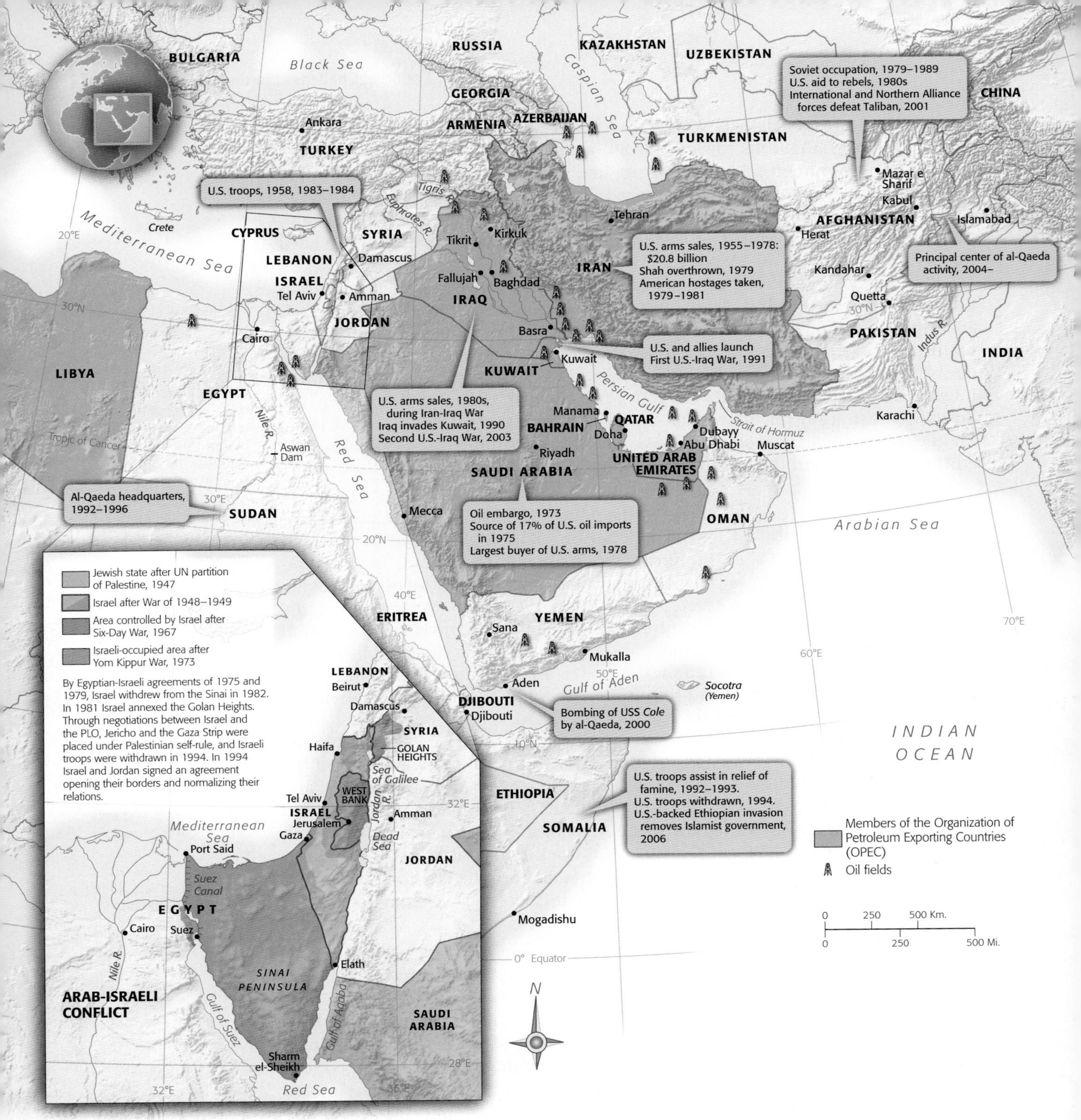

Map 31.2 Middle East Oil and the Arab-Israeli Conflict Not all Arabs and Arab states benefit from Middle Eastern oil reserves, which are highly concentrated in Saudi Arabia and the Persian Gulf. Farther west, Israel, born into a state of war when attacked by its Arab neighbors in 1948, ruled over significant Palestinian populations after taking the West Bank from Jordan and the Gaza Strip from Egypt during the Six-Day War in 1967. Whatever their other disagreements, Arabs have been unified in their denunciation of the Israeli occupation of the West Bank.

The Palestine Liberation Organization (PLO), under the leadership of Yasir Arafat (yah-SEER AHR-ah-FAT) (1929–2004), felt justified in using any means to resist the Israeli occupation, including terrorist attacks on civilians. In 1982, Israel invaded Lebanon to root out PLO bases, driving the group's leadership into North African exile. The savagery of the attacks on their refugee camps, combined with the retreat of the secular PLO, now led many Palestinians to switch their support to Islamist organizations: the Iranian-supported Hezbollah ("Party of God") in Lebanon, and in Palestine, Hamas (the "Islamic Resistance Movement"), a Sunni group related to Egypt's Muslim Brotherhood.

Violence flared again in Palestine in 1987 with the beginning of the first *intifada*, "ceaseless struggle," against the Israeli occupation of Gaza and the West Bank. The Israelis responded with security regulations restricting Palestinian mobility. Even as the intifada and the harsh Israeli response increased tensions on the ground, however, diplomatic initiatives were starting to bear some fruit.

In 1991, under European and American sponsorship, Israeli and Palestinian diplomats met to discuss possibilities for compromise, and in 1993 the Oslo

Hope for Middle East Peace This 1993 handshake between Israeli Prime Minister Yitzhak Rabin and Yasir Arafat, chairman of the Palestine Liberation Organization, gave the world hope for a Middle East peace. However, negotiations for an Israeli-PLO peace accord, mediated by U.S. President Bill Clinton, proved unsuccessful. (Reuters/Corbis)

Accords laid out a mutually agreed-upon "road map" for peace based on the idea of two separate and secure nations living side by side. President Clinton then invited Yasir Arafat and Israeli Prime Minister Yitzhak Rabin (YIT-shak rah-BEEN) to Washington for direct talks. As in South Africa at the very same time, it seemed that the post–Cold War climate meant the possibility of a new beginning.

The outcome dashed those hopes, however, when Arafat refused to accept an Israeli land-for-peace offer more generous than any previously discussed. The status of Jerusalem was one sticking point, with Israelis and Palestinians both laying claim to the city as their capital. In addition, the Israelis would not accept the Palestinian demand for a "right of return" for Arabs to the homes within Israel they had abandoned in the war of 1948. The "road map" had led nowhere.

Globalization and Its Discontents

The fall of the Soviet Union put economic globalization front and center on the world's agenda. Expanding global trade led to unprecedented growth and international economic integration. Some Asian economies surged, with the so-called "Asian Tigers," leading the way. Overcoming the disruptions of the Cultural Revolution (see Chapter 30), the People's Republic of China became the world's fastest-growing economy by adopting market principles.

When the European Economic Community transformed into the European Union (EU) in the 1990s, western Europe instantly became the world's largest single market. Expanding into the former Soviet sphere, the EU integrated parts of eastern Europe more fully into the world economy.

Amid the growth in trade and the incorporation of millions into global networks of consumption, it was also becoming clear that economic globalization brought increasing inequality. Both within nations and between them, the benefits of economic growth were not shared equally, as the gap between the global haves and have-nots increased. *Neoliberalism*, a belief in unfettered markets and unhindered international trade, proved popular with policymakers, but controversial to those who emphasized the more damaging effects of globalization.

Japan and the "Asian Tigers"

While Japan led the way in Asian economic growth in the 1950s, over the next three decades a number of other Asian economies would take off. Counted among these "Asian Tigers" were South Korea, Taiwan, and Singapore.

Japan rose quickly from the battering it took in 1945. Under occupation by the United States, Japanese leaders renounced militarism and accepted the democratic constitution Americans drafted for them. The energy and drive that had earlier gone into empire building was now focused on domestic rebirth. Fukuzawa Yûkichi (see Chapter 24) would have been proud as Japanese products came to surpass those of Europe and the United States in both quality and price.

Several factors facilitated Japanese economic success. American military protection relieved the country of the financial burden of military spending, and close collaboration between the government bureaucracy and large corporations brought planning and coordination to the national economy. Old corporations, like Mitsui, and new ones, like Sony, developed organizational structures that emphasized long-term loyalty between employers and Japanese employees, famous for their work ethic. However, company loyalty entailed endless work hours, and many Japanese women lived confining lives, raising children while rarely seeing their husbands.

- **CONTEXT&CONNECTIONS** In Japan, close coordination between large conglomerates and government civil servants began during the *Meiji Restoration*, when the government cultivated close relations with the large economic combines known as *zaibatsu* (Chapter 24). ●

In the 1970s, Japan enjoyed a rapid increase in automobile exports, especially to the United States. Japanese models first targeted consumers of inexpensive yet well-built cars. Meanwhile, manufacturers in the United States built large vehicles of indifferent quality. After oil prices surged following the OPEC oil boycott in 1973, demand for the more fuel-efficient Japanese cars skyrocketed.

At the same time, the rising price of oil revealed vulnerabilities in the Japanese economy. In addition to being dependent on food and energy imports, Japan was subject to competition from other Asian nations that began to follow the same industrial export strategy with lower labor costs. Japan responded by shifting from heavy industry toward knowledge-intensive sectors such as computers and telecommunications. Backed by large government subsidies for research and development, Japanese corporations in the 1980s increasingly focused on such high-profit activities while relocating many of their factories to other countries.

Then, even as American executives studied the Japanese model for business success, the bubble burst. In 1989, the Tokyo Stock Exchange collapsed. Real estate speculation, political corruption, and a banking crisis caused by bad loans were to blame. Demographics also played a role: Japan's low birth rate and stagnant population limited the expansion of domestic markets. To reignite the economy, the government began to emphasize leisure and consumption over savings, hoping that the country could spend its way out of crisis. While the Japanese economy stabilized, Asian growth moved elsewhere.

The South Korean government emulated the Japanese model, including close coordination between the state administration and the emerging Korean *chaebols*, economic conglomerates such as Samsung and Hyundai. It was also fiercely anticommunist, led by authoritarian personalities with close ties to the military, and paramilitary police often met student and worker protests with fatal force. The South Korean formula of authoritarian rule plus economic growth lasted until 1988, when public revulsion over the violent treatment of student protestors finally led to free elections and political liberalization.

- **CONTEXT&CONNECTIONS** In South Korea, the Summer Olympics of 1988 proved a spur to democratization, with the government anxious to showcase progressive reforms after its earlier harsh suppression of protests. That was the opposite of what had happened in Mexico twenty years earlier, when government suppression of protests leading up to the 1968 summer games culminated in the *Tlatelolco Massacre* (Chapter 30). ●

In Taiwan as well, anticommunism had led to a stern authoritarian political order dominated by Nationalist Party exiles from the mainland (see Chapter 30). As in South Korea, political liberty to match economic gains came to Taiwan only when global circumstances changed in the late 1980s, with the decline of the Soviet Union and the growth of trade with a now market-oriented Chinese mainland. In Taiwan's newly democratic political culture of the 1990s it was even possible to openly debate the previously forbidden topic of whether to declare Taiwanese independence rather than aspire to eventual reunification with the mainland. The liberal equation of rule of law, democratic processes, and free markets was being achieved.

The city-state of Singapore was the quintessence of an "Asian Tiger," its single-minded emphasis on economic growth bringing results that made it the envy of its neighbors. The success of tightly regimented Singapore led some analysts to speak of "Confucian capitalism," based on group consensus and hierarchy rather than individualism and class conflict, as an alternative to the individualistic Western model. But no generalizations about Asian capitalism could be made without taking into account the transformation of the People's Republic of China.

Deng Xiaoping's China and Its Imitators

At the start of the nineteenth century China produced about one-third of the world's industrial output (see page 685). But in 1949, after a century and a half of European economic dominance, that percentage had shrunk to less than 3 percent. The country's astonishing economic growth in the last two decades of the twentieth century restored China's historical role as a global center of manufacturing. More people were lifted out of poverty than at any previous stage in human history.

Deng Xiaoping (1904–1997) Chinese Communist Party leader who brought dramatic economic reforms after the death of Mao Zedong.

That turnabout resulted from the policies of **Deng Xiaoping** (1904–1997). After Mao's death (see Chapter 30), Deng put China on a new economic path by adopting market incentives. The first step was to grant peasants their own farm plots for private cultivation. Food production surged. Deng became a hero to millions of Chinese farming families, who could now afford small luxuries for the first time. When asked how he, a lifelong communist, justified adopting capitalist principles, Deng replied: *"It does not matter whether the cat is black or white, as long as she catches mice." "To get rich,"* he added, *"is glorious."*

• **CONTEXT&CONNECTIONS** During the *Great Leap Forward* (Chapter 30), Deng Xiaoping was among the "experts" Mao Zedong derided for putting pragmatism above ideology. In the 1960s Deng was "sent down" to work in a tractor factory during the Great Proletarian Cultural Revolution, before re-emerging in the 1970s to defeat the radical "Gang of Four." •

AP® THEMES

What allowed for the growing presence of multinational corporations in China?

The second stage in Deng's reforms was development of the industrial sector. In the southern region of Guangzhou, near the British-controlled territory of Hong Kong, foreign investors were invited to build manufacturing plants in an embrace of international capitalism unthinkable under Mao. Many multinational corporations moved their manufacturing operations to Guangzhou to take advantage of China's cheap labor.

Chinese banks funded local investors with connections to the Communist Party. The Red Army itself became a major economic power, controlling one of the world's largest shipping lines. As manufacturing spread from Guangzhou throughout eastern and central China, a vast flow of finished goods crossed the Pacific destined for American markets. China's cities experienced a huge construction boom, attracting millions of rural migrants. The coastal city of Shanghai became a glittering cosmopolitan center, as traffic jams and billboards replaced bicycles and moralistic party posters.

Although Deng Xiaoping resigned from his post in 1987, he remained a dominant power behind the scenes until his death in 1997. During that period, both the costs and benefits of his policies became more and more apparent. A great success was the return of Hong Kong in 1997 from British to Chinese control. Communist leaders promised that under their "one country, two systems" policy the people of Hong Kong would retain their accustomed civil liberties such as rights of free speech and assembly

The biggest test of Deng's career came in 1989. Student activists, yearning for political change to match the economic transformation of their country, organized a large antigovernment rally, erecting a replica of the Statue of Liberty in the heart of Beijing to symbolize their goals of greater freedom and an end to corruption. This student-led prodemocracy movement ended with the **Tiananmen Massacre**, in which hundreds, perhaps thousands, of student activists were killed and many more arrested.

Some Chinese officials had advocated a moderate approach and reconciliation with the students, but hardliners wanted to crush the student demonstrations. Ultimately the decision was up to Deng, who remembered the chaos caused by student rebels during the Cultural Revolution and backed the hardliners. Aware of how Mikhail Gorbachev's policy of glasnost was undermining the Soviet Union, China's communist hardliners were unwilling to put their own political monopoly at risk.

Dylan Martinez/AFP/Getty Images

Hong Kong, 1997 The return of Hong Kong to China ended more than 150 years of British rule. As in India and dozens of other former colonies in prior decades, the Union Jack was lowered and "God Save the Queen" played for the final time; the flag of the People's Republic of China was then raised to mark the transfer of sovereignty

Entering the 1990s, China's economic transformation was generating other challenges as well. Environmental problems multiplied. The gap between rich and poor increased, as did imbalances between wealthier coastal regions and China's interior. As corruption spread, protests increased among the same rural population that Mao had made the center of his revolution. Still, the economic policies of Deng Xiaoping had raised China to the status of a great power. Many Chinese felt that their country had returned to its proper historical place after two centuries of humiliation by Western powers and Japan.

Tiananmen Massacre

Massacre in a public square in Beijing where, in 1989, students and workers demanded freedom and democracy. On order from the Communist Party, the Chinese military cleared Tiananmen Square with tanks and gunfire.

China's competitive advantage was its political stability combined with low-cost labor. By the 1990s other Asian countries were also able to build up export-oriented manufacturing centers. American consumers hardly even noticed that much of their clothing and other commodities were now produced in places like Thailand, Malaysia, Indonesia, and Vietnam. For much of the twentieth century, nationalist leaders in these countries had dreamed of catching up with the West through industrialization. Now, like China, they were moving toward that goal.

The industrial path to prosperity was now complicated, however, by the changing nature of the global economy. Manufacturing was being overtaken by marketing, financial services, and other "knowledge industries" as the highest value-producing activities. In fact, for many Asian workers, industrialization brought little benefit. Young women with few skills other than manual dexterity made up much of the industrial workforce, and child labor was all too common. As global consumers demanded ever-cheaper products, wages remained low in China, Southeast Asia, and other industrial economies. Even in richer countries, industrial workers began to see their wages decline, or their jobs disappear, in the face of competition from low-cost Asian labor.

The European Union

Beginning in the 1980s, western European leaders, especially in France and Germany, sought to deepen cooperation throughout the European Economic Community. A European Parliament, with little real authority but great symbolic importance, was elected. Negotiations began to open borders, create a single internal market free of tariffs, and move toward a common European currency. As the Soviet Union began to dissolve, talk turned to the possibility of incorporating new members from the former Eastern bloc.

AP® THEMES
What is the relationship between the European Union and individual governments of member nations?

In 1992, the Treaty on European Union was signed at the Dutch city of Maastricht. It set a date of January 1, 1999, for the introduction of the euro (the EU's proposed currency), limited the amount of public debt that a nation could hold to be admitted to the union, and created a European Central Bank to coordinate monetary policy.

Some complained that a European "superstate" run by faceless bureaucrats in Brussels would undermine national sovereignty, and Great Britain, Denmark, and Sweden all rejected the euro, refusing to surrender control of their own currencies. But the signatories approved the open market provisions of the Maastricht Treaty, and with an internal market larger than that of the United States and members who represented complementary economic and human resources, the European Union was launched as a major success (see Map 31.3).

By century's end, the European Union accounted for over 18 percent of global exports. Growth rates were especially high in poorer, more agricultural countries. Spain, Greece, and Portugal, all of which had suffered from authoritarian governments, became modern democracies with significantly more educated populations. Ireland was dubbed the "Celtic Tiger" for its transformation from an agrarian society to one based on strong educational foundations and prowess in high technology (See the feature "Movement of Ideas Through Primary Sources: The End of History?").

• **CONTEXT&CONNECTIONS** Global recession in 2008 would reveal that much of the impressive growth in Ireland and the Mediterranean had been based on property speculation and irresponsible government spending. Tensions then developed between northern European governments, especially Germany, and the Mediterranean countries of the European Union, Greece in particular, over monetary policy and the need for austerity (see Chapter 32). •

Even while pursuing market integration, some Europeans rejected what they saw as the excesses of unfettered American-style capitalism and consumerism. In Italy, partisans of the "slow food" movement focused on fresh local ingredients, careful preparation, and leisurely dining with family and friends, a direct contrast with American "fast food" culture. In France, the government reflected popular feeling when, concerned that the "new world order" really meant cultural Americanization, it subsidized French film productions to fend off domination by Hollywood. In Germany, public support for state-run pension and health care systems

Map 31.3 The European Union The European Union (EU) developed from the more limited European Economic Community, dominated by France and the Federal Republic of Germany. The United Kingdom, Ireland, Denmark, Spain, Portugal, and Greece were added in the 1970s and 1980s. The collapse of the Soviet Union led to a dramatic EU expansion into eastern Germany, central and southeastern Europe, and the Nordic and Baltic countries. Turkey's application for membership proved controversial, while Russia has resisted the inclusion of Georgia and Ukraine.

remained nearly universal, even as some economists in the United States touted the supposed advantages of "free market" alternatives.

Neoliberalism, Inequality, and Economic Globalization

Even as economists celebrated the virtues of expanding free trade, citing persistent growth, critics continued to rail against the new global economic regime of **neoliberalism**, the emphasis on free markets not only for their stimulation of trade, but also for their supposed efficiency in dealing with social issues, like education and health care,

neoliberalism
The renewed emphasis on free-market policies that accompanied globalization at the end of the Cold War.

The End of History?

No longer able to use the familiar compass points of East-West conflict, scholars and political analysts at the end of the Cold War struggled to find ways to describe the "new world order" and to anticipate its future direction. One of the most discussed contributions to this literature in the early 1990s was Francis Fukuyama's essay "The End of History."

Fukuyama, a Japanese American, was employed by the U.S. state department when he wrote this article. At that time, in 1989, he was associated with neoconservatism, a movement that stressed the right and responsibility of the United States to unilaterally assert its power across the globe in the defense of American interests, including the promotion of American values of political freedom and economic enterprise. After the neoconservatives achieved great political influence under the administration of George W. Bush, however, Fukuyama broke with them over the issue of the Iraq War (see Chapter 32).

❯ Historical Thinking Skill:

PERIODIZATION According to Fukuyama, what will be different about the history of the world from the late twentieth century and beyond from before the end of the Cold War? What will remain the same?

Source: Francis Fukuyama, "The End of History," *The National Interest*, Summer, 1989.

In watching the flow of events over the past decade or so, it is hard to avoid the feeling that something very fundamental has happened in world history. The past year has seen a flood of articles commemorating the end of the Cold War, and the fact that "peace" seems to be breaking out in many regions of the world.... [T]he century that began full of self-confidence in the ultimate triumph of Western liberal democracy seems at its close to be returning full circle to where it started ... to an unabashed victory of economic and political liberalism....

What we may be witnessing is not just the end of the Cold War ... but the end of history as such: that is, the end point of mankind's ideological evolution and the universalization of Western liberal democracy as the final form of human government.... [T] he victory of liberalism has occurred primarily in the realm of ideas or consciousness and is as yet incomplete in the real or material world. But there are powerful reasons for believing that it is the ideal that will govern the material world in the long run....

The state that emerges at the end of history is liberal insofar as it recognizes and protects through a system of law man's universal right to freedom; and democratic insofar as it exists only with the consent of the governed.... [H]istory ended ... in the ideals of the French or American Revolutions: while particular regimes in the real world might not implement these ideals fully, their theoretical truth is absolute and could not be improved upon....

In the past century, there have been two major challenges to liberalism, those of fascism and of communism. The former saw the political weakness, materialism, anomie, and lack of community of the West as fundamental contradictions in liberal societies that could only be resolved by a strong state that forged a new "people" on the basis of national exclusiveness. Fascism was destroyed as a living ideology by World War II. This was a defeat, of course, on a very material level, but it amounted to a defeat of the idea as well....

The ideological challenge mounted by the other great alternative to liberalism, communism, was far more serious. Marx ... asserted that liberal society contained a fundamental contradiction that could not be resolved within its context, that between capital and labor, and this contradiction has constituted the chief accusation against liberalism ever since. But surely, the class issue has actually been successfully resolved in the West.... [T]he egalitarianism of modern America represents the essential achievement of the classless society envisioned by Marx. This is not to say that there are not rich people and poor people in the United States, or that the gap between them has not grown in recent years. But the root causes of economic inequality do not have to do with the underlying legal and social structure of our society, which remains fundamentally egalitarian and moderately redistributionist....

[T]he power of the liberal idea would seem much less impressive if it had not infected the largest and oldest culture in Asia, China.... China could not now be described in any way as a liberal democracy.... But anyone familiar with the outlook and behavior of the new technocratic elite now governing China knows that Marxism and ideological principle have become virtually irrelevant as guides to policy.... The student demonstrations in Beijing that broke out... recently... were only the beginning of what will inevitably be mounting pressure for change in the political system as well.... The central issue is the fact that the People's Republic of China can no longer act as a beacon for illiberal forces around the world.... Maoism, rather than being the pattern for Asia's future, became an anachronism....

Important as these changes in China have been, however, it is developments in the Soviet Union ... that have put the final nail in the coffin of the Marxist-Leninist alternative to liberal democracy.... What has happened in the four years since Gorbachev's coming to power is a revolutionary assault on the most fundamental institutions and principles of Stalinism, and their replacement by other principles which do not amount to liberalism per se but whose only connecting thread is liberalism....

[A]re there any other ideological competitors left? ... The rise of religious fundamentalism in recent years within the Christian, Jewish, and Muslim traditions has been widely noted.... In the contemporary world only Islam has offered a theocratic state as a political alternative to both liberalism and communism. But the doctrine has little appeal for non-Muslims, and it is hard to believe that the movement will take on any universal significance....

This does not by any means imply the end of international conflict per se.... There would still be a high and perhaps rising level of ethnic and nationalist violence.... This implies that terrorism and wars of national liberation will continue to be an important item on the international agenda. But large-scale conflict must involve large states still caught in the grip of history, and they are what appear to be passing from the scene.

The end of history will be a very sad time. The struggle for recognition, the willingness to risk one's life for a purely abstract goal, the worldwide ideological struggle that called forth daring, courage, imagination, and idealism, will be replaced by economic calculation, the endless solving of technical problems, environmental concerns, and the satisfaction of sophisticated consumer demands. In the post-historical period there will be neither art nor philosophy, just the perpetual caretaking of the museum of human history.... Perhaps this very prospect of centuries of boredom at the end of history will serve to get history started once again.

previously dominated by governments. For neoliberal economists, government intrusions into markets, no matter how well intended, decrease efficiency, increase corruption, and lead to unintended consequences such as diminished availability of services in high demand. For their part, critics of neoliberalism emphasize that without the regulatory oversight of democratically elected governments, neoliberal policies lead to sharpening inequalities in income and access to services, while undercutting labor, environmental, and consumer protections.

• **CONTEXT&CONNECTIONS** What are called "conservative" economic policies in the United States (limiting the size of government, balancing budgets, freeing markets from constraints) are, in most of the world, described as "liberal" or "neoliberal," in accordance with the original nineteenth-century meaning (see Chapter 23). Pressures on governments to allow companies to more easily dismiss workers, for example, might thus be described as moves to "liberalize" labor markets (see Chapter 32). •

Neoliberalism appeared in the 1980s in the guise of "structural adjustment programs" imposed on indebted nations seeking its fiscal help by the International Monetary Fund (IMF), established as part of the *Bretton Woods* accords in 1944 (Chapter 29). After the OPEC oil boycott caused surging petroleum prices in the mid-1970s, "petrodollars" flooded the world's financial institutions, making it easy for poorer nations to borrow money for development projects. Much of that money was poorly invested, or even stolen by corrupt officials. When a global recession struck in 1980 and lenders called in those loans, many Third World nations were unable to pay.

The IMF, as the international "lender of last resort," was willing to offer emergency loans to keep those nations solvent, but only if debtors met "structural adjustment" criteria requiring sharp cuts in government spending. IMF economists argued that state interference in markets was constraining economic activity and that only by slashing state expenditures could developing countries reach sustainable levels of growth.

• **CONTEXT&CONNECTIONS** The IMF was established as part of the *Bretton Woods* accords in 1944 (Chapter 29) specifically to keep debtor nations solvent and thus to avoid the type of international credit crisis that had deepened the *Great Depression* (Chapter 28). •

Structural adjustment programs caused suffering. In Mexico, structural adjustment meant cutting government subsidies on the price of maize meal, causing a sharp rise in the price of tortillas, and thus more hungry children. In the East African nation of Tanzania, education was put at risk after the country accepted an IMF loan in 1987 and was then forced to lay off thousands of teachers to help balance its books. Nevertheless, advocates of structural adjustment argued that, in the long term, the "magic of the market" would align production and consumption and lead to greater prosperity, the only way to create abundance for the people of countries like Mexico and Tanzania.

In the 1990s, the economics of neoliberalism dominated discussions of the many free trade pacts then being negotiated, such as the North American Free Trade Association (NAFTA) of 1994, uniting Canada, the United States, and Mexico in a market even larger than that of the European Union. NAFTA was controversial. In the United States, critics warned that the removal of tariffs on Mexican imports would mean the loss of high-paying industrial jobs as manufacturers seeking to pay lower wages moved south of the border. In Mexico, farmers worried that they would be ruined by open competition with U.S. farmers, who were heavily subsidized by their government. Even as previously high-wage industrial jobs moved south, rural Mexicans would flee north because of falling crop prices.

In the southern state of Chiapas, rebels calling themselves Zapatistas (after the Mexican revolutionary Emiliano Zapata; see Chapter 25) declared "war on the Mexican state" in 1994, with NAFTA as one of their principal grievances. The Zapatistas were part of a global movement of people who sought to reassert their collective welfare against the free-market onslaught and to protect their culture and identity against the wave of globalization. But the Zapatistas faded from the headlines, while the conservative National Action Party (PAN) advocated even greater economic liberalization, broke the monopoly of the ruling party in the Mexican presidential elections of 2000.

In South Africa after 1994, a deep irony marked the policies of the Mandela administration. That government's neoliberal emphasis on free markets, though aligned with global trends, represented a sharp break with the ANC's long advocacy of state ownership of major industries as a means of achieving social justice and racial equality. Nelson Mandela himself, always a pragmatist, understood that market-led growth was the only way to enlarge the South African economic pie and provide more opportunity for those who had historically been excluded. Part of Mandela's great political achievement, and his lasting legacy, was his ability to convince his people that while political democracy could come quickly, patience was required to move the country toward social and economic equality.

Whether economists cheered the neoliberal expansion of free trade or critiqued it as a cruel system that built equity for a few on the backs of the many, one question was no longer at issue. Socialism, in its classic twentieth-century formulations, was gone. For better or worse, capitalism was now the only game being played in the global economy. (See the feature "Movement of Ideas Through Primary Sources: The End of History?")

CONTEXT AND CONNECTIONS

Beyond the "Age of Extremes"?

Eric Hobsbawm, a prominent British historian, referred to twentieth-century world history as the "Age of Extremes." Like Nelson Mandela, Hobsbawm was born while the First World War still raged, and like Mandela he could reflect back from the year 2000 on a lifetime during which rapid and unpredictable change seemed the only constant.

When Mandela and Hobsbawm were young, radio was still a new invention, telephones were a luxury, commercial aviation was in its infancy, and the British empire was the framework for the world around them, a world in which European domination was taken for granted. At the end of the century, both men had lived long enough to witness the development of instantaneous global telecommunications, a thoroughly integrated global economy, and a population that had grown from less than 2 billion to over 6 billion persons.

In the interim, momentous events had rocked the world: the Great Depression; the rise of communism and fascism; the Second World War and the Holocaust; the development of nuclear weapons and the Cold War; the collapse of the European and Soviet empires; the transformation of China and other Asian economies; and the re-creation of a brutally racist South Africa into a beacon of post–Cold War democracy and racial reconciliation. An "Age of Extremes" indeed!

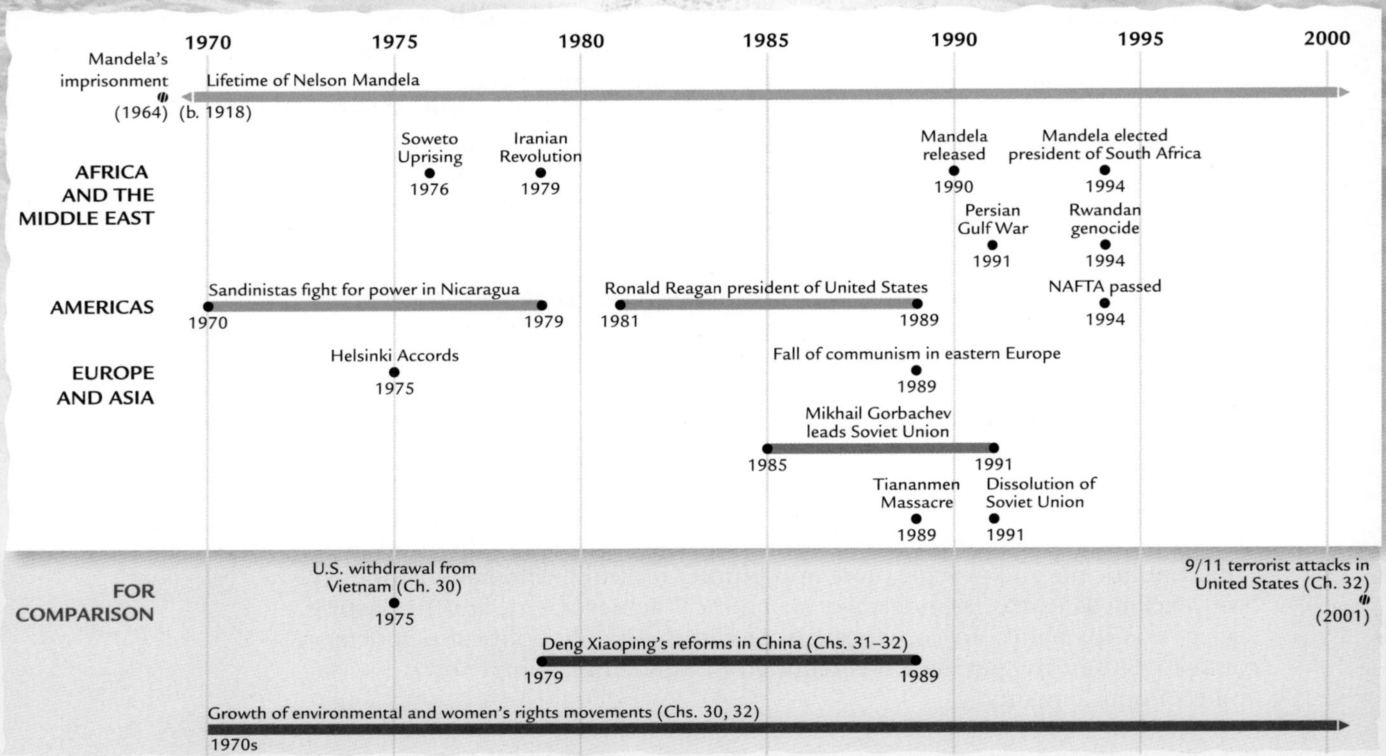

The entire history of the rise and fall of the Soviet Union took place during these single lifetimes. True, communism persisted. But China and Vietnam had transformed their economies using market principles, hardly an advertisement for the superiority of Karl Marx's economic philosophy (see Chapter 23). In North Korea and Cuba, it became doubtful that communism could long survive the economic failure of their leaders. Everywhere else communism had retreated: just a handful of nations were all that was left of the great hopes and the great fears raised by communism in the twentieth century—a paltry legacy. The retreat was seen even in South Africa, where the Communist Party, close allies of Nelson Mandela and the African National Congress in the struggle against apartheid, now advocated private enterprise rather than state control as the key to economic growth and improvements in the lives of the African majority.

However, even as the world celebrated the dawn of a new millennium and U.S. President Bill Clinton talked of "*building a bridge to the twenty-first century*," new challenges appeared. Genocide in Rwanda and other human rights abuses driven by ethnicity and religion had shown that the extreme hatreds of the old century had not been entirely left behind. More broadly, commentators observed the rise of religious extremism as a menace to secular and Enlightenment traditions. Such fears were magnified after the attacks by Islamic militants on the World Trade Center in New York and the Pentagon in Washington on September 11, 2001, and by the highly controversial U.S. invasion of Iraq a few years later. These events are too recent for proper historical analysis, but in the final chapter of this book we will attempt a survey of twenty-first-century realities in a world that has become smaller and smaller thanks to the political, economic, technological, and cultural dynamics of accelerating globalization.

Key Terms

Nelson Mandela (934)
Ronald Reagan (935)
Helsinki Accords (936)
Mikhail Gorbachev (937)
Solidarity (938)
Boris Yeltsin (939)
Bantustans (945)
Soweto Uprising (945)
Organization of Petroleum Exporting Countries (949)
Islamists (949)
Ayatollah Khomeini (949)
Persian Gulf War (951)
Osama bin Laden (951)
Deng Xiaoping (956)
Tiananmen Massacre (957)
neoliberalism (959)

For Further Reference

Barber, Benjamin. *Jihad vs. McWorld: How Globalism and Tribalism Are Reshaping the World.* New York: Times Books, 1995.

Garthoff, Raymond. *The Great Transition: American-Soviet Relations at the End of the Cold War.* Washington, D.C.: Brookings, 1994.

Gerlach, Christian. *Extremely Violent Societies: Mass Violence in the Twentieth Century World.* New York: Cambridge University Press, 2010.

Iriye, Akira, Petra Goedde, and William I. Hitchcock, eds. *The Human Rights Revolution: An International History.* New York: Oxford University Press, 2012.

Judt, Tony. *Thinking the Twentieth Century.* New York: Penguin, 2012.

Kagan, Robert. *Of Paradise and Power: America and Europe in the New World Order.* New York: Knopf, 2003.

Kenney, Padraic. *1989: Democratic Revolutions at the Cold War's End: A Brief History with Documents.* New York: Bedford/St. Martin's, 2009.

Mamdani, Mahmood. *Good Muslim, Bad Muslim: America, the Cold War, and the Roots of Terror.* New York: Crown, 2005.

Mandela, Nelson. *Long Walk to Freedom: The Autobiography of Nelson Mandela.* Boston: Little, Brown, 1996.

Marti, Michael. *China and the Legacy of Deng Xiaoping: From Communist Revolution to Capitalist Evolution.* Washington, D.C.: Potomac, 2002.

Sebestyn, Sebastian. *Revolution 1989: The Fall of the Soviet Empire.* New York: Vintage, 2010.

Smith, Charles D. *Palestine and the Arab-Israeli Conflict.* 7th ed. New York: Bedford/St. Martin's, 2009.

Smith, Peter H. *Democracy in Latin America: Political Change in Comparative Context.* 2d ed. New York: Oxford University Press, 2011.

AP® Review Questions for Chapter 31

Multiple-Choice Questions

QUESTIONS 1–3 REFER TO THE FOLLOWING PASSAGE.

The student demonstrations in Beijing that broke out . . . recently . . . were only the beginning of what will inevitably be mounting pressure for change in the political system as well. . . . The central issue is the fact that the People's Republic of China can no longer act as a beacon for illiberal forces around the world. . . . Maoism, rather than being the pattern for Asia's future, became an anachronism. Important as these changes in China have been, however, it is developments in the Soviet Union . . . that have put the final nail in the coffin of the Marxist-Leninist alternative to liberal democracy. . . . What has happened in the four years since Gorbachev's coming to power is a revolutionary assault on the most fundamental institutions and principles of Stalinism, and their replacement by other principles which do not amount to liberalism per se but whose only connecting thread is liberalism.

—Francis Fukuyama, U.S. State Department official, "The End of History," 1989

1. Which of the following factors contributed to the decline of Stalinism in the Soviet Union according to Francis Fukuyama?
   (A) The European Economic Community
   (B) The fascist corporatist economy
   (C) The *perestroika* and *glasnost* reforms
   (D) Socialism in One State

2. With regard to the late twentieth century, the processes involved with the passage above are best understood in the context of
   (A) increased government encouragement of free-market policies.
   (B) government control of national economies.
   (C) movements to protest growing economic inequality.
   (D) implementation of transnational trading networks.

3. Which of the following was an important continuity underlying the changes described in the passage above?
   (A) China and the Soviet Union continued to closely collaborate on political and economic affairs.
   (B) Despite setbacks, communism continued to spread throughout Southeast Asia and Latin America.
   (C) Both the Soviet Union and China refused involvement in the United Nations.
   (D) The communist parties in both China and the Soviet Union maintained primary economic control.

QUESTIONS 4–6 REFER TO THE FOLLOWING PASSAGE.

With only a few exceptions, Africa's present leaders are broadly agreed on the direction of economic policy, and the requirements for its success. They have unanimously endorsed a program accepting that successful economic development is linked to democracy; they have accepted the need for an enlarged private sector and the shrinking of the state sector; they have come to terms with multinational corporations; and they have agreed to limit budget deficits to 3 percent per annum even though it usually involves reductions in spending on education, health, and welfare. All these policies are in line with the neo-liberal doctrines preached by the West. . . . Irrespective of the individual merits of each of the policies in current Western "economic correctness," collectively they reflect acceptance of, or submission to, the neo-liberal economic doctrines of the Western industrialized nations. They have been driven to accept, under internal and international pressure, that the price to be paid for foreign aid, possible relief from their heavy foreign debt, and attracting foreign capital investment, is to follow the West's prescription for economic growth.

—Colin Legum, journalist and political activist, *Africa Since Independence*, 1999

4. Which of the following conditions best explains Africa's political and economic transition described in the passage above?
   (A) African economies began to play a leading role in global commerce.
   (B) Globalization efforts had relative success within Africa.
   (C) African economic and political systems were unstable.
   (D) Former colonial powers developed the economies of their former possessions.

5. Which of the following organizations was instituted to facilitate the sort of economic development indicated in the passage above?
   (A) The International Monetary Fund
   (B) The United Nations
   (C) North Atlantic Treaty Organization
   (D) Multinational corporations

6. Which of the following conclusions about late-twentieth-century economic development in Africa is supported by the passage above?
   (A) Governments took a strong role in guiding economic life.
   (B) African states became less interdependent with the global economy.

(C) Free-market policies and economic liberalization were increasingly common techniques for growth.
(D) African states rejected regional trade agreements and focused on self-strengthening movements.

QUESTIONS 7–8 REFER TO MAP 31.2 *MIDDLE EAST OIL AND THE ARAB ISRAELI CONFLICT* ON PAGE 952.

7. Which of the following was a *direct* cause of the proliferation of oil fields shown on the map?
   (A) Increased prosperity that led to increased global demand for petroleum products
   (B) OPEC's attempt to monopolize the global oil market
   (C) The presence of Al-Qaeda, which had a destabilizing economic effect
   (D) A substantial increase of private enterprise in the region

8. Which of the following led directly to the political units shown on the map?
   (A) Ethnic and religious conflict that shaped present political borders
   (B) The borders that represented Ottoman administrative regions
   (C) Frequent American involvement in the region
   (D) The mandate system implemented after World War I

QUESTIONS 9–10 REFER TO THE FOLLOWING PASSAGE.

As it became clear that quantity and transport were the keys to profit in a modern salt industry, small producers began disappearing, and companies such as Morton began buying them out to become bigger. In the nineteenth century, more than a dozen salt companies operated in the southern end of San Francisco Bay. During the twentieth century, these companies were consolidated by the Leslie Salt Company. In 1978, Cargill bought Leslie, and today there are only two companies involved in San Francisco Bay salt, Cargill and Morton. . . . It was Morton's 1996 acquisition of Salinas du Midi, owners of the Aigues-Mortes saltworks, producers of France's leading brand, La Baleine, that made Morton the world's largest salt company.

—Mark Kurlansky, historian, *Salt: A World History*, 2002

9. The processes indicated in the passage above are most clearly an example of which of the following?
   (A) Economic isolationism
   (B) Globalization
   (C) Strict economic regulation
   (D) Expanding regional trade agreements

10. Based on your knowledge of world history, which of the following contributed LEAST to the economic changes described in the passage?
   (A) The development of regional trading coalitions
   (B) Increased global population due to improved food output and medical care
   (C) The thawing of relations between the West and former communist bloc states
   (D) Popular and consumer culture becoming more global

Short-Answer Questions

QUESTION 1 REFERS TO MAP 31.1 *DISSOLUTION OF THE SOVIET UNION* ON PAGE 938.

1. Answer parts A and B.
   A. Identify and explain TWO changes caused by the dissolution of the Soviet Union shown on the map.
   B. Identify and explain ONE continuity that was unaffected by the dissolution of the Soviet Union shown on the map.

2. Answer parts A, B, and C.
   A. Explain ONE cause of economic globalization.
   B. Explain ONE effect of economic globalization on the developed world.
   C. Explain ONE effect of economic globalization on the developing world.

32 Voyage into the Twenty-First Century

Ai Weiwei

Peter Macdiarmid/Getty Images

The experiences of Chinese artist **Ai Weiwei** (b. 1957) exemplify some of the best and some of the worst of contemporary China. On the one hand, Ai is a global face of the "new China," a highly respected creative talent whose works are internationally admired and whose innovative contributions to the design of the Beijing National Stadium for the 2008 Summer Olympics helped the People's Republic make a strong impression on the world. More recently, however, Ai Weiwei (eye way way) has been subjected to constant police surveillance: authorities shut down his influential blog, demolished his Shanghai studio, and in 2011 detained him for almost three months. Ai is a firm believer in freedom of speech and the rule of law, and his willingness to spread those beliefs through social media has led the government to tightly restrict his freedom of expression.

As of this writing, Ai is still barred from foreign travel, but he continues to work internationally. His site-specific exhibit @Large, exploring the theme of incarceration, was mounted in 2015 at the former Alcatraz Prison in San Francisco. *"The misconception of totalitarianism is that freedom can be imprisoned,"* he says on the exhibition website. *"This is not the case. When you constrain freedom, freedom will take flight and land on a windowsill."* Meanwhile, his reaction to house arrest is characteristically creative: *"every morning I am putting a bouquet of flowers in the basket of a bicycle outside the front door,"* Ai tweets, *"until I win back the right to travel."**

His father, Ai Qing (eye CHING), was one of China's leading poets, having traveled to Paris as a young man in the 1920s. He joined the Communist Party, was imprisoned by the Guomindang, and achieved fame in the 1950s before Mao declared an "anti-rightist" campaign and sent Ai Qing with his family into exile near the Gobi Desert. For twenty years his poetry was forbidden while he cleaned toilets at a "re-education" camp. His son, Ai Weiwei, grew up in bleak circumstances.

---

*For-Site Foundation, "@Large: Ai Weiwei on Alcatraz," http://www.for-site.org/project/ai-weiwei-alcatraz/.

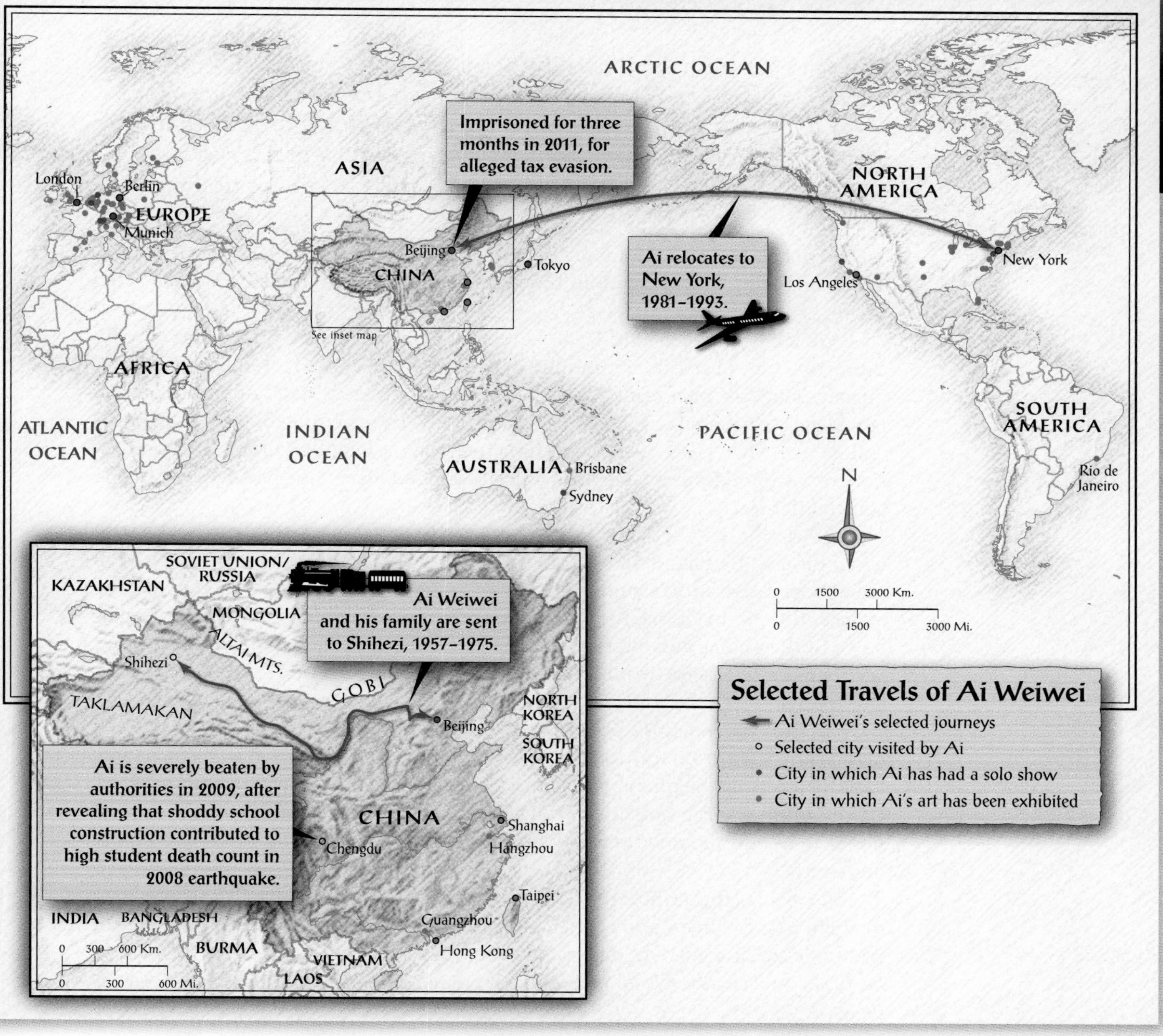

Even the thaw that came with Mao's death, and the return of his father to official favor, did not create the space Ai needed for his art. In 1981, at age twenty-four, he fled toward freedom:

In my mind I already thought New York was the capital of contemporary art. And I wanted to be on top. On the way to the airport my mom said things like "Do you feel sad because you don't speak English? . . .

Ai Weiwei

(b. 1957) A Chinese artist, blogger, and critic of the Communist government. His arrest and detention in 2011 focused global attention on the slow pace of democratization in China.

*You have no money" (I had thirty dollars in my hand).... I was so naïve, but I had so much confidence. I left because the activists from our same group were put in jail. The accusation was that they were spies from the West, which was total nonsense.... [W]e all got mad and even scared—you know, "this nation has no hope."**

Menial labor and financial hardship were part of Ai's New York experience, but so was freedom to explore, energized by the East Village artist scene.

When his father fell ill in 1993, Ai Weiwei returned home with the idea of replicating that type of artistic community in Beijing. A rapid rise to international success quickly followed, then came repression by the communist state. After schools collapsed in an earthquake, Ai angered the authorities by searching for the names of the children who had been killed, publishing them on his blog, and urging an investigation of corrupt dealings between officials and builders that had led to shoddy construction.

The timing of Ai's arrest in 2011 was not a coincidence. That was the year when protests broke out across the world. From the Arab Spring, to Occupy Wall Street, to massive anticorruption demonstrations in India, millions rose up to challenge authority. In China, the government clamped down harshly, fearing a recurrence of the Tiananmen protests of 1989 (see Chapter 31). Elsewhere, hopes rose, but then crashed as the world's elite regained their balance and fended off systematic change.

Did the events of 2011 point toward a different future, or were they just a flash in the pan? There is no way to be sure. Our survey of world history has given us some tools for assessing the recent past, but lacking adequate perspective, we cannot evaluate the most recent events historically. In this final chapter, therefore, our conclusions can be only tentative as we address some of the core issues facing contemporary humanity.

Meanwhile, the authors hope that as you read this, Ai Weiwei will have regained the right to travel freely and further enrich us all with his creative vision. A master at the use of social media, Ai's blogs and tweets have kept his story alive: "*Without the Internet, I would not even be Ai Weiwei today. I would just be an artist somewhere doing my shows.*"†

KEY CONCEPT QUESTION

› How have attitudes toward cultural and economic globalization, the environment, gender relations, and global security changed during the twenty-first century? **(Key Concept 6.3)**

---

*"Hans Ulrich Obrist in conversation with Ai Weiwei," in Ai Weiwei, Karen Smith, Hans Ulrich Obrist, and Berhard Fibicher, *Ai Weiwei* (New York: Phaidon, 2009), pp. 14–15.

†"Ai Wei Wei: Shame on Me," SPIEGEL International, 11, 24, 2011; http://www.spiegel.de/international/world/0,1518,799302,00.html.

Emerging Economic Players

Much of the discussion about the global economy in the early twenty-first century focused on rapid economic growth rates in emerging economies in Asia, Latin America, and Africa, a phenomenon that one analyst called "the rise of the rest."* Economists paid special attention to the exceptionally strong performance of Brazil, Russia, India, and China—the so-called **BRIC** nations—though Turkey, South Africa, and other countries were part of the conversation as well. To some, an equalization of centers of world economic activity seemed to be under way.

BRIC
"Brazil, Russia, India, and China," a shorthand reference to the fast-growing emergent economies of the twenty-first century. BRIC was formalized into an international organization, with the addition of South Africa in 2010, making it BRICS.

After 2014, the picture became somewhat more clouded as the United States regained momentum, Chinese growth slowed, and plunging commodity prices damaged export-dependent economies in Russia, Brazil, and elsewhere. Yet European and Japanese economies stagnated, and with China now the world's second largest economy and Brazil in sixth place, it still seemed that the longer-term trend was toward a more multicentered global economy.

China's economic rise and the story of contemporary economic globalization go hand in hand. When Ai Weiwei was a child in the 1960s, China's contributions to the global economy were meager. In 1981, when Ai left for the United States, the country had only just begun to benefit from Deng Xiaoping's market-oriented policies (see Chapter 31). Then a startling change took place. From the early 1990s until 2010, China's economy grew at an average annual rate of nearly 10 percent a year. (By contrast, Japan's annual growth rates since 1992 have never exceeded 3 percent and have often dipped into the negative range.)

Since the Communist Party takes credit for this economic juggernaut, it must also take responsibility for the less attractive side effects. Lax environmental standards and a reliance on high-sulfur coal have made the air toxic in Beijing and other urban manufacturing centers. Millions experienced social dislocation as the government forced them from ancestral villages into hastily constructed apartment towers in mushrooming cities. Endemic corruption leads to a cynical attitude, while government attempts to restrict access to information collide with China's agenda of participating in the global knowledge economy.

India is also rising to prominence as an emerging economy, though its vibrant multiparty democracy differs sharply from China's one-party totalitarianism. And while Chinese government and business leaders focused on industrial development for export, Indians have put a greater emphasis on high technology and their huge domestic market.

Economic liberalization in the early 1990s meant the lowering of business taxes and the lifting of government restrictions, leading to an onrush of Indian entrepreneurial activity. As in China, annual economic growth rates surged toward 10 percent. Earlier, under socialist policies, Indians might wait for years to have a telephone installed or to become eligible to purchase a car. Now members of the greatly expanded middle class buy the latest-model cars and electronics on credit, take foreign holidays, and get mortgages on newly constructed homes. Such is the "new India," with globally prominent high-technology and telecommunications sectors, the world's largest film industry, and large and influential expatriate communities around the globe.

*Fareed Zakaria, *The Post-American World, Release 2.0* (New York: Norton, 2011), p. 1.

Sajjad Hussain/AFP/Getty Images

Two Indias Mumbai is the largest city in India, with over 18 million inhabitants. The gleaming skyscrapers seen in the background provide both commercial space for the city's booming economy and residences for its fast-growing middle class. That new prosperity stands in stark contrast to the city's slums. Dharavi, shown in the foreground, might be the most crowded place on earth.

Yet amid the undeniable economic transformation, reliance on free markets has left many Indians behind. Corruption is endemic, with billions stolen through fraudulent contracts and many rural Indians losing their land through real estate swindles. Glistening new suburbs are protected by high walls and tight security from the noise and filth of overcrowded slums, while hundreds of millions of rural Indians live without access to clean water or basic sanitation, let alone computers.

Indeed, data from India, China, Brazil, the United States, and elsewhere show a strong correlation between global economic growth and rising inequality. Critics contend that in their haste to liberalize their economies, governments have abandoned the health and educational needs of their citizens. As one economist has argued, "The ancient question of how market forces need to be tempered for the greater good of the economy and the society is now a global one"* (see Map 32.1).

Vladimir Putin
The Russian leader who served from 2000 as either president or prime minister. Putin re-established state control over the largest sectors of the Russian economy and stimulated nationalism by reasserting the country's great power status.

In Russia, economic inequality escalated with the collapse of the Soviet Union. The rapid privatization of state assets in the 1990s benefited economic insiders, instant billionaires who formed a new economic oligarchy, while ordinary workers suffered (see Chapter 31). These post-Soviet oligarchs' lavish displays of wealth angered many, and in the early 2000s President **Vladimir Putin** played on that popular disgust to reassert state control over important sectors like energy, media, and telecommunications.

---

*Robert Kuttner, "The Role of Governments in the Global Economy," in *Global Capitalism*, ed. Will Hutton and Anthony Giddens (New York: New Press, 2000), p. 163.

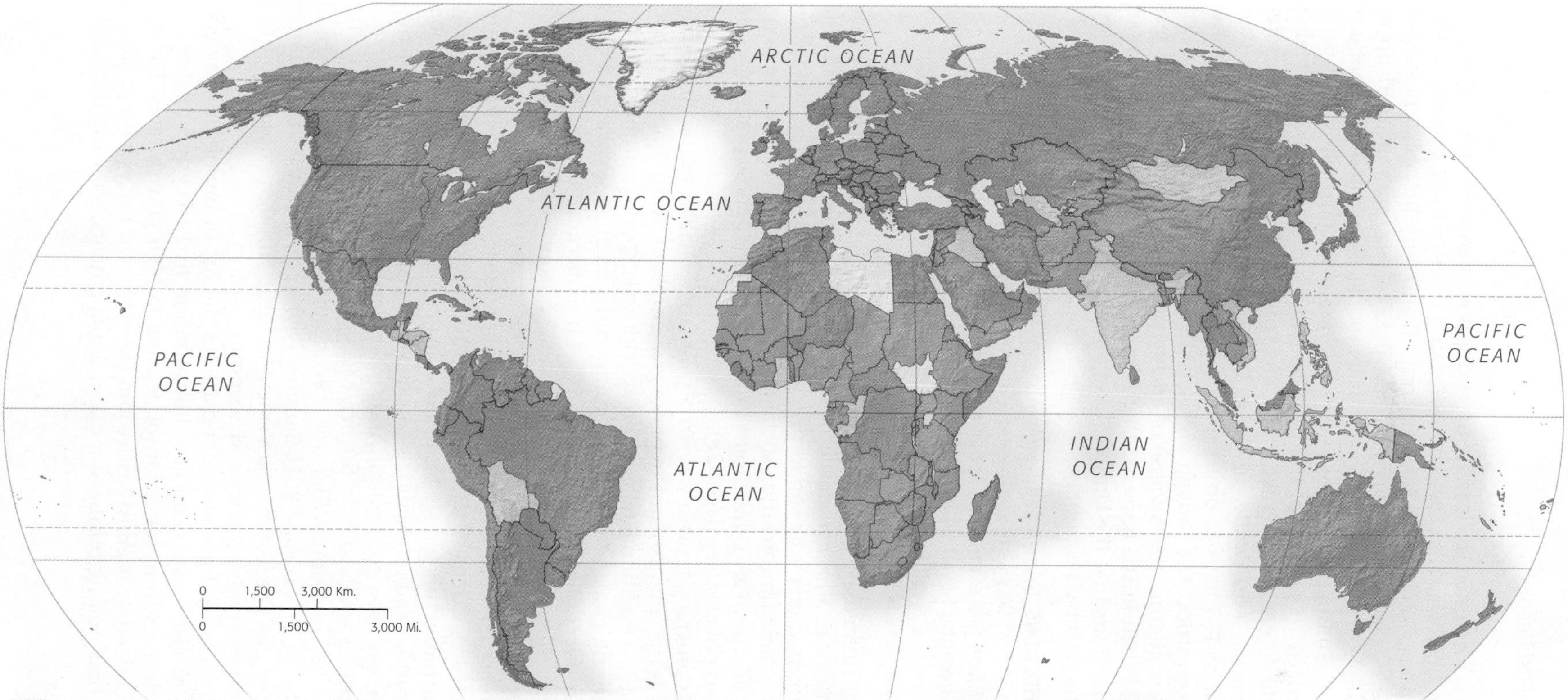

Map 32.1 Per Capita Income Despite recent surges in the economies of countries such as India, China, Russia, and Brazil, the global economy is still dominated by the United States, western Europe, Canada, Australia, and Japan. Per capita income gives only a rough estimate of people's quality of life, however. The United Nations Development Program (UNDP) uses a Human Development Report that takes account of a variety of factors in addition to income—such as education, health care, environmental standards, and gender equality—in its rankings. According to the UNDP, the island nation of Iceland ranks first in human development, Canada fourth, Japan eighth, France tenth, and the United States twelfth.* (Caption data from http://hdr.undp.org/en/statistics. Map data from *The World Almanac and Book of Facts, 2008*, ed. C. Alan Joyce (World Almanac Books, 2008).

Putin was less interested in cleaning up corruption than in eliminating political competition, however. His reassertion of state power put key economic and telecommunications sectors under his own control, and once he had dispossessed and jailed those oligarchs who opposed him, Putin's own cronies lined up to benefit. For example, a government review of textbooks eliminated most options other than those published by one of Putin's billionaire friends, whose company was thus guaranteed 70 percent of the market. Though information about such dealings is available on the Internet, most Russians get their news from state-controlled television. Meanwhile, in 2014 Transparency International ranked Russia 136th out of 175 nations on its Corruption Perception Index, well below the other BRIC countries. And though high oil and gas prices had once burnished Russia's economic gilding, the collapse of energy prices in 2014 revealed its less impressive core. When Russia annexed the Crimean peninsula in the same year, the economic sanctions that the United States and the European Union imposed also damaged the country's economy.

• **CONTEXT&CONNECTIONS** Crimea had become part of the Russian empire at the time of *Catherine the Great* (key term in Chapter 20) and has served as a vital naval station on the Black Sea ever since. It had reverted to Ukraine after that country's independence from the Soviet Union (see Chapter 31), only to be occupied by Russian troops after a revolt in the Ukrainian capital of Kiev unseated an unpopular pro-Russian leader in 2014. •

In Brazil, the immensely popular President Luiz Inácio Lula da Silva (in office 2003–2010) came from a background of labor organization and advocacy for the poor, but he surprised many by supporting growth through economic liberalization, while at the same time creating social programs as a safety net for the poor. Lula's successor and protégé, Dilma Rousseff, has maintained these pragmatic and socially conscious policies (see page 928).

AP® THEMES

What have been the social and environmental effects of the economic policies the leaders of the BRIC nations have implemented in the twenty-first century?

Under Lula's program, growth was strong in many Brazilian sectors, including manufacturing, as the country came to play a greater role in South America's interregional trade. Still, a traditional reliance on agricultural exports continued, further stimulated by strong global demand for commodities such as soybeans (though in 2014 soybean prices plunged; see page 759). China became a huge market for Brazilian exports, showing the rising importance of "south to south" economic transactions among emerging economies in the BRIC grouping.

As elsewhere, rapid economic growth had a dark side in Brazil. Environmental concerns mounted as extensive Amazonian territories were cleared for farm and pasture land, intruding on forests that play a major role in cleaning the global atmosphere of surplus carbon. Scandals ensued when fast money tempted officials and business people into corruption. And, in spite of Lula's s social programs, Brazilian inequalities widened even further. Mass protests in the summer of 2013 accentuated the key question: What use is economic growth, or the prestige of hosting the 2014 World Cup and 2016 Summer Olympics, if only a small number of people benefit? (See the feature "Movement of Ideas Through Primary Sources: The Piketty Controversy: Inequality and Economic History.")

Turkey also seems to have earned a place on the list of important new economic players. As elsewhere, economic liberalization in Turkey has unshackled markets and industries from state control, leading to high growth rates. The ruling party, the moderately Islamist Justice and Development Party, has established a strong social base among businessmen and entrepreneurs, showing that social conservatism grounded in religious beliefs can be compatible with strong economic performance in a predominantly Muslim society. However, social and political tensions have also escalated, as shown by police assaults on youthful protestors in the summer of 2013 and the jailing of journalists who uncovered evidence of high-level government corruption.

• **CONTEXT&CONNECTIONS** Recent crackdowns in Turkey demonstrate once again that free market policies do not always lead to political openness, as had been predicted by nineteenth century liberal ideology (see Chapter 23). The Mexico of *Porfirio Diáz* (Chapter 25) and Chile under Augusto Pinchot (see Chapter 30) are Latin American examples where political repression accompanied free markets. •

The emergence of former "Third World" nations as new economic players also extends to Africa. Though the continent had been seen as a venue for charity rather than investment, some African countries are now experiencing rapid growth. In 2010 South Africa, with its strong mining and industrial sectors, was formally invited to join what, as a result, became the BRICS group, while oil-rich Nigeria became the continent's largest economy.

Situations in Africa vary widely, of course, and in some regions, economic growth is precluded by the absence of rule of law (including war zones). More generally, poor infrastructure for public health, transport, and education is an impediment to growth. Still, away from the limelight, some African nations have improved dramatically in all these areas. Young, dynamic, and urbanizing populations brought a strengthened middle class to the fore. Improved telecommunications allowed many to skip landline telephones and go straight to cellular services, stimulating African economies through more efficient financial transactions via mobile banking apps.

In Ethiopia, for example, the economy grew at an annual rate of over 10 percent from 2005 to 2013, with construction cranes transforming Addis Ababa. Officials describe their country as an "African lion" equivalent to the "Asian tigers" of the 1980s (see Chapter 31). Indeed, the Ethiopian government, like those of South Korea and Taiwan earlier, has played a central role, channeling investments from China, India, Turkey, and Europe to the private sector through state banks. Remittances from Ethiopian migrants living in the United States, Europe, and the Persian Gulf have also provided an economic lift. Of course, as in other emerging economies, costs and benefits are not equally shared. The government has organized the dispossession of the poor when they "stand in the way" of development projects and has jailed the journalists who investigate and make known such human rights abuses.

• **CONTEXT&CONNECTIONS** For Ethiopian nationalists, the recent record of economic success reinforces a sense of exceptionalism tracing back to their long line of Christian kings (see Chapter 16) and the defense of Ethiopian sovereignty during the "scramble for Africa" with the defeat of Italian invaders by the armies of Emperor *Menelik II* (Chapter 26). •

Perhaps the most startling economic transition in Africa has been the trend away from traditional Western sources of aid and investment and the debut of China as a leading player. In the first decade of the new century, over 1 million Chinese relocated to Africa to engage in a broad range of economic activities. Questions have been raised, however, about Chinese business methods and possible ulterior motives. Chinese tend to monopolize the higher-skilled positions

The Piketty Controversy: Inequality and Economic History

Few economic history books make the bestseller list, but Thomas Piketty's *Capital in the Twenty-First Century* was one of the most commented upon publications of 2014. The French economist used centuries of economic data to investigate the issue of inequality in market-driven societies.

Piketty's conclusion is that the structures of capitalism trend toward increasing inequality over time. In his analysis, the *decrease* in inequality found in developed industrial economies between roughly 1914 and 1970 was largely the result of noneconomic exigencies (wars and economic depressions) that liquidated much of the capital stock of the world's wealthiest families, as well as political factors that led to social and taxation policies favoring the middle and working classes.

But over the broader arc of history, Piketty argues, rates of return on capital have routinely exceeded rates of return on labor, meaning that everything else being equal, inherited wealth will outpace income from employment. Rates of return on capital (such as stocks, bonds, or real estate investments) might be a modest 5 percent and still far exceed national growth rates. (The last time the growth rate of the United States surpassed 5 percent was in 1984; for France, 1973.)

Piketty's work made a strong impression on liberal and progressive economists and policymakers, but was also challenged by more conservative, market-oriented analysts. One such rejoinder, from the staunchly conservative U.S. news magazine, *American Spectator*, is excerpted below. Full engagement with this debate would, of course, require a full reading of Piketty's argument and analysis of his extensive data, available at his webpage at the Paris School of Economics (http://piketty.pse.ens.fr/fr/capitalisback).

❯ Historical Thinking Skill:

COMPARISON What are the differences in the opinions of Piketty and the author of the conservative critique about economic inequality?

❯ Historical Thinking Skill:

SYNTHESIS Taking into account both perspectives presented here, what can you conclude about the effects of the development of capitalism as a dominant economic system, and what historical data do you think would assist you in proving your conclusions?

Sources: Thomas Piketty, *Capital in the Twenty-First Century*, trans. Arthur Goldhammer (Cambridge, Mass.: Belknap, 2014), pp. 571–578; James Piereson, "Thomas Piketty's 'Le Capital': Providing Intellectual Cover for Punishing the Rich," *American Spectator*, June 2014.

Thomas Piketty: *Capital in the Twenty-First Century*

The overall conclusion of this study is that a market economy based on private property, if left to itself, contains powerful forces of convergence [reduction of inequalities] associated in particular with the diffusion of knowledge and skills; but also powerful forces of divergence [sharpening of inequalities] which are potentially threatening to democratic societies and to the values of social justice on which they are based.

The principal destabilizing force has to do with the fact that the private return on capital, r, can be significantly higher for long periods of time than the rate of growth of income and output, g. The inequality $r > g$ implies that wealth accumulated in the past grows more rapidly than output and wages. This inequality expresses a fundamental logical contradiction. The entrepreneur inevitably tends to become a rentier [making money by renting out property or investing funds at interest] more and more dominant over those who own nothing but their labor. Once constituted, capital reproduces itself faster than output increases. The past devours the future. The consequences for the long-term dynamics of the wealth distribution are potentially terrifying, especially when one adds ... that the divergence in the wealth distribution is occurring on a global scale.

The problem is enormous, and there is no simple solution. Growth can of course be encouraged by investing in education, knowledge, and nonpolluting technologies. But none of these will raise the growth rate to 4 or 5 percent a year. History shows that only countries that are catching up with more advanced economies—such as Europe during the three decades after World War II or China and other emerging economies today—can grow at such rates. For countries at the world technological frontier—and thus ultimately for the planet as a whole—there is ample reason to believe that the growth rate will not exceed 1-1.5 percent in the long run, no matter what economic policies are adopted.

With an average return on capital of 4-5 percent, it is therefore likely that $r > g$ will again become the norm in the twenty-first century, as it had been throughout history until the eve of World War I. In the twentieth century, it took two world wars to wipe away the past and significantly reduce the return on capital, thereby creating the illusion that the fundamental structural contradiction of capitalism ($r > g$) had been overcome.

To be sure, one could tax capital income heavily enough to reduce the private return on capital to less than the growth rate. But if one did that indiscriminately and heavy-handedly, one would risk killing the motor of accumulation and thus further reducing the growth rate....

A Conservative Critique

Piketty's estimates of wealth and income shares over the generations are probably as reliable and accurate as he or anyone else can make them, but even so they are estimates based upon imperfect and inexact data. His estimates of wealth, for example, do not take into account assets held by pension funds and retirement accounts, which in the United States today add up to close to $20 trillion, or around one-third of the total value of U.S. stocks and bonds.... These funds are typically not owned by members of the "top one percent" but by middle-class workers. If we could throw that $20 trillion into the pool of total wealth, Piketty's graph might look quite different.

Piketty's great fear, and one that is largely overstated, is that the concentrated ownership of wealth will create a new form of "patrimonial" capitalism in which a small number of families control the wealth of the society and pass it along to their heirs. This idea conflicts with the known tendency of wealthy families to disburse their assets over generations and to be replaced at the top by new entrepreneurs and owners of recently created capital.

It also conflicts with the dramatic rise in salaries for "super-managers" since the 1980s, which Piketty discusses. These are, as he writes, "top executives of large firms who have managed to obtain extremely high and historically unprecedented compensation packages for their labor." The "rich" today are increasingly salaried executives and managers rather than owners of stocks, bonds, and real estate, as was the case a century ago. Piketty doubts that the new "super-managers" earn these extravagant salaries on the basis of merit or contributions to business profits. He points instead to cozy and self-serving relationships they establish with their boards of directors. All that aside, the rise of "super-managers" should actually help alleviate intergenerational inequality, since people can pass on to heirs their wealth but not their high-paying jobs....

[Piketty] claims that the differential returns on capital versus labor are the driving forces of the system, but that is a partial and misleading view. The driving force of the capitalist system is relentless innovation that improves productivity and raises living standards.... Over a span of two and a half centuries, since roughly 1750, the traditional regime transformed itself through an accumulating process of technological innovation and widening circles of trade. Workers and consumers have benefited generation on generation from less burdensome forms of work and access to ever more inexpensive products that make life easier. Widely shared progress—not exploitation—is the story of the past two centuries.

in their enterprises, often employing Africans for the lowest-paying jobs without training them for higher positions. Even more troubling is China's support of certain African leaders with poor human rights and corruption records in its drive to secure the African raw materials, especially metals and fossil fuels, necessary for further industrial growth. One proposed solution is to stimulate inter-African trade through regional trading blocs, which would then strengthen overall African bargaining power in the world economy.

Such regional trade compacts became common during the 1990s, though experience has shown it is never easy to balance national interests with regional goals. The United States, Canada, and Mexico, for example, have all had complaints about the North Atlantic Free Trade Association (NAFTA) (see Chapter 31), while political disputes have hampered the effectiveness of a proposed South American common market (see page 670). The European Union (EU), by far the largest regional bloc, has struggled to balance the interests of more developed countries such as Germany and France with the needs of weaker members such as Portugal and Greece.

World Trade Organization

Organization founded in 1995 to establish rules for international trade, with an emphasis on lowering tariffs and other barriers to the free movement of goods.

More ambitious than regional agreements was the drive by the **World Trade Organization** (WTO) to foster international free trade. WTO members, which have included China since 2001, accept international monitoring to assure that they maintain a level playing field by avoiding state subsidies and tariffs. The virtue of WTO policies, from a neoliberal standpoint, is the elimination of the reduction in international economic efficiency that occurs when political distortions are introduced into markets. For critics of neoliberalism, however, the regional trade blocs and the WTO regime have handicapped governments in restraining negative consequences of capitalism such as sharpening inequality and environmental degradation. For these critics, deregulation favors multinational corporations over people.

Muhammad Yunus

(b. 1940) Bangladeshi pioneer of microfinance whose Grameen ("Village") Bank gives small loans to the poor, usually women, to start small enterprises. His bank became a global model for microfinance, and in 2006, he was awarded the Nobel Peace Prize.

While defenders and opponents debated the merits of neoliberal globalization, the Nobel-prize winner **Muhammad Yunus** (b. 1940) of Bangladesh was thinking of practical solutions for those left behind. His Grameen ("Village") Bank pioneered microfinance, lending small amounts of money. Poor borrowers proved to be trustworthy clients even when they had no collateral to secure the loans, and small investments often led to big returns when they pooled their resources, energy, and ideas to start new enterprises. In Africa and elsewhere, it has been shown that women are particularly apt to make good use of such small infusions of capital, stimulating local economies while also addressing gender inequality. Still, such "bottom-up" approaches are dwarfed by the power and resources of the world's largest financial institutions.

Global Finance: Collapse and Consequences

In the autumn of 2008, panic spread across world markets at the prospect of the insolvency of the interconnected global banking and brokerage systems. The use of complex financial instruments called "derivatives" had allowed banks to bundle and sell inflated mortgages to third parties while masking the high risks involved, infecting the financial system and creating a domino effect when the housing bubble burst. The New York Stock Exchange lost 22 percent of its value in a single week and, along with other international stock exchanges, continued to plunge thereafter. Memories of the Great Depression, when a stock market crash led to a decade of economic misery, seemed ominously relevant.

• **CONTEXT&CONNECTIONS** As painful as the 2008 financial crisis was, it was by no means as catastrophic as the *Great Depression* (Chapter 28), when the U.S. stock market crash led to a cascading series of global bank failures. For one thing, in 2008, governments had much more powerful tools of monetary intervention than in 1929. Moreover, 2008 witnessed no rush to raise national tariffs, which in the 1930s had deepened the depression by hindering international trade. •

Most economists and government leaders determined that in the short term state intervention would be necessary to prevent more banks and brokerages from going bankrupt. Thus the outgoing administration of U.S. President George W. Bush proposed and Congress passed a program to make $700 billion available to stabilize the financial services industry. In Britain as well, where the City of London parallels New York as a global financial services center, the government organized an emergency rescue operation. Many were appalled that the very people whose risky business decisions had brought the world to the brink of ruin were being "bailed out," but the measures did forestall further financial contagion.

Still, economic recession struck. The United States and Europe faced high unemployment, and global markets were shrinking. A fundamental question of economic theory then took center stage. Was the best medium-term solution for governments to borrow money and cut taxes, running deficits in order to stimulate a broader economic recovery? Or were government deficits at the very root of the slump, meaning that fiscal austerity, cutting spending while raising taxes, was necessary to restore prosperity?

Responses varied. The United States under President Barack Obama took a Keynesian "stimulus" approach (see Chapter 28). In the United Kingdom, a conservative-led government determined that government indebtedness was the root problem and risked deflation by slashing spending while raising taxes. The French implemented a modest stimulus plan, but the Irish government took the path of austerity, implementing harsh spending cuts.

Divided responses by European Union members revealed a lack of the institutional means to coordinate national fiscal policies. The 2011 financial meltdown of Greece forced the issue. In Greece, relatively low economic productivity was paired with generous social welfare benefits. Amid the global economic crisis, with its credit rating in decline, the Greek government could no longer borrow enough money to sustain that structural imbalance. The Greek parliament passed sharp spending cuts as a condition for an emergency fiscal support package, a move opposed by the Greek voters who in 2015 voted in an anti-austerity government charged to negotiate a better deal.

• **CONTEXT&CONNECTIONS** Tensions between fiscally conservative Germans and Greeks tired of endless austerity were central to European fiscal debate. While many economists argued that *deflation* (falling prices and wages) was the nemesis of post-2008 recovery, Germans still tend to focus on *inflation* (rising prices and wages) as a perennial economic danger seeing excessive borrowing as a fiscal, and even as a moral, failure. That reflexive attitude, dating back to the great inflation of the early Weimar Republic (see Chapter 28), affected German public opinion and thus German negotiations with Greece. •

The euro currency itself was now at risk. It seemed that only stronger fiscal coordination by the European Central Bank would allow euro-zone countries to find fiscal policies balancing their divergent national interests. Yet voters in most countries were reluctant to give up the reins of national finance to Pan-European bureaucracies.

Meanwhile, youth unemployment, especially in southern Europe, began to seem like a structural, perhaps permanent cost of deflation. In Italy, an extreme example, the youth unemployment rate in 2015 was over 41 percent. As ambitious young people left such moribund economies for opportunity elsewhere, the International Labor Office called for attention to what it called a "generation at risk."

To some it seemed that the prolonged slump of mature economies following from 2008 signaled a structural readjustment in the world economy. With U.S., Japanese, and European economies teetering on the edge of recession from 2009 to 2012, and with continued growth in much of Asia, Africa, and Latin America, it seemed that two centuries of Western economic predominance might be coming to an end. By late 2013, China had amassed foreign currency reserves of $366 *billion* dollars, much of it in U.S. Treasury bonds.

Still, by 2015 it appeared that the relative decline of more established economies might have been overstated. Although Europe and Japan continued to struggle, the American dollar remained the world's favored reserve currency, a hedge against instability elsewhere. Growing U.S. energy production (much of it resulting from environmentally controversial hydraulic fracturing technology) added to the U.S. recovery. Meanwhile China's housing boom, which had underwritten the country's recent growth, began to cool. Even though it was unlikely that the "rise of the rest" would be reversed, and while many analysts still looked to emerging markets for future growth, it seemed that zigzags would complicate the future path of the international economy.

● **CONTEXT&CONNECTIONS** Though China's rate of industrial growth has been unprecedented, the resulting contribution to global manufacturing can be viewed as a return to the historic norm. After all, *Qing dynasty* China (Chapter 20) had accounted for a full 33.1 percent of all the world's manufacturing production in 1750 (see Table 23.1, page 685). That figure had fallen to just 6.3 percent in 1900. Now the People's Republic of China accounts for an estimated 22 percent of the world's industrial output. ●

Global Security

The optimism for a safer world that followed from the end of the Cold War did not last long. While wars between nations had indeed become less frequent, societies across the world now found themselves threatened and destabilized by non-state organizations, especially terrorist groups motivated by extreme religious ideologies, such as al-Qaeda (see Chapter 31).

September 11, 2001
Date of the al-Qaeda terrorist attacks on the United States in which two hijacked jetliners destroyed the twin towers of the World Trade Center in New York City. Another hijacked plane crashed into the Pentagon, and a fourth fell in a Pennsylvania field.

Hopeful expectations for the new millennium were shattered on **September 11, 2001**, when operatives of al-Qaeda hijacked four jetliners in the United States and turned them into weapons of destruction. Thousands of New Yorkers were killed in the destruction of the Twin Towers (though the terrorists' plans to destroy the Pentagon and Congress were averted). International sympathy for the people of the United States was nearly universal.

In response, President George W. Bush declared a "war on terror," first sending U.S. forces in October 2001 to invade Afghanistan, where the Islamist Taliban government had given sanctuary and support to Osama bin Laden, and then into

Saddam Hussein's Iraq in 2003. The invasion of Afghanistan had broad international support. An international coalition, working with local anti-Taliban fighters, quickly removed the Taliban from power. The subsequent U.S. invasion of Iraq, however, generated considerable controversy. Many Americans, and even more members of the international community, knew that Iraq had no connection to al-Qaeda or 9/11.

Bush ordered the invasion in 2003, lacking United Nations sanction and with Great Britain as his only major ally. Saddam Hussein was deposed, and later tried and executed. Evidence of Hussein's violent misrule was abundant, but his supposed stockpiles of "weapons of mass destruction," used by the United States to justify its invasion, were never found.

Two years of internecine strife followed, with U.S. soldiers contending with both Shi'ite militias (supported by neighboring Iran) and Sunni terrorists backed by al-Qaeda. In the north of the country, battle-hardened Kurdish forces staked out terrain that would remain virtually autonomous even after elections created a new government in Baghdad (see Map 32.2).

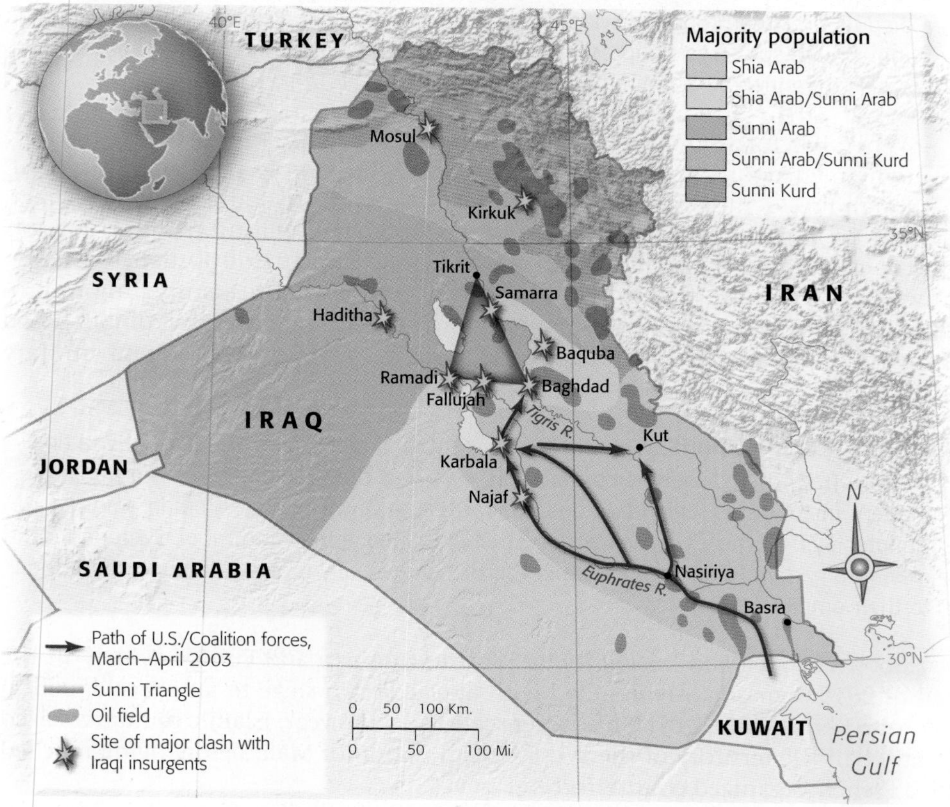

Map 32.2 Iraq in Transition Two Bush presidential administrations invaded Iraq—in 1991 to protect its oil-producing ally Kuwait from invasion, and in 2003 to oust Saddam Hussein and bring democracy to the Arab world. The first mission was successful, the second much less so. After Hussein's fall, some of the Sunnis displaced from power took up arms against the U.S. coalition, against independent Shia Arab militias, and against the now Shi'ite-dominated Iraqi government itself. Even after 2007 elections inaugurated a compromise government—with a Shi'ite prime minister, Kurdish president, and Sunni leader of parliament—it was impossible to reconcile the country's regional, religious, and ethnic divisions.

With Iraq's political future unresolved, in 2011, the United States (following the lead of its ally, Great Britain) began to withdraw its troops. Americans were now ready to end this difficult conflict after eight years and thousands of casualties, especially with the sense of closure that came with Osama bin Laden's death in a smoothly executed Navy Seals operation.

Even so, the U.S. invasion had stirred up a hornet's nest, and the world learned just how fragile Iraq still was. By 2015, the power vacuum left behind by the American invasion of Iraq was being filled by an even more extreme group, the Islamic State of Iraq and Syria (ISIS), taking advantage of regional instability to grab territory as the nucleus of a restored Sunni caliphate. With its bloodstained record of cruelty, that idea made for a chilling prospect.

• **CONTEXT&CONNECTIONS** The term *caliph* in Arabic means "successor" and is used in reference to leaders who inherited the earthly power of the prophet Muhammad. The last of the great Arab caliphates ended in 1258 when the Mongols sacked Baghdad, though Ottoman sultans also claimed the title until 1924, when the office was abolished by the new Turkish republic under *Mustafa Kemal* (Chapter 28). Since a dispute over the proper line of succession to the Prophet was central to the original Sunni-Shi'ite split (see Chapter 17), Shi'ites are especially threatened by the ISIS promise to renew the Sunni caliphate. •

When ISIS forces moved east from their original bases in war-torn Syria, they overwhelmed poorly motivated Iraqi troops, who simply fled from the fight. Although President Barack Obama was clearly anxious to address the ISIS threat, neither he nor the war-weary American people were willing to return "boots on the ground." Neighboring countries, such as Turkey and Jordan, were also unwilling to commit themselves to combat. Only the Kurds, struggling to protect their own homeland, and Iran, for which the Sunni extremists of ISIS posed an existential threat, were proactive in backing up Iraq's subsequent military offensive.

• **CONTEXT&CONNECTIONS** When ISIS insurgents claimed areas of eastern Syria and western Iraq, they dissolved borders that were less than a century old. For most of modern history, this region had been under the authority of the Ottoman empire (see Chapter 17). At the *Paris Peace Conference*, France gained control of Syria under the *mandate system* (Chapter 27), while the British casually drew up Iraq as an addition to their empire. •

Soon violence and instability had spread to Africa and Europe as well. In the fall of 2013 Somali gunmen allied with al-Qaeda laid siege to an upscale mall in Nairobi, Kenya, killing 67. On a larger scale the same year, Islamic militants seized nearly half the territory of the West African nation of Mali, before being repelled by a French-organized counterforce.

• **CONTEXT&CONNECTIONS** The Islamist forces in Mali, like those of al-Qaeda and ISIS, are Salafists who stress a return to the purity of Islam at its founding. That is why, when they took over territories of the former *Songhai empire* (Chapter 19), they demolished ancient shrines and destroyed documents from age-old libraries, claiming that African adaptations of Islam were idolatrous. In West Africa, as elsewhere, the terrorism of Salafist fanatics is most often directed at other Muslims, especially *Sufis* and Shi'ites (Chapter 17). •

Gokhan Sahin/Getty Images

The Islamic State in Syria and Iraq (ISIS) The northern Syrian city of Kobani, a gateway to neighboring Turkey, was attacked by ISIS militants in late 2014. The city was successfully defended by Kurdish militias backed by U.S. airstrikes, though 200,000 refugees fled the area, part of the exodus of 4 million who fled Syria's civil war.

In Paris in 2015, two gunmen shouting *"Allahu Akbar!"* ("God is great!") stormed into the offices of a French satire magazine and opened fire, killing eleven and wounding eleven more: the magazine had published cartoons using caricatures of the Prophet Muhammad to mock Islamic terrorists. Later an accomplice took hostages in a Jewish grocery store and murdered four more people. While the French people then came together across lines of religion and ethnicity to condemn the attacks and the assault on their freedom of speech, feelings of anxiety persisted.

And what if militant groups were able to lay their hands on weapons of mass destruction? What if nuclear devices entered the global arms trade and found their way into the hands of extremist organizations or irresponsible governments? That was a real fear after Pakistan's top nuclear scientist shared his expertise with Iran and North Korea.

The United States, the European Union, and leaders of Sunni-dominant Muslim countries like Saudi Arabia imposed economic sanctions on Iran in an attempt to halt its progress toward enrichment of weapons-grade uranium. While Teheran claimed merely to be advancing a civilian energy program, the global consensus was that strict international supervision must guarantee that the Iranian program did not cross the line to military applications. With the election in 2013 of a reformist Iranian government, anxious first and foremost to address economic issues, international negotiations finally began to move in a positive direction, though a right-wing Israeli government contested U.S. efforts to mediate a diplomatic solution.

AP® THEMES
What elements of governance began to fall under the jurisdiction of international organizations, such as the United Nations, since the mid-twentieth century?

North Korea was equally worrisome. In 2006, the communist government had snubbed international opinion by openly testing a bomb and beginning to develop a nuclear arsenal. A wild card came with the death of long-time dictator Kim Jong-Il and the accession to power of his little known son Kim Jong-Un. While the younger Kim struggled to consolidate power, brutally executing his own uncle and provoking conflict with South Korea, nuclear negotiations were called off. With North Korea otherwise impenetrable, it seemed that only the People's Republic of China might have the influence to subdue the more dangerous tendencies of the Kim dynasty.

Meanwhile, a long simmering nuclear fault line separated India and Pakistan. With a history of animosity and saber-rattling, both countries (along with Israel) had developed nuclear weapons in defiance of the international Treaty on the Non-Proliferation of Nuclear Weapons. Indeed, international regulation of nuclear materials and technology is at least as important today as it was when atomic Armageddon threatened humanity at the height of the Cold War.

• **CONTEXT&CONNECTIONS** Starting in 1947, the Bulletin of the Atomic Scientists has shown a "doomsday clock" on its masthead estimating the danger of nuclear war. The original setting was seven minutes to midnight, dropping to seventeen minutes in 1991, when the United States and the tottering Soviet Union signed an arms control pact (see Chapter 31). Ominously, between 2012 and 2015, the doomsday clock was set back from five minutes to three minutes, the atomic scientists' most imminent warning of nuclear conflict since the Cold War. •

Health and the Environment

In 2014, the virulent Ebola virus spread across the West African nations of Guinea, Liberia, and Sierra Leone. The handful of the cases that developed outside of West Africa were easily contained, but global panic still followed. In the United States, a state governor ordered a nurse who had returned from Sierra Leone to be held in quarantine, even though there was no medical rationale for doing so. Morocco reneged on its offer to host the 2015 African Cup of Nations soccer tournament, citing public health dangers that defied medical logic. The grave suffering Ebola caused was almost entirely limited to the countries first affected, and as successful measures were taken, both the disease and the panic receded.

Though people around the world overreacted to Ebola, their instinct to recognize the global nature of such health threats was not misplaced. International mobility does indeed increase the risk of pandemics, as shown earlier by the global spread of H1N1, or swine flu, itself a close relative of the flu strain that killed millions across the world in 1918–1919 (see Chapter 27 and the feature "World History in Today's World: World Historians and Disease History").

Virulent new strains of traditional killers like malaria, which until recently were confined to small geographic areas, now hop from continent to continent courtesy of mosquito hosts that find their way aboard jet airplanes. Other new strains of influenza, such as the avian flu virus from East Asia, threaten recurrent global epidemics. Meanwhile, overreliance on antibiotics in both humans and

USAID/Alamy

Fighting Ebola The rapid spread of Ebola in Guinea, Liberia, and Sierra Leone overwhelmed their health care systems and threatened the lives of thousands of African health care workers. Finally an intensive international effort was made to provide up-to-date facilities, such as the World Health Organization clinic shown here in Monrovia, Liberia.

domestic animals has spawned resistant strains of bacteria. Such developments overtax health-care systems around the world.

HIV/AIDS is, of course, another case in point. When it was first diagnosed in the 1980s, the disease was associated with two particular groups, homosexual men and intravenous drug users. Today, Africa has the largest number of AIDS victims, and more women are infected than men. For those who can afford it, medical advances have decreased suffering and extended life spans, but most of the world's HIV victims die without the benefit of effective medical intervention.

While HIV infection rates have stabilized in wealthier nations, many global health experts fear for India and China. In India, where hundreds of millions lack access to the most basic health care, the number of people living with HIV/AIDS has soared past 2.5 million. In China, even a low infection rate of 0.1 percent means that over a million people are infected. If HIV were to spread in Asia as it did in South Africa (where the infection rate grew to 25 percent of the population by 2005), those societies would be overwhelmed. Unlike most epidemic diseases, which are deadliest for the very young and very old, AIDS carries people away in the prime of their productive and reproductive lives, adding huge social and developmental costs.

Some health threats are compounded by global climate change. Scientists point to the huge cyclones that hit Burma in 2008 and the Philippines in 2013, and unprecedented drought and flooding in many parts of the world as examples. Climatologists worry that melting polar ice caps will soon disrupt the world's highly populated coastal areas, especially Bangladesh, where 55 million people

World Historians and Disease History

How has disease transmission affected world history? Since viruses and bacteria do not recognize political, cultural, or civilizational boundaries, we can only answer that question by increasing our scale of analysis to take in wider vistas of the human past. Over the past three decades, world historians have been paying greater attention to such transregional phenomena.

Studies of the fourteenth-century Black Death, for example, had too often focused solely on Europe. Today world historians pay closer attention to the epidemic's Central Eurasian origins by examining how the Mongol political ascension led to increased intercontinental exchange, possibly facilitating long-distance disease transmission. Historians are also providing a more balanced pan-Eurasian assessment of the plague's impact by looking at its effects on Chinese and Arab societies.

Analysis of European competition for control of the "new world" (see Chapters 15 and 18) provides another example. Here world historians have recognized the importance of different levels of immunity among Amerindians, Europeans, and Africans to deadly diseases, with susceptibility to malaria, smallpox, and yellow fever helping to determine the characteristics of populations and even political outcomes. A "national" view of the competing European powers and their fiscal, military, and leadership capabilities, while important, cannot achieve the more balanced assessments offered by historians who consider environmental and disease factors within larger spatial frames such as "the Atlantic world."

The story of the Spanish influenza outbreak of 1918–1919 is another historical incident where transnational approaches are required. While local histories bring us close to victims and their lives, a fuller picture requires a global view, since the disease showed no respect for national or imperial boundaries while spreading to every continent.

Disease transmission is one example of how the work of world historians has contemporary relevance. By demonstrating the transnational character of epidemic disease, world historians remind us that international health challenges require more than simply national solutions.

would be displaced by even a modest rise in sea levels. Global warming, notes one commentator, is taking the form of *"global weirding,"* where extreme weather conditions—too much or not enough rain and extremes of heat and cold—have become annual events.*

Global climate change is also affecting the spread of infectious diseases. The director general of the World Health Organization, Dr. Margaret Chan, argues: *"Many of the most important global killers are highly sensitive to climatic conditions. Malaria, diarrhea and malnutrition kill millions of people every year, most of them children. Without effective action to mitigate and adapt to climate change, the burden of these conditions will be greater, and they will be more difficult and more costly to control."*†

Some nations have taken climate challenge seriously and have made significant investments in renewable sources of energy to replace carbon-emitting fossil fuels. Germany, for example, has committed itself to a comprehensive plan for most of its energy to come from renewable sources by 2020. Both conservatives and socialists supported this initiative, and the large investments in wind and solar energy that came with it.

---

*Thomas L. Friedman, "Global Weirding Is Here," *New York Times*, February 17, 2010.

†Dr. Margaret Chan, "Health in a Changing Environment," http://www.who.int/mediacentre/news/statements/2007/s11/en/index.html.

It has proven very difficult, however, to reach a binding international agreement to limit carbon emissions. A promising start came as far back as 1992, when the United Nations instituted the talks leading in 1997 to the **Kyoto Protocol**. By 2005, for the first time, many nations agreed to mandatory limits on emissions of "greenhouse gases." The treaty lapsed in 2012, however, and has not been renewed, with India, China, and the United States stating that they will not accept legally binding reductions on carbon emissions.

Kyoto Protocol
(1997) International agreement adopted in Kyoto, Japan, under the United Nations Framework Agreement on Climate Change in an effort to reduce greenhouse gas emissions linked to global warming.

A global rift pits environmentalists in the developed world against advocates for economic growth in emerging economies. China and India have depended on the burning of high-sulfur coal to fuel economic growth, and environmentalists have logically called for them to reduce emissions. The Chinese and Indian governments have argued, however, that developed countries, having *already* benefited from profligate use of fossil fuels, can *afford* cutbacks, while their own people still need accelerated growth, even at environmental expense, to lift them out of poverty.

Of course, China and India have their own reasons for cleaning up. A so-called "airpocalypse" in Beijing during the summer of 2013 made breathing painful and dangerous; it has long been true that most Chinese cancer deaths are attributable to pollution. (And the effects are not just local. A toxic cloud of coal smoke drifts from China over neighboring countries and sometimes across the Pacific Ocean. Coal shipped from the United States to China thus returns as air pollution.) The official response has been to downplay the problem but also to invest heavily in renewable energies, especially wind and solar. As bad as the air might be in China's cities, recent studies show that it is even worse in India. There, 660 million people live in areas where small airborne particles (2.5 micrometers or less) routinely cause severe lung damage. The result is a dire public health situation, especially for children.

While several countries have put a greater investment in renewable energies, the goal of **sustainable development**, of increasing economic output and productivity without severe damage to the environment, is still far away. The most immediate alternative to fossil fuels is nuclear power. However, many remain wary of its health and environmental consequences. In the spring of 2011, an earthquake in Japan reignited the global debate when the resulting tsunami led to the release of radiation from the Fukushima electricity plant, the worst nuclear incident since Chernobyl (see Chapter 31). Germany subsequently decided to shut down its nuclear energy program, gambling that enough clean energy would be available as a replacement.

sustainable development
Means of increasing economic output and productivity without severe damage to the environment; for example, in the search for alternatives to fossil fuels.

Deforestation magnifies the effect of the world's rising output of greenhouse gases. Tropical forests play a large role in cleansing the atmosphere of carbon dioxide and replenishing it with oxygen. With high demand for tropical hardwoods from Central Africa and Indonesia, however, lumber companies fell vast areas of forest, sometimes bribing politicians to evade environmental regulations. In Brazil, as we have seen, farmers clear the forests for agriculture, with huge tracts of sugar cane and soybeans displacing biologically diverse ecosystems.

AP® THEMES
What have been the environmental consequences of globalization?

This section has touched on only a few of the health and environmental challenges of our times. Work is needed on every front as rising population, urbanization, and global migration make the search for solutions all the more urgent. With many geologists now agreeing that we are two centuries into the Anthropocene epoch, when human activity has dominant effects on our biosphere (see page 687), we can no longer shirk responsibility for environmental solutions.

Population Movement and Demography

AP® THEMES

How have migrations of the twentieth and twenty-first centuries contributed to changing social structures in both the sending and receiving societies?

People are on the move, both within countries and between them, usually seeking opportunity at the focal points of wealth and economic growth. That means cities. China, for example, has a staggering forty-five cities with over 2 million residents each. For the planet as a whole, 2008 was the first year when the majority of humankind lived in urban areas.*

Globally, prospects of higher wages drive millions each year to leave their homes, though they often send back much of their pay back home to support their families and intend to return. Of course, for millions of others, terrible conditions at home are the tragic inducement for movement across international borders: poverty and war drive some Africans to risk their lives crossing the Mediterranean on overcrowded boats, and desperate, low-wage migrant workers are subjected to systematic abuse in some wealthier regions, such as the Persian Gulf.

Immigration policies are controversial all around the world. In 2015, South African gangs attacked immigrants from other African countries, claiming that the outsiders were taking their jobs. In Italy, the government cracked down on illegal Roma (Gypsy) immigrants from southeastern Europe, claiming that they were responsible for an increase in crime. In the United States, immigration from Latin America has shifted the cultural and linguistic balance, generating an anti-immigrant backlash.

Religious differences can magnify concerns about immigration (see Map 32.3). Many western Europeans, for example, have been alarmed by large-scale Muslim immigration stimulated by political unrest in the Arab world. In Germany, a furious debate raged after a prominent politician wrote, *"If the birth rate of the [Muslim] migrants continues to remain higher than the indigenous population, within a few generations the migrants will take over the state and society and create a nation of dunces."*† Such harsh rhetoric was on the rise in many European countries. Questions of whether and how to accept immigrants, and how best to create cultural and linguistic bridges to host societies, are thus matters of global concern.

Total world population recently surpassed 7 billion persons, a worrisome figure if we consider the resources it takes to give each of these individuals the chance at a decent life. But demographers (experts in population science) focus as much on the distribution of populations as their total size. When we consider the ratio of young to old in different societies, we find a striking imbalance. While the populations of wealthier countries grow older, Latin America, Africa, and Asia have enormous adolescent populations. Tapping into the creativity and intelligence of these hundreds of millions of young people would benefit all of us.

Back in the 1980s, worried about too many hungry mouths to feed, leaders of the People's Republic of China adopted a radical **One Child Policy** that punished parents who had a second child. Fertility declined and population growth plummeted. Now the Chinese government is relaxing the One Child Policy, worrying that there will soon be too few people of working age to support a growing number of the elderly.

One Child Policy
In China, most parents are restricted by this policy to a single child to curb population growth. The policy has led to a significant gender imbalance.

---

*United Nations, *World Urbanization Prospects* (New York: Author, 2006).

†Cited in "In a Rich Irony, German Jews Defend Muslims," *The Jewish Daily Forward*, January 28, 2011; http://www.forward.com/articles/134701/.

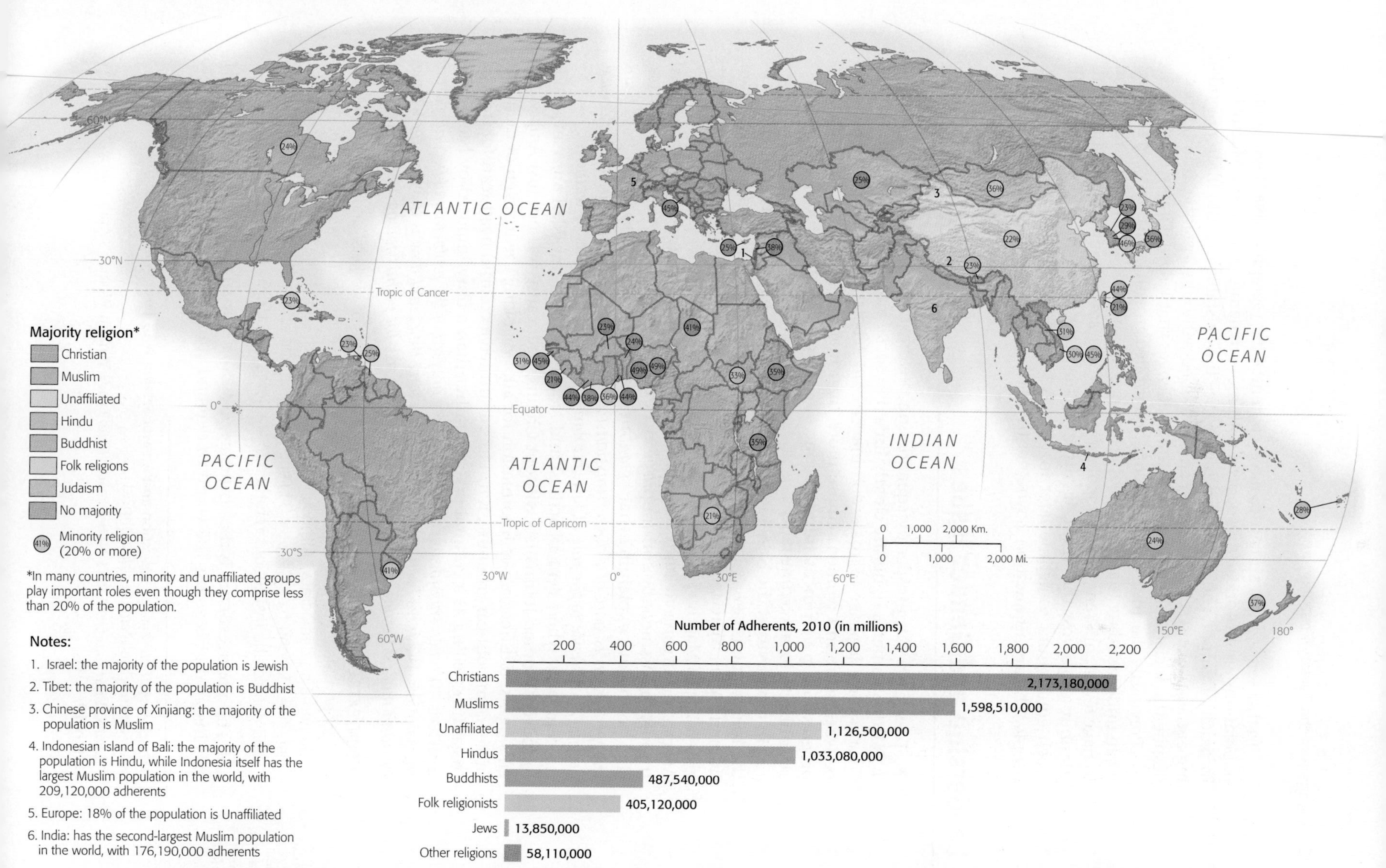

Map 32.3 World Religions Christianity, Islam, Hinduism, and Buddhism are the four major world religions, with "atheists/nonreligious" forming a majority in Communist-ruled China. The religious map of Africa is especially complex. While Muslims predominate in the north and west, and Christians in the east and south, there is a great deal of mixing along the boundaries between them, and local religions are still strong in many areas. In much of Europe and Russia, where Christian majorities are indicated, secularism is also strong and rates of church attendance quite low. While Islam predominates in North Africa and the Middle East, the nation with the largest Muslim population in the world is Indonesia, in Southeast Asia.

In that sense, India and Africa have a potential demographic advantage: younger populations are historically associated with more dynamic economies. Meanwhile, in much of Europe and Japan, it is hard to see how a stable mix of children, working-age adults, and senior citizens can be attained without substantial immigration, despite the social, cultural, and political challenges that will inevitably result.

Previously alarming predictions of uncontrolled growth have now been replaced by an understanding that when people attain greater wealth and security, they tend to have fewer children. Today, population growth is slowing not just in richer countries but also across the world. If current trends hold, total global population will reach equilibrium sometime later in this century, perhaps at a level of 9 billion people. The urgent question is whether the earth can sustain that number.

Women's Leadership and Gender Issues

No society can prosper by squandering the creative talent of half its population: women's rights are closely linked to social and economic advancement. Overcoming legacies of male dominance and rebalancing power more evenly between men and women require more than material prosperity, technological progress, or government intervention. Addressing patriarchal attitudes requires attention to local circumstances.

In recent years, the Nobel Peace Prize committee has paid special attention to the role women leaders have played in improving not only women's rights, but human rights. One twenty-first century Nobel Prize winner, the Kenyan biologist Wangari Maathai (2004), was alarmed by environmental degradation in East Africa, and organized rural women into collectives to plant trees. She persisted through harassment by corrupt property developers and imprisonment by patriarchal politicians, explaining that *"planting trees or fighting to save forests from being chopped down is part of a larger mission to create a society that respects democracy, decency, adherence to the rule of law, human rights, and the rights of women."**

Similarly, when Yemeni activist and Nobel Laureate Tawakkol Karman (2011) founded "Women Journalists without Chains," her cause was not just Arab women's rights, but freedom of information for all. Provoking the ire even of members of her own political grouping, Karman substituted a colorful head scarf for her veil (regarding veiling as a cultural practice rather than a duty imposed by Islam) and insisted: *"Women should stop feeling that they are part of the problem and become part of the solution. We have been marginalized for a long time, and now is the time for women to stand up and become active without needing to ask for permission or acceptance."*†

● **CONTEXT&CONNECTIONS** In 1992, an earlier advocate of workers' and women's rights, Rigoberta Menchú, was awarded the Nobel Peace Prize for her work in restoring Guatemalan democracy. Although government death squads had targeted union activists like Menchú (see Chapter 31) she persisted and attained global influence. Peace and democratic institutions returned to Guatemala in 1996. ●

Malala Yousafzai
(b. 1997) Pakistani Nobel Prize winner and advocate for children's rights, especially for girls' access to education.

The youngest-ever Nobel Laureate, **Malala Yousafzai** of Pakistan (2014), has inspired girls across the world to demand equal education and the power to

---

**The Greenbelt Movement*, "Question and Answer Session with Prof. Wangari Maathai," http://www.greenbeltmovement.org/a.php?id=27.

†"Tawakul Karman Gets 2011 Nobel Peace Prize, Leads Yemeni Women's Arab Spring," Asianews.it, July 10, 2011.

pursue their dreams. In 2009, eleven-year-old Yousafzai began blogging about life under the Islamist Taliban, who threatened to close girls' schools while imposing their severe form of Islamic law. Her blog gave her international prominence but incited revenge from the Taliban: one of their fighters stopped her school bus and shot her in the head.

Yousafzai went to Britain for surgery, and then launched her ongoing campaign for children's rights. After traveling to Oslo, Norway, to receive her award, Malala ended her speech to great applause by saying: *"Let this be the last time that a girl or a boy spends their childhood in a factory. Let this be the last time that a girl is forced into early child marriage. Let this be the last time that a child loses life in war. Let this be the last time that we see a child out of school. Let this end with us."**

Malala Yousafzai Just twelve years old when she was attacked by militants for her stand in favor of girls' education in Pakistan, Nobel-prize winner Malala Yousafzai attained international prominence as a campaigner for children's rights while still a teenager.

Meanwhile in Pakistan's neighbor, India, globalization and technological change have presented new possibilities for women, at least for those fortunate enough to have an education and employment in rapidly growing sectors like information technology. Still, patriarchal attitudes remain, as shown by the persistence of the ancient **dowry system**. A girl's dowry has traditionally been the largest expense faced by Indian parents, sometimes leading the poor to lifelong indebtedness. Now the greater availability of consumer goods has had an inflationary effect, with families demanding ever-greater payments in return for marriage to their sons. Newspapers abound with reports of young brides murdered by their in-laws after their dowry payments have been made.

dowry system Traditional Indian marriage system in which a bride brings substantial gifts to the household of her new husband. Though illegal, it has expanded as the country's wealth has grown, leading to chronic indebtedness and the frequent murder of young brides.

Because of the dowry system, the birth of a girl can seem like a tragedy, ruining the family's financial prospects. Across India, medical clinics advertise sonogram services to determine the gender of a fetus, leading to selective abortions. In the state of Punjab today, there are fewer than eight hundred girls for every thousand boys. Women's rights activists estimate that 50 million females are "missing" from the population because of selective abortion and female infanticide.

Overall disrespect for women in India has also led to an epidemic of rape, with government officials and police officers usually protecting male perpetrators while blaming the victims. Finally, in 2014, there were signs that Indian women, and Indian men of conscience, had seen enough. Huge crowds protested sickening incidents of gang rape, putting pressure on national and community leaders to finally address the issue.

In China gender discrimination remains rampant, despite strong legal and constitutional guarantees of equality and a much broader range of opportunities for educated women in the booming middle class. Lower pay for identical work is as common in China as elsewhere. Moreover, the gender ratio in China is almost as unbalanced as in India. Chinese parents, under the pressure of the One Child Policy and feeling the need for a male heir, have also practiced selective abortion.

*Malala Yousafzai, http://www.nobelprize.org/nobel_prizes/peace/laureates/2014/yousafzai-lecture_en.html.

Demographers estimate that there are as many as 70 million more males than females in the country.

Unequal access to education, unequal pay for identical work, sex trafficking, and high female death rates in childbirth are still all too common. But if women's leadership is key to overcoming such deep-seated gender inequalities, there is hope in the examples of Wangari Maathai, Tawakkol Karman, and Malala Yousafzai.

In her Nobel acceptance speech, Yousafzai also paid tribute to the 1991 winner, the Burmese democracy advocate Aung San Suu Kyi (awng san soo CHEE). For decades, Suu Kyi has been a model of persistence and patience in the difficult struggle for freedom in Burma (or Myanmar, as it was renamed by the secretive military officers who have ruled the country since 1962). After overturning election results that would have made Suu Kyi president of the country in 1990, the Burmese regime subjected her to years of house arrest. Suu Kyi was finally released in 2011 and elected to parliament in 2012, when the military allowed relatively fair elections. Still, the Burmese military holds the keys to power, allowing only gradual reform from the top down, and preventing Suu Kyi from becoming a candidate in 2015 presidential elections. In Burma and across the world, the struggles for democracy and for women's rights are inextricably linked.

A Year of Protest, Then Counter-Reactions

In 2011, hopes for expanded democracy ran high. The spark came from an unlikely place: a young Tunisian street vendor, tired of constant harassment by the police and by the corruption of municipal officials, burned himself to death in a public market. His act sparked a worldwide year of protest.

As protests spread across North Africa and the Middle East, many international observers found inspiration in the street demonstrations that became known as the Arab Spring. The massive prodemocracy encampment at Tahrir Square in Cairo was the epicenter of the movement. As in past revolutions, young people played a central role, their ability to organize and sustain massive demonstrations now greatly increased through the power of the Internet and social networking. Then came disappointment, as the military and political elites of Egypt restored control, a counter-reaction that was repeated across the Arab world and around the world.

● **CONTEXT&CONNECTIONS** As in Europe in the summer of 1848, the Arab world in 2011 saw street protests leapfrog from one capital to another, bringing high hopes for rapid and radical change. But just as in the Europe in the 1850s, those hopes were usually dashed when conservative leaders retook the initiative. Indeed, some Arab protesters would be able to relate to the travails of the Russian anarchist *Mikhail Bakunin* (Chapter 23) when, after organizing for democracy, they faced imprisonment or exile. ●

In Egypt, democratic elections in 2012 voted in the long-banned Islamist Muslim Brotherhood. However, when the Brotherhood seemed incapable of forming policies acceptable to the revolution's diverse constituencies, or even of organizing basic government services, the military stepped in, deposing the elected president and suspending the constitution. Many Egyptians applauded as the forces of "law and order" reasserted control and restored the long-standing proscription of the Muslim Brotherhood.

The greatest disappointment in the wake of the Arab Spring was unquestionably in Syria. Here the regime of Bashir Al-Assad, who became president in 2000

The Arab Spring Cairo has long been the political and intellectual center of the Arab world, and Tahrir Square in the center of Cairo was the focal point of the Arab Spring. Protesters, including many students, used social media to organize massive demonstrations that toppled the regime of Hosni Mubarak and cleared the way for free elections. The result, however, was a further military intervention in Egyptian politics after the Muslim Brotherhood, victors in those elections, proved deeply unpopular. In 2014, an Egyptian judge cleared Mubarak of all charges, including culpability in the death of hundreds at Tahrir Square. (Peter Macdiarmid/Getty Images)

with promises of reform, refused to countenance any meaningful change. A broad array of rebel groups then took up arms. While the international community disagreed over how to respond, civil war made refugees of over 4 million Syrians. It was into this power vacuum that the ruthless ISIS fighters stepped, as what had once seemed a promising chance at democratization in Syria degraded into a living hell.

While protests in the Arab world were intended to provoke fundamental constitutional change, popular movements elsewhere were less extreme, directed toward influencing existing governmental policies. In India, for example, an anticorruption activist named Anna Hazare mobilized millions using Gandhian tactics of nonviolent protest to call the country's political and business elite to account for squandering the nation's resources. Despite an anticorruption bill that finally passed in 2013 and the election of Hazare and his party to the majority in the Delhi state legislature in 2015, corruption remained deeply entrenched.

In the European Union, especially in Spain and Greece, the cause of protest was fiscal austerity. High unemployment and steep cuts to education brought students and recent graduates out into the streets, though cuts in wages, pensions, and government employment brought older workers out as well. Social benefits and free education, taken for granted for several generations, were now being withdrawn. The fault for the troubled economies, protesters argued, lay not with the ordinary people who were being hurt, but with the political and corporate elites who had mismanaged both national and international finances.

In the United States the issue was similar: in the wake of war and financial collapse, who should be held accountable for high unemployment, foreclosed homes, and the cuts in funding that led to increased college tuition? Two radically different movements emerged in response. Members of Tea Party organizations claimed that government itself was to blame and argued for a radically smaller federal government and sharp cuts in spending. "Occupy Wall Street" demonstrators, in contrast, focused on corporate greed and malfeasance as the root of the problem. While the Tea Party was absorbed into the Republican Party, and pushed it rightward, Occupy Wall Street remained outside the mainstream and had virtually no effect on public policy.

China remained relatively quiet. True, unrest was intense among some ethnic minorities, most dramatically in western China, where dozens of Tibetan monks set themselves on fire to protest government restrictions (see page 597), while tensions escalated between Han Chinese immigrants and the largely Muslim Uighur people of Xinjiang. But those protests did not affect the core areas of the Chinese population and economy. During the Arab Spring, Chinese leaders, ever fearful of a repeat of the Tiananmen demonstrations of 1989 (see Chapter 31), clamped down even further on freedom of communication.

Such was the global context for the arrest and detention of Ai Weiwei. The official media limited its coverage of events in Tahrir Square; authorities prevented the translation of foreign news reports and even blocked the word *Egypt* from search engines. It was Ai Weiwei's facility in the use of new media that made him dangerous enough to be detained after he launched an investigation into children's deaths following the Sichuan earthquake of 2008. (See the feature "Visual Evidence in Primary Sources: The Art of Ai Weiwei.")

Thus the 2011 "year of protest" passed with no major challenge to the political monopoly of the Chinese Communist Party. But hundreds of small eruptions had become common, often in out-of-the-way places with little media coverage. Will the Communist Party be able to put out all of those small fires one by one, while keeping the lid on larger-scale urban protest? Perhaps, as long as the economy continues to grow. But the lessons of history, and even the logic of Marxist philosophy, indicate that the emerging Chinese middle class will not remain content with economic benefits alone.

Once-in-a-decade changes at the top of the Communist hierarchy in 2012 led to even more draconian limits on expression. College textbooks, for example, came under scrutiny: "*Strengthen management of the use of original Western teaching materials*," said the education minister. "*By no means allow teaching materials that disseminate Western values in our classrooms.*"* (Of course, there is *no* chance that Communist authorities will allow a book featuring Ai Weiwei into Chinese classrooms!)

But it is likely that China's booming middle class, long obsessed with the material benefits of economic growth, will sooner or later increase demands for

---

*Chris Buckley, "China Warns Against 'Western Values' in Imported Textbooks," *New York Times*, January 30, 2015.

basic freedoms, government transparency, and the rule of law. In 2014, protestors in Hong Kong briefly rekindled memories of the 2011 "year of protest" when they took to the streets to demand free elections. So far, it seems that the "one country, two systems" formula (see Chapter 31) has meant that Communist rulers in Beijing would increasingly impose their legal and political frameworks on relatively liberal Hong Kong. In 2014, they easily outmaneuvered the protestors. Who knows what the future will bring?

Global Art and Culture

Globalization has had mixed results. Myriad opportunities are offset by political confusion, economic anxiety, and increasing inequality. In the cultural domain, however, globalization seems more like an unmixed blessing.

Even in China, the barren propaganda of the Mao Zedong era has been replaced by a vibrant, globally connected art scene. Studios and galleries abound, especially in Beijing and Shanghai. Art schools are booming, and tens of thousands of Chinese art students study abroad.

Visual artists now push the envelope of social commentary, with ironic images of Mao Zedong and sly critiques of the Communist bureaucracy abounding. But everyone knows there are lines that must not be crossed: once artists follow Ai Weiwei's example and enter the public arena as advocates of change, the hammer falls.

Media and film are also areas where we find innovative national trajectories amid increasing transnational fertilization. The two most influential players are still Hollywood and Bollywood (the Indian industry that began in Bombay, today's Mumbai). In Africa, the rapidly expanding "Nollywood" industry of Nigeria is also becoming a regional player, with its audience globalizing as Africans move around the world (in both 2014 and 2015 Afro-British actors were nominated for Academy Awards).

AP® THEMES

How has popular culture been affected by globalization and advances in communication?

- **CONTEXT&CONNECTIONS** An example of expanding transnational media is the Turkish phenomenon *Muhteşem Yüzyıl* (*The Magnificent Century*), a dramatization of life at the Ottoman court of Sultan *Süleyman* (Chapter 17). The show is one of the most popular *telenovelas* across Latin America, where it is shown in Spanish and Portuguese translation. *The Magnificent Century* is also a big hit dubbed into Arabic, inspiring Arab tourists to visit Istanbul's Topkapi Palace, where the show's intrigues actually took place.

For many people, spectator sports are a part of daily life, and here again we find the impact of globalization. Football (or soccer as it is called in the United States) is a prime example. Its modern rules developed in nineteenth-century Britain, and then traveled across the empire and beyond to become part of the texture of life around the world, feeding the hopes and dreams of young boys (and now girls, too). All across Europe, Latin America, and Africa, and increasingly Asia and North America as well, football is king. As one writer notes on the cultural globalization evident on the football pitch: "*Basque teams, under the stewardship of Welsh coaches, stocked up on Dutch and Turkish players; Moldavian squads imported Nigerians. Everywhere you looked, it suddenly seemed, national borders and national identities had been swept into the dustbin of soccer history.*"* Even if some fans bring

*Franklin Foer, *How Soccer Explains the World: An Unlikely Theory of Globalization* (New York: HarperCollins, 2004), pp. 2–3.

The Art of Ai Weiwei

Ai Weiwei practices conceptual art, with a predominant idea underlying artistic execution and materials and aesthetics embodying that driving concept. It is always relevant to ask of Ai's work: What does it mean?

Photography is one medium Ai has explored since his New York years (1981–1993). Here we see one of his most famous (and infamous) works, *Dropping a Han Dynasty Urn* (1995). Another series of photographs make up *Study of Perspective* (1995–2003), where each picture is framed at eye level with Ai's middle finger held up toward famous sites, such as Rome's Colosseum, the White House, Tiananmen Square, the Sydney Opera House, and the *Mona Lisa*. Search for *Study of Perspective* online and consider what concept underlies the images.

Ai is also famous for large-scale public works, such as *Remembering* (2009) (shown opposite), a tribute to the children killed in the Sichuan earthquake. Another is 2011's *Sunflower Seeds* (seen with the artist in this chapter's opening), which featured millions of hand-crafted ceramic sunflower seeds strewn on the floor of London's Tate Gallery, provoking the viewer to question the relationship between nature and artifice, and between individuals and masses. The gallery's website (http://www.tate.org.uk/whats-on/tate-modern/exhibition/unilever-series-ai-weiwei/video) includes a video in which Ai Weiwei explains his rationale behind the piece:

Ai's goal is to make the viewer think. With this image, what thoughts and feelings might he be intending to provoke?

The vase Ai is dropping was genuine, two thousand years old, and quite valuable.

Ai's works question the destruction of cultural heritage in China's rush to modernize.

AP Images/Smithsonian's Hirshhorn Museum

Ai's works often confuse our assumptions about what we see as "real" and what we take to be "artificial." He often juxtaposes old materials and new forms, ideas of progress with emblems of tradition, and themes of perishing and persisting. For *Colored Vases* (2007–2010), Ai painted over valuable imperial vases with brightly colored industrial paints. In Miami, a disgruntled viewer, protesting at the globalization of art, smashed those painted vases.

to adapt an ancient porcelain technique to modern expression and to help maintain the traditional ceramics industry by employing sixteen hundred people in the production of the sunflower seeds.

Viewing the documentary film *Ai Weiwei: Never Sorry* is an excellent way to learn more about the artist. Even better would be viewing an exhibit of Ai's artwork.

Ai's work is especially appreciated in Germany, where many exhibits of his work have been launched. In *Remembering*, thousands of backpacks were fixed to the walls of Munich's *Haus der Kunst* (House of Art), one for each child killed in the Sichuan earthquake.

The backpacks are colored and arranged to spell out "*She lived happily for seven years in this world*" in Chinese characters.

Censors shut down the blog where Ai posted the kids' names, and the police severely beat him when he went to Sichuan to file a complaint. ***Why were the Chinese authorities so angered by Ai's collection and dissemination of these children's names?***

Joerg Koch/AFP/Getty Images

Remembrance (2010) is a related piece, achieving a similar effect in a smaller space: one after another the children's names appear in Chinese script on a computer screen, with a voice reading each name aloud. The experience lasts for 3 hours 41 minutes before looping back to the beginning.

Ai purchased twisted steel rebar from the destroyed schools and had workers hammer it straight. His sculpture "Straight" used that reclaimed material in an undulating 38-ton steel carpet with a seam running up its center: "*The tragic reality of today is reflected in the true plight of our spiritual existence,*" he said. "*We are spineless and cannot stand straight.*"

their racism and xenophobia (fear of foreigners) into soccer stadiums, the world is still richer for the global crosscurrents displayed on the field.

When South Africa hosted the World Cup in 2010, it was a triumphant celebration for the African continent, as hundreds of millions learned more about contemporary African arts, rhythms, and cultures while watching the games. Likewise, Brazil's World Cup in 2014, although not without controversy, gave the country a chance to showcase the vibrant cultural mix in cuisine, music, clothing, and communication arising from the country's melding of African, Amerindian, and European influences.

Indeed, from soccer to basketball, from film to fashion, from home design to graphic novels, from hip hop to classical music—across the artistic landscape, the creative potential of cultural borrowing and mixing seems limitless. True, technology now allows us to experience the power of global culture from home. But as the story of Ai Weiwei and this book's entire series of travelers reminds us, *voyages* are still the best way to satisfy our curiosity and stimulate our creativity.

CONTEXT AND CONNECTIONS

Our Future Voyage

World historians need to be adept at moving across various temporal and spatial scales, from a single moment in time to the sweep of millennia, from individual lives, like that of Ai Weiwei and other travelers featured in *Voyages in World History*, to the development and interaction of global civilizations. In this chapter, we have narrowed the temporal dimension to the beginning of the twenty-first century, while attempting to keep the entire world in view. Now, in conclusion, we may widen our lens briefly to contextualize contemporary events in broader temporal perspective.

In these terms, the key issues are undoubtedly the interrelated ones of population, environment, and energy use. Though only 6.5 percent of the human beings who have ever lived were alive in 2011, they were having an unprecedented impact on the earth and its resources: land, water, and atmosphere. Our preindustrial ancestors relied principally on the power of their own muscles and those of domesticated animals, occasionally harnessing water, wind, and, in small quantities, coal. Since the Industrial Revolution, such constraints have been left behind. In just the past two decades, global energy use has skyrocketed by 39 percent, with growth rates highest in China (146 percent), India (91 percent), and Latin America (66 percent). While European energy consumption grew by just 7 percent during that period, the United States maintained its position as the largest per capita consumer of energy, each American using four times more than the global average. Are such rates of energy consumption sustainable? Will future conflicts be sparked by competition for dwindling energy and water resources?

An optimistic view of humankind's ability to support 7 billion and more people at reasonable levels of prosperity might come from reflection upon the mistake of Thomas Malthus, an early-nineteenth-century pioneer of population studies. Malthus believed that Britain was headed for an inevitable crisis as population growth came to outstrip the food supply. "*The power of population,*" he wrote, "*is indefinitely greater than the power in the earth to produce subsistence for man.*"* Yet Britain escaped the Malthusian trap by harnessing new technologies and energy sources. It remains to be seen, of course, whether an equivalent burst of technological progress can replicate that success on a global scale, where the stakes are much higher than in Malthus's time.

At any rate, the human story is about more than just production, consumption, and reproduction. Culture

*Thomas Malthus, *An Essay on the Principle of Population*, Oxford World's Classics (New York: Oxford University Press, 2008), p. 61.

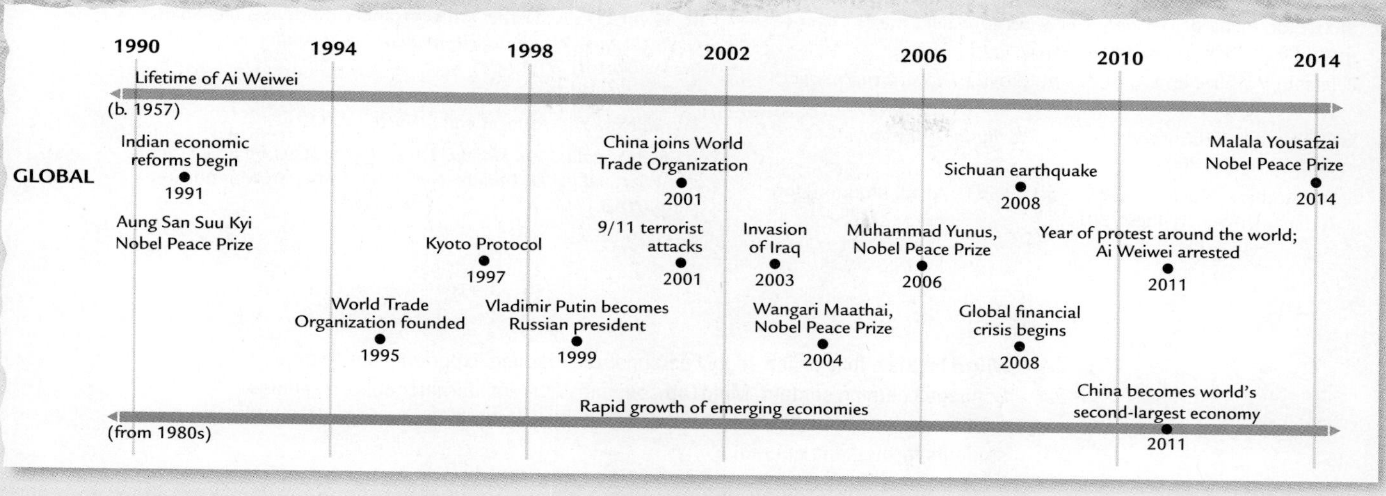

matters, and at least since the Enlightenment, a vision of political, intellectual, and artistic liberation has inspired dreams of a better future. Yet progress is usually charted using only mundane economic indicators, as if increased consumption alone is the key to human fulfilment. In addition to material satisfaction, other measures were used in the United Nation's 2013 *World Happiness Report*, which found that the people of Denmark, Norway, and Switzerland were the most satisfied with their lives. Canadians ranked sixth. The United States came in at seventeenth, just below Mexico and just above Ireland.

As the human voyage continues, the African continent, where the human story began some 160,000 years ago, points the way forward. For all the challenges they have dealt with in their modern history, recent polls show that Africans are the most optimistic people on the planet. Perhaps Africans' persistent belief in and commitment to a better future for themselves and their children is a lesson for the world.

Key Terms

Ai Weiwei (968)
BRIC (969)
Vladimir Putin (970)
World Trade Organization (976)
Muhammad Yunus (976)
September 11, 2001 (978)
Kyoto Protocol (985)
sustainable development (985)
One Child Policy (986)
Malala Yousafzai (988)
dowry system (989)

For Further Reference

Ai, Weiwei. *Evidence*. Catalog of a 2014 exhibition at the Martin-Gropius Bau, Berlin. Edited by Gereon Sievernich. Munich: Prestel, 2014.

Appiah, Kwame Anthony. *Cosmopolitanism: Ethics Is a World of Strangers*. New York: W. W. Norton, 2007.

Bourguignon, François. *The Globalization of Inequality*. Thomas Scott-Railton, trans. Princeton, N.J.: Princeton University Press, 2015.

Farlow, Andrew. *Crash and Beyond: Causes and Consequences of the Global Financial Crisis*. New York: Oxford University Press, 2012.

Friedman, Thomas. *Hot, Flat and Crowded: Why We Need a Green Revolution*. Rev. ed. New York: Picador, 2009.

Klein, Naomi. *This Changes Everything: Capitalism vs. the Climate*. New York: Simon & Schuster, 2014.

Lynch, Mark. *The Arab Uprisings Explained: New Contentious Politics in the Middle East*. New York: Columbia University Press, 2014.

McGregor, Richard. *The Party: The Secret World of China's Communist Rulers*. New York: Harper, 2012.

Peterson, V. Spike, and Anne Sisson Runyan. *Global Gender Issues in the New Millennium*. 3d ed. Boulder, Colo.: Westview, 2009.

Sen, Amartya. *Identity and Violence: The Illusion of Destiny*. New York: Penguin, 2008.

Staab, Andreas. *The European Union Explained*. 2d ed. Bloomington: Indiana University Press, 2011.

Toft, Monica Duffy, Daniel Philpott, and Timothy Samuel Shah. *God's Century: Resurgent Religion and Global Politics*. New York: W. W. Norton, 2011.

Wright, Robin. *Rock the Casbah: Rage and Rebellion Across the Islamic World*. New York: Simon and Schuster, 2011.

Yousafzai, Malala. *I Am Malala: The Girl Who Stood Up for Education and Was Shot by the Taliban*. New York: Little, Brown and Company, 2013.

AP® Review Questions for Chapter 32

Multiple-Choice Questions

QUESTIONS 1–4 REFER TO MAP 32.1 *PER CAPITA INCOME* ON PAGE 971.

1. Which of the following led most directly to the distribution of incomes shown on the map?
   (A) World War I
   (B) World War II
   (C) The Cold War
   (D) The Industrial Revolution

2. Most of Africa remains economically underdeveloped
   (A) due to recurrent political instability, corruption, and economies dominated by raw materials exports.
   (B) as a result of massive population losses to diseases such as AIDS and Ebola.
   (C) because overproduction of agricultural exports has damaged the environment.
   (D) since many nations have abandoned capitalism in favor of communal, subsistence agriculture.

3. The inclusion of Japan and South Korea in the upper income bracket is primarily the result of
   (A) a return to traditional Confucian practices with its focus on filial piety and the larger group.
   (B) the discovery of unique manufacturing processes that revolutionized factory production.
   (C) active economic development in export goods to the United States during the Cold War.
   (D) Soviet and Chinese investment into Japan and Korea following World War II.

4. Which of the following is an important *direct* effect of the income distribution indicated in the map?
   (A) Popular and consumer culture has become more global.
   (B) Political and professional roles have become less inclusive in terms of race, class, and gender.
   (C) Movements, such as Green Belt in Kenya, have arisen to protest the economic inequality of global integration.
   (D) Global economic institutions, such as the World Bank, have focused their activities on the most developed regions.

QUESTIONS 5–7 REFER TO THE FOLLOWING PASSAGES.

The principal destabilizing force has to do with the fact that the private return on capital, *r*, can be significantly higher for long periods of time than the rate of growth of income and output, *g*. The inequality $r > g$ implies that wealth accumulated in the past grows more rapidly than output and wages. . . . The entrepreneur inevitably tends to become a rentier [making money by renting out property or investing funds at interest] more and more dominant over those who own nothing but their labor.

—Thomas Piketty, economist, *Capital in the Twenty-First Century*, 2014

[Piketty] claims that the differential returns on capital versus labor are the driving forces of the system, but that is a partial and misleading view. The driving force of the capitalist system is relentless innovation that improves productivity and raises living standards. . . . Workers and consumers have benefited generation on generation from less burdensome forms of work and access to ever more inexpensive products that make life easier.

—James Piereson, historian, "Thomas Piketty's 'Le Capital,'" 2014

5. The tone of the *second* passage best reflects which of the following developments in the early twenty-first century?
   (A) Marxian-Socialism as an economic system failed to provide the necessary means of support for populations under its sway.
   (B) Over the long term, capitalism will lead to greater economic equality as the rate of return on investments exceeds the rate of return for labor.
   (C) Despite some economic inequality, capitalist globalization has generally led to more prosperous people than any other system.
   (D) Some environmental degradation is a necessary outcome for healthy economic development.

6. Both passages best support which of the following conclusions?
   (A) Free-market economic policies always work more to separate than to equalize the rich and the poor.
   (B) The spread of free-market economics has had both positive and negative outcomes.

(C) Political stability is necessary for economic growth.
(D) The poor are largely responsible for their own economic condition.

7. The debate between Piketty and Piereson as reflected in these passages is best understood in the context of which of the following?
   (A) Rights-based discourse affirming old assumptions about class
   (B) Globalization of popular and consumer culture
   (C) Education as an inclusive force
   (D) Inequality as an economic consequence of global integration

QUESTIONS 8–10 REFER TO THE FOLLOWING PASSAGE.

We agree under this BRICS STI [Science, Technology, Innovation] framework the main areas of cooperation shall include: exchange of information on policies and programmes and promotion of innovation and technology transfer; food security and sustainable agriculture; climate change and natural disaster preparedness and mitigation; new and renewable energy; energy efficiency; nanotechnology; high performance computing; basic research; space research and exploration, aeronautics, astronomy and earth observation; medicine and biotechnology; biomedicine and life sciences (biomedical engineering, bioinformatics, biomaterials); water resources and pollution treatment; high tech zones/science parks and incubators; technology transfer; science popularization; information and communication technology; clean coal technologies; natural gas and con-conventional gases; ocean and polar sciences; and geospatial technologies and its applications.

—BRICS [Brazil, Russia, India, China, South Africa] Science and Technology Cooperation Framework, 2014

8. Which of the following conclusions about the twenty-first century is most directly supported by this passage?
   (A) International cooperation was facilitated by new international organizations.
   (B) Principles of free-market economics spread throughout the world.
   (C) Governments began to take a less active role in economic life.
   (D) Militarized states responded to conflicts in ways that intensified the conflicts.

9. Despite the ambitious goals indicated in the framework above, several BRICS nations continue to struggle
   (A) because of the command nature of their centralized economies.
   (B) in controlling pollution and income inequality.
   (C) due to civil unrest caused by economic inequality.
   (D) because their focus remained primarily agricultural.

10. Which of the following was an important continuity underlying the use of technology in the twentieth and twenty-first centuries illustrated by the passage?
   (A) Improved military technology led to increased wartime casualties.
   (B) Governments became less concerned over the environmental impact of economic activity.
   (C) Cultural differences and nationalism impeded international cooperation.
   (D) Technology was used to enhance the effectiveness of both agriculture and medicine.

Short-Answer Questions

1. Answer parts A and B.
   A. Identify and explain ONE challenge faced by women in the developing world.
   B. Identify and explain ONE way women have responded to challenges in the developing world.

2. Answer parts A, B, and C.
   A. Identify and explain ONE cause of global warming.
   B. Identify and explain ONE effect of global warming other than increased global temperatures.
   C. Identify and explain ONE reason why some are resistant to stricter environmental regulations.

Document-Based Questions (DBQs)

Introduction to the Document-Based Question (DBQ)

Think of a document-based question (DBQ) as a mini-research paper or a mini-investigation. It is a chance to show that you, like a professional historian or detective, can read the documents, question your sources, understand the backgrounds and motivations of the writers, and produce a good interpretation and synthesis. In the words of the AP® World History curriculum framework, a DBQ "emphasizes the [student's] ability to analyze and synthesize historical evidence, including textual, quantitative, or visual materials."[1] The DBQ is scored using a set of guidelines that assesses the historical thinking skills in the curriculum framework. Each DBQ will emphasize one or two of the skills, but all of the DBQ essays will touch on Argumentation, Analyzing Evidence: Content and Sourcing, Contextualization, and Synthesis. Your essay can receive a maximum of 7 points as scored by an AP® reader. Your classroom teacher may use a different system of grading, but she or he will be looking to see if you demonstrate the same skills as outlined in the framework. The DBQs in this section mirror the format of the AP® World History exam and feature five to seven documents each. Each question is designed to be completed in 55 minutes; this time includes a suggested 15-minute reading period.

When working with documents, try the following:

1. **Plot summary:** Underline key words in the prompt. What is this document's basic subject matter and content? What is its date? Where was it written? What are some other events that occurred during the same time period?
2. **Thesis** (1 point): Does the thesis explicitly address all parts of the prompt? Do not simply restate the prompt but explain how and why you have chosen to make a specific argument. Remember that it is okay for the thesis to consist of multiple sentences.
3. **Use as many documents as possible;** however, if you are unsure how to interpret a document, it is best not to use that particular document.
4. **Analysis of historical evidence and support of your argument** (up to 3 points):
   Be sure to analyze explicitly each of the documents to support your thesis. Additionally, you need to address at least one of the following for each document used:
   - Audience
   - Purpose
   - Historical context
   - The author's point of view
5. **Some questions to ask yourself while analyzing the documents:**
   - "Who produced it?" What was his or her gender, age, location, ethnicity, social status, religion, or intellectual approach?
   - "Who was the intended audience?" Was it written privately, written to be read or heard by others (who?), an official document for a ruler to read, a commissioned painting, or some other type of document?

[1]2016–2017 AP® World History Curriculum Framework (© 2014 The College Board). P. 94. Available online at www.apcentral.collegeboard.com.

- "Why?" What is the motivation of the writer or producer of the document, based on the information you have about him or her?

  When you put the answers to these questions together, you have a strong analysis of the historical evidence: why this person would be producing this piece of information at this time. Then you can evaluate how much you "trust" the information in the document and perhaps determine what you think was really going on. It is useful to consider the tone or vocabulary of the document. It will sometimes convey the intent or the point of view of the author, such as anger, disdain, admiration, confusion, and so on.

6. **Other examples not included in the documents to support the thesis or argument** (1 point): You will need to add evidence not included in the documents to further support the thesis.
7. **Contextualization** (1 point): One requirement is that you connect the specific historical events supportive of the thesis to a broader historical context, such as a major social movement, war, or political change.
8. **Synthesis** (1 point): Finally, you will need to synthesize the argument, that is, to combine the argument, evidence, analysis, and context in a well-developed essay that does at least one of the following:
   - Extends or modifies the thesis
   - Recognizes contradictory evidence
   - Appropriately connects the topic of the question to other historical periods and circumstances (for example, connecting a DBQ on the Mughal empire to the general theme of State Consolidation and Imperial Expansion from 1450 to 1750)

Directions: The following question is based on the accompanying documents. The documents have been edited for the purpose of this exercise.

In your response, you should do the following:

- State a relevant thesis that directly a ddresses all parts of the question.
- Support the thesis or a relevant argument with evidence from all, or all but one, of the documents.
- Incorporate analysis of all, or all but one, of the documents into your argument.
- Focus your analysis of each document on at least one of the following: intended audience, purpose, historical context, and/or point of view.
- Support your argument with analysis of historical examples outside the documents.
- Connect historical phenomena relevant to your argument to broader events or processes.
- Synthesize the elements above into a persuasive essay that extends your argument, connects it to a different historical context, or accounts for contradictory evidence on the topic.

DBQ 1: Atlantic Revolutions

Question: Using the documents and your knowledge of world history, analyze the reasons people in regions touching the Atlantic Ocean revolted between 1775 and 1820.

Document 1
Source: Letter from a woman from Philadelphia written shortly after the Battle of Lexington, April 1775

> It is plain truth which the most ignorant peasant knows and is clear to the weakest capacity, that no man has a right to the take their money without their consent. The supposition is ridiculous and absurd—my friend, reconcile it with your own good sense—that a body of men in Great Britain, who have little intercourse with America and, of course, know nothing of us, nor supposed to see or feel the misery they would inflict upon us, shall invest themselves with a power to command our lives and properties at all times and in all cases whatsoever.

Document 2
Source: Declaration of Independence of the United States, July 1776

> We hold these truths to be self-evident, that all men are created equal, that they are endowed by their Creator with certain unalienable Rights, that among these are Life, Liberty and the pursuit of Happiness. –That to secure these rights, Governments are instituted among Men, deriving their just powers from the consent of the governed, –That whenever any Form of Government becomes destructive of these ends, it is the Right of the People to alter or to abolish it, and to institute new Government, laying its foundation on such principles and organizing its powers in such form, as to them shall seem most likely to effect their Safety and Happiness.

Document 3
Source: Declaration of the Rights of Man and the Citizen, issued by the National Assembly of France in August 1789

> The representatives of the French people, organized as a National Assembly, believing that the ignorance, neglect, or contempt of the rights of man are the sole cause of public calamities and of the corruption of governments, have determined to set forth in a solemn declaration the natural, unalienable, and sacred rights of man, in order that this declaration, being constantly before all the members of the Social body, shall remind them continually of their rights and duties; in order that the acts of the legislative power, as well as those of the executive power, may be compared at any moment with the objects and purposes of all political institutions and may thus be more respected, and, lastly, in order that the grievances of the citizens, based hereafter upon simple and incontestable principles, shall tend to the maintenance of the constitution and redound to the happiness of all. Therefore the National Assembly recognizes and proclaims, in the presence and under the auspices of the Supreme Being, the following rights of man and of the citizen:

Articles:

1. Men are born and remain free and equal in rights. Social distinctions may be founded only upon the general good.
2. The aim of all political association is the preservation of the natural and imprescriptible rights of man. These rights are liberty, property, security, and resistance to oppression.
3. The principle of all sovereignty resides essentially in the nation. No body nor individual may exercise any authority which does not proceed directly from the nation. . . .
6. Law is the expression of the general will. Every citizen has a right to participate personally, or through his representative, in its foundation. It must be the same for all, whether it protects or punishes.

Document 4

Source: Anonymous cartoon depicting the three estates of French society: clergy, nobility, and commoners, 1789

Document 5

Source: Letter from Jean-François Papillon and Georges Biassou, leaders of the Haitian rebel slaves, to a newly arrived French commission, carrying a decree of general amnesty for political activity during the uprising of the previous years, December 1791

> We are inspired by your proclamation and admire its moderation and wisdom, but we must tell you that you do not understand our position and that you have inaccurate ideas about the nature of the revolution that has made us, along with the whites, its sad victims. In ordering us each to return our own homes, you are demanding something both impossible and dangerous. A hundred thousand men are in arms, we make up 80 percent of this population, which is a lot. Most of us are fathers, and you must understand that because of this we depend entirely upon the general will. And whose will is it? That of a multitude of *nègres* from Africa, most of whom can barely say two words in French but who, at the same time, were accustomed to fighting wars in their own countries.

Document 6

Source: Miguel Hidalgo, Mexican Catholic priest and leader in Mexican independence movement, decrees issued after the capture of Guadalajara, December 1810

> By these presents I order the judges and justices of the district of this capital to proceed immediately to the collection of the rents due to this day by the lessees of the lands belonging to the Indian communities, the said rents to be entered in the national treasury. The lands shall be turned over to the Indians for their cultivation, and they may not be rented out in the future, for it is my wish that only the Indians in their respective towns shall have the use of them.
>
> From the moment that the courageous American nation took up arms to throw off the heavy yoke that oppressed it for three centuries, one of its principal aims has been to extinguish the multitude of taxes that kept it in poverty. Since the critical state of our affairs does not permit the framing of adequate provisions in this respect, because of the need of the kingdom for money to defray the costs of the war, for the present I propose to remedy the most urgent abuses by means of the following declarations. First: All slaveowners shall set their slaves free within ten days, on pain of death for violation of this article. Second: The payment of tribute by all the castes that used to pay it shall henceforth cease, and no other taxes shall be collected from the Indians.

Document 7

Source: Simon Bolivar, Venezuelan landowner and general in multiple revolutions against Spanish rule in South America, letter to governor of Jamaica, September 1815

The role of the inhabitants of the American hemisphere has for centuries been purely passive. Politically they were nonexistent. We are still in a position lower than slavery, and therefore it is more difficult for us to rise to the enjoyment of freedom. . . . States are slaves because of either the nature or the misuse of their constitutions; a people is therefore enslaved when the government, by its nature or its vices, infringes on and usurps the rights of the citizen or subject.

We have been harassed by a conduct which has not only deprived us of our rights but has kept us in a sort of permanent infancy with regard to public affairs.

Americans today, and perhaps to a greater extent than ever before, who live within the Spanish system occupy a position in society no better than that of serfs destined for labor, or at best they have no more status than that of mere consumers. Yet even this status is surrounded with galling restrictions, such as being forbidden to grow European crops, or to store products which are royal monopolies, or to establish factories of a type the Peninsula itself does not possess.

Despite the convictions of history, South Americans have made efforts to obtain liberal, even perfect, institutions, doubtless out of that instinct to aspire to the greatest possible happiness, which, common to all men, is bound to follow in civil societies founded on the principles of justice, liberty, and equality.

DBQ 2: British–Chinese Relations

Question: Using the documents and your knowledge of world history, analyze the relationship between the British and the Chinese between 1750 and 1850.

Document 1

Source: Letter from Henry Dundas, president of East India Company (EIC), to George Macartney, representative of King George III, outlining British goals and advice for a trading mission to China to ease some of the restrictions of the Canton System, January 4, 1792

The measures lately taken by the Government [of Great Britain] respecting the tea trade, having more than trebled the former legal importation of this article into Great Britain, it [has] become particularly desirable to cultivate a friendship, and increase the communication with China, which may lead to such a vent [market] throughout that extensive empire, of the manufactures of the mother country.

You should fairly state, after repeating the general assurances of his majesty's friendly and peaceful inclinations towards the Emperor . . . first the mutual benefit be derived from a trade between the two Nations, in the course of which we receive besides other articles to the amount of twenty millions of pounds weight of Chinese tea . . . and for which we return woolens, cottons, and other articles useful to the Chinese, but a considerable part is actually to China in bullion.

It is necessary you should be on your guard against one stipulation which, perhaps, will be demanded from you: which is that of the exclusion of the trade of opium from the Chinese dominions as being prohibited by the Laws of the Chinese Empire; if this subject should come into discussion, it must be handled with the greatest caution. It is beyond a doubt that no inconsiderable portion of the opium raised within our Indian territories actually finds its way to China: but if it should be made . . . any article of any proposed commercial treaty, that none of that drug should be sent by us to China, you must accede to it, rather than risk any essential benefit by contending for a liberty in this respect

Document 2

Source: Chinese emperor Qianlong's response to King George III's request to change the Canton System, September 23, 1793

Yesterday your Ambassador petitioned my Ministers to memorialize me regarding your trade with China, but his proposal is not consistent with our dynastic usage and cannot be entertained. Hitherto, all European nations, including your own country's barbarian merchants, have carried on their trade with Our Celestial Empire at Guangzhou. Such has been the procedure for many years, although Our Celestial Empire possesses all things in prolific abundance and lacks no product within its own borders. There was therefore no need to import the manufactures of outside barbarians in exchange for our own produce. But as the tea, silk, and porcelain which the Celestial Empire produces are absolute necessities to European nations and to yourselves, we have permitted, as a signal mark of favor, that foreign *hongs* [Chinese business associations] should be established at Guangzhou, so that your wants might be supplied and your country thus participate in our beneficence. . . . Our dynasty, influencing the many races of the globe, extends the same benevolence toward all. Your England is not the only nation trading at Guangzhou. If other nations, following your bad example, wrongfully importune my ear with further impossible requests, how will it be possible for me to treat them with easy indulgence? Nevertheless, I do not forget the lonely remoteness of your island, cut off from the world by intervening wastes of sea, nor do I overlook your excusable ignorance of the usages of Our Celestial Empire. I have consequently commanded my Ministers to enlighten your Ambassador on the subject, and have ordered the departure of the mission.

Document 3

Source: British merchant in background entering warehouse in Guangzhou where Chinese workers are packing porcelain and tea, unknown artist from Guangzhou, ca. 1825

Document 4

Source: Data about British trade in opium and tea

Year	Average amount of tea exported from China by the EIC (pounds)	Estimated amount of opium shipped from India to China (pounds)
1765	6,000,000	140,000
1775	4,521,000	140,000
1785	18,460,000	140,000
1795	20,360,000	280,000
1805	22,360,000	630,000
1810	32,590,000	630,000
1815	29,640,000	700,000
1820	28,770,000	630,000
1825	29,960,000	1,736,000
1830	31,450,000	2,660,000
1835	—	4,200,000

Compiled from *Selected Statistical Material on China's Modern Economic History*, 1955, and Carl A. Trocki, *Opium, Empire, and the Global Political Economy*, 1999.

Document 5

Source: Thomas Dealtry, Anglican Archdeacon of Calcutta, conclusion to an antiopium pamphlet published in Guangzhou, 1836

> Our sin is growing, and encouraging the trade in opium is, indeed, one of the darkest that ever invoked the wrath of the most high God upon a people. Where are the preachers of the gospel, where is the spirit of the common humanity fled, that this sin should till this moment exist unrebuked? Oh what a wail of misery would awaken your remorse and compassion, could the dying agonies of one poor opium-victim reach your soul! Think then of THE MILLIONS who have already thus perished, and then ask yourself how long is this to continue and no man in a Christian land regard it? How long is a British government to be seen drawing revenue from this source, admitting the misery, and excusing itself for abetting, by a fallacy, the most contemptible and insulting even to common sense? How long is a whole community of British merchants to be content with earning the price of blood, because if they do not, others will in their stead?

Document 6

Source: Edict to Foreigners, Lin Zexu, Chinese commissioner to deal with the opium trade, March 18, 1839

> Foreign ships that have come to Guangzhou for trade have profited heavily. No matter what merchandise was imported, it all sold. No matter what merchandise was desired, it was procured. . . . Our Great Emperor treats everyone equally, permitting all to trade and make a profit. . . . Allowing you to trade every year without tight control is a grace upon you. To show gratitude you should respect our laws.
>
> Now I publicly declare the following edict and all foreign merchants should, upon receiving this edict, abide by its instructions without delay and to surrender to the imperial officials all the opium on your ships. The Chinese merchants are responsible for inventorying how many cases are confiscated, examined, registered, and destroyed. Eliminate the harmful substance with absolutely no exception.

Document 7

Source: Response to claims in a Parliament debate about the immorality of the opium trade and compensating the British traders whose opium was seized by Commissioner Lin, Sir George Stanton, April 4, 1843

> However pernicious and impolitic the traffic in opium may be, and whatever opinion this House may pronounce to-night against its further continuance, we ought to recollect that these persons engaged in this traffic under the full sanction, and indeed encouragement, both of the Indian and the home Government; that they were deprived of their property by an act of violent and unjustifiable outrage on the part of the Chinese authorities; and that they received, at the same time, from her Majesty's Superintendent of Trade, on behalf of the Government, a distinct and specific pledge of reimbursement. I think, therefore, whatever may be the fate of the present motion, these individuals are clearly entitled to full, fair, and entire indemnification for their losses.

DBQ 3: Europeans in the Indian Ocean

Question: Using the documents and your knowledge of world history, analyze how Europeans viewed the peoples of the Indian Ocean between 1498 and 1730.

Document 1

Source: First Portuguese description of Calicut, India, by Vasco da Gama, 1498

> The city of Calicut is inhabited by Christians. They are of a tawny complexion. Some of them have big beards and long hair, whilst others clip their hair short or shave the head, merely allowing a tuft to remain on the crown as a sign that they are Christians. They also wear moustaches. They pierce the ears and wear much gold in them. They go naked down to the waist, covering their lower extremities with very fine cotton stuffs. But it is only the most respectable who do this, for the others manage as best they are able. The women of this country, as a rule, are ugly and of small stature. They wear many jewels of gold round the neck, numerous bracelets on their arms, and rings set with precious stones on their toes. All these people are well-disposed and apparently of mild temper. At first sight they seem covetous and ignorant.

Document 2

Source: Description of the inhabitants of Cambay by Tomé Pires, Portuguese doctor and diplomat who traveled in the Indian Ocean, ca. 1515

> I now come to the trade of Cambay. These [people] are [like] Italians in their knowledge of and dealings in merchandise. All the trade in Cambay is in the hands of the heathen. Their general designation is Gujaratis, and then they are divided into various races. There is no doubt that these people have the cream of the trade. They are men who understand merchandise; they are so properly steeped in the sound and harmony of it, that the Gujaratis say that any offense connected with merchandise is pardonable. There are Guajaratis settled everywhere [around the Indian Ocean]. They work some for some and others for others. They are diligent, quick men in trade. They do their accounts with figures like ours and with our very writing. They are men who do not give away anything that belongs to them, nor do they want anything that belongs to anyone else; wherefore they have been esteemed in Cambay up to the present, practicing their idolatry, because they enrich the kingdom greatly with the said trade. There are also some Cairo merchants settled in Cambay, and many merchants from Aden and Ormuz, all of whom do a great trade in the seaport towns of Cambay; but none of these count in comparison with the heathens, especially in knowledge. Those of our people who want to be clerks and factors ought to go there and learn, because the business of trade is a science in itself which does not hinder any noble exercise, but helps a great deal.

Document 3

Source: Illustration of an encounter between a Portuguese man and an Indian woman, ca. 1540, unknown Portuguese artist

Album/Art Resource, NY

Document 4

Source: Description of inhabitants of Calicut by Pietro della Valle, Roman traveler, ca. 1620

After dinner, I landed also with the captain of my ship, and some other soldiers; we went to see the bazar, which is near the shore; the houses, or rather cottages, are very narrow, but indifferently long; the market was full of all sorts of provision, and other things necessary to the livelihood of that people, conformable to their custom; for as for clothing, they need little, both men and women going quite naked, saving that they have a piece either of cotton or silk hanging down from the girdle to the knees, and covering their shame; the better sort are wont to wear it either all blue, or white striped with azure, or azure and some other color; a dark blue being most esteemed amongst them.

Moreover, both men and women wear their hair long, and tied about the head; the women, with a lock hanging on one side under the ear becomingly enough, as almost all Indian women do; the dressing of whose head is, in my opinion, the most gallant that I have seen in any other nation: The men have a lock hanging down from the crown of the head, sometimes a little inclined on one side; some of them use a small colored head-band, but the women use none at all. Both sexes have their arms full of bracelets, their ears of pendants, and their necks of jewels; the men commonly go with their naked swords and bucklers, or other arms in their hands.

Document 5

Source: Description of the inhabitants of Melaka and their trade links by Ralph Fitch, English merchant, ca. 1600

And so I came to Melaka on 8 February, where the Portuguese have a castle which stands near the sea. And the country outside the town belongs to the Malays, who are a kind and proud people. They go naked with a cloth about their middle, and a little roll of cloth about their heads. Hither come many ships from China and from the Moluccas, Banda, Timor, and from many other Indonesian islands, which bring great store of spices and drugs, and diamonds and other jewels. The voyages into many of these lands belong to the captain of Melaka; so that none may go thither without his license: which yield him great sums of money every year. The Portuguese here have often warred with the king of Aceh, which stands on the island of Sumatra: from which comes great stores of pepper and other spices every year to Pegu [in Burma] and Mecca within the Red Sea, and other places.

Document 6

Source: Description of British and Dutch merchants in Surat, India, by Jean-Baptiste Tavernier, French merchant, 1675

As soon as merchandise is landed at Surat it has to be taken to the custom-house, which adjoins the fort. The officers are very strict and search persons with great care. Private individuals pay as much as four and five percent duty on all their goods; but as for the English and Dutch Companies, they pay less. But, on the other hand, I believe that, taking into account what it costs them in diplomatic missions and presents, which they are obliged to make every year at court, the goods cost them nearly the same as they do private persons.

As regards gold, the [British and Dutch] merchants who import it use so much cunning in order to conceal it, that but little of it comes to the knowledge of the customs officers. The former do all they can to evade paying the customs, especially as they do not run so much risk as in the custom-houses of Europe.

The English, seeing that the custom of searching them had been adopted, had recourse to little stratagems in order to pass the gold, and the fashion of wearing wigs having reached them from Europe, they bethought themselves of concealing the gold coins in the nets of their wigs every time they left their vessels to go on shore.

Document 7

Source: Description of Burmese women by Alexander Hamilton, Scottish trader in the Indian Ocean, 1727

The Women are very courteous and kind to strangers, and are very fond of marrying with Europeans, and most part of the strangers who trade thither, marry a wife for the term they stay.

They prove obedient and obliging wives, and take the management of affairs within doors wholly in their own hands. She goes to market for food, and acts the cook in dressing his victuals, takes care of his clothes, in washing and mending them; if their husbands have any goods to sell, they set up a shop and sell them by retail, to a much better account than they could be sold for by wholesale, and some of them carry a cargo of goods to the inland towns, and barter for goods proper for the foreign markets that their husbands are bound to, and generally bring fair accounts of their negotiations. If she proves false to her husband's bed, and on fair proof convicted, her husband may carry her to the Rounday, and have her hair cut, and sold for a slave, and he may have the money; but if the husband goes astray, she'll be apt to give him a gentle dose [of poison], to send him into the other world a sacrifice to her resentment.

DBQ 4: European and American Justifications for Imperialism

Question: Using the documents and your knowledge of world history, analyze European and American motives and justifications for imperialism in the nineteenth and early twentieth centuries.

Document 1

Source: British Rule in India, Karl Marx, June 25, 1853

We must not forget that this undignified, stagnatory, and vegetative life, that this passive sort of existence evoked on the other part, in contradistinction, wild, aimless, unbounded forces of destruction and rendered murder itself a religious rite in Hindostan [India]. We must not forget that these little communities were contaminated by distinctions of caste and by slavery, that they subjugated man to external circumstances instead of elevating man the sovereign of circumstances, that they transformed a self-developing social state into never changing natural destiny, and thus brought about a brutalizing worship of nature, exhibiting its degradation in the fact that man, the sovereign of nature, fell down on his knees in adoration of Hanuman, the monkey, and Sabbala, the cow [Hindu gods].

England, it is true, in causing a social revolution in Hindostan, was actuated only by the vilest interests, and was stupid in her manner of enforcing them. But that is not the question. The question is, can mankind fulfil its destiny without a fundamental revolution in the social state of Asia? If not, whatever may have been the crimes of England she was the unconscious tool of history in bringing about that revolution.

Document 2

Source: Speech to the National Assembly supporting French imperialism, Jules Ferry, French politician, July 28, 1883

In the area of economics, I allow myself to place before you, with the support of some figures, the considerations which justify a policy of colonial expansion from the point of view of that need, felt more and more strongly by the industrial populations of' Europe and particularly those of our own rich and hard working Country: the need for export markets. Is this some kind of chimera? Is this a view of the future or is it not rather a pressing need, and, we could say, the cry of our industrial population? I will formulate only in a general way what each of you, in the different parts of France, is in a position to confirm. Yes, what is lacking for our great industry, drawn irrevocably on to the path of exportation by the (free trade) treaties of 1860, what it lacks more and more is export markets. Why? Because next door to us Germany is surrounded by barriers, because beyond the ocean, the United States of America has become protectionist, protectionist in the most extreme sense, because not only have these great markets, I will not say closed but shrunk, and thus become more difficult of access for our industrial products, but also these great scares are beginning to pour products not seen heretofore into our own markets. It is not necessary to pursue this demonstration any further.

Document 3

Source: History of British rule in East Africa, Frederick Dealtry Lugard, British soldier and imperial administrator, 1893

There are some who say we have no right in Africa at all, that "it belongs to the natives." I hold that our right is the necessity that is upon us to provide for our ever-growing population—either by opening new fields for emigration, or by providing work and employment which the development of over-sea extension entails—and to stimulate trade by finding new markets, since we know what misery trade depression brings at home.

While thus serving our own interests as a nation, we may, by selecting men of the right stamp for the control of new territories, bring at the same time many advantages to Africa. Nor do we deprive the natives of their birthright of freedom, to place them under a foreign yoke. It has ever been the key-note of British colonial method to rule through and by the natives, and it is this method, in contrast to the arbitrary and uncompromising rule of Germany, France, Portugal, and Spain, which has been the secret of our success as a colonizing nation, and has made us welcomed by tribes and peoples in Africa, who ever rose in revolt against the other nations named. In Africa, moreover, there is among the people a natural inclination to submit to a higher authority. That intense detestation of control which animates our Teutonic races does not exist among the tribes of Africa, and if there is any authority that we replace, it is the authority of the Slavers and Arabs, or the intolerable tyranny of the "dominant tribe."

Document 4

Source: Defense of U.S. imperialism after the Spanish-American War of 1898 and the conquest of Cuba, Puerto Rico, and the Philippines, Senator Albert Beveridge, 1898

Have we no mission to perform, no duty to discharge to our fellow-man? Has God endowed us with gifts beyond our deserts and marked us as the people of His peculiar favor, merely to rot in our own selfishness, as men and nations must, who take cowardice for their companion and self for their deity—as China has, as India has, as Egypt has?

Hawaii is ours; Porto Rico is to be ours; at the prayer of her people Cuba finally will be ours; in the islands of the East, even to the gates of Asia, coaling stations are to be ours at the very least; the flag of a liberal government is to float over the Philippines, and may it be the banner that Taylor unfurled in Texas and Fremont carried to the coast.

The Opposition tells us that we ought not to govern a people without their consent. I answer, The rule of liberty that all just government derives its authority from the consent of the governed, applies only to those who are capable of self-government. We govern the Indians without their consent, we govern our territories without their consent, we govern our children without their consent. How do they know that our government would be without their consent? Would not the people of the Philippines prefer the just, humane, civilizing government of this Republic to the savage, bloody rule of pillage and extortion from which we have rescued them?

Document 5

Source: "Does Colonization Pay?" O. P. Austin, Chief of the U.S. Bureau of Statistics, *The Forum*, 1900

Probably the most striking example, however, of the advantages accruing to a population from a government supplied by experienced people of other blood and climate is in the case of India. From the very beginning of British control there came a gradual end to the bloody and devastating wars between native rulers or by foreign invaders, which had sacrificed so many [Indian] lives and destroyed cities and homes from the earliest history of that great and densely populated peninsula.

With this, and especially with the direct British control of the last half-century, came other improvements. One of the first improvements undertaken was the construction and maintenance of roads. "No native prince in India ever built a road," says a distinguished writer on the history and conditions of that country; and when the British Government assumed control, it found communication between the various sections [of India] almost impossible, by reason of an absence of routes of travel over which vehicles could pass. Now there are 150,000 miles of roads in India maintained by the government, of which no less than 35,000 miles are "metalled," or macadamized, as the term is used in this country. In 1854, there were in India twenty-one miles of railway, and in 1899, 22,000 miles—uniting province with province, city with city, penetrating the native states, bringing them into closer relationship with the territory under direct control of the British Government, carrying the native products to the seaboard, and, in turn, bringing to the natives the products of other parts of the world and proving especially useful in distributing supplies in famine years.

Document 6

Source: Explanation for Britain's conquest of Egypt in 1882, Earl of Cromer, British diplomat, 1908

> There can be no doubt of the force of these arguments. The answer to them is that it was impossible for Great Britain to allow the troops of any other power to occupy Egypt. When it became apparent that some foreign occupation was necessary, that the [Ottoman] Sultan would not act save under conditions which were impossible of acceptance, and that neither French nor Italian cooperation could be secured, the British government acted with promptitude and vigor. A great nation cannot throw off the responsibilities which its past history and its position in the world have imposed upon it. English history affords other examples of the government and people of England drifting by accident into doing what was not only right, but was also most in accordance with British interests.

Document 7

Source: Road building in Dutch Indonesia, ca. 1900–1910

Roger-Viollet/The Image Works

DBQ 5: Mexico 1880–1910

Question: Between 1876 and 1911, Mexican president Porfirio Díaz wanted to modernize Mexico. Using the documents and your knowledge of world history, analyze the effects of Diaz's modernization program on Mexico from 1880 to 1910.

Document 1

Source: Description of new railway track in Mexico City newspaper, Ignacio Manuel Altamirano, early 1880s

The railroad tracks had arrived!

The two ribbons of steel that began at the eastern edge of Mexico City and extended eastward to Texcoco were destined to continue east, to Puebla, and beyond, until reaching the waves of the Gulf of Mexico. The ribbons of steel were like a gold ring symbolizing a marriage, a marriage uniting the high valley of Mexico with European civilization on the other side of those waves and with the prosperous future that Mexico deserves.

The arrival of the railroad was Texcoco's first intimation of what the future holds in store. This is what moved the city's people to rejoice upon hearing the whistle of the locomotive that brought the first train from Mexico City. Interestingly, the entrepreneurs who are carrying out the construction of the rail line are Spanish. If the first arrival of the Spanish in Texcoco brought missionaries of Christianity, this second Spanish mission brings a gospel of Science and nineteenth-century civilization.

Document 2

Source: A letter to striking workers, Matías Romero Avendaño, Minister of Finance for Mexican president Porfirio Díaz, 1892

The Executive branch of government is not, nor can it be indifferent to the evils afflicting the working class of the Republic: if their wages are inadequate, if their needs are many, if it is impossible for them to save money, if they lack employment, the first one to regret this and fully concern himself is the President. However, there are private ills that, while clamoring for all kinds of sympathy, fall largely beyond administrative action; such is the case of those that afflict the class you so honorably represent.

The Government has the law as its norm and justice as its aspiration. Given the institution that govern us, it is unfeasible to restrict freedom of hiring or to intervene directly in the improvement of basic working conditions. No legal document authorizes this, nor do any economic interests oblige the Government to dictate salaries, or prices, or working hours. Our institutions, founded on the high principles freedom and regard for property, ban the Government from meddling directly in labor-management relations and will not allow any action whatsoever other than enforcing each party's legitimate and recognized rights. The Government can only contribute to improving labor conditions by indirect means such as keeping the peace, the promotion of industry, and the investment of both national and foreign capital in native elements of the country's wealth, and thus ensure national credit.

Document 3

Source: Making cigarettes in Mexico City, 1903

Library of Congress Prints and Photographs Division[LC-USZ62-121395]

Document 4

Source: Manifesto of the Mexican Liberal Party, 1903

Is there equality in our country? No.

The capitalist, the priest and the senior official, whether civilian or military, are not treated in Mexico like the humble worker or any other member of the village.

Employees drag a life of humiliation and misery. Privileges and charters into force have plagued us in a kind of useless and vicious, we can call the drones of the social whole.

Are there individual freedoms in our country? No.

Say that these unfortunates who faint in the estates under the whip of the overseer and exploited in the company stores; those unfortunates who are transported to the National Valle, Yucatan, and other places and sometimes not represent more value than ten or twenty pesos.

Does trade thrive in our country?

Yes, it thrives for two or three wealthy; the two or three millionaires and generally foreigners.

Encomendero [large landowners] thrives, prospers the moneylender.

These titans' monopolies go unchecked and are driving up the prices of basic necessities and driving down wages of those who make these items.

With this corrupt administration, the banker, the railroad owner, the contractor, those representing shipping companies, etc., are favored and privileged, enjoying champagne consumed in conjunction with a corrupt government official, improvising outrageous fortunes at the expense of tears and sweat of the people.

Document 5

Source: Assessment of Porfirio Díaz's rule by his advisor, Francscio Bulnes, 1906

A fact which no one can doubt or deny is that during the dictatorship of General Diaz twenty thousand kilometers of railways were constructed in Mexico.

The construction work at the port of Vera Cruz, is also well known to the world. Under the dictatorship a splendid system of sewers was built; water was brought from the springs of Xochimilco, and distributed according to the most scientific modern methods; streets were well paved and good pavements were laid.

Under the same regime splendid buildings were erected in the City of Mexico. Among these may be mentioned the Opera House, not yet completed, which would have competed in magnificence with the Grand Opera of Paris; the Law Courts building, also in course of construction; the Post Office building, undoubtedly one of the finest buildings in the world; the General Hospital; the Insane Asylum; the Department of Railways building, classic and refined in its style of architecture; the monument commemorating the centennial of Mexico's independence, which has been praised by many foreign artists. Besides the sums devoted to luxurious buildings destined for political and administrative purposes, several million pesos were devoted to the construction of training-schools for teachers.

Document 6

Source: Workers' demands from the Cananea copper mine strike, 1906

1. Working people declare a strike.
2. The workers will labor only under the following conditions:
   i. The firing of Luis the overseer.
   ii. Minimum wage for a worker will be five pesos for an eight-hour workday.
   iii. The Cananea Consolidated Copper Co., throughout its entire work force, will employ 75% Mexicans and 25% foreigners, for the former have the same aptitude as the latter.
   v. All Mexicans employed to work by this company will have the right to promotions as long as they are qualified.

Mexican workers: A government elected by the peoples so that it guides them and satisfies their needs in as much as possible: Mexico does not have this.

Furthermore: A government that is made up of ambitious men who tire the patience of the people with their criminally self-interested activities, elected by the worst of them in order to help them get rich Mexico does not need this.

People, rise up and go forward. Learn what it seems that you have forgotten. Gather together and discuss your rights. Demand the respect that is owed you.

Each Mexican who is mistreated by foreigners is worth the same or more than them, if he unites with his brothers and demands his rights.

Document 7

Source: Description of Porfirio Díaz's government in *Barbarous Mexico*, John Kenneth Turner, American journalist, 1910

The slavery and peonage of Mexico, the poverty and illiteracy, the general prostration of the people, are due, in my humble judgment, to the financial and political organization that at present rules that country—in a word, to what I shall call the "system" of General Porfirio Diaz.

I say the "system of Diaz" rather than Diaz personally because, though he is the keystone of the arch, though he is the government of Mexico more completely than is any other individual the government of any large country on the planet, yet no one man can stand alone in his iniquity. Diaz is the central prop of the slavery, but there are other props without which the system could not continue upright for a single day. For example, there is the collection of commercial interests which profit by the Diaz system of slavery and autocracy, and which puts no insignificant part of its tremendous powers to holding the central prop upright in exchange for the special privileges that it receives. Not the least among these commercial interests are American, which, I blush to say, are quite as aggressive defenders of the Diaz citadel as any. These American interests undoubtedly form the determining force in the continuation of Mexican slavery. Thus does Mexican slavery come home to us in the full sense of the term. For the horrors of Yucatan and Valle Nacional, Diaz is to blame, but so are we; we are to blame insofar as governmental powers over which we are conceded to have some control are employed under our very eyes for the perpetuation of a regime of which slavery and peonage are an integral part.

DBQ 6: Argentina 1870–1920

Question: Between approximately 1870 and 1920, Argentina's economy was transformed. Using the documents and your knowledge of world history, analyze the effects of Argentina's economic transformation during this time period.

Document 1

Source: Description of Buenos Aires harbor, Edwin Clark, English civil engineer, *Visit to South America*, 1878

Buenos Aires being the focus of a large foreign trade, the absence of docks, or harbor, or even of large vessels, which lie several miles away in the roads, is at first sight surprising, but the construction of a port is surrounded with engineering difficulties of the highest order. . . . The town pier, which runs outs a considerable distance, is often left entirely dry during low water. The loading and unloading of sea-going ships is therefore performed by means of lighters between the ship and the shore. The cargo is then transferred to carts on high wheels drawn by horses, which are not unfrequently drowned in bad weather. In this rude manner this large trade is carried on, employing a very large population and an immense number of horses and carts. . . . It is, however, no easy task to devise any better means of dealing with the subject under present circumstances, for carts must be employed in any case to fetch and deliver the goods, and once loaded they now proceed direct to their destination without further delay, whether it is the lighter or the warehouse. It is evident from what we have already said that the possibility of dredging and maintain such a deep channel in an estuary subject to such incessant change must be a problem that requires most careful thought, and there are no data at present that could warrant any thoughtful engineer in expressing a positive opinion on the subject, although all evidence, as far as it goes, is against its feasibility.

Document 2

Source: First electoral manifesto of the Argentine Socialist Workers' Party, 1896

A rich, inept, and rapacious class oppresses and exploits the Argentine public. The owners of the land, plantations, factories, transportation—capital in all its forms—forces the dispossessed working class to suffer all the weight of their privileges, aggravated by the weight of their ignorance and greed. This exploitation will grow more barbaric and cruel every day, if the people do not wake up and prepare to resist it.

All of the parties of Argentina's rich class are of a piece when it comes to increasing profits of capital at the cost of working people, even as it stupidly compromises the country's general development. Inundating the country with paper money, they have increased the value of gold, which enormously has increased the price of products and reduced wages. They have seized public lands, expelling primitive peoples, the only ones with a right to occupy them. . . . And to complete this barbaric system of exploitation, they use taxes on consumption, internal taxes, and customs duties to take away a large share of what little workers earn. A worker pays as much tax to feed and dress himself as a farmer who owns three miles of countryside.

Document 3
Source: Port of Buenos Aires, Argentina, after 1890s excavation project

National Geographic Stock/Vintage Collection/Granger, NYC

Document 4
Source: Presidential Address, Julio Argentino Roca, President of Argentina, 1903

> In our brief and eventful existence as a nation we have traveled through civil wars, tyranny and disorder, an enormous distance, and today we can look to the future without the uncertainties and anxieties of earlier times. . . . Without doubt there remain for us . . . many conquests to be made over ourselves, who have such a propensity to set ourselves lofty ideals and to demand of the government, political parties and constitutional practice the last word in political wisdom which supposes a degree of perfection . . . which has still not been attained even by peoples with a centuries-old history. More than on written laws, a republican form of government is founded on public habits and customs.

Document 5
Source: Argentina as Latin American Avant-Garde, Rubén Darío, Nicaraguan poet who spent many years in Argentina, 1911

> Among the events that history must celebrate in the early years of the twentieth century is the emergence of "the new and glorious nation" of which the Argentine national anthem sings. This is not a hymn about the free and independent political life of the country; instead it praises the life of its remarkable people for their work and peaceful prosperity. On the balance scales of the American continent, it is the Argentine Republic that gives us the counterweight to Yankee power [the United States]. This is the country that will rescue the spirit of our race and put an end to present and future imperialist ambition. Today, for these reasons, the world looks to this great country of the South. . . . Argentina takes good care of its schools and universities, spreads culture and progress, raises up the parliamentary system, and sees that its greatest riches lie in the heart of the country. It is preoccupied by economic matters that are vital. . . . Flourishing under, and protected by, policies of economic growth, Argentina is becoming strong.

Document 6

Source: Description of Argentina, James Bryce, British historian, 1912

Buenos Aires is something between Paris and New York. It has the business rush and the luxury of the one, the gaiety and pleasure-loving aspect of the other. Everybody seems to have money, and to like spending it, and to like letting everybody else know that it is being spent.

Twenty years ago sea-going vessels had to lie two or three miles off Buenos Aires, discharging their cargo by lighters and their passengers partly by small launches and partly by high-wheeled carts which carried people from the launches ashore through the shallow water. Now a long, deep channel has been dug, and is kept open by dredging, up which large steamers find their way to the very edge of the city. Docks many miles in length have been constructed to receive the shipping, and large stretches of land reclaimed, and huge warehouses erected and railway lines laid down alongside the wharves.

If the best parts of Buenos Aires are as tasteful as those of Paris, there is plenty of ugliness in the worst suburbs. On its land side, the city dies out into a waste of scattered shanties, or "shacks" (as they are called in the United States), dirty and squalid, with corrugated iron roofs, their wooden boards gaping like rents in tattered clothes. These are inhabited by the newest and poorest of the immigrants from southern Italy and southern Spain, a large and not very desirable element among whom anarchism is rife.

Document 7

Source: Argentina Economic Indicators, 1875–1930

Argentina: Economic Indicators, 1875–1930
(GDP per Capita and Industrial Output, base year 1900 = 100.00)

	Population	Exports (gold pesos)	Imports (gold pesos)	GDP	GDP per Capita	Industrial Output
1875	2,161,000	52,009,113	57,624,481	17.45	55.82	14.46
1880	2,492,000	58,380,787	45,535,880	21.78	53.02	14.57
1885	2,880,000	83,879,100	92,221,969	44.70	82.64	22.40
1890	3,377,000	100,818,993	142,240,812	58.59	88.25	31.26
1895	3,956,000	120,067,790	95,096,438	82.69	115.32	60.37
1900	4,607,000	154,600,412	113,485,069	100.00	100.00	100.00
1905	5,289,000	322,843,841	205,154,420	164.35	159.26	169.56
1910	6,586,000	389,071,360	379,352,515	197.43	162.95	217.85
1915	8,148,000	558,281,000	305,488,006	216.30	137.63	235.14
1920	8,968,000	1,044,085,000	963,123,000	231.73	135.50	271.50
1925	10,500,000	867,930,000	877,973,000	304.94	162.10	389.66
1930	12,046,000	614,104,000	740,088,000	326.93	149.15	417.35

Source: Fernando Rocchi, *Chimneys in the Desert: Industrialization in Argentina during the Export Boom Years, 1870–1930*, 2005

DBQ 7: Views of Mongols

Question: Using the documents and your knowledge of world history, analyze the different views of the Mongols in the thirteenth century.

Document 1
Source: Description of Mongol attacks on Central Asia, Ibn al-Athir, Arab scholar, ca. 1220

For some years I continued averse from mentioning this event, deeming it so horrible that I shrank from recording it. . . . I say, therefore, that this thing involves the description of the greatest catastrophe and the most dire calamity (of the like of which days and nights are innocent) which befell all men generally, and the Muslims in particular. . . . For indeed history does not contain anything which approaches or comes near unto it. . . . For truly those whom they [the Mongols] massacred in a single city exceeded all the children of Israel. Nay, it is unlikely that mankind will see the like of this calamity, until the world comes to an end and perishes. . . .

For even Antichrist will spare such as follow him, though he destroy those who oppose him, but these Mongols spared none, slaying women and men and children, ripping open pregnant women and killing unborn babes. . . . The hurt was universal; and which passed over the lands like clouds driven by the wind. For these were a people who emerged from the confines of China, and attacked the cities of Turkestan.

Document 2
Source: Description of Mongols capturing Russian cities, Chronicle of Novgorod, anonymous Orthodox Christian monks, 1238

[In 1238] foreigners called Mongols came in countless numbers, like locusts, into the land of the Ryazan, and on first coming they halted at the river Nukhla, and took it, and halted in camp there. And thence they sent their emissaries to the Knyazes of Ryasan, a sorceress and two men with her, demanding from them one-tenth of everything: of men and Knyazes and horses—of everything one tenth. . . . And the Knyazes said to them: "Only when none of us remain then all will be yours." . . . And the Knyazes of Ryazan sent to Yuri of Volodimir asking for help or him to come. But Yuri neither went himself nor listed to the request of the Knyazes of Ryasan, but he wished to make war separately. But it was too late to oppose the wrath of God. . . . And then the pagan foreigners surrounded Ryazan and fenced it in with a stockade. And the Mongols took the town on December 21, and they had advanced against it on the 16th of the same month. They likewise killed the Knyaz and the Knyaginya, and men, women, and children, monks, nuns and priests, some by fire, some by sword, and violated nuns, priests' wives, good women and girls in the presence of their mothers and sisters. . . . And who, brethren, would not lament over this, among those of us alive when they suffered this bitter and violent death?

Document 3
Source: *History of the Mongols*, Rashid al-Din, Persian historian and government official for the Mongols, 1241.

During the seven years [between 1235 and 1241] Ogedei [the son of Chinggis Khan] enjoyed life and amused himself. He moved from summer to winter camp and vice versa, serene and happy, and took permanent delight in beautiful women and moonfaced enchantresses.

At every opportunity, he allowed his sublime thoughts to overflow lavishly into the most just and charitable of good deeds, into the eradication of injustice and enmity, into the development of cities and districts, as well as into the construction of various buildings. He never neglected any measure designed to strengthen the framework of peace, and to lay the foundation of prosperity.

Document 4

Source: *Persian History of Chinggis Khan*, Juvaini, Persian historian, 1256

When the extent of their [Mongol] territories became broad and vast and important events fell out, it became essential to ascertain the activities of their enemies, and it was also necessary to transport goods from the West to the East and from the Far East to the West. Therefore throughout the length and breadth of the land they established yams [rest stops] and made arrangements for the upkeep and expenses of each yam, assigning thereto a fixed number of men and beasts as well as food, drink and other necessities. Thus, in accordance with the census, they so distribute and exact the charge, that messengers need make no long detour in order to obtain fresh mounts while at the same time the peasantry and the army are not placed in constant inconvenience. Moreover strict orders were issued to the messengers with regard to the sparing of the mounts, etc., to recount all of which would delay us too long. Every year the yam are inspected, and whatever is missing or lost has to be replaced by the peasantry.

Document 5

Source: Chinese scholar's description of Mongol official Menggu on his death, 1274

In the fourth month of 1236, the court deemed Menggu capable of handling Zhangde [province], so promoted him . . . to be its governor. . . . Because regulations were lax, the soldiers took advantage of their victory to plunder. Even in cities and marketplaces, some people kept their doors closed in the daytime. As soon as Menggu arrived, he took charge. Knowing the people's grievances, he issued an order, "Those who oppress the people will be dealt with according to the law. Craftsmen, merchants, and shopkeepers, you must each go about your work with your doors open, peaceably attending to your business without fear. Farmers, you must be content with your lands and exert yourselves diligently according to the sea- sons. I will instruct or punish those who mistreat you." After this order was issued, the violent became obedient and no one any longer dared violate the laws. Farmers in the fields and travelers on the roads felt safe, and people began to enjoy life.

Document 6

Source: Description of Mongol roads, Marco Polo, 1280s

You must know that the city of Khan-balik is a center from which many roads radiate to many provinces, one to each, and every road bears the name of the province to which it runs. The whole system is admirably contrived. When one of the Great Khan's messengers sets out along any of these roads, he has only to go twenty-five miles and there he finds a posting station, which in their language is called *yamb* and in our language may be rendered as "horse post." At every post the messengers find a spacious and palatial hostelry for their lodging. These hostelries have splendid beds with rich coverlets of silk and all that befits an emissary of high rank. If a king came here, he would be well lodged. Here the messengers find no less than 400 horses, stationed here by the Great Khan's orders and always kept in readiness for his messengers when they are sent on any mission. And you must understand that posts such as these, at distances of twenty-five or thirty miles, are to be found along all the main highways leading to the provinces of which I have spoken. And at each of these posts the messengers find three or four hundred horses in readiness awaiting their command, and palatial lodgings. And this holds good throughout all the provinces and kingdoms of the Great Khan's empire.

Document 7
Source: Drawing of a Mongol archer from Italian eyes, ca. thirteenth century

DBQ 8: Abolition of Slavery

Question: Using the documents and your knowledge of world history, analyze the reasons that peoples in the regions touching the Atlantic called for the abolition of the slave trade and slavery from around 1775 to 1860.

Document 1

Source: *Thoughts upon Slavery*, John Wesley, Methodist preacher, 1774

> Are you *a man?* Then you should have a *human* heart. But have you indeed? What is your heart made of? Is there no such principle as compassion there? Do you never *feel* another's pain? Have you no sympathy? No sense of human woe? No pity for the miserable? When you saw the flowing eyes, the heaving breasts, the bleeding sides and tortured limbs of your fellow-creatures, was you a stone, or a brute? Did you look upon them with the eyes of a tiger? When you squeezed the agonizing creatures down in the ship, or when you threw their poor mangled remains into the sea, had you no relenting? Did not one tear drop from your eye, one sigh escape from your breast? Do you feel no relenting *now?* If you do not, you must go on, till the measure of your iniquities is full. Then will the great GOD deal with *you*, as you have dealt with *them*, and require all their blood at your hands. And at that day it shall be more tolerable for *Sodom* and *Gomorrah* than for you!

Document 2

Source: Petition to British Parliament by the Society of Friends (Quakers), 1783

> To the Commons of Great Britain, in Parliament assembled.
>
> The Petition of the People called Quakers, Sheweth—
>
> That your Petitioners met in this their annual assembly, having solemnly considered the state of the enslaved negroes, conceive themselves engaged in religious duty, to lay the suffering situation of that unhappy people before you, as a subject loudly calling for the humane interposition of the Legislature.
>
> Your Petitioners regret, that a nation professing the Christian Faith, should so far counteract the principles of humanity and justice as by a cruel treatment of this oppressed race, to fill their minds with prejudices against the mild and beneficent doctrines of the Gospel.
>
> Under the countenance of the laws of this country, many thousands of these our fellow-creatures, entitled to natural rights of mankind, are held, as personal property, in cruel bondage; and your Petitioners being informed, that a Bill for the regulation of the African trade is now before the House, containing a clause which restrains the officers of the African Company from exporting Negroes. Your Petitioners, deeply affected with a consideration of the rapine, oppression, and bloodshed attending this traffic, humbly request that this restriction may be extended to all persons whatsoever, or that the House would grant such other relief in the premises, as in its wisdom may seem meet.

Document 3
Source: Plan of the *Brooks* slave ship, Society for Effecting the Abolition of the Slave Trade, 1788

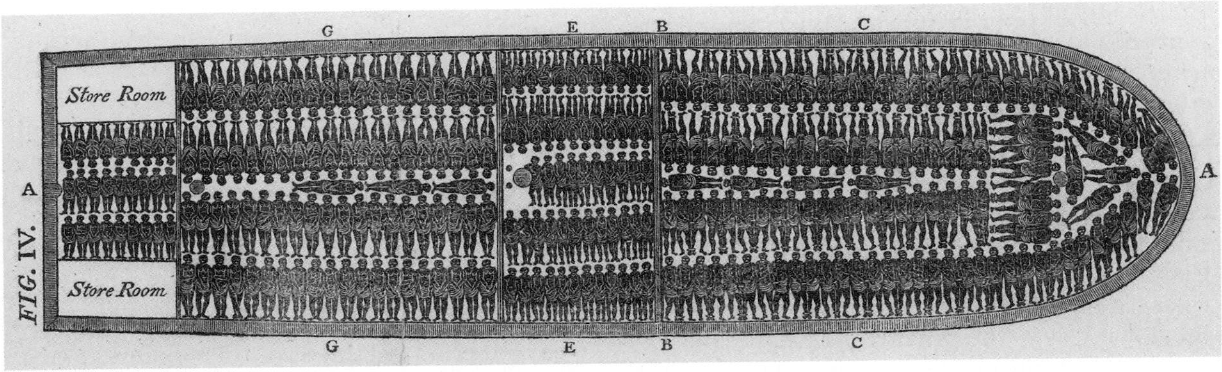

Document 4
Source: "The Negro's Complaint," poem by William Cowper, 1788

FORCED from home and all its pleasures
    Afric's coast I left forlorn,
To increase a stranger's treasures
    O'er the raging billows borne.
Men from England bought and sold me,
    Paid my price in paltry gold;
But, though slave they have enrolled me,
    Minds are never to be sold.

Still in thought as free as ever,
    What are England's rights, I ask,
Me from my delights to sever,
    Me to torture, me to task?
Fleecy locks and black complexion
    Cannot forfeit nature's claim;
Skins may differ, but affection
    Dwells in white and black the same.

Why did all-creating nature
    Make the plant for which we toil?
Sighs must fan it, tears must water,
    Sweat of ours must dress the soil.
Think, ye masters iron-hearted,
    Lolling at your jovial boards,
Think how many backs have smarted
    For the sweets your cane affords.

Document 5

Source: Engraving of Captain John Kimber standing next to the African slave he whipped to death, 1792

Document 6

Source: British Parliamentary debate about sugar purchases, Samuel Wilberforce, 1846

We believe that in the long run, as a commonly admitted principle, free trade will do away with the slave and slavery. The proof is attempted in this way—it is stated that slave labor is dearer than free, and that if the countries cultivated by slave labor are brought into competition with those where free labor is used, they will, by the necessity of that competition, be forced to adopt the free system. You say the emancipationists and abolitionists were always telling us free labor is cheaper than that of slaves, but what is really the argument? It is this, that free labor, other things being held equal, is cheaper than slave labor; that if put together, the lash on the one hand, and the inducements to work furnished by a domestic and family existence on the other, then the free man will do more work than the slave.

Document 7

Source: Argument against slavery in the southern United States, Hinton Rowan Helper, *The Impending Crisis of the South*, 1857

It is not so much in its moral and religious aspects that we propose to discuss the question of slavery, as in its social and political character and influences. To say nothing of the sin and the shame of slavery, we believe it is a most expensive and unprofitable institution; and if our brethren of the South will but throw aside their unfounded prejudices and preconceived opinions, and give us a fair and patient hearing, we feel confident, that we can bring them to the same conclusion. . . . By taking a sort of inventory of the agricultural products of the free and slave States in 1850, we now propose to correct a most extraordinary and mischievous error into which the people of the South have unconsciously fallen. Agriculture, it is well known, is the sole boast of the South; and, strange to say, many pro-slavery Southerners, who, in our latitude, pass for intelligent men, are so puffed up with the idea of our importance in this respect, that they speak of the North as a sterile region, unfit for cultivation, and quite dependent on the South for the necessaries of life! Such rampant ignorance ought to be knocked in the head! We can prove that the North produces greater quantities of bread-stuffs than the South! Figures shall show the facts. Properly, the South has nothing left to boast of; the North has surpassed her in everything, and is going farther and farther ahead of her every day.

DBQ 9: Middle Eastern Modernization

Question: Using the documents and your knowledge of world history, analyze how Middle Eastern states reformed and modernized their societies in the 1800s and early 1900s.

Document 1

Source: French military officer's description of the recently built Egyptian textile factories, Baron de Boislecomte, 1833

The linen cloth factories not only satisfy the country's internal consumption, but supply an export commodity of some value. In 1833 they provided 1,000,000 pieces of narrow cloth in the range of 2.50 to 5 francs. Half was used up within the country, the other half was exported. These same factories produced 30,000 pieces of wide cloth in the range of 12 to 16 francs, and worth 450,000 francs, which in its totality represent one twelfth the value of our production.

They [Egyptians] have generally managed to satisfy local consumption and to produce commodities at the same price that the Europeans normally sell theirs on the market.

Document 2

Source: Hatt-I-Serif Decree, beginning of Tanzimat Reforms of the Ottoman empire, 1839

Tax assessment is also one of the most important matters to regulate. A state, for the defense of its territory, manifestly needs to maintain its borders, the costs of which can be defrayed only by taxes levied on its subjects. . . . It is therefore necessary that from now on every subject of the Empire should be taxed according to his fortune and his means, and that he should be saved from any further exaction. It is also necessary that special laws should fix and limit the expenses of our land and sea forces.

Military matters, as already pointed out, are among the most important affairs of state, and it is the inescapable duty of all the people to provide soldiers for the defense of the fatherland. It is therefore necessary to frame regulations on the contingents that each locality should furnish according to the requirement of the time, and to reduce the term of military service to four or five years.

Document 3

Source: Reform Edict, Sultan Abdulmejid, 1856

Every distinction or designation tending to make any class whatever of the subjects of my Empire inferior to another class, on account of their religion, language, or race shall be forever effaced.

As all forms of religion are and shall be freely professed in my dominions, no subject of my Empire shall be hindered in the exercise of the religion that he professes. . . . No one shall be compelled to change their religion . . . and . . . all the subjects of my Empire, without distinction of nationality, shall be admissible to public employments. . . . All the subjects of my Empire, without distinction, shall be received into the civil and military schools of the government. . . . Moreover, every community is authorized to establish public schools of science, art, and industry.

Document 4

Source: Concession for a tobacco monopoly in Persia granted by the Persian government to a British company headed by Major Talbot, 1890

The monopoly of buying, selling, and manufacturing all the tobacco in the interior or exterior of the Kingdom of Persia is granted to Major Talbot by us for fifty years from the date of the signing of this Concession, in accordance with the following stipulations:

1. The concessionnaires will have to pay 15,000 Pound Sterling per annum to the exalted Imperial Treasury whether they benefit or lose by this business, and this money shall be paid every year, five months after the beginning of the year.
2. In order merely to ascertain the quantities of tobacco produced in the protected provinces (of Persia) the concessionnaires will keep a register of the cultivators who wish to work under the conditions of this Concession,

and the Persian Government will issue strict orders to the local Governors to compel the cultivators of tobacco to furnish such a registration.

Permission for sale of tobacco, cigars, cigarettes, snuff, etc., is the absolute right of the concessionnaires, and no one but the proprietors of this Concession shall have the right to issue the abovementioned permits.

3. After deducting all the expenses appertaining to this business and paying a dividend of 5 percent on their own capital to the proprietors of this Concession, one quarter of the remaining profit will yearly be paid to the exalted Imperial Treasury, and the Persian Government will have the right to inspect their (the concessionnaires') yearly books.

Document 5

Source: Persian Constitution, 1907

Article 8: The people of the Persian Empire are to enjoy equal rights before the Law

Article 9: All individuals are protected and safeguarded in respect to their lives, property, homes, and honour, from every kind of interference, and none shall molest them save in such case and in such way as the laws of the land shall determine.

Article 27: The powers of the Realm are divided into three categories.

First, the legislative power, which is specially concerned with the making or amelioration of laws. This power is derived from His Imperial Majesty, the National Consultative Assembly, and the Senate, of which three sources each has the right to introduce laws, provided that the continuance thereof be dependent on their not being at variance with the standards of the ecclesiastical law, and on their approval by the Members of the two Assemblies, and the Royal ratification. The enacting and approval of laws connected with the revenue and expenditure of the kingdom are, however, specially assigned to the National Consultative Assembly. The explanation and interpretation of the laws are, moreover, amongst the special functions of the above mentioned Assembly.

Second, the judicial power, by which is meant the determining of rights. This power belongs exclusively to the ecclesiastical tribunals in matters connected with the ecclesiastical law, and to the civil tribunals in matters connected with ordinary law.

Third, the executive power, which appertains to the King, that is to say, the laws and ordinances are carried out by the Ministers and State officials in the august name of His Imperial Majesty in such manner as the Law defines.

Document 6

Source: Advocating for educational and economic rights for Egyptian women, Bahithat al-Badiya, female Egyptian teacher, writer, and feminist, 1909

We must pursue an education . . . but that is what men wish to prevent us from doing under the pretext of taking their jobs away. Obviously, I am not urging women to neglect their home and children to go out and become lawyers or judges or railway engineers. But if any of us wish to work in such professions our personal freedom should not be infringed. It might be argued that pregnancy causes women to leave work, but there are unmarried women, others who are barren or have lost their husbands or are widowed or divorced or those whose husbands need their help in supporting the family. It is not right that they should be forced into lowly jobs. These women might like to become teachers or doctors with the same academic qualifications. Is it just to prevent women from doing what they believe is good for themselves and their support?

Men criticize the way we dress in the street. They have a point because we have exceeded the bounds of custom and propriety. We claim we are veiling but we are neither properly covered nor unveiled. I do not advocate a return to the veils of our grandmothers because it can rightly be called being buried alive, not *hijab*, correct covering. The woman used to spend her whole life within the walls of her house not going out into the street except when she was carried to her grave. I do not, on the other hand, advocate unveiling, like Europeans, and mixing with men, because they are harmful to us.

Document 7
Source: Female workers in a Turkish silk textile factory, 1910

DBQ 10: Roman Views of Christianity

Question: Using the documents and your knowledge of world history, analyze the relationship between Christians and non-Christians in the Roman empire from to 50 C.E. to 380 C.E.

Document 1

Source: Letter to Romans, Paul of Tarsus, 57 C.E.

> To all Gods beloved in Rome, who are called to be saints . . . I am eager to preach the gospel to you also who are in Rome. For I am not ashamed of the gospel: it is the power of God for salvation to every one who has faith, to the Jew first and also the Gentile [non-Jews]. Is God the God of Jews only? Is he not the God of gentiles also? Yes, of gentiles also, since God is one; and he will justify the circumcised on the ground of their faith and the uncircumcised because of their faith.

Document 2

Source: Description of Christians in Rome, Tacitus, Roman historian, 64 C.E.

> In order to put an end to these rumors Nero provided scapegoats and visited most fearful punishments on those popularly called Christians, a group hated because of their outrageous practices. The founder of this sect, Christus, was executed in the reign of Tiberius by the procurator Pontius Pilatus. Thus the pernicious superstition was suppressed for the while, but it broke out again not only in Judaea, where this evil had its origin, but even in Rome, to which all obnoxious and disgraceful elements from everywhere in the world and receive a large following. . . . A vast multitude was convicted . . . because of their hatred of humanity. Their executions were made into a sport in that they were covered with skins of wild beasts and torn to pieces by dogs, or they were fastened to crosses or wrapped with inflammable materials so that . . . they could be burned to serve as torches in the night.

Document 3

Source: Exchange between Pliny, Roman provincial governor, and the Emperor Trajan, 111 C.E.

Pliny to Trajan

> Meanwhile, in the case of those who were denounced to me as Christians, I have observed the following procedure: I interrogated these as to whether they were Christians; those who confessed I interrogated a second and a third time, threatening them with punishment; those who persisted I ordered executed. For I had no doubt that, whatever the nature of their creed, stubbornness and inflexible obstinacy surely deserve to be punished. There were others possessed of the same folly; but because they were Roman citizens, I signed an order for them to be transferred to Rome.

Trajan to Pliny

> You observed proper procedure, my dear Pliny, in sifting the cases of those who had been denounced to you as Christians. For it is not possible to lay down any general rule to serve as a kind of fixed standard. They are not to be sought out; if they are denounced and proved guilty, they are to be punished, with this reservation, that whoever denies that he is a Christian and really proves it—that is, by worshiping our gods—even though he was under suspicion in the past, shall obtain pardon through repentance. But anonymously posted accusations ought to have no place in any prosecution. For this is both a dangerous kind of precedent and out of keeping with the spirit of our age.

Document 4

Source: Description of potential challenges in a marriage between a Christian wife and a non-Christian husband, Tertullian, Christian writer, early 200s C.E.

> She is engaged in a fast; her husband has arranged a banquet. It is her Christian duty to visit the streets and the homes of the poor; her husband insists on family business. She celebrates the Easter Vigil throughout the night; her husband expects her in his bed.

Document 5

Source: Edict of Toleration, Emperor Galerius, 311 C.E.

After the publication, on our part, of an order commanding Christians to return to the observance of the ancient [Roman] customs, many of them, it is true, submitted in view of the danger, while many others suffered death. Nevertheless, since many of them have continued to persist in their opinions and we see that in the present situation they neither duly adore and venerate the gods nor yet worship the god of the Christians, we, with our wonted clemency, have judged it is wise to extend a pardon even to these men and permit them once more to become Christians and reestablish their places of meetings; in such manner, however, that they shall in no way offend against good order. We propose to notify the magistrates in another mandate in regard to the course that they should pursue.

Whereof it should be the duty of the Christians, in view of our clemency, to pray to their god for our welfare, for that of the Empire, and for their own, so that the Empire may remain intact in all its parts, and that they themselves may live safely in their habitations.

Document 6

Source: Medallion of the Emperor Constantine with a Chi-Rho symbol above his head, 315 C.E.

Byzantium Italy/akg-images

Document 7

Source: Proclamation by Emperor Theodosius, late 380 C.E.

It is our desire that all the various nation which are subject to our clemency and moderation, should continue to the profession of that religion which was delivered to the Romans by the divine Apostle Peter, as it has been preserved by faithful tradition and which is now professed by the Pope Damasus and by Peter, Bishop of Alexandria, a man of apostolic holiness. According to the apostolic teaching and the doctrine of the Gospel, let us believe in the one deity of the father, Son and Holy Spirit, in equal majesty and in a holy Trinity. We authorize the followers of this law to assume the title Catholic Christians; but as for the others, since in our judgment they are foolish madmen, we decree that they shall be branded with the ignominious name of heretics, and shall not presume to give their meetings the name of churches. They will suffer in the first place the chastisement of divine condemnation and the second the punishment of expulsion, in accordance with the will of heaven shall decide to inflict.

DBQ 11: East Africa versus West Africa

Question: Using the documents and your knowledge of world history, compare the views of East Africa (the Swahili Coast) and West Africa between circa 900 and circa 1500.

Document 1
Source: Arab trader's description of the Swahili Coast, Abul-Hasan Ali al-Mas'udi, 900s

The pilots of Oman pass by the channel [of Berbera] to reach the island of Kanbalu, which is in the Zanj sea. It has a mixed population of Muslims and Zanj idolaters. . . . The aforesaid Kanbalu is the furthest point of their voyages on the Zanj sea, and the land of Sofala and the Waqwaq, on the edge of the Zanj mainland and at the end of this branch of the sea. The people of Siraf [in Persia] also make this voyage, and I myself have sailed on this sea, setting off from Sanjar, the capital of Oman, in company with a number of Omani shipowners

Elephants are extremely common in the land of the Zanj; but they are wild and none are kept in captivity. The natives do not employ them in warfare nor for any other purpose, but they hunt them merely to kill them. . . . The Zanj rush upon them, armed with very long spears and kill them for their ivory. It is from this country that large elephant tusks weighing fifty pounds and more are obtained. They usually go to Oman, and from there are send on to China and India. This is the chief trade route, and were it otherwise, ivory would be very abundant in Muslim lands.

Document 2
Source: Spanish Muslim's description of the Kingdom of Ghana, al-Bakri, Spanish Arab writer, late 1000s

The city of Ghana consists of two towns situated on a plain. One of these towns, which is inhabited by Muslims, is large and possesses twelve mosques, in one of which they assemble for the Friday prayer. There are salaried imams and muezzins [Muslims who sing the call to prayer], as well as jurists and scholars. In the environs are wells with sweet water, from which they drink and with which they grow vegetables. The king's town is six miles distant from this one and bears the name of Al-Ghaba. Between these two towns there are continuous habitations. The houses of the inhabitants are of stone and acacia wood. The king has a palace and a number of domed dwellings all surrounded with an enclosure like a city wall. In the king's town, and not far from his court of justice, is a mosque where the Muslims who arrive at his court pray.

On every donkey-load of salt when it is brought into the country their king levies one golden dinar, and two dinars when it is sent out. From a load of copper the king's due is five mithqals, and from a load of other goods ten mithqals. The best gold found in his land comes from the town of Ghiyaru, which is eighteen days' traveling distant from the king's town over a country inhabited by tribes of the Sudan whose dwellings are continuous.

The nuggets found in all the mines of his country are reserved for the king, only this gold dust being left for the people. But for this the people would accumulate gold until it lost its value. The nuggets may weigh from an ounce to a pound. It is related that the king owns a nugget as large as a big stone.

Document 3
Source: Description of Mombasa and Kilwa on the Swahili Coast, Ibn Battuta, Muslim scholar and traveler, 1340s

We came to Mombasa, a large island two days' journey by sea between it and the land of the Swahili. It possesses no territory on the mainland. They have fruit trees on the island, but no cereals, which have to be brought to them from the Swahili. Their food consists chiefly of bananas and fish. The inhabitants are pious, honorable, and upright, and they have well-built wooden mosques. At every door of the mosques there are one or two wells. He who wants to enter the mosques washes his feet and enters.

We stayed one night in this island and then pursued our journey to Kilwa, which is a large city on the coast. The majority of its inhabitants are Zanj, jet-black in color, and with tattoo marks on their faces. Kilwa is amongst the beautiful cities and most elegantly built. All its buildings are of wood. Its inhabitants are constantly engaged in military expeditions, for their country is contiguous to the heathen Zanj.

The sultan at the time of my visit was Abu'l-Muzaffar Hasan, who was noted for his gifts and generosity. He used to devote the fifth part of the booty made on his expeditions to pious and charitable purposes, as is prescribed in the Qur'an, and I have seen him give the clothes off his back to a mendicant who asked him for them.

Document 4

Source: Description of the people of Mali, Ibn Battuta, Muslim scholar and traveler, 1350s

The Sudanese possess some admirable qualities. They are seldom unjust, and have a greater abhorrence of injustice than any other people. The sultan shows no mercy to anyone who is guilty of the least act of it. There is a complete security in their country. Neither traveler nor inhabitant in it has anything to fear from robbers or men of violence. They do not confiscate the property of any Arab trader who dies in their country, even if it be accounted wealth. On the contrary, they give it into the charge of some trustworthy person among the whites, until the rightful heir takes possession of it. They are careful to observe the hours of prayer, and assiduous in attending them in congregations, and in bringing up their children to them. On Fridays, if a man does not go early to the mosque, he cannot find a corner to pray in, on account of the crowd. It is a custom of theirs to send each man's boy (to the mosque) with his prayer-mat; the boy spreads it out for his master in a place befitting him and remains on it (until his master comes to the mosque).

Yet another is their zeal for learning the Qur'an by heart. They put their children in chains if they show any backwardness in memorizing it, and they are not set free until they have it by heart. I visited the *qadi* in his house on the day of the festival. His children were chained up, so I said to him, "Will you not let them loose?" He replied, "I shall not do so until they learn the Qur'an by heart."

Document 5

Source: Spanish map of Spain, North Africa, and West Africa showing Mansa Musa in bottom left, 1375

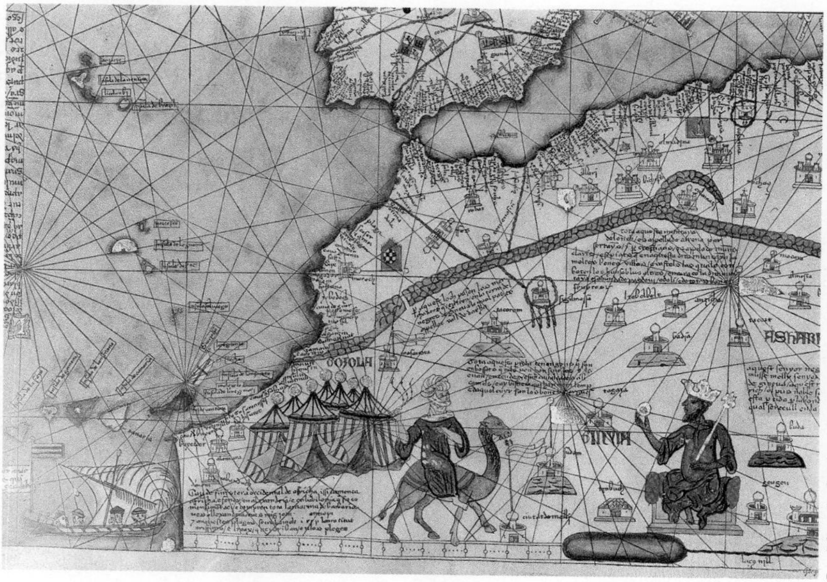

Detail from the Catalan Atlas, 1375 (vellum), Cresques, Abraham (1325–87)/Bibliotheque Nationale, Paris, France/The Bridgeman Art Library

Document 6
Source: Portuguese description of Kilwa, Duarte Barbosa, Portuguese government officer, 1505

Going along the coast from the town of Mozambique, there is an island which is called Kilwa, in which is a Muslim town with many fair houses of stone and mortar, with many windows after our fashion, very well arranged in streets, with many flat roofs. The doors are of wood, well carved, with excellent joinery. Around it are streams and orchards and fruit-gardens with many channels of sweet water. It has a Muslim king over it. From this place they trade with Sofala, whence they bring back gold. Before the King our Lord sent out his expedition to discover India, the Muslims of Sofala, Cuama, Angoya and Mozambique were all subject to the King of Kilwa, who was the most mighty king among them. And in this town was great plenty of gold, as no ships passed toward Sofala without first coming to this island. Of the Muslims there are some fair and some black, they are finely clad in many rich garments of gold and silk and cotton, and the women as well; also with much gold and silver in chains and bracelets, which they wear on their legs and arms, and many jeweled earrings in their ears. These Muslims speak Arabic and follow the creed of the Qur'an.

Document 7
Source: Description of Timbuktu, Leo Africanus, Spanish Arab scholar, 1526

The houses of Timbuktu are huts made of clay-covered wattles with thatched roofs. In the center of the city is a temple built of stone and mortar, and in addition there is a large palace, where the king lives. The shops of the artisans, the merchants and especially weavers of cotton cloth are very numerous. Fabrics are also imported from Europe to Timbuktu, borne by Berber merchants.

The women of the city maintain the custom of veiling their faces, except for the slaves who sell all the foodstuffs. The inhabitants are very rich, especially the strangers who have settled in the country; so much so that the current king has given two of his daughters in marriage to two brothers, both businessmen, on account of their wealth.

The king has about 3,000 horsemen and infinity of foot-soldiers armed with bows made of wild fennel which they use to shoot poisoned arrows. This king makes war only upon neighboring enemies and upon those who do not want to pay him tribute. When he has gained a victory, he has all of them—even the children—sold in the market at Timbuktu.

Only small, poor horses are born in this country. The merchants use them for their voyages and the courtiers to move about the city. But the good horses come from North Africa. They arrive in a caravan and, ten or twelve days later, they are led to the ruler, who takes as many as he likes and pays appropriately for them.

DBQ 12: Governing Ancient States

Question: Using the documents and your knowledge of world history, analyze how rulers between 600 B.C.E. and 100 C.E. were expected to govern their populations.

Document 1

Source: Persian emperor Darius discussing three types of governance, according to the Greek historian Herodotus, ca. 520 B.C.E.

Take these three forms of government—democracy, oligarchy, and monarchy—and let them each be at their best, I maintain that monarchy far surpasses the other two. What government can possibly be better than that of the very best man in the whole state? The counsels of such a man are like himself, and so he governs the mass of the people to their heart's content; while at the same time his measures against evil-doers are kept more secret than in other states. Contrariwise, in oligarchies, where men vie with each other in the service of the commonwealth, fierce enmities are apt to arise between man and man, each wishing to be leader, and to carry his own measures; whence violent quarrels come, which lead to open strife, often ending in bloodshed. Then monarchy is sure to follow; and this too shows how far that rule surpasses all others. Again, in a democracy, it is impossible but that there will be malpractices: these malpractices, however, do not lead to enmities, but to close friendships, which are formed among those engaged in them, who must hold well together to carry on their villainies. And so things go on until a man stands forth as champion of the commonalty, and puts down the evil-doers. Straightway the author of so great a service is admired by all, and from being admired soon comes to be appointed king; so that here too it is plain that monarchy is the best government. Lastly, to sum up all in a word, whence, I ask, was it that we got the freedom which we enjoy? Did democracy give it us, or oligarchy, or a monarch? As a single man recovered our freedom for us, my sentence is that we keep to the rule of one. Even apart from this, we ought not to change the laws of our forefathers when they work fairly.

Document 2

Source: Plato's vision of the ideal government, Plato, *The Republic*, ca. 380 B.C.E.

And this was what we foresaw, and this was the reason why truth forced us to admit, not without fear and hesitation, that neither cities nor States nor individuals will ever attain perfection until the small class of philosophers whom we termed useless but not corrupt are providentially compelled, whether they will or not, to take care of the State, and until a like necessity be laid on the State to obey them; or until kings, or if not kings, the sons of kings or princes, are divinely inspired with a true love of true philosophy. That either or both of these alternatives are impossible, I see no reason to affirm: if they were so, we might indeed be justly ridiculed as dreamers and visionaries. Am I not right?

Quite right.

If then, in the countless ages of the past, or at the present hour in some foreign clime which is far away and beyond our knowing, the perfected philosopher is or has been or hereafter shall be compelled by a superior power to have the charge of the State, we are ready to assert to the death, that this our constitution has been, and is—yea, and will be whenever the Muse of Philosophy is queen. There is no impossibility in all this; that there is a difficulty, we acknowledge ourselves.

Document 3

Source: Description of how to govern, Mencius, Confucian philosopher, 300s B.C.E.

Mencius said, All people possess within them a moral sense that cannot bear the suffering of others. The former kings had such a moral sense and thus they devised means of government that would not allow people to suffer. If a ruler were to employ the moral sense that makes human suffering unendurable in order to implement such humane government, he would find bringing the entire empire into order to be simple, as though he were turning the world in his hand.

Document 4
Source: Edict from the Mauryan emperor Ashoka of India, 200s B.C.E.

For a long time in the past, for many hundreds of years have increased the sacrificial slaughter of animals, violence toward creatures, unfilial conduct toward kinsmen, improper conduct toward Brahmins and ascetics. Now with the practice of morality by King [Ashoka], the sound of war drums has become the call to morality. . . . You [government officials] are appointed to rule over thousands of human beings in the expectation that you will win the affection of all men. All men are my children. Just as I desire that my children will fare well and be happy in this world and the next, I desire the same for all men. . . . King [Ashoka] . . . desires that there should be the growth of the essential spirit of morality or holiness among all sects. . . . There should not be glorification of one's own sect and denunciation of the sect of others for little or no reason. For all the sects are worthy of reverence for one reason or another.

Document 5
Source: A view of Chinese government, Huan Kuan, Chinese scholar, ca. 50 B.C.E.

Thus the son of Heaven [the Emperor] should not speak about much and little, the feudal lords should not talk about advantage and detriment, ministers about gain and loss, but they should cultivate benevolence and righteousness, to set an example to the people, and extend wide their virtuous conduct to gain the people's confidence. Then will nearby folk lovingly flock to them and distant peoples submit to their authority. Therefore, the master conqueror not fight, the expert warrior needs no soldiers; the truly great commander requires not to set his troops in battle array. Cultivate virtue and temple in the hall, then you need only show a bold front to the enemy and your troops will return home in victory. The Prince who practices benevolent administration should be matchless in the world; for him what use is expenditure.

Document 6
Source: Description of how Roman government should behave, Cicero, Roman politician and lawyer, ca. 50 B.C.E.

Some men want to become known as popular politicians and for this reasons they engage in making revolutionary proposals about land [governments seizing land from owners and redistributing it to their supporters], with the result that owners are driven from their homes and money lent out by creditors is simply given free to the borrowers with no need for repayment. Such men are shaking the very foundations of the state. First of all, they are destroying that goodwill and sense of trust which can no longer exist when money is simply taken from some people and given to others [by the state]. And then they take away fairness, which is totally destroyed if each person is not permitted to keep what is his own. For, as I have already said, it is the peculiar function of the state and local government to make sure that each person should be able to keep his own things freely and without any worry.

Document 7

Source: The Roman government built aqueducts, such as this one in Spain, across the empire, ca. 10 C.E.

Nito/Shutterstock.com

DBQ 13: Development in Newly Industrialized States

Question: Using the documents and your knowledge of world history, analyze the role of the state in economic policies of newly independent states between circa 1950 and circa 1975.

Document 1

Source: Speech by Mao Zedong, opening speech from the National Congress of the Communist Party of China, 1955

It is no easy job to build a socialist society in a large country like ours with its complicated conditions and its formerly very backward economy. We may be able to build a socialist society over three five-year plans, but to build a strong, highly industrialized socialist country will require several decades of hard work, say, fifty years, or the entire second half of the present century. Our task requires us to handle the relations among the people well, particularly those between the working class and the peasantry; it requires us to handle the relations among our different nationalities well. At the same time, it requires us to do a good job in furthering close co-operation with the Soviet Union, which is a great and advanced socialist country, and with the People's Democracies and also to promote co-operation with all the peace-loving countries and people in the capitalist world.

Comrades, we are now in a new historical period. For a country in the Orient with a population of 600 million to make socialist revolution, to change its face and the course of its history, to accomplish its basic industrialization and the socialist transformation of agriculture, handicrafts and capitalist industry and commerce . . . and to catch up with or surpass the most powerful capitalist countries in the world in several decades—in doing all this it will inevitably encounter difficulties as numerous as or perhaps even greater than those encountered in the period of the democratic revolution.

Document 2

Source: Speech by Jawaharlal Nehru, first prime minister of India, initiating the discussion on the Second Five-Year Plan, 1956

We have said that our objective is a socialistic pattern of society. Broadly speaking, we mean a society in which there is equality of opportunity and the possibility for everyone to live a good life. Obviously, this cannot be attained unless we produce the wherewithal to have the standards that a good life implies. We have, therefore, to lay great stress on equality, on the removal of disparities, and it has to be remembered always that socialism is not the spreading out of poverty. The essential thing is that there must be wealth and production.

One has always to remember that the primary function of a growing society is to produce more wealth; otherwise it will not grow, and one will have nothing to distribute. Whether it is in industry or agriculture, the one and the primary test is whether you are adding to the wealth of the country by increasing the production of the country If not you become stagnant in that field. In order to reach equality, as I hope we shall, we need to follow a hundred paths which gradually take us there.

All over the world the idea, of planning is being appreciated more and more. For an under-developed country, particularly, planning is essential. It may not be so necessary in developed countries; they can perhaps do without it. But there is no other way but planning for an under-developed country like ours.

Document 3

Source: Fidel Castro, leader of Cuba, speech to representatives of Cuban tobacco industry, 1959

When we took over the government of the nation we found the nation absolutely disorganized and in a precarious condition in all respects. The preoccupation of the Revolutionary Government is directed fundamentally to the economy of the nation. To overcome the economic crisis in which the country was found the Revolutionary Government has two essential purposes: the agrarian reform and the industrialization of the nation.

We plant tomatoes here, we send it up there and then they sell it back to us converted into juice or paste. We will produce everything possible in Cuba. We are even investigating and studying whether wheat can be grown here, this being one of the products that meets with the greatest obstacles here. If in Cuba we produce everything that it is possible to produce of those things that we now import, we will provide work for more than 300,000 persons; 300,000 Cuban families that are suffering want and misery.

Cuba will buy abroad what it needs to buy and what it wishes to buy not what they want to sell us at all events. Cuba is a country full of brush, grassy plains and marabu plants that we are going to plant and put in production. We will buy tractors, machinery and machine tools for our industrialization from abroad. We must buy factories in order not to be an underdeveloped country.

Document 4

Source: Revolutionary Council of Burma, group that overthrew the Burmese government in 1962; treatise on vision for the new government, 1962

The Union of Burma is an economically backward agricultural country. The national productive forces need to be continually developed to build up socialist economy. That is why various productions that would be compatible with existing conditions and time will have to be planned and developed. While modernizing the agricultural production which forms the main basis of the national economy such industries as would be commensurate with the natural resources and capabilities of the country will also be developed. In doing so national private enterprises which contribute to national productive forces will be allowed with fair and reasonable restrictions.

On the full realization of socialist economy the socialist government, far from neglecting the owners of national private enterprises which have been steadfastly contributing to the general well-being of the people, will even enable them to occupy a worthy place in the new society in the course of further national development.

Document 5

Source: Indian workers at newly built telephone factory, Bangalore, India, 1950

Dinodia Photos/Hulton Archive/Getty Images

Document 6

Source: Speech by Kwame Nkrumah, first president of Ghana, to the speaker and members of the National Assembly on launching the Seven-Year Plan, 1964

I have come here today to present our Seven-Year Development Plan, which when completed, will bring Ghana to the threshold of a modern state based on a highly organized and efficient agricultural and industrial program. The main tasks of the Plan are: firstly, to speed up the rate of growth of our national economy. Secondly, it is to enable us to embark upon the socialist transformation of our economy through the rapid development of the State and cooperative sectors. Thirdly, it is our aim, by this Plan, to eradicate completely the colonial structure of our economy.

This Seven-Year Development Plan embodies a long view of the path which should lead to a self-sustaining economy, based on socialist production and distribution. An economy balanced between industry and agriculture, providing a sufficiency of food for the people, and supporting secondary industries based on the products of our agriculture. In other words, an economy founded securely on the basis of socialist production and distribution.

Our aim, under this Plan, is to build in Ghana, a socialist State which accepts full responsibility for promoting the well-being of the masses. Our national wealth must be built up and used in such a way that economic power shall not be allowed to exploit the worker in town or village, but be used for the supreme welfare and happiness of our people. The people, through the State, should have an effective share in the economy of the country and an effective control over it.

Document 7

Source: Anwar Sadat, second president of Egypt, delivering a speech to the National Assembly in which he outlines three economic goals, 1970

1. To complete the base of heavy industry as a principal aim. This is being done now, represented in the iron and steel complex that is under construction, the new petroleum chemicals complex, the phosphates complex, and the aluminum complex. In addition, there is the Suez-Alexandria pipeline which will soon be put into effect.

   The completion of the heavy industry base is the guarantee for rendering our economy an industrial one in the first instance, which is the true yardstick of progress in our age.
2. The fulfillment of the big process of the transformation of scientific agriculture. The first indications of this process already appeared in our output of grains, and we must continue in order to realize self-sufficiency in this field. I believe this can be reached in a period ranging between three and five years. Besides the completion of the process of transformation in scientific agriculture, we must also pay attention to the industrialization of agriculture. Moreover we have a vital duty to carry out in the process of reclaiming new lands, beside exploiting the land which has already been during the last years since we started our organized work in conquering the desert. In this respect, every drop of the water of the High [Aswan] Dam must leave its effect on our land, fertile, good and prosperous.
3. The electrification of the whole of Egypt must be one of the most cherished of our goals. For electricity will illuminate the face of Egypt and push the wheel of action on every part of it. Our present production of electric power is on par with the European rate, but our consumption of the energy which we produce is not yet complete.

DBQ 14: Nonviolence in the Twentieth Century

Question: Using the documents and your knowledge of world history, analyze how individuals and groups protested during the twentieth century.

Document 1

Source: Speech by Gandhi on the night before setting out on the Salt March protest, 1930

From what I have seen and heard during the last fortnight, I am inclined to believe that the stream of civil resisters will flow unbroken. But let there be not a semblance of breach of peace even after all of us have been arrested. We have resolved to utilize all our resources in the pursuit of an exclusively nonviolent struggle. Let no one commit a wrong in anger. This is my hope and prayer. I wish these words of mine reached every nook and corner of the land. My task shall be done if I perish and so do my comrades. . . . Wherever possible, civil disobedience of salt should be started. These laws can be violated in three ways. It is an offence to manufacture salt wherever there are facilities for doing so. The possession and sale of contraband salt, which includes natural salt or salt earth, is also an offence. The purchasers of such salt will be equally guilty. To carry away the natural salt deposits on the seashore is likewise violation of law. So is the hawking of such salt. In short, you may choose any one or all of these devices to break the salt monopoly.

We are, however, not to be content with this alone. . . . I stress only one condition, namely, let our pledge of truth and nonviolence as the only means for the attainment of Swaraj [self-rule] be faithfully kept.

Document 2

Source: Dorothy Day, Catholic activist from New York City, on pacifism, 1936

The Catholic Worker is sincerely a *pacifist* paper.

We oppose class war and class hatred, even while we stand opposed to injustice and greed. Our fight is not "with flesh and blood but principalities and powers."

We oppose also imperialist war.

We oppose, moreover, preparedness for war, a preparedness which is going on now on an unprecedented scale and which will undoubtedly lead to war. The Holy Father Pope Pius XI said, in a pastoral letter in 1929:

"And since the unbridled race for armaments is on the one hand the effect of the rivalry among nations and on the other cause of the withdrawal of enormous sums from the public wealth and hence not the smallest of contributors to the current extraordinary crisis. We cannot refrain from renewing on this subject the wise admonitions of our predecessors which thus far have not been heard."

"We exhort you all, Venerable Brethren, that by all the means at your disposal, both by preaching and by the press, you seek to illumine minds and open hearts on this matter, according to the solid dictates of right reason and of the Christian law."

"Why not prepare for peace?"

1. Let us think now what it means to be neutral in fact as well as in name.
2. American bankers must not lend money to nations at war.
3. We must renounce neutral rights at sea.

Document 3

Source: Martin Luther King, Jr., speech given at Western Michigan University, December 1963

There are certain things in our nation and in the world which I am proud to be maladjusted and which I hope all men of good-will will be maladjusted until the good societies realize. I say very honestly that I never intend to become adjusted to segregation and discrimination. I never intend to become adjusted to religious bigotry. I never intend to adjust myself to economic conditions that will take necessities from the many to give luxuries to the few. I never intend to adjust myself to the madness of militarism, to self-defeating effects of physical violence. But in a day when sputniks and explorers are dashing through outer space and guided ballistic missiles are carving highways of death through the stratosphere, no nation can win a war. It is no longer the choice between violence and nonviolence. It is either nonviolence or nonexistence, and the alternative to disarmament. The alternative to absolute suspension of nuclear tests. The alternative to strengthening the United Nations and thereby disarming the whole world may well be a civilization plunged into the abyss of annihilation.

Document 4

Source: Adam Michnik, leader in Polish Solidarity movement that helped to end Communist rule in Poland, 1985

Why did Solidarity renounce violence? This question returned time and again in my conversations with foreign observers. I would like to answer it now. People who claim that the use of force in the struggle for freedom is necessary must first prove that, in a given situation, it will be effective, and that force, when it is used, will not transform the idea of liberty into its opposite.

No one in Poland is able to prove today that violence will help us to dislodge Soviet troops from Poland and to remove Communists from power. The USSR has such enormous military power that confrontation is simply unthinkable. In other words: we have no guns. Napoleon, upon hearing a similar reply, gave up on pursuing further questions. However, Napoleon was above all interested in military victories, and not in building democratic, pluralistic societies. We, by contrast, cannot leave it at that.

In our reasoning pragmatism is inseparably intertwined with idealism. Taught by history, we suspect that by using force to storm the Bastilles of old we shall unwittingly build new ones.

Document 5

Source: Chinese protestor standing in front of a column of tanks approaching Tiananmen Square during democracy protests in 1989

AP Images/Jeff Widener

Document 6

Source: Indian author Arundhati Roy, "War Is Peace," *The Guardian*, October 29, 2001

Nothing can excuse or justify an act of terrorism, whether it is committed by religious fundamentalists, private militia, people's resistance movements—or whether it's dressed up as a war of retribution by a recognised government. The bombing of Afghanistan is not revenge for New York and Washington. It is yet another act of terror against the people of the world. Each innocent person that is killed must be added to, not set off against, the grisly toll of civilians who died in New York and Washington.

People rarely win wars, governments rarely lose them. People get killed. Governments moult and regroup, hydra-headed. They first use flags to shrink-wrap peoples' minds and suffocate real thought, and then as ceremonial shrouds to cloak the mangled corpses of the willing dead. On both sides, in Afghanistan as well as America, civilians are now hostage to the actions of their own government. Unknowingly, ordinary people in both countries share a common bond—they have to live with the phenomenon of blind, unpredictable terror. Each batch of bombs that is dropped on Afghanistan is matched by a corresponding escalation of mass hysteria in America about anthrax, more hijackings and other terrorist acts.

Document 7

Source: "How Nonviolent Struggle Works," Gene Sharp, nonviolent theorist, 2013

When people refuse their cooperation, withhold their help, and persist in their disobedience and defiance, they are denying their opponents the basic human assistance and cooperation which any government or hierarchical system requires. If people do this in sufficient numbers for long enough, that government or hierarchical system will no longer have power. This is the basic political assumption of nonviolent action.

DBQ 15: Women's Rights in the Twentieth Century

Question: Using the documents and your knowledge of world history, analyze how women around the world in the twentieth century have struggled for women's rights.

Document 1

Source: Editorial from *Revista Feminina*, Brazilian women's magazine, 1921

The growing success of feminism around the world proves that we are dealing with a human evolutionary fact that would be foolish to restrain. The progress of human phenomenon is governed by incontestable laws. . . . That Brazilian feminism exists is an indisputable fact. We need only to visit our departments of science, literature, education, commerce, [and] business, and our offices and industries, to see the Brazilian woman transformed into a useful and productive force after twenty centuries of inaction.

Document 2

Source: "Suffrage Song," Akiko Yosano, 1920s

Women, we are steadfast, honest and upright!
Let us shoulder our duty as human beings,
Be wise mothers and sisters to our people,
And spread women's love throughout our land.

Let us scrub away the age-old corruption
Of a politics run by men and for men,
And transform the wealth built from the sweat of our people
Into a bright and happy future for all.

Our labor, our love and our grace
Over dissension and hatred must prevail;
Wherever the power of women is found,
The light of peace will dawn at last.

Document 3

Source: "No More Miss America!" by New York Radical Women, September 1968

We Protest:

The Degrading Mindless-Boob-Girlie Symbol . . .

The Pageant contestants epitomize the roles we are all forced to play as women. The parade down the runway blares the metaphor of the 4-H Club county fair, where the nervous animals are judged for teeth, fleece, etc., and where the best "Specimen" gets the blue ribbon. So are women in our society forced daily to compete for male approval, enslaved by ludicrous "beauty" standards we ourselves are conditioned to take seriously.

Racism with Roses . . .

Since its inception in 1921, the Pageant has not had one Black finalist, and this has not been for a lack of test-case contestants. There has never been a Puerto Rican, Alaskan, Hawaiian, or Mexican-American winner. Nor has there ever been a *true* Miss America—an American Indian.

Miss America as Military Death Mascot . . .

The highlight of her reign each year is a cheerleader—tour of American troops abroad—last year she went to Vietnam to pep-talk our husbands, fathers, sons and boyfriends into dying and killing with a better spirit. She personifies the "unstained patriotic American womanhood our boys are fighting for." The Living Bra and the Dead Soldier. We refuse to be used as Mascots for Murder.

Document 4

Source: A statement on genital mutilation, Association of African Women for Research and Development (AAWORD), 1980

AAWORD, whose aim is to carry out research which leads to the liberation of African people and women in particular, *firmly condemns* genital mutilation and all other practices—traditional or modern—which oppresses women and justify exploiting them economically or socially, as a serious violation of the fundamental rights of women.

However, as far as AAWORD is concerned, the fight against genital mutilation, although necessary, should not take such proportions that the wood cannot be seen for the trees. Young girls and women who are mutilated in Africa are usually among those who cannot even satisfy their basic needs and who have to struggle daily for survival. This is due to the exploitation of developing countries which is manifested especially through the impoverishment of the poorest social classes. In the context of the present world economic crisis, tradition with all of its constraints becomes more than ever a form of security for the peoples of the Third Worlds and especially for the "wretched of the earth." For these people, the modern world which is primarily Western and bourgeois, can only represent aggression at all levels—political, economic, social and cultural. It is unable to propose viable alternatives for them.

Document 5

Source: Gladys Acosta, Peruvian feminist, 1990s

It is obvious that foreign debt is one of the most inhuman forms of exploitation in our countries when one considers the ratio between work necessary for workers' needs and work producing profit for employers. The experts have already explained how the prevailing exchange and investment structures have created international finance systems which keep whole populations in inhuman conditions. Women in every household are suffering every day as a result of impoverished economies and those who are most exposed to the effects of foreign debt are women.

When it comes to shopping, caring for sick children or the impossibility of meeting their schooling costs, the illusion of "leaving poverty behind" evaporates. Yet the problem is not only of an economic nature because under such circumstances the constant tension leads to grave, often lasting exhaustion. The psychosocial damage is alarming. The adoption of austerity measures means a curtailment of the state's commitment to social services with a direct effect on women. Daily life becomes hell for them. The lack of even minimal state welfare presents women (and obviously children too) with crushing working days.

Document 6

Source: "My Anti-Feminist Manifesto," Aaminah Hernandez, 2007

1. Being a woman, and being a woman of color, and being a Muslim, I choose to not be a feminist or in any way have the term feminist applied to my person, my choices, my thoughts, my writings or my art. I reserve the right to self-identify as I see fit and to define myself in relation to my culture and my ideals. I do not wish to take on the terminology of another's movement nor bend it or re-invent it to suit my own.
   a. As a Muslim, I believe that Islam is the answer for everything. I believe that we have been given the tools with which to free ourselves from oppression here on earth, and I do not find those tools lacking.
   b. I do not feel compelled to look to other cultures to find the answers to my problems. Feminism as it began in a movement by and for middle and upper class white women offers me nothing. It is not my desire to take their movement and somehow prove that my movement is the same. It is not. Theirs has its role in their lives, and mine is different.

Document 7

Source: Filipina women protesting the Japanese government, 2003

Jay Directo/AFP/Getty Images

Introduction to the Long Essay Question (LEQ)

The long essay question is a chance for you to "demonstrate what you know best." You will choose between two comparable long essay options. These questions will measure the use of historical thinking skills to explain and analyze significant issues in world history as defined by the thematic learning objectives.[2]

The LEQ is scored using a set of guidelines that assesses how well you are able to apply the historical thinking skills of the Curriculum Framework. All of the LEQs will assess Argumentation, Analyzing Evidence: Content and Sourcing, Interpretation, and Synthesis. On the exam, the two options will both emphasize ONE of the following skills: Causation, Patterns of Continuity and Change over Time, Periodization, Comparison, or Contextualization. Your essay can receive a maximum of 6 points as scored by an AP reader. Your classroom teacher may use a different system of grading, but she or he will be looking to see if you demonstrate the same skills as outlined in the framework.

The LEQs in this section mirror the format of the AP World History exam; you will have 35 minutes to complete your essay.

When writing your LEQs, try the following:

1. **Read the prompt carefully and create an outline or graphic organizer:** Underline key words. What is the particular skill that will be assessed? What are some other events that occurred during the same time period? (Try to put the prompt into historical context.) Create an outline or graphic organizer that links your response directly to the prompt.
2. **Write a good thesis** (up to 1 point): Does the thesis explicitly address all parts of the prompt? Do not simply restate the prompt, but explain how and why you have chosen to make a specific argument. Remember that it is okay for the thesis to consist of multiple sentences.
3. **Use evidence to support your argument** (up to 2 points): Be sure that your evidence is specific and that it clearly and consistently supports the thesis. Clear linkage between the evidence and the thesis is indicative of a good analytical essay.
4. **Apply the targeted skill being assessed** (Causation, Patterns of Continuity and Change over Time, Periodization, Comparison, or Contextualization) (up to 2 points): Use specific examples that illustrate the historical thinking skill.
5. **Write a synthesis** (up to 1 point): Finally, you will need to synthesize the argument, that is, to combine the argument, evidence, analysis, and context in a well-developed essay that does at least one of the following:
   - Extends or modifies the thesis
   - Employs an additional appropriate category of analysis beyond what the prompt requires; for example, if the overall direction of the prompt is economic history, you might connect it to some political evidence
   - Appropriately connects the topic of the question to other historical periods and circumstances; for example, you might connect an LEQ on the spread of Buddhism to the spread of other universal religions

[2]2016–2017 AP® *World History Curriculum Framework* (© 2014 The College Board). P. 94. Available online at www.apcentral.collegeboard.com.

Long Essay Questions (LEQs)

1. Using specific examples, analyze similarities and differences in techniques of imperial administration between the Roman empire (300 B.C.E.–400 C.E.) and one of the following:
   - Persian empires (600 B.C.E.–600 C.E.)
   - Han empire (200 B.C.E.–220 C.E.)
   - Maurya empire (325 B.C.E.–185 C.E.)

2. Using specific examples, analyze similarities and differences in techniques of imperial administration between the Russian empire (1500 C.E.–1750 C.E.) and one of the following:
   - Manchu Qing empire (1650 C.E.–1800 C.E.)
   - Mughal empire (1525 C.E.–1700 C.E.)
   - Ottoman empire (1400 C.E.–1700 C.E.)

3. Using specific examples, analyze changes and continuities in how rulers of states in Afro-Eurasia maintained control over subject populations during the period circa 2000 B.C.E. to circa 200 C.E.

4. Using specific examples, analyze the causes of the industrialization during the period circa 1700 to circa 1850.

5. Using specific examples, analyze changes and continuities in the beliefs and practices of ONE of the following religions during the period circa 1000 B.C.E. to 200 C.E.
   - Hinduism
   - Judaism

6. Using specific examples, analyze the causes of the collapse of ONE of the following empires in the early twentieth century:
   - Ottoman empire
   - Russian empire
   - Qing empire

7. Using specific examples, analyze factors that contributed to the spread of free-market economics in the twentieth century

8. Using specific examples, analyze similarities and differences in the patterns of exchange between the Eurasian Silk Road and the Indian Ocean sea lanes during the period 200 b.c.e. to 1000 c.e.

9. Using specific examples, analyze changes and continuities in the patterns of exchange on the Mediterranean Sea from 600 B.C.E. to 1000 C.E.

10. Using specific examples, analyze similarities and differences between the outcome of the Haitian Revolution (1791–1804) and the outcome of ONE of the following revolutions:
    - North American (1775–1785)
    - French (1789–1815)
    - Latin American (1810–1830)

Index

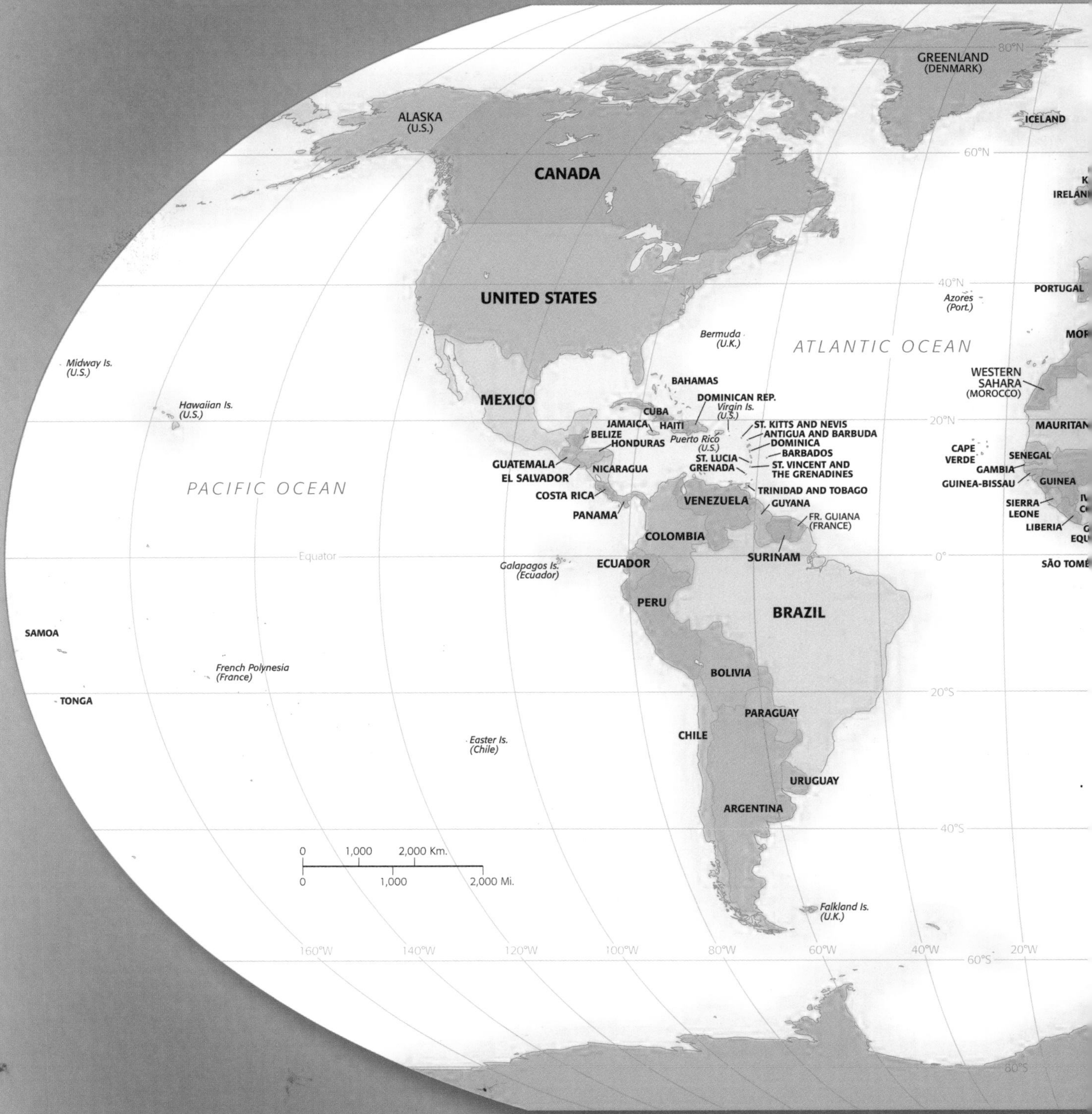

GREENLAND
(DENMARK)
ICELAND
ALASKA
(U.S.)
CANADA
IRELAN
UNITED STATES
PORTUGAL
Azores
(Port.)
Bermuda
(U.K.)
ATLANTIC OCEAN
Midway Is.
(U.S.)
WESTERN
SAHARA
(MOROCCO)
Hawaiian Is.
(U.S.)
BAHAMAS
DOMINICAN REP.
MEXICO
CUBA
Virgin Is.
(U.S.)
JAMAICA
HAITI
ST. KITTS AND NEVIS
ANTIGUA AND BARBUDA
MAURITAN
BELIZE
HONDURAS
Puerto Rico
(U.S.)
DOMINICA
BARBADOS
CAPE
VERDE
SENEGAL
GUATEMALA
ST. LUCIA
GRENADA
ST. VINCENT AND
THE GRENADINES
GAMBIA
NICARAGUA
EL SALVADOR
GUINEA-BISSAU
GUINEA
PACIFIC OCEAN
TRINIDAD AND TOBAGO
COSTA RICA
VENEZUELA
GUYANA
SIERRA
LEONE
PANAMA
FR. GUIANA
(FRANCE)
LIBERIA
COLOMBIA
Equator
Galapagos Is.
(Ecuador)
ECUADOR
SURINAM
SÃO TOMÉ
PERU
BRAZIL
SAMOA
BOLIVIA
French Polynesia
(France)
TONGA
PARAGUAY
CHILE
Easter Is.
(Chile)
URUGUAY
ARGENTINA
0 1,000 2,000 Km.
0 1,000 2,000 Mi.
Falkland Is.
(U.K.)
80°N
60°N
40°N
20°N
0°
20°S
40°S
60°S
80°S
160°W
140°W
120°W
100°W
80°W
60°W
40°W
20°W